HPLC OF PEPTIDES, PROTEINS, AND POLYNUCLEOTIDES

ANALYTICAL TECHNIQUES IN CLINICAL CHEMISTRY AND LABORATORY MEDICINE

Editor

Gary D. Christian, University of Washington

Associate Editors

Margaret Kenny, University of Washington
E. C. Toren, Jr.,[‡] University of South Alabama

CURRENT TITLE

Joseph Wang, *Electroanalytical Techniques in Clinical Chemistry and Laboratory Medicine*

FORTHCOMING TITLES

T. Hadjiioannou, *Quantitative Calculations in Pharmaceutical Practice and Research*

David E. Normansell, *Principles and Practice of Diagnostic Immunology*

[‡]Deceased

Milton T. W. Hearn

HPLC *of* PROTEINS PEPTIDES *and* POLYNUCLEOTIDES

Contemporary Topics and Applications

Dr. Milton T. W. Hearn
Department of Biochemistry and
Centre for Bioprocess Technology
Monash University
Clayton, Victoria 3168
Australia

Library of Congress Cataloging-in-Publication Data

HPLC of peptides, proteins, and polynucleotides : contemporary topics and applications / editor, Milton T. W. Hearn.
p. cm.
Includes bibliographical references and index.
ISBN 0-89573-295-5
1. High performance liquid chromatography. 2. Proteins—Separation. 3. Peptides—Separation. 4. DNA—Separation. 5. RNA—Separation. I. Hearn, Milton. T. W.
QP519.9.H53H536 1991
574.19'245—dc20 91-14525
CIP

British Library Cataloguing in Publication Data

HPLC of peptides, proteins, and polynucleotides.
I. Hearn, Milton T. W.
574.19245

ISBN 3-527-26951-7

Printed in the United States of America
ISBN 0-89573-295-5 VCH Publishers
ISBN 3-527-26951-7 VCH Verlagsgesellschaft

Printing History:
10 9 8 7 6 5 4 3 2 1

Published jointly by:

VCH Publishers, Inc.
220 East 23rd Street
Suite 909
New York, NY 10010

VCH Verlagsgesellschaft mbH
P.O. Box 10 11 61
D-6940 Weinheim
Federal Republic of Germany

VCH Publishers (UK) Ltd.
8 Wellington Court
Cambridge, CB1 1HZ
United Kingdom

SERIES PREFACE

This volume represents the second volume in the continuing series "Analytical Techniques in Clinical Chemistry and Laboratory Medicine." The inaugural volume was "Electroanalytical Techniques," by Joseph Wang, an outstanding overview of modern electroanalytical techniques. The goal of the series is to present analytical methods and techniques that are used to determine and characterize medically relevant substances, and to cover specific problems of current interest. Emphasis is on the techniques and procedures and the interpretation of results obtained, with adequate theory only for understanding of the fundamentals of a particular technique. Authors are encouraged to make generous use of example applications. In this format, the practitioner should be provided the breadth of knowledge and expertise that will be most helpful in utilizing a technique.

The separation and measurement of biologically important substances has become increasingly important and critical for advances in biological sciences. High-performance liquid chromatography (HPLC) is one of the most important arsenals for the analysis of increasingly complex materials, and significant advances have been made in recent years. Professor Hearn has assembled an impressive list of leaders and practitioners in preparing this volume on modern HPLC techniques for proteins and peptides. Starting with sample and column preparation, chapters deal with various types of column materials, protein interactions, preparative and purification chromatography, multimode and microscale chromatography, affinity chromatography, and high-performance electrophoresis. The substances dealt with include protein hormones, membrane hormones, viral proteins, monoclonal antibodies, amino acids, oligonucleotides, plasmids, DNA fragments, and RNA transcripts. All chapters are well documented with key references. There is a wealth of information for both the experienced practitioner and the beginner. The reader should find valuable information on nearly any desired application!

Gary D. Christian
Department of Chemistry
University of Washington
Seattle, WA 98195

CONTENTS

INTRODUCTION

The decade of the 1980s has witnessed the emergence of biochemical separation sciences as mature intellectual and practical endeavors. These developments have largely been responsible for the unprecedented growth in sophistication of the life sciences and biotechnology enabling these disciplines progressively to enunciate biological phenomena more precisely in terms of their molecular origins. Consequently, the biochemical separation sciences—and biochromatography in particular—can now be clearly perceived as the powerhouse that supplies not only the experimental methods and tools of analysis and isolation, but also the sources of much of the intellectual drive to evaluate in quantitative physicochemical terms such diverse biological phenomena as biorecognition, protein folding, or protein transport and packaging in cellular organelles.

Various techniques constitute the arsenal of procedures now available as biochemical separation methods. All are based on the principle of differential migration of the bioanalytes under a defined set of conditions. The process can be achieved using a single, or a combination of different, applied forces. Some chromatographic, electrophoretic, or centrifugational techniques have historically been the mainstay of the biological sciences, yet how many biologists have intimate understanding of the potential of recent significant advances in concept, application, and instrumentation? For example, low-, high-, and ultrahigh-speed centrifugation methods are techniques familiar to most biochemists and biologists, yet how many are familiar with field flow fractionation methods as pioneered by Giddings and co-workers? Similarly, major research progress in university and industrial laboratories in the chromatographic sciences is increasingly being translated into an expanding range of analytical and preparative products and instrumentation on which modern biology depends.

This interdependence between the modern biochemical separation sciences and modern biology currently finds its greatest expression in the field now anecdotally known as high-performance liquid chromatography or HPLC. Who would, for example, have anticipated when the first seminal publications appeared in 1973/1974 on the use of chemically modified silicas for peptide analysis, that today over 3000 laboratories would be routinely using these techniques? The speed, the resolving power, and the experimental flexibility that these methods engender have resulted in one of the major, multidisciplinary success stories in the biological sciences over the subsequent 15 or so years. The fusion of skills from biochemists, chromatographers, analytical chemists, and biologists over the past 20 years now means that to a large extent the separation and analysis of biomacromolecules are not simply based on empirical recipes and intuition of the experimental scientist but increasingly on a rational, strategic framework incorporating structural and functional knowledge on the molecular properties, attributes, and vagaries of the particular biosubstances. Consequently, modern biochromatographic methods have taken on a dimension much larger than other separation methods because of their versatility as ultramicroanalytical procedures through to large process scale preparative procedures.

This book addresses these issues in a number of ways through a detailed examination of contemporary topics and applications of high-performance liquid chromatography and related techniques in the analysis and purification of biomolecules, such as peptides, proteins, and polynucleotides. The general concepts, applications, and physicochemical consequences of these high-resolution separation procedures are presented with the aim to provide students, teachers, and researchers in all facets of the life sciences, and biomedicine and biotechnology in particular, with a concise, yet comprehensive assessment of the essential issues and their solutions. Just as the early phase of chromatography and electrophoresis provided the essential tools of molecular biology, we are now at the verge of the next phase of ultra-high-resolution chromatographic and electrophoretic techniques that will form the basis of atomic biology and rational protein "engineering."

In the preparation of the 22 chapters of this book, leading scientists, all of whom have made seminal contributions to the field, have provided insight into their collective experience. I would like to thank the authors very much for their cooperation throughout all stages of the preparation of this volume. I would also like to thank VCH Publishers, New York, Professor Gary Christian, Series Editor, and Dr. Edmund H. Immergut for their assistance in the realization of this substantial volume. In addition, the tireless efforts of my research colleague, Dr. Marie-Isabel Aguilar and Secretary, Mrs. Joan Carne, are also gratefully acknowledged. In addition, the continued support of the Australian Research Council and the National Health and Medical Research Council of Australia, two Commonwealth competitive peer-review research funding agencies, is gratefully acknowledged, particularly with regard to various aspects of the recent research publications from the Centre for Bioprocess Technology, Monash University.

Finally, I trust all who read this volume will find reconfirmation of the immortal statement of M.S. Tswett that "every scientific advance is an advance in method" and use the knowledge, experience, and insight encapsulated by the authors in each of the 22 chapters to great profit in their studies, teaching, or research.

Milton T. W. Hearn

CONTRIBUTORS

M. I. Aguilar, *Centre for Bioprocess Technology, Monash University, Clayton, Victoria 3168, Australia*

Andreas Becker, *Instutut fur Molekularbiologie und Biochemie, Freie Universität Berlin, Arnimallee 22, D-1000 Berlin 33 (Dahlem), Germany*

Y. D. Clonis, *Enzyme Technology Laboratory, Department of Biology and Biotechnology, Agricultural University of Athens, GR-118-55-Athens, Greece*

Steven C. Goheen, *Battelle Pacific Northwest Laboratory, P8-08 PO Box 999, Richland, WA 99352, U.S.A.*

Karen M. Gooding, *SynChrom, Inc., PO Box 310, Lafayette, IN 47902-0310, U.S.A.*

B. Hansen, *Hagedorn Research Laboratory, Niels Steensensvej 6, DK-2820 Gentofte, Denmark*

Milton T. W. Hearn, *Centre for Bioprocess Technology and Department of Biochemistry, Monash University, Clayton, Victoria 3168, Australia*

K. R. Hejnæs, *Nordisk Gentofte A/S, DK-2820 Gentofte, Denmark*

Michael P. Henry, *J T Baker Inc., 222 Red School Lane, Phillipsburg, NJ 08865, U.S.A.*

Stellan Hjertén, *Institute of Biochemistry, Biomedical Center, University of Uppsala, PO Box 576, S-751 23 Uppsala, Sweden*

A. N. Hodder, *Centre for Bioprocess Technology and Department of Biochemistry, Monash University, Clayton, Victoria 3168, Australia*

Robert S. Hodges, *Department of Biochemistry and the Medical Research Council of Canada Group in Protein Structure and Function, University of Alberta, Edmonton, Alberta T6G 2H7, Canada*

Toshiaki Isobe, *Department of Chemistry, Faculty of Science, Tokyo Metropolitan University, 2-1-1 Fukazawa, Seta Gaya-Ku, Tokyo 158, Japan*

Alain Jaulmes, *Centre National de la Recherche Scientifique, Laboratoire de Physico-Chimie des Biopolymers, U.M. 27 - C.N.R.S., B.P. 28, 94320 Thiais, France*

Djuro Josić, *Fachbereich Medizinische Grundlagenfächer, WE 3, Freie Universität Berlin, Arnimallee 22, D-1000 Berlin 33, Germany*

S. Linde, *Hagedorn Research Laboratory, Niels Steensensvej 6, DK-2820 Gentofte, Denmark*

K. D. Lork, *Institut for Anorganische und Analytische Chemie, Johannes Gutenberg Universität, D6500 Mainz, Germany*

Colin T. Mant, *Department of Biochemistry and the Medical Research Council of Canada Group in Protein Structure and Function, University of Alberta, Edmonton, Albert T6G 2H7, Canada*

Larry W. McLaughlin, *Department of Chemistry, Boston College, Chestnut Hill, MA 02167, U.S.A.*

David R. Nau, *J T Baker Inc., 222 Red School Lane, Phillipsburg, NJ 08865, U.S.A.*

Bohdan Pavlu, *Protein Biochemistry Analysis, Research and Development, Kabi Pharmacia Peptide Hormones, S-112 87 Stockholm, Sweden*

Frank W. Putnam, *Department of Biology, Indiana University, Bloomington, IN 47405 U.S.A.*

G. Ali Qureshi, *Karolinska Institutet, Institutionen för medicinska njursjukdomar, K56 Huddinge, University Hospital, S-141 86 Huddinge, Sweden*

Werner Reutter, *Institut fur Molekularbiologie und Biochemie, Freie Universität Berlin, Arnimallee 22, D-1000 Berlin 33 (Dahlem), Germany*

Detlev Riesner, *Institut für Physikalische Biologie, Universität Düsseldorf, Universitätsstr. 1, D-4000 Düsseldorf 1, Germany*

Mary Nell Schmuck, *SynChrom, Inc., PO Box 310, Lafayette, IN 47902-0310, U.S.A.*

Bernard Sebille, *Centre National de la Recherche Scientifique, Laboratoire de Physico-Chimie des Biopolymers, U.M. 27 - C.N.R.S., B.P. 28, 94320 Thiais, France*

H. H. Sørensen, *Nordisk Gentofte A/S, DK-2820 Gentofte, Denmark*

Nobuhiro Takahashi, *Corporate Research & Development Laboratory, Tonen K.K., 1-3-1 Nishitsurugaoka, Ohi-machi, Iruma-gun, Saitama 354, Japan*

K. K. Unger, *Institut für Anorganische Chemie und Analytische Chemie, Johannes Gutenberg Universität, 6500 Mainz, Germany*

Claire Vidal-Madjar, *Centre National de la Recherche Scientifique, Laboratoire de Physico-Chimie des Biopolymers, U.M. 27 - C.N.R.S., B.P. 28, 94320 Thiais, France*

Timothy C. Wehr, *Varian Instrument Group, Walnut Creek Instrument Division, 2700 Mitchell Drive, Walnut Creek, CA 94598, U.S.A.*

B. S. Welinder, *NOVO Nordisk A/S, Department of Structural Chemistry, 1 Niels Steensensvej, DK-2820 Gentofte, Denmark*

Gjalt W. Welling, *Laboratorium voor Medische Microbiologie, University of Groningen, Oostersingel 59, 9700 RB Groningen, The Netherlands*

Sytske Welling-Wester, *Laboratorium voor Medische Microbiologie, University of Groningen, Oostersingel 59, 9713 EZ Groningen, The Netherlands*

H.-J. Wirth, *Institut fur Anorganische Unemie und Analytische Chemie, Johannes Gutenberg Universität, 6500 Mainz, Germany*

CHAPTER 1

Current Status and Future Challenges of High-Performance Liquid Chromatographic Techniques for Biopolymer Analysis and Purification

Milton T. W. Hearn

CONTENTS

1.1 INTRODUCTION

There can now be little doubt that the high-resolution or high-performance liquid chromatographic techniques, which have evolved over the past 15 years or so from their less sophisticated antecedents, are the unsung heroes of the modern biological sciences. In practically every niche of current life science research and development, high-performance chromatographic methods are pervasive. Irrespective of whether the investigator resides in a molecular biology laboratory associated with the cloning of a new gene, is responsible for a biopharmaceutical or biotechnological quality control laboratory, is involved in vaccine development programs for animals, humans or plants, is working in the food industry, or is associated with the biodegradation of waste materials with environmental consequences, the exquisite sensitivity, speed, and resolving power of high-performance liquid chromatography (HPLC) finds application. In fact, HPLC techniques in their various selectivity modes can rightly be considered the experimental bridge that links biology as practiced today and the emerging fields of biological research that collectively can be termed "atomic biology."

These exciting trends are evolving from the application of instrumental methods that are capable of quantitatively determining changes in composition, topology, and dynamics of biomacromolecules as they interact at liquid–solid and liquid–liquid interfaces. Full application of these methods will provide the essential experimental strategies for scientists to describe biological phenomena at a precise atomic level. Central to these research developments is the link offered by high-resolution separation methods such as HPLC. Extension of current HPLC capabilities can be anticipated to provide a very significant catalyst for the revolution in our understanding of the physicochemical principles of biological phenomena. Progressively, the current one-dimensional view of biological processes provided by molecular biology will be surmounted over the next two decades by more descriptive and quantitative interpretations of the procession of cellular functions and the manner in which proteins and other biomacromolecules interact at the three-dimensional atomic level. It can thus be strongly argued that HPLC currently provides and will continue to provide the most potent expression of the pervasive experimental capabilities needed for these developments. As prophetically experienced[1] in a related context by Oliver Lowry, one of the great biochemists of this century and an investigator whose name is now immortalized in one of the most widely used techniques in quantitative biochemical analysis, namely, the Lowry method for protein quantification, the current generation of research scientists involved with the interface of HPLC and modern biology "will have all the fun and get paid too!"

High-performance liquid chromatographic methods in the broadest context of their application now permit many fundamental questions of modern biology to be approached. In their present format these innovative techniques are pointing the way for us to enunciate with atomic descriptions the complex myriad of biological processes that are involved in integrated cellular responses, from the most simple prokaryotic cell system to the most complex eukaryotic organism—man. At one level, the reason for the versatility and importance of HPLC is relatively simple to appreciate. In practical terms, HPLC is a cornucopia of analytical and preparative methods that now require relatively little experience on the part of the investigator to achieve a significant result. In this context, our scientific colleagues of the mid-1970s through the mid-1980s did their job well, since the methodologies and principles enunciated during this period can be directly applied by an immunologist, a plant biologist, or an animal physiologist to indicate three application areas, in their studies on their particular biological factor, protein, or functional activity. In conceptual terms, HPLC is also a cornucopia of physicochemical principles since buried within the chromatographic retention data and peak width characteristics are Aladdin's caves of quantitative information, on the size, shape, and electronic features of the biomacromolecules. Deciphering this information will enable important new insights into many quantitative structure–function relationships (QSARs), the prediction of protein folding and domain assembly, the processes of protein and biopolymer aggregation, and the fundamental rules of biorecognition.

Just as the 1980s was the decade of the wide, generalist, and mainly empirical application of HPLC in the life sciences, the 1990s and early part of the next century can be expected to become the years in which HPLC facilitates major advances where the three-dimensional structure of a biosolute, its retention behavior, and its biological function at the atomic level are quantitatively established. Recognition of the opportunities that HPLC thus offers is what now drives synthetic chemists involved with sophisticated research programs in sorbent development, theoreticians interested in the modeling of chromatographic processes, and the various multidisciplinary groups who are engaged at the interfaces of surface chemistry, protein engineering, information science, and instrument development including spectroscopy. What features then underpin the current extraordinary popularity of HPLC for the analysis and purification of biomacromolecules? What aspects set HPLC apart from the earlier, more classical aspects of liquid chromatography in its various modes of separation selectivity? This chapter examines these issues and from an assessment of current status attempts to identify several future challenges.

1.2 GENERAL CHROMATOGRAPHIC CONSIDERATIONS

The extraordinary popularity of HPLC for the analysis and purification of biomacromolecules can be attributed to a number of factors:

- the excellent resolution that can be achieved for closely related as well as structurally disparate substances under a large variety of chromatographic conditions;
- the experimental ease with which chromatographic selectivity can be manipulated through changes in mobile phase composition;
- the generally high recoveries, even at ultramicroanalytical levels;

- the excellent reproducibility of repetitive separations carried out over long periods of time, due in part to the stability of the various stationary phases to many aqueous mobile phase conditions;
- the relatively rapid nature of the separation, e.g., seconds to hours rather than days;
- the high productivity in terms of cost parameters;
- the potential, which is only now beginning to be addressed, for evaluating different physicochemical aspects of solute–eluent or solute–stationary phase interactions and their structural consequences from chromatographic data.

All modern high-performance chromatographic procedures lend themselves to the requirements of either analytical or "scaled-up" preparative separations. By combining the capabilities of the various separation techniques, it is now feasible to achieve by a combination of HPLC methods purification factors between 100,000- and 500,000-fold for active substances, an essential requirement if the compound of interest is present in only trace amounts in biological fluids.

The conventional approach of analytical separation, ultramicro-, and small-scale HPLC purification of proteins and other biomacromolecules has largely been predicated on the ability of chromatographic scientists to design and develop laboratory systems that exhibit very high resolution. Although extremely good selectivity and efficient bandwidth may be achieved by these methods, the biological activity of the solutes may be lost. With preparative experimental approaches, it is essential to first specifically address the issue of bioactivity recovery in any process recovery stream. By proper attention to the physicochemical and biological consequences of biopolymer dynamic behavior in bulk solution and at liquid–solid interfaces, these requirements can be systematically addressed. Problem solving associated with loss of bioactivity or mass recovery in process HPLC is still largely based on empirical, or in a limited number of cases (e.g., large-scale purification of human albumin[2,3,88]), on more specific experience on the behavior of a particular biomacromolecule in a chemically defined solution or within the macro- and microenvironment of a stationary phase surface. With recovery of bioactivity the major goal in process purifications, any limitations in instrumental design, system engineering, or process development will lead to inadequate resolution, lower purification factors, and the potential for trace contaminants to adulterate the final product or confuse the quality data analysis. Although these issues are relatively straightforward to identify, they are much more difficult to remedy. Central to overcoming these difficulties is a proper understanding of the purpose for which the (bio)product is being separated or purified. Definition of the purpose of the separation task defines the level of sophistication required for the chromatographic procedures in terms of the minimum level of resolving power, cost, and expertise that will be compatible with the task.

Chromatographic analytical options, based on linear and nonlinear mathematical optimization approaches (see for example references 4–6) have a number of features in common with the preparative methods of biopolymer purification. In particular, both analytical and preparative HPLC methods involve an interplay of secondary equilibrium and nonequilibrium processes with the consequence that retention and band broadening phenomena rarely (if ever) exhibit ideal behavior over a wide range of experimental conditions, i.e., linear or first-order dependencies as predicted from chromatographic theory based on near-equilibrium assumptions are observed only over relatively narrow ranges of conditions. Identification of those secondary parameters that contribute mostly to the nonideality thus represents important objectives for both analytical and process HPLC applications. In process applications a further complication, associated with the high concentration or loading volume of the feed, is involved. These overload considerations in process HPLC impact on product throughput in a manner not relevant in most analytical HPLC procedures, namely through their effect on the preservation of bioactivity. Because biological function is the major endpoint, i.e., maximizing product bioactivity and minimizing degradation are the dominant requirements in process biochromatography, this parameter introduces another dimension to the optimization triangle (speed, capacity, and resolution) not usually experienced with the process chromatography of low-molecular-weight substances. With the emergence of the modern biotechnologies for protein production, the need for precise deterministic models that fuse the chromatographic behavior of biopolymers with their biophysical/structural behavior is thus more pressing than ever before. Various approaches to such deterministic models have been established around modern chromatographic theory and experimental practice, which differentiates the thermodynamics and kinetics of the separation process. Rational improvements in separation performance can thus arise from detailed analysis of the adsorption consequences of the physical (e.g., particle size, flow rate, column configuration, pore size, bed packing quality) or chemical (e.g., sorbent type, eluent composition) characteristics of a particular chromatographic system.

Improvement in bioseparation performance according to more quantitatively predictive approaches has traditionally flowed from data accumulated largely from nonchromatographic measurements such as spectroscopic studies on structure–function stability of the biosolute. In addition, procedures are now at hand to evaluate changes in biological/immunological activities of a protein in response to changes in the separation variables commonly used in static, batch, or dynamic chromatographic experiments. Experimental methods that allow the kinetics of biopolymer adsorption–desorption behavior or the kinetics associated with conformational, ion-binding or solvent hydration phenomena with proteins have special importance in these evaluations.[7–14]

Such approaches are essentially based on chemical equilibrium concepts with the major challenge being the proper understanding of the factors controlling the stabilization of the tertiary structure(s) of biopolymer(s). To permit experimental control over resolution it is essential that the biosolutes manifest only a limited set of preferred conformations and orientations in the distribution process during separation. When these criteria are achieved, high mass and bioactivity recovery can often be realized following desorption. Attention to system residency and dwell effects,[15] the nature of the heterogeneity of the distribution process,[16,17] and minimization of large changes in the entropy of the interaction associated with the biosolute binding to the stationary phase surfaces or permeation through the pores of the sorbent[13–16] are all important parameters in this regard and find ample expression in preparative high-performance liquid chromatographic separations.

From recent trends, it is also evident that empirical models for the retention and mass transfer of biopolymers with microparticulate stationary phases are now the subject of increasing scrutiny in order to address[18–23] more precisely the propensity of biomacromolecules to undergo slow conformational equilibria in solution or at liquid–solid interfaces. The combination of these experimental and theoretical studies on biopolymer folding is thus forming the basis of development of new separation sorbents,[24–27] some of which are now finding their way into the biotechnology industry. In addition, the utility of modern chromatographic methods coupled with new detection methods, e.g., on-line photodiode array detection, optical rotary dispersion—circular dichroism (ORD-CD), laser-activated light scattering, and derivative spectroscopy, to assess bioactivity profiles has important ramifications for the future way biochemists and engineers deal with various biorecovery problems and select alternative strategies in protein purification.

A further consequence of recent developments is the rate at which quantitative data can be acquired with high-performance chromatographic systems. Thus, to carry out in this laboratory optimization experiments investigating the influence on protein recovery and resolution of two different salts at three different pH values with 10 different gradient options, a little over 48 h experimental time was required using modern high-performance ion-exchange support materials while performing comparable experiments with soft gel ion exchangers requires in excess of 800 h of experimental time.

In common with classical liquid chromatography, the different modes of HPLC can be classified according to the selectivity of the sorbent. In size exclusion, the biosolute, in principle, does not interact with the sorbent in any way, with retention controlled solely according to the hydrodynamic properties of the system. In all other modes of chromatography, an adsorption isotherm is established between the biosolute and the sorbent. This adsorption can involve both specific interactions, e.g., protein–ligand binding, or nonspecific interactions mediated by other classes of binding sites. In an ideal system only a single class of interactions will occur, i.e., only protein–ligand binding, but even here binding heterogeneity must be anticipated.[7,8,16,17] The dynamic process involved in biopolymer HPLC can be considered as a convection–diffusion mass transfer event, which generally is associated with mass conservation. However, in the situation of biopolymer folding and unfolding, the chromatographic system effectively behaves as an adsorption–desorption chemical reactor in which mass and activity conservation of a particular species cannot be assumed. From a microscopic point of view, such secondary kinetic processes lead to adsorption isotherms that are more complex than predicted by the Langmuirean description of adsorption, and require much more sophisticated numerical solutions to the mass balance equations to accommodate the influence of the nonlinear behavior of the isotherms, particularly with multicomponent samples.[28–30]

It is important to recall that chromatographic methods per se are only part of the arsenal available for the analysis and purification of a particular biomacromolecule. What sets HPLC apart in its various preparative modes, e.g., ultramicropreparative through process applications, is the speed of the separation that can be achieved without sacrificing the magnitude of the purification factor (resolution). Table 1–1 summarizes some of the comparative capabilities that HPLC offers in this regard over other alternatives.

TABLE 1–1. Separation Parameters Used in Large-Scale High-Performance Protein Purification and Typical Purification Factor Ranges and Time Required per Unit Operation

Parameter	Process	Typical Purification Factor Ranges	Typical Time Requirement[a] (h)
Temperature	Heat denaturation	2–20	2–40
Solubility	Salt precipitation		
	Solvent precipitation		
	Polymer precipitation	2–20	10–100
	Isoelectric precipitation		
	Aqueous partitioning		
	Two-phase systems		
Size and shape	Gel filtration	2–20	40–80
	Ultrafiltration	2–5	4–20
	Gel electrophoresis	2–10	100+
Net charge	Free electrophoresis	2–5	100+
	Ion exchange chromatography	2–40	2–50
Isoelectric point	Chromatofocusing	2–10	10–20
Hydrophobicity	Hydrophobic interaction chromatography	2–30	2–10
	Reversed-phase chromatography	2–200	2–10
Function	Biospecific affinity chromatography	50–1000	2–10
Antigenicity	Immunosorption (e.g., monoclonal antibodies)	20–100	2–20
Carbohydrate content	Lectin affinity chromatography	2–10	2–10
Content of free SH	Covalent chromatography	2–10	2–10
Exposed histidine	Metal chelate affinity chromatography	2–10	2–10
Exposed metal ion	Chelate affinity chromatography	2–10	2–10
Group specific	Hydroxyapatite chromatography	2–10	2–20
	Dipolar chromatography	2–40	2–10
	Dye affinity chromatography	2–40	2–10
	Charge transfer chromatography	2–40	2–10

[a] Based on fractionation data for hen egg white proteins including lysozyme, ovalbumin, and avidin.

In high-resolution chromatographic analysis and purification full knowledge of the mechanistic processes underlying the selectivity and the kinetics of biosolute adsorption, desorption, and mass transport under the separation conditions is an ideal scenario rarely attainable in practice. Much of the research effort associated with the development of new chromatographic separation media has nevertheless addressed questions central to the physicochemical nature of the separation selectivity and kinetics of different classes of biopolymers. Particularly with adsorptive chromatographic systems, the molecular dynamics, associated with multisite interactions between the biopolymers and the stationary phase surface, control not only the retention and zone broadening behavior but also the mass and bioactivity recovery. For several practical reasons, e.g., cost or difficulties with column regenerability, high-resolution purification methods are usually not brought into play with sub-25 μm microparticulate adsorption media of narrow particle diameter distributions and narrow pore size distributions until clarification of the feedstock is complete and partial fractionation has been carried out. To expand these capabilities, considerable activity is now underway at both academic and industrial centers, exploring different options to improve stationary phase characteristics, with the purpose of enhancing separation selectivity and improving kinetics with mesoparticulate sorbents (d_p >30 μm) in preparative separations of biopolymers.[17,24,26,28,30]

Because interactive sorbents have the potential to probe the topography of a biopolymer, and in particular to assess surface accessible regions or binding sites unique to the protein or other biomacromolecule of interest, purification stratagems based on a rational mix of ion-exchange chromatography, biospecific or biomimetic affinity chromatography, and hydrophobic interaction chromatography represent the core methods for high-resolution separation. Figure 1–1 illustrates, as a schemata, the more common modes of protein–ligand interaction used in the adsorption modes of HPLC. Exploitation of the interplay between two or more modes present with one sorbent, e.g., combi-

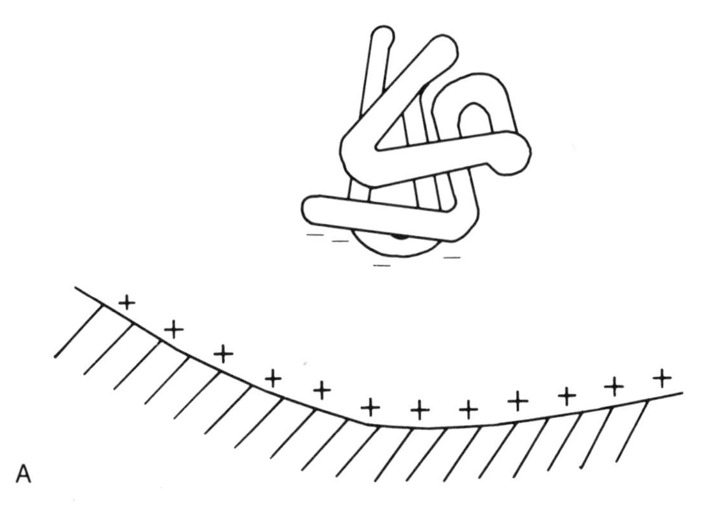

FIGURE 1–1. Schemata representing the more common modes of interaction between a protein and an immobilized chemical ligand; (A) ion exchange: interaction between oppositely charged ionic groups at the surface of the protein and the stationary phase;

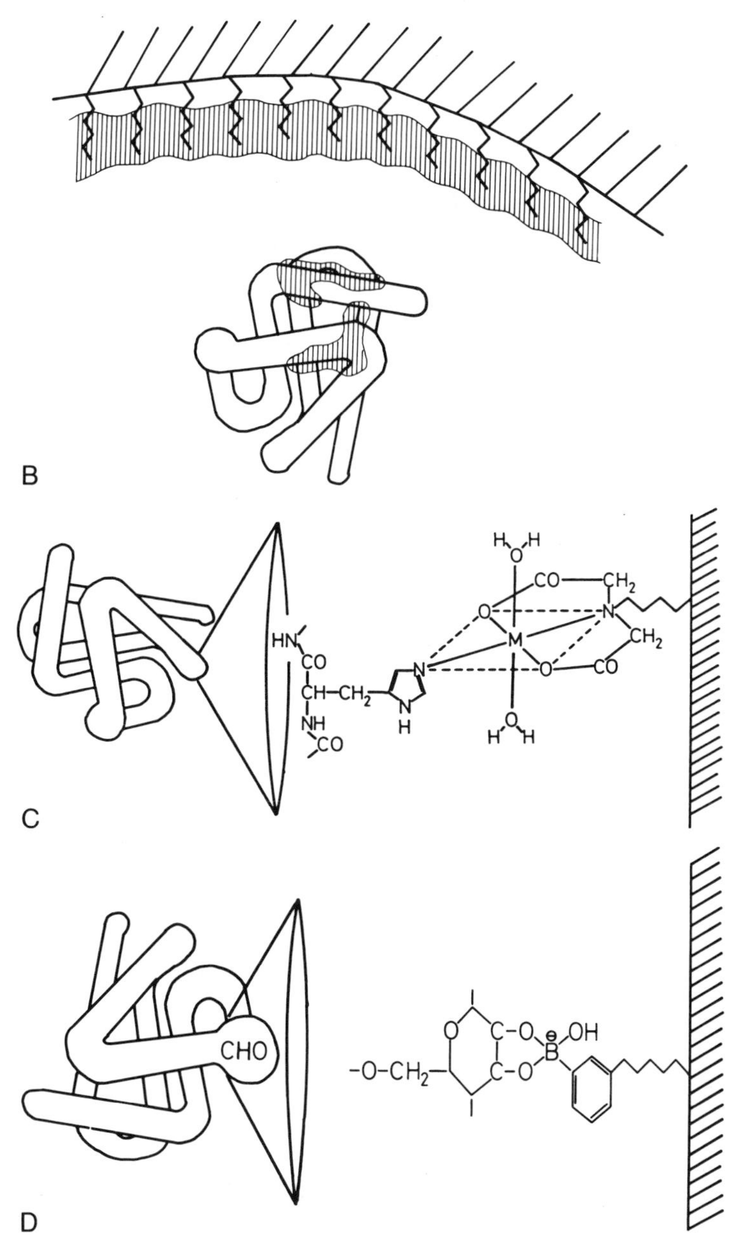

(B) reversed-phase and hydrophobic interaction: interaction of mainly hydrophobic moieties of proteins and stationary phases; (C) metal chelate: exposed functional groups of amino acids (e.g., imidazole from histidine) are involved in an immobilized metal–chelate complex; (D) group-specific interaction such as phenylboronic acid affinity: *cis*-diol groups of carbohydrate side chains of proteins form complexes with boronic acid;

(*continued*)

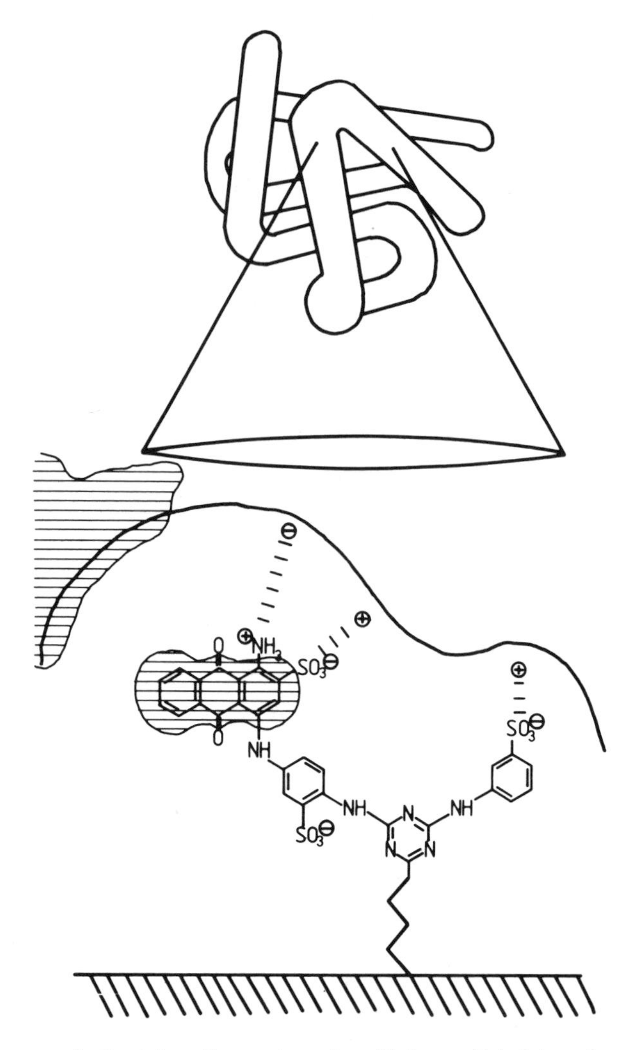

(E) group-selective interaction such as dye affinity: multiple interaction of ionic and hydrophobic moieties of proteins with the dye matrix (e.g., Cibacron Blue F3GA).

nation of hydrophobic and coulombic interactive phenomena, forms the basis of the so called "mixed mode" chromatographic procedures. For example, under appropriately chosen eluent conditions, proteins can be efficiently separated on stationary phases with immobilized coulombic ligands with hydrophobic selectivity, i.e., separation is achieved[31] in order of increasing solute hydrophobicity under conditions of decreasing displacing salt concentration from high ionic strengths ranging typically from $\mu = 3.5$ down to $\mu = 0.1$. Similarly, under appropriately chosen solvent conditions, hydrophobic sorbents such as *n*-alkylsilicas can be induced to exhibit polar phase and even coulombic selectivity with peptides and proteins eluting in order of increasing polarity. As a consequence, retrogradients based on eluents ranging from high solvent content down to lower solvent content, i.e., with organic solvent mole fraction decreasing from $\varphi = 0.9$ to $\varphi = 0.5$, can be used to separate hydrophobic peptides and proteins on reversed-phase packing materials with polar phase selectivity.[32–34,89,90]

The composite interplay between size exclusion phenomena, hydrophobic, and coulombic interactions processes is a feature of all current chromatographic materials. Depending on the magnitude of these interdependencies, the retention and kinetic behavior of biosolutes in interactive systems can be formalized (see Section 1.5) in terms of the summation of the corresponding size exclusion, hydrophobic coulombic, and polar contributions to the overall retention and kinetic process. Which of these parameters makes the greatest overall contribution to the chromatographic behavior of biopolymers depends not only on the permeability, ligand composition, and ligand density of the stationary phase, but also on the mobile phase characteristics in terms of water content, pH, ionic strength, organic solvent type, buffer composition, and whether such additives as ion pairing reagents, organic dissociating reagents, or surfactants and detergents are present in the eluent.

1.3 CHROMATOGRAPHIC MODES

Over the past 15 years, a large amount of developmental effort has been expended to transfer knowledge gained with chemically modified, deformable polymeric gels such as the cross-linked dextrans, agaroses, or acrylate copolymers to the selection and chemical modification of chemically and physically more robust stationary phases with narrower particle and pore size distributions. Many of the criteria now recognized as essential for the selection of chromatographic media and listed in Table 1–2 apply equally to analytical separations as they do to large-scale preparative separations. Clearly, in the latter case the issues of column productivity, in terms of kilograms of product resolved at a defined purity level per unit time per unit cost of operating the

TABLE 1–2. Criteria for the Selection of Chromatographic Media

1. Chemical and physical stability
2. Particle uniformity
3. Mechanical strength and resistance to deformation
4. Hydrophilicity and wettability
5. Sterilizability and regenerability
6. Cost
7. Reproducibility between batches
8. High capacity
9. High resolution or selectivity
10. High mass and biological recoveries
11. High product throughput
12. Potential for GMP scale-up

overall separation system, is of fundamental importance. The potential of the purification approach to satisfy good manufacturing practice (GMP)-scale-up procedures, and thus meet governmental regulatory agency guidelines, is also of major relevance in the selection of a particular sorbent for use in an industrial application for the purification of a peptide or protein.

It has been appreciated for many years that the so-called "noninteractive" modes of chromatographic separation (e.g., size exclusion, gel permeation, and hydrodynamic modes) are incapable of exhibiting the same level of resolution as adsorption techniques. Consequently, the most successful separation techniques are those capable of selective interaction by probing the topography of the desired biopolymer. Ion-exchange chromatography separations take advantage of charge distribution and anisotropy of the charge potential over different regions of the surface of the biopolymer. Ion-exchange HPLC has been the mainstay of the purification of many enzymes, and other proteins in active state. The place of ion-exchange HPLC in the repertoire of separation methods for the resolution of different proteins and polynucleotides is discussed in detail in Chapters 5, 6, 7, 11, 18, 20, and 21 of this volume. Hydrophobic interaction chromatography in comparison exploits the accessibility and surface distribution of lipophilic or nonpolar residues. The term "hydrophobic interaction chromatography" is frequently attributed to separations affected by a decreasing salt concentration while the term "reversed-phase chromatography" has become identified with separations involving an increasing concentration of organic solvent in the eluent. The physicochemical basis for these hydrophobic interaction and reversed-phase separation methods is largely a result of incremental changes in the microscopic surface tension associated with the solute–solvent–stationary phase interaction. The application of these HPLC procedures is described in greater detail in Chapters 6, 8, 9, and 10.

Further examples of separation techniques that exploit the asymmetric distribution of amino acid residues at the surface of folded proteins, for example, access to exposed histidine residues or a coordination site of a metal ion cofactor, include ligand-exchange chromatography and metal chelate affinity chromatography. Similar regioselective discrimination is also observed with hydroxyapatite chromatography, with group-specific affinity chromatography such as the triazine dye affinity (see also Chapters 12 and 13) and borate affinity chromatography as well as other forms of ligand interactions based on generic biological ligands, i.e., biotin–avidin system, protein A–IgG system, or oligosaccharide–lectin systems.

The final group of separation procedures, and the ones that potentially give the highest selectivity, represents methods that exploit functional properties of a biopolymer such as a specific ligand-binding site, an antigenic determinant, or a structural element such as a lipid-binding amphipathic (nonpolar) domain in lipoproteins or subunit contact region of a multimeric protein complex. Applications of these biospecific affinity modes are further discussed in Chapters 14 and 17. With appropriate immobilization chemistries and choice of the ligand, biospecific affinity chromatography and immunoaffinity chromatography both have the potential to generate separation peak capacities more than two orders of magnitude greater than observed with adsorption methods based on simple chemical ligands such as those typically employed for ion-exchange or reversed-phase chromatography.

Table 1–1 summarized examples of the separation parameters used in protein purification and the ranges of purification factors that can be expected as a typical single stage procedure. Because of the inherent requirements for high resolution in biopolymer purification, it is routine to utilize combinations of all of the separation parameters listed in Table 1–1 at different stages and with different objectives during the isolation strategy or analysis. Sequential use of two or more of these different separation modes in a particular application study is known as *multidimensional HPLC* while manifestation of more than one mode of separation with a particular class of sorbent is known as *multimodal HPLC*. To allow fully predictive and integrated separation strategies to evolve with both multidimensional and multimodal HPLC systems, greatly expanded databases on the behavior of proteins and other biomacromolecules in various physical or chemical environments are required, and related to mass-transport and associated mechanistic parameters. Such databases are currently being assembled,[35,36] thus permitting methods of principal component analysis to be applied as part of the development of computer-assisted separation strategies for the HPLC of biomacromoles.

1.4 BASIC CHROMATOGRAPHIC TERMS AND CONCEPTS

The decade of the 1980s represented a period of major advances and consolidation in chromatographic theory and its application to biomacromolecules. The full impact of these developments on biopolymer HPLC has yet to be realized, although their underlying consequences are providing directions for instrument miniaturization as well as integrated process modeling. In particular, developments associated with nonlinear elution and displacement chromatography have special relevance for process HPLC. It is not the intention of this chapter to introduce and describe these various significant developments in chromatographic theory in detailed mathematical terms. The interested reader is referred to other chapters elsewhere in this volume and chapters in several excellent monographs[8,9,37–40] and other publications[41–50] for the current status of these important aspects. Rather, this section examines the practical application of the basic chromatographic terms as an aide to investigators wishing to improve the performance of their HPLC procedures.

The separation of a mixture of polar, ionizable biosubstances, such as peptides and proteins, in a packed chromatographic column is a consequence of two events. The first event, which controls the average solute retention, is embodied in the concept of mass distribution of the biosolute as it migrates along a chromatographic bed (or column) of length L, operated at a mobile phase flow rate, F. As the biosolutes move down the column, individual components interact with the mobile phase and stationary phase to different extents. When the interaction of a specific biosolute with the stationary phase is very strong, that is when the *equilibrium distribution coefficient*, K, is large, then that solute will be retained to a greater extent than another component that interacts less strongly. Solute zones corresponding to each component will therefore migrate through the column at different velocities. This differential migration is thus a function of the equilibrium distribution coefficients established by the solutes between the stationary and mobile phase, the effective diffusivities of the solutes, their linear flow (or so called superficial) velocities, and related physicochemical properties. Depending on the nature of the mass transport characteristics, the isothermal kinetics and the level of heterogeneity of the sorbent, such differential retention behavior may approximate linear or nonlinear adsorption processes.

In the case of size-exclusion HPLC, selectivity still arises from differential migration but in this case it is a consequence of the extent to which the solutes can permeate, by diffusion from the bulk mobile phase, to within the pore chambers of the stationary phase. Ideally, the stationary phase in size-exclusion HPLC has been so prepared that the surface does not itself retard the transport of the biosolutes through chemical equilibrium interactions. This mode thus contrasts to the adsorption modes of HPLC, where the surface of the stationary phase has purposely been chemically modified to allow selective retardation of the solutes. Ideally, the sorbent surface in adsorption HPLC permits separation to occur by only one retention process, i.e., the chromatographic material functions as a monomodal sorbent. In practice, this is rarely achieved with the consequence that most adsorption HPLC sorbents exhibit multimodal characteristics. These differences in retention behavior that constitute the basis of selectivity of the chromatographic system thus depend on the nature and magnitude of a complex interplay of intermolecular forces established between the solutes, the stationary phase, and the mobile phase. In addition, retention behavior will be affected by the hydrodynamic characteristics and fluid dynamic properties of the chromatographic system as well as those manifested by the biosolutes themselves in solution.

The second event involved in biosolute migration in chromatographic beds is associated with the broadening of all solute peaks or zones. This dispersion occurs in both static and flowing liquid systems and is mediated, inter alia, by the respective diffusivities of the biosolutes. The concept of zone dispersion thus incorporates all the kinetic processes associated with the mass transport motion of the solutes through the pore and interstitial spaces within and around the stationary phase as well as those involved with adsorption and desorption. As the individual biosolute zones move, for example, down the column, a number of dispersive effects come into play as a consequence of the inhomogeneities of the column bed, nonlinear flow characteristics, resistance to diffusion, and inappropriate kinetics of solute distribution between the mobile and the stationary phase. These dispersion effects collectively give rise to zone broadening, which progressively increases throughout the total period of time the solute spends traversing the chromatographic bed.

The time taken for a solute to completely pass through a chromatographic bed is called the *retention time*, t_r. The retention time, t_r, is measured as the time taken for the biosolute to move from one end of the column following injection, to emerge from the other end of the column, and be immediately detected as an eluted zone with a peak maximum. To enable comparisons to be made between columns of different dimensions or selectivities, the retention time, t_r, of a biosolute is usually compared with reference to the time taken for a different solute (or solvent) molecule to move through the column bed *without* any interaction, i.e., compared to the time taken for an inert component to be eluted through the void volume of the column, t_0. The void volume of a chromatographic bed represents the total volume occupied by the mobile phase and typically corresponds to 0.3–0.6 of the total column volume. This comparison permits normalization of the retention behavior of any biosolute in the form of a (unitless) *capacity factor*, k', for a particular sorbent, such that

$$k' = (t_r - t_0)/t_0 \quad (1\text{–}1)$$

or

$$t_r = t_0(1 + k') \quad (1\text{–}2)$$

Alternatively, the capacity factor can be expressed in terms of elution volumes since the retention times, t_r and t_0, are related to the elution volumes and flow rate (F) of the chromatographic system through the relationships

$$V_r = t_r(F), \qquad V_0 = t_0(F) \quad (1\text{–}3)$$

hence

$$k' = (V_r - V_0)/V_0 \quad (1\text{–}4)$$

or

$$V_r = V_0(1 + k') \quad (1\text{–}5)$$

The *selectivity*, α, in all chromatographic modes can be defined as the relative separation achieved between adjacent solute peaks and will thus reflect the overall performance of the chromatographic system. In particular, selectivity, α, is given by the ratio of capacity factors for adjacent peaks, i.e.,

$$\alpha = k'_i/k'_d \quad (1\text{–}6)$$

The capacity factor, k', can also be defined as the ratio n_s/n_m, where n_s is the total number of moles of the biosolute associated with the stationary phase and n_m the total number of moles of the biosolute in the mobile phase, i.e.,

$$k' = n_s/n_m \quad (1\text{–}7)$$

or alternatively

$$k' = \frac{[X]_s V_s}{[X]_m V_m} \quad (1\text{–}8)$$

where $[X]_s$, $[X]_m$ refer to the concentrations (in moles/liter) of the solute in the stationary and mobile phase, respectively, and V_s, V_m refer to the volumes of the stationary and mobile phases, respectively, within the column of length, L, and diameter, d_c. The ratio $[X]_s/[X]_m$ is the *equilibrium distribution coef-*

ficient, K, while the ratio V_s/V_m defines the *phase ratio*, Φ, of the chromatographic system.

Hence the capacity factor can also take the form

$$k' = \Phi[X]_s/[X]_m \qquad (1\text{–}9)$$

or

$$k' = \Phi K \qquad (1\text{–}10)$$

Research over the past decade has focused on the development and evaluation of a very large number of different elution conditions and types of stationary phases for peptide, protein, and other biopolymer separations in attempts to maximize column selectivities. The central task was the achievement of an optimal k' value by selecting conditions with the most appropriate K values, although clearly manipulation of the phase ratio, Φ, also permits additional fine tuning, e.g., manipulation of ligand densities permits further control over selectivity and throughput. The reader is referred to other chapters in this volume for compendia of the different options that have resulted from these investigations.

One of the most important decisions an investigator can make with regard to a particular chromatographic system is the choice of the k' range over which the separation is to be achieved. Often the first action of an investigator should be an examination of chromatographic conditions that provide the smallest value of k' without a loss of selectivity. From practical considerations, the range $0 < k' < 10$ is recommended for all chromatographic separations with peptides and proteins. As the value of α approaches unity, selectivity will decline. An equally important task of selecting chromatographic conditions thus centers on the choice of α values that must be achieved for a particular set of k' values.

Since the equilibrium distribution coefficient, K, is related through the Gibbs equation to the overall energy change, ΔG°_T, for the separation event, then the capacity factor also takes on a fundamental thermodynamic complexion through the dependencies:

$$\Delta G^\circ_T = -RT \ln K \qquad (1\text{–}11)$$

$$\ln k' = \ln \Phi - \frac{\Delta G^\circ_T}{RT} \qquad (1\text{–}12)$$

where R is the gas constant and T the absolute temperature.

The capacity factor, k', thus allows a particular chromatographic separation process to be defined both in empirical as well as thermodynamic terms. Differences in the molecular characteristics and interactive behavior of biosolutes can thus be revealed in chromatographic separations, through quantitative evaluation of thermodynamic differences in unitary free energies of the biosolutes. Such evaluations are the basis of the determination of retention coefficients,[33,51,52] characterization of binding sites,[20,53] and elucidation of biopolymer folding and conformational processes.[13,15,18,19,22,36] In fact, ΔG°_T represents the composite of all the unitary free energy changes associated with electrostatic, hydrophobic, solvational, hydrogen bonding, and aggregational interactions and thus can be rewritten in the form

$$\Delta G^\circ_T = \Delta G^\circ_{es} + \Delta G^\circ_{vdw} + \Delta G^\circ_{sol} + \Delta G^\circ_k + \Delta G^\circ_{assoc} + \Delta G^\circ_{red} \qquad (1\text{–}13)$$

where ΔG°_{es}, ΔG°_{vdw}, ΔG°_{sol}, ΔG°_k, ΔG°_{assoc}, and ΔG°_{red}, are the free energy differences associated with electrostatic effects, van der Waals interactions, solvational effects, formation of a solvent cavity of dimensions of the biosolute, self-association or heterogeneous association in the absence of solvent, and reduction in free energy due to nonideal effects. The intimate relationship between $\ln k'$ and ΔG°_T thus represents the basis of the composite interplay between size exclusion phenomena, solvophobic, and coulombic interaction processes that are involved as the dominant features of all current HPLC stationary phases. Depending on the magnitudes of these individual retention dependencies, the retention behavior of a biosolute with an interactive ligand system can be formalized in terms of the summations of the overall retention process. A common relationship[7,33] by which this formalism is expressed is given by

$$\ln k' = \ln[\delta_{sec} k'_{sec} + \delta_{vdw} k_0 e^{-S\xi} + \delta_p k'_p e^{-D(1-\xi)} + \cdots] \qquad (1\text{–}14)$$

where $\delta_{sec} k'_{sec}$ corresponds to the size exclusion term, $\delta_{vdw} k'_{vdw}$ $(= \delta_{vdw} k_0 e^{-S\xi})$ to the solvophobic term, and $\delta_{es} k'_{es}$ $(= \delta_p k'_p e^{-D(1-\xi)})$ to the polar coulombic term for different values of the mole fraction, ξ, of the solvent or ionic modifier. The coefficients S and D correspond to solute-specific parameters and are derived from the slope of the plots of the logarithmic capacity factor, $\ln k'$, for a particular biopolymer versus the reciprocal logarithmic concentration of organic solvent modifier in the case of reversed-phase separations, or versus reciprocal logarithmic concentration of displacing ion in the case of hydrophobic interaction and coulombic separations, while the k'_0 and k'_p correspond to the (hypothetical) solute capacity factors in neat water, e.g., at zero ionic strength and zero organic solvent content.

Depending on the magnitude of the S, D, k'_0, and k'_p parameters a variety of solute retention versus mobile phase eluotropic strength scenarios can be calculated. Figure 1–2 represents four limiting cases of such retention dependencies. Case (b) is typified by shallow $\log k'$ versus ξ [or $\log 1/[c]$(dependencies with small $\log k'_0$ values at ξ(or$[c]$) = 0] and represents a commonly observed situation with small polar peptides separated under reversed-phase HPLC and some small proteins in ion-exchange HPLC conditions. Case (c), which again exhibits shallow dependencies in terms of the $\log k'$ versus ξ (or $\log 1[c]$) dependency but with large values of $\log k'_0$ values, is representative of situations

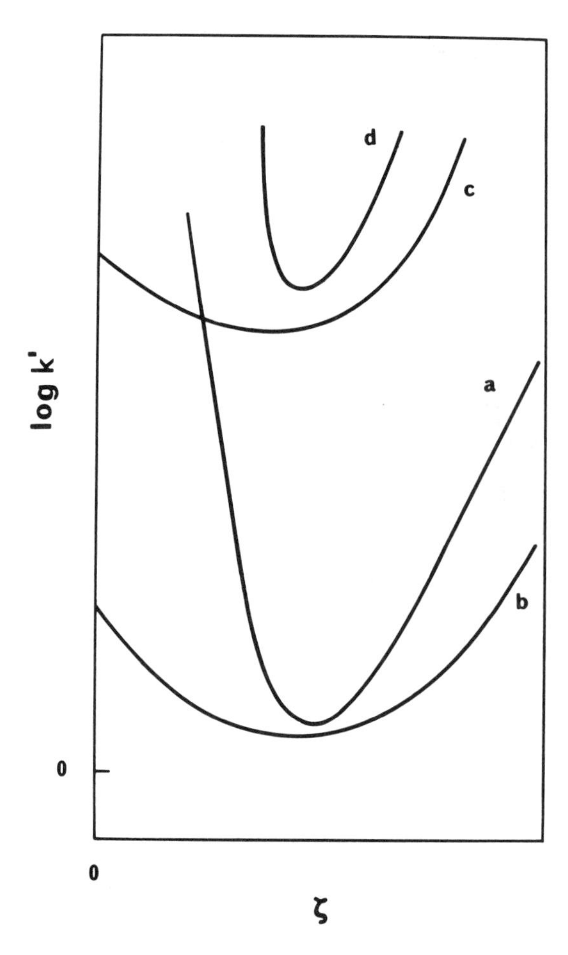

FIGURE 1–2. Schematic representation of the retention dependencies for peptides or proteins chromatographed on mixed-mode support media. The figure illustrates four case histories for the dependency of the logarithmic capacity factor (log k') on the mole fraction, n, of the displacing species. As the contact area associated with the solute–ligand interaction increases, the slopes of the log k' versus n plots increase resulting in a narrowing of the elution window over which the solute will desorb. Cases (a) and (b) are typically observed for the RP-HPLC and HPIEX of polar peptides and small, polar globular proteins while cases (c) and (d) are more representative of the RP-HPLC and HPIEX behavior of highly hydrophobic polypeptides and nonpolar globular proteins including membrane proteins, respectively.

found with middle molecular weight proteins and very hydrophobic peptides under some reversed-phase conditions, in affinity displacement ion-exchange and substrate (or analogue elution) displacement in affinity chromatography of monomeric enzymes where the displacing ionic species or substrate/analogue is again typically of low molecular weight. Some examples of peptide displacement reversed-phase chromatography correspond also to case (c). Because log k_0' values are large with case (c) biosolutes, significant secondary retention effects may occur in response to small changes in a secondary mobile phase component, e.g., pH or salt type. Case (a) represents a typical scenario for polypeptide and globular protein purification in reversed-phase and hydrophobic interaction HPLC techniques and with most polymer- and silica-based anion and cation HPLC support media. From practical considerations the limiting chromatographic conditions are frequently chosen such that the minima of the plot of the logarithmic k' versus ξ (or log $1/[c]$) corresponds to k' values equal to or less than unity. Typically this criterion is easier to achieve in ion-exchange than reversed-phase separations. In situations associated with the purification of large globular proteins or hydrophobic proteins, e.g., multimeric membrane proteins, retention behavior characterized by cases (a–c) with reversed-phase, ion-exchange, or affinity HPLC are rarely seen. With these protein classes retention dependencies approaching case (d) are much more common, i.e., a narrow desorption window, with significant secondary high-affinity sorption effects.

From the point of view of a generalized analytical or preparative purification strategy, obviously it is desirable to select chromatographic conditions in which the retention dependencies approximate case (a) or case (b) rather than cases (c) and (d) where clearly with the two latter cases the affinity of the biosolute for the stationary phase is too high, the elution window feasible for desorption too narrow, the range of solubility parameters of the biosolute too low, and the mass (or bioactivity) recovery potentially impaired. However, from a selectivity point of view situations characterized as case (a) or (d) should not necessarily be excluded out of hand. Exploitation of the potential offered by the case (a) and case (d) scenarios has proved very useful for the removal of undesirable contaminants during the purification of a number of therapeutic proteins by exploiting the so called "negative" adsorption strategy. For example, in this laboratory a method has been developed for the removal of trace components of Hageman factor and associated plasminogen activator/prekallikrein proteins from therapeutic grade human immunoglobulins based on a tandem dye-affinity and anion-exchange HPLC chromatographic method based on these concepts.

Because of the pronounced dependencies of retention and zone broadening phenomena on chromatographic conditions, the most commonly adopted method for elution of biopolymers from adsorptive media involves gradient or step elution procedures. Such conditions take advantage of the severity of the log k' versus ξ (or log $1/[c]$) dependencies but do not necessarily address the important requirements of desorption kinetics and conformational dynamics of the biosolute. However, important progress has recently been made[9,33,35,51,54–57] in the application of gradient elution theory that allows gradient retention data for peptides and proteins to be more accurately predicted with RP– and IEX–HPLC systems. Furthermore, it is feasible in circumstances of so-called regular retention and recovery behavior, e.g., with peptides that satisfy case (b), and small globular proteins [case (a)] to apply data derived[16,58] from small-scale or analytical experiments as normalized integral of the elution volume, column performance etc., to scale up the chromatographic bed configuration and the choice of the physical characteristics of the separation media, to process purification levels.

The extent of zone broadening of a biosolute in a chromatographic system is reflected in the column efficiency, usually expressed in terms of the number of theoretical plates, N, or the height equivalent, H, of a theoretical plate (the H value $= L/N$ where L is the column length).

The value of N is dependent on a variety of chromatographic and solute parameters including the column length, L, the particle diameter, d_p, the linear flow velocity, u (equivalent to L/t_r), and the solutes' diffusivites (D_m and D_s) in the bulk mobile phase and within the stationary phase respectively. The theoretical plate number, N, of a column can be defined as

$$N = \left(\frac{t_r^2}{\sigma_t^2}\right) \qquad (1\text{–}15)$$

or

$$N = 16\left(\frac{t_r}{t_w}\right)^2 \qquad (1\text{–}16)$$

where t_r is the elution time, and σ_t^2 the peak variance of the eluted zone in time units. For practical convenience the peak variance, σ_t^2, is often replaced by the peak width, t_w, at baseline (e.g., the detector response line for zero sample concentration). For Gaussian peaks, t_w approximately corresponds to 4σ (4 $\times$ peak standard deviation). It should, however, be appreciated that by taking t_w as equal to 4σ, only ~95% of the true peak area of a Gaussian peak will be integrated.

Since t_r and k' are interrelated, the theoretical plate number, N, can also be expressed in terms of k' such that

$$N = 16\left[\frac{(1+k')}{t_w}\, t_0\right]^2 \qquad (1\text{–}17)$$

A major task of experimental practice with HPLC techniques is to choose conditions that maximize the N value and minimize the H value. This task necessitates adequate control over the various mass transport processes that control zone broadening (or peak spreading) (see Figure 1–3). These processes include (1) eddy diffusion, (2) mobile phase mass transfer, (3) longitudinal molecular diffusion, (4) stagnant mobile phase mass transfer, and (5) stationary phase mass transfer. From a practical standpoint, some but not all of these processes can be controlled by the quality of the column bed packing procedures using particles of narrow particle size and pore size distributions. Because most biopolymers have small effective diffusivities in HPLC systems (compared to low-molecular-weight organic analytes), the major problems as-

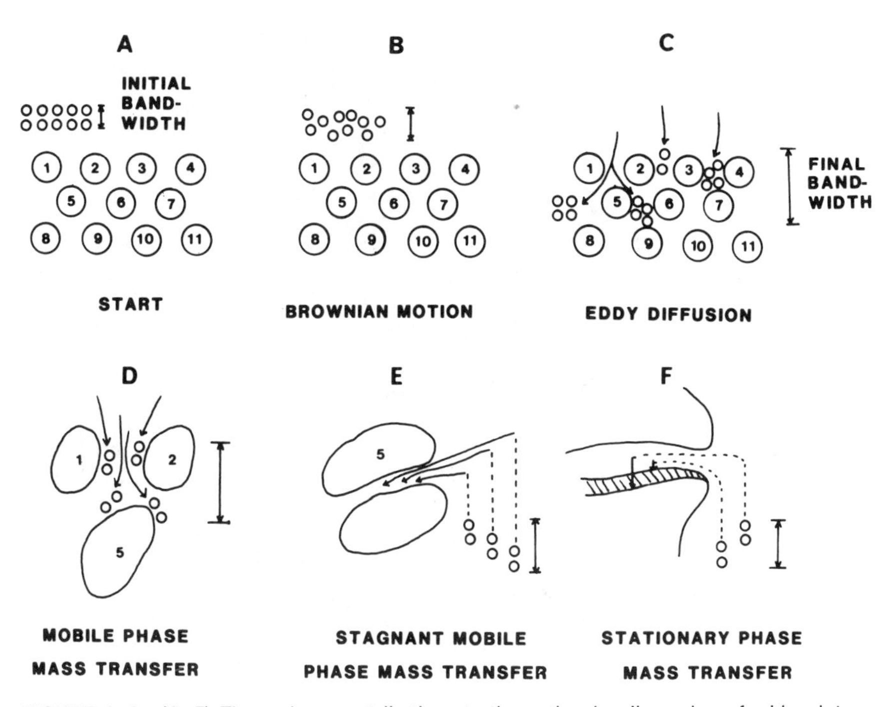

FIGURE 1–3. (A–F) The various contributions to the molecular dispersion of a biosolute following injection into a chromatographic bed packed with a porous HPLC sorbent.

sociated with achieving high efficiencies, particularly with the adsorption modes of HPLC, invariably can be traced to inadequate control over the stagnant mobile phase mass transfer, film diffusion, and stationary phase mass transfer kinetics. Since these kinetics are associated with important convective and diffusive mass transport events, improvements in the physical characteristics and surface chemistry of the sorbent are essential. The recent interest[59,60] in sorbents of very large pore diameter (e.g., porous sorbents with $P_d >$ 2000 Å) underlies one possible solution to these limitations. The so-called tentacle sorbents provide[26] an alternative solution to this problem. In the extreme case of sorbents with very large pores, convective flow conditions can in principle be employed with very high linear flow velocities without sacrificing column capacity and biosolute retention due to relatively slow adsorption kinetics.

To permit comparison of column efficiencies with columns of identical bed dimensions packed with sorbent particles of different physical or chemical characteristics, e.g., different average diameter, the height equivalent H is usually redefined in terms of the reduced plate height, h, while the linear flow velocity, u, $(= L/t_0)$, can also be redefined in terms of a reduced velocity such that

$$h = H/d_p \qquad \text{and} \qquad \nu = ud_p/D_m \tag{1–18}$$

The contributions of the various mass transport effects illustrated in Figure 1–3 that cause zone broadening have been formalized in terms of the dependency of h on ν through the well-known van Dempter–Knox equations, which take the form

$$h = A\nu^{1/3} + B/\nu + C\nu \quad (1\text{–}19)$$

where the A term expresses eddy diffusion and mobile phase mass transfer effects and is a measure of the packing quality of the chromatographic bed, the B term encompasses the longitudinal molecular diffusion effects, while the C term incorporates mass transfer resistances within the stationary phase microenvironment. With well-packed columns, operating at optimal flow rates and carefully selected elution conditions, h values approaching two to five times the particle diameter, d_p, should be realizable by most investigators. The major challenge today for very high efficiency separations of peptides, proteins, and other biomacromolecules with available HPLC packing technology remains proper control of the C term effects. The challenge here is to decrease the impact of the C term on h, either through the use of advanced nonporous sorbents, or to use sorbents that show very shallow h versus ν dependencies. In this regard sorbents capable of exhibiting no change in h over a high range of ν values, would permit very high superficial velocities to be employed. In process applications, this feature would be most attractive. The synthesis of various nonporous sorbents in the particle size range 0.7 to 2.5 μm has been achieved.[61,62] As expected, these sorbents exhibit very high efficiencies and very short analysis times.

Zone broadening of solutes in chromatographic systems arise from two causes, an intracolumn cause as discussed above, and an extracolumn cause due to the instrumentation characteristics. For this reason, it is not typically feasible to achieve the theoretical minimum h value anticipated on the basis of solely considering the chromatographic bed (or column) characteristics. Rather it is necessary to include a system (or instrumental) effect such that

$$\sigma_t^2 = \sigma_{column}^2 + \sigma_{extra}^2 \quad (1\text{–}20)$$

where σ_{column}^2 and σ_{extra}^2 are the peak variances arising due to column broadening induced by column effects and by extracolumn effects, respectively. Careful attention to extracolumn influences (choice of tubing, type of injector, design of the flow through detector cell, etc.) can reduce the impact of σ_{extra}^2 on the overall h value. With microbore HPLC, in particular, it is essential that $\sigma_{extra}^2 \ll \sigma_{column}^2$ otherwise high-speed, sensitive analysis becomes a meaningless exercise.

1.5 FACTORS THAT CONTROL PERFORMANCE

As evident from the above discussion, biosolute retention as expressed in terms of the capacity factor, k' is governed by thermodynamic considerations while zone broadening or peak dispersion, which is most conveniently expressed in terms of the reduced plate height h, arises from kinetic, time-dependent phenomena. When no secondary effects (e.g., slow chemical equilibria, pH effects, conformational changes) impinge on the chromatographic process, *resolution*, R_s, between components separated under equilibrium or near-equilibrium HPLC conditions can be expressed as

$$R_s = \frac{1}{4}\left(\frac{L}{hd_p}\right)^{1/2}(\alpha - 1)\left(\frac{1}{1 + k'}\right) \tag{1–21}$$

or

$$R_s = \frac{1}{4}(N)^{1/2}(\alpha - 1)\left(\frac{1}{1 + k'}\right) \tag{1–22}$$

The importance of Eqs. (1–21) and (1–22) resides in the linkage of the three essential parameters that dictate the quality of a chromatographic separation, namely relative retention (k'), relative selectivity (α), and the extent to which zone spreading (h) causes loss of performance. Larger values of R_s per unit time correspond to separations of higher system performances, while separations with low R_s values are a consequence of poorer system performances. Performance in HPLC separations can also be evaluated in terms of the throughput per system cost. In the analytical mode this translates to the cost per analysis while in the process mode, performance can be measured in terms of the cost of separating a kilogram of product at a predefined purity level.

As is evident from Eqs. (1–21) and (1–22), R_s can be varied by changing N (and h) or k' (and α). The power of current instrumental HPLC methods permits the investigator to implement a wide range of different conditions that very effectively and often very simply modulate k' (or α) changes. Changes in N (or h) are often (technically) much more demanding to address. To provide efficient high-resolution separations, R_s values ≥ 1 are required. Since peak broadening of adjacent zones often represents the major analytical or preparative difficulty that limits resolution and product purity, it is thus important to optimize these parameters whenever possible. Three strategies can be employed to enhance resolution, e.g., either (1) by increasing α, (2) by varying k' over an operational range such as $1<k'<10$, i.e., by ensuring the biosolute elutes in a discrete zone between 2 and 11 column volumes, or (3) by increasing N and thus decreasing h. For a particular column and flow rate, each biosolute in an analytical separation will have an optimal k' value for maximum resolution. Similar criteria apply in preparative (overload) chromatography with multicomponent mixtures. With low-molecular-weight solutes, the conventional approach to process purification has been based on linear scale-up extensions of analytical column systems that exhibit very high resolution following optimization of chromatographic selectivity and zone bandwidth. When similar methods are applied to proteins, their biological activity may be lost. In preparative approaches where subsequent biological uses are contemplated it is, as noted previously, mandatory that the design of the separation system specifically addresses the issues of recovery of bioactivity. By proper attention to the physicochemical and biological consequences of the dynamic behavior of the biosolute in bulk solution and at liquid–solid interfaces the criterion of high recovery of bioactivity can usually be satisfied.

Where conformational requirements impinge on a purification strategy then availability of other data, gained from nonchromatographic measurements, such as evaluation of biological/immunological activity profiles in response to changes in separation variables in batch experiments, is an essential prerequisite. The major challenge here is to obtain sufficient information to allow a detailed understanding of the factors controlling the stability of the biopolymer structure during the chromatographic distribution process. Table 1–3 lists a variety of factors that influence mass and bioactivity recovery as well as resolution behavior of proteins and other biomacromolecules in HPLC systems. System residency effects, the nature of the binding heterogeneity associated with the overall distribution process, the participation of enthalpic and entropic effects associated with biosolute ligand binding or permeation through the stationary phase internal surfaces are all important parameters in preparative HPLC separations. These comments are particularly relevant to proteins if these substances are to be recovered in bioactive form. If these parameters are to be adequately included in the chromatographic optimization process then clearly quantitative structure–retention relationships must be developed. Such mechanistic approaches based on stochastic models require an extensive database before adequate response function and factor design analyses can be carried out. Ultimate success of a chromatographic strategy in process applications hinges very much on the ability of the investigator to integrate response function analysis of the structure–function and structure–retention data into the overall chromatographic optimization scheme.

From a chromatographic point of view the assessment of the quality of the separation in response to changes in chromatographic variables, such as the mobile phase composition, stationary phase particle diameter, or column configuration, or, alternatively, a solute variable such as net charge or charge distribution, can be based on evaluation of the system peak capacity and system productivity in terms of bioactive mass throughput per unit time. Since the peak capacity (PC) depends on both the relative selectivity and bandwidth, i.e., for a chromatographic system with an average resolution of $R_s = 1$, the peak capacity can be defined as $PC = (t_g - t_0)/4\sigma_t$ where t_g is the solute elution

TABLE 1–3. Factors Controlling Chromatographic Resolution and Recovery of Proteins and Other Biomacromolecules

Mobile phase	Stationary phase
Organic solvents	Ligand composition
pH	Ligand density
Metal ions	Surface heterogeneity
Chaotropic reagents	Surface area
Oxidizing or reducing reagents	Pore diameter
Temperature	Pore diameter distribution
Buffer composition	Particle size
Ionic strength	Particle distribution
Loading concentration and volume	

time, t_0 is the column dead time, and σ_t the average standard deviation of the peak, then optimization of peak capacity must of necessity take into account knowledge of kinetic behavior associated with mass transport as well as conformational and other secondary chemical equilibrium processes mediated by the stationary phase surface or, alternatively, components in the mobile phase.

Biopolymer conformational interconversion associated with unfolding and refolding pathways represents a unique set of resolution challenges, which are, from both theoretical and experimental aspects, not experienced with low-molecular-weight, conformationally rigid solutes. Although at present empirical "recipe" approaches dominate most purification studies with peptides, proteins, and other biopolymers, the trend is already evident for more systematic approaches based on computer-aided analysis of retention and kinetic data in terms of different mechanistic models for biopolymer retention in high-resolution adsorption chromatography. Preliminary work on the classification of retention and kinetic data in terms of different mechanistic pathways has already been published[63] for the reversed-phase and ion-exchange HPLC of a number of enzymes and globular proteins. The ability of modern HPLC techniques to yield quantitative data on rate constants for protein folding and unfolding transitions as well as to resolve conformers with relaxation half-times of similar magnitude to the mass transport time (i.e., $\tau_{conf} \approx \tau_{mass\ transfer}$) also has important ramifications in the selection of a purification procedure.

The impact of these kinetic processes escalates rapidly in multistep purification procedures where the disastrous effect of low repetitive yields can result in unacceptable purification productivities. For example, if the average bioactivity/mass yield per step in a 10-step purification method of a particular protein was 60% (a relatively favorable situation) then the overall yield would be only 0.6%. Should the average yield per step drop to 30% due to partial denaturation, then the overall recovery would reach a disastrous value with 1024 times as much raw material needed to be processed simply to yield the same mass of purified protein.

As is evident from Table 1–3 a large variety of mobile phase and stationary phase factors can influence the chromatographic stability and recovery of proteins and other biomacromolecules. The effect of many mobile characteristics such as the nature and concentration of organic solvent or ionic additives, the temperature or the pH can be ascertained very readily from batch "test tube" pilot experiments. Similarly, the influence of many stationary phase variables, including ligand composition, ligand density, surface heterogeneity, surface area, and pore diameter distribution can be ascertained from small-scale batch experiments. However, more subtle chromatographic effects such as the influence of loading concentration on the stability of the protein, or the influence of other protein components at the solid–liquid interface are much harder at this stage of development to quantitatively anticipate.

Moreover, various investigations over the past decade have shown that the behavior of many biosolutes in static batch systems can vary significantly from that observed in dynamic systems as usually employed in column chromatography. This behavior is not only related to issues of different accessibility[3,8,16,17,26,64–66] of the biosolute to the stationary phase surface area but also involves the complex relationships present with multicomponent systems where nonlinear effects[3,8,17,28–30,41] influence the diffusion and adsorption kinetics of the overall mass transport phenomenon. All of these effects impact on the loading capacity of a particular sorbent, which can exhibit subtly different properties for different classes of biosolutes. Various studies[3,8,65,66] have documented such behavior for enzymes and other proteins. For example, when conformational reordering of a protein structure occurs in both the mobile phase and stationary phase,[13–19] this will lead to multizoning of the component into active and/or inactive zones, the abundance of which will be time, concentration, and temperature dependent.

Other phenomena, besides conformational processes, can also lead to multizoning of a biopolymer with adsorptive chromatographic stationary phases. Probably the easiest of these phenomena to identify and remedy is the so-called "split peak breakthrough" effect, very often seen in affinity chromatography and to lesser extent in the ion-exchange and hydrophobic interaction HPLC of proteins.[67–69] This effect is manifested as a nonretained (or weakly retained) peak and a retained peak with the bound-to-free ratio dependent on the solute's diffusion kinetics and adsorption kinetics. The amount of protein in the breakthrough zone is influenced by the flow rate, stationary phase nominal pore diameter and ligand density, and the injection volume. This effect can be circumvented by the choice of a lower flow rate, the selection of stationary phases with better surface area–ligand accessibility characteristics for the particular protein (or biopolymer) of interest, and more appropriate loading volumes and concentrations. A further type of multizoning phenomenon is associated with nonlinear isotherm behavior due to matrix heterogeneity and nonuniformity of the ligand distribution over the stationary phase surface. This effect is most noticeable between "virgin" and "conditioned" columns and can be problematic during the first few cycles of use of a particular column at preparative loadings. At the micropreparative level this effect can lead to catastrophic results where irreproducible recoveries may occur. Other forms of multizoning, associated with slow aggregation and self-assembly equilibria between the monomeric forms of the protein and high oligomers, also are known[15,21,70,71] to significantly affect resolution and recovery.

Since multiple chromatographic steps are the norm in biopolymer purification strategies, the stage at which a particular chromatographic selectivity mode is introduced requires careful planning. Previous experience with the systematic optimization or resolution for low-molecular-weight solutes based on the solvent selectivity triangle concept[7,8] can be used as the basis for a multistep chromatographic approach with single column or multicolumn systems.

Importantly, these approaches offer considerable potential for the optimization of resolution of very complex mixtures of proteins and other biopolymers using the same stationary phase operating under different elution conditions. Such methods have been widely used as multidimensional techniques in reversed-phase HPLC of peptides and proteins for a number of years. Integral to these RP-HPLC approaches have been the application of mobile phases of different composition, notably different ion-pairing systems.[32–34,51,52,61,62,72–74] Similar procedures are equally pertinent to ion-exchange and hydrophobic interaction HPLC separations using displacing ions of different solvated radii and electronegativities.[20,45,49,53–55,75–81]

One avenue of current research that offers considerable versatility in preparative applications with tandem columns is the so-called "positive–negative" adsorption mode. In this stratagem, the chemical characteristics of the immobilized ligand are selected so that components of interest are either adsorbed very strongly, i.e., large K_{assoc}, or not absorbed, i.e., elute in the breakthrough, by sequential or tandem columns. Such approaches are particularly suited to group-specific affinity, metal chelate systems, and also form the basis of some of the immobilized dye affinity approaches. Typical of this approach has been the integration by my co-workers[82] of dye affinity and ion-exchange methods as positive–negative modes into automated protocols for the preparation of immunoglobulins from Cohn fractions, which has led to the development of general stratagems for the purification of other plasma proteins. With such methods the effective peak capacity may be relatively modest, e.g., only between 2 and 10 per stage. However, intercalation of batch methods with gradient elution techniques, where peak capacities in excess of 200 can be realized, has many desirable features for biopolymer fractionation. Tandem batch methods when used at the initial stages of purification scheme may also improve overall recoveries because of the early removal of contaminants. Because greatly decreased protein masses are loaded onto chromatographic beds following batch fractionation, their use also allows substantially higher peak capacities to be achieved at subsequent chromatographic stages. Such batch methods can be readily incorporated into a purification strategy using both chemically modified silica-based sorbents as well as with polymer-based sorbents.

Whether a particular stationary phase functions in a single elution mode is clearly not an essential requirement for its successful application in high-resolution chromatographic analysis or preparative purification of biomacromolecules. The logical extension of mixed mode (multimodal) interactions is, of course, the design of chemical ligands that mimic biospecific chromatography and its immunological counterpart, immunoaffinity chromatography. With such ligands, computer modeling methods[83] can be employed to replicate the composite interplay of coulombic, hydrogen bonding, and hydrophobic forces that determine the magnitude and nature of the association and dissociation phenomena. As currently manufactured, all micro- and mesoparticulate chromatographic media, irrespective of the nature of the ligand or the chemical functionality of the matrix, exhibit separation features characterized by these composite phenomena. Biomolecular modeling and computer graphic procedures can be expected to play an increasing role in sorbent design during the next decade, thus expanding the range of selectivities available.

1.6 SCALING-UP: A HEURISTIC APPROACH

In all chromatographic work the first and arguably the most important step is the choice of an appropriate sorbent material. Since the result of a chromatographic process can never be better than the selectivity that the sorbent allows, it is very important that the mass transport characteristics established between the biosolute, the eluent, and the bed material must be maintained if at all possible as the scale is increased from the analytical to the process level. The choice of appropriate sorbent materials and the optimization of the basic operating conditions have traditionally been made by laboratory trials prior to scale-up. The key questions that thus have to be addressed in scale-up go to the core of process synthesis and the design of a purification strategy. To answer these questions and solve the problems inherent to the synthesis of optimal separation trains, rapid methods to screen alternative pathways are required. These rules—called *heuristics*—are based on scientific intuition, experience, and common sense. Heuristic methods for the synthesis of a separation train and the subsequent scale-up of the process can be subdivided according to whether the rules are based on separation constraints, e.g., the physicochemical characteristics of the system, or on mass or volume constraints, e.g., the quantities of the material to be processed. The advantage of heuristic approaches is that they allow alternative unit operations to be contrasted, potential design conflicts identified, and deficiency areas of knowledge highlighted as limitations that require short- or long-term investigation. Arising out of heuristic approaches, which have their origins in industrial distillation, the following rules can be proposed for the fractionation of biopolymers by HPLC procedures:

1. Choose separation processes based on different physical, chemical, or biochemical properties that are synergistic, i.e., hydrophobic interaction chromatography after ion-exchange chromatography; biomimetic chromatography before biospecific affinity chromatography, etc.
2. Choose those processes that exploit the largest differences in the physicochemical properties of the products and impurities in the most economical manner.
3. Separate out the most plentiful impurities first using the positive–negative strategy.
4. Use a high-resolution step as soon as possible. This is in accord with the "use of the minimum number of separation steps" rule, which anticipates that product yields decline exponentially.
5. Perform the most expensive step last.

An advantage of heuristic approaches is their ability to thus reconcile theory with practice. In addition, heuristic approaches allow qualitative information to be either directly and indirectly used to establish more specific rules that anticipate more quantitatively the design requirements of the large-scale purification process. For example, according to theory, optimum resolution is expected when a sorbent with the smallest possible average particle size is used. Especially in large-scale chromatography, the choice of particle size is, however, more governed by the necessity to use high and constant flow rates. With soft chromatographic materials, these conditions will lead to particle deformation even at relatively low hydrodynamic pressures. How can these conflicts be reconciled? With rigid particles, such as silica-based sorbents, the relationship between the obtained pressure drop and the flow rate is linear and inversely proportional to the square of the particle size, that is

$$\Delta p = \frac{\mu_0 h L}{\epsilon_0 d_p^2} \quad (1\text{–}23)$$

where Δp is the pressure drop over the bed, μ_0 the linear velocity of the eluent, η the eluent viscosity, L the bed height, ϵ_0 the specific permeability of the column (typically 1×10^{-3}–1.3×10^{-3}), and d_p the average particle diameter. For nonrigid or deformable particles, like the soft polysaccharide gels, the observed pressure drop relationship is logarithmic rather than linear and is a function of the bed height and diameter as well as the water regain of the gel. The following empirical equation has been found to fit best with the experimental data:

$$\Delta p = \frac{L}{a} \ln(k_0/k) \tag{1–24}$$

where a is a function of the bed height and diameter and the gel solvent regain. The decision to use a sorbent based on silica versus a polysaccharide or other organic polymer will thus hinge on the prioritization list of the designer of the process, e.g., whether the constraint is time, cost, mass throughput, or pressure drop. Similarly, when using rigid particles, the finest grade possible should be used considering the pressure limits of the whole chromatography system. In practice, however, there may be very little choice for economic reasons and particles of broader distribution will be used. When using nonrigid particles the limiting parameter is the particle size. This choice will compromise the limits of the inlet pressure to a value that must be exceeded by the maximum operational flow velocity otherwise catastrophic collapse of the bed may ensue. Again, the choice of particle size can be made on the basis of the heuristic criteria. For example, in any chromatographic column, the force that is exerted on the lowest part of the bed is the sum of the weight of the packing material, and the drag force acting on it, minus the friction force of the column wall. The tendency for deformation of the nonrigid gel materials, conventionally used in protein chromatography until recently, decreases with decreasing bed height of the column. Consequently, "pancake" columns of large width-to-depth aspect ratio will be favored. However, even in this column configuration a sudden increase in hydrostatic pressure can lead with soft gel sorbents to bed compression and a drop in flow rate, which may be reversible within some pressure limit range but usually results in bed hysteresis. Subsequent operational cycles of the column will show different capacity and resolution characteristics as a consequence. This effect is apparent even with very short columns and is very noticeable with non-cross-linked wide pore organic or polysaccharide polymer-based gels. In contrast, column configuration is not as critical a consideration with pressure stable sorbents, and other criteria, e.g., the cost, biocompatibility, regenerability, sterilizability, come under scrutiny. Even in this case, the choice of column configuration can be made on the basis of a set of heuristic rules where the process design priority is dictated by whether the process task hinges on the ease of the separation, the volume of feed stock to be processed, the complexity of contaminants, or the need for aseptic operational conditions.

There are clearly several practical criteria that have to be taken into account when choosing the most suitable column packing material for a specific chromatographic process. Since the aim is to achieve a cost-effective preparative separation of a complex biological mixture with high mass recovery and maintenance of biological activity considerable effort has been devoted to the selection of the most appropriate sorbent for the process. Clearly, the process design should contemporaneously establish conditions that allow high resolution and short separation times. Does it follow then that sorbents with the highest ligand densities will provide the highest throughput, assuming that other features, such as good pressure stability, compatibility with industrial sterilization methods, etc. are satisfied? A number of academic and industrial research groups have addressed this issue through the preparation of tailor-made sorbents based on various soft gels, such as agarose, dextrans, polyacrylamide or trishydroxymethylpolyacrylamide resins, or on rigid sorbents such as the chemically modified silicas as well as the new polymer-based supports, e.g., polystyrene–divinyl benzene sorbents. It is clear from these studies that sorbents with the highest ligand density are not synonymous with sorbents that achieve maximal throughput. For example, various studies[3,64,66] have shown that there is little to be gained by attempting to immobilize saturation levels of antibodies onto porous supports to generate very high-density immunoaffinity sorbents. Similar observations have been made[8,16,32,74,80,84–86] with reversed-phase, triazine dye, and biospecific sorbents for polypeptide and enzyme purification. Again, heuristic criteria can be used to aid the design selection.

In preparative chromatography, methods to determine the relationship between mass loadability and productivity, i.e., the product throughput in terms of grams (or kilograms) per cycle per currency unit per unit time, are highly relevant. The early recognition of unacceptable system effects associated with time-dependent denaturation or degradation of the protein in question or arising from secondary equilibria such as protein aggregation will also have an important impact on the outcome of a purification approach. Although some proteolytic degradation can be minimized by the use of generic inhibitors for serine or thiol proteases, such procedures may not achieve the inhibition of much more specific degradative enzymes. Such specific enzymes are often present in trace amounts and packaged as copurifying cell debris, lipid membrane micelles, or adsorptively bound to the protein of interest. Careful inspection of the analytical data generated during the purification stratagem, e.g., objective assessment of the SDS–PAGE or analytical HPLC data, can, however, give early warning of such difficulties and suggest likely remedies. For example, the use[8,87] of the multiple "tea bag" affinity chromatographic approach for the removal of cell proteases, antitoxins, nucleic acid fragments, or particles can be particularly effective at the initial stages of procedures involving scale-up. Such application choices flow directly from the application of the heuristic rule 4.

Extension of these heuristic approaches into knowledge-based algorithmic procedures is one of the avenues from which computer intuitive methods for the modelling of scale-up requirements will evolve. Subsequent stages of these developments may lead to so-called expert computer driven systems[91–95] capable of controlling on-line process streams. To be effective, such expert systems would have to exploit advances in chemometrics, multicomponent error function analysis, principal component analysis, as well as the more mundane issues of system monitoring, and control loop feedback. Substantially enlarged databases on biopolymer adsorption behavior will be required to achieve these ends. Collation and classification of the existing knowledge base, arising largely from empirical applications, will in its own right be a formidable undertaking—

worthy of an international cooperative effort. Although such an undertaking may not engender a similar presence in the popular press as, for example, the human genone project, the practical consequences of such research initiative would be of enormous benefit to industry and academe, linking together essential threads of research and development in the life sciences. The ability of scientists to develop and adapt HPLC procedures over the next decade into knowledge-based systems will certainly sustain HPLC in its current dominant position in the biochemical separation sciences.

1.7 SUMMARY

In this chapter, an overview of the current status and future challenges of HPLC techniques for biopolymer analysis and purification is given. A didactic approach to these important issues was purposely taken. As a consequence, this chapter has not introduced a detailed exposé of the theoretical basis of HPLC operating under linear and nonlinear conditions in the analytical or the overload situation. Nor has this chapter embarked on a detailed discussion on the ways biochemical engineering, computer science, and industrial process development interface with HPLC capabilities. To examine these issues, the interested reader is referred elsewhere, in this volume and other recent publications and books.[3,4–7,20,28–30,35–39,41,53,57,58,83,96–98] Rather, this chapter has attempted to provide for our biological colleagues an introduction to the principles, terms, and concepts that are central to current HPLC research and development.

The success of an analytical or preparative chromatographic strategy is predicated on the ease of resolving to a predefined level the desired component from other substances, many of which may exhibit similar separation selectivities, but are usually present at different abundance levels. For high-resolution purification procedures to be carried out efficiently, it is self-evident that rapid, multistage, high recovery methods must be utilized. To minimize losses and improve productivity, on-line evaluation of each of the recovery stages is an important objective. Furthermore, overall optimization and automation of the individual unit operations must be achieved. Similar criteria but with different end points apply in high-resolution analytical application.

For these steps to be properly integrated, detailed assessment of the fractionation data using computer-aided methods for factor analysis are (ideally) required at each stage. This knowledge provides the essential insight into the atomic and molecular basis of the separation selectivity and biorecovery contours of the preparative and/or analytical procedures. The development and application of new generations of on-line detectors capable of monitoring these structure–function–retention characteristics of biopolymers represent a pressing challenge for spectroscopists and chromatographic scientists. Already prototype instrumentation is available for on-line laser-activated light scattering (LALS), optical rotary dispersion (ORD), enhanced laser fluorescence (ELF), and laser raman spectroscopy (LARS) for use in the analytical modes of HPLC of biopolymers. The next decade will certainly witness further significant developments in this area.

If the progress of the past decade is any prognostic indicator, further significant development in sorbent design and their use in high-resolution chromatographic analysis and preparative isolation of bioproducts will be a hallmark of the next decade. These developments will be driven in part by the public and government perception of the requirements of product purity and quality, by underlying commercial considerations of greater efficiency and reproducibility in process purification, and also by the lay curiosity and scientific inquisitiveness of researchers themselves. To a significant extent, the "winners" in modern biotechnology have up to now been the industry sector servicing and manufacturing the equipment and chromatographic supplies used by the processors and manufacturers of bioproducts. All the indicators suggest this pattern will persist, thus ensuring further novel chromatographic products and procedures to tantalize and assist the researcher, the engineer, or the business executive in the biotechnological, pharmaceutical, food, chemical, and environmental industries, well into the twenty-first century.

ACKNOWLEDGMENTS

The support of the Australian Research Council, the National Health and Medical Research Council of Australia, and the Monash University Research Foundation is gratefully acknowledged.

REFERENCES

1. O. Lowry, *Annu. Rev. Biochem.*, 59 (1990) 1.
2. J. C. Janson, in Affinity Chromatography and Related Techniques (T. C. J. Gribnau, J. Visser, and R. J. F. Nivard, eds.). Elsevier, Amsterdam, 1983, pp. 503–520.
3. A. Johnston and M. T. W. Hearn, *J. Chromatogr.*, (1991) in press.
4. P. J. Schoenmakers, in Optimisation of Chromatographic Selectivity. Elsevier, Amsterdam, 1986, pp. 1–333.
5. J. C. Berridge, in Techniques for Automated Optimisation of HPLC Separations. Wiley, Chichester, 1985, pp. 1–267.
6. L. R. Snyder, J. L. Glagch, and J. J. Kirkland, Practical HPLC Method Development, Wiley, New York, 1989, pp. 1–40.
7. M. T. W. Hearn, in Chemical Separations (J. Navratil and C. T. King, eds.). Litarvan Press, 1986, pp. 71–88.
8. M. T. W. Hearn, in Protein Purification, Principles, High Resolution, Methods and Applications (J-C. Janson and L. Ryden, eds.). VCH Press, New York, 1990, pp. 175–206.
9. Snyder, High Performance Liquid Chromatography: Advances and Perspectives, Vol. 1 (Cs. Horvath, ed.). Academic Press, New York, 1980, pp. 208–356.
10. W. R. Melander and Cs. Horvath, High Performance Liquid Chromatography: Advances and Perspectives, Vol. 2 (Cs. Horvath, ed.). Academic Press, New York, 1980, pp. 114–319.
11. F. E. Regnier, *Science*, 238 (1987) 319.

12. T. A. Horbett and H. L. Brash, in Proteins at Interfaces: Physicochemical Aspects and Biochemical studies (J. L. Brash and T. A. Horbett, eds.). American Chemical Society, Washington, D.C., 1987, pp. 1–135.
13. B. L. Karger and R. Blanco, in Proteins, Structure, Folding and Design (T. W. Hutchens, ed.). Alan R. Liss, New York, 1989, pp. 141–146.
14. J. D. Andrade, in Surface and Interfacial Aspects of Biomedical Polymers, Vol. 2 (J. D. Andrade, ed.). Plenum, New York, 1985, pp. 1–62.
15. M. T. W. Hearn, A. N. Hodder, and M. I. Aguilar, *J. Chromatogr.*, 327 (1983) 47.
16. H. J. Wirth, K. K. Unger, and M. T. W. Hearn, *J. Chromatogr.*, 525 (1990), in press.
17. A. Johnston and M. T. W. Hearn, *J. Chromatogr.*, 512 (1990) 101.
18. K. Benedek, S. Dong, and B. L. Karger, *J. Chromatogr.*, 317 (1984) 227.
19. S. L. Wu, A. Figueroa, and B. L. Karger, *J. Chromatogr.*, 371 (1986) 227.
20. A. Hodder, K. J. Machin, M. I. Aguilar, and M. T. W. Hearn, *J. Chromatogr.*, 507 (1990) 33.
21. P. Oroszlan, R. Blanco, X-M Lu, D. Yarmush, and B. L. Karger, *J. Chromatogr.*, 500 (1990) 481.
22. M. Fridman, M. I. Aguilar, and M. T. W. Hearn, *J. Chromatogr.*, 512 (1990) 57.
23. J. D. Andrade and V. Hlady, *Adv. Polym. Sci.* 79 (1986) 1.
24. K. K. Unger, in Chromatographic Techniques, Dekker, New York, 1989, pp. 1–605.
25. V. A. Davankov, A. A. Kurganov, and K. K. Unger, *J. Chromatogr.*, 500 (1990) 519.
26. R. Janzen, K. K. Unger, W. Muller, and M. T. W. Hearn, *J. Chromatogr.*, 522 (1990) 77.
27. K. K. Unger, R. Janzen, and G. Jilge, *Chromatographia*, 24 (1987) 144.
28. B. Lin, Z. Ma, S. Golshan-Shirazi, and G. Guiochon, *J. Chromatogr.*, 500 (1990) 1875.
29. Q. Mao and M. T. W. Hearn, *J. Chromatogr.*, (1990), in press.
30. Q. Yu and N. J. L. Wang, *Computers Chem. Engrg.*, 13 (1989) 915.
31. M. T. W. Hearn, A. N. Hodder, P. G. Stanton, and M. I. Aguilar, *Chromatographia*, 24 (1987) 769.
32. M. T. W. Hearn, in High Performance Liquid Chromatography: Advances and Perspectives, Vol. 3. (Cs. Horvath, ed.). Academic Press, New York, 1983, pp. 87–155.
33. M. T. W. Hearn and M. I. Aguilar, in Modern Physical Methods in Biochemistry (A. Neuberger and L. L. M. van Deenen, eds.). Elsevier, Amsterdam, 1988, pp. 107–142.
34. R. J. Simpson, R. L. Moritz, E. C. Nice, and B. Grego, *Eur. J. Biochem.* 165 (1987) 21.
35. M. Wilce, M. I. Aguilar, and M. T. W. Hearn, *J. Chromatogr.*, (1991), in press.
36. M. T. W. Hearn, M. I. Aguilar, and M. Wilce, *Biochemistry*, (1991), in press.
37. E. Grushka, Preparative Scale Chromatography. Dekker, New York, 1989, pp. 1–324.
38. R. W. Rousseau, Handbook of Separation Process Technology. Wiley, New York, 1987, pp. 1–1010.
39. J. F. P. Hamel, J. B. Hunter, and S. K. Sikdar, Downstream Processing and Bioseparation. American Chemical Society, Washington, D.C., 1990, pp. 1–312.
40. J. Frenz and Cs. Horvath, in High Performance Liquid Chromatography: Advances and Persectives, Vol. 5 (Cs. Horvath, ed.). Academic Press, San Diego, 1988, pp. 212–314.
41. S. Golshan-Shirazi and G. Guiochon, *J. Chromatogr.*, 506 (1990) 495.
42. P. J. Schoenmakers, A. Peeters, and R. J. Lynch, *J. Chromatogr.*, 506 (1990) 45.
43. H. Poppe, *J. Chromatogr.*, 506 (1990) 45.
44. W. W. Yau, J. J. Kirkland, and D. D. Bly, Modern Size Exclusion Liquid Chromatography. Wiley-Interscience, New York, 1979, pp. 1–405.
45. A. N. Hodder, M. I. Aguilar, and M. T. W. Hearn, *J. Chromatogr.*, 512 (1990) 41.
46. X. Geng, L. Guo, and J. Chang, *J. Chromatogr.*, 507 (1990) 1.
47. S. Xamamoto, M. Nomura, and Y. Sano, *J. Chromatogr.*, 512 (1990) 77.
48. G. Stegeman, R. Oostervink, J. C. Kraak, H. Poppe, and K. K. Unger, *J. Chromatogr.*, 506 (1990) 547.

49. W. R. Melander, D. Corradini, and Cs. Horvath, *J. Chromatogr.*, 317 (1984) 67.
50. J. H. Knox and H. M. Pyper, *J. Chromatogr.*, 363 (1986) 1.
51. M. Wilce, M. I. Aguilar, and M. T. W. Hearn, *J. Chromatogr.*, 536 (1990) 165.
52. C. T. Mant and R. S. Hodges, in Separation, Analysis and Conformation of Peptides and Proteins (C. T. Mant and R. S. Hodges, eds.). CRC Press, Boca Raton, 1990, in press.
53. M. T. W. Hearn, A. N. Hodder, K. J. Machin, and M. I. Aguilar, *J. Chromatogr.*, 517 (1990) 317.
54. S. Yamamoto, K. Nakanishi, and R. Matsuno, Ion Exchange Chromatography of Proteins. Dekker, New York, 1988, pp. 1–467.
55. A. N. Hodder, M. T. W. Hearn, and M. I. Aguilar, *J. Chromatogr.*, 458 (1988) 27.
56. M. A. Stadalius, H. S. Gold, and L. R. Snyder, *J. Chromatogr.*, 296 (1984) 3.
57. P. Jandera and J. Churacek, in Gradient Elution in Column Liquid Chromatography. Elsevier, Amsterdam, 1985, pp. 1–410.
58. L. R. Snyder, G. B. Cox, and P. E. Antle, *J. Chromatogr.*, 24 (1987) 82.
59. S. Hjetten, *J. Chromatogr.*, (1990), in press.
60. F. E. Regnier, *J. Chromatogr.*, (1990), in press.
61. R. Janzen, K. K. Unger, H. Geische, J. N. Kinchel, and M. T. W. Hearn, *J. Chromatogr.*, 397 (1987) 91.
62. N. F. Maa and Cs. Horvath, *J. Chromatogr.*, 445 (1988) 71.
63. M. T. W. Hearn and B. Anspach, in Separation Processes in Biotechnology (J. A. Asenjo, ed.). Dekker, New York, 1990, pp. 17–64.
64. J. W. Eveleigh and D. E. Levy, *J. Solid Phase Biochem.*, 2 (1977) 67.
65. M. T. W. Hearn, *J. Chromatogr.*, 376 (1986) 245.
66. M. T. W. Hearn and J. R. Davies, *J. Chromatogr.*, 512 (1990) 23.
67. D. S. Hage, R. R. Walters, and H. W. Heathcote, *Anal. Chem.*, 58 (1986) 274.
68. P. J. Hogg and D. J. Winzor, *Arch. Biochem. Biophys.*, 240 (1985) 70.
69. F. L. de Vos, D. M. Robertson, and M. T. W. Hearn, *J. Chromatogr.*, 392 (1987) 17.
70. H. P. Jennisen, in Surface and Interfacial Aspects of Biomedical Polymers, Vol. 2 (J. D. Andrade, ed.). Plenum, New York, 1985, pp. 295–319.
71. K. Benedek, S. Dong, and B. L. Karger, *J. Chromatogr.*, 317 (1984) 227.
72. M. T. W. Hearn, in Ion Pair Chromatography (M. T. W. Hearn, ed.). Dekker, New York, 1985, pp. 1–294.
73. W. S. Hancock, in CRC Handbook of HPLC for the Separation of Amino Acids, Peptides and Proteins (W. S. Hancock, ed.). CRC Press, Boca Raton, FL, 1984, pp. 1–605.
74. M. T. W. Hearn, *Adv. Chromatogr.*, 20 (1982) 1.
75. M. T. W. Hearn, A. N. Hodder, and M. I. Aguilar, *J. Chromatogr.*, 443 (1988) 97.
76. M. T. W. Hearn, A. N. Hodder, and M. I. Aguilar, *J. Chromatogr.*, 458 (1988) 45.
77. A. N. Hodder, M. I. Aguilar, and M. T. W. Hearn, *J. Chromatogr.*, 476 (1989) 113.
78. A. N. Hodder, M. I. Aguilar, and M. T. W. Hearn, *J. Chromatogr.*, 506 (1990) 17.
79. W. R. Melander and Cs. Horvath, *Arch. Biochem. Biophys.*, 183 (1977) 200.
80. F. E. Regnier and I. Mazsaroff, *Biotechnol. Prog.*, 3 (1987) 22.
81. J. L. Fausnaugh and F. E. Regnier, *J. Chromatogr.*, 359 (1986) 131.
82. M. T. W. Hearn and J. R. Davies, patent pending.
83. I. Cosic and M. T. W. Hearn, *Eur. J. Biochem.*, (1990), in press.
84. I. Mazsaroff, S. Cook, and F. E. Regnier, *J. Chromatogr.*, 443 (1988) 119.
85. M. T. W. Hearn, H. J. Wirth, Q. Mao, and K. K. Unger, *J. Chromatogr.*, in press.
86. M. T. W. Hearn and B. Grego, *J. Chromatogr.*, 282 (1983) 541.
87. B. Evsson, L. Ryden, and J. C. Janson, in Protein Purification, Principles, High Resolution, Methods and Applications (J. C. Janson and L. Ryden, eds.). VCH Press, New York, 1989, pp. 1–32.
88. G. Leaver, J. R. Conder, and J. A. Howell, in Preparative Scale Chromatography (E. Grushka, ed.). Dekker, New York, 1989, pp. 245–267.
89. R. J. Simpson and R. L. Moritz, *J. Chromatogr.*, 474 (1989) 418.

90. R. J. Simpson, L. D. Ward, G. E. Reid, M. P. Batterham, and R. L. Moritz, *J. Chromatogr.*, 476 (1989) 345.
91. R. N. S. Rathore, K. A. Van Wormer, and G. J. Powers, *AIChE J.*, 20 (1974) 491.
92. M. A. Duran and I. E. Grossmann, *AIChE J.*, 32 (1986) 592.
93. J. A. Asenjo, L. Herrera, and B. Byrne, *J. Biotechnol.*, 11 (1989) 275.
94. A. C. Kenney and D. J. Wormald, *Am. Lab.*, (1988) 82–84.
95. A. Nishida, G. Stephanopoulos, and A. W. Westerberg, *AIChE J.*, 27 (1981) 321.
96. M. R. Ladish, R. C. Willson, C. C. Painton, and S. E. Builder, eds., Protein Purification from Molecular Mechanism to Large Scale Processes. ACS Symposium Series No. 427, Washington, D.C., 1990, pp. 1–288.
97. S. Stein, (ed.), Fundamentals of Protein Biotechnology, Vol. 7. Dekker, New York, 1990, pp. 1–620.
98. Cs. Horvath and J. G. Nikelly, eds., Analytical Biotechnology. ACS Symposium Series No. 434. Washington, D.C., 1990, pp. 1–218.

CHAPTER 2

Sample Presentation and Column Hygiene

C. Timothy Wehr

CONTENTS

2.1 INTRODUCTION

In the design of cost-effective separation methods, achieving good chromatographic performance, rapid sample throughput, and minimum equipment downtime requires proper sample preparation and column maintenance. Best column performance will be obtained only when the sample is introduced in a suitable form, and in worst cases inadequate sample preparation leads to equipment failure and reduced column lifetimes. For "clean" samples, e.g., relatively pure polypeptides, preparation may include simple procedures such as filtration, concentration, or dilution. However, high-performance liquid chromatographic (HPLC) methods are increasingly used early in purification schemes where complex samples require more sophisticated manipulations. Here, sample preparation can be the most time-consuming and labor-intensive element of the purification process. Hence, sample handling techniques that lend themselves to automation are highly desirable in manufacturing environments. Of equal importance in achieving good chromatographic performance and day-to-day reliability are adequate procedures for column protection, preventive maintenance, and regeneration. This chapter reviews the commonly used methods and devices for sample preparation in protein chromatography, and procedures for ensuring maximum performance and lifetime for the packings currently employed for protein separations.

2.2 SAMPLE PREPARATION

Table 2–1 summarizes some of the typical operations in preparing a sample for injection onto a high-performance LC column. Traditional methodologies for these operations are laborious and often provide poor recovery. Fortunately, improved procedures are available for most steps that are rapid, simple, and improve yields. In many cases commercial products are available for parallel processing of multiple samples. In certain cases, sample processing devices are available that perform one or more of these operations on-line as part of an automated chromatographic method.

TABLE 2–1. Objectives in Sample Preparation

Sample extraction and prefractionation
Removal of contaminants
Solubilization
Detergent removal
Desalting
Concentration
Dilution
Removal of particulates

2.2.1 Prefractionation

The objectives of sample prefractionation are 2-fold. First, the target class of polypeptides can be separated from unwanted protein, or a complex protein mixture can be fractionated into subclasses for separate processing. The goal is to simplify the separation task such that it is within the peak capacity of available HPLC columns. Second, sample prefractionation can serve to remove protein or nonprotein material that would bind irreversibly to the stationary phase, changing column selectivity or otherwise degrading chromatographic performance. The common sample prefractionation techniques are listed in Table 2–2.

2.2.1.1 Liquid Extraction

Liquid extraction can be used in cases in which very hydrophobic proteins or protein aggregates are soluble only in organic solvents or aqueous organic solvent mixtures. A single solvent extraction can be used to obtain the desired protein or protein class, or a series of extractions with different organic solvents or aqueous organic mixtures can be employed to effect class separations based on solubility. This approach is often used for fractionation of very hydrophobic membrane proteins and structural proteins. For example, the four major classes of cereal proteins (albumins, globulins, prolamines, and glutelins) can be sequentially extracted with water, dilute salt, and ethanol:water.[1] Similarly, the four small subunits of yeast cytochrome *c* oxidase (a seven-subunit oligomeric membrane protein) have been selectively extracted from the holoenzyme with 60:40 water:acetonitrile followed by 50:25:25 water:acetonitrile:isopropanol.[2]

2.2.1.2 Solid-Phase Batch Extraction

Batch extraction with solid-phase sorbents has been used for purification of small proteins and peptides such as immunomodulator peptides from crude mixtures. The technique is inexpensive, can be applied to large volumes, and

TABLE 2–2. Prefractionation Techniques

Liquid extraction
Solid-phase batch extraction
Solid-phase cartridge extraction

is amenable to handling of viscous samples that would plug solid-phase cartridges or analytical HPLC columns. The steps in batch extraction are listed in Table 2–3. As with all sorbent extraction techniques, the selected sorbent must first be conditioned with a suitable solvent to wet the phase (methanol is commonly used for bonded-phase sorbents, hexane for silica sorbents). The conditioned sorbent is then mixed with the sample and polypeptides are allowed to bind to the solid phase. This may require several hours and is typically done with gentle stirring in the cold. Characteristically, low-molecular-weight species (e.g., peptides less than 40,000 AMU) bind more tightly than large species. Binding can be followed with one or more extraction steps with suitable solvents (e.g., aqueous salt solutions, aqueous organic solvent mixtures). Final elution of the desired polypeptide can be achieved batchwise in a small volume of a strong eluent. Alternatively, the sorbent can be packed into a column and the desired peptide eluted in a very small volume with step or gradient elution. Solid-phase batch extraction has been applied to purification of human immune interferon,[3] gibbon interleukin-2,[4] and murine B cell stimulatory factor.[5]

2.2.1.3 Solid-Phase Cartridge Extraction

Solid-phase extraction employing fully porous microparticulate silica or silicas with covalently bonded stationary phases has been used in the analysis of low-molecular-weight compounds in clinical, environmental, and food/agricultural samples for over a decade. Typically, up to a few hundred milligrams of 20- to 50-μm porous silica is packed into a minicolumn or syringe barrel, or sealed in a plastic cartridge that can be fitted to a tuberculin or Luer-lock-type syringe. Sample application, extraction, and elution are achieved by passage of liquids through the cartridge bed by positive pressure or vacuum applied to the cartridge outlet. The advantage of solid-phase extraction is the wide variety of commercially available sorbents and cartridge types, permitting selection of the appropriate phase for a particular sample preparation problem. Also, vacuum and pressure manifolds are available for simultaneous processing of multiple samples.[6,7] Rapid solid-phase cartridge fractionation is advantageous for recovery of bioactive peptides or intermediates in peptide metabolism, which might be lost or degraded in more extensive isolation procedures.

The steps in solid-phase cartridge extraction are the same as those listed in Table 2–3 for batch extraction. The choice of the sorbent is dependent on the nature of the fractionation desired. Compounds may be discriminated on the basis of charge using weak or strong cation- or anion-exchange sorbents. Similarly, retention and elution based on relative surface hydrophobicities are accomplished using one of a variety of alkyl, aromatic, or nitrile phases. Some

TABLE 2–3. Steps in Solid-Phase Extraction

Steps
Sorbent selection
Sorbent conditioning
Sample binding
Extraction of interferences
Sample elution

of the commercially available sorbents are shown in Table 2–4, with sorbents in each class listed in order of decreasing retentiveness.[8]

Approaches to developing a solid-phase sample cleanup method have been defined for low-molecular-weight compounds such as therapeutic drugs,[8] and the principles should be generally applicable to polypeptides except as noted. It is appropriate to begin development of the extraction procedure with the analytical chromatographic method (column, mobile phase, gradient parameters, etc.) in hand so that the effectiveness of the extraction method can be determined. The first step is to decide on the general cleanup strategy (e.g., selective retention of sample and removal of interferences, or selective retention of interferences), and to compile all available information about the sample and matrix. At this point any constraints dictated by the sample chemistry or HPLC method on the extraction method should be identified. These might include the desired final sample concentration and volume, or the desired final solvent composition (e.g., pH, ionic strength, organic modifier concentration, volatility). Chromatographic data on the sample are useful in predicting the behavior of the sample in solid-phase extraction. It is desirable that the final sample volume be small (a minimum of two bed volumes is generally required to elute sample from the sorbent) and that the sample solvent be of weak eluent strength relative to the HPLC mobile phase.

The next step is selection of the appropriate sorbent. The variety of amino acid side chain groups provides opportunity for selective interaction based on polar, nonpolar, aromatic, and anion- or cation-exchange mechanisms. In principle, any of the four classes of sorbents listed in Table 2–4 could be used for polypeptide prefractionation. In practice, the choice will depend on the relative proportion of the various side chains on the interactive surface of the desired peptide or peptide class compared to interferences. For example, polypeptides with surface-available basic side chains can be selectively retained on a sulfopropyl phase and selectively excluded from a trimethylaminopropyl phase. For peptides with significantly hydrophobic contact regions, octyl and phenyl phases would be appropriate. Very hydrophobic polypeptides that are soluble in organic solvents may be retained on polar sorbents in the presence of non-

TABLE 2–4. Commercially Available Sorbents for Solid-Phase Extraction

Nonpolar	Anion exchange
Octadecyl	Trimethylaminopropyl
Octyl	Diethylaminopropyl
Ethyl	Ethylenediamine-*N*-propyl
Cyclohexyl	Aminopropyl
Phenyl	Cation exchange
Nitrile	Sulfonylpropyl
Polar	Propylbenzenesulfonyl
Silica	Carboxymethyl
Diol	
Aminopropyl	
Ethylenediamine-N-propyl	
Diethylaminopropyl	

polar organic solvents. Matrix considerations also affect choice of sorbent, particularly when matrix components are in high enough concentration to interfere with sample binding. For example, the presence of concentrated salts should reduce sample retention on ion-exchange sorbents and enhance retention on nonpolar sorbents; desalting or sample dilution may be required prior to sorbent extraction. Detergents may reduce polypeptide binding by competing for active sites on ion-exchange sorbents, and by reducing surface tension when applying samples to nonpolar sorbents. It may be advantageous to select a sorbent class different from that of the analytical column for reasons of solvent strength. For example, the aqueous salt solutions used to elute samples from ion-exchange sorbents are weak solvents in reversed-phase systems, and permit sample fractions to be introduced directly onto a reversed-phase HPLC column with no intermediate manipulations.

Once the sorbent type has been selected, retention of the sample by the phase should be confirmed. The cartridge should be conditioned by passage of 1–2 bed volumes of a solvating solvent such as methanol, then prepared for sample introduction by passage of 10–20 bed volumes of the sample solvent. If an ion-exchange phase is used, it should first be converted to the proper counterion, then equilibrated at the appropriate pH. Because of the slow diffusion rates of macromolecules, samples should be applied at reduced flow rates, preferably less than 10 ml/min. After sample application, the bed is washed twice with 10–20 bed volumes of sample solvent and both washes analyzed by HPLC. Absence of sample components in the chromatogram indicates adequate retention on the sorbent, while appearance of samples in the wash suggests a more retentive sorbent should be used. The final steps are to elute interferences with suitable wash solvents, then to elute the sample in a small volume with a final strong solvent. Typical wash solvents and sample elution solvents are given in Table 2–5. Because proteins interact at multiple sites with chromatographic supports, the transition from complete sorption to full desorption occurs over an extraordinarily narrow range of solvent strengths.[9] Therefore

TABLE 2–5. Solvents for Sorbent Extraction

Sorbent Class	Weak Solvents	Strong Solvents
Nonpolar	Water Low ionic strength buffers Low percentages of organic solvents in water or buffers	High percentages of polar organic solvents (methanol, propanol, acetonitrile) in water or buffer
Polar	Nonpolar organic solvents (hexane, methylene chloride)	Polar organic solvents Aqueous buffers or acids Water
Ion exchange	Water Low ionic strength buffers Low pH (cation exchange) High pH (anion exchange)	2 pH units above sample p*K* (cation exchange) 2 pH units below sample p*K* (anion exchange) High ionic strength Higher selectivity counterion

it should be possible in most cases to find elution conditions in which the desired protein or protein class is recovered while unwanted material is initially removed by washing or strongly retained on the sorbent. Similarly, sequential elution steps can be used to fractionate a complex protein sample into subfractions. In both ion-exchange and nonpolar interactions, retention depends strongly on the ionic state of the sample, and manipulation of solvent pH provides a powerful tool for modulating retention of both interferences and the protein of interest. In addition, release of strongly retained samples from ion-exchange sorbents may be achieved by use of a counterion with stronger selectivity; for example, a protein strongly retained in chloride buffer may be eluted with phosphate. Most commercially available sorbents use silica as the support material, and this may contribute to protein retention on nonpolar phases. Proteins with basic groups on the surface may bind strongly due to silanol interactions. In such cases, addition of a competing base such as triethylamine or tetramethylammonium salt to the eluent may improve recovery. Sorbent supports usually have pore diameters in the 6–10 nm range; most proteins will therefore be excluded from the majority of the sorbent surface, and protein capacity of these materials may be quite low.

A number of automated sample processing systems are available that used bonded-phase sorbent technology. In some cases, sample wash and elution steps are performed automatically off-line by a standalone processor, and eluted samples are transferred to HPLC autosampler vials. In other systems the processor functions as an on-line autosampler by employing sorbents packed in cartridges compatible with high-pressure operation. This permits samples to be eluted from the sorbent directly onto the LC column via an automated injection valve. Conditioning and wash steps may be performed manually off-line, or sample introduction and wash steps may be performed automatically by the processor or an autosampler interfaced to it. In all devices where the sample is eluted from the sorbent by the HPLC mobile phase, the choice of sorbent and extraction solvents will depend strongly on the HPLC method. The initial mobile phase composition of the LC method must quantitatively transfer the sample from the sorbent to the head of the analytical column; hence it must be both a strong eluent for the sorbent and a weak eluent for the LC column. This requires careful tailoring of the sorbent to the column chemistry. For example, if an octadecyl analytical column is used, a less hydrophobic sorbent will be required, e.g., C_8 or C_3. Ion-exchange prefractionation should be ideal for automated processing prior to a reversed-phase separation since the typical initial mobile-phase composition (dilute aqueous acid with low percentages of organic modifier) will effectively strip sample from the sorbent. The requirement for correct matching of sorbent and column chemistries suggests that manual off-line methods may not be easily adapted to on-line processing.

The use of bonded-phase sorbents for extraction and fractionation of pituitary peptides from biological tissues has been described by Bennett.[10,11] Reversed-phase C_{18} cartridges were used initially to remove bulk hydrophobic protein from the acid extract. The eluent was then adjusted to an appropriate pH and passed through tandem ion-exchange cartridges. Basic peptides bound to a carboxymethyl weak cation-exchange cartridge and acidic peptides bound to a quarternary methylammonium strong cation-exchange cartridge; neutral peptides passed unretained through the cartridge set. Following fractionation, the cartridges were eluted separately with aqueous salt to recover the two retained peptide classes. In this way a complex tissue extract was resolved into three fractions that could be conveniently resolved by reversed-phase HPLC, without damage to the column by unwanted protein. Optimum fractionation in such a system will be achieved by proper selection of the phases and eluent pH. For example, recovery of a peptide in a particular fraction will depend on its charge at the eluent pH. In the case described, weakly basic peptides failed to bind to the carboxymethyl sorbent at pH 7, and eluted with the unretained neutral fraction.

Reversed-phase fractionation of peptides generated from chymotryptic cleavage of the α-subunit of human class II histocompatibility antigen, a membrane glycoprotein, has been reported by Kratzin et al.[12] Peptides in 60% formic acid were bound to an octadecyl cartridge and selectively eluted with formic acid containing increasing concentration of propanol. The hydrophobic intermembrane peptides eluted at a propanol concentration of 80%.

A direct approach for removal of contaminants from proteins excised from two-dimensional electrophoresis gels has been developed by Pearson.[13] The gel material containing the isolated protein is packed into an empty cartridge connected to a short reversed-phase cartridge column. Passage of 0.1% aqueous TFA through the coupled columns elutes protein from the gel, which binds to the reversed-phase column while gel contaminants, buffer, and stain elute in the void volume. Protein is then recovered by gradient elution with TFA-acetonitrile. This procedure works well for recovery of small peptides that are often lost in electroblotting.

2.2.2 Solubilization

Solubilization is required in the special case of membrane proteins. Integral membrane proteins are very hydrophobic species that lie embedded in the lipid bilayer of cell membranes. They consist of relatively hydrophilic regions located on the membrane surfaces and one or more hydrophobic sequences spanning the interior of the membrane in association with the hydrophobic portions of the membrane lipid. Disruption of this organization during purification can lead to aggregation and precipitation. To prevent this, a detergent is typically added that can compete with lipids for interaction with the hydrophobic regions of the protein and maintain it in a soluble state in aqueous environments, usually in the form of protein–detergent micelles or mixed protein–lipid–detergent micelles. In a typical purification scheme, loosely associated hydrophilic peripheral proteins are removed from the membrane with salt or chaotropic agents, then integral membrane proteins are liberated by the addition of the detergent.

A wide variety of detergents have been used for purification of membrane proteins, and the choice of the detergent depends on the protein and the method of purification. The common detergents are listed in Table 2–6; their applications in membrane protein purification have been previously reviewed.[14–16] A systematic approach to the design of a solubilization procedure has been described by Hjelmeland and Chrambach.[17] This approach includes

TABLE 2–6. Common Detergents Used for Solubilization of Membrane Proteins[a]

Detergent	CMC (mM)
Ionic detergents	8.13 (water)
Sodium dodecyl sulfate	2.30 (0.5 M NaCl)
	0.51 (0.5 M NaCl)
Sodium cholate	13–15
Sodium deoxycholate	4–6
Sodium taurodeoxycholate	2–6
Nonionic detergents	
Triton X-100	0.24–0.30
Nonidet P40	0.29
Triton X-114	0.2
Tween 80	0.012
Emulphogen BC-720	0.087
Octylglucoside	25.0
Brij 35	0.091
Dodecyl dimethylamineoxide	2.2
Amphoteric	
CHAPS	4–6
Zwittergent 3-12	3.6

[a]Adapted from ref. 16.

three steps: selecting the detergent, selecting the buffer and temperature conditions, and testing for solubilization.

The guiding considerations in selecting a detergent are the constraints imposed by the chromatographic method to be used for purification following solubilization and any requirements for recovery of biological activity. If the detergent must be removed by dialysis following solubilization, use of a detergent with a high critical micelle concentration (CMC) is recommended. If absorbance detection at 280 nm or shorter wavelengths is to be used during chromatography, UV active detergents such as Triton, Nonidet, Berol, Emulgen, or Renex may interfere with detection if not removed.[16] A hydrogenated version of Triton X-100 is available that has the detergent properties of the aromatic compound but is compatible with 280 nm detection.[18] If ion-exchange chromatography is to be used, ionic detergents should not be used as they could compete for ion-exchange sites on the stationary phase. Most detergents will bind to reversed-phase and gel permeation columns via hydrophobic interactions and, if not removed prior to chromatography, may gradually alter the selectivity of the column. If a column is to be used frequently for chromatography of detergent-containing materials, it may be necessary to dedicate the column for this application. Sodium dodecyl sulfate binds strongly to proteins and is one of the most effective solubilizing agents. However, it tends to irreversibly denature proteins with loss of biological activity. Similarly, if divalent cations are required for maintenance of biological activity, the detergent sodium cholate should be avoided. Bile salts (e.g., sodium cholate and deoxycholate) and their derivatives such as CHAPS are known for their gentleness, and are often used when solubilization without denaturation is desired. In general, solubilization at high ionic strength (0.1–0.5 *M* salt) is recommended, with buffering capacity of 25 m*M* and a pH close to the *pK*. If ion-exchange chromatography is used subsequent to solubilization, the buffer ion should not have greater selectivity than the mobile-phase counterion. Solubilization is typically carried out at reduced temperature.

Once the detergent, salt, and buffer conditions have been selected, solubilization effectiveness can be determined by incubating the sample under these conditions, followed by centrifugation to separate solubilized from insoluble material for subsequent assay. A range of detergent concentrations (e.g., 0.01–3% final concentration in the protein/salt/buffer solution) should be tested with gentle stirring in the cold for 1 h. Successful solubilization in specific cases will depend on finding the optimal detergent/protein ratio by the above procedure. Protein solubilization occurs at or near the CMC for most detergents. Bile salts have been found to be more effective than nonionic detergents in dissociating protein complexes. If biological activity is lost on detergent solubilization, addition of a stabilizer such as glycerol, dithiothreitol, or EDTA may be necessary.

Effective solubilization of a membrane protein may require a detergent that is incompatible with subsequent steps in the purification process. Initially, a high concentration of a detergent with low CMC and high aggregation number such as Triton may be necessary to compete with membrane lipids to form protein–detergent micelles. Since removal of this detergent by dilution or dialysis prior to chromatography could be difficult, it may be useful to exchange the detergent for one more tractable, such as a bile salt. A strategy for detergent exchange has been described by Furth et al.[19] First, protein–detergent micelles are separated from detergent micelles, detergent–lipid micelles, and detergent monomers on the basis of size by passage through a gel permeation column. Detergent exchange is then accomplished by introduction of the detergent–protein fraction onto a gel permeation column followed by elution with a mobile phase containing a detergent of high CMC and low aggregation number. The mobile-phase detergent will disperse the solubilization detergent into monomers and replace it in a smaller protein–detergent micelle.

2.2.3 Concentration

Commonly used techniques for sample concentration are listed in Table 2–7. Conventional techniques such as lyophilization and evaporative concentration

TABLE 2–7. Sample Concentration Techniques

Lyophilization
Vacuum evaporation
Precipitation
Dialysis against concentrator resins
Ultrafiltration
Chromatographic concentration

are lengthy and may cause chemical modification and loss of sample by nonspecific adsorption if the sample is taken to near dryness. Similarly, sample loss can occur during precipitation by formation of insoluble aggregates. Ultrafiltration and chromatographic concentration are rapid and gentle methods that minimize the problems encountered in conventional approaches.

Ultrafiltration is based on the selective passage of low-molecular-weight sample components through a membrane filter of appropriate porosity; high-molecular-weight sample components such as proteins are excluded from the pores and become concentrated during the ultrafiltration process. Commercial products are available[20,21] that use centrifugation as the driving force; they consist of membrane filters with cutoffs in the range of 10,000–30,000 AMU held in centrifuge tube assemblies. Ultrafiltration devices that are designed for use in fixed angle rotors permit unrestricted solvent flow through the membrane and prevent the sample from reaching complete dryness. These devices permit milliliter samples to be rapidly concentrated up to 80-fold with low nonspecific adsorption and good recovery.

In chromatographic concentration, the principles of sorbent extraction are employed using chromatographic columns and packings; the sample in a large volume of a weak solvent is concentrated on the column, then eluted in a small volume of strong solvent. This technique has been used with low-pressure gels such as DEAE cellulose packed into minicolumns to concentrate samples up to 30-fold prior to gel permeation chromatography.[22] It is important that the sample be introduced in a solvent of low ionic strength to allow quantitative binding of protein to the ion exchanger; initial dilution of the sample may be necessary. The same approach can be used with high-performance columns, and short HPLC columns of 3–10 cm in length are ideal for rapid sample concentration. Short microbore reversed-phase HPLC columns have been used for preconcentration of proteins prior to microsequence analysis.[23] Milliliter fractions collected from chromatography on conventional HPLC columns can be diluted and injected onto 1- or 2-mm-i.d. microbore columns. Gradient elution at low rates (0.1–0.2 ml/min for 2-mm-i.d. columns, 0.02–0.04 ml/min for 1-mm-i.d. columns) permits recovery of proteins in volumes as small as 25 μl, with concentration factors of up to 80-fold. The high capacity of microparticulate packings enables 50–100 μg to be loaded onto microbore columns as long as the sample is introduced in a weak solvent. This technique requires an HPLC solvent delivery system capable of gradient elution at reduced flow rates.

2.2.4 Detergent Removal

Removal of detergents used to extract or solubilize hydrophobic proteins may be necessary prior to subsequent purification steps. Detergent micelle formation may complicate concentration procedures, and detergents can degrade column performance or interfere with UV detection in HPLC separations. Techniques for removal of detergents from proteins are listed in Table 2–8.

Dialysis can be used following dilution of the detergent below the CMC. This technique is time consuming and may not be practical for detergents with low CMC values. Chloroform extraction has been used to remove sodium dodecyl

TABLE 2–8. Methods for Detergent Removal

Dialysis
Solvent extraction
Ion pair extraction
Adsorption on polystyrene resin
Adsorption on ion-retardation resin
Binding to affinity matrix

sulfate from proteins electroeluted from SDS polyacrylamide gels;[24] eluted aqueous fractions are mixed with methanol and solvent extracted. Extracted protein is washed extensively with methanol and dried to remove chloroform. Ion-pair extraction has also been used to remove SDS from detergent–protein complexes.[25,26] Dry samples are extracted with a solution of ion-pairing agent in an organic solvent, such as acetone–triethylamine–acetic acid–water or heptane–tributylamine–acetic acid–butanol. Sufficient water must be present in the extractant or protein sample to promote formation of the alkylammonium–SDS ion pair. In the case of the second solvent system, water must be added to about 1%. A single extraction removes up to 95% of total SDS, while protein is recovered as a precipitate that can be separated from extractant by low-speed centrifugation and washed with acetone or heptane to remove residual extractant or SDS. Salts present in the sample may interfere with SDS removal and should be removed prior to extraction. This procedure can be adapted to extraction of small volumes of aqueous protein–SDS solutions by mixing sample and extractant in a 1:20 ratio using extractant prepared without water. A two-step extraction will quantitatively remove the detergent with good recovery of protein (generally 80% or better). This extraction procedure also removes the Coomassie blue stain in proteins recovered from SDS polyacrylamide gels.

Adsorption on neutral polystyrene resins is a popular technique for removal of surfactants from aqueous solutions of proteins, either by batch adsorption or by passage through a resin-packed column for rapid detergent removal. This technique apparently removes only detergent micelles so will reduce the detergent concentration to the CMC. Amberlite XAD-2 resin (Rohm and Haas, Philadelphia, PA) has been used for removal of Triton X-100 by both batch and column methods.[27–29]

Ion retardation resins have also been applied to removal of SDS from proteins.[30,31] These materials consist of acrylic acid polymerized inside a strong anion-exchange resin composed of quaternary ammonium groups attached to a polystyrene–divinylbenzene matrix.[32] Passage of a protein–SDS complex through the resin results in complete retention of SDS and elution of protein with 80–90% recovery. The resin has an SDS capacity of over 2.2 mg of SDS per gram and passage of aqueous SDS–protein complexes through an ion-retardation column can reduce the SDS level to less than one molecule of SDS bound per protein molecule. However, adsorption of SDS is reduced in the presence of buffers, resulting in incomplete removal of detergent from the protein. This can be circumvented by prior removal of buffer by gel filtration or, more conveniently, by the addition of a few grams of a size exclusion gel to the head of the ion-retardation resin bed to retard the buffer. Since SDS binds tenaciously to the resin, it cannot be removed and the resin must be discarded after use.

An affinity matrix for detergent removal has been developed that carries a proprietary ligand bound to a gel matrix.[33] The mechanism is based on selective permeation of the detergent into the gel matrix where it can bind to the affinity ligand, while proteins above 10,000 AMU are excluded from the matrix and pass through in the void volume. Operation in the column mode rather than batch format is recommended. This technique cannot be used for polypeptides below the 10,000 AMU exclusion limit since they can permeate the matrix and bind to the ligand. Also, poor recovery due to nonspecific binding is a problem when dilute protein solutions of 50 μg/ml or less are passed through the matrix. In such cases it is recommended that a carrier protein such as bovine serum albumin be added to the sample to saturate active binding sites. This product has been used for removal of ionic detergents such as SDS[34] and Zwittergent 3-12,[35] and nonionic detergents such as Triton X-100[36] and octyl glucoside.[37]

2.2.5 Desalting

Removal of salt from a protein solution may be necessary to obtain satisfactory chromatography; for example, high concentrations of salt would be incompatible with reversed-phase chromatography using aqueous–organic solvent mobile phases. Also, injection of samples with concentrated salts in ion-exchange chromatography can be a source of irreproducibility for early eluting peaks. The common desalting techniques are listed in Table 2–9.

Dialysis is the traditional method for removing salts and other low-molecular-weight material such as chaotropic agents or detergents from protein fractions. However, it can be quite time consuming. Gel filtration is a rapid alternative to dialysis, and desalting is typically done with cross-linked dextran or polyacrylamide gels with porosities that allow protein to pass through in the excluded volume while salts are retarded by permeation into the bed. Desalting gels are available as prepacked columns that facilitate rapid salt removal.[38,39] Desalting gels can also be packed in centrifuge tubes, and centrifugation used as the driving force to elute protein in attached collection tubes.[40] High-performance gel permeation columns can also be used for rapid desalting. However, these columns can exhibit absorptive interactions with proteins when operated with low ionic strength mobile phases, and recovery may be poor, especially when attempting to desalt basic proteins at neutral pH using silica-based gel permeation columns.

TABLE 2–9. Desalting Techniques

Dialysis
Gel filtration
Reversed-phase sorbent desalting
Ion retardation
Ultrafiltration

Reversed-phase sorbents are used frequently for desalting aqueous protein fractions. The success of this approach is based on the strong interactions of proteins with hydrophobic phases such as octyl and octadecyl under conditions where salts and chaotropic agents are unretained. After sample application, salts and other low-molecular-weight polar compounds can be washed from the sorbent, followed by elution of protein with an aqueous–organic solvent mixture. Desalting can be performed manually with reversed-phase sorbents packed in minicolumns or cartridges, or can be included as the first step in an HPLC gradient elution method in which desalting is accomplished by elution with the weak eluent prior to initiating the organic solvent gradient. Desalting with reversed-phase sorbents is advantageous when it must be followed by a concentration step, since the elution solvent is generally volatile.

Ion retardation resins employed for detergent removal are also used for desalting.[41,42] As mentioned earlier, the resin copolymer consists of adjacent fixed anionic and cationic sites that, in the absence of counterions, exist in a self-adsorbed state. On application of a protein–salt solution to the resin packed in a column, ionic species in the sample adsorb to the resin in an ion-exchange process, disrupting the resin self-association. Salts of monovalent ions (sodium chloride, potassium chloride, Tris-HCl) will be retained while proteins can be readily eluted with water. Sodium acetate, sodium citrate, sodium phosphate, and ammonium sulfate do not compete as effectively with self-adsorption and may not be completely resolved from protein. After desalting, the resin can be regenerated by treatment with 1 *M* hydrochloric acid followed by 1 *M* ammonium hydroxide containing 0.5 *M* ammonium chloride, and finally by extensive washing with water.

The ultrafiltration devices use for sample concentration can also be used for desalting.[43] To desalt a sample that has been concentrated by ultrafiltration, it should be diluted 10-fold in buffer or water and subjected again to ultra-filtration; each ultrafiltration cycle removes about 90% of the salt, and two or three cycles can reduce salt concentration by 99%.

2.3 COLUMN MAINTENANCE AND REPAIR

A survey of HPLC practitioners has indicated that the most common problems in column performance are elevated operating pressure, poor sample recovery, and loss of resolution.[44] The typical causes of poor column performance are listed in Table 2–10. Many of these problems can be minimized by use of adequate sample preparation techniques described above and by the use of

TABLE 2–10. Causes of Poor Column Performance

Frit blockage
Bed compaction
Bed dissolution
Stationary-phase loss
Stationary-phase contamination

guard columns and careful column maintenance procedures.[45–47] When column performance does degrade to unacceptable levels, recovery can often be achieved with the techniques described below.

2.3.1 Bed Repair

Peak broadening, appearance of split peaks, and tailing or fronting peaks are all indications of the formation of bed irregularities such as voids or channels. All peaks in the chromatogram should exhibit the symptom, and a gradual or rapid rise in operating pressure may accompany the degradation in peak shape.[48] Bed irregularities may arise from exposure to excessive pressure or from dissolution of the bed support. Column overpressure caused by use of viscous mobile phases or high flow velocities may generate voids by compaction of less dense regions of the bed; this can be avoided by judicious use of overpressure protection features found on most modern HPLC pumps. Bed dissolution of silica-based columns most often occurs as a result of exposure of the column to alkaline samples or mobile phases. Dissolution will in time lead to fracture and collapse of the silica microparticles as indicated by a large increase in operating pressure. The rate of dissolution will be significantly increased by operation at elevated temperature and by the addition of alkyl amines to the mobile phase. These species are used as ion-pairing agents or to enhance peak shape and recovery in reversed-phase chromatography of basic polypeptides; they also promote silica dissolution at mobile phase pH values above 6. If chromatography under these conditions cannot be avoided, installation of a silica-packed precolumn has been recommended to presaturate the mobile phase with dissolved silicate.[49] Although this has been demonstrated to improve column lifetime, use of a silica saturator column can cause poor reproducibility in gradient elution due to changing gradient delay volumes as the silica degrades. Also, gelation of saturated silicates in the mobile phase may cause plugging downstream from the precolumn, and silicates will be present in sample fractions collected during chromatography. A number of reversed-phase, ion-exchange, and gel permeation HPLC columns are now available based on polystyrene, polymethacrylate, or polyether resins, which are compatible with alkaline mobile phases and which exhibit good resolution and recovery of proteins.

Small voids formed at the column head can be repaired by topping off with bulk packing, and recovery of adequate performance can usually be achieved. If the void is deeper than a few millimeters, topping off will probably not be successful. Internal voids and channels cannot be repaired. In these cases, the column must be repacked or discarded.

2.3.1.1 Topping Off Voids

To verify that void formation is the cause of poor column performance, the inlet terminator should be carefully removed, taking care not to disturb the column bed (it is safest to secure the column in a bench vise for this and successive operations). The bed should be level and flush with the end face of the column tube. If there is any indication of a void, the following top-off procedure is often successful (50):

1. Level the bed using a square blade; a small laboratory spatula with a flat tip works well. Any darkly discolored packing should be removed during this operation.
2. Choose an appropriate packing to fill the void. This can be either a porous or pellicular microparticulate material with a phase that closely matches that of the column packing. If an exact match cannot be made, the void filler should be less retentive than the column packing to minimize efficiency loss. Unbonded silica or unsilanized glass beads should not be used, as proteins will adsorb strongly to these materials.
3. Affix a small plastic tube to the end of the column to serve as a reservoir; a disposable pipettor tip can be easily modified for this purpose.
4. Fill the reservoir with an organic solvent and prepare a slurry of the void filler in the same solvent. Using a transfer pipet, add the slurry dropwise to the reservoir until the void is slightly overfilled.
5. Remove the excess solvent and reservoir, then carefully remove any solvent and void filler from the face of the column tube. Replace the terminator and test the column for efficiency and peak shape.

Settling often occurs after the first top-off operation, and the process may have to be repeated two or three times to obtain a stable bed with good performance.

2.3.1.2 Repacking HPLC Columns

A variety of methods have been described for packing HPLC columns;[51] balanced density slurry packing is the traditional method, but viscosity slurry and nonbalanced density slurry methods have also been used. Many variables affect the preparation of an efficient and stable column, including the type and quality of the support material, the stationary phase ligand and bonding procedure, the column dimensions and wall surface characteristics, and the slurry preparation and packing procedure. Verzele and Dewaele[52] evaluated column packing techniques and make the following recommendations for packing silica-based microparticulate materials:

1. High-quality silica must be used; high-quality silica will tend to remain suspended in the slurry and settle slowly.
2. Highest purity solvents should be used; polar impurities in the packing solvent will promote particle aggregation.
3. Sonication of the slurry helps to disperse aggregates.
4. Column efficiency is highest when the diameter of the packing vessel is the same as that of the column.
5. Slurry concentrations of 20–30% will pack rapidly to yield high efficiency beds.
6. For 10 μm polar particles, downward packing at 300–400 bar with a 10:90 water:methanol slurry is recommended; for nonpolar packings, carbon tetrachloride is suggested.
7. For particles with diameters of 5 μm and smaller, upward packing with low-viscosity solvents is recommended; for nonpolar particles, ether or pentane slurries work well, although acetone was found to be a good solvent for packing 5 μm octadecyl silica.

Reuse of column hardware and packings has also been studied by the same authors.[53] They demonstrated that column hardware could be successfully repacked with fresh material but wall defects limit the number of times a column can be repacked. This limit depends upon the wall thickness and tube dimensions; 8-mm and 21-mm-i.d. preparative columns may have a lower success rate for repacking. Other workers have found that 4.6-mm-i.d. analytical columns could be repacked up to four times with acceptable recovery of performance.[54] The following precautions should be taken if columns and packings are to be reused:[54]

1. The upper centimeter of packing material at the column head should be discarded to prevent contamination of the repacked column.
2. Fines should be eliminated by flotation.
3. Since extrusion of packing from the column tube may expose fresh silica surfaces, the material may require endcapping or rebonding with an appropriate silanization reagent.
4. The packing should be conditioned by sonication to disrupt aggregates. This precaution is very important in the case of polymeric gels, which, because of their semirigid nature, tend to form aggregates during packing.
5. The pressure limit of the packing should be obtained from the manufacturer. The macroporous supports used for chromatography of proteins have pore diameters of 30 nm and larger; they are more fragile than conventional small-pore supports, and may fracture if packed at high pressures.

Acquiring the equipment and expertise for repacking used columns may be a worthwhile investment in cases in which column lifetimes are short and column usage is high. Alternatively, there are repacking services that will repack most commercial HPLC columns at a fraction of the original cost.

2.3.2 Frit Repair

Most commercial HPLC columns incorporate stainless-steel frits in the inlet and outlet terminators to contain and protect the column packing. These frits can contribute to poor chromatographic performance because of blockage, protein adsorption, or corrosion.

A gradual rise in system operating pressure that is not accompanied by a loss of efficiency may indicate blockage of the inlet frit. This will occur if the sample or mobile phase has not been adequately filtered. If the geometry of the inlet terminator is such that solvent flow is not distributed evenly across the frit surface, the central part of the frit may become partially plugged; impeded flow in the frit center relative to the annulus can produce multiple flow paths, giving rise to asymmetric or split peaks. Frit blockage can be prevented by installation of a guard column or low-volume in-line filter with disposable frit. Devices of both types are commercially available that, if properly installed, should not introduce excessive band broadening. If a frit does become blocked, it can be backflushed to remove the blockage or replaced with a new frit.

2.3.2.1 Backflushing Column Frits

Backflushing the column in the inverted flow position is the simplest remedy for a blocked frit. However, the following precautions should be observed:

1. The manufacturer's operating instructions should be consulted to verify that the column can be operated in the inverse flow mode.
2. Verify that elevated pressure is not accompanied by efficiency loss; the appearance of both symptoms suggests void formation, in which case backflushing might further disrupt bed integrity.
3. Elevated pressure during operation of silica columns with alkaline mobile phases or with cationic ion pairing agents at neutral pH may indicate that the outlet frit has become blocked by fines generated by silica dissolution. Backflushing in this case will produce only a temporary reduction in pressure.
4. Disconnect the column from the detector to prevent particulates or contaminants from being swept into the detector flow cell or transfer lines.

If backflushing does not reduce column pressure, the terminator can be removed and installed on an empty column; it can then be backflushed under more vigorous conditions with aggressive solvents (e.g., 20% aqueous nitric acid) with no risk to the analytical column. A spare terminator should be installed on the analytical column during this operation to prevent drying of the bed.

2.3.2.2 Frit Replacement

Frit replacement is indicated if aggressive backflushing fails to reduce pressure. If the terminator is fitted with a pressed-in frit, the entire terminator must be replaced. Achieving a leak-free connection with a replacement terminator may be difficult if the ferrule has been deformed. If column pressure remains high after installation of a new frit, contaminants have probably penetrated into the bed matrix. In this case, a few millimeters of packing can be removed and repacked using the procedures outlined in Section 2.3.1.1.

Adsorption of proteins to stainless-steel surfaces has been observed in certain cases,[55,56] and since the column frits account for the majority of stainless-steel surface area exposed to the sample, it is not surprising that they have been implicated in poor protein recovery.[57] In addition, corrosion of frits by some aqueous mobile phases may cause leaching and deposition of metal ions onto the stationary phase, altering column selectivity or capacity. Stainless steel frits can be passivated with aqueous nitric acid to minimize these problems, or replaced with nonferrous or nonmetallic frits.

2.3.3 Stationary-Phase Regeneration

Degradation of column efficiency, capacity, and selectivity can all arise from changes in the chemical characteristics of the stationary phase. These changes include loss of bonded phase ligands, chemical alteration of the bonded phase, or adsorption of sample or mobile-phase contaminants. Selection of the proper phase regeneration procedures requires diagnostic tools to identify which of these three possibilities are responsible for deterioration of column performance. Table 2–11 lists a series of low-molecular-weight test probes that can aid in column diagnosis; it is advisable to obtain benchmark data with a new column to enable unambiguous fault diagnosis. In addition to these small molecule probes, protein standards are also useful in monitoring column per-

TABLE 2–11. Test Compounds for Silica-Based Columns

Compound	Examples	Detects	Tests for
Neutral aromatics	Toluene Naphthalene Anthracene Alkyl phenones	Efficiency capacity	Voids, channels, phase loss
Chelating agents	Acetylacetone Tetracycline Benzoin	Metals	Metals contamination of stationary phase
Aromatic amines	*N,N*-Diethylanaline Thiamine	Silanols	Phase loss, degree of endcapping

formance. Synthetic peptide standards for HPLC column evaluation are also commercially available;[58,59] These are sequence variants with amino acid replacements designed to probe selected peptide–stationary phase interactions.

2.3.3.1 Stationary-Phase Loss

Gradual reduction in the retention of all sample components is indicative of loss of the stationary phase. Cleavage of bonded phase ligands from silica supports is favored by operation at low pH, high ionic strength, and low concentration of organic modifiers.[60] In reversed-phase chromatography, the stability of long alkyl ligands such as C_8 and C_{18} to hydrolytic cleavage is good. However, short chain bonded phases such as C_1–C_4 are more susceptible to cleavage, and it has been reported that under typical polypeptide elution conditions (water:acetonitrile gradients with low concentrations of TFA) up to 80% of the bonded phase is lost within a few days of operation.[61]

If column performance has deteriorated due to loss of stationary phase, the column may be regenerated by passage of an appropriate silane reagent through

TABLE 2–12. Protein Stripping Solvents for HPLC Columns[a]

Solvent	Composition
Acetic acid	1% in water
Formic acid	60% in water
Trifluoroacetic acid (TFA)	1% in water
0.1% TFA in water:propanol	40:60
Triethylamine phosphate:propanol	40:60
Aqueous urea or guanidine	5–8 *M*
Aqueous sodium chloride, sodium phosphate, or sodium sulfate	1–2 *M*
Dimethyl sulfoxide	100%

[a] Propanol and dimethyl sulfoxide are highly viscous and should be pumped at a reduced flow rate to prevent overpressure. Triethylamine phosphate is prepared by adjusting 0.75 *M* phosphoric acid to pH 2.5 with triethylamine. Manufacturer's column operating instructions should be consulted before introducing aggressive wash solvents.

the column bed.[60,62] Mant et al.[63] described the following procedure for *in situ* rebonding of C_8 and C_{18} columns used for peptide separations with aqueous TFA mobile phases:

1. Wash column sequentially with 15 column volumes each of water, acetonitrile, and dichloromethane.
2. Pump 10 column volumes of 10% (v/v) chlorodimethyloctylsilane in dichloromethane containing 7.5% pyridine at 0.2 ml/min (pyridine neutralizes HCl liberated during reaction of the silane reagent with the stationary phase). The silane reagent can be introduced via a large volume injector loop.
3. Wash column successively with 15 column volumes each of dichloromethane, toluene, and acetonitrile.
4. Equilibrate the column with aqueous 0.1% TFA, and remove any residual reagents or impurities with three rapid linear gradients from 100% aqueous 0.1% TFA to 100% aqueous 0.05% TFA in acetonitrile at 5% per minute.

2.3.3.2 Stationary-Phase Alteration

Chemical reaction of the stationary phase is suspected to occur when cyano columns are used in the reversed-phase mode with aqueous eluents. Cyano columns prepared from trimethoxyalkylsilanes exhibit a gradual reduction in retention times under these conditions, probably due to silanol-catalyzed hydrolysis of the nitrile to hydroxylamine.[60] For reversed-phase chromatography of peptides, the use of cyano columns prepared with a dimethylmethoxyalkylsilane reagent is recommended, since this bonded phase can no longer assist in the hydrolysis.

2.3.3.3 Stationary-Phase Contamination

Contamination of the stationary phase with strongly retained species may modify the chemical characteristics of the phase, resulting in selectivity changes, asymmetric peaks, and reduced column capacity. Protein aggregates can partially block inlet frits or interstitial spaces in the column bed, resulting in elevated operating pressure and multiple flow paths. To strip contaminants from the phase, it is necessary to identify a solvent or series of solvents that will displace strongly adsorbed species. Hydrophobic contaminants such as lipids can generally be removed with nonpolar solvents such as acetonitrile, tetrahydrofuran, or hexane. Metals can be removed by chelating agents such as EDTA, phosphoric acid, or citric acid (exposure of silica bonded phases to low pH conditions should be brief, however). Removal of strongly adsorbed proteins will require a displacing agent that can disrupt the mixed hydrophobic and hydrophilic interactions that are typically involved in protein binding to stationary-phase surfaces. Therefore protein solubilizing agents such as concentrated salts, chaotropic agents, and surfactants have been used. For reversed-phase columns, repetitive gradient–retrogradient cycles with aqueous:organic solvent systems such as TFA:water:propanol have been effective, and this approach has also been successful in regenerating gel permeation and ion-exchange columns.[64] Several wash solvents that have been used in regeneration of HPLC columns are provided in Table 2–12. Dilute base such as 0.01 *M* ammonium hydroxide should be effective in removing basic proteins adsorbed to HPLC columns, but can be used with silica columns only as a last report. Protease treatment of protein-contaminated columns has also been suggested, but the effectiveness of this approach has not been reported.

For difficult contamination situations, several wash solvents may be used in sequence, with 20–30 column volumes of solvent per step. If smaller volumes can be used, wash solvents can be conveniently introduced via a large volume injector loop. Two precautions should be observed in column decontamination. First, washing should be done with the column in the backflush position. Second, sequential wash solvents should be miscible or, if not, be interspersed with a mutually miscible solvent. Washes with salts or chaotropic agents cannot be used before or after organic solvents without an intervening water wash.

The above approaches are designed to prolong column lifetime and return moribund columns to useful performance levels. From an economic standpoint, the cost of lengthy regeneration procedures must be weighed against the advantages of using inexpensive cartridge-type analytical columns that can be discarded when performance becomes unacceptable.

REFERENCES

1. F. E. Regnier, *J. Chromatogr.*, 418 (1987) 115.
2. S. D. Power, M. A. Lochrie, and R. O. Poyton, *J. Chromatogr.*, 266 (1983) 585.
3. R. A. Wolfe, J. Casey, P. C. Familletti, and S. Stein, *J. Chromatogr.*, 296 (1984) 277.
4. L. E. Henderson, J. F. Hewetson, R. F. Hopkins III, R. C. Sowder, R. Neubauer, and H. Rabin, *J. Immunol.*, 131 (1983) 810.
5. J. Ohara, S. Lahet, J. Inman, and W. E. Paul, *J. Immunol.*, 135 (1985) 2518.
6. R. E. Majors, *LC, Liquid Chromatogr. HPLC Mag.*, 4 (1986) 972.
7. R. E. Majors, *LC-GC, Liquid Gas Chromatogr. Mag.*, 5 (1987) 292.
8. K. C. Van Horne, (ed.), Sorbent Extraction Technology. Analytichem International, Harbor City, CA, 1985, p. 6.
9. R. V. Lewis, A. Fallon, S. Stein, K. D. Gibson, and S. Udenfriend, *Anal. Biochem.*, 104 (1980) 153.
10. H. P. J. Bennett, *J. Chromatogr.*, 359 (1986) 383.
11. S. James and H. P. J. Bennett, *J. Chromatogr.*, 326 (1985) 329.
12. H. D. Kratzin, T. Kruse, F. Maywald, F. P. Thinnes, H. Gotz, G. Egert, E. Pauly, J. Friedrich, C.-Y. Yang, P. Wernet, and N. Hilschmann, *J. Chromatogr.*, 297 (1984) 1.
13. J. D. Pearson, D. B. DeWald, H. A. Zurcher-Neely, R. L. Heinrikson, and R. A. Poorman, in Proceedings of the Sixth International Conference on Methods in Protein Sequence Analysis, Seattle, WA, Aug. 17–21, 1986 (K. A. Walsh, ed.). Humana Press, Clifton, NJ, 1986, pp. 295–302.
14. L. M. Hjelmeland and A. Chrambach, in Membranes, Detergents and Receptor Solubilization (J. C. Venter and L. C. Harrison, eds.). Liss, New York, 1984, p. 35.
15. S. Goheen, *LC, Liq. Chromatogr. HPLC Mag.*, 4 (1986) 624.
16. G. W. Welling, R. van der Zee and S. Welling-Wester, *J. Chromatogr.*, 418 (1987) 223.
17. L. M. Hjelmeland and A. Chrambach, *Methods Enzymol.*, 104 (1984) 305.
18. G. E. Tiller, T. J. Mueller, M. E. Dockter, and W. G. Struve, *Anal. Biochem.*, 141 (1984) 262.
19. A. J. Furth, H. Bolton, J. Potter, and J. D. Priddle, *Methods Enzymol.*, 104 (1984) 318.
20. Bio-Rad Technical Bulletin 1322, Bio-Rad Labs., Richmond, CA.
21. Amicon Technical Bulletin 522, Amicon Division, W.R. Grace & Co., Danvers, MA.

22. P. C. Billings and A. R. Kennedy, *BioTechniques*, 5 (1987) 210.
23. E. C. Nice, C. J. Lloyd, and A. W. Burgess, *J. Chromatogr.*, 296 (1984) 153.
24. D. Wessel, and U. I. Flugge, *Anal. Biochem.*, 138 (1984) 141.
25. L. E. Henderson, S. Oroszlan, and W. Konigsberg, *Anal. Biochem.*, 93 (1979) 153.
26. W. Konigsberg and L. Henderson, *Methods Enzymol.*, 91 (1983) 254.
27. C. A. Kruse, E. B. Spector, S. D. Cederbaum, B. J. Wisnieski, and G. Popjak, *Biochim. Biophys. Acta*, 645 (1981) 339.
28. P. W. Holloway, *Anal. Biochem.*, 53 (1973) 304.
29. Bio-Rad Technical Bulletin 1077, Bio-Rad Labs., Richmond, CA.
30. O. H. Kapp and S. N. Vinogradov, *Anal. Biochem.*, 91 (1978) 230.
31. S. N. Vinogradov and O. H. Kapp, *Methods Enzymol.* 91 (1983) 259.
32. Bio-Rad Technical Bulletin 1005, Bio-Rad Labs., Richmond, CA.
33. Extractigel D Technical Bulletin, Pierce Chemical Co., Rockford, IL.
34. M. Elzinga and J. J. Phelan, *Proc. Natl. Acad. Sci. U.S.A.*, 81 (1984) 6599.
35. P. C. Necessary, P. A. Humphrey, P. B. Mahajan, and K. E. Ebner, *J. Biol. Chem.*, 259 (1984) 6942.
36. H. A. Berman, J. Yguerabide, and P. Taylor, *Biochemistry*, 24 (1985) 7140.
37. R. A. Cerione, J. Codina, J. L. Benovic, R. J. Lefkowitz, L. Birnbaumer, and M. G. Caron, *Biochemistry*, 23 (1984) 4519.
38. M. Dyson, S. Gibson, and R. I. Penny, presented at the Sixth International Symposium on HPLC of Proteins, Peptides and Polynucleotides, Baden-Baden, Oct. 20–22, 1986, Abstract No. 944.
39. Bio-Rad Technical Bulletin 2068, Bio-Rad Labs., Richmond, CA.
40. R. I. Christopherson, *Methods Enzymol.*, 91 (1983) 278.
41. Bio-Rad Technical Bulletin 1005, Bio-Rad Labs., Richmond, CA.
42. M. L. Reis, W. Draghetta, and L. J. Greene, *Anal. Biochem.*, 81 (1977) 346.
43. Amicon Technical Bulletin 522, Amicon Division, W.R. Grace & Co., Danvers, MA.
44. R. E. Majors, *LC-GC, Liquid Gas Chromatogr. Mag.*, 5 (1987) 86.
45. C. T. Wehr, *Methods Enzymol.*, 104 (1984) 133.
46. J. W. Dolan and L. R. Snyder, Troubleshooting HPLC Systems. Humana Press, Clifton, NJ, 1987.
47. F. M. Rabel, *J. Chromatogr. Sci.*, 18 (1980) 394.
48. S. R. Abbot, *LC, Liquid Chromatogr. Mag.*, 3 (1985) 568.
49. J. G. Atwood, G. J. Schmidt, and W. Slavin, *J. Chromatogr.*, 171 (1979) 109.
50. C. T. Wehr, *LC, Liquid Chromatogr. Mag.*, 1 (1983) 270.
51. R. E. Majors, *J. Chromatogr. Sci.*, 18 (1980) 488.
52. M. Verzele and C. Dewaele, *LC-GC, Liquid Gas Chromatogr. Mag.*, 4 (1986) 614.
53. C. Dewaele, M. DeConinck, and M. Verzele, *LC, Liquid Chromatogr. Mag.*, 4 (1986) 218.
54. N. C. Avery and N. Light, *J. Chromatogr.*, 328 (1985) 347.
55. H. J. Van Enckevort, D. V. Dass, and A. G. Langdon, *J. Colloid Interface Sci.*, 98 (1984) 138.
56. C. N. Trumbore, R. D. Tremblay, J. T. Penrose, M. Mercer, and F. M. Kelleher, *J. Chromatogr.*, 280 (1983) 43.
57. P. C. Sadek, P. W. Carr, L. D. Bowers, and L. C. Haddad, *Anal. Biochem.*, 144 (1985) 128.
58. C. T. Mant and R. S. Hodges, *LC, Liquid Chromatogr. HPLC Mag.*, 4 (1986) 250.
59. D. Guo, C. T. Mant, A. K. Taneja, J. M. R. Parker, and R. S. Hodges, *J. Chromatogr.*, 359 (1986) 499.
60. S. R. Abbott, *LC, Liquid Chromatogr. HPLC Mag.*, 4 (1986) 12.
61. J. Glajch, J. J. Kirkland, and J. Kohler, *J. Chromatogr.*, 384 (1987) 81.
62. T. D. Wilson, *J. Chromatogr.*, 253 (1982) 260.
63. C. T. Mant, J. M. R. Parker, and R. S. Hodges, *LC-GC, Liquid Gas Chromatogr. Mag.*, 4 (1986) 1004.
64. F. E. Regnier, *Methods Enzymol.*, 104 (1984) 188.

CHAPTER 3

Development of Advanced Silica-Based Packing Materials

K. K. Unger, K. D. Lork, and H.-J. Wirth

CONTENTS

3.1 INTRODUCTION

During the last decade the design of packings for biopolymer separations has undergone remarkable improvements, which in turn has had a major impact on the application of high-performance liquid chromatography (HPLC) to the analysis, structure elucidation, isolation, and purification of biopolymers. Packings designed for these purposes should meet a number of requirements, such as[1]

- high selectivity and specificity,
- high flexibility to accommodate a variety of analytes,
- adequate column efficiency,
- preservation of biological activity together with high mass recovery,
- high bed stability and low flow resistance,
- high chemical stability during use and storage to tolerate aqueous eluents,
- fast and complete regeneration and reequilibration,

- adequate lot-to-lot consistency, and
- minimum fouling when used in preparative isolation.

Historically, the classical packings were soft gels based on polysaccharides,[2,3] e.g., agarose and dextrans, and hydrophilic synthetic polymers, e.g., polyamides and polyacrylamides. Inorganic packings such as porous glasses played a minor role, which was mainly due to their undesired adsorption behavior toward biopolymers even when coated with biocompatible liquids as protective layers, e.g., poly(ethyleneglycol).[4]

At the end of the 1960s column liquid chromatography started an era of rapid development in the separation of low-molecular-weight compounds as microparticulate 6- to 15-nm pore size silicas became available.[5] The silanization of these packings yielded reversed-phase (RP) silicas. The introduction of RP silicas substantially expanded the application of HPLC into the analysis of polar and ionic solutes.[6] This rapid expansion appeared to reach a certain extent of saturation at about 1980. At this point in time research efforts started on the design, development, and manufacture of bonded silicas for biopolymer separation by HPLC. Two factors were responsible for this development. First, the soft hydrophilic organic gels suffering from limited rigidity were not suitable for fast high-resolution separations of biopolymers. Second, the knowledge accumulated in the bonding chemistry of silica, particularly in the attachment of protective polymer coatings of desired functionality, opened a new avenue to overcome the problems of residual adsorptivity and limited chemical stability of bonded silicas.

To adapt to the molecular size of biopolymers, and to provide a sufficiently accessible interactive stationary surface in the chromatographic separation, so-called wide-pore silicas of about 30 nm of nominal pore diameter were introduced into the market whereas the traditional microparticulate silicas had pore sizes between 6 and 15 nm. Studies on the chromatographic behavior of biopolymers on these packings, e.g., in reversed-phase chromatography, revealed that peak dispersion and biorecovery were not as good as expected.[7] These effects have been found to be associated with slow mass transfer kinetics and with the involvement of secondary equilibria (conformational changes, pH-dependent deprotonation–protonation, dimerization, aggregation, etc.) in the separation process that impaired the chromatographic performance. The kinetics of mass transfer and interactions of biopolymers in porous silicas are mainly determined by the tortuous nature and the connectivity of the pore system, and the energetic and geometric heterogeneity of the silica surface even when covered with a bonded phase. To achieve a favorable kinetic pattern and a homogeneous surface for interaction the focus was on macroporous silicas with a defined pore structure and porosity and on nonporous silicas. Thus, both types of packings have been a subject of extensive research and find increasing access to the market as commercial products.[8,9] The results obtained so far clearly evidence the superior chromatographic performance of macroporous and nonporous materials over the traditional wide-pore 30 nm pore size silicas.

This chapter discusses the basic structural characteristics of silicas relevant to the chromatographic application of biopolymers in HPLC. Emphasis is placed on the various concepts and designs of stationary phases made by surface modification of silicas. The major aspects of the chromatographic properties of bonded silicas in size exclusion, reversed-phase, hydrophobic interaction, ion-exchange, and affinity chromatography are discussed.

3.2 STRUCTURAL CHARACTERISTICS OF SILICAS AND THEIR RELEVANCE TO BIOPOLYMER SEPARATION

Although silica merely serves as a support for bonded phases, some of its properties have been found to exert a major effect on the chromatographic performance and to a large extent determine the success of the separation and isolation of biopolymers. An enormous amount of literature exists on the physicochemical characterization of porous and finely dispersed silicas.[5,10,11] However, the majority of the studies deal only with a detailed aspect of the complex structure of specific silica brands that do not allow any generalization to all products. Moreover, the results are of little relevance to the use of bonded silicas with aqueous eluents in HPLC of biopolymers. The essence of the problem is that the chemical and physical structure of silica is so complex to describe, that its complete evaluation in quantitative terms with respect to biopolymer separations is not feasible. Thus, for the purpose of clarity we will discuss some of the most important and comprehensible features related to the chemical and physical structure of silica.

3.2.1 The Chemical Bulk Composition and Surface Structure

Porous silica is an industrial product and used as desiccant and adsorbent. The starting materials are water glass solution and sulfuric acid.[11] Chromatographic grade silicas are manufactured in kilogram or 100 kg batches according to specific reaction routes that allow to produce spherical particles of desired size and size distribution.[12]

Pure silica has a bulk composition of $[SiO_2 \cdot m \cdot H_2O]_n$ and is X-ray amorphous. Commercial silicas contain inorganic impurities such as alumina, titania, alkali and earth alkali metals, traces of acids, bases, and salts in the bulk structure as well as at the surface depending on the manufacturing process and the mode of after-treatment.

The surface of silica behaves in a weakly acidic manner due to the presence of hydroxyl groups that have a pK_a of about 7.[5] Thus, a suspension of silica in 0.1 *M* sodium chloride solution shows a pH between 5 and 7 as a result of the ion-exchange reaction between the protons of the hydroxyl groups and the sodium cations. The surface impurities of silica give rise to deviations of the expected pH of 5 to 7 and shift the pH of silica suspensions either into the acidic or alkaline regime.[13,14]

On account of the amorphous bulk structure the surface also exhibit a heterogeneous character that leads to surface hydroxyl groups of different reactivity.[5] The bonding of ligands and the deposition of polymer coatings remove most of the active hydroxyl groups. Another route to reduce the heterogeneity of the silica is to subject the product prior to modification to a combined acidic and hydrothermal treatment whereby crystalline surface domains are formed.[15]

The major drawbacks in the application of bonded silicas with aqueous buffered eluents in HPLC are (1) the solubility of the silica matrix in alkaline solutions of a pH in excess of 9 and (2) the hydrolytic cleavage of the siloxane bonds, which anchor the bonded groups to the surface. In neat water the solubility of amorphous silica amounts to about 100 ppm. This value increases exponentially with pH above 10 attributed to the formation of soluble silicates.[16] Solubility is known to be reduced by doping the silica surface with alumina[17] and zirconia,[18] respectively, or by adding trace amounts of aluminum into the alkaline mobile phase.[19]

The most important chemical properties are summarized as follows:

- The surface of silica behaves in a weakly acidic manner. As a consequence, silica functions as a weak cation exchanger. The ion-exchange capacity increases with the pH and becomes notable at pH > 8. The isoelectric point of silica is between 2 and 3. Consequently, the surface of silica and the silica particles bear a negative charge at a pH in excess of 4.
- The solubility of silica increases drastically at pH > 9. It is substantially reduced by doping the silica with alumina, or zirconia, or by adding traces of aluminum ions into the alkaline mobile phase.

The question remains: How do the intrinsic properties affect the chromatographic performance?

The remaining hydroxyl groups or negatively charged siloxanyl (SiO^-) sites at the silica surface being in equilibrium with an aqueous mobile phase give rise to undesired adsorption of biopolymers in the separation at bonded silicas.

The negatively charged surface of silica repels negatively charged solutes and as a consequence they are totally or partially excluded from entering the particles.

The ion-exchange capability of the silica surface may lead to a decline of the pH of the mobile phase when strong electrolyte solutions are applied in non-buffered eluents.

The chemical reactivity of the accessible native silica surface as well as the solubility can severely limit the life time of a bonded silica column (compare ref. 20).

3.2.2 The Physical Structure

The physical structure comprises a set of parameters including particle shape, size, and size distribution, pore size and size distribution, porosity, and surface area. The bead size can be controlled between 1 and 100 μm and even larger following sophisticated shaping processes.[12] The particles possess an open pore system made of channels and cavities. The mean pore size of silica can be adjusted between 1 and 1000 nm and is assessed by nitrogen adsorption and mercury penetration techniques applying corresponding computation methods.[21] The pores generate a large internal surface area between 1 and 1000 m^2/g. The internal surface area, a_s, is inversely proportional to the pore size (see Table 3–1). The porosity of the particles expressed by the ratio of the internal pore volume to the total volume of the particles generally amounts to about 80%. To suggest an image of the pore structure of a porous silica each particle can be considered as an aggregate of spherical particles of submicron size ordered in a randomly packed structure. As a result the pore structure is built up by connected constrictions and openings through the particle. By means of an aftertreatment the aggregate structure changes and may convert into a spongy-like system as illustrated in Figure 3–1 for a macroporous silica. It becomes evident from these considerations that a measured pore size distribution gives a rather poor description of the real pore structure. More realistic parameters that characterize the connectivity of porous network are the tortuousity factor and the pore diffusion coefficients of solutes.[22] Depending on the ratio of molecular size of solute to the pore size of packing the mass transfer into and out of the pores can become a limiting factor in the chromatographic separation of biopolymers. Strictly speaking, it is a combined effect of steric hindrance at the pore entrances, the restricted diffusion within the pores, and the fractional accessibility of the stationary surface.[23] Table 3–2 lists the calculated molecular diameters of random coil and globular proteins. Using nonporous packings these effects are eliminated a priori and only film diffusion and axial column dispersion effects have to be considered. The various elements of the physical structure of silica packings are schematically sketched in Figure 3–2.

The physical properties of the silica packings are linked to the chromatographic properties in a manifold way:

- Spherical particles when properly packed into columns generate a much more stable and homogeneous column bed than irregular ones. This leads to the expected column performance and a long column life time.

- The mean particle size, d_p, determines the number of plates of a column, which equals two to five times of d_p at optimum flow rate.

TABLE 3–1. Relation between Average Pore Diameter, p_d, and Specific Surface Area, a_s, of Silicas

p_d (nm)	a_s ($m^2\ g^{-1}$)	a_s ($m\ ml^{-1}$) of column volume
10	~ 250	~ 125[a]
30	~ 100	~ 50[a]
50	~ 50	~ 25[a]
100	~ 20	~ 10[a]
400	~ 5–10	~ 3–5
Nonporous		
d_p ~ 1 μm	3	5

[a]Assuming a packing density of 0.5 g ml^{-1}.

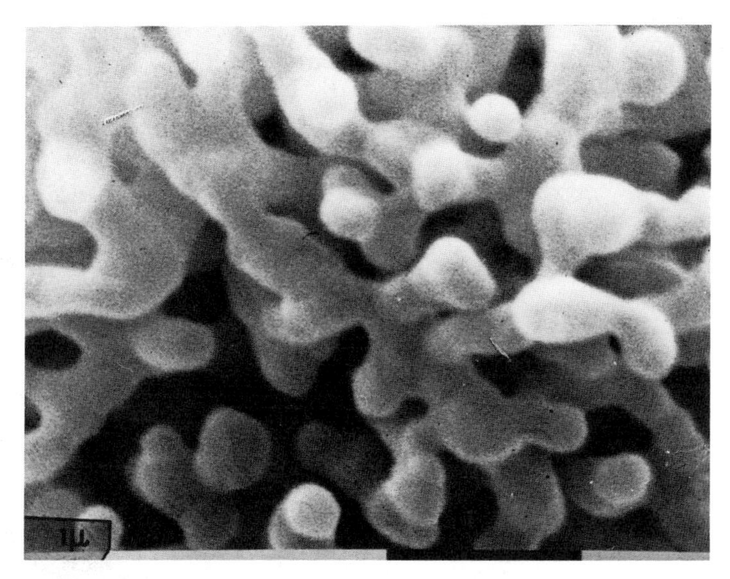

FIGURE 3–1. Electron scanning micrograph of LiCrospher Si 4000. (Courtesy of E. Merck, Darmstadt, FRG.)

- The mean particle size also controls the column pressure drop, Δp. At constant flow rate, column length, viscosity of eluent, and constant packing density Δp is inversely proportional to d_p^2.
- At a first approximation the retention of solutes in interactive HPLC is proportional to the surface area of the silica provided its value remains unchanged after surface modification and the surface is totally accessible to the solutes.
- The choice of the mean pore diameter, p_d, of a silica is dependent on the solute size. While packings of $p_d = 15$ nm are most suitable to chromatograph peptides up to 20 kDa,[25] larger pore sizes are required for proteins. The given p_d of a commercial packing is often a nominal value and does not reflect the actual width of the pore size distribution curve. Nowadays, bonded silicas are marketed with graduated pore sizes of 30, 50, 100, and 400 nm

TABLE 3–2. Molecular Diameter, *d*, of Proteins as a Function of Molecular Weight[a]

M / kilodalton	diameter of random coil proteins / nm	diameter of globular proteins / nm
1	2.6	1.6
10	3.2	3.5
100	25.8	7.6
1000	81.6	16.3

[a]From ref. 24, reprinted with permission of the publisher.

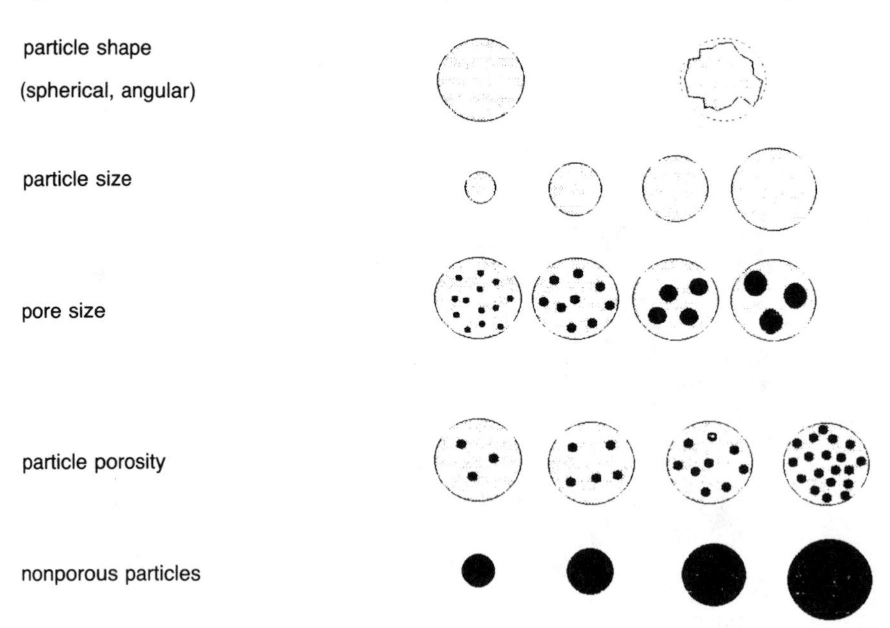

FIGURE 3–2. Physical structure parameters of silica packings.

pore size, and also as nonporous materials. As a general rule the ratio of the molecular diameter of solute to the mean pore diameter should be ≤ 0.1 to eliminate restricted pore diffusion.[26]

- The porosity of packings should be as high as possible. Particles with an internal porosity higher than 80% show a limited rigidity when packing pressures in excess of about 50 MPa and high flow rates of > 5 ml/min are applied. High particle porosities are usually generated by packings with large pores of $p_d > 50$ nm.

3.3 DESIGN, PREPARATION, AND CHARACTERIZATION OF BONDED SILICAS

3.3.1 Introduction

Porous silica provides an optimum support for HPLC of biopolymers due to its rigidity, variation, and control of the physical structure parameters. However, the polar and heterogeneous surface puts severe limitations on the use of native silicas, which is known to result in irreversible adsorption and denaturation of biopolymeric solutes. A promising means out of this dilemma is to chemically modify the surface. Modification serves three purposes. First, by covalent bonding of functional groups through surface reactions with appropriate reagents a novel stationary phase is created. In this way the stationary phase can be tailored to match the structure of analytes to be separated and leads to maximum and selective interactions. Second, in the course of the surface reaction the most active surface centers are removed or covered by a protective layer. As a result, matrix effects are drastically reduced. Third, the attachment of dense layers can substantially improve the chemical stability of a bonded silica toward aqueous mobile phases.

Typically, reagents employed for surface reactions are organosilanes with reactive chloro or alkoxy groups and terminating groups that permit further substitution, addition, and polymerization reactions. Also monomeric and oligomeric organic reagents have been deposited at silica held by adsorption or electrostatic forces, which are then subjected to polymerization and crosslinking. Nowadays, with the knowledge and experience accumulated in organosilicon and polymer chemistry one is able to design stationary phases according to the requirements set by the application in HPLC.

3.3.2 Design of Bonded Silicas

The general approach in bonded phase design is primarily to match the interactions between the solute and the stationary phase in such a way that they become highly discriminative and reversible. To maintain the biological activity of biopolymers the interactions must be "soft," meaning that the free energy of adsorption is low. The discrimination arises from selective single or multisite attachment between certain functional groups of the stationary phase and the solution. Its effectiveness is dependent on the accessibility and spatial arrangement of the interaction sites or the domains. The interactions stem from various attractive and repulsive forces as Lifshitz–van der Waals, hydrogen-bonding, and electrostatic forces. Stationary phases have been designed according to these types of interactions. Those carrying hydrophobic, ionic, and complexating functionalities as in reversed-phase, hydrophobic interaction, ion-exchange, and metal chelate chromatography are collectively termed broad range stationary phases, whereby those with biospecific functionalities (e.g., for antigen recognition) are considered single-client stationary phases, an expression introduced by Pirkle.[27] Another important property of stationary phases (and mobile phases) is that they can induce themselves changes in the conformation of biopolymers, which might result in an enhancement of selectivity. Molecular modeling of the biopolymeric solutes and the surface as well as of solute–surface interactions are in its initial phase and will help to a great extent to better understand the retention principles and the resulting selectivities in the future.

There are various ways to build up a structure of a stationary phase of bonded silicas (see Figure 3–3).

Monolayer type. Functional groups are linked by covalent bonds to the surface and form a fraction up to a complete monolayer. When the functional groups extend in length they become more and more mobile. Furthermore, depending on the extent of solvation by the eluent, the layer can expand or be compressed controlled by choice of solvent. The monolayer type is often met in RP silica packings where silanes with varying n-alkyl chain length are linked to the surface. Although peptides are able to penetrate the solvated n-alkyl chains, the excess of the chains for larger proteins is sterically hindered.

Polymer layers and coatings. Monomers are physically adsorbed or chemically bonded to the surface of a silica and then subjected to polymerization, cross-linking, and additional reactions. Attachment of monomers and oligomers is facilitated on already functionalized silicas such as diol and amino phases. Adhesion can also occur through electrostatic attraction forces when the surface and the reagent to be held bear opposite charges. In the formation of polymer layers onto the silica surface it is essential to control the thickness of the layer, so that pore blocking is avoided and rapid mass transfer is ensured. Furthermore, cross-linking has been found to be an effective means to increase the chemical stability of the polymeric bonded phase. A survey on polymeric layers and coatings was recently given by Schomburg.[28]

Sandwich structure. This principle was mainly advocated by Horvath and co-workers[29] and aims at a better protection of the native silica surface and the generation of "soft surface–solute interactions." The layer-by-layer buildup permits a high degree of flexibility in the design of bonded phases and the binding of functional groups at the top layer with a desired spacing.

Mixed-mode structures. The intention was to prepare bonded phases with a controlled spacing of functional groups, e.g., hydrophobic and ionic, to better utilize the distribution of interacting domains at a biopolymeric solute for higher selectivity.[30–32] The bonded phases offer the chance to operate the column in either one or another mode by simply adjusting the eluent composition.

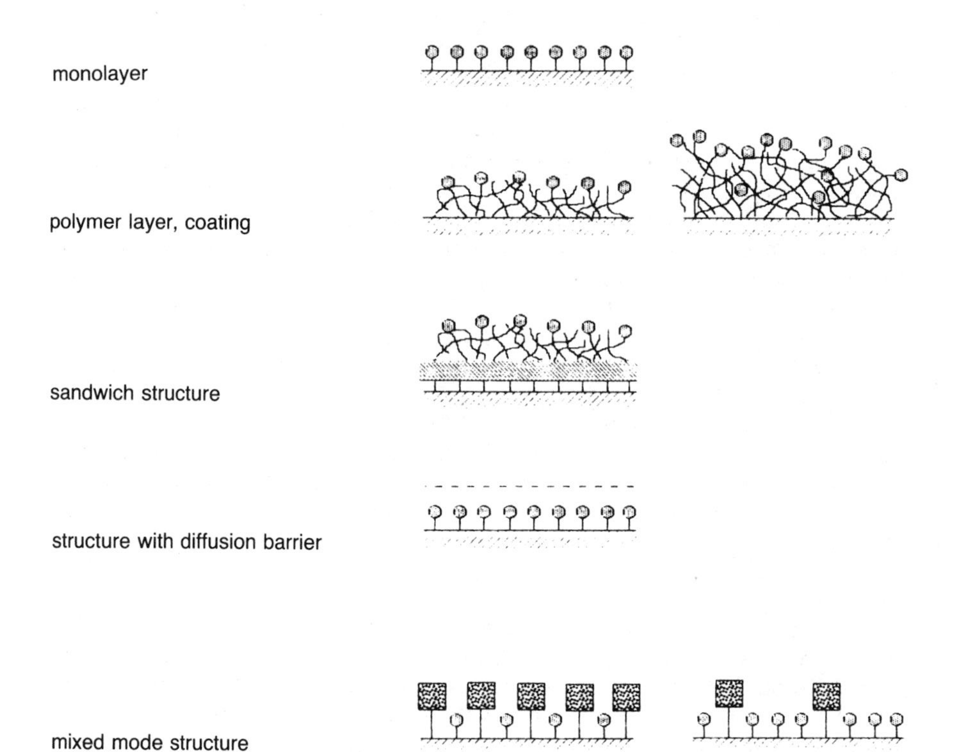

FIGURE 3–3. Structures of bonded silica stationary phases.

Bonded phases with diffusion barriers. In drug analysis in biological fluids it is essential to remove proteins associated with the drug. This has been performed by bonded phases with different functional groups at the external and the internal surface of the silica. The Pinkerton column might serve as a typical example. The particles contain a hydrophilic outer layer and *n*-alkyl functional groups at the internal surface.[33] The proteins elute quickly because they are not adsorbed and unable to penetrate the 6-nm pore size silica. The drug solutes are capable of entering the pores and interact by hydrophobic interactions.

Another concept recently introduced by Desilets and Regnier[39] is to use poly(oxyethylene) sorbitan monoalkylate surfactants that were adsorbed on the surface of a conventional reversed-phase packing and establishes a semipermeable hydrophilic layer over the silanized surface. This layer sterically hinders the protein to access the hydrophobic stationary phase.

3.3.3 Preparation of Bonded Silicas

The principles and procedures of the synthesis of bonded silicas are discussed groupwise according to the modes of HPLC applied to biopolymer separation. A more detailed review is given by Unger et al.[8]

3.3.3.1 Bonded Silicas in Size-Exclusion Chromatography (SEC)

The primary goal in the bonding chemistry of silica packings for SEC is to graft dense layers or coatings with hydrophilic polar, nonionic functional groups, thus minimizing solute–surface interactions and chemically protecting the native silica surface. As the chromatographic resolution in SEC is proportional to the internal porosity of the column it is essential to avoid major losses of the internal porosity of the particle by too thick coatings.

By far the most used silanes in the synthesis of bonded silicas for SEC of biopolymers are β-glycidoxypropyltriethoxysilane (Glymo), γ-substituted aminopropyltriethoxysilane and its derivatives, and silanes of a type such as $R\text{-}(CH_2—CH_2—O)_n—O—(CH_2)_3—Si—(OC_2H_5)_3$.[35] The surface modification is carried out with solutions of the respective silanes at elevated temperatures in various ways:

- under strictly anhydrous conditions with unpolar solvents,
- by adding traces of water to the suspension, which are assumed to act as a catalyst, and
- in aqueous suspensions.

In the latter case the pH controls whether intra- or intermolecular condensation and polymerization occur. Polymerization can lead to a high carbon load and consecutively to a drastic reduction in the pore volume of particles.

For the synthesis of polymeric phases vinylpyrrolidone, vinylimidazole, and vinylether have been applied.[28] Modification is accomplished either by polymerization of the adsorbed monomer without or with a co-monomer or the depositing polymer from aqueous solutions. It has been found that crosslinking of deposited poly(vinylpyrrolidone) reduces the pore volume.[36]

The degree of protection of the native silica surface is best monitored by measuring the elution volume of basic proteins having an isoelectric point of >9, e.g., lysozyme or chymotrypsinogen with buffered eluents of pH 7 and low ionic strength of <0.3. When the native surface is accessible the positively charged protein is attracted by the negative surface charges and thus retained. The elution volume then is larger than the dead volume of the column v_m. The adsorption can be suppressed by increasing the ionic strength of the eluent.

3.3.3.2 Bonded Silicas in Reversed-Phase Chromatography (RPC)

Bonded silicas used for RPC possess hydrophobic functional groups and retain biopolymers primarily through reversible hydrophobic association. Typical functional groups are *n*-octadecyl, *n*-octyl, *n*-butyl, and phenyl. Also cyano-bonded silicas have been employed where the propyl spacer brings about the hydrophobic character. The hydrophobicity of the RP packings is proportional to the carbon load, which arises from the number of carbon atoms per ligand and from the ligand density. Strong hydrophobic interactions might cause considerable losses in the bioactivity of proteins.

RP silicas belong to the monomeric and polymeric types. The surface modification can occur via a chemical bonding of reactive silane and by simple immobilization.

For the synthesis of monomeric type organosilanes such as R_3SiX, R_2SiX_2, and $RSiX_3$ are employed where X is chloro or alkoxy. Other reactive groups are dimethylamino, trialkyltrifluoroacetoxy, and enolate. Under comparable conditions the silanes follow the reactivity scale $C_8Si(CH_3)_2N(CH_3)_2$ > $C_8Si(CH_3)_2OCOCF_3$ > $C_8Si(CH_3)_2$ Cl >> $C_8Si(CH_3)_2OH$ ~ $C_8Si(CH_3)_2OCH_3$ ~ $C_8Si(CH_3)_2OC_2H_5$ and C_8SiCl_3 > $C_8CH_3SiCl_2$ > $C_8(CH_3)_2SiCl$ where C_8 stands for an *n*-octyl group.[37]

The silica is reacted with the silane either under anhydrous or hydrous conditions. In the latter case defined amounts of water are added to the suspension. Unpolar solvents such as toluene or aprotic polar, e.g., dimethylformamide, are used. In the reaction of chloroorganosilanes bases such as 2,6-lutidine[37] and morpholine[38] are added as catalysts and acid scavengers. Before modification the silica is subjected to a treatment by which the surface is activated and impurities are removed. Reaction is either accomplished in suspension with a solution of the corresponding silane or using a fluidized bed reactor where the silane is vaporized.[39] The latter procedure is claimed to give better results in terms of surface homogeneity and batch-to-batch consistency. The silane is added in excess and the suspension is subjected to reaction at elevated temperatures over a prolonged period of time. In the reaction of trichlorosilanes with silicas water can be added to generate a polymeric phase by inter- and intramolecular condensation.[40]

Polymeric phases are prepared by depositing prepolymers of poly(organomethylsiloxanes) at the surface and polymerization and cross-linking is induced by thermal treatment, γ-radiation, and addition of peroxides.[28] Also poly(butadiene) has been deposited to silica. These polymeric phases have an excellent pH stability but have not yet found widespread application for RPC of biopolymers.

3.3.3.3 Bonded Silicas in Hydrophobic-Interaction Chromatography (HIC)

HIC is carried out on weakly hydrophobic stationary phases with a descending salt gradient at neutral pH. The solute–surface interactions as well as the elution conditions are so mild that most of the proteins maintain their biological activity.[41–44]

Apart from organic-based supports such as cross-linked agarose, vinyl- and methacrylate copolymers macroporous silicas have gained considerable interest.[8] The weak hydrophobic character of bonded silicas for HIC relative to reversed-phase silicas is achieved either by reducing the *n*-alkyl chain length or the ligand density. Typically, ligands are pentyl, neopentyl, butyl, propyl, hydroxypropyl, ethyl, and methyl. There are two alternatives to synthesize bonded silicas for HIC. First, suitable organosilanes with *N*-acetyl, glycerol, and alkyldiethylene glycol groups are reacted with silicas.[45,46] Second, a protective hydrophilic polymer layer is immobilized at the surface followed by acetylation or alkylation of the top layer.[47] The latter type have found widespread application in HIC of proteins.

3.3.3.4 Bonded Silicas in Ion-Exchange Chromatography (IEC)

In IEC of biopolymer solutes are retained by electrostatic interactions between the ionogenic functional groups of the ion exchangers and the charged domains of a biopolymeric solute. Thus, the retention is controlled by the net charge and the charge distribution of a protein or nucleic acid at otherwise constant conditions. As the isoelectric points of proteins vary between 4 and 10 anion as well as cation exchangers are required.

The ionogenic functional groups of ion exchangers for biopolymer separations are the same as for classical ion exchangers. They are grouped into weak and strong according to their p*K* values as

cation exchangers:	—SO_3H	p*K* < 1	(SCX)
	—COOH	p*K* 4–6	(WCX)
anion exchangers:	—NR_3OH	p*K* > 13	(SAX)
	—NHR_2Cl —NH_2RCl —NH_3Cl	p*K* 5–9	(WAX)

The functional groups are linked via hydrophobic spacers to the support surface. Thus, there are three major variables in stationary-phase design of ion exchangers: the type(s) and p*K* of ionic functional group(s), the ligand density or the charge density, and the hydrophobic spacer.

To provide access to the stationary phase for proteins the pores must be sufficiently large. For proteins of 50 kDa a pore diameter of 50 nm is adequate. Larger proteins require 100 nm pore diameter packings.[48]

As silica itself acts as a weak cation exchanger it is mandatory to cover the surface properly by an appropriate layer or coating.

There are various approaches in the manufacture of silica-based ion exchangers.

First, an appropriate organosilane, e.g., Glymo is bonded to silica and zirconia-stabilized silica. The epoxy group is then cleaved to yield a diol phase. Amination of the diol-bonded silica yields an anion exchanger.[49,50]

Second, a polymer layer with desired functionalities is deposited at bare silica or a bonded silica with charged groups held by electrostatic interactions. The polymer that attracted the most widespread application in this respect is poly(ethyleneimine) (PEI) pioneered by Regnier and co-workers. Another type of polymeric coating is based on poly(aspartic acid).[51]

Third, a novel type of silica-based ion exchangers is made by a grafting polymerization of acrylamide derivates on diol-bonded macroporous silicas. The ion exchanger constitutes grafted linear polyacrylamide chains with 15 to 25 monomer units and charged functional groups bonded to the chains. The material is called "tentacle" type because of the similarity to the tentacles of the octopus. Ion exchangers are claimed to provide a better performance and maintenance of biological activity than conventional types.[52]

3.3.3.5 Bonded Silicas in Liquid–Liquid Partition Chromatography

Two phase aqueous–aqueous systems composed of water-soluble poly(ethyleneglycol) and dextran have been used by Albertsson[53] to isolate cells and cell fragments by a simple partitioning process. The major breakthrough of this method occurred as suitable polymeric organic and silica supports were developed that enabled immobilization of the dextran-rich phase, thus, permitting high-resolution separations of proteins and nucleic acids under mild conditions.[54–57]

The approach is based on grafting of linear polyacrylamide chains by means of radical polymerization of acrylamide on the surface of a diol-bonded macroporous silica. The same reaction has been carried out with hydrophilic macroporous methacrylate polymers, e.g., Fractogel (E. Merck, Darmstadt). The grafted linear polyacrylamide chains of 15 to 25 monomer units in length immobilize the dextran-rich phase, which is assumed to be attributed to the strong incompatibility between poly(acrylamide) and poly(ethyleneglycol). Although the amount of bonded polyacrylamide decreases with the increase of the pore size, the low surface area of the diol-bonded silicas of 100 and 400 nm nominal pore size has been found not to be a critical parameter in immobilizing a sufficient amount of the dextran-rich phase.

The principle of installing the phase system is illustrated in Figure 3–4. The column is first run with the dextran-rich phase where immobilization occurs. The excess of the dextran-rich phase is removed by rinsing the column with the poly(ethyleneglycol) phase. Preimmobilized packings on the basis of Fractogel are commercially available as LiPar Gel 650 and 750 (E. Merck, Darmstadt). To obtain reproducible results, the mobile phase and the column should be thermostated.

3.3.3.6 Bonded Silicas in Affinity Chromatography (AC)

During the last 5 years silica has gained considerable interest as support in biospecific and biomimetic affinity chromatography due to its rigid pore and particle structure and the control and adjustment of pore size and surface area.[58,59] Recently, the advantages of nonporous over porous silica supports

1.) Chemical modification: grafting polymeristation of acrylamide[1]
on premanufactured hydrophilized beads'
(e.g., Fractogel, LiChrospher® Diol)

CH_2OH, $R-CHOH$ $\xrightarrow[CH_2=CH-C(=O)NH_2]{Ce^{IV}}$ $-CHOH-(CH_2-CH(CONH_2))_n-CH_2-CH_2-C(=O)NH_2$; $R-CH-(CH_2-CH(CONH_2))_n-CH_2-CH_2-C(=O)NH_2$ (n≈15-25)

2.) "Installation" of the aqueous PEG-Dx two-phase system
2.1) adsorption of the Dx-rich bottom phase

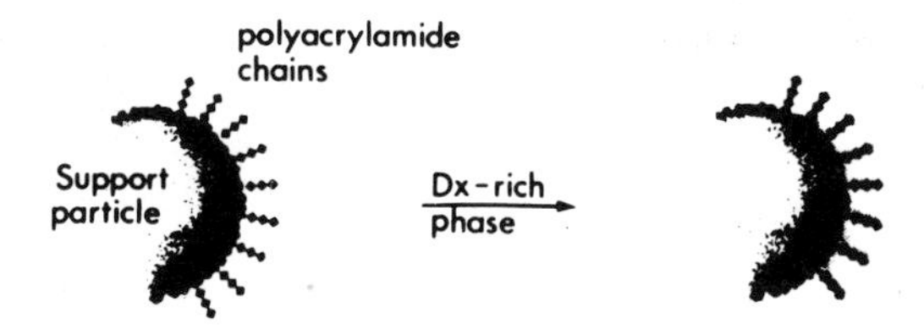

2.2) removal of the excess of the Dx-rich phase by the PEG-rich top phase

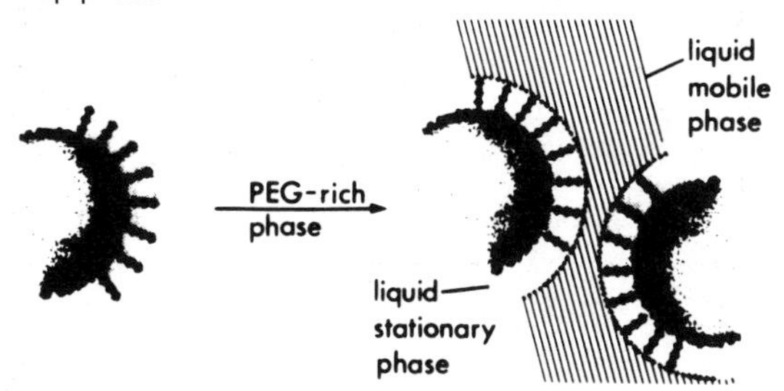

packing of coated support particles (suspended in the mobile top phase) into thermostated glass columns

FIGURE 3–4. Formation of a poly(acrylamide) bonded phase and its function in liquid–liquid partitioning chromatography. (Courtesy of W. Müller, E. Merck, Darmstadt, FRG.)

have been demonstrated in high-performance liquid affinity chromatographic purification and analysis of a variety of biologically active substances.[60,61]

Activation is the first step in the manufacture of any affinity support. The aim is a covalent binding of a ligand at the surface carrying a reactive terminating group, the latter enabling the attachment of the desired biomimetic or biospecific ligand. Activation chemistry up to 1982 has been reviewed by Larsson et al.[62] By far the most commonly used silane was 3-glycidoxypropyltrimethoxysilane (Glymo). Glymo offers various options to obtain activated silicas (see Figure 3–5).

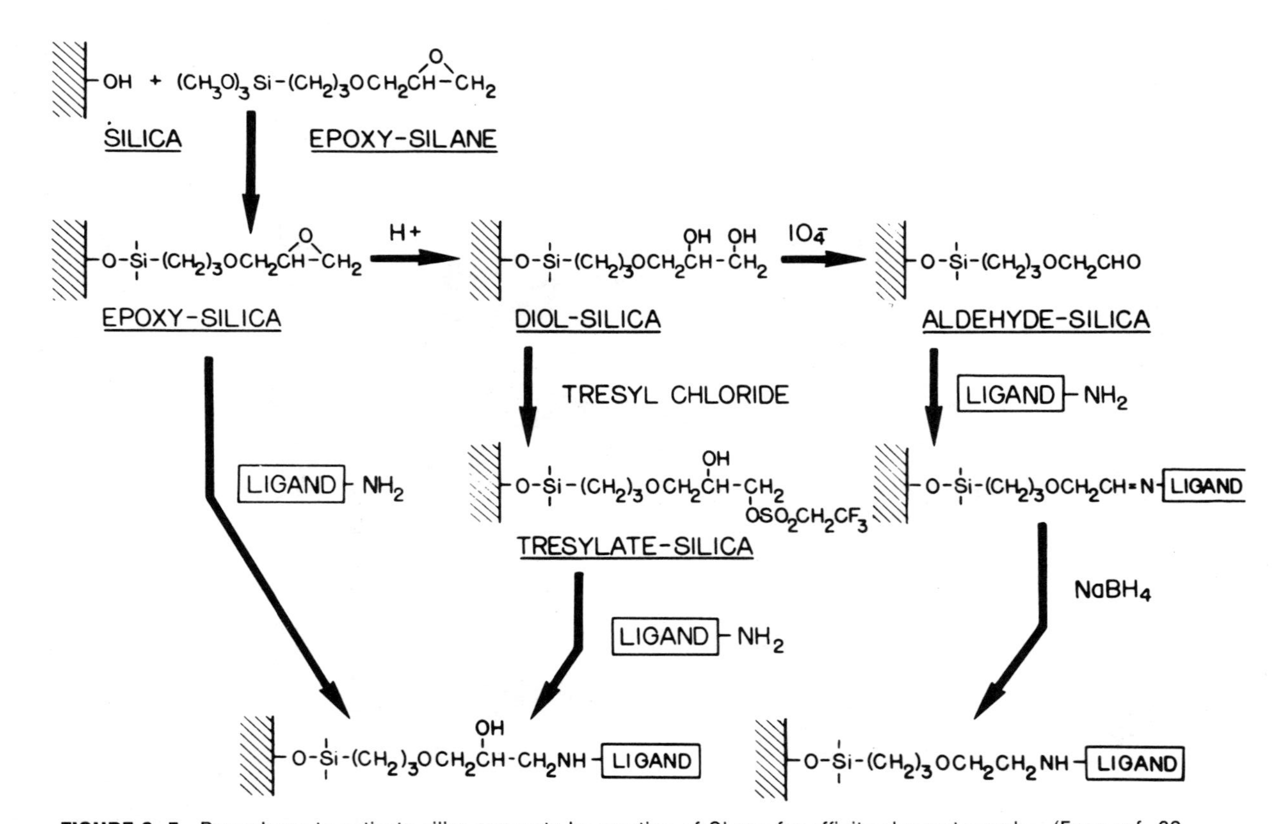

FIGURE 3–5. Procedures to activate silica supports by reaction of Glymo for affinity chromatography. (From ref. 62, reprinted by permission of the publisher.)

The epoxy-activated silica can react directly with the ligand. The oxirane ring can be cleaved by acids yielding a diol silica, which thereafter is converted to an aldehyde silica by addition of iodate. The diol groups themselves can be aminated, tresylated, and sulfhydrated.

Other popular silanes for activation are 3-aminopropyl-, 3-mercaptopropyl-, 3-isocyanatopropyl-, and 3-isothiocyanatopropylsilane. Of these the 3-isothiocyanatopropyl (–NCS) activated silicas have been frequently employed, because they react with primary and secondary amino functional groups of the ligand only at moderate pH values between 5 and 8.[61]

Ligands that have been bound to activated silicas range from low- to high-molecular-weight compounds up to monoclonal antibodies (see Table 3–3). The conditions of binding vary from substrate to substrate and are also dependent on the type of activated silica.

Comparative studies using activated silicas of various pore sizes have clearly demonstrated that the kinetics of the uptake of a substrate of about 50 kDa are slow at 30 nm of nominal pore size. To avoid slow kinetics associated with restricted pore diffusion activated silicas of 100 or more than 400 nm pore size are recommended.[63] The loss in internal surface area and in binding capacity with increasing pore size is not a critical parameter in affinity chromatography. Even 2-μm nonporous silicas with surface areas of about 3 m^2/ml of packing yielded loading capacities of more than 0.6 nmol of protein per ml of immobilized dye supports.[61] Moreover, it has been shown that nonporous silica supports provide a ligand accessibility in excess of 50% of total ligands bound.[64] Further studies are directed toward the utilization of ligands and to the elimination of nonspecific interactions caused by the silica matrix.

Metal chelate chromatography (MCC) pioneered by Porath and co-workers on agarose[65–67] was adapted to bonded silicas with metal complexing groups.[68,69] Hydrolytically stable bonded silicas with metal complexing ligands including iminodiacetate (IDA) were synthesized by Gimpel and Unger,[70] Feibush et al.,[71] Fanou-Ayi and Vijayalaksami,[72] and El Rassi and Horvath.[73] MCC was performed on IDA-bonded silicas mainly in the Cu^{2+} complexed form.

3.3.4 Characterization of Bonded Silicas

There have been numerous studies directed toward the characterization of bonded silicas elucidating their structural and chromatographic properties (for comparison see refs. 164 and 165). The studies aim at widely different purposes:

- to establish the physical and chemical structure of bonded silicas relative to the parent material,
- to control the reproducibility of the properties of bonded silicas in manufacturing processes,
- they serve to improve the chromatographic properties of bonded silicas,
- to assess the chromatographic properties, e.g., retention, selectivity, efficiency, under standardized elution conditions,
- to determine the mass and biorecovery of biopolymers in chromatographic use, and
- to evaluate the life time of bonded silica columns.

TABLE 3–3. Silica-Based Affinity Systems

Activation	Immobilized ligand	Substrate	Reference
	Anti-interferon-α	Interferon-α	74
	Human IgG	Protein G	75
	Human serum albumin		
	Concanavalin A	Glycoproteins	76
Amino	Neomycin sulfate	Anionic phospholipids	77
	L-Lysine		
Epoxy	Anti-human IgG	Human IgG	78
Dialdehyde	Glucose oxidase		
Amino			
CNBr	Asialofetuin	Pertussis toxin	79
Iminodiacetic acid–Cu(II) complex	Concanavalin A	Peroxidase α_1-Acid glycoprotein	80
	Cibacron Blue F3GA	Polynucleotide kinase	81
	Bright Red 6 C		
	Procion Red HE-3B		
	Red Brown 2K		
	Bright Yellow 53		
	Stable Light-Yellow 2KT		
	Orange 5K		
	Dextran Blue		
	L-Lysine	Human thrombin	82
	L-Arginin		
	Hexamethylendiamine		
	Gramicidin S		
	Bacitracin		
Glutaricaldehyde	Gramicidin S	Pepsin	83
p-Benzoquinone		Proteolytic complex	
Carbodiimide			
	Protein A	Immunoglobulin	84
		Stroma free hemoglobin	85
		Receptor proteins	86
		Antibodies	
		Active enzymes	
	Procion Blue MX-R	L-Lactade dehydrogenase	87
N-Hydroxy-succinimide ester	Protein A	Proteins, enzymes IgG, etc.	88
	Concanavalin A		
	Melittin		
	6-Aminohexyl-Cibacron		
	2-(Trifluoromethyl)-10-(3-aminopropyl) phenothiazine		
Diol	Leucoagglutinating phytohemagglutinin	Oligosaccharides	89
	Concanavalin A		
	Datura stramonium agglutinin		

TABLE 3–3. Silica-Based Affinity Systems (*continued*)

Activation	Immobilized ligand	Substrate	Reference
	Vicia villosa agglutinin		
Epoxy	BSA		90
Methacrylate	Trypsin		
Amino	Bovine pancreatic trypsin inhibitor	Trypsin	
Epoxy	Melittin	Calmodulin	91
Adipic acid	ATP	Hemoglobin	92
		Oxyhemoglobin	
Amino	Diaza[2.2]-18-crown-6	tRNA	93
Amino	Phenylboronic acid	Peptides	94
	Protein A	Monoclonal antibodies	95
Epoxy	Gramicidin S	Thrombin	96
	Bacitracin	Plasma serine proteinase	
Mercapto	Tresyl chloride activated	Lactate dehydrogenase	97
	Dextran		
N-Hydroxysuccimide	TXB_2 antibody	Thromboxane B_2	98
	Concanavalin A	Anti-blood group A antibody	99
	Concanavalin A	*p*-Nitrophenyl-α-D-mannopyranoside	100
Carbodiimidazole	Antigen	Antibody	101
	Trypsin inhibitor	Trypsin	
	Trypsin	Trypsin inhibitor	
Aminoaryl	5-Hydroxyuridine 2′(3′)5′-diphosphate	Exonuclease A5	102
	Iminodiacetic acid–metal complex	Proteins with histidine on the surface	103
Epoxy	Steroid dexamethasone	Antidexamethasone AB	104
	2-(Trifluoromethyl)-10-(3′-aminopropyl) phenothiazine	Calmodulin	105
	p-Aminophenyl-α-D-mannopyranoside	Concanavalin A	106
	D-Glucosamine		
	Procion Blue MX-R	L-Lactate dehydrogenase	107
	Tomatine	Sterols	108
Chloromethyl benzene	Adenine	Purine	109
	Uracil		
	Nitrobenzene boronic acid		
	Protein A	Igs G	110
	Concanavalin A	Membran glycoproteins from human lung	111
	Pisum sativum agglutinin	Fibroblast	

(*continued*)

TABLE 3–3. Silica-Based Affinity Systems (*continued*)

Activation	Immobilized ligand	Substrate	Reference
N-*p*-Nitrobenzoyl-β-alanin	5-Hydroxypyridine 2′(3′)5′-diphosphate N_4-(2-Aminoethyl) cytidine 2′(3′)5′-diphosphate	Exonuclease A5	112
Amino		Glucoamylase	113
Epoxy	Mannitol Glucitol Xylitol Glucose	Glucose isomerase	114
Amino	Polygalacturonic acid	Pectinase	115
Diol	Diverse sugars	Concanavalin A	116
Amino	*p*-Diazoniumbenzylate		117
	12-Crown-4	Na^+	118
Amino	Enzymes, antigens, antibodies, lectins, cells, etc.		119
	Bovine serum albumin	α-Chymotrypsin	120
—N═C═S Amino	Procion triazine dyes	Hydrophobic plasma membrane proteins	121
Epoxy	Lysine Albumin IgG Protein A	Plasminogen Bilirubin Protein A IgG	122
	Boric acid	Ribonucleoside	123
Diol	D-Glucosamine Trypsin inhibitor	Concanavalin A Trypsin	124
	Organomercury	Sulfhydryl-containing compounds	125
	Concanavalin A	Sugar derivates	126
	Phytohemagglutinin	Human serum glycoprotein	127
	Boronic acid	Ribonucleotides	128
Amino	γ-Globulin	Influenza virus Rabies virus	129
Epoxy	Alcohol dehydrogenase	Adenine nucleosides Adenine nucleotides Triazine dyes	130
Chloro	*m*-Aminobenzene-boronic acid	Polyols Nucleosides	131
	Procion Blue MX-R	Lactate dehydrogenase	132
Diol	Protein A	IgG	133
	Anthraquinone, phthalocyanine, or aromatic Azo Dye in connection with a metal ion	Enzymes, e.g., carboxypeptidase G_2	134

TABLE 3–3. Silica-Based Affinity Systems (*continued*)

Activation	Immobilized ligand	Substrate	Reference
Amino	*p*-Aminophenyl-aminooxoacetic acid linked with pentadialdehyde	Sialidase	135
Amino	Antraquinone Phthalocyanine Aromatic Azo Dye	Diverse enzymes	136
Epoxy	*N*-Methylolacrylamide	Diverse proteins	137
Diol	Glucosamine	Concanavalin A	138
	2.2-Bis(4-epoxy-propylhydroxyphenyl) propan	Microbial lipase	139
	Boronic acid	Ribo- and deoxyribonucleotides and nucleosides	140
	Concanavalin A	Peroxidase Glucose oxidase	141
	Dextran Blue	Luciferase	142
Epoxy	5-Hydroxyuridine 2′(3′)5′-diphosphate	Exonuclease A5	143
	Triazine dyes	Enzymes	144(rev.)
	Heparin Antithrombin III	Antithrombin III Heparin	145
Amino	Bacitracin Bacillioquin Gramicidin	Carboxylic proteinases *Russula decolorans* *Trichoderma lignorum* Serine proteases from *Thermoactinomyces vulgarus, T. koningii, T. lignorum*, and bacilli (subtilisins)	146
Aldehyde	Aromatic Diamine	Hemin	147
Epoxy	Procion Blue MX-R Procion Yellow H-A Procion Green H-4G Procion Red H-8BN Procion Brown MX-5BR Cibacron Blue F3G-A	Lactate dehydrogenase Hexokinase Alkaline phosphatase carboxypeptidase G_2 Tryptophanyl-tRNA synthetase	148
Epoxy	Cibacron Blue F3G-A	Dehydrogenases Isoenzymes Kinases Pancreatic RNase A	149
Amino	Digitonin	Cholesterol	150
Polydiazo	Antigen	Antibody	151

(*continued*)

TABLE 3–3. Silica-Based Affinity Systems (*continued*)

Activation	Immobilized ligand	Substrate	Reference
Epoxy	3-Aminobenzeneboronic acid	Nucleosides Nucleotides Carbohydrates	152
Amino	Ovomucoid	Trypsin	153
Aldehyde	Phospholipid	Phospholipidase D	154
Amino	Modified lectin	Phospholipidase A_2	155
Amino	*p*-Benzoquinone linked with bacitracin	Proteolytic enzymes	156
	Antibody	Protein antigen	157
DEAE-Dextran	Ganglioside GM_1	Cholera toxin	158
Amino	Lysoganglioside GM_1	γ-Globulins Albumin Cholera toxin	159
Aldehyde	N_6-(6-Aminohexyl)-AMP	Lactate dehydrogenase Alcohol dehydrogenase	160
Chloro	Uracil Thymine Cytosin	Uridine Cytidine Guanosine Adenine	161
Amino	D-Asparagine	L-Asparaginase	162
Amino	Adenine Adenylyl imidodiphosphate NAD	Alcohol dehydrogenase	163

The object subjected to a given measurement is either the bulk powder, the suspended powder, or the column packed with the material of interest. To obtain reliable information on the chemical and physical structure of bonded silicas as powders a large number of physicochemical methods have been applied. According to the underlying principle they are grouped into spectroscopic, adsorption, thermal analysis. Each method yields information on a specific surface or bulk property of the material. To assess a general valid structural view several methods have to be applied in combination to the same sample. Furthermore, the structural properties derived by surface analysis where samples are pretreated in high vacuum and at high temperature might not reflect the situation of the material when used in chromatography equilibrated with a mobile phase. Chromatographic tests with mixtures of selected standard probes are certainly more useful and informative. Again, the test conditions are far from the real world where biopolymers in serum or plasma have to be analyzed after an extensive cleanup procedure.

Following these considerations the researcher faced with any kind of characterization and testing should answer the following questions:

What kind of information is essentially required?

Does the information derived by a certain method have a distinct relevance to the problem posed?

What are the limitations of the method applied?

This section will briefly deal with the collective physical, chemical, and chromatographic properties that can be assessed on bonded silicas.

Methods Applied for Characterization of Bonded Silicas A survey of the most relevant methods is given in Table 3–4. The more interested reader is referred to the special literature. The methods are grouped into those applied to powders and to bonded silicas packed into columns. The former range from simple techniques such as elementary analysis to highly sophisticated techniques in which the surface structure of bonded silicas is examined, e.g., by means of ^{13}C and ^{29}Si CP MAS NMR spectroscopy. The column experiments are mainly thought to check the quality of separation and to help optimize the conditions with respect to resolution, speed, and recovery.

Brief Summary of the Physical and Chemical Structure of Bonded Silicas Hydroxyl groups such as isolated, geminal, and vicinal have been identified at the silica surface by means of ^{29}Si CP MAS NMR spectroscopy[164] and infrared spectroscopy in combination with deuterium exchange.[166] The total content of hydroxyl groups and physisorbed water has been measured by ^{1}H NMR spectroscopy with deuterated trifluoroacetic acid,[167] by thermal analysis,[164] and by titration with *n*-butylamine in aprotic solvents.[168]

Quantitation of single hydroxyl group species has been accomplished by ^{29}Si CP MAS NMR spectroscopy by varying the contact time.[169] Surface impurities have been monitored by electron spectroscopic methods.[170] On account of the amorphous bulk structure the surface of silica has been viewed as energetically and geometrically heterogeneous. The fractal dimension of porous silicas has been found to be close to 3.[171]

Most efforts in the surface studies of bonded silicas have been centered on reversed-phase materials using infrared (transmission and DRIFT)[164] and solid-state CP MAS NMR spectroscopy.[172–174] The latter method has been shown to be a sensitive means to estimate the short-range structure of silicon atoms. In this way one is able to discriminate between different structures of bonded phases, e.g., monomeric and polymeric. By measuring the proton relaxation times, $T_{1\rho H}$, the mobility of *n*-alkyl groups has been estimated and correlated to chromatographic retention of solutes.[175] A phase transition of bonded *n*-alkyl groups has been identified by differential scanning calorimetry and by measuring the retention–temperature dependencies of solutes on reversed-phase silicas.[176,177]

Such a phase transition occurs when the chain length of the ligand, n, is larger than 16, the ligand density $\alpha > 3$ µmol/m^2, and the mean pore diameter of silica $d_p >> 6$ nm.[178] So far, little information is available on the structure and mobility of polymer chains in polymer coatings at the silica surface.

The application of modern surface analytic methods has substantially improved knowledge of the surface structure of bonded silicas. The gap between the measurement and operation conditions has become partially overcome by *in situ* column spectroscopic measurements as demonstrated by NMR image analysis[179] and fluorescence spectroscopic studies.[180]

TABLE 3–4. Survey of Methods to Characterize Bonded Silicas

Method	Property
Applied to powders, suspensions etc.	
Sieving	Particle shape, particle size, particle size distribution[184]
Sedimentation	
Light microscopy	
Electron scanning microscopy	
Light scattering	
Coulter counter	
Gas adsorption (nitrogen, 77K)	Specific surface area according to BET, specific pore volume
Mercury porosimetry	Pore size distribution, mean pore diameter[21]
Adsorption from solution	Sorption isotherm, maximum uptake, kinetics of adsorption distribution constant[185]
Titration with bases or acids	Ion-exchange capacity[186]
Titration with *n*-butylamine and acrymethanols as indicators	Total acidity and acidity strength distribution[168]
Elementary analysis	C, H, N content (load, ligand density)
Thermal analysis[187]	
Thermogravimetry (TG)	Weight loss during ignition
Differential thermal analysis (DTA)	
Differential scanning calorimetry (DCS)	Exothermic, endothermic changes during ignition
Spectroscopy	
Inductively coupled plasma-atomic emission spectroscopy (ICP-AAS)	Content of elements in the bulk phase
Nuclear magnetic resonance spectroscopy (NMR)	
Suspension	Types of hydroxyl groups and *n*-alkyl groups, polymer–monomer grafting, ligand density, mobility of functional groups
Solid-state	
Cross-polarization magic angle spinning (CP MAS ^{1}H, ^{13}C, ^{29}Si	
^{1}H NMR spectroscopy following deuterium exchange using CF_3COOD	Content of hydroxyl groups and physisorbed water
Infrared spectroscopy (IR)[188–190]	Types of hydroxyl groups, types of bonded groups, and their interactions with probe molecules
Diffuse reflection infrared fourier transform spectroscopy (DRIFT)[191]	
Treatment with HF followed by GC analysis of fluorosilanes[192]	Types and content of *n*-alkyl groups of reversed phase silicas

TABLE 3–4. Survey of Methods to Characterize Bonded Silicas (*continued*)

Method	Property
Applied to columns	
Isocratic elution mode	Solute capacity factor, k'
	Selectivity coefficient, α
	Standard deviation of solute peak in time units, σ_t
	Column plate height, H
	Column plate number, N
	H as a function of linear velocity of eluent, u
	Column pressure drop as a function of the flow rate of the eluent, F
	Calibration curve in SEC: logarithm of molecular weight as a function of elution volume of solute
	Distribution constant of solute in SEC, K_{SEC}
	Chromatographic resolution, R_s
	S, solute parameter in gradient elution RPC
	Z, solute parameter in gradient elution IEC
	λ, solute parameter in gradient elution HIC
	Lifetime of column = dependence of k', α, H, R_s, and Δp as a function of column usage
Gradient elution mode	Solute capacity factor, $\bar{k}$
	Standard deviation of solute peak in time units, σ_t
	S, solute parameter in gradient elution RPC
	Z, solute parameter in gradient elution IEC
	Distribution constant of solute in IEC, K_{IEC}
	Chromatographic resolution in gradient elution, R_s
	Peak capacity, PC
Fluorescence spectroscopy of column effluent that contains biopolymers labeled with polar sensitive fluophors[193,194]	Conformational changes of proteins and their interactions with the surface of bonded silicas
Elution of radioactive-labeled compounds	Mass recovery of proteins

(*continued*)

TABLE 3–4. Survey of Methods to Characterize Bonded Silicas (*continued*)

Method	Property
Application of bioassays to the eluate	Biological recovery
Zonal elution, frontal analysis[196]	Effective ligand density, binding capacity, ligand accessibility, association constant of the ligand–substrate complex, K_{assoc}

Brief Description of the Chromatographic Properties of Bonded Silicas It is general consensus that spherical particles offer a better chromatographic performance than irregular particles, taking column efficiency, column pressure drop, and column life time as decisive criteria into account. The mean particle diameter of bonded silicas ranges between 3 and 10 μm meeting the requirements for analytical separations, while for preparative isolations particles of $d_p > 10$ μm are preferred. Columns packed with 2–3 μm have been designed for fast separations. They are packed in short columns and run with specifically designed instruments (low injection volume, low volume of the detector cell, minimum extracolumn contributions, response time of detector in the order of 50 msec).

To generate the expected column efficiency the ratio of the mean particle diameter $d_{p_{90}}/d_{p_{10}}$ should amount to 1.5 to 2.0 where $d_{p_{90}}(d_{p_{10}})$ is the particle diameter at 90% (10%) of the cumulative particle size distribution.

The column performance in terms of plate height is measured as a function of the flow rate of the eluent under isocratic elution conditions.

For comparison of columns with different particle diameter reduced parameters are used as the reduced plate height

$$h = \frac{H}{d_p} \tag{3–1}$$

and the reduced linear velocity of eluent

$$\nu = \frac{u d_p}{D_{im}} \tag{3–2}$$

where D_{im} is the solute diffusion coefficient in the mobile phase.[181] The experimental curves h against ν have been fitted with the equation

$$h = A\nu^{1/3} + B/\nu + C\nu \tag{3–3}$$

where A, B and C are constants.

The column packing quality is reflected by the term A, which varies between 0.5 and 0.8. C represents the mass transfer kinetics and is in the order of

0.01 and is mainly dictated by the stationary-phase properties and the pore structure of bonded silicas.[182]

The function h against ν goes through a minimum at $h = 2\text{–}5$ and $\nu = 5\text{–}10$. This means that at optimum flow rate the plate height corresponds to 2 to 5 times of the particle diameter of the bonded silica.

Biopolymers require larger pore size packings than low-molecular-weight compounds. As a general rule the pore diameter, p_d, should be three times larger than the Stokes diameter of the solute.[183] To avoid restricted diffusion of the solute into the pore space of the particles the p_d should be at least 10 times larger than the solute Stokes diameter. Packings with pore sizes of 15 nm thus match solutes up to 20 kDa, whereas larger proteins require macroporous silicas of p_d of 50 nm and larger. As a consequence, nonporous bonded silicas have been developed as packings in interactive HPLC of biopolymers with particle sizes between 1 and 2 μm. The lack of internal surface and pores leads to a drastic reduction of the surface area to about 5 m^2/ml of column volume at 1–2 μm packings. The retention of solutes on these packings then corresponds to those obtained on 100- to 400-nm pore size silicas.

A general model of the HPLC separation of large molecules including biopolymers has been worked out by Snyder and Stadalius.[184] The approach includes a discussion of the retention relationships and band broadening effects in large molecule HPLC by means of RPC, HIC, IEC, and SEC and provides guidelines to optimize a separation.

Retention in RPC is usually presented as a plot of logarithm of $\bar{k}$ against the mobile phase composition $\bar{\Phi}$. From the initial part of the curve the slope S can be derived. The solute parameter, S, is related to the molecular weight, M, of the solute as follows:

$$S = 0.48M^{0.44} \qquad (3\text{–}4)$$

Equation (3–4) permits S values to be predicted for given biopolymeric solutes without carrying out experiments.

In IEC the solute parameter Z and the distribution constant of a given protein is derived from the plot logarithm of k' against the reciprocal of the salt concentration of the eluent at isocratic conditions. The data are equivalent to those derived from gradient elution.

In SEC of biopolymers the calibration curve (logarithm of M against the elution volume) provides the most valuable information, namely on the fractionation range and resolution power of an SEC column.

As in isocratic elution the bandwidth expressed by σ_t is related to column plate number, N, in gradient elution by

$$\sigma_t = (2.3 + 1)Gt_0/2.3bN^{1/2} \qquad (3\text{–}5)$$

where G is the gradient compression factor, to the column dead time, and b the gradient steepness parameter.

Calculated σ_t values have been compared to experimentally derived σ_t values in RPC, HIC, and IEC to validate the model. Equations to calculate the band broadening of proteins on SEC columns have been proposed, permitting comparison similar to the interactive modes.

The concept of chromatographic resolution, R_s, in isocratic elution can be also adapted to gradient conditions by substituting k' with $\bar{k}$. A more useful separation parameter in gradient elution is the peak capacity, *PC*, which is proportional to R_s. *PC* is related to the gradient time, t_g, the flow rate, F, the column length, L, and the particle diameter of packing, d_p, as

$$PC \propto R \propto t_g^{0.5} F^0 L^0 d_p^{-1} \quad (3\text{–}6)$$

According to Eq. (3–6) peak capacity and resolution increase with the gradient time and are not much affected by the flow rate and the column length. *PC* is inversely proportional to the particle diameter of packing.

The peak height, *PH*, is inversely proportional to the band broadening expressed by σ_t and related to t_g, F, L, and d_p as follows

$$PH \propto t_g^{-0.5} F^{-1} L^0 d_p^{-1} \quad (3\text{–}7)$$

According to Eq. (3–7) *PH* decreases with t_g and F and is not affected by L. The smaller d_p is the larger *PH* will be.

At optimized gradient conditions an increase in column length results in an enhancement of *PC* and R_s. Long columns used in gradient elution of interactive HPLC of biopolymers might create problems with respect to biorecovery of solutes. If this is the case the column length has to be correspondingly reduced.

In biomimetic and biospecific affinity chromatography the binding capacity, the ligand utility, and the extent of nonspecific interactions are the most relevant parameters to judge the performance of an affinity packing apart from resolution and biorecovery.

3.4 CHROMATOGRAPHIC PROPERTIES OF BONDED SILICAS IN NONINTERACTIVE AND INTERACTIVE HPLC OF BIOPOLYMERS

3.4.1 Size-Exclusion Chromatography

Size-exclusion columns elute biopolymers in the sequence of decreasing molecular size and shape on the basis of a selective permeation in the intraparticle column volume, V_i.[196] The limits of the elution volume, V_e, are set. V_e varies between V_0, the interstitial or interparticle column volume, and V_m, the column dead volume, which is the sum of V_0 and V_i. This holds only in the case of a pure size-exclusion mechanism when secondary phenomena contributing to retention are negligibly small. Using V_e, V_i, and V_m a solute distribution coefficient, K_{SEC}, can be calculated that varies between zero and unity. Cases in which $K_{SEC} > 1$ indicate that additional retention takes place caused by solute–surface electrostatic and hydrophobic interactions.

When attempting an SEC separation of biopolymers the primary decision is to choose a column with a fractionation range that matches the molecular weight range of the biomacromolecules to be resolved.[197] This information is drawn from the calibration curve of the SEC column, which is a plot of the logarithm of the molecular weight of biopolymer against the elution volume, V_e. Calibration curves are usually available from the supplier or can be experimentally measured using a set of standard proteins with known molecular weights. Figure 3–6a and b shows such curves for two commercial columns, the Zorbax Bio Series Columns GF 250 and 450. The number 250 and 450 indicate the nominal pore size of silica packings in Ångström units.

Essential for the SEC separation of biopolymers is the linear part of the calibration curve and its width. The linearity is determined by the mean pore size and pore size distribution of the packing. As a general rule, 10- and 50-nm pore size silicas generate a fractionation range between 10 and 2000 kDa. It should be emphasized that V_e is not only a function of the molecular weight but is also dependent on the molecular shape. Thus, a globular protein when denaturated gives a smaller elution volume than in its native form. Deviations from the linearity of the calibration curve are often associated with a multimodal pore size distribution of the packing, the occurrence of electrostatic (attractive or repulsive) and hydrophobic (attractive) solute–surface interactions. The latter can be manipulated by adjusting the pH and the ionic strength of the eluent.[197]

Chromatographic resolution, R_s, related to the molecular weight difference of biomacromolecules, is controlled by two packing properties: the internal column volume V_i, which corresponds to the specific pore volume per ml packing in the column ($R_s \propto V_i$), and the mean particle size, d_p, of the packing, $R_s \propto d_p^{-1}$. First, V_i relative to V_o, called the phase ratio, determines the width of the abscissa of the calibration curve at which the fractionation occurs. The phase ratio of commercial bonded silica SEC columns varies between 0.6 and 1.7.[197] Second, the particle size controls the peak dispersion in terms of the column plate number, N, according to the equation

$$N = \frac{L}{2d_p} \tag{3–8}$$

where L is the column length. In other words, the peaks become sharper and higher when reducing the particle diameter, d_p. Thus, high resolution SEC columns are now packed with 5-μm particles as compared to 10-μm particles in traditional columns. However, to gain the expected column performance as given in Eq. (3–8) the eluent flow rate should be kept at optimum. At constant d_p the optimum flow rate is proportional to the molecular weight of biopolymer via the solute diffusion coefficient [see Eq. (3–2)]. In comparison to the separation of low-molecular-weight compounds in interactive HPLC where optimum flow rates of columns of 4 mm i.d. are in the order of 0.5 to 2.0 ml/min, the optimum flow rates for SEC separations of biopolymers of 10 to 1000 kDa range between 7 and 300 μl/min.[198] As the flow rate dictates the analysis time, t, by the equation

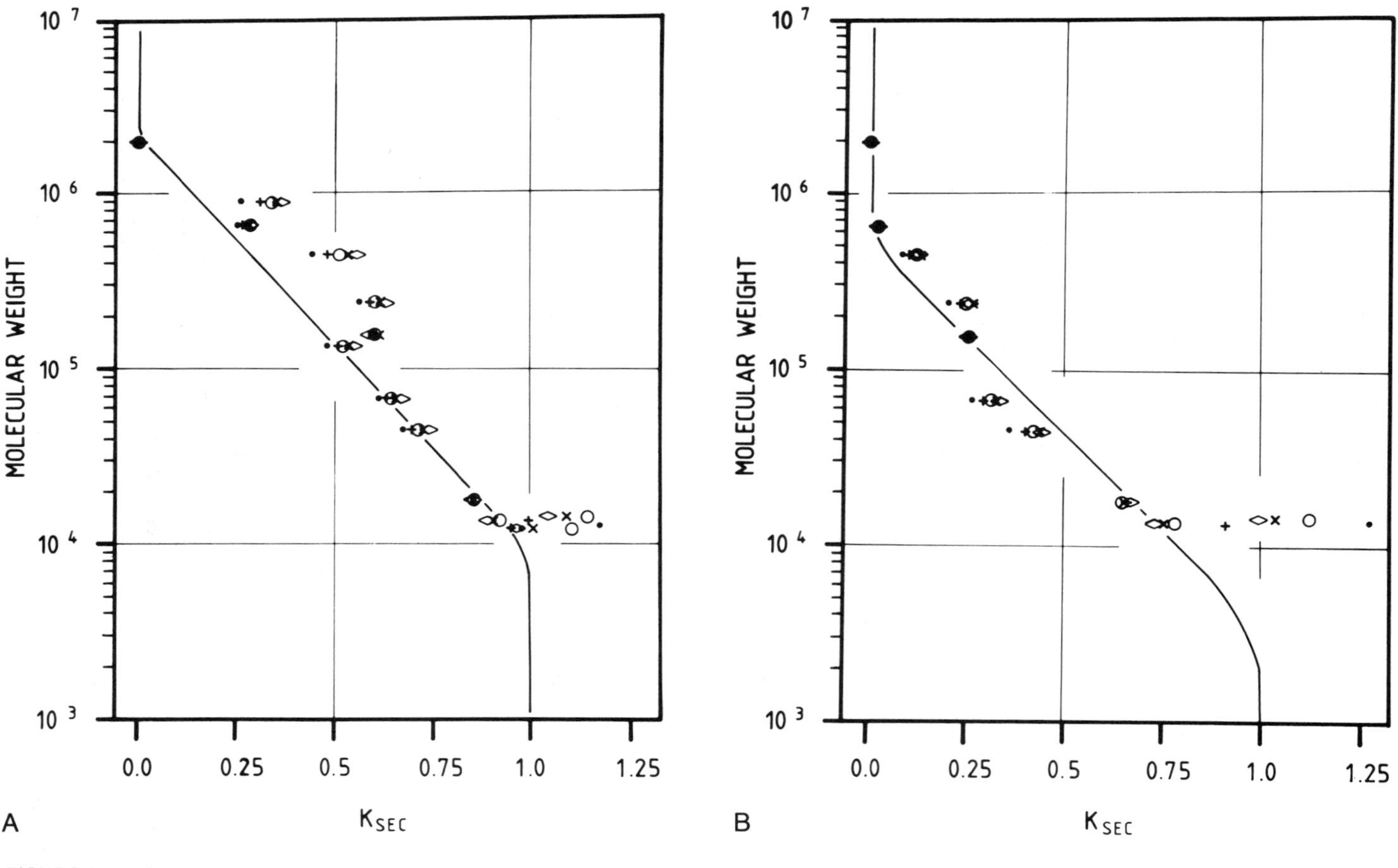

FIGURE 3–6. Calibration curves of standard proteins on Zorbax Bio Series columns GF 250 (A) and GF 450 (B). (From ref. 199, reprinted by permission of the publisher.)

$$V_e = Ft \tag{3–9}$$

such low flow rates generate analysis times of several hours. Thus, a compromise has to be made between chromatographic resolution and analysis time. It should be mentioned in this context that most common HPLC pumps do not provide a reproducible flow below 100 μl/min and hence special pumps must be used as in micro-HPLC.

Chromatographic resolution of SEC columns is defined as

$$R_s = \frac{V_{e(2)} - V_{e(1)}}{2(\sigma_{V(1)} + \sigma_{V(2)})(\log M_1/M_2)} \tag{3–10}$$

where $V_{e(2)} > V_{e(1)}$ yields values up to 7 for a given pair of biopolymers. Simply expressed, biopolymers are resolved that differ in their molecular weight ratio by less than two. Highest R_s values are obtained for biopolymers eluted in the middle part of the calibration curve.

The performance of SEC columns is often expressed in terms of the peak capacity, n, which is defined as

$$n = 1 + \frac{\overline{N}^{1/2}}{4} \ln (V_{e(2)}/V_{e(1)}) \tag{3–11}$$

where $\overline{N}$ is the average column plate number of solute 1 and 2. Particle columns of 5 μm provide peak capacities between 20 and 30.[198]

Bonded silica SEC columns are run with 50 to 100 m*M* buffers (phosphate, Tris-HCl) of pH 5 to 8 having an ionic strength of $\mu > 0.2$ adjusted by adding salts. The mass and biorecovery have been reported to be in the order of 80–100%. Mass loadabilities range between 0.1 and 10 mg per column of 300 mm in length and 10 mm inner diameter. Membrane proteins have been resolved on SEC columns using acetonitrile and formic acid up to 50% (v/v). Eluents to separate proteins under denaturated conditions are sodium dodecyl sulfate (SDS), 6 *M* urea, and 6 *M* guanidine-hydrochloride.

3.4.2 Reversed-Phase Chromatography

Reversed-phase chromatography of proteins is carried out on *n*-alkyl bonded silicas with an acidic low ionic strength mobile phase as starting eluent and applying a gradient of organic solvent.[199] Retention is based on hydrophobic association between the nonpolar domains of the protein and the lipophilic surface of the RP packing. Solutes are eluted in the sequence of increasing hydrophobicity. In addition, electrostatic solute–surface interactions may contribute to retention. Several stationary-phase variables have an impact on resolution and biorecovery of proteins.

First the pore diameter of the RP silica should be at least 30 nm for proteins greater than 15 kDa to provide access to the stationary phase and to ensure rapid mass transfer. Larger pore size packings of 50, 100, and 400 nm nominal pore diameter have been also employed. At a constant type of *n*-alkyl group, ligand density, and mobile-phase composition the retention decreases with increasing pore diameter, p_d, of RP silica due to the inverse relationship between p_d and the specific surface area, a_s, of the stationary phase. The values given in Table 3–1 may serve as a guideline. Retention on nonporous 2-μm RP silicas free of any internal surface area is comparable to that observed on a 200-nm porous RP silica. As the surface area of stationary phase is proportional to the mass loadability, the mass loadability declines from about 100 mg per ml of a 30-nm pore size packing to about 1 mg per ml of a 2-μm nonporous packing.

The second variable is the n-alkyl chain length of the RP silica. Retention studies of proteins on n-alkyl and phenyl bonded silicas at constant ligand density revealed that the retention follows the sequence ethyl $<$ n-butyl $\sim$ phenyl $\sim$ n-octyl $\leq$ n-octadecyl at otherwise constant conditions.[200] This finding supports the view that large proteins are not capable of intercalating to a large extent the n-alkyl layer as small molecules do. There is a preference to use n-butyl and n-octyl-bonded silicas in RPC of proteins over longer n-alkyl derivatives. The shorter the chain length the lesser the probability of denaturation of the native protein by surface-induced effects. The biological activity of horseradish peroxidase chromatographed on RP silicas with 0.1% TFA and 2-propanol/water was lowest at the n-octadecyl, n-octyl, and n-butyl-bonded silicas and highest at the ethyl and phenyl derivatives. Karger and coworkers[201,202] have shown that a number of proteins can be separated by RPC maintaining their native conformation. The loss of biological activity is proportional to the residence time the protein spends in the column. Thus, long columns and long gradient times are not favorable in this aspect.

RP silicas with very short n-alkyl groups suffer from facile hydrolytic cleavage of the anchoring siloxane bond of the n-alkyl group.

In conclusion, the choice of n-butyl and n-octyl-bonded silicas of intermediate lipophilic character is a compromise between retention, biorecovery, and column stability.

The third parameters are the carbon load and ligand density at a given type of RP silica. Usually there is a linear increase of retention with these parameters up to a limiting value. RP silicas with low carbon load and ligand density might pose problems to basic proteins due to silanol–solute interactions.

In reality, RP silicas even with the same pore diameter and type of ligand might show widely different retention and selectivity patterns for proteins from each other, which is attributed to the bonding chemistry.

The bonding chemistry also comes into play when one attempts to transfer a separation on an RP silica of a different particle size. Column and packing manufacturers have put some effort into the production of RP silicas of various particle size showing the same retention behavior. The particle size of RP silica is a decisive factor in the decision on whether an analytical or preparative work is intended to be carried out. Analytical separations are performed on columns of 100 to 250 mm length and 4 mm inner diameter packed with 5-μm particles. Larger particles in the range between 10 and 30 μm serve for preparative purposes. Fast high-resolution separations and isolations of proteins are done on 2- to 3-μm nonporous and porous RP silicas packed in columns shorter than 50 mm.

To gain in efficiency proteins are often chromatographed at higher column temperatures up to 80°C.[203] In view of the limited stability of proteins at higher temperature this approach does not seem to be very successful.

The starting eluent is a 10 m*M* acid, e.g., trifluoroacetic acid, phosphoric acid, perchloric acid, and heptafluorobutyric acid of pH 2 to 5. The displacing eluent contains an organic solvent such as methanol, acetonitril, or 1- or 2-propanol. Linear gradients are run up to 70% (w/w) of the organic solvent within 20 to 60 min. Typically, flow rates are about 2.0 ml/min with changes of the organic modifier of 0.2–1%/min. With increasing solvent strength the retention of protein decreases as exemplified by the plot of the logarithm of the capacity factor against the content of organic solvent in the eluent. Retention is further regulated by the ionic strength employing buffers such as triethylammonium phosphate, ammonium acetate, and pyridinium acetate and by ion pairing reagents.[204–206]

Mass and biorecovery of proteins are often found to be less than 100% in RPC. Losses of the bioactivity are caused by both surface-induced and mobile-phase-mediated phenomena, which have to be examined for any specific protein. Irreversible adsorption of proteins also occurs at the frits of the column. As a completely inert material does not exist, such surfaces have to be saturated with proteins before use.

Peak capacities in RPC of proteins are reported to be in the order of 100 and higher depending on the gradient time. Retention relationships of proteins in RPC have been predicted by Snyder and Stadalius based on a general model.[183] The same concept was applied to band broadening predictions. Calculated bandwidths of proteins have been compared with experimentally obtained values and were found to be in good agreement.

3.4.3 Hydrophobic-Interaction Chromatography

In HIC biopolymers are resolved on weakly hydrophobic packings with a buffer of neutral pH applying a descending salt gradient. At the initial high salt concentration proteins are adsorbed at the surface by hydrophobic interactions maintaining their tertiary structure. Elution with the descending salt gradient weakens the solute–surface interactions and proteins are eluted according to their hydrophobic nature.

A variety of bonded silicas have been examined in HIC, which vary in pore size and hydrophobicity. As mentioned in Section 3.4.2 a bonded silica with an appropriate pore size should be chosen to match the size of protein and to provide sufficient retention. Retention is proportional to the hydrophobicity of the ligand and the ligand density at a given type of hydrophobic ligand and at constant eluent composition. As shown by Alpert[47] and Gooding[207] the solute retention increased in the sequence of methyl < propyl < hydroxypropyl < *n*-butyl < *n*-pentyl < phenyl as ligands. Irreversible binding of proteins at the stationary phase often takes place with ligands longer than *n*-butyl.

Eluents in HIC are 10–100 m*M* buffers of pH 5 to 8. Displacing salts are ammonium or sodium sulphate. Linear descending salt gradients are run with salt concentrations from 1 to 2 *M* down to zero.

3.4.4 Ion-Exchange Chromatography

Proteins and nucleic acids are separated on ion exchangers on the basis of electrostatic interactions. To achieve a significant degree of retention the pH of the eluent must be one unit away from the isoelectric point (p*I*) of the protein. Proteins are usually chromatographed on anion exchangers at a pH > p*I*. When the pH of the eluent is below the p*I* cation exchangers are employed. To manifest the retention pattern of proteins it is advisable to measure the retention value as a function of the pH of the mobile phase.[208] For a given protein the retention increases with the charge density of the stationary phases. Although the charge density for strong ion exchangers remains constant over the entire pH range, weak ion exchangers show a strong dependency of the charge density on the pH. Moreover, the topography of the ionogenic groups at the stationary phase plays an important role in retention. At a first approximation the charge density of an ion exchanger determines its mass loadability provided the ionogenic surface sites are accessible to biomacromolecules. For proteins of 30–100 kDa a pore diameter of 50 nm of the ion exchanger provides a good compromise between maximum access and adequate mass loadability.[48] The retention of proteins on a given ion exchanger of polymeric type of bonded silica can be enhanced by simply increasing the layer thickness as in the case of a poly(ethyleneimine) coating.

Starting eluents are 10–20 m*M* phosphate and Tris-HCl buffers of pH 5–8. Displacing solvents are 0.5–1.0 *M* salt solutions. Proteins and nucleic acids are chromatographed with a linear ascending salt gradient. Column mass loadability amounts to about 10–100 mg of protein per ml of ion exchanger. Biorecovery is in the order of 80–100%. Bonded silica ion exchangers are cleaned by rinsing the column with a concentrated salt solution. Column temperature is usually kept at room temperature.

IEC is the most applied interactive mode of HPLC in the separation of proteins and nucleic acids due to its high selectivity. Even isoforms of proteins, e.g., lysozyme, have been resolved by IEC.[209]

Selectivity at a given type of bonded silica ion exchanger cannot be predicted and has to be assessed by trial and error. Often hydrophobic solute–surface interactions contribute to retention and cause unique selectivities.

3.4.5 Affinity Chromatography

AC covers a variety of techniques such as biomimetic, biospecific, metal chelate, charge-transfer, and covalent chromatography.[195] The noncovalent binding of a substrate S to a ligand L bound to an affinity support is formally described by

$$\mathrm{L} + \mathrm{S} \underset{k_2}{\overset{k_1}{\rightleftharpoons}} \mathrm{LS} \qquad (3\text{–}12)$$

where k_1 and k_2 denote the rate constants of the adsorption and desorption steps. The equilibrium is described by the association constant, K_{assoc}, which varies between 10^4 and 10^{10}. The association constant as well as the overall rate constants k_1 and k_2 are derived from batch experiments and frontal analysis.[195,210] By means of modeling the biospecific adsorption the overall rate constant of the adsorption step k_1 can be divided into the rate constants of the kinetics of mass transfer (pore diffusion, film diffusion) and into the rate constant of the kinetics of the adsorption.[211,212]

The most decisive stationary phase variables in AC are the pore size of the support and the ligand density. Both parameters affect the effective binding capacity for a given substrate and also have a major impact on the kinetics of mass transfer of biopolymers. Furthermore, the extent of unspecific interactions between the substrate and the support surface is also controlled by the ligand density.

The pore size of a support in AC is a much more critical parameter than in other modes of interactive chromatography for two reasons. First, the ligands bound to the support are often quite bulky in case of high molecular weight. Second, the substrate that is associated with the ligand can also vary in size. As shown by Hossain et al.[214] the pore diffusion is not only controlled by the ratio of the size of the biopolymer solute relative to the pore diameter of the support but is also a function of the ligand density. Due to restricted access phenomena and steric hindrance of substrates in AC a high ligand density does not provide the highest binding capacity, and the ligand utility might be lower than expected. A ligand density lower than the maximum increases significantly the degree of utilization. Usually the Scatchard plot is used to discriminate between specific and nonspecific bindings. The ratio of the concentration of bound to the free ligand $[L_B]/[L_F]$ is plotted against the bound fraction $[L_B]$.[214] Studies of this kind have been performed with the following system: Cibacron blue F3GA as ligand and lysozyme, hSA, ADH as substrates on porous silicas and glass beads.[215]

Kinetic effects are most noticeable when using silica supports of pore sizes smaller than 30 nm and proteins of more than 10 kDa. The results are tailed peaks and impaired column performance. With larger pore size of silica the binding capacity decreases, but the kinetics become faster. Pore diffusion is completely eliminated on nonporous silica supports in AC. Nonporous microparticulate silica-based affinity packings preferably find use for very rapid analytical and micropreparative AC.[60,61]

3.5 CONCLUSION

In this chapter the various aspects of bonded silicas synthesized and applied for the separation of biopolymers by means of HPLC are discussed, such as structural characteristics, design, preparation, and characterization as well as the impact of stationary phase on the column performance.

During the last decade notable progress in the synthesis of tailor-made bonded silicas was achieved, yielding highly selective stationary phases. Further efforts will be directed toward the improvement of silica-based ion exchangers and affinity supports for analytical, preparative, and large-scale separations of biopolymers.

3.6 APPENDICES

Appendix I: Glossary of Symbols

AC	Affinity chromatography
a_s	Specific surface area of packing (m^2/g or m^2/ml of packing)
b	Gradient steepness parameter
A, B, C	Constants in Knox equation
c	Concentration of salt in the mobile phase (ion exchange)
d	Molecular diameter of solute molecule
d_c	Column inner diameter (cm)
DCS	Differential scanning calorimetry
d_p	Column packing particle diameter (μm)
D_{im}	Solute diffusion coefficient in bulk mobile phase (cm^2/sec)
DRIFT	Diffuse reflection infrared Fourier transmission (spectroscopy)
D_s	Solute diffusion coefficient in stationary phase (cm^2/sec)
DTA	Differential thermal analysis
F	Mobile phase flow rate (ml/min)
G	Gradient compression factor
h	Reduced plate height
H	Plate height; $H = L/N$ (μm)
HIC	Hydrophobic interaction chromatography
ICP-AAS	Inductively coupled plasma-atomic emission spectroscopy
IEC	Ion-exchange chromatography
$\bar{k}$	Value of k' in gradient elution when band has reached column midpoint
k'	Solute capacity factor
k_1, k_2	Rate constants of the adsorption and desorption steps in AC
K	Equilibrium constant
K_{assoc}	Association constant of the ligand–substrate complex in AC
K_{SEC}	SEC distribution constant
k'_w	Capacity factor of solute in RPC with neat water as mobile phase
L	Column length (cm)
L	Ligand in affinity chromatography
L_B, L_F	Concentration of bound to free ligand in AC
M	Solute molecular weight
MCC	Metal chelate chromatography
n	Peak capacity in SEC
N	Column plate number
NMR	Nuclear magnetic resonance (spectroscopy) CP MAS: Cross-polarization magic angle spinning
PC	Peak capacity
p_d	Pore diameter of packing (nm)

PH	Peak height
pK	p$K = -\log_{10}K$
RPC	Reversed-phase liquid chromatography
R_s	Chromatographic resolution
S	Solute parameter in reversed phase gradient elution
S	Substrate in affinity chromatography
SEC	Size exclusion chromatography
t_g	Retention time in gradient elution (min)
t_G	Gradient time (min)
TG	Thermal analysis
t_m	Retention time for nonretained solute (min)
t_R	Solute retention time (min)
u	Mobile phase velocity (cm/sec)
V_e	Elution volume of solute (ml)
V_G	Gradient volume, equal to (t_GF) (ml)
V_i	Volume of mobile phase inside pores (ml)
V_m	Column dead volume (ml)
V_o	Volume of mobile phase outside of pores (ml)
v_p	Specific pore volume (ml/g)
V_R	Solute retention volume (ml)
Z	In ion exchange, the effective charge on the solute ion divided by the charge on the mobile phase ion
α	Selectivity coefficient, equal to ratio of k' values for two adjacent bands
α	Ligand density of functional groups grafted at the surface
Δp	Column pressure drop (bar)
$\Delta\Phi$	Change in Φ during gradient elution
η	Mobile phase viscosity (cP)
λ	Solute parameter in gradient elution (HIC)
ν	Reduced mobile-phase velocity
Φ	In reversed-phase HPLC, the volume fraction of organic solvent in the mobile phase
$\Phi(\Phi')$	Column resistance factor
σ_t	Bandwidth (1 sigma) measured in min
σ_v	Bandwidth (1 sigma) measured in ml

Appendix II: Equations

Solute capacity factor k' $$k' = t_R - t_m/t_m$$

Selectivity coefficient $$\alpha = k'_2/k'_1 \quad (k'_2 > k'_1)$$

Column plate height $$H = \frac{1}{16}\left(\frac{4\sigma_t}{t_R}\right)^2$$

Column plate number $$N = L/H$$

$H(h)$ as a function of $u(\nu)$	$H = A\nu^{1/3} + B/\nu + C\nu$
Column pressure drop	$\Delta p = \eta u L \Phi(\Phi')/d_p^2$
Chromatographic resolution	$R_s = \frac{1}{4}(\alpha - 1)\, N^{1/2} \left(\frac{k'}{1 + k'}\right)$
Distribution constant of solute in SEC	$K_{SEC} = \frac{V_e - V_o}{V_m - V_o}$
Solute parameter S	$\log k' = \log k'_w - S\Phi$ $S = 0.48M^{0.44}$
Solute parameter Z	$\log k' = \log K - Z \log C$
Solute capacity factor $\bar{k}$	$\bar{k} = t_g \Pi F/(1.15\Delta\Phi S V_m)$
Chromatographic resolution in gradient elution	$R_s = \frac{1}{4}(\alpha - 1)\, N^{1/2} \left(\frac{\bar{k}}{1 + \bar{k}}\right)$
Peak capacity	$PC = t_g/\sigma_t$ $R_s = (\text{constant}) \cdot PC/\Delta\Phi$

Appendix III: Survey of Bonded Silica Packings for Biopolymer Separation by HPLC

Trade name	Supplier	d_p (μm)	p_d^a (nm)	Comments
		A. Size-exclusion packings		
Aquapore	Brownlee Labs			
OH-100		10	10	
OH-300		10	30	
OH-500		10	50	
OH-1000		10	100	
OH-4000		10	400	
Bio-Sil TSK	Bio-Rad			
125		10±2	12.5	
250		10±2	25	
400		13±3	40	
Chromegapore	ES Industries	10	6, 10, 30, 50, 100, 400	Available in plain silica, TMS- and diol-deactivated, respectively
LiChrospher	E. Merck			
100 Diol		5, 10	10	
500 Diol			50	
1000 Diol			100	
4000 Diol			400	
μ-Bondagel	Millipore/Waters			
E-125		10	12.5	
E-500		10	50	
E-1000		10	100	
E-High Å		10	>100	
μ-Porasil GPC	Millipore/Waters	10		
PROTEIN-PAK	Millipore/Waters	10	6, 12.5, 30	

(continued)

Appendix III: Survey of Bonded Silica Packings for Biopolymer Separation by HPLC (*continued*)

Trade name	Supplier	d_p (μm)	$p_d{}^a$ (nm)	Comments
Protein	Showa-Denko			
WS-802.5		9	15	Hydrophilic modified silica
WS-803		9	30	Hydrophilic modified silica
WS-802.5F		9	15	Hydrophilic modified silica
WS-803F		9	30	Hydrophilic modified silica
WS-804F		9	50	Hydrophilic modified silica
Serva Polyol = Si	Serva	3, 5	6, 10, 30, 50	
Shim-pack	Shimadzu			
Diol-150		10	15	
Diol-300		10	30	
Shodex	Showa Denko			
WS-800 F				
Spherogel TSK	Beckman			
2000 SW		13 ± 2	200	
3000 SW		13 ± 2	300	
4000 SW		13 ± 2	400	
Supelcosil SEC	Supelco			
LC-1		5	10	C_1 bonded silica
301		5	30	C_1 bonded silica
501		5	50	C_1 bonded silica
LC-Diol		5	10	3-Glycerylpropylsilyl
LC-3Diol		5	30	3-Glycerylpropylsilyl
SynChropak	SynChrom			
GPC		10	10, 30, 50, 100 and 400	Silica bonded with a carbohydrate phase
CATSEC		10		Polymerized polyamine coating

TSKgel	Tosoh			
G2000SW		10	12.5	
G3000SW		10	25	
G4000SW		10	40	
YMC-PAK PSA	YMC	5	30	Hydrophobic coating
Zorbax	Du Pont			
GF-250		4	25	
GF-450		6	45	
		B. Reversed-phase packings		
Aquapore	Brownlee Labs			
butyl, BU 300		10	30	
octyl, RP 300		10	30	
phenyl, PH 300		10	30	
Bakerbond	Baker			
Octadecyl		10	15	
WP-Butyl		5, 15, 40	27.5, 30	
WP-Octyl		5, 15, 40	27.5, 30	
WP-Octadecyl		5, 15, 40	27.5, 30	
WP-Cyanopropyl		5, 15, 40	27.5, 30	
WP-Diphenyl		5, 15, 40	27.5, 30	
Bio-Sil	Bio-Rad			
HiPore RP-304		5	33	C_4 bonded silica
HiPore RP-318		5	33	C_{18} bonded silica
Chromegabond	ES Industries			
TMS		3, 5, 10	30	C_1 bonded silica, polymeric
C3		3, 5, 10	30	Polymeric
C4		3, 5, 10	30	Polymeric
M-C8		3, 5, 10	30	Monomeric
M-C18		3, 5, 10	30	Monomeric

(continued)

Appendix III: Survey of Bonded Silica Packings for Biopolymer Separation by HPLC (*continued*)

Trade name	Supplier	d_p (μm)	$p_d{}^a$ (nm)	Comments
DP		10	30	Diphenyl, polymeric
HD-GEL	Orpegen			
RP-300		7, 40–80	30	C_3/C_4 bonded silica
18-300		7, 40–80	30	C_{18} bonded silica
HP-	HP-Chemicals			
2205		5	15	Available as propyl-, butyl-, octyl-, octadecyl-, and phenylphase, end-capped
2210		10	15	
2215		15	15	
2220		20	15	
3205		5	25	
3210		10	25	
3215		15	25	
3220		20	25	
Hypersil WP 300	Shandon			
Butyl		5, 10	30	End-capped
Octyl		5, 10	30	End-capped
ICN Silica	ICN			
RP (6–8)			30	C_6/C_8 bonded silica
RP 18			20–30	
Isco	Isco			
MP C_4		5	30	
MP C_{18}		5	30	
LiChrospher	E. Merck			
500 RP-8		10	50	
1000 RP-8		10	100	
4000 RP-8		10	400	

Matrex Silica	Amicon			
C8		5, 10, 15, 20	25	
C18		5, 10, 15, 20	25	
μ-Bondapak	Millipore/Waters			
C_{18}		10	12.5 (pore size distribution to 45 nm)	
Nucleosil	Macherey-Nagel			
300–7 Protein RP		7	30	No residual silanols
300 C_4		5, 7, 10	30	End-capped
300 C_8		5, 7, 10	30	Not end-capped
300 C_{18}		5, 7, 10, 15–25	30	End-capped
300 C_6H_5		5, 7, 10	30	Not end-capped
500 C_4		7	50	End-capped
500 C_8		7	50	Not end-capped
500 C_{18}		7, 15–25	50	End-capped
500 C_6H_5		7	50	Not end-capped
1000 C_4		7	100	End-capped
1000 C_{18}		7	100	End-capped
1000 C_6H_5		7	100	Not end-capped
4000 C_4		7	400	End-capped
4000 C_{18}		7	400	
Polygosil	Macherey-Nagel			
300 C_4		7, 25–40	30	End-capped
300 C_{18}		7, 25–40	30	End-capped
500 C_4		7, 25–40	50	End-capped
500 C_{18}		7, 25–40	50	End-capped
Pro RPC	Pharmacia-LKB	5	30	C_8, C_1 bonded silica
Protesil	Whatman			
300 Octyl		10	30	

(continued)

Appendix III: Survey of Bonded Silica Packings for Biopolymer Separation by HPLC (*continued*)

Trade name	Supplier	d_p (μm)	p_d[a] (nm)	Comments
300 Diphenyl		10	30	
Serva	Serva			
Butyl = Si300		5, 10	30	
Diphenyl = Si300		3, 5, 10	30	
Octadecyl = Si300		3, 5, 10	30	
Octyl = Si300		3, 5, 10	30	
Butyl = Si500		10, 30	50	
Octadecyl = Si500		10	50	
Octyl = Si500		10	50	
Spherisorb	Phase Separations			
S5XC1		5	30	C_1 bonded silica
S5XC3		5	30	C_3 bonded silica
S5XC6		5	30	C_6 bonded silica
S5XC18		5	30	C_{18} bonded silica
S10XC1		10	30	C_1 bonded silica
S10XC3		10	30	C_3 bonded silica
S10XC6		10	30	C_6 bonded silica
S10XC18		10	30	C_{18} bonded silica
Supelcosil	Supelco			
LC-PAH		5	30	C_{18} bonded silica (polymeric)
LC-304		5	30	C_4 bonded silica
LC-308		5	30	C_8 bonded silica
LC-318		5	30	C_{18} bonded silica
LC-DP		5	30	Diphenylsilyl bonded silica

SynChropak RP-P	SynChrom	5, 6.5, 10	30, 50, 100, 400	C_{18} bonded silica (C_1, C_4, and C_8 bonded silica are also available)
TSK gel	Tosoh			
TMS-250		10	25	C_1 bonded silica
Versapack C18	Alltech	10	15	End-capped
Vydac TPB 10-	Separations Group			
201		10	30	C_{18}, not end-capped
218		10	30	C_{18}, end-capped
214		10	30	C_4, end-capped
219		10	30	Phenyl, end-capped
C_8		5–30	30	pH stable (to pH 10) due to a polymer coating
Diphenyl		5–30	30	
YMC	YMC			
300 A ODS		5	30	C_{18} bonded silica
300 A Butyl		5, 15	30	C_4 bonded silica
Zorbax Bio Series	Du Pont			
PEP RP-1		10	15	C_8, end-capped
Protein PLUS			30	
C. Hydrophobic-interaction packings				
Bakerbond WP-HI-Propyl	Baker	5, 15, 40		
PolyMETHYL A	PolyLC	5, 7, 15–20	30	Polypeptide-coated silica
PolyETHYL A		5, 7, 15–20	30	
PolyPROPYL A		5, 7, 15–20	30	
Spherogel CAA-HIC	Beckman	5		

(continued)

Appendix III: Survey of Bonded Silica Packings for Biopolymer Separation by HPLC (*continued*)

Trade name	Supplier	d_p (μm)	$p_d{}^a$ (nm)	Comments
SynChropak	SynChrom			
Propyl		5, 6.5, 10	30, 50, 100, 400	
Hydroxypropyl		5, 6.5, 10	30, 50, 100, 400	
Benzyl		5, 6.5, 10	30, 50, 100, 400	
		D. Ion-exchange packings		
Adsorbosphere	Alltech			
SAX		5, 10	10	N,N,N-Trimethylaminopropylsilane
SCX		5, 10	10	Phenethyldimethylsilane sulfonic acid
NH_2		3, 5, 10	8	Aminopropylsilane, WAX
Aquapore	Brownlee Labs			
AX-300		10	30	WAX
CX-300		10	30	WCX
Bakerbond	Baker			
1°, 2° Amino		10	10, 15	WAX
Polyethylene imine		5	33	WAX
N^+		5, 10	6, 12, 15	Quaternary amine, SAX
NH_2		5, 10	6, 12, 15	Aminopropyl, WAX
SO_3H		5, 10	6, 12, 15	Aliphatic sulfonic acid, SCX
COOH		5, 10	6, 12, 15	Aliphatic carbon acid, WCX
WP-PEI		5, 15, 40	6, 30	Polyethylene imine, WAX
WP-QUAT		5, 15, 40	6, 30	Quaternary amine, SX
WP-CBX		5, 15, 40	6, 30	WCX
WP-CARBOXY-SULFON		5, 15, 40	6, 30	Weak/strong cation exchange
Bio-Sil TSK	Bio-Rad			

CM-2-SW		5	12.5	Functional group: —COO—, WCX
CM-3-SW		10	25	Functional group: —COO—, WCX
DEAE-2-SW		5	12.5	Functional group: —N^+HEt_2, WAX
DEAE-3-SW		10	25	Functional group: —N^+HEt_2, WAX
Chromegabond	ES Industries			
P-SCX		5, 10	6, 10, 30	Phenyl sulfonate
A-SCX		5, 10	6, 10, 30	Alkyl sulfonate
P-WCX		5, 10	6, 10, 30	Phenyl carboxylate
A-WCX		5, 10	6, 10, 30	Alkyl carboxylate
SAX		5, 10	6, 10, 30	SAX
RP-SCX		5, 10	6, 10, 30	Hybrid RP/SCX
RP-SAX		5, 10	6, 10, 30	Hybrid RP/SAX
M-WAX		5, 10	6, 10, 30	Mono WAX
D-WAX		5, 10	6, 10, 30	Di WAX
T-WAX		5, 10	6, 10, 30	Tri WAX
HP	HP Chemicals			
Amine		10, 15–20	6, 15, 25	Aminopropyl, WAX
CM		30–70		Carboxymethyl, WCX
DEAE		10, 15–20	6, 15, 25	Diethylaminoethyl, WAX
Aromatic sulfonic acid		30–70		SCX
Hypersil-APS	Shandon	3, 5, 10	12	WAX
Isco				
QA^+		5	8	SAX
SO_3^-		5	8	SCX
Ionosphere™ A	Chrompack	5		SAX
LiChrosorb	E. Merck			
Kat		10		Sulfonic acid, SCX
NH_2		5, 7, 10		Amino functional, WAX
AX-W		10		Diethanolamine, WAX
CX-W		10		Carboxymethyl, WCX

(*continued*)

Appendix III: Survey of Bonded Silica Packings for Biopolymer Separation by HPLC (*continued*)

Trade name	Supplier	d_p (μm)	p_d[a] (nm)	Comments
Mikropak	Varian			
AX		5, 10		Phosphate modificated, WAX
SAX		10		Phosphate modificated, SAX
NH_2		10		WAX
μ-Bondapak NH_2	Millipore/Waters	5		WAX
Nucleogen	Macherey-Nagel			
DEAE 60		7	6	Diethylamino, WAX
DEAE 500		10	50	Diethylamino, WAX
DEAE 4000		10	400	Diethylamino, WAX
Nucleosil	Macherey-Nagel			
SA		5, 10		Sulfonic acid, SCX
SB		5, 10		Quaternary amine, SAX
$N(CH_3)_2$		5, 10		Dimethylamino, WAX
NH_2		5, 10		Aminopropyl, WAX
Partisil	Whatman			
10 SAX		10		SAX
10 SCX		10		SCX
Perisorb SCX	E. Merck	30–40	—	
Poly	PolyLC			
CAT A		5, 7, 15–20	30	Polypeptide-bonded silica, cation exchanger
SULFOETHYL A		5, 7, 15–20	30	SCX
WAX LP		5, 7, 15–20	30	WAX
RoSil NH_2	Alltech	3, 5, 10	8	Aminopropylsilane, WAX
Sepralyte	Analytichem			

SCX		5, 10, 40		Benzenesulfonylpropyl
PRS		5, 10, 40		Sulfonylpropyl
CBA		5, 10, 40		Carboxymethyl
DEA		5, 10, 40		Diethylaminopropyl
SAX		5, 10, 40		Trimethylaminopropyl
Serva	Serva			
Carboxymethyl =Si 300		5, 10	30	Cation exchanger
DEAE = Daltosil		4	10	Anion exchanger
DEAE = Si100		5, 10	10	Anion exchanger
DEAE = Si300		5, 10	30	Anion exchanger
DEAE = Si500		10	50	Anion exchanger
Sulfopropyl = Si100 Polyol		5	10	WCX
TEAP = Si100 Polyol		5, 10		SAX
Spherogel TSK-	Beckman			
CM-3SW		10		
DEAE-3SW		10		
Supelcosil	Supelco			
SAX		5	10, 30	SAX
SCX		5	10, 30	SCX
LC-IC		5	10, 30	WAX
SynChropak	SynChrom			
AX 100		5	10	Polyamine polymer coating on silica;
AX 300		6.5	30	WAX
AX 500		6.5	50	WAX
AX 1000		6.5	100	WAX
Q 300		6.5	30	SAX
CM 300		6.5	30	WCX
Thomaspher	Reichelt			

(continued)

Appendix III: Survey of Bonded Silica Packings for Biopolymer Separation by HPLC (*continued*)

Trade name	Supplier	d_p (μm)	p_d[a] (nm)	Comments
Si 100 SA		5, 10	10	SCX
Si 100 SB		5, 10	10	SAX
Si 100 NH_2		5, 10	10	WAX
Si 100 $N(CH_3)_2$		5, 10	10	WAX
Thomasorb	Reichelt			
Si 60 NH_2		5, 10	6	WAX
Si 60 $N(CH_3)$		5, 10	6	WAX
TSK-IEX	Tosoh			
SP Sil		5	12.5	Propyl sulfonic acid, SCX
CM Sil		5, 10	12.5, 25	Carboxymethyl, WCX
DEAE Sil		5, 10	12.5, 25	Diethylaminoethyl, WAX
Vydac	Separations Group			
301 TP		10	8, 30	SAX
401 TP		10	8, 30	SCX
Zorbax Bio Series	Du Pont			
SAX		7	30	Based on zirconia stabilized silica
WAX		7	30	
SCX		7	30	
WCX		7	30	
NH_2		5, 7	6, 10	Aminopropyl, WAX
E. Affinity packings				
Bakerbond WP-MAb	Baker	5, 15, 40		Anion exchanger for ascites

ABx		5, 15, 40	27.5, 30	Antibody exchanger
(activated silica supports)		40	27.5, 30 27.5	*p*-Nitrophenyl or diazofluoroborate bonded silica
Cibacronblue F3GA = Si300	Serva	5		
SelectiSpher-10	Pierce			
Protein A		10	50	For the separation of immunoglobul.
Cibacron Blue		10	50	For the separation of enzymes
Boronate		10	50	For the separation of nucleosides, nucleotides, glycoproteins etc.
Concanavalin A		10	50	For the separation of carbohydrates, and glycoproteins
Activated Tresyl		10	50	For the immobilization of amine and thiol-containing ligands
Ultraffinity	Beckman	10		Glycidoxy bonded silica

[a] Exclusively silicas with pore diameters $p_d > 12$ nm were taken into account in this table.

F. List of suppliers

Company	Address
Alltech	Alltech Associates Inc., Applied Science Labs, 2051 Waukegan Road, Deerfield, IL 60015, USA Alltech Europe, Begoniastraat, B-9731 Eke, Belgium
Amicon	Amicon Corporation, 17 Cherry Hill Drive, Danvers, MA 01923, USA Grace AG, Amicon-Schweiz, Av. Moutchoisi 35, CH-1001 Lausanne, Switzerland
Baker	J. T. Baker, Research Products, 222 Red School Lane, Phillipsburgh, NJ 08865, USA Baker Chemikalien, Postfach 1661, D-6080 Gross-Gerau, FRG

(continued)

Appendix III: Survey of Bonded Silica Packings for Biopolymer Separation by HPLC (continued)

Beckman	Beckman Instruments Inc., 2350 Camino Ramon, P.O. Box 5101, San Ramon, CA, USA Beckmans Instruments GmbH, Frankfurter Ring 115, D-8000 München 40, FRG
Bio-Rad	Bio-Rad Laboratories, 2200 Wright Avenue, Richmond, CA 94804, USA Bio-Rad Laboratories GmbH, Dauchauer-strasse 364, D-8000 München 50, FRG
Brownlee	Brownlee Labs Inc., 2045 Martin Ave., Santa Clara, CA 95050, USA
DuPont	DuPont Company, Analytical Instruments Division, McKean Bldg.-Concord Plaza, Wilmington, DE 19801, USA DuPont GmbH, Postfach 1509, Dieselstrasse 18, D-6350 Bad Nauheim 1, FRG
ES Industries	ES Industries, 8 South Maple Ave., Marlton, NJ 08053, USA
HP Chemicals	HP Chemicals Inc., 4221 Forest Park Blvd., St. Louis, MO 63108, USA
ICN Biomedicals	ICN Biomedicals GmbH, Postfach 369, D-3440 Eschwege, FRG
ISCO	ISCO Inc., P.O. Box 5347, Lincoln, Nebraska 68505, USA
Macherey-Nagel	Macherey-Nagel, Neumann-Neander-Strasse 6–8, Postfach 307, D-5160 Düren, FRG
Merck	E. Merck, Frankfurter Strasse 250, D-6100 Darmstadt, FRG E. M. Science, 111 Woodcrest Road, P.O. Box 5018, Cherry Hill, NJ 08034-0395, USA
Millipore-Waters	Millipore-Waters Associated, Milford, MA 01757, USA Millipore-Waters Chromatographie, Hauptstrasse 71-79, D-6236 Eschborn, FRG
Orpegen	Orpegen, Czernyring 22, D-6900 Heidelberg, FRG
Pharmacia LKB	Pharmacia LKB Biotechnology AB, Box 175, S-75104 Uppsala 1, Sweden Deutsche Pharmacia LKB Biotechnologie GmbH, Munziger Strasse 9, D-7800 Freiburg, FRG

Phase Separations	Phase Separations Ltd., Deeside Industrial Estate, Queensferry, CLWYD CH5 2LR, UK
Pierce	Pierce Chemical Company, P.O. Box 117, Rockford, IL, USA Pierce GmbH, Daimlerstrasse 15–17, D-6054 Rodgau 6, Weiskirchen, FRG
Poly LC	Poly LC, 9052 Bellwart Way, Columbia, MD 21045, USA
Reichelt	Reichelt Chemie Technik, Euglerstrasse 18, D-6900 Heidelberg 1, FRG
Separations Group (Vydac)	Separations Group, 17434 Mojave Street, P.O. Box 867, Hesperia, CA 92345, USA
Serva	Serva, Carl-Benz-Strasse 7, Postfach 105260, D-6900 Heidelberg, FRG
Shandon	Shandon Southern Instruments Inc., 515 Broad Street, Drawer 43, Sewickley, PA 15143-0043, USA Shandon Labortechnik GmbH, Karl von Prais Str. 18, Postfach 501029, D-6000 Frankfurt 50, FRG
Shimadzu	Shimadzu (Europe) GmbH, Ackerstr. 11, D-4000 Düsseldorf, FRG
Showa Denko	Showa Denko K. K., 13-9 Shiba Daimon 1-chome, Minato-Ku, Tokyo 105, Japan Showa Denko (Europe) GmbH, Niederkasseler Lohrweg 8, D-4000 Düsseldorf 11, FRG
Supelco	Supelco Inc., Supelco Park, Bellefonte, PA 16823-0048, USA Supelchem, Am Laubach 3, Postfach 1127, D-6231 Sulzbach/Taunus, FRG
SynChrom	SynChrom Inc., P.O. Box 110, Linden, IN 47955, USA
Tosoh	Tosoh Manufacturing Co. Ltd., 1-7-7 Akasaka, Minato-Ku, Tokyo 107, Japan
Varian	Varian, 220 Humboldt Court, Sunnyvale, CA 94089, USA Varian GmbH, Alsfelder Strasse 6, D-6100 Darmstadt 11, FRG
Whatman	Whatman Inc., 9 Bridgewell Place, Clifton, NJ 07014, USA
YMC	YMC Inc., P.O. Box 492, Mt. Freedom, NJ 07970, USA

REFERENCES

1. K. Unger, R. Janzen, and G. Jilge, *Chromatographia*, 24 (1987) 144.
2. S. Hjertén, in Protides of the Biological Fluids, Vol. 30 (H. Peeters, ed.). Pergamon Press, Oxford, 1983, pp. 9–17.
3. J.-C. Janson, *Chromatographia*, 23 (1987) 361.
4. O. Mikeš (ed.), HPLC of Biopolymers and Biooligomers, J. Chrom. Library, Vol. 41 A. Elsevier, Amsterdam, 1988, A 128–A 131.
5. K. Unger, Porous Silica, J. Chrom. Library, Vol. 16. Elsevier, Amsterdam, 1979.
6. W. Melander and Cs. Horvath, in HPLC: Advances and Perspectives, Vol. 2 (Cs. Horvath, ed.). Academic Press, London, 1980, pp. 114–303.
7. M. T. W. Hearn, A. N. Hodder, and M. I. Aguilar, *J. Chromatogr.*, 327 (1985) 47.
8. K. K. Unger, B. Anspach, R. Janzen, G. Jilge, and K. D. Lork, in HPLC: Advances and Perspectives, Vol. 5 (Cs. Horvath, ed.). Academic Press, London, 1988, pp. 2–88.
9. K. K. Unger and G. Jilge, *8th Int. Symp. HPLC Proteins, Peptides, Polynucleotides*, October 30–November 2, 1988, Copenhagen, Denmark, paper 101.
10. R. K. Iler, The Chemistry of Silica. Wiley, New York, 1979.
11. D. Barby, in Characterization of Powder Surfaces (G. D. Parfitt and K. S. W. Sing, eds.). Academic Press, London, 1978, pp. 353–419.
12. K. K. Unger, in Packings and Stationary Phases in Chromatographic Techniques (K. K. Unger ed.). Dekker, New York, 1990, pp. 334–340.
13. H. Engelhardt and H. Müller, *J. Chromatogr.*, 218 (1981) 395.
14. St. Hansen, P. Helboe, and M. Thomsen, *J. Chromatogr.*, 368 (1986) 39.
15. K. D. Lork and K. K. Unger, *J. Chromatogr.*, in print.
16. R. K. Iler (ed.), Chemistry of Silica. Wiley, New York, 1979, pp. 3–104.
17. Yu. S. Nikitin and T. D. Khokhlova, *5th Danube Symp. Chromatogr.*, Yalta, U.S.S.R., November 11–18, 1985, paper 074.
18. R. W. Stout and J. J. De Stefano, *J. Chromatogr.*, 326 (1985) 63.
19. E. A. Pfannkoch and W. Kopaciewicz, *7th Int. Symp. HPLC Proteins, Peptides, Polynucleotides*, 2–4 November 1987, Washington, D.C., paper 140.
20. C. T. Wehr and R. E. Majors, *LC/GC Int. Mag.*, 1 (1988) 10.
21. S. J. Gregg and K. S. W. Sing (eds.), Adsorption, Surface Area and Porosity. Academic Press, London, 1982.
22. J. H. Petropolous, N. K. Kanellopolous, and A. I. Liapis, *2nd Conf. Fund. Adsorption*, Sonthofen, FRG, May 1989.
23. A. I. Liapis, in Proceedings of the Second Conference on Separation Technology Engineering Foundation (N. L. Li (ed.). New York, 1988.
24. G. Guiochon and M. Martin, *J. Chromatogr.*, 326 (1985) 3.
25. M. A. Stadalius, H. S. Gold, and L. R. Snyder, *J. Chromatogr.*, 327 (1985) 27.
26. A. I. Liapis, private communication.
27. W. H. Pirkle and Th. C. Pochapsky, in Packings and Stationary Phases in Chromatographic Techniques (K. K. Unger, ed.). Dekker, New York, 1990, pp. 783–814.
28. G. Schomburg, *LC/GC Int. Mag.*, 1 (1988) 34.
29. Z. El Rassi and Cs. Horvath, *Chromatographia*, 19 (1989) 9.
30. J. B. Crowther and R. A. Hartwick, *Chromatographia*, 16 (1982) 349.
31. R. Bischoff and L. W. McLaughlin, *J. Chromatogr.*, 270 (1983) 117.
32. L. A. Kennedy, W. A. Kopaciewicz, and F. E. Regnier, *J. Chromatogr.*, 359 (1986) 73.
33. I. H. Hagestam and Th. C. Pinkerton, *Anal. Chem.*, 57 (1985) 1757.
34. C. Desilets and F. E. Regnier, *12th Int. Symp. Column Liquid Chromatogr.*, June 19–24, 1988, Washington, D.C., paper W-P 326.
35. K. K. Unger and J. N. Kinkel, in Aqueous Size Exclusion Chromatography, J. Chromatogr. Libr. Vol. 40 (P. L. Dubin, ed.). Elsevier, Amsterdam, 1988, pp. 193–234.

36. B. Sebille, private communication.
37. K. D. Lork, K. K. Unger, and J. N. Kinkel, *J. Chromatogr.*, 352 (1986) 199.
38. B. Buszewski, A. Jurašek, J. Garaj, L. Nondek, I. Novak, and D. Berek, *J. Liquid Chromatogr.*, 10 (1987) 2325.
39. T. M. Khong and C. F. Simpson, *Chromatographia*, 24 (1987) 385.
40. L. C. Sander and S. A. Wise, *J. Chromatogr.*, 316 (1986) 163.
41. Y. Kato, T. Kitamura, and T. Hashimoto, *J. Liquid Chromatogr.*, 9 (1986) 3209.
42. H. Engelhardt and U. Schön, *J. Liquid Chromatogr.*, 9 (1986) 3225.
43. Z. El Rassi and Cs. Horvath, *J. Liquid Chromatogr.*, 9 (1986) 3245.
44. N. T. Miller and C. H. Shieh, *J. Liquid Chromatogr.*, 9 (1986) 3269.
45. H. Engelhardt and D. Mathes, *J. Chromatogr.*, 142 (1977) 311.
46. K. Benedek, S. Dong, and B. L. Karger, *J. Chromatogr.*, 317 (1984) 227.
47. A. J. Alpert, *J. Chromatogr.*, 359 (1986) 85.
48. F. E. Regnier, *Chromatographia*, 24 (1986) 241.
49. W. Jost, K. K. Unger, R. Lipecky, and H. E. Gassen, *J. Chromatogr.*, 185 (1979) 403.
50. R. W. Stout, S. I. Sivakoff, R. D. Ricker, H. C. Palmer, M. A. Jackson, and T. J. Odiorne, *J. Chromatogr.*, 352 (1986) 381.
51. A. J. Alpert, *J. Chromatogr.*, 266 (1983) 23.
52. W. Müller, *8th Int. Symp. HPLC Proteins, Peptides, Polynucleotides*, October 31–November 2, 1988. Copenhagen, Denmark, paper 121.
53. P. Å. Albertsson, Partition of Cell Particles and Macromolecules. Almquist & Wiksell, Stockholm, Sweden, 1971.
54. W. Müller, *Eur. J. Biochem.*, 155 (1986) 213.
55. W. Müller, *Kontakte (Darmstadt)*, 3 (1986) 3.
56. W. Müller, *Kontakte (Darmstadt)*, 1 (1987) 45.
57. W. Müller, Liquid–Liquid Partition Chromatography of Biopolymers. GIT Verlag, Darmstadt, FRG, 1988.
58. P. O. Larsson, *Methods Enzymol.*, 104 (1984) 212.
59. R. R. Walters, *Anal. Chem.*, 57 (1985) 1099A.
60. B. Anspach, K. K. Unger, J. Davies, and M. T. W. Hearn, *J. Chromatogr.*, 457 (1989) 195.
61. B. Anspach, H.-J. Wirth, K. K. Unger, P. Stanton, J. R. Davies, and M. T. W. Hearn, *Analyt. Biochem.*, 179 (1989) 171.
62. P. O. Larsson, M. Glad, L. Hansson, M. O. Månsson, S. Ohlsson, and K. Mosbach, in Advances in Chromatography, Vol. 21 (J. C. Giddings, E. Grushka, J. Cazes and P. Brown, eds.). Dekker, New York, 1983, pp. 41–85.
63. B. Anspach, to be published.
64. H.-J. Wirth, F. B. Anspach, M. T. W. Hearn, and K. K. Unger, *8th Int. Symp. HPLC Proteins, Peptides, Polynucleotides*, October 30–November 2, 1988, Copenhagen, Denmark, paper 511.
65. J. Porath, J. Karlsson, I. Olsson, and G. Belfrage, *Nature (London)*, 258 (1975) 598.
66. J. Porath, B. Olin, and B. Graustrand, *Arch. Biochem. Biophys.*, 225 (1983) 543.
67. E. S. Hemdan and J. Porath, *J. Chromatogr.*, 323 (1985) 255.
68. B. Feibush, B. L. Karger, and A. Figueroa, *9th Int. Symp. Column Liquid Chromatogr.*, Edinburgh, United Kingdom, 1985, Lecture L 10.1.
69. Z. El Rassi and Cs. Horvath, *J. Chromatogr.*, 359 (1986) 241.
70. M. Gimpel and K. K. Unger, *Chromatographia*, 17 (1983) 200.
71. B. Feibush, M. J. Cohen, and B. L. Karger, *J. Chromatogr.*, 282 (1985) 3.
72. L. Fanou-Ayi and M. Vijayalakshmi, *Ann. N.Y. Acad. Sci.*, 413 (1983) 300.
73. Z. El Rassi and Cs. Horvath, *J. Chromatogr.*, 359 (1986) 241.
74. T. Motokubota and Y. Morise, Japan Jpn. Kokai Tokkyo Koho JP 62/244441 A2 [87/244441], 24 October 1987, 5pp.
75. C. Falkenberg, L. Bjoerck, B. Aakerstroem, and S. Nilsson, *Biomed. Chromatogr.*, 2(5) (1987) 221.

76. D. Josic, W. Hofmann, R. Habermann, and W. Reutter, *J. Chromatogr.*, 444 (1988) 29.
77. I. V. Mezhova, B. A. Klyashchitskii, and V. I. Shvets, *Khim.-Farm. Zh.*, 22(4) (1988) 455.
78. M. Nakamura, T. Kumazawa, and E. Kogure, Japan Eur. Pat. Appl. EP 239079 A2, 30 September 1987, 13 pp.
79. M. J. Quentin-Millet and F. Arminjon, Eur. Pat. Appl. EP 242302 A1, 21 October 1987, 12 pp. Designated.
80. Z. El Rassi, Y. Truei, Y. F. Maa, and Cs. Horvath, *Anal. Biochem.*, 169(1) (1988) 172.
81. R. Marcisauskas, D. Karalite, I. Barilkaite, O. Sudziuviene, and I. Pesliakas, *Biotekhnologiya*, 4(1) (1988) 97.
82. A. V. Gaida, V. A. Monastyrskii, Yu. V. Magerovskii, S. M. Staroverov, and G. V. Lisichkin, *J. Chromatogr.*, 424(2) (1988) 385.
83. A. P. Ignatchenko, V. I. Bogomaz, V. A. Tugai, and A. A. Chuiko, *Ukr. Biokhim. Zh.*, 59(6) (1987) 28.
84. S. Ohlson and U. Niss, *J. Immunol. Methods*, 106(2) (1988) 225.
85. J. C. Hsia, Eur. Pat. Appl. EP 229696 A1, 22 July 1987, 13 pp. Designated.
86. D. F. Hollis, S. Ralston, E. Suen, N. Cooke, and R. G. L. Shorr, *J. Liquid Chromatogr.*, 10(11) (1987) 2349.
87. Y. D. Clonis, *J. Chromatogr.*, 407 (1987) 179.
88. H. W. Jarrett, *J. Chromatogr.*, 405 (1987) 179.
89. E. D. Green, R. M. Brodbeck, and J. U. Baenziger, *Anal. Biochem.*, 167(1) (1987) 62.
90. K. Ernst-Cabrera, and M. Wilchek, *J. Chromatogr.*, 397 (1987) 187.
91. W. S. Foster and H. W. Jarrett, *J. Chromatogr.*, 403 (1987) 99.
92. J. C. Hsia, PCT Int. Appl. WO 87/177 A1, 15 January 1987, 29 pp. Designated.
93. U. Klussmann and V. A. Erdmann, Ger. Offen. DE 3644346 A1, 21 May 1987, 6 pp.
94. M. L. Stolowitz, U.S. US 4665037 A, 12 May 1987, 12 pp.
95. S. Ohlson and J. Wieslander, *J. Chromatogr.*, 397 (1987) 207.
96. A. V. Gaida, Yu. V. Magerovskii, and V. A. Monastyrskii, *Biokhimiya (Moscow)*, 52(4) (1987) 569.
97. P. Wikstroem and P. O. Larsson, *J. Chromatogr.*, 388(1) (1987) 123.
98. H. L. Hubbard, T. D. Eller, D. E. Mais, P. V. Halushka, R. H. Baker, I. A. Blair, J. J. Vrbanac, and D. R. Knapp, *Prostaglandins*, 33(2) (1987) 149.
99. J. Dakour, A. Lundblad, and D. Zopf, *Anal. Biochem.*, 161(1) (1987) 140.
100. J. L. Wade, A. F. Bergold, and P. W. Carr, *Anal. Chem.*, 59(9) (1987) 1286.
101. K. Ernst-Cabrera and M. Wilchek, *Anal. Biochem.*, 159(2) (1986) 267.
102. V. P. Varlamov, G. E. Bannikova, S. A. Lopatin, and S. Rogozhin, *Symp. Biol. Hung.*, 31 (*Chromatography '84*) (1986) 127.
103. A. Figueroa, C. Corradini, B. Feibush, and B. L. Karger, *J. Chromatogr.*, 371 (1986) 335.
104. P. Formstecher, H. Hammadi, N. Bouzerna, and M. Dautrevaux, *J. Chromatogr.*, 369(2) (1986) 379.
105. H. W. Jarrett, *J. Chromatogr.*, 363(2) (1986) 456.
106. D. J. Anderson, J. S. Anhalt, and R. R. Walters, *J. Chromatogr.*, 359 (1986) 369.
107. Y. D. Clonis, K. Jones, and C. R. Lowe, *J. Chromatogr.*, 363(1) (1986) 31.
108. I. Csiky and L. Hansson, *J. Liquid Chromatogr.*, 9(4) (1986) 875.
109. M. Akashi, T. Tokiyoshi, N. Miyauchi, and K. Mosbach, *Nucleic Acids Symp. Ser.*, 17 (*Symp. Nucleic Acids Chem. 13th*) (1985) 41.
110. D. S. Hage, R. R. Walters, and H. W. Hethcote, *Anal. Chem.*, 58(2) (1986) 274.
111. D. Renauer, F. Oesch, J. Kinkel, K. K. Unger, and R. J. Wieser, *Anal. Biochem.*, 151(2) (1985) 424.
112. G. E. Bannikova, V. P. Varlamov, S. A. Lopatin, and S. Rogozhin, *Nukleazy: Biol. Rol Prakt. Ispol'z.*, (1985) 51.
113. I. Miedziak, G. Jozefaciuk, and A. Waksmundzki, *Chem. Anal. (Warsaw)*, 30(2) (1985) 275.

114. I. V. Ulezlo, A. V. Ananichev, and A. M. Bezborodov, *Prikl. Biokhim. Mikrobiol.*, 21(4) (1985) 445.
115. J. Lobarzewski, J. Fiedurek, G. Ginalska, and T. Wolski, *Biochem. Biophys. Res. Commun.*, 131(2) (1985) 666.
116. M. Nakajima, K. Kimura, E. Hayata, and T. Shono, *J. Liquid Chromatogr.*, 7(11) (1984) 2115.
117. J. Zemek, I. Novak, D. Berek, and L. Kuniak, Czech. CS 211176 B, 15 March 1984, 4 pp.
118. S. Allenmark, B. Bomgren, and S. Andersson, *Prep. Biochem.*, 14(2) (1984) 139.
119. J. N. Kinkel, B. Anspach, K. K. Unger, R. Wieser, and G. Brunner, *J. Chromatogr.*, 297 (1984) 167.
120. A. K. Roy and S. Roy, *Affinity Chromatogr. Biol. Recog.*, [*Proc. Int. Symp.*], 5th (1983) 257.
121. E. Hagemeier, K. Kemper, K. S. Boos, and E. Schlimme, *J. Clin. Chem. Clin. Biochem.*, 22(2) (1984) 175.
122. R. R. Walters, *Affinity Chromatogr. Biol. Recog.*, [*Proc. Int. Symp.*], 5th (1983) 261.
123. N. R. Tzodikov, U.S. US 4432877 A, 21 February 1984, 6 pp.
124. A. J. Muller and P. W. Carr, *J. Chromatogr.*, 284(1) (1984) 33.
125. C. A. K. Borrebaeck, J. Soares, and B. Mattiasson, *J. Chromatogr.*, 284(1) (1984) 187.
126. E. Hagemeier, K. Kemper, K. S. Boos, and E. Schlimme, *J. Chromatogr.*, 282 (1983) 663.
127. A. V. Kiselev, V. M. Kolikov, B. V. Mchedlishvili, Yu. S. Nikitin, and T. D. Khokhlova, *Dokl. Akad. Nauk USSR*, 272(5), (1983) 1158 [*Phys. Chem.*].
128. K. Nilsson and P. O. Larsson, *Anal. Biochem.*, 134(1) (1983) 60.
129. E. Hagemeier, K. S. Boos, E. Schlimme, K. Lechtenboerger, and A. Kettrup, *J. Chromatogr.*, 268(2) (1983) 291.
130. D. A. P. Small, T. Atkinson, and C. R. Lowe, *J. Chromatogr.*, 266 (1983) 151.
131. S. C. Crowley and R. R. Walters, *J. Chromatogr.*, 266 (1983) 157.
132. P. Hughes, C. R. Lowe, and R. F. Sherwood, Eur. Pat. Appl. EP 64378 A2, 10 November 1982, 33 pp. Designated.
133. D. Zhang and C. Zhang, *Beijing Yixueyuan Xuebao*, 14(4) (1982) 323.
134. A. Atkinson, C. R. Lowe, D. A. Philip, and K. Mosbach, Brit. UK Pat. Appl. GB 2097280 A, 3 November 1982, 16 pp.
135. N. V. Akzo, Jpn. Kokai Tokkyo Koho JP 57/38937 A2 [82/38937], 3 March 1982, 18 pp.
136. R. R. Walters, *J. Chromatogr.*, 249(1) (1982) 19.
137. N. N. Lestrovaya, Zh. D. Lebedeva, I. M. Volkova, A. K. Aren, V. U. Bukbarde, I. V. Gruzin, and E. L. Ruban, U.S.S.R. SU 943278 A1, 15 July 1982. Otkrytiya, Izobret., Prom. Obraztsy, Tovarnye Znaki 1982, (26), 124.
138. S. M. Payne and B. N. Ames, *Anal. Biochem.*, 123(1) (1982) 151.
139. A. Borchert, P. O. Larsson, and K. Mosbach, *J. Chromatogr.*, 244(1) (1982) 49.
140. S. Rajgopal and M. Vijayalakshmi, *J. Chromatogr.*, 243(1) (1982) 164.
141. G. E. Bannikova, V. P. Varlamov, O. L. Samsonova, and S. V. Rogozhin, *Bioorg. Khim.*, 8(2) (1982) 212.
142. A. Atkinson, J. E. McArdell, M. D. Scawen, R. F. Sherwood, D. A. P. Small, C. R. Lowe, and C. J. Bruton, *Anal. Chem. Symp. Ser.*, 9 (*Affinity Chromatogr. Relat. Tech.*) (1982) 399.
143. J. Schutyser, T. Buser, D. Van Olden, H. Tomas, F. Van Houdenhoven, and G. Van Dedem, *Anal. Chem. Symp. Ser.*, 9 (*Affinity Chromatogr. Relat. Tech.*) (1982) 143.
144. V. M. Stepanov, G. N. Rudenskaya, A. V. Gaida, and A. L. Osterman, *J. Biochem. Biophys. Methods*, 5(3) (1981) 177.
145. A. V. Brykalov, V. N. Postnov, S. I. Kol'tsov, V. I. Koval'kov, V. P. Tel'bukh, and V. I. Smyshlyaeva, Otkrytiya, Izobret., Prom. Obraztsy, Tovarnye Znaki 1981, (31), 120.

146. D. A. P. Small, T. Atkinson, and C. R. Lowe, *J. Chromatogr.*, 216, (1981) 175.
147. C. R. Lowe, M. Glad, P. O. Larsson, S. Ohlson, D. A. P. Small, T. Atkinson, and K. Mosbach, *J. Chromatogr.*, 215 (1981) 303.
148. I. V. Berezin, Yu. M. Lopukhin, I. P. Andrianova, Ya. I. Lapuk, L. B. Alekseeva, V. I. Sergienko, E. A. Borodin, E. M. Khalilov, and A. I. Archakov, *Vopr. Med. Khim.*, 26(6) (1980) 843.
149. U.S.S.R. SU 762916, 15 September 1980. Otkrytiya, Izobret., Prom. Obraztsy, Tovarnye Znaki 1980, (34).
150. M. Glad, S. Ohlson, L. Hansson, M-O. Maansson, and K. Mosbach, *J. Chromatogr.*, 200 (1980) 254.
151. D. Daija, R. Berzina-Berzite, V. Kirse, and A. Arens, U.S.S.R. SU 777041, 7 November 1980. Otkrytiya, Izobret., Prom. Obraztsy, Tovarnye Znaki 1980, (41), 90.
152. M. M. Rakhimov, R. Akhmedzhanov, M. U. Babaev, Sh. R. Mad'yarov, U. Z. Muratova, and B. A. Tashmukhamedov, *Uzb. Biol. Zh.*, (5) (1980) 7.
153. N. G. Evstratova, I. A. Vasilenko, N. Yu. Kondrat'eva, G. A. Serebrennikova, R. P. Evstigneeva, V. P. Varlamov, N. N. Semenova, and S. V. Rogozhin, *Bioorg. Khim.*, 6(9) (1980) 1355.
154. A. V. Gaida, V. M. Stepanov, V. K. Akparov, and G. N. Rudenskaya, Brit. UK Pat. Appl. GB 2031432, 23 April 1980, 11 pp.
155. J. R. Sportsman and G. S. Wilson, *Anal. Chem.*, 52(13) (1980) 2013.
156. J. L. Tayot and M. Tardy, *Adv. Exp. Med. Biol.*, 125 (Struct. Funct. Gangliosides) (1980) 471.
157. J. L. Tayot and M. Tardy, Fr. Demande FR 2422699, 9 November 1979, 18 pp. Division of Fr. Demande 2,403,098.
158. I. V. Berezin, A. M. Egorov, E. M. Gavrilova, B. B. Dzantiev, and Y. Ya. Mokeev, U.S.S.R. SU 651814, 15 March 1979. Otkrytiya, Izobret., Prom. Obraztsy, Tovarnye Znaki 1979, (10), 18.
159. S. Ohlson, L. Hansson, P. O. Larsson, and K. Mosbach, *FEBS Lett.*, 93(1) (1978) 5.
160. J. Langer and Z. Kornetka, *Pol. J. Chem.*, 52(6) (1978) 1303.
161. A. S. Karsakevich, G. Ya. Migla, and R. Zagats, *Khim. Prir. Soedin.*, (1) (1978) 118.
162. V. Kh. Akparov, and V. M. Stepanov, *Prikl. Biokhim. Mikrobiol.*, 13(1) (1977) 141.
163. H. Mazarguil, F. Meiller, and P. Monsan, Ger. Offen. DE 2614405, 14 October 1976, 10 pp.
164. J. Köhler, D. B. Chase, R. D. Farlee, A. J. Vega, and J. J. Kirkland, *J. Chromatogr.*, 352 (1986) 275.
165. J. Köhler and J. J. Kirkland, *J. Chromatogr.*, 385 (1987) 125.
166. A. V. Zhuravlev, *Langmuir*, 3 (1987) 316.
167. M. Holik and B. Matějkova, *J. Chromatogr.*, 213 (1981) 33.
168. U. Kittelmann and K. K. Unger, *Progr. Colloid Polym. Sci.*, 67 (1980) 19.
169. B. Pfleiderer, K. Albert, E. Bayer, L. van de Ven, J. de Haan, and C. Cramers, *J. Phys. Chem.*, 94 (1990) 4189.
170. H. P. Boehm and H. Knözinger, in Catalysis, Vol. 4 (J. A. Anderson and M. Boudart, eds.). Springer Verlag, Heidelberg, 1983, pp. 39–207.
171. D. Farin, Sh. Peleg, D. Yavin, and D. Avnir, *Langmuir*, 1 (1985) 399.
172. G. A. Maciel and D. W. Sindorf, *J. Am. Chem. Soc.*, 102 (1980) 7606.
173. D. W. Sindorf and G. E. Maciel, *J. Am. Chem. Soc.*, 103 (1981) 4263.
174. E. Bayer, K. Albert, J. Reiners, M. Nieder, and D. Müller, *J. Chromatogr.*, 264 (1983) 197.
175. B. Pfleiderer, K. Albert, E. Bayer, K. D. Lork, K. K. Unger, and H. Brückner, *Angew. Chem.*, 101 (1989) 336.
176. R. K. Gilpin and J. A. Squires, *J. Chromatogr. Sci.*, 19 (1981) 195.
177. D. Morel, J. Serpinet, J. M. Letoffe, and P. Claudy, *Chromatographia*, 22 (1988) 103.
178. J. Serpinet, personal communication.
179. E. Bayer, K. Albert, and B. Pfleiderer, *12th Int. Symp. Column Liquid Chromatogr.*, June 19–24, 1988, Washington, D.C., paper M-L-3.

180. B. L. Karger, *17th Int. Symp. Chromatogr.*, September 25–30, 1988, Vienna, Austria, paper L-1.
181. J. H. Knox, *J. Chromatogr. Sci.*, 15 (1977) 352.
182. P. A. Bristow and J. H. Knox, *Chromatographia*, 10 (1977) 279.
183. L. R. Snyder and M. A. Stadalius, in HPLC: Advances and Perspectives, Vol. 4 (Cs. Horvath, ed.). Academic Press, New York, 1986, pp. 195–312.
184. T. Allen, Particle Size Measurement. Chapman and Hall, London, 1981.
185. G. D. Parfitt and C. H. Rochester, Adsorption from Solution at the Solid/Liquid Interface. Academic Press, London, 1983.
186. F. Helfferich, Ion Exchange. McGraw-Hill, New York, 1962.
187. R. C. Machenzie, Differential Thermal Analysis, Vols. 1 and 2. Academic Press, London, 1972.
188. M. Bavarez and J. Bastick, *Bull. Soc. Chim. Fr.*, (1964) 3226.
189. M. L. Hair, Infrared Spectroscopy in Surface Chemistry. Dekker, New York, 1967.
190. L. H. Little, Infrared Spectra of Adsorbed Species. Academic Press, London, 1966.
191. D. E. Leyden and R. S. S. Murthy, *Trends Anal. Chem.*, 7 (1988) 164.
192. S. D. Fazio, S. A. Tomellini, H. Shih-Hsien, J. B. Crowther, T. V. Raglione, T. R. Floyd, and R. A. Hartwiek, *Anal. Chem.*, 57 (1985) 1559.
193. C. H. Lochmüller and S. S. Saavedra, *J. Am. Chem. Soc.*, 109 (1987) 1244.
194. C. H. Lochmüller and S. S. Saavedra, *Langmuir*, 3 (1987) 433.
195. P. G. D. Dean, W. S. Johnson, and F. A. Middle, Affinity Chromatography—A Practical Approach. IRL Press, Oxford, 1985.
196. W. W. Yau, J. J. Kirkland, and D. D. Bly, Modern Size Exclusion Chromatography. Wiley, New York, 1979.
197. K. K. Unger, *Methods Enzymol.*, 104 (1984) 154.
198. B. Anspach, H. U. Gierlich, and K. K. Unger, *J. Chromatogr.*, 443 (1988) 45.
199. W. S. Hancock and J. T. Sparrow, in HPLC: Advances and Perspectives, Vol. 3 (Cs. Horvath, ed.). Academic Press, New York, 1983, pp. 50–83.
200. R. Janzen, K. K. Unger, H. Giesche, J. N. Kinkel, and M. T. W. Hearn, *J. Chromatogr.*, 397 (1987) 81.
201. S. A. Cohen, K. P. Benedek, S. Dong, Y. Tapuhi, and B. L. Karger, *Anal. Chem.*, 56 (1984) 217.
202. K. Benedek, S. Dong, and B. L. Karger, *J. Chromatogr.*, 317 (1984) 227.
203. Cs. Horvath, *17th Int. Symp. Chromatogr.*, September 25–30, 1988, Vienna, Austria, paper L-4.
204. M. T. W. Hearn, in Advances in Chromatography, Vol. 20 (J. C. Giddings, E. Grushka, J. Cases, and Ph. Brown, eds.). Academic Press, London, 1982, pp. 87–155.
205. M. T. W. Hearn, in HPLC: Advances and Perspectives, Vol. 3 (Cs. Horvath, ed.). Academic Press, New York, 1983, pp. 87–155.
206. M. T. W. Hearn, *Methods Enzymol.*, 104 (1984) 190.
207. D. L. Gooding, M. N. Schmuck, M. P. Nowlan, and K. M. Gooding, *J. Chromatogr.*, 359 (1986) 331.
208. W. Kopaciewicz, M. A. Rounds, J. Fausnagh, and F. E. Regnier, *J. Chromatogr.*, 266 (1983) 3.
209. M. L. Heinitz, L. K. Kennedy, W. Kopaciewicz, and F. E. Regnier, *J. Chromatogr.*, 443 (1988) 173.
210. L. W. Nichol, A. G. Ogsten, D. J. Winzor, and W. H. Sawyer, *Biochem. J.*, 143 (1974) 435.
211. B. H. Arve and A. I. Liapis, *AIChE J.*, 33 (1987) 179.
212. B. H. Arve and A. I. Liapis, in Proceedings of the Second International Conference on Fundamentals of Adsorption Engineering Foundation (A. I. Liapis, ed.). New York, 1987.
213. M. M. Hossain, D. D. Do, and J. E. Bailey, *AIChE J.*, 32 (1986) 1088.
214. G. Scatchard, *Ann. N.Y. Acad. Sci.*, 51 (1949) 660.
215. F. B. Anspach, A. Johnston, H.-J. Wirth, M. T. W. Hearn, and K. K. Unger, *8th Int. Symp. HPLC Proteins, Peptides, Polynucleotides*, October 30–November 2, 1989, Copenhagen, Denmark, paper S12.

CHAPTER 4

High-Performance Agarose-Based Chromatographic Media and Their Application in Biopolymer Separation

Stellan Hjertén

CONTENTS

4.1 INTRODUCTION

From the different chapters in this book it is evident that high-performance liquid chromatography (HPLC) during the last decade has become a widely used analytical and preparative method for the separation of biopolymers, particularly proteins. Typical of HPLC is that smaller and more rigid beads are used than in conventional, low-pressure chromatography. In principle, there are no other differences between these two chromatographic versions, which means that the results of theoretical as well as experimental studies of the latter version are directly applicable on HPLC. This is not fully realized, however, to judge from the many HPLC investigations that are mere reiterations of earlier performed low-pressure chromatographic investigations. On the other hand, it is understandable that the higher resolution and the shorter run times in HPLC give a feeling that it is a new technique also from a theoretical point of view.

The main reason why smaller beads give a higher resolution is that the diffusion paths in both the stationary and mobile phases are shorter, which favors a more rapid partition of the solute between the two phases (see also Chapters 3 and 5–8). Theoretically, the highest resolution is obtained when both of these diffusion paths are close to zero. This ideal case can in practice be approached if nonporous beads are used and if the beads—after packing—are deformed to decrease the average distance between them (nonporous beads cannot, of course, be used in molecular-sieve chromatography, since its separation mechanism is based on diffusion of the solutes into and out of the beads).

Silica is still the most commonly used packing material in HPLC. However, due to its instability above pH 8 and relatively high nonspecific adsorption there is a trend to replace it with matrices that are more inert and biocompatible and more stable at basic pH. From this point of view, beads from carbon materials, synthetic polymers, and agarose are highly interesting. This chapter will exclusively deal with agarose-based HPLC on porous as well as nonporous beads and such beads deformed by compression of the column bed. Deformed, nonporous agarose beads have the unique property to give a resolution that is independent of, or sometimes increases with an increase in flow rate. The resolution is also very little dependent on the bead size. These important properties are at variance with the general theory of chromatography (see Chapters 3, 7, and 8).

Agarose as an HPLC matrix is commercially available only for molecular-sieve chromatography and hydrophobic-interaction chromatography on porous beads. Readers who wish to take advantage of the great potential of the many different forms of agarose-based HPLC, mentioned in Section 4.11.1, must accordingly themselves prepare the bed materials. Therefore, the preparation and sizing of both porous and nonporous agarose beads and synthesis of their derivatives will be described in some detail. The uninitiated reader can, however, find more information in the references given.

In Chapter 22 I have emphasized the analogies between chromatography and electrophoresis and have described a method that is defined as the electrophoretic counterpart of HPLC. This new, high-resolution method (high-performance electrophoresis) is very convenient for rapid analyses of HPLC fractions.

4.2 THE STRUCTURE AND PROPERTIES OF AGAROSE

In 1937 Araki published a paper[1] showing that agar consists of two types of polysaccharides, agarose and agaropectin and 19 years later a paper on the structure of agarose.[2] The former component was stated to be nonionic and the latter acidic. I could confirm by repeating his experiments that agar contains an almost nonionic gel-forming moiety (Araki kindly translated his paper from Japanese to English on my behalf). The method Araki developed for the preparation of agarose for his structural studies was not suitable for the manufacture of agarose on a larger scale.[1,3] Therefore, other methods were developed.[4–6]

According to Araki, agarose is a polysaccharide built up of alternate residues of 3,6-anhydro-L-galactose and D-galactose.[2] Because of the studies of Rees and collaborators,[7] we know that the polysaccharide chains form double helices that are collected in bundles, which confers a very porous structure on the agarose gels even when their concentration is as high as 15% (Figure 4–1). Cross-linking occurs chiefly between the chains in these bundles or/and in the junctions.[8] Therefore, cross-linking of agarose beads to make them more rigid only slightly reduces the size of the pores created by the polysaccharide bundles.[8]

Although twenty-five years have passed since agarose gels were introduced as matrices for electrophoresis,[3] immunoelectrophoresis,[9] and chromatography,[10] they are still widely used for the same purpose.

4.3 PREPARATION AND SIZING OF AGAROSE BEADS

Agarose beads are prepared by a suspension–gelation procedure. Since this method has been treated in ref. 11, only a brief description will be given here.

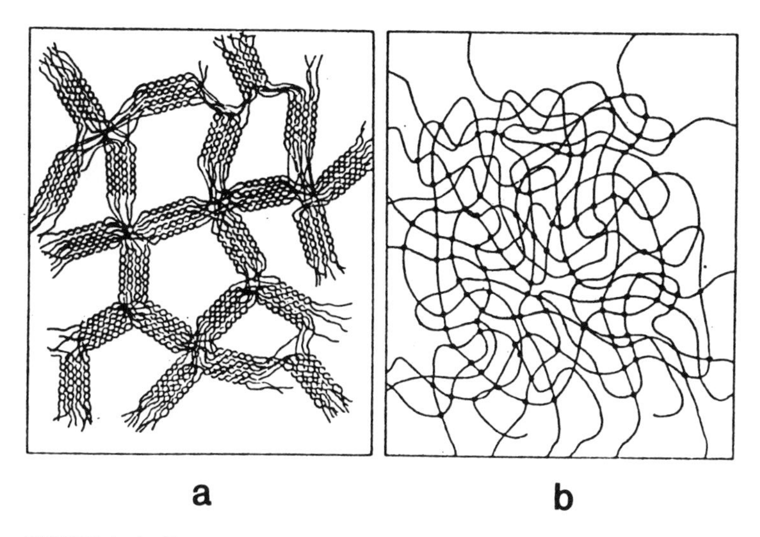

FIGURE 4–1. The structures of agarose gels (a) and cross-linked dextran and polyacrylamide gels (b). The aggregates of the helical agarose chains actually contain 10 to 10^4 helices rather than the smaller numbers shown here. (Reproduced from ref. 7, with permission.)

To give the beads the mechanical stability required for HPLC they are prepared from solutions of relatively high agarose concentrations (often 10–15 g of agarose per 100 ml of water). For complete dissolution of agarose at these concentrations boiling at an overpressure of 2 bar is recommended (for this purpose an ordinary pressure cooker can be used). An organic solvent at a temperature of 50°C and containing a stabilizer is added to the warm agarose solution. On vigorous stirring beads of agarose solution are formed in the organic phase (the stabilizer, for instance polyoxyethylene sorbitan monostearate, prevents the beads from coalescing). When the temperature is lowered, gelation starts. The organic solvent is removed by washing on a Büchner funnel.

The gel beads are sized by elutriation in distilled water in the equipment shown in Figure 4–2. The suspension of agarose beads is poured into tube A and water is continuously fed into it from the bottom with the aid of pump P. The suspension is agitated occasionally with the magnetic stirrer S if a layer of larger sedimented beads forms on the porous disc M.

For a mathematic treatment of the elutriation procedure we consider an agarose sphere of radius r in any of the tubes A and B. The following forces act upon the gel sphere:

$$\text{gravitational force } F_1 = 4/3\ \pi r^3 \rho_a g$$

$$\text{buoyancy force } F_2 = 4/3\ \pi r^3 \rho_w g$$

$$\text{frictional force } F_3 = 6\ \pi \eta r v \qquad \text{(Stokes' law)}$$

where ρ_a and ρ_w are the densities of the agarose spheres and water, respectively, g is the gravitational acceleration, η is the viscosity of water, and v is the linear

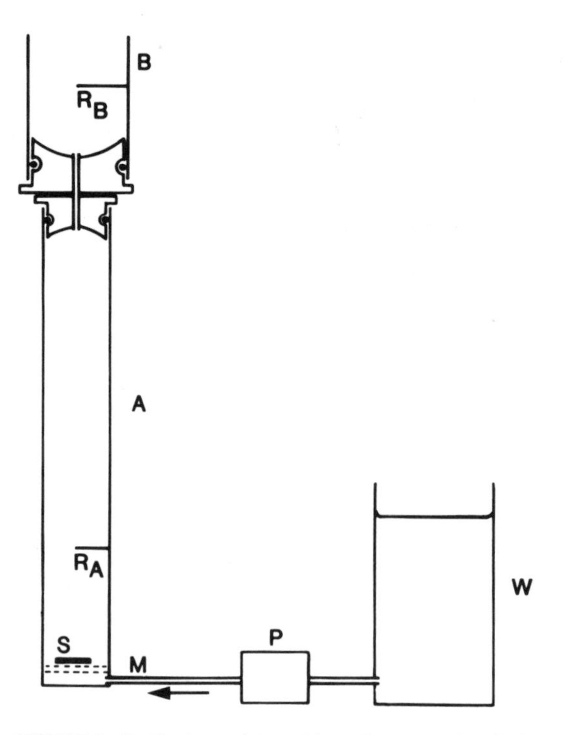

FIGURE 4–2. Equipment for sizing of agarose beads by elutriation. W, water reservoir; P, peristaltic pump; M, porous polyethylene disc; S, stirrer; A, Plexiglas tube with radius R_A; B, Plexiglas tube with radius R_B. An aqueous suspension of agarose beads with different diameters is poured into tube A. Water is fed into tube A with the aid of pump P. Beads with radii equal to and above a critical value (r_A) will collect in tube A, whereas beads with radii below this value will pass into tube B (for beads with radius r_A the sedimentation velocity is equal to the flow velocity in tube A). Since the linear flow velocity is lower in tube B than in tube A, smaller particles will collect in tube B rather than in tube A. In tube C, not shown in the figure, but positioned on top of tube B, still smaller beads collect. The radii of the beads in tube B are determined by the radii R_A and R_B in accordance with Eq. (4–8).

sedimentation velocity of the gel spheres relative to the tube wall. The equilibrium condition $F_1 = F_2 + F_3$ gives

$$v = \frac{2r^2(\rho_a - \rho_w)g}{9\eta} \tag{4–1}$$

If the pump speed is S (cm^3/min), the linear flow velocities f_A (cm/min) in tube A and f_B in tube B are determined by the relations

$$f_A = S/\pi R_A^2 \tag{4–2}$$

$$f_B = S/\pi R_B^2 \tag{4–3}$$

Assume that a gel sphere in tube A has a radius r_A such that the gel sphere is stationary with respect to the tube wall, i.e., the sedimentation velocity v_A is equal to the flow velocity, or

$$v_A = f_A \tag{4–4}$$

Similarly we assume the existence of a gel sphere with radius r_B in tube B fulfilling the condition

$$v_B = f_B \tag{4–5}$$

Gel spheres with a radius $< r_A$ will then enter tube B and spheres with a radius $< r_B$ will leave it. Therefore, gel spheres with radii r smaller than r_A but larger than (and equal to) r_B are collected in tube B ($r_A > r \geqslant r_B$).

A combination of Eqs. (4–1), (4–2), and (4–4) gives

$$S = \frac{\pi R_A^2 2 r_A^2 (\rho_a - \rho_w) g}{9\eta} \tag{4–6}$$

This equation gives the pump speed S required for spheres with radius r_A to be stationary in tube A. At this pump speed spheres with the radius r_B will be stationary in tube B if the following condition is fulfulled:

$$S = \frac{\pi R_B^2 2 r_B^2 (\rho_a - \rho_w) g}{9\eta} \tag{4–7}$$

From Eqs. (4–6) and (4–7) one gets

$$R_A/R_B = r_B/r_A \tag{4–8}$$

For instance, if tube B has a radius equal to 4 cm and a column is to be packed with non-crosslinked 12% agarose beads with diameters ranging from 8 to 10 μm then the pump speed S must be [Eq. (4–7)]: $[\pi 4^2 \cdot 2(0.0004)^2 \cdot (1.12 - 1.00) 981]/(9 \cdot 0.01) = 0.025$ cm³/min and the radius R_A of tube A [Eq. (4–8)]: $(0.0004/0.0005) \cdot 4 = 3.2$ cm.

For the calculation of ρ_a, the density of a 12% agarose sphere, we have made the approximation that there is no increase in volume when 12 g of agarose are dissolved in 100 ml of water.

Even if much attention is paid to the design of the connection between tubes A and B the linear flow velocity close to the wall of tube B in its bottom part is often so low that gel beads with radii smaller than r_B sediment and accordingly never leave tube B. Therefore we often reelutriate the beads that collect at the bottom of this tube.

The elutriation is not performed in buffer but in distilled water since the repulsion between the slightly negatively charged agarose beads then is larger and the risk of aggregation of gel spheres is negligible.

4.4 CROSS-LINKING

To get high flow rates when a column is packed with macroporous agarose beads of a small diameter (10 μm or less) it is important that the beads are mechanically stable. This rigidity can be obtained if the agarose concentration is high and the agarose chains are cross-linked. As mentioned above neither high agarose concentrations nor cross-linking makes the beads impenetrable for macromolecules (cf. cross-linked dextran and polyacrylamide gels; Figure 4–1b).

4.4.1 Cross-Linking with Epoxides

Epichlorohydrin and bisepoxides have been used for cross-linking of cellulose, starch, and dextran for many years. For cross-linking of agarose gels to be used in the form of beads for HPLC bisepoxides (and trisepoxides) are preferable since they give the agarose beads the rigidity required. The reaction scheme is shown in Figure 4–3a.[12] Although the description given in Section 4.5 refers to 1,4-butandiol diglycidyl ether, it is applicable with many other cross-linkers of the epoxide type. A mixture of bis- and trisepoxides of different chain lengths—or succesively used—can sometimes give a still higher rigidity. There are accordingly many possibilities to vary the structure of the cross-linkers and thus the rigidity of the agarose beads.[13] Cross-linking with epoxides is ideal from a theoretical point of view: a pH-stable ether bond is formed and no net loss in hydrophilic OH groups occurs (an OH group in the agarose is lost but a new one is created during the cross-linking, see Figure 4–3a). However, in practice the bisepoxide cross-linked beads often become relatively hydrophobic, which is a great disadvantage, since this may lead to undesirable, sometimes irreversible, interactions between the bed and the macromolecules to be separated. This disturbing hydrophobicity is understandable when the cross-linker is relatively nonpolar. However, a cross-linker such as triglycidoxyglycerol, which ought to give a hydrophilic bridge also renders the agarose beads somewhat hydrophobic. Possibly the hydrophobicity is caused by contaminants in the epoxide solutions. For methods to reduce hydrophobic interactions, see Section 4.11.2.

The cross-linking can be performed in either an aqueous solution at alkaline pH in the presence of sodium borohydride to prevent hydrolysis of the glucosidic bonds in the agarose chains[12] or in an organic solvent with boron trifluoride diethyl etherate (or stannic chloride[14]) as catalyst. The latter alternative will later be described in detail, since it is used for the preparation of nonporous beads (Section 4.5).

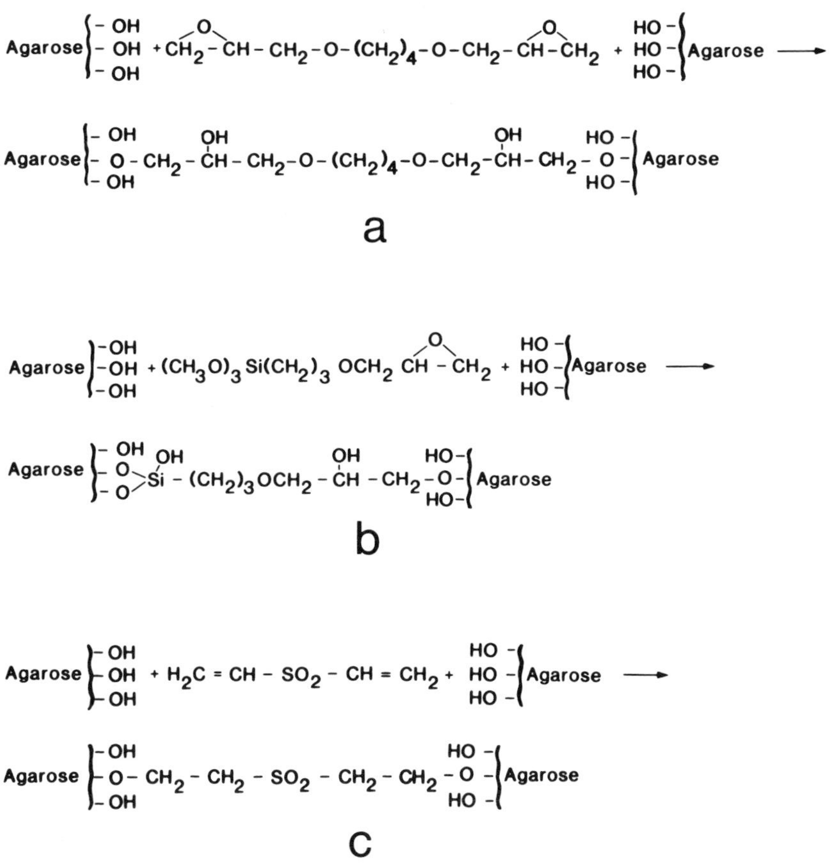

$$\text{Agarose}\begin{cases}-OH\\-OH\\-OH\end{cases} + \overset{O}{\overbrace{CH_2-CH}}-CH_2-O-(CH_2)_4-O-CH_2-\overset{O}{\overbrace{CH-CH_2}} + \begin{cases}HO-\\HO-\\HO-\end{cases}\text{Agarose} \longrightarrow$$

$$\text{Agarose}\begin{cases}-OH\\-O-CH_2-\underset{}{\overset{OH}{CH}}-CH_2-O-(CH_2)_4-O-CH_2-\overset{OH}{CH}-CH_2-O-\\-OH\end{cases}\begin{matrix}HO-\\ \\HO-\end{matrix}\text{Agarose}$$

a

$$\text{Agarose}\begin{cases}-OH\\-OH\\-OH\end{cases} + (CH_3O)_3Si(CH_2)_3\,OCH_2\,\overset{O}{\overbrace{CH-CH_2}} + \begin{cases}HO-\\HO-\\HO-\end{cases}\text{Agarose} \longrightarrow$$

$$\text{Agarose}\begin{cases}-OH\\-O\\-O\end{cases}\!\!>\overset{OH}{Si}-(CH_2)_3OCH_2-\overset{OH}{CH}-CH_2-O-\begin{cases}HO-\\ \\HO-\end{cases}\text{Agarose}$$

b

$$\text{Agarose}\begin{cases}-OH\\-OH\\-OH\end{cases} + H_2C=CH-SO_2-CH=CH_2 + \begin{cases}HO-\\HO-\\HO-\end{cases}\text{Agarose} \longrightarrow$$

$$\text{Agarose}\begin{cases}-OH\\-O-CH_2-CH_2-SO_2-CH_2-CH_2-O-\\-OH\end{cases}\begin{matrix}HO-\\ \\HO-\end{matrix}\text{Agarose}$$

c

FIGURE 4–3. Simplified reaction schemes for the cross-linking of agarose with bis-epoxides (a), γ-glycidoxypropyltrimethoxysilane (b), and divinyl sulfone (c).

4.4.2 Cross-Linking with γ-Glycidoxypropyltrimethoxysilane

The cross-linking reaction in a simplified version is shown in Figure 4–3b.[15] The cross-linked beads show no indications of hydrophobic interactions with proteins[16] and are stable at pH 10 during a period of at least 2 months.[14] The cross-linking procedure described below is very attractive due to its simplicity.[17]

A suspension of 12% agarose beads is centrifuged at 500 × 8 for 10 min. About 5 g of the sedimented beads are suspended in an Erlenmeyer flask containing 2 ml of γ-glycidoxypropyltrimethoxysilane and 50 mg of sodium borohydride. With stirring, 6 ml of 2 *M* potassium hydroxide is added dropwise. After stirring for 20 h at room temperature the suspension is centrifuged. The beads are washed four times with 6 ml of 0.1 *M* potassium hydroxide and then with deionized water until the washings are neutral. Repetition of the cross-linking further increases the rigidity of the beads.

4.4.3 Cross-Linking with Divinyl Sulfone (DVS)

DVS has long been used as a cross-linking agent, for instance of cellulose.[18] The reaction scheme in Figure 4–3c[18] shows that the two OH groups in an agarose chain that are lost during the cross-linking are not compensated by the formation of new OH groups. It is therefore not surprising that DVS-cross-linked agarose beads exhibit hydrophobic interactions. These can, however, be strongly suppressed or nullified by coupling mannitol, dextrans, or other OH-rich substances to the cross-linked beads.[19] The presence of sodium borohydride at an appropriate concentration during the cross-linking has two positive effects (excessively high concentrations of sodium borohydride should be avoided, since the rigidity of the beads then decreases): (1) the nonspecific (hydrophobic) interaction decreases and (2) the pH stability of the beads increases.[19] Agarose beads cross-linked with DVS as described below were exposed to pH 13 during a test period of 15 days without any loss in flow rate (if the cross-linking is performed in the absence of sodium borohydride the bisethylene sulfone bridges are hydrolytically cleaved at pH above 9[8]). For a more detailed study of cross-linking with DVS, see ref. 19 from which the following formulation is taken.

About 10 g of sedimented 12% agarose beads are suspended in 10 ml of 0.5 *M* sodium phosphate buffer, pH 12.5. Sodium borohydride (0.20–0.24 g) is immediately added with stirring followed by 3 ml of DVS. The stirring is continued for 16 h at room temperature. The agarose beads are then washed several times with deionized water by centrifugation at 500 × g for 10 min until the supernatant has a pH of 7–8. The sedimented beads are then suspended in 10 ml of 1 *M* sodium hydroxide containing 0.1 g of sodium borohydride and 2 g of D-mannitol (or other OH-rich compounds). After stirring for 6 h the gel beads are washed with water by centrifugation until the pH of the gel suspension is about 7.

The pore size of the beads can be varied by replacing the mannitol by dextrans of different molecular weights.[19]

4.5 PREPARATION OF NONPOROUS AGAROSE BEADS BY SHRINKAGE OF THE BEADS AND SUBSEQUENT CROSS-LINKING

The structure of agarose shown in Figure 4–1a refers to an aqueous medium. When the water is exchanged for a nonpolar solvent one would expect this structure to collapse to form shrunken, nonporous gel beads. If the shrunken beads are cross-linked in the nonpolar solvent the agarose retains its collapsed structure and the beads will swell only slightly when this solvent is exchanged for water. The beads will thus be nonporous also in an aqueous medium. These considerations form the basis for the following method for the preparation of shrunken, nonporous, cross-linked agarose beads.[15,20]

About 1 g of agarose beads shrunken in chloroform is suspended in 20 ml of chloroform. With stirring 3.2 ml of 1,4-butanediol diglycidyl ether is added followed by 0.3 ml of boron trifluoride diethyl etherate diluted with 12 ml of chloroform. After cross-linking for 30 min the beads are transferred to water via a solvent of medium polarity.

If a higher rigidity of the beads is desired an additional cross-linking is recommended.

4.6 THE DESIGN OF THE COLUMN TUBE

The column tube C in Figure 4–4 is made from Plexiglas and is thus transparent, which is an obvious advantage in comparison with stainless-steel tubes. By using colored solutes one can easily see whether the packing is satisfactory. Any void space between the upper plunger and the surface of the bed is readily

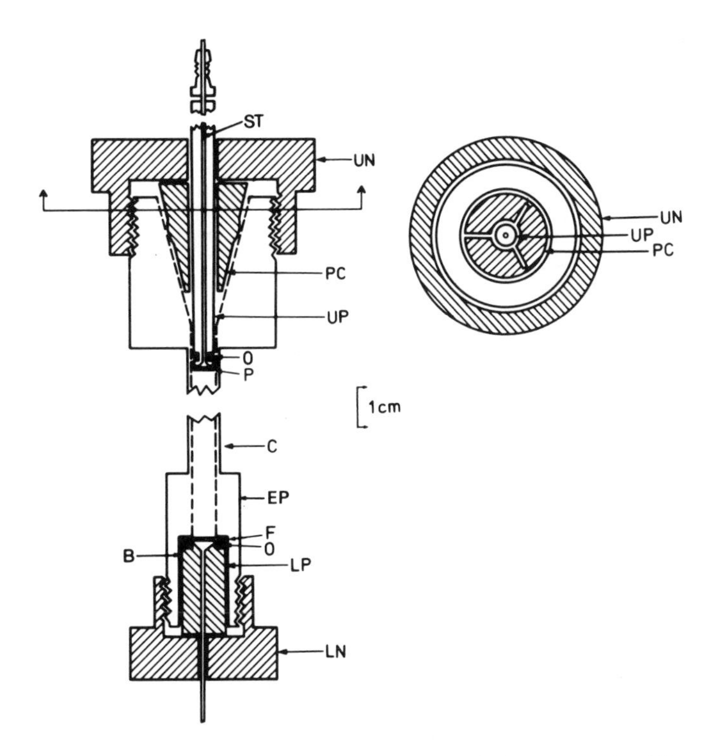

FIGURE 4–4. The design of the column tube. C, Plexiglas tube; UP, LP, upper and lower plungers, respectively; UN, LN, upper and lower nuts, respectively; P, porous polyethylene disc; EP, end piece with bore B; PC, cone made of PVC; ST, stainless-steel tubing; F, frit; O, O-ring.

observable; the plunger is movable and can then be lowered to touch the bed. By screwing the lower nut LN upward the O-ring O will be pressed against the metal frit F and at the same time expand and seal against the wall of the bore B in the end piece EP. With the aid of the upper nut UN the PVC cone PC is forced downward to make close contact with the rough surface of the upper plunger UP (made from a metal tube). This plunger can thus be firmly fixed in any position. The same Plexiglas column can accordingly be used for beds of any desired height. Plexiglas columns with an inner diameter of 6 mm and a wall thickness of 2 mm stand a pressure of 50–60 bar.

4.7 AN INCREASE IN RESOLUTION BY INCREASING THE RATIO V_i/V_o (DECREASING V_o)

The resolution R_s of a chromatographic bed is determined by the following expression[21,22]:

$$R_s = \frac{\sqrt{N}}{2} \frac{\frac{V_i}{V_o} \cdot K''\left(\frac{K''}{K'} - 1\right)}{2 \cdot \frac{K''}{K'} + \frac{V_i}{V_o} \cdot K''\left(\frac{K''}{K'} + 1\right)} \qquad (4\text{–}9)$$

where N is the number of theoretical plates, V_i is the inner volume, V_o is the void volume, and K' and K'' are the distribution coefficients of two solutes.

The equation shows that the higher the ratio V_i/V_o the higher is the resolution. It might be impossible to increase this ratio by increasing the inner volume (V_i) but the void volume (V_o) of the column can be decreased by compressing the bed. For soft gels like Sephadex™, Sepharose™, and Bio-Gel A and P™ this approach decreases the flow rate so strongly that it has been utilized only by a few researchers.[23,24] However, for more rigid cross-linked agarose beads used in HPLC, the method is very attractive as is evident from Figure 4–5, which is based on data taken from ref. 22. The column was packed at a relatively low pressure with such macroporous beads. The V_i and V_o values were then determined at a somewhat higher pressure (flow rate). This procedure was repeated for several different pressures (flow rates). With each increase in pressure the bed was automatically compressed, i.e., the void volume decreased. The great increase in V_i/V_o (in the experiment shown in Figure 4–5 from 1.4 to 2.8) on compression of a bed of cross-linked, porous agarose beads increases the resolution considerably according to Eq. (4–9). (The primary reason why compression of the bed (decrease in void volume) causes an increase in resolution is that after compression the beads are deformed and closer to each other, which means shorter diffusion paths between the beads. The partition of a solute between the mobile and stationary phases then proceeds faster, which decreases the zone broadening and therefore increases the resolution.)

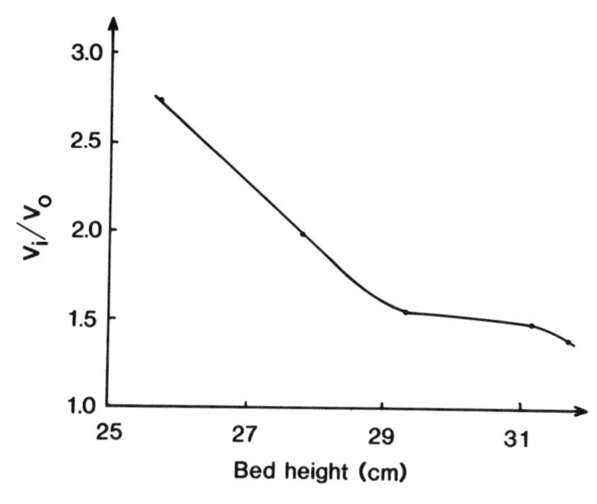

FIGURE 4–5. V_i/V_0 as a function of the degree of compression of the agarose bed, expressed in terms of the bed height. Bed material: cross-linked, macroporous 12% agarose beads with diameters ranging from 3 to 10 μm. The column was packed at increasing flow rates (pressures). For each increase in flow rate the bed became automatically compressed and the ratio V_i/V_0 was determined. V_i = inner volume. V_0 = void volume. The diagram shows that V_i/V_0 increases when the bed is compressed; at the same time the resolution increases according to Eq. (4–9).

In the experiment described the agarose beads were macroporous, i.e., penetrable for proteins. As expected, a decrease in void volume has a favorable effect on the resolution also for nonporous agarose beads, as illustrated in Figure 4–6 with an ion-exchange chromatography experiment.[15] The conditions were as follows. A Plexiglas column was packed at a flow rate of 0.2 ml/min with cross-linked, shrunken, nonporous beads (diameter: 10–50 μm) of 3-diethylamino-2-hydroxypropyl agarose synthesized as described in refs. 15 and 25. The bed height was 6 cm. The column was equilibrated with 0.02 *M* Tris-HCl, pH 8.5. A 100-μl sample, containing the proteins mentioned in the legend to Figure 4–6, was applied. The elution was performed with a 5-ml linear gradient formed from the equilibration buffer and the same buffer containing 0.3 *M* sodium acetate. The flow rate was 0.2 ml/min. It was then increased to 0.5 ml/min, which caused compression of the bed. Before application of the sample the movable upper plunger (UP in Figure 4–4) was adjusted to make contact with the gel bed. At a flow rate of 0.5 ml/min and with monitoring at 280 nm the left chromatogram in Figure 4–6 was obtained. The experiment was then repeated with the flow rates 1, 2, and 4 ml/min. On each increase in flow rate the gel was compressed and the plunger was therefore pressed down prior to application of the sample. The 5-ml gradient was used in all runs. The recorder chart speed was increased proportional to the flow rate. This facilitates visual comparison of the chromatograms, since they then acquire the same width (Figure 4–6).

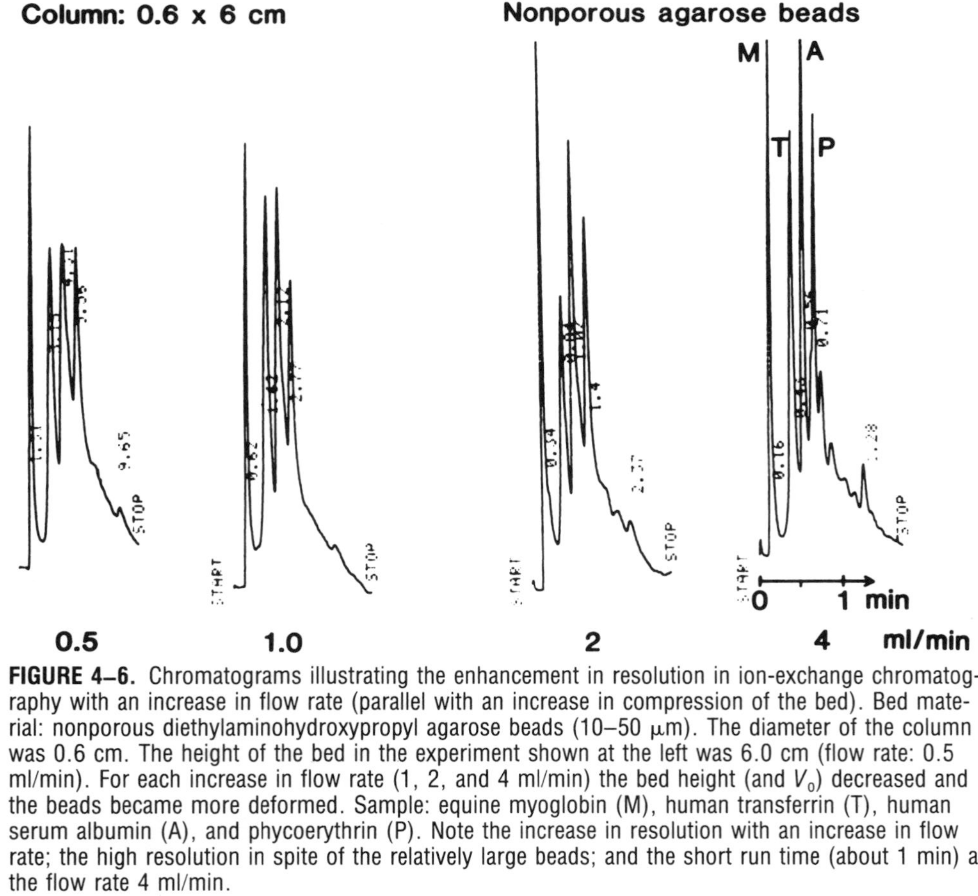

FIGURE 4–6. Chromatograms illustrating the enhancement in resolution in ion-exchange chromatography with an increase in flow rate (parallel with an increase in compression of the bed). Bed material: nonporous diethylaminohydroxypropyl agarose beads (10–50 μm). The diameter of the column was 0.6 cm. The height of the bed in the experiment shown at the left was 6.0 cm (flow rate: 0.5 ml/min). For each increase in flow rate (1, 2, and 4 ml/min) the bed height (and V_0) decreased and the beads became more deformed. Sample: equine myoglobin (M), human transferrin (T), human serum albumin (A), and phycoerythrin (P). Note the increase in resolution with an increase in flow rate; the high resolution in spite of the relatively large beads; and the short run time (about 1 min) at the flow rate 4 ml/min.

4.8 THE RESOLUTION AS A FUNCTION OF FLOW RATE IN HYDROPHOBIC-INTERACTION CHROMATOGRAPHY ON A COMPRESSED BED OF NONPOROUS BEADS

The nonporous beads (diameter: 10–20 μm), prepared from 11% macroporous agarose beads by a method different from that described herein (see ref. 5 on p. 148) were packed in a 0.6-cm Plexiglas column at a constant pressure of about 45 bar. At this pressure the beads became deformed. The bed height was 4.8 cm. A 25-μl sample of ovalbumin (120 μg) and α-chymotrypsinogen A (25 μg) was applied and eluted at a flow rate of 0.06 ml/min with a 3.2-ml linear gradient from 0.01 *M* sodium phosphate (pH 6.8) containing 3.0 *M* ammonium sulfate (the equilibration buffer) to 0.01 *M* sodium phosphate (pH 6.8) containing 0.25 *M* ammonium sulfate.

The resolution R_s between the two proteins was calculated from the following equation:

$$Rs = \frac{t_2 - t_1}{0.5(t_{w2} - t_{w1})} \qquad (4\text{–}10)$$

where t_{w1} and t_{w2} are the peak widths at half the peak heights and t_1 and t_2 are the retention times. The experiment was repeated at a series of increasing flow rates. The result is presented in Figure 4–7. The gradient volume was the same in all runs whereas the recorder chart speed was increased proportional to the flow rate to give the same width of the chromatograms. Figure 4–7 shows that the resolution increases somewhat with an increase in flow rate.

4.9 APPLICATIONS—BEDS OF MACROPOROUS BEADS

4.9.1 Estimation of Peptide/Protein Molecular Weights by Molecular-Sieve Chromatography in 6 *M* Guanidine Hydrochloride

For the separation of peptides the pores in the gel beads should be relatively small. The beads were therefore prepared from a solution of a high agarose concentration (20%). (Later experiments have shown, however, that the pore size of agarose gels in the presence of guanidine hydrochloride is almost independent of the agarose concentration in the range 6–20%.[26]) The bed dimensions were 0.6 × 34.5 cm. The diameters of the agarose beads varied between 5 and 15 μm. Divinyl sulfone was used as cross-linker.[19] To get a high resolution the flow rate was low (0.1 ml/min), corresponding to a run time of about 100 min (see Section 4.11.5). The experiment was carried out in 0.1 *M* sodium phosphate (pH 6.5),[26] containing 6 *M* guanidine hydrochloride purified according to Fohlman et al.[27] The model substances used—which were reduced and alkylated[27,28]—are given in the legend to Figure 4–8a. A plot of $-\log K_D$ against $MW^{2/3}$ is shown in Figure 4–8b (K_D = the distribution coefficient, MW = the molecular weight). This way of plotting is based on a thermodynamical treatment of molecular-sieve chromatography,[29] which has the great advantage that it does not require any assumption about the separation mechanism.

Figure 4–8a and b shows that the operational separation range extends from proteins with molecular weights from about 90,000 and unexpectedly down to peptides with very low molecular weights (about 1000). Figure 4–8b also illustrates that the size of glycoproteins cannot be estimated with the same accuracy as carbohydrate-free proteins.

An inherent weakness of molecular-sieve chromatography is that only the volume $V_t - V_o$ (see Figure 4–8a) can be utilized for separation, i.e., the column permits but a relatively limited number of proteins to be separated (the peak capacity is low).

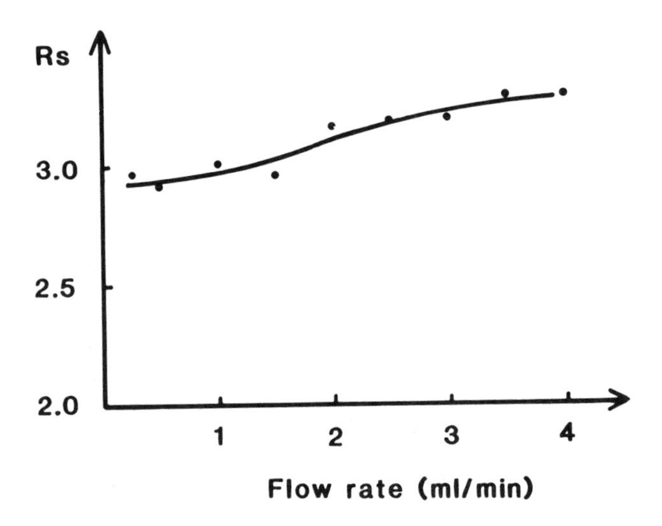

FIGURE 4–7. The resolution Rs in hydrophobic-interaction chromatography on a compressed bed of nonporous agarose beads as a function of the flow rate. Bed dimensions: 0.6 (i.d.) × 4.8 cm. Bead diameter: 10–20 μm. The diagram shows that the resolution increases somewhat with an increase in flow rate. The experiment was performed by Dr. K.-O. Eriksson and Mr. J. Mohammad in the author's laboratory.

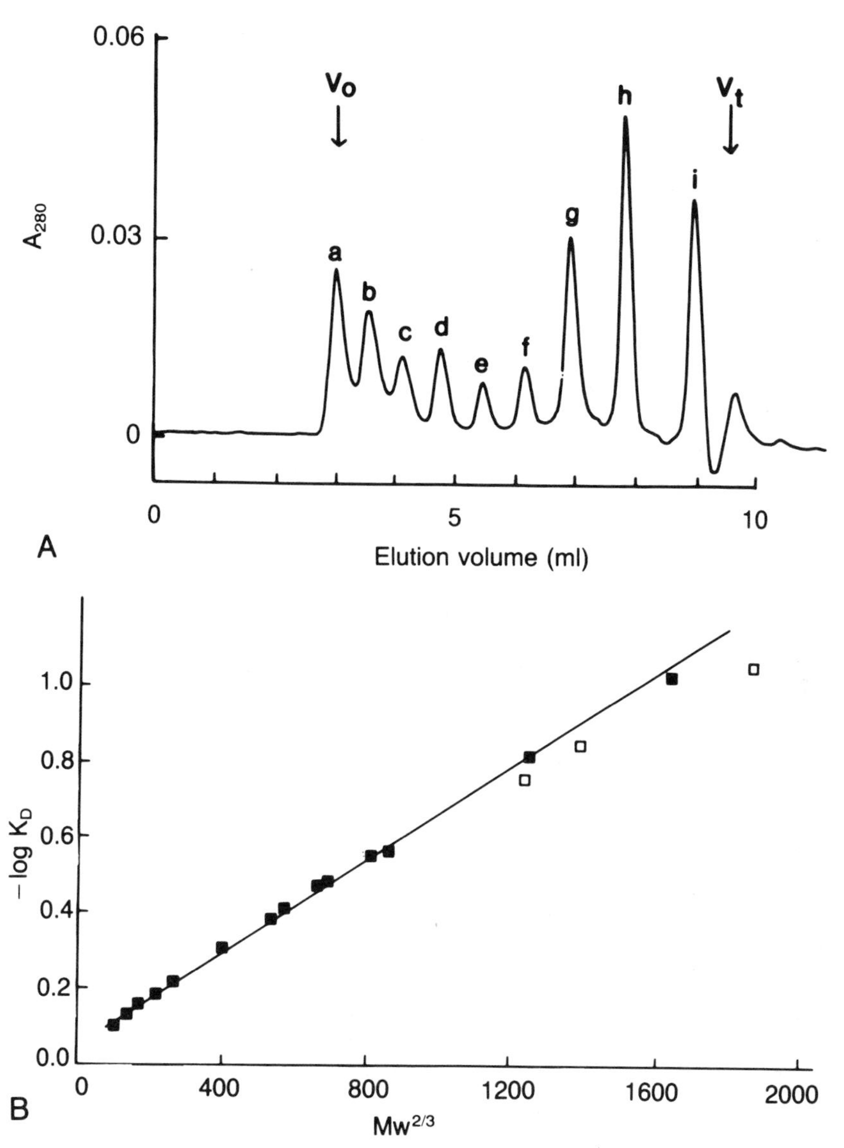

FIGURE 4–8. Estimation of peptide and protein molecular weights in 6 *M* guanidine-hydrochloride by molecular-sieve chromatography on macroporous agarose beads. Bed dimensions: 0.6 (i.d.) × 30 cm. The cross-linked 20% agarose beads had a diameter ranging from 5 to 15 μm. Flow rate: 0.1 ml/min. (a) Blue Dextran (MW about 2,000,000); (b) transferrin (80,000); (c) ovalbumin (43,000); (d) chymotrypsinogen A (25,000); (e) ribonuclease A (13,700); (f) notechis III:4 (8050); (g) ACTH (4500); (h) neurotensin (1670). Data from the chromatogram (A)—and similar chromatograms—gave the plot (B). (■) Carbohydrate-free peptides/proteins; (□) glycoproteins. (Reproduced from ref. 26, with permission.)

4.9.2 Gradient and Isocratic Separation of Proteins in a Cellulase Fraction by Ion-Exchange Chromatography

The ion-exchanger, 3-diethylamino-2-hydroxy-propyl-agarose (DEAHP-agarose), was synthesized from 12% agarose beads (diameters: 5–10 μm), 1.4-butanediol diglycidyl ether, and diethyl-amine as described in ref. 25. The long spacer arm increases the accessibility of the ion-exchanging tertiary amino groups. The column (0.6 × 8 cm) was equilibrated with 0.02 *M* ammonium acetate, pH 4.5. After application of 100 μl of the cellulase fraction the proteins were eluted with a linear gradient from 0.02 to 0.1 *M* ammonium acetate (pH 4.5) in 50 min (Figure 4–9a). The experiment was then repeated with the difference that the column was equilibrated with 0.44 *M* ammonium acetate (pH 4.5) and the proteins were eluted isocratically with this buffer (Figure 4–9b). Observe that gradient elution and isocratic elution gave similar chromatograms.

4.9.3 Separation of Glycoproteins by Boronate Chromatography

Fifteen percent agarose beads (diameters: 15–20 μm) were cross-linked with divinyl sulfone.[19] Dihydroxyboryl-agarose was prepared by coupling *m*-aminophenylboronic acid to these beads via γ-glycidoxypropyltrimethoxysilane[14]; for other coupling methods see ref. 30. This adsorbent primarily interacts with molecules with two vicinal hydroxy groups in the *cis* configuration. An increase

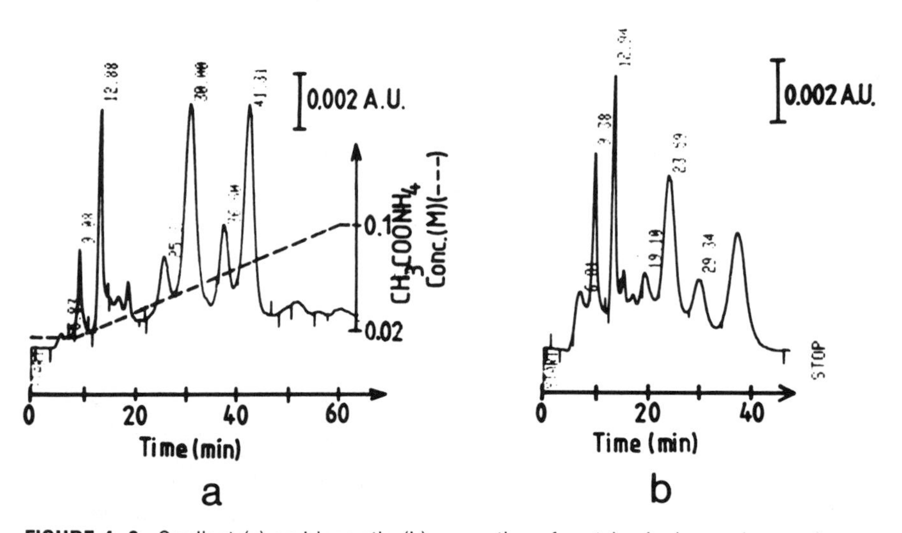

FIGURE 4–9. Gradient (a) and isocratic (b) separation of proteins by ion-exchange chromatography on macroporous agarose beads. Bed dimensions: 0.6 × 8 cm. The bed material comprised cross-linked 12% 3-diethylamino-2-hydroxypropyl agarose beads with diameters varying from 5 to 10 μm. The sample, a cellulase fraction (Endo II, pI ca 4.5), was obtained from Dr. Göran Pettersson of this institute. Flow rate: 0.2 ml/min. Reproduced with permission.[25]

in pH to increase the concentration of the anionic form of the dihydroxyboryl group (pK ~ 9) should increase the adsorption of the solutes, since it is the anionic form that is active in the formation of complexes with *cis*-diols. Desorption can accordingly be achieved by lowering the pH or by including in the buffer sorbitol or other compounds which easily form complexes with borate.

Quantitative determination of glycosylated hemoglobin by low-pressure chromatography on columns of dihydroxyboryl-agarose is gaining increasing use in the management of patients with diabetes. However, as emphasized by Walters,[31] "A similar high-performance affinity method would be faster and more convenient to use." Figure 4–10 shows such an HPLC experiment on a 0.6 × 11 cm column of dihydroxyborylagarose, synthesized as described above. A 2-μl sample of hemolysate of erythrocytes from a diabetic patient was applied. Nonadsorbed material (peak I, Figure 4–10a) was washed out during 5 min at a flow rate of 1 ml/min with 0.05 *M* HEPES (*N*-2-hydroxyethylpiperazine-*N*-2-ethanesulfonic acid) containing 0.05 *M* magnesium chloride (the same buffer was used for equilibration of the column). This buffer supplemented with 0.1 *M* sorbitol was employed to displace the glycosylated hemoglobin (peak II, Figure 4–10a). The area of peak II was considerably lower when the experiment was repeated with a hemoglobin sample from a nondiabetic individual (Figure 4–10b).

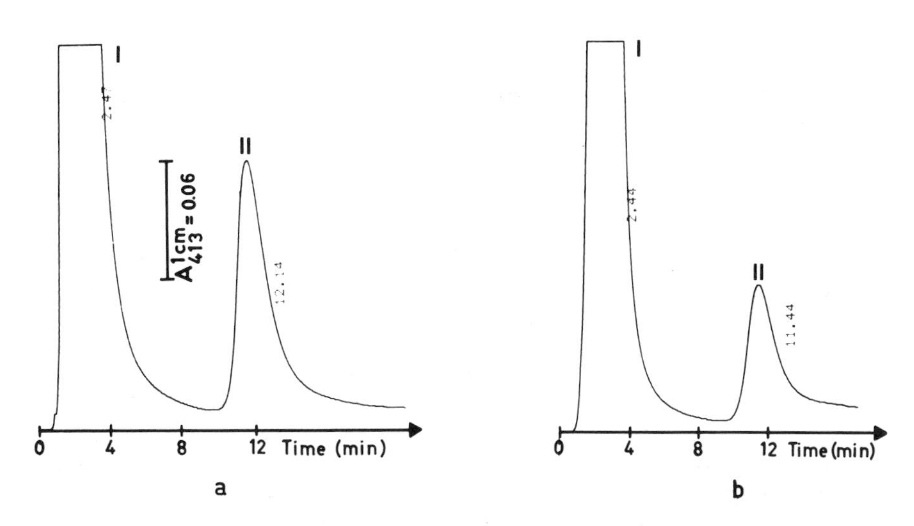

FIGURE 4–10. Separation of non-glycosylated (peak I) from glycosylated (peak II) hemoglobin by boronate chromatography on macroporous agarose beads. Bed dimensions: 0.6 × 11 cm. Bed material: 15–20 μm beads of 15% cross-linked dihydroxyboryl-agarose. Sample: hemoglobin from a diabetic (a) and a nondiabetic (b) individual. Flow rate: 1 ml/min. The glycosylated protein (peak II) was displaced with sorbitol. Observe that the area of peak II is larger in chromatogram (a) than in chromatogram (b). Reproduced with permission.[30]

4.10 APPLICATIONS—COMPRESSED BEDS OF NONPOROUS BEADS

4.10.1 Ion-Exchange Chromatography of Proteins at Low and High Flow Rate

The ion-exchanger (3-dimethylamino-2-hydroxypropyl-agarose) was synthesized by coupling dimethylamine to nonporous 11% agarose beads with a diameter of about 15 μm, as described in ref. 32. The beads were packed in a Plexiglas column with a diameter of 0.6 cm, at a flow rate of 2 ml/min. When the flow rate was increased to 5 ml/min the bed was compressed some millimeters to a final height of 6.2 cm. The sample consisted of about 30 μg of each of the proteins horse skeletal myoglobin (1), human hemoglobin (2), human transferrin (3), ovalbumin (4), bovine serum albumin (5), and phycoerythrin (6), dissolved in 20 μl 0.01 *M* Tris-HCl, pH 8.5. The same buffer was used for equilibration of the column. The proteins were eluted at a flow rate of 0.25 ml/min. The chromatogram is shown in Figure 4–11a. At the same gradient volume (10 ml), the experiment was repeated at a flow rate of 4 ml/min (Figure 4–11b). The recorder chart speed was 16-fold higher to get the same width of the chromatograms. A comparison between Figure 4–11a and 4–11b indicates that the resolution is about the same in spite of the 16-fold higher flow rate in the experiment shown in Figure 4–11b. More information about ion-exchange chromatography on compressed beds of nonporous agarose beads is given in ref. 32.

4.10.2 Hydrophobic-Interaction Chromatography (HIC) of Proteins

Agarose-based bed materials for this chromatographic method are usually synthesized by coupling nonpolar ligands to the cross-linked, hydrophilic agarose beads.[14,33,34] However, if the cross-linker is somewhat hydrophobic it can serve the dual function of making the beads more rigid and at the same time more hydrophobic, i.e., the step involving coupling of a nonpolar ligand to the beads can be omitted. One can thus take advantage of the otherwise undesirable property of certain bisepoxides to confer to the agarose beads a slightly hydrophobic nature (see Section 4.4.1). The shrunken agarose beads were therefore crosslinked with butanediol diglycidyl ether as described in Section 4.5.

Before shrinkage and cross-linking the bead diameter was about 30 μm and afterward about 20 μm. The shrunken beads were not penetrable to cytochrome *c* (MW 12,400) as was evident from a molecular-sieve chromatography experiment. They can accordingly be considered nonporous for proteins—and probably also for smaller substances. Before shrinkage the concentration of agarose in the beads was 11%, corresponding to an exclusion limit of about 500,000.

The cross-linked, nonporous beads were packed in deionized water at a flow rate of 5 ml/min in a Plexiglas tube with an inner diameter of 0.6 cm. At this high flow rate the bed was compressed to a height of 5.5 cm (at the same time the beads were deformed). The upper plunger (UP in Figure 4–4) was pressed

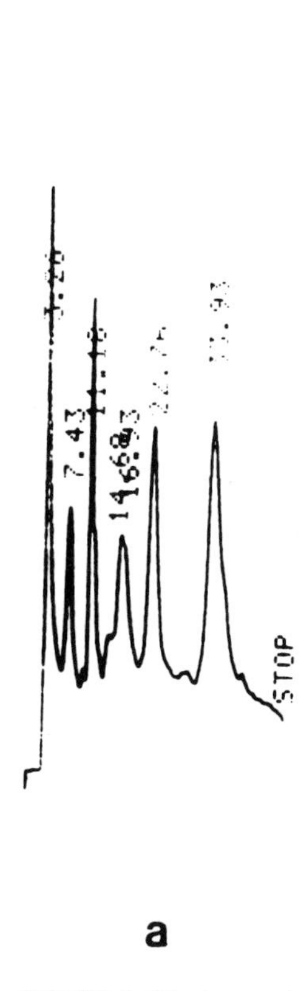

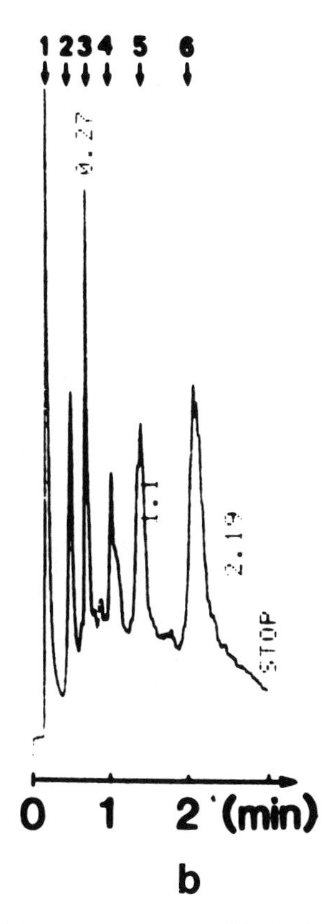

FIGURE 4–11. Ion-exchange chromatography of proteins on a compressed bed of nonporous agarose beads at low (a) and high (b) flow rate. Bed material: nonporous 15-μm agarose beads. Bed dimensions: 0.6 (i.d.) × 5.5 cm. A linear salt gradient was used for elution. The flow rate was 0.25 ml/min in (a) and 4 ml/min in (b). Observe that the resolution is virtually independent of the flow rate. The experiment was performed by Mr. Jia-li Liao in the author's laboratory.

down to make contact with the bed. The column was equilibrated with 0.02 *M* sodium phosphate buffer (pH 6.8) containing 2.12 *M* ammonium sulfate. A 20-μl sample was applied consisting of 20 μg of each of the proteins listed in the legend to Figure 4–12. The elution was performed with a linear, negative 0.8-min gradient formed from the equilibration buffer and 0.02 *M* sodium phosphate (pH 6.8) containing 0.25 *M* ammonium sulfate. The flow rate was 4 ml/min. In spite of the relatively large size of the beads and the high flow rate the resolution was high (see Figure 4–12). In a control experiment a more hydrophilic cross-linker was used (γ-glycidoxypropyltrimethoxysilane[15]). The beads were as expected not hydrophobic enough to be useful for hydrophobic-interaction chromatography of proteins. See ref. 20 for more information about hydrophobic-interaction chromatography on compressed beds of nonporous agarose beads.

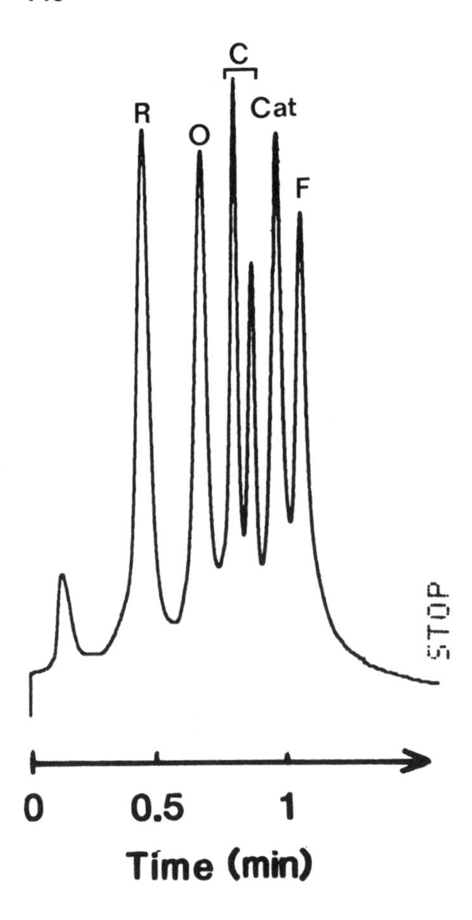

FIGURE 4–12. Hydrophobic-interaction chromatography of proteins on a compressed bed of nonporous agarose beads. Bed material: nonporous 20-μm agarose beads. Butanediol diglycidyl ether was chosen as a cross-linker to make the beads both rigid and amphiphilic (in this way the coupling of a nonpolar compound to the matrix could be omitted). Bed dimensions: 0.6 (i.d.) × 5.5 cm. Flow rate: 4 ml/min. A linear negative salt gradient was used for elution. R, ribonuclease; O, ovalbumin; C, α-chymotrypsinogen A; Cat, catalase; F, ferritin. The figure shows that deformed, nonporous agarose beads give a high resolution even if the beads are relatively large and the flow rate is very high. The experiment was performed by Mr. Jiali Liao in the author's laboratory. Observe the short run time.

4.10.3 Chromatofocusing

Nonporous 15–20 μm agarose beads cross-linked with γ-glycidoxypropyltrimethoxysilane were derivatized with polyethyleneimine, essentially as described in ref. 25. The agarose concentration prior to shrinkage was 11%. This ion-exchanger was packed in a Plexiglas column (i.d. = 0.6 cm) at a flow rate of 2 ml/min. The upper plunger UP (Figure 4–4) was pressed down in order to compress the column 3–4 mm. The bed, the height of which was 3 cm, was equilibrated with 0.025 *M* bis(2-hydroxyethyl)imino-tris(hydroxymethyl)methane (BIS-TRIS), adjusted to pH 6.5 with hydrochloric acid (starting buffer). A sample consisting of 0.5 mg of human transferrin dissolved in 0.1 ml of the starting buffer was applied. The elution was performed at a flow rate of 4.8 ml/min with Polybuffer 74™ (Pharmacia AB, Laboratory Separation Division, Uppsala, Sweden) diluted 1:80 with deionized water. Monitoring at 280 nm gave the chromatogram shown in Figure 4–13. The experiment was finished within 5 min. The deformed, nonporous beads thus permit a high resolution also at run times shorter than those normally used in chromatofocusing (which hitherto has been performed only on porous beads). Another advantage is that only 1–2 bed volumes of the starting buffer is required for equilibration, in this experiment corresponding to about 1 min (cf. columns of porous beads which require about 10–15 bed volumes). A paper on chromatofocusing on a compressed bed of nonporous agarose beads is in preparation.[35] The chromatographic properties of this bed is in that paper compared with those of a noncompressed bed of macroporous agarose beads.[36]

4.10.4 Adsorption Chromatography of Proteins on Compressed Beds of Nonporous Agarose Beads Covered with Ferric (Hydr)Oxide

The nonporous 7–10 μm agarose beads were covered with ferric (hydr)oxide by a method which is described in ref. 37 (before shrinkage the agarose concentration in the beads was 12%). Following compression, the bed height was 6 cm (diameter of the column: 0.6 cm). The sample [25 μg of ovalbumin (1), 25 μg of human hemoglobin A_{1C} (2), 100 μg of human transferrin (3), 50 μg of bovine carbonic anhydrase (4), 50 μg of bovine pancreas α-chymotrypsinogen A (5), and 25 μg of chicken egg white lysozyme (6)] was dissolved in 55 μl of the equilibration

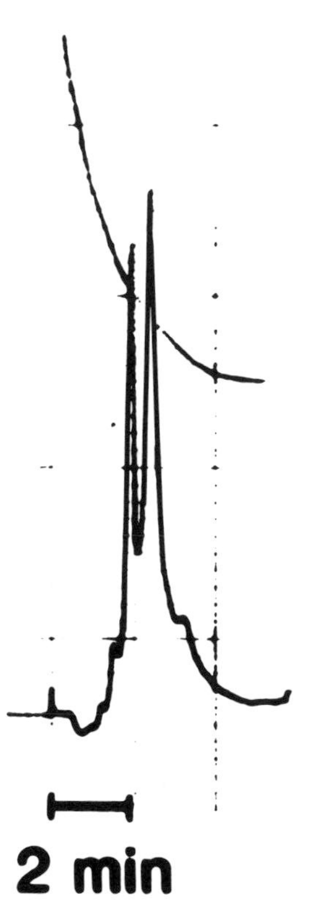

FIGURE 4–13. Chromatofocusing of human transferrin on a compressed bed of nonporous polyethyleneimine-agarose beads. Bed dimensions: 0.6 (i.d.) × 3.0 cm. Bead diameter: 20–40 μm. Thanks to the use of deformed, nonporous beads the run was much faster (completed within 5 min) than conventional electrofocusing experiments on porous beads (without loss in resolution). The time for regeneration was also much shorter. The experiment was performed by Mrs. Jin-ping Li in the author's laboratory.

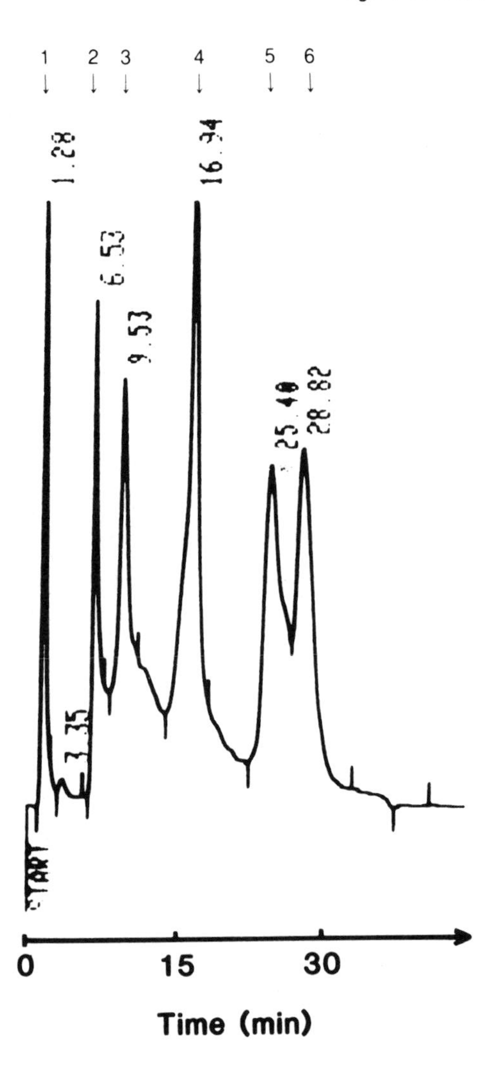

FIGURE 4–14. Adsorption chromatography of proteins on a compressed bed of nonporous beads, covered with iron (hydr)oxide. Bed material: nonporous agarose beads with diameters in the range 7–10 μm. Bed dimensions: 0.6 (i.d.) × 6.0 cm. Flow rate: 1 ml/min. The experiment was performed by Mr. I. Zelikman in the author's laboratory.

buffer (0.01 *M* sodium cacodylate, pH 6.0). At a flow rate of 1 ml/min the column was eluted first with a 15-min salt gradient from this buffer to 0.01 *M* sodium cacodylate (pH 6.0) containing 0.05 *M* potassium phosphate (pH 6.0) and then with a 20-min gradient from the latter buffer mixture to 0.01 *M* sodium cacodylate (pH 6.0) containing 0.2 *M* potassium phosphate (pH 6.0). The chromatogram is shown in Figure 4–14.

4.11 DISCUSSION AND COMMENTS

4.11.1 The Application Range of Agarose-Based HPLC Matrices

Agarose is the most widely used gel matrix for low-pressure chromatography of biopolymers. This inert, biocompatible polysaccharide has thus been employed for chromatographic experiments based on molecular sieving (size exclusion), ion-exchange, hydrophobic interaction, bioaffinity, complex formation with borate, metals and triazine dyes, and focusing in a pH gradient (chromatofocusing). However, following the introduction of new methods for the preparation of more rigid porous and nonporous agarose beads all of these chromatographic techniques can also be designed as HPLC experiments, i.e., with higher resolution and shorter run times than are possible with classical low-pressure chromatography. In this chapter I have given examples of most of these techniques. A new method based on the interaction of proteins with metal (hydr)oxides is also presented.[37]

4.11.2 Suppression of Electrostatic and Hydrophobic Side Interactions between the Polymers to Be Separated and the Agarose Matrix

Different types of agar contain agarose chains of somewhat different structures. For the preparation of agarose one should select an agar, the agarose moiety of which has a low methoxy content (to suppress hydrophobic interactions) and few carboxylic groups (to suppress electrostatic interactions). The sulfur content is not so important, since most of the sulfate groups can be removed easily at high pH in the presence of sodium borohydride.[12,38] Observe that these conditions are also used for cross-linking of agarose in an aqueous medium as described in Section 4.4. This cross-linking technique therefore gives as an extra bonus a desulfatation. A method for decarboxylation of agarose has been described,[39] but since it is rather cumbersome it is more practical to start the preparation of agarose from an agar type which contains agarose chains with few carboxylic groups.

However, it is not only the quality of the agarose that is of importance for the design of an ideal inert matrix. Equally important is that the cross-linking does not reduce the hydrophilicity of the agarose beads. From this point of view, beads cross-linked with γ-glycidoxypropyltrimethoxysilane are ideal, since they do not exhibit any hydrophobic interaction—not even in the presence of 1 *M* ammonium sulfate.[16] Nor does the protein adsorption to these beads show any time-dependence.[16] The appearance of a chromatogram is therefore not dependent on the duration of an experiment (compare reversed-phase chromatography treated in another chapter of this volume). The pH stability of the beads is also an important parameter: agarose cross-linked with bisepoxides stands pH 14,[13] with divinyl sulfone pH 13[19] and with γ-glycidoxypropyltrimethoxysilane pH 10–11.[14,16] These three cross-linkers give the beads roughly the same rigidity, i.e., the same maximal flow rate.

The hydrophobicity of cross-linked agarose beads can be suppressed by coupling glycidol[40] or OH-rich compounds, such as mannitol and dextran (see ref. 19 and Section 4.4.3). The attachment of glycidol and dextran—but not mannitol—causes a decrease in the porosity of the agarose gel.

In ideal hydrophobic-interaction chromatography (HIC)—a term introduced in 1973 by the author[41]—it is extremely important that the methods chosen for cross-linking and for coupling of the nonpolar ligands do not introduce charged groups into the matrix. Otherwise, there is a risk that the ionic strength at which the hydrophobic bonds between a protein and the adsorbent are broken is too low to break electrostatic bonds, resulting in an irreversible interaction of the protein with the adsorbent[42] (hydrophobic interactions decrease and electrostatic interactions increase when the ionic strength decreases).

4.11.3 Estimation of Molecular Weights by Molecular-Sieve Chromatography with the Aid of the Formula $-\log K_D = R \cdot MW^{2/3} + S$

A thermodynamic treatment of molecular-sieve chromatography does not require any knowledge about the structure of the gel beads. Accordingly, we need not employ physical models based on the assumption that the gel contains cones,[43] cylinders,[44] etc. into which the solutes, depending on their size, can diffuse more or less restricted, or rods, partially or totally excluding the solutes.[45] Since it is difficult to know whether it is justified to use these simplified models of the gel structure (and therefore the formula derived) it is safer to treat molecular-sieve chromatography thermodynamically as a partition chromatography experiment. Upon doing so the above formula[29] could be derived (R and S are constants). A plot of $-\log K_D$ (or $-\log (V_e - V_o)$) against $MW^{2/3}$ should accordingly give a straight line, provided that the different proteins have the same conformation. The latter requirement is very often fulfilled if the experiments are performed in 6 M guanidine hydrochloride, since in this medium most proteins behave as randomly coiled homopolymers, i.e., they have the same conformation, which explains why all points (except those corresponding to glycoproteins) fall on a straight line in Figure 4–8b. Estimation of peptide or protein molecular weights should therefore be done in a buffer containing guanidine hydrochloride.

4.11.4 Isocratic Elution

There are many reports in the literature on successful isocratic separations by ion-exchange chromatography of low-molecular-weight compounds, such as amino acids, but very few of macromolecules, for instance proteins. The cause of this difference in chromatographic behavior between amino acids and proteins is not that the type of interaction between amino acids and adsorbent differs from that between proteins and adsorbent, since proteins are built up of amino acids. The main difference is that amino acids can interact with the adsorbent only via one or two binding sites and proteins via many more sites.

For isocratic separation of a mixture of proteins it is accordingly necessary to approach the condition for isocratic elution of amino acids, i.e., to decrease the number of points of attachment between the proteins and the adsorbent. This can be achieved by synthesizing beds with a low ligand density. When the ligand density is high macromolecules are either adsorbed (R_f = 0) or migrate with R_f = 1, i.e., without retention[46,47] ("all or none effect"). In other words: it is then impossible to find such a composition of the eluent that it permits the different proteins in a sample to migrate with different velocities on the column, which is equivalent to isocratic elution.

High-resolution isocratic runs of macromolecules require not only low ligand density but also that (1) the column is eluted at relatively low flow rates and packed with small beads to minimize zone broadening (cf. gradient elution where the zone-sharpening effect permits the use of higher flow rates and larger beads); (2) the peaks are symmetrical, i.e., that the adsorption isotherms are linear (which often is the case when the ligand density is low; and (3) nonspecific side interactions to the adsorbent are very small, since they otherwise can compete with the specific interaction which must be weak in any isocratic separation of macromolecules, as discussed above [condition (1) is not as important for nonporous as it is for macroporous packing materials]. In the experiment shown in Figure 4–9b all of these three requirements are fulfilled. Observe that the height of the column bed in this experiment was only 8 cm; yet the resolution is satisfactory. Since the resolution increases with the square root of the bed height isocratic runs should, however, in general be performed on longer columns. In molecular-sieve chromatography experiments—which always are conducted in the isocratic mode—bed heights far above 8 cm must be used for satisfactory separations, since in these experiments one cannot utilize elution volumes exceeding the total volume (V_t; see Figure 4–8a). As mentioned in Section 4.9.1, this is the basic reason why molecular-sieve chromatography in comparison with many other separation methods has a low resolution.

4.11.5 Porous, Nonporous, and Deformed Beads

In columns of nonporous beads the separations are based on diffusion of the biopolymers only in the mobile phase, i.e., between the beads, whereas in porous beads also a diffusion into and out of the beads is operating. Therefore, the zone broadening is smaller (and accordingly the resolution higher) in a column packed with nonporous beads than in the same column packed with porous beads. This faster mass transfer in nonporous packing materials explains why they exhibit a resolution that decreases less with an increase in flow rate than do porous beads.

If the nonporous beads are deformed by compression they come closer to each other, i.e., the diffusion paths of the solutes between the beads decreases, which partly may explain why the resolution is virtually constant when the flow rate increases (Figure 4–11). In some experiments the resolution may even increase with an increase in flow rate (see Figure 4–7 and ref. 15); we have no unambiguous explanation for this observation.[15] There are consequently, although nonlaminar flow may be a contributing factor, no disadvantages to run columns packed with these beads at high flow rates to cut down the run times (Figures 4–6, 4–7, 4–11, 4–12, 4–13, and 4–14). One should note that the diameters of the beads used in the experiments shown in these figures (except in Figure 4–14) are relatively large (in the range 10–50 μm). The preparation of such beads is simple and cost-effective. They are therefore attractive for large-scale columns. The lower capacity of nonporous beads in comparison with porous ones is compensated—at least partially—by the higher flow rates (shorter run times) and the considerably shorter time for regeneration of the column.

Nonporous beads of synthetic resins[48–51](diameter 2.5–7 μm) and of silica[52–55] (diameter 1.5 μm) have with great success been used for HPLC separations of proteins. These references are recommended.

4.11.6 Adsorption Chromatography of Proteins on Metal (Hydr)oxides Fixed to the Surface of Nonporous Agarose Beads—A New Separation Method

We have previously described the use of metal (hydr)oxides, embedded in cross-linked macroporous agarose beads, as adsorbents for chromatographic purification of proteins.[56] The (hydr)oxides can also be attached to the surface of nonporous agarose beads.[37] These adsorbents have the same attractive features as the other nonporous agarose adsorbents discussed in this chapter. Even if the adsorption mechanism of the metal (hydr)oxide/agarose beads has not been elucidated we know it differs from that of more conventional chromatographic separation methods, such as ion-exchange, molecular-sieve, and hydrophobic-interaction chromatography. A combination of these latter methods and methods based on metal (hydr)oxide interactions can therefore be expected to give a high resolution. We have also prepared adsorbents where the ferric (hydr)oxide is replaced by (hydr)oxides of titanium, zirconium, chromium, and aluminium (see ref. 2 on p. 148). The appearance of the chromatograms sometimes varies with the metal used, which means that consecutive use of agarose beads with different metal (hydr)oxides may be an efficient approach for the purification of proteins.

Acknowledgments

The author is much indebted to the following co-workers for contribution in different forms to the development of agarose-based high-performance liquid chromatography of macromolecules: Kjell-Ove Eriksson, Jin-ping Li, Jia-li Liao, Zhao-quian Liu, Jamil Mohammad, Bo-liang Wu, Duan Yang, Kunquan Yao and Ilya Zelikman. The work has financially been supported by the Swedish Natural Science Research Council and the Knut and Alice Wallenberg and the Carl Trygger Foundations.

REFERENCES

1. C. Araki, *J. Chem. Soc. Jpn.*, 58 (1937) 1338.
2. C. Araki, *Bull. Chem. Soc. Jpn.*, 29 (1956) 543.
3. S. Hjertén, *Biochim. Biophys. Acta*, 53 (1961) 514.
4. S. Hjertén, *Biochim. Biophys. Acta*, 62 (1962) 445.
5. B. Russell, T. H. Mead, and A. Polson, *Biochim. Biophys. Acta*, 86 (1964) 169.
6. S. Hjertén, *J. Chromatogr.*, 61 (1971) 73.
7. S. Arnott, A. Fulmer, W. E. Scott, I. C. M. Dea, R. Maorhouse, and D. A. Rees, *J. Mol. Biol.*, 90 (1974) 269.
8. J. Porath, T. Låås, and J.-C. Janson, *J. Chromatogr.*, 103 (1975) 49.
9. S. Brishammar, S. Hjertén, and B. v. Hofsten, *Biochim. Biophys. Acta*, 53 (1961) 518.
10. S. Hjertén, *Arch. Biochem. Biophys.*, 99 (1962) 466.
11. S. Hjertén, *Biochim. Biophys. Acta*, 79 (1964) 393.
12. J. Porath, J.-C. Janson, and T. Låås, *J. Chromatogr.*, 60 (1971) 167.
13. T. Andersson, M. Carlsson, L. Hagel, J.-C. Janson, and P.-Å. Pernemalm, *J. Chromatogr.*, 326 (1985) 33.
14. S. Hjertén, K. Yao, Z.-q. Liu, D. Yang, and B.-I. Wu, *J. Chromatogr.*, 354 (1986) 203.
15. S. Hjertén, K. Yao, and J.-I. Liao, *Makromol. Chem.*, 17 (1988) 349.
16. S. Hjertén, K. Yao, K.-O. Eriksson, and B. Johansson, *J. Chromatogr.*, 359 (1986) 99.
17. S. Hjertén, B.-I. Wu, and J.-I. Liao, to be published.
18. J. P. Schroeder and D. C. Shroeder, in Vinyl and Diene Monomers, Vol. 24, Part 3, (E. C. Leonard, ed.). Wiley-Interscience, New York, 1971, pp. 1357–1612.
19. S. Hjertén, B.-I. Wu, and J.-I. Liao, *J. Chromatogr.*, 396 (1987) 101.
20. S. Hjertén and J.-I. Liao, *J. Chromatogr.*, 457 (1988) 165.
21. S. H. Chang, K. H. Gooding, and F. E. Regnier, *J. Chromatogr.*, 125 (1976) 103.
22. S. Hjertén, Z.-q. Liu, and D. Yang, *J. Chromatogr.*, 296 (1984) 115.
23. V. E. Edwards and J. M. Helft, *J. Chromatogr.*, 47 (1970) 490.
24. M. L. Fishman and R. A. Barford, *J. Chromatogr.*, 52 (1970) 494.
25. K. Yao and S. Hjertén, *J. Chromatogr.*, 385 (1987) 87.
26. K.-O. Eriksson and S. Hjertén, *J. Pharm. Biomed. Anal.*, 4 (1986) 63.
27. J. Fohlman, D. Eaker, E. Karlsson, and S. Thesleff, *Eur. J. Biochem.*, 68 (1976) 457.
28. P. Lind and D. Eaker, *Toxicon* 19 (1981) 11.
29. S. Hjertén, *J. Chromatogr.*, 50 (1970) 189.
30. S. Hjertén and D. Yang, *J. Chromatogr.*, 316 (1984) 301.
31. R. R. Walters, *TrAC*, 2 (1983) 282.
32. J.-I. Liao and S. Hjertén, *J. Chromatogr.*, 457 (1988) 175.
33. S. Hjertén, J. Rosengren, and S. Påhlman, *J. Chromatogr.*, 101 (1974) 281.
34. F. Maisano, M. Belew, and J. Porath, *J. Chromatogr.*, 321 (1985) 305.
35. S. Hjertén, J.-p. Li, and J.-I. Liao. *J. Chromatogr.*, 475 (1989) 177.
36. S. Hjertén and J.-p. Li, *J. Chromatogr.*, 475 (1989) 167.
37. S. Hjertén, I. Zelikman, J. Lindeberg; J.-I. Liao, K.-O. Eriksson, and J. Mohammad, *J. Chromatogr.*, 481 (1989) 175.
38. K. B. Guiseley, *Carbohydrate Res.*, 13 (1970) 247.
39. T. Låås, *J. Chromatogr.*, 66 (1972) 347.
40. K.-O. Eriksson, *J. Biochem. Biophys. Methods*, 15 (1987) 105.
41. S. Hjertén, *J. Chromatogr.*, 87 (1973) 325.
42. L. Hammar, S. Påhlman, and S. Hjertén, *Biochim. Biophys. Acta*, 403 (1975) 554.
43. J. Porath, *J. Pure Appl. Chem.*, 6 (1963) 233.
44. P. G. Squire, *Arch. Biochem. Biophys.*, 107 (1964) 471.
45. T. Laurent and J. Killander, *J. Chromatogr.*, 14 (1964) 317.

46. A. Tiselius, *Arkiv kemi*, 7 (1954) 443.
47. A. Tiselius, S. Hjertén, and Ö. Levin, *Arch. Biochem. Biophys.*, 65 (1956) 132.
48. D. J. Burke, J. K. Duncan, L. C. Dunn, L. Cummings, C. J. Siebert, and G. S. Ott, *J. Chromatogr.*, 353 (1986) 425.
49. D. J. Burke, J. K. Duncan, C. J. Siebert, and G. S. Ott, *J. Chromatogr.*, 359 (1986) 533.
50. J. K. Duncan, A. J. C. Chen, and C. J. Siebert, *J. Chromatogr.*, 397 (1987) 3.
51. Y. Kato, T. Kitamura, A. Mitsu, and T. Hashimoto, *J. Chromatogr.*, 398 (1987) 327.
52. K. K. Unger, G. Jilge, J. N. Kinkel, and M. T. W. Hearn, *J. Chromatogr.*, 359 (1986) 61.
53. G. Jilge, R. Janzen, H. Giesche, K. K. Unger, J. N. Kinkel, and M. T. W. Hearn, *J. Chromatogr.*, 397 (1987) 71.
54. R. Janzen, K. K. Unger, H. Giesche, J. N. Kinkel, and M. T. W. Hearn, *J. Chromatogr.*, 397 (1987) 81.
55. R. Janzen, K. K. Unger, H. Giesche, J. N. Kinkel, and M. T. W. Hearn, *J. Chromatogr.*, 397 (1987) 91.
56. S. Hjertén, I. Zelikman, J. Kourteva, and J. Lindeberg, *Proc. 6th Int. Symp. HPLC of Proteins, Peptides Polynucleotides*, October 20–22, 1986, Baden-Baden, Germany, paper 113.

RECENT ACHIEVEMENTS

Additional information on the chromatographic behavior of compressed beds of nonporous agarose beads is given in the references below. The titles of the papers are inserted to enable the reader to select papers which are of personal interest. Ref. 5 shows that also silica-based beads can be deformed and that such beads—even if they are as large as 30–45 μm—afford the same high resolution as do non-compressible 1.5-μm silica beads. Ref. 7 deals with a new, simple and cost-effective method to design a chromatographic bed without a prepreparation of beads.

1. S. Hjertén, M. Sparrman, and J.-I. Liao, "Purification of membrane proteins in SDS and subsequent renaturation." *Biochim. Biophys. Acta* 939 (1988) 476.
2. S. Hjertén, I. Zelikman, J. Lindeberg, and M. Lederer, "High-performance adsorption chromatography of proteins on deformed non-porous agarose beads coated with insoluble metal compounds. II. Coating: Aluminum and zirconium (hydr)oxide with stoichiometrically bound phosphate." *J. Chromatogr.*, 481 (1989) 187.
3. S. Hjertén and J.-p. Li, "High-performance liquid chromatography of proteins on deformed non-porous agarose beads. Fast boronate affinity chromatography of haemoglobin at neutral pH." *J. Chromatogr.*, 500 (1990) 543.
4. J.-p. Li, K.-O. Eriksson, and S. Hjertén, "High-performance liquid chromatography of proteins on deformed nonporous agarose beads. Affinity chromatography of dehydrogenases based on Cibacron Blue-derivatized agarose." *Prep. Biochem.*, 20(2) (1990) 107.
5. S. Hjertén, J. Mohammad, K.-O. Eriksson, and J.-I. Liao, "General methods to render macroporous stationary phases nonporous and deformable, exemplified with agarose and silica beads and their use in high-performance ion-exchange and hydrophobic-interaction chromatography of proteins." *Chromatographia* 31 (1991) 85.
6. J.-p. Li and S. Hjertén, "High-performance liquid chromatography of proteins on deformed nonporous agarose beads. Immuno-affinity chromatography, exemplified with human growth hormone as ligand and a combination of ethylene glycol and salt for desorption of the antibodies." *J. Biochem. Biophys. Methods*, in press.
7. S. Hjertén, J.-I. Liao, and R. Zhang. "High-performance liquid chromatography on continuous polymer beds." *J. Chromatogr.* 473 (1989) 273.

CHAPTER 5

The Development of High-Performance Multimode and Mixed-Mode Polyethyleneimine-Based Chromatographic Media

Michael P. Henry

CONTENTS

5.1 INTRODUCTION

5.1.1 Definitions

PEI is a commonly used abbreviation for polyethyleneimine or poly(iminoethylene) (IUPAC). The polymer may be branched (Figure 5–1) or linear (Figure 5–2). In practice a useful molecular weight is 600, which corresponds to 14 repeating units.

All chromatographic media that are the focus of this chapter are PEI based and high performance. That is, they consist of PEI and/or its derivatives attached to a substrate, the latter providing the structural integrity required of chromatographic media for HPLC. Substrates may be inorganic (silica, alumina), organic (polystyrene, polyacrylate), or biopolymeric (cellulose), in nature. These are discussed in Section 5.3. High performance generally implies the use of media of a microparticulate (<20 μm) nature. However, for the purposes of this chapter, this term can be defined as that chromatographic system in which bands broaden at a rate which keeps the height equivalent to a theoretical plate less than 40 μm.

5.1.2 Mechanisms in Chromatographic Processes

Solution- and Surface-Mediated Interactions The concepts of mixed-mode and multimode chromatographic media (or bonded phases) have their origin in the major forms of interaction among solute, solvent, and stationary phase. These interactions include steric effects (size exclusion) and solvophobic, dispersive, and coulombic forces. The overall interaction will often be a complex

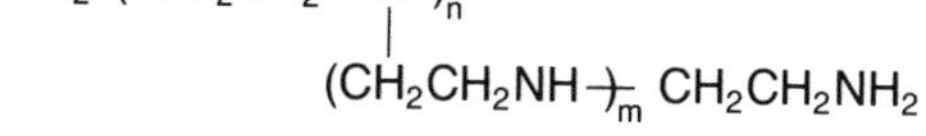

$$NH_2\text{-}(CH_2CH_2\text{—}N)_n\text{-} \quad | \quad (CH_2CH_2NH)_m\,CH_2CH_2NH_2$$

FIGURE 5–1. General structure of branched polyethyleneimine.

$NH_2\text{-}(CH_2CH_2NH)_n\text{-}CH_2\text{—}CH_2\text{—}NH_2$

FIGURE 5–2. General structure of linear polyethyleneimine.

combination of these forces. The magnitude of the contribution of each to overall chromatographic retention will depend on almost every property of the system[1]: pore size distribution, ligand type, ligand density, pH, ionic strength, temperature, organic solvent content, and buffer type, and the content of additives such as ion-pair reagents, dissociating agents, or surfactants.

Separation Mechanisms All of the above aspects of the chromatographic system may determine the so-called mechanisms of separation, broadly classified as size-exclusion, reversed-phase, hydrophobic-interaction, anion-exchange, and cation-exchange chromatography. Bonded phases generally resolve components in a mixture through the participation of several major interactions; but the mechanism of a separation process is defined by the nature of the predominant interaction. Table 5–1 gives a list of these mechanisms and the major associated interaction types.

Both the nature and elucidation of separation mechanisms that occur during the chromatographic process are often complicated by the indirect nature of the information that a chromatographer normally collects; in other words, the time-related UV absorption profiles of the material that elutes from the column under a variety of chromatographic conditions. Hearn[2] and Karger[3] and their co-workers have described the broad and often multiple peaks that are obtained in the reversed-phase and hydrophobic interaction chromatography of single proteins (see Figure 5–3). These phenomena are due to the tendency of these polymers to unfold partially in solution or at a liquid–solid interface, and thereby create a multiplicity of altered forms, each with their own sorptive properties. The meaning of a capacity factor, k', in these cases is lost among the broad humps and sharp peaks that often characterize the chromatographic journey of a single protein along a hydrophobic column.

Surface-mediated aggregation effects also alter the chromatographic profiles of biopolymers and their mixtures. Englehardt and co-workers[4] explained the increased retention of certain proteins on a weak anion exchanger as concentration is increased as due to reversible surface polymerization. The detailed work by Kopaciewicz and Regnier,[5] and most recently Nau,[6] in observing bonded phase selectivity changes under altered conditions of pH and buffer ion type, implicate the more subtle effects of multiple interactions on retention. These phenomena complicate the attempts to determine mechanisms on the basis of chromatographic information alone. The ideas of multimode and mixed-

TABLE 5–1. Mechanisms and Interaction Forces

Mechanism	Major Interaction
Size exclusion	Steric
Cation exchange	Coulombic
Anion exchange	Coulombic
Reversed phase	Dispersive
Hydrophobic interaction	Solvophobic

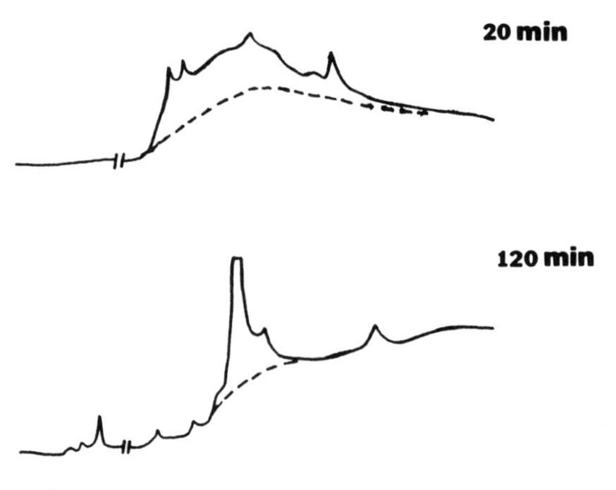

FIGURE 5–3. UV absorbance profile (215 nm) of bovine trypsin chromatographed on a 10-μm, 300 Å, *n*-butyl column, under nonoptimized conditions, illustrating the effects of multiple interactions involving the protein, the stationary phase, and mobile phase. Linear gradient: 15 m*M* orthophosphoric acid + 50 m*M* sodium phosphate, pH 2.3 to 15 m*M* orthophosphoric acid + 50 m*M* sodium phosphate, pH 2.3/acetonitrile (1/1 v/v), in 20 or 120 min. Flow rate: 1 ml/min. The dashed lines show the optical density profile for a subsequent blank gradient. (From Hearn et al.[2] with permission.)

mode concern the nature of the binding of a biopolymer to a surface during chromatography, and, as defined broadly in the following discussion, they are quite valid amid the many processes that may occur at or near that surface.

Mixed-Mode and Multimode Chromatography Reviews of this topic have been written by Floyd and Hartwick[7] and most recently by Berkowitz.[8] In mixed-mode chromatography more than one interaction type plays a significant role in the separation process within a single bonded phase. In multimode chromatography one interaction type predominates under a given set of mobile phase conditions, and a second interaction type predominates under a different set of conditions. These concepts are illustrated in an idealized form in Figure 5–4. The figure represents a retention map of a single biopolymer chromatographed isocratically at various ionic strengths.

The bonded phase may be an anion exchanger for example, containing hydrophobic groups. At low ionic strength (μ) (region A), retention decreases with increasing ionic concentration. The slope is a measure of the number of attachment points between the solute and stationary phase,[9] and its linearity is indicative of a single ion-exchange mechanism. At high ionic strength (region C) retention increases with salt concentration. Retention in this case is caused by the preference of the polymer to be desorbed from a solution of increasing surface tension. Since negatively charged ions are present in solution at high concentration they effectively screen the positive sites on the bonded phase, allowing adsorption of the biopolymer to occur via nonpolar

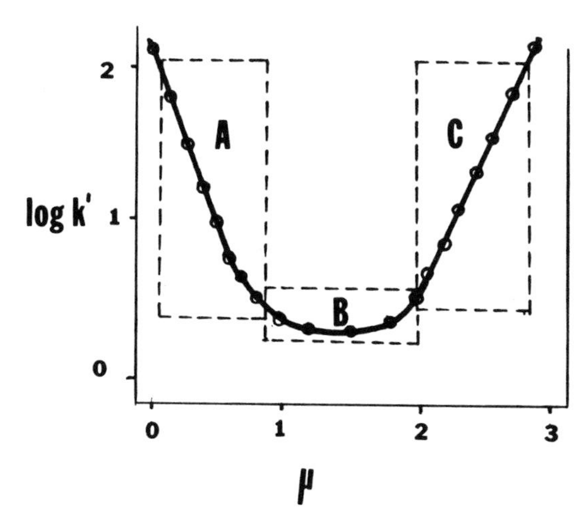

FIGURE 5–4. Idealized retention map of a single, unspecified protein chromatographed isocratically on a hydrophobic interactor/anion exchanger at various ionic strengths. Region A: Largely ion exchange. Region B: Mixed ion exchange and hydrophobic interaction. Region C: Largely hydrophobic interaction.

groups on the surface of the bonded phase and solute. In this region of the retention map a linear relationship is indicative of the solvophobic interaction being predominant; in other words the mechanism is hydrophobic interaction.

For region B both ion-exchange and hydrophobic-interaction mechanisms are present. Although ionic displacing power increases with μ, so does surface tension, so that their combined effect has a moderately constant effect on retention over a short range of ionic strengths. In region B the biopolymer is significantly retained at all values of μ.

Thus the bonded phase exhibits multimode properties since there can be two distinctly different mechanisms operating under distinctly different mobile phase conditions (A and C). The chromatographic medium also exhibits mixed-mode behavior in region B (ion exchange and hydrophobic interaction).

The retention map illustrated in Figure 5–4 is just one of several limiting cases described by Hearn[1] for proteins. The shape and position of these curves depend on the protein, the mobile phase, and the stationary phase. Careful choice of the last two is important in determining resolution and recovery.[1] An example of multimode chromatography is given in Figure 5–5 and chromatography on a mixed-mode ion exchanger is given in Figure 5–6.

Figure 5–5 illustrates how a commercially available PEI column can be used in two chromatographic modes: ion exchange and hydrophobic interaction. Where these modes overlap in a bonded phase, reduced or zero recoveries of certain proteins may be observed (see Section 5.4.2.1).

Figure 5–6 shows the effect of introducing a hydrophobic group into a cross-linked PEI bonded phase. The proteins are retained longer due to added dispersive and other interactions that are present on the surface. The chroma-

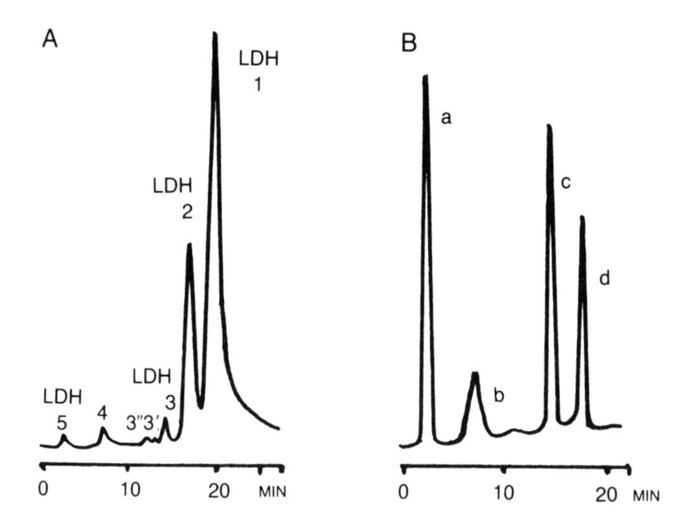

FIGURE 5–5. Chromatography of proteins on a commercially available 6.5-μm, 300 Å PEI column (4.1 × 250 mm) illustrating multimode behavior. (A) Anion exchange of LDH isoenzymes. Linear gradient: 0.02 *M* Tris-acetate, pH 7.9 to 0.02 *M* Tris-acetate plus 0.4 *M* sodium acetate, pH 7.9 over 25 min. Flow rate: 1.5 ml/min. Detection: Postcolumn reactor. Sample: Heart tissue supernatent. (B) Hydrophobic-interaction chromatography of standard proteins. Linear gradient: 2.0 *M* ammonium sulfate + 25 m*M* potassium phosphate, pH 7.0 to 25 m*M* potassium phosphate, pH 7.0 over 15 min. Flow rate: 1 ml/min. Detection: UV at 280 nm. Sample: (a) cytochrome *c*, (b) myoglobin, (c) lysozyme, (d) α-chymotrysinogen A.

tography illustrates that multiple forces of interaction are present during normal anion-exchange processes on this column.

Determination of the Presence of Multiple Mechanisms Several methods of obtaining evidence for the existence of multiple interactions in PEI-based bonded phases during chromatographic processes, have been described.

1. The potential for multiple interactions can often be qualitatively assessed from a knowledge of the functional groups present at the surface of a bonded phase. For example, cross-links used in the Alpert/Regnier PEI-coated silicas, which contain more than 2 carbons, show evidence of both anion-exchange and hydrophobic-interaction mechanisms.[10] On the other hand, Fausnaugh and co-workers[11] found no evidence for ion-exchange character in an acylated form of PEI silica that is known to have 10–20% of its nitrogens in the amino form. Presumably proteins may be sterically hindered from binding to these basic groups.
2. Retention maps under extremes of ionic strength can often be used to demonstrate multiple interactions, as described in Section 5.1.1.
3. The effect on retention of the addition of small amounts of organic solvents such as acetonitrile or 2-propanol has been observed by Gupta[12] and Bischoff[13]

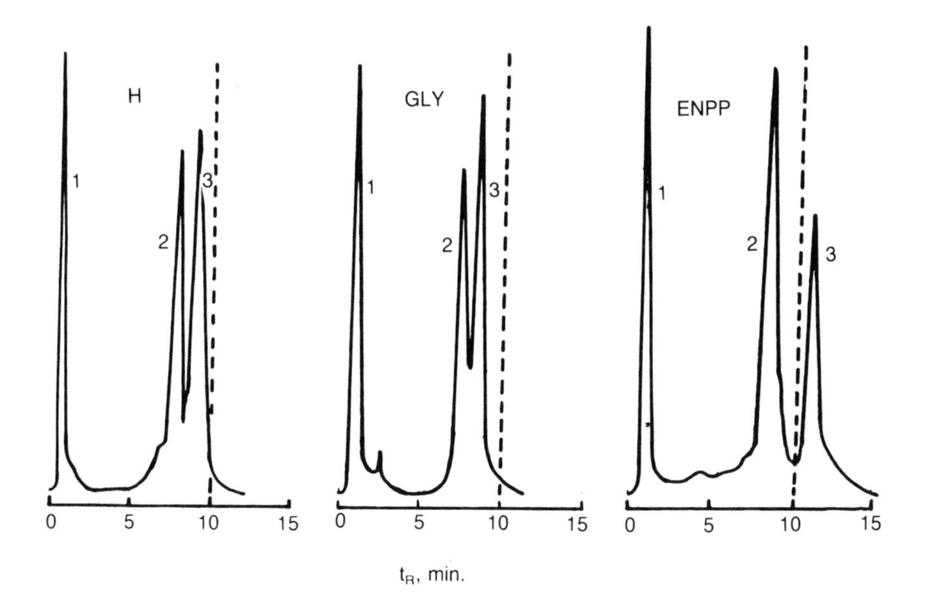

FIGURE 5–6. Separations of standard proteins on three 6.5-μm, 300 Å PEI-coated stationary phases (in 4.1 × 50 mm columns) of equal ligand density, but varying hydrophobicity. The hydrophobic character was obtained by reacting the cross-linked base coating (H) with 1,2-epoxy-3-hydroxypropane (GLY) and 1,2-epoxy-3-(*p*-nitrophenoxy)propane (ENPP). Chromatographic conditions were the same for each bonded phase. Linear gradient: 10 m*M* Tris-HCl, pH 8.0 to 10 m*M* Tris-HCl + 500 m*M* NaCl, pH 8.0 over 20 min. Flow rate: 1 ml/min. Detection: UV at 254 nm. (From Kopaciewicz et al.[10])

and their co-workers. Where 1 or 2% solvent cause no more than 5% retention time decrease, these authors considered that a negligible hydrophobic effect was present in the anion-exchange chromatography of biopolymers. Conversely, in several extreme cases of mixed-mode anion-exchange chromatography, Kopaciewicz and co-workers[9,10] noted that the elution of hydrophobically bound hemoglobin required high concentrations of 2-propanol containing 0.1% trifluoroacetic acid.

4. Kopaciewicz and co-workers[10] noted empirically that where the retention of a proteins is sensitive to small changes in pH then a hydrophobic effect is playing a significant role in binding. Where retention changes significantly over a broad pH range in PEI-based media, then the major interaction changes from an electrostatic one to one of an ion-dipolar nature. Where retention is independent of pH, the mechanism is probably unchanged (as in strong ion exchangers) and a single interaction type predominates.
5. Hofstee and co-workers[14,15] have shown that where the chromatographic profile of the elution of a protein in an ion exchanger is independent of dwell time, then hydrophobic effects in the bonded phase will be absent. The converse is not necessarily true, however, since strong ionic adsorptive effects can cause protein denaturation. In addition, time-dependent protein

association processes may occur on the surface, altering the retention characteristics with dwell time.

5.1.3 Aims and Scope of This Review

This chapter aims to describe all major classes of chromatographic media that are high performance, PEI based, and that exhibit multiple forms of interactions with biopolymers (largely proteins). The work encompasses a brief and qualitatively descriptive overview of separation mechanisms and their relation to the concepts of mixed- and multimode chromatography. The chapter reviews the nature of PEI and the substrates to which it has been attached and describes the modes of binding the basic polymer and its chemical derivatization and cross-linking. A discussion of PEI-based affinity bonded phases will not be given in this chapter. A selected list of applications concludes the chapter.

5.2 NATURE OF PEI

Aspects of the structural and chemical properties of PEI are described by Foster[16] and Ise and Okubo.[17] A review of the general physical and chemical properties of both linear and branched PEI has been written by Molyneux[18] and Davis.[19]

Linear PEI consists almost entirely of secondary amines (see Figure 5–2). Commercial grades of this polymer are highly branched, however, and contain primary, secondary, and tertiary amines in the ratio 1:2:1, approximately. There must be equal numbers of primary and tertiary nitrogens, if the general formula C_2H_5N is to be preserved, but the ratio of either of these to the number of secondary nitrogens is variable.

The commercial, and therefore economic, method of synthesizing PEI is by the acid-catalyzed polymerization of ethyleneimine. This leads to highly branched structures due to reactions of the type shown in Figure 5–7.

Linear PEI can be synthesized via isomerization polymerization of 2-oxazolines, as shown in Figure 5–8.

In dilute aqueous solution at pH 7, 10% of nitrogens (predominantly the primary type) are protonated while at pH 10.5 ionization is still 2.5%.[18] In more concentrated aqueous solutions (for example, 5%) of PEI the ionization is suppressed due to the difficulty of increasing positive charge density. There is a wide variety of basicities of the nitrogens in PEI leading to a very poorly defined end-point under normal aqueous titration conditions.[20] A well-defined end-point is achieved by titrating with *p*-toluene sulfonic acid in glacial acetic acid.[20] This method of analysis, however, indicates that only about 80% of the nitrogens are protonated, due to high positive charge density in the molecule.

As a consequence of steric hindrance the relative basicities of the three types of nitrogens are tertiary < secondary < primary. Electrophoretic mobility measurements indicate that a maximum of about 75% of nitrogens can be protonated, due to intramolecular charge repulsions mentioned above. This number is in close agreement with that obtained by nonaqueous titration.

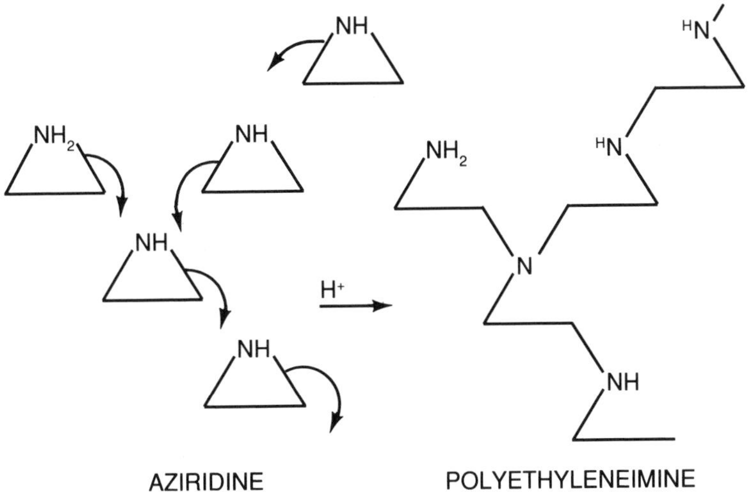

FIGURE 5–7. Synthesis of branched PEI.

Solutions of PEI exhibit low values of intrinsic viscosity, $[\eta]$, and a low value (0.39) of the Mark–Houwink–Sakurada (MHS) index, a. Since the value of $[\eta]$ is a direct measure of hydrodynamic volume of a polymer, a low value indicates that PEI is a relatively compact molecule in solution (pH 12, ionic strength 0.02 M). A fully extended rod shaped polymer will give in theory an MHS index value of 2.0.

Reactions of a linear PEI such as acylations and alkylations can in principle occur at every nitrogen in the molecule. The tertiary nitrogens in branched PEI can undergo only quaternization reactions. Klotz and co-workers[22,23] have prepared several acyl and alkyl derivatives of PEI, which have biocatalytic activity.

Polyethyleneimine has several useful properties as an immobilized ligand for protein binding:

1. Flexibility: This results in a chromatographic surface that is soft and allows a different type of ionic interaction with the surface of a protein, when compared to small point-charged groups such as diethylaminoethyl.

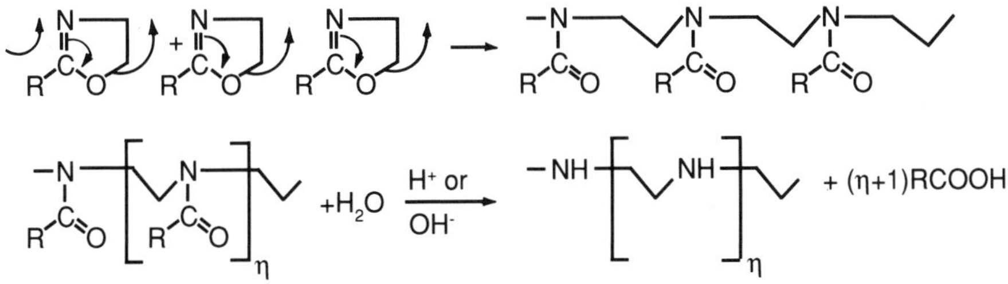

FIGURE 5–8. Synthesis of linear PEI.

2. Size: The long polymer chains that extend into solution provide a large number of possible interaction sites for protein binding, thereby increasing the effective surface area and capacity. Furthermore, proteins are held away from surfaces such as silica, preventing unwanted adsorption to such substructures.
3. Hydrophilicity: PEI exhibits little or no discernible hydrophobic properties. Mechanisms of separation on this polymer, when immobilized, and when it carries no cross-links, are therefore relatively pure and free from mixed- and multimode effects.
4. Viscosity: The concentration of PEI chains at the surface of a substrate increases the localized viscosity and reduces diffusion rates of basic ions to the substructure. This improves the stability of PEI-based bonded phases toward base-catalyzed hydrolysis.
5. Reactivity: The reactive amino groups provide the potential for almost unlimited numbers of different functional groups to be incorporated into a PEI-based chromatographic medium. If this is done correctly, single-mode bonded phases can be prepared having cation-exchange, hydrophobic-interaction, and reversed-phase mechanisms (see Section 5.4.2).

5.3 SUBSTRATES

Supports for the PEI polymer include silica,[24,25] alumina,[26] polymethylmethacrylate,[27] polystyrene/divinyl benzene,[28,29] cellulose,[30] and polyvinyl chloride-silica[31] and a polyol ester copolymer (Hydrophase™ see ref. 32).* The general properties of these supports are given in Table 5–2. Each support has its own advantages and limitations, and the major criteria for the selection of a general substrate material are given in Table 5–3 (ref. 1, p. 7).

The general chromatographic properties of porous versus nonporous particles have been the subject of significant investigation[33,34] and will not be reviewed in this chapter. The influence of the substrate on the chromatography of bonded phases, however, has been less studied and mainly with respect to acid stability of the phase,[35] the ability to resolve basic compounds,[35] and the separation of polynuclear aromatic hydrocarbons.[36] In the chromatography of proteins, studies have been made of the influence of silica type[37,38] and pore size[39] on resolution and capacity.

The influence of particle diameter on resolution is well established,[40] of course. The intrinsic properties of nonporous particles in chromatography have been measured[25,27,29,34] and compared with the same properties of porous particles.

*Trademarks: BAKERBOND Wide-Pore is a trademark of J. T. Baker Inc. Microanalyzer™ is a trademark of Bio-Rad Laboratories. MEMSEP™ is a trademark of Millipore Corp. FAST-CHROM™ is a trademark of Amerace, Inc. Hydrophase™ is a trademark of Interaction Chemicals, Inc. Gen-Pak™ is a trademark of Waters™ Chromatography. Waters™ is a trademark of Millipore Corp. Hydropore™ is a trademark of Rainin Instrument Company, Inc. SynChropak CATSEC™ is a trademark of SynChrom, Inc. SynChropak® is a registered trademark of SynChrom, Inc. Matrex™ is a trademark of W. R. Grace & Co. PolyWAX™ is a trademark of Poly LC. Amicon® is a registered trademark of W. R. Grace & Co. Mono Q® is a registered trademark of Pharmacia LKB.

The importance of the nature of the substrate in determining mixed-mode or multimode characteristics of the bonded phase has only occasionally been addressed. For example, the pore size distribution of chromatographic medium may exert size-exclusion effects on selectivity.[41] As an added complication, the size exclusion effect will usually vary with elution conditions.[42] Thus in gradient elution where ionic strength and pH may change during chromatography, so also may the size exclusion effect.

For PEI-based media, there is no published evidence for any influence of the adsorptive properties of the substrate on their chromatographic properties. The absorbed or covalently bound polymer effectively prevents the biopolymer from approaching the substrate. It is assumed, of course, that sufficient PEI is bound to cover fully the surface of the substrate, whether porous or nonporous. In the case of the Hydropore™ group of chromatographic media from Rainin, the exposed coating on the silica substrate exerts a hydrophobic effect at high ionic strength. This gives the anion exchangers based on this phase multimodal properties (see Section 5.4.1.2).

The cellulose and polyvinyl chloride-silica substrates that have been included in this chapter are particularly interesting. The former is the basis of the MEMSEP™ group of products and the latter is the substrate for the FASTCHROM™ chromatographic media. MEMSEP can be described as high performance according to the definition given in Section 5.1.1. FASTCHROM is included as a high-performance medium since it exhibits efficiencies approaching those of the 2.5-μm, nonporous Gen-Pak™ FAX (Waters™) when used to separate polynucleotides up to 12,000 base pairs.

MEMSEP consists of circular sealed stacks of regenerated, derivatized, cellulose membranes. They have a very open structure, through which biopolymers flow with normal buffered mobile phases. Adsorption–desorption occurs at the external surface of submicron particles. PEI and other ion exchange groups are bound to the cellulose molecule.

FASTCHROM also consists of circular stacks of membranes. They are composed of a polyvinyl chloride-silica composite material, prepared by blending PVC and silica in the presence of solvents. The mixture is then extruded at 120°F, and rolled into sheets. Silica particles, held in place by PVC within large, flowthrough pores, are derivatized by adsorbing high-molecular-weight PEI, for example. In both cases, sample is applied evenly over the disc via a distributor, and the sample components separate within 0.5–5 cm path lengths.

5.4 PEI-BASED CHROMATOGRAPHIC MEDIA

5.4.1 Bonding

PEI may be bound covalently or adsorbed to the substrate directly or attached to a coating on the substrate.

5.4.1.1 Direct Bonding of PEI to Substrate

Horvath et al.[25] adsorbed PEI directly to nonporous glass spheres. The polymer was cross-linked at 130°C with dibromomethane. Although these authors

TABLE 5–2. General Properties of Substrates That Have Been Used To Prepare PEI-Based Bonded Phases

Property[a]	Silica[b]	Alumina[c]	Polymethyl-methacrylate[d]	Polystyrene/divinyl benzene[e]	Cellulose[f]	Polyvinyl chloride-silica[g]	Hydrophase[h]
Mechanical strength	High	High	High	High	Moderate	Moderate	High
Minimum HETP (small molecules) (μm)	10	15	100	10	30	NA	30
Chemical reactivity	Good	Good	Good	Very good	Very good	Good	NA
Pore size ranges (Å)	150, 300 500, 1000	150, 300 500, 100	Nonporous	Nonporous or about 1000	About 10,000	About 2000	About 500
Pore size distribution	Narrow	Wide	Nonporous	Wide	Narrow	10^2–10^6	Wide
Common particle sizes (μm)	5, 10, 20, 40	5, 10, 20, 40	7	3(nonporous) 8 (porous)	Nonparticulate	Nonparticulate (but see ref. 29)	10
Particle shape	Spherical Irregular	Spherical Irregular	Spherical	Spherical	Nonparticulate	Nonparticulate	Spherical

Surface areas (m^2/g)	50–300	About 70	~1	~2 (nonporous) NA (porous)	300	80	4
Pore volumes (ml/g)	0.5–1.8	About 0.5	Nonporous	Zero (nonporous) NA (porous)	3.5	1.3	NA
pH stability	2–7.5	4–11	2–12	1–14	2–13	4–8	2–12
Organic solvent compatibility	All solvents	All solvents	Most solvents	Most solvents	Few solvents	Most solvents	Some solvents
Degree of nonspecific binding	High	High	Moderate	High	Very low	High	Low
Biodegradability	No	No	No	No	Yes	No	No

[a]These properties are those of the substrate and not the ion exchanger.
[b]PEI silicas from SynChrom, Poly LC, J. T. Baker, Inc., Rainin Instrument Co., Inc., Amicon, Inc.
[c]See ref. 26.
[d]Microanalyzer™ from Bio-Rad, Chemical Division.
[e]Nonporous, see ref. 29; porous, see ref. 28.
[f]MEMSEP™, from Domnick Hunter Filters, Ltd.
[g]FASTCHROM™, from Amerace, Inc.
[h]Hydrophase™, from Interaction Chemicals, Inc.

TABLE 5–3. Criteria for the Selection of Chromatographic Media[a]

1. Chemical and physical stability
2. Particle uniformity
3. Mechanical strength and resistance to deformation
4. Hydrophilicity and wettability
5. Sterilizability
6. Cost
7. Reproducibility between batches
8. High capacity
9. High resolution or selectivity
10. High mass and biological recoveries
11. High product throughput
12. Potential for good manufacturing practice scale-up

[a]From Hearn,[1] with permission.

reported that the chromatography of proteins on this bonded phase was "useful," they did not provide details.

Haynes and Walsh[43] describe a process whereby PEI is adsorbed to silica, cross-linked with glutaraldehyde, and then reduced with $NaBH_4$. This surface, described for colloidal silica only, was subsequently used to immobilize enzymes rather than as an anion-exchange medium.

Alpert and Regnier[24] in their important 1979 paper described the preparation, properties, and use of adsorbed PEI-based, porous silica chromatographic media for high-performance ion-exchange chromatography of proteins. In view of the steric protection of tertiary nitrogens mentioned in Section 5.2, and, as a consequence, the decreased basicity of these atoms, it seems likely that the primary amines of PEI will be preferentially adsorbed (see Figure 5–9). Cross-linking of the PEI was considered necessary to prevent desorption of the polymer during chromatography. Alpert and Regnier[24] chose several cross-linkers to achieve this, including pentaerythritoltetraglycidyl ether, glyceryldiglycidyl ether, and epichlorohydrin.

The above authors determined that an optimized packing material could be reproducibly prepared using conditions that resulted in a thin layer of PEI adsorbed to the silica surface. The layer was cross-linked under conditions that did not desorb the amine, and permitted the cross-linker to react at the surface. The conditions involved the choice of solvent (usually methanol) for adsorption, the determination of the correct amount of washing and drying, and the choice of cross-linking solvent (dioxane).

The Matrex™ PAE-300, PAE 1000, and PAE 1000L bonded phases[44] from Amicon® consist of branched PEI adsorbed and cross-linked to silica, probably in a similar fashion to that described by Alpert and Regnier.[24]

Kopaciewicz et al.[10] prepared adsorbed PEI-based anion exchangers of varying ligand density by binding different amounts of the polymer to silica using the same cross-linker. Theories were proposed by these authors to explain the relationship between ligand density and protein selectivity and recovery. Further discussion of this work is given in Section 5.4.2.3. In summary, Kopa-

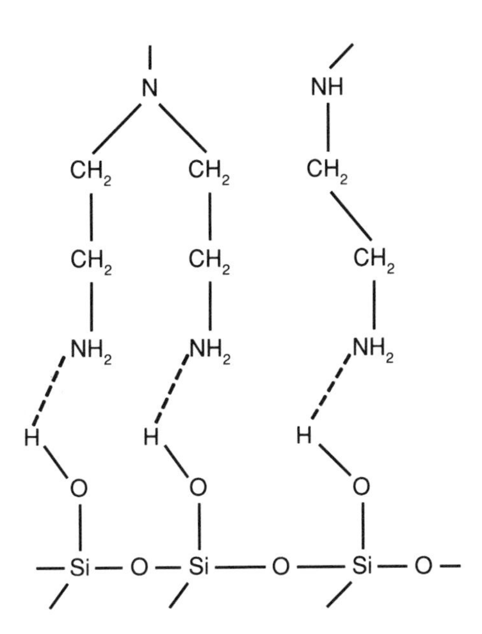

FIGURE 5–9. Probable orientation of branched PEI at a hydroxylated silica surface.

ciewicz and co-workers provided evidence for the existence of hydrophobic effects in determining selectivity. The hydrophobic component is due to the nonpolar cross-linkers used to stabilize the absorbed PEI.

Linear PEI has been used to prepare the weak anion exchanger PolyWAX™ LP.[45] It is believed that the basic polymer is adsorbed to silica and cross-linked using methods similar to those of Alpert and Regnier.[24]

Ramsden[46] described a method of covalently bonding PEI to a silica surface using trimethoxypolyethyleneiminopropyl silane. The reaction may be carried out in toluene at room temperature. The PEI does not require cross-linking and consequently has been shown[47] to be completely hydrophilic, even in very high ionic strength solutions. The silicon of the reagent is covalently bound to the silica via an oxygen bridge. This method of binding PEI to a substrate has been commercialized by J. T. Baker Inc., as the BAKERBOND Wide-Pore PEI family.

Sulfonated polystyrene cross-linked with divinyl benzene has been used by Rounds et al.[28] and Rounds and Regnier[29] as a substrate for PEI adsorption, cross-linking, and quaternization. The porous[28] and nonporous[29] particles, when so treated, behaved as strong anion-exchange supports. Sulfonation of the aromatic hydrocarbon polymer was accomplished with chlorosulfonic acid. PEI was coated in methanol, then cross-linked with triglycidylglycerol, then quaternized with methyl iodide in the presence of 1,2,2,6,6-pentamethylpiperidine and dimethylformamide.

PEI is adsorbed to particulate silica embedded in polyvinylchloride, in the FASTCHROM™ products from Amerace, Inc.[31] Strong adsorption of a 50,000 MW polymer to PVC-silica occurs in water over a 1-h period at room temperature. No cross-linking was necessary since the PEI was bound irreversibly at pH values from 3 to 9 and ionic strengths up to 1 *M* KH_2PO_4.

High-performance 10 μm alumina has been treated with PEI by Alpert and Regnier.[24] However, the small pore size of this substrate (100 Å) makes it unsuitable for protein chromatography. Chicz and co-workers[26] described several properties of anion-exchange packings in which PEI is adsorbed and cross-linked to alumina and zirconia-coated silica. The general process of Alpert and Regnier[24] was used.

The methods by which PEI is bound to polymethylmethacrylate,[27] cellulose,[30] and in Hydrophase[32] are not published. In all cases, however, bonding is covalent. PEI has been covalently bound to cellulose[48] via an iminocarbonic acid ester intermediate as shown in Figure 5–10. Hydroxyl groups in the polyolester polymer are the attachment points for PEI in Hydrophase HP-PEI.[32]

5.4.1.2 Bonding of PEI to a Coated Substrate

In this process a multifunctional reagent is bonded to the surface of a rigid substrate (usually silica). PEI is then covalently attached to this reagent. The result is a double-layered anion exchanger that does not require separate cross-linking to maintain its integrity.

For example, Gupta and co-workers[49] reacted 2-(carbomethoxy)ethyltrichlorosilane with 300 Å pore silica to form a moderately polar esterified surface. This was reacted with branched PEI of molecular weight 600 to form a layer that was covalently bound at several surface points.

Kagel[50] described in general terms the nature of the Hydropore group of chromatographic media. A hydrophilic polymer is covalently bound to macroporous silica, and branched PEI is covalently bound to this polymer at a low ligand density. The resulting medium has the properties of a weak anion exchanger, size excluder, and hydrophobic interactor, depending on the mobile phase conditions used.

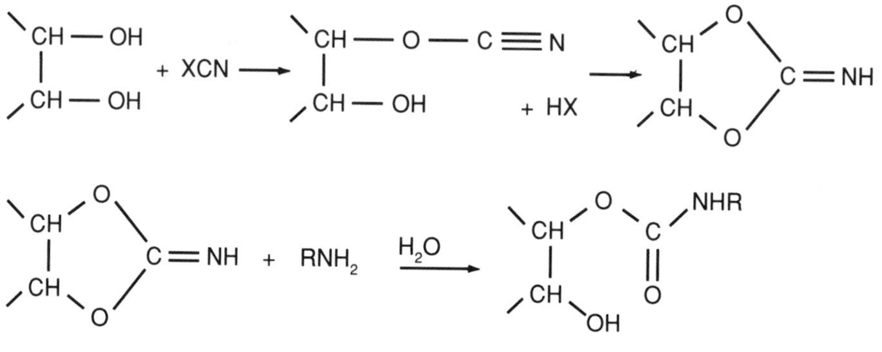

X = Halogen

RNH_2 = PEI

FIGURE 5–10. Reactions in the covalent bonding of amines to cellulose.

5.4.2 Derivatization and Multiple Mechanisms

Acylation[22,23] and alkylation[22–24] of the reactive nitrogen atoms in PEI have already been mentioned. Polyfunctional cross-linkers have been used in general to stabilize adsorbed PEI, although Kopaciewicz and Regnier[51] used a polyacid anhydride to cross-link PEI and simultaneously introduce carboxyl groups. Further reactions of the bound PEI, whether cross-linked or not, can be used to introduce hydrophobic, carboxyl, and sulfonic acid groups.

Whether the PEI is non-cross-linked[27,30,31,32,46,50] or cross-linked and/or derivatized,[10,24,25,28] multiple separation mechanisms (including size exclusion) will exist to influence selectivity and band width with derivatized PEI. Acylations, in which basic nitrogen atoms are rendered neutral, produce the greatest change in the balance of the various adsorptive effects. The surface can be made nonpolar or negatively charged,[10] changing the anion exchanger into a hydrophobic interaction column or cation exchanger. Alkylations generally do not alter the anion exchange character of the surface except in degree. Large alkyl groups would be expected to increase hydrophobic character, and bulky alkyl groups would reduce nitrogen basicity and prevent close approaches of peptides and proteins. Exhaustive methylation of a PEI-based bonded phase produces a quaternary ammonium strong anion exchanger, which would retain its positive charge at any pH. Cross-linking introduces a hydrophobic character that depends on the nature of the cross-linker.

Glutaraldehyde has been reacted with PEI[30] to produce a substrate for an affinity bonded phase. However, there will be no description of PEI-based affinity media in this work.

5.4.2.1 Cross-Linking

The works of Regnier and co-authors[24,26,28,29] and Horvath et al.[25] involve the use of a wide range of cross-linker reagents. They include tri- and diepoxides, alkyldihalides, reactive diols, chloroalchohols, and reactive diimides. One result of most cross-linking reactions is to convert primary amines to secondary; and secondary amines to tertiary (see Figure 5–11). The effect of this will most likely be to decrease the basicity of each reactive nitrogen, since there is

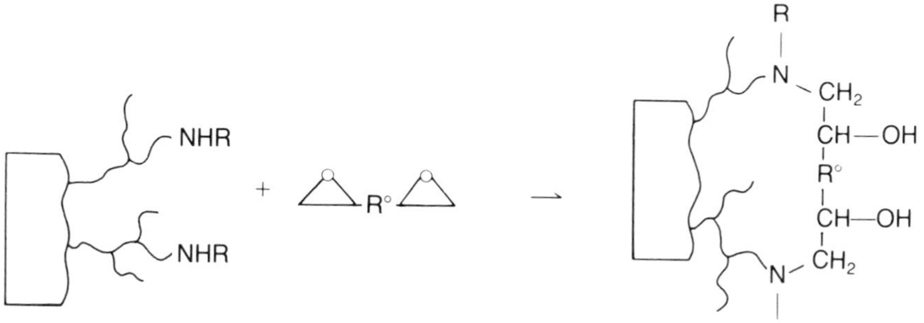

FIGURE 5–11. Cross-linking of PEI with a diepoxide.

more steric hindrance to solvation about each basic atom (see Section 5.2). Alpert and Regnier[24] estimated that between three and four amine groups per 600 MW PEI molecule react in a typical cross-linking reaction.

The choice of a particular cross-linker was made[24] depending on the size of the picric acid ion pair capacity of the resulting PEI-based medium (see Section 5.4.3). This choice will also determine the protein binding capacity[24] and hydrophobic character of the support. The last of these properties is important in determining the degree of mixed-mode and multimode character of these anion exchangers. The more hydrophobic the cross-linker, the greater the likelihood of there being a hydrophobic component of retention of a given protein. Kennedy et al.[52] demonstrated that an extensively cross-linked PEI bonded phase could be operated both as an anion exchanger and hydrophobic interactor (in multimode chromatography). A hydrophobic effect may occur during ion-exchange chromatography (mixed-mode) or mainly under high salt conditions (multimode). Kennedy et al.[52] suggested that a mixed-mode mechanism operated in their cross-linked PEI, since the acidic protein ovalbumin was retained longer than lysozyme due to binding to positive residual amines. In SynChropak Propyl, however, a presumably neutral phase, ovalbumin eluted sooner than lysozyme. This proposal cannot be conclusive, however, since the cross-linkers used by Kennedy and co-workers produces polar hydroxy and other groups that may exert their own preferential binding effect on ovalbumin over lysozyme.

In an extreme case of mixed-mode behavior on a multimode column, Berkowitz[47] observed complete loss of the acidic, hydrophobic protein, calmodulin on a commercial PEI-based column. The bonded phase consists of cross-linked PEI adsorbed to a wide-pore silica. The cross-links impart sufficient hydrophobic character to the anion exchanger, that one protein-binding force (hydrophobic interaction) replaces another (coulombic) as the ionic strength increases. On the other hand, the PEI phase of another commercially available column (BAKERBOND Wide-Pore PEI), where no cross-linking is present, gave over 90% recovery of this protein.[47]

5.4.2.2 Simple Acylations

These reactions are generally carried out using an acid chloride or acid anhydride in the presence of a basic catalyst (see Figure 5–12). Each primary or secondary amino group that is acylated is converted to a secondary or tertiary amide group, respectively, thereby neutralizing the nitrogens. Secondary amides can react further to produce tertiary amides (Figure 5–13).

Not all primary and secondary nitrogens may react with the acylating reagent; and tertiary nitrogens will not react at all. Thus a residual proportion of basic

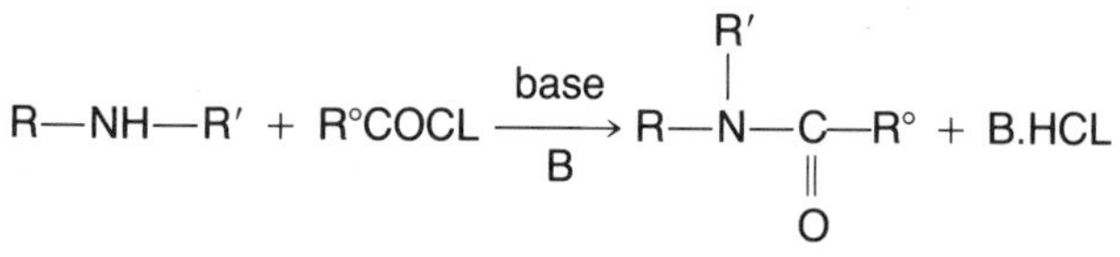

$$\mathrm{R{-}NH{-}R' + R^{\circ}COCL \xrightarrow[\text{B}]{\text{base}} R{-}N(R'){-}C({=}O){-}R^{\circ} + B.HCL}$$

R′ may be H, alkyl; R° may be alkyl or aryl groups

FIGURE 5–12. Acylation reaction of amines.

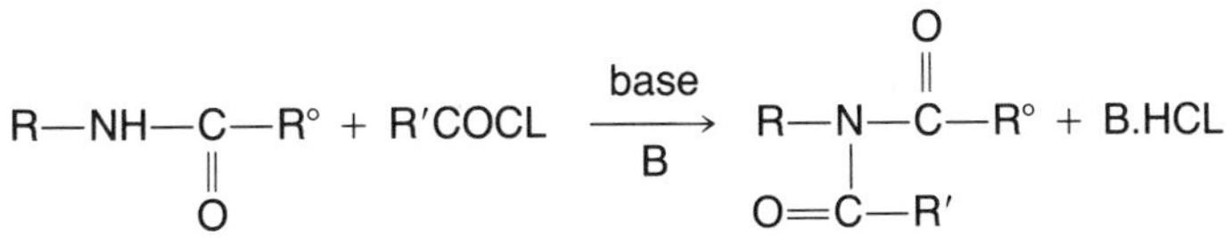

$$R{-}NH{-}\underset{\underset{O}{\|}}{C}{-}R^{\circ} + R'COCL \xrightarrow[B]{base} R{-}\underset{\underset{O{=}C{-}R'}{|}}{N}{-}\overset{\overset{O}{\|}}{C}{-}R^{\circ} + B.HCL$$

FIGURE 5–13. Acylation reaction of secondary amides.

groups will always be present, even after extensive acylation of branched PEI. Linear PEI can in principle be fully reacted, resulting in a more clearly defined product.

Kennedy et al.[52] prepared acyl derivatives of covalently bound polyamines and observed hydrophobic interaction effects at high salt concentrations. There will be a potential for anion exchange as well as hydrophobic interaction in such acylated, less polar derivatives of branched PEI (see Section 5.4.2.1). Kennedy and co-workers[52] demonstrated the bimodal nature of such chromatographic media. Familiar U-shaped retention maps were observed (see Figure 5–4), in which retention was significant at both low concentrations (<0.5 *M*, anion-exchange mode) and high concentrations (>1 *M*, hydrophobic-interaction mode).

In earlier work Fausnaugh et al.[11] prepared a covalently attached pentamine-based bonded phase containing secondary amines only. Acylation of these amines was 80–90% complete, but no detectable electrostatic binding of proteins was observed to the remaining secondary amines.

Kopaciewicz and Regnier[51] prepared weak cation-exchange stationary phases by reacting adsorbed PEI with cyclic acid anhydrides. Each nitrogen that reacts is converted to an amide, and the cyclic reactant breaks open to form a terminal carboxyl group. Although these authors estimated that 30% of the amino groups were not acylated, they found no evidence for a weak anion-exchange interaction. On the other hand, Kopaciewicz and Regnier[51] demonstrated the presence of a cooperative hydrophobic–ionic interaction in this bonded phase. In a similar study, Gupta et al.[49] prepared a weak cation exchanger from a silica-based covalently attached PEI. Reaction with diglycolic anhydride introduced a relatively hydrophilic acyl group containing a terminal carboxyl. The authors suggested the possible presence of hydrophobic contributions to the overall retention mechanism.

Fausnaugh and co-workers[11] synthesized hydrophobic interactors by covalently bonding a pentamine to silica, and then reacting this with hexanoic and benzoic anhydrides. The resulting nonpolar bonded phases eluted proteins only at low ionic strength and preferably in the presence of alcoholic modifiers. This behavior is indicative of a chromatographic medium that is at the point of crossover between hydrophobic-interaction and reversed-phase mechanisms. The addition of trifluoroacetic acid to the mobile phase in this case would most likely have increased peak sharpness.

5.4.2.3 Alkylations

These reactions may be used to prepare PEI bonded phases containing only tertiary nitrogens[10] or to quaternize the nitrogen atoms. In both cases, the existence of a hydrophobic effect has been observed in addition to the anion-exchange mechanism.

Kopaciewicz et al.[10] alkylated cross-linked PEI-based phases using monofunctional epoxides having a variety of aliphatic and aromatic functional groups. Both retention and recovery varied depending on the nature of the functional group and the protein. For example, a trichloromethyl (ETP) and phenoxy (EPP) group markedly increased retention of soybean trypsin inhibitor (STI) and caused nonelution of ferritin (FER) with respect to a cross-linked, but nonalkylated reference bonded phase. On the other hand, alkyl groups such as isopropoxy (EIP) and ethoxy (EP) caused decreased retention of STI and FER. The effect on the retention of ovalbumin (OVA) was relatively minor.

The nature of hemoglobin-binding capacity was also found to change depending on the alkyl group. This protein binds both electrostatically and hydrophobically to a cross-linked, nonalkylated PEI bonded phase. In this reference case, the proportion is 50:50. With the more hydrophobic alkyl groups (ETP, EPP) the percentage of hemoglobin bound ionically drops to about 15% of the total. The less hydrophobic alkyl groups (EIP, EB) boost this figure back to 50% of the total. Total hemoglobin binding capacity drops by about 15% on average for all alkyl groups. Removal of the nonionically bound hemoglobin can be achieved only using solvents such as 0.1% trifluoroacetic acid in 2-propanol.

The explanation of these observations is considered by Kopaciewicz and co-workers[10] to be due to a combination of increases in hydrophobicity of the anion exchanger and increases in steric inhibition of protein binding. The latter phenomenon by itself will cause decreased capacity and decreased retention. The former property will be associated with increased nonelectrostatic binding, increased retention, and decreased recovery, as the alkyl functional group becomes more hydrophobic.

The final selectivity, recovery, and capacity will therefore be caused by a combination of hydrophobic, electrostatic, and steric effects of the alkyl groups at each nitrogen.

Quaternized Supports Full quaternization of all nitrogen atoms on branched or linear PEI may not be possible due to the high charge densities that would be present in each molecule (see Section 5.2). However, quaternization can be accomplished to the extent that the retention of proteins will either be independent of[10] or increase with pH.[53] The quaternization of PEI has been described by Rounds and co-workers[28] using the reagents mentioned in Section 5.4.1.1. The selection of the solvent (dimethylformamide) was on the basis of maximum reaction rate, and that of the basic catalyst (1,2,2,6,6-pentamethylpiperidine) was on the basis of this compound's very high basicity (pK_a = 11.25) and sterically assisted resistance to self-quaternization.

Gooding and Schmuck[53] compared the retention of several proteins on a PEI-based weak anion exchanger with that on an exhaustively quaternized derivative. Similar or shorter retention times were observed with the quaternized ion exchanger. This indicated the presence of some steric inhibition to binding on the latter, although these authors considered that the weak ion exchanger was intrinsically more hydrophobic than the strong ion exchanger. Rounds and co-workers,[28] in assessing the hydrophobic component of retention on a quaternized PEI-based polystyrene resin, observed a 10% decrease in retention of concanavalin, OVA, and STI when 10% acetonitrile was used in the mobile phases. These authors ascribed this decrease to the hydrophobic effects of the added methyl groups and the cross-links. In comparing various quaternized supports using this method, Rounds et al.[28] indicated that Mono Q® (Pharmacia LKB) was the least hydrophobic, their polystyrene-based strong anion exchanger the next most hydrophobic, and their silica-based medium the most hydrophobic. The last two are extensively cross-linked, which will account for most if not all of their hydrophobic properties. On the other hand, it has been shown[54] that a non-cross-linked PEI support quaternized with methyl groups has no hydrophobic properties. (At high salt concentrations in the mobile phase of 2.0 *M* ionic strenth proteins are unretained.) Methyl groups, therefore, contribute no more hydrophobicity to a stationary phase than hydrogen atoms as far as protein chromatography is concerned.

Evidence obtained by Pungor[55] indicates that Mono Q® exhibits hydrophobic properties under certain conditions. He found that in the chromatography of hydrophobic membrane proteins in the presence of 6 *M* urea (used as a solubilizer), mass recovery was low as evidenced by the presence of ghost peaks. In this case, the polystyrene/divinyl benzene substrate is sufficiently hydrophobic to cause significant reductions in mass recovery under normal ion-exchange chromatographic conditions. No ghosting was observed with the hydrophilic BAKERBOND Wide-Pore PEI and recovery was much higher. Furthermore Hearn and co-workers[56] observed complex relationships between retentions and salt concentrations for cytochrome *c* and lysozyme on Mono Q. These authors explained this behavior in terms of a hydrophobic-interaction mechanism that plays a predominant role even at low ionic strength. Thus in the chromatography of very hydrophobic proteins and/or under conditions where denaturation may occur, it is important to use media that are as hydrophilic as possible.

5.4.3 General Properties

Table 5–4 lists several properties of PEI-based chromatographic media for HPLC of proteins when operated in the anion-exchange mode. Recovery of

TABLE 5–4. General Properties of PEI-Based Media for HPLC of Proteins

Phase Type or Name	Capacity (mg/ml)	pH range	P_{max} (bar)	Hydrophobic Character
BAKERBOND Wide-Pore PEI	120	2–10	300	No
SynChropak® AX300	107	2–8	300	Yes
PolyWAX™ LP	200	2–8	300	Yes
Hydropore™ AX	100	2.5–8	300	Yes
Hydrophase™	40	2–12	300	No
Matrex™	108	2–8	400	Yes
MEMSEP™	45	2–13	7	No
FASTCHROM™	1–2	4–8	3	No
Microanalyzer™	0.6	2–12	50	No
Alumina based[26]	25	4–12	100	Yes
Polystyrene based (porous[28])	75	1–14	300	Yes
Polystyrene based (nonporous[29])	0.35	1–14	300	Yes

biological enzymic activity is generally greater than 95% for all the media in this table. Mass recoveries usually lie in the range 85–100%, except for the more acidic, hydrophobic proteins such as calmodulin. Cross-linked PEI media exhibit poor recoveries of such proteins, since hydrophobic effects are present that prevent desorption. Recoveries of hemoglobin by ion exchange are also very low (sometimes less than 15%) on cross-linked PEI. (The non-cross-linked BAKERBOND Wide-Pore PEI exhibits 97% recovery of this protein, due to the negligible hydrophobicity of this medium.) Mass and activity recoveries, under conditions that promote hydrophobic interaction (high ionic strength), are generally similar to the values mentioned above. Only half of the chromatographic media in this table will exhibit hydrophobic properties.

Those PEI-based media that can be operated under conditions where biopolymers do not bind (medium to high ionic strength or using positively charged proteins) act as bonded phases for size-exclusion chromatography. This property generally requires either a very hydrophilic surface (for example that of BAKERBOND Wide-Pore or Hydrophase) or a low ionic capacity (Hydropore AX). SynChropak CATSEC™ (see ref. 57), which contains hydrophilic cross-links, can be used as a size excluder of cations such as polyvinylpyridines. In this case the vinyl polymer may be sufficiently hydrophilic and positively charged to eliminate any hydrophobic effects.

5.5 APPLICATIONS

Several examples of chromatography on multimode and mixed-mode, PEI-based chromatographic media have already been given (see Figures 5–5 and 5–6). It is considered that in general pure hydrophilic bonded phases (see Table 5–4) will not exhibit multiple mechanisms (with the exception of size exclusion) during any chromatographic mode in which they are operated. The size-exclusion effect (see Section 5.4.3), however, will be observed for the majority of the PEI-based media in Table 5–4 when they are used to separate cationic polymers. Published and unpublished work illustrating multiple interactions is available for SynChropak AX300 (see Figure 5–5), Hydropore AX,[50] and Matrex PAE-1000L.[44] The covalently bound pentamine and adsorbed, cross-linked PEI phases and their derivatives of Regnier and co-workers[7,10,11,24,28] also exhibit multiple mechanisms (see Section 5.4). Further selected chromatograms are given in this section.

Figure 5–14 illustrates the separation of proteins in mouse ascites fluid using a Hydropore AX column in both anion-exchange mode (A) and hydrophobic-interaction mode (B). Here there is the usual change in elution order with change in chromatographic mode. Albumin, for example, elutes later than the monoclonal antibody in the anion-exchange mode (p*I* of IgG is greater than that of albumin), but earlier than the immunoglobulin molecule in the hydrophobic interaction mode (this particular monoclonal IgG is more hydrophobic on its surface than albumin). It should be noted that monoclonal antibodies can differ in their p*I* and hydrophobic character, resulting in different elution patterns in both anion exchange and hydrophobic interaction.[58]

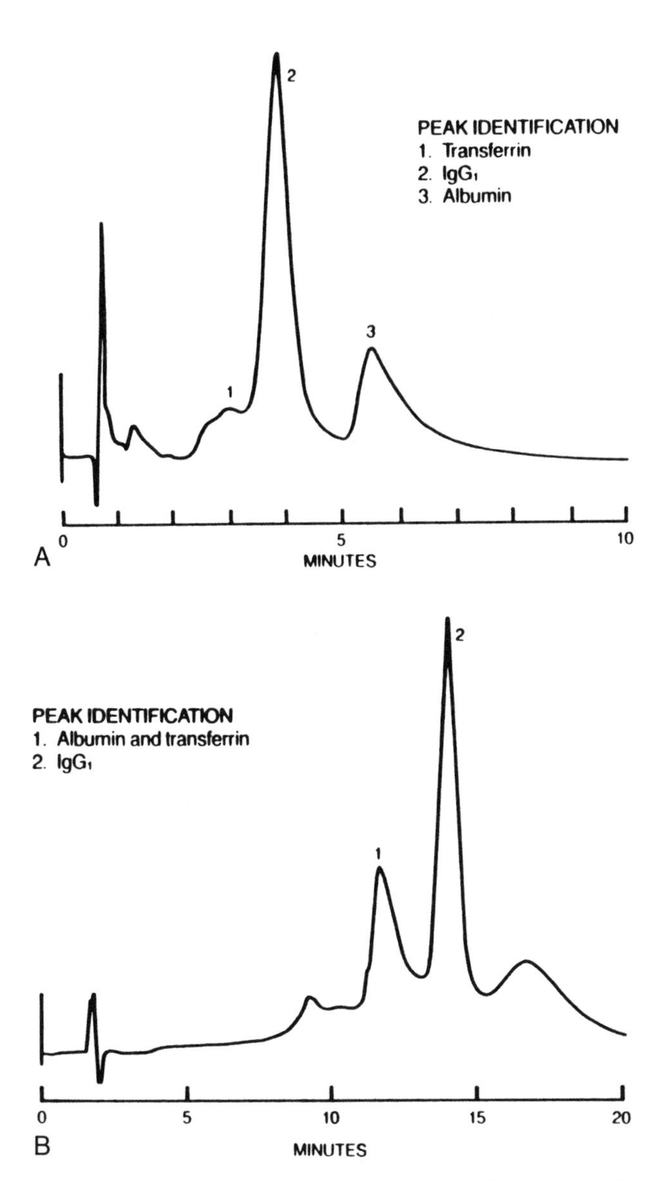

FIGURE 5–14. Chromatography of MOPC-21 IgG, mouse ascites fluid on 12-μm 300 Å Hydropore-AX (4.6 × 100 mm column), illustrating multimode behavior. (A) Anion exchange mode. Linear gradient: 10 m*M* potassium phosphate, pH 7.0 to 0.5 *M* sodium chloride + 10 m*M* potassium phosphate, pH 7.0 over 10 min. Flow rate: 2 ml/min. Detection: UV at 280 nm. Sample: (1) transferrin, (2) IgG, (3) albumin. (B) Hydrophobic interaction mode. Linear gradient: 3.0 *M* ammonium sulfate + 100 m*M* potassium phosphate, pH 7.0 to 100 m*M* potassium phosphate, pH 7.0 in 20 min. Flow rate: 1.0 ml/min. Detection: UV at 280 nm. Sample: See A. (From Kopaciewicz and Regnier.[50])

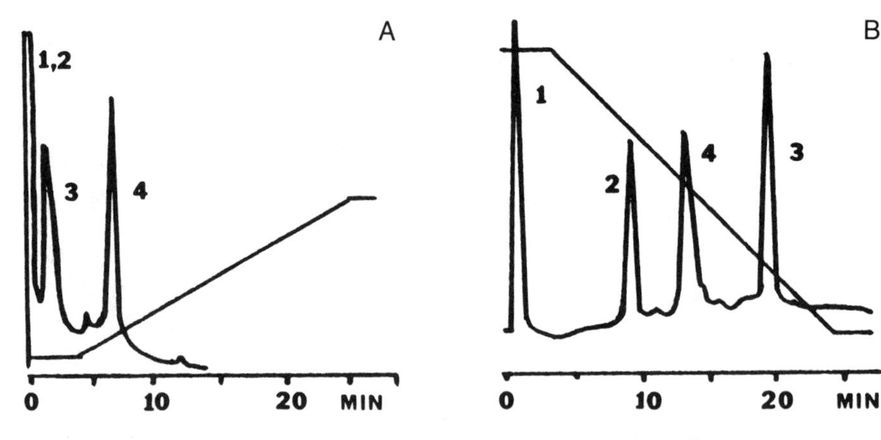

FIGURE 5–15. Chromatography of standard proteins on 10-μm, 1000 Å Matrex PAE-1000L column (4.6 × 100 mm) illustrating multimode behavior. (A) Anion exchange of proteins. Linear gradient: 2 m*M* Tris-HCl pH 8.0 to 2 m*M* Tris-HCl + 0.5 *M* sodium chloride, pH 8.0 in 20 min. Flow rate: 1 ml/min. Detection: UV at 280 nm. Sample: (1) cytochrome *c*, (2) ribonuclease A, (3) α-chymotrypsinogen A, (4) ovalbumin. (B) Hydrophobic interaction chromatography of proteins. Linear gradient: 2.0 *M* ammonium sulfate + 2 m*M* Tris-HCl, pH 8 to 2 m*M* Tris-HCl, pH 8.0 in 20 min. Other conditions as for A. (From Matrex Silica PAE.[44])

Figure 5–15 gives the anion-exchange elution pattern and the hydrophobic-interaction chromatography of four protein standards on Matrex PAE-1000L. Elution is rapid and resolution is poor in the anion-exchange mode, which is probably due to the low charge density of this bonded phase. The excellent resolution under hydrophobic-interaction conditions indicates that the bonded phase is more suited to this mode. Retention maps of both Hydropore AX, Matrex PAE-1000L, and Kennedy's polyamine phase V[52] will be the typical U-shape illustrated in Figure 5–4. The PEI-based media designed by Regnier and co-workers[7,10,11,24,28] exhibit both multimode behavior and the more subtle mixed-mode chromatography. A discussion of some of this work was given in Section 5.4.2.

Table 5–5 summarizes reference sources of information in which chromatography of biopolymers on mixed- and multimode PEI-based chromatographic media can be found.

5.6 CONCLUSIONS AND SUMMARY

Polyethyleneimine when adsorbed or bonded to a substrate has several unique properties as a positively charged material for the HPLC of biopolymers (Section

TABLE 5–5. Chromatography of Biopolymers on Multiply Interactive PEI-Based Chromatographic Media

Proteins	Reference
Myoglobin (MYO), ovalbumin (OVA), soybean trypsin inhibitor (STI), Ferritin (Fer)	10
α-Chymotrypsinogen (CHYGN), bovine serum albumin (BSA), lysozyme (LYZ), ribonuclease (RNase)	52
Cytochrome *c* (CYTc), RNase CHYGN, OVA mouse ascites	44
fluid, β-lactoglobulin, CHYGN, lactalbumin	50
MYO, conalbumin (CON), OVA, STI (BSA, CHYGN, CYTc, LYZ), and cyanobacteria extract	28, 29, 49, 51

5.2). When it is covalently bound to a substrate, without cross-linking, the resultant bonded phase is highly hydrophilic (see Section 5.4.1.1). If the substrate itself has hydrophobic properties, these can sometimes be detected in the anion-exchange chromatography of the bonded phase (see Figure 5–4). Cross-linked PEI-based bonded phase usually exhibits hydrophobic character, in addition to anion exchange (see Figures 5–5 and 5–6). In these cases hydrophobicity plays a more important role in a separation as higher ionic strengths are used. Alkylation reactions of PEI-based media increase hydrophobicity to an extent that depend on the nonpolar nature of the alkyl group. This type of reaction retains the anion-exchange character of the bonded phase (see Section 5.4.2). Acylation reactions, on the other hand, eliminate the ability of primary and secondary amines to become ionized (see Figures 5–12 and 5–13). Exhaustive acylation, in which nonpolar and negatively charged groups are incorporated into the bonded phase, can produce media exhibiting no residual anion-exchange properties for proteins. By careful synthesis, PEI-based bonded phases may be prepared that have surface charges ranging from highly positive (strong anion exchangers) to highly negative (strong cation exchangers). Mildly nonpolar, single-mode hydrophobic interactors, and a virtually unlimited combination of all these surface types, can also be prepared. In addition, most of these chromatographic media will exhibit some form of size exclusion under the appropriate mobile-phase conditions.

The reproducibility of the various properties of chromatographic media is of great importance, both from a fundamental scientific viewpoint as well as for commercial reasons. Tight control over every aspect of the manufacture of these media must be exercised. This is especially important when processes are designed to prepare PEI-based bonded phases of a variety of particle sizes, but having the same chromatographic selectivity for example. Work in our laboratories has been conducted to achieve reproducibility as a major goal. The more steps that are required in the synthesis of a bonded phase (imparting predictable, consistent multi- or mixed-mode properties), the more difficult is the task of manufacture. Reproducibility is, and will continue to be, of critical importance in the continued value of mixed- and multimode chromatographic media.

Acknowledgments

The author gratefully acknowledges discussions with Drs. Laura Crane, Steve A. Berkowitz, and David R. Nau of J. T. Baker Inc. The chromatography in Figure 5–5B was carried out by Dr. Berkowitz. The assistance of Louise Crivellaro in manuscript preparation is gratefully acknowledged.

REFERENCES

1. M. T. W. Hearn, *J. Chromatogr.*, 418 (1987) 3.
2. M. T. W. Hearn, A. N. Hodder, and M. I. Aguilar, *J. Chromatogr.*, 327 (1985) 47.
3. S-L. Wu, A. Figueroa, and B. L. Karger, *J. Chromatogr.*, 371 (1986) 3.
4. H. Engelhardt, M. Czok, and E. Schweinheim, Paper TH-L-2, *Twelfth Int. Symp. Column Liquid Chromatogr.*, Washington, D.C., June 19–24, 1988.
5. W. Kopaciewicz and F. E. Regnier, *Anal. Biochem.*, 133 (1983) 251.
6. D. R. Nau, Chapter 11, this volume.
7. T. R. Floyd and R. A. Hartwick, in High Performance Liquid Chromatography: Advances and Perspectives, Vol. 4. (C. Horvath, ed.). Academic Press, Orlando, FL, 1986, p. 45.
8. S. A. Berkowitz, in Advances in Chromatography, Vol. 29. (J. Calvin Giddings, E. Grushka, and P. Brown, eds.). Dekker, New York, 1989, p.175.
9. W. Kopaciewicz, M. A. Rounds, J. Fausnaugh, and F. E. Regnier, *J. Chromatogr.*, 266 (1983) 3.
10. W. Kopaciewicz, M. A. Rounds, and F. E. Regnier, *J. Chromatogr.*, 318 (1985) 157.
11. J. L. Fausnaugh, E. Pfannkoch, S. Gupta, and F. E. Regnier, *Anal. Biochem.*, 137 (1984) 464.
12. S. Gupta, E. Pfannkoch, and F. E. Regnier, *Fed. Proc.*, 41 (1982) 875 (Abstract 3541).
13. R. Bischoff and L. W. McLaughlin, *J. Chromatogr.*, 270 (1983) 11.
14. B. H. J. Hofstee and N. Catsimpoolas (eds.), Methods of Protein Separation, Vol. 2. Plenum, New York, 1976, Chapter 7.
15. B. H. J. Hofstee and N. F. Otillio, *J. Chromatogr.*, 159 (1978) 57.
16. W. A. Foster, in Water-Soluble Polymers, Polymer Science and Technology, Vol. 2 (N. M. Bikales, ed.). Plenum, New York, 1973, p. 3.
17. N. Ise and T. Okubo, in Water-Soluble Polymers, Polymer Science and Technology, Vol. 2 (N. M. Bikales, ed.). Plenum, New York, 1973, p. 243.
18. P. Molyneux, Water-Soluble Synthetic Polymers: Properties and Behaviour, Vol. I (Chapter 2) and Vol. II (Chapter 1). CRC Press, Boca Raton, FL., 1983.
19. L. E. Davis, in Water-Soluble Resins, 2nd ed. (R. L. Davidson and M. Sittig, eds.). Van Nostrand Reinhold, New York, 1968, Chapter 11.
20. C. R. Dick and G. E. Ham, *J. Macromol, Sci. Chem.*, A4 (1970) 1301.
21. J. W. A. van der Berg, C. J. Bloys van Tresland, and A. Polderman, *Recl. Trav. Chim. Pays-Bas*, 92 (1973) 3.
22. G. P. Royer and I. M. Klotz, *J. Am. Chem. Soc.*, 91 (1969) 5885.
23. H. C. Kiefer, W. I. Cangdon, I. S. Scarpa, and I. M. Klotz, *Proc. Natl. Acad. Sci. U.S.A.* 69 (1972) 2155.
24. A. J. Alpert and F. E. Regnier, *J. Chromatogr.*, 185 (1979) 375.
25. C. G. Horvath, B. A. Preiss, and S. R. Lipsky, *Anal. Chem.*, 39 (1967) 1422.
26. R. M. Chicz, Z. Shi, and F. E. Regnier, *J. Chromatogr.*, 359 (1986) 121.

27. D. J. Burke, J. K. Duncan, L. C. Dunn, L. Cumming, C. J. Siebert, and G. Sott, *J. Chromatogr.*, 353 (1986) 425.
28. M. A. Rounds, W. D. Rounds, and F. E. Regnier, *J. Chromatogr.*, 397 (1987) 25.
29. M. A. Rounds and F. E. Regnier, *J. Chromatogr.*, 443 (1988) 73.
30. M. S. Lee, J. P. Robertson, and K. L. Gollan, *Int. Labmate*, 12 (1984).
31. B. S. Goldberg, U.S. Pat. 4,102,746, July 1978.
32. N. Kitagawa, *J. Chromatogr.*, 443 (1988) 133.
33. L. R. Snyder and J. J. Kirkland, Introduction to Modern Liquid Chromatography. Wiley-Interscience, New York, 1979.
34. K. K. Unger, G. Jilge, J. N. Kinkel, and M. T. W. Hearn, *J. Chromatogr.*, 359 (1986) 61.
35. J. Kohler, D. B. Chase, R. D. Farlee, A. J. Vega, and J. J. Kirkland, *J. Chromatogr.*, 352 (1986) 275.
36. L. C. Sander and S. A. Wise, in Advances in Chromatography, Vol. 25 (J. C. Giddings, exec. ed.). Dekker, New York, 1986, Chapter 4.
37. J. D. Pearson, N. T. Lin, and F. E. Regnier, *Anal. Biochem.*, 124 (1982) 217.
38. M. A. Rounds, W. Kopaciewicz, and F. E. Regnier, *J. Chromatogr.*, 362 (1986) 187.
39. W. Kopaciewicz, S. Fulton, and S. Y. Lee, *J. Chromatogr.*, 409 (1987) 111.
40. G. J. Kennedy and J. H. Knox, *J. Chromatogr. Sci.*, 10 (1972) 549.
41. L. R. Snyder, M. A. Stadalius, and M. A. Quarry, *Anal. Chem.*, 55 (1983) 1413A.
42. E. Pfannkoch, K. C. Lu, F. E. Regnier, and H. G. Barth, *J. Chromatogr. Sci.*, 18 (1980) 430.
43. R. Haynes and K. A. Walsh, U.S. Patent Number 3,796,634, March 12, 1974.
44. Matrex Silica PAE, Technical Data Sheet, Amicon, Danvers, MA.
45. Technical Data Sheet, Poly LC, Columbia, MD.
46. H. E. Ramsden, U.S. Pat. 4,540,486.
47. S. A. Berkowitz, *J. Liquid Chromatogr.*, 10 (1987) 2771.
48. L. E. Weeks, C. Coeur, and J. H. Reynolds, U.S. Pat. 3,741,871, June 26, 1973.
49. S. Gupta, E. Pfannkoch, and F. E. Regnier, *Anal. Biochem.*, 128 (1983) 196.
50. R. Kagel, The Retention Times (Rainin Instrument Company, Inc.) 1 (1987) 1.
51. W. Kopaciewicz and F. E. Regnier, *J. Chromatogr.*, 358 (1986) 107.
52. L. A. Kennedy, W. Kopaciewicz, and F. E. Regnier, *J. Chromatogr.*, 359 (1986) 73.
53. K. M. Gooding and M. N. Schmuck, *J. Chromatogr.*, 327 (1985) 139.
54. D. R. Nau, J. T. Baker Inc., personal communication.
55. E. Pungor, personal communication.
56. M. T. W. Hearn, A. N. Hodder, and M. J. Aguilar, *J. Chromatogr.*, 443 (1988) 97.
57. D. L. Gooding, M. N. Schmuck, and K. M. Gooding, *J. Liquid Chromatogr.*, 5 (1982) 2259.
58. S. A. Berkowitz and M. P. Henry, *J. Chromatogr.*, 389 (1987) 317.

CHAPTER 6

Comparative Performance of Silica-Based Adsorbents for Ion-Exchange and Hydrophobic-Interaction Chromatography

Karen M. Gooding and Mary Nell Schmuck

CONTENTS

6.1 ION-EXCHANGE CHROMATOGRAPHY

6.1.1 Historical Development

In the mid-1970s, protein purification was revolutionized when Regnier and co-workers developed silica-based adsorbents for high-performance size exclusion[1] and ion-exchange[2–4] chromatography. Rapid analyses could be achieved on these HPLC supports because their silica backbones were rigid and able to withstand high flow rates, in contrast to carbohydrate-based gels, which were easily compressed and whose volumes could change under different mobile phase conditions. Figure 6–1 exemplifies the dramatic improvement in both resolution and speed of analysis that can be achieved by HPLC on a

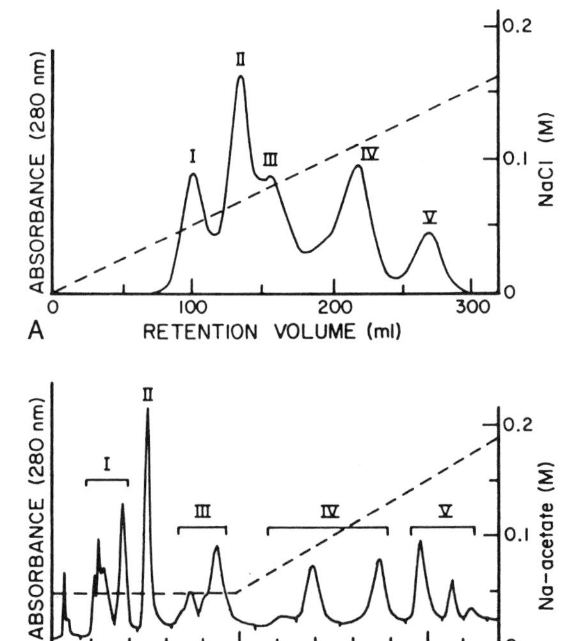

FIGURE 6–1. Analysis of dogfish total γ-crystallins. Column A: SP-Sephadex; column B: SynChropak CM300. Flow rate: (A) 12 ml/h; (B) 1 ml/min. Buffer column A: sodium acetate, pH 4.8; column B: Tris-acetate, pH 6.0. (Reprinted from ref. 5, with the permission of Elsevier Science publishers.)

silica-based cation exchanger compared to analysis on a gel column by traditional techniques.[5]

Although several ionic functional groups for high-performance ion-exchange chromatography were utilized in the early studies, the most successful were weak anion-exchange functionalities, in particular, diethylaminoethanol (DEAE).[2–4] Figure 6–2 illustrates a 6-min separation of lactate dehydrogenase isoenzymes on a DEAE glycophase column developed by Regnier et al.[4] Because weak anion exchange had been historically the most popular ion-exchange mode for protein purification, synthesis of similar anion exchangers was emphasized during the early years of development of silica-based supports. Supports that substituted polyethyleneimine (PEI) for DEAE as functional groups were seen[6] to give similar chromatographic performance to DEAE, but better reproducibility and higher protein binding capacity (see Chapter 5).

Although cation-exchange silica-based supports were marginally successful in the mid-1970s,[3] it was not until the 1980s that they achieved the same quality of performance as anion-exchange packing materials.[9–11] A major explanation for this lag time was the superb surface coverage gained from synthesizing anion-exchange layers on silica due to ion pairing of the amino functional groups with anionic residual silanol groups on the silica surface. Cation exchange coatings did not have the appropriate cation-pairing groups and in the prototypes of the 1970s, there were sometimes patches of exposed silica.

Both the thickness of the polymeric layer and the pore diameter of the silica can be varied to achieve different chromatographic effects.[7,8] Resolution can be changed by substituting a thick or "fuzzy" coating for a thin pellicular layer.[8] Loading capacity can be maximized by choosing the smallest pore diameter into which a protein can penetrate in order to maximize effective surface area and access a large number of ion-exchange functionalities. Generally, 300 Å pores have been seen to be optimum in terms of capacity and recovery for proteins under 300 kDa.[8] Silica-based anion- and cation-exchange supports with 300 Å pores have dynamic loading capacities of 10–20 mg of protein (albumin or chymotrypsinogen) on a standard 250 × 4.6-mm i.d. HPLC column.[9] The dynamic capacity is the amount of solute that increases peak width.

6.1.2 General Methods

Ion-exchange chromatography of proteins is usually achieved by forcing interaction between proteins and packing materials in a buffer of low ionic strength at a pH at which the proteins and supports are suitably ionized and oppositely charged. The proteins are then selectively eluted during a gradient to an ionic strength of 0.5–1 *M* salt. Although it is generally true that the pH of the mobile phase should be lower than the isoelectric point of a protein for cation exchange and higher than the isoelectric point for anion exchange, such generalities have many exceptions. The unpredictable behavior of proteins during ion exchange is due both to the complex amino acid compositions of proteins and to the fact that in nondenaturing mobile phases, the ion-exchange interactions occur only with ionic groups on the outer surface of a protein.[12,13] When Kopaciewicz et al.[14] plotted retention maps for numerous proteins on both anion

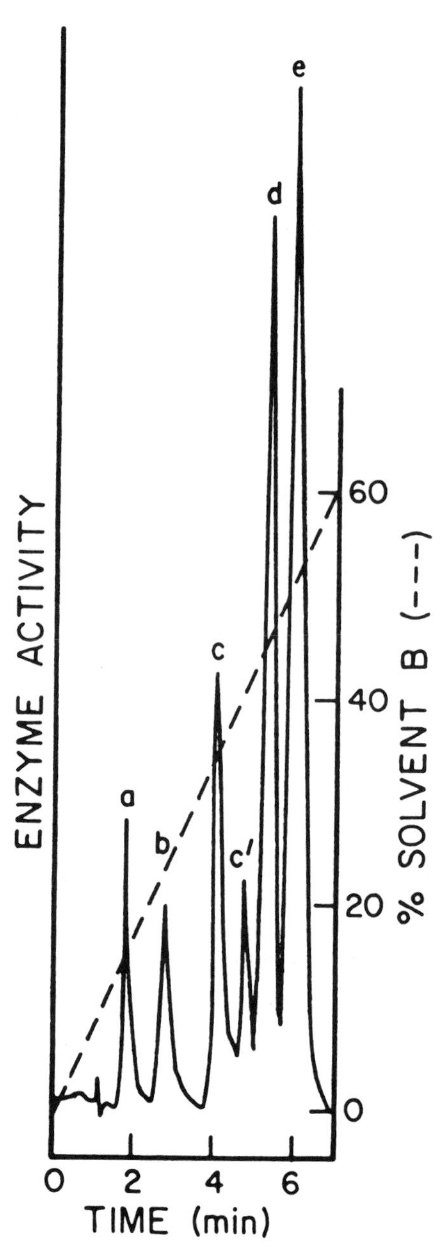

FIGURE 6–2. Analysis of LDH isoenzymes. Column: DEAE Glycophase/CPG (250 Å), 250 × 4 mm i.d. Flow rate: 3 ml/min. Buffer A: 0.025 *M* Tris, pH 8; B: 0.025 *M* Tris, 0.2 *M* NaCl, pH 8. (Reprinted from ref. 4, with the permission of Elsevier Science Publishers.)

and cation exchangers, they found that virtually none of the proteins behaved as predicted (no binding at the isoelectric point, anionic behavior above and cationic behavior below). With this unpredictability in mind, it is generally recommended that proteins with low isoelectric points be run on anion exchangers, those with high isoelectric points be run on cation exchangers, and those with intermediate isoelectric points be run on either type of ion exchanger.

If only the functionality of the packing material is considered, the pH of the mobile phase should be critical to the operation of weak ion-exchange packings, but unimportant for strong. However, the presence of ionizable groups on the proteins means that their net charge is likewise determined by the pH of the solution. The retention maps of Kopaciewicz et al. illustrate this phenomenon because the studies were carried out on strong ion-exchange supports that should be immune to pH effects. Gooding and Schmuck[15] saw variance in retention for ovalbumin and bovine serum albumin with mobile phase pH on both weak and strong anion-exchange materials, as seen in Figure 6–3. Silica-based ion exchangers generally have a pH limit of 8 due to the solubility of the silica, however, the polymeric layer on the support imparts some pH resistance, allowing mobile phases with higher pH to be used.[16]

The salts used for gradient formation are critical to the retention characteristics of proteins. In two different studies, it was found that the selectivity, as well as the retention, was dependent on the nature of the anion and the cation used.[14,17] Kopaciewicz et al. found that the resolution of trypsin inhibitor and ovalbumin on a quaternized anion-exchange support was maximal in citrate and minimal in chloride, whereas for cations, the difference in selectivity was greatest for sodium and least for calcium (Table 6–1).[14] On the weak cation exchanger, SynChropak CM 300, it was found that the resolution of lysozyme and ribonuclease was greatest for sulfate and least for chloride, whereas for cations, the difference in selectivity was greatest for calcium and least for barium (Table 6–2).[17] From the studies cited above, it is obvious that it is possible to replace a salt to alter selectivity, making any given ion-exchange column very versatile as an analytical tool. Two of the most commonly used salts for gradient development in ion exchange have been sodium chloride and sodium acetate. When buffer volatility has been desired, ammonium acetate has been used.

Many silica-based ion exchangers can be used as multimodal columns because high concentrations of salts promote hydrophobic interactions of proteins with the supports.[18,19] These phenomena result from the hydrophobic properties of cross-linkers used in the synthesis of the polymeric layers of the supports. For further information, see Chapters 5 and 7.

Silica-based ion-exchange supports are compatible with many mobile phase additives that can increase stability, solubility, or recovery of proteins and enzymes. Wittliff et al.[20,21] used glycerol and molybdate to increase the stability and recovery of estrogen and progestin receptors during the resolution of isoforms by anion-exchange on SynChropak AX1000. Urea and nonionic detergents such as Genapol X-100 have been utilized to increase the solubility of apolipoproteins[22] and membrane proteins[23] during ion-exchange chromatography. In an extreme example of insolubility, water was almost totally omitted from the mobile phase when a subunit of chloroplast coupling factor was

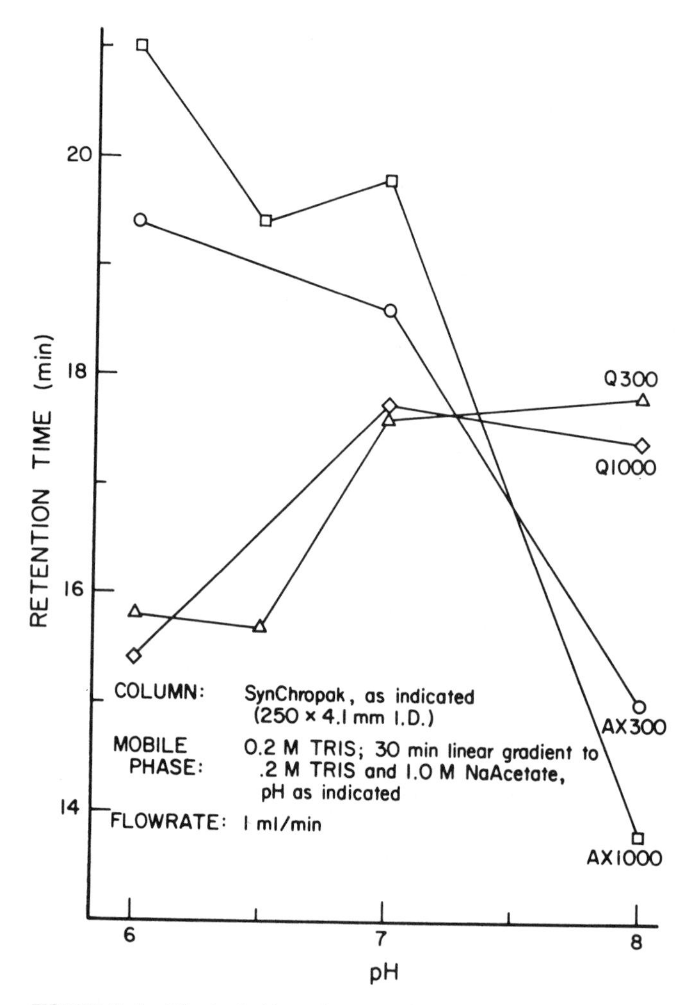

FIGURE 6–3. Effect of pH on the retention of ovalbumin. SynChropak IEC columns as indicated, 250 × 4.1 mm i.d. Flow rate: 1 ml/min. Pressure: 80 atm. Buffer: 0.02 *M* Tris, 30 min gradient from 0–1 *M* sodium acetate. (Reprinted from ref. 15, with the permission of Elsevier Science Publishers.)

purified by an ammonium acetate gradient in mixtures of chloroform and methanol.[24] The rigid silica matrix of the ion exchangers permits their compatibility with many solvents and additives without negative effects.

Anion- and cation-exchange supports can be used in series or in a mixed bed to further enhance separations of complex mixtures.[25] Stringham and Regnier[26] used a mixed bed and selected pH to isolate the immunoglobulin, IgG_1, from bovine serum by adsorbing virtually all other components from the complex mixture. Josic et al.[23] used a mixed bed column to isolate a glycoprotein from a mixture of liver membrane proteins.

TABLE 6–1. Influence of Various Ions on the Retention of Ovalbumin (OVA) and Soybean Trypsin Inhibitor (STI) on a Strong Anion-Exchange (SAX) Column[a]

	Relative retention[b] on SAX[c] Column		Retention Ratio[d]
	OVA	STI	STI/OVA
Anion[e] (sodium salt)			
Chloride	0.83	0.64	1.50
Bromide	0.72	0.56	1.46
Perchlorate	0.62	0.64	1.93
Bicarbonate	0.82	0.71	1.63
Formate	1.00	0.72	1.73
Acetate	1.00	0.95	1.91
Propionate	1.00	1.00	1.89
Sulfate	0.68	0.79	2.20
Tartrate	0.72	0.80	2.09
Citrate	0.50	0.69	2.61
Cation[e] (chloride salt)			
Lithium	1.00	0.82	1.52
Sodium	0.83	0.65	1.47
Potassium	0.85	0.68	1.49
Ammonium	0.81	0.64	1.46
Magnesium	0.68	0.50	1.38
Calcium	0.68	0.47	1.28
Sodium[f]	0.67	1.00	1.92
Magnesium[f]	0.83	0.82	1.91

[a]Reprinted from Kopaciewicz et al.[14] with the permission of Elsevier Science Publishers.
[b]Unity refers to the longest retention time obtained with a 20-min gradient.
[c]SAX column refers to a silica-based strong anion-exchange column.
[d]Ratios were calculated from the actual retention times.
[e]Chromatography was performed at pH 8. The ionic strength of Buffer B was 0.5.
[f]Acetate salts.

6.1.3 Applications

6.1.3.1 Isoenzymes

Among the first protein separations to be performed by HPIEC were the resolution of isoenzymes of creatine kinase, hexokinase, alkaline phosphatase, and lactate dehydrogenase (Figure 6–2) by Regnier et al.[4,6,27] Both the high enzymatic recoveries and the excellent resolution of HPIEC were aptly demonstrated by these analysis. Further studies of lactate dehydrogenase[28–30] and creatine kinase[30–32] extended the HPLC techniques to clinical usage. Rudolph et al.[33,34] used HPIEC to purify a multitude of enzymes, including adenosine deaminase and adenylosuccinate synthetase, with high resolution and recovery. There are numerous other examples of isoenzyme analyses in the literature including those of lipoxygenase,[35] cytochrome P-450,[36] aldehyde dehydrogenase,[37] amylase,[38] lysozyme,[16] and glutathione S-transferase.[39]

TABLE 6–2 Relative Retention of Proteins on a Weak Cation-Exchange Column[a,b]

Ion	Retention Ratio			
	Lys/Ribo	Lys/Cyt *c*	Lys/Chym	Lys/Chymogen
Anions (sodium salt)				
MOPS	1.23	—	1.11	1.06
Acetate	1.33	1.19	1.19	1.08
Chloride	1.20	1.16	1.16	1.10
Sulfate*	1.42	1.13	1.16	1.07
Phosphate*	1.33	—	1.17	1.14
Cations (chloride salt)				
Sodium	1.20	1.16	1.16	1.10
Potassium	1.22	1.22	1.22	1.16
Ammonium	1.25	1.21	1.19	1.09
Magnesium*	1.37	1.28	1.25	1.13
Calcium*	1.43	1.43	1.35	1.21
Barium*	1.16	1.13	1.10	1.06

[a]Reprinted from Gooding and Schmuck[17] with the permission of Elsevier Science Publishers.

[b]Conditions for the analyses were column, SynChropak CM300, 250 × 4.1 mm i.d.; flow rate, 1 ml/min; 30- or 60*-min gradient, from 0 to 0.5 *M* salt; Lys, lysozyme; Ribo, ribonuclease A; Cyt *c*, cytochrome *c*; Chym, α-chymotrypsin; Chymogen, chymotrypsinogen A.

6.1.3.2 Hemoglobins

The separation and identification of hemoglobin variants were other early applications of HPIEC that quickly progressed to usage in clinically related areas. The early analyses of several common variants, including Hb A, S, F, and A_2[4,40] prompted the use of HPLC for a broad spectrum of hemoglobins. Wilson and Huisman pioneered the use of HPIEC to quantify variant hemoglobins for clinical determination[41–44] and for assessment of cellular distribution.[45] Figure 6–4 illustrates their technique in the quantification of hemoglobin variants in the blood of a person with sickle cell anemia. Other laboratories have also used HPIEC on silica-based cation-exchange supports to quantify variant hemoglobins.[10,46]

A related analysis to that of variant hemoglobins is the determination of glycated hemoglobins by high-performance cation-exchange chromatography. These hemoglobins differ by their attached carbohydrate groups and are used to assess insulin and diet control in diabetes. Huisman and Wilson[42] were among the first groups to pioneer this technique, in the context of elucidating variant hemoglobins. Abraham et al.[47–49]and David and Shihabi[50] investigated the use of HPLC to quantify glycated hemoglobins to monitor diabetic control clinically.

6.1.3.3 Other Proteins

An interesting and important application of HPIEC has been the purification of monoclonal antibodies from biological fluids. Figure 6–5 illustrates the separation of IgG_1 from mouse on a DuPont Bio Series SAX column. As men-

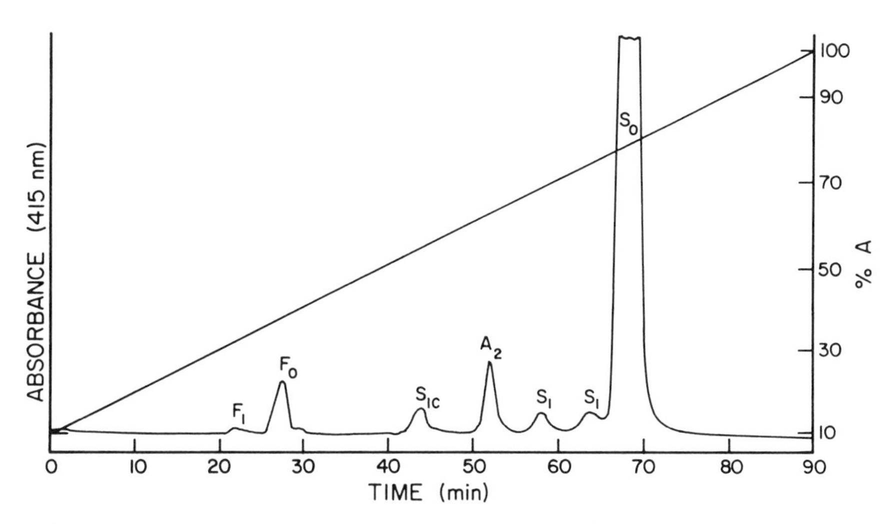

FIGURE 6–4. Analysis of abnormal hemoglobins. Column: SynChropak CM300, 250 × 4.1 mm i.d. Flow rate: 1.0 ml/min. Mobile phase: A: 0.03 *M* Bis-Tris, 0.15 *M* sodium acetate, and 0.0015 *M* potassium cyanide, pH 6.40; B: 0.03 *M* Bis-Tris and 0.0015 *M* potassium cyanide, pH 6.40. Sample: hemolyzed sickle cell anemia blood. (Printed with the permission of J. B. Wilson and T. H. J. Huisman.)

tioned previously, Stringham and Regnier[26] successfully purified IgG_1 by selective nonadsorption on a mixed bed column containing SynChroprep Q300 and S300. Chen et al.[51] purified IgM monoclonal antibodies to a purity of 99% on a mixed mode Baker ABx column.

Wittliff et al.[20,52,53] extensively used anion exchange on silica-based supports to study steroid hormone receptors through resolution of their isoforms. Another chapter discusses these analyses in more detail; however, the ability to successfully resolve isoforms of the extremely labile estrogen and progestin receptors with high recoveries aptly illustrates the unsurpassed capabilities of HPIEC. In the course of their studies, this group also used HPIEC to elucidate other proteins related to receptors and cancer, including topoisomerase[54] and monoclonal antibodies.[55]

Siezen et al.[5,56] effectively used high-performance cation-exchange chromatography to study the presence of various forms of crystallins in eye lenses from several species. The excellent resolution of the different crystallin forms was illustrated in Figure 6–1.[5]

6.1.3.4 Peptides

Although reversed-phase chromatography has been overwhelmingly the most popular method for peptide analysis, strong cation-exchange chromatography can be successfully used as a complementary technique. Mant and Hodges[57] showed the feasibility of using cation exchange on SynChropak S300 to separate peptide standards that they had developed. Figure 6–6 shows the excellent resolution of peptides that was obtained by Alpert and Andrews[58] on a PolySULFOETHYL Aspartamide column using acetonitrile in the mobile phase. Crimmins et al.[59] showed the utility of the same silica-based cation-exchange

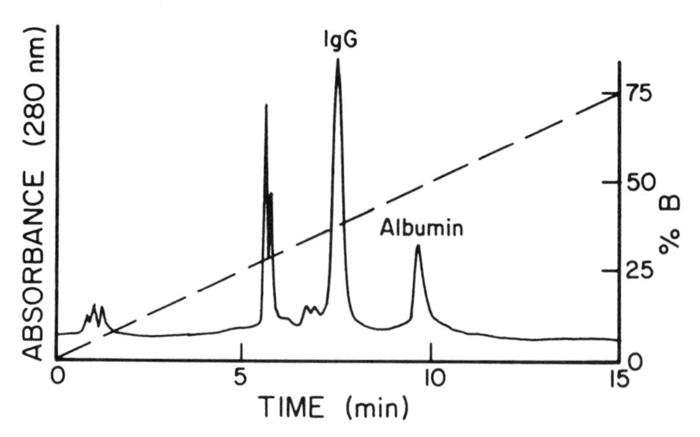

FIGURE 6–5. Separation of IgG, from mouse ascites. Column: Du Pont BioSeries SAX, 80 × 6.2 mm i.d. Flow rate: 2 ml/min. mobile phase: A: 0.02 M Bis-Tris, pH 7.0; B: 0.02 *M* Bis-Tris, 1.0 *M* NaCl, pH 7.0. Gradient: 0–100% B in 20 min. Temperature: ambient. Sample size: 20 μl. (Printed with the permission of S. S. Sivakoff.)

support in the characterization of peptides by a different selectivity from reversed phase chromatography.

6.2 HYDROPHOBIC-INTERACTION CHROMATOGRAPHY

6.2.1 Historical Development

Hydrophobic-interaction chromatography (HIC) was developed as a result of the observation that variations from predicted retentive behavior of samples were observed during affinity chromatography.[60] These differences in retention were seen to be dependent on the length of the hydrophobic spacer arm that held the functional group on the matrix and, thus, the proteins were being separated by differences in their hydrophobic character. The name, "hydrophobic-interaction chromatography," was subsequently introduced by Hjertén[61] to describe salt-mediated separations of proteins on weakly hydrophobic carbohydrate gel matrices.

The feasibility of high performance HIC was first demonstrated by Chang et al.[2] in 1976 using controlled pore glass derivatized with heptanol and polyethylene oxide. The elution behavior of proteins on this weakly hydrophobic matrix was similar to that described on carbohydrate gel analogs. Since 1983, a number of high-quality silica-based matrices have been developed for high performance HIC of proteins. Regnier et al.[62,63] reacted a polyamine-coated silica with a series of acid anhydrides or chlorides to produce HIC supports with different ligands. Gooding et al.[64] likewise prepared a series of silica-based HIC supports in which various ligands were attached to a polymeric

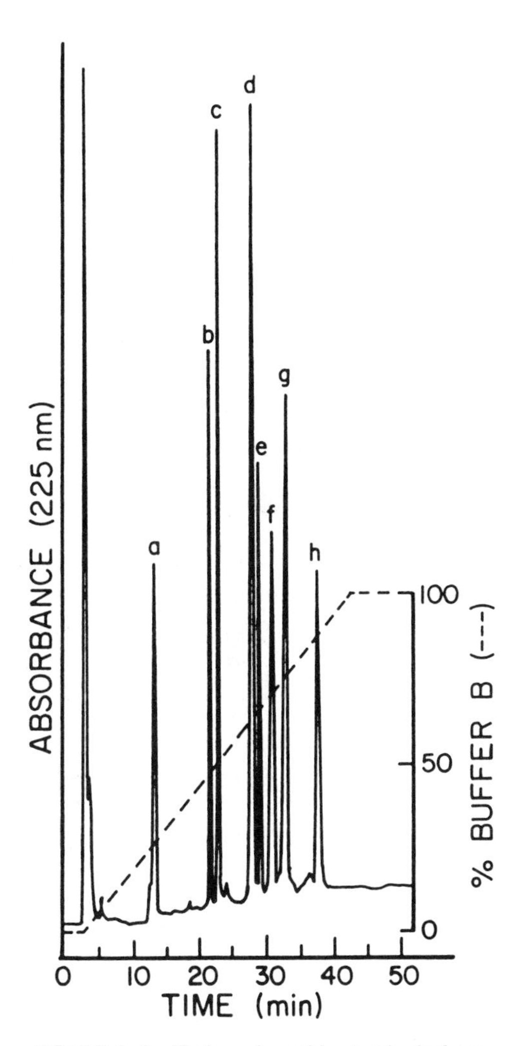

FIGURE 6–6. Elution of peptide standards from a PolySULFOETHYL Aspartamide column, 200 × 4.6 mm i.d. Flow rate: 0.7 ml/min. Buffer A: 0.005 *M* potassium phosphate (pH 3.0) and 25% acetonitrile. Buffer B: 0.005 *M* potassium phosphate (pH 3.0), 25% acetonitrile, and 0.25 *M* potassium chloride. Sample: 50 μl (initial mobile phase), containing ~ 5 μg of each peptide. Peptides (net charge pH 3): (a) oxytocin (+1); (b) [Arg^8]-vasopressin (+2); (c) somatostatin (+3); (d) substance P, free acid (+3); (e) substance P (+3); (f) bovine pancreatic polypeptide (+5); (g) anglerfish peptide Y (+6); (h) human neuropeptide Y (+7). (Reprinted from ref. 58, with the permission of Elsevier Science Publishers.)

coating. Karger et al.[65] synthesized a polyether HIC support on silica and Horvath et al.[66] bonded silica with a hydrophobic layer covered by a hydrophilic coat. In 1986, Alpert[67] introduced a silica-based HIC support which made use of a poly(alkyl aspartamide) layer.

6.2.2 Hydrophobic-Interaction versus Reversed-Phase Chromatography

Two distinct modes of chromatography separate compounds by their hydrophobic physical properties, namely, reversed-phase (RPC) and hydrophobic-interaction chromatography (HIC). Although the basic retention principles may be the same, the two methods are very different in their selectivities.

RPC employs gradients composed of acidic and/or organic mobile phases, whereas HIC makes use of salt solutions. As a result, RPC frequently denatures proteins and exposes interior hydrophobic sights, while HIC leaves proteins intact and separates by surface hydrophobicity. Table 6–3 shows a study by Fausnaugh et al.[74] in which they compared retention on an HIC phenyl-acetyl column with that on an RPC column for 12 proteins. Several major differences were noted: Cytochrome *c* and myoglobin, which behave in a hydrophilic manner on the HIC column, are both strongly retained by the RPC column. In contrast, β-glucosidase is strongly retained by the HIC column but weakly retained by the RPC column. Intermediately, ovalbumin elutes about halfway through the gradient in HIC, but is strongly retained by the RPC column. These differences can be explained by examining the hydrophobicity of the protein's exterior. For example, cytochrome *c* and myoglobin have hydrophilic

TABLE 6–3. HIC and RPC Selectivity[a,b]

HIC		RPC	
Protein	t_R (min)	Protein	t_R (min)
Cytochrome	0.6	β-Glucosidase	5.3
Myoglobin	0.8	RNase	10.7
RNase	1.6	Cytochrome *c*	12.6
Concanavalin A	6.3	α-Chymotrypsin	13.6
Ovalbumin	6.5	Lysozyme	14.3
Lysozyme	8.5	Myoglobin	14.6
β-Glucosidase	15.6	Ferritin	16.6
α-Chymotrypsin	16.6	α-Chymotrypsinogen A	16.8
α-Chymotrypsinogen A	18.1	Bovine serum albumin	17.1
Lactoperoxidase	19.5	Concanavalin A	17.3
Bovine serum albumin	20.5	Ovalbumin	18.5
Ferritin	20.8	Lactoperoxidase	20.3

[a]Reprinted from Fausnaugh et al.[74] with the permission of Elsevier Science Publishers.

[b]*Conditions* HIC: column: phenyl-acetyl; Buffer A: 1.0 *M* sodium sulfate in B; Buffer B: 10 m*M* potassium phosphate, pH 7; 20 min gradient from 100% A to 100% B; flow rate: 1 ml/min. RPC: column: SynChropak RP8; 20 min linear gradient from 0.1% TFA in water to 0.1% TFA in 2-propanol–water (60/40); flow rate: 1 ml/min.

exterior amino acids and hydrophobic interior ones and they thus interact strongly during RPC, but weakly during HIC.

A noteworthy physical difference between RPC and HIC matrices is the density of the alkyl or aryl hydrophobic groups. RPC packings commonly have very high ligand density and HIC matrices usually have low ligand density. As a result, proteins are eluted using less severe conditions in HIC than in RPC. Because proteins retain their structures under normal HIC operating conditions, it is especially suitable for studies in which enzymatic activity is of prime importance.

6.2.3 Methods Development

HIC supports generally have hydrophilic polymeric layers into which short hydrophobic ligands are incorporated.[63–67] Some hydrophobic ligands that have been used for protein analysis are hydroxypropyl, methyl, propyl, butyl, pentyl, benzyl, phenyl, polyether, poly(ethylene glycol), and poly(alkyl aspar-

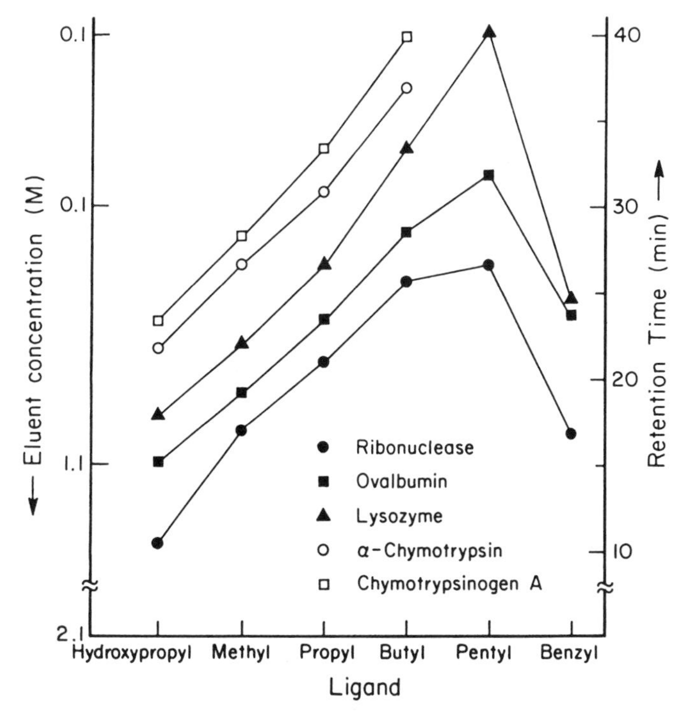

FIGURE 6–7. Effect of ligand arm on retention. SynChropak HIC columns as indicated, 250 × 4.1 mm i.d. Flow rate: 1 ml/min mobile phase, 0.1 *M* potassium phosphate (pH 6.8); 30-min gradient from 2 *M* to 0 *M* ammonium sulfate; t_0, 2.1–2.4 min. Proteins: (●) Ribonuclease, (■) ovalbumin, (▲) lysozyme, (○) α-chymotrypsin, and (□) chymotrypsinogen A. (Reprinted from ref. 77, with the permission of Elsevier Science Publishers.)

tamide). Of the first six ligands, hydroxypropyl is the least hydrophobic and pentyl is the most. There are definite retentive differences between ligands, as can be seen in Figure 6–7. Of this series, the propyl ligand, which is mid-range in hydrophobicity, is an excellent choice to begin HIC analysis because most proteins have some retention, yet elute under normal operating conditions. If the protein of choice has extremely long retention on the column, notwithstanding adjustments in salt, pH, and temperature, a shorter chain, such as hydroxypropyl, should be tried. Likewise, if the protein has inadequate retention on the propyl, a longer ligand, such as a pentyl, may be appropriate.

In HIC, proteins are usually eluted with a gradient of decreasing salt concentration (e.g., 2–0 *M*) at neutral pH. The effectiveness of salts for HIC is generally correlated with the lyotropic or Hofmeister series.[68] Ammonium sulfate is well suited for HIC and has commonly been used in the mobile phase. The popularity of ammonium sulfate is due to its high salting-out abilities, its high solubility, and its commercial availability in high purity. Ammonium acetate has been used to a lesser extent and it is weaker in promoting hydrophobic interactions.[69] Surfactants, such as Genapol X-100[23] or CHAPS[70,71] have been used successfully with HIC to increase protein solubility or to change the elution characteristics by its interaction with the support. In an extensive study by Wetlaufer et al. to determine the effect of CHAPS on protein elution in HIC, they observed that the effects were protein specific. For example, Figure 6–8 illustrates that during the isocratic separation of bovine pancreatic trypsin inhibitor (BPTI) and yeast enolase, both proteins elute more rapidly in the presence of CHAPS; however, the effect is much greater for enolase than BPTI, with a resulting reversal in elution order of the two proteins.[78] Organic solvents, such as acetonitrile, can also be added to the mobile phase to aid in elution.[72] Care must be taken, however, to keep the concentration of organics at a low enough level to prevent precipitation of the high concentrations of salt in the mobile phase.

Temperature[73] has also been seen to influence the selectivity in HIC. In HIC, shorter retention times are observed at lower temperatures, in contrast to reversed-phase or ion-exchange chromatography, where elevated temperatures shorten retention. Subambient temperature can increase the stability of labile proteins; however, the effects of lower salt solubility must be considered.

The relationship between protein retention and pH has also been studied by several groups.[61,69,74,77,79] In general, changes in pH produce some selectivity differences but have less effect on protein retention than ligand chain, nature of the salt, or temperature. These pH effects may be due in part to changes in solubility or conformation of the proteins, especially near their p*I* or at extreme pH. Because different HIC columns and mobile phases were used in these studies, the results have not been totally conclusive.

As mentioned previously, HIC has also been employed on weak anion-exchange supports that have multimodal properties.[18,19,75] Although these columns have some selectivity differences from other HIC supports, similar methods can be used for their operation. See Chapters 5 and 8 for an in-depth discussion of this subject.

HIC supports are available in a variety of particle sizes so that they can be used for both analytical and preparative purposes. Because resolution and capacity on 6.5- and 30-μm particle sizes have been seen to be comparable if

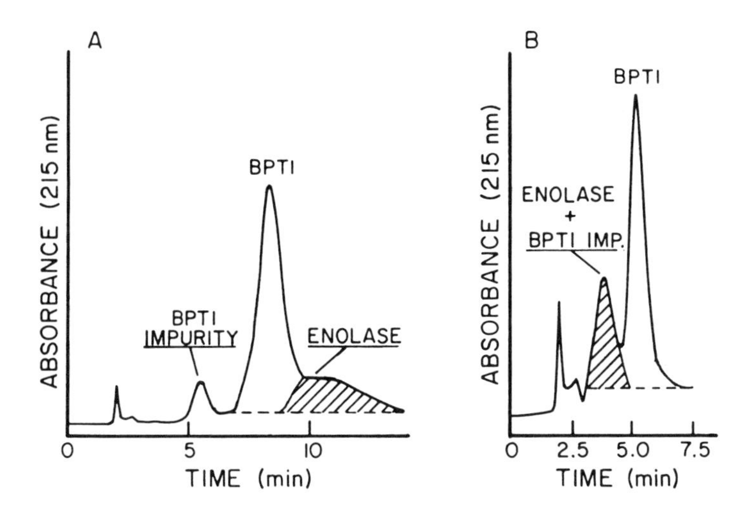

FIGURE 6–8. Effect of CHAPS on protein elution in HIC. Column: SynChropak Propyl. Flow rate: 1 ml/min. Mobile phase: isocratic 1.4 *M* $(NH_4)_2SO_4$, 0.02 *M* phosphate, pH 6.0. (A) Without CHAPS; (B) with 0.82 m*M* CHAPS. Sample: bovine pancreatic trypsin inhibitor (BPTI) and yeast enolase. (Printed with the permission of D. Wetlaufer, J. Buckley and J. Gehas.)

conditions are adjusted appropriately, scaling-up can be achieved with relative ease.[76,77,80] The dynamic loading capacities of HIC supports are high and similar to those of ion exchange (approximately five times as great as those of reversed phase supports). A 250 × 4.6-mm SynChropak Propyl column has a dynamic loading capacity of 20 mg for ovalbumin.[76]

6.2.4 Applications

As HIC has become more popular, scientists have begun to recognize its potential to separate macromolecules with minor compositional and conformational differences by their surface hydrophobicity. The nondenaturing feature of HIC has further enhanced its potential in biochemistry because of the high retention of biological activity after elution.

6.2.4.1 Proteins

HIC has been used for several years by Wittliff et al.[72,81–83] at the Hormone Receptor Laboratory of the University of Louisville as a separations technique for steroid receptors that is complementary to ion exchange. In one study, they used HIC to examine the DNA binding domain of estrogen receptors by selectively modifying the amino acids and/or the receptor and observing the effect on HIC differentiation of the isoforms.[84] In the course of these studies, and others investigating the effect of the stabilizing agent sodium molybdate, on the structure of steroid receptors, several commercial HIC columns have been used effectively to separate the isoforms of estrogen receptors. Figure 6–9 illustrates the excellent resolution obtained on two different columns. The gradients are not identical, due to the difference in hydrophobicity between the two columns.

The pharmaceutical industry has welcomed HPLC assays for stability testing to complement costly and time-consuming biological assays. Such methods aid protein drug formulation by allowing rapid, and potentially more accurate, evaluation of the stability of drug forms based on their tertiary structure. The assays can also determine changes in a protein's chemical and physical properties upon long-term storage. Withka et al.[85] used HIC as one of their HPLC methods to determine structural changes associated with exposure of albumin to urea. They concluded that the data about conformational changes gained by HIC correlate well with classical physical and biochemical methods, such as fluorescence and enzyme activity.

Since HIC is a mild hydrophobic procedure, some proteins that have been considered difficult to analyze because of their strong hydrophobicity in RPC can be separated successfully by HIC. Figure 6–10 illustrates the excellent resolution of ferritin and transferritin with retention of 95% radioactivity by Bischoff.[86]

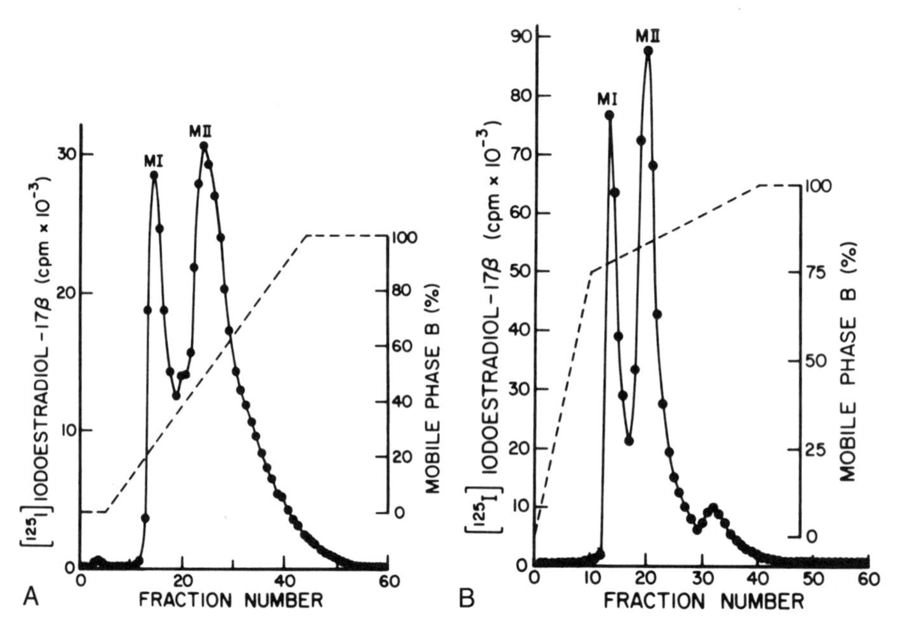

FIGURE 6–9. Analysis of estrogen receptor isoforms by HIC on two columns. Column A: Spherogel CAA-HIC; B: SynChropak Propyl, 100 × 4.6 mm i.d. Buffer A: 2 *M* ammonium sulfate in Buffer B; Buffer B: 10 m*M* phosphate, 1.5 m*M* EDTA, 1 m*M* DTT, 10 m*M* sodium molybdate, 10% v/v glycerol, pH 7.4. Flow rate: 1 ml/min. Gradient: 0–75% B in 10 min, then 75–100% B in 30 min. Sample: Estrogen receptors from human breast cancer labeled with [^{125}I]iodoestradiol. [(A) Reprinted from ref. 84, with the kind permission of Elsevier Science Publishers. Both figures printed with the permission of James Wittliff and Salman Hyder.]

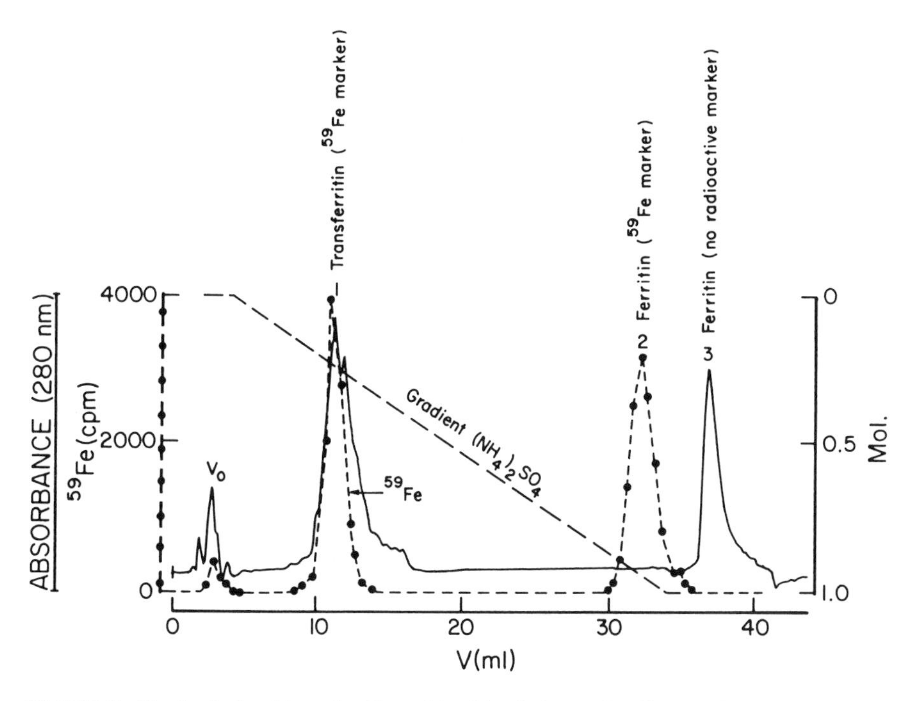

FIGURE 6–10. Analysis of transferritin and ferritin. Column: SynChropak Propyl, 80 × 4.2 mm. Flow rate: 0.5 ml/min. Mobile phase: buffer A: 1 *M* $(NH_4)_2SO_4$ in 0.1 *M* KH_2PO_4, pH 7.0; buffer B: 0.1 *M* KH_2PO_4, pH 7.0. Sample: (1) human transferritin, (2) human ferritin, and (3) bovine ferritin. Note: Recovery = 95% radioactivity. (Reprinted from ref. 86, with the permission of *Labor. Praxis.*)

6.2.4.2 Peptides

Alpert[87,88] investigated the utility of HIC as an alternative or a complementary technique to RPC for peptide separations. In Figure 6–11, it can be seen that peptides with differences of a single hydrophobic residue can be separated easily by HIC.[87] Alpert[88] also found that HIC is broadly applicable to the purification of other peptides, including large polypeptides such as those found in snake venom.

Because the biological activity of calcitonin has been shown to be related to structural features, particularly the spacing of hydrophobic and hydrophilic residues in positions 8–22, Heinitz et al.[89] examined its structure by HIC. Figure 6–12 exemplifies the high sensitivity of HIC to changes in the polypeptide primary structure because most of the modified analogues are well separated from the parent compound, salmon calcitonin. No direct relationship was found between amino acid composition and chromatographic retention; however, a correlation does seem to be dependent upon the position of the residue in the molecule.[89]

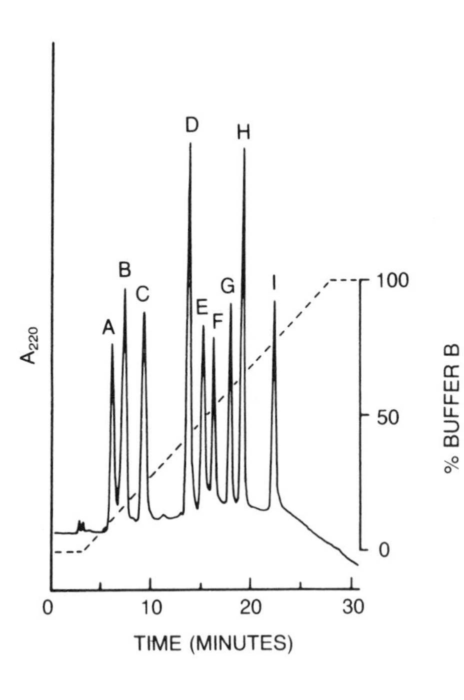

FIGURE 6–11. Resolution of a mixture of peptide standards by HIC. Column: PolyPROPYL Aspartamide, 5 μm, 200 × 4.6 mm i.d. Flow rate: 1.0 ml/min. Buffer A: 2 *M* ammonium sulfate and 0.025 *M* potassium phosphate, pH 6.5; Buffer B: 0.025 *M* potassium phosphate, pH 6.5. Sample, 5–10 μg of each peptide in 25 μl of a 1:2 mixture of Buffer A and Buffer B. Samples: (A) substance P(1–9); (B) [Arg⁸]-vasopressin; (C) oxytocin; (D) substance P, free acid; (E) [Tyr⁸]-substance P; (F) substance P; (G) [Tyr¹¹]-somatostatin; (H) somatostatin; (I) [Tyr¹]-somatostatin. (Reprinted from ref. 88, with the permission of Elsevier Science Publishers.)

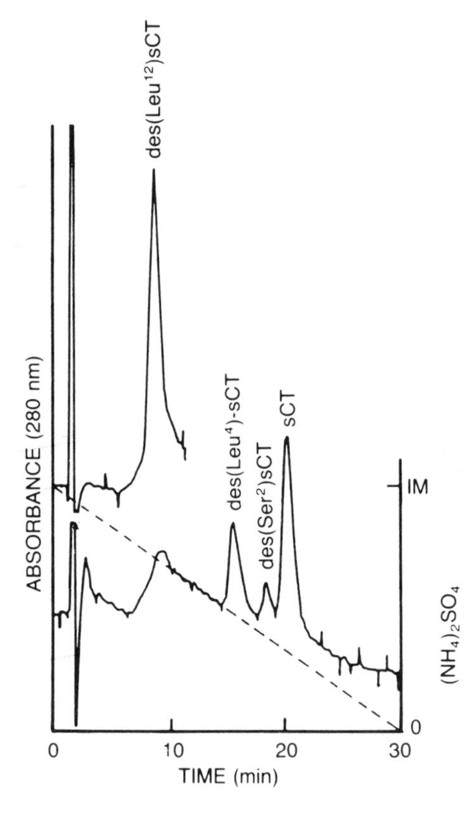

FIGURE 6–12. Separation of modified calcitonins by HIC. Column: SynChropak Propyl, 100 × 4.6 mm i.d. Flow rate: 1 ml/min. Mobile phase: Buffer A: 1 *M* $(NH_4)_2SO_4$, 0.02 *M* phosphate, pH 7; Buffer B: 0.02 *M* phosphate, pH 7.0. (Printed with the permission of M. Heinitz, E. Flanigin, and F. Regnier.)

6.3 CONCLUSIONS

Silica-based HPLC supports, in both the ion-exchange and hydrophobic-interaction modes, have proven to be very well-suited for protein analysis. The generally high quality of HPLC-grade silica results in well-packed columns of high efficiencies and resolution. The rigid matrix allows a wide range of flow rates to be feasible, as well as compatibility with most solvents and additives. The reactivity of the silica makes derivatization by many synthetic routes to be relatively simple. The availability of appropriate pore diameters, in particular, 300 Å, enables high loading capacities for proteins to be achieved, along with excellent resolution. The wide range of important applications cited in this paper and in the current literature emphasizes the invaluable contribution of silica-based supports to the advancement of biochemical research.

REFERENCES

1. F. E. Regnier and R. Noel, *J. Chromatogr. Sci.*, 14 (1979) 316.
2. S. H. Chang, K. M. Gooding, and F. E. Regnier, *J. Chromatogr.*, (1976) 321.
3. S. H. Chang, R. Noel, and F. E. Regnier, *Anal. Chem.*, 48 (1976) 1839.
4. S. H. Chang, K. M. Gooding, and F. E. Regnier, *J. Chromatogr.*, 125 (1976) 103.
5. R. J. Siezen and E. D. Kaplan, *J. Chromatogr.*, 444 (1988) 239.
6. A. J. Alpert and F. E. Regnier, *J. Chromatogr.*, 185 (1979) 375.
7. G. Vanecek and F. E. Regnier, *Anal. Biochem.*, 109 (1980) 345.
8. G. Vanecek and F. E. Regnier, *Anal. Biochem.*, 121 (1982) 156.
9. K. M. Gooding and M. N. Schmuck, *J. Chromatogr.*, 266 (1983) 633.
10. A. Alpert, *J. Chromatogr.*, 266 (1983) 23.
11. S. Gupta, E. Pfannkoch, and F. E. Regnier, *Anal. Biochem.*, 128 (1983) 196.
12. F. E. Regnier, *Science*, 238 (1987) 319.
13. R. M. Chicz and F. E. Regnier, *J. Chromatogr.*, 443 (1988) 193.
14. W. Kopaciewicz, M. A. Rounds, J. Fausnaugh, and F. E. Regnier, *J. Chromatogr.*, 266 (1983) 3.
15. K. M. Gooding and M. N. Schmuck, *J. Chromatogr.*, 327 (1985) 139.
16. J. Fausnaugh-Pollitt, G. Thevenon, L. Janis, and F. E. Regnier, *J. Chromatogr.*, 443 (1988) 221.
17. K. M. Gooding and M. N. Schmuck, *J. Chromatogr.*, 296 (1984) 321.
18. M. L. Heinitz, L. Kennedy, W. Kopaciewicz, and F. E. Regnier, *J. Chromatogr.*, 443 (1988) 173.
19. L. A. Kennedy, W. Kopaciewicz, and F. E. Regnier, *J. Chromatogr.*, 359 (1986) 73.
20. D. M. Boyle, R. D. Wiehle, N. A. Shahabi, and J. L. Wittliff, *J. Chromatogr.*, 327 (1985) 369.
21. L. A. Van Der Walt and J. L. Wittliff, *J. Chromatogr.*, 425 (1988) 277.
22. G. S. Ott and V. G. Shore, *J. Chromatogr.*, 231 (1982) 1.
23. D. Josic, W. Hofmann, and W. Reutter, *J. Chromatogr.*, 371 (1986) 43.
24. N. E. Tandy, R. A. Dilley, and F. E. Regnier, *J. Chromatogr.*, 266 (1983) 599.
25. Z. El Rassi and C. Horvath, *J. Chromatogr.*, 359 (1986) 255.
26. R. W. Stringham and F. E. Regnier, *J. Chromatogr.*, in press.

27. T. D. Schlabach, S. H. Chang, K. M. Gooding, and F. E. Regnier, *J. Chromatogr.*, 134 (1977) 91.
28. J. A. Fulton, T. D. Schlabach, J. E. Kerl, and E. C. Toren, Jr., *J. Chromatogr.*, 175 (1979) 269.
29. T. D. Schlabach, A. J. Alpert, and F. E. Regnier, *Clin. Chem.*, 24 (1978) 1351.
30. W. D. Bostick, M. S. Denton, and S. R. Dinsmore, *Clin. Chem.*, 26 (1980) 172.
31. A. H. B. Wu and T. G. Gornet, *Clin. Chem.*, 31(4) (1985) 25.
32. A. H. B. Wu, T. G. Gornet, V. H. Wu, R. E. Brockle, and A. Nishikawa, *Clin. Chem.*, 33(3) (1987) 358.
33. F. B. Rudolph and S. W. Clark, *Anal. Biochem.*, 127 (1982) 193.
34. F. B. Rudolph, B. F. Cooper, and J. Greenhut, in Progress in HPLC, Vol. 1 (Parves et al., eds.). VNU Science Press, 1985, p. 133.
35. C. S. Ramadoss and B. Axelrod, *Anal. Biochem.*, 127 (1982) 25.
36. Y. Funae, A. N. Kotake, and K. Tamamoto, in Progress in HPLC, Vol. 1 (Parves et al., eds.). VNU Science Press, 1985, p. 59.
37. C. T. Johnson, W. F. Bosron, C. A. Harden, and T. K. Li. *Alcoholism, Clin. Exp. Res.*, 11(1) (1987) 60.
38. J. E. Baker, *Insect Biochem.*, 17(1) (1985) 37.
39. S. V. Singh, G. A. S. Ansari, and Y. C. Awasthi, *J. Chromatogr.*, 361 (1986) 337.
40. K. M. Gooding, K. C. Lu, and F. E. Regnier, *J. Chromatogr.*, 164 (1979) 506.
41. T. H. J. Huisman, M. B. Gardiner, and J. B. Wilson, in Advances in Hemoglobin Analysis (S. M. Hanash and G. J. Brewer, eds.). Liss, New York, 1981, p. 69.
42. T. H. J. Huisman, J. B. Henson, and J. B. Wilson, *J. Lab. Clin. Med.*, 102(2) (1983) 163.
43. J. B. Wilson, M. E. Headlee, and T. H. J. Huisman, *J. Lab. Clin. Med.*, 102(2) (1983) 174.
44. T. H. J. Huisman and J. B. Wilson, *Protides Biol. Fluids*, 32 (1985) 1029.
45. A. Kutlar, F. Kutlar, J. Wilson, M. Headlee, and T. Huisman, *Am. J. Hematol.*, 17(1) (1984) 39.
46. C. N. Ou, G. J. Buffone, and G. L. Reimer, *J. Chromatogr.*, 266 (1983) 197.
47. M. Stallings and E. C. Abraham, *Hemoglobin*, 8(5) (1984) 509.
48. E. C. Abraham, A. Abraham, and M. Stallings, *J. Lab. Clin. Med.*, 104(6) (1984) 1027.
49. E. Bisse, A. Abraham, M. Stallings, R. E. Perry, and E. C. Abraham, *J. Chromatogr.*, 374 (1986) 259.
50. R. M. David and Z. K. Shihabi, *J. Liquid Chromatogr.*, 7(14) (1984) 2875.
51. F. M. Chen, G. S. Naeve, and A. L. Epstein, *J. Chromatogr.*, 444 (1988) 153.
52. J. L. Wittliff, *LCGC*, 4(11) (1986) 1092.
53. L. A. Van Der Walt and J. L. Wittliff, *J. Chromatogr.*, 425 (1988) 277.
54. S. M. Hyder, A. Baldi, M. Crespi, and J. L. Wittliff, *J. Chromatogr.*, 359 (1986) 433.
55. N. Sato, S. M. Hyder, L. Chang, A. Thais, and J. L. Wittliff, *J. Chromatogr.*, 359 (1986) 475.
56. R. J. Siezen, E. D. Kaplan, and R. D. Anello, *Biochem. Biophys. Res. Commun.*, 127 (1985) 153.
57. C. T. Mant and R. S. Hodges, *J. Chromatogr.*, 327 (1985) 147.
58. A. J. Alpert and P. C. Andrews, *J. Chromatogr.*, 433 (1988) 85.
59. D. L. Crimmins, J. Gorka, R. S. Thoma, and B. D. Schwartz, *J. Chromatogr.*, 443 (1988) 63.
60. S. Shaltiel and Z. Er-el, *Proc. Natl. Acad. Sci. U.S.A.*, 70 (1973) 778.
61. S. Hjertén, *J. Chromatogr.*, 87 (1973) 325.
62. F. E. Regnier and J. Fausnaugh, *LC Mag.*, 1 (1983) 402.
63. J. L. Fausnaugh, E. Pfannkoch, S. Gupta, and F. E. Regnier, *Anal. Biochem.*, 137 (1984) 464.
64. D. L. Gooding, M. N. Schmuck, and K. M. Gooding, *J. Chromatogr.*, 296 (1984) 107.

65. N. J. Miller, B. Feibush, and B. L. Karger, *J. Chromatogr.*, 316 (1984) 519.
66. Z. El Rassi and C. Horvath, *Chromatographia*, 19 (1985) 9.
67. A. J. Alpert, *J. Chromatogr.*, 359 (1986) 85.
68. W. R. Melander, D. Corradini, and C. Horvath, *J. Chromatogr.*, 317 (1984) 67.
69. M. N. Schmuck, M. P. Nowlan, and K. M. Gooding, *J. Chromatogr.*, 371 (1986) 55.
70. D. B. Wetlaufer and M. R. Koenigbauer, *J. Chromatogr.*, 359 (1986) 55.
71. J. J. Buckley and D. B. Wetlaufer, *J. Chromatogr.*, 464 (1988) 61.
72. S. M. Hyder, R. D. Wiehle, D. W. Brandt, and J. L. Wittliff, *J. Chromatogr.*, 327 (1985) 237.
73. S. L. Wu, K. Benidek, and B. L. Karger, *J. Chromatogr.*, 359 (1986) 3.
74. J. L. Fausnaugh, L. A. Kennedy, and F. E. Regnier, *J. Chromatogr.*, 317 (1984) 141.
75. M. D. Potter, B. R. Coryell, S. P. Fulton, and W. Kopaciewicz, *1987 Int. Symp. HPLC*, paper #12 (1987).
76. M. N. Schmuck, K. M. Gooding, and D. L. Gooding, *LC Mag.*, 3(9) (1985) 814.
77. D. L. Gooding, M. N. Schmuck, M. P. Nowlan, and K. M. Gooding, *J. Chromatogr.*, 359 (1986) 331.
78. J. Buckley, J. Gehas, and D. Wetlaufer, personal communication.
79. N. J. Miller and B. L. Karger, *J. Chromatogr.*, 326 (1985) 43.
80. N. J. Miller and C. H. Shiek, *J. Liquid Chromatogr.*, 9 (1986) 3269.
81. S. M. Hyder, N. Sato, and J. L. Wittliff, *J. Chromatogr.*, 397 (1987) 251.
82. S. M. Hyder and J. L. Wittliff, *Current Protocols in Molecular Biology*, Green Publ. Assoc., New York, 1987, p. 10.15.1.
83. S. M. Hyder and J. L. Wittliff, *Biochromatography*, 2 (1987) 121.
84. S. M. Hyder and J. L. Wittliff, *J. Chromatogr.*, 444 (1988) 225.
85. J. Withka, P. Morcuse, A. Baziotis, and R. Maskiewiecz, *J. Chromatogr.*, 398 (1987) 175.
86. K. Bischoff, *Labor Praxis*, January–February (1986) 58.
87. A. J. Alpert, *Biochromatography*, 2 (1987) 131.
88. A. J. Alpert, *J. Chromatogr.*, 444 (1988) 269.
89. M. L. Heinitz, F. Flanigan, R. Orlowski, and F. E. Regnier, *J. Chromatogr.*, 443 (1988) 229.

CHAPTER 7

High-Performance Ion-Exchange Chromatography of Proteins

M. I. Aguilar, A. N. Hodder, and Milton T. W. Hearn

CONTENTS

7.1 INTRODUCTION

High-performance ion-exchange chromatography (HPIEC) is now extensively used in the high-resolution analysis of peptides, proteins, and polynucleotides and represents an integral part of the battery of chromatographic regimes available for biomacromolecular purification. The early stages of a purification strategy generally utilize solubility parameters to carry out initial fractionation based on such techniques as salt or solvent precipitation. Differences in size and shape of biopolymers are then exploited through application of gel permeation and preparative electrophoretic techniques (e.g., preparative free flow electrophoresis). Adsorptive techniques, such as HPIEC and reversed-phase high-performance liquid chromatography (RP-HPLC), however, enable separation protocols to be introduced that enable rapid increases in the level of resolution, recovery, and product purity.

The success of these interactive modes of chromatography is due to the ability of the specific technique to probe the surface topography of a biopolymer, such as the asymmetry of coulombic charge by HPIEC methods or the regional hydrophobicity by RP-HPLC procedures, through selective interaction between an immobilized liquid on the surface of the stationary phase and the biopolymer in question. A significant advantage of HPIEC over other adsorptive modes is the nondenaturing effects of the solutions used in the elution of proteins from ion-exchange sorbents. While gross conformational changes are often associated with RP-HPLC, these effects are less evident or not generally observed in HPIEC of peptides, proteins, and polynucleotides.

The wide utility of HPIEC for protein purification is demonstrated by reference to the selected examples listed in Table 7–1. However, the enormous potential for the optimization of solute selectivity in HPIEC through rational, predictive manipulation of protein surface charge distribution has yet to be fully exploited. Recent advances in the preparation of pressure-stable, microparticulate ion-exchange sorbents with pore diameters greater than 200 Å,[1–4] together with the development of theoretical models to describe protein retention behavior in ion-exchange systems[5–7] are now enabling this situation to be redressed.

Protein retention to an ion-exchange surface is believed to predominantly arise from electrostatic interactions between the protein surface and the charged stationary phase. Accordingly, the conventional "net-charge" concept has been widely used[8,9] as a predictive basis to anticipate the retention characteristics of proteins with both anion- and cation-exchange resins. Commercially available materials are often characterized and marketed on the basis of this principle. The hypothetical relationship between protein net charge and chromatographic retention is depicted in Figure 7–1. According to this classical model, a protein will be retained on a cation-exchange column if the solvent pH is lower than the known p*I* value of the protein, since under these conditions the protein will carry net positive charges. Conversely, a protein will be retained on an anion-exchange resin when the eluent pH is above the protein's p*I*. Furthermore, with mobile phases operating at a pH equal to the protein's p*I*, the surface of the protein is considered to be overall electrostatically neutral.

TABLE 7–1. Selected Examples of Proteins Purified by HPIEC

Protein	Column	Mobile Phase	Reference
Transferrin	AX-300	0.004 *M* Na_2PO_4, pH 7.8, 0.06 *M* NaCl, 40 min, 0.7 ml/min	71
Red cell membrane Proteins	Mono-Q	50 m*M* $CH_3CH_2NH_2$, pH 9.0, 1 ml/min	72
Estrogen receptor	KH_2PO_4	pH 7.4, 1 ml/min	73
Lipoxidase	DEAE-5PW	0.01 *M* Tris, pH 8, 0–0.5 *M* NaCl, 60 min, 1 ml/min	74
Superoxide dismutase	DEAE-5PW	0.02 *M* Tris, pH 7.5, 0–0.3 *M* NaCl, 30 min, 1 ml/min	74
Growth hormone	DEAE-5PW	0.02 *M* glycine, pH 8, 0.075–0.5 *M* NaCl, 60 min, 1 ml/min	74
α-Toxin	Mono-Q	20 m*M* bis-Tris, pH 6, 0.1 *M* NaCl, 20 min, 1 ml/min	75
Gelatinase	Mono-Q	0.01 m*M* Tris, pH 8.4, 0.005 *M* CaCl, 20% glycerol, 0.03% Brij 35, 0.03 *M* NaCl, 55 min, 1 ml/min	76
Progesterone receptor	Mono-Q	0.01 *M* Tris, pH 7.5, 0.015 *M* EDTA, 0.1 *M* NaCl, 60 min, 1 ml/min	77
Dopamine β-hydroxylase	AX-300	0.02 *M* KH_2PO_4, pH 6.8, 0.04–0.76 NaCl, 45 min, 1 ml/min	78
Papaya latex proteotylic enzymes	SP-5PW	0.02–1.0 *M* NaOAc, pH 5, 75 min, 1 ml/min	79
Uridine specific acid nuclease	Mono-S	0.01 *M* KH_2PO_4, pH 6, 0–0.14 *M* KCl, 2 min, 1 ml/min	80
Estrogen synthetase	Mono-Q	0.02 *M* Tris-acetate, pH 7.5, 0.02 *M* EDTA, 20% glycerol, 0.5%	81
Immunoglobulin G	DEAE-545	0.05 *M* Na_2HPO_4, pH 7, 0.05 *M* NaCl, step gradient, 1 ml/min	82
Calmodulin	PEI	0.025 *M* KH_2PO_4, pH 7, 0–1 *M* $(NH_4)_2SO_4$, 15 min, 1 ml/min	83
Immunoglobulin M	Mono-Q	0.02 *M* histidine, pH 6, 0–0.5 *M* NaCl, 25 min, 1 ml/min	84
Epidermal growth factor	IEX-545k	0.05 *M* Tris, pH 8, 0–0.5 *M* NaCl, 30 min, 1 ml/min	85

(*continued*)

TABLE 7–1. Selected Examples of Proteins Purified by HPIEC (*continued*)

Protein	Column	Mobile Phase	Reference
Milk proteins	Mono-Q	0.02 *M* Tris, pH 7, 0–0.35 *M* NaCl, 20 min, 1 ml/min	86
Milk proteins	Mono-S	0.05 *M* NaHCOOH, 0–0.3 *M* NaCl, 20 min, 1 ml/min	86
Topoisomerase I	CM-300	0.01 *M* Na_2HPO_4, 0.0015 M EDTA, 0.001 *MDTT*, 10% glycerol 0–0.5 *M* NaCl, 40 min, 1 ml/min	87
Progestin receptor	AX-1000	0.01 *M* sodium molybdate, 0.0015 *M* EDTA, 0.001 *M* DTT, 10% glycerol, pH 7.4, 0.01–0.3 *M* KH_2PO_4, 49 min, 1 ml/min	88
Glycoprotein hormones	Mono-Q	0.02 *M* Tris, pH 7.6, 0–0.3 *M* NaCl, 33 min 1 ml/min	89
Adenovirus hexon proteins	Mono-Q	0.05 *M* bis-Tris, pH 6.5, 0–0.5 *M* NaCl, 60 min, 4 ml/min	90
Lutropin	Mono-Q	0.02 *M* piperazine, pH 9.6, 0.01–0.3 *M* NaCl, 34.3 min, 1 ml/min	91
Estrogen receptor	AX-1000	0.01–0.5 *M* Na_2HPO_4, 40 min, 1 ml/min	92
Glycoproteins	Mono-Q	0.02 *M* bis-Tris, pH 7.5, 0–0.35 *M* NaCl, pH 9.5, 40 min, 10 ml/min	93
Glucose oxidase	DEAEHP-A	0.03 *M* Tris, pH 7.6, 0–0.3 *M* NaOAc, 30 min, 0.2 ml/min	94
Catalase	DEAEHP-A	0.03 *M* Tris, pH 7.6, 0–0.16 *M* NaOAc, 30 min, 0.2 ml/min	94
Ribosomal 30 S proteins	Mono-S	6 *M* urea, 0.05 *M* MES, pH 6.5, 0–0.7 KCl, 43 min, 2 ml/min	95
Cardiodilatin	Mono-S	0.02–0.5 *M* NH_4HCO_3, pH 7, 4 ml/min	96
Acetohydroxy acid synthase	Mono-Q	0.025 *M* Na_2HPO_4, pH 7, 0.005 *M* pyruvate, 0.005 *M* EDTA, 0–0.5 *M* KCl, 20 min, 1 ml/min	97
Pituitary extract	Poly-A	0.005 *M* KH_2PO_4, pH 3, 25% CH_3CN, 0–0.2 *M* KCl, 40 min, 1 ml/min	98
Pollen extract	DEAE-545	0.02–0.5 *M* NaOAc, 45 min, 1 ml/min	99
Heat shock protein	Mono-Q	0.02 *M* Na_2HPO_4, 0.001 *M* EDTA, pH 7.4, 0.2–0.6 *M* NaCl, 30 min, 1 ml/min	100

TABLE 7–1. Selected Examples of Proteins Purified by HPIEC (*continued*)

Protein	Column	Mobile Phase	Reference
High mobility group protein	Mono-S	0.01 *M* $NaBO_4$, pH 8.8, 0.2–0.44 *M* NaCl, 10 min, 4 ml/min	101
Aldehyde dehydrogenase isoenzymes	DEAE-5PW	0.005–0.25 *M*, Na_2HPO_4, pH 7, 30 min, 0.5 ml/min	102
Adrenal medulla endopeptidase	Mono-Q	0.02 *M* Tris, 0.001 *M* DTT, 0.001 *M* EDTA, pH 8, 0–1 *M* NaCl, 50 min, 2 ml/min	103
Monoclonal Fab fragment	Mono-S	0.062–0.366 m*M* NaOAc, pH 4.0, 40 min, 1 ml/min	104
1,4,5-Inositol	Part-SAX	0.15 *M* NH_4OAc, pH 4, 1.5 ml/min	105
Adenosine deaminase	Mono-Q	0.02 *M* Tris, pH 7.5, 0.05–0.5 *M* KCl, 45 min, 0.5 ml/min	106
Lysozyme	CM-2-SW	0.2–1 *M* NH_4OAc, pH 3.5, 70 min, 1 ml/min	107
Restriction endonuclease	Mono-Q	0.02 *M* Tris, pH 7.4, 5% glycerol, 0–0.7 *M* NaCl, 24 min, 1 ml/min	108
Growth hormone	Mono-Q	0.05 *M* Tris, pH 8.0, 30% CH_3CN, 0–0.3 *M* NaCl, 25 min, 1 ml/min	109
Serum albumin	Polyol	0.005 *M* KH_2PO_4, pH 7.0, 0.05 *M* NaCl, 30 min, 2 ml/min	110

Under these conditions the protein should not be retained on either cation- or anion-exchange resins.

Because of the progress made over the past decade in terms of greater insight into the relationship between structure, surface topography, and chromatographic retention, this classical model is now recognized as representing a simplistic approach to describing protein retention in HPIEC. The amphoteric nature of proteins results in the existence of localized areas of interactive electrostatic charge potential as the pH of the mobile phase is manipulated. These localized coulombic areas in turn gives rise to the ability of the protein to undergo electrostatic interactions even though the protein may be at its isoelectric point.

In various recent investigations[5,10–17] the influence of mobile phase composition on the chromatographic behavior of proteins separated on several different ion-exchange resins has been extensively documented. Studies from various laboratories have examined the effect of ionic strength, pH, buffer type, and concentration and also the nature of the counterion and coion on the chromatographic behavior of several proteins in HPIEC. What these studies have revealed is that the magnitude of electrostatic interactions between the

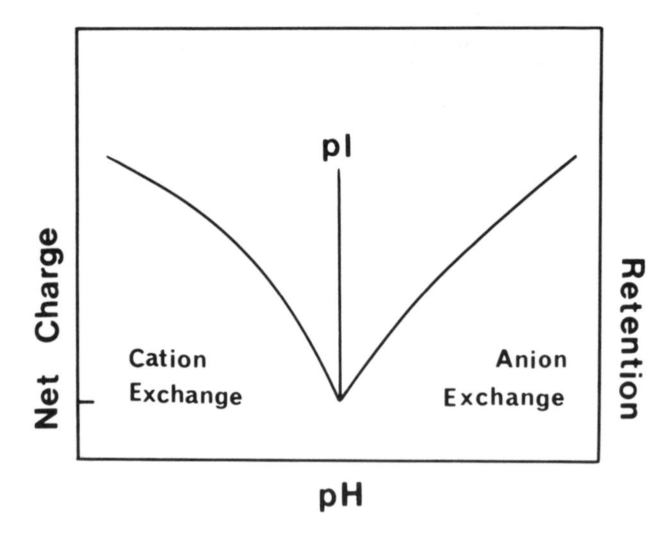

FIGURE 7–1. The theoretical relationship between protein net charge and chromatographic retention in ion-exchange chromatography.

solute and the sorbent surface in HPIEC is dependent on several key structural and chromatographic factors. These include

1. the number and distribution of charged sites on the solute molecule that define the surface topography and electrostatic contact area of the protein that interact with the stationary phase,
2. the charge density of the stationary phase, and
3. the mobile phase composition.

Thus, variation of the chromatographic experimental parameters alters the affinity of the solute for the stationary phase. This occurs through changes in the overall electrostatic surface charge ratio by protonation/deprotonation or through specific electrostatic interactions of the displacer coions and counterions with surface charge groups on the protein solute or the coulombic ligand. Furthermore, it is often assumed that these interactions will take place at the surface of a conformationally intact protein. However, subtle changes in the three-dimensional structure of the protein, which may result from time-dependent exposure of the protein to certain chemical environments present in the mobile phase and/or at the stationary phase surface, will also have significant effects on solute retention characteristics.

The concept of a regionally dominant coulombic interaction site, the ionotope, as depicted in Figure 7–2, and the ability to identify the location of these sites within the surface structure of specific proteins is central to elucidating the mechanistic basis of HPIEC of proteins. An overall picture of the vagaries of structure–retention relationships is required if appropriate selection of mobile phase composition is to be made based on experimental procedures that adequately manipulate the molecular forces involved in the elution process. This chapter therefore reviews recent experimental and theoretical develop-

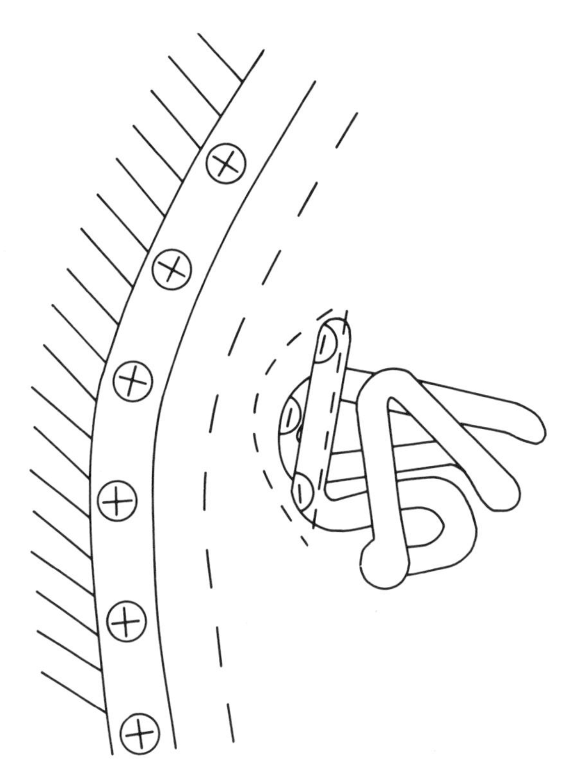

FIGURE 7–2. Schematic representation of the ionotope, the charged interactive binding site on the protein surface. This diagram shows a negatively charged section of the protein surface that is interacting with a positively charged anion-exchange stationary phase.

ments that characterize HPIEC of proteins, and describes recent advances in the evolution of fully mechanistic models that describe, in physicochemical terms, the nature of the interaction between biological macromolecules and charged biological and synthetic surfaces. These developments hold important implications for the future development of computer-aided optimization models for solute elution as well as the manner in which preparative HPIEC in the overload mode will be carried out with optimal efficiency. The reader is also referred elsewhere to several seminal articles or chapters that have specifically addressed these issues in recent years.[5–7,10,12,14]

7.2 RETENTION RELATIONSHIPS OF PROTEINS IN HPIEC

Insight into the mechanistic behavior of proteins at an ion-exchange surface can be obtained from a number of experimental methods, including (1) evaluation of the molecular characteristics of structure–retention behavior, (2) analysis of isothermal behavior and adsorption–desorption kinetics, and (3) physicochemical treatments that provide quantitative information on protein volume or area occupancy at the surface or data on the minimum approach distance. Despite the enormous extent of the applications literature available for peptide, protein, or polynucleotide IEC, the extent of systematic experimentation, which could form the data base needed for the above three requirements, is currently limited to a small group of "model" proteins, e.g., serum albumin and dehydrogenases. These limitations restrict the general application of optimization routines at both the analytical and the preparative (process) levels. These limitations also restrict the thermodynamic interpretation of biosolute behavior in the vicinity of a coulombic surface. For example, studies on the adsorption of polyelectrolytes at charged surfaces[18] established that the structure of adsorbed solute layers is governed by a subtle balance between enthalpic and entropic factors. For homopolymers, such as polylysine with a repeating segmental unit, these factors include the segmental adsorption energy, the chain conformation entropy, the entropy of mixing segments in a defined solvent, and the interaction between segments and solvent components. Application of similar theoretical treatments to heteropolymers (e.g., proteins) has yet to reach a generalized stage that can describe the behavior at coulombic interfaces of biopolymers. Such a generalized theoretical treatment would have to accommodate biopolymers with asymmetric charge distribution and compositionally different segments, which do not behave like statistical coils. In addition, the unique tertiary or quaternary hierarchical structures such as those found for globular proteins or membrane proteins, would have to be accommodated if a generalized thermodynamic treatment of biopolymer adsorption was to have wide applicability.

The extension of these similar physicochemical approaches to the dynamic interactive systems of chromatographic separations has also not been established. Several recent advances[5,19–21] in both theoretical and experimental aspects of interactive modes of HPLC have resulted in the empirical development of optimization models for protein separation on microparticulate stationary phases. These models were generally adapted from retention models for small-molecular-weight solutes and modified to account for multivalent attachment sites. Originally, these theoretical treatments provided a useful basis for assessing the retention[22,23] and bandwidth behavior[24,25] of proteins separated under both isocratic and gradient elution conditions in reversed-phase HPLC. These developments stimulated more detailed investigations[26,27] on the physicochemical phenomena associated with the interaction of biomacromolecules with hydrophobic surfaces. More recently, similar theoretical models have also been extended[5,6,10,14–17] to describe protein retention phenomena with multivalent charged interactions, on modern HPIEC materials.

The physicochemical basis of all modes of liquid chromatography can be described by the solvophobic theory[28–30] where the isocratic retention factor, k', can be expressed as

$$\ln k' = -1/RT\,\Delta G^\circ + \ln(RT/PV) + \Phi \qquad (7\text{–}1)$$

where ΔG° is the overall difference between mobile and stationary phase in unitary Gibbs free energy and Φ represents a functional relationship to the system phase ratio. The terms V and P are the mean molar volume of solvent and the operating pressure, respectively. The Gibbs free energy change, ΔG° is represented by

$$\Delta G^\circ = \Delta G^\circ_{cav} + \Delta G^\circ_{es} + \Delta G^\circ_{vdw} + \Delta G^\circ_{assoc} + \Delta G^\circ_{red} \qquad (7\text{–}2)$$

where ΔG°_{cav}, ΔG°_{es}, and ΔG°_{vdw} are the differences between mobile and stationary phases in free energy associated with formation of a cavity of molecular dimensions of the solute, electrostatic effects, and van der Waals interactions, respectively. ΔG°_{assoc} is the free energy change for ligand–eluite association in the absence of surrounding solvent, i.e., in the gas phase. ΔG°_{red} expresses the reduction in free energy due to solvent–ligand and solvent–solute interactions not treated in the first three terms and represents a correction factor for non-ideal behavior.

Retention in HPIEC is largely dependent on the degree of electrostatic interaction between the solute molecules and the stationary phase surface. The electrostatic free energy change associated with the chromatographic retention process can then be expressed as

$$\Delta G^\circ_{es} = \Delta G^\circ_{es,s} - \Delta G^\circ_{es,m} \qquad (7\text{–}3)$$

where s and m refer to the stationary and mobile phases, respectively. In the simplest case, the magnitude of the electrostatic force, F, between two point charges, Q_1 and Q_2, separated by distance, r, is given by

$$F = \frac{Q_1 Q_2}{\epsilon_m r^2} \qquad (7\text{–}4)$$

where ϵ_m is the dielectric constant of the medium. The theoretical dependence of electrostatic energy on the distance between two charged bodies is shown in Figure 7–3. The increasing electrostatic attractive energy of a system where two species of opposite charge are brought progressively closer together until a minimum separation distance is reached is illustrated on the right side of Figure 7–3. This region corresponds to the adsorption phase of HPIEC. Conversely, the energy associated with the repulsion between two molecules of similar charge is illustrated on the left side of Figure 7–3, where a decrease in the separation distance results in an increase in the repulsive energy. As solute retention in HPIEC arises from attractive electrostatic interactions the degree of repulsion depicted in Figure 7–3 can be assessed only indirectly from ion-exchange chromatographic data, e.g., from deviations in the hydrodynamic elution volume. However, these conditions will exist, for example, when proteins are chromatographed in anion-exchange systems at pH levels well below their known pI, i.e., when the surface of the protein assumes an overall positive charge resulting in repulsion between the solute and cationic groups at the surface of the stationary phase.

In the HPIEC of proteins, the stationary phase and solute cannot be represented as point interacting charges. In particular, the amphoteric nature of proteins significantly complicates their treatment as a single charged species.

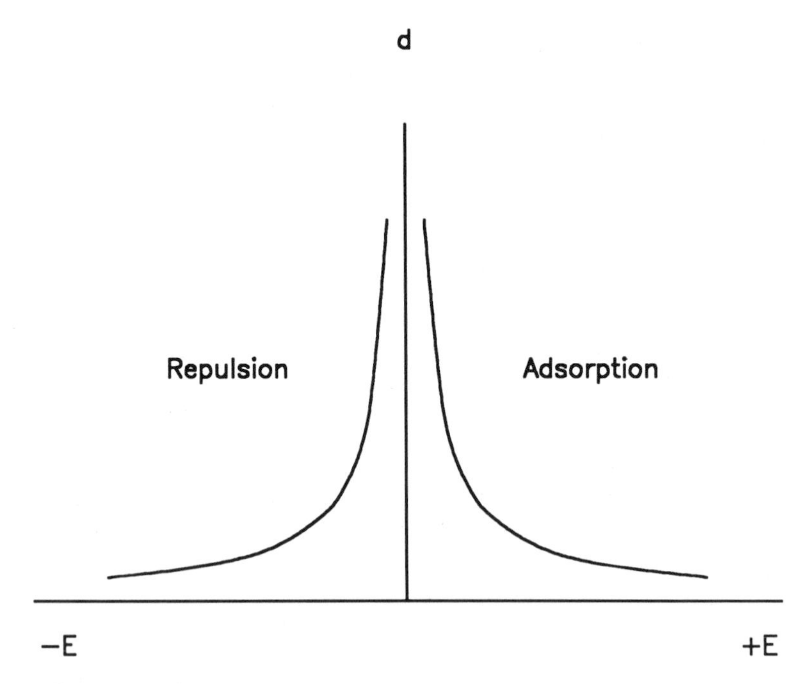

FIGURE 7–3. Plot of the theoretical dependence of the distance between two oppositely or similarly charged particles on the electrostatic energy of attraction (+E) or repulsion (−E).

In high-performance anion-exchange chromatography, for example, it is often assumed that protein solutes interact with the stationary phase exclusively through the surface anionic groups. In this case, the magnitude of the electrostatic interaction will depend on several factors. These include (1) the number of charged sites on the solute molecule that interact simultaneously with the packing, (2) the charge density of the packing, i.e., its zeta (ζ) potential, and (3) the mobile phase composition.

Over 30 years ago, Boardman and Partridge described a theoretical treatment for ion-exchange chromatography of polyelectrolytes on conventional weak cation exchangers.[8] In this model, polyelectrolytes in equilibrium at the ion-exchange surface with smaller displacing ions were assumed to be bound to the surface at multiple sites. A nonmechanistic stoichiometric equation similar to that proposed by Boardman and Partridge can be written for the mass balance distribution of a solute molecule, $P^{\pm a}$ of charge $\pm a$, in HPIEC as follows

$$(P^{\pm a})_{\mathrm{m}} + (a/b)(D^{\pm b})_{\mathrm{s}} \rightleftharpoons (P^{\pm a})_{\mathrm{s}} + (a/b)(D^{\pm b})_{\mathrm{m}} \qquad (7\text{–}5)$$

where $D^{\pm b}$ is the displacer counterion and subscripts m and s represent the mobile and stationary phase, respectively. From the above equation, the equilibrium constant for the interaction of a protein with an ion-exchange surface under static (near equilibrium) conditions can be represented as

$$K_b = \frac{[P^{\pm a}]_s \, [D^{\pm b}]_m^{Z_t}}{[P^{\pm a}]_m \, [D^{\pm b}]_s^{Z_t}} \tag{7–6}$$

where Z_t for large molecules, such as proteins, represents the stoichiometric charge ratio (a/b), of the charges associated with the adsorption–desorption process. If near-equilibrium conditions can be assumed for an isocratic chromatographic process associated with the transport of a protein along an ion-exchange support, then the following form of the Taylor series expression can also be employed to represent the relationship between retention of the polyelectrolyte solute and the concentration, c, of the displacer salt,

$$\log k' = \alpha + \beta[\log(1/c)] + \gamma[\log(1/c)]^3 + \delta[\log(1/c)]^2 \cdots \tag{7–7}$$

where k' is the capacity factor and α, β, γ, and δ are coefficients dependent on the solubility parameter of the solute, the stationary phase ζ-potential and the mobile phase composition, polarizability, and dielectric properties. Over a limited range of salt concentrations the relationship between log k' and log 1/ c is often approximated to a linear dependency given in the familiar empirical form

$$\log k' = \log K_0 + Z_c \log(1/c) \tag{7–8}$$

where K_0 is the distribution coefficient, which incorporates several terms including the binding constant K_b, the phase ratio Φ, and the stationary phase ligand concentration, L, in the following manner:

$$K_0 = \frac{K_b \Phi L Z_0}{ab} \tag{7–9}$$

where a and b adjust for solute and salt valency. Under linear elution conditions, values for Z_c and log K, which can be used to characterize the retention behavior of a particular solute, can be determined for a narrow range of ionic strengths by linear regression analyses of plots of log k' versus log$(1/c)$. The Z_c coefficient defined in Eq. (7–8) is not formally equivalent in mathematical or physicochemical terms to the Z_t term of Eq. (7–6) or indeed the Z_0 term as defined in Eq. (7–9). The Z_c term is an experimentally determined parameter that reflects the apparent number of ionic charges associated with the adsorption–desorption process at the chromatographic surface of a specific sorbent. Consequently, the Z_c term is an important "reporter" parameter, not only of the topography of the biopolymer, but also of the surface characteristics of the sorbent.

While isocratic elution conditions offer an additional dimension for high-resolution protein purification, complex mixtures of proteins are commonly separated under gradient-elution conditions, where advantage can be taken of band compression effects. The fundamental principles of gradient elution of low-molecular-weight solutes are now well established.[19] Various mathematical expressions have been developed that relate isocratic and gradient elution parameters under a wide range of experimental conditions. In some instances these relationships also allow the accurate prediction of solute retention and bandwidth properties in ion-exchange,[6,16] reversed-phase,[22–25] and hydrophobic interaction[31] chromatography. For example, the retention time, t_g, of a conformationally rigid solute under linear solvent strength (LSS) gradient-elution conditions can be expressed as

$$t_g = (t_0/b)[\log 2.3k_0b] + t_0 + t_e \qquad (7\text{–}10)$$

where t_0 is the column dead time, k_0 is the capacity factor for the solute under the initial gradient conditions, t_e is the time taken for eluent B to reach the column inlet and b is the gradient steepness parameter. Evaluation of b can be easily achieved by several experiments in which different gradient times or flow rates are used. Thus, for elution conditions with fixed column, mobile phase composition and flow rate, the gradient steepness parameter, b, can be derived from the relationship

$$b_1 = t_0 \log \beta/[t_{g1} - (t_{g2}/\beta) + (t_{G1} - t_{G2})/t_{G2}] \qquad (7\text{–}11)$$

where t_{g1} and t_{g2} are the solute gradient retention times at gradient times t_{G1} and t_{G2}, respectively, and β is the ratio of the gradient times (t_{G2}/t_{G1}). If chromatographic data are obtained at flow rates F_1 and F_2, while the gradient time is maintained constant, then b values may be obtained from

$$b_1 = \log(F_2/F_1)/[X_1 - X_2(F_1/F_2)] \qquad (7\text{–}12)$$

where

$$X_1 = (t_{g1} - t_{0,1})/t_{0,1} \qquad (7\text{–}13)$$

and

$$X_2 = (t_{g2} - t_{0,2})/t_{0,2} \qquad (7\text{–}14)$$

If it is assumed that the salt gradient in gradient elution HPIEC approximates LSS conditions during the time that a solute molecule migrates through a column, experimental t_g values can then be used to obtain a solution for b from Eqs. (7–11) or (7–12). The median capacity $\bar{k}$ for a particular solute, eluted under these gradient conditions, can then be obtained from

$$\bar{k} = 1/1.15b \qquad (7\text{–}15)$$

where the value of $\overline{k}$ corresponds to the capacity factor for a solute band at the column midpoint. Similarly, the concentration, $\overline{c}$, of the eluting salt when the sample band has reached the column midpoint is given by

$$\overline{c} = c_0 + [t_g - t_0 - t_e - 0.30(t_0/b)]\Delta C/t_G \qquad (7\text{–}16)$$

where $\Delta c = c_f - c_0$ and c_0 and c_f are the initial and final salt concentration. Gradient Z_c values can then be readily determined from iterative analysis of plots of log $\overline{k}$ versus log $1/\overline{c}$.

The LSS model provides a useful method for the optimization of ion-exchange separations of protein samples. However, a limitation of the LSS method is that experimental conditions are still arbitrarily selected. The LSS method optimizes separations from the standpoint of analytical criteria, i.e., minimum bandwidth, linear $\overline{k}$ dependencies over the range $1 < \overline{k} < 20$, and assumed insensitivity of k' to loading conditions. Under preparative conditions, the minimum bandwidth may not be synonymous with the optimal bandwidth, i.e., the recovery of a particular component in bioactive form may require the choice of elution conditions that do not yield minimal peak widths. Optimal efficiency can be obtained only by manipulation of chromatographic parameters based on a fully mechanistic model that accounts for protein structural properties as well as the contribution of both the mobile phase and stationary phase to the separation process.

As indicated above the experimentally derived Z_c value represents a valuable parameter with which to probe the physicochemical basis of protein interactions with charged surfaces through analysis of the influence of different experimental conditions on protein retention behavior. The following sections therefore outline recent studies on characterizing the contribution of both stationary phase and mobile phase properties to macromolecular retention in HPIEC.

7.3 EFFECT OF pH AND IONIC STRENGTH ON PROTEIN RETENTION

7.3.1 Ionic Strength Effects

The magnitude of electrostatic interactions between protein solutes and the sorbent surface in HPIEC is dependent on several key structural and chromatographic factors associated with the protein structure, the charge density of the stationary phase, and the mobile phase composition. Of these factors, the mobile phase composition is the easiest and most convenient to manipulate systematically. It is known that the mobile phase constituents can be changed in a number of ways to influence protein retention. These include variation in displacer ion concentration, the type of displacer ion, the solvent pH, and also the nature and concentration of the buffer species.

The most straightforward method of altering protein retention is through manipulation of the ionic interaction equilibrium through changes in the concentration of the displacing salt. This is illustrated in Figure 7–4, which shows the elution profiles of myoglobin, carbonic anhydrase and ovalbumin at two different sodium chloride concentrations. Figure 7–5 represents the corresponding plots of log k' versus log $1/c$ for these and other globular proteins with sodium chloride again as the displacer salt. The well-documented rapid increase in k' with decreasing salt concentration is clearly evident. In common with similar multisite interaction processes found in reversed-phase HPLC of proteins, curvilinear plots of log k' versus log $1/c$ are also observed. In HPIEC, these curves arise from the existence of mixed mode retention processes that can occur with certain protein solutes. The shape of these plots are typical of peptide, protein, and polynucleotide retention behavior in HPIEC. Representative of this behavior is the hypothetical HPIEC retention curve depicted in

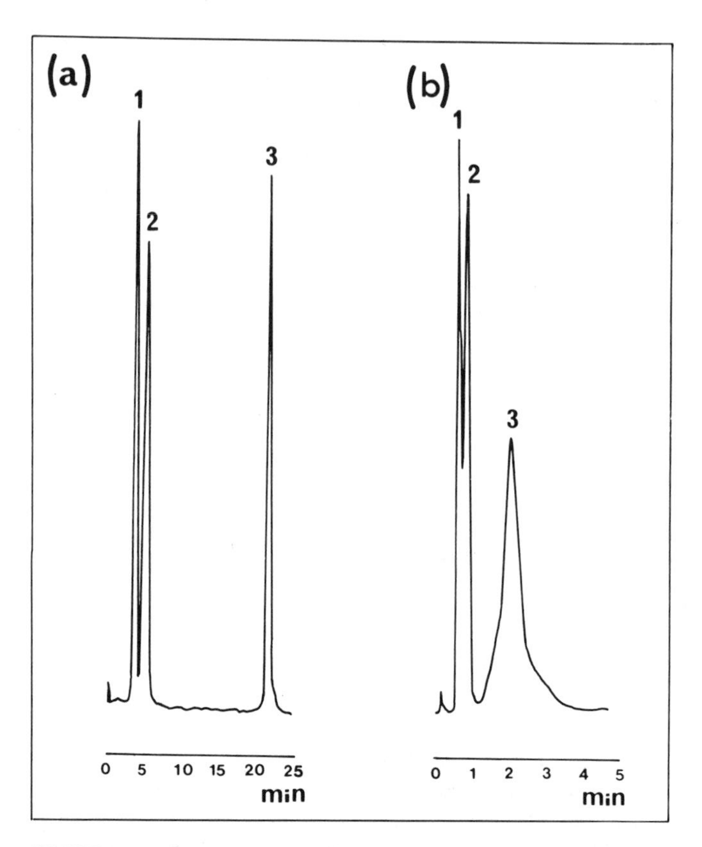

FIGURE 7–4. Elution profile of (1) myoglobin, (2) carbonic anhydrase, and (3) ovalbumin separated isocratically on a Mono-Q anion-exchange stationary phase at a flow rate of 1 ml/min. Mobile phase consisted of 0.02 *M* piperazine at pH 9.60 with sodium chloride as the displacer salt at a concentration of (a) 60 m*M* and (b) 180 m*M*.

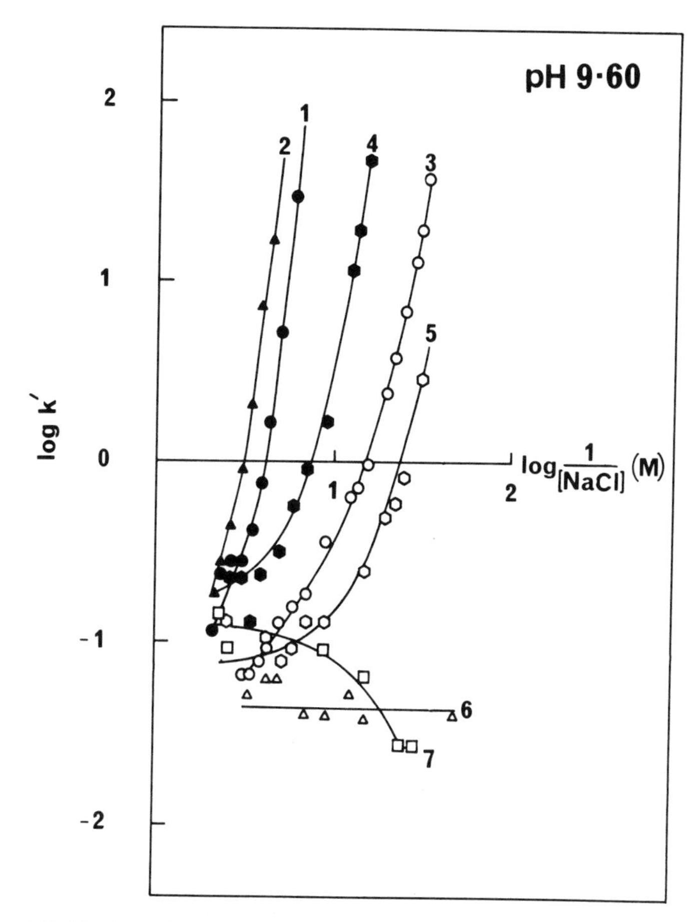

FIGURE 7–5. Plots of log k' versus log 1/[NaCl] for several proteins separated isocratically on a Mono-Q anion-exchange resin. Mobile phase consisted of 0.02 *M* piperazine at pH 9.60 and a flow rate of 1 ml/min. The key to protein identity is given in Table 7–2.

Figure 7–6. The number, Z_c, of charged interactive sites involved with the binding of the ionotopic region(s), of, for example, the protein solute and the stationary phase is determined by regression analysis of linear portions of the log k' versus log $1/c$ plots as defined in section (1) of Figure 7–6. Over this region of ionic strength the interaction is dominated by electrostatic forces. As the salt concentration increases, a point is reached in section (2) where there is minimal interaction between the solute and the sorbent, and size exclusion phenomena tend to dominate the retention process. Further increases in ionic strength will then result in two further retention phenomena. One phenomenon involves ion exclusion effects where the solute is effectively repelled from the surface and will lead to a further decrease in k' as shown in section (3). Alternatively, high salt concentrations can lead to reduced protein

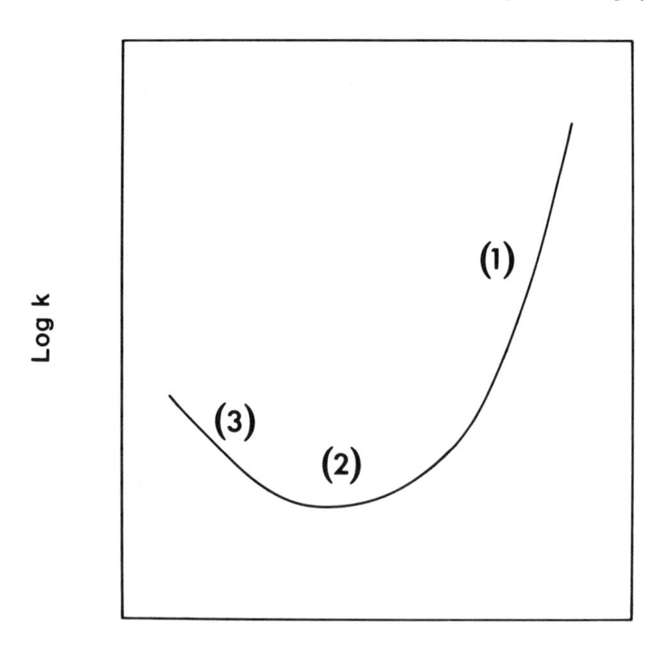

FIGURE 7–6. General dependence of the retention on the salt concentration for proteins separated by HPIEC illustrating (1) electrostatic, (2) size-exclusion, and (3) hydrophobic interactions.

solubility in the mobile phase, with the protein "salted out" onto the stationary phase surface through intervention of hydrophobic effects. As a result, the capacity factors are seen to increase with increasing ionic strength, as can be seen for lysozyme in Figure 7–5.

7.3.2 pH Effects

Proteins are amphoteric molecules. The titration curve of a particular protein reveals that at a unique pH value, the p*I*, a zero net charge is manifested where the ratio of anionic to cationic groups reaches unity. As the mobile phase pH is decreased below the protein p*I*, the protein gains increasing cationic character due to protonation of accessible amino groups. Similarly, as the pH is increased, the protein acquires more anionic character through carboxyl group ionization. Manipulation of the mobile phase pH therefore represents an attractive method for regulating the degree of protein interaction with a particular sorbent in HPIEC.

Figure 7–7 represent plots of protein retention to a strong anion and a strong cation exchanger as a function of mobile phase pH.[5] It is evident from these data that protein retention decreases with an anion exchanger as the pH is

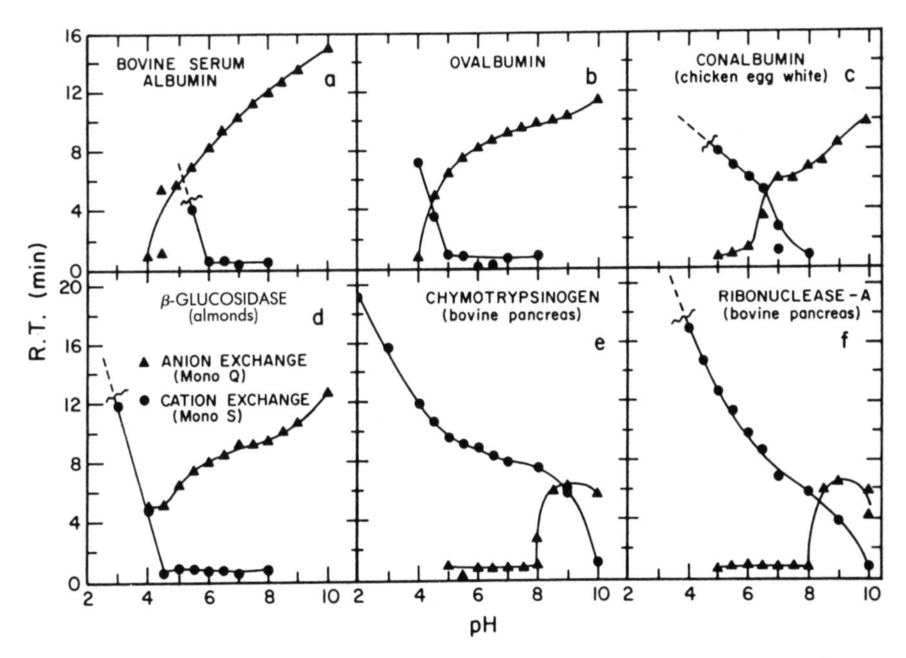

FIGURE 7–7. Plots of retention versus mobile phase pH for a range of proteins (a–f) separated isocratically on a Mono-Q anion-exchange resin or a Mono-S cation-exchange resin. (Reproduced with permission from ref. 5.)

lowered. However, contrary to the prediction of the net charge concept, some degree of retention can be ascertained for some proteins at mobile phase pHs equal to and below the p*I* of the protein. Similar observations are also apparent with cation-exchange resins[5] where a number of proteins showed significant retention at pHs above the known protein p*I* value. Several explanations can be considered for this phenomenon. First, the vectorial sum of all interacting charge potentials for a highly curved porous coulombic surface will be different from that generated by an infinitely flat electrostatic surface. An incremental Donnan potential will, as a result, exist between surface charges located inside and outside the pores. As a consequence of this phenomenon, the pH of the solvent contained within the pores will be different from that of the bulk mobile phase. These small differences in microscopic pH may be sufficient to allow significant protein retention even though the bulk pH of the mobile phase is equivalent to the protein p*I* value.

Second, the heterogeneous distribution of charged groups on the protein surface is capable of generating localized electrostatic potentials, allowing specific site or domain interactions with the stationary phase, even when the bulk ionization state of the protein corresponds to the p*I* condition. Steric restrictions imposed by the protein structure can also reduce the potential number of interactions between the protein and stationary phase. Such anomalies which may be attributed to charge asymmetry are evident in the data shown in Figure 7–7 where ovalbumin and β-glucosidase both show retention on the anion exchanger with mobile phase pHs well below their p*I* values.

The experimental Z_c values obtained from plots of log k' versus log $1/c$ for a range of proteins are shown in Table 7–2. It can be seen that increased suppression of carboxyl group ionization leads to the lowering of the Z_c value for each protein and concomitantly shorter elution times. The precise physicochemical significance of Z_c remains to be determined. As is evident from the data in Table 7–2, on a strong anion-exchange column, Z_c increases with pH. A generalized sigmoidal dependence of Z_c on pH, as shown in Figure 7–8 can be envisaged, which represents three distinct situations for protein interaction with the stationary phase. In the first situation, the maximum number of charged binding sites on the protein surface will be reached at pH values that greatly exceed the protein's pI. At this point, further increases in pH will have no influence on the retention properties of the solute. As the pH is reduced and approaches the pI of the protein, the concomitant decrease in the number of interactive surface charges will result in a marked dependence of Z_c on pH. Finally at pHs well below the pI of the protein, repulsion between the positively charged stationary phase and the fully protonated protein will lead to minimal binding where Z_c values approach zero over a certain pH range. In Figure 7–9, plots of protein Z_c values as a function of eluent pH for ovalbumin, human serum albumin, carbonic anhydrase, and myoglobin eluted on the anion-exchange resin Mono-Q with sodium chloride as the displacer salt are shown. The trends observed here are representative of solute-specific effects shown by other globular proteins both in terms of the magnitude of the experimentally determined Z_c values and the pH range over which these Z_c values are seen to vary. This behavior presumably arises as a consequence of the amino acid composition and tertiary structure of the solutes, which impart a unique surface charge distribution that determines the interactive properties at particular pH conditions.

In reversed-phase chromatography it has been shown that the corresponding S value, i.e., the slope of the plot of log k' versus φ, not only relates to the hydrophobic contact area established between the protein solute and the stationary phase, but is also dependent on the polarity and disposition of surface amino acids.[32,33] The experimental Z_c values in HPIEC is the result of an analogous complex interplay between the relative distribution of charged groups on the protein with varying affinities for the stationary phase and the displacing properties of the mobile phase constituents. In this context, Z_c thus reflects the magnitude of the coulombic contact area rather than the total number of surface charges on a protein. Support for this conclusion can be found in a variety of recent studies, for example, the retention behavior of various dehydrogenases. In particular, the retention mechanism of lactate dehydrogenase (LDH) isoenzymes in anion-exchange chromatography has been extensively examined.[34] The LDH isoenzymes were composed of heart (H) and muscle (M) subunits. The studies demonstrated that Z_c increased incrementally as the number of heart subunits increased up to a total of 3 while both the MH_3 and H_4 isoenzymes had the same Z_c indicating the role of steric factors in the adsorption process. In this and other cases, the interactive potential of surface accessible charged groups also appears to be influenced by interactions with other ionic species in solution. For example, the resolution of 7 closely related lysozyme variants by cation-exchange chromatography has been reported, although very similar Z_c values were obtained.[35] Further insight into

TABLE 7–2. Protein Physical Parameters

No.	Protein (Source)	p*I*	MW	Z_c value at pH			
				5.50	6.50	7.50	9.60
1.	Ovalbumin (egg white)	4.70	43,500	4.12	6.01	6.69	7.73
2.	Albumin (human serum)	5.85	69,000	2.34	5.57	4.81	11.14
3.	Carbonic anhydrase (bovine erythrocyte)	5.89	30,000	0.33	0.92	1.37	2.16
4.	Hemoglobin (bovine blood)	6.80	64,500	—	—	—	5.04
5.	Myoglobin (sperm whale muscle)	7.68 8.18	17,500	0.00	0.16	−0.06	2.76
6.	Cytochrome *c* (horse heart)	9.40	12,400	—	—	—	—
7.	Lysozyme	11.0	14,300	—	—	—	—

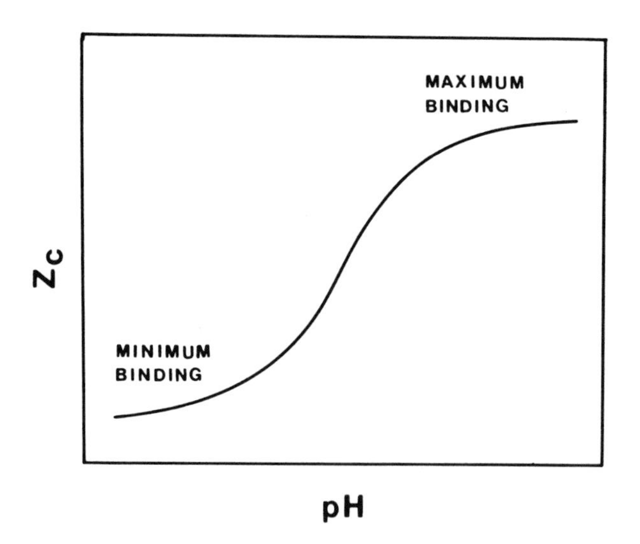

FIGURE 7–8. Hypothetical relationship between experimentally derived Z_c value and mobile phase pH.

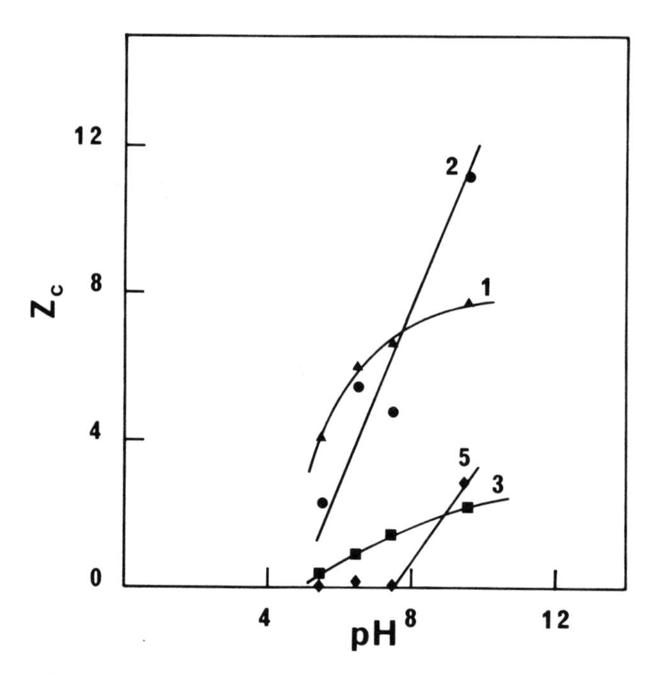

FIGURE 7–9. Plot of Z_c versus pH for ovalbumin, human serum albumin, carbonic anhydrase, and myoglobin eluted isocratically on a Mono-Q column at 1 ml/min with NaCl as the displacer salt. (Reproduced with permission from ref. 14.)

the mechanism of HPIEC of proteins can therefore be derived from studies of proteins eluted with different displacer salts.

7.4 EFFECT OF DISPLACER SALT ON PROTEIN RETENTION

The previous section demonstrated that the selectivity of proteins eluted in HPIEC can be manipulated by variation in solution pH and ionic strength and the bulk pH thereby capitalizing on changes in the electrostatic surface potentials of the proteins via changes in protonic equilibria. An alternative method of optimizing selectivity in HPIEC involves changes in the chemical nature of the displacer ion. However, the roles that different salt species can play in the retention behavior of proteins in the HPIEC has not been fully rationalized in thermodynamic terms to permit comprehensive predictability. Nevertheless, extensive application studies have been completed with classical ion-exchange resins to allow guidelines to be proposed for the effect of different salts on protein retention in HPIEC. For example, it can be anticipated that the well-documented effect of different salts on protein solubility and stability, known as the Hofmeister effect,[36] will have a significant influence on the chromatographic behavior of proteins in HPIEC. Formal relationships between the Hofmeister coefficients and the electrostatic displacing strength of different ions have not yet been established. However, sufficient empirical data are available to suggest the validity of the following conclusions, namely the Hofmeister effects become important at moderate concentrations in the range 0.01–1.0 *M* in bulk solution and tend to be dominated by anion effects that are approximately additive for many polyionic or amphoteric species in solution.

In more complex systems such as ion-exchange chromatography, the effect of counterions on protein stability will not simply be manifested through their presence in the bulk mobile phase but will also arise due to time-dependent protein interactions with anions complexed at the stationary phase–mobile phase interface. These charge and concentration gradients, which form to neutralize the charged stationary phase surface, are referred to as double layers and are believed to exist predominantly at relatively low ionic strengths.[5] Similarly, the role of coions and the influence of the double layer in the mechanism of protein retention in HPIEC have not been fully defined in thermodynamic terms. It is generally considered that the coions complex with the accessible protein surface as proposed in the ion-condensation theory.[37–39] As these thermodynamically favorable interactions may exert significant effects on protein structure and stability, the appropriate choice of both the anion and cation species therefore represents an important consideration for the optimization of protein separations in terms of both resolution and biorecovery.

According to Eq. (7–8), for eluents of fixed mobile phase pH, the logarithmic capacity factor of a protein separated in HPIEC is linearly related to the inverse of the logarithm of the concentration of displacer ion. In addition, solute desorption from HPIEC supports is anticipated to be closely associated with the affinity that the displacer ions exhibit with the support surface. At fixed ionic strengths, anions can be ranked in terms of their affinity for the quaternary ammonium anion-exchange resin, Dowex-2, as follows[40]:

$$ClO_4^- > SCN^- > (CH_3)_3CH_2COO^- > p\text{-tosyl}^- > I^- > Br^- >$$

$$NO_3^- > Cl^- > H_2PO_4^- > CH_3COO^- > F^-$$

Experimentally, under normal HPIEC operating conditions, smaller elution volumes are observed for low-molecular-weight samples when the elution is carried out with displacer ions with higher affinities for the stationary phase. For example, simple organic acid molecules are typically eluted from anionic resins with much smaller retention times using thiocyanate than fluoride ions. Similar trends are observed when small organic bases and other positively charged low-molecular-weight molecules are separated using cation-exchange chromatography. Under these conditions, retention times are found to increase with the choice of the displacing cation in the following manner[41]:

$$Ba^{2+} < Ca^{2+} < Mg^{2+} < K^+ < NH_4^+ < Na^+ < Li^+$$

However, there is generally less variation in retention times of low-molecular-weight solutes eluted in cation-exchange than in anion-exchange chromatography. This difference arises from the interplay of two phenomena. First, the range in the magnitude of the distribution coefficients and cation affinities for the support surface is much narrower than observed for anions due to smaller variations in the size and charge characteristics of the solvated cation compared to solvated anion. Second, significant differences exist in the solvated characteristics of the complementary immobilized ionic ligand in terms of the double layer structure of an anionic versus cationic ligand.

According to the stoichiometric model for HPIEC of proteins as given by Eq. (7–5), and on the basis of ion affinities for the stationary phase, the relative selectivity of protein solutes can be anticipated to be directly related to the number of interacting point charges and the displacing power of the counter-ion. However, it is now well established that different salts can, in bulk solution, influence the stability, solubility, and biological activity of macromolecules. These effects will have profound implications for the chromatographic behavior of proteins in HPIEC.

The effects of various salts were originally documented by Hofmeister[36] and has since been extensively reviewed.[42–45] Generally, anionic species with stronger affinities than chloride (Cl^-) for the anion-exchange medium are classified as chaotropes or water-structure breakers. These ions interact with the first layer of adjacent water molecules less strongly than bulk water and are known to destabilize protein structure. Those anions which have a weaker affinity than Cl^- are referred to as polar kosmotropes or water-structure makers. These ions interact with the first layer of adjacent water molecules more strongly than bulk water and have a stabilizing effect on protein structure. The chloride ion has little effect on water structure and in the range of molarities commonly used in HPIEC (e.g., 0.1–0.7 *M*) usually has little influence on protein conformational stability. The effectiveness of chaotropic ions as displacing species in HPIEC and their destabilizing effect on protein three-dimensional structure can therefore be associated[46,47] with the energetically favorable loss of loosely held water molecules from the first hydrated shell of ions as they preferentially complex with either the sorbent or protein molecules. The loss of water molecules from the hydration layer(s) of polar kosmotropes does not readily occur and consequently these ions tend to stabilize protein structure and complex less readily with HPIEC sorbents.

Based on the above considerations, the HPIEC retention properties of proteins will be strongly influenced by the presence of different salts. This conclusion has been documented[5,10,14–17] in various studies on the influence of monovalent alkali metal halides on protein retention in anion- and cation-exchange systems. These studies have indicated that the chaotropic and kosmotropic properties of various salts significantly alter the interactive properties of protein solutes in anion- and cation-exchange systems. For example, the influence of both the counterion and the coion on protein retention with Mono-Q sorbents has been extensively studied[17] using LiCl, LiBr, NaF, NaCl, NaBr, KF, KCl, and KBr as displacing salt. Table 7–3 shows the Z_c values obtained for carbonic anhydrase, ovalbumin, myoglobin, and lysozyme eluted with each salt under conditions of varied gradient time. The ions used can be classified according to their chaotropic (e.g., Br^- and K^+), kosmotropic (e.g., F^- and Li^+), or neutral (e.g., Cl^- and Na^+) properties. For a particular solute species separated under normal HPIEC conditions, it can be argued that the use of different displacer ions of the same valency should result in parallel retention plots if the Z_c term simply reflects the stoichiometry of the solute–stationary phase interaction. However, identical Z_c values for a particular protein eluted with different salts are not always observed. Several general trends in the changes in Z_c values are apparent in Table 7–3. For example, the value of Z_c increased as the anion and cation of the displacer salt both became more chaotropic in nature. Similarly, the value of Z_c also increased as the anion and cation of the displacer salt became more kosmotropic in nature. However, the value of Z_c decreased when the displacer salt contained a combination of a chaotropic and kosmotropic ion. A change in Z_c value suggests that the ionotopic region of the protein is altered in the presence of different ions. Thus, the influence of these salts on protein interactive behavior, which is experimentally manifested as changes in Z_c, can be considered to be additive in the presence of salts comprised of only chaotropes (KBr) or kosmotropes (LiCl). However, a combination of a chaotropic and kosmotropic ion (e.g., KF, LiBr) results in opposing effects on the magnitude of Z_c.

From a practical standpoint, variation in the chemical characteristics of the desorbing salt can be used to optimize both resolution and recovery of proteins separated by HPIEC. The dependency between Z_c and a logarithmic distribution coefficient, $\log K_c$, is shown in Figure 7–10 for ovalbumin and carbonic anhydrase eluted from a strong anion-exchange column with different salts. For these calculations values of $\log K_c$ were determined by extrapolation of the $\log k$ versus $\log 1/c$ plots to the limit case of $c \rightarrow 10^{-6}$ mol/liter. While these $\log K_c$ values are not equivalent to the true $\log K_o$ value, which by definition is constant for a particular protein solute, $\log K_c$ values provide some indication of the relative influence of various experimental parameters on protein reten-

TABLE 7–3. Z_c Values Obtained by Linear Regression of Varied Gradient Time Data

Salt	Protein			
	Carbonic anhydrase	Ovalbumin	Myoglobin	Lysozyme
LiF	Not done	Not done	Not done	Not done
LiCl	5.60 ± 2.12(0.78)[a]	9.92 ± 2.90(0.80)	17.75 ± 3.23(0.97)	2.50 ± 0.26(0.98)
LiBr	3.14 ± 0.71(0.80)	7.30 ± 0.46(0.98)	1.96 ± 0.66(0.69)	4.21 ± 0.66(0.93)
NaF	3.55 ± 0.45(0.91)	6.56 ± 0.71(0.95)	5.49 ± 1.71(0.78)	2.99 ± 0.31(0.96)
NaCl	3.07 ± 0.21(0.99)	9.40 ± 0.50(0.99)	4.61 ± 1.57(0.90)	1.48 ± 0.17(0.97)
NaBr	2.92 ± 0.17(0.99)	7.83 ± 0.47(0.99)	1.43 ± 0.02(1.00)	2.41 ± 0.44(0.94)
KF	2.37 ± 0.25(0.95)	6.37 ± 0.57(0.97)	1.98 ± 0.27(0.93)	3.58 ± 0.14(1.00)
KCl	3.84 ± 0.05(1.00)	8.40 ± 0.76(0.98)	4.54 ± 0.51(0.99)	1.16 ± 0.15(0.95)
KBr	5.60 ± 0.75(0.92)	9.48 ± 0.69(0.97)	4.84 ± 0.75(1.89)	3.28 ± 0.24(0.98)[b]
				0.98 ± 0.14(1.00)[c]
LiF	Not done	Not done	Not done	Not done
NaF	3.55 ± 0.45(0.91)	6.56 ± 0.71(0.95)	5.49 ± 1.71(0.78)	2.99 ± 0.31(0.96)
KF	2.37 ± 0.25(0.95)	6.37 ± 0.57(0.97)	1.98 ± 0.27(0.93)	3.58 ± 0.14(1.00)
LiCl	5.60 ± 2.12(0.78)	9.92 ± 2.90(0.80)	17.75 ± 3.23(0.96)	2.50 ± 0.26(0.98)
NaCl	3.07 ± 0.21(0.99)	9.40 ± 0.50(0.99)	4.61 ± 1.57(0.90)	1.48 ± 0.17(0.97)
KCl	3.84 ± 0.05(1.00)	8.40 ± 0.76(0.98)	4.54 ± 0.51(0.99)	1.16 ± 0.15(0.95)
LiBr	3.14 ± 0.71(0.80)	7.30 ± 0.46(0.98)	1.96 ± 0.66(0.69)	4.21 ± 0.66(0.93)
NaBr	2.92 ± 0.17(0.99)	7.83 ± 0.48(0.99)	1.43 ± 0.02(1.00)	2.41 ± 0.44(0.94)
KBr	5.60 ± 0.75(0.92)	9.48 ± 0.69(0.97)	4.84 ± 0.75(0.89)	3.28 ± 0.24(0.98)[b]
				0.98 ± 0.14(1.00)[c]

[a] Coefficient of determination in parentheses.
[b] Z_c determined at low log $1/\bar{c}$ values.
[c] Z_c determined at high log $1/\bar{c}$ values.

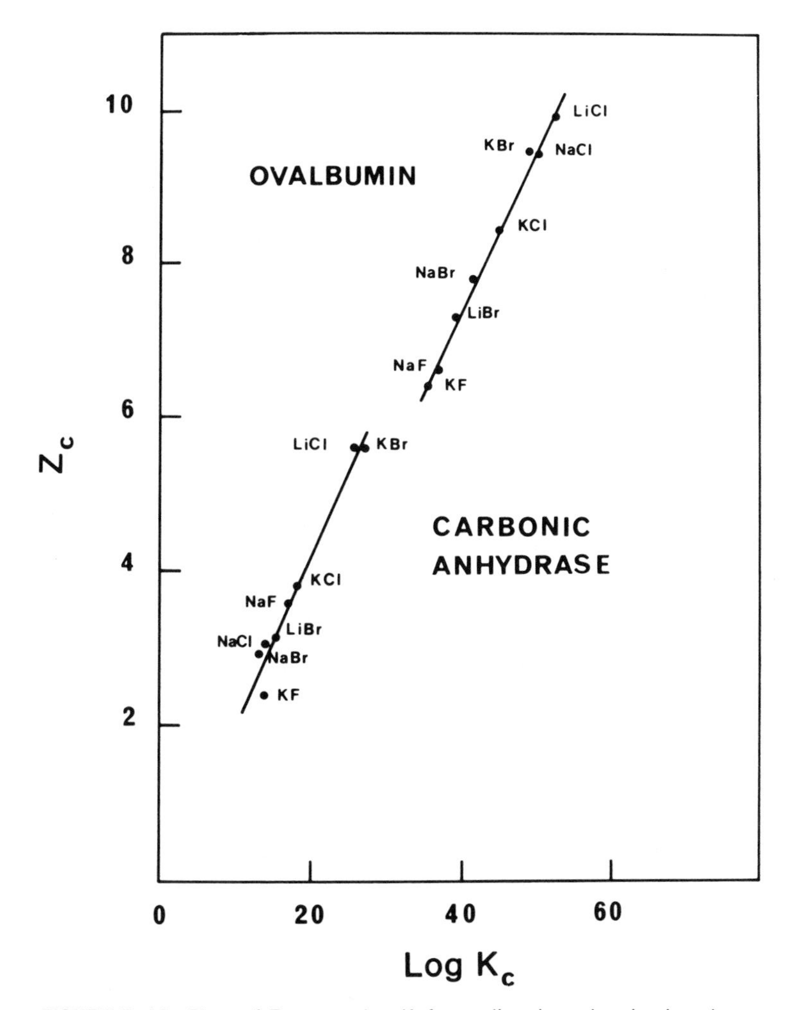

FIGURE 7–10. Plots of Z_c versus log K_c for ovalbumin and carbonic anhydrase separated under conditions of varied gradient time with a range of displacer salts on a Mono-Q anion-exchange resin at 1 ml/min. (Reproduced with permission from ref. 17.)

tion behavior. This kind of experimental data demonstrates that guidelines based on consideration of chaotropic and kosmotropic properties of different salts can result in obtaining predictable retention and selectivity patterns for protein solutes.

The mechanism of protein desorption in HPIEC involves an ionic displacement hierarchy as the protein is desorbed from the charged stationary phase, in which certain charged centers on the solute surface dominate the interaction. These unique areas on the surface of the protein can be represented as a contour surface or ionotope. The influence of solvent conditions on the interactive nature of these areas will thus not be solute specific per se, but rather will be dependent on the specific orientation and electrostatic contact area. These electrostatic contact areas or ionotopes will define the structure–retention dependency for different proteins. It thus follows that structurally different proteins with the same ionotopic contact area can have the same apparent retention under a particular HPIEC condition.

Conversely, closely related protein variants that may differ only in a very small number of amino acids will also be separated if these differences occur within the chromatographic binding region. This has been recently demonstrated by several studies.[34,35,48,49] The example of the resolution of the LDH-MH_3 and LDH-H_4 isozymes has already been given.[34] As a further example, it has been demonstrated that chromatographic resolution of several isoforms of bovine carbonic anhydrase and ovalbumin can be manipulated in HPIEC by variation of the displacer salt. Figure 7–11 shows plots of log $\bar{k}$ versus log

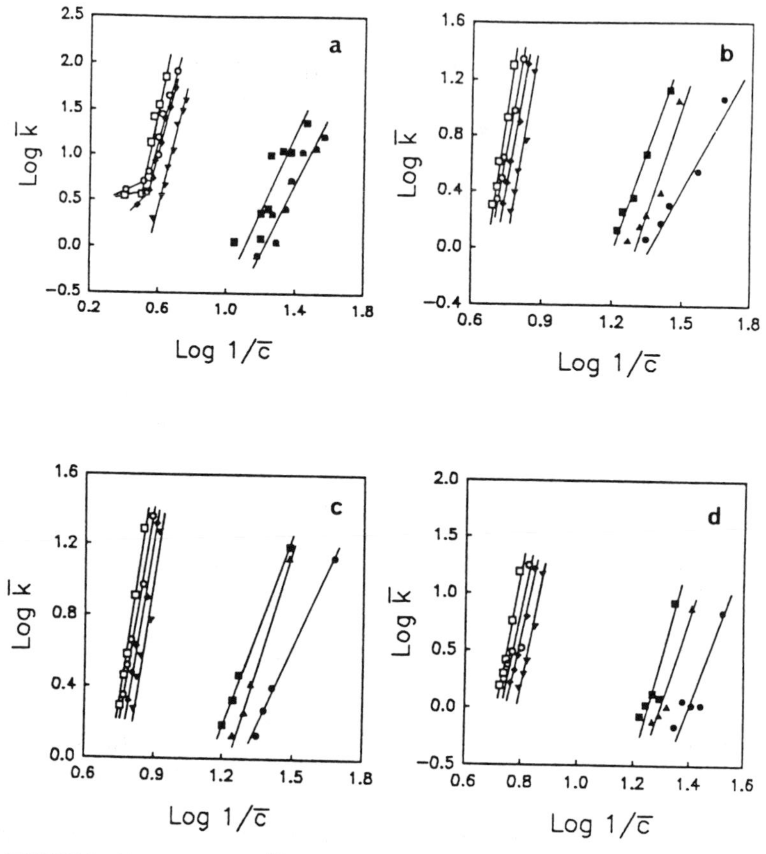

FIGURE 7–11. Plots of log $\bar{k}$ versus log(1/$\bar{c}$) for isoforms of carbonic anhydrase and ovalbumin separated under conditions of varied gradient times on a Mono-Q anion-exchange resin at 1 ml/min. Mobile phase consisted of 0.02 *M* piperazine at pH 9.60 with (a) KF, (b) KCl, (c) KBr, and (d) LiBr as displacer salts. (Reproduced with permission from ref. 48.)

($1/\bar{c}$) for these proteins separated with KF, KCl, KBr, and LiBr. These data indicate that subtle changes in experimental conditions can result in significant changes to the interactive properties of extremely similar proteins. Furthermore, this level of resolution control has important implications in studies on protein microheterogeneity and demonstrates the utility of HPIEC to complement other techniques such as isoelectric focusing and chromatofocusing for the characterization of microheterogeneous proteins derived from natural or recombinant DNA sources.

7.5 COMPARISON OF ISOCRATIC AND GRADIENT ELUTION

As noted above, application of the linear solvent strength system[19] has proved useful for the analysis of macromolecular retention data in reversed-phase chromatographic systems. Similarly, extension of the LSS model to HPIEC can provide a useful basis to compare isocratic and gradient elution data. If the physicochemical basis of isocratic and gradient elution in HPIEC is assumed to be the same, the LSS model predicts that plots of log $\bar{k}$ versus log $1/\bar{c}$ should be superimposable. However, if the interactive properties of the protein solute are sensitive to time-dependent sorption changes, including changes mediated by the displacer salt concentration, conformational effects, ion binding, and salt bridging effects or other secondary equilibria, the experimental values of Z_c and log K_o, derived according to the LSS model, will not coincide with the values determined isocratically.

Both scenarios, e.g., agreement with and divergence from the LSS model, have been encountered in the HPIEC of proteins. For example, Figure 7–12 shows plots of log k versus log $1/c$ for ovalbumin and carbonic anhydrase separated under isocratic conditions and by gradient elution with either varied gradient time or varied flow rate. The slopes of the individual curves Z_{ISO}, Z_{VTG}, and Z_{VF} together with the slope of the combined data, Z_{comb}, and the correlation coefficient, r^2, are listed in Table 7–4. Values of r^2 approaching unity, as observed for ovalbumin ($r^2 = 0.95$), indicate that both isocratic and gradient data can be highly congruent for some proteins and that the LSS theory provides an accurate model of gradient elution behavior for these types of proteins. Similar observations have also been made for the elution of ribonuclease A, α-chymotrypsinogen A, cytochrome c, and lysozyme in weak cation-exchange systems.[6,50] As evident from Table 7–4, lower r^2 values for Z_{comb} are seen for carbonic anhydrase ($r^2 = 0.87$) and myoglobin ($r^2 = 0.74$) indicating that other protein examples can exhibit different behavioral effects. Regular, or ideal, behavior for a protein clearly involves no retention dependencies on secondary equilibrium effects, e.g., time-dependent conformational changes or ligand-induced reorientation. At the opposite extreme irregular or non-ideal behavior involves complete retention dependency on secondary equilibrium effects with the protein typically undergoing denaturation during the chromatographic process. A formal classification of such extremes in retention

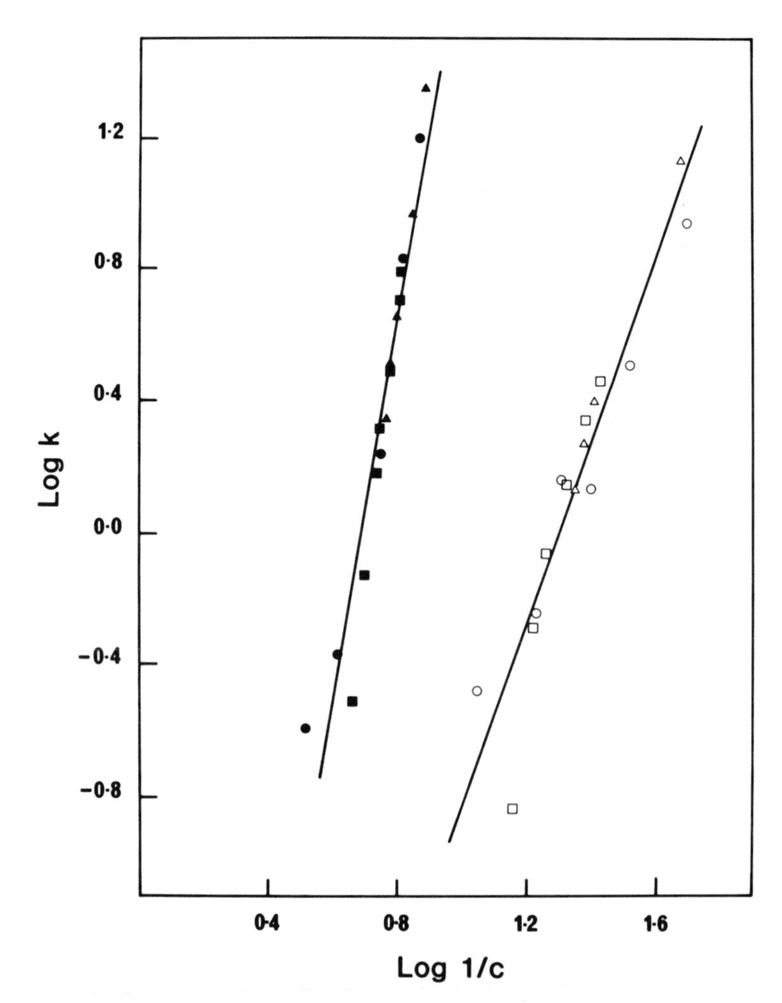

FIGURE 7–12. Retention plots for isocratic (log k' versus log $1/c$) and gradient experiments (log $\bar{k}$ versus log $1/\bar{c}$) for ovalbumin and carbonic anhydrase eluted with sodium bromide using a Mono-Q anion-exchange resin. For ovalbumin: (●) isocratic; (▲) varied gradient time; (■) varied flow rate. For carbonic anhydrase; (○) isocratic; (△), varied gradient time; (□) varied flow rate. (Reproduced with permission from ref. 17.)

behavior has been described elsewhere for all modes of adsorption behavior with proteins.[51]

While gradient and isocratic elution processes can be mathematically related through such theoretical treatments as the LSS model, experimental data often indicate that the two modes of elution are not directly comparable for protein solutes separated by these two HPIEC methods. The main reason for these divergences is that different sorption–desorption dynamics will occur in each process. For example, solutes eluted isocratically are exposed throughout col-

TABLE 7–4. Z_c Values Obtained by Linear Regression of Combined Retention Data

	Protein			
Salt	Carbonic anhydrase	Ovalbumin	Myoglobin	Lysozyme
NaF	2.24 ± 0.27(0.78)[a]	4.52 ± 0.46(0.88)	1.84 ± 0.36(0.62)	−0.81 ± 0.63(0.09)
NaCl	2.41 ± 0.35(0.77)	7.37 ± 0.47(0.95)	1.70 ± 0.32(0.74)	0.37 ± 0.21(0.11)
NaBr	2.72 ± 0.25(0.90)	5.85 ± 0.44(0.92)	1.93 ± 0.23(0.85)	1.26 ± 0.31(0.55)
LiCl	3.63 ± 0.48(0.80)	9.97 ± 1.80(0.74)	0.92 ± 0.50(0.26)	0.66 ± 0.14(0.58)
NaCl	2.41 ± 0.35(0.77)	7.37 ± 0.47(0.95)	1.70 ± 0.32(0.74)	0.37 ± 0.21(0.11)
KCl	2.14 ± 0.19(0.90)	5.61 ± 0.38(0.94)	0.85 ± 0.25(0.39)	−0.14 ± 0.86(0.00)

[a] Coefficient of determination in parentheses.

umn migration to a constant salt concentration. In contrast, under conditions of gradient elution, solutes are initially immobilized at low ionic strength and then subjected to either varying rates of change in the salt concentration and/or varying flow rates. An assumption inherent in the derivation of the LSS equations, which relate isocratic and gradient retention data, is that each k value is measured at equilibrium or near-equilibrium conditions. However, if the interactive properties of the protein solute are dependent on the mobile phase composition, then time-dependent changes in the protein tertiary structure, due to changes in the salt concentration associated with varied gradient times, may not result in an interactive system that is at equilibrium.

Some proteins will behave with regular properties and others with much more divergent characteristics. The influence of different salts on the stability, solubility, and biological activity of proteins in solution has attracted considerable attention.[46,47,52,53] At present, the implications of these effects for the chromatographic of proteins in HPIEC have not yet been incorporated into a general retention model. While sodium chloride is known not to greatly influence protein structure and stability, it has been found[16] that even changes in the concentration of this salt over a range of gradient times can modify the interactive properties of different solutes. Furthermore, conformational changes induced by the type or concentration of the salt or pH changes in the microenvironment of the protein would be expected to give rise to changes in the Z_c parameter. Where such changes are discrete rather than monotonously continuous, breaks in the log k versus log $1/c$ plots will occur, leading to more than one apparent Z_c value. Such behavior can be seen for lysozyme[17] shown in Figure 7–13, and has also been observed for subtilisin variants.[49]

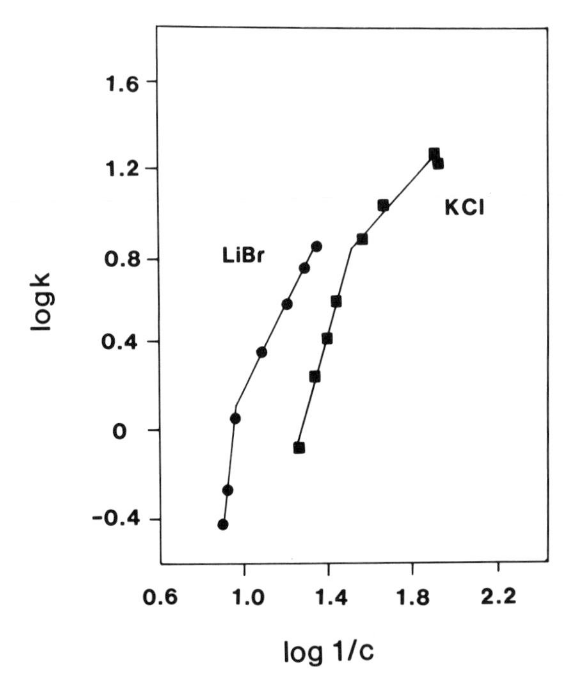

FIGURE 7–13. Retention plots for lysozyme eluted under gradient conditions with LiBr or KF as the displacer salt using a Mono-Q anion-exchange resin. (Reproduced with permission from ref. 17.)

The degree of solute exposure to mobile phase constituents represents an important factor contributing to noncoincident retention behavior for proteins eluted by gradient and isocratic HPIEC methods. The mechanism of protein desorption is closely dependent on the nature of the complex interaction between the protein, the displacing salt species, and the charged stationary phase surface. If the Z_c term does represent a measure of the electrostatic interaction area, A_c, larger values of Z_{VTG} can be anticipated as the solute is initially sorbed in the absence of displacer salt, which should promote maximum interaction. Furthermore, if the protein surface structure is not influenced by the nature or the concentration of the displacer salt, similar Z_c values will be obtained for both isocratic and gradient experiments. However, if the interactive potential of the charged centers, which constitute the coulombic interaction area, is diminished or enhanced in the presence of displacer salts, the desorption process will clearly differ between isocratic and gradient elution conditions. This will give rise to subtle but important selectivity differences, which can be exploited in both analytical and preparative applications.

7.6 THE SOLUTE-SURFACE APPROACH DISTANCE

In ion-exchange chromatography, the affinity of the solute for the stationary phase is reflected in the retention behavior, which will be dependent on the relative charge distribution at the surface of both the protein and the stationary phase. Changes in these affinity dependencies will also be reflected in the distance to which the protein is able to approach the stationary phase through the contribution of mutually attractive and repulsive forces and steric bulk. Under normal pH conditions, the nonuniform charge distribution at the surface of the protein will result in localized areas of high electrostatic potential. These regions arise as a consequence of either continuous (i.e., sequentially linked amino acids) or discontinuous (i.e., topographic through space interactions) clustering of charged amino acids. These ionotopic regions represent the sites of highest interactive potential, which orient or direct the approach of the protein to the charged surface of the stationary phase. They thus act as "docking" sites of definable surface contract area, A_c, and charge anisotropy, Z_{anis}.

If it is assumed that the retention process is governed by electrostatic interactions, then the Debye–Hückel theory for spherical impenetrable ions can be adapted to evaluate the behavior of the ionized protein at an HPIEC packing surface. Since chromatographic retention data measure the free energy of interaction between the solute and stationary phase, the influence of experimental conditions on the approach distance and orientation of a protein solute at the charged surface thus can be assessed through calculation of the electrostatic potential of the protein, which, in turn, allows an average approach distance to be determined.

Figure 7–14 shows a simplified graphic representation of the Debye–Hückel theory for spherical impenetrable ions, as adapted for a macroionic ionotope at an ion-exchange packing surface.[54] The model assumes that the topographic

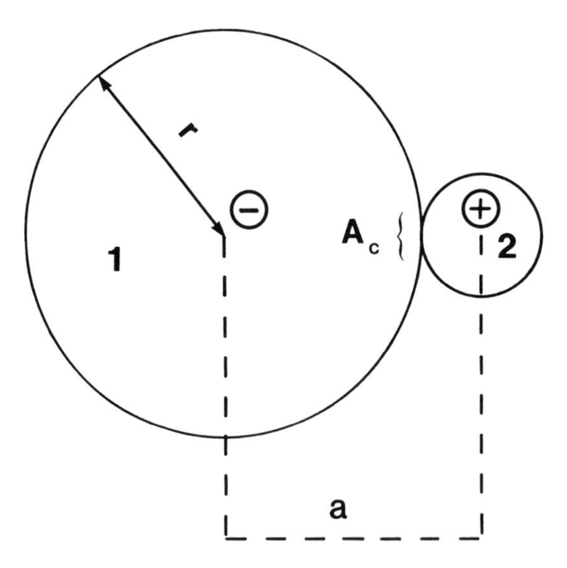

FIGURE 7–14. Theoretical model used to calculate the solvent approach distance. For anion-exchange systems the model consists of the anionic macroion (1) of radius r, and the cationic stationary phase ligand (2), which interact through the coulombic interaction area A_c.

region on the protein surface that interacts with the HPIEC ligands to create the coulombic contact area, A, can be represented by a charged surface with effective radius, r, and is located at the fixed center of a coordinate system. Both the protein ionotope and those ions present at the solute–stationary phase interface are found in a solvent with a dielectric constant, D. The charge vector, q, associated with the ligand–solute interaction established between the stationary phase and the protein is assumed to be either evenly distributed over the macroionic ionotope surface or spherically symmetrical in its location. The distance, a, in Figure 7–14 thus represents the average distance of closest approach between the vectorial center of the ionotopic surface and the point charge of the ligand ion at the solute–stationary phase interface.

The approach distance, a, can also be related to chromatographic retention data as follows. The electrical work in placing charges on the central ion is the product of potential and charge. The work involved in adding a charge, dq, to a point with electrical potential, ψ, is

$$dW_e = \psi dq \tag{7–17}$$

Hence, the electrostatic free energy, W_e, can be defined in terms of a hypothetical discharge state of the protein ion such that

$$W_e = \int_0^q \psi dq \tag{7–18}$$

The potential at the surface where the charge is located may then be represented as

$$\psi = \left(\frac{q}{Dr}\right)\left(1 - \frac{\kappa r}{1 + \kappa a}\right) \tag{7–19}$$

Substitution of Eq. (7–18) into Eq. (7–17) followed by integration assuming that Z_q is the final effective charge at the macroion surface gives

$$W = \left(\frac{Z^2 q^2}{2Dr}\right)\left(1 - \frac{\kappa r}{1 + \kappa a}\right) \tag{7–20}$$

By solving Eq. (7–20) for the a term, the value for the average distance between the protein ion and the charged ligands at the solute–stationary phase interface is obtained as follows:

$$a = \left(\frac{Z^2 q^2}{Z^2 q^2 - 2DrW_e}\right)\left(\frac{1}{\kappa}\right) \tag{7–21}$$

where Z and q are the magnitude and sign of the charge, respectively. The protein radius, r, is calculated from molecular weight, M_w, according to the relationship

$$r = (0.39 M_w)^{1/3} \tag{7–22}$$

The quantity κ^{-1} has the dimensions of length and is referred to as the Debye length. It is a measure of the thickness of the ionic atmosphere or the distance over which the electrostatic field of an ion extends with appreciable strength, and is determined according to

$$\kappa^2 = \left(\frac{Ne^2 \cdot 1000}{\epsilon_o DkT}\right)(\Sigma\, c_i Z_i) \tag{7–23}$$

where N is Avogadro's number, e is the protonic charge, ϵ_o is the permitivity in vacuum, k is the Boltzmann constant, and T is the temperature (K). The $\Sigma\, c_i Z_i$ term represents the summation of all charged species of concentration, c, and charge, Z.

If solute elution is carried out under conditions that maximize electrostatic interactions, then the electrostatic free energy term, ΔG_e, for ion-exchange solute retention can be considered to be equivalent to W_e. Thus, in the absence of other secondary retention phenomena, the a term from Eq. (7–21) may be calculated by the following substitution:

$$W_e = \Delta G_e = -RT \ln K_d \tag{7–24}$$

The equilibrium constant, K_d, for the ion-exchange process can be expanded to give

$$\Delta G_e = -RT(\ln k' - \ln \Phi) \tag{7-25}$$

where R is the gas constant, k' is the chromatographic capacity factor, and Φ is the dimensionless phase ratio, equal to the ratio of the volume of the stationary phase (V_s) to the volume of the mobile phase (V_m).

Figure 7–15a and b shows plots of the approach distance, a, as a function of k' for ovalbumin and human serum albumin (HSA) separated isocratically

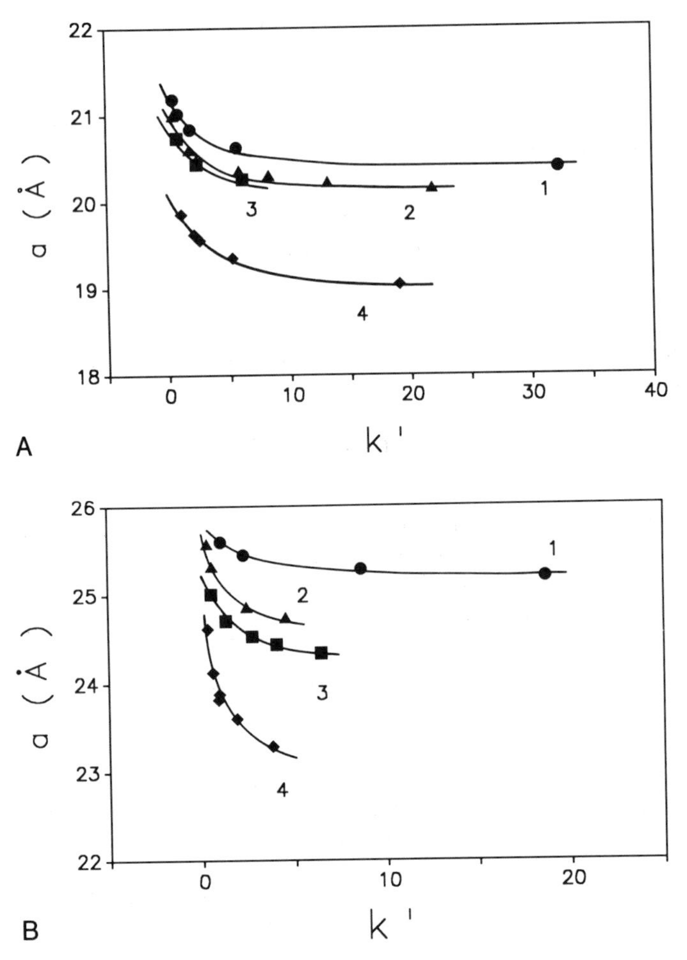

FIGURE 7–15. Plots of approach distance, a versus the isocratic capacity factor k' for (a) ovalbumin and (b) human serum albumin. The data were derived using the Mono-Q anion-exchange resin at a flow rate of 1 ml/min and solvent pH values of (1) 9.6, (2) 7.5, (3) 6.5, and (4) 5.5. (Reproduced with permission from ref. 55.)

at different pHs with sodium chloride as the displacer salt.[55] For HSA, there is an inverse relationship between the approach distance and k'. Thus as k' is systematically increased, a minimum a value is reached where the protein ion is thermodynamically restricted from moving any closer to the packing surface, regardless of further decreases in displacer ion concentration (i.e., further increases in k' values). Furthermore, the minimum a value decreases with decreasing solvent pH. These results indicate that the protein ion orients itself progressively closer to the sorbent surface as the overall anionic charge on the solute surface diminishes and as the dominant interactive charge groups become more spatially isolated.

HSA and carbonic anhydrase (CA) have very similar p*I* values of 5.85 and 5.89, respectively. On the basis of the net charge concept, similar dependencies of the a value on k' would be anticipated for these two proteins. However, associated studies have indicated that HSA exhibits significant retention with Mono-Q sorbents over the entire pH range, while there is little electrostatic interaction between CA and the Mono-Q sorbents at pH 5.50 and 6.50. In these cases, as the solvent pH approaches and passes through the solute p*I*, both protein solutes become increasingly positively charged and this results, in the case of CA, in lower k' values. However, the distribution of carboxylic side chains is significantly different and changes in net charge are not translated to significant changes in k' for serum albumin. It is apparent from these data that the interactive sites or ionotopes for CA and HSA are significantly different in structure, resulting, in the case of HSA, in a closer apparent distance of approach to the stationary phase over a wide range of pH condition.

The differences between the minima of plots of a versus k' for different proteins, i.e., the a versus k' function, provide an indication of the types of molecular changes that may occur at the protein–stationary phase interface as a result of a change in buffer pH or composition. For example, under conditions where the same buffer composition is used at pH 9.6 and 5.5, the distance changes derived from asymptotes for ovalbumin in HSA correspond to 1.4 and 2.0 Å, respectively.[55] Such distances are similar to those calculated for nearest-neighbor hydrogen-bonding effects of 0–H distances (1.86 Å) in liquid water.[56] This change in approach distance indicates that there is a difference in the thickness of the layer of solvating water molecules present at the interactive surface of either the protein macroion or the stationary phase as a consequence of the change in ionization state. Changes in the degree of protein solvation have significant implications in the conformational stability of protein solutes during HPIEC. Furthermore, substantial repulsive or hydration forces are known to occur when solvated surfaces are brought within close proximity of each other.[57,58] For example, with mica,[59,60] competitive adsorption between metal ions, such as Na^+, and H^+ ions produces a pH-dependent switching mechanism. In HPIEC, with NaCl or other sodium salts as displacers, a Na^+/H^+ ion switching mechanism may also be active at the solute–stationary phase interface, whereby the lowering of buffer pH from 9.6 to 5.5 causes the sorbed sodium ions at the protein surface to be replaced by hydrogen ions. This process will then promote a change in the hydrated radii, and consequently the approach distance, a. The analysis of chromatographic retention data in terms of a modified Debye–Hückel theory therefore provides a quantitative approach to studying the behavior of proteins at charged surfaces in the presence of solvated ions. Clearly, small changes in the charge of the interactive or ionotopic surface of the solute can strongly influence the retention behavior of proteins through changes in the electrostatic potential. Furthermore, in the absence of displacer salt, the chromatographic capacity factor, K_o, will be related to the interactive affinity of the protein solute for the charged stationary phase surface. This, in turn, is related to the area and charge density of the interactive region. According to Gauss' law, the electrical intensity, E, of a spherically symmetrical ion, as depicted in Figure 7–15, with a surface charge and potential φ_s, respectively, is given by

$$E = \frac{Z_t \epsilon}{Dr^2} = \frac{4\pi Z_t \epsilon}{DA_t} = \frac{-d\psi_s}{dr} \qquad (7\text{–}26)$$

where ϵ is the protonic charge and A_t is the total surface area of the charged sphere. For a protein solute with a single ionotopic region that dominates the coulombic interaction with an ion-exchange surface, the electrical intensity of the ionotopic surface can be given by

$$E = \frac{Z_c \epsilon}{D \Sigma\, r_i r_j} = \frac{C_c Z_c \epsilon}{DA_c} \qquad (7\text{–}27)$$

where $\Sigma\, r_i r_j$ accounts for the ionotopic surface area, A_c, of the three-dimensional coordinates r_i, r_j, r_z while C_c is a constant. If it is assumed that the distance, a, between the ionotope and the charged ligand corresponds to the distance of closest approach between the vector centers of the protein ion and the charged ligand of radius r_p and r_1, respectively, integration of Eq. (7–18) with respect to r yields

$$\psi = \frac{C_c Z_c \epsilon r_z}{D} \frac{1 + F}{A_c}, \quad r_p \leq r \leq a \qquad (7\text{–}28)$$

where F is given by

$$F = \frac{-Z_c \epsilon}{D} \frac{k}{1 + \kappa a} \qquad (7\text{–}29)$$

and

$$\kappa^2 = \frac{4\pi\epsilon^2}{DkT} \Sigma\, c_i Z_i^2 \qquad (7\text{–}30)$$

The term, F, corresponds to the potential due to the ion atmosphere surrounding the ionotope and is proportional to the charge of the ionotope. For a particular ligand type and mobile phase composition, F will be constant for a defined protein in ionization state, Z_i. Once again, if solute elution is carried out under conditions that maximize electrostatic interactions, the electrostatic free energy term ΔG_e can be equated with W_e according to

$$W_e = \frac{Z_c Z_i \epsilon^2}{2D}\left(\frac{r_p}{A_c} - \frac{\kappa}{1 + \kappa a}\right) = \frac{-RT \log K_0}{2.303} \qquad (7\text{–}31)$$

Hence, if the above assumptions apply, it follows that $\log K_0$ will be proportional to the ionotopic contact area, A, and a linear dependency of $\log K_0$ on Z_c is anticipated. Figure 7–10 shows plots of Z_c versus $\log K_c$ for ovalbumin and carbonic anhydrase for a variety of different displacing ion systems, at extrapolated values of $K_c \rightarrow K_0$. As evident from Figure 7–10, linear dependencies between Z_c and $\log K_0$ exist with the ion effect following the expected behavior assuming that Hofmeister-like properties prevail.

7.7 BANDWIDTH RELATIONSHIPS IN HPIEC

Changes in the experimentally derived Z_c values reflect changes in the effective surface area of the solute's coulombic binding site. Provided that the average coulombic area remains constant over a range of experimental conditions, it is feasible for two different proteins to exhibit identical Z_c values. Similarly, a particular protein could exhibit a constant Z_c value with a selection of ionic displacers, despite the fact that mechanistically different retention processes may prevail. Double-layer-mediated orientational or conformational changes may give rise to differences in the affinity of the protein for the stationary phase surface. To distinguish the various contributions of mobile phase constituents to the mechanism of protein retention in HPIEC, reliance must also be made on the analysis of experimental bandwidth behavior.

The efficiency of a well-packed column can be assessed in terms of the well-known van Dempter–Knox relationship[61]

$$h_{eff} = A\nu^{1/3} + B\nu^{-1} + C\nu \qquad (7\text{–}32)$$

where ν is the reduced velocity, h_{eff} is the effective reduced plate height obtained from the peak zone second moment data, the A term is related to eddy diffusion, and interparticle mass transfer, while the B term accommodates longitudinal diffusion effects. When operating at high flow rates (where ν is typically > 100) with a well-packed ion-exchange column, the dependency of the reduced plate height on the reduced velocity can usually be approximated to

$$h_{eff} = C\nu \qquad (7\text{–}33)$$

where C is the intraparticulate mass transfer coefficient and includes the resistance to mass transfer at the stationary phase surface inside the pores of the column packing material. Giddings[62] represented the dependency of C on the separation conditions as follows:

$$C = \frac{1}{30} \frac{k''}{(1 + k'')^2} \frac{D_m}{D_{sz}} \tag{7–34}$$

where D_m and D_{sz} are the solute diffusion coefficients in the mobile phase and stationary phase zone, respectively, and k'' is the zone capacity factor equivalent to

$$k'' = \frac{\text{mass of solute in stationary phase}}{\text{mass of solute in mobile phase}} \tag{7–35}$$

In addition, k' can be related to k'' through the parameter β, which is the fraction of the mobile phase present in the stagnant pools within the pores as follows:

$$k' = k''(1 - \beta) - \beta \tag{7–36}$$

If it is assumed that the ratios of D_m and D_{sz} for a particular protein in the presence of different salt systems remain constant, then the contribution of the diffusion processes associated with mass transfer of the solute to the overall kinetics of the separation would, according to Eq. (7–33), be reduced to the dependence of the C term on the zonal capacity factor.

Central to these considerations are the assumptions that the experimental capacity factors are exclusively dependent on the concentration of the displacer ion and the kinetics of solute migration are independent of the mobile phase composition in terms of pH or the ions present. Under these circumstances, superimposable plots of h_{eff} versus k' for a specific protein at either different pH values or with different displacer salts would be anticipated. Conversely, when the degree of protein ionization or the exposure to different salts does influence the diffusional properties and binding kinetics of a protein solute then nonsuperimposable plots of h_{eff} versus k' are expected. The experimental results shown in Figure 7–16a and b illustrate that there can be a marked variation in h_{eff} values over a given pH range[14] or with various displacer salts,[15] respectively. The dependence of h_{eff} on k' also varies considerably with the choice of anion or cation. For example, as shown by Hodder et al.,[15] in anion-exchange systems using the alkali halide salts as displacers, h_{eff} values were closely dependent on the protein solute, and, in some cases, increased in the order $F^- < Cl^- < Br^-$, which is consistent with their relative positions in the Hofmeister series.

The formation of double layers and diffuse boundary layers at charged surfaces results in a gradient of both charge potential and ionic concentration between the solid phase and the bulk solution. The magnitude of this electrostatic potential gradient is dependent on the pH and the nature of the ionic and nonionic species in the medium. Ion exclusion studies[5] using HPIEC media have shown that double layer formation is greatest at lower ionic strength. Furthermore, current evidence indicates that only a small portion of the total

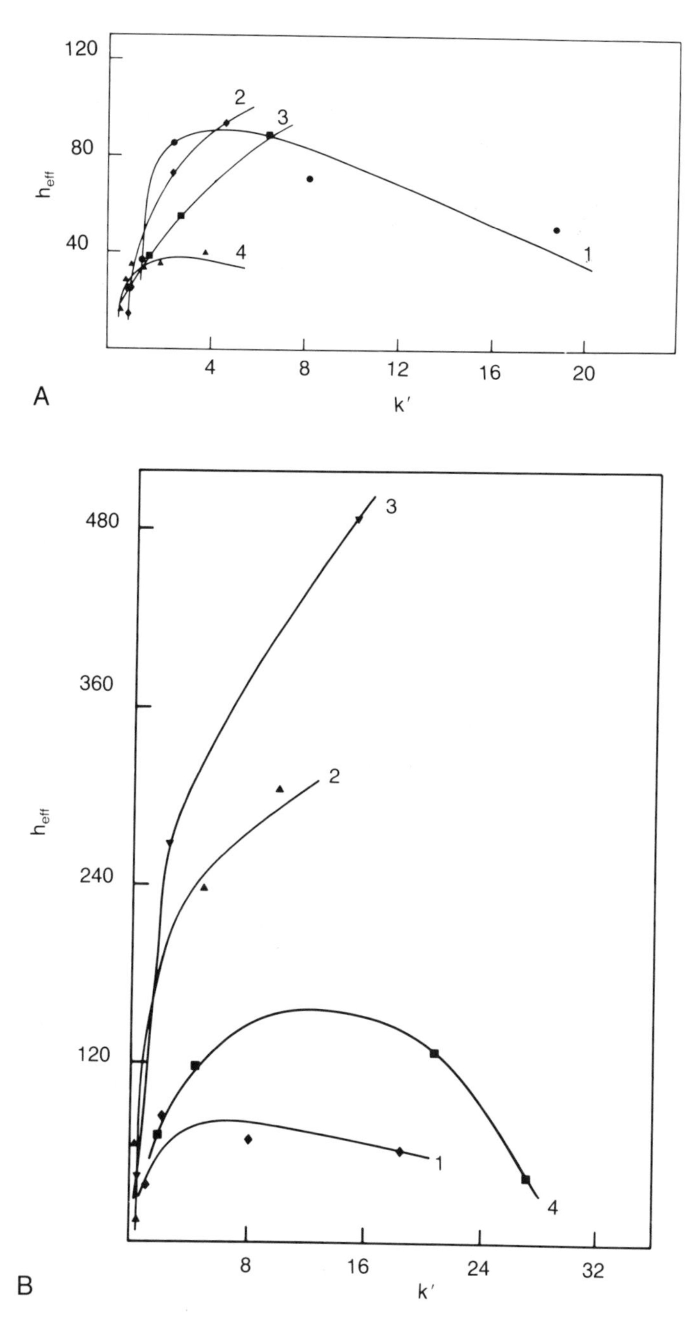

FIGURE 7–16. (a) Plots of h_{eff} versus [NaCl] for human serum albumin eluted isocratically with a Mono-Q anion-exchange resin at (1) pH 9.6, (2) pH 7.5, (3) pH 6.5, and (4) pH 5.5. (b) The influence of anion and cation type on the dependence of h_{eff} versus k' for human serum albumin eluted isocratically with a Mono-Q anion-exchange resin at pH 9.6 with (1) NaCl, (2) NaBr, (3) LiCl, and (4) KCl as displacer salts.

surface area of a protein surface will dominate the equilibrium interaction, but other areas of lower potential could kinetically participate in molecular orientation of the protein solute at the support surface or tumbling motions as the protein traverses the sorbent. Prolonged exposure of the solute to the anion gradient at the double layer-diffuse boundary layer interface may then lead to increased band broadening with longer column residence time. The effect of the presence of double layers formed with different types of anions that influence protein stability will also be reflected in changes in the D_m/D_{sz} ratio, and thus a change, according to Eqs. (7–32) and (7–33) in both the C and h_{eff} terms.

As discussed earlier, complex protein mixtures are commonly separated by gradient elution methods. However, the comparison of retention properties of proteins separated by isocratic and gradient elution conditions demonstrates that the mechanistic details of the desorption process can differ between these two modes of elution. Thus, while protein selectivity can be manipulated through changes in a number of experimental parameters, including gradient time, salt type, and mobile phase pH, the variation in solute bandwidth associated with these changes in experimental conditions in terms of resolution and peak capacity must also be routinely assessed. This can be most conveniently achieved through evaluation of the overall chromatographic resolution in the gradient systems.

A method for predicting solute bandwidths has been developed by Snyder through a combination of retention parameters derived from the LSS model and the general plate height theory for small molecules.[19] The peak capacity, PC, for a chromatographic separation of gradient time t_G, flow rate, F, with average resolution equal to one for all adjacent peaks, i.e., $R_s = 1$, can be expressed by

$$PC = \frac{(t_G - t_0)F}{4\sigma_v} \quad (7\text{–}37)$$

where σ_v is the bandwidth measured in volume units. The relationship between σ_v and $\bar{k}$ for linear solvent systems can be expressed as

$$\sigma_{v,calc} = \frac{(0.5\bar{k} + 1)GV_m}{\sqrt{N}} \quad (7\text{–}38)$$

where V_m is the column void volume ($V_m = t_0F$) and G is the band compression factor that arises from the increase in solvent strength across the solute zone as the gradient develops along the column and is given by the expression

$$G^2 = [(1 + 2.3b) + (2.3b^2/3)]/(1 + 2.3b)^2 \quad (7\text{–}39)$$

Under normal flow rate conditions in gradient elution, the plate number, N, can be approximated by

$$N = \frac{D_m t_0}{Cdp^2} \quad (7\text{–}40)$$

where d_p is the particle diameter and D_m is the diffusion coefficient of the solute in the mobile phase, which can be expressed[63] in terms of solute molecular weight (M_w) as

$$D_m = \frac{8.34 \times 10^{-10} T}{\eta M_w^{1/3}} \qquad (7\text{–}41)$$

where T is the absolute temperature and η is the eluent viscosity. The Knox equation parameter, C, which accounts for resistance to mass transfer at the stationary phase surface can be estimated by

$$C = \frac{[(1 - x + \bar{k})/(1 + \bar{k})]^2}{15\rho^* a' + 15\rho^* b' \bar{k} - 19.2\rho^* x} \qquad (7\text{–}42)$$

where x is the interstitial column fraction, and a' and b' are surface diffusion parameters.

Although the above bandwidth relationships provide reasonable correlations with experimental data of conformationally rigid, low-molecular-weight, solutes, it has been found in, for example, reversed-phase HPLC[27,64–66] that the chromatographic band broadening behavior of proteins is typically much more complex than described by these equations. Application of these relationships assumes that the solute migrates as a single interactive species with an invariant surface charge distribution and shape. Divergences between experimental and theoretical bandwidths will arise when changes in surface structure occur as a result of preferential salt interactions, which, in turn, may or may not lead to more specific conformational changes. If it is assumed that these secondary equilibrium processes are either very rapid or very slow compared to the solute chromatographic separation time, then the ratio between the experimentally observed bandwidth, $\sigma_{v,exp}$, and the calculated bandwidth, $\sigma_{v,calc}$, should approach unity over an optimal range of retention values, i.e., $1 < \bar{k} < 10$.

There is an increasing number of examples where the average relaxation times associated with solute-dependent secondary equilibrium process, such as conformational effects, are of a magnitude comparable to the mass transfer time. In such cases where the shape and surface characteristics of the polypeptide molecule are changing in a relatively slow, time- or condition-dependent manner, the corresponding changes in the diffusional and interactive properties of the solute will lead to differential zone migration. These increases or decreases in the kinetics of solute mass transfer properties will ultimately be revealed as experimental bandwidths that deviate significantly from values predicted by Eq. (7–38).

Figure 7–17 shows plots of $\sigma_{v,exp}/\sigma_{v,calc}$ versus $1/b$ for ovalbumin, carbonic anhydrase, and myoglobin eluted with NaCl under gradient conditions.[16] In these plots, the bandwidth ratio increases with decreasing b and then approaches a plateau limit. As is evident from Figure 7–17, the variation in the rate of change of displacer salt concentration, associated with different gradient times, dramatically affects the kinetic processes for protein solutes at lower b values or longer column residence times. Values of $\sigma_{v,exp}/\sigma_{v,calc}$ in re-

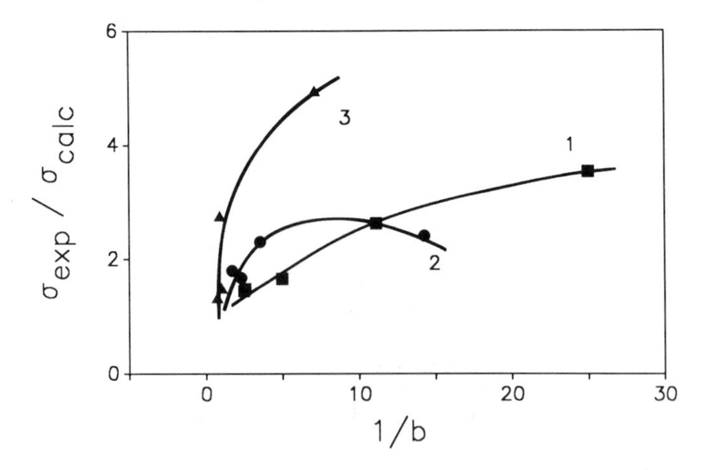

FIGURE 7–17. Plots of $\sigma_{v,exp}/\sigma_{v,calc}$ versus 1/*b* for (1) ovalbumin, (2) carbonic anhydrase, and (3) myoglobin separated under conditions of varied gradient time on a Mono-Q anion-exchange resin at 1 ml/min with NaCl as the displacer salt. (Reproduced with permission from ref. 16.)

versed-phase systems with proteins deviate much less from unity over similar *b* value ranges.[25,32,33] The influence of different displacer salts on the bandwidth properties of several proteins separated by gradient elution[67] is shown in Figure 7–18. At high *b* values, the plots often intersect and no trends are evident. However, at low *b* values, the data for ovalbumin, carbonic anhydrase, and myoglobin are illustrative of a general trend observed for other proteins. For example, the bandwidth ratio generally increased in the order $Br^- \leq Cl^- < F^-$ for anions, while for cations, the ratio increased $K^+ \leq Na^+ < Li^+$.[67]

The larger $\sigma_{v,exp}/\sigma_{v,calc}$ values in HPIEC clearly relate to the physicochemical nature of the kinetics of interaction between solute and sorbent surface. The solute–stationary phase electrostatic interactions in HPIEC are much stronger in terms of free energy changes than the changes mediated by van der Waals interactions that dominate reversed-phase separations, i.e., ΔG_{IEC} versus ΔG_{vdw} of ~40 and 4 kJ/mol, respectively.[68] As a result, the differences in affinity of the interacting groups in HPIEC will be much larger than in reversed-phase systems. This will impact on the bandwidth through the dependency on k' associated with the differential zonal migration of the solute band. However, other effects associated with solute transport within the microenvironment of a coulombic versus a hydrophobic pore must also be invoked and will contribute to anomalous bandbroadening behavior, particularly at longer column residence times.

Overall, in HPIEC, protein bandwidths can be strongly influenced by the mobile phase composition and other operating parameters such as the gradient time or flow rate. Careful manipulation of these conditions is therefore important in the optimization of biomolecule separations by ion-exchange and indeed hydrophobic-interaction chromatography.

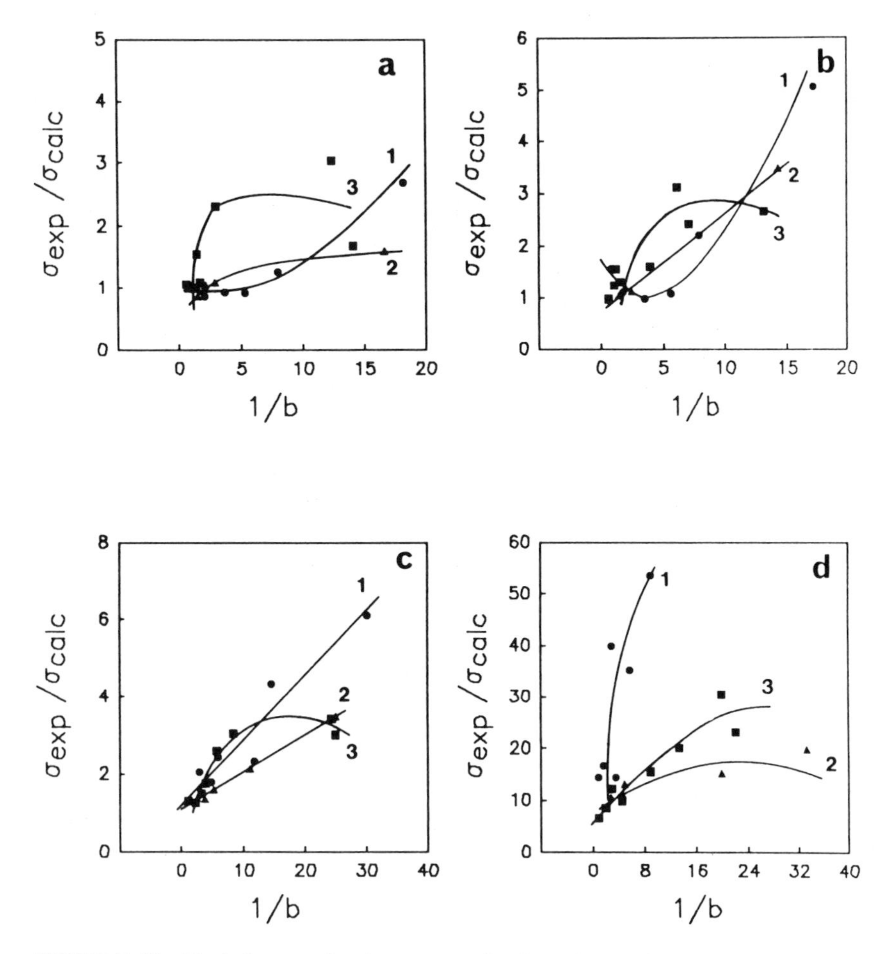

FIGURE 7–18. The influence of cation type on the dependence of $\sigma_{v,exp}/\sigma_{v,calc}$ versus 1/*b* for (a) carbonic anhydrase, (b) myoglobin, (c) ovalbumin, and (d) lysozyme separated by anion-exchange chromatography at pH 9.6. The displacer salts used were (1) LiBr, (2) NaBr, and (3) KBr. (Reproduced with permission from ref. 67.)

7.8 CONCLUSION

This chapter has reviewed the current status in the development of the mechanistic description of the HPIEC of proteins. In particular, the derivation and interpretation of various physicochemical parameters, which describe the interaction of proteins with charged surfaces, have been outlined. The interactive process between charged sites on the protein surface and the stationary phase can be quantitatively characterized by the Z_c value. Various studies on the influence of several experimental parameters on protein Z_c values have culminated in the development of the concept of the electrostatic interactive area or ionotope through which the protein binds to the stationary phase. This model has allowed a detailed characterization of the processes that control the approach to and adsorption and desorption of a biopolymer from charged surfaces.

The next stage in providing a more fundamental understanding of the retention processes in HPIEC will be the definition of the precise interactive topography of the protein ionotope. A number of recent studies[35,69,70] have provided the initial impetus toward fulfilling this goal, through correlation of chromatographic Z_c values with protein structural features. For example, Z_c values for lysozyme separated by anion-exchange chromatography range between 1 and 4 depending on the mobile phase composition and elution conditions. Examination of the X-ray crystal structure of lysozyme by computer graphics reveals that between 1 and 4 negatively charged groups are located in the region encompassing the catalytic cleft.[69] This suggests that these charges may be involved in the interaction of this protein with the positively charged stationary phase surface. These types of studies provide a general approach to characterizing the mechanism by which proteins approach and orient themselves at the sorbent surface through the analysis of the spatial disposition of specific amino acid residues.

Until recently, little was known about the environmental and structural parameters that are important in understanding mobile phase-induced changes in protein retention behavior. However, this chapter has demonstrated how our understanding of HPIEC and indeed chromatographic processes in general has developed to a sophisticated level that has provided significant insight into the interaction of biopolymers at synthetic surfaces. The future derivation of retention models that will accurately predict the HPIEC behavior of biopolymers is dependent on establishing general relationships that describe the complex interactions that occur between the solute and both the mobile phase and stationary phase.

ACKNOWLEDGMENTS

The support of the Australian Research Council, the National Health and Medical Research Council, the Monash University Special Research Grants Committee, the Potter Foundation, and the W. Buckland Foundation is gratefully acknowledged.

REFERENCES

1. O. Mikes, in New Comprehensive Biochemistry, Vol. 8 Separation Methods (Z. Reyl, ed.). Elsevier, Amsterdam, 1984, p. 215.
2. M. A. Rounds, W. D. Rounds, and F. E. Regnier, *J. Chromatogr.*, 397 (1987) 25.

3. R. W. Stout, S. I. Sivakoff, R. D. Ricker, H. C. Palmer, M. A. Jackson, and T. J. Odiorne, *J. Chromatogr.*, 352 (1986) 381.
4. R. M. Chicz, Z. Shi, and F. E. Regnier, *J. Chromatogr.*, 359 (1986) 121.
5. W. Kopaciewicz, M. A. Rounds, J. Fausnaugh, F. E. Regnier, *J. Chromatogr.*, 266 (1983) 3.
6. R. W. Stout, S. I. Sivakoff, R. D. Ricker, and L. R. Snyder, *J. Chromatogr.*, 353 (1986) 439.
7. M. T. W. Hearn, A. N. Hodder, and M. I. Aguilar, *J. Chromatogr.*, 458 (1988) 45.
8. N. K. Boardman and S. M. Partridge, *Biochem. J.*, 59 (1955) 543.
9. S. R. Himmelhoch, *Methods Enzymol.*, 22 (1971) 273.
10. W. Kopaciewicz and F. E. Regnier, *Anal. Biochem.*, 133 (1983) 251.
11. K. M. Gooding and M. N. Schmuck, *J. Chromatogr.*, 296 (1984) 231.
12. M. A. Rounds and F. E. Regnier, *J. Chromatogr.*, 283 (1984) 37.
13. K. M. Gooding and M. N. Schmuck, *J. Chromatogr.*, 327 (1985) 139.
14. M. T. W. Hearn, A. N. Hodder, P. G. Stanton, and M. I. Aguilar, *Chromatographia*, 24 (1987) 769.
15. M. T. W. Hearn, A. N. Hodder, and M. I. Aguilar, *J. Chromatogr.*, 443 (1988) 97.
16. M. T. W. Hearn, A. N. Hodder, and M. I. Aguilar, *J. Chromatogr.*, 458 (1989) 27.
17. A. N. Hodder, M. I. Aguilar, and M. T. W. Hearn, *J. Chromatogr.*, 476 (1989) 391.
18. J. Papenhuijzen, G. J. Fleer, and B. H. Bijsterbosch, *J. Colloid Interface Sci.*, 104 (1985) 553.
19. L. R. Snyder, in High Performance Liquid Chromatography, Vol. 1 (Cs Horvath, ed.). Academic Press, New York, 1980, p. 208.
20. X. Geng and F. E. Regnier, *J. Chromatogr.*, 296 (1984) 15.
21. Cs Horvath and W. Melander, *J. Chromatogr. Sci.*, 15 (1977) 393.
22. M. I. Aguilar, A. N. Hodder, and M. T. W. Hearn, *J. Chromatogr.*, 327 (1985) 115.
23. M. A. Stadalius, H. S. Gold, and L. R. Snyder, *J. Chromatogr.*, 296 (1984) 31.
24. M. A. Stadalius, H. S. Gold, and L. R. Snyder, *J. Chromatogr.*, 327 (1985) 27.
25. M. T. W. Hearn and M. I. Aguilar, *J. Chromatogr.*, 352 (1986) 35.
26. M. T. W. Hearn, A. N. Hodder, and M. I. Aguilar, *J. Chromatogr.*, 327 (1985) 47.
27. W. R. Melander, H-J. Lin, and Cs Horvath, *J. Phys. Chem.*, 88 (1984) 4527.
28. Cs Horvath, W. R. Melander, and I. Molnar, *J. Chromatogr.*, 125 (1976) 129.
29. W. R. Melander and Cs Horvath, *Arch. Biochem. Biophys.*, 183 (1977) 393.
30. W. R. Melander, D. Corradini, and Cs Horvath, *J. Chromatogr.*, 317 (1984) 67.
31. N. T. Miller and B. L. Karger, *J. Chromatogr.*, 326 (1985) 45.
32. M. T. W. Hearn and M. I. Aguilar, *J. Chromatogr.*, 359 (1986) 31.
33. M. T. W. Hearn and M. I. Aguilar, *J. Chromatogr.*, 392 (1987) 33.
34. R. R. Drager and F. E. Regnier, *J. Chromatogr.*, 406 (1987) 237.
35. J. Fausnaugh-Pollit, G. Thevenon, L. Janis, and F. E. Regnier, *J. Chromatogr.*, 443 (1988) 221.
36. F. Hofmeister, *Naunyn-Schmiedebergs Arch. Exp. Pathol. Pharmacol.*, 24 (1988) 247.
37. M. Daune, *Stud. Biophys.*, 24/25 (1970) 287.
38. R. M. Clement, J. Sturn, and M. P. Daune, *Biopolymers*, 12 (1973) 405.
39. G. S. Manning, *Q. Rev. Biophys.*, 11 (1978) 179.
40. S. Peterson, *Ann. N.Y. Acad. Sci.*, 57 (1954) 144.
41. L. R. Snyder and J. J. Kirkland, Introduction to Modern Liquid Chromatography. Wiley, New York, 1979, p. 421.
42. E. H. Bycher, *Chem. Weeblblad*, 39 (1942) 402.
43. F. A. Long and W. F. McDevit, *Chem. Rev.*, 51 (1952) 119.
44. B. E. Conway, *Adv. Colloid Interface Sci.*, 8 (1977) 91.
45. W. A. P. Luck, in Water and Ions in Biological Systems (A. Pullman, V. Vasileui, and L. Packer, eds.). Plenum, New York, 1985, p. 95.
46. K. D. Collins and M. W. Washabaugh, *Q. Rev. Biophys.*, 18 (1985) 323.
47. M. W. Washabaugh and K. D. Colins, *J. Biol. Chem.*, 261 (1986) 12477.

48. A. N. Hodder, M. I. Aguilar, and M. T. W. Hearn, *J. Chromatogr.*, 506 (1990) 17.
49. R. M. Chicz and F. E. Regnier, *J. Chromatogr.*, 443 (1988) 193.
50. E. S. Parente and D. B. Wetlaufer, *J. Chromatogr.*, 355 (1986) 29.
51. M. T. W. Hearn, A. N. Hodder and M. I. Aguilar, J. Chromatogr., 327 (1985) 47.
52. T. Arakawa and S. N. Timasheff, *Biochemistry*, 21 (1982) 6545.
53. T. Arakawa and S. N. Timasheff, *Biochemistry*, 23 (1984) 5912.
54. C. Tanford, Physical Chemistry of Macromolecules. Wiley, New York, 1961, p. 457.
55. M. T. W. Hearn, A. N. Hodder, and M. I. Aguilar, *J. Chromatogr.*, 458 (1988) 45.
56. A. H. Harten, W. E. Theissen, and L. Blum, *Science*, 217 (1982) 1033.
57. D. M. LeNeve, R. P. Rand, V. A. Parsegian, and D. Gingell, *Biophys. J.*, 18 (1977) 209.
58. D. F. Evans and B. W. Ninham, *J. Phys. Chem.*, 90 (1986) 226.
59. R. M. Pashley and J. N. Israelachvili, *J. Colloid Interface Sci.*, 101 (1984) 511.
60. R. M. Pashley, *J. Colloid Interface Sci.*, 83 (1981) 531.
61. G. J. Kennedy and J. H. Knox, *J. Chromatogr. Sci.*, 10 (1972) 549.
62. J. C. Giddings, in Dynamics of Chromatography (J. C. Giddings and R. A. Keller, eds.). Dekker, New York, 1965, p. 13.
63. R. Chang, Physical Chemistry with Applications to Biological Systems, 2nd Ed. Macmillan, New York, 1981, p. 487.
64. M. T. W. Hearn and M. I. Aguilar, in Separation Methods (Z. Deyl, ed.). Elsevier, Amsterdam, 1988, p. 107.
65. K. Benedek, S. Dony, and B. L. Karger, *J. Chromatogr.*, 317 (1984) 227.
66. S. A. Cohen, K. Benedek, Y. Tapuhi, J. C. Ford, and B. L. Karger, *Anal. Biochem.*, 144 (1985) 275.
67. A. N. Hodder, M. I. Aguilar, and M. T. W. Hearn, *J. Chromatogr.*, 512 (1990) 41.
68. D. E. Metzler, Biochemistry; The Chemical Reactions of Living Cells. Academic Press, New York, 1977, p. 182.
69. A. N. Hodder, M. I. Aguilar, and M. T. W. Hearn, *J. Chromatogr.*, 517 (1990) 317.
70. A. N. Hodder, M. I. Aguilar, and M. T. W. Hearn, *J. Chromatogr.*, 507 (1990) 33.
71. J. R. Strahler, *J. Chromatogr.*, 266 (1983) 281.
72. P. Lundahl and E. Greijer, *J. Chromatogr.*, 297 (1984) 129.
73. R. D. Weihle and J. L. Wittuff, *J. Chromatogr.*, 297 (1984) 313.
74. K. Nakamura and Y. Kato, *J. Chromatogr.*, 333 (1985) 29.
75. C. Eloy, G. Faudel, and J. P. Flandrois, *J. Chromatogr.*, 321 (1985) 235.
76. J. L. Seltzer, M. L. Eichbach, and A. Eisen, *J. Chromatogr.*, 326 (1985) 147.
77. A. Heubner, B. Manz, H. J. Grill, and K. Pollow, *J. Chromatogr.*, 297 (1984) 301.
78. M. K. Speedie, O. L. Wong, and R. D. Ciaranello, *J. Chromatogr.*, 327 (1985) 351.
79. D. H. Calam, J. Davidson, and R. Harris, *J. Chromatogr.*, 326 (1985) 103.
80. B. Ellis and J. Jolly, *J. Chromatogr.*, 326 (1985) 157.
81. N. Muto and L. Tan, *J. Chromatogr.*, 326 (1985) 137.
82. M. F. Schmerr, K. R. Goodwin, H. D. Lehmkuhl, and R. C. Cutlip, *J. Chromatogr.*, 326 (1985) 225.
83. S. A. Berkowitz, *J. Chromatogr.*, 398 (1987) 288.
84. P. Clezardin, G. Bougro, and J. L. McGregor, *J. Chromatogr.*, 354 (1986) 425.
85. J. A. Smith and J. J. O'Hare, *J. Chromatogr.*, 345 (1985) 168.
86. A. T. Andrews, M. D. Taylor, and A. J. Owen, *J. Chromatogr.*, 348 (1985) 177.
87. S. M. Hyder, A. Baldi, M. Crespi, and J. Wittliff, *J. Chromatogr.*, 359 (1986) 433.
88. S. M. Hyder, F. P. Kohrs, and J. L. Wittliff, *J. Chromatogr.*, 397 (1987) 269.
89. R. C. Johnston, P. G. Stanton, D. M. Robertson, and M. T. W. Hearn, *J. Chromatogr.*, 397 (1987) 389.
90. M. Waris and P. Halonen, *J. Chromatogr.*, 397 (1987) 321.
91. P. G. Stanton and M. T. W. Hearn, *J. Chromatogr.*, 397 (1987) 379.
92. D. W. Brandt and J. L. Wittliff, *J. Chromatogr.*, 397 (1987) 287.
93. A. M. Cox, R. Turner, and E. H. Cooper, *J. Chromatogr.*, 397 (1987) 213.

94. K.-O. Eriksson, I. Kourteva, K. Yao, J-L Liao, F. Kilar, and S. Hjerten, *J. Chromatogr.*, 397 (1987) 289.
95. J. R. Grun and R. Reinhardt, *J. Chromatogr.*, 397 (1987) 327.
96. D. Hock, U. Schriek, E. Fey, W. C. Forssmann, and W. Matt, *J. Chromatogr.*, 397 (1987) 347.
97. B. K. Singh, M. A. Stidham, and P. L. Shaner, *J. Chromatogr.*, 444 (1988) 251.
98. A. J. Alpert and P. C. Andrews, *J. Chromatogr.*, 443 (1988) 85.
99. E. Bolzacchini, G. DiGregorio, M. Nali, B. Rindone, S. Tollari, P. Falagiani, G. Riva, and G. Crespi, *J. Chromatogr.*, 397 (1987) 299.
100. M. Denis, *Anal. Biochem.*, 173 (1988) 405.
101. D. P. Bofinger, N. W. Fucile, and S. W. Spaulding, *Anal. Biochem.*, 170 (1988) 9.
102. C. G. Sanny and K. Rymas, *Anal. Biochem.*, 172 (1988) 51.
103. G. E. Marver and J.-L. Fauchere, *Anal. Biochem.*, 172 (1988) 248.
104. J. D. Orbell, L. W. Guddat, K. J. Machin, and N. W. Isaacs, *Anal. Biochem.*, 170 (1988) 390.
105. M. M. Van Lookeren Campagne, C. Erneux, R. Van Eijk, and P. J. M. Van Huastert, *Biochem. J.*, 254 (1988) 313.
106. J. R. McLachlin, S. C. Bernstein, and W. Frend Anderson, *Anal. Biochem.*, 163 (1987) 143.
107. A. J. M. van Den Eijden-van Raaij, I. Koornneef, Tn.MJ van Oostwaard, S. W. de Laac, and E. J. J. van Roelen, *Anal. Biochem.*, 163 (1987) 263.
108. V. Bouriotis, A. Zafeiropoulos, and Y. D. Clonis, *Anal. Biochem.*, 160 (1987) 127.
109. R. M. Riggin, G. K. Dorulla, and D. J. Miner, *Anal. Biochem.*, 167 (1987) 199.
110. J. Frank, A. Braat, and J. A. Diune, *Anal. Biochem.*, 162 (1987) 105.

CHAPTER 8

Reversed-Phase and Hydrophobic-Interaction Chromatography of Proteins

M. I. Aguilar and Milton T. W. Hearn

CONTENTS

8.1 INTRODUCTION

High-resolution analytical and preparative separation of proteins can now be routinely carried out through a combination of high-performance reversed-phase (RP-HPLC), hydrophobic-interaction (HP-HIC), and ion-exchange chromatography (HPIEC). Recent advances in the fractionation of biomacromolecules by HPIEC, which is based on electrostatic interactions between the protein solute and a charged stationary phase, has been reviewed elsewhere in Chapters 5–7 in this volume. This chapter outlines theoretical and experimental aspects of RP-HPLC and HP-HIC and the important impact these related techniques has had, and will continue to make, on modern biochromatography.

The term hydrophobic-interaction chromatography is now attributed to separations carried out with hydrophobic sorbents with elution usually involving a decrease in salt concentration. Reversed-phase chromatography refers to separations with mobile phases involving an increasing concentration of organic solvent in the eluent again with a hydrophobic sorbent. The concept of hydrophobic interaction in modern biochromatographic separations can be traced back to the classical work of Howard and Martin in 1950[1] when these workers reported one of the first applications with paraffin-impregnated paper for the resolution of organic metabolites. However, it was not until the work of various imaginative investigators, notably Shaltiel,[2,3] Hjertén,[4] and Hoftsee,[5] in the early 1970s that hydrophobic interaction chromatography came to assume importance for the separation of peptides and proteins in the context that the technique is now understood, i.e., the use of chromatographic stationary phases with chemically immobilized ligands of hydrophobic character.

The physicochemical basis of separation selectivity for both hydrophobic-interaction and reversed-phase methods is largely associated with the incremental changes in the microscopic surface tension involved with the solute–solvent–stationary phase interaction.[6,7] Chromatographic sorbents in RP-HPLC typically contain octadecyl groups or octyl groups chemically bonded, for example, to porous silica particles.[8] HP-HIC column packings feature more weakly hydrophobic surfaces based on immobilized acetyl, propyl, butyl, phenyl, poly(ethylene glycol), or poly(alkylaspartamide) groups.[9–13] Selectivity in both systems can be influenced by many eluent factors including the type of salt or organic modifier present in the eluent,[14–17] the addition of surfactants,[18,19] and operating temperature.[17,20] Protein separations can also be manipulated through changes in stationary phase variables such as the particle size,[21] the chain length,[15,22] and density of the hydrophobic ligand.[23]

Despite the current wide usage of both chromatographic techniques in the purification and analysis of peptides, proteins, and other biopolymers, the selection of a particular type of chemically bonded HIC or RP stationary phase with a compatible mobile phase composition has been frequently based on empirical criteria. Such arbitrary choices rarely result in fully optimized systems in terms of chromatographic resolution, band shape, or solute recovery. In particular, it is now well established that the separation of proteins in all the adsorptive modes of chromatography, but RP-HPLC and HP-HIC in particular, involves chromatographic distribution and kinetic processes that are much more complex than those shown by small polar molecules. In reversed-phase and hydrophobic-interaction chromatography these differences are now known to arise from (1) specific solute–solvation equilibria,[24] (2) multisite interaction with a heterogeneous stationary phase surface,[25] (3) solute aggregation in the bulk mobile phase or at the packing surface,[26] (4) sol-gel equilibria,[27] (5) specific ion-interaction equilibria involving ions present in the mobile phase or adsorbed on the nonpolar stationary phase surface,[28] and (6) specific pH-dependent ionization equilibria,[28] which reflect the unique isoelectric point characteristics of the zwitterionic protein solutes. Furthermore, the dynamic effects of conformational equilibria established by proteins and polypeptides[29] both in the bulk mobile phase and at the stationary phase surface have yet to be also incorporated into fully mechanistic, and predictive descriptions of protein chromatographic behavior. Recent advances in both the theoretical understanding and the experimental design of high-performance chromatographic systems have allowed various physicochemical aspects of solute–eluent and solute–stationary phase interactions to be quantitatively evaluated from chromatographic data. This chapter documents the application of these developments, which can be used to characterize in thermodynamic and extrathermodynamic terms hydrophobic interactions of peptides and proteins in RP-HPLC and HP-HIC. In addition, selected case studies are introduced to illustrate the potential that these methods offer for both analytical as well as preparative separation of biomacromolecules.

8.2 RETENTION RELATIONSHIPS IN SOLVOPHOBIC CHROMATOGRAPHY

Solvophobic liquid chromatography, which is based on exploiting the hydrophobic interactions between polar solutes and a nonpolar stationary phase surface, has its origin in a study reported in 1948,[30] on the separation of long chain fatty acids on a column of rubber powder using mobile phases composed of aqueous methanol or acetone. In 1950, Howard and Martin employed liquid paraffin and *n*-octane as stationary phases in the liquid–liquid chromatography of fatty acids. These investigators referred to the technique as "reversed-phase" chromatography to distinguish it from conventional partition chromatography. The term "solvophobic separations" is derived from the extensive theoretical investigations of Sinanoglu and his co-workers,[31,32] and more recently the studies of Horvath et al.[6,7] Solvophobic chromatography encapsulates both reversed-phase and hydrophobic-interaction chromatography. Simply stated, solvophobic chromatography is achieved through a decrease in the microscopic surface tension associated with the solute–sorbent interface. This can be achieved through changes in the water content by variation of the mole fraction of a soluble organic solvent modifier or salt.

Over the intervening decades reversed-phase techniques with aquoorganic solvent eluents have gained wide acceptance for the analysis of polar analytes but have only been successfully applied in the general context to the separation of proteins during the last decade following the development of high-performance stationary phase packings. The technique known as "hydrophobic-interaction chromatography" originates from Tiselius' concept of "salting-out" chromatography.[33] This technique has evolved almost exclusively as a method utilizing eluents with decreasing salt concentration to effect the desorption and the purification of proteins, initially with classical soft gels[2,3] and more recently with more stable silica-based packings.[12,34–38] The use of RP-HPLC for protein separation has often been identified with the irreversible binding of the solute to the stationary phase, and solute denaturation due to protein interactions with the mobile phase constituents or, in particular, the stationary phase surface. This is not necessarily the case and remedies to this difficulty with RP-HPLC have been suggested. The use of decreasing salt gradients in HP-HIC with weekly hydrophobic stationary phases generally avoids the problems of protein denaturation.

The physicochemical basis of both modes of solvophobic chromatography, i.e., the nonpolar interaction between a protein and a hydrophobic matrix, can be described in terms of the solvophobic theory where the isocratic retention factor, k', can be expressed as

$$\ln k' = -\frac{1}{RT}\Delta G^\circ + \ln(RT/PV) + \Phi \qquad (8\text{–}1)$$

where ΔG° is the overall difference in free energy of the solute between the mobile phase and the stationary phase, V is the mean molar volume of the solvent, P is the operating pressure, R and T are the gas constant and temperature, respectively, and Φ, the phase ratio, is a constant related to the density of accessible ligands on the stationary phase surface. The ΔG° term can be further represented by

$$\Delta G^\circ = \Delta G^\circ_{\mathrm{cav}} + \Delta G^\circ_{\mathrm{es}} + \Delta G^\circ_{\mathrm{vdw}} + \Delta G^\circ_{\mathrm{assoc}} + \Delta G^\circ_{\mathrm{red}} \qquad (8\text{–}2)$$

where $\Delta G^\circ_{\mathrm{cav}}$, $\Delta G^\circ_{\mathrm{es}}$, and $\Delta G^\circ_{\mathrm{vdw}}$ are the differences between mobile phase and stationary phase in free energy associated with cavity formation, electrostatic effects, and van der Waals interactions, respectively. The term $\Delta G^\circ_{\mathrm{assoc}}$ is the free energy change for ligate–eluite association in the absence of surrounding solvent, i.e., in the gas phase. The term $\Delta G^\circ_{\mathrm{red}}$ expresses the reduction in free energy due to solvent–ligand and solvent–solute interactions not treated in the first three terms and is essentially a correction factor of Eq. (8–2) for nonideal behavior.

In solvophobic chromatography, with a particular column and eluent composition, the capacity factor of a solute can be obtained according to the solvophobic theory by the following expression

$$\ln k' = A' + B'\left(\frac{1-\lambda}{2\lambda}\right)\frac{\mu_s^2}{v_s}\frac{1}{1-(\alpha_s/v_s)} + C'\Delta A \qquad (8\text{–}3)$$

where the constants A', B', and C' are given by

$$A' = \varphi - \frac{\Delta G_{\text{vdw, assoc}}}{RT} + \frac{\Delta G_{\text{vdw, s}}}{RT} + \frac{4.836N^{1/3}(\kappa^{e} - 1)V^{2/3}\gamma}{RT} + \ln \frac{RT}{P_0 V} \tag{8–4}$$

$$B' = ND/RT \tag{8–5}$$

and

$$C' = N\gamma/RT \tag{8–6}$$

The parameter λ is defined by the expression

$$\upsilon_{SL} = \lambda \upsilon_{S} \tag{8–7}$$

where υ_{SL} and υ_S are the molecular volumes of the solute–ligand complex and the unbound solute, respectively. The term D is the dielectric constant of the medium, while μ_s and α_s refer to the static dipole moment and the polarizability of the solute, respectively. Experimentally it has been shown that the solvophobic forces that have the greatest influence on k' are those that are dependent on surface tension, γ. Thus Eq. (8–3) can be simplified to

$$\ln k' = A'' + B''\gamma \tag{8–8}$$

where A'' is the sum of all terms present in Eq. (8–3), which do not contain the surface tension parameter and

$$B'' = \frac{N\Delta A_{\text{h}} + 4.836N^{1/3}(\kappa^{e} - 1)V^{2/3}}{RT} \tag{8–9}$$

where N is Avogadro's number and ΔA_h is the hydrophobic contact surface area of the associated species. The parameter κ is defined as the ratio of the energy required to create a cavity for a solvent molecule to the energy required to extend the planar surface of the liquid by the surface area of the molecules.

The dependency of log k' on both surface tension, γ, and hydrophobic contact area, ΔA_h, predicted by the solvophobic theory has been validated for a wide range of small-molecular-weight solutes including carboxylic acids, amines, and amino acids.[39,40] However, extension of this model to accurately describe the retention of protein solutes on hydrophobic stationary phases is significantly more complicated due to the complex nature of protein secondary and tertiary structure. For example, the parameters related to the dipole moment, μ_s, the molecular volume, υ_s, and the polarizability, α_s, of a protein can be readily estimated only if it is assumed that the protein is a rigid sphere of uniform surface charge and shape. This assumption is clearly untenable for many classes of proteins. Furthermore, derivation of thermodynamic parameters that are capable of describing the solute–stationary phase interaction must also account for the influence of multisite attachment and conformational equilibrium on the experimental capacity factor. Again, the lumped form of Eq. (8–9) does not readily allow these effects to be segregated.

The manipulation of retention by surface tension changes is carried out in RP-HPLC through the use of either aquoorganic solvent mixtures and by the variation in inorganic salt concentrations in HP-HIC. As a result, the influence of these additives on the protein hierarchical structure and interactive behavior must also be incorporated into retention models. The following sections therefore describe the current theoretical and experimental approaches to the elucidation and characterization of these factors that control the interaction of proteins with hydrophobic surfaces.

8.3 THE DEPENDENCE OF PROTEIN RETENTION ON ORGANIC SOLVENT MIXTURES

The number of applications of RP-HPLC and HP-HIC in protein purification continues to expand at a rapid rate. However, the development of fully mechanistic models, capable of describing the underlying thermodynamic and kinetic processes involved in the interaction of proteins with nonpolar stationary phases, has been impeded by the complex nature of protein structure. In the absence of rigorous approaches capable of predicting the effect on retention and bandwidth dependencies of experimental conditions, several empirical, nonmechanistic models for the isocratic and gradient elution of peptide solutes by RP-HPLC have been described.[25,41–44]

According to the solvophobic theory, the solute capacity factor should decrease with decreasing surface tension of the solvent. Thus in RP-HPLC, maximal retention of proteins to nonpolar sorbents will occur with neat aqueous eluents as water has the highest surface tension among the common solvents. Indeed, by analogy with Eq. (8–8), in RP-HPLC, the isocratic k' values of proteins typically have their largest value with neat water, which decreases as the content of a water miscible solvent increases. This behavior has been expressed as a linear function of the mole function, φ, of the organic solvent such that over a defined range of $\Delta\varphi$ values,

$$\log k' = \log k'_0 - S\varphi \qquad (8\text{–}10)$$

An analogous equation can be utilized for hydrophobic chromatography, namely

$$\log k' = \log k'_0 - H\xi \qquad (8\text{–}11)$$

where ξ is the mole fraction of salt present in the mobile phase. Depending on the magnitude of the S, H, and $\log k'_0$, parameters, a variety of dependencies of solute retention on mobile phase eluotropic strength can be anticipated as depicted in Figure 8–1. Cases (c) and (d) represent typical scenarios for the RP-HPLC of highly hydrophobic polypeptides and globular proteins, while cases

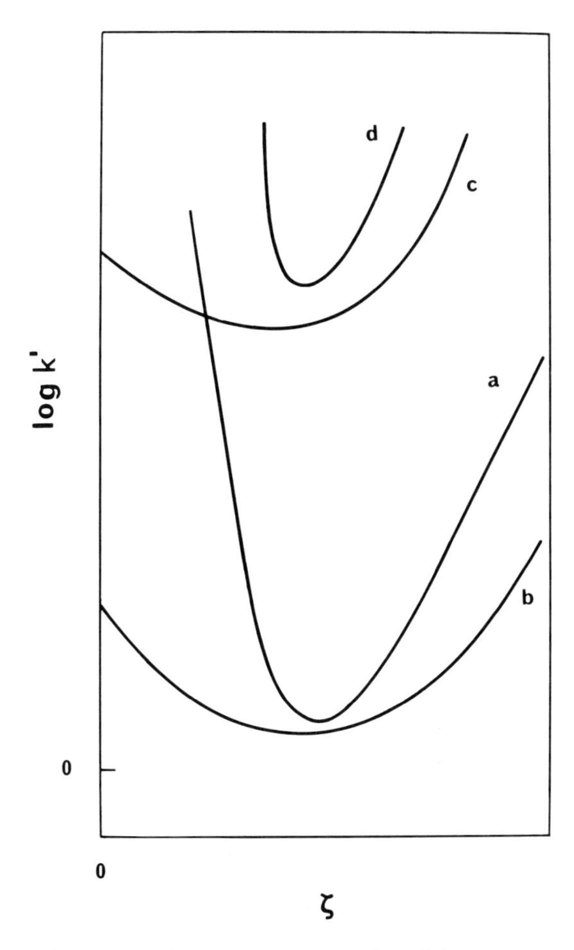

FIGURE 8–1. Schematic representation of the retention dependencies of proteins chromatographed on mixed-mode support media. The figure illustrates four case histories for the dependency of the logarithmic capacity factor (log k') on the mole fraction, ζ the displacing species. (Reproduced with permission from ref. 43.)

(a) and (b) are more representative of the RP-HPLC behavior of polar peptides and small polar globular proteins. Plots of log k' versus φ for proteins separated on n-alkylsilicas with aquoorganic solvent eluents are generally found from experimental studies to be curved rather than linear. Examples of the plots of experimental logarithmic capacity factors against organic solvent strength for several hormonal proteins are shown in Figure 8–2.[45] In cases such as these, the tangent, S, to the curve can be calculated at a particular value of k' and the value of log k' at $\varphi = 0$ (log k'_0) obtained by extrapolation using linear or nonlinear regression analysis. Similarly with HP-HIC separations, plots of log

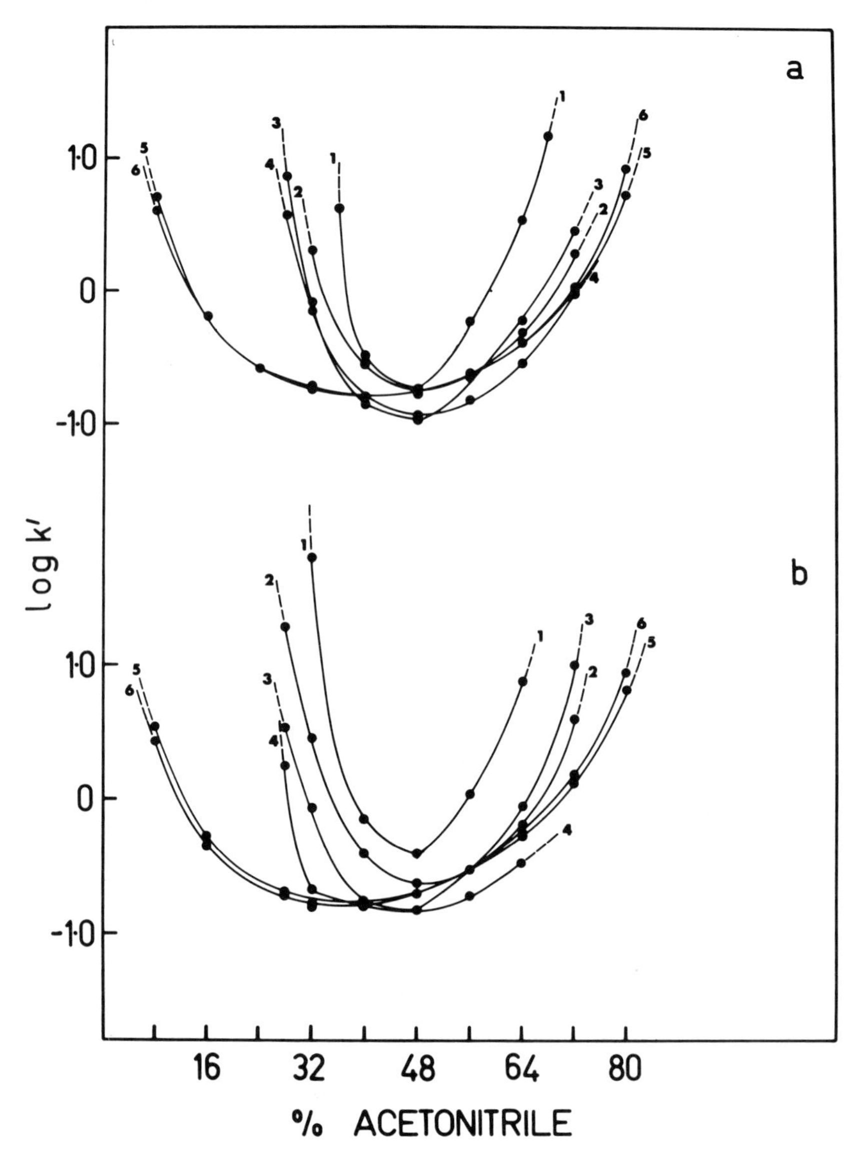

FIGURE 8–2. Plots of the logarithmic capacity factors for hen lysozyme and several hormonal polypeptides against the volume fraction, φ, of the organic solvent in water–acetonitrile isocratic mobile phases. Conditions, μ-Bondapak C_{18}, flow rate, 2.0 ml/min; primary mobile phases, (a) water–4 m*M* sodium sulfate–15 m*M* orthophosphoric acid, pH 2.2 and (b) water–4 m*M* sulfuric acid–15 m*M* orthophosphoric acid–15 m*M* triethylamine with the acetonitrile content adjusted over the φ range 0.0–0.8. The polypeptides 1, hen lysozyme; 2, porcine glucagon; 3, bovine insulin; 4, bovine insulin β-chain; 5, arginine vasopressin; 6, lysine vasopressin. (Reproduced with permission from ref. 45.)

k' versus ξ are often curvilinear, although again over a narrow operational range linear dependencies of slope H can be observed (see *Figure 8–3*).

The determinations of S, H, and log k'_0 values for proteins from isocratic chromatographic data can on occasions be time-consuming and requires high experimental precision. Furthermore, many proteins exhibit skewed peaks when eluted from n-alkylsilicas under isocratic conditions. As a consequence, accurate determinations of the average elution time and peak variance require more precise methods such as the calculation of the first and second moments of the peak zone. To overcome these experimental difficulties, complex mixtures are now typically separated under gradient elution conditions. Several studies on the development of optimization models for gradient elution of low- and high-molecular-weight solutes by RP-HPLC have recently been described.[41–43,47] In particular, concepts derived from the linear solvent strength (LSS) gradient model[42] have been shown to provide a useful basis for evaluating the retention behavior of polypeptides and proteins. If it is assumed that the

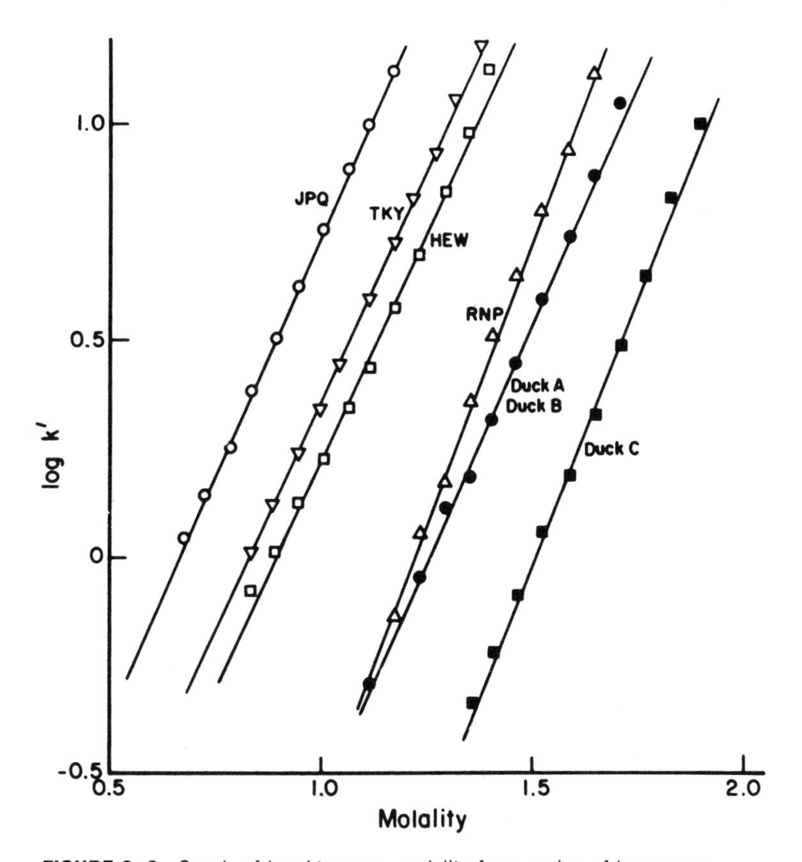

FIGURE 8–3. Graph of log k' versus molality for a series of lysozymes. Each lysozyme was chromatographed on a TSK gel Phenyl-5PW column in 10 mM potassium phosphate buffer (pH 7.0) at increasing ammonium sulfate concentrations. (Reproduced with permission from ref. 46.)

same chromatographic variables that control retention, resolution, and bandwidth in isocratic elution are also relevant in the gradient elution modes of RP-HPLC and HP-HIC then solute S and $\log k_0'$ values can be determined through application of the LSS theory. If all secondary solution equilibria remain constant under gradient conditions of varying gradient time, t_G, flow rate, F, or organic modifier volume fraction, φ, then the retention time, t_g, for a protein chromatographed under gradient elution conditions can be expressed according to the LSS model as

$$t_g = (t_0/b)\,[\log 2.3k_0'b + 1] + t_0 + t_d \tag{8–12}$$

where t_0 is the column dead time, t_d is the time required for the mobile phase to reach the column inlet as the volume fraction of the B solvent increases, and b is the gradient steepness parameter. When solutes are chromatographed over a range of gradient times in the same column with the same mobile phase system, the gradient steepness parameter can be derived according to

$$b = \frac{t_0 \log \beta}{t_{g1} - (t_{g2}/\beta) + t_0\,(t_{G1} - t_{G2})/t_{G2}} \tag{8–13}$$

where t_{g1} and t_{g2} are the gradient retention times of the solute at gradient times t_{G2}/t_{G1}. Evaluation of the b values from retention data determined over various gradient times allows the calculation of a range of median capacity factors, $\bar{k}$, and the corresponding organic volume fraction, $\bar{\varphi}$, as follows:

$$\bar{k} = 1/1.15b \tag{8–14}$$

and

$$\bar{\varphi} = [t_{g,1} - t_0 - (t_0/b)\log 2]/t_G^0 \tag{8–15}$$

where $t_G^o = t_{G1}/\Delta\varphi$. The values of $\bar{k}$ and $\bar{\varphi}$ can therefore be related by analogy with Eq. (8–9) through the empirical expression

$$\log \bar{k} = \log k_0' - S\bar{\varphi} \tag{8–16}$$

The S, H, and $\log k_0'$ values can then be derived by regression analysis of plots of $\log \bar{k}$ versus $\bar{\varphi}$ or $\log \bar{k}$ versus ξ as shown in *Figures 8–4* and *8–5*, respectively.

The evaluation of S, H, and $\log k_0'$ values is central to the optimization of separation and characterization of protein retention behavior in both RP-HPLC and HP-HIC. For example, availability of these parameters provides the basis for the enhancement of resolution via optimization procedures with a particular chromatographic system through the determination of resolution as follows:

$$R_s = \left(\frac{1}{4}\right)\left(\frac{R_2'}{R_1'}\right)\sqrt{N}\left(\frac{k'}{1 + k_1'}\right) \tag{8–17}$$

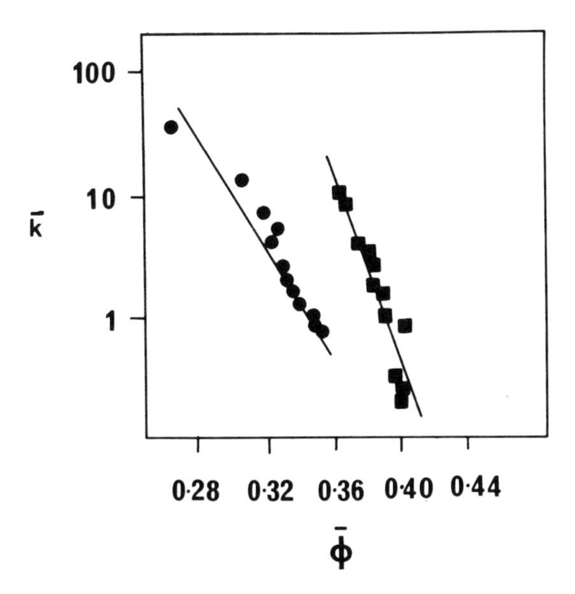

FIGURE 8–4. Plots of log $\bar{k}$ versus $\bar{\varphi}$ for (●) lysozyme and (■) insulin eluted from a 5-μm, 15-nm pore octyl-silica stationary phase.[51] Gradient elution was carried out with acetonitrile–water mixtures with 0.1% morpholine and 0.125% trifluoroacetic acid.

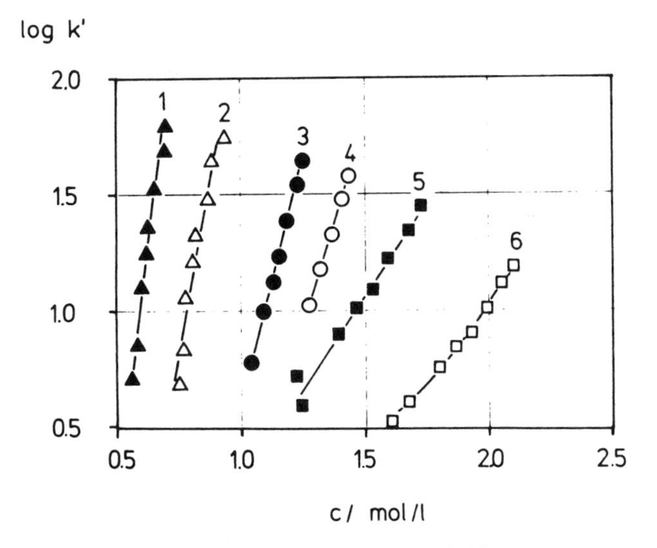

FIGURE 8–5. Dependence of log k' on $(NH_4)_2SO_4$ concentration during linear descending $(NH_4)_2SO_4$ gradients, using a nonporous 1.5-μm amide bonded silica. Proteins: 1, ferritin; 2, catalase; 3, lactate dehydrogenase; 4, ovalbumin; 5, lysozyme; 6, ribonuclease. (Reproduced with permission from ref. 59.)

where N is the separation efficiency and the selectivity, α, between the two solutes P_1 and P_2, i.e., k'_2/k'_1, is determined by

$$\alpha = \log(k'_2/k'_1) = \log\left(\frac{k'_{0,2}}{k'_{0,1}}\right) - \varphi(S_2 - S_1) \qquad (8\text{–}18)$$

These relationships provide the fundamental basis of iterative computational assessment of microprocessor-controlled approaches to the optimization of chromatographic selectivity. Whether this optimization is achieved by Simplex routines, or more demanding algorithms, depends in part on the complexity of the separation task, but also on the investigator's access to sophisticated microprocessor-driven systems. Analysis of S, H, and $\log k'_0$ values also provides practical quantitative guidelines for the design and preparation of improved hydrophobic stationary phases through the characterization of different stationary phase topographies and the effect of different column configurations on protein retention behavior.

Knowledge of the S, H, and $\log k'_0$ values also assists in the determination of physicochemical relationships underlying selectivity–function dependencies. The chromatographic behavior and biological activity of a protein are closely dependent on its three-dimensional structure. The application of the above expressions allows quantitative structure–activity relationships to be correlated with chromatographic retention data via linear free-energy relationships. Chromatographic selectivity increments ($\bar{\tau}$) can therefore be formally related to functional coefficients through expressions such as

$$\log \alpha = \bar{\tau} = f(K) \qquad (8\text{–}19)$$

where K is a measure of biological function. Where the data base is extensive, the correlation of protein structure with chromatographic retention and biological activity can be thus approached, e.g., in the case of calcitonin[48] the retention behavior of analogues was correlated with function and similar methods have been applied to enzyme substrates.[49]

The S, H, and $\log k'_0$ values of proteins are usually large when compared to those of simple organic molecules. This feature of protein retention behavior is believed to be a consequence of multisite ligand-solute interactions. According to Eqs. (8–8) and (8–9), these parameters can be directly related to the magnitude of the hydrophobic contact area established between the solute and the hydrocarbonaceous ligand. Thus changes in retention processes that are mediated through different classes of binding sites on the heterogeneous stationary phase surface or through different topographic regions of the exposed solvated surface structure of the protein solute will lead to different values of S, H and $\log k'_0$ for the protein or peptide in question. For example, marked differences in experimentally observed S values for a series of closely related interleukin-2 muteins have been reported that reflect the differences in the interactive sites on the protein surface.[50]

Correlation of protein S values with molecular weight (MW) has been assessed[24,41,49,51] through the empirical relationship

$$S = (MW)^b \qquad (8\text{–}20)$$

where the coefficients a and b have varied according to the set of peptides and proteins and chromatographic conditions. Analogous expressions can also be derived for the HP-HIC of proteins. Although the hydrophobic contact area and the number of interaction sites should increase in number with increasing molecular weight and size of the protein, it is not the molecular weight per se but rather the polarity and spatial disposition of the surface amino acid residues involved in the interaction with the stationary phase that will ultimately control the mechanistic pathway of the binding process and thus the magnitude of the S or H term.

8.4 THE DEPENDENCE OF PROTEIN RETENTION ON SALT CONCENTRATION

The purification of proteins by RP-HPLC often results in poor recovery in terms of both total mass and biological activity. These observations are due to their strong interactions with the hydrophobic stationary phase and/or the acidic eluents containing organic solvents. HP-HIC has therefore become increasingly popular for the separation and purification of proteins, whereby the protein is eluted from a weakly hydrophobic surface by a decreasing salt gradient. Melander and Horvath[52,53] extended the use of the solvophobic theory to describe the effects of neutral salts on protein solubility and retention in HIC. The magnitude of the free energy change ΔG°_{es}, due to electrostatic interactions between the protein solute and the mobile phase varies with the salt concentration, m, according to a modified Debye–Hükel equation as

$$\Delta G^\circ_{es} = A - \frac{B(m^{1/2})}{1 + (CM^{1/2})} - D\mu m \qquad (8\text{–}21)$$

where μ is the dipole moment of the protein, A and B are proportional to the net charge on the protein, and C and D are constants that are dependent on the size of the protein solute. The surface tension, γ, of aqueous salt solution is a function of the salt concentration according to

$$\gamma = \gamma^\circ + \sigma m \qquad (8\text{–}22)$$

where γ° is the surface tension of neat water and σ is the molal surface tension increment.

The following expression is thus obtained for the overall energy of cavity formation

$$\Delta G^\circ_{cav} = -[N\Delta A_h + 4.8N^{1/3}(\kappa^e - 1)V^{2/3}]\sigma m + \text{constant} \qquad (8\text{–}23)$$

which can be simplified to

$$\Delta G^{\circ}_{\mathrm{cav}} = -N\Delta A_{\mathrm{h}}\sigma m + \mathrm{constant} \tag{8–24}$$

The free energy change, $\Delta G^{\circ}_{\mathrm{vdw}}$, due to van der Waals interactions, is assumed to be approximately linear in salt concentration according to

$$\Delta G^{\circ}_{\mathrm{vdw}} = Vm + \mathrm{constant} \tag{8–25}$$

Thus, combination of Eqs. (8–1) and (8–21)–(8–23) yields an expression for the dependence of the logarithmic capacity factor on salt concentration for isocratic elution as follows:

$$RT\ln(k'/k'_0) = \frac{-Bm^{1/2}}{(1 + Cm^{1/2})} - D\mu m + N\Delta A\sigma m + \upsilon m + \mathrm{constant} \tag{8–26}$$

where k'_0 is the capacity factor at zero salt concentration. At high ionic strengths, the Debye term on the right-hand side approaches a constant value and the logarithmic capacity factor becomes linear with respect to salt concentration according to

$$\log k'/k'_0 = (-D\mu + \upsilon + NA\sigma)m/RT \tag{8–27}$$

The terms $D\mu$ and υ, which are related to the dielectric constant of the medium, the dipole moment of the protein, and van der Vaals interactions are assumed to be constant for a particular protein solute and chromatographic system. Thus, the free energy of interaction of a protein with HP-HIC stationary phases is dependent on contact surface area, ΔA_{h}, established between the solute and the sorbent and the molal surface tension increment, σ, of the eluting salt solution.

The retention behavior of proteins separated by gradient elution with a linear decrease in salt concentration can also be analyzed in terms of retention volume V_{R} according to

$$V_{\mathrm{R}} = V_{\mathrm{a}}/\lambda m \log\left[\frac{\lambda m[V_{\mathrm{R,0}}\exp(\lambda m)] - V_1}{V_{\mathrm{G}} + \exp(\lambda m V_1/V_{\mathrm{G}})}\right] \tag{8–28}$$

The linear dependency of protein retention on salt concentration is illustrated in plots (shown in Figure 8–6) of the logarithmic retention volume, $\log V_{\mathrm{R}}$ of eight proteins, versus the concentration of $(NH_4)_2SO_4$ in the starting eluent in gradient elution.[53] The slopes of these curves are termed the hydrophobic interaction parameter, λ, which, according to Eq. (8–27) is equal to

$$\lambda = -(D\mu + \upsilon + NDA\sigma)/RT \tag{8–29}$$

This relationship can be further simplified if it is assumed that for proteins of similar size, net charge, and charge distribution, the term $(D\mu + \upsilon)$ is similar for a particular set of chromatographic conditions, to give

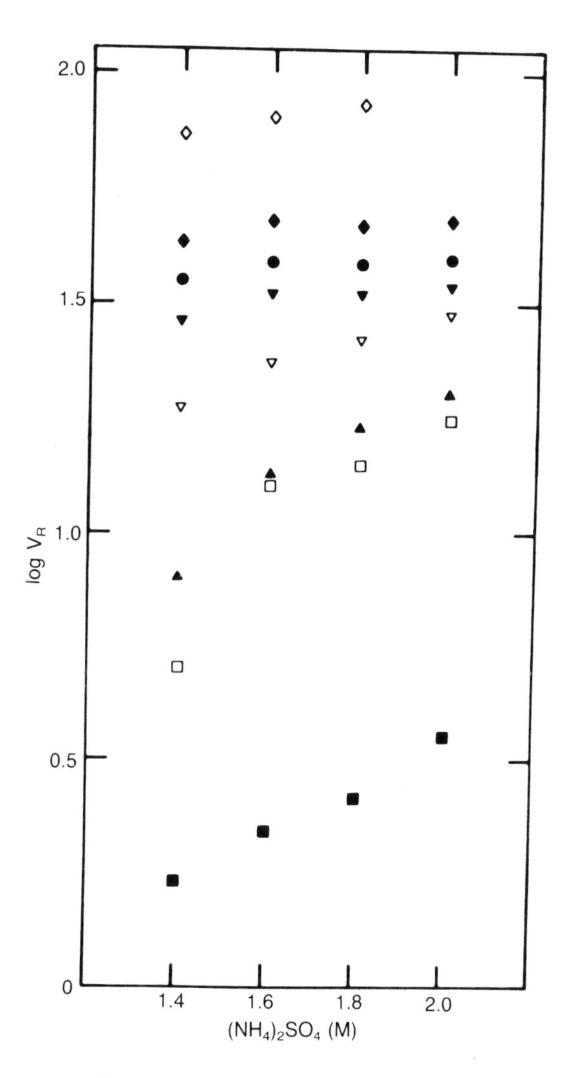

FIGURE 8–6. Plots of logarithmic retention volume, log V_R, versus the concentration of $(NH_4)_2SO_4$ in the starting eluent with gradient elution for eight proteins. (◇) Insulin, (◆) insulin β-chain, (●) trypsin inhibitor, (▼) trypsinogen, (▽) insulin α-chain, (▲) ribonuclease, (□) myoglobin, and (■) cytochrome *c*. (Reproduced with permission from ref. 53.)

$$\lambda = \text{constant} + NDA\sigma/RT \tag{8–30}$$

This relationship allows a number of predictions about protein retention behavior in HP-HIC to be made. First, if the adsorption of the protein solute onto the stationary phase surface arises solely from hydrophobic interactions, then

λ will be directly proportional to the molal surface tension increment, σ. However, if specific interactions such as electrostatic effects occur between the protein and either the stationary phase or the salt, a nonlinear dependency between λ and σ will be observed. Both scenarios are evident in Figure 8–7, which represents plots of λ versus σ for a number of proteins separated on a propyl bonded phase in 50 m*M* phosphate buffer with descending concentration gradients of a range of salt types.[53] Second, according to Eq. (8–29), λ

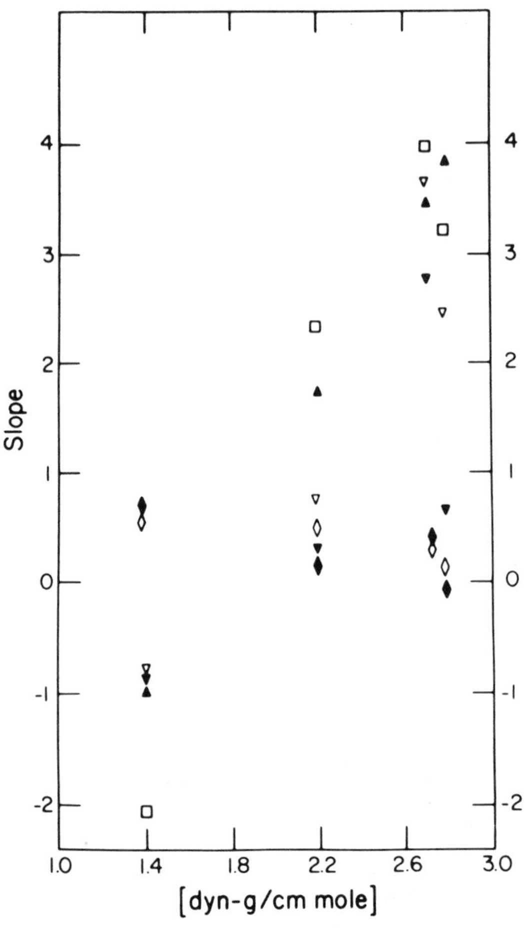

FIGURE 8–7. Graphs of the hydrophboic interaction parameter λ derived from the slope of plots of logarithmic retention factor versus salt molality, plotted against the molal surface tension increment of the corresponding salt. For identification of symbols see Figure 8–6. (Reproduced with permission from ref. 53.)

will also be dependent on the hydrophobic interaction area, ΔA_h, which should also be proportional to the accessible surface area, A_{max}, according to

$$\Delta A_h = qA_{max} \tag{8–31}$$

where q is a proportionality constant. If it is assumed that the tertiary structure and surface characteristics of a protein in solution are similar to the structure determined by X-ray crystallography, then A_{max} can be estimated from known atomic coordinates. Combinations of Eqs. (8–30) and (8–31) yields

$$\lambda = \text{constant} + qA_{max}N\sigma/RT \tag{8–32}$$

which predicts that λ will be linearly related to the surface area determined from crystallography, provided A_{max} can be estimated from crystallographic data. Plots of λ measured on a phenyl-linked stationary phase against A_{max} for proteins determined with a 4.0 Å diameter probe are shown in Figure 8–8. While the results have been obtained with only three proteins, the data demonstrate that the hydrophobic interaction parameter is closely related, as predicted by the solvophobic theory, to the potential hydrophobic contact area.

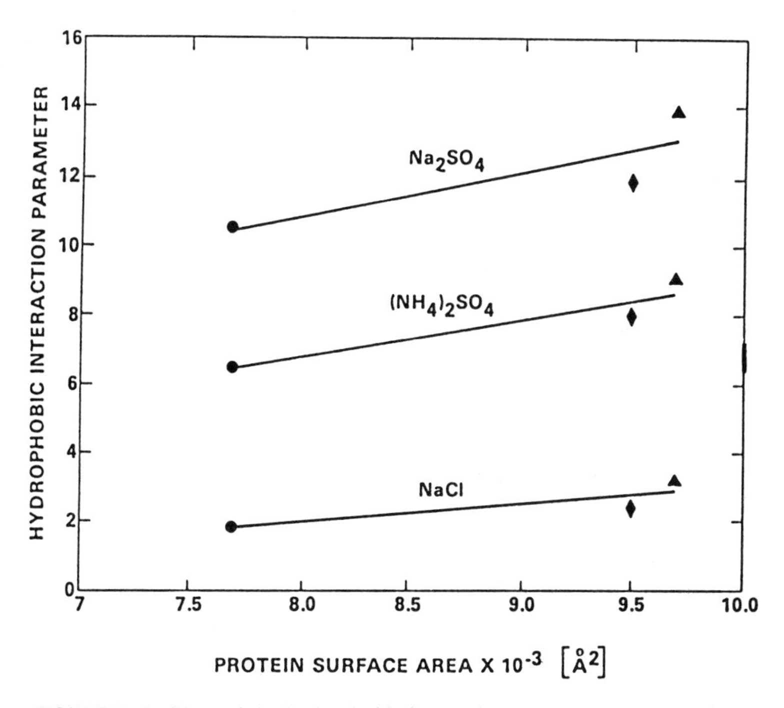

FIGURE 8–8. Plots of the hydrophobic interaction parameter λ versus the surface area of the proteins calculated with a 4.0 Å diameter probe. Proteins used were (●) lysozyme, (◆) trypsinogen, and (▲) α-chymotrypsinogen. (Reproduced with permission from ref. 54.)

8.5 KINETIC RELATIONSHIPS OF PROTEINS IN SOLVOPHOBIC CHROMATOGRAPHY

The adsorption of proteins on hydrophobic sorbents has been shown in the previous sections to arise from solvophobic expulsion of the solute from the polar mobile phase onto the nonpolar stationary phase surface. As a consequence, the hydrophobic contact area occupied by the protein at the stationary phase–mobile phase interface determines the extent of interaction under normal operating conditions. The relatively large contact surface areas of proteins also gives rise to the pronounced dependency of retention and bandwidth on the concentration of the eluting species, which is often observed for proteins eluted in either RP-HPLC or HP-HIC. Smaller N values than those obtained for low-molecular-weight solutes would be anticipated for proteins separated under equivalent elution conditions due to the low diffusion coefficients of biomacromolecules in solution. However, other effects mediated by the matrix (e.g., silanophilic) properties of the heterogeneous stationary phase surface, by specific solvation or buffer interaction equilibria, or by conformational phenomena also contribute to the bandwidth dependencies of protein solutes on experimental conditions.

While the use of gradient elution for protein purification reduces separation time, decreases peak volumes, and allows the more accurate prediction of retention behavior in selected cases for the optimization of experimental parameters, these approaches do not address the practical requirements central to the description of the kinetics and conformational dynamics of the solute. In particular, current theoretical approaches, which describe the thermodynamic and kinetic processes of macromolecular solute migration in interactive HPLC in terms of a conformationally rigid solute interacting with a homogeneous ligand surface system, do not quantitatively address the implications of a single solute capable of manifesting multiple interacting sites or varying diffusional properties and molecular shape as a consequence of time-dependent exposure to a particular chromatographic environment. For example, the derivation of the equation for the chromatographic bandwidth[55,56] σ_v, namely

$$\sigma_v = [(\bar{k}/2) + 1]Gt_0FN^{-0.5} \tag{8–33}$$

is based on the assumption that the surface area of a peptidic or protein solute of a defined molecular weight can be characterized in terms of a constant hydrodynamic shape with fixed chemical topography throughout the chromatographic separation. Under these conditions it would be anticipated that the ratio of the experimentally observed bandwidths to the calculated bandwidths should approach unity over the normal operational range of $\bar{k}$ values. Often the experimental bandwidths have been found to significantly exceed the values predicted on the basis that the solute behaves as a conformationally rigid species that interacts with a single class of binding sites during its passage along the column. In these cases, the chromatographic behavior has been interpreted in terms of residence time effects, which result in changes in protein conformation or when other secondary equilibrium effects operate.

Band-broadening relationships can be further analyzed through the comparison of experimental and calculated peak capacity (*PC*) data. The peak capacity for a chromatographic separation of gradient time t_G and average resolution equal to unity (e.g., $R_s = 1$) for all solute pairs is given by

$$PC = t_G F / 4\sigma_{v,exp} \tag{8–34}$$

Substitution of Eq. (8–33) into (8–34) results in the expression

$$PC = \frac{0.5}{k^{-0.25} dp} \left(\frac{D_m t_G \Delta\varphi S}{C} \right)^{0.5} \tag{8–35}$$

where D_m is the solute diffusion coefficient in the mobile phase and C is the Knox equation parameter that accounts for resistance to mass transfer at the stationary phase surface. This relationship allows further optimization of a separation through maximizing peak capacity by manipulation of experimental conditions. For example changes in the gradient time t_G in both RP-HPLC and HP-HIC systems have been shown to lead to an increased peak capacity up to a maximum value of ~250 depending on column configuration. Further, according to Eq. (8–35), peak capacity is inversely proportional to the stationary phase particle diameter, *dp*. Exploitation of this dependency has formed the basis for the recent development of nonporous particles.[57–59]

However, although the dependencies of peak capacity on experimental parameters as predicted by Eq. (8–35) are generally observed, the magnitude of the experimental peak capacity values is often significantly lower than the calculated value, particularly under experimental conditions associated with longer residence times and with low flow rates or long gradient times. Thus, if the molecular dimensions and secondary structure of the protein change during its passage along the column in a relatively slow, time-dependent manner, corresponding changes in the diffusional and interactive properties of the solute will lead to differential zone migration. These changes in diffusional properties, manifested as changes in D_m, C, and other parameters associated with the kinetics of solute interaction will ultimately be revealed as experimentally observed bandwidths and peak capacities that deviate from the theoretical values predicted by Eqs. (8–33) and (8–35). Ovalbumin[61] (*Figure 8–9*), and β-endorphin[56] (*Figure 8–10*) provide examples of ideal and nonideal band-broadening behavior, as analyzed in terms of the LSS zone spreading equations.

The molecular composition of the interactive segment of the solute, which presents itself to the chromatographic surface, ultimately determines the magnitude of the experimentally observed bandwidth behavior. The ability to detect and resolve intermediate kinetic steps of a multistep conformational transition will depend on the sensitivity of the on-line spectroscopic measurements, the relaxation times associated with the different phenomena, the magnitude of the differences in retention times for the different species, and the peak variance of each species. Recent studies on the conformation of proteins adsorbed onto various reversed-phase and hydrophobic-interaction sorbents in the presence of aquoorganic and salt containing solvents using fluorescence,[62] Fourier

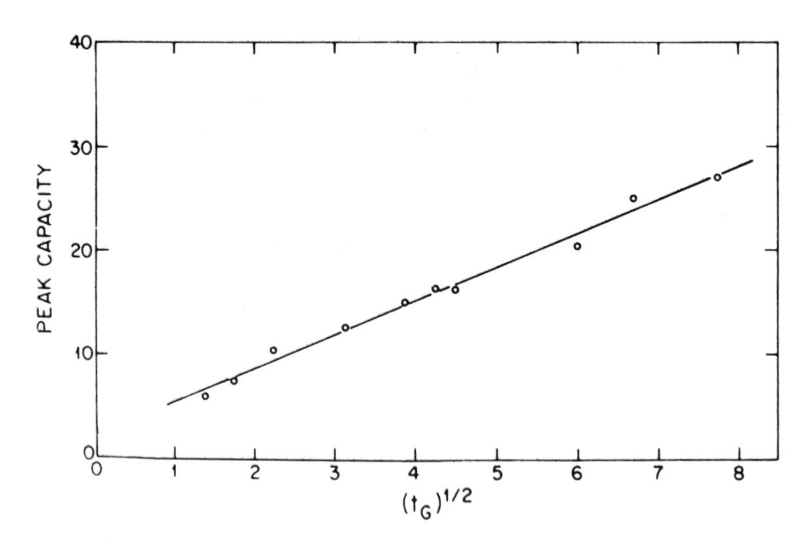

FIGURE 8–9. Influence of gradient time, t_G, on peak capacity of ovalbumin under HP-HIC gradient elution conditions with an ether-bonded silica-based stationary phase. Solvent A consisted of 0.5 *M* NH_4OAc and 3 *M* $(NH_4)_2SO_4$ (pH 6.0) and solvent B 0.5 *M* NH_4OAc. (Reproduced with permission from ref. 61.)

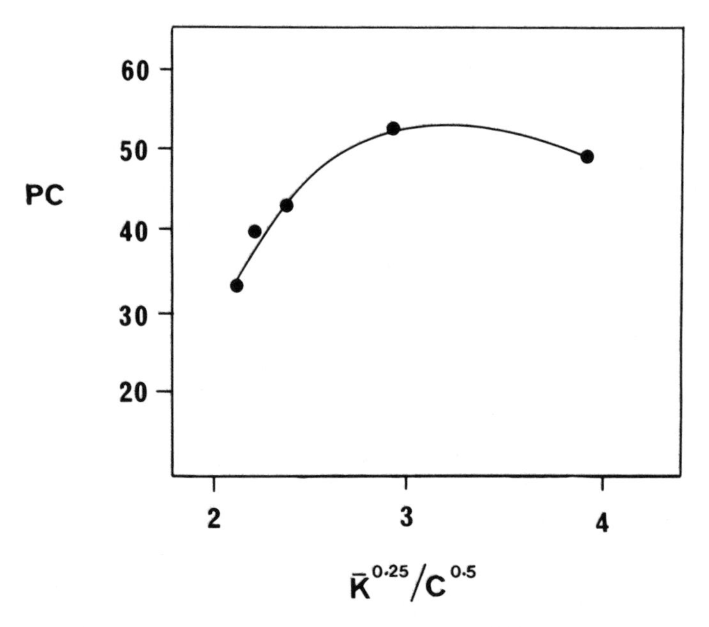

FIGURE 8–10. Plot of peak capacity (*PC*) versus $\bar{k}^{0.25}/C^{0.5}$ for human β-endorphin eluted under gradient conditions on a 6-μm 13-mm pore size octadecyl silica stationary phase. Solvent A consisted of 0.1% TFA/water and B 0.1% TFA/60% acetonitrile.

transform infrared,[63] and low-angle laser light scattering procedures[26] have demonstrated the existence of surface-associated protein conformational changes that are induced by the stationary phase ligand or the mobile phase constituents. The ability of the current multiwavelength detectors to detect gross changes in protein conformations in chromatographic systems is illustrated in Figure 8–11, which shows the thermal denaturation of β-lactoglobulin as monitored by changes in retention volume and spectral properties.[64]

Accurate quantitation of the more subtle effects associated with small shifts in conformational equilibria that may be induced by interaction with nonpolar surfaces requires more sophisticated approaches to the analysis of chromatographic data. Recent studies on the characterization of conformational equilibria for biopolymers at liquid–solid interfaces have provided a theoretical framework for the treatment of multizoning phenomena.[65,66] For example, if a protein undergoes a two-stage interconversion in both the mobile phase and at the stationary phase surface, then a retention cycle that represents the distribution of the native protein $P_{m,0}$ and two unfolded forms $P_{m,1}$ and $P_{m,2}$ between the two chromatographic phases can be written as follows:

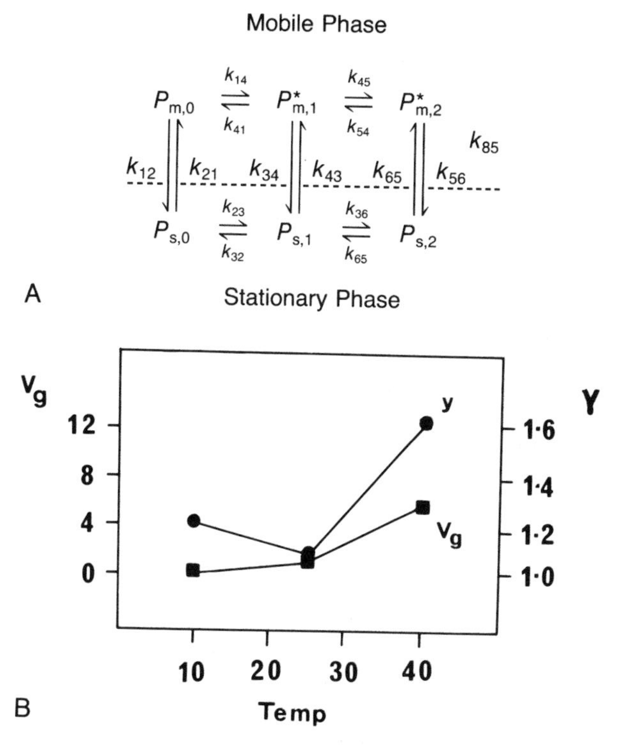

FIGURE 8–11. Effect of temperature on retention and on-line spectroscopic properties of β-lactoglobulin on an ether-bonded silica-based stationary phase.[64] Solvent A consisted of 2 *M* $(NH_4)_2SO_4$, 0.5 *M* NH_4OAc (pH 6) and (B) 0.5 *M* NH_4OAc (pH 6). Elution was carried out with a 20 min linear gradient from 100% A to 100% B at a flow rate of 1 ml/min.

If the rate-determining step for the pathway is associated with the unfolding of $P_{m,1} \rightleftharpoons P_{m,2}$, then the distribution can be approximated by a four-component cycle. The resolution of the interconverting species can then be given by

$$R = \frac{t_0\Phi(k_{12}/k_{21} - k_{43}k_{34})(1 - e^{-D_a})}{4D_a(\sigma_1 + \sigma_2)} \qquad (8\text{–}36)$$

where D_a is the Damkohler number and given by

$$D_a = \frac{L(\Phi k_{12}k_{23} + k_{14}k_{21})(k_{14} + k_{41})}{(k_{14}k_{21})u_0} \qquad (8\text{–}37)$$

and k_{ij} are the respective rate constants for adsorption, desorption, unfolding, and refolding, σ_i is the peak width of component i, L is the column length, and u_0 is the linear velocity. The plate height increment due to slow kinetics of interconversion, H_{se}, can be determined by

$$H_{se} = \frac{2A}{D_a}\left(\frac{1 + e^{a^{-D}} - 1}{D_a}\right) \qquad (8\text{–}38)$$

where

$$A = [L(k_0 - k_1)^2/K_m]/[1 + k_1 + (1 + k_0)/k_n]^2 \qquad (8\text{–}39)$$

where k_0 and k_1 are the capacity factors for the two interconverting forms. The Damkohler number represents the ratio of the time taken by the protein or peptide to passage along the column in the mobile phase to the overall relaxation time for all conformational interconversions. The influence of the Damkohler number on a chromatographic profile is shown in Figure 8–12. When the value is small, the chromatogram for a four-component cycle will reflect the average retention behavior of a fully unfolded form or, alternatively, two peaks separated by a time interval equivalent to $(k_{12}/k_{21} - k_{43}/k_{34})$. Conversely, when D_a is very large, kinetic effects associated with conformational interconversion essentially vanish. However, at intermediate reaction rates where $1 < D_a < 10$, complex elution profiles are anticipated that are dependent on the equilibrium distribution of the two species, the rate of interconversion, the chromatographic conditions, and the column efficiency. For example, the asymmetric peak observed for ribonuclease A separated on an n-butylsilica sorbent[67] corresponded to a D_a value of 0.85.

There are currently very few reports that describe the detailed analysis of the adsorption–desorption kinetics or conformational interconversion of proteins chromatographed on hydrophobic stationary phases. Nevertheless, the graphic representations derived from numerical solutions of the mass balance equations with various combinations of selected values for the rate constants, equilibrium constants, and as selectivities can be used to simulate elution profiles, and to provide visual comparison with experimentally observed chromatograms. The availability of the various kinetic parameters involved in the re-

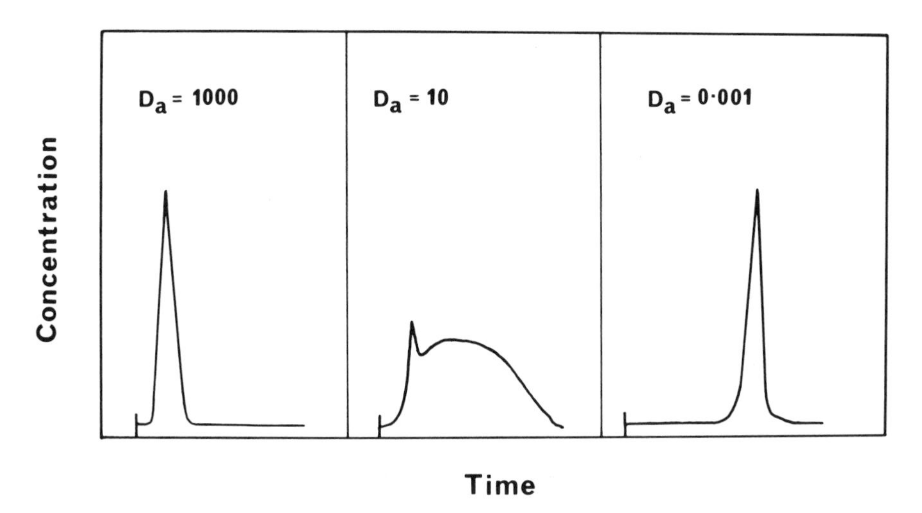

FIGURE 8–12. Computer simulation of the influence of the magnitude of the Damkohler number on the elution profile of a protein undergoing a 4-cycle interconversion. (Reproduced with permission from ref. 43.)

versed-phase and hydrophobic-interaction behavior of proteins will provide fundamental insight into the mechanistic basis of the interaction of proteins with hydrophobic surface in the presence of inorganic salts or aquoorganic solvents.

8.6 APPLICATIONS

Over the past decade, the scientific community has shown a substantial fondness for the resolving power of HP-HIC and RP-HPLC techniques in their quest for the isolation and analysis of exotic peptides and proteins. Consequently, the research literature at multiple levels—chromatographic sciences, protein chemistry, biochemistry, molecular biology, biomedical sciences, and biotechnology—is now rich with many thousands of applications based on the original observations and concepts pioneered in the mid-1970s for high-resolution and high-performance separation in the "hydrophobic" selectivity mode. Constant refinements have been introduced since these pioneering investigations, but the basic strategies and application protocols have remained largely unchanged. The selected examples given in other chapters in this volume as well as in Table 8–1 provide a flavor of the versatility, range, and relevance of the HP-HIC and RP-HPLC methods in the whole gambit of the life sciences. Clearly, the stage is at hand when our understanding of the molecular mechanism of retention and kinetic behavior of peptides and proteins with hydrophobic sorbents will usher in a new era of even more discriminatory separation techniques addressing *in situ* definition of the conformational properties and

TABLE 8–1. Selected Examples of Proteins Purified by RP-HPLC and HP-HIC

Protein	Column	Mobile phase	Reference
gag gene product p18	Vydac C_{18}	0.1% TFA, 7–63% CH_3CN, step, 0.6 ml/min	68
Hirudin	Nucleosil C_8	0.1% TFA, 15–30% CH_3CN, 15 min, 1 ml/min	69
Estrogen receptor	SynChropak C_3	10 m*M* KH_2PO_4, 1.5 m*M* EDTA, 1 m*M* DTT, 10% glycerol, 2–0.5 *M* $(NH_4)_2SO_4$, 10 min, 1 ml/min	70
Neuromedin U	Techsil C_{18}	0.05% TFA, 20–50% CH_3CN, 90 min, 1 ml/min	71
IL-2 receptor fragments	Supelco C_{18}	0.1% TFA, 0.70% CH_3CN, 1 ml/min	72
Valyl-tRNA synthetase	Phenyl-Sepharose	100 m*M* KH_2PO_4, pH 7.2, 1 m*M* DTT, 0.1% Triton X-100, 10% glycerol	73
Gramicidin A	C_{18}	CH_3OH:H_2O:CH_3CN (68:12:20), 1 ml/min	74
Histone H3	Ultrasphere C_8	0.1% TFA, 0–100% CH_3CN, 110 min, 1 ml/min	75
Myelin proteins	Ultrapore C_3	0.1% TFA, 10–70% *i*PrOH, 60 min, 1 ml/min	76
Glucocerebrosidase	Phenyl-5PW	10 m*M* Na_2PO_4, pH 6.0, 100 m*M* NaCl, 1.06–0 *M* $(NH_4)_2SO_4$, 5 ml/min	77
Insulin	Zorbax C_8	0.1 *M* Na_2HPO_4, pH 2.1, 0–50% CH_3CN, 120 min, 1 ml/min	78
Retinal protein peptide M	Delta Pak C_{18}	0.1% TFA, 0–50% CH_3CN, 40 min, 0.5 ml/min	79
Factor X	Proteosil diphenyl	0.1% TFA, 20–45% CH_3CN, 25 min, 1 ml/min	80
α_2-Microglobulin	Novapak C_{18}	0.1% TFA, 0–50% CH_3CN, 0.5 ml/min	81
Malaria antigen	Aquapore C_4	0.1% TFA, 20–50% CH_3CN, 25 min, 1 ml/min	82
Renin	Phenyl-5PW	50 m*M* Tris-HCl, pH 8.0, 1.5–0 *M* NaCl, step, 1 ml/min	83
Prorenin	Phenyl-5PW	50 m*M* Tris-HCl, pH 8.0, 1.5–0 *M* NaCl, step, 1 ml/min	83
Cytochrome *c* oxidase	LC-HINT	50 m*M* Na_2HPO_4, pH 7.2, 0.1% Tween 20, 0.5 ml/min	84
Estrogen receptor	Spherogel-CAA-HIC	10 m*M* Na_2HPO_4, 1.5 m*M* EDTA, 1 m*M* DTT, 10% glycerol, pH7.4, 2–0 *M* $(NH_4)_2SO_4$, 40 min, 1 ml/min	85
Glycinin	Vydac C_{18}	0.1% TFA, 20–45% CH_3CN, 90 min, 1 ml/min	86
Insulin	Ultrasphere C_{18}	5 m*M* H_3PO_4, 20 m*M* triethylamine, 150 m*M* $NaClO_4$, pH 3, 30% CH_3CN, 1 ml/min	87
Leukemia inhibitory factor	YMC-C_4	0.1% TFA, 0–60% CH_3CN, 45 min, 0.8 ml/min	88

Bitistatin	Delta Pak C_{18}	0.1% TFA, 0–30% CH_3CN, 60 min, 100 ml/min	89
GRP cyclohydrolase I	Toyopearl C_4	50 m*M* K_2HPO_4, pH 7.5, 0.1 m*M* EDTA	90
Arial nutriuretic factor prohormone	Aquapore C_8	0.1% TFA, 0–100% CH_3CN, 100 min, 1 ml/min	91
Secretin	Vydac C_{18}	10 m*M* HCl, 20–36% CH_3CN, 40 min, 1 ml/min	92
Bone growth factor	Vydac C_4	0.1% TFA, 14–42% CH_3CN, 70 min, 1 ml/min	93
Heparin binding growth factors	Vydac C_4	0.1% TFA, 30–50% CH_3CN, 80 min, 0.6 ml/min	94
Rec. interferon-1	Cosmosil C_{18}	0.1% TFA, 0–70% CH_3CN, 100 min, 1 ml/min	95
Caldesman	Vydac C_{18}	0.1% TFA, 5–38% CH_3CN, 60 min, 1 ml/min	96
Fibroblast growth factor	YMC-C_4	0.1% TFA, 20–50%, CH_3CN, 50 min, 1 ml/min	97
Insulin-like growth factor I	C_{18}	0.05% TFA, 0–60% CH_3CN, 60 min, 1 ml/min	99
Scorpion α-toxin derivative	C_8	0.15 *M* NH_4HCOOH, pH 2.7, 10–40%, CH_3CN, 30 min, 1 ml/min	100
Fasciatoxin	Vydac C_4	0.07% TFA, 10–60%, CH_3CN, 70 min, 1 ml/min	101
Lipoprotein lipase-inhibiting protein	Aquapore C_8	0.1% TFA, 0–53% CH_3CN, 45 min, 0.2 ml/min	102
Methylated calmodulin	Vydac C_4	10 m*M* MES, 0.1 m*M* $CaCl_2$, pH 6.12, 5–100%, CH_3CN, 1 ml/min	103
Inhibin α-Subunit monomer	Ultrapore C_{18}	0.1% TFA, 10–60% CH_3CN, 50 min, 0.5 ml/min	104
Betaine aldehyde dehydrogenase	Phenyl Superose	10 m*M* Tris-HCl, pH 7.8, 1 m*M* DTT, 10% v/v glycerol, 1–0 *M* $(NH_4)_2SO_4$	105
Phospholipase A_2	Vydac C_4	0.1% TFA, 0–75% CH_3CN, 45 min, 1 ml/min	106
Carnitine dehydratase	Phenyl Sepharose	50 m*M* KH_2PO_4, pH 7.5, 25–15% Sat. $(NH_4)_2SO_4$, step, 0.8 ml/min	107

associated functional features of these biomacromolecules. Table 8–1 thus should be viewed as a representative selection of a technique whose full impact has yet to traverse the teenage years.

8.7 CONCLUSION

Protocols for the high-resolution purification of protein samples generally incorporate RP-HPLC and/or HP-HIC. However, fully mechanistic models that accurately describe protein retention behavior in HPLC systems based on hydrophobic interactions have still to be fully developed. Nevertheless, the empirical models now available to analyze retention and bandwidth behavior have allowed significant advances to be made over the last decade in our understanding of the physicochemical processes that are involved in the interaction of proteins with hydrophobic stationary phases. The ultimate goal of the chromatographer is to be able to completely define the functional status of the protein by a detailed analysis of the relative retention, band shape, and online spectroscopic properties. In this regard, the ability to characterize and quantitate the interactive process in terms of contact surface areas and the strength of the interaction represents the first major steps in providing a mechanistic basis in terms of structure–retention relationships. These advances in defining the conformational integrity of proteins as they elute from the stationary phase also provide the foundations, both experimentally and theoretically, for new insight into surface–surface interactions and interfacial phenomena in general, which are intimately involved in the control of biological systems. In particular, identification and analysis of the chromatographic contact region will provide information on the nature of the strong (electrostatic and hydrogen-bonding) and weak (hydrophobic and dipole) forces that control all interactive processes.

ACKNOWLEDGMENTS

The support of the Australian Research Council, the National Health and Medical Research Council, the Monash University Research Excellence Fund, and the Commonwealth Industrial Research and Development Board is gratefully acknowledged.

REFERENCES

1. G. A. Howard and A. J. P. Martin, *Biochem. J.*, 46 (1950) 532.
2. S. Shaltiel and Z. Er-el, *Proc. Natl. Acad. Sci. U.S.A.*, 70 (1973) 778.
3. S. Shaltiel, *Methods Enzymol.*, 34 (1974) 142.

4. S. Hjertén, *J. Chromatogr.*, 87 (1973) 325.
5. B. H. J. Hoftsee, *Anal. Biochem.*, 52 (1973) 430.
6. Cs. Horvath, W. Melander, and I. Molnar, *J. Chromatogr.*, 125 (1976) 129.
7. W. R. Melander, D. Corradini, and Cs. Horvath, *J. Chromatogr.*, 317 (1984) 67.
8. K. K. Unger, in HPLC–Advances and Perspectives, Vol. 5 (Cs. Horvath, ed.). Academic Press, New York 1988, p. 1.
9. J. L. Fausnaugh, E. Pfannkoch, S. Gupta, and F. E. Regnier, *Anal. Biochem.*, 137 (1984) 464.
10. A. J. Alpert, *J. Chromatogr.*, 359 (1986) 85.
11. S. C. Goheen and S. C. Engelhorn, *J. Chromatogr.*, 317 (1984) 55.
12. N. T. Miller, B. Feibush, and B. L. Karger, *J. Chromatogr.*, 316 (1984) 519.
13. Y. Kato, T. Kitamura, and T. Hashimoto, *Anal. Biochem.*, 360 (1986) 260.
14. J. L. Fausnaugh, L. A. Kennedy, and F. E. Regnier, *J. Chromatogr.*, 317 (1984) 41.
15. M. N. Schmuck, N. P. Nowlan, and K. M. Gooding, *J. Chromatogr.*, 371 (1986) 55.
16. M. T. W. Hearn and B. Grego, *J. Chromatogr.*, 218 (1981) 497.
17. K. A. Cohen, K. Schelenberg, K. Benedek, B. L. Karger, B. Grego, and M. T. W. Hearn, *Anal. Chem.*, 140 (1984) 223.
18. D. B. Wetlaufer and M. R. Koenigbauer, *J. Chromatogr.*, 359 (1986) 73.
19. M. T. W. Hearn and B. Grego, *J. Chromatogr.*, 296 (1984) 309.
20. S-L. Wu, K. Benedek, and B. L. Karger, *J. Chromatogr.*, 359 (1986) 3.
21. M. Verzele, Y-B Yang, C. Dewaele, and V. Berry, *Anal. Chem.*, 60 (1988) 1329.
22. A. J. Alpert, *J. Chromatogr.*, 359 (1986) 85.
23. D. Wu and R. R. Walters, *Anal. Chem.*, 60 (1988) 1517.
24. M. T. W. Hearn and M. I. Aguilar, *J. Chromatogr.*, 359 (1986) 33.
25. X. Geng and F. E. Regnier, *J. Chromatogr.*, 296 (1984) 15.
26. N. Grinberg, R. Blanco, D. M. Yarmush, and B. L. Karger, *Anal. Chem.*, 61 (1989) 514.
27. H. P. Jennisen, in Affinity Chromatography and Biological Recognition (I. Chaiken, M. Wilchek, and I. Parikh, eds.). Academic Press, New York, 1983, p. 281.
28. M. T. W. Hearn (ed.), Ion Pair Chromatography. Dekker, New York, 1984.
29. M. T. W. Hearn, A. N. Hodder, and M. I. Aguilar, *J. Chromatogr.*, 327 (1985) 47.
30. J. Boldingh, *Experientia*, 4 (1948) 270.
31. O. Sinanoglu in B. Pullman (ed.), Molecular Associations in Biology. Academic Press, New York, 1968, p. 427.
32. O. Sinanoglu, *Theor. Chim. Acta*, 33 (1974) 279.
33. A. Tiselius, in Chromatographic Analysis, Discussion of the Faraday Society, No. 7. Hazell, Watson and Winey, London, 1949, p. 9.
34. J. D. Pearson, M. Mitchell, and F. E. Regnier, *J. Liquid Chromatogr.*, 6 (1983) 1441.
35. Y. Kato, T. Kitamura, and T. Hashimoto, *J. Chromatogr.*, 266 (1983) 49.
36. D. L. Gooding, M. N. Schmuck, and K. M. Gooding, *J. Chromatogr.*, 296 (1984) 107.
37. J.-P. Chang, Z. El Rassi, and Cs. Horvath, *J. Chromatogr.*, 396 (1985) 399.
38. Z. El Rassi and Cs. Horvath, *J. Liquid Chromatogr.*, 9 (1986) 3245.
39. Cs. Horvath, W. Melander, and I. Molnar; *J. Chromatogr.*, 125 (1976) 129.
40. Cs. Horvath, W. Melander, and I. Molnar, *Anal. Chem.*, 49 (1977) 142.
41. M. I. Aguilar, A. N. Hodder, and M. T. W. Hearn, *J. Chromatogr.*, 327 (1985) 115.
42. L. R. Snyder, in HPLC—Advances and Perspectives, Vol. 1 (Cs. Horvath, ed.). Academic Press, New York, 1980, p. 208.
43. M. T. W. Hearn and M. I. Aguilar, in Modern Physical Methods in Biochemistry, Part B (A. Neuberger and L. L. M. Van Deenen, eds.). Elsevier, Amsterdam, 1988, p. 107.
44. D. W. Armstrong and R. E. Boehm, *J. Chromatogr. Sci.*, 22 (1984) 378.
45. M. T. W. Hearn and B. Grego, *J. Chromatogr.*, 255 (1983) 125.
46. J. L. Fausnaugh and F. E. Regnier, *J. Chromatogr.*, 359 (1986) 131.
47. R. Van Der Zee, T. Hoekzema, S. Welling-Wester, and G. W. Welling, *J. Chromatogr.*, 368 (1986) 283.

48. M. L. Heinitz, E. Flanigan, R. C. Orlowski, and F. E. Regnier, *J. Chromatogr.*, 443 (1988) 229.
49. M. T. W. Hearn and M. I. Aguilar, *J. Chromatogr.*, 392 (1987) 33.
50. M. Kunitani, P. Hirtzer, D. Johnson, R. Halenbeck, A. Boosman, and K. Koths, *J. Chromatogr.*, 359 (1986) 391.
51. M. A. Stadalius, H. S. Gold, and L. R. Snyder, *J. Chromatogr.*, 296 (1984) 31.
52. W. Melander and Cs. Horvath, *Arch. Biochem. Biophys.*, 183 (1977) 200.
53. W. R. Melander, D. Corradini, and Cs. Horvath, *J. Chromatogr.*, 317 (1984) 67.
54. A. Katti, Y.-F. Maa, and Cs. Horvath, *Chromatographia*, 24 (1987) 646.
55. M. A. Stadalius, H. S. Gold, and L. R. Snyder, *J. Chromatogr.*, 327 (1986) 27.
56. M. T. W. Hearn and M. I. Aguilar, *J. Chromatogr.*, 352 (1986) 35.
57. K. K. Unger, J. N. Kinkel, B. Anspach, and H. Giesche, *J. Chromatogr.*, 296 (1984) 3.
58. K. K. Unger, G. Jilge, J. N. Kinkel, and M. T. W. Hearn, *J. Chromatogr.*, 359 (1986) 61.
59. R. Jansen, K. K. Unger, H. Giesche, J. N. Kinkel, and M. T. W. Hearn, *J. Chromatogr.*, 397 (1987) 91.
60. G. Jilge, R. Janzen, H. Giesche, K. K. Unger, J. N. Kinkel, and M. T. W. Hearn, *J. Chromatogr.*, 397 (1987) 71.
61. N. T. Miller and B. L. Karger, *J. Chromatogr.*, 326 (1985) 45.
62. A. J. Sadler, R. Micanovic, G. E. Katzenstein, R. V. Lewis, and C. R. Middaugh, *J. Chromatogr.*, 317 (1984) 93.
63. G. E. Katzenstein, S. A. Vrona, R. J. Wechsler, B. L. Steadman, R. V. Lewis, and C. R. Middaugh, *Proc. Natl. Acad. Sci. U.S.A.*, 83 (1986) 4268.
64. S.-L. Wu, K. Benedek, and B. L. Karger, *J. Chromatogr.*, 359 (1986) 3.
65. W. R. Melander, H. J. Lin, J. Jacobson, and Cs. Horvath, *J. Phys. Chem.*, 88 (1984) 4536.
66. J. Jacobson, W. R. Melander, G. Vaisnys, and Cs. Horvath, *J. Phys. Chem.*, 88 (1984) 4.
67. X. M. Lu, K. Benedek, and B. L. Karger, *J. Chromatogr.*, 359 (1986) 19.
68. H. V. J. Kolbe, F. Jaeger, P. Lepage, C. Roitsch, G. Lacaud, M-P Kieny, J. Sabatie, S. W. Brown, J-P Lecocq, and M. Girard, *J. Chromatogr.*, 476 (1989) 99.
69. A. Bischoff, D. Clesse, O. Whitechurch, P. Lepage, and C. Roitsch, *J. Chromatogr.*, 476 (1989) 245.
70. S. M. Hyder and J. L. Wittliff, *J. Chromatogr.*, 476 (1989) 455.
71. J. Domin, Y. Yiangou, R. A. Spokes, A. Aitken, K. B. Parmar, B. J. Chrysanthou, and S. R. Bloom, *J. Biol. Chem.*, 264 (1989) 20881.
72. M. C. Miedd, J. D. Hulmes, and Y-C E. Pan, *J. Biol. Chem.*, 264 (1989) 21097.
73. G. Bec and J. P. Waller, *J. Biol. Chem.*, 264 (1989) 21138.
74. C. J. Stankovic, J. M. Delfino, and S. L. Schreiber, *Anal. Biochem.*, 184 (1990) 100.
75. L. P. Kurochkina and G. Y. Kolomijtsera, *Anal. Biochem.*, 178 (1989) 88.
76. D. A. Bizzozero, T. S. Odykirk, J. F. McGarry, and M. B. Lees, *Anal. Biochem.*, 180 (1989) 59.
77. F. Y. M. Choy, *Anal. Biochem.*, 179 (1989) 312.
78. E. P. Kroeff, R. A. Owens, E. L. Campbell, R. D. Johnson, and H. I. Marks, *J. Chromatogr.*, 461 (1989) 45.
79. M. Knight, M. P. Strickler, M. J. Stone, L. Chiodetti, S. Gluch, and T. Shinohara, *J. Chromatogr.*, 459 (1988) 366.
80. K. T. Shitanishi and S. W. Herring, *J. Chromatogr.*, 444 (1988) 107.
81. J. Escribano, R. Matas, and E. Mendez, *J. Chromatogr.*, 444 (1988) 165.
82. K. Benedek, B. Hughes, M. B. Seaman, and J. K. Swadesh, *J. Chromatogr.*, 444 (1988) 191.
83. C. T. Carilli, L. Cameron-Wallace, L. M. Smith, M. A. Wong, and J. A. Lewicki, *J. Chromatogr.*, 444 (1988) 203.

84. N. Parris, H. A. Gruber, S. M. Mozersky, and R. A. Barford, *J. Chromatogr.*, 444 (1988) 219.
85. S. M. Hyder and J. L. Wittliff, *J. Chromatogr.*, 444 (1988) 225.
86. R. E. Peterson and W. J. Wolf, *J. Chromatogr.*, 444 (1988) 263.
87. C. J. Rhodes and P. A. Halban, *Biochem. J.*, 251 (1988) 23.
88. H. Gascan, A. Godard, C. Ferenz, J. Naulet, V. Praloran, M-A Peyrat, R. Hewick, Y. Jacques, J-F Moreau, and J. P. Soulillon, *J. Biol. Chem.*, 264 (1989) 21509.
89. R. J. Shebuski, D. R. Ramjit, G. H. Bencen, and M. A. Polokoff, *J. Biol. Chem.*, 264 (1989) 21550.
90. K. Hatakeyma, T. Harada, S. Suzuki, Y. Watanabe and H. Kayamijama, *J. Biol. Chem.*, 264 (1989) 21660.
91. J. K. Gierse, P. O. Olins, C. S. Devine, J. D. Marlay, M. G. Obukowicz, L. H. Mortensen, E. G. McMahon, E. H. Blaine, and R. Seetharan, *Arch. Biochem. Biophys.*, 271 (1989) 441.
92. D. Gossen, A. Vandermeers, M-C. Vandermeers-Piret, J. Rathe, A. Cauvin, P. Robberecht, and J. Christophe, *Biochem. Biophys. Res. Commun.*, 160 (1989) 862.
93. H. Mayer and K.-G. Kukoschke, *Eur. J. Biochem.*, 181 (1989) 409.
94. W. Quinkler, M. A. Aspberg, S. Bernotat-Daniebuski, N. Luthe, H. S. Sharma, and W. Schaper, *Eur. J. Biochem.*, 181 (1989) 67.
95. J. Utsumi, Y. Mizuno, K. Hosoi, K. Okanoi, R. Sawada, M. Kajitani, I. Sakai, M. Naruto, and H. Shimizu, *Eur. J. Biochem.*, 181 (1989) 545.
96. J. Leszyk, D. Mornet, E. Audemard, and J. H. Collins, *Biochem. Biophys. Res. Commun.*, 160 (1989) 210.
97. T. Ohtaki, K. Wakamatsu, M. Mori, Y. Ishibush, and T. Yasuhara, *Biochem. Biophys., Res. Commun.*, 161 (1989) 169.
98. T. Suzuki, T. Takagi, and S. Ohta, *Biochem. J.*, 260 (1989) 177.
99. K. Tamura, M. Kobayashi, Y. Ashi, T. Tamura, K. Hashimoto, and S. Nakamura, *J. Biol. Chem.*, 264 (1989) 5616.
100. R. Kharrat, H. Darbon, H. Rochat, and C. Granier, *Eur. J. Biochem.*, 181 (1989) 153.
101. C.-S. Lin, P.-W. Hsiao, C.-S. Chang, M.-C. Tzeng, and T.-B. Lo, *Biochem. J.*, 259 (1989) 153.
102. M. Mori, K. Yamaguchi, and K. Abe, *Biochem. Biophys., Res. Commun.*, 160 (1989) 1085.
103. I. M. Ota and S. Clarke, *J. Biol. Chem.*, 264 (1989) 54.
104. K. Sugino, T. Nakamura, K. Takio, K. Titani, K. Miyamoto, Y. Haseyawa, M. Igarashi, and H. Sugino, *Biochem. Biophys. Res. Commun.*, 159 (1989) 1323.
105. E. A. Weretilnyk and A. P. Hanson, *Arch. Biochem. Biophys.*, 271 (1989) 56.
106. R. M. Kramer, C. Hession, B. Johansen, G. Hayes, P. McGray, P. Chow, R. Tizard, and R. B. Pepinsky, *J. Biol. Chem.*, 264 (1989) 5678.
107. H. Jung, K. Jung, and H-P. Kleber, *Biochim., Biophys, Acta*, 1003 (1989) 270.

CHAPTER 9

Optimization and Prediction of Peptide Retention Behavior in Reversed-Phase Chromatography

Colin T. Mant and Robert S. Hodges

CONTENTS

9.1 INTRODUCTION

In the years since its introduction, reversed-phase high-performance liquid chromatography (RPC) has become the predominant HPLC technique for peptide separations. The versatility of RPC is reflected in its successful application to the isolation of peptides from a wide variety of sources. In protein sequencing and peptide mapping techniques, it is often necessary to separate all the peptides from a complex chemical or proteolytic digest, while in other structure–function studies of proteins only a few particular peptides may require isolation. Many biologically active peptides, including those with hormonal, antibiotic, or toxic properties, are often found in only small quantities and may require extensive purification. The wide use of automated solid-phase peptide synthesis in recent years has also called for efficient isolation of peptides from various impurities, often closely related to the peptide of interest (deletion, terminated or chemically modified peptides).

Optimum resolution of peptides during RPC generally involves a compromise between satisfactory separation of peptide components and a reasonable run time. This optimization may be achieved by a systematic manipulation of both the stationary phase (type of support, hydrophobic functionalities, etc.) and the mobile phase (pH, temperature, solvent composition, gradient rate, flow rate, etc.) or a combination of the two. Although the desired peptide separation may be obtained by trial and error, this may take many attempts, with subsequent loss of time and final peptide yield. This could be a particular problem where only limited amounts of sample are available. Prior knowledge of the effect of varying chromatographic parameters on a peptide elution profile obtained under one particular set of conditions would greatly benefit researchers in the protein-peptide field. In addition, where peptide composition is known, knowledge of the relative hydrophobicities of the amino acid side chains can be a guide to estimating both the elution order and retention times of the desired peptide(s).

The choice of mobile phase for RPC must be dictated not only by its effect on the components of a peptide mixture, but also by its effect on the hydrophobic stationary phase. The most favored RPC columns for separation of peptides are silica-based supports containing octyl (C_8) or octadecyl (C_{18}) functionalities. These columns may contain surface silanols that act as weak acids and have pK_as about pH 3.5–4.0. These weak acids may interact with the basic residues of peptides and have an adverse effect on resolution. For accurate prediction of the effects of chromatographic parameters on peptide retention behavior in RPC, it is necessary to eliminate or suppress any nonhydrophobic interactions between the column matrix and the peptide solutes. Thus, although excellent resolution of peptide mixtures may be obtained at acidic or neutral pH, the majority of researchers carry out RPC at pH values <3.0. Apart from the suppression of silanol ionization under these conditions, silica-based columns are more stable at low pH. Although reversed-phase peptide separations have been demonstrated on pH-stable polymer-based columns,[1–4] these supports have not yet seen widespread use.

In the authors' experience, the best approach to most peptide separations is to employ aqueous trifluoroacetic acid (TFA) to TFA-acetonitrile linear gradients (pH 2.0) at room temperature. Acetonitrile is the favored organic solvent for most purposes[5,6] and the ion-pairing properties of TFA are effective in separating complex peptide mixtures.[6–8] It is often advantageous to carry out an initial run with a mixture of basic peptide standards on the selected reversed-phase column.[9,10] This has the advantage of both testing column performance (efficiency, selectivity and resolving power)[9] and detecting any undesirable ionic, as opposed to hydrophobic, interactions.[10] Having subsequently subjected the peptide sample of interest to RPC, examination of the resultant elution profile will provide information about the need for further optimization of the mobile phase. The use of peptide standards can be invaluable in suggesting the suitability of the reversed-phase column to the researcher's needs prior to losing valuable samples on an inappropriate column.

Once a suitable column has been found, manipulation of ion-pairing reagent, flow rate, and gradient rate are common approaches to optimizing peptide separations. Although changes in ion-pairing reagent will often offer the more powerful peptide-resolving capability, varying the flow rate and steepness of the gradient can be very effective in improving peptide separations. It can be very time consuming to test the effect of all permutations of these mobile phase parameters. Hence the need for more rapid, predictive methods.

9.2 PREDICTION OF PEPTIDE RETENTION TIMES FROM OBSERVED VALUES WHEN VARYING CHROMATOGRAPHIC PARAMETERS

9.2.1 Ion-Pairing Reagents

9.2.1.1 Effect of Ion-Pairing Reagents on Peptide Separations

Since peptides are charged molecules at most pH values, the presence of different counterions will influence their chromatographic behavior. Differences in the polarities of peptides in a peptide mixture can be maximized through careful choice of ion-pairing reagent. Favored models for the mechanism of ion-pair separations either involve formation of ion pairs with the sample solute in solution, followed by retention of the solute molecules on a reversed-phase column,[11,12] or a dynamic ion-exchange event in which the ion-pairing reagent is first retained by the reversed-phase column and then solute molecules exchange ions with the counterion associated with the sorbed ion-pair reagent.[13–16] Whatever the mechanism, the resolving power of ion-pairing reagents is effected by its interaction with the ionized groups of a peptide. Anionic counterions (e.g., alkylsulfonates, phosphate, trifluoroacetate, heptafluorobutyrate) will interact with the protonated basic residues of a peptide; cationic counterions (e.g., trialkylammonium and tetraalkylammonium ions) will show affinity for ionized carboxyl groups.

The use of cationic ion-pairing reagents is limited to pH values above the pK_as of acidic side-chain groups (~pH 4.0), necessitating the use of buffered, generally nonvolatile, mobile phases. The most widely used ion-pairing reagents at present still remain perfluorinated carboxylic acids, particularly TFA and the more hydrophobic heptafluorobutyric acid (HFBA).[7,8,17–20] These anionic reagents are excellent solvents for most peptides, are completely volatile, enabling simple sample recovery, and allow detection at wavelengths below 220 nm due to their low UV transparency. Despite being nonvolatile, phosphoric acid has proved useful as a hydrophilic ion-pairing reagent for hydrophobic peptides and proteins.[8,17,21–25]

The actual effect on retention time of a peptide will depend strongly on both the hydrophobicity of the anionic ion-pairing reagent and the number of positively charged groups on the peptide. Various studies on the use of perfluorinated carboxylic acids as ion-pairing reagents, for instance, have demonstrated increasing retention times of basic peptides with increasing hydrophobicity of the anionic counterion.[7,8,17–19] Guo et al.[8] examined the effect of phosphoric acid, TFA, and HFBA on the reversed-phase elution profile of a mixture of peptides (5–14 residues) containing 1–6 positively charged groups (Figure 9–1). Increasing the hydrophobicity of the anionic counterion from phosphate (Figure 9–1A) to trifluoroacetate (Figure 9–1B) and, finally, to heptafluorobutyrate (Figure 9–1C) resulted in increasing retention times of all the peptides (the number of a peptide also denotes the number of positively charged groups it contains). However, the effect of increasing counterion hydrophobicity on peptide retention became more pronounced with increasing numbers of positively charged groups in the peptides. Thus, the elution order of the peptides

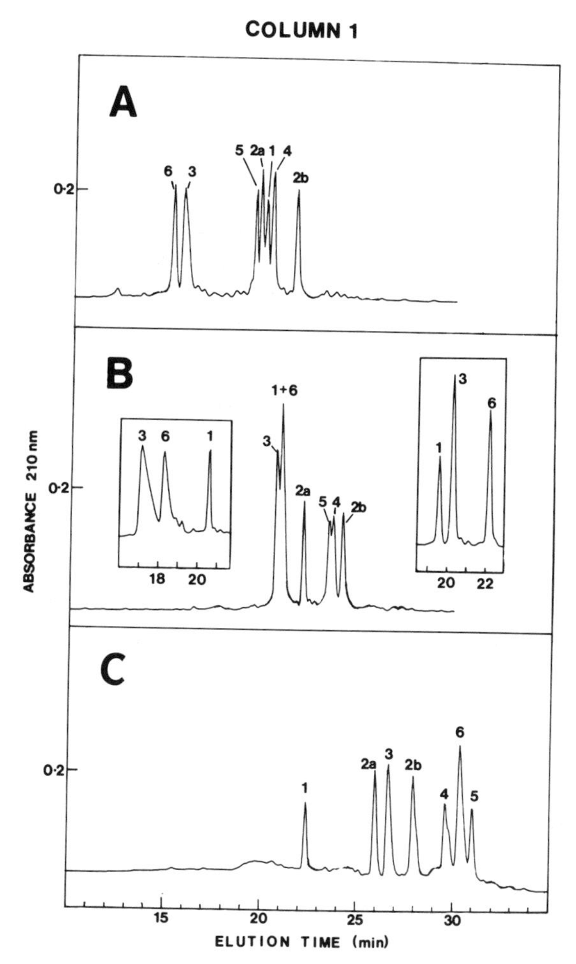

FIGURE 9–1. Effect of ion-pairing reagent on the separation of a mixture of basic peptides in RPC. Column: SynChropak RP-P C_{18} (250 × 4.1 mm i.d.; SynChrom, Linden, IN). Mobile phase: linear AB gradient (1% B/min), where solvent A is water and solvent B is acetonitrile, both solvents containing 0.1% (v/v) H_3PO_4 (A), TFA (B), or HFBA (C); flow rate, 1 ml/min; 26°C (B, insets). Left, 0.01% TFA in solvents A and B; right, 0.4% TFA in solvents A and B. Peptide numbers denote the number of positively charged residues the peptides contain.

changed from one counterion to another. For instance, the elution order of peptides 1, 3, and 6 (containing one, three, and six positively charged residues, respectively) was reversed as the counterion changed from $H_2PO_4^-$ (Figure 9–1A) to $HFBA^-$ (Figure 9–1C). Figure 9–1 demonstrates that no single ion-pairing reagent will necessarily produce perfect separation of a given peptide mixture, although a particular reagent (HFBA in this case) may work better than others. It is also apparent from Figure 9–1 that considerable flexibility of peptide elution profiles may be achieved through manipulation of ion-pairing reagents.

A number of researchers have demonstrated increasing peptide retention times with increasing concentrations of anionic counterions in the mobile phase.[17,18,26,27] This counterion concentration effect on peptide retention time is illustrated in Figure 9–1B. As the concentration of TFA in the mobile phase increased from 0.01% (inset, left) to 0.1% (main panel) to 0.4% (inset, right), there was a concomitant increase in retention times of peptides 1, 3, and 6 (one, three, and six positively charged residues, respectively). The more basic the peptide, the greater the effect of TFA concentration on its retention time. Thus, the elution order of these three peptides changed from 3, 6, and 1 in 0.01% TFA (left inset) to 1, 3, and 6 in 0.4% TFA. It is interesting to note that this change in peptide elution order is different from that observed when increasing the hydrophobicity of the counterion, i.e., 6, 3, and 1 with $H_2PO_4^-$ (Figure 9–1A) to 1, 3, and 6 with $HFBA^-$ (Figure 9–1C). These results clearly demonstrated the importance of consistency in the concentration of ion-pairing reagent in the mobile phase for accurate run-to-run comparisons of peptide separations.

Despite the desirability of a simple predictive method to gauge the effect of varying ion-pairing reagents on peptide resolution, researchers have noted that there are difficulties in predicting the effects of different chromatographic systems, particularly if the overall selectivities of the different systems diverge.[24,25] In a study designed to provide a clearer understanding of the effect of changing counterion hydrophobicity on peptide retention, Guo et al.[8] examined the retention behavior, on reversed-phase columns, of a series of model synthetic basic peptides and commercially available basic synthetic peptide standards. Using a water–acetonitrile mobile phase containing phosphoric acid, TFA, or HFBA, it was clearly shown that these reagents effected changes in peptide retention solely through interaction with the basic residues in the peptide. In general, each positive charge, whether originating from a lysine, arginine, or histidine side chain, or from an N-terminal α-amino group, exerted an essentially equal effect on peptide retention. In addition, increasing concentrations of a specific counterion had an essentially equal effect per positively charged residue. These effects of counterion and counterion concentration on peptide retention behavior were also found to be column dependent (*n*-alkyl chain length and ligand density). These results, demonstrating a simple relationship between peptide retention in different ion-pairing systems, enabled the determination of rules for prediction of peptide retention times in one ion-pairing system from observed or predicted retention times in another system.

9.2.1.2 Prediction When Varying Ion-Pairing Reagents

The following rules for prediction of peptide retention in one anionic counterion system from the results of another system were proposed by Guo et al.,[8] and require two basic assumptions: first, only basic, positively charged residues contribute to shifts in peptide retention; second, each positive charge, whether originating from a lysine, arginine, or histidine side chain, or from an N-terminal α-amino group, exerts an equal effect on peptide retention.

The contribution of each positively charged residue to shifts in peptide retention is determined by chromatographing a basic peptide standard with both the desired counterion system and the counterion system employed initially. The average contribution of each basic residue to a change in retention time is denoted by Δ/N, where Δ is the shift (in minutes) in retention time of the standard between the two counterion systems, and N equals the number of positively charged residues in the standard. The counterion correction factor (t_i) for a peptide of interest is then obtained by multiplying the number of positively charged residues of the peptide (n) by Δ/N for the standard,

$$t_i = n(\Delta/N)$$

This correction factor will have a negative value for a change from a more hydrophobic to a less hydrophobic counterion, while the reverse will require a positive correction factor.

When the retention time of a peptide of interest is known in the presence of one counterion, its predicted position in another counterion system is described by the expression,

$$\tau = t_R^{obs} + t_i$$

where τ is the predicted peptide retention time in the desired counterion system, t_R^{obs} is the observed retention time in the initial counterion system, and t_i is the counterion correction factor. The concept of a simple correction factor to relate peptide elution times in different ion-pairing systems was at variance with studies carried out by Browne et al.[20] who applied linear regression analysis to estimate the contribution of each residue to peptide retention in two ion-pairing systems and presented different sets of retention coefficients for all the amino acid residues in both systems. The discrepancy between the results of Browne et al.[20] and those of Guo et al.[8] was due to the former researchers not identifying that the increased retention times of the peptides were solely a result of increased hydrophobicity of the peptides through ion-pair formation with the basic residues.

The above prediction rules were applied to the separation of the mixture of basic peptides of varying net positive charge demonstrated in Figure 9–1. The retention times of the peptides in H_3PO_4, TFA, and HFBA were predicted (τ) from the observed values t_R^{obs} in each of the three ion-pairing systems on two different columns (columns 1 and 2) (Table 9–1). The counterion correction factor (t_i) was obtained by chromatographing a synthetic, 10-residue basic peptide standard (S4; available from Synthetic Peptides Inc., Department of Biochemistry, University of Alberta, Edmonton, Alberta, Canada T6G 2H7), containing two positively charged residues, in all three ion-pairing systems. The average contributions of a basic residue to a change in retention time (Δ/N or $\Delta/2$ for S4) between two counterion systems were, for the $H_3PO_4 \leftrightarrow$ TFA systems, 1.0 min (Column 1) and 1.2 min (Column 2); for the TFA $\leftrightarrow$ HFBA systems, the values were 1.9 min (Column 1) and 2.7 min (Column 2); for the $H_3PO_4 \leftrightarrow$ HFBA systems, the values were 2.9 min (Column 1) and 3.9 min (Column 2). These values indicate that the difference in hydrophobicity between the TFA and HFBA systems is greater than between the H_3PO_4 and TFA systems. In addition, the difference in the values obtained on the two reversed-phase columns for identical changes in ion-pairing systems highlights the column dependence of counterion effects on the retention behavior of ionized peptides. Examination of the results presented in Table 9–1 illustrates the accuracy of this predictive method for the peptides examined. The average deviations of predicted and observed values for the seven peptides were ± 0.7 min for the $H_3PO_4 \leftrightarrow$ TFA systems, 1.0 min for the TFA $\leftrightarrow$ HFBA systems, and 1.5 min for the $H_3PO_4 \leftrightarrow$ HFBA systems, indicating a generally good predictive

TABLE 9–1. Comparison of Predicted and Observed Retention Times in RPC Using Different Anionic Ion-Pairing Reagents[a]

Peptide[b]	H_3PO_4			TFA			HFBA		
	τ_T[c]	t_R^{obs}[d] (min)	τ_H	τ_P	t_R^{obs} (min)	τ_H	τ_P	t_R^{obs} (min)	τ_R
Column 1									
1	20.0	20.1	19.5	21.1	21.0	20.5	23.0	22.4	22.9
2a	20.1	19.8	20.2	21.8	22.1	22.2	25.6	26.0	25.9
2b	22.1	21.7	22.2	23.7	24.1	24.2	27.5	28.0	27.9
3	17.8	15.8	18.0	18.8	20.8	21.0	24.5	26.7	26.5
4	19.6	20.4	18.0	24.4	23.6	22.0	32.0	29.6	31.2
5	18.5	19.5	15.9	24.5	23.5	20.9	34.0	30.4	33.0
6	15.0	15.3	13.6	21.3	21.0	19.6	32.7	31.0	32.4
Column 2									
1	19.3	19.8	19.8	21.0	20.5	21.0	23.7	23.7	23.2
2a	20.1	19.3	21.1	21.7	22.5	23.5	27.1	28.9	27.9
2b	23.2	21.9	22.6	24.3	25.6	25.0	29.7	30.4	31.0
3	17.7	15.6	18.2	19.2	21.3	21.8	27.3	29.9	29.4
4	19.2	19.3	16.6	24.1	24.0	21.4	34.9	32.2	34.8
5	17.7	17.6	16.1	23.6	23.7	22.1	37.1	35.6	37.2
6	13.3	12.6	12.2	19.8	20.5	19.4	36.0	35.6	36.7
Average error	±0.7		±1.5	±0.7		±1.0	±1.5		±1.0

[a]Conditions: Column 1, SynChropak C_{18} (250 × 4.1 mm i.d.); Column 2, Aquapore C_8 (220 × 4.6 mm i.d.); linear gradient (1% B/min), where solvent A is water and solvent B is acetonitrile, both solvents containing 0.1% orthophosphoric acid, TFA, or HFBA as ion-pairing reagent; flow rate, 1 ml/min; 26°C; absorbance at 210 nm.

[b]Peptide number also denotes number of positively charged residues the peptide contains.

[c]τ_P, τ_T, τ_H denote predicted peptide retention times from observed values in H_3PO_4, TFA, and HFBA ion-pairing systems, respectively.

[d]Observed peptide retention time in a particular ion-pairing system.

accuracy. It is apparent that the wider the difference in hydrophobicity between two ion-pairing systems, the greater the average deviation between predicted and observed values. This discrepancy may be due to slightly unequal contributions of the basic residues. It is also possible that the close proximity of charged groups may produce anomalous results. It has already been demonstrated, for instance, that a charged α-amino group on a basic N-terminal residue has a different effect on peptide retention at pH 2 and 7 than an α-amino group on an N-terminal residue with an uncharged side chain.[5,28] However, the small average deviation of predicted and observed peptide retention time values justifies, for most practical purposes, the assumptions required to simplify peptide retention prediction in anionic ion-pairing systems, i.e., only basic residues need be taken into account and each residue exerts an essentially equal effect on retention. Of course, further investigation into any subtle effects on peptide retention behavior of different basic residues and/or peptide sequence can only serve to enhance the value of this already useful predictive method.

9.2.2 Flow Rate and Gradient Rate

9.2.2.1 Effect of Flow Rate on Peptide Retention

The resolution between two peaks is described quantitatively by the expression $2\Delta t/(w_1 + w_2)$, where Δt is the difference (minutes) between the retention times of the two retained components at their peak maxima, and w_1 and w_2 are the baseline peak widths (minutes). This expression was applied by Guo et al.[29] to the resolution of two synthetic peptide standards (S4 and S5) on a reversed-phase semipreparative column with a linear gradient (aqueous TFA to TFA–acetonitrile) of 0.5–4% B/min, at flow rates of 0.3–5.0 ml/min (Figure 9–2). The peptides demonstrated increasing resolution with increasing flow rate. The tendency for peptides to diffuse decreased as the flow rate increased, producing smaller peak widths (w_1, w_2) and, hence, improved resolution.

If the researcher desires to vary flow rate in order to manipulate the resolution of a peptide mixture, it is important to gauge the effect of flow rate on peptide retention time. A number of researchers have suggested that, under gradient elution conditions, flow rate changes generally have little effect on peptide retention, provided gradient steepness is kept low.[23,29–32] Thus, under ideal conditions, subtraction of gradient delay time, t_g (time for the gradient to reach the detector from the proportioning value via pump, injection loop, and column), from observed peptide retention times (t_R) and plotting this difference against flow rate should result in straight-line plots with zero slope. Guo et al.[29] examined the effect of flow rate on RPC of peptides by comparing the separation of five synthetic peptide HPLC standards (S1–S5) and four alkylphenone HPLC standards (A1–A4) on a semipreparative C_{18} column with a linear gradient (aqueous TFA to TFA–acetonitrile) of 1% B/min at flow rates of 0.3–5.0 ml/min. The composition of the peptides varied as follows: peptide S2, -Gly^3-Gly^4-; S3, -Ala^3-Gly^4-; S4, -Val^3-Gly^4-; S5, -Val^3-Val^4-. All peptides contained an N$^\alpha$-acetylated N-terminal and a C-terminal amide, except peptide S1, which was identical to S3 but had a free α-amino group (available from Synthetic Peptides Inc., Department of Biochemistry, University of Alberta,

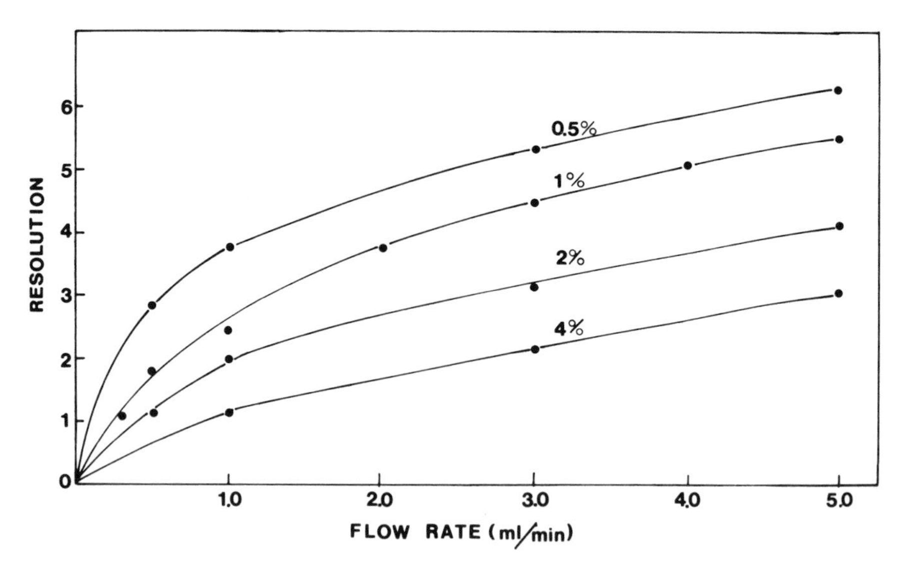

FIGURE 9–2. Effect of flow rate and gradient rate on resolution of two synthetic decapeptide RPC standards (S4, S5). Column: SynChropak RP-P C_{18} (250 × 10 mm i.d.; SynChrom, Linden, IN). Mobile phase: linear AB gradient (0.5, 1, 2, or 4% B/min), where solvent A is 0.1% aqueous TFA and solvent B is 0.1% TFA in acetonitrile (pH 2.0); flow rate, 0.3–5.0 ml/min; 26°C; absorbance at 210 nm. Between S4 and S5, there is a difference of one isopropyl group (see text).

Edmonton, Alberta, Canada, T6G 2H7). The relationship between ($t_R - t_g$) and flow rate for the alkylphenone (A1–A4) and peptide (S1–S5) standards, derived from these runs, is demonstrated in Figure 9–3. The contrast between the alkylphenone and peptide standards is quite dramatic. Flow rate is seen to have little effect on retention time of the peptides, once the value for gradient elapsed time is taken into account. In contrast, the alkylphenones are exhibiting increasingly longer retention times (after the correction for t_g) as the flow rate decreases, supporting the view that alkylphenones are separated mainly by a partitioning mechanism. Although the slightly negative slope of the peptide plots may be due to some increase in peptide partitioning as the flow rate decreases, the very small deviation from zero slope highlights the mainly adsorption–desorption mechanism of peptide separation by RPC. In addition, despite these slight deviations from absolute zero slope, the plots for all five peptides are essentially parallel, i.e., the differences in retention time between the peptides remain constant, regardless of the flow rate.

9.2.2.2 Effect of Gradient Rate on Peptide Retention

Variations in gradient steepness affect both the resolution and retention behavior of peptides and, thus, generally have a more profound effect on the separation of peptide mixtures than flow rate changes. Figure 9–2 illustrates that the resolution of the two peptide standards, S4 and S5, increased with decreasing gradient rate. This improved resolution was obtained because the resulting increase in Δt between the two peptides more than compensated for any concomitant increase in peak widths as the gradient was shallowed.

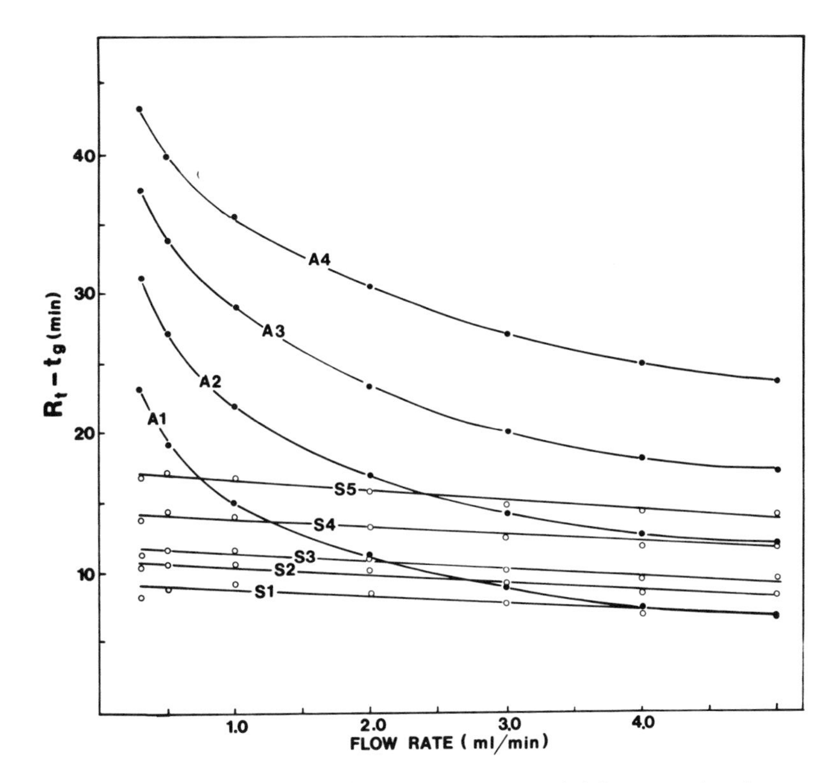

FIGURE 9–3. Effect of subtracting gradient delay time (t_g) from retention time (t_R) of alkylphenone and synthetic decapeptide RPC standards at different flow rates. Column: SynChropak RP-P C_{18} (250 × 10 mm i.d.; SynChrom, Linden, IN). Mobile phase: linear AB gradient (1% B/min), where solvent A is 0.1% aqueous TFA and solvent B is 0.1% TFA in acetonitrile (pH 2.0); flow rate, 0.3–5.0 ml/min; 26°C; absorbance at 210 nm. Sequence variations of peptide standards S1–S5 are described in the text. A1–A4 denote acetophenone, propiophenone, *n*-butyrophenone, and valerophenone, respectively.

The retention times of peptides are inversely related to gradient steepness.[29,33–36] Variations in gradient rate affect different peptides to different extents, hence the significant effect gradient rate may have on peptide separations. Under ideal conditions, a linear relationship should exist between peptide retention and the reciprocal of the gradient slope, with the plots for all five peptides intercepting at the gradient delay time (t_g). A study by Mant et al.[37] examined the effect of gradient steepness on the reversed-phase separation of five synthetic peptide standards on a semipreparative C_{18} column with linear gradients (aqueous TFA to TFA–acetonitrile) of 0.5–5.0% B/min at flow rates of 1–5 ml/min. Figure 9–4 demonstrates the results of plotting peptide retention time against the reciprocal of gradient slopes (0.5–5.0% B/min) for flow rates of 1.0 and 5.0 ml/min. An increase in peptide partitioning as the gradient rate decreased probably caused a deviation from strict linearity, resulting in larger retention times than expected. Nevertheless, Figure 9–4 demonstrates that, for most practical purposes, the inverse relationship be-

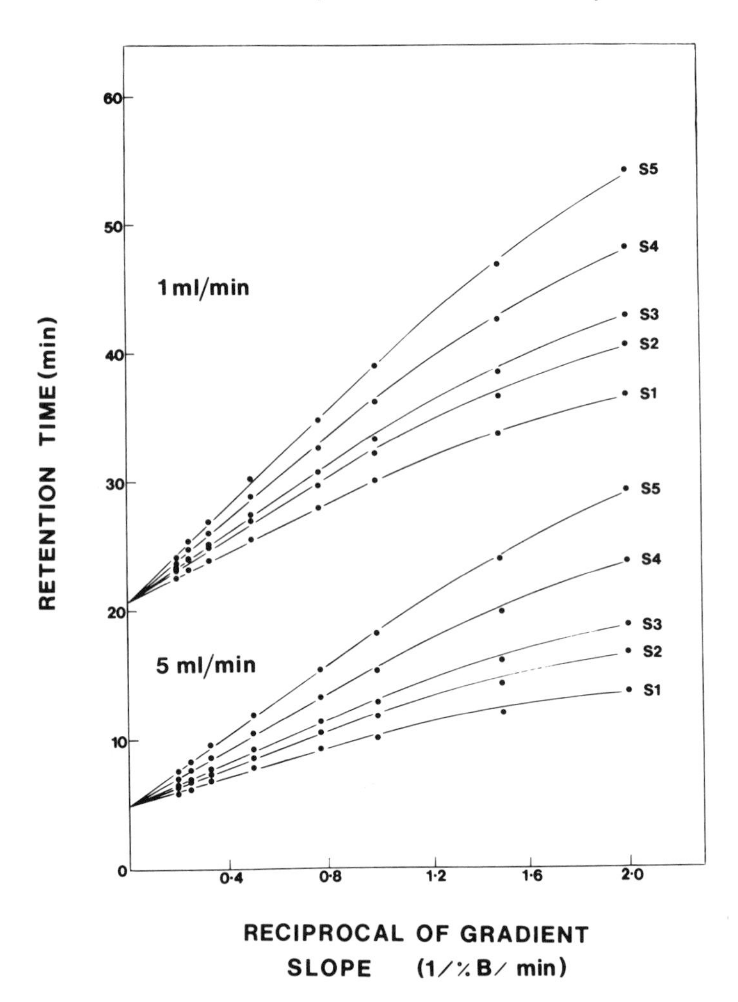

FIGURE 9–4. Plots of retention times of five synthetic decapeptide standards versus the reciprocal of the gradient slope (1% B/min). Column: SynChropak RP-P C_{18} (250 × 10 mm i.d.; SynChrom, Linden, IN). Mobile phase: linear AB gradient (0.5–5.0% B/min), where solvent A is 0.05% aqueous TFA and solvent B is 0.05% TFA in acetonitrile (pH 2.0); flow rate, 1 and 5 ml/min; 26°C; absorbance at 210 nm. Sequence variations of peptide standards S1–S5 are described in the text.

tween peptide retention time and gradient slope may be considered linear for the usual working range of gradient rates (1–5% B/min).

9.2.2.3 Prediction When Varying Gradient Rate

Assuming an inverse linear relationship between peptide retention time and gradient steepness, the predicted retention time of a peptide at varying gradient rates and fixed flow rate may be calculated by the expression:

$$\tau^{(y\%)} = [t_R^{obs_{(x\%)}} - g][x\%/y\%] + g$$

where $\tau^{y\%}$ is the predicted retention time at the desired gradient steepness (y% B/min), $t_R^{obs_{(x\%)}}$ is the observed retention time at an initial gradient steepness, and g is the column- and flow rate-dependent gradient correction factor.[36] This parameter can be simply determined for any column by running a peptide standard, or a peptide from the mixture under investigation, at two different gradient rates (1 and 3% B/min are recommended) and extrapolating the plot of retention times versus the reciprocal of gradient slope to obtain the intercept on the ordinate. This factor is related to the value for gradient delay time, t_g, but is generally larger. Thus, from Figure 9–4, the gradient correction factors for the semipreparative column were 5 and 20.8 min for flow rates of 1 and 5 ml/min, respectively.

This approach to prediction of peptide retention times at different gradient rates was applied to the gradient elution separation (0.05% aqueous TFA to 0.05% TFA in acetonitrile) of five synthetic peptides (S1–S5) on an analytical C_8 column (Table 9–2). Predicted retention values for peptides S1–S5 were calculated, at a fixed flow rate, for five gradient rates (1.0–4.0% B/min) from observed retention times of the four peptides at all five gradient rates. These calculations were carried out for all four flow rates. The gradient correction factors (obtained with S4 as a peptide standard) were 17.5, 9.7, 7.0, and 5.6 min for flow rates of 0.5, 1.0, 1.5, and 2.0 ml/min, respectively. From Table 9–2, the average error between all predicted and observed retention times of the peptides was 0.3 min for peptides S1 and S2, and 0.4 min for each of peptides S3, S4, and S5. This represents a satisfactory accuracy for most practical purposes, particularly since peptide retentions varied by as much as 21–28 min. This predictive approach serves as a useful method of screening rapidly the effect of a wide range of flow rate and gradient rate permutations on peptide separations.

9.2.2.4 Prediction When Varying Flow Rate and Gradient Rate

If a greater, and more consistent, accuracy of peptide retention prediction on varying gradient rates and/or flow rates is required, the following expression may be utilized:

$$\tau^{(y\%,\ y\ \mathrm{ml})} = t_R^{(x\%,\ x\ \mathrm{ml})} \times (x\%/y\%) + f$$

where τ is the predicted retention time at the desired gradient rate (y% B/min) and flow rate (y ml/min), t_R is the observed retention time at an initial gradient rate (x% B/min) and flow rate (x ml/min), and f is a gradient rate and/or flow rate correction factor. This factor is determined from the expression,

$$f = t_R^{std_{(y\%,\ y\ \mathrm{ml})}} - (t_R^{std_{(x\%,\ x\ \mathrm{ml})}} \times [x\%/y\%])$$

where t_R^{std} is the observed retention time of a peptide standard at the desired run conditions (y% B/min, y ml/min) and at the initial run conditions (x% B/min, x ml/min). Thus, accurate prediction of peptide retention times at various gradient rates, flow rates, or a combination of the two simply requires

TABLE 9–2. Comparison of Predicted versus Observed Peptide Retention Times[a]

Flow Rate (ml/min)	Gradient Rate (% B/min)	Peptide S1[b]			Peptide S2			Peptide S3			Peptide S4			Peptide S5		
		t_R^{obs} (min)	Δt^c (min)	Δ%B[d]	t_R^{obs}	Δt	Δ%B	t_R^{obs}	Δt	Δ%B	t_R^{obs}	ΔT	Δ%B	t_R^{obs}	ΔT	Δ%B
0.5	1	28.6	0.7	0.7	30.2	0.7	0.7	31.3	0.8	0.8	34.1	0.8	0.8	37.0	0.7	0.7
	1.33	26.5	0.7	0.9	27.6	0.6	0.8	28.4	0.7	0.9	30.6	0.8	1.1	32.8	0.7	0.9
	2	23.9	0.8	1.6	24.8	0.9	1.8	25.2	0.8	1.6	26.6	0.8	1.6	28.0	0.7	1.4
	3	21.2	0.2	0.6	21.8	0.2	0.6	22.0	0.3	0.9	22.9	0.3	0.9	23.9	0.3	0.9
	4	20.2	0.2	0.8	20.6	0.2	0.8	20.8	0.3	1.2	21.6	0.2	0.8	22.3	0.2	0.8
1	1	18.6	0.4	0.4	20.2	0.4	0.4	21.3	0.4	0.4	24.1	0.5	0.5	27.0	0.5	0.5
	1.33	16.7	0.3	0.4	17.8	0.2	0.3	18.7	0.3	0.4	20.8	0.4	0.5	23.0	0.6	0.8
	2	14.4	0.2	0.4	15.2	0.2	0.4	15.7	0.2	0.4	17.1	0.3	0.6	18.4	0.2	0.4
	3	12.8	0.1	0.3	13.3	0.1	0.3	13.6	0.1	0.3	14.4	0.2	0.6	15.4	0.2	0.6
	4	11.8	0.2	0.8	12.2	0.2	0.8	12.4	0.2	0.8	13.1	0.2	0.8	13.7	0.4	1.6

1.5	1	14.8	0.4	0.4	16.3	0.4	0.4	17.4	0.5	0.5	20.2	0.6	0.6	23.0	0.6	0.6
	1.33	13.0	0.4	0.5	14.1	0.3	0.4	14.9	0.4	0.5	17.1	0.5	0.7	19.2	0.6	0.8
	2	10.9	0.2	0.4	11.7	0.2	0.4	12.3	0.3	0.6	13.6	0.2	0.4	15.1	0.4	0.8
	3	9.5	0.2	0.6	10.0	0.2	0.6	10.3	0.2	0.6	11.3	0.2	0.6	12.2	0.2	0.6
	4	8.6	0.4	1.6	9.1	0.2	0.8	9.3	0.3	1.2	9.9	0.4	1.6	10.6	0.4	1.6
2	1	12.7	0.3	0.3	14.1	0.4	0.4	15.2	0.4	0.4	18.0	0.3	0.3	20.9	0.4	0.4
	1.33	11.2	0.4	0.5	12.3	0.3	0.4	13.1	0.4	0.5	15.2	0.4	0.5	17.4	0.4	0.5
	2	9.2	0.1	0.2	10.1	0.2	0.4	10.6	0.2	0.4	11.9	0.2	0.4	13.4	0.2	0.4
	3	8.0	0.1	0.3	8.5	0.2	0.6	8.8	0.1	0.3	9.7	0.2	0.6	10.6	0.2	0.6
	4	7.2	0.2	0.8	7.6	0.2	0.8	7.8	0.2	0.8	8.5	0.2	0.8	9.3	0.2	0.8
Average error			0.3	0.6		0.3	0.6		0.4	0.7		0.4	0.7		0.4	0.8

[a]The observed retention times were obtained at four flow rates (0.5, 1, 1.5, 2 ml/min), with five gradient rates (1, 1.33, 2, 3, 4% B/min) performed at each flow rate. From the observed retention time at each flow rate and gradient rate, predicted retention times were calculated for the remaining gradient rates at the same flow rate. These predicted times were then compared to the actual observed times. An analytical reversed-phase column (Aquapore RP-300 C_8, 220 × 4.6 mm i.d., 300 Å, 7 μm particle size, from Pierce Chemical Co., Rockford, IL was used for all separations.

[b]The five peptides contain 10 residues each, with varying sequence as described in text.

[c]Each Δt value is the average error between the observed retention time and the four predicted retention times.

[d]ΔB% is the average error in % organic modifier; for example, a Δt value of 0.1 min at a gradient rate of 2% B/min gives an average error in % organic modifier of 0.2%.

chromatographing a peptide standard under two sets of conditions (initial and desired) in addition to an initial reversed-phase separation of the peptide sample mixture. The number of reversed-phase runs may be reduced even further if, under the initial chromatographic conditions, the standard is included in the peptide sample mixture.

Application of the above equation allows the researcher not only to predict rapidly the effect of gradient rate and flow rate variations on peptide retention, but also to allow for changes in column parameters (column dimensions, *n*-alkyl chain length, and/or ligand density). The accuracy of this predictive approach was examined by its application to the gradient elution separation (0.05% aqueous TFA to 0.05% TFA in acetonitrile) of the five peptide standards, S1–S5. With S4 as the internal standard, predicted retention values for peptides S1, S2, S3, and S5 were calculated for all combinations of eight gradient rates (0.5–5.0% B/min) and five flow rates (1–5 ml/min) on a semipreparative C_{18} column, from observed retention times of the peptides at all combinations of the eight gradient rates and four flow rates (0.5–2.0 ml/min) on an analytical C_8 column. It was felt that a simultaneous change in column dimensions and packing while varying gradient rates and flow rates would be the most demanding test of the efficiency of this predictive method and extremely practical for scale up to a preparative separation on a semipreparative column from the analytical profile on an analytical column. The predictive accuracy of this approach is demonstrated in Table 9–3. The average error between all predicted and observed retention times of the peptides was 0.3 min for peptide S1, 0.2 min for peptide S2, and only 0.1 min for peptides S3 and S5. This impressive accuracy was obtained with variations of as much as ~46 min in retention for any one peptide on either column.

The best resolution of a peptide mixture is usually obtained between concentrations of 15 and 40% of the organic solvent in the mobile phase gradient.[6,31] The results from Tables 9–2 and 9–3 clearly show that accurate prediction of the effects of flow rate and gradient rate on peptide retention behavior within this range of acetonitrile concentration is both possible and straightforward.

9.3 PREDICTION OF PEPTIDE RETENTION TIMES USING AMINO ACID HYDROPHOBICITY PARAMETERS

Even though peptides derived from various sources differ widely in size and polarity, it is now recognized that, unless a peptide is subject to conformational restraints, its chromatographic behavior in RPC can be correlated with its amino acid composition and, in particular, with the summated relative hydrophobic contribution of each amino acid residue. Knowledge of the contribution of individual amino acids to peptide retention on hydrophobic stationary phases, enabling prediction of elution profiles of known composition, greatly enhances the value of RPC. A major advantage of peptide retention predictions, for instance, is that the position of a peptide(s) of interest in the elution profile of a peptide mixture will be narrowed down to a small section of the chromatogram, saving much time and effort in subsequent purification. In addition, information about the relative order of peptide elution from a complex mixture may be obtained. In conjunction with detection by UV absorbance of aromatic residue-containing peptides, fluorescence detection and/or amino acid-specific color reactions, the identification of specified peptides in a complex mixture may be greatly simplified.

9.3.1 Non HPLC-Derived Parameters

When alanine oligomers up to six residues were subjected to isocratic RPC on a silica-based C_{18} column[38] or porous copolymer stationary phases,[1,2] the peptides were eluted in order of increasing peptide length, i.e., the contribution of each alanine residue was essentially additive. In contrast, glycine oligomers showed little appreciable retention on silica-based C_8[39] or C_{18}[27,38] bonded phases in acidic aqueous or aqueous-organic eluents, suggesting that the polypeptide chain itself makes little or no contribution to the retention process at low pH.

Molnár and Horváth[38] noted that it should be possible to obtain quantitative estimates of the hydrophobicity of the amino acids contained in a peptide, which will then reflect the retention behavior of the peptide on a reversed-phase column. These researchers, employing increasing acetonitrile concentrations to elute peptides from a C_{18} stationary phase, found that the adjusted retention times of phenylalanine and its oligomers were a linear function of the number of residues. In addition, a good correlation was obtained between peptide retention times and the sum of the side chain "hydrophobicity numbers" of Recker, based on the partition coefficients of free amino acids between water and octanol.[40] A number of researchers[23,27,33,38,41,42] have reported fairly good correlation, under both gradient and isocratic elution conditions, between observed order of elution of peptides and their relative hydrophobicities expressed as the sum of Recker's constants of the individual amino acids. However, several researchers[23,27,33,42,43] have also reported significant deviations between observed peptide elution order and peptide hydrophobicity expressed as the sum of Recker's constants for the constituent amino acids. In addition, absolute peptide retention times, as opposed to relative retention times, are difficult to gauge through the use of these constants. This is, perhaps, not surprising considering that retention on an octadecylsilyl silica gel is a quite different process from octanol/water partition, on which Recker's constants are based. Thus, a very accurate set of HPLC retention coefficients is required to predict both relative elution order and absolute retention times.

9.3.2 HPLC-Derived Parameters

9.3.2.1 Parameters Derived by Computer-Calculated Regression Analysis of Peptide Retention

An important paper by Meek[44] attempted to show that retention indices or coefficients, describing the effective contribution of each amino acid side chain and end groups to the retention process, could be derived directly from HPLC

TABLE 9–3. Comparison of Predicted versus Observed Peptide Retention Times[a]

Flow Rate (ml/min)	Gradient Rate (% B/min)	Peptide S1[b]			Peptide S2			Peptide S3			Peptide S5		
		t_R^{obs} (min)	Δt^c (min)	Δ%B[d]	t_R^{obs}	Δt	Δ%B	t_R^{obs}	Δt	Δ%B	t_R^{obs}	ΔT	Δ%B
1	0.5	36.8	0.8	0.4	40.7	0.2	0.1	42.9	0.2	0.1	54.1	0.2	0.1
	0.67	33.7	0.9	0.6	36.8	0.2	0.1	38.5	0.1	0.1	46.9	0.2	0.1
	1.0	30.1	0.8	0.8	32.4	0.1	0.1	33.5	0.1	0.1	39.1	0.1	0.1
	1.33	27.8	0.7	0.9	29.6	0.1	0.1	30.4	0	0	34.6	0.1	0.1
	2.0	25.8	0.5	1.0	27.0	0.1	0.2	27.6	0.1	0.2	30.3	0.1	0.2
	3.0	24.0	0.3	0.9	24.9	0.1	0.3	25.2	0	0	27.0	0.1	0.3
	4.0	23.3	0.2	0.8	24.2	0.3	1.2	24.2	0.1	0.4	25.4	0.2	0.8
	5.0	22.6	0.1	0.5	23.3	0.3	1.5	23.3	0.1	0.5	24.3	0	0
2	0.5	24.4	0.3	0.2	27.8	0.3	0.2	30.0	0.4	0.2	40.8	0.3	0.2
	0.67	21.3	0.4	0.3	24.0	0.2	0.1	25.7	0.2	0.1	33.9	0.2	0.1
	1.0	18.8	0.4	0.4	20.6	0.1	0.1	21.7	0.1	0.1	27.2	0.2	0.2
	1.33	17.0	0.3	0.4	18.6	0.1	0.1	19.3	0.1	0.1	23.4	0.1	0.1
	2.0	15.1	0.4	0.8	16.2	0.1	0.2	16.8	0.1	0.2	19.5	0.1	0.2
	3.0	13.6	0.3	0.9	14.4	0	0	14.7	0	0	16.5	0.1	0.3
	4.0	12.9	0.1	0.4	13.5	0.1	0.4	13.8	0.1	0.4	15.0	0.1	0.4
	5.0	12.3	0.1	0.5	13.0	0.2	1.0	13.0	0	0	14.1	0	0
3	0.5	19.0	0.2	0.1	22.3	0.4	0.2	24.4	0.4	0.2	35.1	0.3	0.2
	0.67	16.8	0.2	0.1	19.4	0.3	0.2	21.0	0.3	0.2	29.1	0.2	0.1
	1.0	14.3	0.2	0.5	16.1	0.1	0.1	17.2	0.2	0.2	22.6	0.1	0.1
	1.33	12.9	0.2	0.3	14.3	0.1	0.1	15.1	0.1	0.1	19.2	0.1	0.1
	2.0	11.2	0.2	0.4	12.3	0.1	0.2	12.7	0	0	15.5	0	0
	3.0	10.0	0.2	0.6	10.7	0	0	11.0	0.1	0.3	12.9	0	0
	4.0	9.4	0.1	0.4	9.9	0.1	0.4	10.1	0	0	11.5	0	0
	5.0	8.9	0.1	0.5	9.3	0	0	9.5	0	0	10.6	0	0

4	0.5	16.1	0.4	0.2	19.2	0.4	0.2	21.3	0.4	0.2	31.8	0.4	0.2
	0.67	14.1	0.2	0.1	16.6	0.3	0.2	18.2	0.3	0.2	26.2	0.2	0.1
	1.0	11.8	0.1	0.1	13.5	0.1	0.1	14.6	0.2	0.2	19.9	0.2	0.2
	1.33	10.4	0.2	0.3	11.8	0.1	0.1	12.6	0.1	0.1	16.7	0.1	0.1
	2.0	9.0	0.2	0.4	10.0	0.1	0.2	10.6	0.2	0.4	13.3	0.1	0.2
	3.0	8.0	0.1	0.3	8.8	0.2	0.6	9.0	0	0	10.8	0	0
	4.0	7.4	0.1	0.4	7.9	0	0	8.2	0	0	9.6	0	0
	5.0	7.0	0.1	0.5	7.4	0	0	7.6	0	0	8.8	0.1	0.5
5	0.5	13.6	0.5	0.3	16.7	0.5	0.3	18.8	0.5	0.3	29.2	0.3	0.2
	0.67	11.8	0.2	0.1	14.3	0.3	0.2	16.0	0.3	0.2	23.9	0.2	0.1
	1.0	10.1	0.1	0.1	11.8	0.2	0.2	12.9	0.2	0.2	18.3	0.1	0.1
	1.33	9.2	0.1	0.1	10.4	0.1	0.1	11.3	0.2	0.3	15.2	0.1	0.1
	2.0	7.8	0.1	0.2	8.8	0.1	0.2	9.3	0.1	0.2	12.0	0	0
	3.0	6.8	0.2	0.6	7.5	0.1	0.3	7.9	0.1	0.3	9.7	0	0
	4.0	6.2	0.2	0.8	6.8	0	0	7.0	0	0	8.4	0	0
	5.0	5.9	0.1	0.5	6.4	0.1	0.5	7.5	0.1	0.5	7.7	0	0
Average error[e]			0.3	0.4		0.2	0.3		0.1	0.2		0.1	0.1

[a]The observed retention times were obtained using a semipreparative reversed-phase column (Synchropak RP-P C_{18}, 250 × 10 mm i.d., 300 Å, 6.5 μm particle size,with approximately 10% carbon loading from SynChrom, Linden, IN). The predicted retention times were calculated from observed values on an analytical reversed-phase column (Aquapore RP-300 C_8, 220 × 4.6 mm i.d., 300 Å, 7 μm particle size from Pierce Chemical Co., Rockford, IL). The flow rates on the analytical column were 0.5, 1.0, 1.5, and 2.0 ml/min. At each flow rate, eight different gradient rates were performed (0.5, 0.67, 1.0, 1.33, 2, 3, 4, and 5% B/min where B = 0.05% TFA in acetonitrile).

[b]The four peptides contain 10 residues each, with varying sequence as described in text.

[c]Each Δt value is the average error between the observed retention time and the 32 predicted retention times calculated from 8 gradient rates at each of 4 different flow rates.

[d]ΔB% is the average error in % organic modifier; for example, a Δt value of 0.1 min at a gradient rate of 2% B/min gives an average error in % organic modifier of 0.2%.

[e]Each average represents an average of 1280 predictions for each peptide.

data. Retention times of 25 peptides were determined at two pH values on a silica-based C_{18} column with gradients from aqueous 0.1 *M* sodium perchlorate to 60% aqueous acetonitrile containing 0.1 *M* sodium perchlorate. For separations at pH 7.4, the starting buffer contained 5 m*M* phosphate buffer; for separations at pH 2.1, both starting and final solvents contained 0.1% H_3PO_4. Retention coefficients for the amino acids were computed by regression analysis, where the retention coefficients of all the amino acids were changed sequentially to obtain a maximum correlation between actual and predicted retention times. When actual peptide retention times were plotted against the times predicted by summing the appropriate retention coefficients for each peptide, correlations of 0.9970 (pH 2.1) and 0.9996 (pH 7.4) were obtained. When determining amino acid retention coefficients, and during their subsequent application to prediction of peptide retention times, it was important to ensure that any nonhydrophobic interactions between the peptides and the hydrophobic stationary phase were suppressed or eliminated. As has been stated previously, acidic pH values suppress ionization of unreacted silanol groups on the silica surface. The addition of salts, such as sodium perchlorate (a chaotropic reagent), to the mobile phase helps to suppress ionic interaction between the peptides and column packing material at pH values above the pK_a of silanol groups (pH 3.5–4.0).[6,44] Meek and Rossetti[32] later increased the number of peptides examined to 100 in order to obtain more accurate values for their retention coefficients. Though the elimination of nonspecific interactions is a requirement for the accurate determination of hydrophobicity coefficients, the mobile phases used by these workers are not in common use. In addition, there are difficulties in predicting peptide retention values for a particular chromatographic system using coefficients derived from a different chromatographic system.

A similar regression analysis approach to determination of amino acid side chain retention coefficients has been undertaken by several other researchers. Browne et al.[20] obtained their coefficients by chromatographing a series of 25 peptides from the rat neurointermediary lobe on a C_{18} column. They employed identical linear gradients of aqueous acetonitrile containing 0.1% TFA or 0.13% HFBA throughout. The retention coefficients of all the amino acid side chains were changed on proceeding from the TFA system to the HFBA system in order to account for the changes in the retention times and relative elution order of the peptides. As previously stated, these researchers apparently did not identify that the variation of peptide retention times between the two systems was solely a result of the effects of ion-pair formation between basic residues and the anionic trifluoroacetate and heptafluorobutyrate counterions. Wilson et al.[33] determined retention coefficients by employing pyridine–formate–acetate buffers (pH 3.0) with propan-1-ol as organic modifier during gradient elution of 96 peptides, ranging in length from 2 to 65 residues, on C_8 and C_{18} columns. Su et al.[45] analyzed group retention contributions for RPC through gradient elution of 57 different peptides, including a variety of peptide hormones, on a C_{18} column at pH 2.65 (50 m*M* NaH_2PO_4–15 m*M* H_3PO_4 to 50% aqueous acetonitrile–50 m*M* NaH_2PO_4–15 m*M* H_3PO_4). These researchers determined the retention contribution of each amino acid by two different methods of numerical analysis, namely multiple regression analysis and by a mathematical routine for solving linear equations. Sasagawa et al.[46] developed a set of coefficients from an exponential relationship between the observed retention times of 100 peptides and their relative hydrophobicities, expressed as the sum of modified Recker coefficients of their constituent amino acids.

All of these researchers applied their hydrophobicity parameters to retention time prediction of the peptides originally used to derive their coefficients; thus, the generally good correlation between observed and predicted retention times of peptides up to about 20 residues is not surprising because of bias. The only fair test of the accuracy of the coefficients is to use them to predict retention behavior of peptides unrelated to those used to derive the coefficients. However, these results did support the view that composition is the major factor determining retention of small peptides in RPC.

Guo et al.[5] compared four series of retention coefficients determined by Sasagawa et al.,[46] Browne et al.,[20] Su et al.,[45] and Meek and Rossetti[32] from regression analysis of the retention times, at acidic pH, of a wide range of peptides of varied composition. Retention coefficients were normalized relative to leucine (assigned a value of 100) to allow a direct comparison. Large discrepancies were noted both in the relative order of hydrophobicities of the amino acid side chains, and in the magnitude of the contributions of specific residues. A possible explanation for these discrepancies is that certain residues did not appear often enough in the various peptide mixtures used to enable an accurate determination of their contributions. Other possible explanations are unknown nearest-neighbor and polypeptide chain-length dependence effects, since the peptides used to determine the coefficients were of a wide range of size, composition, and sequence. Polypeptide chain-length effects on retention behavior can be eliminated if peptides of identical size are used to determine the coefficients.

9.3.2.2 Parameters Derived from Model Synthetic Peptides

Determination of Retention Coefficients The approach of Guo et al.[5] of using model synthetic peptides overcomes the problems associated with the computer-calculated regression analysis approach. These researchers examined the contribution of individual amino acid residues to peptide retention on reversed-phase columns by measuring their effect on retention of a model synthetic peptide: Ac-Gly-X-X-$(Leu)_3$-$(Lys)_2$-amide, where X was substituted by the 20 amino acids found in proteins. These researchers felt this to be a more precise method for determining retention coefficients than regression analyses of the retention times of a wide range of peptides of varied composition. Two residues were substituted each time in the model peptide to amplify their effect on peptide retention time and enable those residues with only small effects to be evaluated more accurately. The effect of polypeptide chain length on retention is relatively unimportant in small peptides and is eliminated in this model peptide approach, where single amino acid substitutions were made in an eight-residue peptide. This approach offers the most accurate method of determining retention coefficients. The peptide analogues were subjected to linear gradient elution (1% acetonitrile/min) at 1 ml/min on C_8 and C_{18} reversed-phase columns at pH 2.0 (0.1% aqueous TFA to 0.1% TFA in acetonitrile) and pH 7.0 (aqueous 10 m*M* $[NH_4]_2HPO_4$–0.1 *M* sodium perchlorate to 0.1 *M* sodium perchlorate in 60% aqueous acetonitrile). Retention coefficients for pH 2.0 and 7.0 were then determined by two approaches; first, a "core" approach, where the observed retention time for the "core" peptide, Ac-Gly-$(Leu)_3$-$(Lys)_2$-amide, was subtracted from the observed retention times of all 20 peptides, this result then being divided by two; second, a linear equation approach, where the retention times of the model peptides substituted with glycine, leucine, and lysine were applied to simultaneous equation analysis, the resulting retention values for these three residues then being applied to the other model peptides, to determine coefficients for the remaining 17 amino acids. The retention coefficients determined by each approach were very similar, and the final values (shown in Table 9–4) were an average of those obtained by the two approaches. Retention coefficients for N- and C-terminal groups (Table 9–4) were determined from the separation of a mixture of model peptides with the sequence Y-$(Leu)_5$-$(Lys)_2$-Z, where Y = N^{α}-acetyl or α-amino, and Z = C^{α}-amide or α-carboxyl.

The pH 2.0 system used in this study (linear aqueous TFA to TFA–acetonitrile gradient) was chosen because it is the most commonly used solvent system for the reversed-phase separation of peptides.

The pH 7.0 system was used to derive a new set of hydrophilicity–hydrophobicity parameters for predicting surface regions (antigenic sites) in proteins.[47] These parameters are the first reported hydrophilicity–hydrophobicity parameters derived from amino acid residues in synthetic peptides.

The relative hydrophilicity–hydrophobicity values of the retention coefficients determined at pH 2.0 and 7.0 were very logical and did not show the large discrepancies for various amino acid side chains observed in previous studies. For instance, the retention data (Table 9–4) showed that the aromatic and large bulky aliphatic side chains are the most hydrophobic among the 20 amino acid side chains. In addition, the neutral amino acids had very similar hydrophilicity–hydrophobicity values at pH 2.0 and 7.0, as expected, even though they were determined using drastically different chromatographic conditions. At pH 2.0, amino acids with basic side chains (positively charged) have a negative contribution to retention, while protonated, acidic side chains (uncharged) make little or a slightly negative contribution.

The relative elution order of the peptides was as expected. For example, the -$(Glu)_2$- peptide was more hydrophobic than the -$(Asp)_2$- peptide. Similarly, -$(Ala)_2$- > -$(Gly)_2$, -$(Thr)_2$- > -$(Ser)_2$-, -$(Ile)_2$- > -$(Val)_2$-, and -$(Gln)_2$- > $(Asn)_2$-. All of these peptides differed by two methylene groups. Interestingly, the differences in the values of the retention coefficients of alanine compared to glycine, and isoleucine compared to valine were 2.2 and 2.4 min, respectively. In both cases, an additional methylene group has been added to the side chain of glycine or valine, and this group was accessible to interact with the hydrophobic stationary phase. In contrast, the retention coefficients for glutamic acid and aspartic acid, glutamine and asparagine, and threonine and serine differed by only 0.9, 0.6, and 0.8 min, respectively, on adding the extra methylene group. This can be explained by the fact that the extra methylene group was not as accessible when added to the amino acid side chain between the peptide backbone and the hydrophilic functional groups. The -$(Leu)_2$- peptide was more hydrophobic than the -$(Ile)_2$- peptide, although these peptides contained the same number of carbon atoms. Since isoleucine is β-branched, the β-carbon is close to the peptide backbone and not as available to interact with the hydrophobic stationary phase compared to the conformation of the leucine side chain.

TABLE 9–4. Retention Coefficients of Amino Acid Residues[a]

Amino Acid Residue	Retention Coefficient (min)	
	pH 2.0	pH 7.0
Trp	8.8	9.5
Phe	8.1	9.0
Leu	8.1	9.0
Ile	7.4	8.3
Met	5.5	6.0
Val	5.0	5.7
Tyr	4.5	4.6
Cys	2.6	2.6
Pro	2.0	2.2
Ala	2.0	2.2
Glu	1.1	−1.3
Thr	0.6	+0.3
Asp	0.2	−2.6
Gln	0.0	0.0
Ser	−0.2	−0.5
Gly	−0.2	−0.2
Arg	−0.6	+0.9
Asn	−0.6	−0.8
His	−2.1	+2.2
Lys	−2.1	−0.2
α-amino	−6.9, −3.0[b]	−2.4, 0[b]
α-COOH	−0.8	−5.2

[a]The retention coefficients (minutes) were determined from retention times in RPC. The predicted retention time for a peptide equals the sum of the retention coefficients for the amino acid residues and end groups (ΣR_c) plus t_0 (the time for elution of unretained compounds) plus t_s (the time correction for the peptide standard). All parameters are calculated for N^{α}-acetylated and C-terminal amide peptides; only the values of the end groups shown above need be considered.

[b]The charged α-amino group had a smaller effect in an N-terminal Arg residue than an N-terminal residue with an uncharged side chain.

The most striking changes in the retention coefficients in raising the pH from 2 to 7 were seen in the values for Glu, Asp, His, Arg, and Lys. At pH 7.0, the side chains of the acidic residues (Glu, Asp) are completely ionized, making their relatively large shift in retention reasonable. The largest shift was seen for histidine, which loses its positive charge above pH 6–6.5. At pH 2.0, the positive charge contributed by a free α-amino group was seen to have a large negative effect on retention, whereas, at pH 7.0, this effect was seen to be somewhat smaller. It is very common for the pK_a of a peptide α-amino group to be near 7, and this partial deprotonation would explain why the effect at pH 7.0 is smaller than that at pH 2.0. The C-terminal α-carboxyl group would be highly protonated (COOH) at pH 2.0 and had only a small effect on retention under these conditions. In contrast, this group would be completely ionized (COO−) at pH 7.0, producing a large, negative effect on retention. Thus, at pH 7.0, the α-carboxyl group is fully ionized, and at pH 2.0 the α-amino group is fully protonated. These charged end groups, in contrast to blocked and uncharged end groups, can drastically affect the retention time of a peptide.

Rules for Prediction of Peptide Retention Times These rules apply to linear gradients: starting composition of 100% A, followed by increasing concentrations of B at 1%/min (A = 0.1% aqueous TFA; B = 0.1% TFA in acetonitrile), a flow rate of 1 ml/min, and a temperature of 20°C.

The predicted retention time (τ) for a peptide equals the sum of the retention coefficients (ΣR_c) for the amino acid residues and end groups (Table 9–4), plus the time for elution of unretained compounds (t_0) and the time correction for the peptide standard (t_s),[5]

$$\tau = \Sigma R_c + t_0 + t_s$$

The value t_0 is the time after injection needed for an unretained compound to reach the detector. Compounds such as TFA or 2-mercaptoethanol, which are detectable at 210 nm, can be used. The value t_s is obtained by subtracting the sum of the retention coefficients for the peptide standard (ΣR_c^{std}) plus t_0 from the observed retention time of the same peptide ($[t_R]_{std}^{obs}$):

$$t_s = (t_R)_{std}^{obs} - (\Sigma R_c^{std} + t_0)$$

combining these equations gives

$$\tau = \Sigma R_c + (t_R)_{std}^{obs} - \Sigma R_c^{std}$$

Both Meek[44] and Guo et al.[5] noted that there are differences in peptide retention on different columns that will affect retention time prediction. However, the use of an internal peptide standard allows the researcher to use (1) reversed-phase columns of any length or diameter, (2) reversed-phase packings of any particle size, *n*-alkyl chain length, and ligand density, and (3) any HPLC apparatus, making the use of retention coefficients practical.[5,29]

Accuracy of Peptide Retention Time Prediction The value of a predictive method in RPC should be assessed by its accuracy in predicting the retention times of peptides not used to derive the retention coefficients. Hence, the amino acid residue coefficients derived from the retention times of synthetic model octapeptides were applied to retention time predictions of 58 peptides.[29] The peptides were chromatographed on reversed-phase C_8 and C_{18} columns, under the conditions used to determine the coefficients[5] (linear gradient, where solvent A was 0.1% aqueous TFA and solvent B was 0.1% TFA in acetonitrile [pH 2.0]; 1% B/min, 1 ml/min, 26°C). Differences in peptide retention arising from different column packings (C_8, C_{18}) or from column aging were corrected by chromatographing an internal, 10-residue, synthetic peptide standard, S4, along with the peptides under investigation. By deliberately using columns of different age, *n*-alkyl chain length, and ligand density, it was hoped to lessen any favorable bias in the comparison of observed and predicted retention times. The small average deviation of predicted values from observed retention times (1.3 min) and the high degree of correlation (Figure 9–5; correlation = 0.98, calculated by linear least squares fitting) indicated that the coefficients derived from model synthetic peptides produced excellent predictive accuracy under the stringent test conditions for the range of peptides studies (2–16 residues).

9.3.2.3 Deviations from Predicted Peptide Retention Behavior

The application of amino acid side chain hydrophobicity parameters to peptide retention in RPC assumes that peptide retention is mainly or solely de-

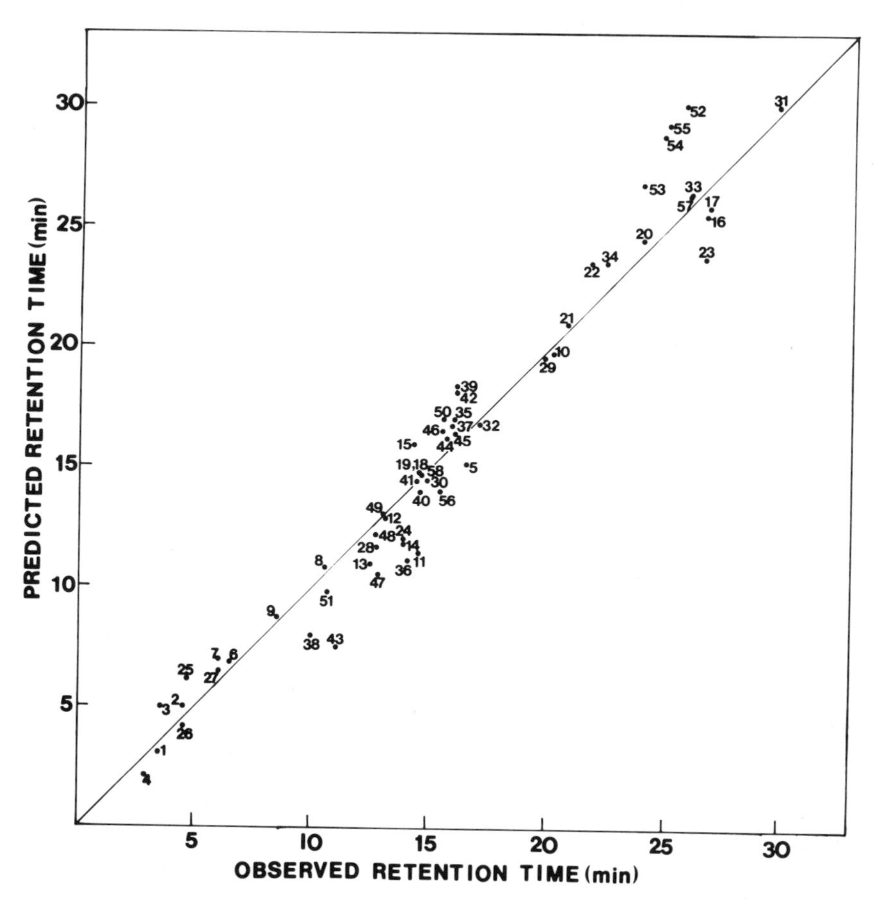

FIGURE 9–5. Correlation of predicted and observed peptide retention items in RPC. Columns: SynChropak RP-8 C_8 and RP-P C_{18} (250 × 4.1 mm i.d.; SynChrom, Linden, IN). Mobile phase: linear AB gradient (1% B/min), where solvent A is 0.1% aqueous TFA and solvent B is 0.1% TFA in acetonitrile (pH 2.0); flow rate, 1 ml/min; 26°C; absorbance at 210 nm. The peptides were 2–16 residues in length. The predicted peptide retention times were obtained by summation of retention coefficients for amino acid residues and end groups as described in the text under "Rules for prediction of peptide retention times."

pendent on amino acid composition. Although this assumption holds well enough for small peptides (up to ~20 residues), anomalies do occur. A number of researchers,[1–3,39,48–50] for instance, have presented examples of peptides with identical compositions but different sequences (i.e., positional isomers) having different retention times during RPC. Pietrzyk's group has shown that, for small, highly ionized peptides, the position of an aromatic side chain relative to a charged site may have a significant effect on retention.[1–3,39] It has been stated previously that the negative contribution to peptide retention of a protonated α-amino group is greater in an uncharged N-terminal residue than an N-terminal arginine residue.[5,28] The separation of diastereomers has also been described by several researchers.[1–3,39,49,51]

Deviations from predicted retention times and/or elution order for small peptides are generally explained in terms of sequence-specific conformational differences, leading to preferential interaction sites, or anomalous stationary phase interactions.[27,32,45,48,50,52–56] In addition, a nonpolar environment, such as a hydrophobic stationary phase, may induce helical structures in potentially helical molecules.[6] If a molecule becomes helical on binding, then obviously some residues may not be interacting with the sorbent that would result in a deviation from a predicted retention time calculated assuming denaturing conditions. Recently, Zhou *et al*[54] demonstrated the effect of preferred binding domains on peptide retention behavior. These authors demonstrated that it is possible not only to predict the retention behavior of amphipathic helices during RPC, but also to deduce the presence of amphipathic α-helical structures in peptides based upon their retention data. Unknown, nearest-neighbor interactions may also have an effect on peptide retention. However, although strict predictive accuracy may not always be possible, reported discrepancies between observed and predicted retention behavior of small peptides have generally been small and in no way negate the inherent practical value to researchers of retention coefficients.

Several researchers have noted that peptides larger than 15–20 residues tended to be eluted more rapidly than predicted from hydrophobic considerations alone.[6,23,33,34,42,43,45,52] This nonideal behavior is generally assumed to be due to stabilized secondary and tertiary structures in the polypeptide removing certain amino acid residues from contact with the hydrophobic stationary phase. It is also possible that there is a peptide chain length effect on retention behavior of polypeptides independent of any conformational considerations. Lau et al.[56] reported a linear relationship between $\log_{10}$ MW and peptide retention time during RPC for a series of five peptide polymers of 8–36 residues. Mant and Hodges[6] demonstrated a similar exponential relationship for a series of five peptide polymers of 10–50 residues (Figure 9–6). The effect on peptide retention of increasing peptide length decreased progressively with each 10-residue addition.

9.4 FUTURE PROSPECTS FOR USE OF RETENTION COEFFICIENTS

A more complete understanding of the various effects that peptide chain length, peptide conformation, and amino acid nearest-neighbor interactions (perhaps

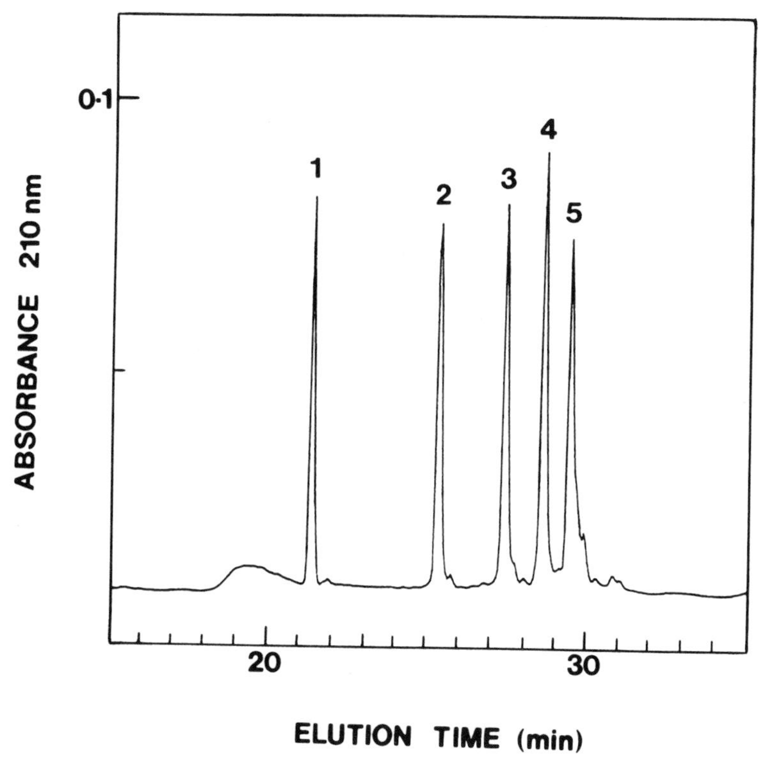

FIGURE 9–6. RPC of a mixture of synthetic peptide polymers. Column: Aquapore RP300 C_8 (220 × 4.6 mm i.d.; Brownlee Labs., Santa Clara, CA). Mobile phase: linear AB gradient (1% B/min), where solvent A is 0.1% aqueous TFA and solvent B is 0.1% TFA in acetonitrile (pH 2.0); flow rate, 1 ml/min; temperature, 26°C. Peptide standards 1, 2, 3, 4, and 5 contain 10, 20, 30, 40, and 50 residues, respectively.

the most difficult effect to gauge) have on peptide retention behavior during RPC would undoubtedly be beneficial for retention time predictions. The use of model synthetic peptide analogues offers a very promising approach to examining these effects. It may be possible, for instance, to produce a set of "pure" retention coefficients, i.e., values determined from model peptides with no conformation and no significant nearest-neighbor interactions. Deviations from expected retention behavior of a particular peptide would then allow the researcher to gain an insight into its structural and conformational characteristics.

The effect of peptide chain length, as opposed to the effects of polypeptide secondary or tertiary structure, may be ascertained by examining the retention behavior of a peptide polymer series, based on repeating units of a conformationless model peptide. Work in this direction has already been carried out and early results appear promising.[57]

Conformation and/or nearest-neighbor effects can be induced in a conformationless model peptide by addition, deletion, or rearrangement of amino acid residues, followed by examination of their reversed-phase retention behavior. Thus, in the future, not only will it be possible to predict peptide retention times more and more accurately, but also the conformation of a peptide (e.g., % α-helix) will be predicted from its retention behavior.

ACKNOWLEDGMENTS

This work was supported by the Medical Research Council of Canada and equipment grants from the Alberta Heritage Foundation for Medical Research. We also thank Dawn Oare and Vicki Luxton for typing the manuscript.

REFERENCES

1. E. P. Kroeff and D. J. Pietrzyk, *Anal. Chem.*, 50 (1978) 502.
2. Z. Iskandarini and D. J. Pietrzyk, *Anal. Chem.*, 53 (1981) 489.
3. D. J. Pietrzyk, R. L. Smith, and W. R. Cahill, Jr., *J. Liquid Chromatogr.*, 6 (1983) 1645.
4. T. Sasagawa, L. E. Ericsson, D. C. Teller, K. Titani, and K. A. Walsh, *J. Chromatogr.*, 307 (1984) 29.
5. D. Guo, C. T. Mant, A. K. Taneja, J. M. R. Parker, and R. S. Hodges, *J. Chromatogr.*, 359 (1986) 499.
6. C. T. Mant and R. S. Hodges, in High-Performance Liquid Chromatography of Biological Macromolecules: Methods and Applications (K. Gooding and F. Regnier, eds.). Dekker, New York, 1990, p. 301.
7. H. P. J. Bennett, C. A. Browne, and S. Solomon, *J. Liquid Chromatogr.*, 3 (1980) 1353.
8. D. Guo, C. T. Mant, and R. S. Hodges, *J. Chromatogr.*, 386 (1987) 205.
9. C. T. Mant and R. S. Hodges, *LC, Liquid Chromatogr. HPLC Mag.*, 4 (1986) 250.
10. C. T. Mant and R. S. Hodges, *Chromatographia*, 24 (1987) 805.
11. Cs. Horváth, W. Melander, I. Molnár, and P. Molnár, *Anal. Chem.*, 49 (1977) 2295.
12. Cs. Horváth, W. Melander, and I. Molnár, *J. Chromatogr.*, 125 (1976) 129.
13. J. C. Kraak, K. M. Jonker, and J. F. K. Huber, *J. Chromatogr.*, 142 (1977) 671.
14. N. E. Hoffman and J. C. Liao, *Anal. Chem.*, 49 (1977) 2231.
15. P. T. Kissinger, *Anal. Chem.*, 49 (1977) 883.
16. J. L. M. Van de Venne, J. L. H. M. Hendrikx, and R. S. Deelder, *J. Chromatogr.*, 167 (1978) 1.
17. A. N. Starratt and M. E. Stevens, *J. Chromatogr.*, 194 (1980) 421.
18. W. M. M. Schaaper, D. Voskamp, and C. Olieman, *J. Chromatogr.*, 195 (1980) 181.
19. D. R. K. Harding, C. A. Bishop, M. F. Tarttelin, and W. S. Hancock, *Int. J. Peptide Protein Res.*, 18 (1981) 214.
20. C. A. Browne, H. P. J. Bennett, and S. Solomon, *Anal. Biochem.*, 124 (1982) 201.
21. W. S. Hancock, C. A. Bishop, R. L. Prestidge, D. R. K. Harding, and M. T. W. Hearn, *Science*, 200 (1978) 1168.
22. E. C. Nice and M. J. O'Hare, *J. Chromatogr.*, 162 (1979) 401.
23. M. J. O'Hare and E. C. Nice, *J. Chromatogr.*, 171 (1979) 209.
24. B. Grego, F. Lambrou, and M. T. W. Hearn, *J. Chromatogr.*, 266 (1983) 89.
25. H. Gaertner and A. Puigserver, *J. Chromatogr.*, 350 (1985) 279.

26. M. T. W. Hearn, B. Grego, and W. S. Hancock, *J. Chromatogr.*, 185 (1979) 429.
27. M. T. W. Hearn and B. Grego, *J. Chromatogr.*, 203 (1981) 349.
28. C. T. Mant, P. D. Semchuk, and R. S. Hodges, Abstract 504, 10th International Symposium on HPLC of Proteins, Peptides and Polynucleotides, Oct. 29–31, 1990, Wiesbaden, F.R.G.
29. D. Guo, C. T. Mant, A. K. Taneja, and R. S. Hodges, *J. Chromatogr.*, 359 (1986) 519.
30. M. T. W. Hearn, *J. Liquid Chromatogr.*, 3 (1980) 1255.
31. W. C. Mahoney and M. A. Hermodson, *J. Biol. Chem.*, 255 (1980) 11199.
32. J. L. Meek and Z. L. Rossetti, *J. Chromatogr.*, 211 (1981) 15.
33. K. J. Wilson, A. Honegger, R. P. Stötzel, and G. J. Hughes, *Biochem. J.*, 199 (1981) 31.
34. T. Sasagawa, T. Okuyama, and D. C. Teller, *J. Chromatogr.*, 240 (1982) 329.
35. M. T. W. Hearn and B. Grego, *J. Chromatogr.*, 255 (1983) 125.
36. M. T. W. Hearn, M. I. Aguilar, C. T. Mant, and R. S. Hodges, *J. Chromatogr.*, 438 (1988) 197.
37. C. T. Mant and R. S. Hodges, *J. Liquid Chromatogr.*, 12 (1989) 139.
38. I. Molnár and Cs. Horváth, *J. Chromatogr.*, 142 (1977) 623.
39. D. P. Kroeff and D. J. Pietrzyk, *Anal. Chem.*, 50 (1978) 1353.
40. R. F. Rekker, The Hydrophobic Fragmental Constant. Elsevier, Amsterdam, 1977, p. 301.
41. M. T. W. Hearn, C. A. Bishop, W. S. Hancock, D. R. K. Harding, and G. D. Reynolds, *J. Liquid Chromatogr.*, 2 (1979) 1.
42. C. T. Wehr, L. Correia, and S. R. Abbott, *J. Chromatogr. Sci.*, 20 (1982) 114.
43. K. J. Wilson, A. Honegger, and G. J. Hughes, *Biochem. J.*, 199 (1981) 43.
44. J. L. Meek, *Proc. Natl. Acad. Sci. U.S.A.*, 77 (1980) 1632.
45. S-J. Su, B. Grego, B. Niven, and M. T. W. Hearn, *J. Liquid Chromatogr.*, 4 (1981) 1745.
46. T. Sasagawa, T. Okuyama, and D. C. Teller, *J. Chromatogr.*, 240 (1982) 329.
47. J. M. R. Parker, D. Guo, and R. S. Hodges, *Biochemistry*, 25 (1986) 5425.
48. S. Terabe, R. Konaka, and K. Inouye, *J. Chromatogr.*, 172 (1979) 163.
49. R. A. Houghten and S. T. DeGraw, *J. Chromatogr.*, 386 (1987) 223.
50. M. T. W. Hearn and M. I. Aguilar, *J. Chromatogr.*, 392 (1987) 33.
51. B. Larsen, B. L. Fox, M. F. Burke, and V. J. Hruby, *Int. J. Peptide Protein Res.*, 13 (1979) 12.
52. E. C. Nice, M. W. Capp, N. Cooke, and M. J. O'Hare, *J. Chromatogr.*, 218 (1981) 569.
53. M. T. W. Hearn and M. I. Aguilar, *J. Chromatogr.*, 359 (1986) 31.
54. N. E. Zhou, C. T. Mant, and R. S. Hodges, *Peptide Research*, 3 (1990) 8.
55. K. K. Lee, J. A. Black, and R. S. Hodges, in High Performance Liquid Chromatography of Peptides and Proteins: Separation, Conformation and Analysis (C. T. Mant and R. S. Hodges, eds.), CRC Press, Boca Raton, FL, 1991 (in press).
56. S. Y. M. Lau, A. K. Taneja, and R. S. Hodges, *J. Chromatogr.*, 317 (1984) 129.
57. C. T. Mant, T. W. L. Burke, J. A. Black, and R. S.Hodges, *J. Chromatogr.*, 458 (1988) 193.

CHAPTER 10

Multidimensional, Microscale HPLC Technique in Protein Sequencing

Nobuhiro Takahashi, Toshiaki Isobe, and Frank W. Putnam

CONTENTS

10.1 INTRODUCTION

Protein sequencing is a central technology in modern biological science. Amino acid sequence data generated from direct protein sequencing can be used (1) for identification of the protein by computational sequence analysis using NBRF, GenBank, and EMBL data banks, etc., (2) for gene isolation through the use of synthetic oligonucleotides or through the use of antisera against a synthetic peptide, (3) for definition of active site and domain boundaries, and posttranslational modification, (4) for confirmation of the amino acid sequence deduced from DNA sequence analysis, and (5) for establishment of the amino acid substitutions in genetic variants.

For successful protein sequencing, the protein must first be isolated in a pure form, and second, many peptides generated by chemical or enzymatic digestion of a protein have to be separated. Generally speaking, the purification of protein and peptide samples for sequence analysis has been achieved by multidimensional column chromatography. In many cases, HPLC technique is applied at the final stage of purification, which is combined with several conventional column chromatographies using Sephadex, Sepharose, or cellulose columns. Especially in recent years, HPLC technique tends to be applied directly from the beginning of the purification steps. For example, many combinations, such as gel filtration, followed by reversed-phase HPLC (RP-HPLC), a cation- or an anion-exchange column with RP-HPLC, RP-HPLC at two different pH values, and RP-HPLC with two different ion-pairing agents, have been used for multidimensional HPLC techniques. These procedures are usually carried out manually, i.e., the eluent from the first column is collected in many fractions and then each fraction is applied to the second column separately. However, manual operation of multidimensional HPLC may cause many problems such as precipitation during concentration of samples, sample loss by multihandling, increased time and labor, chance of human error, and decreased reproducibility through accumulation of experimental errors.

At present there is no universal purification method applicable to all proteins because, in nature, there are numerous proteins with different characteristics. Therefore, the method for protein purification tends to be an individual one, which is applied for only one of the proteins. Thus, it seemed to be very difficult to develop a universal and systematic purification method applicable to many proteins. However, recent progress in high-performance liquid chromatography (HPLC) has greatly improved the efficiencies of the protein and peptide separations.[1] Many commercially available systems for HPLC are now able to program many different elution modes and to control many conditions for chromatography by means of a computer control system. In addition, many HPLC columns, not only reversed-phase columns, but also ion-exchange, gel filtration, and hydroxyapatite columns, now have high resolution power sufficient to separate at least several dozen components in a single operation. Furthermore, although silica-based columns tend to be unstable at higher pH range (over pH 7), some polymer-based columns have high stability even at high pH, which permits washing out with alkaline solution. This type of column can be used repeatedly for direct application of crude protein mixtures, such as serum and tissue extracts.

By taking advantage of recent progress in HPLC as described above, it seemed reasonable to try to develop a universal high-resolution technique that is applicable to many proteins and peptides. One approach to developing such a technique is the automation of multidimensional HPLC. The idea is somewhat similar to that of two-dimensional (2D) electrophoresis that is performed by the combination of isoelectric focusing and SDS-polyacrylamide gel electrophoresis, represented by O'Farrell's method.[2] The 2D method seems to have the highest separation power and universality in the current technologies for protein or peptide separation. Methods for sample preparation from the two-dimensional acrylamide gel by electroelution[3] or blotting techniques,[4,5] have also been developed for microscale protein sequencing. However, these are tedious and complicated methods, and there are still some limitations on sample preparation, including blocking of amino-terminal residues during electrophoresis, poor extraction efficiency for some proteins, and difficulty in further chemical or enzymatic treatment for analyzing internal amino acid sequence, etc.

Automated systems for multidimensional HPLC technique have been developed, which perform sequential chromatography on two different columns. These systems are composed of either two independent HPLC assemblies, or one HPLC assembly with valve control equipment for buffer change. In each case programmed elution is carried out by a computer-assisted controller. Typically, a sample mixture is applied to an ion-exchange column and eluted in a stepwise manner. The eluent from the first column is introduced directly into the second column, which is a reversed column connected in tandem through a tee tube. After application of the eluent, reversed-phase chromatography is performed by a linear gradient elution. Stepwise elution for ion-exchange chromatography and the gradient elution for reversed-phase chromatography are synchronized by a computer program.

These automated systems have been extensively applied to systematic protein mapping and purification of tissue extracts, and to peptide mapping of extremely complex peptide mixtures. For example, the cytosol fraction from bovine cerebellum has been resolved into about 200 peaks; not only were many known proteins isolated in a pure form, but also several new proteins were purified by a single operation of the chromatography. The technique has also been used to isolate the peptides with amino acid substitutions in many genetic variants of human serum albumin, and for study of proteolytic modification or carbohydrate variants of ceruloplasmin. Because of the high resolution and excellent reproducibility of the method, the automated multidimensional HPLC technique is very useful for systematic protein purification from tissue extracts and for comparative peptide mapping of extremely complex peptide mixtures from very large proteins.

This chapter describes the continuing effort to develop automated multidimensional HPLC techniques applicable to systematic separation of very complex protein or peptide mixtures. The automation of multidimensional HPLC has several advantages not only over manual operation of the technique, but also over two-dimensional electrophoresis. These include high resolution, reproducibility, ease of sample handling and recovery, and quantification. Because of the high resolution and excellent reproducibility of the automated method, the system can also be applied to comparative peptide mapping for identification of peptides with microheterogeneity, e.g., in the study of amino acid substitutions in genetic variants, proteolytic modifications, and carbohydrate variants. The automated method can also be used to prepare peptides in the strategy for protein sequencing of very large proteins.

10.2 PRINCIPLE OF THE METHOD

The technique of automated multidimensional HPLC described here is a sequential chromatography on two different kinds of columns that are connected in tandem. The separation mode of the two kinds of columns differs. The resolution power of the columns is multiplied by a combination of the two columns with different specificity. In principle, if each column is capable of resolving peptide mixture into, for example, 50 peaks, the theoretical separation capacity of the combination is $50 \times 50 = 2500$ peaks.

One approach to perform automated multidimensional HPLC is that the eluent from the first column is collected in many fractions and then each fraction is applied to the second column separately.[6] In this case, automated sample injection equipment has to be coupled with a fraction collector between the first and second columns.

Another approach is that the eluent from the first column is applied directly to the second column without pooling the eluent fractions and/or pretreatment. In this case two different kinds of columns are connected in tandem. There are two methods for this approach. In one method many columns with the same mode are connected in parallel after the first column through a column change valve. For this system the elution of the first column is performed completely by the end of the chromatography without any interruption. During the chromatography the eluent is continuously applied little by little to all of the second columns by changing the valve automatically. The chromatography of each of the second columns, then, is performed sequentially. In order to perform this method the number of the second columns should probably exceed an order of ten, and all of the second columns must be of the same quality. In another method only one second column is connected in tandem after the first column through a tee tube.[7] In this case the elution of the first column is interrupted in the midst of the chromatography in order to perform chromatography with the second column, to which the eluent from the first column is applied. After the completion of the chromatography of the second column, the elution of the first column is started again and the eluent is applied to the second column. The chromatography of the second column is repeated exactly as performed in the first step. Their steps are repeated over and over again.

In the three methods described above the first two probably give better resolution than the last method because they do not interrupt the elution in the midst of the chromatography of the first column. However, the last method does not require the excessive equipment that the other two do. Therefore, in our laboratory we have chosen the last method to perform automated multidimensional HPLC because the technique is relatively simple and can be done easily in many laboratories that have one or two ordinary HPLC assemblies with a computer-assisted controller.

The system for our multidimensional technique is composed of either two independent HPLC assemblies, or one HPLC assembly with valve control equipment for buffer change. In each case programmed elution is carried out by a computer-assisted controller. A sample mixture is applied to an ion-exchange column and eluted in a stepwise manner. The eluent from the first column is introduced directly into the second column, which is a reversed-phase column connected in tandem through a tee tube. After application of the eluent, reversed-phase chromatography is performed by a linear gradient elution. Stepwise elution for ion-exchange chromatography and the gradient elution for reversed-phase chromatography are synchronized by a computer program.

10.3 EXPERIMENTAL PROCEDURES

10.3.1 Apparatus and Performance of Two-Dimensional HPLC with One HPLC Assembly

The 2D-HPLC assembly is illustrated in Figure 10–1. The system consists of two HPLC columns (C1 and C2) of different separation modes that are con-

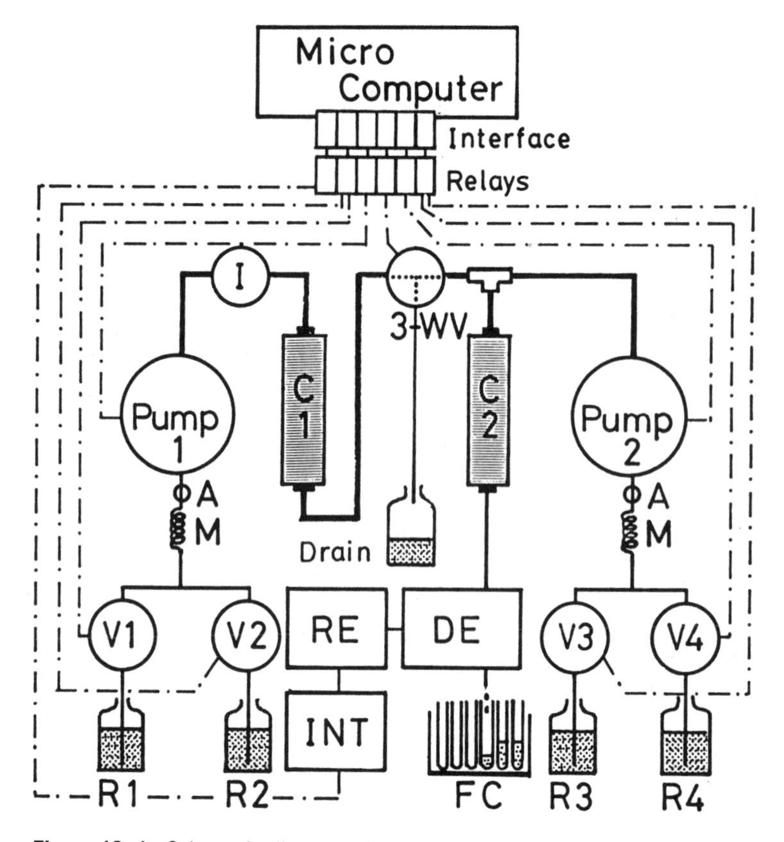

Figure 10–1. Schematic diagram of the 2D-HPLC system with one HPLC assembly for protein mapping. The assembly is explained in the text.

nected in tandem through a three-way electrical column switching valve (3WV), and two independent flow systems each equipped with a high pressure pump (Pump 1 and Pump 2), two pairs of solenoid valves (V1/V2 and V3/V4), and a coil solvent mixer (M). A system controller, composed of an 8-bit microcomputer connected to electrical relays through an interface, controls pumps 1 and 2 (on/off), the column switching valve (connect/disconnect C1 and C2), and the two pairs of solenoid valves to perform a series of stepwise elutions for C1 and to perform a repetitive linear gradient elution for C2. A wavelength-tunable UV detector (DE) connected to an integrator-recorder (RE) is set to monitor the eluent and to quantitate the peaks from the HPLC. For our standard system focused particularly on the separation of brain acidic proteins, a polymer-based anion-exchange TSK-gel DEAE-5PW (Tosoh, Tokyo) was combined with a polymer-based reversed-phase TSK-gel Phenyl-5PWRP for C1 and C2, respectively. However, in principle, other types of packing material can also be coupled for the first and the second dimensional separations.

The computer program processes the 2D-HPLC as follows. By starting the program the columns C1 and C2 are equilibrated with B1(e.g., with 0.025 *M* Tris-HCl buffer, pH 7.5) and B3 (e.g., with 20% acetonitrile in 0.1% trifluoroacetic acid), respectively, at a flow rate of 1.0 ml/min. After equilibration for 40 min, pump 2 is stopped, and the column switching valve moves to connect C1 and C2. A protein mixture is applied to column C1 through a sample injector (I) and eluted with buffer B1 for the time t_1 (20 min as standard) at a flow rate of 1.0 ml/min. After the eluate from C1 is applied directly into the reversed-phase column C2, pump 1 is stopped; simultaneously, the second chromatography begins as pump 2 starts pumping at a flow rate of 1.0 ml/min with a linear gradient from B3 to B4 (e.g., with 20–60% of acetonitrile in 0.1% trifluoroacetic acid) during the time t_2 (40 min as standard). Column C2 is equilibrated again with B3 for 10 min after the linear gradient elution is finished; then pump 2 is stopped. By this step, the first cycle of the 2D-HPLC is completed. Then, pump 1 for the first chromatography starts again to elute proteins stepwise from the ion-exchange column C1 by introducing and mixing a portion of the buffer B2 (e.g., with 0.4 *M* NaCl in 0.025 *M* Tris-HCl buffer, pH 7.5) into B1. After applying the eluate to C2, the second chromatography is repeated exactly as described above. These procedures are repeated for a number of cycles (n) changing the mixture ratio of B1 and B2 with computer-assisted, time-dependent control of solenoid valves V1 and V2. For versatility, the computer program has been made open for the elution times of C1 and C2 (t_1 and t_2), the cycle number (n), and the mixing ratio of B1/B2 in each cycle, so that an operator is able to input these parameters depending on the complexity and ionic distribution of a protein mixture.

10.3.2 Apparatus and Performance of Two-Dimensional HPLC with Two HPLC Assemblies[7]

The 2D-HPLC assembly is illustrated in Figure 10–2. As employed in our laboratory an anion-exchange Spherogel-TSK IEX-540 DEAE column (30 × 0.4 cm i.d., Altex, Berkeley, CA) (C1) (System 1) is connected in tandem with a reversed-phase Ultrasphere ODS column (15 × 0.4 cm i.d., Altex, Berkeley, CA) (C2) (System 2) through a tee tube (T). Other solvent systems and column configurations can also be used. In each system, programmed elution is performed with a 421 CRT controller (Controllers 1 and 2) (Models 334 and 344 Gradient HPLC Systems, Beckman, Berkeley, CA). Controller 1 regulates two pumps (P1 and P2) of System 1 (Model 334) to perform a series of stepwise elutions, synchronized with Controller 2. Buffers B1 (0.02 *M* Tris-acetic acid, pH 8.0) and B2 (0.4 or 1.0 *M* ammonium hydroxide-methanesulfonic acid–0.02 *M* Tris-acetic acid, pH 8.0), pumped by P1 and P2 respectively, are combined in a mixing chamber (M1) and flow into the anion-exchange column (C1) after passing through the sample injector (SI). Controller 2 regulates the flow rates of two pumps (P3 and P4) in System 2 (Model 344) to perform a repetitive linear gradient elution, synchronized with System 1. Buffers B3 [0.1% trifluoroacetic acid (TFA)] and B4 (acetonitrile containing 0.1% TFA), pumped by P3 and P4, respectively, are combined in a mixing chamber (M2) and flow into the reversed-phase column (C2) through the tee tube after the stepwise elution from the column (C1) is stopped.

For the first chromatography a peptide mixture is applied in System 1 to the anion-exchange column (C1) for 15 min at a typical flow rate of 0.5 ml/min only with buffer B1. At this step, P2 does not pump buffer B2 (0% B2). After the eluate from C1 is applied directly into the reversed-phase column C2, System 1 is stopped; simultaneously, the second chromatography begins as System 2 starts pumping typically at a flow rate of 1.0 ml/min with a linear gradient from e.g., 0 to 45% of acetonitrile during 60 min. Column C2 is equilibrated again with B3 for 5 min after the linear gradient elution is finished; then the flow in System 2 is stopped. By this step the first cycle of the 2D-chromatography is completed. Then, System 1 for the first chromatography starts again to elute peptides stepwise from the anion-exchange column (C1) with 5% B2. After the application of the eluate to C2, the second chromatography is repeated exactly as described above. The pumping ratio of B2 for the first chromatography is increased in a stepwise manner as follows: 0, 5, 10, 15, 20, 25, 30, 35, 40, 50, and 100% B2. The stepwise elution for anion-exchange chromatography and the linear gradient elution for reversed-phase chromatography are synchronized by computer programs of controllers 1 and 2.

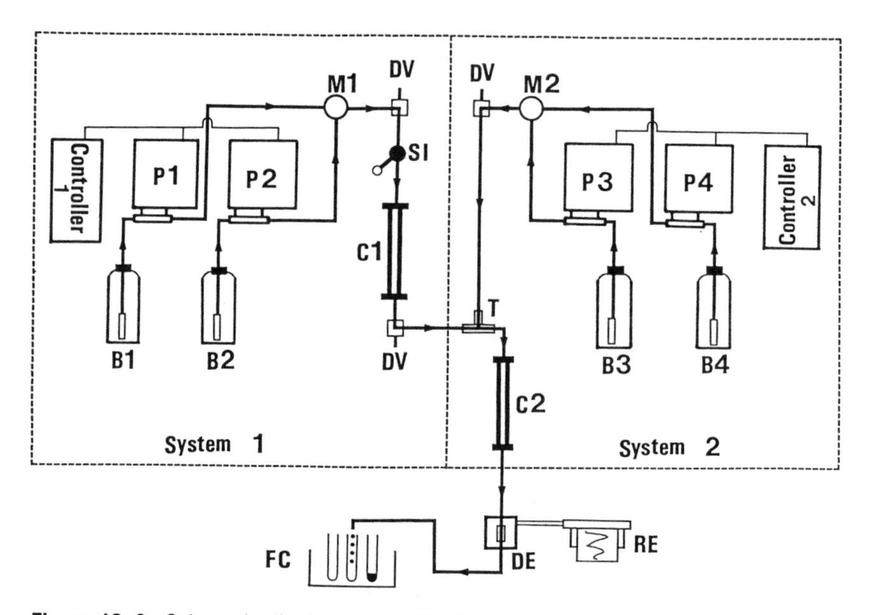

Figure 10–2. Schematic diagram of the 2D-HPLC system with two HPLC assemblies for peptide mapping of very large protein.[7] The assemblies are explained in the text. DV, drain value; FC, fraction collector; DE, wavelength-tunable UV detector; RE, recoder.

10.4 PROTEIN MAPPING BY TWO-DIMENSIONAL HPLC WITH REFERENCE TO CEREBELLAR EXTRACTS

10.4.1 Separation of Soluble Proteins in Extracts of Bovine Cerebellum

The following example is representative of the application potential of the method. Soluble proteins were extracted from bovine cerebellum (40 g wet weight) with a 4-fold volume of 0.1 *M* potassium phosphate buffer, pH 7.1, containing 1.6 *M* ammonium sulfate and 1 m*M* EDTA, and the extracted proteins were precipitated by addition of solid ammonium sulfate to 85% saturation at pH 4.7. After centrifugation, the precipitate was dissolved in 0.1 *M* potassium phosphate buffer, pH 7.1, containing 1 m*M* EDTA and dialyzed against the buffer B1 for the 2D-HPLC. A portion of the cerebellar extracts was applied directly to the automated 2D-HPLC system under the programmed conditions given in the legend to Figure 10–3A.

Figure 10–3A shows a three-dimensional visualization of the 2D-HPLC profile, in which each horizontal profile corresponds to one cycle in the chromatography. The NaCl concentration of elution buffer for a series of stepwise elutions of the first-dimensional anion-exchange column is shown at the right side of each horizontal profile which, then, represents the result of the second-dimensional reversed-phase chromatography of a protein fraction eluted from the first column. Thus, the programmed number of cycles (n) was set at 10 in this separation, which required the total analysis time of 12 h.

When these conditions are applied to the cerebellar extracts containing 6 mg of protein, ca. 200 peaks are detected. Quantitative analysis indicated that each of these peaks contained 0.5–60 μg of protein, suggesting that our system could detect proteins present at a level of more than 0.01% of the total soluble proteins in bovine cerebellum with the detector sensitivity used (220 nm, 0.64 AUFS). The number of peaks resolved by the 2D-HPLC separation of the extracts increased to ca. 250, if the cycle number of the first chromatography was increased to 20. Although it is difficult to estimate the actual number of proteins present in the extracts within this range of abundance, we have noticed that the number of proteins separated by the 2D-HPLC system compares to ca. 400 protein spots detected by two-demensional electrophoresis of this preparation followed by Coomassie blue staining.[8]

By the analysis described below, it is noticed that among 15 proteins identified in the cerebellar extracts only two proteins, albumin and HMG-1, are found in duplicated peaks eluted in the adjacent, first-dimensional separation.

10.4.2 Analysis of Separated Proteins

To evaluate the efficiency as a separation method of proteins, 25 peaks containing 5–60 μg of protein were collected from the 2D-HPLC and analyzed for purity by SDS-polyacrylamide gel electrophoresis. Twelve peaks analyzed contained proteins with suffucient purity for subsequent protein chemical anal-

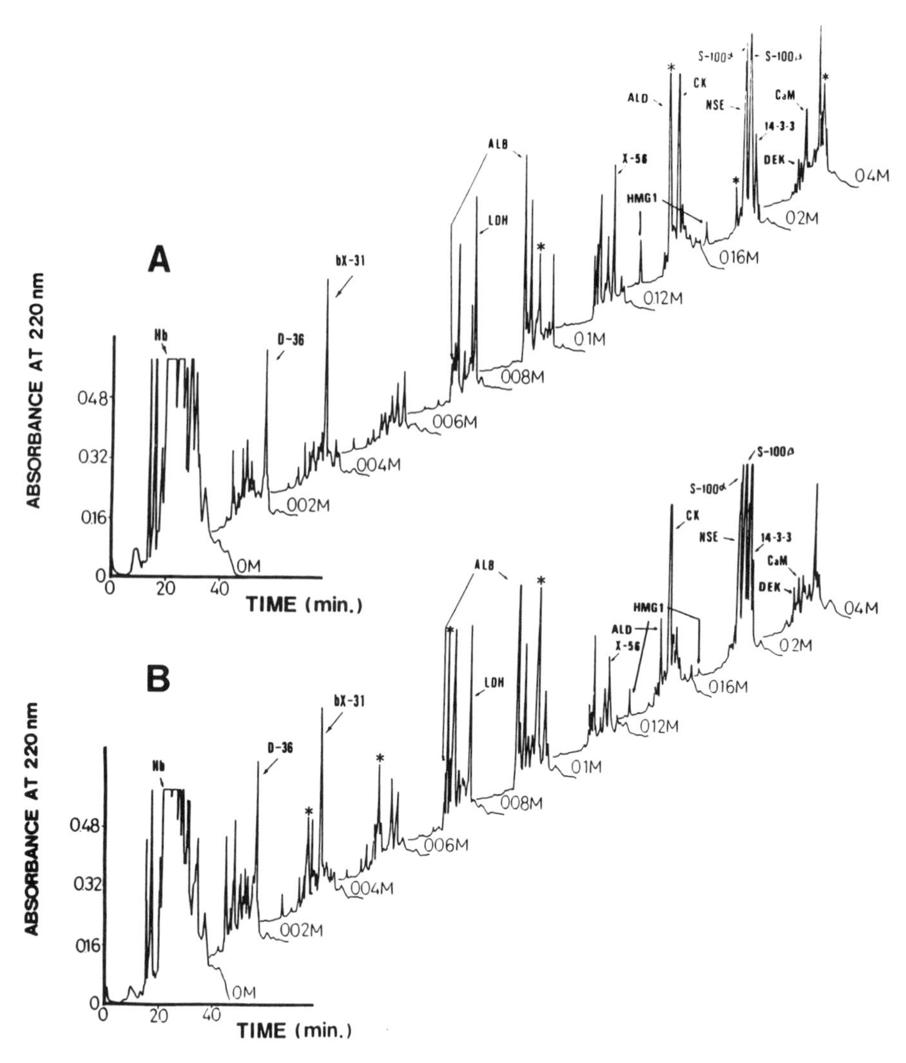

Figure 10–3. Three-dimensional representation of the protein maps of bovine cerebellum (A) and cerebrum (B). The 2D-HPLC was done as described in the text. Peaks identified are designated as Hb, hemoglobin; ALB, albumin; LDH, lactate dehydrogenase; ALD, aldolase; HMG-1, high mobility group I protein: CK, creatine kinase; NSE, neuron specific enolase; S100α, alpha-subunit of S100 protein; S100β, beta-subunit of S100 protein; 14-3-3, 14-3-3 protein; CaM, calmodulin. D-36, BX-31, X-56, and DEK are new proteins found by this method. Asterisks indicate the proteins present in either cerebellum or cerebrum.

ysis. Although other peaks contained two or three proteins or contained some impurities giving rise to smeared bands in polyacrylamide gel, most of these peaks could be purified by an additional reversed-phase chromatography eluted with a gentle gradient of acetonitrile, or using 0.08% heptafluorobutyric acid in place of trifluoroacetic acid.

The isolated proteins were analyzed for amino acid composition by the conventional procedure, or where only a small quantity of sample was available, by the precolumn phenylthioisocyanate derivatization method following gas-phase HCl hydrolysis.[9] Portions of the protein samples were also subjected to micro-amino-terminal sequence analysis on a gas-phase sequenator. Although many of these brain proteins were found to have blocked amino-terminal residues, several proteins analyzed yielded an amino-terminal sequence of 15–25 residues by this direct protein analysis. Proteins with blocked amino terminals were cleaved by cyanogen bromide, the fragments were separated on a reversed-phase ODS-120T column (Tosoh), and the purified fragments analyzed for sequence determination as described above. The partial sequence resulting from either of these procedures was subjected to computer-assisted analysis for the search of possible identity or homology to proteins of known amino acid sequence using a SEARCH program of the NBRF-IDEAS protein database. Figure 10–4 illustrates an example of such a protein chemical analysis of a peak obtained by the 2D-HPLC technique, from which the proteins could be identified as brain-type creatine kinase.[10] For a protein found to have a unique amino acid sequence, the sequence analysis can be extended further by protein chemical techniques, or by molecular cloning techniques after synthesizing a specific oligonucleotide probe or producing a specific antiserum against a polypeptide synthesized for the partial sequence. The latter cloning approach is in progress to determine the complete sequence of one of the proteins that we refer to as DEK in Figure 10–3A.

Other analytical methods applied to the purified proteins include micro-two-dimensional electrophoresis,[11] which provided isoelectric points and molecular weight values of the separated proteins with less than 0.1 μg of proteins, and also dot-blot immunochemical analysis on a nitrocellulose membrane[12] using peroxidase-labeled second antibodies. The dot-blot analysis served to confirm the identification of several proteins such as neuron-specific enolase and S100 proteins for which the specific antisera are available. Alternatively, 12 brain proteins that we purified by our conventional large-scale procedure and characterized by various means[13] were analyzed by the 2D-HPLC system and their peaks identified in the protein map shown in Figure 10–3A.

As the result of the analyses described above, 15 peaks obtained from the 2D-HPLC of bovine cerebellar soluble proteins have been characterized so far. These peaks include most of the major peaks detected in the 2D-HPLC, and contain many known brain proteins such as the brain-type isozymes of glycolytic enzymes lactate dehydrogenase, aldolase C, creatin kinase, and neuron-specific enolase, the "EF-hand" type calcium-binding proteins calmodulin and the S100 protein, and the kinase II-dependent tyrosine and tryptophan hy-

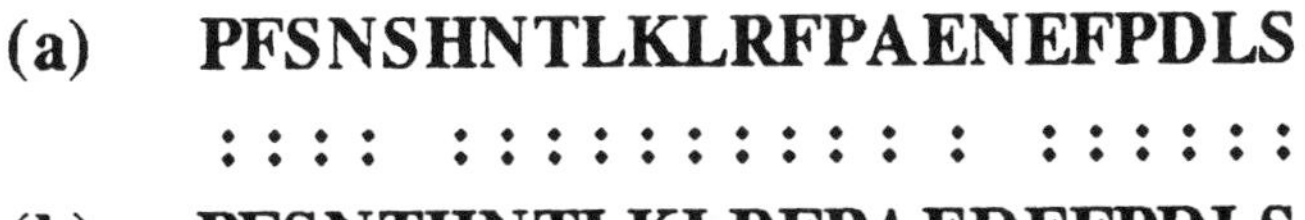

Figure 10–4. Amino terminal sequence of (a) dog brain creatine kinase and (b) a protein isolated by the 2D-HPLC method.

droxylase activator protein 14-3-3.[14] Serum albumin and hemoglobin, which probably originated from the peripheral blood, and the nonhistone protein HMG-1[15] were also identified. Not only were these known proteins isolated, but also several new proteins were purified by the chromatography. All of these proteins, designated tentatively as DEK, X-56, and so on in Figure 10–3A, are relatively abundant in the cerebellum; they have acidic isoelectric points (ca. pH 6.0–4.2) and exhibit a relative molecular mass of 50,000–80,000 Da on SDS-polyacrylamide gel electrophoresis.

10.4.3 Reproducibility and Stability

The 2D-HPLC system showed excellent reproducibility when the analysis of standard proteins or the protein mapping of cerebellar soluble proteins was repeated. This is, of course, attributable to the reliability of the total system employed including the computer program used for the valve control, but the chemical stability of polymer-based columns is particularly important. We have used this 2D-HPLC system at least 100 times for various purposes, mainly for protein separations of crude tissue extracts. After 20–25 analytical runs, the back pressure of the first-dimensional anion-exchange column rises from 20 to 80 kg/cm^2 probably due to accumulation of lipids, nucleic acids, and very large proteins of low solubility, etc. However, the column could be regenerated after washing with 30 ml of 0.5 *M* NaOH in 50% aqueous acetone without detectable deterioration in peak resolution.

10.4.4 Comparison of the Protein Maps of the Bovine Cerebellar and Cerebral Extracts

When the 2D-HPLC system was applied to the separation of the extracts prepared from bovine adrenal medulla, the resulting protein map was very different and clearly distinguishable from that of the cerebellar extracts because the adrenal tissue lacked the known brain proteins such as neuron-specific enolase and S100 (Uchida et al., unpublished results). To further examine whether the method is applicable to the detection of differences between the protein compositions of tissues of a closer ontogenetic origin, bovine cerebral extracts were prepared and analyzed by the 2D-HPLC system. As shown in Figure 10–3B, the cerebral extracts gave rise to a protein map very similar to that of the cerebellar extracts. Here, we find ca. 200 peaks, and most of these peaks seem to be equivalent to the cerebellar counterparts. The cerebral extracts contained all of the 15 proteins assigned in the protein map of cerebellum, except one protein that we identified as aldolase C. This indicates that the protein compositions of cerebellum and cerebrum are very similar as expected from their close ontogenetic relationship. However, both these maps are still distinguishable in containing many proteins in different quantities. In particular, the distribution of several proteins is significantly different between the cerebellar and cerebral extracts, i.e., there are proteins such as aldolase C that are much more abundant in the cerebellar extracts than in the cerebral extracts, and likewise, several other proteins appear to be specific to the cerebral extracts. These proteins are indicated by asterisks in Figure 10–3A and B. Most of these proteins have not yet been characterized, and the regional distribution of aldolase C within the brain is not reported in detail. However, our result for aldolase C is consistent with the observation of a previous immunohistochemical study in that this brain type isozyme is strongly associated with Purkinje cells in human cerebellum.[16] These results suggest that the 2D-HPLC system could be useful for the protein mapping of very complex protein mixtures such as crude tissue extracts and for the detection of differences in the protein compositions of various tissues and cells.

10.4.5 Sensitivity of the Method

The 2D-HPLC system described above is equipped with a 7.5-mm-i.d. column for the first anion-exchange separation and a 4.6-mm-i.d. column for the second reversed-phase separation. This system has a sample loading capacity of about 10 mg. When this amount of the extracts is applied for the systematic purification of cerebellar proteins, ca. 1–100 μg each of purified protein can be isolated by a single operation of the chromatography. On the other hand, the same system allows one to perform an analytical protein mapping with less than 100 μg of the extracts (derived from 10 mg of cerebellum tissue) simply by increasing the detector sensitivity (210 nm, 0.16 AUFS), without introducing a significant problem in the baseline. We are able to obtain a protein map of cultivated hybridoma cells using 5×10^6 cells grown in a single well of a conventional 24-well plastic plate.

If the amount of sample is smaller than this, both columns can be replaced by smaller diameter columns; and conversely, larger diameter columns will allow larger scale purification of proteins. We anticipate that such a flexibility will be an important feature of the 2D-HPLC system, so that it may serve for both analytical and preparative protein separations.

10.4.6 Limitation of the Method

We have selected an anion-exchange column for the first separation, because our initial interest in developing the 2D-HPLC system was the systematic separation of proteins in brain, the tissue characterized specifically by a high content of acidic proteins. Based on the analysis of a series of proteins with known acidity, the anion-exchange column absorbs proteins having an isoelectric point below pH 6.5 under the solvent condition employed (0.025 *M* Tris-HCl, pH 7.5). Thus, more basic proteins elute together in the first cycle of the chromatography, and this decreases the number of peaks in the subsequent cycles. Complementary to the present system would be the use of a cation-exchange support for the first separation, and in fact, a cation-exchange TSK-gel CM-5PW or a spherical hydroxyapatite column (Tonen K.K., Saitama, Japan) was found to be more effective than the present system in separating basic proteins. It is advantageous, therefore, to select either an anion- or a cation-exchange column depending on the charge distribution of the protein mixture. Of course, a tandem system of anion- and cation-exchange columns or a mixed-bed ion-exchange column can be used for the first separation in order to decrease the number of proteins eluted in the first cycle.

The second separation was performed on a reversed-phase column taking advantage of its high resolution; however, this introduces two limitations. First, very hydrophobic proteins will bind to the reversed-phase column too tightly and may not be recovered from the column during the chromatography. The reversed-phase column selected is the one that, in our experience, has the lowest hydrophobicity among the commercial columns tested, and is able to separate relatively large proteins such as serum amine oxidase (subunit M_r = 95,000). The column is stable even after 100 analyses of the tissue extracts, suggesting that most, if not all, of proteins are eluted from the column. Yet, we cannot exclude the possibility of incomplete elution when the method is applied to very hydrophobic and poorly soluble proteins. Second, the reversed-phase separation will cause a decrease or loss of the biological activities of proteins that are labile in high acetonitrile concentration and an acidic pH. In general, small proteins can be easily renatured after the chromatography. However, the renaturation of large protein molecules may be relatively difficult. Also, proteins composed of noncovalently bound structural factors such as subunits, metals, and prosthetic groups have to be reconstituted after the chromatography in order to recover their activities. Therefore, the 2D-HPLC system presented is thought to be most suitable as a preparative method for protein chemical studies such as microscale protein sequencing, although a similar 2D-HPLC system constructed without the reversed-phase separation will reduce most of these limitations.

10.5 PEPTIDE MAPPING BY TWO-DIMENSIONAL HPLC

The columns used for peptide mapping are different from those for protein mapping because the separation range must be targeted to peptides, and these are much smaller than proteins. The peptide mixture used for mapping is usually produced by chemical or enzymatic digestion of a purified protein; thus, it does not contain unknown contaminants such as lipid and nucleic acid as the samples for protein mapping do. Therefore, silica-based columns can be routinely selected for peptide mapping because it is not necessary to be very concerned about cleaning the columns after running the chromatography. In addition, there are two other reasons why silica-based columns can be selected. First, the chromatographic behavior of peptides is relatively well studied for both ion-exchange and reversed-phase columns; second, high chromatographic resolution for small peptides is well established, at least for silica-based reversed-phase columns.[1]

If the complete amino acid sequence of the protein is known, the recovery and the retention time of the expected peptides can be predicted to some extent. That is, it is now widely accepted that the retention time in reversed-phase chromatography is linearly related to the natural logarithm of the sum of the hydrophobicity.[17] As an example, Figure 10–5 shows the distribution of charge and hydrophobicity of all of the tryptic peptides expected from a completely

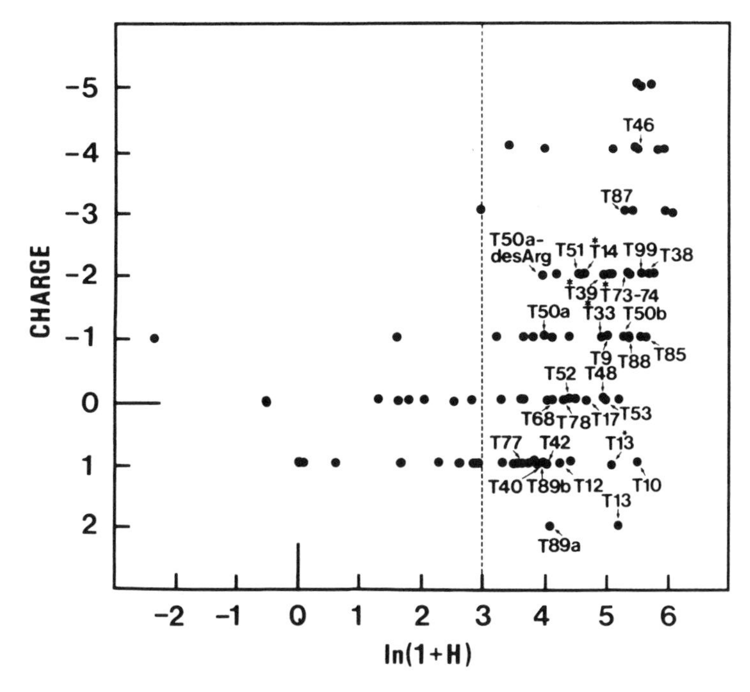

Figure 10–5. Distribution between charge and ln (1 + *H*) of the tryptic peptides of human ceruloplasmin.[7] The peptides identified are designated as described in ref. 7. Glycopeptides are indicated by an asterisk. A dotted line is drawn at ln (1 + *H*) = 3.

specific cleavage of human ceruloplasmin.[7] In the figure, the charges of the theoretical peptides are plotted against ln (1 + H), in which H indicates the hydrophobicity of the peptides, calculated by the method of Sasagawa et al.[17] using their list of nonweighted retention constants. The charges of the peptides at pH 8.0 can be estimated from the constituent amino acids of the peptide by the microcomputer method of Manabe.[18] The charges of the tryptic peptides of ceruloplasmin range from +2 to −5, and the values of ln (1 + H) range from −2.3 to 6.1. Thus, although ceruloplasmin has a molecular weight of 135,000 and is the second largest plasma protein for which the complete amino acid sequence has been determined by direct protein sequencing, the charge and hydrophobicity of all of the theoretical tryptic peptides distribute within a relatively narrow range compared to the distribution for proteins occurred naturally.[7] When this calculation is applied to the theoretical tryptic peptides of many other proteins, the charges of the peptides range from +5 to −5, and in most cases the values of ln (1 + H) are within the same range as for ceruloplasmin. Thus, although the selection of the ion-exchange column may differ depending on whether the sample used is a basic protein or an acidic protein, the reversed-phase column may generally be applied to many proteins. This is because the values of ln (1 + H) of the most hydrophobic peptides fall around

6 for most proteins, and peptides with a value around 6 can be recovered from most silica-based reversed-phase columns.

10.5.1 Separation of the Tryptic Peptides of Human Ceruloplasmin[7]

Human ceruloplasmin contains 1046 amino acids and has a potential for yielding 103 tryptic peptides. Although we have determined the complete amino acid sequence of ceruloplasmin by protein sequencing,[19] we never considered purifying the peptides from the tryptic digest of the entire protein as part of the strategy of sequence determination because at that time there was no method efficient enough to effect the separation of such a complex peptide mixture. If we had attempted to do so, it would probably have taken a year just to purify the peptides. Even today it is still difficult to separate the theoretical 100 peptides expected from a tryptic digest of ceruloplasmin. Furthermore, the peptide mixture produced from such a large protein by enzymatic cleavage becomes even more complex because of incomplete and nonspecfic cleavage.

When the tryptic digest of the carboxymethylated single-chain ceruloplasmin was separated by the automated 2D-HPLC system using the program described for two HPLC assemblies in Section 10.3, about 260 peaks were obtained (Figure 10–6) compared with the expected 103 theoretical tryptic peptides. The separation clearly shows the excellent resolution of the chromatography. Of course, the number of peaks exceeds the expected 103 theoretical peptides, because some peptides are duplicated in the adjacent stepwise elutions, and also because of incomplete and/or nonspecific cleavage. To evaluate the efficiency of the 2D-HPLC system as a separation method for peptides, many peaks selected randomly were analyzed by amino acid analysis. At least 70% of the peaks analyzed contained pure peptides that were identified in the sequence of ceruloplasmin. Although some of the peaks contained two peptides, these could be also identified in the sequence. Some of the peaks identified are indicated in Figure 10–6.

The other notable feature of human ceruloplasmin is that it is a glycoprotein exhibiting four sites of attachment for glucosamine oligosaccharides. Earlier, Ryden and Eaker[20] expended much effort in isolating the glycopeptides from three sites by use of conventional methods; yet they could not isolate the fourth glycopeptide because of the complexity of the peptide mixture. By a combination of gel filtration and reversed-phase chromatography we were able to isolate all four glycopeptides in good yield, but this manual procedure was tedious and lengthy. However, all four glycopeptides were easily purified from the tryptic digest of the whole ceruloplasmin molecule in 16 h by use of our automated 2D-HPLC system. The yields of the four glycopeptides T14, T33, T39, and T73-74 were 53, 32, 55, and 40%, respectively; these values are higher than those we obtained earlier by a manual combination of gel filtration and reversed-phase chromatography.[7] Thus, the 2D-HPLC method has proved to be effective for purifying all of the major glycosylated peptides of ceruloplasmin from the very complex peptide mixture by means of a single operation of the chromatography system.

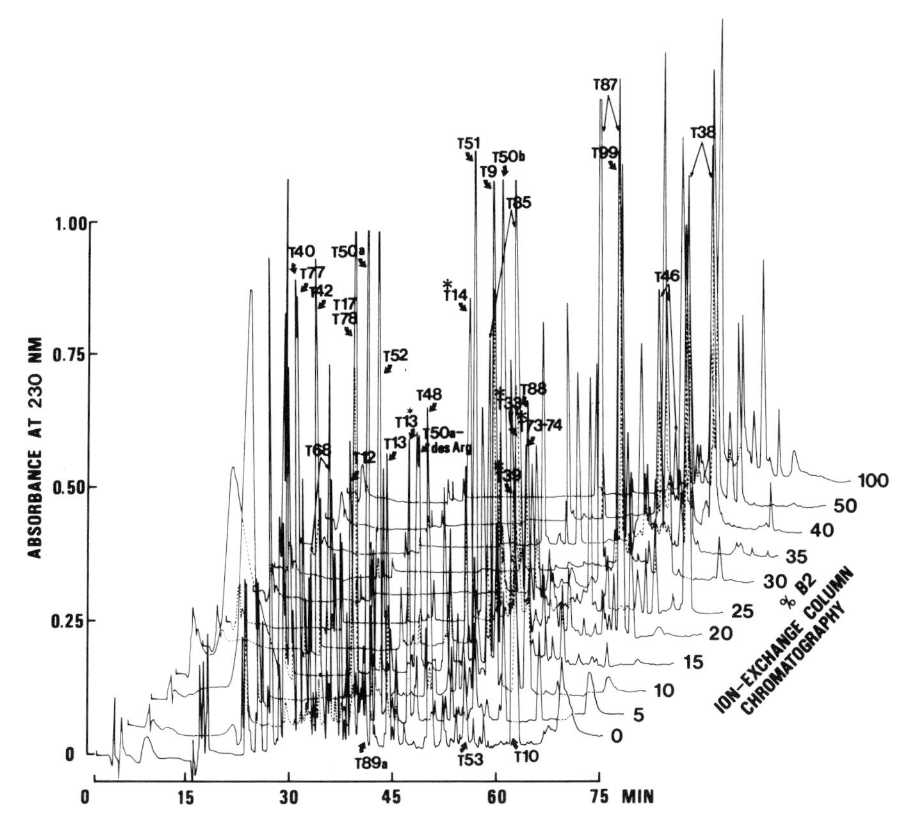

Figure 10–6. A three-dimensional visualization of peptide map of human ceruloplasmin.[7] The 2D-HPLC was done as described in the text. Some of the peptides identified in the chromatogram are indicated by the nomenclature used in ref. 7. Peptides identified as two peaks are shown by two fine arrows and peptides identified as a single peak by a thick arrow. Glycopeptides are indicated by an asterisk.

10.5.2 Application of Peptide Mapping to Genetic Variants of Human Serum Albumin[21]

Peptide mapping by conventional high voltage paper chromatography or by reversed-phase chromatography has been used for comparative analysis of closely related proteins such as genetic variants. However, these methods are suitable mainly for small proteins, and in many instances gave ambiguous results when applied to large proteins. In fact, although the complete amino acid sequence of about 60 out of 100 plasma proteins has been determined, the amino acid substitution in genetic variants is not known for most of the plasma proteins because of their high molecular weight.

For example, in the case of human serum albumin, more than 30 apparently different genetic variants have been typed by electrophoretic analysis under various conditions, and up to 80 have been named and described; yet, until recently the structural change had been identified in only a few. This is so despite the fact that albumin is the most abundant protein in serum. Also, in genetic studies of some populations, it is often possible to collect only a small amount of serum containing a rare variant. Hence, we investigated whether our 2D-HPLC technique could be applied successfully to identification of the peptide with an amino acid substitution in genetic variants of such a large protein as albumin, whose availability may be restricted.

We started with the identification of tryptic peptides in the chromatogram of normal albumin A, which is predominant in all populations.[21] The protein was first reduced and carboxymethylated and was then digested with TPCK-trypsin in 0.1 *M* ammonium bicarbonate (enzyme-to-substrate ratio = 1:50) for 16 h at 37° C. The digest was lyophilized to remove the ammonium bicarbonate, and the lyophilizate was dissolved in 0.5 ml of 8 *M* urea and diluted with 0.5 ml of 0.02 *M* Tris-acetate buffer (pH 8.0). The insoluble material was removed by centrifugation, and the supernatant was used as a sample for 2D-HPLC. The pattern of peptide mapping by 2D-HPLC is shown three dimensionally in Figure 10–7. Human albumin with molecular weight of 67,000 has a potential yield of 80 theoretical tryptic peptides. About 100 peaks were obtained. The peptides identified are indicated by the numbers in Figure 10–7. The number of peaks exceeds the expected 80 theoretical peptides, because some peptides are duplicated in the adjacent stepwise elution, and also because of irregular or incomplete cleavage. The sum of the amino acid residues identified was about 80% of the total amino acid residues of the protein.[21]

After the identification of the tryptic peptides of normal albumin A was completed, the chromatogram of a series of genetic variants was compared with that of normal albumin. The variant albumins used were isolated from 0.4–1.0 ml of serum collected during genetic surveys of certain populations. The pretreatment of the protein for peptide mapping was done by the same method as that for normal albumin.

Genetic variant Naskapi, which is found mainly in North American Indians, is one of the few that occur in polymorphic frequency. Although analysis of the CNBr fragments had indicated that the amino acid substitution site in this variant was probably located between residues 330 and 446 in the protein sequence,[22] the site had not been determined. Therefore, 2D-HPLC was applied to peptide mapping analysis of albumin Naskapi in order to test whether a peptide with an amino acid substitution can be detected by the comparison of peptide maps of standard albumin and the Naskapi albumin.

When the profiles of the 2D-HPLC of the standard albumin and the homozygote albumin of Naskapi were compared (Figures 10–7 and 10—8A),[21] five major peaks, corresponding to peptides T10, T11–12, T48, T49, and T50 + T75, disappeared from the chromatogram of the Naskapi homozygote, and three new peaks appeared in the elution pattern of the ion-exchange column at 30, 35, and 40% B2. These peaks were analyzed by both amino acid composition and sequence analysis.

The new peak that was eluted at 30% B2 contained peptide T10–11–12, which was produced by incomplete cleavage between T10 and T11–T12 and which did not have any amino acid substitution in the peptide sequence. However, a peptide that was eluted at 35% B2 (T48–49–50 in Figure 10–8A)

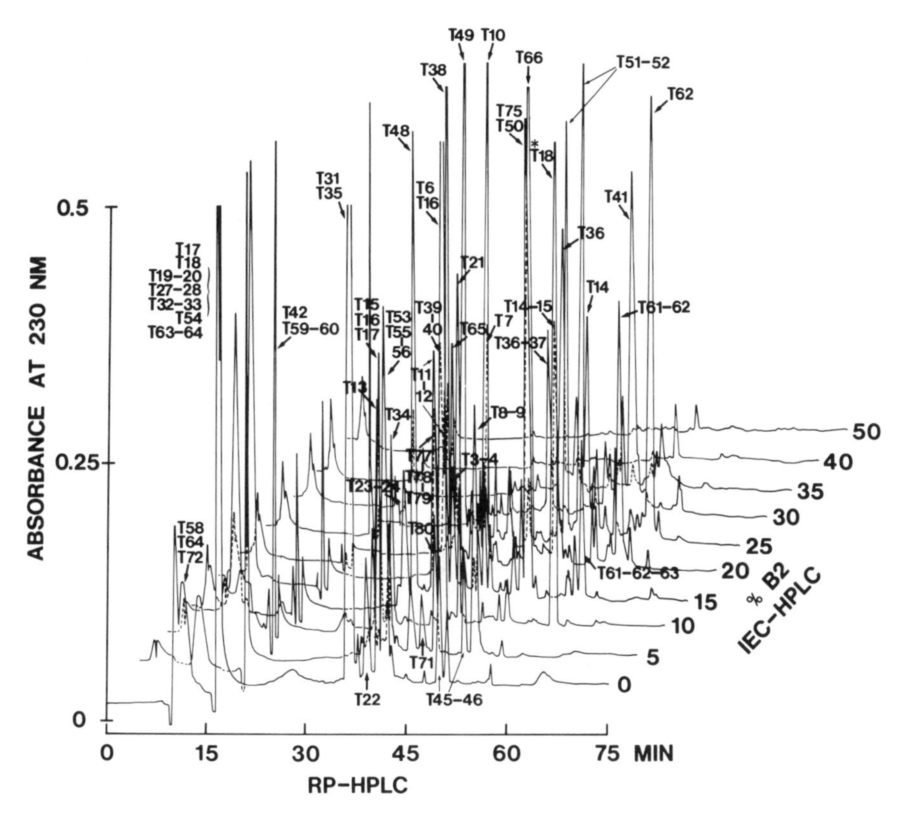

Figure 10–7. A three-dimensional representation of the 2D-HPLC of standard human serum albumin.[21] The nomenclature for peptides, described in ref. 21, is used to illustrate the elution positions of the tryptic peptides identified. The numbers connected by a dash (e.g., T51–52) indicate that the peptides were produced by incomplete cleavage with trypsin. An asterisk shows that the peptide was obtained by chymotrypsin-like cleavage.

was found to cover the region from residues 352 to 389 in the protein sequence and to contain one amino acid substitution at residue 372 where lysine was replaced with glutamic acid.[21,23] This substitution explains why peptides T49 and T50 were not obtained with trypsin, and therefore they disappeared from the chromatogram of the Naskapi homozygote. The lack of cleavage between T48 and T49 is probably caused by the acidic environment around Lys-359 due to the presence of the adjacent glutamic acid at 358 and the two carboxymethylcysteines at 360 and 361. The peak that was eluted at 40% B2 had the same retention time and amino acid composition as peptide T48–49–50. The combined yield of the peptide T48–49–50 was 75%.

Albumin Mersin, found in the Eti Turks of southern Turkey, was assumed to be identical with albumin Naskapi.[23] The corresponding peptides of albumin Naskapi and albumin Mersin from heterozygous individuals were also analyzed by 2D-HPLC. Two peptides, one with and the other without the substitution, were obtained from both the Naskapi heterozygote and the Mersin heterozygote, although the cleavage between T48 and T49 did occur in the case of Mersin (Figure 10–8C). These examples show that once the elution position of a peptide with a substitution has been identified in the chromatogram, it is easy to screen for a known amino acid substitution by use of 2D-HPLC. They also show that the complexity resulting from incomplete cleavage of the protein,

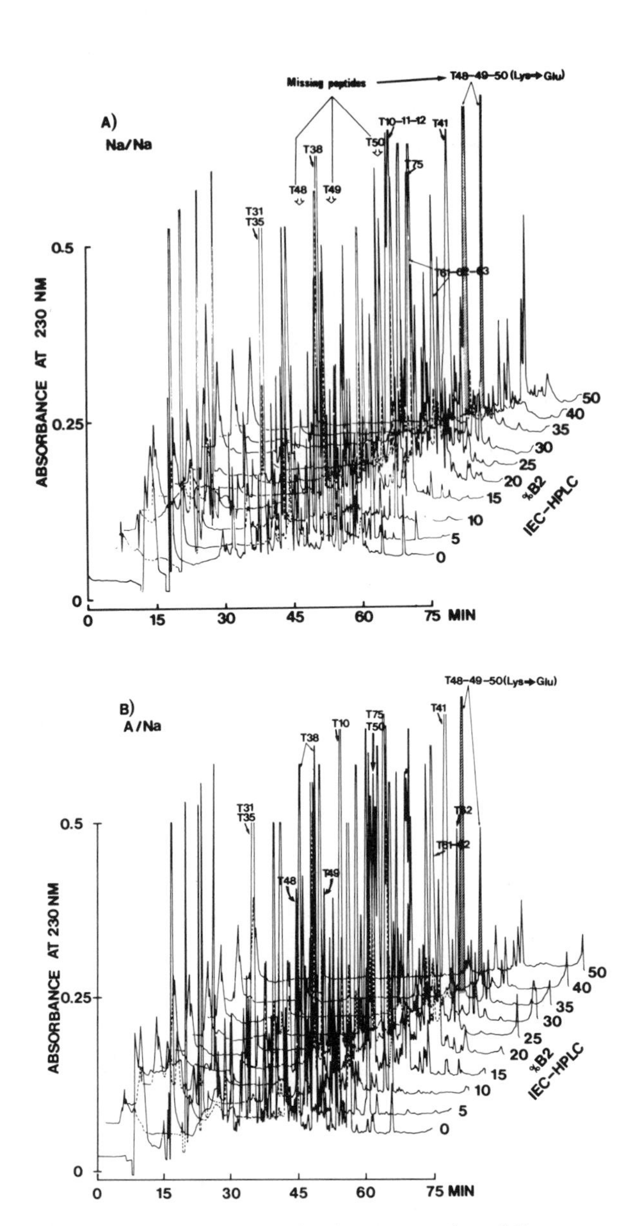

Figure 10–8. Three-dimensional representation of the peptide maps of (A) Naskapi homozygote (Na/Na). (B) Naskapi

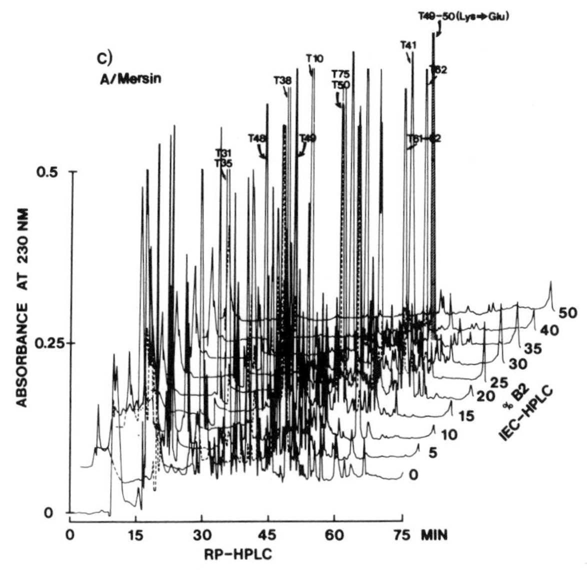

heterozygote (A/Na), and (C) Mersin heterozygote (A/Mersin) albumins. Peptides from the region from residues 352 to 389 in the sequence of human serum albumin are indicated, and the peak containing the peptide with the substitution (Lys → Glu) is shaded. Some of the peaks are indicated as internal markers to facilitate comparison of the chromatograms. In A the missing peptides are indicated by open arrows.

which is observed very often in such large proteins, could be resolved by this method.[7,21]

The 2D-HPLC technique was applied to a total of 11 albumin variants, and the peptide with the amino acid substitution was identified in six, i.e., Naskapi, Mersin, Mexico-2, Nagasaki-1, Nagasaki-2, and Yanomama-2.[2,24] Thus, the method was proven to be effective for detecting the peptide with an amino acid substitution in a series of albumin variants, and, in principle, could be used for a similar investigation of other large proteins.

10.5.3 Limitation of the Two-Dimensional HPLC Method as a Peptide Mapping Procedure

Although we were able to isolate the peptide with an amino acid substitution in more than half of the albumin genetic variants analyzed by the 2D-HPLC technique, we did not succeed in doing so for five other genetic variants. As described in Section 10.5.2, about 80% of the total amino acid residues of the albumin sequence could be identified by the comparison of the 2D-HPLC chromatograms. However, the remaining 20% could not be identified by this technique. Most of the unidentified peptides are small peptides that have a value of ln $(1 + H)$ less than 3, and thus cannot be separated by the second reversed-phase chromatography.[7,21] These small peptides were obtained as several broad peaks during chromatography on the ion-exchange column. In fact, by N-terminal sequence analysis of the whole protein we later identified the amino acid substitution in albumin variant Nagasaki-3 to be Gln instead of His at the third position.[25] The substitution occurred in the tetrapeptide T1, which was not separated in 2D-HPLC because its value of $\ln(1 + H)$ is 2.2. A similar result occurred in the case of albumin Maku, in which the amino acid substitution is Glu for Lys at position 541.[24] This substitution is present in the tripeptide T72 with $\ln(1 + H) = 2.3$, which also was not separated by the 2D-HPLC system. However, for the other three genetic variants we could not find the substitution in peptides representing about 80% of the total amino acid sequence. Therefore, the substitute probably is present in the small peptides or in very hydrophobic peptides; the latter might be removed as a precipitate before chromatography or might not be recovered from the columns. The hydrophobic peptides that could not be identified by the method, include T5, T44, and T67. Their values of $\ln(1 + H)$ are around 6. However, some other hydrophobic peptides with values around 6, including T62, T18, and T41, etc., were recovered in high yields by our method.[21] We still do not know if the unidentified three peptides are present in the precipitate, or if they are bound irreversibly to the columns used.

The main problem encountered during this study was a small degree of irregular or incomplete tryptic cleavage of albumin samples. This occurs most often when an acidic amino acid is adjacent to lysine or arginine, and this is the case at many positions in the sequence of albumin, which has a high content of glutamic and aspartic acids. Therefore, in studies of a variant it was sometimes necessary to analyze several peaks that did not appear in the HPLC profile of the standard albumin, even though the substitution turned out to be present in only one peptide.[21]

Although the silica-based columns we used seem to be suitable for high resolution peptide mapping, we detected some deterioration of the resolution after chromatography for a dozen times. However, we were able to get nearly identical chromatograms even after replacing the deteriorated columns with new columns because the quality of the silica-based columns recently available is well controlled by the column manufacturers. If more stable columns are developed, whose separation power for small peptides matches that of recently available silica-based columns, they would be ideal for our peptide mapping technique.

Although it is very difficult to compare our 2D-HPLC technique with other peptide mapping methods, we believe that our system probably gives the highest resolution of the currently reported peptide mapping methods.

10.5.4 Flexibility of the Method

The major advantages of the automated two-dimensional HPLC technique are not only its high resolution and excellent reproducibility, but also its flexibility. The column for the first chromatography can be changed to a cation-exchange column depending on the charge distribution of the peptide mixture. If the amount of protein is small, both columns can be changed to smaller columns.

The programs for both dimensions also can be changed, depending on how complex the peptide mixture is, and on other characteristics.

10.6 CONCLUSIONS

Although the technique we describe is not yet perfect, it is very powerful as a systematic separation method. The high resolution of the chromatography is achieved by a multidimensional combination of ion-exchange and reversed-phase chromatography, while the reproducibility of the method is maintained by the automation of the chromatography by connecting two columns in tandem through a tee tube that enables us to perform sequential chromatography of two kinds. The applicability of the technique could be demonstrated in the protein mapping of bovine cerebellum and in the peptide mapping of ceruloplasmin and genetic variants of human serum albumin. Although the technique has some limitations in the resolution of large proteins, we propose that it can be an alternative to two-dimensional electrophoresis as a protein mapping method for preparative use in microscale protein sequencing. As a peptide mapping method, the technique is very powerful in the purification of many peptides from a very complex peptide mixture by a single operation of chromatography. Therefore, the technique may be a complementary tool in looking for peptide probe sequence or for sequence confirmation in a strategy for DNA sequencing and, likewise, for the preparative purification of peptides in the strategy for protein sequencing of very large proteins. Furthermore, it will be especially suitable for comparative peptide mapping of very closely related large proteins, such as genetic variants.

REFERENCES

1. M. T. W. Hearn, F. E. Regnier, and C. T. Wehr, High-Performance Liquid Chromatography of Proteins and Peptides. Academic Press, New York, 1983.
2. P. H. O'Farrell, *J. Biol. Chem.*, 250 (1975) 4007.
3. M. W. Hunkapiller, E. Lujan, F. Ostrander, and L. E. Hood, *Methods Enzymol.*, 91 (1983) 227.
4. P. J. Matsudaira, *J. Biol. Chem.*, 262 (1987) 10035.
5. R. H. Aebersold, J. Leavitt, R. A. Saavedra, L. E. Hood, and S. B. H. Kent, *Proc. Natl. Acad. Sci. U. S. A.*, 84 (1987) 6970.
6. I. Kallman, *Pharm. Separation News*, 13 (1986) 1.
7. N. Takahashi, N. Ishioka, Y. Takahashi, and F. W. Putnam, *J. Chromatogr.*, 326 (1985) 407.
8. T. Kadoya, Y. Takahashi, N. Ishioka, T. Manabe, T. Isobe, and T. Okuyama, *Protides Biol. Fluids, Proc. Colloq.*, 30 (1981) 591.
9. T. Hiroi, Y.-I. Fang, and T. Okuyama, *Proc. 7th Conf. Liquid Chromatog.*, 7 (1986) 30.
10. D. Roman, J. Billandello, J. Gordon, A. Grace, B. Sobel, and A. Strauss, *Proc. Natl. Acad. Sci. U. S. A.*, 82 (1985) 8394.

11. T. Manabe, E. Hayama, and T. Okuyama, *Clin. Chem.*, 28 (1982) 824.
12. T. Manabe, Y. Takahashi, and T. Okuyama, *Anal. Biochem.*, 143 (1984) 39.
13. N. Ishioka, T. Isobe, T. Kadoya, and T. Okuyama, *J. Biochem. (Tokyo)*, 95 (1984) 611.
14. T. Ichimura, T. Isobe, T. Okuyama, N. Takahashi, K. Araki, R. Kuwano, and Y. Takahashi, *Proc. Natl. Acad. Sci. U.S.A.*, 85 (1988) 7084.
15. R. Reeves, *Biochim. Biophys. Acta,* 782 (1984) 343.
16. R. J. Thompson, P. A. M. Kynoch, and V. J. C. Willson, *Brain Res.*, 232 (1982) 489.
17. T. Sasagawa, T. Okuyama, and D. C. Teller, *J. Chromatogr.*, 240 (1982) 329.
18. T. Manabe, *Kagaku no Ryoiki*, 36 (1982) 470 (in Japanese).
19. N. Takahashi, T. L. Ortel, and F. W. Putnam, *Proc. Natl. Acad. Sci. U. S. A.*, 81 (1984) 390.
20. L. Ryden, and D. Eaker, *Eur. J. Biochem.*, 44 (1974) 171.
21. N. Takahashi, Y. Takahashi, N. Ishioka, B. S. Blumberg, and F. W. Putnam, *J. Chromatogr.*, 359 (1986) 181.
22. S. G. Franklin, S. I. Wolf, Y. Ozdemir, G. T. Yuregir, T. Isbir, and B. S. Blumberg, *Proc. Natl. Acad. Sci. U. S. A.*, 77 (1980) 5480.
23. N. Takahashi, Y. Takahashi, B. S. Blumberg, and F. W. Putnam, *Proc. Natl. Acad. Sci. U. S. A.*, 84 (1987) 4413.
24. N. Takahashi, Y. Takahashi, T. Isobe, F. W. Putnam, M. Fujita, C. Satoh, and J. V. Neel, *Proc. Natl. Acad. Sci. U. S. A.*, 84 (1987) 8001.
25. N. Takahashi, Y. Takahashi, and F. W. Putnam, *Proc. Natl. Acad. Sci. U. S. A.*, 84 (1987) 7403.

CHAPTER 11

Optimization of Protein Separations on Multimodal Chromatographic Supports

David R. Nau

CONTENTS

11.1 MODERN LIQUID CHROMATOGRAPHY AND BIOTECHNOLOGY

Recent advances in the field of biotechnology have generated considerable interest in improving the effectiveness of protein purification techniques.[1–7] Although modern liquid chromatography has become an indispensable tool for the commercial production of protein pharmaceuticals and other protein-based products, purification remains the "Achilles' heel" of the modern biotechnology industry.[5,8,13]

In some respects, the recent advent of high-performance liquid chromatography (HPLC) has led the way to significant improvements and major advancements in the field of protein separation science, particularly in terms of speed and resolution.[1–5,14,15] However, while often practical for analytical applications and on the relatively small preparative scale, the high cost, high-pressure drop, and low capacity of most high-performance supports have drastically limited their use within the process environment, particularly since high resolution is compromised under the overloaded conditions that are often used for preparative chromatography.[4–16] As a result, HPLC has been relegated to the later stages of downstream processing schemes, in polishing steps; by this point, the enormous volumes of crude sample and total protein loads have been reduced significantly, so that high performance supports can be more effectively utilized, without fear of fouling, and without compromising resolution for capacity;[5,7,15–18] the few protein contaminants that remain at this stage typically exhibit similar physicochemical properties that often necessitate the use of a high-resolution technique such as HPLC.[5,7,15]

As a result of these limitations, HPLC can represent, at best, only a partial solution for improving the separation of proteins within the process environment.[5–8,15] Therefore, many recent advances in protein chromatographic science have focused on improvements in the area of chromatographic selectivity.[5,6,15] One approach toward improving chromatographic specificity involves the logical design of stationary phases by modulating surface chemistry in order to control and manipulate the various physicochemical interactions between the protein and the matrix, and in particular, the development of complex multimodal stationary phases that are sensitive to changes in mobile phase composition due to the presence of multiple functional groups.[5,6,15,18]

Because the manipulation of mobile phase conditions may serve to enhance or attenuate the interactions between a given protein molecule and one or more of the functional groups on the matrix, it is appropriate to begin with a discussion of the known effects of specific salt species, ionic strength, and pH on the conformation and chromatographic retention behavior of proteins. This discussion will be followed by an overview of various multimodal chromatographic supports, the theoretical and mechanistic basis of multimodal interactions, and finally, examples of mixed-bed and column coupling chromatographic techniques.

11.2 EFFECTS OF MOBILE PHASE ON PROTEIN CONFORMATION AND CHROMATOGRAPHIC SELECTIVITY

In the past, most research scientists involved with the purification of proteins were not particularly concerned with the effects of mobile phase on chromatographic profile and purity. However, with the recent advances in biotechnology and the impending commercialization of numerous protein-based products, the economics of protein purification has become an important issue;[5,8,15] this has led to a renewed interest in the area of chromatographic optimization. Furthermore, the advent of high-performance chromatographic matrices based on smaller, more rigid particles, has helped to facilitate rapid method development studies aimed at determining the effects of mobile phase composition, as well as changes in surface chemistry, on resolution and selectivity.[5,15]

Substantial experimental evidence has been gathered in recent years demonstrating the effects of mobile phase composition on selectivity and the ability to manipulate protein elution profiles on reversed-phase matrices.[20,24] However, in certain situations there may be restrictions on solvent type, while in other cases, mobile phase manipulation may not provide the resolution and selectivity that are required.[20–24] Furthermore, the high degree of resolution characteristic of reversed-phase chromatography cannot be exploited in most protein purification schemes, due to the labile nature of larger proteins and the possibility of denaturation induced by organic mobile phases and/or hydrocarbonaceous ligands. As a result, most classical protein purification schemes have involved the use of numerous chromatographic steps on a variety of different supports, including a number of steps on ion-exchange matrices. However, a review of the literature suggests that relatively little work has been conducted on the optimization of buffer species and pH for the separation of proteins on these ion-exchange supports. Even studies conducted on high-performance ion exchangers have often demonstrated minor effects of mobile phase composition on the basic chromatographic profile.[26–36] In some cases, the lack of significant effects were attributable to the minimal differences in the salt species employed, while in other cases, these minor effects appeared to be the result of an inherent inability to manipulate selectivity on conventional ion exchangers, in general. Although manufacturers have made substantial efforts in developing hundreds of ion exchange matrices for protein purification, relatively little attention has been paid to the effects of manipulating mobile phase conditions and the use of retention maps in the optimization of protein separations on these supports.[26–36] This seems surprising, since the complex surface chemistry and topology of proteins make them ideal candidates for chromatographic manipulation, and facilitate the design of chromatographic supports that employ multimodal retention mechanisms to achieve selectivity and specificity.[5,6,15,42,43]

11.2.1 Effects of Mobile Phase on Isoelectric Point and Electrostatic Interactions

Although many of the theoretical relationships between protein structure and chromatographic retention have still not been fully elucidated,[15,19,27,37–42] the ability to manipulate protein retention on ion-exchange matrices by adjusting the mobile phase pH is rather well established.[26–36] According to the "net charge concept" a protein is negatively charged at a pH above its isoelectric point and will bind to an anion exchanger, while below its p*I* the protein is positively charged and will bind to a cation exchanger.[35,44] Although this concept has been used extensively in order to predict protein retention characteristics on ion-exchange supports with some degree of accuracy,[35,44–46] a number of recent studies[5,28,33,44,47–50] clearly indicate that retention also depends on more complex factors, including the number, density, distribution, and steric accessibility of charged sites on the protein surface. Regnier and co-workers[14,44,47,49,53] recently developed a model for ion-exchange retention processes that suggests that, due to charge asymmetry and charge group distribution, only a specific portion(s) of the protein surface, or "face," interacts with the ion exchanger (leading to a particular molecular orientation during adsorption), and that retention properties are proportional to the number and/or density of these interacting sites. This model suggests that isoelectric point may be less important than surface charge distribution in determining the precise retention characteristics of any given protein, and that the "net charge concept" is a gross oversimplification. Several retention mapping studies indicate that p*I* is not an absolute marker for retention behavior on ion exchangers, with each protein exhibiting a unique behavior.[26–35] Work in this laboratory[26,44,50–52] indicates that numerous proteins (e.g., IgM, β-lactoglobulin, and numerous proteases) exhibit a high affinity toward both cation- and anion-exchange supports, suggesting the presence of basic as well as acidic surface regions; other proteins (e.g., IgG antibodies, α-chymotrypsinogen, and calmodulin) have a strong affinity for both HIC and ion-exchange supports,[5,15,43,50,75,154,209–211] suggesting that they contain hydrophobic surface patches as well as highly charged regions. Indeed, several studies[55–57] have shown that different "faces" of a given protein (e.g., lysozyme) are responsible for the binding on different chromatographic matrices.[55–57] These faces on the protein surface are similar to the various epitopes of a given antigen that are bound by antibodies with different specificities. Hearn[58] recently coined the term "ionotope" to describe a particular area on a protein's surface that binds to an ion-exchange support.

The chromatographic retention behavior of a protein is often predetermined by its primary as well as secondary and tertiary structure.[27] However, the differential effects that mobile phase components can exert on protein hierarchical structure must certainly also affect electrostatic and hydrophobic interactions and chromatographic retention. The stoichiometric model for ion-exchange chromatography as well as the differential affinities that various counterions exhibit toward ion-exchange media suggest that chromatographic selectivity might be directly related to the sum of the electrostatic interactions between the protein and the matrix, as well as the relative displacing power of the counterion.[27] However, different salt species are known to have a profound influence on protein conformation, solubility, stability, and activity, and these effects will also undoubtedly affect protein chromatographic behavior. Indeed, Hearn and co-workers[27] observed changes in the stoichiometric charge ratio (z) of proteins that were eluted from a strong anion exchanger with different counterions or coions, indicating the presence of ion-mediated and ion-specific changes in the number of charged interactive sites involved in binding. Conversely, elution with different coions was shown to affect protein retention without affecting the stoichiometric charge ratio (z), suggesting that double-layer-mediated changes in protein conformation or binding orientation may affect a protein's binding affinity.[27] These studies clearly indicate that protein retention on ion-exchange supports is certainly much more complex than that predicted by the net charge concept.

11.2.2 Role of pH in Hydrophobic Interactions

Although there is no general relationship between isoelectric point, mobile phase pH, and retention in hydrophobic interaction chromatography (HIC), pH may affect hydrophobic interactions and thereby modulate retention, either by changing the electrostatic double-layer interactions between the protein and the matrix, intramolecular electrostatic interactions, or other pH-induced changes in protein conformation.[28,52,59–67] Furthermore, the effects of pH on retention become particularly accentuated on multimodal supports that contain both ion-exchange and hydrophobic ligands.[28,52,59]

Hearn and co-workers[27] suggested that as the mobile phase pH approaches the isoelectric point of a given protein, its solubility will be reduced dramatically, and the interplay between hydrophobic and electrostatic interactions will be accentuated such that multimodal retention mechanisms become more dominant. For example, at pH 9.6, the retention of lysozyme (pI ~ 11) and cytochrome *c* (pI ~ 9.4) on an anion-exchange support actually decreased with decreasing salt concentration (from 0.3 *M*), consistent with increased hydrophobic interaction chromatographic and "salting out" behavior.[27] Multimodal ion exchangers that contain hydrophobic ligands also provide enhanced resolution for isozymes and other microheterogeneous protein species when that separation is conducted at or near the isoelectric point (Figures 11–6 and 11–9).

11.2.3 Role of Specific Salt Species

As noted previously, numerous studies have demonstrated the ability to optimize protein selectivity on ion-exchange supports via the manipulation of mobile phase pH, ionic strength, and other factors that affect a protein's electrostatic surface potential.[26–36] In contrast, the specific roles of individual salt species in ion-exchange retention behavior have not been examined extensively, and, until recently, were rather poorly understood, particularly in terms of predicting retention behavior.[27] Indeed, although there are numerous examples of ion-selective influences on protein retention in ion-exchange[27,30,31,33,34,50–52,68] and HIC,[27,50–52,61,66,67,69,71,72,74,75] no formal relationships have been derived to correlate the Hofmeister or Setchenow coefficients and the electrostatic displacing strength of various ions;[27] this, despite the known effects of the different salts in the lyotropic series on protein conformation, stability, and solubility in bulk solution on the one hand, and chromatographic retention on the other. Indeed, the differential effect that various salt species exert on protein conformation in bulk solution are well established.[37–41,76–81] However, translation of these phenomena into predictable effects on protein chromatographic retention behavior will obviously require substantial research.[27]

The stabilization or destablization of the native conformational state of a given protein via the salt species-specific perturbation of ionic strength is exemplified by the "salting out" phenomena (salt precipitation) observed with different lyotropic salts of the Hofmeister or lyotropic series.[79–82] Mobile phases containing salt species with different Hofmeister/Setchenow constants can have dramatic effects on protein retention, as well as recovery, by affecting hydrophobic interactions on chromatographic matrices that contain hydrocarbonaceous ligands; Horvath and co-workers[69,74] have shown that these effects correlate with the classical lyotropic/Hofmeister series numbers and molal surface tension increments of a given salt.[27,69,76,79–82] Indeed, Hearn[6] recently pointed out the similarity between the empirical Setchenow equation and the empirical (chromatographic) retention equation.

According to the solvophobic theory, increasing the salt concentration or changing to a salt of higher molal surface tension increment (higher on the lyotropic series) will result in increased retention in HIC or stronger interactions between a protein and hydrophobic ligands.[25,69,74] Although Melander and Horvath[69] have shown that the correlation between molal surface tension increments and the classical lyotropic numbers provides a theoretical framework to describe the effects of a given salt on hydrophobic interaction chromatography and salt precipitation, the dual and often antagonistic effects that a particular salt exerts on hydrophobic and electrostatic interactions must be considered in order to accurately describe salt species-specific changes in chromatographic behavior.

Although hydrophobic effects are undoubtedly important in determining ion-exchange chromatographic behavior, they are generally dominated by ionic interactions, which are particularly important with large protein molecules because of the additive nature of electrostatic interactions and the highly charged nature of proteins. However, these effects do become increasingly important on multimodal supports that contain hydrophobic ligands. Furthermore, the importance of the particular salt species (and its relative position on the lyotropic/Hofmeister series) in ion-exchange processes is underscored by the relatively low ionic strengths (0.01 *M*) at which these "lyotropic effects" begin to play a role in affecting protein conformation and chromatographic behavior.[5,50–52,57]

Anions can be ranked according to their affinity for (ability to displace simple solutes from) anion-exchange resins ($SCN^- > I^- > Br^- > Cl^- > H_2PO_4^- > CH_3COO^- > F^-$), with shorter retention times being observed with higher affinity displacers such as thiocyanate.[27,83] Likewise, cations may be ranked[27,84] in terms of their affinity for cation exchangers ($Ca^{2+} > Mg^{2+} > K^+ > NH_4^+ > Na^+ > Li^+$) with calcium exhibiting strong displacer properties. However, different cations tend to produce less variation in chromatographic retention (compared to anions), because there is less variation in the size and charge characteristics of the solvated cations and the solvated characteristics of the complementary immobilized ligand in terms of double layer structure.[27]

Hofmeister[81] first reported the effects of various salts on protein solubility and ranked numerous ions into the lyotropic series in terms of their stabilizing or destabilizing effects on protein conformation.[76–81] Perhaps by serendipity, the influence of various salts on protein solubility coincides with the affinity of these ions for anion exchangers.[27] In general, anions with weaker affinities for anion exchangers than chloride may be classified as "polar kosmotropes" or water structure-makers and tend to exhibit a stabilizing effect on protein conformation; in contrast, anions with a stronger affinity than chloride are "chaotropes" or water structure-breakers and tend to destabilize the three-dimensional hierarchical structure of proteins. The destabilizing effect of chaotropic ions as displacers in ion-exchange processes is presumably associated with the enthalpy-driven (energetically favored) loss of water from the ion's outermost hydration layer as they complex with proteins or ion exchangers. In contrast, polar kosmotropes tend not to lose water from their hydration shells, and, therefore, do not disrupt protein structure, and complex less readily with ion-exchange groups.[27]

Regnier and co-workers[28] postulated that the different elution profiles and relative retention orders obtained on multimodal ion-exchange matrices might result from hydrophobic contributions to retention induced by salts (such as sodium sulfate) that are high on the lyotropic series; therefore, retention might be controlled by the choice of elution salt species. Ethylene glycol, a kosmotrope that tends to preferentially hydrate and stabilize the native conformation state of a protein[79,85] can be used to eliminate hydrophobic interactions, and thus, examine the hydrophobic contributions toward ion-exchange chromatographic retention in the presence of particular salt species.[28] Regnier et al.[28] have shown that the addition of ethylene glycol does reduce retention on multimodal ion exchangers significantly, particularly when "hydrophobic" proteins are eluted with salts that are high on the lyotropic series.[28]

Hearn et al.[27] have recently shown that different displacer salts may exert a strong influence on the isocratic retention behavior of proteins on ion-exchange supports. Divergence from ideal ion-exchange retention behavior was observed at both low and relatively high ionic strengths, implicating the involvement of a multimodal, hydrophobic interaction retention mechanism; these ion-specific effects were found to correlate with the position of the salts on the lyotropic series. Hearn's group[27] also suggested that for some proteins, band broadening effects and reduced column efficiencies may often result from aggregation and the relative destabilization of protein conformation, effects that are induced in accordance with the "salting-out" ability of various ions of the Hofmeister series.

The specific effects that individual ions exert on protein structure also result from time-dependent interactions between the charge and concentration gradients of the "double layer," that area in close proximity to the chromatographic surface (mobile phase–stationary phase interface) in which mobile phase counterions complex with and partially neutralize the charges of the ion exchanger.[27,86–88] These ion-specific effects are particularly important at low ionic strengths.[27,47] Likewise, the thermodynamically favorable and salt species-specific interactions between the coions and the proteins surface, as proposed in the ion condensation theory,[27,89–91] may also affect protein conformation and stability, and thus, chromatographic selectivity and recovery.[27] Although coions exert relatively little direct influence on the affinity of proteins for the ion-exchange matrix, they can affect the protein's ionic binding domain (ionotope) and stabilize protein hierarchical structure by neutralizing the repulsive forces between like charges on the protein surface and the matrix.[27]

Several groups[27,30,31,33,52] have recently shown that specific coions can indeed exert a strong influence on chromatographic behavior. Hearn and co-workers[27] proposed that the larger hydrated ionic radius of lithium relative to (>) sodium and (>) potassium indicates that the positive charge of the lithium ion is more delocalized throughout the water molecules of the inner solvation sheath; this might result in a preference for multisite attachments with oppositely charged areas on the protein surface and a concomitant masking of these sites, thereby affecting interactions with anion-exchange supports.

The formation of the double layers of charge extending into the mobile phase results in a gradient of charge potential and ion concentration between the matrix and the mobile phase that is dependent on pH and the ionic species present.[86–88] Hearn and colleagues[27] suggested that prolonged exposure of the protein molecule to this counterion gradient might lead to increased band broadening with increasing residence time, and account for the stabilization or destabilization of protein conformation and activity observed in the presence of specific-salt species.

It should also be noted that specific ions can also favor ion-bridge (salt-bridge) formation and specific ionic interactions that may alter a protein's secondary and tertiary structure, and, thus, its chromatographic behavior. Similar ion-specific intramolecular salt-bridge formation may occur on mixed-mode matrices that contain both anion- and cation-exchange ligands. Certain salt species may induce protein comformational changes that either change the pK_a values or net charges of groups and/or regions that are already exposed, or result in the internalization of surface faces or the exposure of new areas on the protein surface. These mobile phase conditions may alter a protein's overall net charge (isoelectric point), or may alter only local protein topography and electrostatic surface potential. These "regiospecific"/"regioselective" effects may be particularly important, since they may exert a rather selective influence on a given protein's ionotope, and this might have a rather selective effect on the retention of that particular protein molecule.

The presence of specific divalent cations can also induce changes in conformation and chromatographic retention in proteins with specific metal ion-binding sites, particularly those containing multiple sites with different dissociation constants. Karger et al.[52,92] have clearly shown that the presence of Mg^{2+} or Ca^{2+} in hydrophobic interaction chromatographic mobile phases can have specific effects on the retention of individual protein molecules, and on the stabilization or destabilization of native structure, effects that depend on the protein's metal-binding characteristics.[92]

Considering the ability of different salt species to induce characteristic changes in protein conformation, and thus expose or envelop specific amino acid residues, it is not at all surprising that chromatographic retention behavior might also change significantly in the presence of different mobile phases. Furthermore, if the chromatographic matrix itself is modified by changes in mobile phase composition, it becomes even more probable that mobile phase manipulation might alter chromatographic selectivity.

Obviously, the molecular mechanisms that are responsible for mobile phase-induced changes in chromatographic profiles are, like proteins themselves, extremely complex. It may not be imperative that the chromatographer fully understand all of these phenomena in order to put them to practical use. However, the ability to assess the effects of mobile phase pH and salt species on protein conformation and surface interactive properties is important from a scientific, as well as an economic point of view, since it not only provides insight into the mechanistic details of complex chromatographic interactions, but also provides the potential means to optimize the chromatographic separation of proteins in terms of resolution, purity, capacity, and the recovery of mass and biological activity.

11.3 "TRADITIONAL" CHROMATOGRAPHY ON "CONVENTIONAL" SUPPORTS

Over the past several decades a myriad of chromatographic matrices have been developed for the purification and analysis of proteins. However, with relatively few exceptions, these supports have been based on the same surface chemistries that have been used for years in traditional soft gel chromatography. Most modern protein chromatographic supports are "one dimensional" and are designed to function via one predominant "unimodal" chromatographic mechanism. Because these conventional supports typically lack the specificity required to selectively remove a given protein from extremely complex biological mixtures, a variety of separation techniques are usually required to achieve the desired level of purity. As a result, most traditional purification schemes involve the use of numerous independent, discrete purification steps on separate chromatographic supports, each operating via more or less different physicochemical retention mechanisms. This approach requires multiple columns and manual sample manipulation (e.g., dialysis, ultrafiltration, dilution) prior to each chromatographic step. Although tedious and laborious, this is the most common, and often the most practical approach to protein purification.

11.4 MULTIMODAL CHROMATOGRAPHIC SUPPORTS

Although chromatographic supports have traditionally been designed to operate via one predetermined physicochemical mechanism, virtually all chromatographic matrices, regardless of the nature of the functional group, ligand, and base support, exhibit some degree of multimodal chromatographic behavior.[6,15,19] Although often assumed to play a passive role in retention, these groups are often capable of generating secondary retention phenomena. Floyd and Hartwick[19] pointed out that most modern stationary phases have evolved by default around the premise that better chromatographic separations are achieved through simple unimodal retention mechanisms. However, the ability of a particular matrix to operate in a purely one-dimensional mode is certainly not an essential requirement, nor a prerequisite, for its successful application.[6,15,19] As is the case with mobile phase effects, most chromatographers may be unaware of the beneficial aspects or deleterious effects that these multimodal supports may manifest on any particular separation problem. Exploitation of secondary retention capabilities should not simply be discounted out of hand, since it may often provide efficient solutions to difficult separation problems.[6,15,19]

With the recent advances in the area of multimodal liquid chromatography, numerous diverse approaches are now available that offer distinct advantages over conventional chromatographic techniques for increasing the selectivity, specificity, speed, and efficacy of protein separations.[6,15,19] In the broadest sense of their definition, the terms "multimodal" and "mixed-mode" have often been used as interchangable, generic terms, encompassing all separation techniques in which multiple chromatographic mechanisms are utilized within a closed system; these include traditional mixed-bed column chromatography and column coupling techniques (which will be discussed later), and the more specific definitions of multimodal and mixed mode. In many cases there is a fine line between "true" multimodal and "pure" mixed-mode interactions and many supports exhibit both types of behavior; however, it is important to clarify these terms and make the distinction here.

According to Regnier et al.,[28,29] "mixed-mode" interactions involve multiple chromatographic mechanisms operating simultaneously, whereas in multimodal separations, the various chromatographic mechanisms are (more) "segregated" in that any one of these multiple, independent models can be induced by varying mobile phase conditions. For example, multimodal supports containing ion-exchange groups and hydrophobic ligands might operate either in the "ion-exchange mode" under low to high ionic strength gradients with the effects of the ionic ligands predominating, or in the "hydrophobic interaction mode" under high to low ionic strength mobile phase conditions with the hydrocarbonaceous ligands determining the chromatographic profile. One advantage of these "true multimodal" supports is that several steps can be conducted on the same column, in different modes, at multiple points within a given purification scheme (with significantly different results), simply by manipulating mobile phase conditions.[27,28,50–52,93]

In "pure mixed-mode" supports, multiple functional groups operate simultaneously; the possibility that these multiple ligands might interact in a site-specific, geometric orientation with a specific area on a protein's surface offers the opportunity to enhance selectivity. Similar site-specific geometric interactions occur in affinity chromatography[5] and with numerous chiral phases,[94] where complex three-dimensional interactions determine specificity and enhance chromatographic binding and retention. Pure mixed-mode ion exchange supports tend to operate only under ion-exchange conditions, and not in the HIC mode, since proteins fail to bind in the presence of high salt concentrations.[50–52]

In contrast, "true" multimodal supports tend to operate by only one predominant chromatographic mechanism at a time, depending on the mobile phase conditions. In general, the other retention mechanisms and the effects of other ligands of the multimodal chemistry do not predominate, although they may impart some "nonspecific" mixed-mode effects, which may enhance separations in the presence of different elution salts.[27,28] Although true multimodal supports often display some mixed-mode behavior, pure mixed-mode supports do not exhibit true multimodal behavior.

For the sake of simplicity, in this chapter the term multimodal will be used as a generic term to encompass both true multimodal and pure mixed-mode interaction. Although the relative importance of multimodal interactions in enhancing chromatographic selectivity has just recently begun to be fully appreciated and gain widespread acceptance, the existence of multiple retention mechanisms on many "traditional" stationary phases has been known for years.

11.4.1 Affinity Chromatographic Spacer Arms

One well-documented example of multimodal interactions on traditional affinity supports involves the presence of hydrophobic ligands that were originally intended to function as spacer arms or as stabilizing cross-linkers.[95,109] These ligands have been shown to promote "nonspecific binding," and in a number of instances have led to low recoveries of mass and activity.[96,97,101,104,105,108,109] Although less frequently discussed within the literature, charged spacer arms on affinity supports have also been shown to exhibit "nonspecific" electrostatic interactions.[95,96,99–106,110–116] Finally, in other cases, these spacer arms are of the mixed hydrophobic-ionic type and exhibit multimodal behavior even in the absence of the bound affinity ligand itself.[95,97,99–102] Numerous studies have focused on eliminating the secondary interactions imparted by these spacer arms, because with most affinity separations their effects are deleterious.[95,97,99–102] However, in some cases, these ligands have led to the development of new and unique chromatographic techniques.[71,72,95]

11.4.2 Reversed-Phase Supports

The existence of multimodal behavior on traditional reversed-phase supports has also been known for years. The contribution of residual silanol groups to retention and peak tailing in reversed-phase chromatography is well documented.[21–24,117] Numerous reports have focused on the advantages of minimizing exposed silanols by endcapping and other techniques.[19,21–24,118] However, these secondary effects can rarely be eliminated, and, in many cases, the heterogeneity of the support can be responsible for mobile phase-induced changes in selectivity observed in the presence of ion pair reagents, trifluoroacetic acid (TFA), and other mobile phase modifiers that may affect silanol–protein interactions.[19,21–24,118–127] This is particularly true for C_4 and C_8 matrices, since the hydrophilic surface of the silica may be rather accessible and almost certainly plays a substantial role in modifying the separation via mixed-mode interactions.[19,119–121]

Reversed-phase supports containing anion-exchange groups have also been developed to separate various nucleic acids and proteins;[134,135] these supports provide resolution that is enhanced relative to those containing either functional group alone. Recently, Pidgion and co-workers[135] immobilized a phosphatidylcholine (lecithin) analog on silica to form a multimodal matrix that provides unique selectivity. The immobilization of this and other phospholipid analogs, as well as other common membrane components, might provide chromatographic supports that mimic portions of the cellular membrane, and thus, provide rather specific mixed-mode interactions between the support and those proteins that are normally associated with the membrane. For example, cytochrome *P*-450 can be purified from crude microsomal preparations in a single pass over the lecithin column with good recoveries and a hundred-fold increase in specific activity of some of the isozymes, relative to other purification techniques.[135] Furthermore, because phospholipids contain polar headgroups, these supports are much less hydrophobic than most conventional reversed-phase supports; as a result, most peptides can typically be separated without the use of harsh organic solvents or detergents, and thus, with better recovery of biological activity.[135]

11.4.3 Size-Exclusion Chromatography

Multimodal behavior has also been demonstrated on numerous size exclusion chromatographic matrices that contain hydrophobic ligands.[29,73,93,136–146] Although a hydrophobic interaction chromatographic (HIC) mechanism may prevail at high ionic strength, this effect usually diminishes as the salt concentration of the mobile phase is reduced to 0.5 *M*;[29,73,137] however, in many cases, it may be difficult to eliminate these hydrophobic effects totally.[137]

Other size exclusion supports have been shown to exhibit electrostatic interactions with proteins,[136–138,140–142,145,147–149] and in these cases, retention often correlates with isoelectric point.[136,137,140,141,145,147,148] Although anion-exchange groups may be responsible for binding on some of these supports,[137,138,144,149] cationic interactions may also result from the presence of exposed silanol groups.[73,136,140,141,147–148] Santarelli et al.[149] recently used a multimodal approach to design a size exclusion support that minimizes these electrostatic interactions, by coating the silica with dextran containing a small percentage of DEAE (diethylaminoethyl) groups, and adjusting the percentage of these ligands in order to neutralize the residual silanols.

It should be noted, however, that the presence of these secondary multimodal interactions often provides beneficial effects in size exclusion chromatography since they allow separations to be optimized by mobile phase manipulation, particularly on matrices that exhibit both hydrophobic and electrostatic interactions.[136,137] Furthermore, many of these supports exhibit true multimodal behavior and can be used either in the size exclusion mode, as well as the hydrophobic interaction mode[73,138–142,145–146] and/or the ion-exchange mode.[138,141–142,147–149]

11.4.4 Hydrophobic Ion-Exchange Supports

Yon and co-workers[99,150–152] first examined the effects of adding hydrophobic ligands to ion-exchange supports to produce "imphilytes" (amphipathic ampholytes). Similar work was simultaneously being conducted by several other groups[100–102] by coupling various alkylanines, arylamines, or amino acids in order to form mixed hydrophobic–ionic supports. These multimodal supports were used in the purification of numerous proteins, by using mobile phase conditions to control and determine the retention mechanism (i.e., either ion exchange or HIC).

Regnier et al.[28,29,153–156] also demonstrated this type of multimodal behavior with polyethylenimine (PEI) matrices to which cross-linking reagents (which were originally used to enhance stability) impart significant hydrophobic characteristics. These properties allow a single column to be used either in the anion exchange mode or the hydrophobic interaction mode (Figure 11–10G). Furthermore, the chromatography obtained on these cross-linked PEI supports is significantly different from that obtained on non-cross-linked PEI matrices,[15,52,154–155] suggesting that mixed-mode effects also occur on these supports. Henry[155] reviewed the chemistry and the role of various cross-linkers in the multimodal behavior of PEI-based matrices elsewhere within this book.

Similar hydrophobic properties have also been reported on a number of other high-performance anion-exchange matrices.[6,19,27,157,166] The chemistry of several of these supports that were designed for mixed-mode nucleic acid separations has recently been reviewed by Floyd and Hartwick.[19]

Mayheu and Howell[161] first observed hydrophobic interaction chromatographic behavior on DEAE-cellulose in the presence of high concentrations of ammonium sulfate. More recently, Karger[162] demonstrated HIC behavior on high-performance DEAE supports; the hydrophobicity of these bonded phases appears to result from the presence of the two terminal ethyl moieties. More recently, Horvath and co-workers[163] reported similar multimodal behavior on zirconia-treated silica-based ion-exchange supports. Hydrophobic interaction chromatography could be conducted either on these simple ion-exchange matrices alone or on mixed-bed columns containing a mixture of strong and/or weak anion- and cation-exchange resins.[163] Hearn et al.[27] also observed hydrophobic interaction chromatographic effects on Mono Q, a strong anion exchanger; the influence of various salts was shown to correlate with their ranking in the Hofmeister series. Other hydrophobic properties have also been observed on this support.[164,165] Kagel[166] recently demonstrated multimodal behavior on a matrix in which the silica base is coated with a hydrophobic polymer and then derivatized with PEI; either anion-exchange, hydrophobic interaction, or size exclusion chromatographic mechanisms predominate depending on the mobile phase composition.

Hydrophobic effects have also been observed on cation-exchange matrices, particularly those containing aromatic sulfonic acids as the functional group.[19] Previous work in this laboratory indicated that low recovery of protein mass is often obtained on aromatic sulfonic acid supports, particularly with hydrophobic proteins (unpublished observations). Regnier and co-workers[28] have recently shown that a weak cation-exchange matrix based on cross-linked PEI silica could also be used in the hydrophobic interaction mode. The selectivity and elution order obtained in the HIC mode were slightly different than those on a nonionic HIC matrix,[28] suggesting that cooperative hydrophobic–ionic mixed-mode effects were also present.

11.4.5 Ionic HIC Supports

Conversely, ion-exchange properties have been observed on several matrices designated for hydrophobic interaction chromatography. Alpert[167] recently demonstrated a mild cation-exchange effect on a series of hydrophobic interaction supports. However, the relativity low ligand density of the ionic groups on these supports was indicated by their low capacity in the presence of low salt concentrations. It should also be noted that some of the pH effects that have been observed on PEI-based HIC supports[28,50–52,59] may also be due to the presence of residual amine groups. (For a detailed review, see Ref. 66.)

11.4.6 Dye Affinity Chromatography

Dye affinity chromatography on immobilized, multifunctional dyes containing numerous ion-exchange and hydrophobic functionalities has been employed to separate numerous proteins, including nucleotide-dependent oxidoreductases, phosphokinases, glycolytic enzymes, growth factors, immunoglobulins, and numerous other serum proteins.[15,168–189]

Several studies focused on the effects of derivatizing these complex dyes with additional functional groups.[15,182] Berkowitz[15] has shown that Cibacron Blue F3GA bound to PEI-silica displays unique hydrophobic interaction chromatographic properties; the modulation of the HIC properties that are imparted by the dye molecules can be attributed to the presence of residual anion-exchange groups of PEI, since acetylation of these amines results in a chromatographic profile reminiscent of traditional HIC. These supports can also be used in the anion- or cation-exchange mode due to the presence of the PEI as well as the other ionic functional groups on the dye molecules. Similar multimodal supports containing Cibacron Blue F3GA plus diethylaminoethyl (DEAE) or carboxymethyl (CM) groups have also been used to bind specific proteins from serum.[182]

These and other multimodal supports often exhibit unique selectivities in the affinity elution or desorption mode.[184–189] The participation of multiple chromatographic mechanisms of these complex dye affinity separations is indicated by the strong effect of mobile phase on retention; this is certainly not unanticipated, considering the structural heterogeneity of these dyes, which consist of a multitude of functional groups.

11.4.7 Immobilized Metal Affinity Chromatography

Several groups[97,108,190–207] recently developed supports for immobilized metal chelate affinity chromatography (IMAC) in which divalent cations from the first series of transition elements (e.g., Zn^{2+}, Cu^{2+}) are chelated to immobilized iminodiacetic acid or other dicarboxylic acid ligands and subsequently used to selectively adsorb metal binding proteins. These supports are capable of displaying a number of different chromatographic mechanisms depending on the mobile phase conditions. In the absence of a bound metal ion the carboxylic acid moieties may exhibit weak cation-exchange properties,[192,193,199,205] and in some cases, particularly when the base support is fairly hydrophobic, the matrix can be used for hydrophobic-interaction chromatography.[192,193] In the presence of the bound metal ion, several other mechanisms may operate; anion-exchange chromatography is predominant in low ionic strength binding buffers[191,192,193,205,206] and particularly at low pH values,[207] while under high ionic strength binding conditions, particularly with lyotropic salts that enhance the organization of water structure and minimize the contribution of ionic interactions, either a hydrophobic-interaction chromatographic mechanism,[193] or a more selective ligand-exchange (IMAC) mechanism may prevail.[97,192,199] The binding of proteins via the IMAC mechanism apparently results from the ability of electron-rich residues (e.g., histidine, cysteine) to substitute weakly bonded ligands (e.g., water) and form coordination bonds with the metal complex;[195,199] elution may be accomplished by decreasing the pH, or by the addition of competitive complexing ligands[192] or EDTA[97] to the mobile phase. The selectivity that is obtained under either of these elution conditions is strongly dependent on the particular metal ion species that has been immobilized.[97,108,193,199,207] In addition, Porath[97] recently emphasized the importance of the other, additional interactive contributions that might arise from the specific base matrix, the spacer arm, and the chelating ligand. The coordinate covalent bonding interactions displayed by IMAC supports are often so strong that these supports can even be used for immobilizing enzymes.[195] Due to this diversity and specificity, IMAC will undoubtedly become an extremely important and versatile tool for the chromatographic separation of proteins.

11.4.8 Thiophilic-Interaction Chromatography

Porath[71,72,95,97,208] recently discovered a new kind of multimodal chromatographic interaction that exists between immobilized thioethersulfone ligands and some specific types of proteins, including immunoglobulins. These thiophilic adsorbents, or T-gels, bind almost exclusively immunoglobins and α_2-macroglobulin in the presence of both low and high salt concentrations.[71,72] Although thiophilic-interaction chromatography and hydrophobic-interaction chromatography are both promoted by high salt concentrations, the separation mechanisms are apparently not the same, because the two matrices exhibit different affinities and absorption capacities for various serum proteins (such as albumins and antibodies) in the presence of various salts of the Hofmeister series.[71,72] Furthermore, relative to HIC matrices, T-gels seem to show a preference for binding aromatic amino acids.[71] Porath[71] suggested that T-gels may represent an almost universal adsorbent for immunoglobulins because in many cases, these matrices are capable of producing near homogeneous antibody preparations with good recoveries (75–92%). In many respects, the results obtained on T-gels are reminiscent of those obtained in this laboratory with BAKERBOND HI-Propyl (a hydrophobic-interaction support) in the presence of moderately low ionic strength binding buffer conditions;[5,209–211] these similarities are currently being investigated in this laboratory.

Other adsorbents that are similar to the T-gels, but contain a π-electron-rich aromatic or heteroaromatic group, have also been developed by Porath;[97,208] these "thioaromatic" adsorbents exhibit properties and selectivities that are slightly different than those of the T-gels.

11.4.9 Mixed-Mode Ion-Exchange Supports

Many of the multimodal supports that were discussed in the previous section exhibit an "all-or-none" response, in which only one chromatographic mechanism is operational (predominant) under a given set of mobile phase conditions. In contrast, the true utility of pure mixed-mode supports typically resides in the unique selectivity that often reflects the synergistic specificity, above and beyond that exhibited by the individual, composite functional groups alone. This unique selectivity apparently results from an increase in the number or a change in the nature of different potential contact points between the matrix and the protein(s), and/or from the generation of a hybrid surface in which the close spatial proximity of the functional groups causes either affinity-like selectivity with specific proteins, or perturbational effects that can arise from intraligand, interligand, or ligand–support interactions.[5,6,15,19,42]

In contrast to the more conventional multimodal supports discussed in the previous section, in which the mobile phase conditions determine the predominant chromatographic mechanism, these mixed-mode ion-exchange supports tend to operate only in the ion-exchange mode (and not in the HIC mode), but with all or most of the multifunctional ligands affecting the separation simultaneously. In general, the role of the mobile phase in these mixed-mode separations is that of subtle enhancement or mild attenuation of one or more of these chromatographic mechanisms.

As previously noted, the complex structure of individual proteins provides surfaces with numerous sites for physicochemical interactions. Therefore, synthetic mixed-mode supports that contain multifunctional binding ligands offer multiple chromatographic adsorption mechanisms that may be utilized to facilitate mobile-phase-induced changes in selectivity. Physical interactions between any given protein and these complex surfaces may differ substantially in various mobile phases due to the differences in buffering capacity, pH, ionic strength, and ionic composition of various elution and binding buffers, and their effects on protein conformation, as well as the chromatographic matrix itself.

11.4.9.1 Dipolar Adsorbents

Several decades ago, Porath and co-workers[212,213] detailed the synthesis and application of dipolar ion-exchange adsorbents; "complex" supports containing both anion- and cation-exchange ligands, which bound both acidic and basic proteins, but also, exhibited some unique properties toward several human serum proteins. Similar studies conducted by Yon et al.[150–152] confirmed the unique nature of these supports and extended this work.

As early as 1970, Porath's group[212,213] realized that these dipolar adsorbents offered great potential as an alternative to more conventional ion exchangers. Because in many of these supports the entire immobilized ligand is comprised of a single amino acid molecule such as arginine, they can be considered to represent true mixed-mode supports. Indeed, Porath and co-workers[212,213] emphasized the relative importance of (1) the structural and spatial distribution of the amphoteric groups, (2) the matrix density, and (3) the nature of the medium, in determining the chromatographic behavior of proteins on these mixed-mode supports.

Recent work in this and other laboratories has focused on the development of "complex" mixed-mode ion-exchange chromatographic supports for the purification and analysis of proteins. These supports have been shown to exhibit unique characteristics, including high selectivity for specific proteins, and/or enhanced sensitivity to changes in mobile phase composition that may be used to facilitate resolution.

11.4.9.2 Mixed-Mode Weak Cation-Exchange Supports

Some of these mobile phase effects are illustrated by the chromatographic retention behavior of various proteins on BAKERBOND CBX, a "complex" mixed-mode, weak cation-exchange matrix (Figures 11–1 and 11–2). In contrast to conventional weak cation-exchange matrices,[52,219] different elution salts have a strong effect on chromatographic profile and the relative retention behavior of various proteins (Figure 11–3). Furthermore, ligand density can also have major effects on the selectivity of this surface chemistry (compare Figures 11–1 and 11–2), again emphasizing the importance of spatially-specific interactions in mixed-mode separations.

FIGURE 11–1. Effect of elution buffer on the chromatographic profile and elution order of four protein standards on 40-μm BAKERBOND CBX, a "complex" weak cation exchanger. Chromatography was conducted on a column (10 × 100 mm) containing 40-μm CBX with a low ligand density. The mobile phase included an initial (A) buffer of 25 m*M* MES, pH 5.0, and an elution (B) buffer of either 500 m*M* NaOAc, pH 7.0, or 250 m*M* $(NH_4)_2SO_4$ plus 20 m*M* NaOAc, pH 5.6, or 250 m*M* KH_2PO_4, pH 7.0, or 250 NaCl plus 25 m*M* NaOAc, pH 7.0. The gradient was linear from 100% A to 100% B buffer over either 15, 30, or 60 min as indicated above each set of chromatograms. The flow rate was 2.0 ml/min with a back pressure of 10 psi. Proteins were detected by UV absorbance at 280 nm at 0.2 AUFS. The sample injection volume was 1.0 ml and consisted of 10 mg total protein standards; peak 1 was an impurity, peak 2 was ovalbumin (chicken egg), peak 3 was ovalbumin dimer (chicken egg), peak 4 was hemoglobin (bovine blood), peak 5 was reduced cytochrome *c* (horse heart, type VI), peak 6 was oxidized cytochrome *c* (horse heart, type VI), and peak 7 was lysozyme (chicken egg). Changes in elution profiles and the elution order on CBX occur in the presence of various elution buffer systems. Protein separations are facilitated either by optimizing buffer conditions for a single run or by rechromatography of the active fractions on the same column in the presence of a second buffer system.

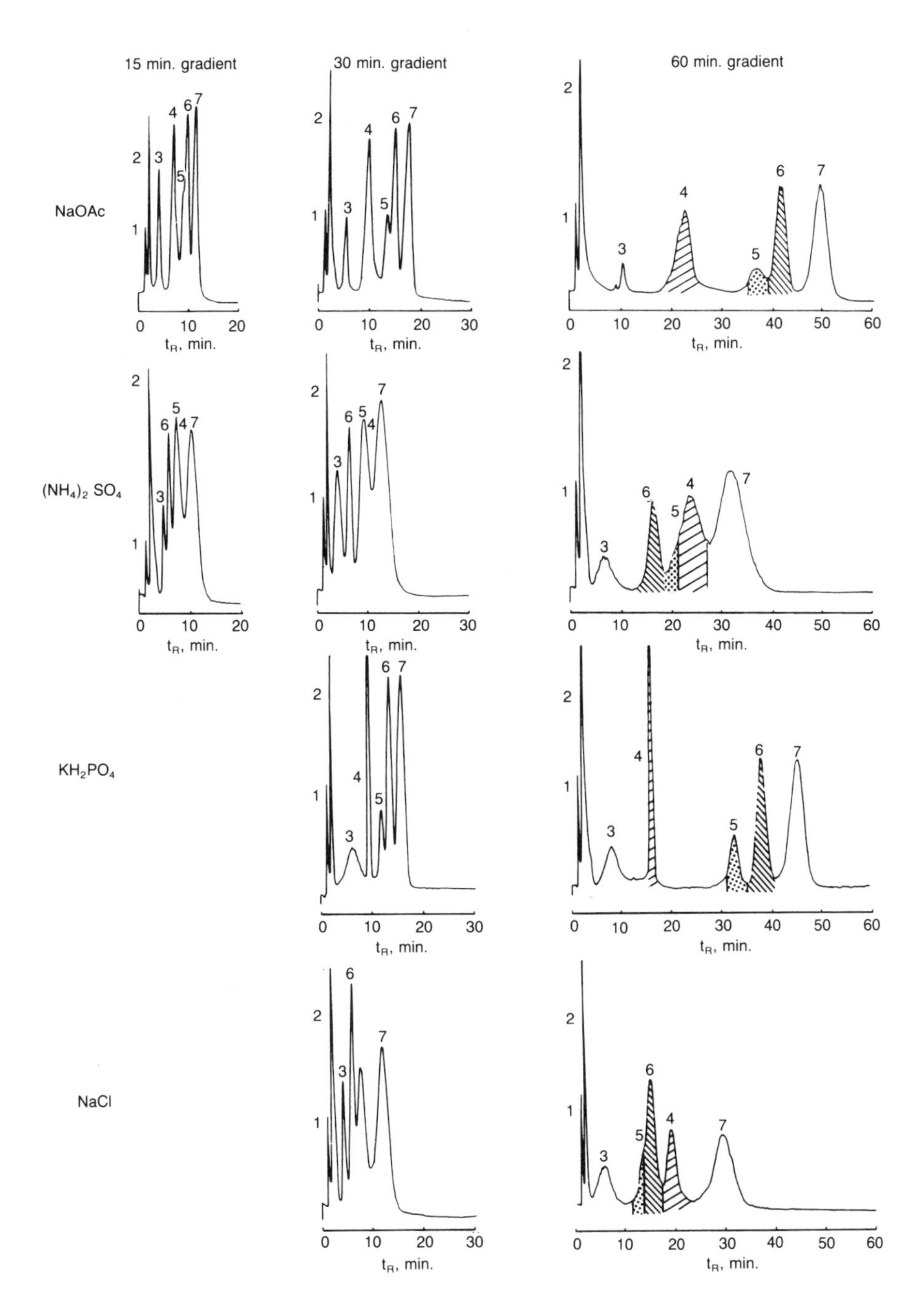
15 min. gradient
30 min. gradient
60 min. gradient
NaOAc
$(NH_4)_2$ SO_4
KH_2PO_4
NaCl
t_R, min.

11.4.9.3 Mixed-Mode Weak–Strong Cation-Exchange Matrices

An alternative approach to the design of mixed-mode matrices is the combination of both strong and weak cation-exchange groups on the same support.[52,211,220] BAKERBOND CARBOXY-SULFON*, a weak–strong cation exchanger, was designed using a surface chemistry similar to CBX in order to exploit the inherent advantages of this mixed-mode predecessor; however, strong cation-exchange (sulfonic acid) groups were also added adjacent to the carboxylic acid groups.[52,211,220] This approach results in a chromatographic matrix that not only exhibits the individual attributes that are inherent to either weak or strong cation exchangers, but also imparts unique characteristics that are not found in either support alone. CARBOXY-SULFON retains the titratable nature and sensitivity to mobile phase conditions exhibited by CBX, although the selectivities obtained with either of these two surface chemistries are unique (Figures 11–4 to 11–7). However, it also exhibits the advantages of strong cation exchangers, including the ability to remain fully ionized and retain high capacity at pH values below 3 or 4, and thus bind proteins with low isoelectric points, or peptides in the presence of TFA.[52,220] CARBOXY-SULFON also exhibits significant advantages over either type of conventional cation exchanger alone, including a higher (more than double) ligand density, and the ability to discriminate between microheterogeneous protein species

FIGURE 11–2. Effect of mobile phase elution buffer species on the relative retention and elution order of 20 protein standards on 40-μm BAKERBOND CBX, a "complex" weak cation exchanger. Chromatography was conducted on a column (10 × 100 mm) containing 40-μm CBX with an intermediate ligand density. The initial (A) buffer was 25 m*M* MES, pH 5.4 and the elution (B) buffer was either 1 *M* NH_4OAc, pH 7.0, or 250 m*M* $(NH_4)_2SO_4$ plus 20 m*M* KH_2PO_4, pH 7.5, or 250 m*M* KH_2PO_4, pH 7.1, or 1 *M* NaCl, plus 30 m*M* NaOAc, pH 5.8, with a linear gradient from 100% A to 50% B over 1 h, at a flow rate of 2.0 ml/min, with a back pressure of 20 psi. Proteins were detected by UV absorbance at 280 nm at various AUFS. The sample injection volume was 2.0 ml and consisted of 5 mg of each of the individual proteins diluted in buffer A. The proteins standards were numbered from 1 to 20 in accordance with their relative elution order in the sulfate buffer; the proteins included (1) ovalbumin (chicken egg), (2) bacitracin (bacterial), (3) α-lactalbumin (bovine milk), (4) trypsin inhibitor (soy bean), (5) β-lactoglobulin A (bovine milk), (6) transferrin (human plasma), (7) conalbumin (bovine milk), (8) aldolase (rabbit skeletal muscle), (9) aldolase (rabbit skeletal muscle), (10) myoglobin (sperm whale skeletal muscle), (11) trypsinogen (bovine pancreas), (12) ribonuclease A (bovine pancreas, type IIIA), (13) hemoglobin (bovine plasma), (14) α-chymotrypsinogen (bovine pancreas, type II), (15) α-chymotrypsin (bovine pancreas, type II), (16) trypsin (bovine pancreas), (17) cytochrome *c* (oxidized; horse heart, type VI), (18) cytochrome *c* (reduced; horse heart, type VI), (19) IgG monoclonal antibody (mouse hybridoma), and (20) lysozyme (chicken egg). The tabulated data indicate the relative elution order of the various proteins in each of the four elution buffers with the crossing lines denoting the relative shifts in elution order. The chromatograms shown indicate the relative elution profile of the 20 protein standards in sulfate (above) and phosphate (below) elution buffers (the profiles in the halide and acetate buffers are not shown); the protein peaks have been arbitrarily segregated into two groups [odd (left) and even (right) numbers] for the sake of clarity. Minor protein contaminants are not indicated, except in the case of aldolase (peaks 8 and 9) and cytochrome *c* (peaks 17 and 18), which both eluted as two major peaks; ribonuclease and trypsin also contained major protein components, which also eluted in the void volume.

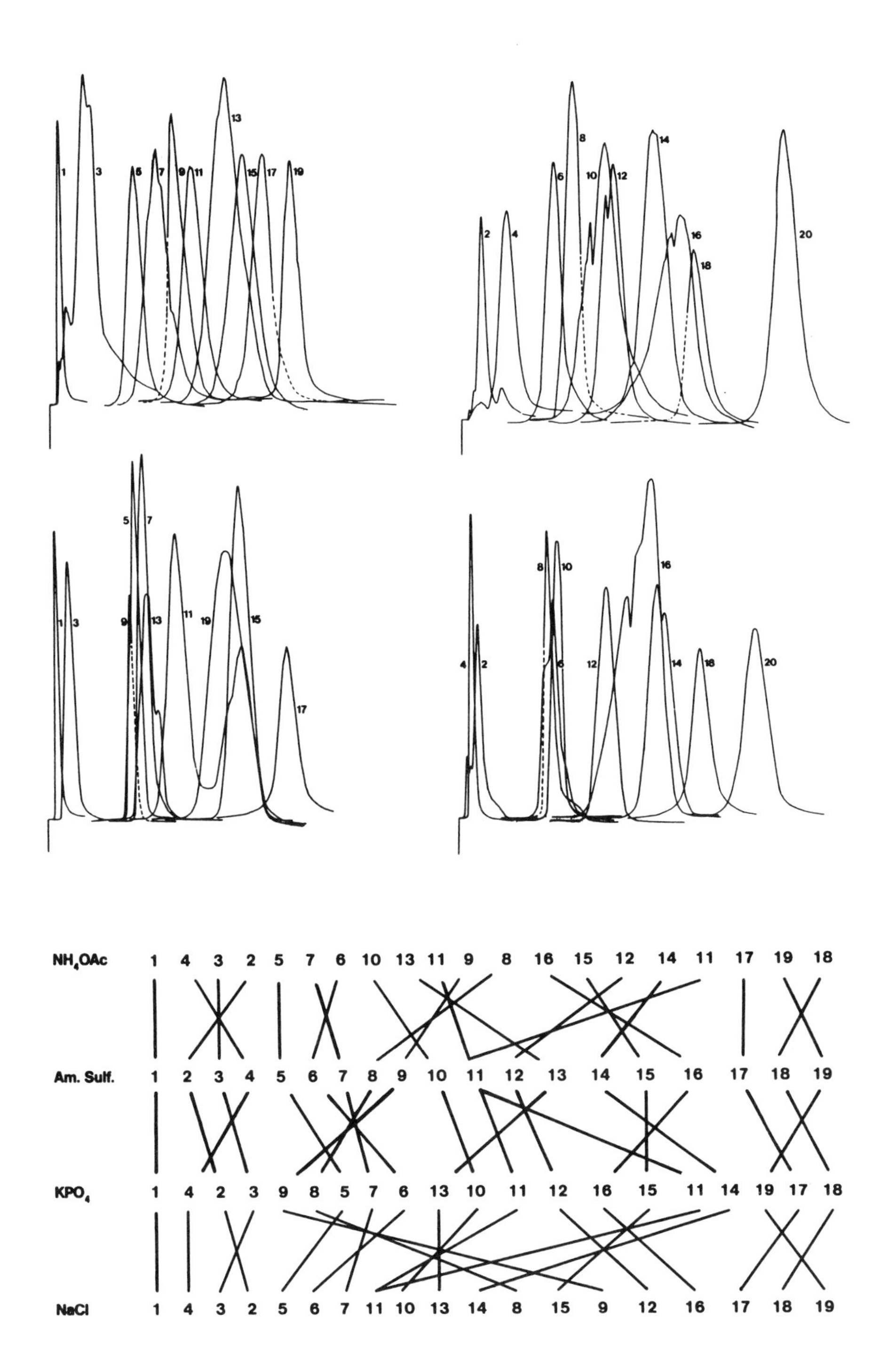
NH4OAc 1 4 3 2 5 7 6 10 13 11 9 8 16 15 12 14 11 17 19 18
Am. Sulf. 1 2 3 4 5 6 7 8 9 10 11 12 13 14 15 16 17 18 19
KPO4 1 4 2 3 9 8 5 7 6 13 10 11 12 16 15 11 14 19 17 18
NaCl 1 4 3 2 5 6 7 11 10 13 14 8 15 9 12 16 17 18 19

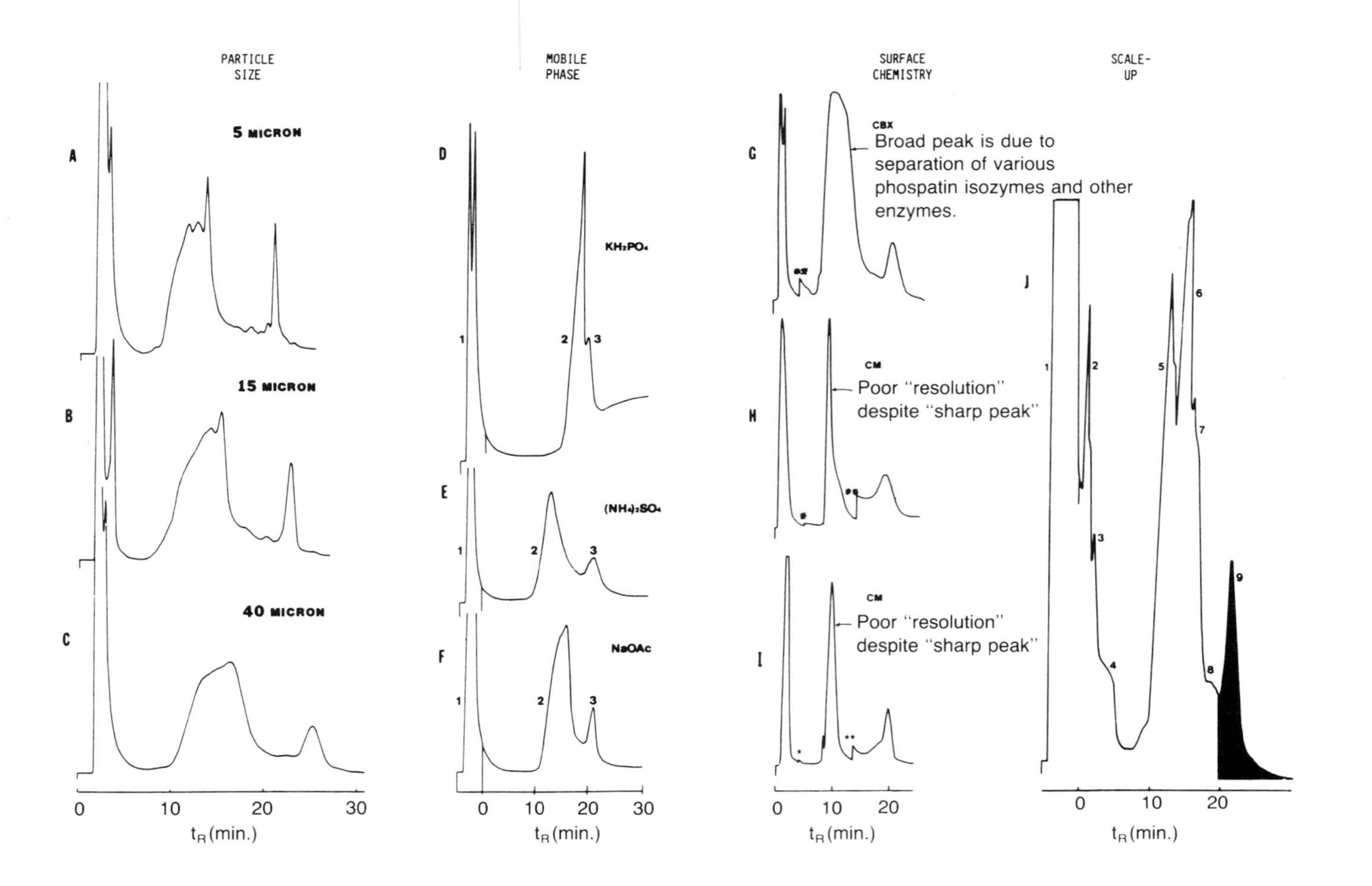
PARTICLE SIZE
A
5 MICRON
B
15 MICRON
C
40 MICRON
0
10
20
30
t_R(min.)
MOBILE PHASE
D
KH2PO4
E
(NH4)2SO4
F
NaOAc
1
2
3
t_R(min.)
SURFACE CHEMISTRY
G
CBX
Broad peak is due to separation of various phospatin isozymes and other enzymes.
H
CM
Poor "resolution" despite "sharp peak"
I
CM
Poor "resolution" despite "sharp peak"
t_R(min.)
SCALE-UP
J
1
2
3
4
5
6
7
8
9
t_R(min.)

FIGURE 11–3. Effect of particle size/column efficiency, mobile phase conditions, surface chemistry, and sample load on the purification of egg white proteins by weak cation-exchange chromatography. In chromatograms A, B, and C, the effects of particles size and column efficiency are examined on 5-, 15-, or 40-μm BAKERBOND CBX, a "complex" weak cation exchanger. Chromatography was conducted on columns (4.6 × 250 mm) containing either 5-, 15-, or 40-μm CBX, with efficiencies of approximately 80,000, 20,000, and 5,000 plates per meter, respectively. The mobile phase consisted of an initial (A) buffer of 10 m*M* MES, pH 5.6, and an elution (B) buffer of 1 *M* NaOAc, pH 7.0 with a linear gradient (begun at time zero) from 100% A to 100% B buffer over 30 min, at a flow rate of 1.0 ml/min, with a back pressure of 1000, 200, and 50 psi (in A, B, and C, respectively). Proteins were detected by UV absorbance at 280 nm at 0.5 AUFS. The sample injection volume was 2.0 ml and consisted of 10 mg of crude chicken egg white diluted in buffer A. In chromatograms D, E, and F, the effects of mobile phase (elution buffer) composition are examined on 40-μm CBX. Chromatography was conducted as detailed in chromatogram C, except that the elution buffer was either 500 m*M* KH_2PO_4, pH 7.0, or, 500 m*M* $(NH_4)_2SO_4$ plus 20 m*M* KH_2PO_4, pH 7.0, or 1 *M* NaOAc, pH 7.0 (in chromatograms D, E, and F, respectively) and the gradient time was only 20 min. Peak 1 contained ovalbumin isozymes, peak 2 contained phospatin isozymes, conalbumin, and other proteins, and peak 3 was lysozyme. The acetate (and also the sulfate) buffer appeared to give the best resolution; this method was scaled-up in chromatogram J. In chromatograms G, H, and I, the effects of surface chemistry (and base support) are examined; chromatography was conducted as detailed in chromatogram C, except that the columns (10 × 100 mm) were packed with either 40-μm BAKERBOND CBX (a "complex" weak cation exchanger), or with (100-μm cross-linked agarose-based or 20-μm "medium performance" polymer-based) "conventional" carboxyl-methyl, weak cation-exchange matrices (chromatograms G, H, and I, respectively). The flow rate was 4.0 ml/min and the concentration of the elution buffer was only 0.7 *M* NaOAc, pH 7.0; the detector sensitivity was changed from 1.0 AUFS to 0.5 (*) and/or 0.2 AUFS (**) following the elution of the void volume peak (in order to better visualize the bound peaks). The broad peak obtained in chromatogram G is due to enhanced resolution of multiple phospatin isozymes, conalbumin, and other proteins, as can be seen by electrophoretic analysis, or in chromatogram A on 5-μm CBX and in chromatogram J under overloaded, frontal chromatographic conditions. In contrast, these proteins coelute as a sharp peak on the "conventional" weak cation exchangers; this poor resolution may result from a rapid change in eluent pH similar to that obtained in chromatogram D (with phosphate) and elsewhere.[50–52,219,220] In chromatogram G, the enhanced resolution may result from the pseudochromatofocusing effect that results from the polyelectrolytic nature of the CBX matrix and the presence of other functional groups. In chromatogram J, the methods detailed in chromatograms A, B, C, F, and G are scaled-up onto a larger column (21 × 150 mm) with a proportionally higher sample load (2.0 g of total egg white protein); chromatography was conducted as detailed in chromatogram C, except the flow rate was 20.0 ml/min. Peaks 1–4 were ovalbumin isozymes, peaks 5, 6, 7, and 8 contained phospatin isozymes, conalbumin, and other minor proteins, and peak 9 was lysozyme. The recovery and purity of the ovalbumin and the lysozyme were both >98% as determined by high-performance hydrophobic interaction, reversed-phase, and anion-exchange chromatography and SDS-PAGE.[50–52,219,220]

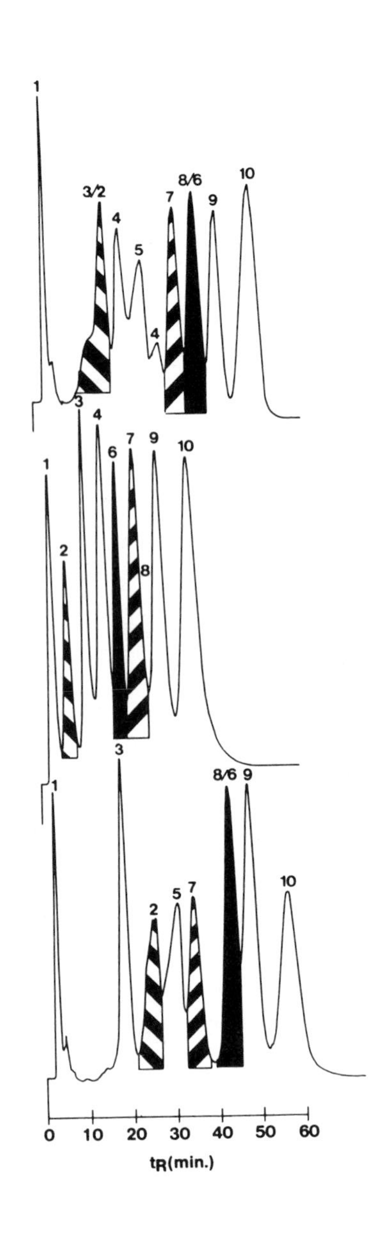

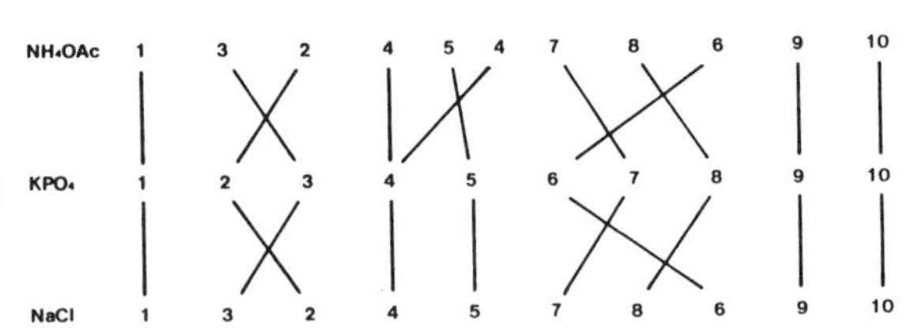

FIGURE 11–4. Effect of elution buffer on the chromatographic retention behavior of protein standards on 40-μm BAKERBOND CARBOXY-SULFON*, a "complex" weak–strong cation exchanger. The relative elution order for several of the protein standards changes in the presence of different elution buffers. Chromatography was conducted on a column (10 × 100 mm) containing 40-μm CARBOXY-SULFON with an initial (A) buffer of 10 m*M* KH_2PO_4, pH 7.15 and an elution (B) buffer of either 500 m*M* KH_2PO_4, pH 7.0 (upper chromatogram), or 500 m*M* NaCl plus 12.5 m*M* KH_2PO_4, pH 5.0 (middle chromatogram), or 1 *M* NH_4OAc, pH 7.0 (lower chromatogram), with a linear gradient from 100% A to 100% B buffer over 1 h; the flow rate was 2.0 ml/min, with a back pressure of 20 psi. Proteins were detected by UV absorbance at 280 nm at 0.5 AUFS. The sample injection volume was 2.0 ml and consisted of 10 mg of total protein diluted in buffer A. Peak 1 was ovalbumin (chicken egg), peak 2 was aldolase (rabbit skeletal muscle), peak 3 was hemoglobin (bovine blood), peak 4 was trypsinogen (bovine pancreas), peak 5 was trypsin (bovine pancreas), peak 6 was ribonuclease A (bovine pancreas), peak 7 was α-chymotrypsinogen (bovine pancreas), peak 8 was cytochrome *c* (oxidized-horse heart, type VI), peak 9 was cytochrome *c* (reduced-horse heart, type VI), and peak 10 was lysozyme (chicken egg).

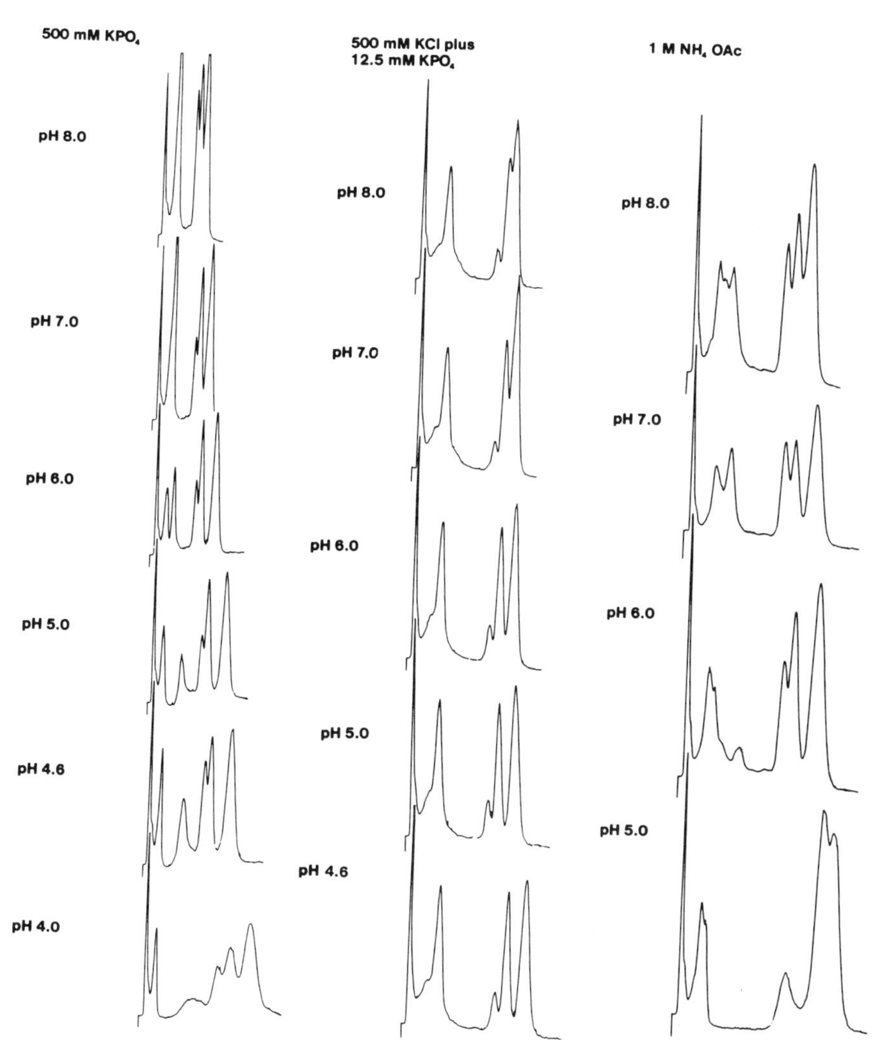

FIGURE 11–5. Effect of elution buffer species and pH on the retention behavior of protein standards on 40-μm BAKERBOND CARBOXY-SULFON, "complex" weak–strong cation exchanger. Chromatography was conducted on a column (10 × 100 mm) containing 40-μm CARBOXY-SULFON with an initial (A) buffer of 10 m*M* KH_2PO_4, pH 7.15 and an elution (B) buffer of either 1 *M* NH_4OAc, 500 m*M* KH_2PO_4, or 500 m*M* KCl plus 12.5 m*M* KH_2PO_4, each at various final pH values (8.0, 7.0, 6.0, 5.0, or 4.0) with a linear gradient from 100% A to 100% B over 1 h; the flow rate was 2.0 ml/min, with a back pressure of 20 psi. Proteins were detected by UV absorbance at 280 nm at 0.2 AUFS. The sample injection volume was 1.0 ml and consisted of 10 mg of total protein diluted in buffer A. Peak 1 was ovalbumin (chicken egg), peak 2 was hemoglobin (bovine blood), peak 3 was cytochrome *c* (oxidized-horse heart, type VI), peak 4 was cytochrome *c* (reduced-horse heart, type VI), peak 5 was lysozyme (chicken egg).

(Figure 11–6). The ability to discriminate between closely related protein species facilitates the analysis and purification of proteins derived from recombinant techniques, as well as proteins that exhibit only minor differences in surface glycosylation or other subtle forms of posttranslational modification.

CARBOXY-SULFON exhibits a unique sensitivity to changes in binding buffer species and pH; for example, the binding and retention of hemoglobin are affected over a full pH unit change in the binding buffer (Figure 11–6a). In contrast, on more conventional cation-exchange supports, binding appears to be an all-or-none response, with proteins losing all affinity for the matrix over one-tenth of pH unit (Figure 11–6b). Therefore, separations on CARBOXY-SULFON are actually less sensitive to minor variations in binding buffer composition, yet, at the same time, are more discriminating in terms of selectivity.[52,220]

Furthermore, the chromatographic retention behavior of specific proteins on CARBOXY-SULFON is even more sensitive to reaction conditions and ligand density than on CBX, enhancing the capability to "tailor" individual batches for the optimal resolution of specific proteins. For example, the particular reaction conditions employed to add the sulfonic acid functionality on to the

FIGURE 11–6. Differential effects of equilibration buffer pH on protein binding and elution characteristics on a "complex" weak–strong cation exchanger versus more "conventional" strong cation-exchange matrices. (a) Effects of equilibration buffer pH on the binding of hemoglobin and other protein standards on 40-μm CARBOXY-SULFON, "complex" weak–strong cation exchanger. Relative to more "conventional" strong cation exchangers (see below in b), the effect of pH on binding on CARBOXY-SULFON is evident over a much wider range of pH values (more than one full pH unit); furthermore, manipulation of pH can have a strong effect on the resolution of multiple forms of a given protein (in this case, hemoglobin). Chromatography was conducted on a column (10 × 100 mm) containing 40-μm BAKERBOND CARBOXY-SULFON with an initial (A) buffer of either 10 m*M* KH_2PO_4 or 25 m*M* MES (each at various pH values) and an elution (B) buffer of 1 *M* NH_4OAc, pH 7.0, with a linear gradient from 100% A to 100% B over 1 h; the flow rate was 2.0 ml/min, with a back pressure of 20 psi. Proteins were detected by UV absorbance at 280 nm at 1.0 AUFS. The sample injection volume was 1.0 ml and consisted of 10 mg of total protein diluted in buffer A. Peak 1 was ovalbumin (chicken egg), peak 2 was hemoglobin (bovine blood), peak 3 was cytochrome *c* (oxidized-horse heart, type VI), peak 4 was cytochrome *c* (reduced-horse heart, type VI), and peak 5 was lysozyme (chicken egg). (b) Effect of equilibration buffer pH on the binding of hemoglobin and other proteins standards on 40-μm BAKERBOND SULFONIC, a "conventional" strong cation exchanger. On strong cation exchangers, large changes in the retention of proteins such as hemoglobin (peak 2) are obtained with only minor changes in binding buffer pH; a change of less than 0.1 pH unit near the isoelectric point of a given protein determines whether binding is total or not at all (compare with a). Chromatography was conducted on a column (7.75 × 100 mm) containing 40-μm BAKERBOND SULFONIC with an initial (A) buffer of 10 m*M* KH_2PO_4, pH 7.05, 7.10, or 7.15 (as indicated above each chromatogram) and an elution (B) buffer of 1 *M* NaOAc, pH 7.0, with a linear gradient from 100% A to 100% B buffer over 60 min, which was initiated at about 3 min after the injection; the flow rate was 1.0 ml/min, with a back pressure of 20 psi. Proteins were detected by UV absorbance at 280 nm at 1.0 AUFS. The sample injection volume was 1.0 ml and consisted of 10 mg of protein standards dilution in buffer A. Peak 1 was ovalbumin (chicken egg), peak 2 was hemoglobin (bovine blood), peak 3 was cytochrome *c* (horse heart; type VI), and peak 4 was lysozyme (chicken egg).

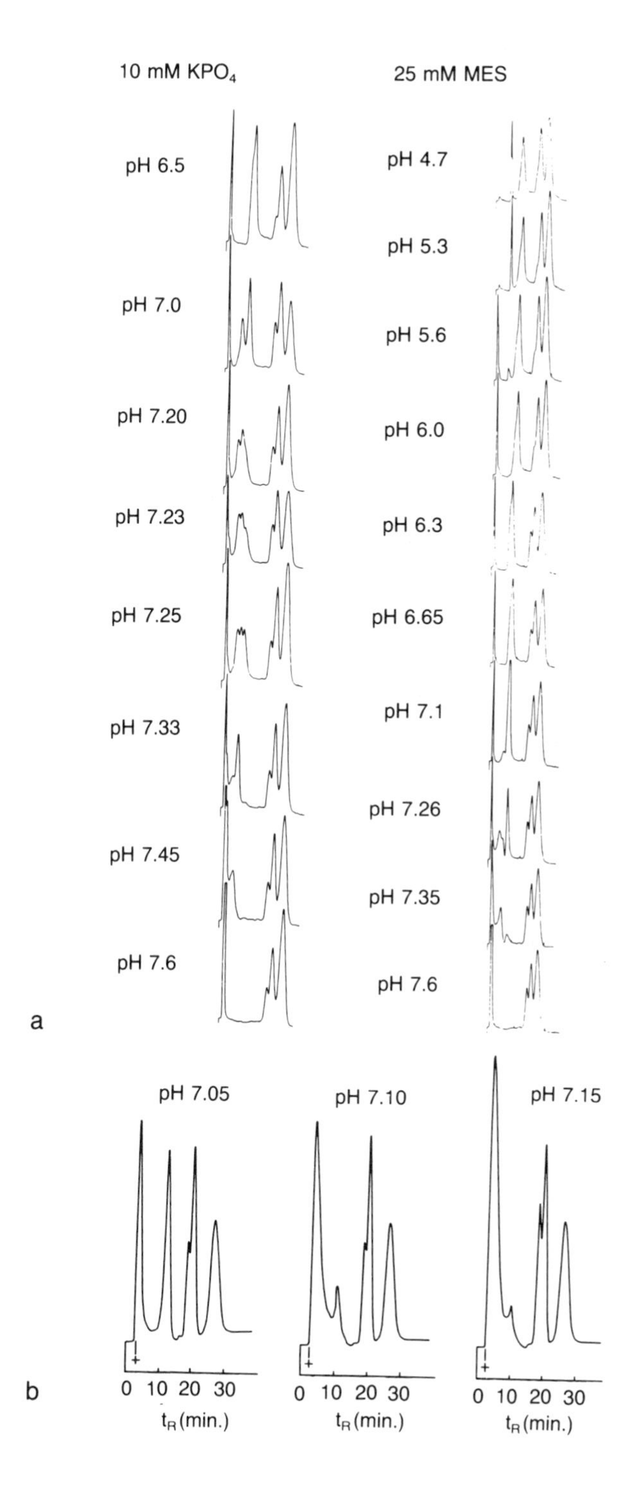
10 mM KPO4
25 mM MES
pH 6.5
pH 7.0
pH 7.20
pH 7.23
pH 7.25
pH 7.33
pH 7.45
pH 7.6
pH 4.7
pH 5.3
pH 5.6
pH 6.0
pH 6.3
pH 6.65
pH 7.1
pH 7.26
pH 7.35
pH 7.6
a
pH 7.05
pH 7.10
pH 7.15
b
0 10 20 30
tR (min.)
0 10 20 30
tR (min.)
0 10 20 30
tR (min.)

main ligand have a major effect on the chromatographic profile, apparently by determining its position (α or β) relative to the carboxylic ligand, thus affecting the spatial orientation of protein binding.

Previous work in this laboratory indicated that ligand density is often more important than intrinsic binding capacity in determining sample load in the presence of the overloaded, frontal chromatographic conditions that are often used in the preparative chromatographic separation of proteins from complex biological mixtures.[5,52,223] The use of both types of cation-exchange moieties on each ligand more than doubles the ligand density of CARBOXY-SULFON relative to other cation-exchange supports, and significantly enhances its ability to bind proteins quantitatively in the presence of overloaded conditions.[5,52,211,223] Although this can lead to a change in specificity (Figures 11–1, 11–2, and 11–14), it is often an advantageous approach.[5,223]

Finally, it should be noted that the complex mixed-mode surface chemistry and polymeric backbone of these cation exchange matrices facilitate the generation of internal pH gradients, which can be used to optimize the purification of specific proteins (Figures 11–8 and 11–9). This is due to the ability to selectively manipulate the titration of the ion-exchange groups on the support as well as those on the protein itself. This "pseudochromatofocusing" system represents an economical alternative to conventional chromatofocusing techniques, without many of the inherent disadvantages.[221] Pseudochromatofocusing is conducted with simple salts, eliminating the need for extensive dialysis and the variability inherent to polyampholyte–polysaccharide-based systems. Furthermore, this system was designed for use with CBX, CARBOXY-SULFON, and ABx*, which, unlike traditional chromatofocusing columns, can also be used in the normal ion-exchange mode. It can also be conducted without instrument constraints, and utilized in large-scale separations, because these

FIGURE 11–7. Effects of mobile phase conditions on the purification of a sugar oxidase from yeast on BAKERBOND CARBOXY-SULFON, a "complex" weak–strong cation exchanger. Methods development experiments were conducted on a SCOUT* column (4.6 × 50 mm) containing 5-μm CARBOXY-SULFON with an initial (A) buffer of 25 m*M* MES, pH 5.6 and an elution (B) buffer of either (1) 1 *M* NaCl plus 20 m*M* NaOAc, pH 6.7, or (2) 500 m*M* NaH_2PO_4, pH 6.7, or (3) 2 *M* NaOAc, pH 6.7 or (4) 1 *M* $(Na)_2SO_4$ plus 50 m*M* NaOAc, pH 6.7, with a linear gradient from 100% A to 75% B buffer over 90 min. The flow rate was 1.0 ml/min with a back pressure of 200 psi. Proteins were detected by UV absorbance at 280 nm at 0.1 AUFS (or 0.2 AUFS in chromatogram 2). The sample injection volume was 3.0 ml and consisted of 1.0 ml of crude yeast extract (10 mg/ml) diluted in buffer A. Initial experiments focused on the optimization of binding conditions under which the majority of the contaminating proteins would not bind, yet provide strong binding of the sugar oxidase, particularly under overloaded conditions (data not shown). Examination of various elution conditions indicated that acetate, sulfate, or chloride buffers provided highly active enzyme at >80% purity, while phosphate gave only 50% purity (by SDS-PAGE). However, the highest purity and resolution were obtained with the chloride elution buffer, and the method shown in chromatogram 1 was transferred to a preparative column (10 × 100 mm) containing 15-μm CARBOXY-SULFON and scaled-up with a proportional sample load (10 ml of yeast diluted to 25 ml in buffer A). This method provided product at a higher purity and activity than that obtained by a three-step procedure on conventional chromatographic supports.[51,52]

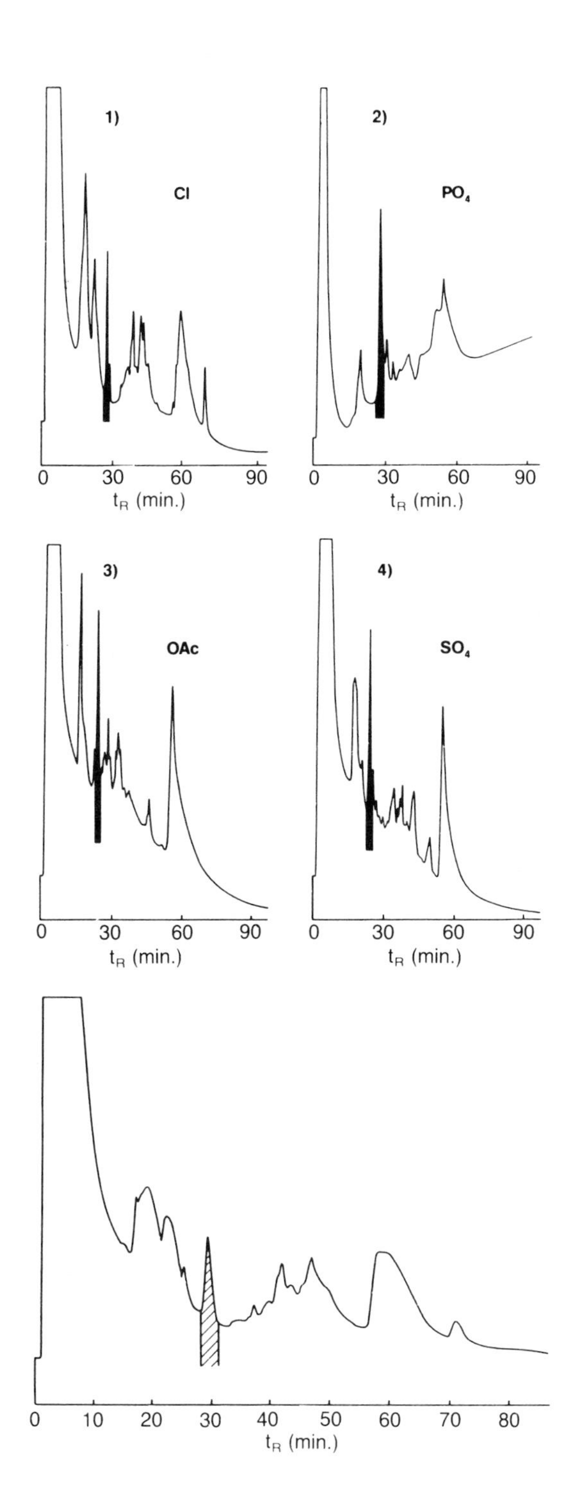
1)
Cl
0 30 60 90
t_R (min.)
2)
PO_4
0 30 60 90
t_R (min.)
3)
OAc
0 30 60 90
t_R (min.)
4)
SO_4
0 30 60 90
t_R (min.)
0 10 20 30 40 50 60 70 80
t_R (min.)

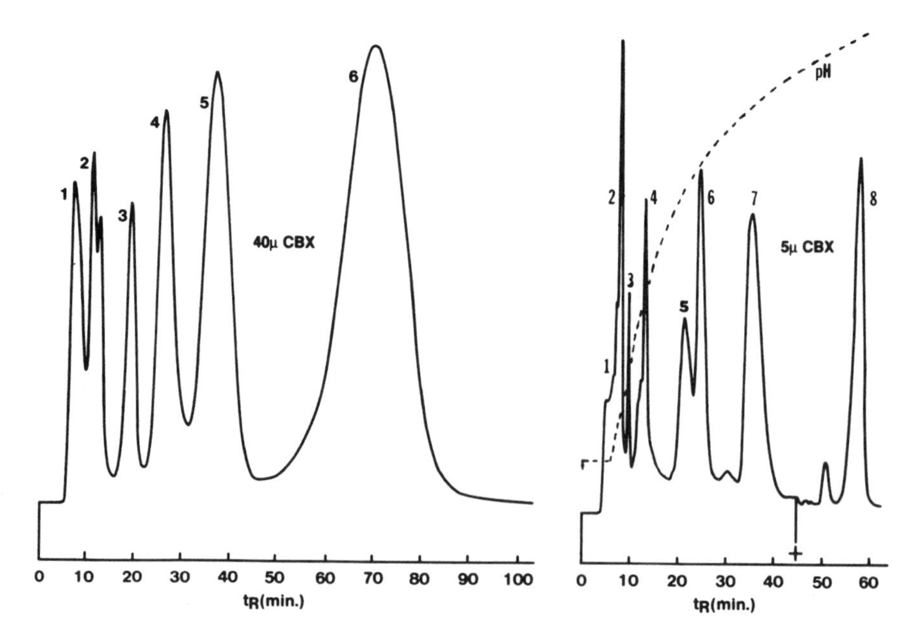

FIGURE 11–8. Pseudochromatofocusing of protein standards on 5- and 40-μm BAKER-BOND CBX, a "complex" weak cation exchanger. Chromatography was conducted on columns (7.75 × 100 mm) containing either 5- or 40-μm CBX with an initial (A) buffer of 25 m*M* MES, pH 4.8 and an elution (B) buffer of 200 m*M* NaOAc, pH 7.0 (on 5-μm CBX) or 400 m*M* NaOAc, pH 7.0 (on 40-μm CBX), with a step gradient from 100% A to 100% B following the injection. The flow rate was 1.0 ml/min (changed to 7 ml/min in the 5-μm run at 44 min), with a back pressure below 200 psi. Proteins were detected by UV absorbance at 280 nm at 1.0 AUFS. The sample injection volume was 1.0 ml and consisted of 10 mg of total protein diluted in buffer A. In the 5-μm chromatogram, peaks 1 through 8 consisted of α_1-acid glycoprotein (human serum; p*I* ~ 4), ovalbumin (chicken egg; p*I* ~ 5), galactose oxidase (yeast; p*I* ~ 6), hemoglobin (bovine blood; p*I* ~ 7), α-chymotrypsinogen (bovine pancreas, type II; p*I* ~ 8), RNase A (bovine pancreas, type IIIA; p*I* ~ 9), cytochrome *c* (horse heart, type VI; p*I* ~ 10), and lysozyme (chicken egg; p*I* > 11), respectively. In the 40-μm run, the protein standards in peaks 1 through 6 were α_1-acid glycoprotein, ovalbumin, ovalbumin plus hemoglobin, hemoglobin, cytochrome *c*, and lysozyme, respectively.

surface chemistries have been bonded to 5, 15, and 40 μm silicas (Figure 11–8). Curvilinear pH gradients have been generated on all of these supports and retention has been shown to correlate directly with isoelectric point (Figure 11–8). Manipulation of the pH and ionic strength of the binding buffer (10–50 m*M* MES, pH 3.6–6.0) and the elution buffer (50–500 m*M* acetate salts, pH 6.0–10.0) can be used to optimize the binding and resolution (Figure 11–9) of any particular protein.[221]

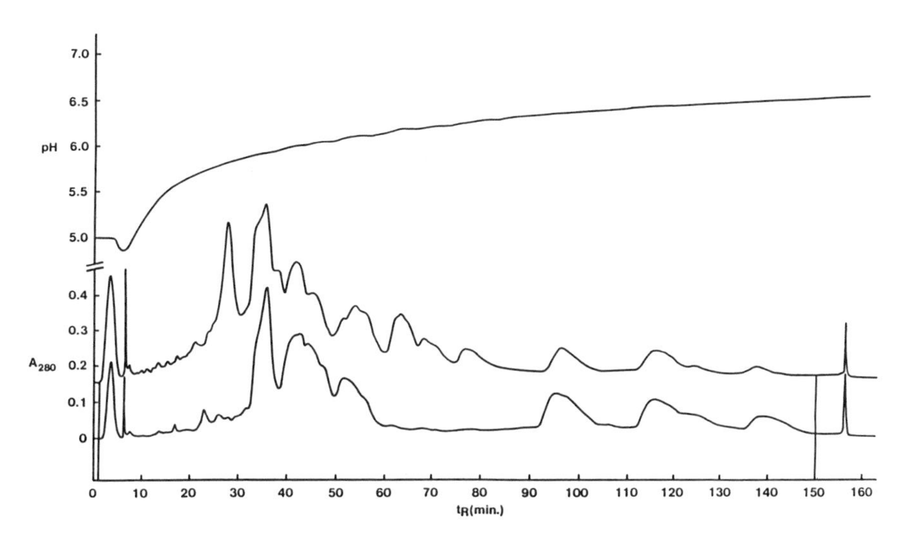

FIGURE 11–9. Pseudochromatofocusing of human hemoglobin variants on 5-μm BAKER-BOND CBX, a "complex" weak cation exchanger. Chromatography was conducted on a column (7.75 × 100 mm) containing 5-μm CBX with an initial (A) buffer of 25 m*M* MES, pH 5.0, an elution (B) buffer of 75 m*M* NaOAc, pH 7.5, and a final wash (C) buffer of 1 *M* NaOAc, pH 7.5, with an initial loading at 100% A buffer for approximately 1 min, followed by an initial step gradient to 100% B buffer, and a second step gradient to 100% C buffer at 150 min; the flow rate was 1.0 ml/min (changed to 2.0 ml/min after 150 min), with a back pressure of 200 psi. Proteins were detected by UV absorbance at 280 nm at 0.2 AUFS. The sample injection volume was 1.0 ml and consisted of approximately 1.0 mg of either AFCS human hemoglobin variants (in the upper chromatogram), or only the AC variants (in the lower chromatogram) diluted in buffer A.

11.4.9.4 Mixed-Mode Anion-Exchange Supports

Non-cross-linked, branched PEI matrices can only provide subtle forms of mixed-mode interactions, due to the presence of 1°, 2°, and 3° amines that exhibit some degree of complex hierarchical structure and mild hydrophobic characteristics.[15,52,219] Although this type of matrix can exhibit enhanced sensitivity to mobile phase composition relative to conventional anion exchangers (Figures 11–10A–C), it does not exhibit true multimodal behavior (Figure 11–10E) as do cross-linked PEI supports (Figure 11–10G). However, quaternization of PEI further can extend the mixed-mode aspects of this support by adding 4° amines via addition of alkyl groups to the basic architectural framework of PEI (Figures 11–11 and 11–12), and, depending on the carbon chain length, may act via a hydrophobic interaction mechanism to provide differential effects on retention.[51] Several investigators have previously shown that variations in the alkyl chain length on anion-exchange supports can influence selectivity via a hydrophobic interaction mechanism;[161,162] work in this laboratory is presently being conducted to expand these studies and characterize these supports.[52,219,224,225]

11.5 DESIGN CONSIDERATIONS FOR MULTIMODAL SUPPORTS

For decades, biochemists have made use of chromatographic matrices that were specifically designed for the purification of proteins. Although these supports were presumably designed to operate via just one chromatographic mechanism, recent studies suggest that many do exhibit multimodal behavior. Although many of these multimodal supports are capable of providing unique and discriminating selectivities that can often be further modulated by mobile phase manipulation, many give poor recoveries and suffer from a number of design flaws and related disadvantages. Recent studies suggest that special care must be taken to reduce or eliminate the problems that are inherent to this type of support.

In the past, serendipity often played a major role in the development of multimodal supports. However, logical design considerations can often lead to

FIGURE 11–10. Multimodal chromatographic behavior on cross-linked and non-cross-linked high-performance PEI matrices. Chromatograms A, B, and C examine the effects of elution buffer species and pH on the purification of calmodulin (CaM) from crude bovine brain extract and the mixed-mode behavior exhibited by 5-μm BAKERBOND PEI (non-cross-linked, covalently bound PEI). Chromatography was conducted on a column (4.5 × 50 mm) containing 5-μm BAKERBOND PEI with an initial (A) buffer of 25 m*M* Tris-OAc, pH 7.0 and an elution (B) buffer of either 1 *M* $(NH_4)_2SO_4$ plus 25 m*M* KH_2PO_4, pH 7.0 (chromatogram A), 2 *M* NaOAc, pH 7.0 (chromatogram B), or 2 *M* NaOAc, pH 5.0 (chromatogram C). The gradient was linear from 100% A to 100% B buffer over 15 min, at a flow rate of 1.0 ml/min, with a back pressure of 200 psi. Proteins were detected by UV absorbance at 280 nm at various AUFS. The sample injection volume was 1.0 ml and consisted of 8 mg of protein diluted in buffer A. Chromatograms D, E, F, and G compare the multimodal behavior of non-cross-linked 5-μm BAKERBOND PEI (chromatograms D and E) and a commercially available 5-μm cross-linked PEI (chromatograms F and G) in the "ion-exchange mode" (chromatograms D and F) and "hydrophobic-interaction mode" (chromatograms E and G). In chromatograms D and F, purified calmodulin (1.0 mg) was chromatographed under anion-exchange conditions, as detailed in chromatogram B above, with an initial buffer (A) of 25 m*M* Tris, pH 7.0 and an elution (B) buffer of 2 *M* NaOAc, pH 7.0, with a linear gradient from 100% A to 100% B buffer over 15 min, at a flow rate of 1.0 ml/min, at 200 psi. The recovery of calmodulin was quantitative on the covalent, non-cross-linked PEI (chromatogram D), but negligible on the cross-linked PEI (chromatogram F). Chromatograms E and G compare the chromatography of four protein standards (a = cytochrome *c*, b = myoglobin, c = lysozyme, and d = α-chymotrypsinogen) obtained under hydrophobic interaction chromatographic conditions, with an initial (A) buffer of 2 *M* $(NH_4)_2SO_4$ plus 25 m*M* KH_2PO_4, pH 7.0 and an elution (B) buffer of 25 m*M* KH_2PO_4, pH 7.0, with a linear gradient from 100% A to 100% B over 15 min, at a flow rate of 1.0 ml/min, at 200 psi. On the non-cross-linked PEI (chromatogram E) none of the proteins was bound by hydrophobic interactions and eluted in the void volume with quantitative recovery; in contrast, the cross-linked PEI (chromatogram G) exhibited multimodal hydrophobic properties and the chromatographic profile was reminiscent of that obtained on normal HIC matrices. (Reprinted from refs. 15 and 154 with the kind permission of the author.)

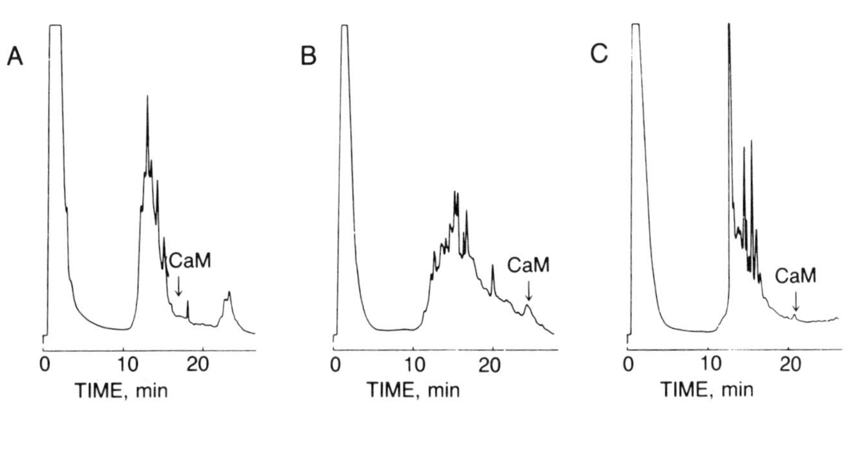
A
CaM
0
10
20
TIME, min
B
CaM
0
10
20
TIME, min
C
CaM
0
10
20
TIME, min

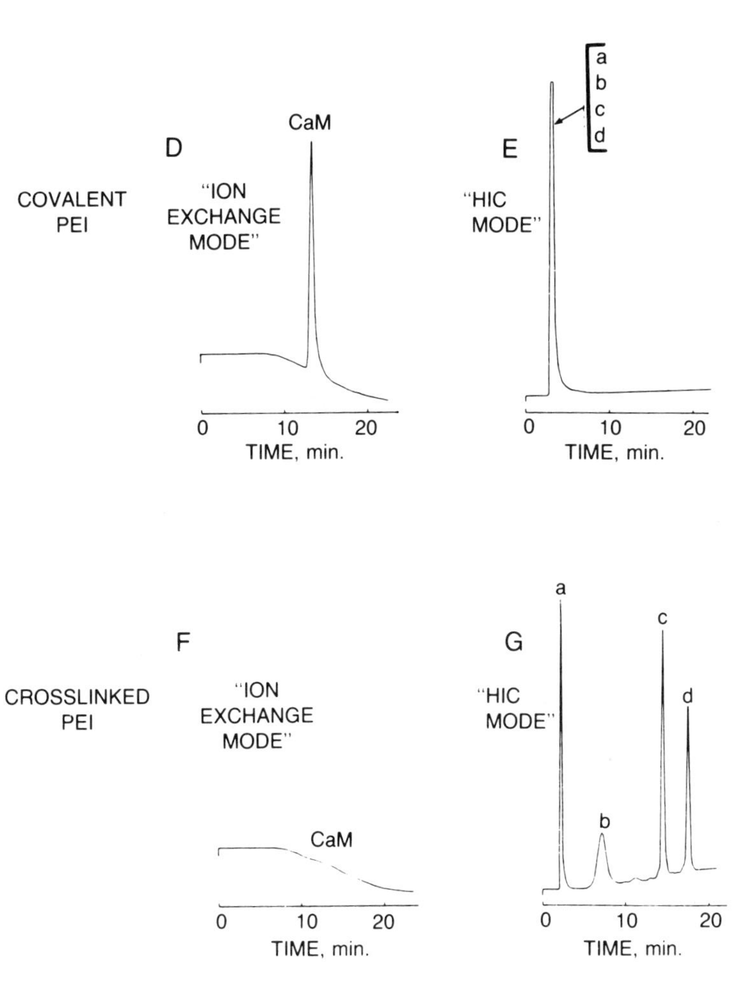
COVALENT
PEI
D
CaM
"ION
EXCHANGE
MODE"
0
10
20
TIME, min.
E
a
b
c
d
"HIC
MODE"
0
10
20
TIME, min.
CROSSLINKED
PEI
F
"ION
EXCHANGE
MODE"
CaM
0
10
20
TIME, min.
G
a
b
c
d
"HIC
MODE"
0
10
20
TIME, min.

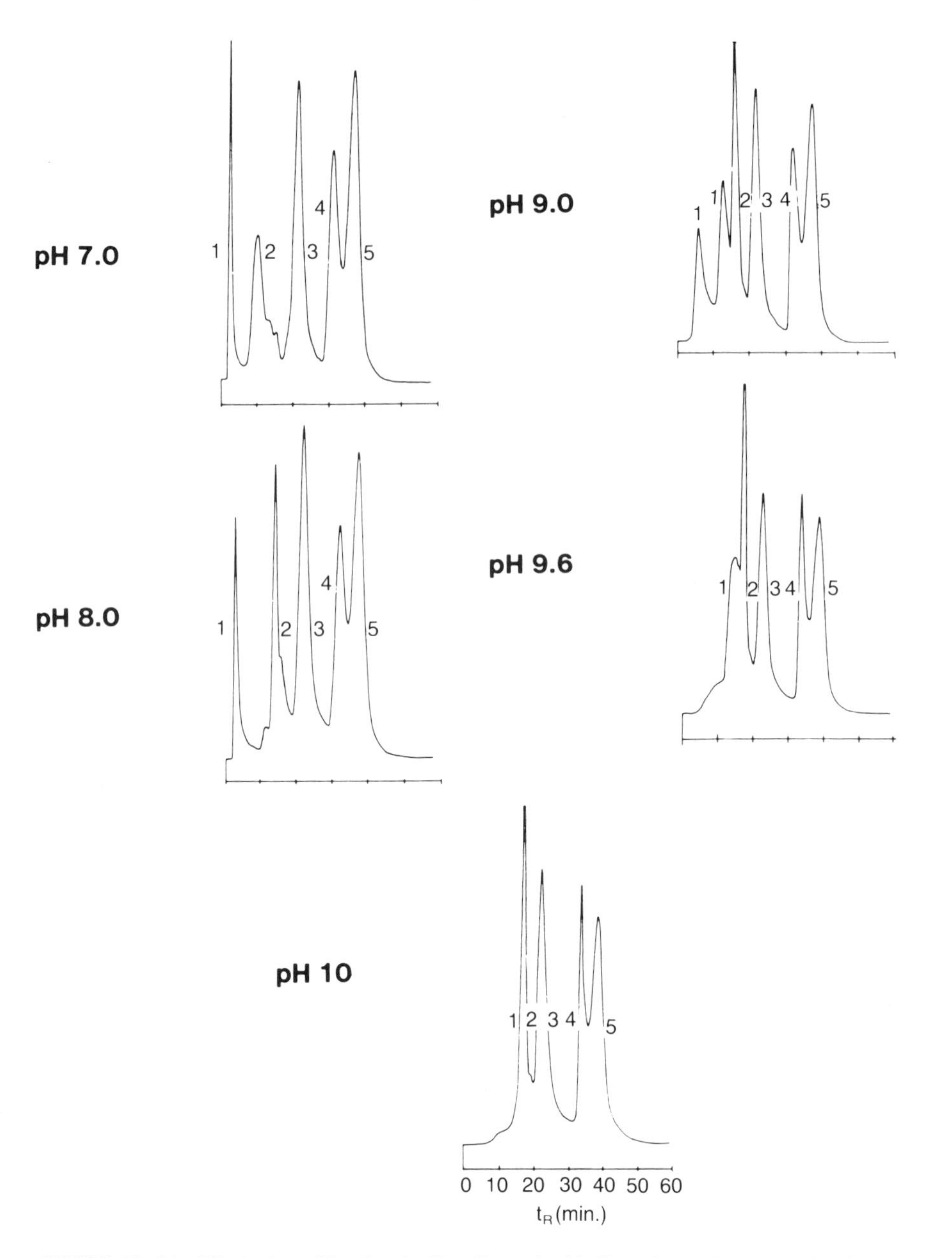

FIGURE 11–11. Effect of equilibration buffer pH on the binding of protein standards of 40-μm BAKERBOND QUAT, a "complex" strong anion exchanger. Chromatography was conducted on a column (4.6 × 250 mm) containing 40-μm QUAT with an initial (A) buffer of 25 m*M* Tris-OAc at various pH values, and an elution (B) buffer of 2 *M* NH_4OAc, pH 5.8, with a linear gradient from 100% A to 100% B over 1 h; the flow rate was 1.0 ml/min with a back pressure of 40 psi. Proteins were detected by UV absorbance at 280 nm at 1.28 AUFS. The sample injection volume was 1.0 ml and consisted of 10 mg of total protein diluted in buffer A. Peak 1 was cytochrome *c* (horse heart, type VI), peak 2 was carbonic anhydrase (bovine erythrocyte), peak 3 was conalbumin II (bovine milk), peak 4 was β-lactoglobulin B (bovine milk) and peak 5 was β-lactoglobulin A (bovine milk).

the generation of useful multimodal chromatographic matrices, provided that several conceptual problems are kept in mind.

One of the problems involved in the development of mixed-mode supports is the proper spatial orientation of the various functional groups; in most cases, this must be dealt with on an empirical basis, since until recently, little has been known about the exact spatial orientation of various amino acids in a given protein. Likewise, the optimization of ligand density is often best accomplished by experimentation, although this too may be conducted in a logical and systematic manner.[5,52]

Another related problem that is particularly important in the design of mixed-mode supports is that of surface microheterogeneity or nonuniformity among the different functional groups, since it can result in reduced capacity, lack of reproducibility, or a single homogeneous protein species being eluted as split or multiple peaks;[5,151,184,211,218] it can also complicate the process of understanding the mechanisms involved in mixed-mode separations. These problems may also arise with mixed-bed supports, or with multimodal supports in which the functional groups are added to the support in separate reactions.[19] Surface microheterogeneity can be avoided by taking a synthetic route in which all the functional groups, or at least those on the surface, are contained on the same major ligand.[5]

Another important design consideration for multimodal supports is the possible interaction of the various functional groups with each other or with the base support; these would, of course, depend on the chemical nature of the various functional groups, their spatial orientation, and steric considerations. In extreme circumstances, these might even include the irreversible chemical reaction of the functional groups.[224,225] However, in most cases, these interactions involve electrostatic or other physicochemical associations in which the chromatographic surface responds to changes in the mobile phase composition; as a result the chromatographic profile is altered, either in a beneficial or a detrimental manner.[224,225]

One advantage of true multimodal supports is that the same column can be used in several different chromatographic modes within the same purification scheme[28] and this may reduce the cost associated with the stationary phase. However, these supports often exhibit a decrease in capacity in either chromatographic mode relative to pure unimodal supports;[28] this may result from the relative decrease in ligand concentration, shielding effects that arise from the presence of the other functional groups, or the direct interactions among the functional moieties.

Perhaps the most important design considerations for multimodal supports are those that affect protein recovery. In many cases, inappropriate secondary retention phenomena can be detrimental and lead to "nonspecific" binding, irreversible adsorption and/or reduced recoveries. For years, this type of behavior has been demonstrated on size exclusion and on affinity supports that contain ionic or hydrophobic groups. Recent work in our laboratories[15,52,154] indicates that proteins that contain both acidic and hydrophobic regions (e.g., ovalbumin, calmodulin, and immunoglobulins) may be bound irreversibly by either anion exchangers with strong hydrophobic ligands or by HIC supports that have anion-exchange characteristics (Figure 11–10G); conversely, proteins that have both basic and hydrophobic faces (e.g., lysozyme, ribonuclease, and most antibodies) may give low recoveries on cation exchangers with excessive hydrophobic areas or on HIC supports containing negative ligands.[52] Recovery of these "sticky" proteins can be low if the salt concentration required for ion-exchange desorption is higher than that required for hydrophobic interactions to predominate, and vice versa. The accumulation of sticky proteins on these supports can lead to changes in elution profile or a lack of reproducibility (since these nonspecifically bound proteins can themselves act as complex multifunctional chromatographic ligands). It can also result in a decrease in column capacity and/or lifetime, and the need for frequent column regeneration. The fact that routine cleaning procedures are required on the vast majority of protein chromatographic supports, in addition to the common complaints about recovery, reproducibility, and column hygiene suggest that these problems are fairly widespread.[15,165] Work in this and other laboratories[15,50–52,154] suggests that it is possible to design mixed-mode chromagraphic supports that are capable of providing quantitative recovery of protein mass and activity (Figures 11–10D and E). Paradoxically, some of these ion exchangers, which were designed to exhibit mild hydrophobic mixed-mode characteristics (e.g., ABx, CBX, CARBOXY-SULFON, etc.), have been used for over 1000 h under preparative conditions with little or no change in performance or capacity and without regeneration, suggesting that nonspecific binding and protein losses are minimal.[5,52,165,219,220] This is supported by numerous reports from this[43,50–52,75,154,209–211,214–223] and other[8,68,93,164–165,226] laboratories that have demonstrated high recoveries of mass and activity for sticky proteins on these supports (Figure 11–10D). These problems clearly illustrate the need for careful design consideration for multimodal supports which utilize combined retention mechanisms that may require different or even opposite conditions for elution.

Proper design and reproducible synthesis of mixed-mode supports require that quantitative methods are available for the accurate analysis and characterization of the surface chemistry. Much of the work conducted in our laboratories has focused on the optimization of reaction conditions in order to create more reproducible chromatographic surfaces,[224] and the development of accurate analytical methods that correlate reaction conditions with mixed-mode chromatographic behavior.[225] Although these studies are beyond the

FIGURE 11–12. Effect of elution buffer on the retention behavior of bovine brain proteins on 40-μm BAKERBOND QUAT, a "complex" strong anion exchanger. Significant changes in the elution profile are obtained in the presence of different elution buffer conditions; this facilitates the optimization of resolution by manipulating buffer conditions and the rechromatography of collected (active) fractions in the presence of a second buffer system in order to remove impurities. Chromatography was conducted on a column (4.6 × 250 mm) containing 40-μm QUAT with an initial (A) buffer of 25 m*M* Tris-OAc, pH 9.0 and an elution (B) buffer of either 1 *M* NaCl plus 20 m*M* NaOAc, pH 7.0, or 1 *M* NaOAc, pH 7.0, or, 500 m*M* NaCl plus 20 m*M* KH_2PO_4, pH 7.0, or 500 m*M* KH_2PO_4, pH 5.0 or pH 7.0; the flow rate was 1.0 ml/min with a back pressure of 40 psi. Proteins were detected by UV absorbance at 280 nm at 1.0 AUFS. The sample injection volume was 2.0 ml and consisted of 10 mg of bovine brain acetone extract diluted in buffer A.

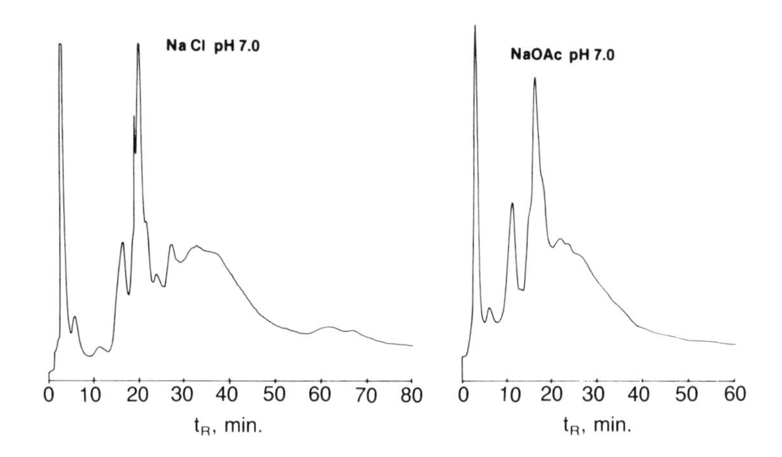
Na Cl pH 7.0
0 10 20 30 40 50 60 70 80
t_R, min.
NaOAc pH 7.0
0 10 20 30 40 50 60
t_R, min.

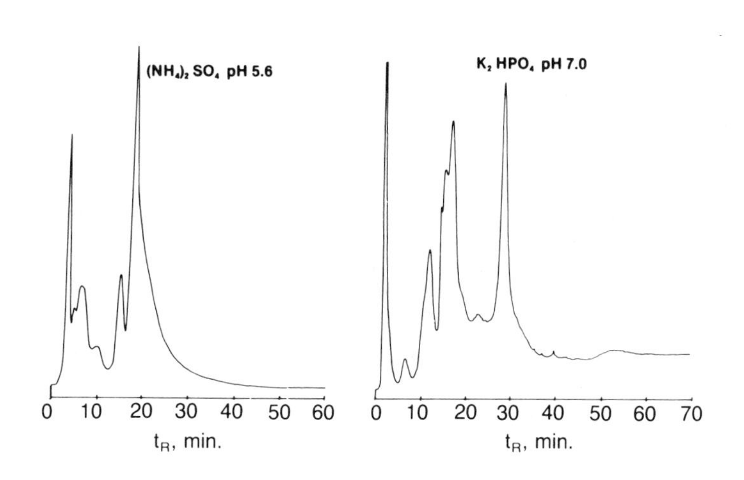
$(NH_4)_2SO_4$ pH 5.6
0 10 20 30 40 50 60
t_R, min.
K_2HPO_4 pH 7.0
0 10 20 30 40 50 60 70
t_R, min.

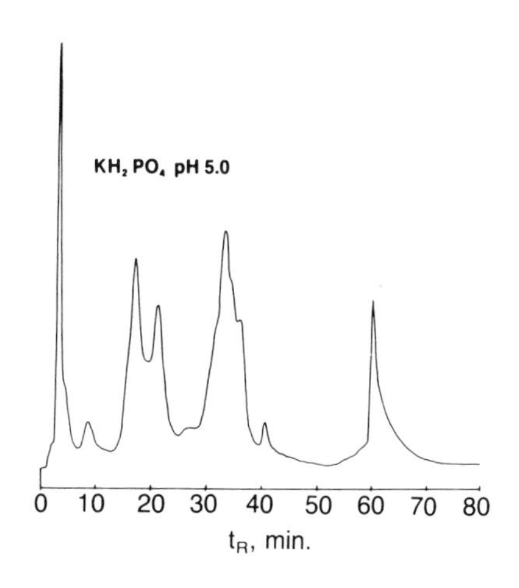
KH_2PO_4 pH 5.0
0 10 20 30 40 50 60 70 80
t_R, min.

scope of this chapter, it should be noted that a number of methods have been used for final product characterization, including Fourier transformed infrared (FTIR) spectroscopy, electronic spectroscopic chemical analysis (ESCA), elemental analysis, titration methods, and a variety of chromatographic use tests; silanes may be characterized via nuclear magnetic resonance (NMR) spectroscopy, gas chromatography (GC), elemental analysis, and titration methods, while the surface areas and pore size distributions of the various silica raw materials can be routinely determined by mercury intrusion porisometry and nitrogen adsorption.[224,225] Some of the chromatographic methods have been detailed elsewhere.[5] Floyd and Hartwick[19] also discussed a number of other techniques used for the characterization of mixed-mode supports.

Considering the problems associated with designing adequate mixed-mode matrices, the labor and fine-tuning that is required, the complex nature of proteins and their interactions with chromatographic surfaces, and the myriad different proteins that must ultimately be purified, it is doubtful that the future will bring about a significant proliferation in the rational design of application-specific chromatographic matrices. However, it is anticipated that, for proteins of significant importance, which will be required in large quantities and high purities, such an approach may prove to be advantageous. Indeed, mixed-mode supports will undoubtedly help the biotechnology and pharmaceutical industries to realize the potential and reap the benefits of modern recombinant technology. Furthermore, the intricate physicochemical interactions involved in these mixed-mode separations will undoubtedly prove to be a fruitful area for understanding chromatographic processes and for optimizing the chromatographic separations of proteins.

11.6 DESIGN OF BAKERBOND ABx*

Previously, Alpert and Regnier[153] adjusted the hydrophobic and hydrophilic characteristics of PEI by manipulating cross-linking chemistry and mobile phase conditions in order to optimize the separation of numerous rat kidney lactate dehydrogenase isozymes. Similar work in this laboratory led to the development of mixed-mode supports that are able to separate protein molecules that differ by only one amino acid or by minor differences in posttranslational modification, as well as other supports that exhibit a high specificity for certain proteins.[5,52,119–121] This section details some of the chromatographic properties that were used to design one of those mixed-mode matrices that was engineered for the purification of antibodies.

The need for an economical chromatographic matrix able to rapidly purify large quantities of antibodies to homogeneity compelled us to investigate synthetic approaches in an attempt to construct a chromatographic surface that would bind antibodies more selectively than conventional ion-exchange matrices. Using mixed-mode interactions, we developed BAKERBOND ABx* (antibody exchanger), a unique chromatographic matrix that behaves like an ion exchanger, in that immunoglobulins may be resolved via the manipulation of buffer pH and ionic strength (Figures 11–13 and 11–14), while at the same time exhibiting an affinity-like sensitivity toward all immunoglobulins, indicative of more complex interactions. ABx may be used to purify pyrogen-free antibodies of any class or subclass, from any source.[5,8,68,93,165,210–211,214,218,223,226]

The effects of mobile phase conditions on selectivity and elution profile on ABx have been discussed in detail elsewhere;[5,43,216–218] therefore, this section will focus on the rationale used to design ABx. However, it should be noted that the ability to manipulate elution order and control selectivity provides a number of different strategies for optimizing purity on ABx. These techniques include (1) the manipulation of binding buffer species, pH, and ionic strength;[5,43,216,217,223] (2) manipulating the relative degree of column equilibrium;[5,68,217,223] (3) the use of frontal chromatography and sample displacement to exploit the differences in the adsorption isotherms of the various protein components and the different elution orders obtained with different elution buffers;[5,43,217,223] (4) manipulating elution buffer species and pH (Figure 11–13) in order to provide an optimized initial purification step;[5,43,214–217] or (5) rechromatography of active fractions with a second elution buffer to remove impurities;[5,43,52,214–217] (6) the use of simple step gradient elution techniques;[5,210,216,217] (7) the use of several low ionic strength step gradients, each composed of different salt species, in order to separate contaminants that might not be removed by a single step gradient alone (e.g., an initial step into sulfate followed by a second step into acetate for pseudo-chromatofocusing; Figure 11–14A); (8) the use of an initial high ionic strength step gradient in order to invoke a hydrophobic-interaction chromatographic (HIC) mechanism to bind the antibody while selectively desorbing the bound contaminants, followed by a second step gradient or a linear gradient to a lower (intermediate) ionic strength to elute the antibody (Figure 11–14B); and (9) various combinations of these techniques. In effect, it is possible to achieve two purification steps in one, by utilizing the techniques detailed above (see 7 and 8 and Figure 11–14).

Although one chromatographic mechanism predominates on ABx (weak cation exchange), the presence of other ligands of the mixed-mode chemistry (mild anion exchange and mild hydrophobic interaction) significantly enhances the selectivity of this matrix.

The construction of ABx is initiated with silica bases of various particle sizes (5, 15, and 40 μm) with an average pore size of 300 Å. This architectural base, which consists of high-quality, closely sized wide-pore chromatographic silicas with a narrow pore size distribution (factors that enhance resolution and efficiency), is then derivatized with a covalently bound hydrophilic polyamine backbone via a patented process; this in turn, is further derivatized with ligands that contain the various functional groups.

Although the functions of the polyamine base are multiple, most of these roles are noninteractive.[5] This polymeric backbone serves seven purposes: (1) it covers up nonspecific interactive sites on the silica surface, leading to quantitative recovery of antibody mass and immunological activity, thereby reducing the need for routine cleaning or regeneration of the matrix; (2) it protects the entire surface of the silica base, thereby increasing chemical and physical stability, and, thus, column lifetime; (3) it increases not only intrinsic binding capacity, but more important, ligand density, and, thus, the capacity of the matrix to quantitatively bind immunoglobulins in the presence of highly overloaded conditions; (4) it enhances the effects of mobile phase composition on resolution, and elution profile, and enhances selectivity control; (5) it reduces the pK_a values of the adjacent weak cation-exchange groups to ensure their ionization at lower pH values; (6) it widens the pK_a range of these carboxylic acid ligands, as well as the amines themselves, and, thus, provides a polyelectrolyte matrix that is ionizable over an extremely wide pH range; and finally, (7) it provides "tentacle-like" polymeric arms which can surround proteins and provide anion-exchange, hydrogen bonding and van der Waals interactions that can work in concert with the rest of the ABx surface chemistry to bind (via multipoint attachments) and resolve immunoglobulins.

Obviously, these amines can function as anion-exchange ligands that are able to bind to acidic regions of both the Fc and the Fab chains of immunoglobulins. However, it is imperative that the relative proportion of anion-exchange groups is carefully controlled and kept to a minimum, because albumins and other acidic proteins begin to bind to the matrix as the level of these anion exchange groups increase.[5] Another function of this polymeric coverage is that it provides amines and carboxylic acids with a wide range of pK_a values, which are ionizable over a wide pH range; this facilitates the generation of internal pH gradients (pseudochromatofocusing) in the presence of various mobile phases, which may be used to enhance resolution.[5,121,214–216]

One of the more important functions of this polyamine base is that the presence of adjacent amines and amides significantly reduces the pK_a values of the weak cation exchange moieties. The ability to reduce the pH of the equilibration buffer and still have a major portion of the carboxylic acid residues fully charged facilitates the binding of immunoglobulins to ABx. Fur-

FIGURE 11–13. Effect of elution buffer on the purification of a mouse IgG monoclonal antibody from a cell culture ultrafiltrate with 5-μm BAKERBOND ABx. Chromatography was conducted on a column (7.75 × 100 mm) containing 5-μm ABx. The mobile phase consisted of an initial (A) buffer of 10 m*M* MOPSO plus 15 m*M* MES, pH 5.6, and a final elution (B) buffer of either 1 *M* NaOAc, pH 5.8, or 1 *M* NaOAc, pH 7.0, or 1 *M* NaCl plus 20 m*M* NaOAc, pH 6.7, or 500 m*M* KH_2PO_4, pH 5.2, or 500 m*M* KH_2PO_4, pH 7.4, or 500 m*M* $(NH_4)_2SO_4$ plus 20 m*M* NaOAc, pH 6.7. The gradient consisted of an initial hold at 100% A followed by a linear gradient from 100% A to 100% B buffer over 26 min. The initial flow rate was 0.7 ml/min for 4 min, then changed to 1.0 ml/min; the back pressure was less than 200 psi. Proteins were detected by UV absorbance at 280 nm at 2.0 AUFS. The sample consisted of either 0.4 ml of fetal bovine serum containing a hormone/peptide supplement ("media blank"), or 0.3 ml of cell culture ultrafiltrate ("culture fluid"), each diluted to 1.0 ml buffer A. The monoclonal antibody (cross-hatched peaks labeled "MAb") eluted as the last major peak and was resolved from most protein contaminants, including the host (fetal bovine serum polyclonal) IgG [cross-hatched peaks labeled "FBS IgG"; note that the cross-hatched area in each of these lower chromatograms is not intended to indicate the shape of the host antibody peak (as most of these peaks are not this sharp), but rather, simply indicates their relative retention times]. The removal of host (bovine) polyclonal IgG, IgA, and IgM was estimated to be greater than 70% in the two chromatograms in which acetate buffer was used, and greater than 90% with the phosphate, halide, and sulfate elution buffer systems. The purity of the monoclonal (determined by SDS-PAGE and high-performance size exclusion chromatography) was between 80% and 99%, as shown above each chromatogram.

thermore, because of the polyelectrolytic nature of the nitrogenous base, the pK_a values of these carboxylic acid groups cover a wide range. One of the disadvantages of conventional cation-exchange matrices is that rather low pH values are often required to bind immunoglobulins, and as a result, many nonimmunoglobulin proteins also bind strongly, thereby reducing capacity, resolution, and selectivity.[5,211] In contrast, higher pH values may be used to

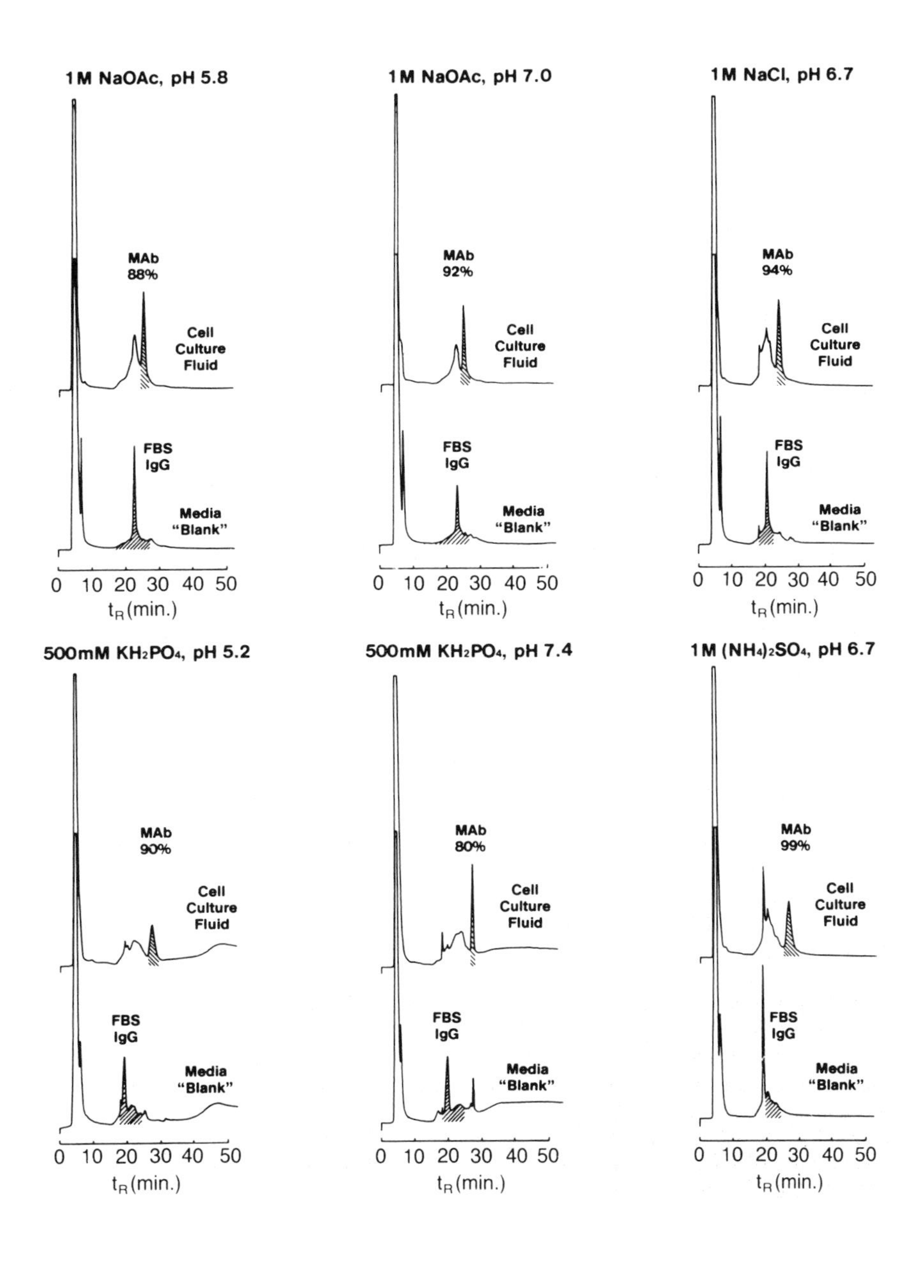

bind antibodies to ABx; this may result from a number of complex factors, including cooperative multisite interactions and the partial contributions to immunoglobulin binding that results from (1) anion-exchange functionalities, (2) hydrophobic interactions, (3) size exclusion mechanisms, (4) increased ligand density, (5) shifts in the pK_a values of the ion-exchange ligands, (6) hydrogen bonding, and (7) the titratable nature of ABx.[5,52]

Ligand density is of crucial importance in optimizing the binding of immunoglobulins to ABx, not only in terms of balancing the relative proportion of anion- and cation-exchange groups, but also, in terms of maximizing the number of carboxylic acid and hydrophobic ligands per unit volume of matrix.[5,52,223] While the density of cation exchange groups on ABx is well above 0.4 meq/ml, the ligand density on most commercially available high performance cation exchangers is below 0.1 or 0.2 meq/ml.[5,211]

FIGURE 11–14. Effect of two different double-step gradient elution protocols to selectively elute bound contaminating proteins from a monoclonal antibody on 40-μm BAKERBOND ABx+, a "complex" mixed-mode cation exchanger for antibody purification. Chromatography was conducted on a column (7.75 × 100 mm) containing 40-μm ABx+ (ABx with a high ligand density, designed to provide maximum binding capacity for acidic antibodies). The initial (A) buffer was 25 m*M* MES, pH 5.6, and the elution buffers were 75 m*M* $(NH_4)_2SO_4$ plus 25 m*M* MES, pH 5.6 (buffer B), 85 m*M* NaOAc, pH 7.5 (buffer C), 2 *M* $(NH_4)_2SO_4$ plus 50 m*M* KH_2PO_4, pH 7.2 (buffer D), and 200 m*M* NaOAc, pH 7.2 (buffer E). The flow rate was 1.0 ml/min with a back pressure of 30 psi. Proteins were detected by UV absorbance at 280 nm at 1.0 AUFS. The sample injection volume was 4.0 ml and consisted of 1.0 ml of a 10% fetal bovine serum-supplemented cell culture ultrafiltrate (a 20-fold concentrate) diluted in 3.0 ml of buffer A, or, 0.5 ml of fetal bovine serum diluted in 3.5 ml of buffer A. In the upper set of chromatograms (A), the bound contaminating proteins were selectively eluted with the use of two low ionic strength step gradients into sulfate and then acetate; following the loading with 100% A buffer for 5 min, elution was conducted with an initial step gradient to 100% B buffer (sulfate) which was held for 25 min and followed by a second step gradient to 100% C buffer (acetate; this produced the "pseudochromatofocusing" effect described within the text). The elution profile is indicated by the solid line (—). The lower dashed line (---) denotes the elution profile at 1.0 ml of fetal bovine serum (diluted to 4.0 ml in buffer A) under identical chromatographic conditions. The middle dashed line indicates the buffer concentration, and the upper dashed line (---) denotes the pH of the column eluent as measured by flow through pH meter. In the lower chromatogram (B), the bound contaminating proteins were selectively eluted with the use of a high ionic strength step gradient, while the antibody remained bound to the column, presumably via hydrophobic interactions; following the loading with 100% A buffer for 5 min, elution was conducted with an initial step gradient (into high ionic strength sulfate buffer) with 100% D buffer for 15 min and followed by a linear gradient of decreasing salt concentration (into an intermediate ionic strength buffer) with 100% E buffer over 10 min, in order to elute the antibody. The dashed line (---) indicates the elution buffer concentration. Purified mouse, human, and bovine polyclonal IgG preparations were run under these chromatographic conditions and the ratio of antibodies eluting at 40 min versus 20 min was approximately 3:1, 1:1, and 1:2, respectively, suggesting that mouse polyclonal IgG contains the largest population of hydrophobic antibodies (~75%) relative to human IgG and particularly bovine IgG [relatively few of the bovine antibodies (~35%) are bound under the high salt conditions]. The active antibody fractions (cross-hatched areas) were greater than 98% (chromatogram A) and 90% (chromatogram B) by SDS-PAGE and high-performance ABx and size-exclusion chromatographic analysis.

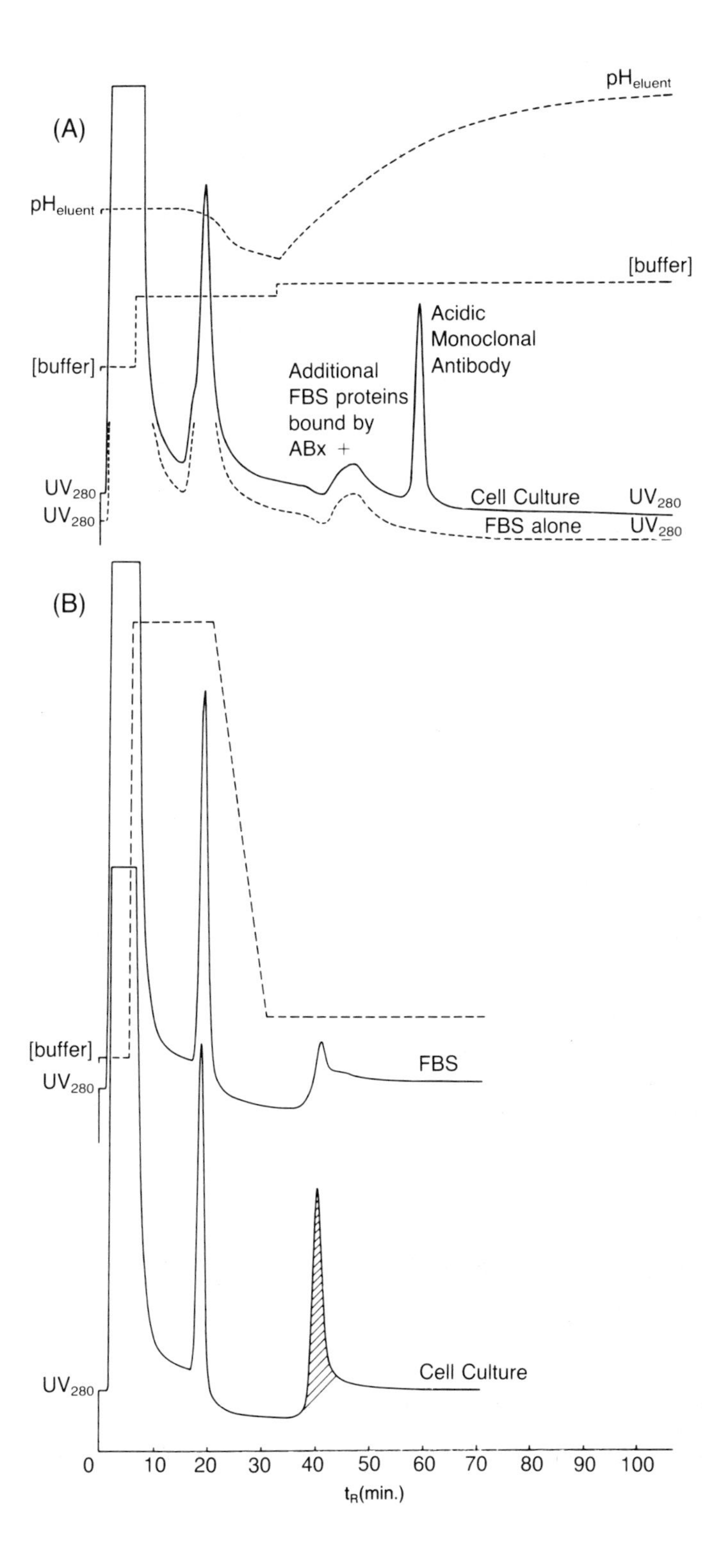
(A)
pH$_{eluent}$
pH$_{eluent}$
[buffer]
[buffer]
Acidic
Monoclonal
Antibody
Additional
FBS proteins
bound by
ABx +
UV$_{280}$
UV$_{280}$
Cell Culture
UV$_{280}$
FBS alone
UV$_{280}$
(B)
[buffer]
UV$_{280}$
FBS
UV$_{280}$
Cell Culture
0
10
20
30
40
50
60
70
80
90
100
t_R(min.)

Another factor that influences the binding of immunoglobulins to ABx is pore size. Larger pores facilitate the binding of large nonimmunoglobulin proteins, such as α_2-macroglobulin (700 kD), which in turn, compete for the binding sites which could otherwise be occupied by IgG.[5,52] Because α_2-macroglobulin can be a major component in crude antibody samples, its exclusion can increase the real-life capacity of ABx significantly.[5,52,223]

The role of a hydrophobic interaction chromatographic mechanism in the selectivity and binding of immunoglobulins to ABx is not completely understood. However, it is possible that hydrophobic ligands might contribute to antibody binding and selectivity via cooperative multisite interactions because immunoglobulins exhibit a highly specific affinity toward some HIC supports.[5,209–211] Although high salt concentrations are usually required for most proteins to be driven onto hydrophobic ligands, the selectivity and binding strength that some HIC matrices exhibit toward immunoglobulins reach a maximum at moderately low salt concentrations.[209–211] Furthermore, since HIC is actually a mild form of reserved-phase chromatography, having the same intrinsic physicochemical basis, some hydrophobic interactions might occur on ABx even at low ionic strengths. This seems possible given the fact that in bulk solution the Hofmeister effect becomes important at moderate salt concentrations.[27]

Garg et al.[8] recently used the hydrophobic nature of ABx to selectively desorb the bound, contaminating proteins with a step gradient to high $(NH_4)_2SO_4$ concentrations; under these conditions many monoclonals still remain bound (presumably via hydrophobic interactions), and may be eluted (free of contaminating proteins) with the use of a lower salt concentration [similar results have been obtained in this laboratory (Figure 11–14B)]. One possible mechanism for this effect will be discussed in the next section.

The complex surface chemistry and topology of proteins make them ideal candidates for chromatographic manipulation and facilitate the design of chromatographic supports, such as ABx, which employ multimodal retention mechanisms to achieve enhanced selectivity and specificity. By properly designing mixed-mode supports and optimizing mobile phase conditions, it is often possible to increase capacity, recovery, purity, and throughput, and at the same time decrease the number of downstream purification steps, chromatographic run time, mobile phase consumption, and the related labor and costs.[52,211] As a result, the design and optimization of multimodal chromatographic separations will undoubtedly be important areas for future research and development in the field of chromatographic science.

11.7 THEORETICAL AND MECHANISTIC BASIS FOR MIXED-MODE INTERACTIONS

Thermodynamic and kinetic analysis of interactions at heterogeneous surfaces has previously been examined in detail.[19,227–232] Theoretical calculations[19] indicate that chromatographic selectivity increases with decreasing adsorption energy differences between (1) two or more solutes with different physicochemical properties and matrices containing a single homogeneous (unimodal) adsorption site, or between (2) solutes with similar properties and matrices with different (multiple) adsorption sites. In other words, the enhanced selectivity of mixed-mode supports would be particularly evident for the separation of "similar" molecules; for example, the separation of virtually identical compounds by chiral phases.[94] In contrast, it is well established that conventional (unimodal) chromatographic supports exhibit the greatest selectivity between solutes that have large differences in structure and physicochemical properties (i.e., p*I*, hydrophobicity, size, etc.). Therefore, mixed-mode supports designed for protein chromatography are inherently well suited for discriminating between extremely similar protein molecules and discerning minute differences in primary structure, surface topology, three-dimensional structure, and posttranslational modification. This is particularly relevant for proteins derived from recombinant DNA techniques; mixed-mode supports may be ideal for separating aberrant protein products containing minor structural differences that arise from genetic defects and faulty processing, including translational errors, incomplete or incorrect posttranslational modification, and improper folding, as well as protein artifacts that result from proteolytic or chemical degradation, and/or the purification process.

Several groups[6,19,42,61,67,212,213] proposed molecular mechanisms by which the heterogeneity of mixed-mode and multimodal supports might affect chromatographic retention; these include:

1. The creation or enhancement of region-specific (regiospecific or regioselective) multipoint interactions between the protein and the support (similar to those that occur in affinity and other pure mixed-mode interactions).
2. The formation of a kind of "ion moderation," by which ionic groups present among hydrocarbonaceous ligands decrease (moderate) the retention of a hydrophobic biopolymer (as opposed to the regiospecific multipoint interactions characteristic of true-mode supports that generally increase retention).
3. Changes in the nature of the ligand–ligand and ligand–solvent interactions, and thus, changes in the overall chemical potential of the stationary phase toward the solute.

All of these mechanisms may act in concert to modulate chromatographic retention although, in some cases, one may predominate over the others.

Adsorption of proteins on ion-exchange, hydrophobic-interaction, and reversed-phase surfaces has been described as a cooperative process occurring between similar ligands on the protein and the matrix.[29,47,61,67,233,234] Cooperative adsorption of proteins onto a chromatographic surface may result from "concentration effects" at the interface in which the interaction between one set of functional groups increases the probability of adsorption or interaction between other groups on that same molecule, and, at the same time, decreases the probability of desorption.[29]

Several investigators have recently proposed a multisite/multiple group interaction hypothesis for chromatographic retention behavior that suggests that strong interactions may result from the combined (possibly even synergistic) effects from numerous weak forces (electrostatic, hydrophobic, hydrogen bonding, etc.), which alone have little or no effect on retention.[6,42] This hypothesis does appear to hold for affinity interactions, and for several synthetic mixed-mode matrices.[209–211,214–223] It also accounts for one of the major differences between multimodal supports, as a general group, and "pure" mixed-mode supports. In pure mixed-mode separations the specific spatial and geometric arrangement of the various ligands determines specificity and/or selectivity. In most multimodal supports, the contribution of these groups may have a dramatic effect on retention behavior in the presence of various mobile phase conditions, although these effects tend to be neither spatially specific nor synergistic.

The most complex type of mixed-mode behavior is found in nature, in affinity interactions. In affinity chromatography, the type and the geometric arrangement of the various functional groups impart high specificity and selectivity via the cooperative and composite interplay of numerous spatially-specific, electrostatic, hydrophilic, hydrophobic, and hydrogen bonding forces; these also determine the magnitude of the interactions, including binding association and dissociation phenomena.[5,6,15,19,52,109,110] In principle, monoclonal antibodies make it possible to construct immunoaffinity chromatographic supports with virtually any specificity. However, due to economic constraints, low recoveries, and a number of other factors,[5,11] affinity chromatography may not always be the best purification technique; one alternative is the use of synthetic mixed-mode chromatographic matrices.

Hartwick's group[19,235] recently conducted mechanistic studies aimed at understanding the behavior of mixed-ligand (capped reversed-phase) supports toward simple model compounds. These studies indicate that "excess retention" above that predicted by theory can result from secondary effects, possibly "ligand–ligand synergism." These investigators[19,235] also demonstrated the utility of van Deempter and van Hoff plots for examining the mechanisms involved in mixed-mode separations.

The eloquent investigations conducted by Hearn's group[27] also provide a rational approach and an experimental design for elucidating the mechanisms involved in multimodal protein chromatographic behavior, as well as some forceful insights into the effects of mobile phase conditions on multimodal chromatographic retention processes. Several other groups have also suggested experimental approaches to identify the presence of multiple chromatographic mechanisms, including the linearity of retention maps plotted as a function of extremes in ionic strength,[6,27,65] and the effect on retention behavior of mobile phase pH,[65,156] organic solvent content,[65,132,155,156] and dwell time.[155]

Porath[97] recently suggested that the term "high performance" should be expanded to include several of the chromatographic separation techniques that exhibit extremely high selectivity as a result of their complex and specific interactions with various proteins. Although mixed-mode separations certainly might also be included in this expanded, broader definition, it should be noted that the efficacy of these two quite different techniques arises from two fundamentally different mechanisms. While the high resolution inherent to "conventional high-performance" supports results from kinetic properties, such as increased column efficiency, the increased selectivity inherent to mixed-mode supports is a thermodynamic property imparted by the surface chemistry. In fact, on some multimodal supports reduced column efficiency and increased peak broadening and peak tailing have been shown to result from the presence of multiple mechanisms that are governed by significantly different rate constants.[19] However, in most cases, multimodal and particularly mixed-mode effects may actually produce sharper peaks,[5,27,52,219–221,217–221] as well as improved selectivity (Figures 11–13 and 11–14), and sensitivity to mobile phase conditions (Figures 11–1 to 11–18 and 11–10 to 11–14). Because this high resolving power is an inherent characteristic of mixed-mode supports, the use of "conventional high performance" particles (i.e., <10 μm) may often be unnecessary.[5,211] This is supported by the high resolution obtained in this laboratory with >40 μm silica-based mixed-mode supports (Figures 11–13 and 11–14), as well as in Porath's laboratory[71,97] on T-gels, IMAC, and affinity supports that are based on soft gels with an even larger particular size distribution (50–150 μm). A similar argument has been made against "high-performance" affinity supports;[5,211] despite differences in column efficiencies of up to several orders of magnitude, similar product purities can often be obtained on 5 and 40 μm particles,[52] since the resolving power of these supports is the result of the high specificity imparted by the surface chemistry.

Of particular importance in mixed-mode and multimodal separation are the relative distances over which the various interactive forces act, and the relative strengths of these interactions under various mobile phase conditions. Although theory suggests that electrostatic interactions are negated at high ionic strength,[26,28] Faunsnaugh and Regnier[54] have shown that ionic interactions do affect some protein separations at high salt concentrations; Bischoff and McLaughlin[236] have also observed this phenomenon with nucleic acid separations. Conversely, Hearn's group[27] demonstrated hydrophobic effects during ion-exchange chromatography at relatively low ionic strength conditions. These effects may be particularly evident when a protein is already in contact with a mixed-mode chromatographic surface, due to the influence of cooperative multipoint interactions in modulating binding and retention behavior.

It should also be emphasized that the differential strength of hydrophobic and coulombic interactions and their relative strength as a function of intermolecular distance and mobile phase conditions might also have profound effects on chromatographic processes and design considerations for multimodal supports. For example, while electrostatic interactions appear to operate over relatively short (<4 Å) distances,[28,237] hydrophobic or Lifshitz–van der Waals interactions may operate over much longer (100 Å) distances.[28,66,238]

The combination of these effects may explain the ability to perform affinity separations at relatively high salt concentrations that reduce random, nonspecific ionic interactions without decreasing the affinity of the antibody for the antigen.[52,113,116,239] It may be possible that once the long-range hydrophobic interactions draw the antigen into close proximity of the support, the ionic interacting may also become operational and facilitate the binding process, retaining specificity, without reducing binding strength.

These factors may also explain the relatively strong hydrophobic characteristics of ion-exchange supports that are based on a hydrophobic polymer[27,68,164,165] or even silica that is coated with a hydrophobic polymer,[28,29,153,156,163,166] despite the addition of hydrophilic ion-exchange groups above. In contrast, on

HIC supports, the presence of charged groups on hydrophilic polymers that are present below the hydrophobic ligands appears to impart little or no ion-exchange characteristics or recovery problems.[19,52,59,65,154,155,167] These properties might have a profound influence on the rational uses of strategies for designing mixed-mode matrices, as well as those used for purely unimodal supports.

These factors may also explain the seemingly paradoxical observations made by Garg[8] that, contrary to those obtained in this laboratory,[5] indicate that the ABx matrix can exhibit hydrophobic binding of antibodies at a high ionic strength. Garg[8] used high ionic strength step gradients to evoke a hydrophobic interaction mechanism by which the adsorbed antibody (which is initially adsorbed to ABx at low ionic strength mostly via ionic interactions) remains bound, while the other, less hydrophobic[5,209–211] protein contaminants elute. These results seem to contradict studies[5,52] that indicate that even hydrophobic proteins fail to bind to ABx when loaded in high salt concentrations. It is tempting to hypothesize that although this high ionic strength step may partially desorb the antibody from the ion-exchange sites, interactions between the hydrophobic antibody molecules[5,165,209–211] and the mild hydrophobic ligands on ABx[5,52] may keep the antibody bound to the support (and/or begin to draw the antibody back towards the surface before it is beyond 100 Å). With the antibody in close proximity of the stationary phase, ionic interactions might still participate in binding despite the high ionic strength. Desorption on the antibody (Figure 11–14B) can be accomplished by reducing the mobile phase salt concentrations to a point ($<0.5\ M$), at which the effects of hydrophobic interactions are relatively small.[28,29,136] These results seem to support the multipoint/multigroup attachment/interaction hypothesis.

11.8 MIXED-BED CHROMATOGRAPHY

In all simultaneous forms of multimodal chromatographic separations, multiple functional groups are contained within the same column; these different functional groups may be attached to the same particle to form mixed-mode supports or contained on separate particles that are mixed to form a "mixed bed."[15,19,163,240–245] Totally different chromatographic selectivities typically result from these two approaches, due to the difference in the spatial and geometric arrangement of the functional groups in each column.

In mixed-bed chromatography, two (or more) different matrices, each containing a different surface chemistry, are "blended" or "mixed" together.[15,163,240–246] Because these different ligands are physically separated on the molecular level (being contained on separate particles), the chromatographic retention mechanisms operate in a more or less independent fashion. However, the presence of ligands, such as titratable ion-exchange groups, which can affect the pH or ionic composition of the mobile phase may alter the local environment of other particles of the mixed bed, and thereby modulate retention on these ligands.

Mixed-bed chromatographic columns containing strong anion- plus strong cation-exchange matrices have been used to selectively bind contaminating proteins from crude biological mixtures, while the protein of interest flows through the column without interacting; this can often be accomplished by adjusting the mobile phase to a pH near the isoelectric point of the protein of interest.[242,246] The advantage of this method is that the recovery of mass and activity is typically high because, in theory, this protein does not interact with the stationary phase. However, the major disadvantage of this approach is that capacity is reduced because most of the contaminating proteins are bound.

In general, mixed-bed columns are also less attractive for initial preparative separation because the amount of a given stationary phase per column is reduced by the presence of the other particles and this generally reduces the binding capacity for any given protein.[5,52] However, Horvath and co-workers[241] noted that the mixing of matrices that have similar retentive properties, but slightly different selectivities (e.g., several different cation exchangers), represents an excellent opportunity for "fine tuning" column selectivity and resolution, without reducing binding capacity. Furthermore, mixed stationary phases offer specific advantages in displacement, frontal, and other nonlinear chromatographic techniques that are often superior to conventional linear elution techniques in terms of capacity, mobile phase consumption, and the ability to concentrate the product without sacrificing resolution.[163,240–241,247–249]

Mixed-bed chromatography may also be particularly advantageous for analytical applications, since it is possible to adjust the "mixing ratio" (bed composition) to optimize resolution and increase selectivity for the protein of interest. Furthermore, on mixed-bed ion-exchange columns, proteins with a wide range of isoelectric points may be bound and quantitated,[163] partially alleviating the "general elution problem" proposed by Snyder, to describe the fundamental difficulties in separating components with widely different retention factors with the use of simple isocratic elution techniques.[250]

Horvath and co-workers[163,241] conducted extensive studies with mixed-bed columns containing "binary" mixtures of both anion- plus cation-exchange particles for "bipolar electrostatic interaction chromatography," as well as "ternary" mixed phases composed of two ion exchangers plus a mildly hydrophobic support. Although the elution pattern on the binary mixed-bed column was similar to that achieved with coupled/tandem column chromatography (two separate columns each containing only one ion-exchange resin), the mixed-bed approach appears to represent a more flexible approach in which bed composition (mixing ratio) may be adjusted to modulate selectivity and maximize resolution.[241] "Ternary" mixed-bed columns composed of anion and cation exchangers plus a "mild" HIC support were found to give slightly different selectivities in the ion-exchange mode relative to the binary phases, and could also be used for hydrophobic interaction chromatography. These studies[163,241] indicate that for some proteins, the dependence of retention on bed composition is linear, regardless of which particles are mixed, or the ionic strength; however, for other proteins these relationships are nonlinear. Although no satisfactory explanation has been found for this nonlinear behavior, Horvath et al.[163] formulated an "empirical mixing rule" that also describes this nonlinear behavior with remarkable accuracy.

Several techniques have been developed for the optimization of bed composition (mixing ratio) for any particular separation problem; these include window diagrams, overlapping resolution maps, or complex computer algorithms.[163,251–255] Almost limitless possibilities exist in this highly unexploited area of protein chromatographic science.

11.9 SEQUENTIAL CHROMATOGRAPHY—COLUMN COUPLING/SWITCHING

In traditional purification schemes, each of the chromatographic mechanisms is utilized "off line," in discrete, individual steps, on separate columns. In contrast, "on line" or multimodal chromatographic approaches involve the use of multiple separation mechanisms contained in a closed system; one alternative for the application of multiple chromatographic mechanisms is sequential chromatography. In sequential chromatography, the columns are physically coupled, "sequentially," in series, as a "bank" of columns. Within the literature, sequential chromatography has also been referred to as tandem chromatography, column coupling, column switching, or less often as multidimensional, multicolumn, column programming, orthagonal or mode sequencing chromatography.[15,241,256–262] Because each of the coupled columns is separated, proteins interact independently with each support, via a separate retention mechanism, as they pass from one column to the next. Coupling arrangements can either be "linear," with direct column coupling and only one chromatographic system, or "nonlinear," with multiple, independent solvent delivery systems with independent fluid pathways and plumbing arrangements. Sophisticated switching values, complex plumbing, and other types of hardware arrangements are often used to control solvent flow and column order, and to determine which fractions are directed to the next, downstream column. Switching values can be particularly useful, allowing sample loading, elution, regeneration, and reequilibration to take place in a more-or-less independent manner; this approach is particularly advantageous in situations that require isocratic elution from the first column.[207,241,261–264] Column switching techniques offer multiple advantages over conventional column coupling, and obviously represent a major advance in this area.

Column coupling often represents an efficient alternative to conventional preparative purification schemes that typically employ a series of independent chromatographic steps. Enormous opportunities exist in this area, particularly for the process-scale purification of protein pharmaceuticals. Because coupled columns represent a closed system, sample handing, sample manipulation, and maintenance of a sterile environment are facilitated; furthermore, these arrangements are easy to automate and control, and often lead to a decrease in chromatographic run time, labor, and costs, and, in many cases, an increase in purity, capacity, recovery, and throughput.[15,52]

In general, column coupling is most effective (in terms of the interactions with each of the individual columns (steps)) when the protein of interest is either bound rather selectively, or passes through the column while most of the impurities are bound. These interactions and the concomitant separation that result on each of the coupled columns are referred to as positive responses (selective binding) or negative responses (no binding).

11.9.1 Positive–Negative Coupling Arrangements

In the positive–negative column arrangement, the protein of interest binds to the first (positive) column and is eluted (along with any contaminants) onto a second column; ideally the protein of interest flows through this second (negative) column while all or most of the remaining contaminants bind. In all coupling arrangements that utilize an initial positive column, sample loading is most effectively conducted with the downstream column(s) off-line, so that the majority of the protein contaminants that do not bind to the positive column are removed from the system (Figure 11–15).

This is generally the most efficient column-coupling arrangement in terms of capacity; in fact, positive–negative column arrangements represent a common strategy for optimizing capacity in all preparative purification schemes, even on noncoupled columns.[5,52,75] Because proteins are typically present at extremely low levels in crude starting materials, the most efficient strategy is to utilize positive initial steps that selectively bind and concentrate the protein of interest; because most of the contaminants flow through without interacting with the support, the capacity of the column is increased. In downstream steps, as the protein of interest becomes the major component, it is more advantageous in terms of capacity to utilize negative interactions by adjusting mobile phase conditions such that that protein does not bind and is selectively eluted in the column void volume, while the few remaining contaminants do bind and bind rather selectively.

This strategy was utilized in a positive–positive–negative–positive, four column coupling arrangement that was recently developed for the purification of therapeutic-grade monoclonal antibodies (Figure 11–15). Details of these experiments have been presented elsewhere.[5,52,209–211,217,219,220]

The use of a noninteractive size-exclusion chromatographic column "downstream," as the negative column, is often advantageous, because it is typically insensitive to mobile phase conditions, allowing almost any type of adsorption chromatography to be used in the positive column. In addition, it has the potential to act as a buffer exchange or desalting step, preparing the active fraction for further downstream purification steps and/or removing labile proteins from harsh mobile phase conditions.[15,52,264] Furthermore, the inherently low capacity of size exclusion chromatography is not as much of a disadvantage in this situation, since the first (positive) step may be used to concentrate the protein of interest and remove it from the vast majority of the total protein mass.[5,211,265,266] This approach has been used advantageously in a number of laboratories.[15,52,267]

11.9.2 Negative–Positive Coupling Arrangements

In negative–positive column coupling arrangements or "differential chromatography," the initial (negative) column binds the contaminating proteins, while the second (positive) column selectively binds the protein of interest.[188]

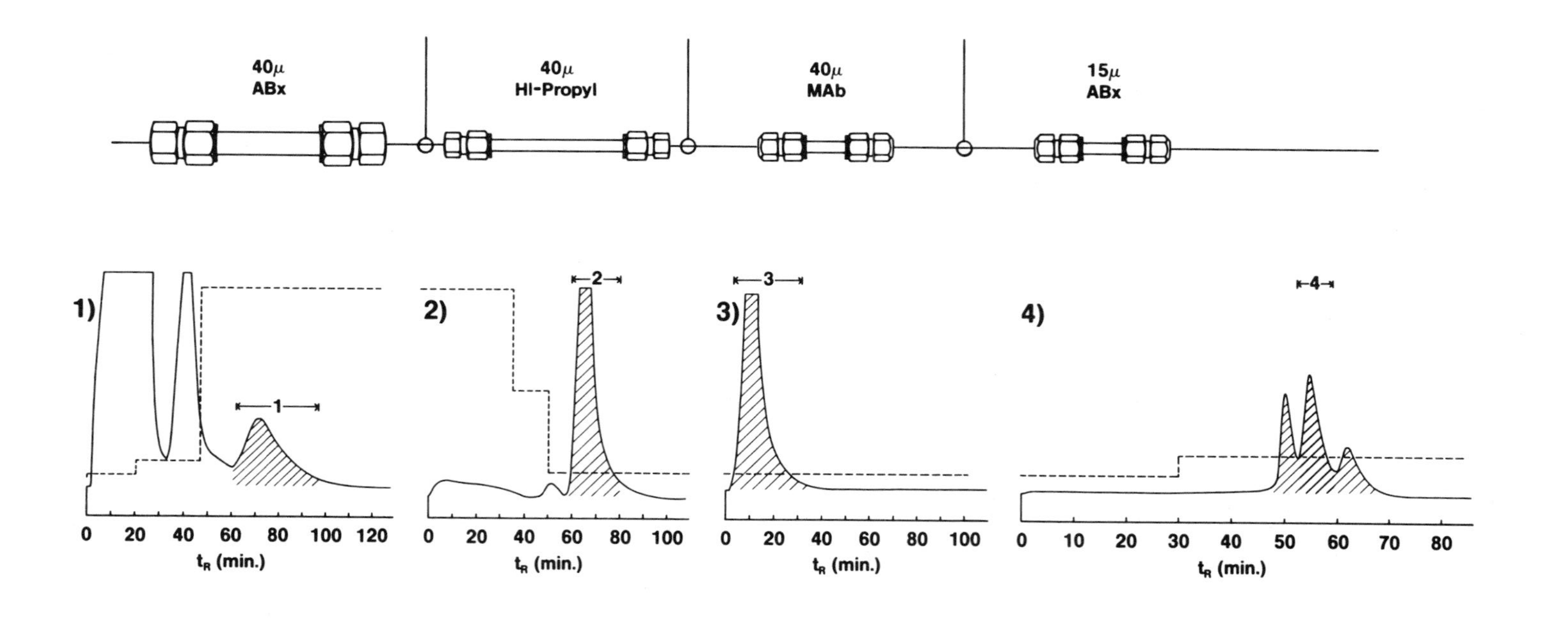
40μ
ABx
40μ
HI-Propyl
40μ
MAb
15μ
ABx
1)
2)
3)
4)
1
2
3
4
0 20 40 60 80 100 120
t_R (min.)
0 20 40 60 80 100
t_R (min.)
0 20 40 60 80 100
t_R (min.)
0 10 20 30 40 50 60 70 80
t_R (min.)

FIGURE 11–15. Column coupling scheme for the purification of therapeutic-grade mouse (or human) IgG monoclonal antibodies from fetal bovine serum-supplemented cell culture fluid by mixed-mode cation exchange, hydrophobic-interaction, and anion-exchange chromatography. Chromatography was conducted on four coupled columns containing either 40-μm BAKERBOND ABx (10 × 100 mm), 40-μm BAKERBOND HI-Propyl (4.6 × 100), 40-μm BAKERBOND MAb (4.6 × 50 mm), or 5-μm BAKERBOND ABx (4.6 × 50 mm), respectively. The buffers included (A) 25 m*M* MES, pH 5.6, (B) 75 m*M* $(NH_4)_2SO_4$ plus 25 m*M* MES, pH 5.6, (C) 700 m*M* $(NH_4)_2SO_4$ plus 25 m*M* KH_2PO_4, pH 6.4, (D) 350 m*M* $(NH_4)_2SO_4$ plus 25 m*M* KH_2PO_4, pH 6.4, (E) 15 m*M* KH_2PO_4 plus 20 m*M* MES, pH 5.6, (F) 70 m*M* NaOAc, pH 7.5, and (G) 1.6M HOAc, pH 2.5 (10% acetic acid). Following initial cleaning with buffer G and buffer C, each column was equilibrated separately and "off-line"; the ABx columns (1 and 4) with buffer A, the HI-Propyl column (2) with buffer C, and the MAb column (3) with buffer E. Each of the columns was kept "off-line" until the antibody peak was about to elute; the active fractions were diverted to the next (downstream) column with the use of column switching values or simply by manual connection of the columns. The initial ABx column (1) was loaded with 75 ml of sample [0.5 liter of original sample; 10% fetal bovine serum-supplemented cell culture fluid that was concentrated 20-fold by ultrafiltration and diluted with 2 volumes (50 ml) of buffer A containing 1 mg of LPS plus 1 mg of DNA]. The initial flow rate was 5.0 ml/min and was changed to 2.0 ml/min after 60 min and to 1.0 ml/min after 120 min. Loading of the sample onto the initial ABx column was conducted for 15 min through a large sample loop and followed by a wash with 100% A buffer for 5 min, and a step gradient to 100% B buffer for 25 min, and a final elution step into 100% C buffer (45 min after the loading began). After 15 min (just before the antibody peak began to elute), the flow rate was changed to 2.0 ml/min and the ABx column eluent (containing the antibody) was loaded onto the HI-Propyl column (2) in 100% C buffer for 35 min. Elution from the HIC column was conducted with an initial step to 100% D buffer for 15 min and a second step to 100% E buffer in order to elute the antibody. After 10 min (just before the antibody peak began to elute from the HIC column), the MAb column (3) and the ABx column (4) were connected. The antibody peak eluted in the void volume of the MAb column was bound and concentrated by the high-performance ABx column (4). Microheterogeneous forms of the antibody were eluted from the ABx column by pseudochromatofocusing with a step gradient to 100% buffer F (after a 30 min loading period). Each of the downstream columns was connected immediately before the active fractions (cross-hatched areas) began to elute from the upstream column. Each of the upstream columns were disconnected immediately following the elution of the active fractions (see areas labeled 1, 2, and 3). Therapeutic-grade antibodies have been purified by variations of this method; in some cases, only the first two steps are required, while in others, the third step may also be required. The fourth step is shown here because it is able to separate various microheterogeneous forms of the antibody. Nucleic acid and pyrogen clearance factors between 10^3 and 10^5 are possible on each of the first three steps alone (except for ABx, which does not remove most of the nucleic acids). Details of each of these techniques have been given elsewhere.[5,43,75,209–211] Lower flow rates or larger columns may be utilized in order to enhance binding capacity and the clearance of pyrogens and nucleic acids.

This technique is commonly used in dye affinity[183,187–189] and salting-out adsorption techniques.[191,196–198] In this arrangement the negative column is often removed following loading (and eluted "off line") so that the protein of interest can be eluted from the positive column without being contaminated by proteins bound to this negative column.

One of the disadvantages of the negative–positive arrangement is that the first column must bind the majority of the protein contaminants; this reduces overall capacity, and if this first column is overloaded, these contaminants will bleed onto the second column and may reduce product purity. However, since the second column has less protein mass to bind (mostly just the protein of interest), this column can typically be much smaller than the first, and elution conditions from this second column can be rather simple. Furthermore, this second step usually has the advantage of concentrating the product.

11.9.3 Negative–Negative Coupling Arrangements

Negative–negative coupling arrangements are almost totally passive with respect to the protein of interest, as it flows through the columns without interacting (or at least without binding). This approach has been taken with strong anion- plus strong cation-exchange chromatography to purify a significant amount of the bovine polyclonal IgG from bovine serum by adjusting the initial mobile phase pH to a value close to the isoelectric point of the antibodies.[242] However, it should be noted that this technique will be inapplicable in many cases, because the presence of both cationic and anionic "faces" (ionotopes) on many proteins will make it impossible to adjust the pH to a point at which neither ion exchanger binds that protein.[52,219,220] In general, negative chromatographic techniques have an inherently low selectivity; because the protein is not bound, elution conditions cannot be manipulated to enhance resolution. Furthermore, although assumed to be totally passive, negative interactions can, paradoxically, provide lower biological activity than positive chromatographic techniques.[68] The major disadvantage of this approach is that the protein of interest is actually diluted following the purification. Ideally, the initial preparative steps should concentrate the product, thereby providing a more stable environment for the product, and reducing engineering difficulties associated with further downstream processing.[15,52,268]

11.9.4 Positive–Positive Coupling Arrangements

Positive–positive coupling arrangements typically provide the highest selectivity of all sequential techniques; this is an inherent feature of these systems, since resolution can be enhanced by the optimization of elution conditions. A major requirement for this arrangement is that the mobile phase used to elute the protein from the first column must be compatible for binding on the second column, in order to eliminate band broadening effects,[269] or the generation of a split peak;[5,151,184,211,218,270] alternatively, on line sample conditioning may be conducted with the use of switching values. Although these problems may occur with coupling arrangements that utilize two ion-exchange columns, numerous examples of this technique have been demonstrated in this and other laboratories.[15,270]

The simplest arrangement for coupled ion exchangers involves the use of supports with the same surface chemistry but on different particle sizes. For example, two columns packed with either 5 or 40 μm CBX have been coupled, with the high-performance column placed downstream in order to enhance the resolution which was achieved on the initial preparative column (Figure 11–16). Similar arrangements can be utilized more effectively with the use of switching values to transfer only the fraction(s) of interest onto the smaller

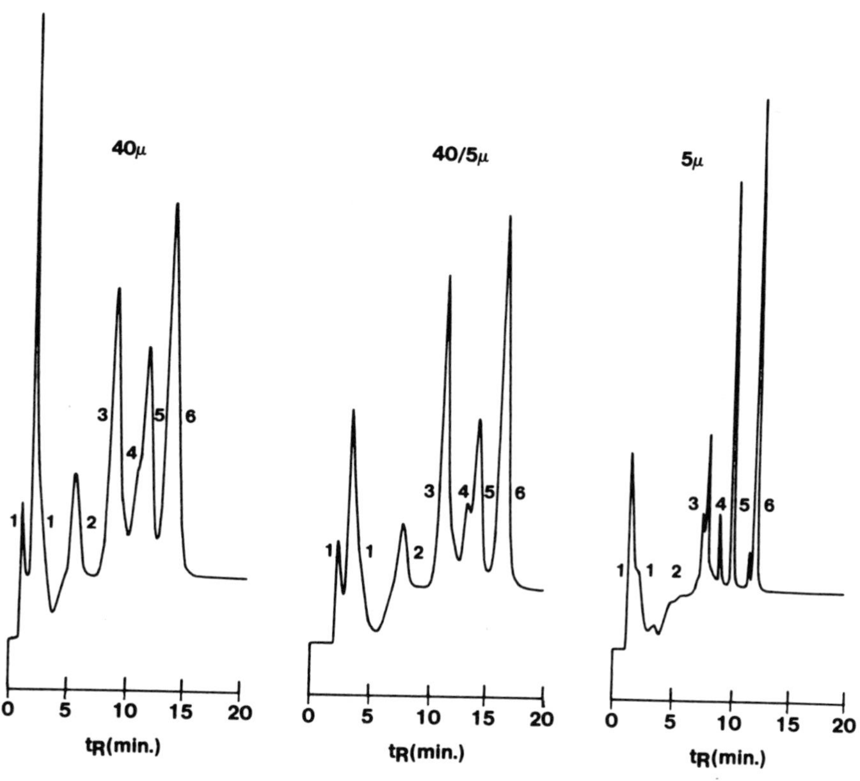

FIGURE 11–16. Tandem chromatography of protein standards on columns containing 5- and 40-μm BAKERBOND CBX, a "complex" weak cation exchanger. This technique can be used to increase capacity and resolution relative to the preparative (40-μm) column alone. Chromatography was either conducted on a column (4.6 × 250 mm) containing 40-μm CBX alone (left), or on a column (7.75 × 250 mm) containing 5-μm CBX alone (right), or with a tandem arrangement with the 5-μm column coupled (downstream) to the 40-μm column (middle chromatogram). In each case, elution was with an initial (A) buffer of 10 m*M* KH_2PO_4, pH 6.0, and an elution (B) buffer of 500 m*M* KH_2PO_4, pH 7.0, with a linear gradient from 100% A to 100% B over 20 min; the flow rate was 1.0 ml/min with a back pressure of 20, 180, or 200 psi on the 40-μm column, the 5-μm column, and the tandem arrangement, respectively. Proteins were detected by UV absorbance at 280 nm at 0.32 AUFS. The sample injection volume was 1.0 ml and consisted of less than 5 mg of total protein diluted in buffer A. Peaks 1 and 2 were ovalbumin (chicken egg), peak 3 was hemoglobin (human blood), peak 4 was cytochrome *c* (oxidized-horse heart, type VI), peak 5 was cytochrome *c* (reduced-horse heart, type VI), and peak 6 was lysozyme (chicken egg).

high-performance column, followed by a more highly resolving elution technique, such as pseudochromatofocusing.[52]

Horvath and co-workers[241,243] used gradient elution to separate protein standards on coupled anion- and cation-exchange columns and found that the selectivity and elution profiles were different depending on the serial order of the columns. These differences apparently arise from the modification of the salt gradient as it passes through the first column, so that the second gradient shape will differ on the downstream column(s). These investigators[241,243] also noted that selectivity can often be further modulated by adjusting the relative dimensions of the coupled columns.

Berkowitz[15,154] demonstrated the utility of coupling hydrophobic interaction plus anion-exchange columns to purify calmodulin from a crude bovine brain extract. Although in this case the reverse column arrangement is possible, and in general, more applicable,[52] calmodulin elutes from the HIC column at a low enough ion strength to be suitable for direct loading and binding on the anion-exchange matrix.[15,154] A similar strategy is shown in Figure 11–15. Several groups[53,272,273] recently developed the technique of ICA (immunological chromatographic analysis), in which an affinity column is coupled to an ion exchange, HIC or reversed-phase column which resolves and "analyzes" the proteins bound to the affinity support.

ICA typically improves the accuracy and the detection limit for analytical applications, because the use of linear gradient elution of the antigen(s) from the second, more efficient high-performance column eliminates the broad peaks and severe tailing that arise from slow desorption kinetics on the affinity support,[53,274] and also, minimizes the baseline disturbance that arise from the use of affinity desorption techniques such as step gradient elution, including changes in mobile phase adsorbance (adsorbtivity) and the coelution of non-specifically bound proteins.

11.10 CONSTRAINTS INHERENT TO COLUMN COUPLING

Although column coupling can result in effective and efficient protein separations, in most cases, extreme caution most be taken to ensure that proper method development experiments are conducted, including an investigation of the retention behavior of the protein(s) on each of the individual supports. This approach will indicate which coupling schemes are possible and which strategies will be most advantageous.

The physical and chemical properties of the individual packing materials may place constraints on the column sequence and may even determine which types of supports can, in fact, be coupled. One of these constraints involves the chemical and physical compatibility of the matrix and the mobile phase; for example, organic solvents may be incompatible with soft gels or resin-based supports, while silica-based supports may not tolerate pH extremes. Furthermore, the pressure limitations on polymeric or soft gels may place strict constraints on the order and/or dimensions of the columns, although the proper use of holding loops and switching values can often be used to relax these limitations.[15]

Perhaps the most important consideration for designing a column-coupling scheme involves the compatibility of the mobile phase; the eluent from the initial column(s) must be conducive to facilitate the selective binding of the protein(s) of interest to the next, downstream column (as discussed in the previous sections).

Likewise, the mobile phase as well as the surface chemistries of the supports must be compatible with labile proteins, in terms of retaining biological activity.

11.11 CONCLUSIONS

The design of multimodal chromatographic systems for protein purification and analysis represents a rational approach to improve selectivity and specificity. The ability to control and modulate surface heterogeneity will undoubtedly provide a means to improve chromatographic separation techniques, as well as our understanding of the physicochemical properties of proteins and their interactions with chromatographic surfaces and other biological molecules. Knowledge of the effects of chromatographic parameters (such as surface chemistry and mobile phase composition) on protein conformation may provide insight into the mechanistic details of the chromatographic process, as well as information on conditions most conducive to maintaining biological activity and the optimization of resolution and selectivity. Endless opportunities exist in these areas.

11.12 APPENDIX: MULTIMODAL CHROMATOGRAPHIC TERMS

In the *off-line* chromatographic approach, each chromatographic step/mechanism is conducted with separate columns in discrete individual steps; an example of this is the "traditional" ("multicolumn") chromatographic approach.

In the *on-line* chromatographic approaches, multiple chromatographic mechanisms are used in a closed system. This closed system can either be a single column, as in simultaneous (e.g., mixed-bed or mixed-mode) chromatography, or within numerous independent columns that are physically coupled, as in "sequential" (or "tandem" or "coupled column" or "column switching") chromatography; all multimodal separations are, by definition, "on-line."

Mixed-bed chromatography typically refers to the physical mixing of two or more different chromatographic matrices with different functional groups into the same column.

Mixed-mode chromatography typically refers to a particular matrix in which multiple functional groups have been attached to a single particle (i.e., in contrast to mixed beds, the particles are homogeneous with respect to surface chemistry); in "true" mixed-mode supports these ligands interact with proteins in a spatially specific manner.

Multimode (or *multimodal*) chromatography may be used as a general term that encompasses all forms of "on-line" separations including mixed-mode, mixed-bed, and column-coupling (switching) arrangements. Although often interchangeable with each of these other, more specific terminologies (in which multimodal refers to any separation in which multiple chromatographic mechanisms are being utilized in a given separation), in its most strict usage, the term refers to a multifunctional adsorbent that functions predominantly via different separation mechanisms depending on the mobile phase conditions.

Multicolumn chromatography implies the use of multiple columns; although multicolumn can refer to any multiple column arrangement and has even been used as a synonym for column coupling (sequential chromatography), it is most often used to describe the traditional, off-line approach.

In *sequential* chromatography two or more separate, independent columns are coupled or physically linked to form a closed system; sequential chromatography is more commonly known as "column switching," "column coupling," or "tandem" column chromatography.

In *simultaneous* chromatography multiple chromatographic mechanisms are operational (simultaneously) within one column; these encompass both mixed-mode and mixed-bed matrices, and to some extent multimodal matrices.

Multidimensional separations involve the use of multiple chromatographic mechanisms, typically as separate discrete steps, as in traditional "off-line" purification schemes with multiple columns (i.e., multicolumn techniques).

ACKNOWLEDGMENTS

The author would like to acknowledge the assistance of the editor and his colleagues (in particular the work presented in ref. 27) for providing eloquent data and ideas that form a basis for some of the discussions concerning the role of mobile phase in ion-exchange chromatographic processes.

The author would like to acknowledge Dr. Stephen Berkowitz for his help in providing some of the historical background information on column coupling techniques, and for the anion-exchange chromatography shown in Figure 11–10 (see refs. 15 and 154).

REFERENCES

1. G. K. Sofer, *Bio/Technology*, 4 (1986) 712.
2. F. E. Regnier, *Pharmaceutical Technology*, Aug., 26 (1985).
3. K. K. Unger and R. Janzen, *J. Chromatogr.*, 373 (1986) 237.

4. D. K. R. Low, in Bioactive Microbial Products 3: Downstream Processing (J. D. Stowell, P. J. Bailey, and D. J. Winstanley, eds.). Academic Press, New York, 1986, p. 121.
5. D. R. Nau, in High Performance Liquid Chromatography in Biotechnology (W. Hancock, ed.). Wiley, New York, 1989, p. 117.
6. M. T. W. Hearn, *J. Chromatogr.*, 418 (1987) 3.
7. W. S. Hancock, *Chromatogr. Forum*, 1 (1986) 57.
8. V. Garg, Use of preparative HPLC in large scale purification of therapeutic grade proteins from mammalian cell culture. Paper number 911 presented at the Seventh International Symposium on HPLC of Proteins, Peptides, and Polynucleotides, November 2–4, 1987, Washington, D.C. and presented at the 1987 annual meeting of the Society for Industrial Microbiology, Baltimore, MD.
9. J. Van Brunt, *Bio/Technology*, 3 (1985) 419.
10. I. Mazsaroff and F. E. Regnier, *J. Liquid Chromatogr.*, 9 (1986) 2563.
11. R. J. Goirgio, *Biopharm Manufacturing*, 1 (5) 1988) 38.
12. J. L. Dwyer, *Bio/Technology*, 957 (1984).
13. N. E. Pfund and K. G. Charles, *Biopharm*, 20 (1987).
14. F. E. Regnier, *Science*, 222 (1983) 245.
15. S. A. Berkowitz, in Advances in Chromatography, Vol. 29. (P. Brown and C. Giddings, eds.). Dekker, New York, 1989, pp. 176–219.
16. G. Guiochon and H. Colin, *Chromatogr. Forum*, 1(3) (1988) 21.
17. P. A. Tice, I. Mazsaroff, N. T. Lin, and F. E. Regnier, *J. Chromatogr.*, 410 (1987) 43.
18. L. R. Snyder and J. J. Kirkland, in Introduction to Modern Liquid Chromatography. Wiley, New York, 1979, p. 615.
19. T. R. Floyd and R. A. Hartwick, in High-Performance Liquid Chromatography, Vol. 4 (Cs. Horvath, ed.), Academic Press, New York, 1986, p. 45.
20. D. D. Nugent, W. G. Burton, T. K. Slattery, B. F. Johnson, and L. R. Snyder, *J. Chromatogr.*, 443 (1988) 10.
21. L. R. Snyder, in High Performance Liquid Chromatography—Advances and Perspectives, Vol. 3 (Cs. Horvath, ed.). Academic Press, New York, 1983, p. 1.
22. W. S. Hancock and J. T. Sparrow, in High Performance Liquid Chromatography—Advances and Perspectives, Vol. 3 (Cs. Horvath, ed.). Academic Press, New York, 1983.
23. M. T. W. Hearn, in High Performance Liquid Chromatography—Advances and Perspecftives, Vol. 3 (Cs. Horvath, ed.). Academic Press, New York, 1983.
24. W. R. Melander and Cs. Horvath, in High Performance Liquid Chromatography—Advances and Perspectives, Vol. 2 (Cs. Horvath, ed.). Academic Press, New York, 1983.
25. W. Melander, D. Corradini, and Cs. Horvath, *J. Chromatogr.*, 317 (1985) 67.
26. L. A. Haff, L. G. Faegerstam, and A. R. Barry, *J. Chromatogr.*, 226 (1983) 409.
27. M. T. W. Hearn, A. N. Hodder, and M. I. Aguilar, *J. Chromatogr.*, 443 (1988) 97.
28. M. L. Heinitz, L. Kennedy, W. Kopaciewicz, and F. E. Regnier, *J. Chromatogr.*, 443 (1988) 173.
29. L. A. Kennedy, W. Kopaciewicz, and F. E. Regnier, *J. Chromatogr.*, 359 (1988) 73.
30. A. N. Hodder, M. I. Aguilar, M. T. W. Hearn, Control of selectivity behavior by co- and counter-ions in preparative high performance ion exchange chromatography of proteins: A reappraisal. Paper 801, presented at HPLC '86 (Tenth International Symposium on Column Liquid Chromatography), San Francisco, CA, May 18–23, 1986.
31. W. Kopaciewicz and F. E. Regnier, *Anal. Biochem.*, 133 (1988) 251.
32. M. P. Strickler and M. J. Gemski, in Commercial Production of Monoclonal Antibodies (S. Seaver, ed.). Dekker, New York, 1987, pp. 217–245.
33. K. M. Gooding and M. N. Schmuck, *J. Chromatogr.*, 296 (1984) 321.
34. W. Anderson and W. Mayhew, Effects of gradient type and composition on monoclonal antibody purification by ion exchange high performance liquid chromatography. Poster 804, presented at Seventh International Symposium on HPLC of Proteins, Peptides and Polynucleotides, Washington, DC, November 2–4, 1987.

35. B. Winter and U. Moberg, The relation between pH and pI in ion exchange chromatography of monoclonal antibodies. Poster 833, presented at the Seventh International Symposium of HPLC of Proteins, Peptides and Polynucleotides, Washington, DC, November 2–4, 1987.
36. J. R. Deschamps, J. E. K. Kildreth, D. Derr, and J. T. August, *Anal. Biochem.*, 147 (1985) 451.
37. P. H. von Hippel and T. Schleich, in Structure and Stability of Biological Macromolecules (S. N. Timasheff and G. D. Fasman, eds.). Dekker, New York, 1969, pp. 417–574.
38. B. E. Conway, *Annu. Rev. Phys. Chem.*, 17 (1966) 506.
39. J. Porath, *J. Chromatogr.*, 376 (1986) 331.
40. R. Arakawa and S. N. Timasheff, *Biochemistry*, 21 (1982) 6545.
41. T. Arakawa and S. N. Timasheff, *Biochemistry*, 23 (1984) 5912.
42. F. E. Regnier, *Science*, 238 (1987) 319.
43. D. R. Nau, *Biochromatography*, 4(3) (1989) 131–143.
44. W. Kopaciewicz and F. E. Regnier, *Anal. Biochem.*, 126 (1982) 8.
45. N. K. Boardman and S. M. Partridge, *Biochem. J.*, 59 (1955) 543.
46. S. R. Himmelhoch, *Methods Enzymol.*, 22 (1971) 273.
47. W. Kopaciewicz, M. A. Rounds, J. Fausnaugh, and F. E. Regnier, *J. Chromatogr.*, 266 (1983) 3.
48. M. T. W. Hearn, A. N. Hodder, P. G. Stanton, and M. I. Aguilar, *Chromatographia*, in press.
49. M. A. Rounds and F. E. Regnier, *J. Chromatogr.*, 283 (1984) 37.
50. D. R. Nau, *Biochromatography*, 4(2) (1989) 62–68.
51. D. R. Nau, New strong anion and cation exchange supports for protein purification and analysis. Poster 135, presented at the Seventh International Symposium on HPLC of Proteins, Peptides and Polynucleotides. Washington, DC, November 2–4, 1987.
52. D. R. Nau, (1991) (in preparation).
53. L. Janis and F. E. Regnier, *J. Chromatogr.*, 444 (1985) 1.
54. J. L. Fausnaugh and F. E. Regnier, *J. Chromatogr.*, 359 (1986) 131.
55. R. R. Drager and F. E. Regnier, *J. Chromatogr.*, 406 (1987) 237.
56. J. Fausnaugh-Pollit, G. Thevenon, L. J. Janis, and F. E. Regnier, *J. Chromatogr.*, in press.
57. F. E. Regnier, personal communication.
58. M. T. W. Hearn, Investigation into non-ideal adsorption behavior of proteins with coulombic and biospecific affinity chromatography media. Lecture Tu-L-16, presented of HPLC 88. The Twelfth International Symposium on Column Liquid Chromatography, Washington, D.C., June 19–24, 1988.
59. M. N. Schmuck, M. P. Nowlan, and K. M. Gooding, *J. Chromatogr.*, 371 (1986) 55.
60. S. Hjerten, *J. Chromatogr.*, 87 (1973) 325.
61. S. Hjerten, J. Rosengren, and S. Pahlman, *J. Chromatogr.*, 101 (1974) 281.
62. N. T. Miller and B. L. Karger, *J. Chromatogr.*, 326 (1985) 45.
63. D. L. Gooding, M. N. Schmuck, M. P. Nowlan, and K. M. Gooding, *J. Chromatogr.*, 359 (1986) 331.
64. Y. Kato, T. Kitamura, and T. Hashimoto, *J. Chromatogr.*, 298 (1984) 407.
65. J. L. Fausnaugh, E. Pfannkoch, S. Gupta, and F. E. Regnier, *Anal. Biochem.*, 137 (1984) 464.
66. R. Srinivasan and E. Ruckenstein, *Sep. Purif. Methods*, 9 (1980) 267.
67. S. Hjerten, K. Yao, K.-O. Eriksson, and B. Johansson, *J. Chromatogr.*, 359 (1986) 99.
68. A. R. Nazareth, C. Mello, and R. P. McPartland, Rapid purification of monoclonal antibodies by anion-exchange HPLC. Poster 3703, presented at HPLC '86—the Tenth International Symposium on Column Liquid Chromatography, San Francisco, CA, May 18–23, 1986.
69. W. Melander and Cs. Horvath, *Arch. Biochem. Biophys.*, 183 (1977) 200.

70. J. L. Fausnaugh, L. A. Kennedy, and F. E. Regnier, *J. Chromatogr.*, 317 (1984) 141.
71. J. Porath and M. Beleu, *TIBTECH*, 5 (1987) 225.
72. T. W. Hutchens and J. Porath, *Anal. Biochem.*, 159 (1986) 217.
73. N. Miller, B. Feibush, and B. L. Karger, *J. Chromatogr.*, 316 (1985) 519.
74. Cs. Horvath, W. R. Melander, and Z. El Rassi, Presented at the 9th International Symposium on Column Liquid Chromatography, Edinburgh, Scotland, July 1–5, 1985.
75. D. R. Nau, Optimization of the hydrophobic interaction chromatographic purification of monoclonal antibodies. Presented at Prep. '89, The Sixth International Symposium on Preparative Chromatography, Washington, DC, May 8–10, 1989.
76. B. E. Conway, *Adv. Colloid Interface Sci.*, 8 (1977) 91.
77. F. A. Long and W. F. McDevit, *Chem. Rev.*, 51 (1952) 119.
78. W. A. P. Luck, in Water and Ions in Biological Systems. (A. Pullman, V. Vasileui, and L. Pakcer, eds.). Plenum, New York, 1985, p. 95.
79. T. Arakawa and S. N. Timasheff, *Biochemistry*, 24 (1985) 6756.
80. E. H. Bycher, *Chem. Weekblad.*, 39 (1942) 402.
81. F. Hofmeister, *Naunyn-Schmiedebergs Arch. Exp. Pathol. Pharmakol.*, 24 (1888) 247.
82. H. P. Jennissen and L. M. G. Heilmeyer, *Biochemistry*, 14 (1975) 754.
83. S. Peterson, *Ann. N.Y. Acad. Sci.*, 57 (1954) 144.
84. L. R. Snyder and J. J. Kirkland, Introduction to Modern Liquid Chromatography. Wiley, New York, 1979, p. 421.
85. H. Inoue and S. N. Timasheff, *Biopolymers*, 11 (1972) 737.
86. A. Guoy, *J. Phys.*, 9 (1910) 4457.
87. H. Helmholtz, *Ann. Phys.*, 7 (1879) 337.
88. O. Stern, *Z. Electrochem.*, 30 (1924) 508.
89. G. S. Manning, *Quart. Rev. Biophys.*, 11 (1978) 179.
90. M. Daune, *Stud. Biophys.*, 24/25 (1970) 287.
91. R. M. Clement, J. Sturn, and M. P. Daune, *Biopolymers*, 12 (1973) 405.
92. S. L. Wu, A. Figueroa, and B. L. Karger, *J. Chromatogr.*, 371 (1966) 3.
93. A. L. Epstein, G. S. Neave, and F. M. Chen, *J. Chromatogr.*, 444 (1985) 153.
94. M. Zeif and L. J. Crane, personal communication.
95. F. Maisano, M. Belew, and J. Porath, *J. Chromatogr.*, 321 (1985) 305.
96. S. Hjerten, *J. Chromatogr.*, 87 (1973) 325.
97. J. Porath, *J. Chromatogr.*, 443 (1988) 3.
98. M. Wilchek and T. Miron, *Biochem. Biophys. Res. Commun.*, 72 (1976) 108.
99. R. J. Yon, *Biochem. J.*, 126 (1972) 765.
100. Z. Er-el, Y. Zaidenzaig, and S. Shaltiel, *Biochem. Biophys. Res. Commun.*, 49 (1972) 3838.
101. B. H. J. Hofstee, *Anal. Biochem.*, 52 (1973) 430.
102. R. A. Rimerman and G. W. Hatfield, *Science*, 182 (1973) 1268.
103. R. Axen, J. Porath, and S. Ernback, *Nature (London)*, 214 (1967) 1302.
104. J. Porath, L. Sundberg, N. Fornstedt, and I. Olsson, *Nature (London)*, 245 (1973) 465.
105. M. Wilchek and T. Miron, *Biochem. Biophys. Res. Commun.*, 72 (1976) 108.
106. J. Porath, *Nature (London)*, 218 (1968) 834.
107. G. Halperin, M. Breitenback, M. Tauber-Finkelstein, and S. Shaltiel, *J. Chromatogr.*, 215 (1981) 211.
108. J. Porath, *J. Chromatogr.*, 376 (1986) 331.
109. C. R. Lowe, in Laboratory Techniques in Biochemistry and Molecular Biology: An Introduction to Affinity Chromatography (T. S. Work and E. Work, eds.). Elsevier North-Holland, Amsterdam, 1979, pp. 319–326, 371–373, 422, 494–498.
110. C. R. Lowe, in Laboratory Techniques in Biochemistry and Molecular Biology: An Introduction to Affinity Chromatography (T. S. Work and E. Work, eds.). Elsevier North-Holland, Amsterdam, 1979, pp. 373–379, 415, 419–421.
111. G. Haperin and S. Shaltiel, *Biochem. Biophys. Res. Commun.*, 72 (1976) 1497.

112. Z. Er-El, Y. Zaidenzaig, and S. Shaltiel, *Biochem. Biophys. Res. Commun.*, (1972).
113. H. F. Hixson and H. A. Nishikawa, *Arch. Biochem. Biophys.*, 154 (1973) 501.
114. A. H. Nishikawa, P. Bailon, and A. H. Ramel, *J. Macromol. Sci. Chem.*, A10 (1976) 149.
115. A. H. Nishikawa, *Chem. Technol.*, (1975) 565.
116. P. O'Carra and S. Barry, *FEBS Lett.*, 21 (1972) 281.
117. A. Nahum and Cs. Horvath, *J. Chromatogr.*, 203 (1981) 53.
118. H. Hemetsberger, M. Kellermann, and H. Ricken, *Chromatographia*, 10 (1977) 726.
119. W. R. Melander, K. Kalghatzi, and Cs. Horvath, *J. Chromatogr.*, 201 (1980) 201.
120. W. R. Melander and Cs. Horvath, *J. Chromatogr.*, 201 (1980) 211.
121. J. H. Knox and R. A. Hartwick, *J. Chromatogr.*, 204 (1981) 3.
122. R. S. Deelder, H. A. J. Linssen, A. P. Kronijnendijk, and J. L. M. van de Venne, *J. Chromatogr.*, 185 (1979) 241.
123. C. P. Terweij-Groen, S. Heemstra, and J. C, Kraak, *J. Chromatogr.*, 161 (1978) 69.
124. P. T. Kissinger, *Anal. Chem.*, 49 (1977) 883.
125. R. P. W. Scott and P. Kucera, *J. Chromatogr.*, 175 (1979) 51.
126. R. A. Bidlingmeyer, S. N. Deming, W. P. Price Jr., B. Sachok, and M. Petrusek, *J. Chromatogr.*, 186 (1979) 419.
127. Z. Iskandarani and D. J. Pietrzyk, *Anal. Chem.*, 54 (1982) 1065.
128. R. N. Nikolov, *J. Chromatogr.*, 286 (1984) 147.
129. J. D. Pearson, N. T. Lin, and F. E. Regnier, *Anal. Biochem.*, 124 (1982) 217.
130. C. Becker, J. Efcavitch, C. Heiner, and N. Kaiser, *J. Chromatogr.*, 326 (1985) 293.
131. T. R. Floyd, L. Yu, and R. A. Hartwick, *Chromatographia*, 21 (1986) 402.
132. R. Bischoff and L. W. McLaughlin, *J. Chromatogr.*, 270 (1983) 117.
133. R. Bischoff and L. W. McLaughlin, *J. Chromatogr.*, 296 (1983) 329.
134. L. W. McLaughlin and R. Bischoff, *J. Chromatogr.*, 418 (1987) 51.
135. W. Worthy, *Chem. Engineer. News*, December 12, (1988) 23.
136. H. Anspach, U. Gierlich, and K. K. Unger, *J. Chromatogr.*, 443 (1988) 45.
137. R. W. Stout and J. J. DeStefano, *J. Chromatogr.*, 326 (1985) 63.
138. E. Pfannkoch, K. C. Lu, F. E. Regnier, and H. G. Barth, *J. Chromatogr. Sci.*, 18 (1980) 430.
139. S. H. Chang, K. M. Gooding, and F. E. Regnier, *J. Chromatogr.*, 120 (1976) 321.
140. H. Engelhardt and D. Mathes, *Chromatographia*, 14 (1981) 325.
141. H. Engelhardt and D. Mathes, *J. Chromatogr.*, 142 (1977) 311.
142. D. E. Schmidt, R. W. Giese, D. Conron, and B. L. Karger, *Anal. Chem.*, 52 (1980) 177.
143. Y. Kato, T. Kitamura, and T. Hashimoto, *J. Chromatogr.*, 266 (1983) 49.
144. F. E. Regnier and R. Noel, *J. Chromatogr. Sci.*, 14 (1976) 316.
145. D. R. Nau and S. Kakodkar, unpublished data.
146. J-P. Bouvet, R. Pires, and J. Pillot, *J. Immunol. Methods*, 66 (1984) 299.
147. P. Roumeliotis and K. K. Unger, *J. Chromatogr.*, 185 (1979) 445.
148. P. Roumeliotis and K. K. Unger, *J. Chromatogr.*, 218 (1981) 535.
149. X. Santarelli, D. Muller, and J. Jozefonvicz, *J. Chromatogr.*, 444 (1985) 1.
150. R. J. Yon, R. J. Simmonds, and J. E. Grayson, in Hydrophobic Ion Exchange and Affinity Methods, Vol. 2 (R. Epton, ed.). Ellis Horwood Ltd, Chichester, England, 1978, p. 67.
151. R. J. Yon, *Biochem. J.*, 126 (1972) 765.
152. R. J. Yon and R. J. Simmonds, *Biochem. J.*, 151 (1975) 281.
153. A. J. Alpert and F. E. Regnier, *J. Chromatogr.*, 185 (1979) 375.
154. S. A. Berkowitz, *J. Liquid Chromatogr.*, 10 (1987) 2771.
155. M. P. Henry, this volume, Chapter 5.
156. W. Kopaciewicz, M. A. Rounds, and F. E. Regnier, *J. Chromatogr.*, 318 (1985) 157.
157. M. Colpan and D. Reisner, *J. Chromatogr.*, 296 (1984) 339.

158. Y. Kato, K. Nakamura, and T. Hashimoto, *J. Chromatogr.*, 266 (1983) 385.
159. Y. Kato, M. Sasaki, T. Hashimoto, T. Murotsu, S. Fukushige, and K. Matsubara, *J. Chromatogr.*, 265 (1983) 342.
160. Z. El Rassi and Cs. Horvath, *Chromatographia*, 19 (1984) 9.
161. S. G. Mayhew and L. G. Howell, *Anal. Biochem.*, 41 (1971) 466.
162. B. Karger, HPLC protein separations with concentrated salt mobile phases. Lecture 405, presented at The Pittsburgh Conference and Exposition on Analytical Chemistry and Applied Spectroscopy, Atlantic City, March 9–13, 1987.
163. Y-F. Maa, F. D. Antia, Z. El Rassi, and Cs. Horvath, *J. Chromatogr.*, 452 (1988) 331.
164. E. Pungor, personal communication, 1989.
165. G. Corleone and B. Swaminathan, personal communication, 1991; manuscript in preparation.
166. R. Kagel, *The Retention Times* (Rainin Instrument Company, Inc.) 1 (1977) 1.
167. A. J. Alpert, *J. Chromatogr.*, 359 (1986) 85.
168. S. K. Roy, and A. H. Nishikawa, *Biotechnol. Bioeng.*, 21 (1979) 775.
169. C. R. Lowe, S. J. Burton, J. C. Pearson, Y. D. Clonis, and V. Stead, *J. Chromatogr.*, 376 (1986) 121.
170. K. D. Kulbe and R. Schuer, *Anal. Biochem.*, 93 (1979) 46.
171. M. D. Scawen, P. M. Hammond, M. J. Corner, and A. Atkinson, *Anal. Biochem.*, 132 (1983) 413.
172. A. Cordes and M. R. Kula, *J. Chromatogr.*, 376 (1986) 375.
173. C. R. Lowe and J. C. Pearson, *Methods Enzymol.*, 104 (1984) 97.
174. P. D. G. Dean and D. H. Watson, *J. Chromatogr.*, 165 (1979) 301.
175. C. R. Lowe, D. A. P. Small, and A. Atkinson, *Int. J. Biochem.*, 13 (1981) 33.
176. S. Subramanian, in Critical Reviews in Biochemistry, Vol. 16 (B. D. Fasman, ed.). CRC Press, Boca Raton, FL, 1984, p. 169.
177. I. Lascu, H. Porumb, T. Porumb, I. Abrudan, C. Tarmure, I. Petrescu, E. Presecan, I. Proinov, and M. Telia, *J. Chromatogr.*, 283 (1984) 199.
178. S. Angal and P. D. G. Dean, *FEBS Lett.*, 96 (1978) 346.
179. E. Gianazza and P. Arnaud, *Biochem. J.*, 201 (1982) 129.
180. E. Gianazza and P. Arnaud, *Biochem. J.*, 203 (1982) 637.
181. A. E. Hanahan, L. Miribel, and P. Arnaud, *J. Chromatogr.*, 397 (1984) 197.
182. *Bio-Rad Laboratories Bulletin* (1984) 1061.
183. R. K. Scopes, *Anal. Biochem.*, 165 (1987) 235.
184. R. J. Yon, *Anal. Biochem.*, 113 (1981) 219.
185. R. K. Scopes, in Affinity Chromatography and Related Techniques (T. C. J. Gribnau, J. Visser, and R. J. F. Nivard, eds.). Elsevier, Amsterdam, 1982, p. 331.
186. R. K. Scopes, *Biochem. J.*, 161 (1977) 253.
187. Y. Hey and P. D. G. Dean, *Biochem. J.*, 209 (1983) 363.
188. R. K. Scopes and K. Griffiths-Smith, *Anal. Biochem.*, 136 (1984) 530.
189. R. K. Scopes, *J. Chromatogr.*, 376 (1986) 376.
190. J. Porath, J. Carlsson, I. Olsson, and G. Belfrage, *Nature (London)*, 258 (1975) 598.
191. N. Ramadan and J. Porath, *J. Chromatogr.*, 321 (1985) 93.
192. A. Figueroa, C. Corradini, B. Feibush, and B. L. Karger, *J. Chromatogr.*, 371 (1986) 335.
193. Z. El Rassi and Cs. Horvath, *J. Chromatogr.*, 359 (1986) 241.
194. L. Fanou-Ayi and M. Vijayalakshmi, *Ann. N.Y. Acad. Sci.*, 413 (1983) 300.
195. P. R. Coulet, J. Carlsson, and J. Porath, *Biotechnol. Bioeng.*, 23 (1981) 663.
196. J. Porath, *J. Chromatogr.*, 376 (1986) 331.
197. J. Porath, *Biotech. Prog.*, 3(1) (1987) 14.
198. J. Porath, *Biopolymers*, 26 (1987) S193.
199. B. Lonnerdal and C. L. Keen, *J. Appl. Biochem.*, 4 (1982) 203.
200. J. Porath and B. Olin, *Biochemistry*, 22 (1983) 1621.

201. P. Mohr and K. Pommerening, in *Affinity Chromatography*, Dekker, New York, 1985, p. 209.
202. E. Sulkowski, *Trends Biotechnol.*, 3 (1985) 17.
203. Cs. Horvath and Z. El Rassi, *Chromatogr. Forum*, Sept.–Oct. (1986) 49.
204. J. Porath, in Modern Methods in Protein Chemistry, Vol. 2 (H. Tschesche, ed.). Walter de Gruyter, Berlin, 1985, p. 83.
205. J. Porath and M. Belew, in Affinity Chromatography and Biological Recognition (I. M. Chaiken, M. Wilchek, and I. Parikh, eds.). Academic Press, New York, 1983, p. 175.
206. N. Ramadan and J. Porath, *J. Chromatogr.*, 321 (1985) 81.
207. J. Porath, B. Olin, and B. Granstrand, *Arch. Biochem. Biophys.*, 225 (1983) 543.
208. J. Porath, F. Maisano, and M. Belew, in The Svedberg Symposium on the Physical Chemistry of Colloids and Macromolecules (B. Ranby, ed.). IUPAC, Blackwell Scientific Publications, Oxford, 1986, Ch. 20, in press.
209. D. R. Nau, *BioChromatography*, 5(2) (1990) 62.
210. D. R. Nau, in Techniques in Protein Chemistry (T. Hugli, ed.). Academic Press, New York, 1988 (in press).
211. D. R. Nau, *BioChromatography*, 4(1) (1989) 4.
212. L. Fryklund and J. Porath, *Nature (London)*, 226 (1970) 1169.
213. J. Porath and N. Fornstedt, *J. Chromatogr.*, 51 (1970) 479.
214. D. R. Nau, *BioChromatography*, 1(2) (1986) 82.
215. D. R. Nau, in Commercial Production of Monoclonal Antibodies: A Guide for Scaling-Up Antibody Production (S. Seaver, ed.). Dekker, New York, 1987.
216. D. R. Nau, in Monoclonal Antibodies and Nucleic Acid Probes (B. Swaminathan and G. Prakash, eds.). Dekker, New York, 1989.
217. D. R. Nau, *BioChromatography*, 4(5) (1989) 266–278.
218. D. R. Nau, *BioChromatography*, 1(2) (1986) 82–94.
219. D. R. Nau, *J. Chromatogr.*, submitted.
220. D. R. Nau, *J. Chromatogr.*, submitted.
221. D. R. Nau, *J. Chromatogr.*, submitted.
222. D. R. Nau, *J. Chromatogr.*, submitted.
223. D. R. Nau, *J. Chromatogr.*, submitted.
224. D. R. Nau, D. Youngs, S. Kakodkar, J. Horvath, and H. Ramsden, unpublished data.
225. D. R. Nau, S. A. Berkowitz, S. Murphy, M. P. Henry, S. Kakodkar, and L. J. Crane, unpublished data.
226. A. H. Ross, D. Herlyn, and H. Kiprowski, *J. Immunol. Methods*, 102 (1987) 227.
227. I. Mazsaroff and F. E. Regnier, (1987), A thermodynamic study of salt effects in ion-exchange chromatography of proteins. Poster 116, presented at the Seventh International Symposium of HPLC of Proteins, Peptides and Polynucleotides, Washington, DC, November 2–4, 1987.
228. J. C. Giddings, *J. Chem. Phys.*, 26 (1957) 169.
229. M. Jaroniec, J. K. Rozylo, and W. Golkiewicz, *J. Chromatogr.*, 178 (1979) 27.
230. R. E. Boehm and D. E. Martire, *J. Phys. Chem.*, 84 (1979) 3620.
231. R. N. Nikolov, *J. Chromatogr.*, 286 (1984) 147.
232. T. Kawasaki, *Biopolymers*, 9 (1970) 277.
233. H. P. Jennissen, *J. Chromatogr.*, 159 (1978) 71.
234. X. Geng and F. E. Regnier, *J. Chromatogr.*, 296 (1984) 15.
235. R. A. Hartwick, S. A. Tomellini, S. Hsu, S. D. Fazio, R. Kaliszan, and K. Osmialowski, A rational approach to the design of HPLC separations on complex stationary phases. Paper presented at the 9th International Symposium on Column Liquid Chromatography, Edinburgh, July, 1985.
236. R. Bischoff and L. W. McLaughlin, *Anal. Biochem.*, 151 (1985) 526.
237. C. J. van Oss, R. J. Good, and M. K. Chaudhury, *Sep. Sci. Technol.*, 22 (1987) 1.
238. E. M. Liftshitz, *Dokl. Akad. Nauk. USSR*, 97 (1954) 643.
239. C. R. Lowe, in Laboratory Techniques in Biochemistry and Molecular Biology: An In-

troduction to Affinity Chromatography (T. S. Work and E. Work, eds.). Elsevier North-Holland, Amsterdam, 1979, pp. 403, 410–415, 420–421.
240. Cs. Horvath and Z. El Rassi, *Chromatogr. Forum*, 1(3) (1986) 49.
241. Z. El Rassi and Cs. Horvath, *J. Chromatogr.*, 359 (1986) 255.
242. R. W. Stringham and F. E. Regnier, *J. Chromatogr.*, 409 (1987) 305.
243. Z. El Rassi, Y-F. Maa, F. D. Antia, and Cs. Horvath, Movement of components in columns packed with mixed stationary phases in biopolymer HPLC with gradient elution. Paper 201, presented at HPLC '86 (Tenth International Symposium on Column Liquid Chromatography), San Francisco, CA, May 18–23, 1986.
244. J. K. Carlton and W. C. Bradbury, *Anal. Chem.*, 27 (1955) 67.
245. S. A. Wise, L. C. Sander, and W. E. May, *J. Liquid Chromatogr.*, 6 (1983) 2709.
246. R. K. Scopes, in Protein Purification: Principle and Practice. Springer Verlag, New York, 1982, p. 90.
247. J. Frenz and Cs. Horvath, *AIChE J.*, 31 (1985) 400.
248. Cs. Horvath, in The Science of Chromatography (F. Bruner, ed.). (Journal of Chromatography Library, Vol. 32). Elsevier, Amsterdam, 1986, pp. 179–203.
249. J. Jacobson, J. Frenz, and Cs. Horvath, *J. Chromatogr.*, 316 (1986) 53.
250. L. R. Snyder, in High Performance Liquid Chromatography—Advances and Perspectives, Vol. 1 (Cs. Horvath, ed.). Academic Press, New York, 1980, pp. 207–316.
251. P. J. Schoemakers, Optimization of Chromatographic Selectivity (Journal of Chromatography Library, Vol. 35). Elsevier, Amsterdam, 1986.
252. R. J. Laub and J. H. Purnell, *J. Chromatogr.*, 112 (1975) 71.
253. J. L. Glajch, J. J. Kirkland, K. M. Dquire, and J. M. Minor, *J. Chromatogr.*, 199 (1980) 57.
254. B. Sachok, R. C. Kong, and S. N. Deming, *J. Chromatogr.*, 199 (1980) 317.
255. R. J. Laub, J. H. Purnell, and P. S. Williams, *J. Chromatogr.*, 134 (1977) 249.
256. L. R. Snyder and J. J. Kirkland, in Introduction to Modern Liquid Chromatography. Wiley, New York, 1979, p. 694.
257. R. E. Majors, *LC-HPLC Mag.*, 2(5) (1984) 358.
258. D. H. Freeman, *Anal. Chem.*, 53 (1981) 2.
259. E. Bollin Jr. and E. Sulkowski, *J. Gen. Virol.*, 52 (1981) 227.
260. E. Bollin Jr. and E. Sulkowski, *J. Gen. Virol.*, 52 (1981) 227.
261. R. J. Dolphin, F. W. Willmontt, A. D. Mills, and L. P. J. Hoogeveen, *J. Chromatogr.*, 122 (1976) 259.
262. K. A. Ramsteiner and K. H. Bohm, *J. Chromatogr.*, 260 (1983) 33.
263. A. Heubner, O. Belovsky, H. J. Grill, and K. Pollow, *J. Steroid Biochem.*, 14 (1986) 207.
264. S. A. Berkowitz and J. Wolf, *J. Biol. Chem.*, 256 (1981) 11216.
265. A. L. Lee, A. W. Liao, and Cs. Horvath, *J. Chromatogr.*, 443 (1983) 31.
266. A. W. Liazo, Z. El Rassi, D. M. Lemaster, and Cs. Horvath, *Chromatographia*, 24 (1987) 881.
267. R. Ehrnstrom and B. Gustausson, *Am. Lab.*, April (1987) 78.
268. E. N. Lightfoot, S. J. Gibbs, M. C. M. Cockrem, and A. M. Athalye, in Protein Purification: Micro to Macro (R. Burgess, ed.). Liss, New York, 1987, p. 475.
269. T. V. Vaglione, N. Sagliano Jr., T. R. Floyd, and R. A. Hartwick, *LC-GC Mag.*, 4(4) (1986) 328.
270. S. Yammamoto, M. Nomura, and Y. Sano, *AIChE J.*, 33 (1987) 1456.
271. N. Takahashi, N. Ishioka, Y. Takaharhi, and F. W. Putnam, *J. Chromatogr.*, 326 (1985) 407.
272. L. Rybacek, M. D'Andrea, and S. J. Tarnowski, *J. Chromatogr.*, 397 (1987) 355.
273. S. K. Roy, D. V. Weber, and W. C. McGregor, *J. Chromatogr.*, 202 (1984) 225.
274. P. W. Carr, A. F. Bergold, D. A. Hanggi, and A. J. Miller, *Chromatogr. Forum*, Sept/Oct. (1986) 31.

CHAPTER 12

Protein–Protein Interactions Studied by Chromatography

Bernard Sebille, Claire Vidal-Madjar, and Alain Jaulmes

CONTENTS

12.1 INTRODUCTION

The use of chromatography for the study of interactions involving proteins has been widely developed because of the reliability of this technique. Moreover the progress of HPLC has opened new possibilities with the reduction of experimentation times. In this report, two distinct ways will be considered for interaction parameter evaluation. The first is referred to stationary phases, which separate the species by a mechanism mainly based on the size; the second one relies on the use of a column grafted with protein or ligand whose affinity to other biological macromolecular compounds is exploited. This latter case corresponds to a particular use of affinity chromatography to determine thermodynamic and kinetics interaction parameters.

These two procedures are roughly equivalent from a theoretical point of view but they differ essentially in practical applications. The choice between these procedures depends essentially on the amounts of the protein available. At the beginning, saturation techniques used large volumes of protein solutions but some progress in reducing the quantitation has permitted an extension of their application domain. Zonal elution on size exclusion, ionic, or affinity columns appears to be a more promising technique when the values of the kinetic nanometers of the system are suitable.

12.2 THE USE OF SIZE EXCLUSION CHROMATOGRAPHY FOR THE MEASUREMENT OF PROTEINS INTERACTIONS

Size exclusion chromatography (SEC) was used like other mass migration techniques (electrophoresis, sedimentation) for the study of interacting proteins. Pioneer works of Nichol and Winzor[1] and Gilbert and Kellett[2] were undertaken with soft gels such as Sephadex only available at that time.

In zonal analysis, which entails the migration of a small zone of solute, a noninteracting mixture is resolved into several peaks. In the case of reversible association between the compounds, the results depend on the interconversion rate between them. When the kinetics is slow enough for no reequilibration to occur during the experiment, the chromatographic behavior is indistinguishable from that of a noninteracting mixture. The case of hemerythrin is an example of a self-associating system with slow attainment of equilibrium[3,4] but in most cases interconversion between oligomeric species is rapid and induces a chromatographic profile similar to that for a system in which association equilibrium is established instantaneously. The major disadvantage of a zonal technique is the dilution that occurs during migration and that favors the monomeric form at the expense of polymer in the case of a rapid reversible self-association. As the migration rate is governed in SEC by the molecular volume of components, the measured elution volumes are strongly dependent on the concentration applied. Moreover the concentration elution volume dependence may result from physical interactions, namely with concentrated solutions. Then quantitative evaluations in term of stoichiometry and equilibrium constant require a better knowledge of the concentrations, that is obtained more easily by frontal analysis. This method will be explained now and some peculiar examples of zonal chromatography reported below.

12.2.1 Frontal Analysis

12.2.1.1 Subunits Association

In this method, a large amount of protein solution is injected onto a column so that the stationary phase is saturated. By recording the effluent composition it appears successively a sharp advancing edge, a plateau whose concentration is that of the injected solution, then a trailing edge (Figure 12–1). Gilbert[5,6]

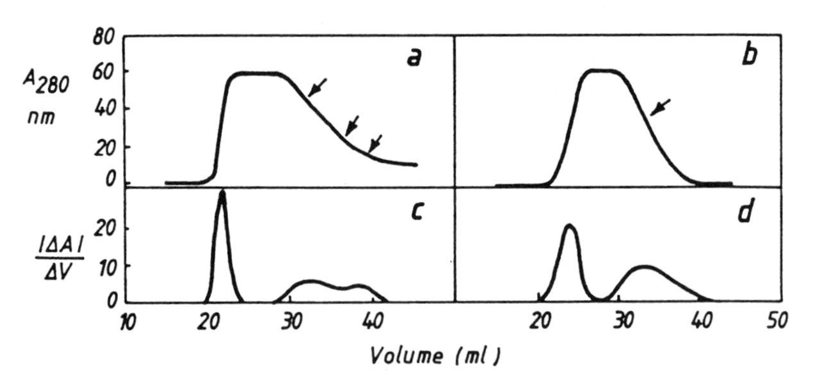

FIGURE 12–1. Elution profiles obtained in the chromatography of (a) α-chymotrypsin (3.8 g/liter) and (b) D.I.P. chymotrypsin (3.2 g/liter) on Sephadex G-100. Patterns c and d are the respective first derivative curves. Arrows indicate the inflection points. (From ref. 7.)

has first introduced the theoretical statements of this process from sedimentation experiments. These results have been illustrated with chromatographic data by Winzor and Scheraga[7] and adapted to the usual chromatographic equations by Ackers and Thompson.[8] Summarizing this later development, a rapid equilibrium is considered between monomeric M and polymeric Mn species:

$$n\mathrm{M} \Leftrightarrow \mathrm{M}n \tag{12–1}$$

with

$$K = \frac{C_{\mathrm{m}}^{n}}{C_{\mathrm{p}}} \tag{12–2}$$

with C_{m} and C_{p} being the concentration of monomer and polymer, respectively. The usual molecular sieve coefficient σ is the ratio of the amount of solute within the gel and the amount in the void volume per unit of column length. Neglecting the variation of σ with concentration, the median bisector front volume is given by

$$V_{\mathrm{e}} = V_{\mathrm{o}} + \sigma V_{\mathrm{i}} \tag{12–3}$$

where V_{o} is the void volume and V_{i} is the internal (or porous) volume. The trailing edge has a descending front at

$$V_{\mathrm{e}}' = V_{\mathrm{o}} + \sigma V_{\mathrm{i}} + S \tag{12–4}$$

where S is the volume of the injected sample.

It is observed that the chromatographic profile reveals a nonenantiography so that the trailing edge is generally less sharp than the advancing boundary. That is evidenced by the plot of the effluent concentration first derivatives.

The theoretical calculation of $\partial C_T/\partial \nu'$ with C_T, total concentration and ν' reduced volume defined by $\nu' = (V - V_o - S)/V_i$ leads to different expressions[8] depending on n values. It is stated that the plot of $\partial C_T/\partial \nu'$ as a function of ν' has a single minimum and two maximums for $n > 2$. For dimerization ($n = 2$) there is only a maximum but no minimum (Figure 12–2).

Winzor and Scheraga[7] have experimentally demonstrated the predictions of Gilbert[5,6] by studying the chromatographic behavior of ovalbumin, chymotrypsin, and diisopropyl-phosphoryl (DIP) chymotrypsin (Figure 12–1).

The derivative patterns of the trailing edge evidence as in Figure 12–3, the presence of two maximums in the curve of $\partial C_T/\partial V'$ as a function of the elution volume V', and the position of one maximum (fast moving peak) depend on the overall protein concentration as predicted by Gilbert[5] from sedimentation techniques. A similar study of ovalbumin reveals the absence of self-association owing to the independence of the shape of the advancing and trailing edges with concentration.

A quantitative analysis of the self-association of carboxyhemoglobin was achieved by Ackers and Thomson[8] by the use of frontal analysis. Considering the centroid volume $\bar{V}$ of the hypersharp leading boundary, it can be written

$$\bar{V} = V_o + \bar{\sigma}_w V_i \qquad (12\text{–}5)$$

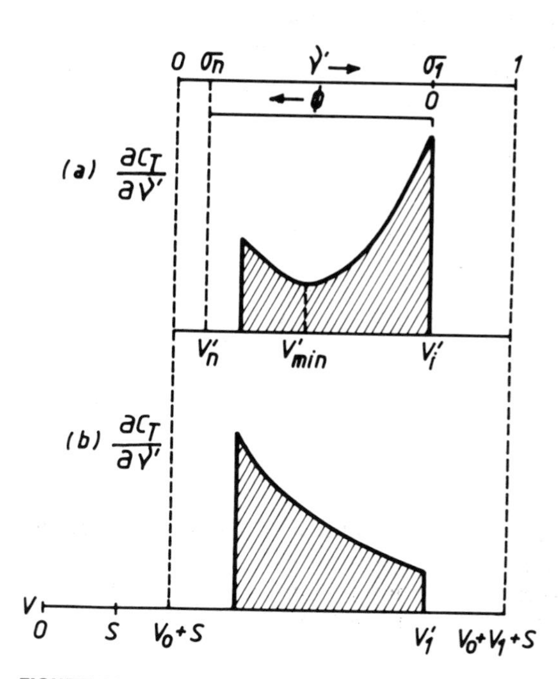

FIGURE 12–2. Ideal concentration gradient patterns for the trailing edge of a solute zone when monomer is in reversible equilibrium with a single polymeric species. (a) corresponds to $n > 2$; (b) $n = 2$. (From ref. 8.)

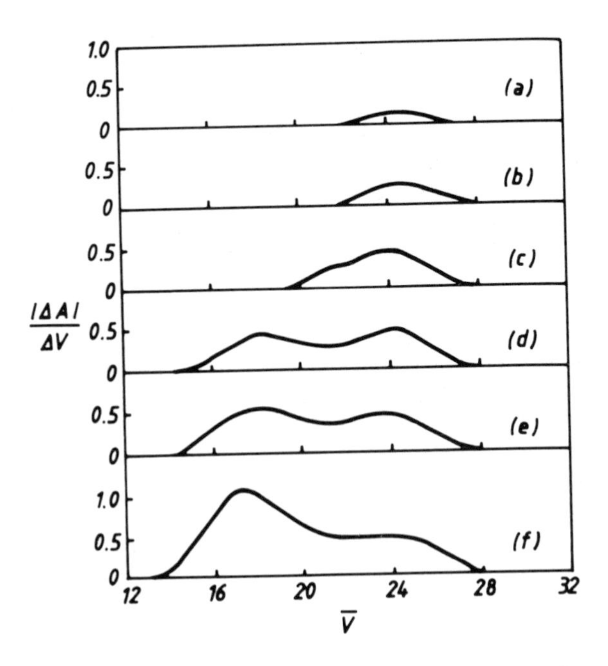

FIGURE 12–3. Derivative patterns of the trailing edge of the protein zone in the chromatography of α-chymotrypsin at various concentrations on Sephadex G-100. (a) 0.6, (b) 1.2, (c) 1.4, (d) 2.8, (e) 3.4, (f) 5.0 g/liter. (From ref. 7.)

$\bar{\sigma}_w$ is the weight average of the molecular sieve coefficient. This coefficient depends on the dissociation by

$$\bar{\sigma}_w = \sigma_p + \alpha(\sigma_m - \sigma_p) \quad (12\text{–}6)$$

where σ_p and σ_m are the polymer and monomer coefficients, respectively, and α is the weight fraction of monomeric species in the plateau region. Then,

$$\bar{V} = V_o + [\sigma_p + \alpha(\sigma_m - \sigma_p)]V_i = \alpha V_m + (1 - \alpha)V_p \quad (12\text{–}7)$$

with V_m and V_p the centroid volume of leading edge for pure monomer or polymer, respectively.

From the experimental measurements of $\bar{V}$, V_m, V_p the fraction is easily obtained and the association constant K is calculated from:

$$K = \frac{\alpha^n C_T^{n-1}}{1 - \alpha} \quad (12\text{–}8)$$

if n is known.

If it is not the case, Winzor et al.[9] have suggested a simple solution. As

$$K = \frac{C_p}{C_m^n} = \frac{C_0 - C_m}{C_m^n} \tag{12–9}$$

$$\log(C_0 - C_m) = n \log C_m - \log K \tag{12–10}$$

C_m is given by

$$C_m = \alpha C_0 = \frac{C_0(\overline{V} - V_p)}{V_m - V_p} \tag{12–11}$$

A plot of $\log(C_0 - C_m)$ versus $\log C_m$ should be linear and gives from the ordinate intercept and slope the values of n and K.

The experimental determination of V_m is very possible from dilute solutions where the protein is fully dissociated or by extrapolation methods. For V_p, the use of high concentration induces sometimes only partial boundary resolution so that Ackers[8] has suggested combining the data from two columns of different bed volumes.

Several examples of applications of these methods have been reported. The following proteins can be mentioned: carboxyhemoglobin dimerization, α-chymotrypsin hexamer–monomer,[9] bovine arylsulfatase tetramer,[10] *E. coli* alkaline phosphatase,[11] and bovine neurophysin dimer associations.[12]

Some additional features of these chromatographic processes must be taken into consideration to avoid any error in the association parameters determination. The more striking point is the slight increase of the leading edge elution volume for highly concentrated protein solutions even for individual species. This is exemplified with chymotrypsin[13] and oxyhemoglobin,[14] whose variation of retention is roughly linearly dependent of the concentration for every monomeric or polymeric subunit (Figure 12–4). The experimental relationship is given by

$$V = V_o(1 + gC) \tag{12–12}$$

where V_o is the V extrapolated value of elution volume species for $C \to 0$, C is the total concentration, and g is positive and generally independent of the n value.

Gilbert[15] had previously introduced a calculation simulating a monomer–dimer association in the case of a gel permeation experiment with the consideration of elution volume–concentration dependence. In the course of a very complete study of oxyhemoglobin behavior including sedimentation and chromatographic experiments, Chiancone et al.[14] concluded that an analysis of the results based on the independence of the g coefficient with n-mer did not permit a decision on a dissociation model involving dimer or tetramer with concentrated solutions. For the more diluted domain (down to 0.009 mg ml^{-1}), where dimer–monomer equilibrium predominates, the authors have determined the association parameters.

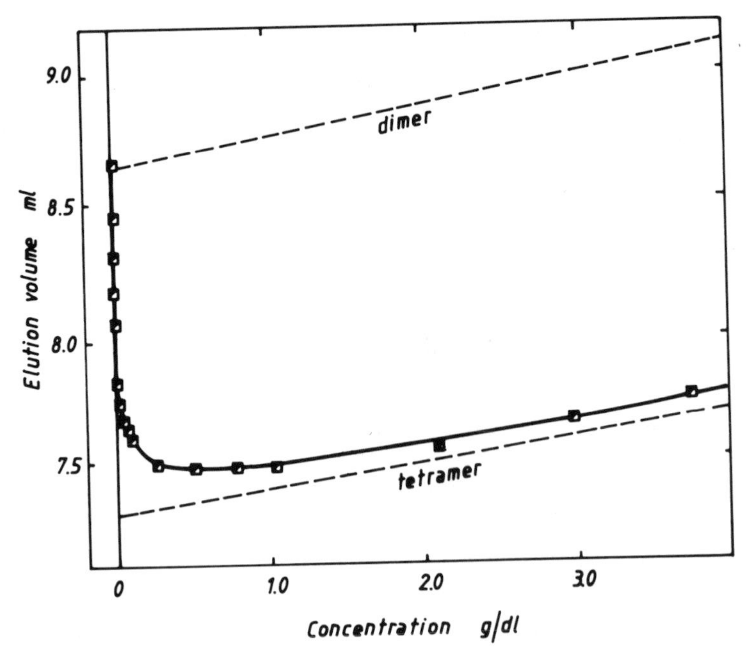

FIGURE 12–4. Elution volume as a function of human hemoglobin concentration. (From ref. 14.)

The concentration dependence of elution volume even in the absence of chemical association has been first traced to osmotic shrinkage of the soft gel beads.[16–18] This physical phenomenon was interpreted in terms of the Flory gel swelling theory[19] from which a simple equation is derived:

$$\frac{C_s^0}{C_s} = 1 - G\left(\frac{\pi_e}{RT}\right) \qquad (12\text{–}13)$$

where C_s is the internal gel concentration (reciprocal of the inner volume per gram), C_s^0 is the internal gel concentration in the absence of external osmotic pressure, and G is a constant that can be measured from experiments with various concentrations of totally excluded solute in order to change the present external osmotic pressure π_e.

This equation evidences the dependence of gel porosity in the presence of increasing protein solution and the consequence on retention volumes. Despite the derivation of accurate calculations,[18] some assumptions limit the validity of this analysis: first, the partition coefficients σ_m and σ_p are considered to be unaffected by the osmotic shrinkage and second, the thermodynamic nonideality of concentration is not taken into consideration. Only a qualitative accordance of the theoretical predictions with experimental results have been obtained in the study of bacterial α-amylase dimerization with BioGel P-150.[20]

To avoid the complications due to osmotic shrinkage, the use of porous rigid glass beads is recommended for a careful study of interactions from chromatography. Several sets of experiments were achieved to characterize the association involving ovalbumin and bovine or human oxyhemoglobin. The results of Nichol et al.[21] on ovalbumin, provided with controlled-pore glass beads, reveal a linear relationship between elution volume of the sharp boundary and protein concentration.

It is therefore recommended that even in the absence of any shrinkage, a variation of the partition coefficient arises. This effect is explained by a variation of the activity coefficient with the total concentration. The partition equilibrium requires chemical potential equality in every phase. It means that the ratio between thermodynamic activities of solute in the stationary and mobile phases is constant.

Owing to the variation of activity coefficient the partition coefficient (concentration ratio in every phase) is expected to vary with concentration. In the case of a single noninteracting solute Nichol et al.[21] have calculated the partition coefficient σ_i:

$$\sigma_i = \sigma_i^0 \exp \frac{\alpha_{ii}}{M_i} C_i(1 - \sigma_i) \qquad (12\text{–}14)$$

where σ_i^0 is the value of σ_i for infinite dilution, M_i is the molecular weight of i species, C_i is the concentration, and α_{ii} is the thermodynamic nonideality coefficient.

From this expression, it appears that σ_i increases with C_i as a consequence of nonideal effects arising from steric and charge interactions. A good agreement between calculated and experimental values was observed.[21]

If self-association of solute occurs, a simplification to the theoretical analysis may be introduced when a stationary phase excluding all polymers is used. This gives a simplified value of the weight-average partition coefficient $\overline{\sigma}$:

$$\overline{\sigma} = \frac{\sigma_1 C_1}{C} \qquad (12\text{–}15)$$

σ_1 and C_1 are monomer partition coefficient and concentration, respectively; C is the total protein concentration.

After a preliminary determination of σ_1 with very dilute solutions, the measurement of C_i is obtained from $\overline{\sigma}$ and C.

The determination of monomer concentration permits fitting several association constants with the experimental results.

Such measurements have been done for glutamate dehydrogenase[21a] and are interpreted as a series of polymers in rapid association equilibrium with the same association constant (isodesmic indefinite self-association) (Figure 12–5). The consequence of this association is to lower the penetration of solute into the gel. The study of oxyhemoglobin has been undertaken by a similar approach[21b] using an evaluation of activity coefficient from Stokes radius of the protein. This study concludes an association of hemoglobin units ($\alpha_2\beta_2$) either on dimeric forms or isodesmic oligomers. In a complementary analysis,[21c] the same authors have concluded that an indefinite association of $\alpha_2\beta_2$ units is favored both for oxy- and deoxyhemoglobin.

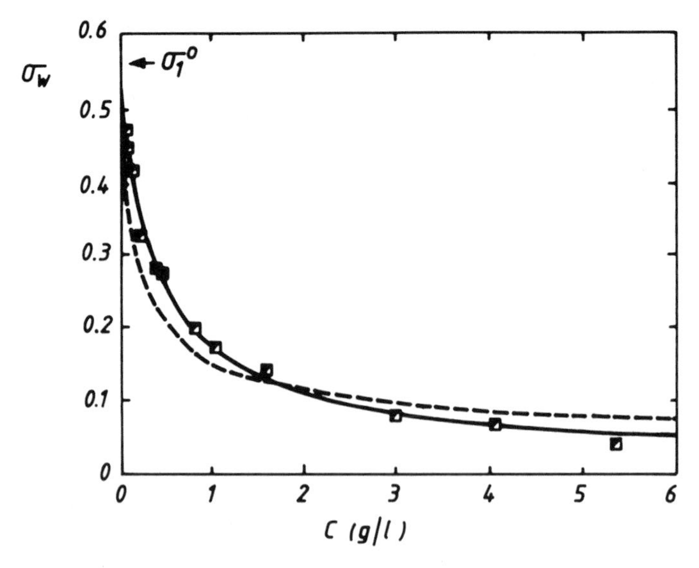

FIGURE 12–5. Dependence of partition coefficient σ_w of bovine liver glutamate dehydrogenase on total protein concentration. Solid line: theoretical curve referring to an isodesmic self-association. Broken line: theoretical curve for a monomer–dimer model. (From ref. 21a.)

Summarizing the Nichol and Winzor developments, it can be said that in the absence of nonideal effects, the self-association causes the partition coefficient to decrease with increasing protein concentration while nonideality effects give rise to an increase of the partition coefficient with protein concentration.

The assignment of the partition coefficient lowering to a protein self-association has been criticized by Minton[22] by taking the model of spherical particle in the vicinity of a hard wall described by Snook and Henderson.[23] In the Minton model, it is considered that the mean density of particles immediately adjacent to the wall is greater than the bulk density of the fluid. It is the case inside the pores that induces an exclusion effect that lowers the partition coefficient. From the data of Nichol and co-workers,[21b] Minton[22] concluded that the change of concentration can be explained only by a surface layer effect that repels the protein molecules by an exclusion volume effect in two rather than three dimensions. This analysis did not permit choosing between surface effect or self-association to explain the hemoglobin chromatographic behavior. Therefore the ability of hemoglobin to gel in highly concentrated phosphate solutions[24] suggests that the multiple association-based model is more realistic.

To measure the self-association of proteins *differential migration techniques* have been introduced for the comparison of very similar associating species. This layer technique in gel filtration is based on velocity migration differences rather than absolute migration rates. This was first described by Gilbert[25] from gel filtration experiments. A steady-state flow of a solution of one hemoglobin (human) is first set up through a gel column, followed by a second flow of another hemoglobin (sheep) at the same concentration. Due to a difference in the association state, the front velocity of the second protein differs from the first, so that a dip appears on the record if the second protein is more dissociated. In the opposite case, a hump is observed. The surface of the dip or hump is given by $C\Delta V$, with C the protein concentration and ΔV the difference of frontal elution volume of each protein. As stated above, frontal elution volumes are proportional to the dissociation degree so that

$$\Delta V = V_a - V_b = \alpha_a - \alpha_b(V_2 - V_4) \qquad (12\text{–}16)$$

α_a and α_b are the degrees of dissociation of the proteins. V_2 and V_4 are elution volumes of dimer and tetramer, respectively.

The experimental determination of ΔV from surface measurements gives a simple way to compare the association state of the two proteins and concludes a higher dissociation of sheep oxyhemoglobin than that of the human analogous protein.

Similar experimentations were reported by Lovell and Winzor[26] for the comparison of rabbit muscle and beef heart lactate dehydrogenase associations. Figure 12–6 refers to the study of Gattoni et al.[27] on *Scaphorca inaequivalvis* (bivalve mollusc) oxyhemoglobin as compared to oxyhemoglobin A. The higher association of the former protein and its relative insensitivity to the salt present in the solution are then evidenced.

The main merit of this technique is to reveal subtle differences of similar protein self-associations. From a qualitative point of view, the method is very sensitive and easily indicates the sign of the difference. Quantitative determinations need accurate measurements of the dip or hump surface. From Figure 12–6 it appears that the dispersion of the experimental points influences the determination of the association constant. The progress of continuous integrating recorders and the use of rigid chromatographic gel could afford decisive improvements.

12.2.1.2 Association between Dissimilar Proteins

Many complexes involving proteins have to be characterized since they occur in several biological processes such as immunochemical, inducer–repressor interactions or association of enzymes with effectors or substrates. Several procedures using chromatography have been developed for the analysis of such systems.

Nichol and Winzor[28] have introduced the results of a study concerning mixtures of ovalbumin and lysozyme. This experimentation is based on the frontal analysis of a protein mixture saturation of a gel filtration column (Sephadex G-100). A typical chromatogram is presented in Figure 12–7. The presence of association is revealed by a change in the advancing front of lysozyme and the lowering of concentration of this protein in the trailing front of the diagram. Moreover a nonenantiography of the advancing and trailing edges of the pattern is revealed.

The theoretical aspects of the problem have been analyzed by Gilbert and Jenkins[29] and demonstrate that, in the absence of a dependence of velocity with protein concentration, the slower boundary represents the pure slow

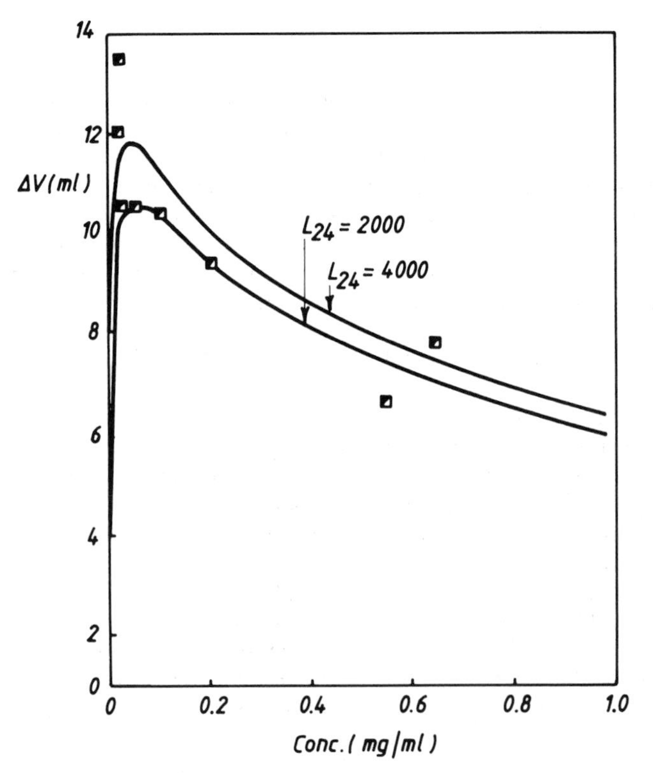

FIGURE 12–6. Difference gel filtration of hemoglobin HbA vs. *S. inaequivalvis* hemoglobin. Δ: experimental elution volume difference. Solid lines: theoretical curves corresponding to the indicated dimer–tetramer association constants in dl/g. (From ref. 27.)

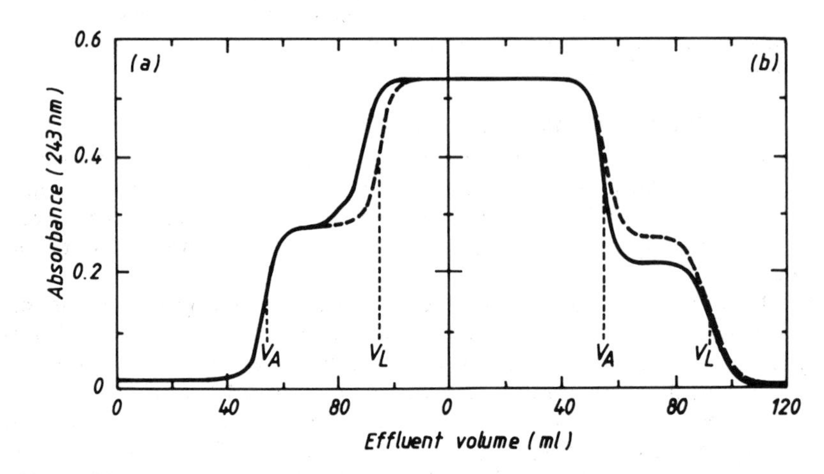

FIGURE 12–7. Frontal gel chromatography of a mixture of ovalbumin (9.6 μM) and lysozyme (9.7 μM) at pH 6.8. Solid lines: experimental profiles for the interacting mixture. Broken lines: corresponding patterns for a noninteracting mixture. V_A and V_L denote the elution volumes of ovalbumin and lysozyme, respectively. (From refs. 28a and 28b.)

reactant. It means that the measurement of lysozyme concentration (Figure 12–7) from the last plateau height (β zone) gives the value of the free protein concentration in the domain of the total mixture, including complex and free components. From a calculation based on the mass conservation of every species and the specific measurement of ovalbumin and lysozyme in the different zones, the complex concentration is given by

$$(\text{complex}) = C^{\alpha}_{\text{LYS}} - C^{\beta}_{\text{LYS}} \qquad (12\text{–}17)$$

so that the association constant is

$$K = \frac{(\text{complex})}{(\text{LYS})\,(\text{OVA})} = \frac{(\text{complex})}{C^{\beta}_{\text{LYS}} - [(C_{\text{OVA}} - \text{complex})]} \qquad (12\text{–}18)$$

This analysis avoids the use of the velocity or elution volume of the different species.

From these measurements, an association constant (2.5×10^4 at pH 6.2) has been measured in good accordance with the results of sedimentation experiments achieved in the same work and based on a similar theoretical approach.

These results have been submitted to a new analysis by the same authors,[30] taking into account the dependence of each species velocity with the total protein concentration. This effect was originally pointed out by Johnson and Ogston,[31] who had noticed that in sedimentation experiments, different velocities pertain to the slower solute when it moves alone or in a mixture. It is the case in chromatographic experiments even with nonchemically interacting solutes as evidenced by Winzor and Nichol[32] in the case of a mixture of ovalbumin with dextran. Figure 12–8 illustrates this behavior and shows clearly that albumin concentration is lower in the α zone (containing all the equilibrium components) than in the β zone where ovalbumin is alone. This observation indicates the overestimation of the amount of slower moving species when based only on the plateau height.

To obtain more precise measurements, Johnson and Ogston[31] suggested considering a linear relationship between the velocity of each species and the overall accompanying protein concentration. Nichol et al.[30] experimentally measured the dependence of elution volume of several proteins with their concentration or the presence of another protein. In most cases, they observed a linear dependence of the elution volume on the sum of protein concentration present in the mixture. Then the experiments concerning ovalbumin–lysozyme interaction were analyzed again by applying corrective factors. The calculations are based on experimental measurements of the elution volume of boundaries for the different species in the presence of increasing protein concentration under conditions in which chemical interactions are present or canceled by changing the pH value.

The elution volumes thus determined permit an interactive calculation of the concentrations at equilibrium and give an association constant that was found to be significantly different from the previous determinations.

By studying ovalbumin–myoglobin interaction, Gilbert and Kellet[33] stated a simple relationship between the concentration of the slower protein (myoglo-

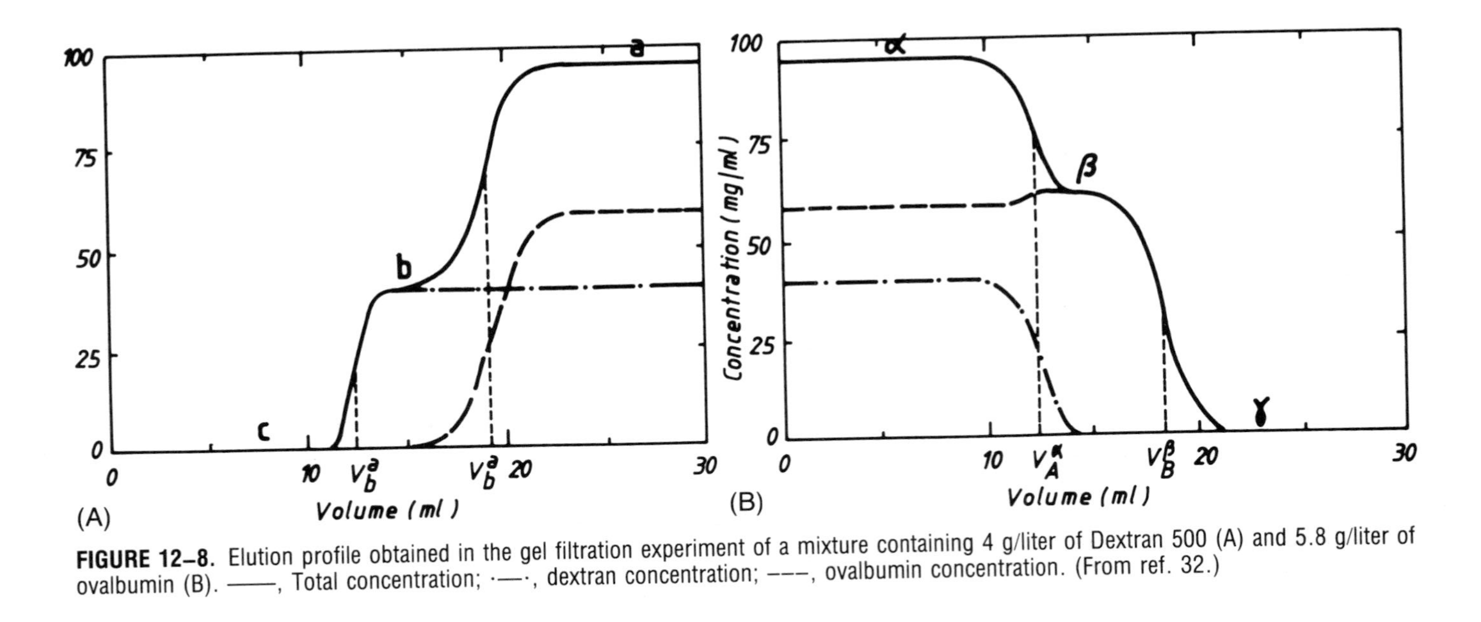

FIGURE 12–8. Elution profile obtained in the gel filtration experiment of a mixture containing 4 g/liter of Dextran 500 (A) and 5.8 g/liter of ovalbumin (B). ——, Total concentration; ·—·, dextran concentration; ---, ovalbumin concentration. (From ref. 32.)

bin) in the complex domain and its concentration in the last plateau where it is alone. This equation is

$$C^{\alpha}(\overline{V} - V^{\alpha}) = C^{\beta}(\overline{V} - V^{\beta}) \tag{12–19}$$

where V^{β} is the elution volume of myoglobin trailing edge, V^{α} is the similar elution volume measured in the absence of interactions with ovalbumin (pH 4), and $\overline{V}$ is the boundary $\alpha\beta$ elution volume.

This equation is similar to that of Johnson and Ogston[31] by replacing the velocity of each compound by its elution volume as theoretically demonstrated by Gilbert.[34]

A calculation of the association constant is then possible[33] from only the concentrations and avoiding the uncertainty of elution volume measurements. By measuring the effluent absorbance at different wavelengths (280 and 409 nm) accurate specific concentration determinations were possible so that the equilibrium constant was calculated easily. A careful study of the influence of concentration on elution volume of each protein alone has revealed a strong dependence as already pointed out.

Moreover the successive injections of differently concentrated solutions as previously described by Chiancone et al.[14] evidence the presence of electrostatic interactions arising with increasing protein concentration and depressed by high ionic strengths. As the contributions of interactions can be considered as separate and additive, the elution volume of each boundary is given by an equation similar to that reported above [Eq. (12–12)] with some difference in g value for the contribution of ovalbumin or myoglobin.[33]

The study of highly concentrated mixtures of myoglobin and ovalbumin reveals the complexity of the problem due to nonideal effects that would necessitate a complete calculation with numerical integration to simulate the experimental profiles. Indeed the assumptions of independent and additive effects should be revised to reach a good coincidence. Nevertheless provided moderately concentrated solutions are used, the frontal analysis method described gives good estimations of association constants.

12.2.2 Saturation Methods

12.2.2.1 Direct Column Scanning

A method for the binding ratio determination between macromolecular components and small ligand species or protein subunits was introduced first by Brumbaugh and Ackers.[35] It is based on the saturation of a gel permeation column and the readings are obtained from the direct optical scanning of a section of the column including both gel and mobile phase. The chromatographic system is equivalent to an equilibrium dialysis with the void volume corresponding to the compartment containing the macromolecular compound and unbound ligand. A schematic diagram of the device is represented in Figure 12–9.

Principle The column is saturated with a solution containing ligand and macromolecule. The gel porosity is chosen so that all the polymer species with bound ligand are excluded. When the binding ratio is high, the ligand does

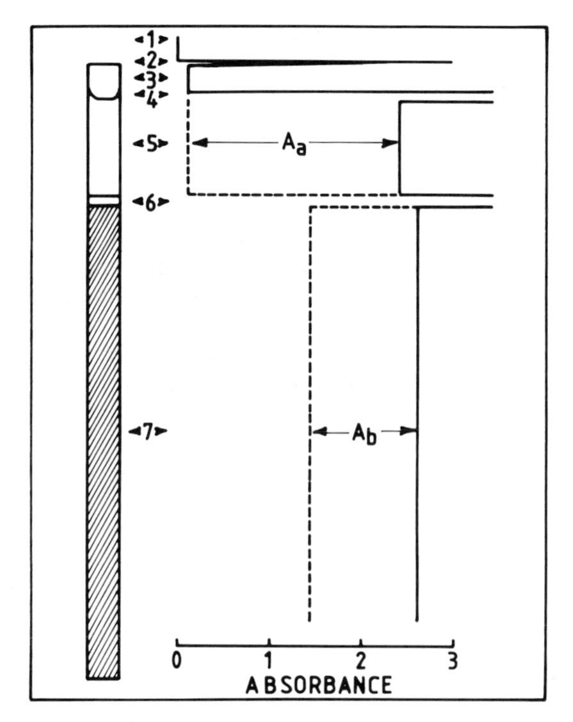

FIGURE 12–9. Schematic diagram of a gel filtration column and idealized scan. Solid trace represents absorbance of column saturated with solution. A_a is the absorbance of solution above column bed. A_b is the absorbance within column bed. (From ref. 35.)

not penetrate the gel and the column absorbance is small. By optically scanning the equilibrated column, the absorbance measurement yields the binding ratio. Two zones of the column are mainly measured: the liquid above gel whose absorbance A_a is related to the initial mixture, and the gel bed absorbance A_b corrected from the line absorbance measured in the absence of protein and ligand. A partition cross section is defined by the solute distribution volume per unit distance along the column axis and measured as $\xi = A_b/A_a$. This permits the free ligand determination after separate measurements of ξ_p and ξ_L for protein and ligand. If necessary, corrections for possible nonspecific binding ligand to the gel must be made.

The Brumbaugh and Ackers method has been extended to the study of subunit hemoglobin associations. The experimental device was modified[36] and contains two cells with gel and one reference (Figure 12–10). The absorbance measurements necessitate a very high accuracy since they have to be applied to very dilute protein solutions (in the case of high association rates) in the presence of absorbing gel (as high as 2 OD units at 215 nm). The apparatus is based on a single photon spectrophotometer with amplifier and computer.

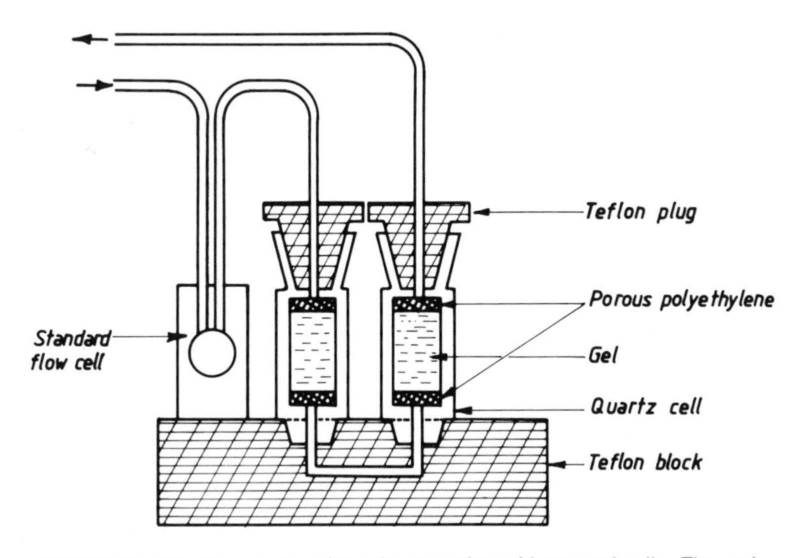

FIGURE 12–10. Flow system for gel permeation with two gel cells. The optical beam is perpendicular to the plane of this diagram. (From ref. 36.)

When several subunits interact to give i-mer with an association constant K_i, due to the different penetration of each species into the gel, a weight average partitioning cross section is observed:

$$\xi_w = \frac{\sum_1^n i\xi_i K_i (m_1)^i}{\sum_1^n i K_i (m_1)^i} \qquad (12\text{–}20)$$

with m_1 molar monomer concentration.

$K_i = (m_i)/(m_1)^i$ is the association constant of i-mer. The partition coefficient $\xi_w = A_b/A_a$ is measured by scanning as described above and plotted as a function of the total concentration $C_T = \Sigma_i(m_i)$. A nonlinear square analysis yields the best fit values of stoichiometry and association constant.

Applications Using this technique, the authors performed several applications. First, the association constant of the dimer–tetramer association is easily determined from the basic equation:

$$\xi_W = \xi_T + f_D(\xi_D - \xi_T) \qquad (12\text{–}21)$$

with ξ_T and ξ_D partition cross sections of tetramer and dimer, respectively, and f_D the fraction of dimer.

Then the dissociation constant is calculated from

$$^4K_2 = \frac{f_D^2 C_T}{(1 - f_D)} \qquad (12\text{–}22)$$

This method has been shown to have an upper limit of determination about $10^9\,M^{-1}$ and was convenient for the dimer–tetramer association of hemoglobin but not deoxyhemoglobin ($K_a = 10^{10}$–$10^{12}\,M^{-1}$). The same method was very able to determine association values for mutant or chemically modified hemoglobin, which presents a large reduction in the stability of the $\alpha_1\beta_2$ contact.

Other examples of application concern the influence of partial oxygen saturation[37] on the dimer–tetramer equilibrium constant and the ligand-linked subunits association of isolated hemoglobin chains.[38]

Despite the originality and usefulness of Brumbaugh and Ackers's technique, it must be emphasized that it necessitates a special device and is restricted to soft gels the transparency of which enables absorbance measurements.

12.2.2.2 Recycle Chromatography

The limitations caused by the sophisticated equipment described above were overcome by Ford and Winzor[39] who introduced a recycle gel partition technique using a common flow cell for the absorbance measurements. This ingenious method is based on recording the mixture of interacting compounds having saturated a stirred gel slurry. The first application was devoted to methyl orange (MO)–bovine serum albumin binding measurements. The apparatus is depicted in Figure 12–11 and for the sake of simplicity we will summarize the principle of the technique with the example of this ligand–protein binding.

The gel is chosen so that the protein is excluded and only MO penetrates the pores. After equilibration with a buffered solution, a volume V_a of MO solution is injected and the absorbance is noted after attainment of a constant value. Further aliquots of MO solution are successively added and the corresponding absorbance is measured. For each experiments the partition coefficient of MO is calculated from

$$\sigma = \frac{V_a(ms)_a - V_m(ms)_m}{V_g(ms)_m} \tag{12–23}$$

where $(ms)_a$ is the concentration of MO solution injected, $(ms)_m$ is the MO concentration in the mobile phase, and V_m and V_g are the respective volumes of mobile phase and gel phase determined by independent experiments.

This calibration gives for all circumstances the ligand concentration in the mobile phase from the amount retained by the gel.

Recycling experiments with a known concentration of bovine serum albumin yield a series of values $(\overline{ms})_m$ for the total ligand concentration in the mobile phase.

The amount of dye within the gel is obtained from mass conservation considerations and the preceding calibration gives the free MO concentration in the mobile phase (ms). The binding function is then

$$\bar{r} = \frac{(\overline{ms}) - (ms)}{m_A} \tag{12–24}$$

where m_A is the protein concentration.

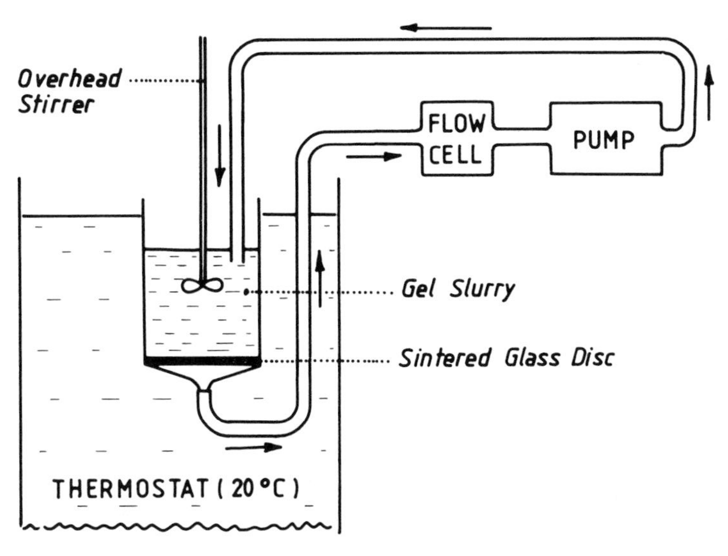

FIGURE 12–11. Recycling gel partition system. (From ref. 39.)

The same technique was recently applied by Hogg and Winzor[40] to the study of dextran–concanavalin A interaction with a column containing porous glass beads (Glyceryl C.P.G.), the porosity of which excludes the dextran so that the protein plays the role of ligand.

According to previous theoretical calculations of Nichol et al.[41] and Winzor et al.[42] the multivalency of the ligand modifies the usual equation of binding ratio, which becomes

$$\bar{r} = \frac{(\overline{ms})^{1/f} - (ms)^{1/f}}{m_A} \qquad (12\text{–}25)$$

where f is the ligand valency.

A similar experimentation was achieved to evaluate the binding of hemoglobin to a monoclonal antibody antihemoglobin by using Sephadex G-100. This gel meets the requirements that the ligand hemoglobin is able to penetrate only the gel.

In both experiments, a generalized Scatchard analysis for multivalent ligand was used and has led to the association constant evaluation. The main merit of this analytical process is to eliminate the curvilinearity of the conventional Scatchard plot when multivalent ligands are concerned and to replace it by a linear format giving the association constant with good accuracy.

It must be stressed that this technique is of value with small amounts of material. For instance the aliquots of antihemoglobin antibody had a volume of 50 μl with a concentration of 196 μ*M* while the concentration of hemoglobin was 0.94 m*M* in 10 ml of mobile phase (gel volume = 0.4 ml).

The main merit of this recycling technique over the others is to achieve the gel saturation with small volumes. The fundamental question remains the validity of the ligand calibration in the presence of the other constituent as already mentioned in frontal analysis.

12.2.2.3 Vacancy Chromatography

The development of rigid supports in high-performance liquid chromatography has incited us to use these materials by saturation methods. As the beads are generally opaque the direct scanning technique is not possible. To avoid the problems of concentration measurements by frontal analysis we preferred a vacancy peak method that we applied to protein ligand[43] and protein subunit association determinations.[44]

In this technique, a small volume of solvent (aqueous buffer) is injected on a size exclusion chromatographic column saturated by the mixture under study, which plays the role of eluent. The effluent absorbance is scanned at the column outside by a photometric detector.

This saturation method was extended to the determination of the association constant of tetramer–dimer subunits of hemoglobin.[44] Indeed in the case of a rapid equilibrium, the saturation of a column by a hemoglobin solution gives one negative peak when a few microliters of solvent are injected (Figure 12–12). The elution volume V of this peak depends on the penetration of the solute into the pore and can be connected to the tetramer dissociation fraction.

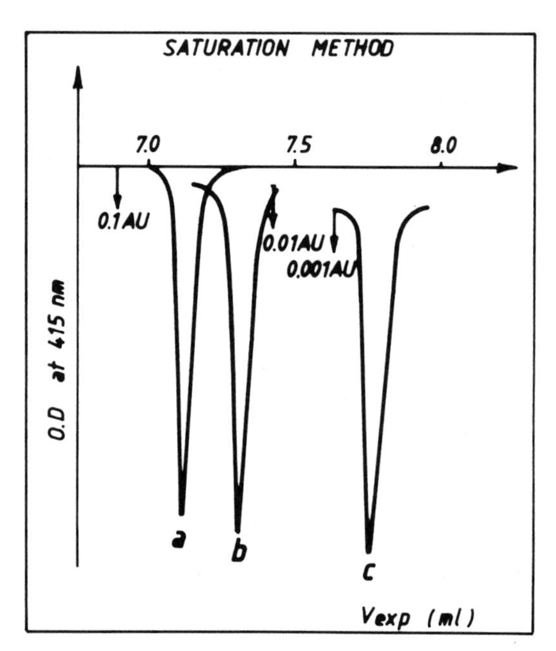

FIGURE 12–12. Saturation method for the measurement of hemoglobin retention volume. (a) $Hb(O_2)$ 10^{-5} M; detector sensitivity $s = 1$; (b) $Hb(O_2)$ 10^{-6} M ($s = 0.1$); (c) Hb (O_2) 10^{-7} M ($s = 0.01$). (From ref. 44.)

As a matter of fact, $V = V_0 + \sigma V_p$ from the usual chromatographic equation and

$$\sigma = (1 - \alpha)\sigma_D + \sigma_T \tag{12–26}$$

σ_D and σ_T are the molecular sieve coefficient of dimer and tetramer, respectively.

This equation theoretically demonstrated[44] is formally identical to that of Ackers and Thomson.[8] From the experimental measurement of V, α is then calculated and gives the dissociation contant:

$$^4K_2 = 4\frac{C_0\alpha^2}{1 - \alpha} \tag{12–27}$$

where C_0 is the concentration of hemoglobin tetramer.

Several successive experiments with differently concentrated hemoglobin solutions led to a mean value of $^4K_2$, in good agreement with the previous values of Ackers.[35]

The main interest of this method is that it can be achieved with standard HPLC equipment. The use of rigid stationary phases reduces the time of experimentation as compared to columns filled with soft gels. Its application is limited by the amount of protein available since the column must be saturated. In the case of our own experience with a 30 × 7.5 cm column, about 50 ml of protein solution is needed. For the measurements with several protein solutions several hundred milligrams of protein is necessary. When highly associated proteins are under study, lesser amounts are convenient since more diluted solutions are sufficient. We discuss below a zonal elution technique that opens the way to the study of a minute amount of protein.

12.2.3 Zonal Chromatography

12.2.3.1 Equilibrium Constants

Zonal chromatography has a major advantage on saturation techniques for it requires only minute amounts of proteins to give a lot of information about the compounds present in the injected sample. For the study of interacting species, the results depend on two factors. First, the dilution that occurs during zonal migration prevents a precise knowledge of the concentration and increases the dissociation of interacting species when they are differently retained by the stationary phase. The second point deals with the kinetics of association–dissociation reactions that compete with the separation process so that the resulting chromatographic pattern depends on the relative kinetic rates of these exchanges.

Experimental determination of protein–protein interaction is divided into two classes according to kinetic characteristics. When complex dissociation is slow as compared to chromatographic exchange it is not distributed by the elution across the column. The use of HPLC made the application of this method easier since the time of residence in the column is smaller than with conventional equipment. Thus the monomer–dimer equilibrium of *Streptomyces* subtilisin was studied by Akasaka et al.[45] A chemical modification (nitration) of the tyrosine residue changes the p*K* of this site so that for a given pH, the electric charge is modified. The chromatographic separation of modified, unmodified, and hybrid protein is achieved on an ion-exchange high-performance column. As the dimeric complex is stable and dissociates very slowly the equilibrium is considered as unchanged by passing onto the column.

The rate constants (assumed to be independent from the chemical modification) are determined from the elution profiles corresponding to successive injections at different times (from 50 to 500 h) after mixing the modified and unmodified protein.

In a similar way Murakami et al.[46] used an SEC HPLC column for the study of a renin–renin binding protein complex. The influence of pH, salts, and temperature was measured after increasing the time of incubation and the percentage of complex conversion was quantified according to these parameters. Ingham[47] applied the same technique for the measurement of different reactions of interacting proteins: dissociation of human chorionic gonadotropin subunits, aggregation of various protein inhibitors, and the ability of antithrombin III to bind heparin.

In every case, the recombination is too slow to cause any significant change in the association during the chromatographic transfer (10–20 min) and the complex kinetic parameters can be measured from chromatographic experiments scanned at different times. However, when rapid equilibria are involved in zonal chromatography, the profiles are influenced by the penetration in the stationary phase and the dilution.

To minimize the dissociating effect during the transfer, Tojo et al.[48] suggested using a short column (75 mm) with a high resolving power (TSK Coll 3000 SW). A correlation between the distribution coefficient and the Stokes radius of several proteins was first stated and the study of the flavoenzyme D-amino-acid-oxidase was then undertaken. No limit for the radius values was observed even for the highest concentration values. On the other hand diluted samples correspond to the apparent molecular volume of the monomeric unit. This qualitative study concerning a rapidly reversible association–dissociation equilibrium indicates the presence of higher polymers than dimers in concentrated solutions. A calculation based on a theoretical evaluation of a friction coefficient has demonstrated the occurrence of hexamers not reported previously.

In the case of tetramer–dimer hemoglobin equilibrium, the zonal elution chromatography on an SEC column gives a single peak whose retention volume leads to an evaluation of the equilibrium rate by using a method we have introduced recently.[44] In this process, the dissociation of an injected sample increases as the sample is transferred through the column due to the dilution and the different penetration of hemoglobin subunits into the pore.

Then we suggested assimilating the equilibrium observed after the transfer to the one obtained from any saturating solution that would have a vacancy peak at the same retention volume as that of the injected sample. Let C_0 and α_0 be the concentration and dissociation rate of tetramer in the injected sample and C_{eq} and α_{eq} the concentration and dissociation rate of the virtual saturating solution. The equilibrium law gives

$$^{4}K_2 = \frac{4C_0\alpha_0^2}{1 - \alpha_0} = \frac{4C_{eq}\alpha_{eq}^2}{1 - \alpha_{eq}} \tag{12-28}$$

Then

$$\frac{C_0}{C_{eq}} = \frac{\alpha_{eq}^2(1 - \alpha_0)}{\alpha_0^2(1 - \alpha_{eq})} = f \tag{12-29}$$

This ratio, called the "elution factor," represents the dissociation ability of the chromatographic equipment including the dilution and penetration into the pores. It is determined with a protein solution available in a large amount (e.g., hemoglobin A). As it is independent of association constants, it can be applied for the determination of other dimerizing protein systems such as modified or mutant hemoglobin. At this time this method is still being studied both in terms of its theoretical aspects and application.

12.2.3.2 Reaction Kinetic Parameters

Problems of subunits reaction in relation to the time of duration of a chromatographic experiment were considered by many authors. Most of the analytical expressions and computer simulations have been done from the assumption of instanteous equilibrium between species. Halvorson and Ackers[49] evaluated kinetic constants for hen egg lysozyme isomerization using zonal elution chromatography with gel filtration columns. The reaction rates were slow (several hours) and the time of experimentation was in the same range (5–6 h).

Complete calculations including axial dispersion and the different cross-sectional area of folded and unfolded lysozyme express the chromatographic profiles according to the rate constants. Then simulated patterns are used for kinetic determinations. The comparison with experiments resulting from UV difference measurements indicates that the chromatography results may be subject to considerable uncertainty since discrepancies as great as 10-fold are observed. Nevertheless this work illustrates clearly the consequence of non-instantaneous equilibrium on chromatographic curves.

A theoretical approach to dimer–tetramer equilibrium was analyzed by Zimmerman[50] who predicted the effect of the passage through a gel chromatographic column on a reversible association at a given initial equilibrium. The calculations concern the frontal profile of the solute concentration as a function of the distance in the column. The main conclusion of Zimmerman is that kinetic control occurs when the equilibrium has a dissociation rate constant giving a half-time within 1–1.5 orders of magnitude of the time the system has been undergoing transport. It means that the use of soft gels restricts this method application to very slow dissociating systems.

More recent experimental results using HPLC columns have been reported by Anbari et al.[51] who studied by zonal chromatography the dissociation of hybrid hemoglobin resulting from the mixture of different hemoglobins. The distinct $\alpha\beta$ dimers combine to form hybrid hemoglobin tetramer. The use of

TSK cationic and anionic columns under anaerobic conditions allows the separation of hybrid from parent hemoglobins by an ion-exchange process. Changing the profile gradient of the eluting solution, the elution times are varied as wished, so that the effect of the time course of reaction during elution is measured. By plotting on a semilogarithmic scale the hybrid percentage as a function of time, the data points fit straight lines (Figure 12–13) indicating first-order reaction kinetics. The extrapolation at zero time of the hybrid percentage gives the fraction of the hybrid in the mixture prior to separation. From those plots, the rate of dissociation of hybrid hemoglobin is calculated. The range of time experimentation is up to 1 h giving dissociation kinetic constants of about 10^{-3} *M*/sec.

12.3 CHARACTERIZATION OF PROTEIN–PROTEIN INTERACTIONS BY QUANTITATIVE AFFINITY CHROMATOGRAPHY

Quantitative affinity chromatography is now a well-recognized method for measuring ligand–protein and protein–protein interactions. Several recent reviews[52–55] have been published that describe in detail the applications of quantitative affinity chromatography. In this chapter, we shall focus our attention on the theoretical basis of the various equilibria that have been con-

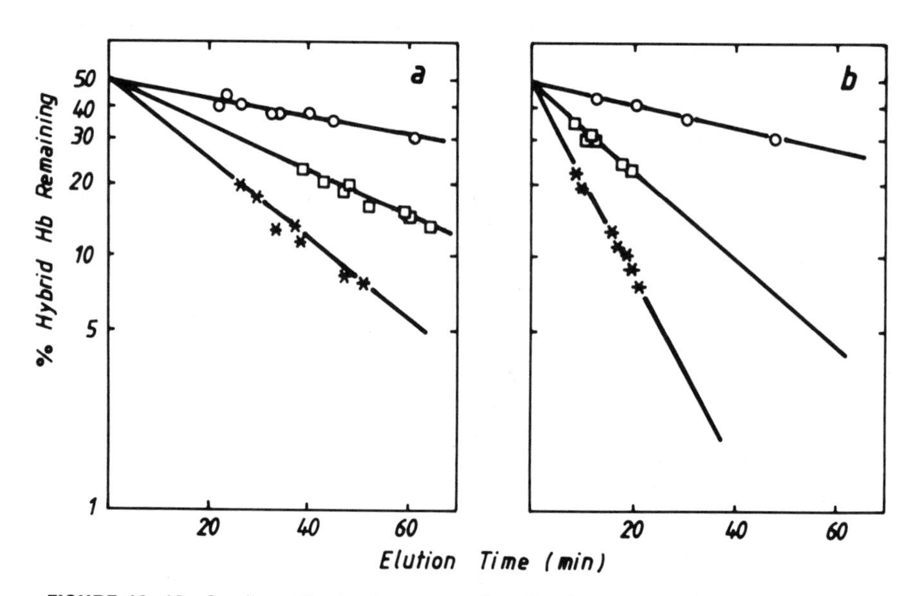

FIGURE 12–13. Semilogarithmic plot representing the time course of the dissociation of hybrid hemoglobin during separation, on a cation-exchange HPLC column. (○) AS hybrid Hb; (□) AY hybrid Hb; (*) SY hybrid Hb. (a) pH 6.1; (b) pH 6.75. (From ref.51.)

sidered to describe the interaction between biopolymeric species and give a general approach to determine the affinity constants by chromatography.

As an analytical tool for measuring molecular interactions, high-performance liquid affinity chromatography (HPLAC)[56] is now rapidly developing. It combines the specificity of the method with the advantage of high-performance liquid chromatography (HPLC) (high sensitivity and speed of analysis). Frontal elution is a powerful technique to determine the equilibrium isotherm, even with kinetic phenomena interfering. However, the injection of a pulse at the column inlet (zonal elution) is generally preferred, because the amount of solute required can be made very small. The analysis of the elution profile could, in principle, give the information needed to determine the equilibrium and kinetic constants, but several difficulties arise in the theoretical treatments with a nonlinear equilibrium isotherm.

12.3.1 Basic Theory of Chromatography

A mobile phase (liquid) flows through a column of uniform diameter, packed with solid porous or nonporous particles and a detection device is set at the outlet of the column to record the concentration of the solute eluting out of the column as a function of the time elapsed from the injection instant.

Two types of chromatographic techniques are generally used that differ by the shape of the input concentration signal: the frontal and the zonal chromatographic methods.

12.3.1.1 Frontal Elution Method

In the frontal elution method the solute concentration is suddenly raised at the moment chosen for the injection, and then maintained at a constant value (Dirac step function).

If one integrates the volumes on the concentration domain of the front (0 to $\overline{C}$), one obtains the quantity of solute P retained on the column added to the amount contained in the whole mobile phase. The average retention volume,[53] independent of the slowness of the adsorption or chemical process, is given by

$$\overline{V} = \frac{1}{\overline{C}} \int_0^{\overline{C}} V(\overline{C}) d\overline{C} \tag{12–30}$$

The solute amount $\overline{\mathcal{Q}}_P$ that has been retained on the solid phase by affinity is measured[57] from the difference between this average retention volume $\overline{V}$ and V^* the one measured without chemical affinity (blank conditions) (Figure 12–14a).

$\overline{\mathcal{Q}}_P$ is a function of the total concentration of the solute in the mobile phase ($\overline{C} = [\overline{P}]$), which is known from experimental conditions:

$$\overline{\mathcal{Q}}_P = (\overline{V} - V^*)\overline{C} = f(\overline{C}) \tag{12–31}$$

This relationship will depend only on the type of binding of solute P onto the solid and on temperature. It is the global partition isotherm of solute P on

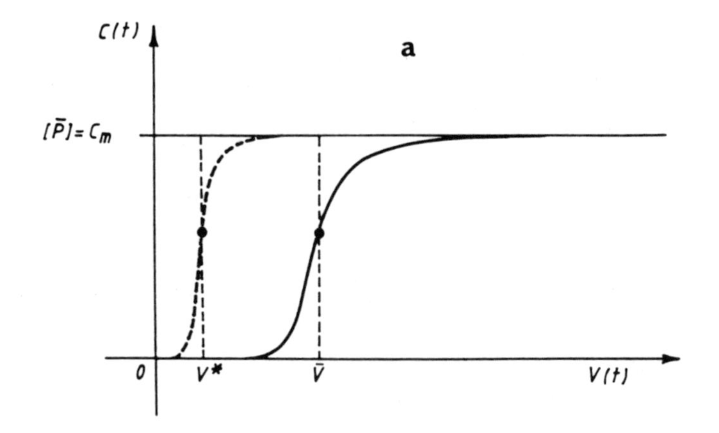

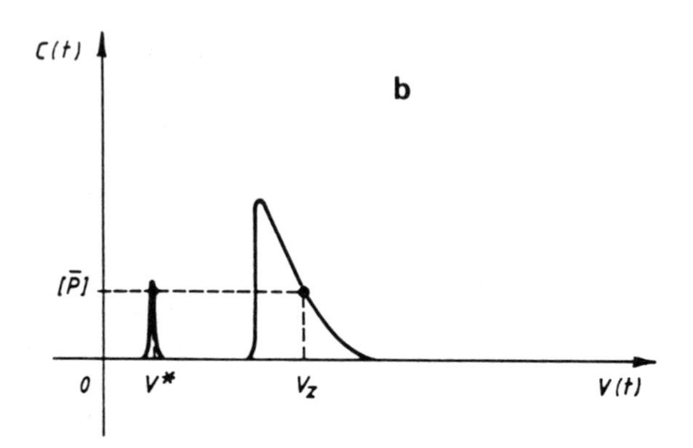

FIGURE 12–14. Chromatographic methods. (a) Frontal elution. (b) Zonal elution.

the solid studied. In the presence of several chemical equilibria, the free solute concentration [P] is not known, but a direct relationship exists between [P] and $[\overline{P}]$.

If one measures the mean occurrence volume of the concentration front at the outlet, one will obtain (Figure 12–14a) mean retention volumes, without chemical affinity V^* and with chemical affinity $\overline{V}$.

V^* is a magnitude depending on the nature of the solute used if the solid particles are porous, since the permeation of the solute is a function of molecule size. Such dependence may be represented by the equation

$$\left.\begin{aligned} V^* &= V_o + \sigma V_i \\ &\text{or} \\ &= V_o(1 + k_o) \end{aligned}\right\} \quad (12\text{–}32)$$

where V_o is the liquid external volume, V_i is the internal pore volume, σ is the permeation coefficient of the solute P, and k_o is the ratio $\sigma V_i/V_o$.

The global retention ratio $\overline{K}$, independent of the quantity packed in the column, is then

$$\overline{K} = \frac{\overline{\mathcal{Q}}_P}{\overline{C}V^*} = \frac{\overline{V} - V^*}{V^*} \qquad (12\text{–}33)$$

12.3.1.2 Zonal Elution Method

In the zonal elution method, the solute concentration is raised at a high value during a short time and is then suddenly lowered back to zero value (Dirac rectangular pulse function) (Figure 12–14b).

The output response in the effluent is most often rounded off by dispersive effects difficult to take into account in the general case, i.e., when $\overline{\mathcal{Q}}_P$ is not proportional to $\overline{C}$. Therefore, to foresee the output response, we will assume instantaneous chemical and physical equilibria. The differential equation describing the propagation process of solute P through the column is[58]

$$\frac{\partial}{\partial t}(\overline{q}_P^{tot}) + u\frac{\partial}{\partial z}\overline{q}_P^0 = D\frac{\partial^2 \overline{q}_P^0}{\partial z^2} \qquad (12\text{–}34)$$

where $\overline{q}_P^0$ is the total amount of P in the mobile liquid phase present in an infinitesimal cross slice of the column (out of the particles).

$\overline{q}_P^{tot}$ is the total amount of P in this slice.

z is the abscissa of the slice along column length. $z = 0$ corresponds to the inlet, $z = L$ to the outlet of the column.

t is the time elapsed from the injection instant.

u is the average velocity of the liquid phase.

D is the dispersive coefficient or global diffusion parameter.

With $\overline{q}_P^{tot} = \overline{q}_P^0 + \overline{q}_P' + \overline{q}_P$, where $\overline{q}_P'$ and $\overline{q}_P$ are, respectively, the total amounts of P in an infinitesimal slice in the pores and fixed on the particles by affinity.

Extending the magnitudes to the whole column length and introducing the concentration of solute in the mobile phase $\overline{C} = \overline{q}_P^0/v^0$, where v^0 is the mobile phase volume corresponding to $\overline{q}_P^0$, the mass balance equation of chromatography can then be written:

$$\frac{\partial \overline{C}}{\partial t} + u\frac{\partial \overline{C}}{\partial z} - D\frac{\partial^2 \overline{C}}{\partial z^2} = -\frac{1}{V_0}\frac{\partial(\overline{\mathcal{Q}}_P + \overline{\mathcal{Q}}_P')}{\partial t} \qquad (12\text{–}35)$$

Assuming that instantaneous equilibrium is achieved at any moment between bulk mobile phase and pore liquid, one can then write the material balance in the form

$$\frac{V^*}{V_o}\frac{\partial \overline{C}}{\partial t} + u\frac{\partial \overline{C}}{\partial z} + \frac{1}{V_o}\frac{\partial \overline{\mathcal{Q}}_P}{\partial t} = D\frac{\partial^2 \overline{C}}{\partial z^2} \qquad (12\text{–}36)$$

since $\overline{\mathcal{Q}}_P' = V_i\sigma\overline{C}$ and $V^* = V_o + V_i\sigma$.

We shall first extract an evaluation of the propagation velocity of a slice of given total concentration in P. It is only simple in the case in which dispersive effects are negligible, i.e., when the second member is considered as zero in Eq. (12–36).

Neglecting the diffusion coefficient, Eq. (12–36) can be written in the form

$$\left(\frac{1}{V^*}\frac{d\overline{\mathcal{Q}}_P}{d\overline{C}} + 1\right)\frac{\partial \overline{C}}{\partial t} + u\frac{V^o}{V^*}\frac{\partial \overline{C}}{\partial z} = 0 \tag{12–37}$$

From this expression one can extract the expression of propagation velocity $U_{\overline{C}}$ of an infinitesimal slice of total concentration $\overline{C}$ in the mobile phase [Eq. (3) in ref. 57]:

$$U_{\overline{C}} = \left.\frac{\partial z}{\partial t}\right|_{\overline{C}=\mathrm{cst}} = -\frac{\partial \overline{C}}{\partial t}\bigg/\frac{\partial \overline{C}}{\partial z} = u\frac{V^o}{V^*}\bigg/\left(\frac{1}{V^*}\frac{d\overline{\mathcal{Q}}_P}{d\overline{C}} + 1\right) \tag{12–38}$$

The propagation velocity for a solute without affinity but the same permeation volume would be uV^o/V^*. As the retention volumes are inversely proportional to these velocities

$$\frac{V_R}{V^*} = \frac{1}{V^*}\frac{uV^o}{U_{\overline{C}}} = 1 + \frac{1}{V^*}\frac{d\overline{\mathcal{Q}}_P}{d\overline{C}} \tag{12–39}$$

where V_R is the retention volume for the concentration $\overline{C}$ in the output signal (Figure 12–14b). Thus one can derive the expression of the apparent capacity factor,[59] often symbolized by k':

$$k' = \frac{1}{V^*}\frac{d\overline{\mathcal{Q}}_P}{d\overline{C}} \tag{12–40}$$

Equation (12–39) can be written in the form

$$V_R(\overline{C}) = V^*[1 + k'(\overline{C})] \tag{12–41}$$

In zonal affinity chromatography the limit retention volume at zero sample size is defined as $V_Z = V_R(0)$. However, according to the approximations made, V_R and $\overline{C}$ must be measured at the outlet in the diffuse edge of the peak, not too near from the baseline or the peak apex (Figure 12–14b).

Let us compare the retention volumes measured by both methods.

Retention volume in frontal chromatography:

$$\overline{V} = V^*[1 + \overline{K}(\overline{C})] \tag{12–42}$$

with

$$\overline{K}(\overline{C}) = \frac{1}{V^*}\frac{\overline{\mathcal{Q}}_P}{\overline{C}} \tag{12–43}$$

Retention volume in zonal chromatography:

$$V_R(\overline{C}) = V^*[1 + k'(\overline{C})] \qquad (12\text{–}44)$$

with

$$k'(\overline{C}) = \frac{1}{V^*}\frac{d\overline{Q}_P}{d\overline{C}} \qquad (12\text{–}45)$$

The retention volume expressions will be different in any nonlinear case, except if $\overline{C} = 0$.

In frontal elution the retention volume is related directly to the equilibrium isotherm $Q_P = f(\overline{C})$, while in zonal elution it is related to its first derivative. Therefore in most cases the equations relating the equilibria to the retention volumes in frontal elution are not to be applied to zonal elution. The zonal case formulas are nevertheless easy to derive.

In frontal elution, equilibrium is reached when the signal reaches the final plateau and thus allows correct measurement of the average volumes, even in the presence of slow exchanges or spreading effects in the column. In zonal elution Eqs. (12–44) and (12–45) may be no more valid with too large spreading or nonequilibrium effects even in a linear case, i.e., when the retention volume is independent of the amount injected.

12.3.2 Equilibrium Measurements

The dependence of the measured retention volumes in affinity chromatography is based on a set of equilibrium equations that describes the interactions between a solute P, the immobilized ligand X and the soluble ligand L.

In this section we shall give the description of the equilibrium equations and the experiments that lead to a methodology for measuring protein–protein interactions. Detailed reviews exist that describe systems involving protein–ligand interactions.[52–55, 61–63]

12.3.2.1 Monovalent Monomeric Solute

The theory was first developed[64–66] to describe situations in which a monomeric solute having a single site interacts with a single site immobilized ligand. The solute is univalent, or, if it is multivalent, should interact with only one site because of steric requirements.

The quantitative treatment of affinity chromatography was developed by Nichol et al.[64] and general relationships are given that include all possible interactions between P, L, and X. The simplest equilibria are those involving interactions of the protein with the mobile and immobilized ligands. There is no interaction between the mobile ligand or the ligand–protein complex and the matrix.

Two equilibria define the interactions of the protein:

$$P + X \rightleftharpoons PX \quad \{PX\} = \{X\}\,[P]K_{PX} \qquad \mathbf{(12\text{–}46)}$$

$$P + L \rightleftharpoons PL \quad [PL] = [L]\,[P]K_{PL} \tag{12–47}$$

where K_{PX} and K_{PL} are the binding constants and the braces represent the surface concentrations in mol/m^2. In this case there is no interaction of the mobile ligand L with the immobilized one X at the surface of the matrix.

The total concentration of protein $[\overline{P}]$ in the liquid phase is related to the free species by:

$$[\overline{P}] = [P](1 + [L]K_{PL}) \tag{12–28}$$

The total amount of immobilized protein $\overline{Q}_P$ is

$$\overline{Q}_P = \{PX\}S = \overline{Q}_X \frac{[P]K_{PX}}{1 + [P]K_{PX}} \tag{12–49}$$

where S is the surface area of the matrix and $\overline{Q}_X$ is the total amount of immobilized ligand. The combination of Eqs. (12–48) and (12–49) yields the partition equilibrium isotherm:

$$\overline{Q}_P = \frac{\overline{Q}_X[\overline{P}]K_{PX}}{1 + [\overline{P}]K_{PX} + [L]K_{PL}} \tag{12–50}$$

This relationship, where $\overline{Q}_P$ is a function of the total concentration of the protein $[\overline{P}]$, can be directly used for frontal chromatographic experiments. Since $\overline{Q}_P/[\overline{P}] = \overline{V} - V^*$, therefore,

$$\overline{V} - V^* = \frac{\overline{Q}_X K_{PX}}{1 + [\overline{P}]K_{PX} + [L]K_{PL}} \tag{12–51}$$

The experiments are carried out at given protein or ligand concentrations and allow the determination of the constants K_{PL}, K_{PX}, and $\overline{Q}_X$ by a nonlinear least-squares fit method or any graphical one.

Frontal chromatography has been used to measure protein–protein interactions.[67] The main advantage over zonal elution chromatography is that one need not make the hypothesis of linear chromatography; the equilibrium is obtained when the steady state is reached (plateau on the chromatogram). The total number of ligand moles $\overline{Q}_X$ that are actually active toward the protein is measurable from these experiments, for large amounts of protein, toward free ligand concentration, since $[\overline{P}](\overline{V} - V^*) \rightarrow \overline{Q}_X$.

The interaction of trypsin with various L-arginine-terminated oligopeptides immobilized on agarose gel was studied by frontal affinity chromatography.[68,69] The effect of the addition of a counterligand was then studied[70] and the dissociation constant for the enzyme-soluble competitive inhibitor determined ($K_i = 1/K_{PL}$). The values obtained are in good agreement with those from kinetic analyses. Further the interaction of β-trypsin immobilized on Sepharose with competitive inhibitors was studied.[71] Frontal chromatography gives two important parameters: the dissociation constant ($K_D = 1/K_{PX}$) and the total amount $\overline{Q}_X$ of active trypsin immobilized on Sepharose. The K_D value for the immobilized trypsin–benzamidine complex is similar to the K_i value. These results show that trypsin activity is hardly affected on immobilization. The chromatographic method can be superior to enzyme kinetics measurements because it is applicable even when the enzyme is no longer active.[67]

The main drawback of frontal chromatography is the large amount of protein required for every measurement, specially when long retention times are needed. Therefore the zonal method is generally preferred. However, this method assumes that local equilibrium is reached throughout the column and is independent of the amount injected. To check linear elution chromatography, the retention volume is to be independent of sample size, while the assumption of local equilibrium is valid if no variation of the retention volume is observed with a change in flow rate.

The retention volume V_Z of the elution peak at infinite dilution is given by

$$V_Z - V^* = \left(\frac{\partial \overline{Q}_P}{\partial [\overline{P}]}\right)_{[\overline{P}]=0} \qquad (12\text{–}52)$$

and is related to the slope of the equilibrium isotherm at origin.

In the absence of dispersive effect, the retention volume $V_R(\overline{C})$ in zonal elution is a function of solute concentration:

$$\sqrt{\frac{1}{V_R - V^*}} = \sqrt{\frac{1 + [L]K_{PL}}{\overline{Q}_X K_{PX}}} + [\overline{P}]\sqrt{\frac{K_{PX}}{\overline{Q}_X(1 + K_{PL}[L])}} \qquad (12\text{–}53)$$

For $\overline{C} = 0$, a linear relationship is obtained when $1/(V_Z - V^*)$ is plotted vs. the total ligand concentration $[\overline{L}]$, and K_{PL} is deduced from the slope to ordinate intercept ratio:[66]

$$\frac{1}{V_Z - V^*} = \frac{1}{K_{PX}\overline{Q}_X} + \frac{K_{PL}}{K_{PX}\overline{Q}_X}[\overline{L}] \qquad (12\text{–}54)$$

This theoretical relationship will not apply if the retention volume depends on the amount of protein injected. It is necessary to inject small sample sizes near from the limit of the detector sensitivity.

Chaiken and Taylor,[72] when studying the ribonuclease–nucleotide interactions, have shown that the retention volume of the ribonuclease peak decreases with increasing amount injected. In the case of a nonlinear isotherm the procedure generally adopted is the extrapolation of retention volumes to zero sample size.

Another drawback of the zonal elution method is that the value of K_{PX}, defining the interaction between the protein and the immobilized ligand, is not directly measurable: the effective amount of immobilized ligand active toward the protein has to be known. If measured from an independent titration method, it may be found considerably lower than the amount originally immobilized on the support. $\overline{Q}_X$ may then be determined by frontal chromatography, measuring the maximum amount of mobile component that binds with the derivatized support.[53]

Malanikova and Turkova[73] compared the zonal and the frontal chromatographic methods of measuring the dissociation constants of the complexes of trypsin with its soluble or immobilized inhibitors. The elution behavior of trypsin on *p*-aminobenzamidine immobilized on hydroxyalkylmethacrylate gel (Spheron) in the presence of mobile ligands (benzylamine, benzoyl-L-arginine, *N*-butylamine, benzamidine, and *p*-aminobenzamidine). The values of the dissociation constants ($K_i = 1/K_{PL}$) obtained by affinity chromatography with zonal or frontal method are in good agreement with the data measured kinetically. The dissociation constant of the complex of trypsin with immobilized *p*-aminobenzamidine (1.6 to 3.7×10^{-6} mol/liter) is lower than the dissociation constant of the complex of trypsin with free *p*-aminobenzamidine (1.9×10^{-5} mol/liter).

Chaiken[74] investigated the interaction of neurophysin with a low capacity neurophysin recognized peptide immobilized on agarose (methionyl-tyrosyl-phenylalanyl-ω-aminohexyl-agarose) in the presence of various amounts of lysine vasopressin in the buffer. The dissociation constants for the interaction of neurophysin with the immobilized ligand ($K_D = 7 \times 10^{-6}$ mol/liter) and the soluble ligand ($K_i = 3.6 \times 10^{-5}$ mol/liter) were calculated from the slope and the ordinate intercept according to Eq. (12–54). It must be noticed that K_D is considerably lower than the value (2×10^{-4} mol/liter) measured by equilibrium dialysis for Met-Tyr-Phe-NH_2 and the tighter binding of neurophysin to the immobilized ligand must be due to specific factors such as divalency and affinity enhancing protein aggregation.

Angal and Chaiken[75] studied the interaction of neurophysin with the various affinity matrices Met-Tyr-Phe-ω-(aminohexyl)- and ω-(aminobutyl)-agarose in the presence of soluble ligands (oxytocin and lysine vasopressin). The plots of $1/(V_Z - V^*)$ vs. $[\bar{L}]$ were linear except near $[\bar{L}] = 0$. Deviation from linearity was specially apparent at high protein concentration. The hypothesis of linear chromatography is contradicted by the experimental results, since an increase in retention volume is observed for high protein concentrations. Although Eq. (12–54) is no more valid for zonal chromatography, it has been applied to calculate the dissociation constants ($K_i = 1/K_{PL}$) that were measured at low and high concentrations of protein injected from the slope to intercept ratio. The value of K_i measured at low protein concentration is similar to that reported for neurophysin monomer, while that of K_i at the highest protein concentration is comparable to literature values given for the dimer. The results can be explained by a model with a protein dimerization equilibrium, where the dimer has a higher affinity for peptide ligands (see Section on Multiple Interaction Equilibria).

The interaction of lipase with a colipase-coupled gel was investigated by Léger and co-workers.[76] They observed that the elution volume of lipase decreases when the amount of lipase injected increases. The mathematical treatment allows the calculation of the mean concentration of the elution peak at the column outlet. Then Eq. (12–51), valid for frontal chromatography, is applied to zonal experiments with $[L] = 0$ and the amount of active ligand $\bar{Q}_X$ and the dissociation constant ($K_D = 1/K_{PX}$) are determined. The lipase–colipase system[77] was further studied by HPLAC, using colipase immobilized on a diol-bonded silica phase. The same dependence of retention volume with concentration was observed. The influence of various chromatographic parameters was studied (temperature, ionic strength, and flow rate). The variation of the apparent dissociation constant K_D with flow rate reveals a kinetic contribution. The value of K_D measured at low flow rates is in good agreement with independent measurements.

12.3.2.2 Evaluation of Protein Multivalency

Divalent Monomeric Solute This type of system was first described by Chaiken et al.,[78,79] but was recently treated in a more rigorous approach by Anderson and Walters,[80] since they introduced surface concentrations in the expression of the interactions with a single-site ligand immobilized on the matrix.

The various equilibria that occur in a divalent system with a single-site immobilized ligand are

$$PX_2 \rightleftharpoons PX \;\; \begin{matrix} & P & \\ \nearrow\!\!\!\swarrow & & \searrow\!\!\!\nwarrow \\ \searrow\!\!\!\nwarrow & & \nearrow\!\!\!\swarrow \\ & PLX & \end{matrix} \;\; PL \rightleftharpoons PL_2 \tag{12-55}$$

The corresponding equilibrium constants are

$$\left.\begin{aligned} K_2 &= \frac{[PL]}{[P]\,[L]} = \frac{[PL_2]}{[PL]\,[L]} = \frac{\{PLX\}}{\{PX\}\,[P]} \\ K_3 &= \frac{\{PX\}}{[P]\,\{X\}} = \frac{\{PLX\}}{[PL]\,\{X\}} \qquad K_4 = \frac{\{PX_2\}}{\{PX\}\,\{X\}} \end{aligned}\right\} \tag{12-56}$$

The equilibrium partition isotherm is then

$$\bar{\mathcal{Q}}_P = S\{X\}\,[\bar{P}]K_3\,\frac{2 + 2[L]K_2 + \{X\}K_4}{(1 + [L]K_2)^2} \tag{12-57}$$

where {X} is the surface concentration of the noncomplexed immobilized ligand and [L] is the concentration of the free ligand in solution. They both depend on the total amount of protein. {X} is related to the total amount of immobilized ligand $\bar{\mathcal{Q}}_X$ by

$$\bar{\mathcal{Q}}_X = S\{X\}\left[1 + \frac{2[\bar{P}](1 + [L]K_2 + \{X\}K_3K_4)}{(1 + [L]K_2)^2}\right] \tag{12-58}$$

When the protein amount is negligible besides that of the ligands, the zonal retention volume is equal to the slope of the equilibrium isotherm at origin:

$$V_Z - V^* = \bar{\mathcal{Q}}_X K_3\,\frac{2 + 2[L]K_2 + \{X\}K_4}{(1 + [L]K_2)^2} \tag{12-59}$$

The limiting cases of this model were discussed by Anderson et al.[81] according to the value of the equilibrium constant K_4.

By the zonal elution method Chaiken et al.[78] measured the interaction of radioisotopically labeled divalent immunoglobulin-A monomer with its antigen (phosphorylcholine) immobilized on Sepharose in the presence of various concentrations [L] of free phosphorylcholine. Although at low density of immobilized phosphorylcholine a linear behavior is observed in agreement with Eq. (12–54). The dissociation constant for protein-immobilized ligand complex ($K_D = 1/K_{AX}$) is lower than that of IgA Fab on the same matrix, indicating that some divalent binding occurs. At high enough immobilized phosphorylcholine concentration deviations from linearity were observed, demonstrating the effect of multivalency. Assuming that $K_4 = K_3 S/V^*$, the values of K_2 and K_3 were determined from the curve fitting of the variation of V_Z with [L] for both high- and low-density ligand matrices. The value of V_Z at $[L] = 0$ was used to obtain an independent estimate of K_3. The dissociation constants for divalent IgA monomer with free phosphorylcholine ($K_i = 1/K_2 = 1.7 \times 10^6\ M$), and for protein-immobilized ligand ($K_D = 1/K_3 = 4.8 \times 10^6\ M$) are in good agreement within experimental errors with those measured by the equilibrium dialysis method ($2 \times 10^6\ M$).

Inman[82] applied the theoretical relationships developed by Hethcote and DeLisi[83,84] to his experimental work, relating the mass center of the elution peak to the three association constants involved in the equilibrium. When elution is carried out with no dissolved ligand, Eq. (12–59) reduces to

$$V_B - V^* = \bar{\mathcal{Q}}_X K_3(2 + K_4\{\bar{X}\}) \qquad (12\text{–}60)$$

Thus, dividing Eq. (12–59) by this expression, one obtains

$$G = \frac{V_Z - V^*}{V_B - V^*} = \frac{a}{1 + K_2[L]} + \frac{1 - a}{(1 + K_2[L])^2} \qquad (12\text{–}61)$$

with $a = 2\mathcal{Q}_X K_3/(V_B - V^*)$.

The parameters a and K_2 can be calculated from a series of chromatographic runs employing various concentrations of ligand L by a least-squares fit method ($a = 0$ corresponds to the complete dominance of divalent binding; $a = 1$ corresponds to a univalent solute). Parameter a is independent of the competitive ligand and has to be determined only once. This method was used to study the interaction of a monoclonal IgB antibody with an anti-2,4-dinitrophenyl monoclonal antibody bound on Sepharose in the presence of a series of ligands of various structures, including alkaloids, drugs, pyrimidine and purine derivatives, antibiotics, enzyme site probes, a lipid, a polysaccharide, and a peptide. It is shown that the method is well adapted to test the hypothesis of multispecificity.

HPLAC was used[80,81] to measure the interaction of divalent concanavalin A with various densities of ligands immobilized on diol silicas [p-aminophenyl-α-D-mannopyranoside (PAPM) and glucosamide]. The competitive inhibitor in the liquid phase was methyl-α-D-mannopyranoside. The conditions of pH and ionic strength were such that concanavalin A was present primarily in the form of a dimer with two identical binding sites. It was observed that, as the density of the ligand increases, the retention law changes from the case of a univalent interaction to the one of a divalent interaction. This is illustrated in Figure 12–15 where the plot of $1/k' = V^*/(V_Z - V^*)$ vs. [L] is a straight line for a purely univalent interaction. The curvature indicates a multivalent interaction. The equilibrium constants K_2, K_3, and K_4 were calculated by a least-squares fit method. The equilibrium constants determined for the competing sugar from the low coverage studies were in good agreement with literature values. The K_3 values for the medium and high coverage PAPM column were larger than expected from the monovalent data.

A recycling partition equilibrium procedure was used by Hogg and Winzor[85] to study the divalent case in their investigation on the interaction of horse liver alcohol-dehydrogenase with Blue Sepharose by frontal chromatography in an imidazole chloride buffer. The model assumes that the successive interactions between the affinity matrix and the divalent solute are governed by a single intrinsic binding constant ($K_3 = K_4V^*/S$).

Although the model [Eq. (12–62) with $n = 2$] is in good agreement with experimental data, a large difference in K_3 values for two different concentrations of immobilized ligand is obtained. It shows that the theoretical treatment based on the equivalence and independence of interactions, which helps in simplifying the mathematical expressions, is not valid for this system.

Multivalent Monomeric Solute Assuming independence and equivalence of the interacting constants,[86] the theory of a monovalent affinity matrix has been extended to describe the equilibrium between a solute P that possesses

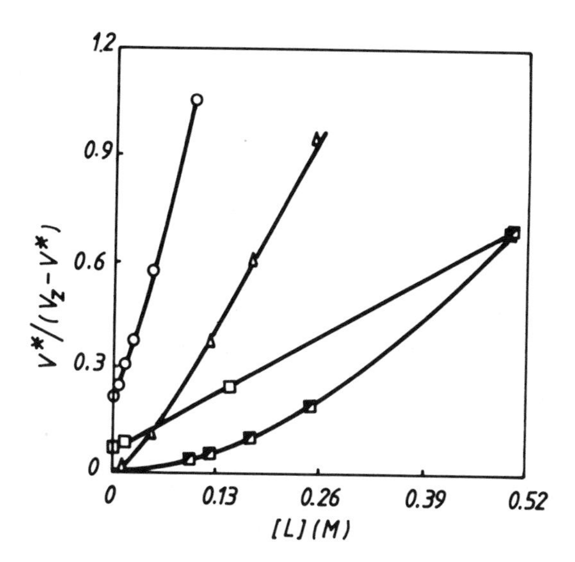

FIGURE 12–15. Plots of $1/k'$ vs. the concentration of methyl-D-mannopyranoside on an immobilized glucosamine column (○) and on a *p*-aminophenyl-D-mannopyranoside column of low (□), medium (△), and high (◪) immobilized ligand densities. (From ref. 81.)

f sites for interaction with either a univalent ligand or a single-site immobilized one.[41,42] This concept was formulated by Chaiken et al.[79] for a divalent solute.

An expression is derived that allows to evaluate the retention volume by frontal chromatography[87]:

$$\left(\frac{\bar{V}}{V^*}\right)^{1/n} - 1 = \frac{K_{PX}Q_X}{V^*(1 + [L]K_{PL})} - n\frac{K_{PX}(\bar{V}/V^*)[\bar{P}][1 - (V^*/\bar{V})^{1/n}]}{1 + [L]K_{PL}} \tag{12–62}$$

If the model and the valency degree of solute n assumed are correct, a plot of $(\bar{V}/V^*)^{1/n} - 1$ vs. $[\bar{P}](\bar{V}/V^*)[1 - (V^*/\bar{V})^{1/n}]$ should yield a straight line (Figure 12–16). The constant K_{PX} can be evaluated if $[L] = 0$, while K_{PL} can be determined from the plots obtained at various concentrations of the ligand L.

This model reduces to the one described previously for a divalent monomeric solute when $n = 2$, $K_3 = K_4 = K_{PX}$ and $K_2 = K_{PL}$.

Frontal affinity chromatography with the recycling procedure was used to study the binding of aldolase to cellulose phosphate in the presence and in the absence of a phosphate ligand.[41] The equilibrium constants were calculated with $n = 4$, a value in agreement with the number of bonds used in the aldolase–cellulose interaction. The value of K_{PL} is in close agreement with that deduced from competitive inhibition studies.

Hogg and Winzor[87] have studied the NADH-dependent elution of lactate dehydrogenase from Blue Sepharose, by frontal chromatography. A valency of 4

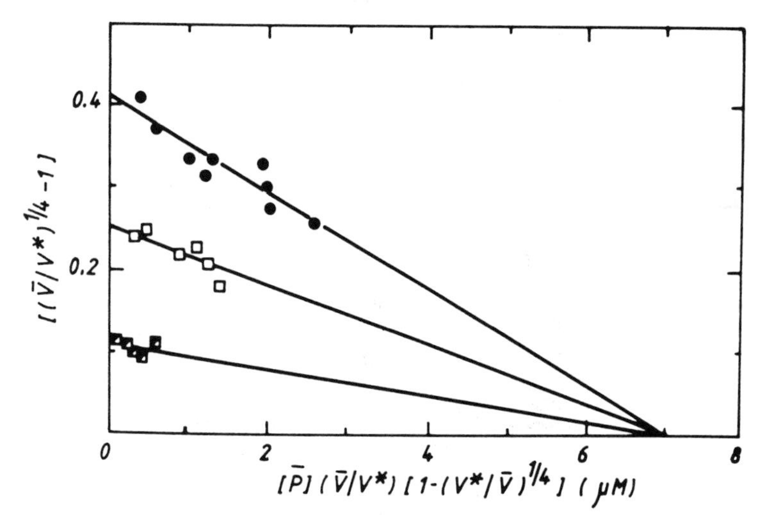

FIGURE 12–16. Graphic analysis, according to Eq. (12–62), of results obtained in a frontal affinity chromatographic study of the NADH-facilitated elution of rabbit muscle lactate dehydrogenase from trinitrophenyl-Sepharose. Experimental points refer to series of experiments with free enzyme concentrations [L], of zero (●); 5 μM (□); 20 μM (◩). (From ref. 89.)

is ascribed to the protein. Graphical analysis in the format of Eq. (12–62) permits the determination of the total concentration of matrix sites from the slope to intercept ratio. The equilibrium constant K_{PL} between NADH and rabbit muscle lactate dehydrogenase is in good agreement with that previously measured for the binding of NADH to mammalian muscle lactate dehydrogenase.[88] The graphical procedure described has the disadvantage that the effective valency of the partitioning solute has to be assigned. Further Bergman and Winzor[89] studied the elution of rabbit muscle lactate dehydrogenase in the presence of NADH on a column of trinitrophenyl Sepharose by frontal and zonal chromatography. They show that zonal chromatography affords a reliable quantitative analysis of solute–ligand interactions if the total amount of matrix sites $\overline{Q}_X$ is much larger than $n \cdot [\overline{P}]$. From Eq. (12–62) a simplified expression is then derived that can be used in frontal or zonal affinity chromatography, when the amount of protein is negligible toward the one of active sites of the matrix.

Another scheme was introduced by Kyprianou and Yon[90] where there is a monovalent binding of the protein but b binding sites of the protein are blocked, unable to associate to any ligand molecule. For a multivalent protein that possesses n identical sites the general equilibria are

$$\begin{array}{lccccccc}
\text{Number of isomers} & 1 & & n & & C_n^b & & C_n^{b-1} \quad\quad 1 \\
 & P & \underset{K_{PL}}{\rightleftharpoons} & PL & \underset{K_{PL}}{\rightleftharpoons} \cdots \underset{K_{PL}}{\rightleftharpoons} & PL_{n-b} & \underset{K_{PL}}{\rightleftharpoons} & PL_{n-b+1} \underset{K_{PL}}{\rightleftharpoons} \cdots \underset{K_{PL}}{\rightleftharpoons} PL_n \\
\text{Equilibria} & K_{PX} & & K_{PX} & & K_{PX} & & \\
 & PX & \underset{K_{PL}}{\rightleftharpoons} & PLX & \underset{K_{PL}}{\rightleftharpoons} \cdots \underset{K_{PL}}{\rightleftharpoons} & PL_{n-b}X & & \\
\text{Number of isomers} & n & & nC_{n-b}^1 & & n & &
\end{array} \tag{12–63}$$

where K_{PL} and K_{PX} are the binding constants.

The equilibrium isotherm is

$$\overline{Q}_P = \overline{Q}_X \frac{nK_{PX}[\overline{P}]}{(1 + [L]K_{PL})^b + nK_{PX}[\overline{P}]} \tag{12–64}$$

The retention volume in frontal chromatography deduced from the equilibrium isotherm equation is then

$$\frac{\overline{Q}_X}{\overline{V} - V^*} = [\overline{P}] + \frac{(1 + [L]K_{PL})^b}{nK_{PX}} \tag{12–65}$$

The elution of rat liver lactate dehydrogenase from 10-carboxydecylamino-Sepharose with NADH as the mobile ligand was studied by frontal chromatography.[90,91] Since the plot of $1/(\overline{V} - V^*)$ vs. [L] is not a straight line, it is necessary to assume a multiple site occlusion.

Lactate dehydrogenase has four NADH binding sites and 1, 2, 3, or all of these sites may be blocked during the elution of the protein through the column. The results show that about two sites are blocked when the molecule of enzyme is adsorbed. Since the data are well fitted by Eq. (12–62) with $n = 4$, Winzor and Yon[92] have shown that these experiments confirm the hypothesis of the four coenzyme binding sites interacting independently with the matrix.

Oda et al.[93] developed a theoretical model for the particular case where $b = 1$. By frontal affinity chromatography they studied the elution of concanavalin A (Con A) on *p*-aminophenyl-β-D-glucopyranoside immobilized on Sepharose. Experiments were carried out under the conditions where Con A exists as a dimer. α-Con A has a stronger affinity than β-Con A. Changes in pH and ionic strength have different effects on the affinity of these proteins.

12.3.3 Self-Associating Proteins

Subunit-Exchange Chromatography The theory of "subunit exchange chromatography" was first introduced by Antonini et al.[94,95] If an equilibrium exists between the biopolymer and the subunits in solution, the subunits P will interact with those covalently bound to the resin X. The simplest case describing the reversible dissociation of a dimer into its monomer is

$$\left.\begin{array}{ll} P + P \rightleftharpoons P_2 & L_1 = [P_2]/[P]^2 \\ X + P \rightleftharpoons XP & L_2 = \{XP\}/\{X\} \cdot [P] \end{array}\right\} \quad (12\text{–}66)$$

The equilibrium isotherm $\bar{Q}_P = f([\bar{P}])$ is then

$$\bar{Q}_P = 2L_2\bar{Q}_X[\bar{P}]/(2L_2[\bar{P}] + 1 + \sqrt{1 + 8[\bar{P}]L_1}) \quad (12\text{–}67)$$

In frontal chromatography the retention volume is given by

$$\frac{\bar{Q}_X}{\bar{V} - V^*} = [\bar{P}] + (1 + \sqrt{1 + 8[\bar{P}]L_1})/(2L_2) \quad (12\text{–}68)$$

Frontal analyses performed with immobilized α-chymotrypsin have shown[95] that, when the concentration of the immobilized protein is relatively low, its associating capacity is very similar to that of the free protein ($L_1 = L_2$).

Figure 12–17 shows that the amount of α-chymotrypsin ($y = \bar{Q}_P/\bar{Q}_X$) immobilized on Sepharose at pH 8 has the same association capacity as the protein in solution.[96] When the protein is immobilized at pH 5, the associating capacity of the immobilized protein is larger than for the protein in solution. The analyses of these data suggest that a tetrameric species is formed.

The reversible dissociation of the $\alpha_2\beta_2$ tetramers of human hemoglobin into αβ dimers was studied by subunit chromatography.[96,97] It is shown that oxyhemoglobin coupled to Sepharose is dimeric and bound to the matrix through α and β chains. Detailed frontal analyses were also performed with glucagon immobilized in its monomeric form onto Sepharose.[98] The extent of self-association was similar to that of free glucagon, which exists in solution in a monomer–trimer equilibrium.

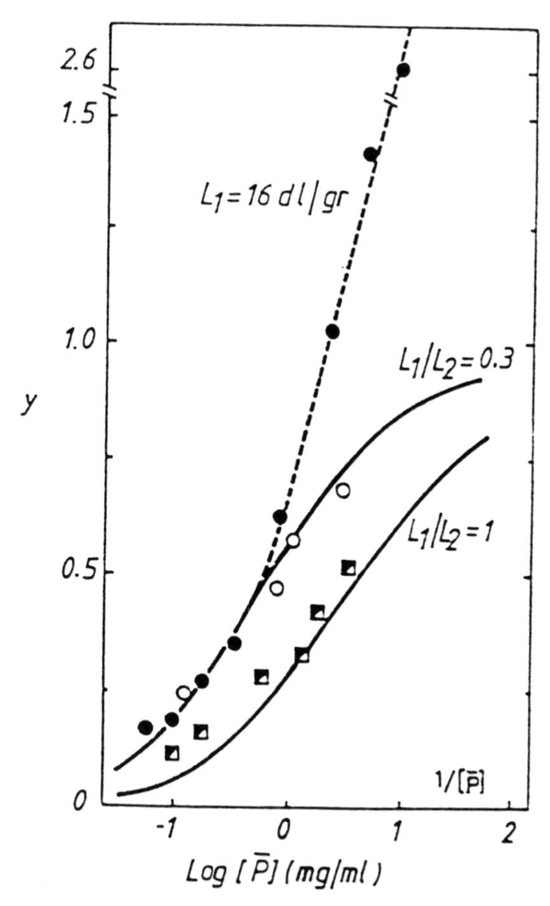

FIGURE 12–17. Binding of α-chymotrypsin in solution to a column of Sepharose-linked α-chymotrypsin as a function of protein concentration. (○) and (◪) refer to two different preparations of α-chymotrypsin immobilized at pH 8.0. (●) refers to α-chymotrypsin immobilized at pH 5.0. Continuous curves are theoretical ones and were computed according to Eq. (12–68). (From ref. 96.)

These experiments show that insoluble subunits have the same associating capacity as the protein in solution, provided that the coupling of the protein is achieved with only one subunit.

Multiple Interaction Equilibria The multiple equilibria were studied by Chaiken et al.[54,55] in pulse zone affinity chromatography and were applied to the measurement of the interaction between the neuropeptide hormones (oxytocin and vasopressin) and the neurophysins. The elution of bovine neurophysin was studied on immobilized peptide ligands or immobilized neurophysin, in the presence of soluble ligands (oxytocin or lysine-vasopressin).

The various equilibria considered in solution are[99]

$$
\begin{aligned}
P + P &\rightleftharpoons P_2 & K_{PP} &= [P_2]/[P]^2 \\
P + L &\rightleftharpoons PL & K_{PL} &= [PL]/[P]\cdot[L] \\
PL + P &\rightleftharpoons PLP & K_{PLP} &= [PLP]/[PL]\cdot[P] \\
P_2 + L &\rightleftharpoons PPL & K_{PPL} &= [PPL]/[P_2]\cdot[L] \\
PL + PL &\rightleftharpoons P_2L_2 & K_{PLPL} &= [P_2L_2]/[PL]^2
\end{aligned}
\qquad (12\text{–}69)
$$

The equilibria with the affinity matrix are

$$
\begin{aligned}
X + P &\rightleftharpoons XP & K_{PX} &= \{XP\}/\{X\}\cdot[P] \\
X + L &\rightleftharpoons XL & K_{XL} &= \{XL\}/\{X\}\cdot[L] \\
XP + L &\rightleftharpoons XLP & K_{XLP} &= \{XLP\}/\{XP\}\cdot[L] \\
XP + L &\rightleftharpoons XPL & K_{XPL} &= \{XPL\}/\{XP\}\cdot[L] \\
XPL + L &\rightleftharpoons XPL_2 & K_{XPLL} &= \{XPL_2\}/\{XPL\}\cdot[L]
\end{aligned}
\qquad (12\text{–}70)
$$

From those equilibria it may be shown that the equilibrium isotherm is

$$
\bar{\mathcal{Q}}_P = 2B'\bar{\mathcal{Q}}_X[\bar{P}]/[2B'[\bar{P}] + (1 + K_{XL}[L])(1 + K_{PL}[L] + \sqrt{(1 + K_{PL}[L])^2 + 8[\bar{P}]B})] \qquad (12\text{–}71)
$$

with

$$
B = K_{PP} + (K_{PLP}K_{PL} + K_{PP}K_{PPL})[L] + K_{PL}^2 K_{PLPL}[L]^2 \qquad (12\text{–}72)
$$

and

$$
B' = K_{PX}(1 + K_{XPL}[L] + K_{XLP}[L] + K_{XPL}K_{XPLL}[L]^2 \qquad (12\text{–}73)
$$

In the absence of soluble ligand L, the isotherm equation reduces to Eq. (12–67) previously established for subunit-exchange chromatography. In zonal elution, with extrapolation to zero sample size and pulse injection, the limit retention volume V_Z is given by

$$\frac{\overline{Q}}{V_Z - V^*} = (1 + K_{XL}[L])\,(1 + K_{PL}[L])/B' \qquad (12\text{–}74)$$

When $[L] = 0$, $B = K_{PP}$, and $B' = K_{PX}$ the limit retention volume in pulse zonal chromatography is given by the equation:

$$\frac{\overline{Q}_X}{V_Z - V^*} = \frac{1}{K_{PX}} \qquad (12\text{–}75)$$

The method of zonal elution was developed to study neurophysin self-assocation and the interaction of neurophysin with neuropeptide hormone.[100–102] Reviews with tables summarizing the dissociation constants measured were recently published.[52,54,55]

High-performance liquid affinity chromatography was successfully used to determine the dissociation constants by the zonal elution method. The protein bovine neurophysin II was immobilized in its monomeric form on several high flow–low compressibiity supports and the zonal elution behavior of the peptide hormone Arg-vasopressin was studied.[99,103,104] Since the elution volume was concentration dependent, the data were extrapolated to zero concentration and the constant K_{PX} was estimated from Eq. (12–75) if the amount of immobilized ligand $\overline{Q}_X$ is known. The values of the dissociation constants were in good agreement with those measured for free soluble species. By extension of the theoretical treatment of analytical affinity chromatography, they evaluated the self-association of a protein by studying the behavior of bovine neurophysin II on its immobilized monomer. The zonal elution profiles (Figure 12–18) were observed to be dependent on the concentration of soluble protein. The dimer dissociation constant (16.6 μmol/liter) could be calculated from extrapolation to zero protein concentration and the result is in good agreement with that derived from equilibrium sedimentation.

12.3.3 Kinetic Measurements

The analysis of the elution profile is of first importance in zonal elution chromatography since it may give information about the equilibrium and kinetic constants. Its theoretical expression is obtained from the solution of the mass balance equations characterizing the chromatographic system:

$$\frac{\partial \overline{C}}{\partial t} + u\frac{\partial \overline{C}}{\partial z} - D\frac{\partial^2 \overline{C}}{\partial z^2} = -\frac{1}{V_o}\frac{\partial(\overline{Q}_P + \overline{Q}'_P)}{\partial t} \qquad (12\text{–}76)$$

where $\overline{C}$ denotes the solute concentration in the bulk mobile phase; $\overline{Q}'_P$ and $\overline{Q}_P$ are, respectively, the total amount of solute (moles) in the pores and the one of solute fixed on the support by affinity.

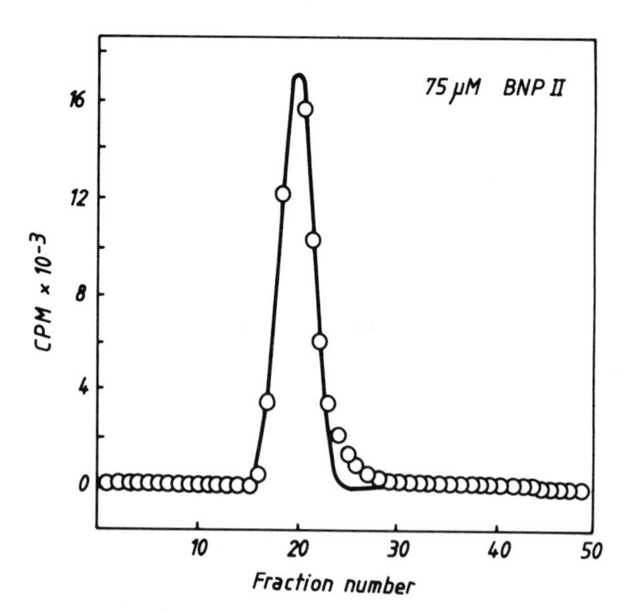

FIGURE 12–18. Zonal elution profile for ^{125}I-labeled bovine neurophysin II (BNP II) at an initial concentration of 75 μ*M* (BNP II) on a column of BNP II immobilized on glass beads. (From ref. 99.)

Taking into account the kinetic effects, a relationship exists between the sum $(\overline{\mathcal{Q}}'_P + \overline{\mathcal{Q}}_P)$ and the value that would have been reached at equilibrium: $(\overline{\mathcal{Q}}'^*_P + \overline{\mathcal{Q}}^*_P)$:

$$\frac{\partial(\overline{\mathcal{Q}}_P + \overline{\mathcal{Q}}'_P)}{\partial t} = \alpha[(\overline{\mathcal{Q}}_P + \overline{\mathcal{Q}}'_P) - (\overline{\mathcal{Q}}'^*_P + \overline{\mathcal{Q}}^*_P)] \qquad (12\text{–}77)$$

where α is the rate constant that may be a complicated function of the solute concentration in the bulk. In the preceding section we assumed instantaneous equilibria, therefore $\overline{\mathcal{Q}}'^*_P = \overline{\mathcal{Q}}'_P = \sigma V_i \overline{C}$, and $\overline{\mathcal{Q}}_P = \overline{\mathcal{Q}}^*_P$ and the rate constant is assumed to be infinite. Therefore, $\overline{\mathcal{Q}}_P$ is expressed as a function of the equilibrium isotherm [Eq. (12–31)].

The mathematical solution of the mass balance equations involves considerable difficulties for the general treatment with a nonlinear adsorption isotherm, when nonequilibrium effects are included. Taking into consideration the diffusion kinetics and the chemical reactions involved, numerical methods could be used, in principle, to modelize the elution profile. Then the physicochemical constants implied in the chromatographic phenomena can be extracted from curve fitting of the model onto the experimental profile.

In affinity chromatography exact analytical solutions have been derived in the case of a linear isotherm or with the nonlinear sorption rate limited model, which leads to an isotherm of the Langmuir type. We saw previously that the equilibrium isotherms are seldom linear, except in a very low and narrow concentration range; furthermore for many systems they will differ from Langmuir type. Therefore the theoretical laws applied to the determination of kinetic constants from peak shape analysis will have to be used with caution since large peak distortions are caused by a nonlinear shape of the equilibrium isotherm.

12.3.3.1 Kinetics with a Linear Sorption Isotherm

Using a stochastic approach,[105] Giddings and Eyring[106] have shown that the elution peak "without dispersion" is given by the product of a modified Bessel function with an exponential step and with the inverse of time square root, which is to be added to a Dirac step function. This statistical approach was applied to affinity chromatography by Denizot and Delaage[107] and the expressions of the moments of the elution peak were derived.

Moment Analysis and Plate Height Method The set of differential equations describing the chromatographic system is difficult to solve analytically, but the moments that characterize the band broadening of the elution peak can be found by using the Laplace transformation and Van der Laan's theorem.

The zeroth moment μ_0 (peak area), the first moment μ_1' (mean retention time), and the second central moment μ_2 (peak variance) are given by the equations

$$\mu_0 = \int_0^\infty \overline{C}(t)\,dt; \qquad \mu_1' = \frac{\int_0^\infty \overline{C}(t)\,t\,dt}{\mu_0};$$

$$\mu_2 = \frac{\int_0^\infty \overline{C}(t)(t - \mu_1')^2\,dt}{\mu_0} \tag{12–78}$$

where $\overline{C}(t)$ is the solute concentration $[\overline{P}]$ at the column outlet.

They may be calculated by numerical integration, but when the peak is gaussian, μ_2 is equal to the variance and may be measured from the peak width at the fraction $e^{-0.5}$ (≈ 0.606) of the peak height.

The integrals of the form $\int_0^\infty \overline{C}(t)t^k\,dt$ can be obtained from the Laplace transform of $\overline{C}(t)$, assuming a Dirac pulse function for the injection signal.[108,109] The first moment is given as a function of the column capacity factor k' [Eq. (12–40)] and the column permeation ratio $k_0 = \sigma(V_i/V_0)$:

$$\mu_1' = \frac{L}{u}(1 + K_0)(1 + k') \tag{12–79}$$

The second moment, or peak variance, is directly related to the plate height:

$$H = L\mu_2/\mu_1'^2 \tag{12–80}$$

Under the usual linear chromatographic conditions, the plate height may be written as a sum of increments[110,111]

$$H = H_D + H_E + H_I + H_K \tag{12–81}$$

The first term H_D expresses the plate height increment due to axial dispersion; the plate height increment H_E is related to the mass transfer resistance at the external particle boundary; the plate height increment H_I is due to diffusion inside the pores. The plate height increment for the mass transfer kinetics is

$$H_K = 2 \frac{k'}{k_d(1 + K_0)(1 + k')^2} u \tag{12–82}$$

where k_d is the desorption rate constant in the linear kinetic process.

Horvath and Lin[110,111] have given the expressions of the plate height contributions corrected for the combined effects of flow velocity and the diffusion in the mobile phase. Hethcote and DeLisi[108] have derived similar expressions for the moments of the elution peak and the plate height equation. In the case of linear zonal chromatography (zero solute concentration) they give the expressions of the moments describing the various equilibria implied in affinity chromatography[83]: univalent and divalent binding, binding to ligands on porous and impenetrable particles. Complex expressions of the first and second moments are derived that involve the various equilibrium and rate constants of the affinity process.

The capacity to determine kinetic constants from the peak band broadening was discussed in detail by Arnold et al.[112] The plate height method can be used to determine the dissociation rate constants, if the other contributions to band broadening are negligible or can be determined and subtracted. It was used by Walters[113] to study the band broadening of the elution peak of proteins on glucosamine bonded to the diol phase. It is shown that the restricted diffusion in the pores causes a large increase in plate height, when the pore diameter is close to the protein molecular one.

Nilsson and Larsson,[114] when studying the interaction of nucleotides with alcohol dehydrogenase immobilized on silica by HPLAC, attempted to measure rate constants from the peak width method. Large discrepancies exist between the rate constants determined by the plate height method and those reported from other determinations. A reasonable explanation of the poor agreement would be that intraparticle diffusion resistance was not properly compensated for. Moreover the rate constants related to silica-bound and free enzyme are not necessarily identical.

Muller and Carr[115] used the plate height method [Eqs. (12–81) and (12–82)] based on Horvath and Lin's approach[111] to determine the dissociation constants by HPLAC. Although the experiments do not lie in the linear region of the isotherms, they have applied the plate height equation to study the kinetics of the interaction between concanavalin A immobilized on silica and several sugar derivatives, noting that the only plate height contribution that does not depend on particle diameter is the kinetic one. These studies were extended to other carbohydrate solutes and the effects of isotherm nonlinearity on thermodynamic and kinetic properties were discussed.[116]

Anderson and Walters[117] studied the same biochemical system consisting of immobilized concanavalin A and various sugars, as free species. Under linear elution conditions, assuming concanavalin A to be homogeneous in nature, it was shown that the contribution to plate height is inadequately described as a function of k'. The method used to determine the dissociation rates was quite inaccurate because of the important diffusion contributions to band broadening, which are difficult to take into account.

Peak Shape Analysis The inaccuracy of the plate height method for measuring kinetic constants due to extracolumn and nonkinetic effects has led to other methods, which are based on the extraction of the kinetic information from peak shape analysis.

An analytical expression of the elution peak can be obtained if a linear kinetic law is assumed for the global mass transfer of the solutes between the mobile phase and the particles.

$$\mathrm{P} \underset{h_{-1}}{\overset{h_1}{\rightleftarrows}} \mathrm{P_g} \tag{12–83}$$

where P is the solute in the bulk liquid phase and P_g the solute inside the grains. h_1 and h_{-1} are global rate constants for entrance into, and exit from the beads.

The solute mass transfer flow from the grains is

$$\frac{\partial(\overline{Q}'_P + \overline{Q}_P)}{\partial t} = h_1 V_o \overline{C} - h_{-1}(\overline{Q}'_P + \overline{Q}_P) \tag{12–84}$$

The solution of the differential system of equations of chromatography [Eqs. (12–76) and (12–84)] using the Laplace transforms yields the equation of the output signal,[109] similar to that derived by Giddings and Eyring[106] from a stochastic approach. In the simplified case studied by DeLisi et al.[109] (ideal conditions for homogeneous molecular population, uniform bed packing, and concentration-independent rate constants), the shape of the theoretical peak presents a tailing part, which, under some particular experimental conditions, can generate a bimodal peak (Figure 12–19).

The theoretical model introduced by Giddings[105,106,118] predicts that the probability for solute molecules to pass through the column without being adsorbed is $e^{-h_1 l/u}$. The theory was further developed by Hage et al.[119] to include the mass transfer at the outer boundary:

$$\mathrm{P} \underset{k_{-1}}{\overset{k_1}{\rightleftarrows}} \mathrm{P_P} \tag{12–85}$$

where P symbolizes the protein in the bulk liquid phase and P_p the protein inside the pores. The surface binding process is then written:

$$\mathrm{P_P} + \mathrm{X} \underset{k_{-3}}{\overset{k_3}{\rightleftarrows}} \mathrm{PX} \tag{12–86}$$

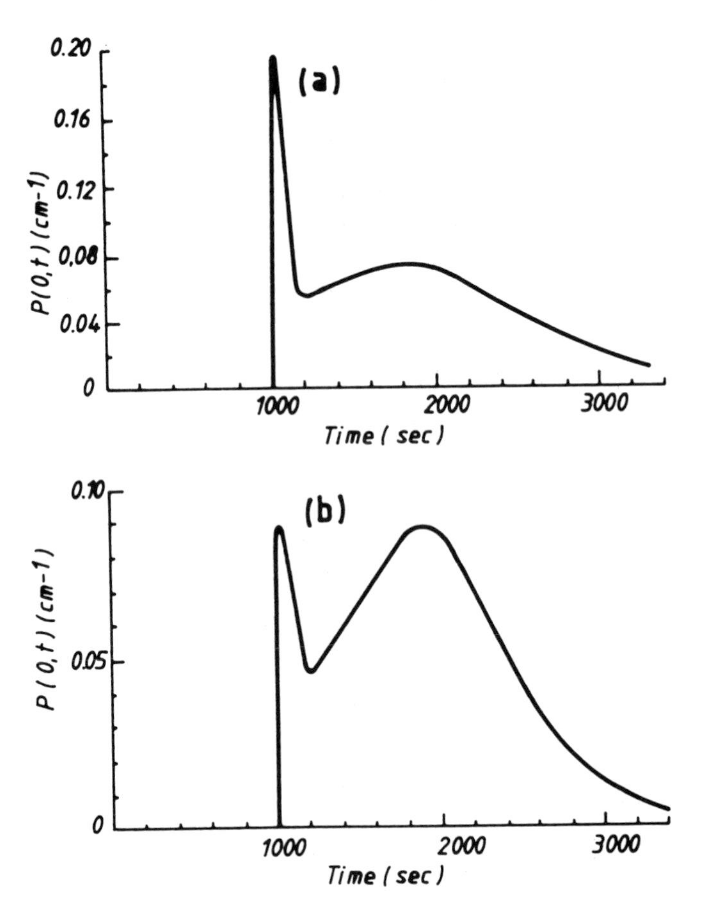

FIGURE 12–19. Bimodal elution peak for a homogeneous population under ideal conditions. $D = 10^{-6}$ cm²/sec; $u = 0.01$ cm/sec; $L = 10$ cm; $h_1/h_{-1} = 1$. (a) $h_1 = 4 \times 10^{-3}$ sec^{-1}; (b) $h_1 = 5 \times 10^{-3}$ sec^{-1}. (From ref. 109.)

With the partial differential equations:

$$\frac{\partial(\overline{Q}'_P + \overline{Q}_P)}{\partial t} = k_1 V_o \overline{C} - k_{-1} \overline{Q}'_P \qquad (12\text{–}87)$$

$$\frac{\partial \overline{Q}_P}{\partial t} = k_3 \frac{\overline{Q}_X}{V_i \sigma_P} \overline{Q}'_P - k_{-3} \overline{Q}_P \qquad (12\text{–}88)$$

where the amount of free immobilized ligand $\overline{Q}_X$ is assumed to be independent of the solute concentration (hypothesis of linear chromatography).

$k_3/k_{-3} = K_{PX}$ and K_{PX} is the equilibrium constant for a monomeric protein interacting with a single site immobilized ligand. The rate constant k_3 (liters $mol^{-1}sec^{-1}$) is relative to a second-order process and the others k_1, k_{-1}, and k_{-3} (sec^{-1}) to first-order ones.

When the adsorption is quasiirreversible toward the time scale of the experiment (k_{-3} very small), it may be shown by solving the system of differential equations [Eqs. (12–76), (12–87), and (12–88)] using Laplace transform that the fraction f of solute that has not been retained by affinity depends on flow rate F:

$$-1/\ln(f) = F\left(\frac{1}{k_1 V_o} + \frac{1}{k_3 Q_x}\right) \qquad (12\text{–}89)$$

The value $f = 0$ is valid for a normal chromatographic behavior, without the appearance of an unretained peak. Equation (12–89) predicts the occurrence of the "split-peak" phenomenon with high enough flow rate values.

The "split-peak"[119] behavior was studied for a chromatographic system consisting of immobilized protein A and immunoglobulin G and the flow rate was varied through short protein columns. When the inverse of the logarithm of the fraction of nonadsorbed protein is plotted as a function of flow rate, straight lines were obtained in agreement with Eq. (12–89). The activity of immobilized protein A was determined from breakthrough curves and an independent estimate of k_1 was obtained from the plate height method [Eq. (12–81)], using a matrix without immobilized protein. For an adsorption limited process, a reasonable value for the association rate constant of protein A with IgG ($k_3 = 1.2 \times 10^5$ liters mol^{-1} sec^{-1}) was measured when protein A was immobilized on a diol-bonded support using the "Schiff base" method.

It was found that the kinetic properties of the protein depend on the immobilization method. The "split-peak" method is particularly useful for studying antibody–antigen reaction when the retention is strong. The derivation of Eq. (12–89) is based on the assumptions of linear elution chromatography. Since a dependence of the retention volume with sample size was observed, an extrapolation to zero sample size was necessary to extract kinetic parameters.

Further Hage and Walters[120] used computer simulations to determine how nonlinear elution conditions affect those measurements. The method was used to estimate the effects due to a nonlinear equilibrium law. Two experimental systems were studied: the retention of hemoglobin on reversed-phase columns and the binding of immunoglobulin to protein A affinity column. This work demonstrates the applicability of the linear extrapolation zero flow rate, as used previously.[119]

Another method of measuring the association and dissociation rate constants of biological materials was introduced by Moore and Walters[121]: the "peak decay" method, based on the analysis of the elution peak shape when only a single dissociation takes place. The model assumes that there are two reversible processes occurring in the column: an adsorption–desorption step and a diffusional mass transport step:

$$\left.\begin{array}{ccc} P\text{–}X & \underset{k_3}{\overset{k_{-3}}{\rightleftarrows}} & P_p + X \\ P_P & \underset{k_1}{\overset{k_{-1}}{\rightleftarrows}} & P \end{array}\right\} \quad (12\text{–}90)$$

The solute adsorbed in the column is eluted with a competing inhibitor, which binds to X rather than to P. Since the inhibitor prevents readsorption and does not cause the dissociation of the complex PX, the value of k_{-3} is not altered. If large competing inhibitor concentrations are used ($k' = 0$), and with a zero length column, it may be shown that the peak profile equation reduces to a simple exponential decay when $k_{-3} \ll k_{-1}$.

The dissociation rate constant could be determined from the slope of the plot of the logarithm of the signal in the tailing part of the peak vs. elution volume. Computed numerical modeling was used to find the best conditions to apply the peak decay method. It was shown that if k_{-1} was 10 times larger or smaller than k_{-3}, the smaller of the two rate constants (k_{-1} or k_{-3}) could be measured.

The experimental system consists in studying the elution of a fluorescent sugar on immobilized concanavalin A. After equilibration of the solute with a weak buffer, the mobile phase was changed for a strong buffer containing mannose. A large flow rate was maintained while the solute peak decay was recorded. The experiments were performed at several flow rates and mannose concentrations. The dissociation rate constant (1.8 ± 0.1 sec^{-1} at 25°C) is in excellent agreement with the value measured by the plate height method (2.0 ± 0.6 sec^{-1}) but approximately half of the one determined from free solution studies (3.4 sec^{-1}). A higher precision is, however, obtained from the peak decay method, which should be useful for measuring rate constants for univalent interactions in the range of 10 to 10^{-3} sec^{-1}.

12.3.3.2 Second-Order Kinetics with a "Langmuir"-Type Isotherm

The interaction between a monomeric univalent solute P with the immobilized binding sites X on the affinity adsorbent can be described by an equilibrium equation of the form:

$$P + X \underset{k_r}{\overset{k_f}{\rightleftarrows}} P\text{–}X \quad (12\text{–}91)$$

where k_f is the second-order rate constant governing the forward reaction and k_r is the first-order rate constant governing the reverse one.

This model assumes instantaneous equilibrium between the pore and bulk liquid phases ($\overline{Q}'_P = \overline{Q}'^{*}_P = V_i\overline{C}\sigma$) and corresponds to a Langmuir-type equilibrium isotherm. At equilibrium one writes

$$\overline{Q}^{*}_{P} = \frac{K_{PX}\overline{C}\,\overline{Q}_X}{1 + K_{PX}\overline{C}} \quad (12\text{–}92)$$

This corresponds to a Langmuir-type equilibrium isotherm. The ratio k_f/k_r is equal to the association constant K_{PX} relative to the chemical equilibrium.

The rate of formation of the affinity complex is described by the relationship

$$\frac{\partial \overline{\mathcal{Q}}_P}{\partial t} = k_f \overline{C}(\overline{\mathcal{Q}}_X - \overline{\mathcal{Q}}_P) - k_r \overline{\mathcal{Q}}_P \qquad (12\text{–}93)$$

Output Signal Analysis The expression of mass balance in the chromatographic system [Eq. (12–76)] is now in the form

$$(1 + k_0)\frac{\partial \overline{C}}{\partial t} + u\frac{\partial \overline{C}}{\partial z} - D\frac{\partial^2 \overline{C}}{\partial z^2} = -\frac{1}{V_o}\frac{\partial \overline{\mathcal{Q}}_P}{\partial t} \qquad (12\text{–}94)$$

The analytical solution of the system of differential equations (12–93) and (12–94) was obtained by Thomas[122] and was adapted by Chase[123] to predict the shape of sorption "breakthrough" curves in affinity chromatography.

The affinity systems investigated to test the validity of the theoretical predictions were the binding of proteins (bovine serum albumin and hen egg lysozyme) to Cibacron Blue Sepharose and the adsorption of *E. coli* β-galactosidase on an immobilized monoclonal antibody.

Taking into account the dispersion effects through the column Arnold et al.[124,125] extended the theoretical model. They described adsorption, wash, and elution processes in liquid chromatography. It is shown that the dispersion contributions (axial dispersion, diffusion inside the pores) are to be added to the mass transfer kinetics.

The theory was further developed by Carr et al.,[126] who gave a rigorous analytical solution of the output signal in elution chromatography. The retention behavior of *p*-nitrophenyl-α-D-mannopyranoside on immobilized concanavalin A was studied. The adsorption–desorption rate constants and the binding site density were obtained for the more populous binding sites. The nonlinear theory reveals heterogeneous affinity adsorption on immobilized concanavalin A.

Displacement Method Sportsman and Wilson[127,128] described a method of extracting kinetic parameters from an unusual chromatographic behavior, in which a part of the solute is eluted like an unretained peak, while the other one is strongly retained.

On a very short column a fraction of the solute yields a nonretained peak (referenced A). Then the mobile phase is changed to elute the retained fraction as a second peak (referenced B) (Figure 12–20). The system studied was the interaction of two antigen proteins: human immunoglobulin and beef insulin with their respective antibodies immobilized on diol-bonded porous glass spheres. With an apparent binding constant K' defined as

$$K' = \frac{\{PX\}}{[\overline{P}]\,\{X\}} \qquad (12\text{–}95)$$

The ratio g of the area of peak B (amount of bound antigen $\overline{\mathcal{Q}}_P = \{PX\} \cdot S$) over the one of peak A (amount of free antigen $[P]V_0$), plotted vs. the amount of bound antigen, yields a straight line:

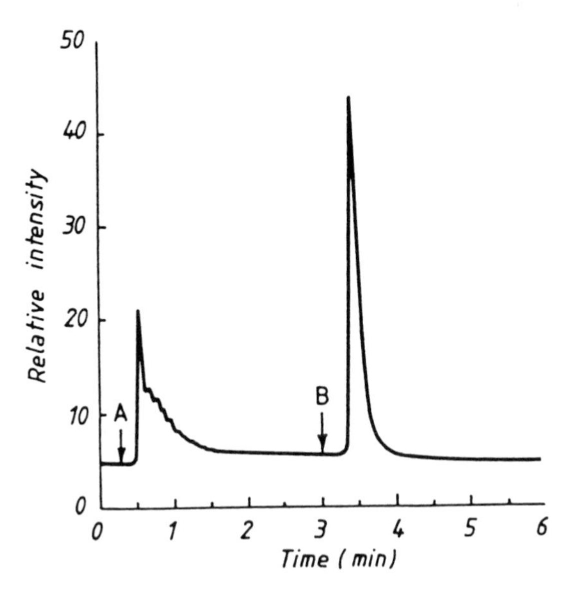

FIGURE 12–20. High-performance immunoaffinity chromatography. Immunosorbent: monoclonal antiinsulin attached to Lichrosphere Si-100; antigen: insulin (volume injected: 50 µl). Column: 2 mm i.d. × 4 cm. Flow rate: 0.30 ml/min. Mobile phase A: phosphate-buffered saline pH 7.4. Mobile phase B: 28% acetonitrile in phosphate-buffered saline. (From ref. 127.)

$$\frac{\overline{\mathcal{Q}}_P}{[\overline{P}]V_o} = \frac{\overline{\mathcal{Q}}_x K'}{V_o} - \frac{\overline{\mathcal{Q}}_P K'}{V_o} \qquad (12\text{–}96)$$

where $\overline{\mathcal{Q}}_x$ is the total amount of active antibodies immobilized on silica.

It is shown that the binding of an antigen (human IgG) with an immobilized antibody (antihuman IgG) may be described by an apparent binding constant K', of which the value depends on flow rate. The value of 7.8 for log K', extrapolated to zero flow rate, is in good agreement with the one obtained from batch experiments (7.6 ± 0.2).

For the insulin–antiinsulin system the value of 8.8×10^5 liters/mol is obtained for K' and a single type of binding is found. The chromatographic method describes adequately the insulin–antiinsulin system since one finds the value of 8.8×10^5 liters/mol for K' with a single type of binding site, close to the value obtained with cold competition radioassay experiments ($K' = 1.5 \times 10^6$ liters/mol).

The method was further investigated to derive kinetic rate constants from these experiments. Sportsman et al.[128] studied the interaction of antigen insulin with an antiserum exhibiting high affinity when immobilized on the diol-bonded silica phase. Equilibrium studies show that the nonspecific interaction of the diol-bonded phase is a significant process that explains why the measured apparent binding constant varies with the amount of antibody immobilized on the matrix.

The dependence of the amount of insulin bound to the column as a function of the flow rate (in the range of 0.1 to 0.5 ml/min) was treated in order to obtain the apparent forward rate constant k_f of the slower process. In chromatographic or batch experiments the data were plotted according to the integrated form of a second-order reversible rate expression, which is a function of the concentration of bound antigen at any time and at equilibrium. The batch mode kinetics indicate the heterogeneity of the antigenic binding sites. The values of k_f obtained for the "slower" process (3.4×10^6 liters/mol^{-1} sec^{-1}) are in good agreement with the values from chromatographic measurements (3.6×10^6 liters/mol^{-1}sec^{-1}).

To study faster rate kinetics chromatographic experiments were carried out at higher flow rates (0.5 to 3.0 ml/min). The forward rate constant (3.0×10^7 liters/mol^{-1}sec^{-1}) observed for fast kinetics is consistent with a diffusion-limited process for the antigen–antibody association. The apparent reverse rate constant k_r (6.0×10^{-3} sec^{-1}) indicates that an essentially irreversible reaction takes place.

12.4 CONCLUSION

The usefulness of size exclusion or ionic chromatography as a tool for protein interaction characterization was demonstrated many years ago. Soft gels available in the 1960s were used first but were progressively replaced by the rigid and small-diameter materials of HPLC columns. As kinetic aspects are not often considered, the saturation methods including frontal analysis, recycle, and vacancy chromatography are preferred to zonal chromatography. In these methods, the measurements based on the components concentration are often more reliable than those obtained from retention volumes. Indeed in this last case, physical interactions between similar or dissimilar protein or gel and protein can alter the confidence of results. The main limitation is due to the amount of material required for the experiments. The recycle technique of Ford and Winzor[39] affords in this respect interesting perspectives.

As with size exclusion chromatography, affinity chromatography is a reliable technique for measuring protein–protein interactions between free species dissolved in the liquid phase. The equilibrium constants are then generally in good agreement with those determined from other techniques. Large differences exist, however, with the constants characterizing the interaction between the free protein and that immobilized on the support, since the capacities of the protein to recognize a specific receptor will depend on the point of attachment of the immobilized species to the matrix. The trend is now to produce immobilized ligands with affinity properties as close as possible to those of the free ones, to decrease the nonspecific interactions of the support itself and, for kinetic measurements, to reduce the contributions due to the diffusion into the pores and the extra-column effects.

The fundamental basis of the equilibrium between the interacting species is now well understood in affinity chromatography. Frontal elution is a powerful tool for measuring the equilibrium constants of complicated systems, since the amount of interacting species at equilibrium is easily related to the chromatographic data. The potentialities of the zonal analysis are advantageous from both theoretical and experimental viewpoints. Experiments are easy and require a small amount of injected protein, while the method could in principle be used to determine equilibrium and kinetic constants. An effort should now be expected to develop the theoretical approaches, since the hypotheses on which the present theory is based, linear chromatography and instantaneous equilibrium, are seldom confirmed experimentally.

As a micro method, zonal chromatography is probably the most promising technique to approach both kinetics and thermodynamic parameters of protein–protein interactions. Some years ago, it was restricted to systems in which the equilibrium was very rapid or the dissociation very slow so that the time of residence in the column had no influence on the equilibrium state.

At the present time, some examples of intermediate kinetics have appeared and theoretical and experimental improvements are expected to develop the use of zonal elution in this field. It is hoped that the growing development of numerical methods to simulate and fit experimental curves in chromatography will provide efficient means to characterize all the parameters of associations involving proteins with minute amounts of samples.

REFERENCES

1. L. W. Nichol and D. J. Winzor, *J. Phys. Chem.*, 68 (1964) 2455.
2. G. A. Gilbert and G. L. Kellett, *J. Biol. Chem.*, 246 (1971) 6079.
3. M. H. Klapper, G. H. Barlow, and J. M. Klotz, *Biochem. Biophys. Res. Commun.*, 25 (1966) 116.
4. N. R. Langerman and I. M. Klotz, *Biochemistry*, 8 (1969) 4746.
5. G. A. Gilbert, *Disc. Faraday Soc.*, 20 (1955) 68.
6. G. A. Gilbert, *Proc. R. Soc. London Ser., A*, 250 (1959) 377.
7. D. J. Winzor and H. A. Scheraga, *Biochemistry*, 2 (1963) 1263.
8. G. K. Ackers and T. E. Thompson, *Proc. Natl. Acad. Sci. U.S.A.*, 53 (1965) 342.
9. D. J. Winzor, J. P. Loke, and L. W. Nichol, *J. Phys. Chem.*, 71 (1967) 4492.
10. L. W. Nichol and A. B. Roy, *Biochemistry*, 4 (1965) 386.
11. D. J. Winzor, *Biochim. Biophys. Acta*, 200 (1970) 423.
12. B. A. Whittaker and N. N. Allewell, *Arch. Biochem. Biophys.*, 234 (1984) 585.
13. D. J. Winzor and H. A. Scheraga, *J. Phys. Chem.*, 68 (1964) 338.
14. E. Chiancone, L. M. Gilbert, G. A. Gilbert, and G. L. Kellett, *J. Biol. Chem.*, 243 (1968) 1212.
15. G. A. Gilbert, *Anal. Chem. Acta*, 38 (1967) 275.
16. E. Edmond, S. Farquhar, J. R. Dunstone, and A. G. Ogston, *Biochem. J.*, 108 (1968) 755.
17. L. W. Nichol, M. Janado, and D. J. Winzor, *Biochem. J.*, 133 (1973) 15.
18. S. A. Baghurst, L. W. Nichol, A. G. Ogston, and D. J. Winzor, *Biochem. J.*, 147 (1975) 575.

19. P. J. Flory, Principles of Polymer Chemistry. Cornell Univ. Press, Ithaca, NY, 1953, pp. 490–540, 577–581.
20. R. Tellam and D. J. Winzor, *Biophys. Chem.*, 12 (1980) 299.
21. (a) L. W. Nichol, R. J. Siezen, and D. J. Winzor, *Biophys. Chem.*, 9 (1978) 47. (b) R. J. Siezen, L. W. Nichol, and D. J. Winzor, *Biophys. Chem.*, 10 (1979) 17. (c) R. J. Siezen, L. W. Nichol, and D. J. Winzor, *Biophys. Chem.*, 14 (1981) 221.
22. A. P. Minton, *Biophys. Chem.*, 18 (1983) 139.
23. J. K. Snook and D. Henderson, *J. Chem. Phys.*, 68 (1978) 2134.
24. K. Adachi and T. Asakura, *J. Biol. Chem.*, 254 (1979) 12273.
25. G. A. Gilbert, *Nature (London)*, 212 (1966) 296.
26. S. J. Lovell and D. J. Winzor, *Biochemistry*, 13 (1974) 3527.
27. M. Gattoni, D. Verzili, E. Chiancone, and E. Antonini, *Biochim. Biophys. Acta*, 743 (1983) 180.
28. (a) L. W. Nichol and D. J. Winzor, *J. Phys. Chem.*, 68 (1964) 2455. (b) D. J. Winzor, in Protein–Protein Interactions (C. Frieden and D. J. Winzor, eds.). Wiley, New York, 1981.
29. G. A. Gilbert and R. C. L. Jenkins, *Proc. R. Soc. London Ser. A*, 253 (1959) 420.
30. L. W. Nichol, A. G. Ogston, and D. J. Winzor, *Arch. Biochem. Biophys.*, 121 (1967) 517.
31. J. P. Johnson and A. G. Ogston, *Trans. Faraday Soc.*, 42 (1946) 789.
32. D. J. Winzor and L. W. Nichol, *Biochim. Biophys. Acta*, 104 (1965) 1.
33. G. A. Gilbert and G. L. Kellet, *J. Biol. Chem.*, 246 (1971) 6079.
34. G. A. Gilbert, *Nature (London)*, 210 (1966) 299.
35. E. E. Brumbaugh and G. K. Ackers, *J. Biol. Chem.*, 243 (1968) 6315.
36. G. K. Ackers, E. E. Brumbaugh, S. H. C. Ip, and H. R. Halvorson, *Biophys. Chem.*, 4 (1976) 171.
37. R. Valdes, L. P. Vickers, H. R. Halvorson, and G. K. Ackers, *Proc. Natl. Acad. Sci. U.S.A.*, 75 (1978) 5493.
38. R. Valdes and G. K. Ackers, *Proc. Natl. Acad. Sci. U.S.A.*, 75 (1978) 311.
39. C. L. Ford and D. J. Winzor, *Anal. Biochem.*, 114 (1981) 146.
40. P. J. Hogg and D. J. Winzor, *Biochim. Biophys. Acta.*, 843 (1985) 159.
41. L. W. Nichol, L. D. Ward, and D. J. Winzor, *Biochemistry*, 20 (1981) 4856.
42. D. J. Winzor, L. D. Ward, and L. W. Nichol, *J. Theor. Biol.*, 98 (1982) 171.
43. N. Thuaud, B. Sebille, M. H. Livertoux, and J. Bessiere, *J. Chromatogr.*, 282 (1983) 509.
44. J. P. Mahieu, B. Sebille, C. T. Craescu, M. D. Rhoda, and Y. Beuzard, *J. Chromatogr.*, 327 (1985) 313.
45. K. Akasaka, S. Fujii, F. Hayashi, S. Rokushika, and H. Hatano, *Biochem. Int.*, 5 (1982) 637.
46. K. Murakami, N. Ueno, and S. Hirose, *J. Chromatogr.*, 225 (1981) 329.
47. K. C. Ingham, T. F. Busby, D. H. Atha, and H. Forastieri, *J. Liquid Chromatogr.*, 6 (1983) 229.
48. H. Tojo, K. Horiike, K. Shiga, Y. Nishina, M. Nozaki, H. Watari, and T. Yamano, *J. Biochem.*, 95 (1984) 1.
49. H. R. Halvorson and G. K. Ackers, *J. Biol. Chem.*, 249 (1974) 967.
50. J. K. Zimmerman, *Biochemistry*, 13 (1974) 2.
51. M. Anbari, K. Adachi, C. Y. Ip, and T. Asakura, *J. Biol. Chem.*, 260 (1985) 1522.
52. I. M. Chaiken, *J. Chromatogr. Biomed. Appl.*, 376 (1986) 11.
53. D. J. Winzor, in Affinity Chromatography. A Practical Approach (P. D. G. Dean, W. S. Johnson, and F. A. Middle, eds.). IRL Press, Oxford, 1984, pp. 149–168.
54. D. M. Abercrombie and I. M. Chaiken, in Affinity Chromatography. A Practical Approach (P. D. G. Dean, W. S. Johnson, and F. A. Middle, eds.). IRL Press, Oxford, 1984, p. 169.

55. G. Fassina and I. M. Chaiken, Advances in Chromatography, Vol. 27 (J. C. Giddings, E. Grushka, and P. R. Brown, eds.). Dekker, New York, 1987, p. 247.
56. P. O. Larsson, M. Glad, L. Hansson, M.-O. Manson, S. Ohlson, and X. Mosbach, Advances in Chromatography, Vol. 21 (J. C. Giddings, E. Grushka, J. Cazes, and P. R. Brown, eds.). Dekker, New York, 1983, p. 41.
57. J. F. K. Huber and R. G. Gerritse, *J. Chromatogr.*, 58 (1971) 137.
58. J. N. Wilson, *J. Am. Chem. Soc.*, 62 (1940) 1583.
59. F. Riedo and E. sz. Kováts, *J. Chromatogr.*, 239 (1982) 1.
60. F. H. Arnold, S. A. Schofield, and H. W. Blanch, *J. Chromatogr.*, 355 (1986) 1.
61. J. Turkova, Affinity Chromatography. Elesevier, Amsterdam, 1978, p. 35.
62. I. M. Chaiken, *Anal. Biochem.*, 97 (1979) 1.
63. B. M. Dunn, *Appl. Biochem. Biotechnol.* 9 (1984) 261.
64. L. W. Nichol, A. G. Ogston, D. J. Winzor, and W. H. Sawyer, *Biochem. J.*, 143 (1974) 435.
65. B. M. Dunn and I. M. Chaiken, *Proc. Natl. Acad. Sci. U.S.A.*, 71 (1974) 2382.
66. B. M. Dunn and I. M. Chaiken, *Biochemistry*, 14 (1975) 2343.
67. K. Kasai, Y. Oda, M. Nishikata, and S. Ishii, *J. Chromatogr. Biomed. Appl.*, 376 (1986) 33.
68. K. Kasai and S. Ishii, *J. Biochem.*, 77 (1975) 261.
69. M. Nishikata, K. Kasai, and S. Ishii, *J. Biochem.*, 82 (1977) 1475.
70. K. Kasai and S. Ishii, *J. Biochem.*, 84 (1978) 1051.
71. K. Kasai and S. Ishii, *J. Biochem.*, 84 (1978) 1061.
72. I. M. Chaiken and H. C. Taylor, *J. Biol. Chem.*, 251 (1976) 2044.
73. M. Malanikova and J. Turkova, *J. Solid-Phase Biochem.*, 2 (1977) 237.
74. I. M. Chaiken, *Anal. Biochem.*, 97 (1979) 302.
75. S. Angal and I. M. Chaiken, *Biochemistry*, 21 (1982) 1574.
76. J. M. Alessandri, C. Léger, and N. Mahe, *Biochimie*, 66 (1984) 663.
77. N. Mahe, C. L. Leger, A. Linard, and J. M. Alessandri, *J. Chromatogr.*, 395 (1987) 511.
78. D. Eilat and I. M. Chaiken, *Biochemistry*, 18 (1979) 790.
79. I. M. Chaiken, D. Eilat, and W. M. McCormick, *Biochemistry*, 18 (1979) 794.
80. D. J. Anderson and R. R. Walters, *J. Chromatogr.*, 331 (1985) 1.
81. D. J. Anderson, J. S. Anhalt, and R. R. Walters, *J. Chromatogr.*, 359 (1986) 369.
82. J. K. Inman, in Affinity Chromatography and Biological Recognition (I. M. Chaiken, M. Wilchek, and I. Parikh, eds.). Academic Press, Orlando, FL, 1983, p. 153.
83. H. W. Hethcote and C. Delisi, *J. Chromatogr.*, 248 (1982) 183.
84. C. Delisi and H. W. Hethcote, in Affinity Chromatography and Related Techniques (T. C. J. Gribnau, J. Visser, and R. J. F. Nivard, eds.). Elsevier, Amsterdam, 1982, p. 63.
85. P. J. Hogg and D. J. Winzor, *Arch. Biochem. Biophys.*, 240 (1985) 70.
86. I. M. Klotz, *Arch. Biochem.*, 9 (1946) 109.
87. P. J. Hogg and D. J. Winzor, *Arch. Biochem. Biophys.*, 234 (1984) 55.
88. R. I. Brinkworth, C. J. Masters, and D. J. Winzor, *Biochem. J.*, 151 (1975) 631.
89. D. A. Bergman and D. J. Winzor, *Anal. Biochem.*, 153 (1986) 380.
90. P. Kyprianou and R. J. Yon, *Biochem. J.*, 207 (1982) 549.
91. R. J. Yon and P. Kyprianou, in Affinity Chromatography and Replated Techniques (T. C. J. Gribnau, J. Visser, and R. J. F. Nivard, eds.). Elsevier, Amsterdam, 1982, p. 143.
92. D. J. Winzor and R. J. Yon, *Biochem. J.*, 217 (1984) 867.
93. Y. Oda, K. Kasai, and S. Ishii, *J. Biochem.*, 89 (1981) 285.
94. E. Antonini and M. R. Rossi Fanelli, in Methods in Enzymology, Vol. 44 (K. Mosbach, ed.). Academic Press, New York, 1976, p. 538.
95. E. Antonini, G. Carrea, P. Cremonesi, P. Pasta, M. R. Rossi Fanelli, and E. Chiancone, *Anal. Biochem.*, 95 (1979) 89.

96. E. Chiancone, M. Gattoni, and E. Antonini, in Affinity Chromatography and Biological Recognition (I. M. Chaiken, M. Wilchek, and I. Parikh, eds.). Academic Press, Orlando, FL, 1983, p. 103.
97. M. R. Rossi Fanelli, G. Amiconi, and E. Antonini, *Eur. J. Biochem.*, 92 (1978) 253.
98. G. Carrea, P. Pasta, and E. Antonini, *Biotechnol. Bioeng.*, 27 (1985) 704.
99. H. E. Swaisgood and I. M. Chaiken, *Biochemistry*, 25 (1986) 4148.
100. I. M. Chaiken, H. Tamaoki, M. J. Brownstein, and H. Gainer, *FEBS Lett.*, 164 (1983) 361.
101. D. M. Abercrombie, T. Kanmera, S. Angal, H. Tamaoki, and I. M. Chaiken, *Int. J. Pept. Prot. Res.*, 24 (1984) 218.
102. T. Kanmera and I. M. Chaiken, *J. Biol. Chem.*, 260 (1985) 8474.
103. H. E. Swaisgood and I. M. Chaiken, *J. Chromatogr.*, 327 (1985) 193.
104. G. Fassina, H. E. Swaisgood, and I. M. Chaiken, *J. Chromatogr. Biomed. Appl.*, 376 (1986) 87.
105. J. C. Giddings, Dynamics of Chromatography, Part I, Principles and Theory. Dekker, New York, 1965.
106. J. C. Giddings and H. Eyring, *J. Phys. Chem.*, 59 (1955) 416.
107. F. C. Denizot and M. A. Delaage, *Biochemistry*, 72 (1975) 4840.
108. H. W. Hethcote and C. Delisi, *J. Chromatogr.*, 240 (1982) 269.
109. C. Delisi, H. W. Hethcote, and J. W. Brettler, *J. Chromatogr.*, 240 (1982) 283.
110. Cs Horvath and H. J. Lin, *J. Chromatogr.*, 126 (1976) 401.
111. Cs Horvath and H. J. Lin, *J. Chromatogr.*, 149 (1978) 43.
112. F. H. Arnold, H. W. Blanch, and C. R. Wilke, *J. Chromatogr.*, 330 (1985) 159; *Chem. Eng. J.*, 30 (1985) B25.
113. R. R. Walters, *J. Chromatogr.*, 249 (1982) 19.
114. K. Nilsson and P. O. Larsson, *Anal. Biochem.*, 134 (1983) 60.
115. A. J. Muller and P. W. Carr, *J. Chromatogr.*, 284 (1984) 33.
116. A. J. Muller and P. W. Carr, *J. Chromatogr.*, 357 (1986) 11.
117. D. J. Anderson and R. R. Walters, *J. Chromatogr. Biomed. Appl.*, 376 (1986) 69.
118. J. C. Giddings, *Anal. Chem.*, 35 (1963) 1999.
119. D. S. Hage, R. R. Walters, and H. W. Hethcote, *Anal. Chem.*, 58 (1986) 274.
120. D. S. Hage and R. R. Walters, *J. Chromatogr.*, 436 (1988) 111.
121. R. M. Moore and R. R. Walters, *J. Chromatogr.*, 384 (1987) 91.
122. H. Thomas, *J. Am. Chem. Soc.*, 66 (1944) 1664.
123. H. A. Chase, *J. Chromatogr.*, 297 (1984) 179.
124. F. H. Arnold and H. W. Blanch, *J. Chromatogr.*, 355 (1986) 13.
125. F. H. Arnold, H. W. Blanch, and C. R. Wilke, *Chem. Eng. J.*, 30 (1985) B9.
126. J. L. Wade, A. F. Bergold, and P. W. Carr, *Anal. Chem.*, 59 (1987) 1286.
127. J. R. Sportsman and G. S. Wilson, *Anal. Chem.*, 52 (1980) 2013.
128. J. R. Sportsman, J. D. Lidll, and G. S. Wilson, *Anal. Chem.*, 55 (1983) 771.

CHAPTER 13

Preparative Dye-Ligand Chromatography

Y. D. Clonis

CONTENTS

13.1 INTRODUCTION

Affinity chromatography[1] is by far the most powerful and effective technique used in enzyme and protein purification. As the quality criteria imposed on fine biomolecules become more stringent the technique finds increasing application in downstream processing.[2,3] Affinity chromatography exploits the formation of specific reversible complexes formed between a ligand immobilized on an insoluble porous support and the complementary biomolecule(s) to be isolated. After the affinity adsorbent has been packed in a column, the sample is applied, nonadsorbed material is washed off with irrigating buffer, and specifically adsorbed compounds then eluted by altering the buffer composition. Depending on the ligand immobilized, affinity adsorbents are distinguished as those of high specificity, typically binding one biomolecule (e.g., antibody–antigen complexes), and those of moderate specificity, the so-called group-specific adsorbents, binding a number of related biomolecules. However, although a respectable number of useful and effective adsorbents/ligands of the latter category are currently available, they often display certain drawbacks. For example, the chemical synthesis of defined affinity ligands requires considerable chemical and biological expertise, and is both laborious and expensive. In addition, the adsorbents based on such ligands often display low binding capacities and are susceptible to both chemical and biological degradation. In contrast, dye ligands[4] offer several advantages over group-specific affinity ligands, for example, they are available in large quantities and at low cost, can easily and safely be immobilized to various supports, and are resistant to chemical and biological degradation. Furthermore, dye adsorbents have high binding capacities for many proteins that can be eluted under mild conditions with good yields. The advantages offered by dye ligands should stimulate workers to employ affinity chromatography with dyes[4,5] at a preparative scale and on a routine basis, since these remarkable molecules can successfully answer the frequently cited problem of ligand cost. Furthermore, dyes, because of their built-in reactivity and ease of immobilization, practically eliminate any hazards during the large-scale coupling procedures that are often encountered with conventional matrix activation and ligand coupling techniques.

13.2 THE DYE MOLECULE AND ENZYME PURIFICATION

Commercial dyes encompass a complete range of shades derived primarily from anthraquinone, azo, and phthalocyanine chromophores bonded to suitable reactive functions such as triazinyl, other polyhalogenyl heterocycles, vinyl sulfone, sulfatoethyl sulfone, or β-chloroethyl sulfones. Anthraquinone dyes produce bright blue and the phthalocyanines bright turquoise shades. Green dyes are produced by structures containing mixed anthraquinone-stilbene, anthraquinone, azo, or phthalocyanine-azo chromophores, while the remainder of the spectral range are derived mainly from the azo class. Black, violet, brown, and rubine dyes are metal complexes of *O,O'*-dihydroxyazo or *O*-hydroxy-*O'*-carboxyazo chromophores. Triazine dyes have been used more than any other dye family in enzyme and protein purifications, and, likewise, the triazine dye Cibacron® Blue F3G-A (Figure 13–1a) has received by far most attention by biochemists. This may well be attributed to a pure historical accident that occurred during an anomalous size exclusion chromatographic run of yeast pyruvate kinase using Blue Dextran as void volume marker. It was later revealed that the blue chromophore, Cibacron Blue F3G-A, was responsible for binding the enzyme and not the dextran carrier itself. A typical triazine dye structure comprises the chromophore linked to a highly reactive dichlorotriazinyl group (Procion® MX range) or to a less reactive monochlorotriazinyl group (Procion® H range) via a —NH— bridge. In the Procion H range the second chlorine has been substituted by a nonlabile terminal group, for example, a sulfoanilino group.

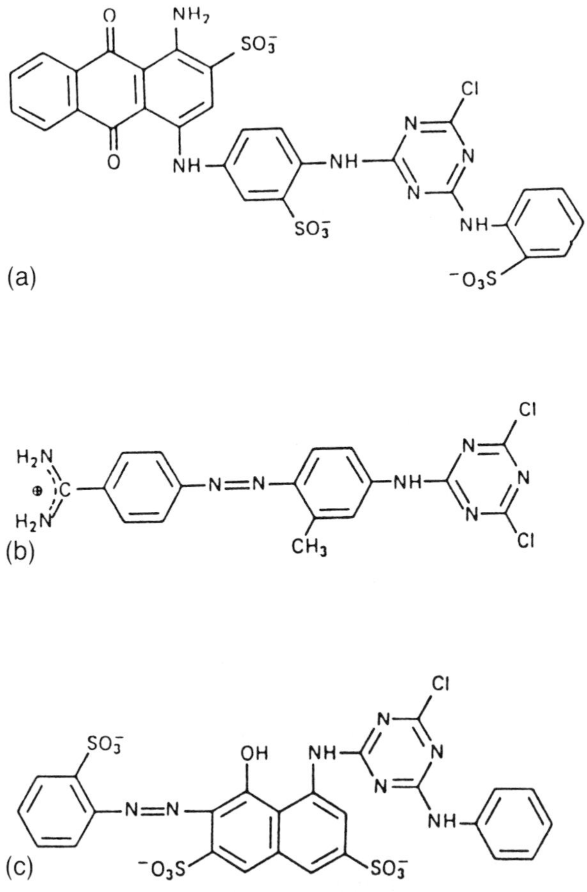

FIGURE 13–1. The chemical structure of some triazine dyes; (a) Cibacron® Blue F3G-A, (b) a cationic triazine dye, (c) Procion® Red H-3B.

After the original observation that led to the use of commercial textile triazine dyes in enzyme and protein purification, a large number of direct studies were performed in order to elucidate the nature and mode of dye–enzyme interactions. The fact that triazine dyes bind to various enzymes is of no surprise since the dye molecule displays a nearly planar arrangement and appears to resemble natural heterocyclic ligands in terms of charges and hydrophobicity. Furthermore, chromatographic, kinetic, absorption spectrum difference, induced circular dichroism, X-ray crystallographic and affinity labeling studies point to the conclusion that the dye molecule binds the enzyme at the binding site(s) of the natural ligands or at regions overlapping such natural binding sites.[6] Such binding phenomena allow for a varying degree of specificity during the formation of the dye–enzyme complex. Although some textile triazine dyes bind certain enzymes in a clearly specific manner, they also bind to other unrelated macromolecules. This universal binding ability of triazine dyes gave rise to a type of pseudoaffinity chromatography called dye-ligand chromatography. However, it is this universal binding of dye ligands that endows these molecules with moderate specificity, a fact that has received most of the criticism. To address this problem, the last few years have seen the introduction of purpose-designed dye ligands of high specificity tailor-made to the target enzyme. In many cases these novel dyes have been built using the principles of computer-aided molecular design. It has been possible to observe dramatic improvement of the dye specificity by defined structural modifications of the parent dye. The following examples are sufficient to demonstrate the potential of this new era in downstream processing. Substitution of the sulfonyl group of the terminal aminobenzylsulfonyl ring of the parent dye Cibacron® Blue F3G-A with an *m*-carboxyl group and insertion of an ethyl spacer between the triazine ring and the bridging diaminobenzene sulfonated ring have increased the affinity of the dye for horse liver alcohol dehydrogenase by several orders of magnitude.[7] The affinity adsorbent based on this purpose-designed dye could resolve commercial samples of the above enzyme into two active components. Notably, the structure of this dye was predicted from molecular design computing to be capable of adopting a similar shape and flexibility to NAD^+.[7] A novel cationic triazine dye bearing a benzamidine group was designed to specifically bind trypsin-like serine proteases (Figure 13–1b). After the dye was immobilized on agarose, it was successfully employed in a facile one-step resolution of trypsin and chymotrypsin from bovine crude pancreatic extract.[8] One-step 330-fold purification of alkaline phosphatase from a crude calf intestinal extract has been achieved with a purpose-designed dye ligand immobilized on agarose support.[9] In this case the terminal ring of the parent dye Cibacron® Blue F3G-A was substituted for a *p*-aminobenzylphosphoric acid ring, and the enzyme alkaline phosphate was recovered from the affinity dye adsorbent with 5 m*M* inorganic phosphate.[9]

13.3 MAKING A DYE ADSORBENT

The reactive part of triazine dyes is a heterocyclic chlorotriazinyl ring that although quite stable at near neutral pH will slowly hydrolyze under acidic conditions initiating an autocatalytic circle. To prevent this happening, a suitable buffer, usually phosphate, is added to the dye solution during the manufacturing process and before isolating the product by precipitating with salt. Additional sodium chloride is added to adjust the dye content together with an antidusting agent such as diodecylbenzene. Dyes made available for biochemical research by various firms are of this quality, although in addition, various amounts of precursor compounds are present. It is possible to purify commercial dye samples or dye ligands synthesized in the laboratory by passing a dye solution through a Sephadex® LH-20 column equilibrated in methanol–water. This is hardly justifiable for crude textile dye samples intended for the preparation of large columns, however, dye purification should be considered for purpose-synthesized dyes of high specificity.

Fixation of a triazine dye on a carbohydrate support is achieved with nucleophilic displacement of the dye chlorine atom(s) under alkaline conditions by the polymer hydroxyls.[5] On addition of a polysulfonic chlorotrazinyl dye to a suspension of carbohydrate polymeric support, the dye remains stable at nearly neutral pH. The addition of sodium chloride will "salt out" the dye onto the polymer by screening the repulsive electrostatic forces, thus bringing into proximity the two species, and it will also help to disintegrate "stacked" dye molecules. When satisfactory adsorption has been achieved (after 30 to 45 min) the pH is raised to 10–11 by adding sodium carbonate in order to initiate the formation of covalent bonds between the dye and the support. Obviously, at this stage, the dye can be attacked either by hydroxyl ions leading to dye hydrolysis or by carbohydrate-O^- ions resulting in dye fixation. Fortunately, the latter reaction is predominant, apparently because the carbohydrate O^- ions react faster than the hydroxyl ions, which are derived from the water, and because the dye molecules are already in proximity ("salted out") with the polymer ions. Acceleration in the rate of dye immobilization may be achieved by increasing the temperature and the pH. The final concentration of immobilized dye will also depend on the reactivity of the dye itself—dichlorotriazine dyes (Procion® MX range) are more reactive than chlorotriazine dyes (Procion® H range), the concentration of free dye in the reaction cocktail, and the reaction time. To couple a triazine dye directly to cross-linked agarose, the favorite support for preparative work, the gel is suspended in a dye solution (20 mg dye per g gel, 5 ml H_2O per g gel) followed by NaCl at a final concentration of 2% (w|v). After the suspension is incubated at room temperature for 30 min under shaking, solid sodium carbonate is added to a final concentration of 0.1 *M* and the reaction is further incubated either for 3 days at ambient/2 days at 30°C (monochlorotriazine dyes) or for 5 h at ambient/3 h at 30°C (dichlorotriazine dyes). Such dye immobilization protocols are straightforward for up to 1 liter or so of adsorbent volume; however, upon scaling-up to a few tens of liters, it is necessary to sample the large-scale reaction and determine the coupling level as the reaction proceeds. This is because mass and heat transfer phenomena important at the large-scale make it impossible to determine the time required to obtain the same substitution level as for the small-scale experiments. Should it be necessary, coupling of a dye to a support via a spacer molecule can be achieved in different ways. The reactive dye is coupled to dextran or some other similar spacer molecule and the conjugate then immobilized to the support material after appropriate activation of one of the species. Alternatively, the reactive dye is caused to react with an excess of diaminoalkane spacer molecule and the resulting aminoalkyl dye is then coupled to an appropriately active support under mild alkaline conditions. At first sight this seems to be uneconomical for preparative scale applications, however, in some instances it may improve the affinity of the dye ligand.[7] The latter immobilization approach is an inevitable choice for coupling monochlorotriazine dyes to silica-based supports, since silica is sensitive in alkaline conditions and this method is extremely mild.[10,11] Nevertheless, where possible, direct coupling of reactive dyes to polyhydroxylic supports still remains the favored approach for reasons of simplicity and economy. This method is also useful with the highly reactive dichlorotriazine dyes and appropriately coated silica, as it has been demonstrated on a large-scale 3.3-liter experiment,[12] as well as with synthetic macroporous rigid high-performance packings,[13] for example, TSK-PW (Toyo Soda, Japan), Separon (LIW, Czechoslovakia), and Dynospheres XP-3507 (Dyno Particles A.S., Norway).

After the accomplishment of the coupling procedure, only dichlorotriazine dye adsorbents should be left at pH 8.5 for 3 days to convert the remaining chlorine residues to hydroxyl functions. At the large-scale, washing protocols to remove unbound dye are more efficient when performed *in situ* in a column, and include 1–2 *M* NaCl, ethylene glycol [20% (v|v)], 6–8 *M* urea, although distilled water alone is probably the best washing medium for hydrophilic dyes.[6] The dye adsorbents should be stored in a solution of bacteriostatic agent (e.g., 0.02% sodium azide) at 4°C.

13.4 DEVELOPING A PURIFICATION PROCEDURE AND SCALING-UP

The initial development of a preparative-scale purification usually features, in the first place, screening of a large number of different dye adsorbents on a laboratory scale[14,15] (1–5 ml adsorbent) in order to determine the purification (fold), the binding capacity (mg protein/ml adsorbent), and the yield (%) and for a set of parameters such as ionic strength, temperature, pH, presence of metal ions, and elution medium. After narrowing the number of adsorbents to a few "possibles" a full study of each dye adsorbent is performed with respect to the above parameters in order to determine the optimal conditions. It is of paramount importance that right from the beginning of method development we use the same starting material/extract as we intend to employ later on at the preparative work. Some practical points are worth remembering: it has been suggested[16] that phosphate buffers be avoided since these can create problems with dye adsorbents. Also, usually, proteins bind anionic dyes more strongly at the lower pH range, and some dyes and proteins bind metal ions, consequently, the effect of metal ions on the dye–protein binding can be very crucial.[17] In most purification protocols relatively low ionic strength buffers (20–100 m*M*) are used for adsorption, whereas higher ionic strengths can be beneficial where the binding contains an element of hydrophobic interaction. Similarly, the effect of temperature on the interaction of immobilized dyes with enzymes is equally important. The operating temperature often may be determined from the stability of the biomolecule to be isolated, however, a temperature increase will strengthen the binding if the predominant forces are hydrophobic, and weaken the binding if the predominant forces are electrostatic.[6,14] Desorption of bound macromolecules can be effected by nonspecific means[8,15]: change of pH, ionic strength, and temperature, inclusion of chaotropic salts, ethylene glycol and glycerol, or by specific means[9,14,18]: inclusion of cofactors, inhibitors, substrates, and chelating agents. One efficient mode of operation is that involving two consecutive dye columns, a "negative" followed by a "positive"; the first column should not bind the protein of interest but other proteins that otherwise would occupy potential sites on the second column that binds preferentially the protein of interest.[19]

Let us now turn to the problem of scaling-up.[2,3] The economics of preparative-scale operations demand that the maximum possible material is processed through the adsorbent per hour. This is known as "throughput" and necessitates the use of high flow rates, which, however, should not exceed a critical value determined by the gel's rigidity and diffusion kinetics. The smaller the bead radius of the support, the larger the interfacial surface area and, also, the shorter the time required for a macromolecule to diffuse and reach the immobilized dye in the interior of the particle. Therefore, the efficiency of the adsorption–desorption process is improved by reducing the particle size. This, on the other hand, will increase the total interfacial support surface area above each unit of column cross section and may lead to bed compression if the support material is soft. Consequently, when scaling-up the particle size should not be small and one should also use a wider diameter column rather than increasing the column length. Obviously always the flow rate should not exceed a critical value determined by the support compressibility. The concept of stacked columns (Pharmacia, Sweden; Amicon, USA) is an excellent solution to the problem of bed compression; this approach comprises short, wide-diameter columns linked together by a small-bore tubing. Developments in chromatography support materials have practically eliminated the problem of bed compression. Natural polymeric supports cross-linked with dibromopropanol under the trade name CL-Sepharose® and Fast Flow Sepharose® are marketed by Pharmacia (Sweden), whereas Amicon (USA) has introduced the range of Matrex Cellufine® that can also tolerate high flow rates. Compression-resistant entirely synthetic beaded supports with functional hydroxyl groups are also available and include, Spheron® (Lachema Brno, Czechoslovakia), Trisacryl® (IBF, France), Toyopearl® (Toyo Soda, Japan), Fractogel TSK (Merck, Germany), and Eupergit® C, which contains active epoxy groups. Composite hydrogels made from agarose (2–6%) on Kieselguhr (diatomaceous earth) are available under the trade name Macrosorb® (Sterling Organics, U.K.). To address the need of high-performance preparative-scale affinity chromatography packings, various manufacturers have recently introduced rigid macroporous beaded hydrophilic supports with narrow particle-size distribution and appropriate functional groups (usually hydroxyl or epoxy) for ligand immobilization. Wide-pore silica has limited potential for preparative-scale high-performance affinity chromatography with dye ligands. Although it has excellent mechanical properties it also possesses two serious drawbacks, poor chemical stability in mild alkaline environments and the need for compulsory coating prior to dye coupling.[11,12] This has led to the introduction of synthetic porous hydrophilic supports[13]: (1) TSK-PW® (Toyo Soda, Japan), particle size in the range of 10 to 20 μm and size exclusion limits from 1×10^3 to 3×10^7 Da, (2) monosized Dynospheres® XP-3507 (Dyno Particles A.S., Norway), particle size 20 μm and pore size up to 0.2 μm, (3) Eupergit® C 30N (Röhm Pharma, Germany), particle size 30 μm and pore size 0.1–0.25 μm, and (4) Separon® HEMA 1000 (LIW/Prague, Czechoslovakia), particle size 10 μm and size exclusion limits between 10^4 and 5×10^6 Da.

It is important to remember that dye adsorbents, as other affinity media, require regular maintenance. The particular procedures vary with the nature of ligand and support. Dye ligands are virtually stable under any conditions of treatment, thus, the support itself is the limiting factor. Cross-linked polysaccharide and synthetic support materials, after they have been used in a protein purification, should be treated with 0.5–1.0 *M* NaOH or 6 *M* urea–0.5 *M* NaOH to free them of proteins, glycoproteins, and protein–lipid complexes. This care will extend the lifetime of the dye adsorbent and provide the production plant with substantial economy.

13.5 APPLICATIONS OF PREPARATIVE DYE-LIGAND CHROMATOGRAPHY

Dye-ligand adsorbents are especially aimed for preparative-scale chromatographic applications. This is because they are not only cheap and stable but also exhibit long lifetimes together with a high protein binding capacity. Table 13–1 summarizes preparative-scale purifications of proteins and enzymes using immobilized dye ligands.

Cibacron Blue F3G-A has been widely examined as a pseudoaffinity ligand for the purification of albumin and other plasma or serum proteins. A three column large-scale process has been described for the purification of IgGs and plasma albumin[20] (Figure 13–2). The first column, 50 liters Trisacryl®, was used to desalt the 17-liter plasma sample with a dilution factor of about 1.1. The second column, 50 liters DEAE-Trisacryl® M, adsorbed all proteins but IgGs in 0.025 *M* Tris-HCl buffer, pH 8.8, containing 0.035 *M* NaCl. Bound plasma proteins after were eluted in 0.05 *M* Tris-HCl buffer, pH 8.0 containing 0.75 *M* NaCl, loaded on a 50-liter Cibacron Blue F3G-A-Trisacryl® column equilibrated in the above buffer. Albumin and lipoproteins were totally bound, whereas all other proteins washed through. Albumin was eluted in 0.05 *M* Tris-HCl buffer, pH 8.0, containing 3.5 *M* NaCl; lipoproteins were afterward desorbed in distilled water. The chromatographic profile obtained from the dye adsorbent shows four main peaks (A_{280}). The first and second peaks represent the fraction washed through and correspond to transferrin (main peak), and α- and β-globulins, as well as traces of albumin, respectively. The third large peak eluted with 3.5 *M* NaCl corresponds to albumin with a purity greater than 99%. The fourth peak obtained after washing the column with distilled water corresponds to α- and β-lipopoteins and traces of albumin.

TABLE 13–1. Preparative-Scale Purifications Using Immobilized Dye Ligands

Protein/Enzyme Purified	Source (with Amount of Starting Material)	Dye ligand	Quantity Processed through Column	Bed (L)	Purification (fold)	Yield (%)	Ref.
Albumin	Human plasma; cryosupernatant 17 liters	Cibacron Blue F3G-A	>20 liters	50	—	—	20
Albumin	Human plasma, Cohn fraction IV, 1 kg paste	Cibacron Blue F3G-A	300 g albumin	16	—	—	21
Alcohol dehydrogenase	Equine liver, 5 kg	Cibacron Blue F3G-A	10.8 liters, 23.6 g protein	1.9	2.9	17	22
Alcohol dehydrogenase	*Bacillus stearothermophilus*, 25 kg cell paste	Procion Blue MX-5BR	—	—	7	70	16
Alkaline phosphatase	Calf intestine	Reactive Blue-2 phosphonate analogue	~300 g powder	1	>300	>90	—
α_1-Antitrypsin	Human serum, 0.5 liter	Cibacron Blue F3G-A	>20 ml	1	—	—	23
Carboxypeptidase-G_2	*Pseudomonas* sp., 5 kg cell paste	Procion Red H-8BN	3.1 g protein	0.2	47	—	24
Glucokinase	*Bacillus stearothermophilus*, 28 kg cell paste	Procion Brown H-3R	79.5 g protein, 60 liters	5.2	3.9	34	25
Glyceraldehyde 3-phosphate dehydrogenase	*Bacillus stearothermophilus*, 28 kg cell paste	Procion Blue H-B or Procion Orange MX-6G	—	5	8	85 and 70	16

(*continued*)

TABLE 13–1. Preparative-Scale Purifications Using Immobilized Dye Ligands (*continued*)

Protein/Enzyme Purified	Source (with Amount of Starting Material)	Dye ligand	Quantity Processed through Column	Bed (L)	Purification (fold)	Yield (%)	Ref.
Glycerokinase	*Bacillus stearothermophilus*, 9.6 kg cell paste	Procion Blue MX-3G	56 g protein, 2.5 liters	3.5	—	79	26
3-Hydroxybutyrate dehydrogenase	*Rhodopseudomonas spheroides*, 1 kg cell paste	Procion Red H-3B and Blue MX-4GD	76.2 and 2.2 g protein	1.8 and 0.4	34 and 6.2	99 and 79	27
Interferon	Human fibroblast, 10–15 liters	Cibacron Blue F3G-A	0.5 g protein, 10–15 liters	0.05	—	—	28
L-Lactate dehydrogenase	Rabbit muscle	Procion Blue MX-R	1.8 g protein, 0.1 liter	3.3	8.6	50	12
Malate dehydrogenase	*Rhodopseudomonas spheroides*, 1 kg cell paste	Procion Red H-3B and Blue MX-4GD	76.2 and 3.1 g protein	1.8 and 0.4	19 and 2.8	79 and 81	27
Phosphofructokinase	*Bacillus stearothermophilus*, 25 kg cell paste	Procion Blue MX-B	—	—	5	75	16
6-Phosphogluconate dehydrogenase	*Bacillus stearothermophilus*, 25 kg cell paste	Procion Red HE-3B	—	—	11	70	16
Phosphoglycerate kinase	*Saccharomyces cerevicae*, 3.5 kg cell paste or 1.0 kg dry paste	Cibacron Blue F3G-A	5.3 g protein	0.5	113	52	29

Phosphotransferase ATP:AMP	Beef heart, 26 kg; mito. 1 liter	Cibacron Blue F3G-A	29 mg protein	0.01	1.0	51	30
Phosphotransferase ATP:AMP	Yeast, 2.3 kg cell paste	Cibacron Blue F3G-A	140 g protein, 3.3 liters	0.04	119	54	31
Phosphotransferase GTP:AMP	Beef heart, 26 kg; mito. 0.5 liter	Blue Dextran	33 mg protein	0.005	1.1	24	32
Protein kinase	Porcine liver, 1.5 kg; muclei, 120 g	Blue Dextran	—	0.15	4	15	33
tRNA synthetase	*Bacillus stearothermophilus*, 25 kg cell paste						16
Methionyl-		Procion Green HE-4BD	—	—	12	70	
Tryptophanyl-		Procion Brown MX-5BR	4 g protein	0.1	137	88	
Tyrosyl-		Cibacron Blue F3G-A		—	13	80	

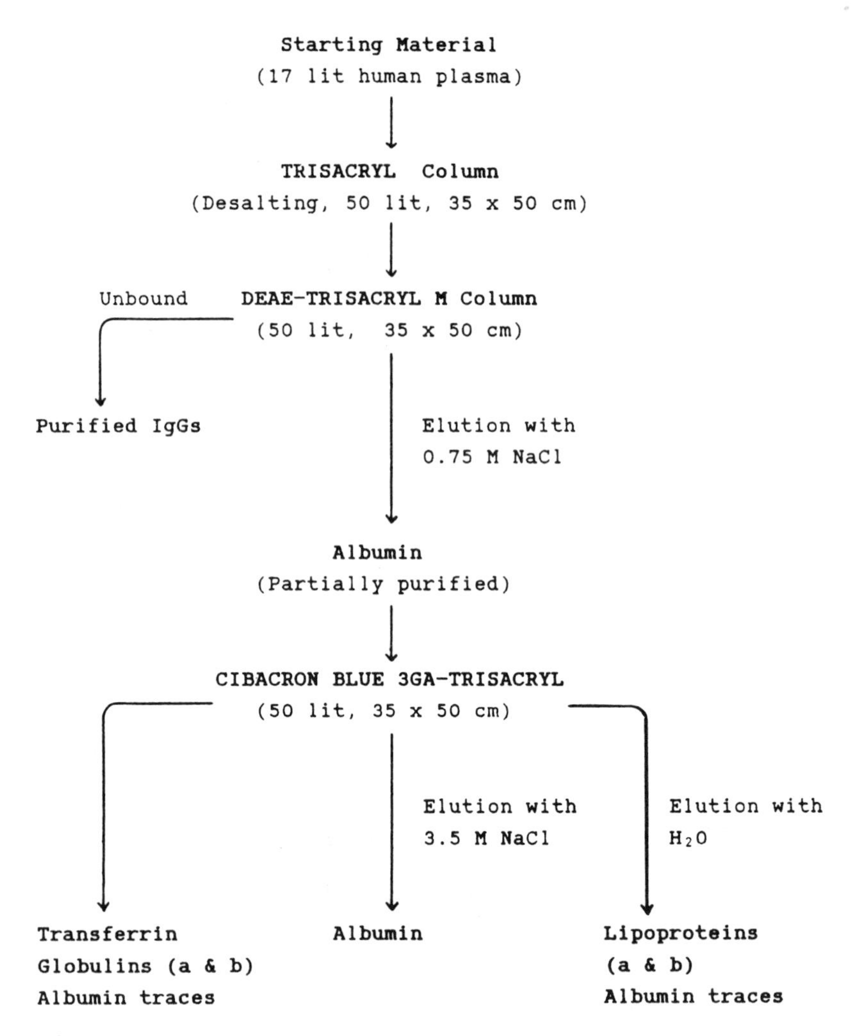

FIGURE 13–2. Flow chart of the large-scale purification of human serum albumin using dye-ligand chromatography.

A spectacular example is the resolution and purification of 3-hydroxybutyrate dehydrogenase (HBDH) and malate dehydrogenease (MDH) from *Rhodopseudomonas spheroides* on Procion® Red H-3B and Blue MX-4GD columns.[27] These two dye adsorbents operate in a complementary fashion for the two enzymes, and providing the right elution conditions are used, both enzymes can be obtained homogeneously (Table 13–2). After the disruption of 1 kg of cells and centrifugation, the cocktail is adsorbed on a 1.8-liter Procion Red H-3B-Sepharose 4B column (Figure 13–1c). HBDH is desorbed with 1 *M* KCl followed by biospecifically eluted MDH with 2 m*M* NADH in 1 *M* KCl. After desalting the HBDH pool it is adsorbed on a 0.8-liter column of Procion® Blue MX-4GD Sepharose 4B. The column was washed with 1 *M* KCl and homoge-

TABLE 13–2. The Resolution and Purification of 3-Hydroxybutyrate Dehydrogenase (HBDH) and Malate Dehydrogenase (MDH) from *R. spheroides* by Dye-Ligand Chromatography

Step	Enzyme	Units	Protein (mg)	Specific Activity (units/mg)	Yield (%)
Cell extract	HBDH	6,900	76,200	0.09	100
	MDH	414,000	76,200	5.4	100
Procion Red H-3B	HBDH	6,800	2,200	3.1	99
	MDH	327,000	3,100	105	79
Procion Blue MX-4GD	HBDH	5,400	280	19.2	78
	MDH	265,000	910	292	64

neous HBDH is recovered with 2 m*M* NADH in 1 *M* KCl. The partially purified MDH obtained from the first column is desalted to remove NADH and then was adsorbed on the "blue" column before recovering pure MDH by salt gradient elution; 0–700 m*M* KCl. Many more examples where dye-ligand chromatography has been successfully employed in the purification of nucleotide-binding enzymes at a preparative scale can be found in the literature (Table 13–1). Carboxypeptidase G_2 from *Pseudomonas* sp. represents the first example of enzyme purification by chelating agent-effected specific elution.[24] This enzyme adsorbs on a Procion® Red H-8BN column in the presence of zinc ions at pH 7.3. Elution of the enzyme by removing the zinc ions with the chelating agent EDTA at the same pH is unsatisfactory because the enzyme desorbs in a large volume. However, by treating the adsorbent first with EDTA at pH 5.8 and then raising the pH to 7.3 homogeneous enzyme is eluted in a sharp peak.

To address the problem of moderate specificity with textile dye ligands, a new family of purpose-designed affinity dye adsorbents has been introduced marking the beginning of a new era. Probably an impressive example is that of 330-fold purification of alkaline phosphatase from crude calf intestinal extract in a single step. The affinity dye ligand employed here was an analogue of Reactive Blue 2 substituted at the terminal aminobenzene ring with phosphoric acid in place of the sulfonic acid.[9] This structural modification of the ligand when combined with specific elution (5 m*M* inorganic phosphate) of the adsorbed enzyme afforded virtually homogeneous alkaline phosphatase equivalent to "high purity" commercial preparations. Typically, 2 g lyophilized powder of crude enzyme (2000 units) was dissolved in 10 ml tricine–NaOH buffer, 10 m*M*, pH 8.5, and purified on 5 g dye adsorbent at 4°C.[9] This system was later shown to work when scaled-up to 1 liter adsorbent, which was loaded with approximately 300 g starting material.

Last, but not least, one should discuss the application of preparative high-performance dye-ligand chromatography in protein/enzyme purifications. This technique, besides the prospect of achieving higher throughput due to adsorbent rigidity, it is of special value when the protein to be purified is unstable in crude extracts and rapid processing is important. The vast majority of HPAC applications in enzyme purification were performed with silica-based adsorbents, a material that always has to be coated with organofunctional silanes prior to ligand coupling.[10,11] Such silica-based packings exhibit low protein binding capacity due to their relatively small pore size (150–1000 Å) and poor stability in alkaline conditions, properties that limit silica's potential for routine large-scale operations.[2,11] For example, a column containing 60 g of silica-Procion® Blue MX-R adsorbent was saturated with 25 ml crude extract containing 348 mg total protein of rabbit muscle. After washing off unbound material and biospecifically eluting lactate dehydrogenase with NADH, only 22 mg of purified enzyme was recovered corresponding to a capacity of 0.33 mg pure enzyme per g silica.[34] Synthetic macroporous hydrophilic packings have been shown[13] to exhibit superior characteristics when compared to silica with regard to certain factors important in protein purification; binding capacity, porosity, ease of ligand immobilization, and chemical stability. Nevertheless, the only published large-scale example of high-performance chromatography with dye ligands was performed with the dye Procion® Blue MX-R immobilized on silica, which had previously been coated with γ-glycidoxypropyltrimethoxysilane.[12] The adsorbent was packed in a stainless-steal column by axial compression to a final volume of 3.3 liters. The column was loaded with 100 ml dialyzed crude extract of rabbit muscle containing 1.8 g total protein. Unbound proteins were washed off with irrigating buffer and bound lactate dehydrogenase was eluted with a pulse of NADH (7 m*M*, 10 ml) in almost one bed volume with 50% overall recovery and 8.6-fold purification.

Dye-ligand chromatography enjoys international acceptance and recognition as a major technique in protein purification. We believe that the future will see an increasing number of applications of this technique in preparative-scale protein purifications.

REFERENCES

1. Y. D. Clonis and C. R. Lowe, in Principles of Clinical Biochemistry (D. L. Williams and V. Marks, eds.). Heinemann Medical Books, Oxford, U.K., 1988, Chap. 25, p. 383.
2. Y. D. Clonis, *Bio/Technology*, 5 (1987) 1290.
3. Y. D. Clonis, in Separation Processes in Biotechnology (J. Asenjo, ed.). Dekker, New York, 1990. Chap. 13, p. 401.
4. Y. D. Clonis, A. Atkinson, C. J. Bruton, and C. R. Lowe (eds.), Reactive Dyes in Protein and Enzyme Technology. Macmillan, Basingstoke, U.K., 1987.
5. Y. D. Clonis, *CRC Crit. Rev. Biotechnol.*, 7 (1988) 263.
6. Y. D. Clonis, in Reactive Dyes in Protein and Enzyme Technology (Y. D. Clonis, A. Atkinson, C. J. Bruton, and C. R. Lowe, eds.). Macmillan, Basingstoke, U.K., 1987, Chap. 3, p. 33.
7. C. R. Lowe, S. J. Burton, J. C. Pearson, Y. D. Clonis, and V. Stead, *J. Chromatogr.*, 376 (1986) 121.
8. Y. D. Clonis, C. V. Stead, and C. R. Lowe, *Biotech. Bioeng.* 30 (1987) 621.
9. N. M. Lindner, R. Jeffcoat, and C. R. Lowe, *J. Chromatogr.*, in press.
10. Y. D. Clonis and D. A. P. Small, in Reactive Dyes in Protein and Enzyme Technology (Y. D. Clonis, A. Atkinson, C. J. Bruton, and C. R. Lowe, eds.). Macmillan, Basingstoke, U.K., 1987, Chap. 5, p. 87.
11. Y. D. Clonis, in HPLC of Macromolecules—A Practical Approach (R. W. A. Oliver, ed.). IRC Press, Oxford, U.K., 1989, Chap. 6, p. 157.
12. Y. D. Clonis, K. Jones, and C. R. Lowe, *J. Chromatogr.*, 363 (1986) 31.
13. Y. D. Clonis, *J. Chromatogr.*, 407 (1987) 179.
14. Y. D. Clonis and C. R. Lowe, *Biochim. Biophys. Acta*, 659 (1981) 86.
15. G. Vlatakis, G. Skarpelis, I. Stratidaki, V. Bouriotis, and Y. D. Clonis, *Appl. Biochem. Biotechnol.*, 15 (1987) 203.
16. M. C. Scawen and T. Atkinson, in Reactive Dyes in Protein and Enzyme Technology (Y. D. Clonis, A. Atkinson, C. J. Bruton, and C. R. Lowe, eds.). Macmillan, Basingstoke, U.K., 1987, Chap. 6, p. 51.
17. P. Hughes and R. F. Sherwood, in Reactive Dyes in Protein and Enzyme Technology (Y. D. Clonis, A. Atkinson, C. J. Bruton, and C. R. Lowe, eds.). Macmillan, Basingstoke, U.K., 1987, Chap. 7, p. 125.
18. Y. D. Clonis, M. J. Goldfinch, and C. R. Lowe, *Biochem. J.*, 197 (1981) 203.
19. F. Qadri and P. D. G. Dean, *Biochem. J.*, 191 (1980) 53.
20. J. Saint-Blancard, J. M. Kirzin, P. Riberon, and F. Petit, in Affinity Chromatography and Related Techniques (T. C. J. Gribnau, J. Visser, and R. J. F. Nivard, eds.). Elsevier, Amsterdam, 1982, p. 305.

21. M. J. Harvey, R. A. Brown, J. Rott, D. Lloyd, and R. S. Lane, in Separation of Plasma Proteins (J. M. Curling, ed.). Academic Press, New York, 1983, p. 80.
22. S. K. Roy and A. H. Nishikawa, *Biotechnol. Bioeng.*, 21 (1979) 775.
23. A. B. Cohen and H. James, DHEW Publication No. 781422, 1978, p. 326.
24. R. F. Sherwood, R. G. Melton, S. M. Alwan, and P. Hughes, *Eur. J. Biochem.*, 148 (1985) 447.
25. C. R. Goward, R. Hartwell, T. Atkinson, and M. C. Scawen, *Biochem. J.*, 237 (1986) 415.
26. M. D. Scawen, P. M. Hammond, M. J. Comer, and T. Atkinson, *Anal. Biochem.*, 132 (1983) 413.
27. M. D. Scawen, J. Derbyshire, M. J. Harvey, and T. Atkinson, *Biochem. J.*, 203 (1982) 699.
28. E. Knight and D. Fahey, *J. Biol. Chem.*, 256 (1981) 3609.
29. K. Kulbe and R. Schuer, *Anal. Biochem.*, 93 (1979) 46.
30. A. G. Tomasselli and L. H. Noda, *Eur. J. Biochem.*, 103 (1980) 481.
31. Y. Ito, A. G. Tomasselli, and L. H. Noda, *Eur. J. Biochem.*, 105 (1980) 85.
32. A. G. Tomasselli, R. H. Schirmes, and L. H. Noda, *Eur. J. Biochem.*, 93 (1979) 257.
33. H. Baydoun, J. Hoppe, W. Freist, and K. Wagner, *J. Biol. Chem.*, 257 (1982) 1032.
34. D. A. P. Small, A. Atkinson, and C. R. Lowe, *J. Chromatogr.* 266 (1983) 151.

CHAPTER 14

Application of High-Performance Affinity Chromatographic Techniques

Djuro Josić, Andreas Becker, and Werner Reutter

CONTENTS

14.1 INTRODUCTION

The use of high-performance affinity chromatography (HPAC) has steadily increased after publication of the pioneering work by Mosbach et al.[1] New commercially available supports for HPAC frequently appear on the market. They are either activated supports for coupling with the desired ligand, or the ligand has already been coupled to them, e.g., protein A, protein G, different lectins, heparin. For use in HPAC such supports have been developed, whose surface is supposed to minimize nonspecific interaction with the sample and whose spacer has been optimized.[2–20]

Recently the development of affinity HPLC has followed two different lines. The first aim is preparative HPAC, where supports with rather large particle diameters, over 20 μm, are used. The supports are less expensive, they have lower back pressure also in preparative columns, and they can therefore be applied on a large scale.

Preparative HPAC has become the center of interest also because it can be used for purification of gene technologically obtained products. The structures of these products are becoming increasingly complicated, e.g., in the case of glycoproteins. Very often small quantities of product have to be isolated from large volumes of matter. This applies to fermentation fluids, supernatants, or lysates of animal or vegetable cells from a cell culture. In these cases preparative HPAC is the best method, as it provides high selectivity of the chromatographic medium, high flow rates, which offer the opportunity to process large volumes in a short time and ultimately allow automization. The application of this method has therefore been the object of several studies recently.[4,16,17,21–23]

The second aim is analytical and micropreparative HPAC. In this field porous and nonporous supports with particle sizes between 1 and 15 μm are used.[1,4,5–7] The use of nonporous supports is particularly promising. These supports are produced either on a silicagel basis or synthetically, and have particle diameters between 1 and 10 μm.[4,6,24–26] The nonporous supports have smaller specific surfaces than the porous supports. Their capacity is correspondingly lower. The important advantage of nonporous supports over porous ones lies in the fact that the smaller specific surface causes less nonspecific binding.[4,6]

This review deals with HPAC application, analytical as well as preparative. It discusses experiments that involve the most popular HPAC methods, that is immunoaffinity HPAC, lectin and heparin HPAC, and some HPAC separations with low molecular ligands. Another subject is the isolation of mono- and polyclonal antibodies by protein A and protein G HPAC. Furthermore high-performance immobilized metal ion-affinity chromatography (HPIMAC) and hydroxylapatite HPLC (HA-HPLC) have to be included. These two methods of biopolymer HPLC, however, follow different rules. In contrast to typical HPAC methods such as lectin HPAC or protein A HPAC, gradient elution can be applied.[27–33]Apart from these differences HPIMAC and HA-HPLC have much in common with the HPAC methods. The latest application of hydroxylapatite HPLC for a very specific separation of B and T lymphocytes suggests that a biospecific interaction takes place between matrix and sample components.[34,35] As both HPIMAC and HA-HPLC are discussed in other chapters of this book, they are not further investigated.

14.2 ISOLATION OF IMMUNOGLOBULINS

14.2.1 General Aspects

The rapid increase in production and use of monoclonal and polyclonal antibodies over the last years has seen a corresponding development of methods for their purification. The simplest and fastest purification of antibodies can be achieved above all by affinity chromatographic methods, such as protein A and protein G HPAC. Protein A, bound to different soft gels, mostly agarose, has been in use for some time for the binding of antibody–antigen complexes in immunoprecipitation. Protein G has recently been used for the same purpose in immunoprecipitation with antibodies, which do not bind to protein A. Protein A and protein G, which are bound to activated porous or nonporous HPLC supports, are used with good results for HPAC purification of antibodies.[4,36–38]

The binding of the antibodies to the protein A or protein G is, however, very strong, and the antibodies can be released only under rather sharp conditions, e.g., with low pH buffers (less than pH 3.0) or with chaotropic reagents such as 3 *N* NaSCN. Therefore, if the antibodies concerned are sensitive and lose their activity under such elution conditions, other isolation methods have to be chosen, such as ion-exchange, hydrophobic-interaction, or hydroxylapatite HPLC.[37]

Despite these limitations, protein A and protein G HPAC have still to be regarded as the most favorable methods for the isolation of antibodies from serum, ascites fluid, or also from the supernatants of antibody-producing cells. Both bacterial proteins bind the antibodies in a highly specific manner.[38–40] As can be seen in Figure 14–1, all the other components of the sample are not supposed to bind to the column. The nonspecifically bound components that stick to the support, e.g., through hydrophobic interaction, are rinsed out with a detergent solution. In the next step the antibody is eluted from the column with a low pH buffer or with chaotropic reagents. In this way highly purified antibodies could be obtained within a short period of time (see Figure

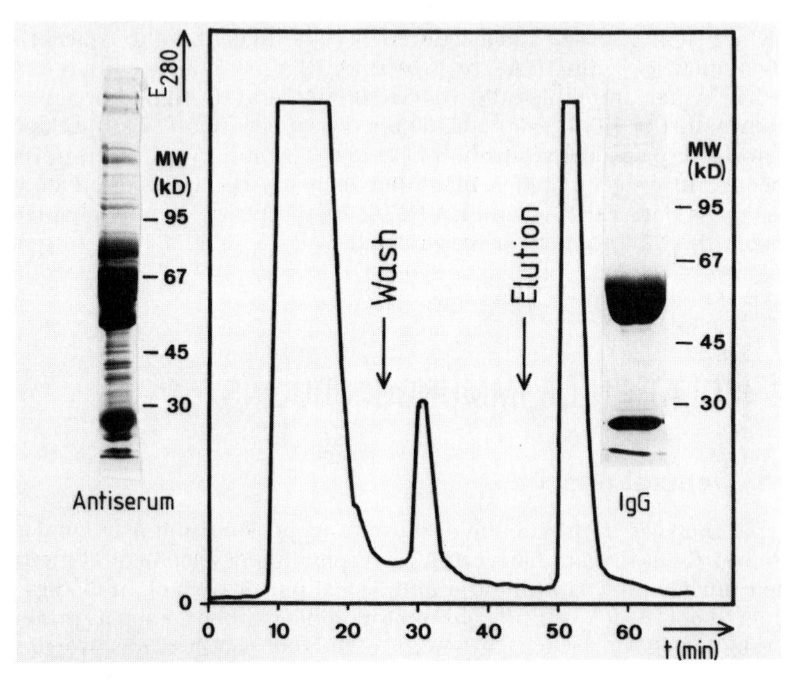

FIGURE 14–1. Isolation of polyclonal antibodies from rabbit antiserum with protein A HPAC. A part of albumin was removed from the antiserum by chromatography on an affi-blue column (cf. ref. 37). The material, about 20 ml, was applied to an 80 × 8.0 mm protein A Eupergit C 30N column. The column was washed with 10 ml of 0.1 *M* sodium borate buffer, pH 8.3, containing 0.1% (v/v) nonionic detergent Genapol X-100 ("wash"). The IgG was eluted with 0.1 *M* sodium citrate buffer, pH 2.4. Other chromatographic conditions, 1.0 ml/min flow rate, 5 bar pressure, room temperature. The purity of the isolated IgG was monitored with SDS-PAGE. (Reprinted from ref. 37 with the permission of Walter de Gruyter, Inc.)

14–1). Immunoglobulin G from several mammals, e.g., goat and some mouse monoclonal IgG subclasses, do not bind to protein A.[41] In these cases protein G has to be used for purification. The purification with immobilized protein G is analogous to the schema shown in Figure 14–1. Neither protein A nor protein G can be used for purification of immunoglobulin M, as this antibody does not bind to either protein. As other bacterial proteins exist, which bind IgG or IgM, their possible use for antibodies of the IgM class is being investigated.[42]

Protein A and protein G bind to the constant, carbohydrate-containing section of the IgG molecule (Fc), so that the Fab, the antigen-binding part, is free. This fact can be useful for the separation of the Fab from the Fc part after enzymatic digestion of isolated antibodies. Such a separation is shown in Figure 14–2. In the experiment the antibody was digested with papain, and applied to a column with immobilized protein A. When the antigen-binding Fab is cleft from the Fc, it does not bind to the column and is subsequently

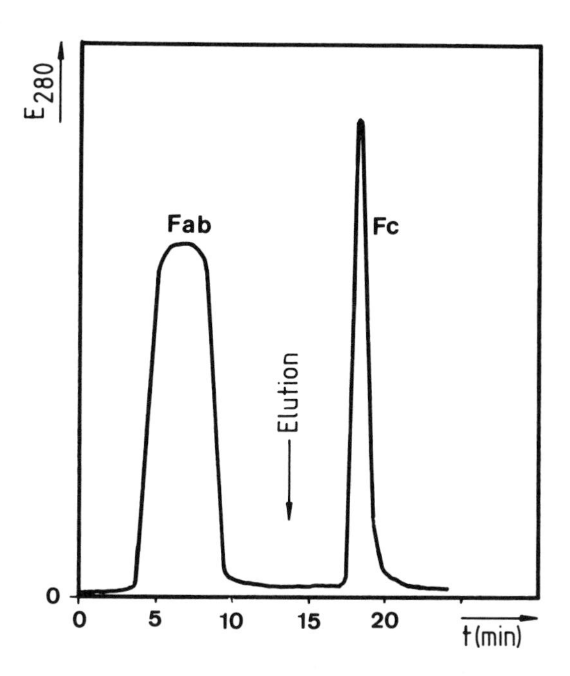

FIGURE 14–2. Separation of Fab and Fc fragments from IgG. The isolated IgG was digested with papain. After digestion the sample was applied to a 60 × 4.6 mm protein A Eupergit C 30N column. The antigen-binding fragment (Fab) does not bind to the column. The Fc fragment, however, binds to the column and can be eluted with 0.1 *M* sodium citrate buffer, pH 2.4. Conditions, 0.5 ml/min flow rate, 2–5 bar pressure, room temperature. (Reprinted from ref. 37 with permission of Walter de Gruyter, Inc.)

separated from the Fc, which is retarded. The Fc can be eluted by a pH step gradient. The column can be reused after equilibration.[37]

Protein A and protein G are very stable substances, so that such HPAC columns have a correspondingly long life, provided the particular support is equally stable. A column with immobilized protein A can be used up to 300 times.[37] The isolation of antibodies with this method thus becomes less expensive than it would be, if soft gels were used. Their limited mechanical stability makes them ineffective after only a few separations.

14.2.2 Affinity Purification of Antibodies with Immobilized Antigen

When a polyclonal antibody is used for screening of cDNA, all nonspecific immunoglobulins have to be removed. The isolation of monospecific antibodies is best achieved by affinity chromatography with immobilized antigen. When polyclonal antibodies are raised against a posttranslationally modified protein, they are not only directed against the polypeptide chain, but also against other epitopes such as carbohydrates (in the case of glycoproteins), fatty acids, and other residues. These antibodies, which are not directed against the polypeptide part, can cause adverse side reactions, when screening a cDNA expression vector library.[43]

To avoid these difficulties, the residues have to be removed, which were posttranslationally attached to the polypeptide chain. The polypeptide chain is subsequently isolated and immobilized. A support like this can be used for "reversed" immunoaffinity chromatography to separate specifically those antibodies, which are directed only against the epitopes on the polypeptide part. This problem will be followed up below in a separate paragraph concerning a membrane glycoprotein.

14.3 IMMUNOAFFINITY HPLC

14.3.1 Immobilization of Antibodies

Antibodies can either covalently or noncovalently be bound to the support. Covalent binding to reactive groups of the support usually takes place through free amino, hydroxy, or sulfhydryl groups.[1,4] The kind of active group on the support and the pH of the surrounding medium determines which of these free groups of the immunoglobulin gets involved in the binding process. The immobilization through free side groups of the amino acids always causes the antibody to lose some of its activity. The reason for this is that amino, hydroxy, or sulfhydryl groups can be located in the antigen-binding part of the antibody molecule. Also, antibody–antigen reaction can be sterically obstructed through this kind of immobilization. By choosing the optimal ligand (IgG) density on the support surface, and by optimizing the spacer carrying the active group,[44] this problem can be eased though not fully eliminated.[37] The second, more elegant solution is the immobilization of the antibody by means of its Fc part. It exploits the fact that the antibody has carbohydrate chains at the Fc. This oligosaccharide can be immobilized to a hydrazide activated support.[45]

14.3.2 HPAC with Immobilized Antibodies

Despite several unsolved problems, as shown above, the use of immunoaffinity HPLC has increased steadily, especially in the case of antigens occurring in low concentrations in complex mixtures.[36,37,46–49] Such an example is shown in Figure 14–3. In a single step a membrane protein could be isolated in a highly purified state by means of an immobilized antibody. In order to isolate 1.2 mg of protein, 750 mg of liver plasma membrane extract was pumped through the column (about 1.2 g of plasma membranes were solubilized). The

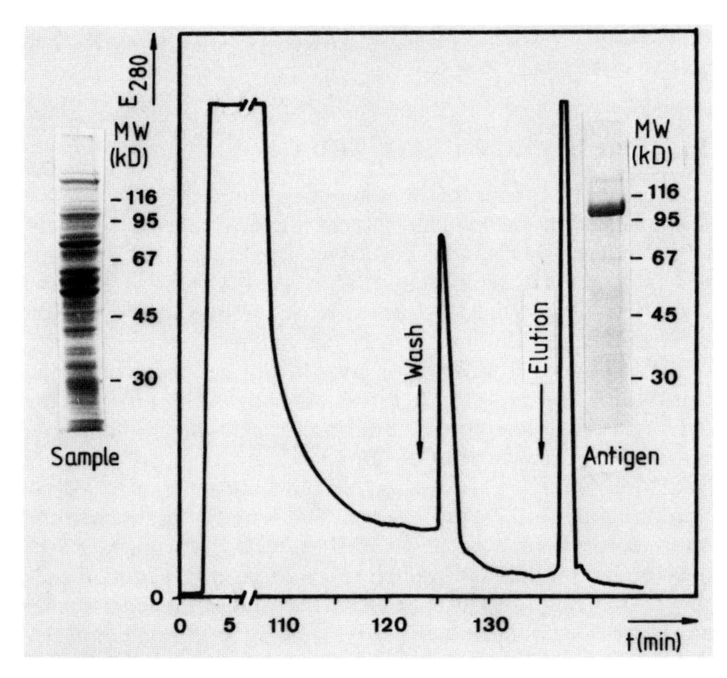

FIGURE 14–3. Isolation of glycoprotein gp105 from liver plasma membranes with immunoaffinity HPLC. Triton X-114 extract from liver plasma membranes was applied to the column with immobilized monoclonal antibodies against gp105. After washing the column with 10 ml of 0.1 *M* sodium borate, pH 8.3, containing 0.1% Genapol X-100 ("wash"), the antigen could be eluted with 0.1 *M* sodium citrate, pH 2.4, containing 1 g/liter CHAPS. Conditions, 40 × 4.6 column, 1 ml/min flow rate, 20 bar pressure, temperature 0°C (on ice). The composition of the applied sample and eluate was monitored by SDS-PAGE and shown in the chromatogram. (Reprinted from ref. 37 with the permission of Walter de Gruyter, Inc.)

quantity of isolated glycoprotein is sufficient to obtain data about its amino acid sequence, and a first insight into its carbohydrate structure, as shown below, where the application of this method is described.

14.3.3 Epitope Mapping

Janis and Regnier[50] propose a combination of immunoaffinity and reversed-phase HPLC for analytical use. Tandem immunoaffinity and reversed-phase HPLC columns are used for the analysis of single and multicomponent antigen samples. Immunoaffinity columns are prepared by hydrophobic adsorption or covalent binding of antibodies on macroporous packing materials. Proteolytic digest of protein is applied. Specific epitopes are bound to the immunoaffinity column and desorbed by low pH buffer and concentrated on a "conventional" analytical reversed-phase column. Gradient elution on the reversed-phase column separates the desorbed antibody-binding epitopes and permits their discrimination from nonbinding parts of antigen molecule. This analysis has been performed on several lysozyme variants, which are very similar in their three-dimensional structures.

14.3.4 Indirect Immunoaffinity HPLC

Immunoaffinity HPLC, though being an elegant and quick method for analytical as well as preparative work, has a severe disadvantage. As antigen elution is carried out under rather sharp conditions, the immobilized antibodies are subjected to gradual denaturing. Column life is quite short as a consequence. This applies above all to analytical work, where frequently large numbers of analyses have to be carried out in quick succession.

Phillips et al.[51] suggest that the antibody be applied to a column with immobilized protein A. By cross-linking, the antibody is then in turn covalently bound to the protein A. Thereby the binding capacity of the immunoglobulin is preserved, because the antigen-binding sites are free. Still the problem of short column life persists. Josić et al.[37,46] have chosen not to crosslink the immunoglobulin after binding to protein A. The principle of this method, called indirect immunoaffinity HPLC, is shown in Figure 14–4. An appropriate amount of antiserum (or ascites fluid) is applied to a column with immobilized protein A or protein G. After washing the column with a buffer that contains detergent, only the antibody is still bound, without any of the proteins being nonspecifically bound. The sample containing the antigen is applied to the column in a second step. Now the antigen binds to the antibodies, the other proteins are excluded. After washing out the nonspecifically bound material with buffer and detergent, the antigen–antibody complex is eluted from the column, e.g., with a low pH buffer.

This method can be used very successfully instead of immunoprecipitation, especially if the antigen is labeled radioactively, as shown in Figure 14–5. The transferrin from rat serum was radioactively labeled with [^{35}S]methionine. Figure 14–5 shows in its left part the control of the eluate from the column by SDS-PAGE. By means of staining with Coomassie blue the antigen transferrin can be seen along with the light and the heavy chain of the used antibody.

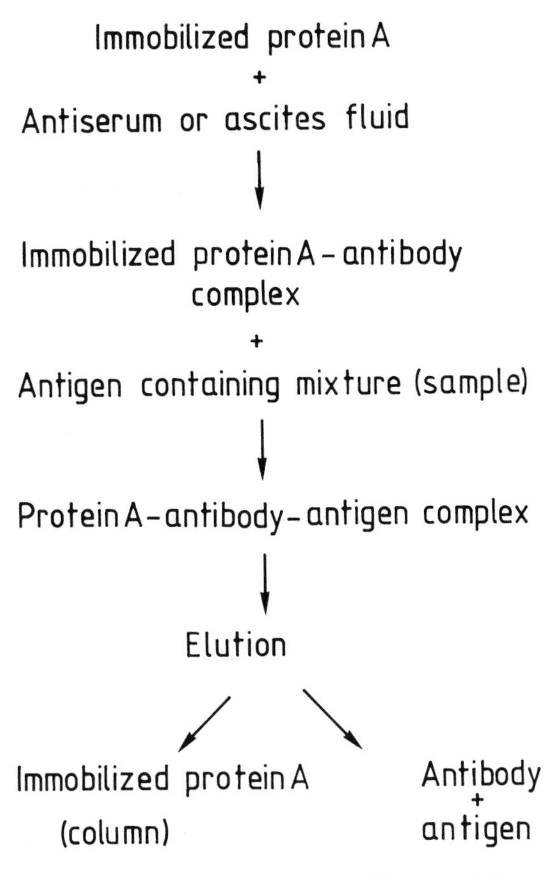

FIGURE 14–4. Principle of "indirect" immunoaffinity HPLC.

If the same gel is autoradiographed, as shown in the right part of Figure 14–5, only the radioactively labeled antigen–transferrin can be seen. In this way the half-lives of the ^{35}S-labeled methionine and the ^{3}H-labeled sugar fucose both in the rat transferrin can be measured quickly.[46]

It is also possible to use several columns packed with different antibodies in a tandem and thereby bind different antigens from the antibody solution in a single run. Subsequent elution has to be performed separately. When indirect immunoaffinity HPLC is applied, it is important to bear in mind that in most cases the protein A HPAC column is not saturated with IgG. Consequently it can bind any immunoglobulin that may exist in the sample. This has to be given proper attention. The immunoglobulins have to be removed from the sample, e.g., by applying a protein A precolumn (without antibodies, cf. ref. 37). The protein A columns required for these experiments, of which only two were used, protein A 5PW (Toyo Soda) and Eupergit C 30N protein A (Röhm Pharma), will yield up to 400 separations without any decrease in the binding capacity of the IgG.[37,46]

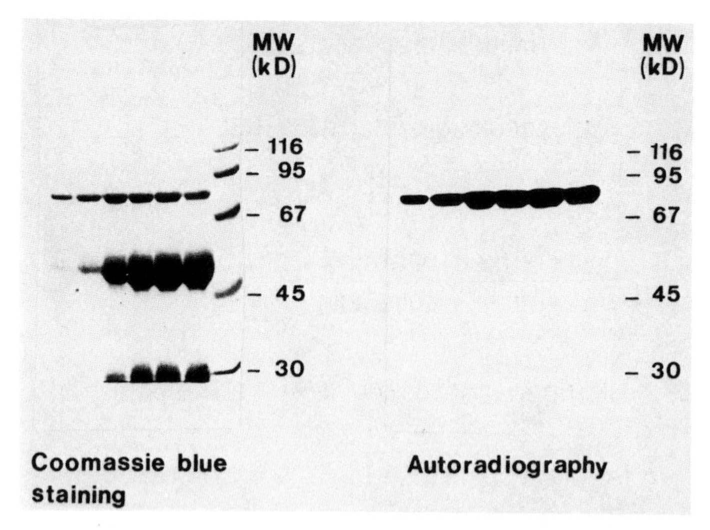

FIGURE 14–5. "Indirect" immunoaffinity HPLC of serum transferrin with antitransferrin antibodies, bound to a protein A HPAC column. The left part of the figure shows that the antigen (transferrin) and antibody were eluted from the column. Consequently both proteins were stained with Coomassie blue. As only the rat serum was labeled with [^{35}S]methionine, only transferrin with an apparent M_r of 78,000 could be detected by autoradiography of the same gel (see the right part of the figure and Figure 14–4). (Reprinted from ref. 37 with the permission of Walter de Gruyter, Inc.)

Another strategy has been proposed by Babashak and Phillips,[52] which is similar to indirect immunoaffinity HPLC as described above. Instead of protein A, bound to the support, they use avidine-coated glass beads, which strongly bind the antibodies that had previously been biotinylated. If the separations are carried out at +4°C, and the column is stored at the same temperature, between 10 and 40 runs are possible within a period of up to 6 months. Generally speaking the avidine–biotin method carries a high risk of misleading results because of the nonspecific binding to the support.[53] However, under HPLC conditions, the problem appears to be much smaller.

14.3.5 Application of Immunoaffinity HPLC, Isolation of Monospecific Antibodies against gp110

The glycoprotein gp110 occurs in rather high concentrations in liver plasma membranes. It seems to play an important part in cell–cell interaction. This protein was isolated and partly characterized.[54] In SDS-PAGE the gp110 has an apparent molecular weight of 110,000 and contains more than 50% carbohydrate.[55]

Monoclonal antibodies were raised against this protein.[54] Further characterization required major amounts of isolated gp110. This was achieved by immunoaffinity HPLC with immobilized monoclonal antibodies. Immunoaffinity HPLC was carried out according to the following protocol.

The monoclonal antibodies were isolated from the ascites fluid with HA-HPLC and immobilized to epoxy-activated support, Eupergit C 30N.[36] The immobilized antibodies (about 3 mg/ml bed volume) were packed into a 4.6 × 40 mm column. The column was rinsed with 10 volumes of Tris-buffered saline, pH 7.8 (TBS), containing 0.1% reduced Triton X-100. Then 20 ml of plasma membrane extract was applied, with a flow rate of 0.2 ml/min during application. It was cycled at least three times through the column. To minimize nonspecific adsorption of proteins via hydrophobic or ionic interactions, especially mediated by divalent cations, the column was washed at a flow rate of 2 ml/min with 10 bed volumes each of the following buffers. Washing buffer #1, 10 m*M* Tris-HCl, pH 7.8, 150 m*M* NaCl, 1 m*M* $MgCl_2$, 1 m*M* $CaCl_2$, 1 m*M* phenylmethylsulfonyl chloride (PMSF), and 0.1% (v/v) reduced Triton X-100. Washing buffer #2, 10 m*M* Tris-HCl, pH 7.8, 500 m*M* NaCl, 1 m*M* EDTA, 1 m*M* PMSF, 0.1% reduced Triton X-100. Washing buffer #3, 10 m*M* Tris-HCl, pH 7.8, 1 m*M* EDTA, 1 m*M* PMSF, 0.1% reduced Triton X-100.

At this point an exchange of detergent is possible, e.g., by introducing CHAPS or octylglucoside for reduced Triton X-100. Elution of specifically bound antigen was achieved with 5 bed volumes of 0.1 *M* Na-citrate, pH 2.3, containing 0.1% reduced Triton X-100. This was immediately neutralized by the addition of 1/10 volume of 1 *M* sodium carbonate. Alternatively a buffer containing 3 *M* sodium thiocyanate and 0.1% reduced Triton X-100, pH 7.2, can be used. The eluted fraction, usually between 0.5 and 1.5 ml volume, was dialyzed extensively against 1/10 phosphate-buffered saline (PBS), pH 7.2, and concentrated with a rotary evaporator. Protein concentration was determined by the BCA method (Pierce), and the purity of the preparation was checked by SDS-PAGE (cf. Figure 14–6).

Purified gp110 was used to immunize rabbits. After 4 injections of 10 μg of purified antigen, a high-titered antiserum to gp110 was produced. Specificity was demonstrated by immunoblotting on rat liver plasma membrane proteins separated by SDS-PAGE.

In preliminary experiments investigating the suitability of the isolated IgG fraction as an antibody probe for screening a cDNA expression vector library,[43] it was noted that it contained cross-reacting antibodies with an undesirably high background. Attempts to absorb these antibodies with an affinity matrix of *Echerichia coli* lysate proteins, coupled to the matrix, failed to produce the expected results. Therefore it became a necessity to construct an antigen-specific affinity matrix.

The first experiment, performed to immobilize native gp110, failed. More than 90% of the protein used for coupling was recovered in the supernatant, indicating that the coupling reaction had not taken place. Since the procedure had been used routinely and successfully before, namely for the immobilization of antibodies and other soluble ligands,[36] it was assumed that its failure was due to specific properties of glycosylated membrane proteins. It is possible that the protein moiety of a heavily glycosylated protein like gp110 is completely covered by carbohydrate. The experiment was therefore repeated with deglycosylated gp110.

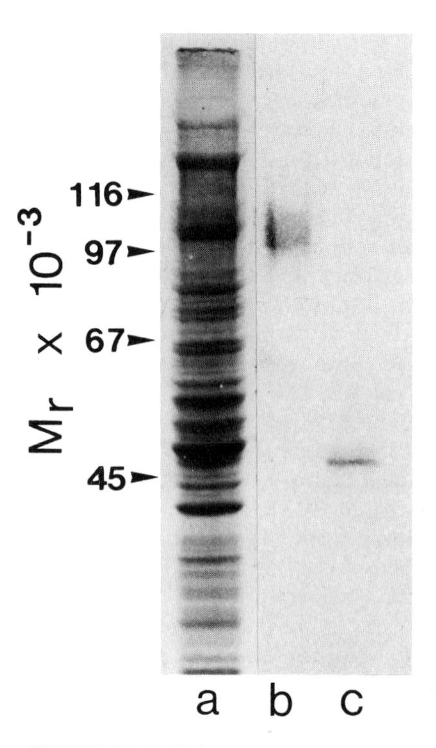

FIGURE 14–6. Preparation of dgp110: a. detergent extract of plasma membranes; b. purified gp110 after immunoaffinity HPLC; c. deglycosylated gp110.

For this sake 250μg of purified gp110 was freeze-dried and resuspended in 40 μl of peptide-*N*-glycanase F (PNGaseF) sample buffer, containing 0.4% (w/v) SDS, 1% (v/v) 2-mercaptoethanol, and 40 m*M* EDTA. After sonication for 5 min, the sample was heated to 90°C for 5 min and placed on ice. Then 70 μl of incubation buffer, 500 m*M* sodium phosphate buffer, pH 8.6, containing 1% (w/v) decanoyl-*N*-methylglucamide (MEGA-10) and 30 μl PNGaseF were added. The removal of oligosaccharide side chains under these conditions is complete (cf. Figure 14–6). These were separated from the polypeptide chain by ultrafiltration, using Centricon filters (for deglycosylation see ref. 56).

Deglycosylated membrane proteins have a strong tendency to aggregate and subsequently precipitate out of the solution. Therefore the sample was freeze-dried and redissolved in 400 μl of coupling buffer (100 m*M* $NaHCO_3$, 1 *M* NaCl, pH 8.3), containing 0.1% SDS and 0.25% 2-mercaptoethanol. After sonication and heating, 100 mg of Eupergit C 30N support was added, until a thick slurry was formed without supernatant. This was left standing for 3 days at room temperature. The slurry was washed twice with 800 μl each of coupling buffer, which was pooled and analyzed for protein in order to estimate coupling efficiency. Unreacted groups on the gel were blocked by incubation for 2 days at room temperature with 1 *M* ethanolamine, pH 8.0 (cf. also ref. 36). Protein determination in the supernatant indicated that more than 95% of the protein had been coupled.

For reversed immunoaffinity HPLC the slurry was packed into a 4.6 × 20 mm column and equilibrated with 100 ml of PBS. One milliliter of purified IgG (see above) was diluted 1:10 in PBS, loaded into the sample injector, and passed over the matrix at a flow rate of 0.2 ml/min. Washing was performed with 15 ml of PBS. Elution was achieved with 10 ml of 0.1 *M* glycin-HCl, pH 2.3. The eluate was collected in tubes that contained 1 *M* sodium carbonate for neutralizing the pH. The ratio between the sodium carbonate and the eluate was 1:10 (v/v).

The antibodies directed to deglycosylated gp110 were detected and quantified in an ELISA with deglycosylated gp110 as antigen (Reutter and Becker, unpublished results). Thus it was determined that an IgG equivalent to 100 μl of antiserum could be purified in a single run under these conditions.

The fractions of the eluate that contained the antibodies were pooled and tested in a dot blot assay for specificity of binding to deglycosylated gp110 in the presence of *E. coli* and/or gt11 proteins. It was found that these antibodies exhibited an approximately 10-fold smaller cross-reactivity with other proteins in the assay, as compared with nonpurified IgG.

The complete isolation schema for the production of monospecific antibodies by different HPAC methods is shown in Figure 14–7.

14.4 LECTIN HPAC

14.4.1 General Aspects

The use of immobilized plant lectins for fractionation and characterization of glycoproteins, glycopeptides, and oligosaccharides is well established.[57–60] Once the surface chemistry and pore size of the support as well as the immobilization procedure of the ligand had been optimized,[12,17,20,36,61] lectin high-performance affinity chromatography became a widespread method. Lectin affinity chromatography has been used in HPLC mode for fractionation and analysis of glycoproteins, glycopeptides, oligosaccharides, and nucleotide sugars.[4,13,62–67] For analytical use, such as fractionation of glycopeptides and oligosaccharides according to their sugar composition,[13,67] and for quantitative estimation of nucleotide sugars, [64,65] different plant lectins have been applied. Most lectins are not used for preparative purposes, because they are too expensive. Initially only concanavalin A (Con A) was used for both analytical and preparative separations. Another lectin, which has recently been applied to preparative isolation of glycoproteins, is wheat germ agglutinin (WGA).[68,69]

14.4.2 Concanavalin A HPAC

Although routinely used for both affinity chromatography with soft gels and for HPAC, the chromatography with immobilized Con A can cause several difficulties such as ligand leakage from the column and poor sample recovery.

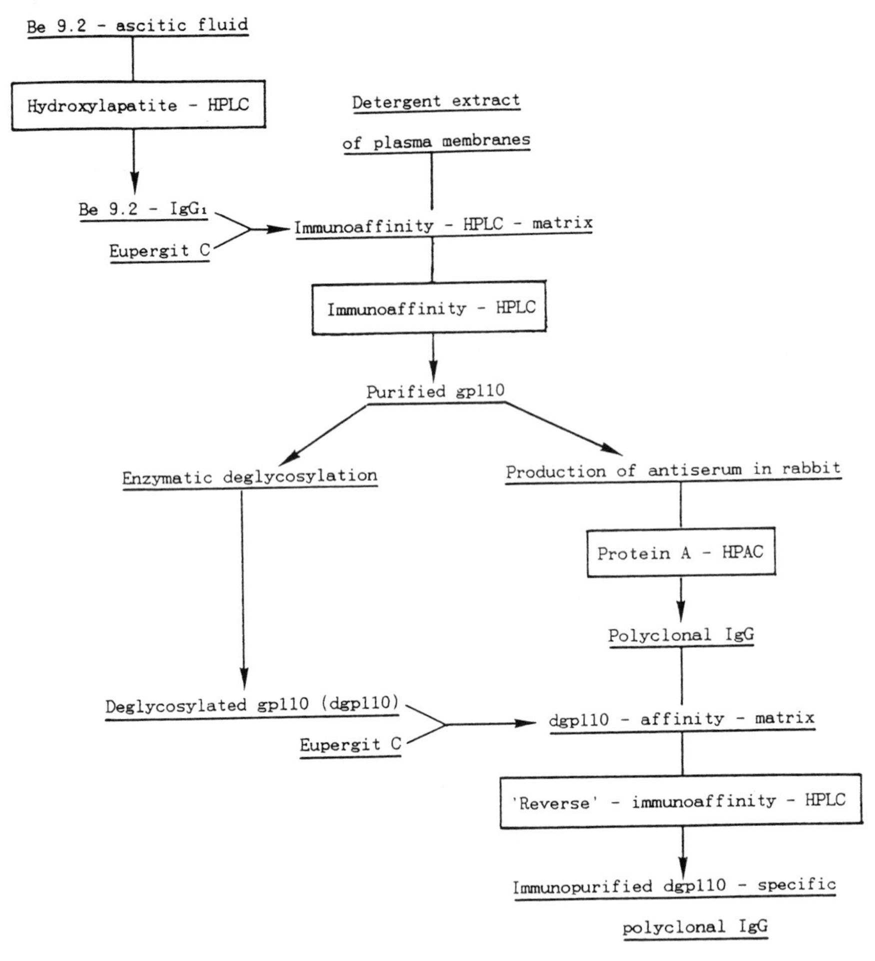

FIGURE 14–7. Purification scheme for dgp110—specific polyclonal IgG.

These problems result from lectin behavior, including the nature of interaction between Con A molecules as well as interaction between lectin and ligand. Con A can often be found in solution as a dimer, tetramer or polymer. The aggregation depends above all on the pH of the medium.[70] Every molecule binds calcium and magnesium, which are in turn required for sugar binding. The Con A molecule also has hydrophobic areas on the surface. Therefore hydrophobic interaction is an important factor in binding to the lectin, especially in the case of large molecules such as glycoproteins, which contain strong hydrophobic domains.[36,62] These aspects have to be considered, when Con A HPAC is used for the separation of hydrophobic biopolymers.

Figure 14–8 shows one of the meanwhile numerous applications of Con A HPAC, the purification of the enzyme peroxidase from horseradish. After applying raw plant extract, the pure enzyme could be eluted with a high yield of α-methyl-glucopyranoside. Once initial difficulties with optimization of lectin-binding and considerable leakage of the columns had been overcome, good progress was made. By binding the lectin at pH 5, the partial binding of aggregates is avoided. They are then washed out under elution conditions. Figure 14–9 shows an example for the analytical use of Con A HPAC. It is based on the fact that the glycoproteins of the so-called high-mannose type have less complex glycosylation and therefore bind more strongly to the column than the glycoproteins, which contain other sugars in their oligosaccharide part. Among these are galactose, fucose, and sialic acid, so-called complex types of glycosylation.[58] The glycoproteins containing oligosaccharides of the complex type either do not bind to the column at all, or they can be eluted with just α-D-methyl-glucopyranoside. The important shift in the glycosylation of the pro-

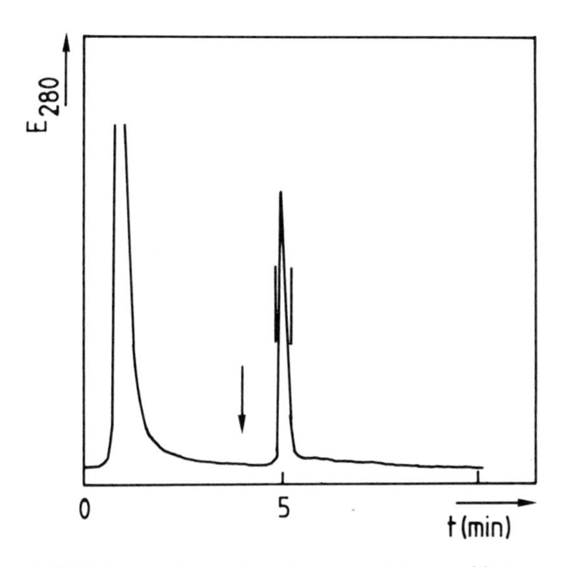

FIGURE 14–8. Separation of horseradish peroxidase with concanavalin A HPAC. Commercial crude sample of peroxydase (1 mg) was dissolved in 0.1 *M* acetate buffer containing 1 *M* sodium chloride, 1 m*M* magnesium, and 1 m*M* calcium chloride, pH 6.0. The peroxidase was eluted by injecting 2 ml of the same buffer, containing 0.025 *M* α-methyl-D-glucopyranoside, using sample injector. Recovery of enzymatic activity was 98%. Other chromatographic conditions, column Con A-5PW (40 × 6 mm), flow rate 1 ml/min, room temperature, 2–5 bar pressure. (The figure was made available by Dr. Y. Kato, Tosohaas Co.)

teins from tumor plasma membranes toward the less complex high-mannose type is clearly demonstrated in Figure 14–9. To reduce the nonspecific, mostly hydrophobic interactions between support and sample components to a minimum, a nonporous support with 1-μm particle size was used here.

Such selective, stepwise elution can be completed further by a combination of detergents with different concentrations and hydrophobic characteristics, so that glycoproteins, e.g., of membrane origin, are fractionated also according to their water solubility.[62]

In some areas a broadening of the peaks will occur because of strong interaction between the ligand and Con A. By using nonporous supports, as shown in Figure 14–9, this problem can be minimized. In the case of preparative isolation, however, the porous supports have to be used, as they have a higher capacity. One option for overcoming peak broadening is to elute the sample at a higher temperature, e.g., at 35–40°C.[71]

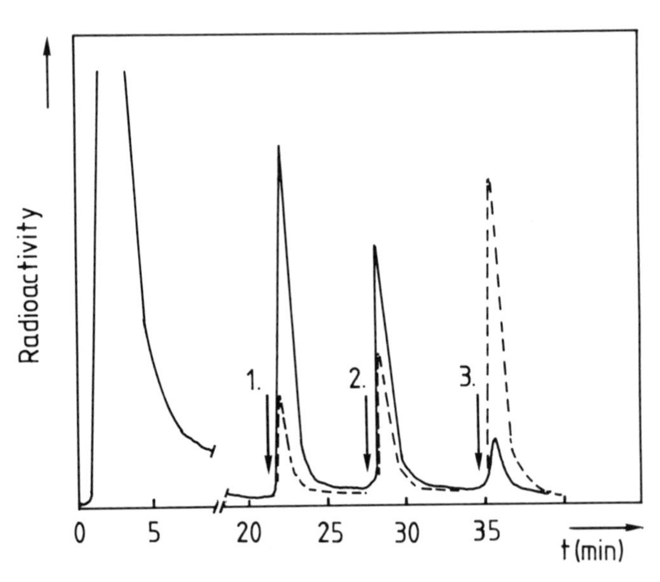

FIGURE 14–9. Analytical application of concanavalin A HPAC. Fractionation of [^{35}S]methionine-labeled extracts from liver and Morris hepatoma 7777 plasma membranes. One milliliter of Triton X-114 plasma membrane extract, containing 1 × 10^6 counts was applied to the Con A HPAC column. The column was washed with 10 ml of sample buffer (cf. Figure 14–9), containing 0.1% (v/v) Triton X-114 and eluted in three steps. Step one, with 0.025 *M* α-methyl-D-glucopyranoside; step two, with 0.2 *M* α-methyl-D-glucopyranoside; step three, with 0.2 *M* α-methyl-D-mannopyranoside. Chromatographic conditions: column, Con A-Eupergit C 1Z, 40 × 6 mm, flow rate 0.5 ml/min, pressure 40 to 60 bar, room temperature. ——, liver plasma membrane extract; ---, Morris hepatoma 7777 plasma membrane extract.

14.4.3 Application of Other Lectins

There is no large-scale use of lectins other than Con A, at least for the time being. The above-mentioned wheat germ agglutinin (*N*-acetylglucosamine specific) and the lens lectin are the most likely candidates for extended use. Despite their high cost, their use in a last purification step in micropreparative isolation of different glycoproteins, e.g., of the membrane-bound enzyme dipeptidyl-peptidase IV[69] or of erythrocyte membrane protein glycophorin,[68] has to be considered. The usual soft gels for lectin affinity chromatography can be replaced without difficulty by high-performance gels, which save time and allow higher yields.[4,66,67]

14.5 HEPARIN HPAC

14.5.1 General Aspects

Immobilized heparin has been used for separating plasma proteins for a long time, especially for the isolation of proteins that are involved in blood coagulation.[4,72,73] The nature of the interaction between heparin and protein is basically ionic. However, some proteins such as fibronectin, have special heparin-binding segments.[74] This suggests a kind of specific interaction between the heparin and the heparin-binding proteins, where not only ionic, but also hydrophobic and other forces play a part.

The chromatographic separation through immobilized heparin is achieved in principle according to the following schema:

The sample is applied to the column with a diluted buffer at low ionic strength;

The column is washed with a diluted buffer, sometimes additionally with a nonionic detergent;

Elution is carried out with concentrated sodium chloride, mostly 1 to 2 *M*, with either a slope or a step gradient.

14.5.2 Applications

Figure 14–10 shows the isolation of antithrombin from human plasma by heparin HPAC. Although being an interesting method for protein purification under mild conditions, heparin HPAC has so far been used very little.[4] Figure 14–11 shows an additional application of heparin HPAC for the isolation of bathrobin, a proteolytic enzyme from poison extract of the snake *Bathrops moojeni*. Separation was carried out by "medium" performance liquid chromatography with a biocompatible version of the equipment, on a 47 × 560 mm column, with about 900 ml bed volume. Two hundred grams of protein in 300 ml volume could be applied to the column. The enzyme could be eluted from the column with 0.25 *M* sodium chloride, the recovery of enzymatic activity was almost complete. The time for one chromatographic run was reduced

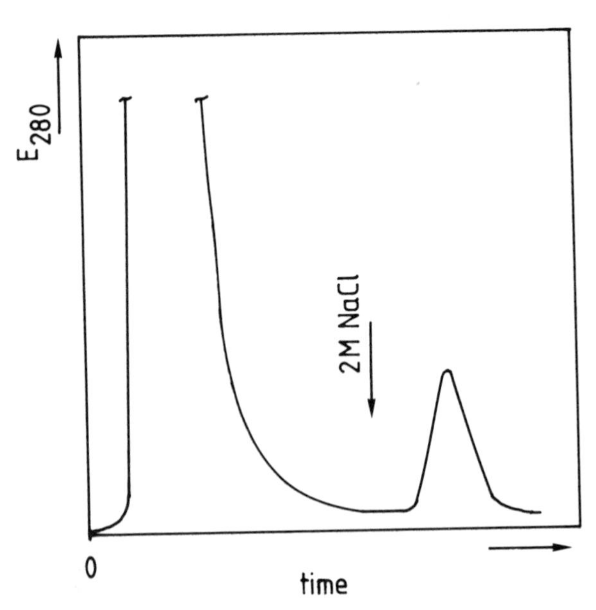

FIGURE 14–10. Affinity purification of antithrombin III (AT III) from human plasma with heparin HPAC. Eupergit-Heparin (30N) was shaken for 4 h with 200 ml of human plasma at 4°C. After packing in a 250 × 8.0 mm column, an elution step with 0.05 *M* Tris-HCl buffer, pH 7.4, containing 5 m*M* EDTA and 20 m*M* sodium chloride, was carried out. Afterward AT III was eluted with 2.0 *M* sodium chloride. Other chromatographic conditions, flow rate 2 ml/min, pressure 2 bar, temperature 4°C.

to one-fifth of the time that would have been required, had the separation been performed on a column packed with soft gel.

Heparin columns have a long life. They can be exposed to extreme pH and high salt concentrations, and they can be sterilized. The latter characteristic makes these columns particularly useful for fractionation of serum proteins.

14.6 OTHER HPAC METHODS

14.6.1 General Aspects

Apart from immunoaffinity, lectin, and heparin HPAC, any kind of biospecific interaction between two molecules can be used for separation. This applies, e.g., to interaction between enzymes and inhibitors, coenzymes (e.g., NAD) and enzymes, and interaction between the amino acid arginine and certain proteases or peptidases (for a review see refs. 75 and 76). In some cases, such

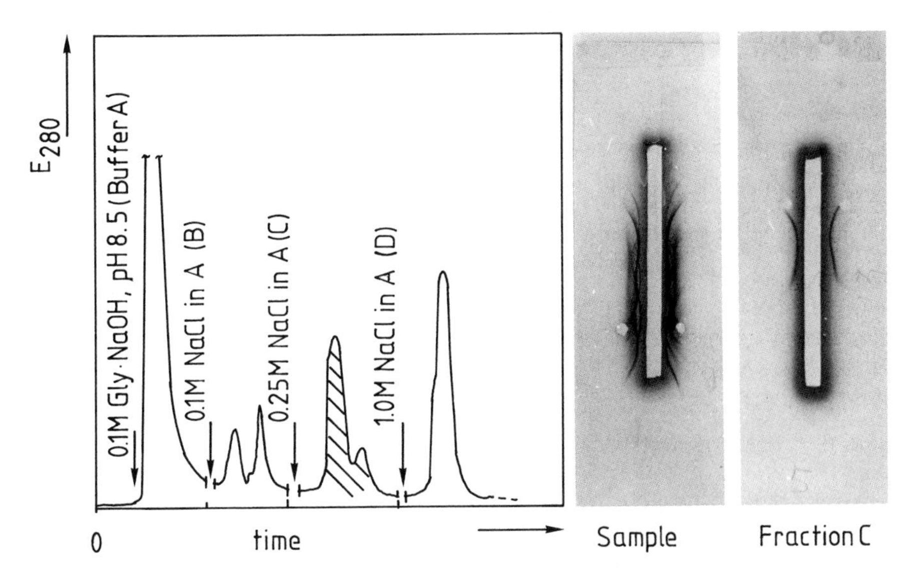

FIGURE 14–11. Isolation of proteolytic enzyme bathrobin with heparin HPAC. A total amount of 200 g of pretreated venom of the snake *Bathrops moojeni* in 300 ml of sample buffer (buffer A) was applied to a 560 × 47 mm chromatographic column, packed with Eupergit-Heparin, particle size 150 μm. The buffers used for step elution are shown in the chromatogram. Immunopherograms of the raw snake venom ("sample") and of the proteolytic enzyme bathrobin after affinity chromatographic purification, eluted with buffer C, are shown on the right side of the figure. (Reprinted from ref. 22 with the permission of Roland Hartl, Labomatic AG.)

as chromatography on immobilized amino acids, metal-affinity chromatography, hydroxylapatite or boronate HPLC, complex interactions occur, which lie somewhere between "bioaffinity," ion-exchange, hydrophobic, and others. Some methods, among them hydroxylapatite or metal-chelating chromatography, are treated as separate methods; others, like boronate and affi-blue chromatography, are called collectively affinity chromatographic methods. In Table 14–1 several low molecular ligands are listed, which have been used for HPAC separations on at least one occasion.

When immobilized to suitable HPLC supports, such ligands can be used for very successful separations. With these methods slope gradient elution can be used along with step gradient elution, the latter being the only option in the case of the other methods.

A small molecule, containing an amino, hydroxy, or sulfhydryl group, can be immobilized to the support, which reacts specifically with different polymers. Mosbach et al.[1] have immobilized NAD to silicagel and used it for the separation of lactate-dehydrogenase isoenzymes. Different immobilized inhibitors can be used for purification of corresponding enzymes.[1,75,76] For the resulting wide variety of ligands, which are not used very often, the producers provide activated supports. The user can then immobilize the ligands according to his individual requirements and pack the columns in his own laboratory.[36] Three kinds of ligands, which are used on a considerable scale in HPAC

TABLE 14–1. Low Molecular Ligands, Which Have Been Used in HPAC of Biopolymers

Immobilized ligand	Interacting biopolymer	References
AMP	Alcohol dehydrogenase	1
NAD	Lactate dehydrogenase	1
Boronic acid	Nucleotides, carbohydrates, proteins	77, 78
Glucosamine, other sugars	Lectins	79
Amino acids, peptides	Proteases, other enzymes	69, 76, 80, 81
Cibachrom Blue F3G-A	Enzymes, other proteins	82
Other dyes	Enzymes, other proteins	83, 84
Serotonin	Sialoglycoproteins	81, 85
Thiamine	Nucleic acids	86
Crown ether	Nucleic acids, proteins	87, 88

of biopolymers, are amino acids or different small peptides, boronate and affiblue. They are therefore the object of a more detailed discussion.

14.6.2 HPAC with Immobilized Amino Acids and Small Peptides

Figure 14–12 shows an experiment with HPAC of membrane proteins on a column with the immobilized amino acid arginine. The serine-protease dipeptidyl-peptidase IV (DPP IV) binds specifically to the column and can be eluted with a salt gradient. The elution of the enzyme from an arginine column was achieved at an NaCl concentration of less than 0.1 mol/liter. When a column with a weak anion-exchange support is used, this protein could be eluted only at a concentration of 0.4 mol/liter (Dj. Josić, unpublished results). This high salt concentration causes a considerable loss of enzymatic activity in DPP IV, whereas it remains unimpaired at 0.1 mol/liter NaCl. The second important advantage of the arginine column is that the enzyme could be enriched to a concentration 20 times higher than that achieved through the use of anion-exchange HPLC.

A number of other amino acids or small peptides can be used for affinity purification of proteins. According to Porath the amino acids lysine, arginine, histidine, and tryptophan are of special interest. They have an additional nitrogen atom, and they are responsible for many interactions among proteins as well as between proteins and other biopolymers (J. Porath, personal communication). The use of immobilized amino acids and polypeptides for the purification of biopolymers may therefore become more widespread in the future. For the time being their potential remains unexploited.

14.6.3 Boronate HPAC

The fact that boronate ions form complexes with monosaccharides, which in turn can be separated on an anion-exchange column, has been used for sugar separation.[77] Similar interaction with the sugars of glycoproteins as well as

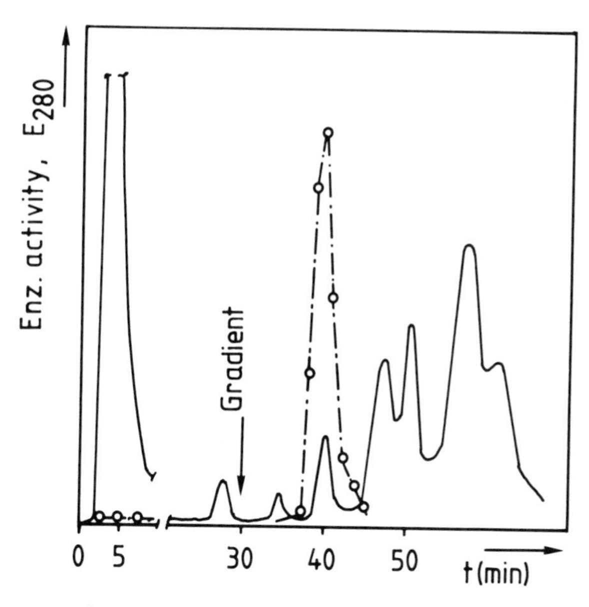

FIGURE 14–12. Isolation of the enzyme dipeptidyl-peptidase IV from kidney plasma membranes with arginine HPAC. One milliliter of Triton X-114 extract from kidney plasma membranes was applied to a 60 × 4.6 mm column, packed with Eupergit C 30N. After washing with 10 ml of 10 m*M* Tris-HCl, pH 8.0, containing 0.1% Triton X-114, the enzyme was eluted by a slope gradient between 0.0 and 0.2 *M* sodium chloride, containing 0.1% Triton X-114 for a period of 30 min. Other chromatographic conditions, flow rate 0.5 ml/min, pressure 2 bar, room temperature. The recovery of enzymatic activity was between 90 and 95%. ——, Absorbance at 280 nm; ○, enzymatic activity (mU/ml).

with other proteins and with nucleotides can be achieved on a column that contains immobilized boronate groups.[78] After application of the sample, the bound components can be eluted with a salt gradient or with the sugar alcohol sorbitol. Figure 14–13 shows the purification of trypsin by boronate HPAC from a sample with enriched enzyme. As can be seen in this experiment, separation is achieved under mild conditions, and the enzymatic activity of the trypsin is almost fully preserved. This purification takes place under much milder conditions than would be the case on a column with immobilized trypsin inhibitor, where elution requires a buffer with a pH of 2.8 (Y. Kato, personal communication).

14.6.4 HPAC Using Immobilized Cibacron Blue F3G-A and Other Dyes

Other low molecular ligands, which are used frequently, are Cibacron Blue F3G-A (affi-blue) and similar dyes.[82–84] Affi-blue HPAC is used above all for

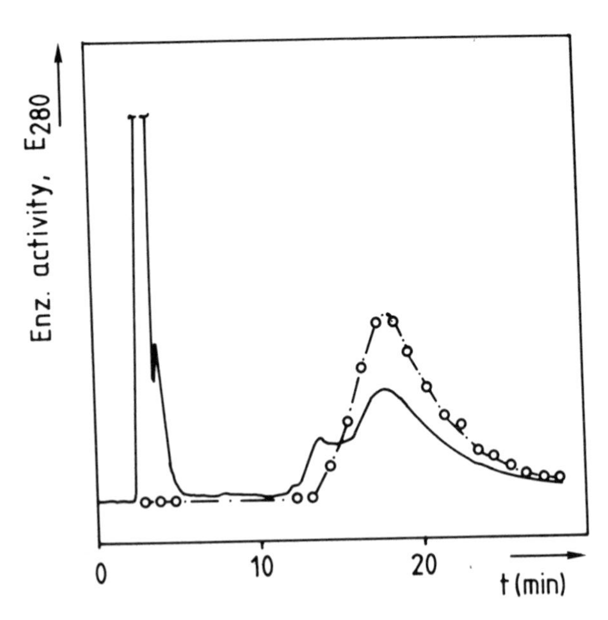

FIGURE 14–13. Separation of trypsin by boronate HPAC. Commercial crude sample of trypsin (10 mg) was dissolved in 1 ml of 20 m*M* HEPES-NaOH buffer, pH 8.5, containing 50 m*M* $MgCl_2$ (buffer A) and applied to a TSK-gel Boronate-5PW (75 × 7.5 mm) column. Elution was performed by a 60 min linear gradient between 0.0 and 100 m*M* sorbitol in buffer A. Recovery of enzymatic activity was 94%. Other chromatographic conditions, flow rate 1 ml/min, pressure 5 bar, room temperature. ——, Absorbance at 280 nm; ○, enzymatic activity. (The figure was made available by Dr. Y. Kato, Tosohaas Co.)

the isolation of serum albumin or the removal of albumin from antiserum, before antibodies have been isolated.[89] Figure 14–14 shows a chromatographic run on an affi-blue HPAC column. An extract from bakers' yeast was applied, which contained six water-soluble enzymes. Elution was carried out with a salt gradient.

As mentioned above, there are differences between boronate and affi-blue HPAC, in some respects also between HPAC with immobilized amino acids and peptides, on the one hand, and the above described HPAC methods, such as lectin and immunoaffinity HPAC, on the other hand. One major discrepancy results from the ligand size and the much improved displacement kinetics, which ensue, if the separation is carried out on columns with immobilized low molecular ligands. Whereas a step gradient is mostly indispensable, if immobilized high molecular ligands are applied, a normal slope gradient can be used in HPAC with immobilized low molecular ligands (see Figures 14–13 and 14–14).

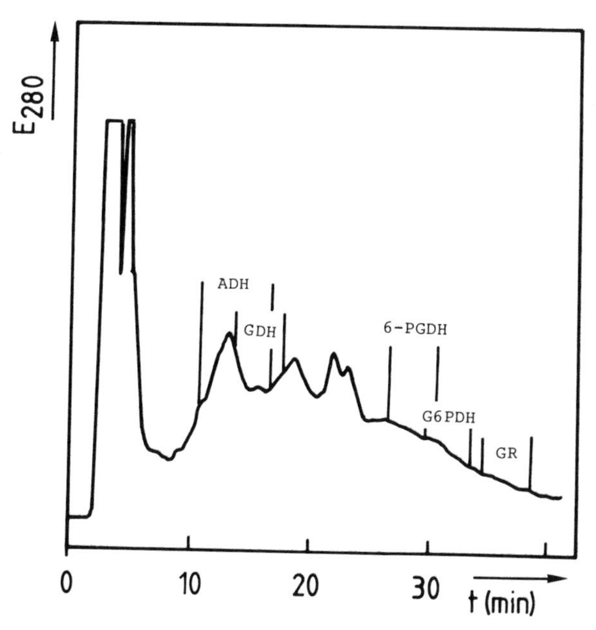

FIGURE 14–14. Separation of different enzymes from bakers' yeast extract by affi-blue HPAC. One milliliter of yeast extract was dialyzed against 20 m*M* bistris-HCl buffer, pH 6.4, containing 5 m*M* $MgCl_2$ (buffer A) and applied to a TSK-gel Blue-5PW (75 × 7.5 mm) column. Elution was performed with a 60 min linear gradient between 0.0 and 1 *M* NaCl in buffer A. Other chromatographic conditions, flow rate 1 ml/min, pressure 4 bar, room temperature, detection at 280 nm. Recovery of single enzymatic activities: alcohol dehydrogenase (ADH), 94%; glutamate dehydrogenase (GDH), 90%; 6-phosphogluconate dehydrogenase (6-PGDH), 64%; glucose-6-phosphate dehydrogenase (G6PDH), 114%; glutathione reductase (GR), 57%. (The figure was made available by Dr. Y. Kato, Tosohaas Co.)

14.7 CONCLUSIONS

Almost all separations achieved on soft-gel-type supports can be accomplished at much higher speed and resolution with mechanically stable, high-performance media. The much quicker separation and the high capacity and resolution are the characteristics that make HPAC an interesting tool for the isolation of large quantities of biopolymers, above all proteins from diluted solutions. This applies, e.g., to gene technolgically produced products such as vaccines, glycoproteins, and antibodies.

A future of HPAC can be seen also on an analytical and micropreparative scale. Here the most important characteristic is its specific interaction between sample and immobilized ligand. This allows, e.g., "indirect" immunoaffinity HPAC instead of the "classic" immunoprecipitation, isolation of monospecific antibodies, or investigation of the interaction between receptor and immobilized ligand.[90]

So far we have seen only the beginning of HPAC development. Neither the supports nor the column hardware and instrumentation have yet been optimized to the point, where their full potential can be exploited. The progress of biotechnology in general and the separation problems arising with the isolation of biologically active molecules have focused attention on the so-called "downstream" processing.[91,92] A new impetus can also be expected from biochemical and clinical-chemical laboratories, covering the whole range of HPAC applications, that is preparative as well as analytical and micropreparative.

REFERENCES

1. S. Ohlsson, L. Hansson, P.-O. Larsson, and K. Mosbach, *FEBS Lett.*, 93 (1978) 5.
2. M. Wilchek, T. Miron, and J. Kohn, *Methods Enzymol.*, 104 (1984) 3.
3. K. Nilsson and K. Mosbach, *Methods Enzymol.*, 104 (1984) 56.
4. Dj. Josić, W. Reutter, and D. Kraemer, *Angew. Makromol. Chem.*, 166 (1989) 249.
5. K. Ernst-Cabrera and M. Wilchek, *Anal. Biochem.*, 159 (1986) 267.
6. K. K. Unger and B. Anspach, *Trends Anal. Chem.*, 6 (1984) 121.
7. L. J. Janis and F. E. Regnier, *J. Chromatogr.*, 444 (1988) 1.
8. R. L. Schnaar, B. G. Langer, and B. K. Brandley, *Anal. Biochem.*, 151 (1985) 268.
9. T. Joergensen, *Proc. 7th Int. Symp. on HPLC of PPP*, Washington, D.C., 1987, Abstr. #506.
10. Z. El Rassi, D. Corradini, G. Guerra, W. Horne, and Cs. Horvath, *Proc. Twelfth Int. Symp. Column Liquid Chromatogr.*, Washington, D.C., 1988, Abstr. M-L-7.
11. R. L. Schnaar, B. G. Langer, and B. K. Brandley, *Anal. Biochem.*, 151 (1985) 268.
12. J. N. Kinkel, B. Anspach, K. K. Unger, R. Wieser, and G. Brunner, *J. Chromatogr.*, 297 (1984) 167.
13. E. D. Green, R. M. Brodbeck, and J. U. Baenziger, *Anal. Biochem.*, 162 (1987) 62.
14. H. Harada, M. Kamei, Y. Seiko, and F. Kogama, *J. Chromatogr.*, 355 (1986) 291.
15. N. Danielson and R. W. Siergiej, *Biotechnol. Bioeng.*, 23 (1981) 1913.
16. A. Kanamori, N. Seno, and J. Matsumoto, *J. Chromatogr.*, 363 (1986) 231.
17. D. Kraemer, *Jahrbuch. Biotechnol.*, (1986/87) 398.
18. R. R. Walters, *J. Chromatogr.*, 249 (1982) 19.
19. K. Nilsson and K. Mosbach, *Biochem. Biophys. Res. Communn.*, 102 (1981) 449.
20. P.-O. Larsson, *Methods Enzymol.*, 104 (1984) 212.
21. V. Saxena, A. E. Weil, R. T. Kawahata, W. C. Mc Gregor, and M. Chander, *Int. Lab.*, #1/2 (1988) 50.
22. K. Stocker and R. Hartl, *GIT Suppl.* 3/88 *Chromatographie* (1988) 20.
23. J. Mazsaroff and F. E. Regnier, *J. Liquid Chromatogr.*, 9 (12/1986) 2563.
24. K. Kalghatgi, L. Varady, and Cs. Horváth, *Proc. Twelfth Int. Symp. on Column Liquid Chromatogr.*, Washington, D.C., 1988, Abstr. M-P-140.
25. L. F. Colwell and R. A. Hartwick, *J. Liquid Chromatogr.*, 10 (12/1987) 2721.
26. Y. Kato, T. Kitamura, A. Mitsui, and T. Hashimoto, *J. Chromatogr.*, 398 (1987) 327.
27. J. Porath and B. Olin, *Biochemistry*, 22 (1983) 1621.
28. J. Porath, *J. Chromatogr.*, 443 (1988) 3.
29. Y. Kato, K. Nakamura, and T. Hashimoto, *J. Chromatogr.*, 354 (1986) 511.

30. Z. El Rassi and Cs. Horvath, *J. Chromatogr.*, 359 (1986) 241.
31. F. E. Regnier, *Chromatographia*, 24 (1987) 241.
32. T. Kawasaki, K. Ikeda, Sh. Takahashi, and Y. Kuboki, *Eur. J Biochem.*, 155 (1986) 249.
33. Y. Kato, K. Nakamura, and T. Hashimoto, *J. Chromatogr.*, 398 (1987) 340.
34. M. J. Gorbunoff and S. N. Timasheff, *Anal. Biochem.*, 136 (1984) 440.
35. S. Tsuru, M. Taniguchi, M. Tsugita, S. Sekiguchi, and K. Nomoto, *J. Immunol. Methods*, 106 (1988) 169.
36. Dj. Josić, W. Hofmann, R. Habermann, A. Becker, and W. Reutter, *J. Chromatogr.*, 397 (1987) 39.
37. Dj. Josić, W. Hofmann, R. Habermann, H.-J. Schulzke, and W. Reutter, *J. Clin. Chem. Clin. Biochem.*, 26 (1988) 559.
38. S. Ohlsson and J. Weislander, *J. Chromatogr.*, 397 (1987) 207.
39. G. Kronvall, *J. Immunol.*, 111 (1973) 1401.
40. L. Bjoerk and G. Kronvall, *J. Immunol.*, 133 (1984) 969.
41. K. J. Reis, H. F. Hansen, and L. Bjoerk, *Mol. Immunol.*, 23 (1986) 425.
42. D. Juergens, B. Sterzik, and F. J. Fehrenbach, *J. Exp. Med.*, 165 (1987) 720.
43. R. A. Young and R. W. Davis, *Science*, 222 (1983) 778.
44. M. T. Hearn and J. D. Davies, *Proc. 7th Int. Symp. on HPLC of PPP*, Washington, D.C., 1987, Abstr. #515.
45. D. W. Sears, S. Young, P. H. Wilson, and Christiaansen, *J. Immunol.*, 124 (1980) 2641.
46. Dj. Josić, R. Tauber, W. Hofmann, J. Mauck, and W. Reutter, *J. Clin. Chem. Clin. Biochem.*, 25 (1987) 869.
47. R. Buelow and P. Overath, *J. Biol. Chem.*, 261 (1986) 11918.
48. T. M. Phillips, and S. C. Frantz, *J. Chromatogr.*, 444 (1988) 13.
49. D. F. Hollis, S. Ralston, E. Suen, N. Cooke, and G. L. Shorr, *J. Liquid Chromatogr.*, 10 (1987) 2349.
50. L. J. Janis and F. E. Regnier, *J. Chromatogr.*, 444 (1988) 1.
51. T. M. Phillips, N. S. More, W. D. Queen, T. V. Holohan, N. C. Kramer, and A. M. Thompson, *J. Chromatogr.*, 317 (1984) 175.
52. J. V. Babashak and T. M. Phillips, *J. Chromatogr.*, 444 (1988) 21.
53. M. Wilchek and E. A. Bayer, *Anal. Biochem.*, 171 (1988) 1.
54. A. Becker, R, Neumeier, C.-S. Park, R. Gossrau, and W. Reutter, *Eur. J. Cell Biol.*, 39 (185) 417.
55. A. Becker, Ch. Hoffmann, and W. Reutter, in Glycoconjugates; Proc. 9th Int. Symp on Glycoconjugates (J. Montreuil, A. Verbert, G. Spik, and B. Fournet, eds.). G 137, Lille, 1987.
56. R. Nuck, M. Zimmermann, D. Sauvageot, Dj. Josić, and W. Reutter, Proc. Japanese-German Symp. on Sialic Acids (R. Schauer and T. Yamakava, eds.). Berlin, 1988, pp. 158–159.
57. I. L. Goldstein and C. E. Hayes, *Adv. Carbohydr. Chem. Biochem.*, 35 (1978) 127.
58. R. D. Cummings and S. Kornfeld, *J. Biol. Chem.*, 257 (1982) 11235.
59. Y. Endo, K. Yamashita, Y. Tachibana, S. Tojo, and A. Kobata, *Biochem. J.*, 85 (1979) 669.
60. R. Tauber, C.-S. Park, and W. Reutter, *Proc. Natl. Acad. Sci. U.S.A.*, 80 (1983) 4026.
61. A. Borchert, P.-O. Larsson, and K. Mosbach, *J. Chromatogr.*, 244 (1982) 49.
62. Dj. Josić, W. Hofmann, R. Habermann, and W. Rutter, *J. Chromatogr.*, 444 (1988) 29.
63. C. A. K. Borrebaeck, J. Soares, and B. Matiasson, *J. Chromatogr.*, 284 (1984) 187.
64. M. Tokuda, M. Kamei, S. Yui, and F. Koyama, *J. Chromatogr.*, 323 (1985) 434.
65. M. Tokuda, M. Kamei, S. Yui, and F. Koyama, *J. Chromatogr.*, 355 (1986) 291.
66. D. Renauer, F. Oesch, J. Kinkel, K. K. Unger, and R. J. Wieser, *Anal. Biochem.*, 151 (1985) 424.
67. E. D. Green, R. M. Brodbeck, and J. V. Benziger, *J. Biol. Chem.*, 262 (1987) 12030.
68. D. Corradini, Z. El Rassi, G. Guerra, W. Horne, and Cs. Horvath, *J. Chromatogr.*, 458 (1988) 1.

69. Dj. Josić, M. Raps, W. Hoffmann, and W. Reutter, Gemeinsame Tagung der Deutschen und Österreichischen Gesellschaft Für Biologische Chemie, Innsbruck, 1988.
70. I. E. Liener, in Concanavalin A as a Tool (H. Bittiger and H. P. Schnebli, eds.). Wiley, London, 1976, pp. 17–31.
71. A. Bergold and P. Carr, *Proc. 7th Int. Symp. on HPLC of PPP*, Washington, D.C., 1987, p. 28.
72. I. Danishefsky, F. Tzeng, M. Ahrens, and S. Klein, *Thromb. Res.*, 8 (1976) 131.
73. W. Kiesiel and W. E. Davie, *Biochemistry*, 14 (1975) 4928.
74. S. K. Akiyama and K. M. Yamada, *Adv. Enzymol.*, 59 (1987) 2.
75. J. Porath, *J. Chromatogr.*, 218 (1981) 241.
76. P. C. Dean and J. N. B. Walker, *Biochem. Soc. Transct.*, 13 (1985) 1055.
77. Dj. Josić, R. Hafermaas, Ch. Bauer, and W. Reutter, *J. Chromatogr.*, 317 (1984) 35.
78. M. Glad, S. Ohlsson, L. Hansson, M.-O. Månsson, and K. Mosbach, *J. Chromatogr.* 200 (1980) 254.
79. R. R. Walters, in Affinity Chromatography and Biological Recognition (I. M. Chaiken, M. Wilcheck, and I. Parikh, eds.). Academic Press, New York, 1983, pp. 261–264.
80. J. Turková, K. Blaká, and J. Adamamová, *J. Chromatogr.*, 236 (1982) 375.
81. Dj. Josić, K. Zeilinger, Y.-P. Lim, M. Raps, and W. Reutter, *J. Chromatogr.*, 484 (1989) 327.
82. C. R. Lowe, M. Glad, P.-O. Larsson, S. Ohlsson, D. A. P. Small, T. Atkinson, and K. Mosbach, *J. Chromatogr.*, 215 (1981) 303.
83. D. A. P. Small, T. Atkinson, and C. R. Lowe, *J. Chromatogr.*, 216 (1981) 175.
84. P. Konečny, M. Smrž, J. Borák, and S. Slováková, *J. Chromatogr.*, 398 (1987) 387.
85. R. J. Sturgeon and C. M. Sturgeon, *Carbohydr. Res.*, 103 (1982) 213.
86. Y. Kato, T. Seita, T. Hashimoto, and A. Shimizu, *J. Chromatogr.*, 134 (1977) 204.
87. J. Reusch, *Labo*, 19 (1988) #7 (in German), 38.
88. Dj. Josić, W. Reutter, and J. Reusch, *J. Chromatogr.*, 476 (1989) 309.
89. Dj. Josić, W. Schuett, J. van Renswoude, and W. Reutter, *J. Chromatogr.*, 353 (1986) 13.
90. Dj. Josić, W. Hofmann, R. Habermann, F. Coenders, and W. Reutter, *Proc. Twelfth Int. Symp. Column Liquid Chromatogr.*, Washington, D.C., 1988, Abstr. M-L-6 (p. 6).
91. Cs. Horváth, *Proc. 4th Int. Symp. Separation Science and Biotechnology*, Gargnano/Garda (Italy), 1988, p. 1.
92. M. Ventilla, *Proc. 4th Int. Symp. Separation Science and Biotechnology*, Gargnano/Garda (Italy), 1988, p. 1.

CHAPTER 15

Stationary and Mobile Phase Effects in High-Performance Liquid Chromatography of Protein Hormones

B. S. Welinder, H. H. Sørensen, K. R. Hejnæs, S. Linde, and B. Hansen

CONTENTS

15.1 INTRODUCTION

A considerable increase in the number of literature reports in the last 5–10 years has documented that the use of high-performance liquid chromatography has been extended from "classical" organic chemistry to biochemistry. The major reason for this evolution has been the introduction of stationary phases free of strong nonspecific binding of polypeptides, which then could be separated with acceptable recovery in a highly efficient manner and in a short time.

The use of a new separation technique with a speed and separation capacity far superior to "classical" open-column chromatography indicated a minor revolution in biochemistry and has been one of the major prerequisites for the introduction of recombinant-derived proteins in the pharmaceutical industry.

Although the technical equipment has been considerably developed (introduction of high-pressure pumps, sample injectors, detectors, etc.) the column developmental work has been the precondition for separation processes involving polypeptides with biological activity. Many protein hormones have been analyzed under the strongly nonphysiological conditions normally used in reversed-phase analyses, and retaining the biological activity seems to be the rule rather than the exception. High-performance ion-exchange chromatography, size-exclusion chromatography, affinity chromatography, and hydrophobic-interaction chromatography may be performed under physiological or close-to-physiological conditions, and remain the choice for the analyses of larger proteins with enzymatic activity, i.e., biomolecules where the activity is strictly dependent on a totally retained three-dimensional structure. Loss of biological activity after these separation principles may occur, but can often be attributed to the strong multipoint binding between the sample molecules and the stationary phase, a phenomena not unknown in classical, open-column chromatography of enzymes.

Due to an unrivaled separation capacity and selectivity, i.e., the ability to distinguish between closely related sample molecules, RP-HPLC* remains the obvious choice for polypeptide analyses. Insulin is a well-documented example on the applicability of the technique, which has been used for analyzing insulin, insulin-related, and non-insulin-related substances present in pancreatic extracts, fermentation liquids from recombinant-derived insulins, or reaction mixtures from enzyme-derived semisynthetic human insulin. Baseline separation of two insulins differing in one of the 51 amino acids or between insulin and monodesamido insulin characterizes the efficiency of the present RP-HPLC analyses.

However, to obtain these sophisticated separations, a considerable amount of developmental work must be undertaken with respect to choice of mobile and stationary phase. In the present chapter we will describe some of this developmental work for insulin (6 kDa) and human growth hormone (22 kDa). RP-HPLC analyses for the separation of insulin and insulin derivatives (desamidoinsulin, iodinated insulins, desalanineinsulin, proinsulin, insulin dimer, etc.) as well as human growth hormone (hGH), hGH impurities, and methionyl-hGH will be presented. HPSEC separations of insulin and hGH from dimers and polymers as well as nonrelated substances with different molecular weight will illustrate the usability of the major commercially available stationary phases for high-performance size-exclusion chromatography. HPIEC of interleukin-1β (IL-1β) will deal exclusively with the stationary phases commercially available from Pharmacia and the possibility to scale up directly (in a linear fashion) from microbore to production columns. Finally, evaluation of a number of HIC stationary phases with 'standards' proteins (including insulin and hGH) as well as membrane proteins from erythrocyte ghosts will be shown in order to elucidate the limits—at present—for HPLC separation of proteins with increasing MW and hydrophobicity.

*Abbreviations: RP-HPLC, reversed-phase high-performance liquid chromatography; HPSEC, high-performance size-exclusion chromatography; HPIEC, high-performance ion-exchange chromatography; HIC, hydrophobic-interaction chromatography; TFA, trifluoroacetic acid; TEAP, triethylammonium phosphate; TEAF, triethylammonium formiate; IL-1β, interleukin 1β; hGH, human growth hormone; phGH, pituitary-derived human growth hormone; bhGH, biosynthetic human growth hormone; SDS, sodium dodecyl sulfate; DTT, dithiothreitol; RIA, radioimmunoassay; DA*P*-1, diamino-peptidyl peptidase.

15.2 MATERIALS AND METHODS

Commercially available HPLC equipment and columns were used throughout. Pumps: M6000A, M510, M45, M590 (Waters), Spectra Physics SP 8700, Gynkotek 300 C. Sample injectors: U6K and WISP 710 A or B, 712 (Waters), 7125 (Rheodyne). Detectors: Pye Unicam UV detector, Waters M440, Lambda Max 481, Hitachi L 4200, Linear UVIS 200. Integrators: Waters M730 Data Module, 840 Chromatography Control Station, Hewlett Packard 3390A. Gradient controllers: Waters M660 and 720 Chromatography Control Station, Gynkotek 250 B, Spectra Physics SP 8700. FPLC equipment (Pharmacia).

All analyses were performed at ambient temperature unless otherwise stated. Acetonitrile, ethanol, methanol, and 2- and *n*-propanol were obtained from Rathburn (HPLC quality). All chemicals were of similar purity. Water was drawn from a Millipore Milli-Q plant. Mobile phases were Millipore filtered (0.45 μm) and degassed (vacuum/ultrasound) before use. During chromatography the mobile phase was degassed continuously with helium sparkling or by passing through an ERMA degasser. Insulins, growth hormones, and IL-1β were obtained from Nordisk Gentofte A/S. Membrane proteins were isolated from blood collected from one of the authors (a healthy male, 42 years old) as described.[170] All other polypeptides used as samples were obtained from Sigma or Aldrich. All HPLC columns used were obtained prepacked from local distributors with the exception of the TSK Phenyl 5 PW and the TSK Ether 5 PW columns, which were obtained directly from Toyo Soda (Japan).

15.3 REVERSED-PHASE HIGH-PERFORMANCE LIQUID CHROMATOGRAPHY OF INSULIN AND GROWTH HORMONE

RP-HPLC analyses of several polypeptide hormones have been published in the last years, covering the MW range from a few hundred to several thousand. We have chosen insulin as an example since a considerable number of reports reflect several strategies for RP-HPLC optimization and because insulin demonstrates the potential of RP-polypeptide analysis when it is most successful. From one extreme to another, human growth hormone, a hydrophobic 22-kDa protein hormone, marks the border for utilizing RP-HPLC in protein chemistry: The developmental work in the design of effective RP-HPLC analyses is very extensive, but in spite of that, RP analyses of hGH remains less successful than those of insulin.

15.3.1 Mobile Phase Effects

In this section we describe the use of a single stationary phase for insulin analyses and two different matrices for hGH analyses, and present the results obtained by changes in buffer components, pH, organic modifier, ion pairing substances, temperature, etc.

15.3.1.1 Insulin

The most common mobile phases used for RP-HPLC of insulin and insulin-related substances published in the period 1978–1988 are given in Table 15–1, and they can be divided into four major groups containing

1. H_3PO_4 or acid phosphates,
2. ammonium salts,
3. alkylammonium salts, and
4. TFA.

This reflects the well-known experience that in order to obtain sharp, symmetrical peaks in silica-based RP-HPLC analyses of polypeptides, it is essential

TABLE 15–1. Mobile Phase Additives Used for RP-HPLC of Insulins and Insulin-Related Substances[a]

	Reference
Phosphoric acid	7, 23, 39, 41, 50, 52, 53, 90
Acid K/Na-phosphates	9, 17, 18, 19, 20, 27, 36, 45, 46, 51, 64, 76, 94, 96, 115
Phosphates + additives[b]	3, 5, 6, 8, 15, 27, 31, 40, 43, 48, 54, 57, 67, 79, 102
Other salts[c]	4, 11, 14, 22, 25, 29, 34, 38, 44, 50, 51, 55, 56, 65, 67, 69, 70, 72, 74, 85, 89, 92, 95, 98, 113, 116, 118, 119, 121, 125, 128
Alkylammonium salts	1, 12, 24, 26, 32, 33, 38, 43, 53, 56, 59, 60, 62, 65, 69, 74, 95, 107, 117, 125, 127, 129
Alkylammonium salts + additives[d]	2, 10, 13, 21, 28, 37, 80, 87, 99, 101, 110, 126
Trifluoroacetic acid	5, 16, 32, 35, 61, 66, 68, 69, 73, 75, 77, 78, 79, 81, 83, 84, 86, 88, 90, 91, 95, 97, 100, 103, 104, 105, 106, 108, 109, 111, 112, 113, 114, 120, 123, 124, 125, 126
Others[e]	30, 47, 49, 58, 59, 60, 63, 71, 72, 82, 93, 122

[a] Desamidoinsulin, arginine insulin, ethylester insulin, insulin dimers, A- and B-chains, iodinated insulins, insulin species, mutant insulins, and hybrid insulins.

[b] Perchlorate and neutral salts.

[c] Ammonium sulfate, sodium sulfate, ammonium acetate, ammonium phosphate, or perchlorates.

[d] Perchlorate.

[e] Hexafluoroacetone,[30] acetic acid,[47] Tris/phosphoric acid,[49] Tris,[58] perchloric acid,[59,60] acetic acid/octanesulfonate,[63] formic acid,[71,122] TFA/octanesulfonate,[72] bicarbonate,[82] sodium sulfate/butanesulfonate.[93]

to minimize the interaction between the sample molecules and the stationary phase by adding ion pairing substances, neutral salts, or chaotropic agents preferably at acidic pH. Acetonitrile was used as organic modifier almost exclusively (101 of 129 references).

In RP-HPLC of insulin and insulin-related substances it is essential to be able to separate closely related polypeptides, i.e., insulin peptide and desamidoinsulin (Asn → Asp or Gln → Glu in a single of the 51 amino acids), insulin species, mutant insulins or hybrid insulins (a single amino acid substitution of the 51), and arginine insulins (one Arg extension). Optimization of such separations can be obtained by proper combinations of stationary and mobile phases, and we hereby present some examples using a single stationary phase (LiChrosorb RP-18) eluted with various mobile phases.

Although it can be seen from Table 15–1 that TFA is a popular mobile phase additive, its use for isocratic elution of insulin and desamidoinsulin often results in miserable peak shape under conditions where TEAP and ammonium sulfate-containing mobile phases elute insulin and desamidoinsulin in sharp, symmetrical peaks (Figure 15–1). However, gradient elution of polypeptides present in rat* pancreatic islets could be performed almost equally well when TFA and TEAP were compared as mobile phase additives. The elution order of the major components was found to be identical but in TFA glucagon was eluted much closer to rat insulin II than in TEAP (Figure 15–2).

Rat proinsulin I and II are eluted later than the insulins, and due to very low content in normal islets, it is generally not possible to obtain a UV-absorbance signal. If rat islets are pulse-labeled with [^{3}H]leucine and [^{35}S]methionine, rat proinsulin I and II can be detected, and it was found that separation of the two proinsulins was possible only if the LiChrosorb RP-18 column was eluted with TFA/CH_3CN. TEAP/CH_3CN will coelute rat proinsulin I and II (Figure 15–3).

The separation between insulin peptide and desamidoinsulin may be improved by replacing ammonium sulfate with acid NaH_2PO_4 or TEAP (see Figures 15–4 and 15–5). On the contrary, the separation between insulin-related substances with MW >6000, i.e., proinsulin and insulin dimers, is improved when TEAP is replaced with $(NH_4)_2SO_4$ (Figure 15–5).

The separation between insulin peptide and des-B30-alanineinsulin (DAI), a common intermediate in insulin degradation with trypsin, is difficult to perform in mobile phases containing phosphate or TEAP, but addition of chaotropic agents, i.e., perchlorate, results in baseline separation of insulin and DAI (Figure 15–6).

pH in the mobile phase is an essential parameter, and a separation may often be possible only in a narrow pH interval. As an example the separation of rat insulin I and II, rat C-peptides I and II, and rat glucagon was performed at pH 3.0, 4.0, 5.0, and 6.0 in TEAP/acetonitrile, and the separation pattern was found to be satisfactory only at pH 4.0 (Figure 15–7). Further, the separation of the four monoiodoinsulins (monoiodinated in Tyr A14, A19, B16, or B26) in TEAF/acetonitrile could be performed only at pH 4.0. At pH 3.0, 5.0, and 6.0, B16 and A14 monoiodoinsulins coeluted (see Figure 15–8).

*Two different insulins (insulin I and II) are synthesized in the rat.

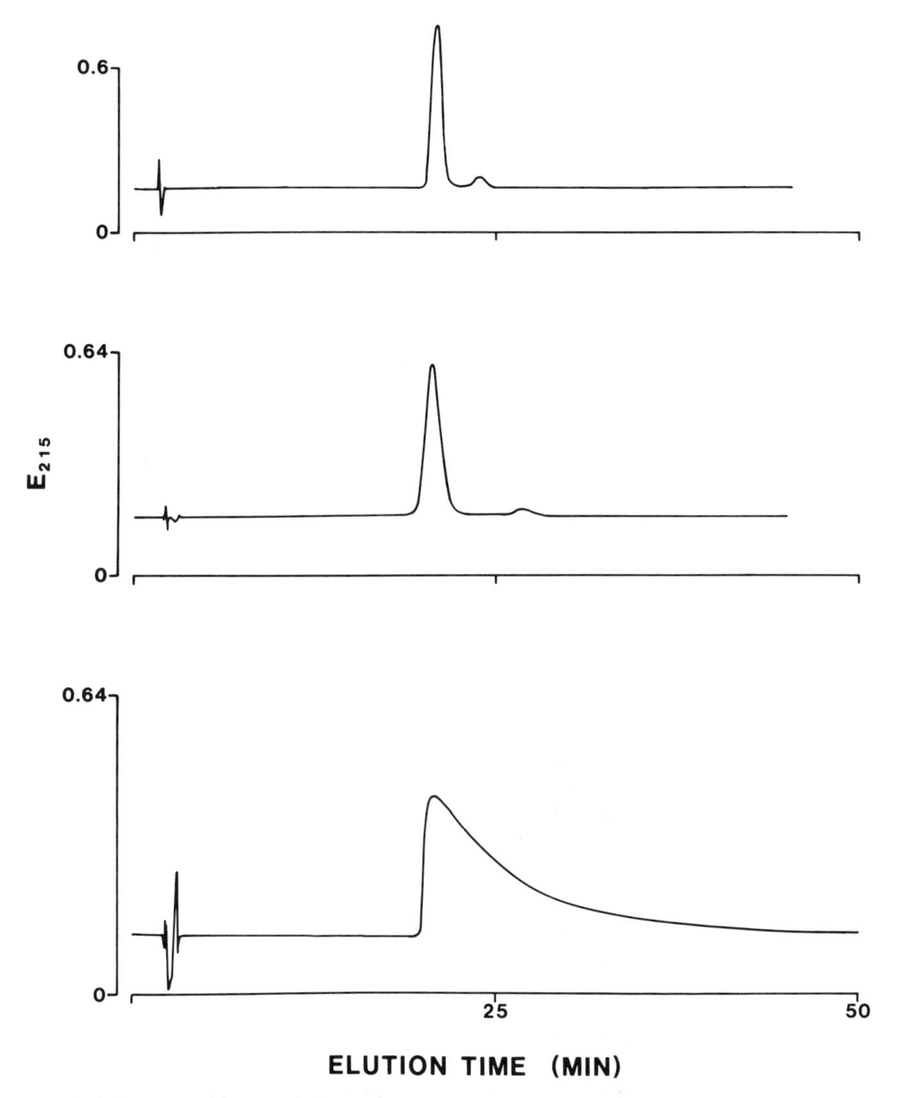

FIGURE 15–1. Isocratic elution of 100 μg crystalline porcine insulin using a 250 × 4.0 mm I.D. LiChrosorb RP-18 column eluted with 0.125 *M* $(NH_4)_2SO_4$, pH 4.0/29.5% acetonitrile, 45°C (upper panel), 0.25 *M* TEAP, pH 3.0/26% acetonitrile (middle panel), and 0.05% TFA/32% acetonitrile (lower panel). Flow rate 1.0 ml/min. (Reproduced with permission from ref. 125.)

As stated above, acetonitrile is the most common organic modifier due to low viscosity, low UV cut-off, and solubilizing properties. However, in the case of the monoiodoinsulins, 2-propanol was found to be a better choice as organic modifier since the separation in TEAF/2-propanol could be performed at three of the four above-mentioned pH values (Figure 15–9) compared to only one of four pH values in TEAF/acetonitrile (Figure 15–8).

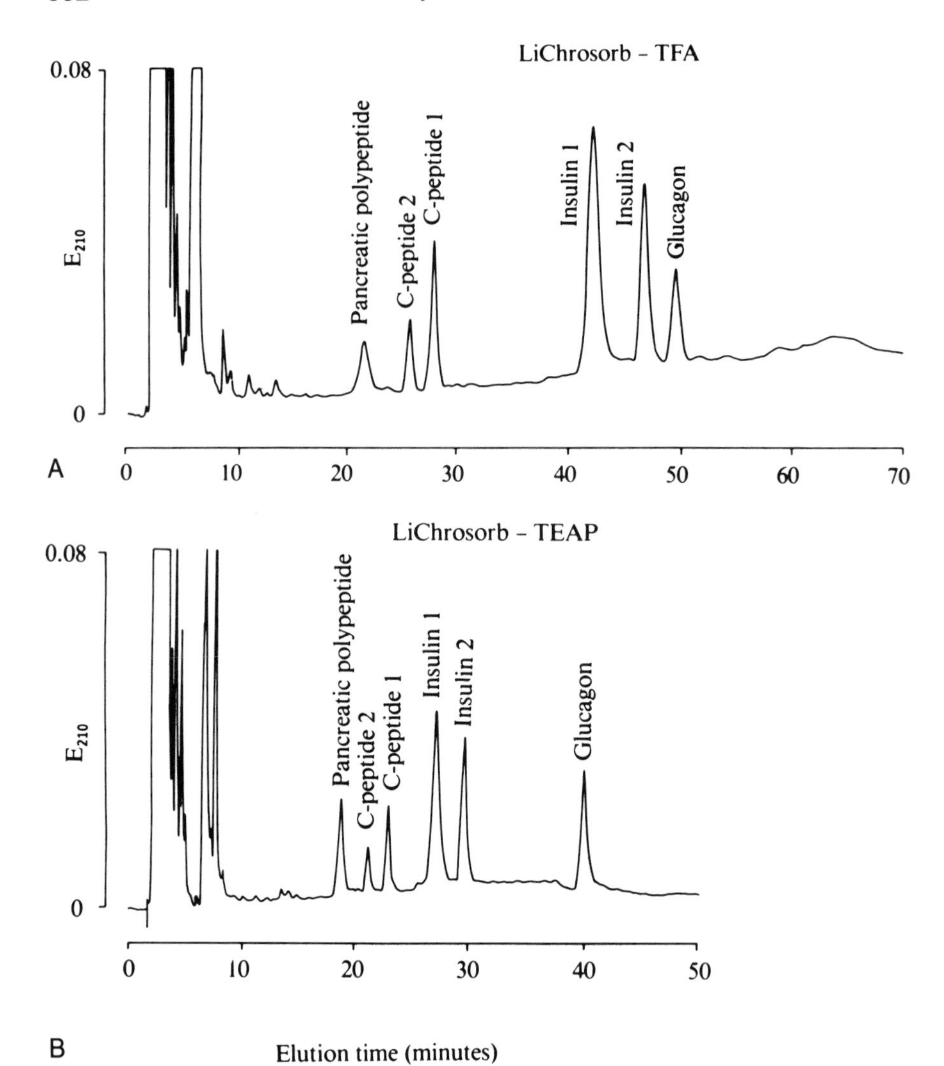

FIGURE 15–2. RP-HPLC separation of rat islet culture medium (containing insulin I and II, C-peptides I and II) plus added glucagon and rat pancreatic polypeptide using a Li-Chrosorb RP-18 column (250 × 4.0 mm I.D.) eluted at 1.0 ml/min with linear acetonitrile gradients. (30 → 36% acetonitrile in 0.1% TFA during 60 min. 25–30% acetonitrile during 30 min in 0.125 *M* TEAP, pH 4.0.)

If the separation at pH 4.0 in acetonitrile (Figure 15–8) is compared to the pH 4.0 separation in 2-propanol (Figure 15–9), it can be seen that the elution order of A14 and B16 monoiodoinsulins is reversed in the two examples, i.e., choice of organic modifier may strongly influence the retention time of closely related polypeptides as well as their overall resolution.

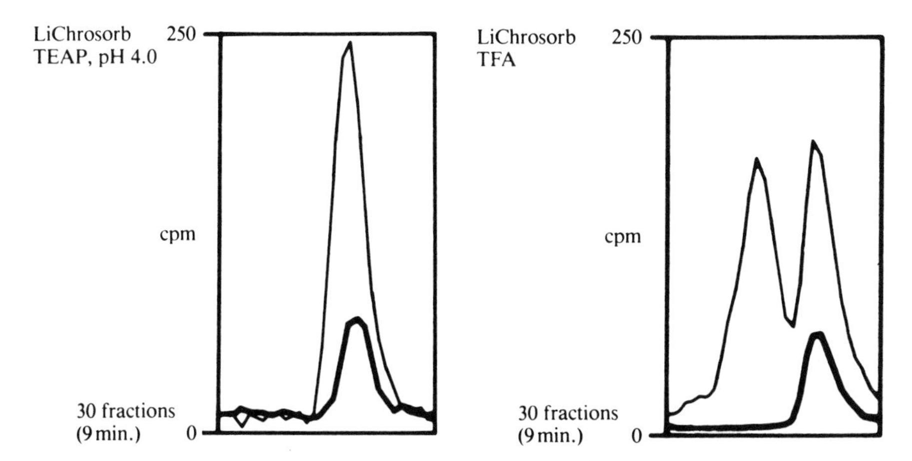

FIGURE 15–3. RP-HPLC separation of labeled rat proinsulin I and II from cultured rat islets using the same conditions as in Figure 15–2. The curves represent the later part of the chromatograms (in the TEAP system from ~35 min, in the TFA system from ~60 min). The thin lines show [^{3}H]leucine incorporated in proinsulin I and II; the thick lines represent [^{35}S]methionine incorporated in proinsulin II only.

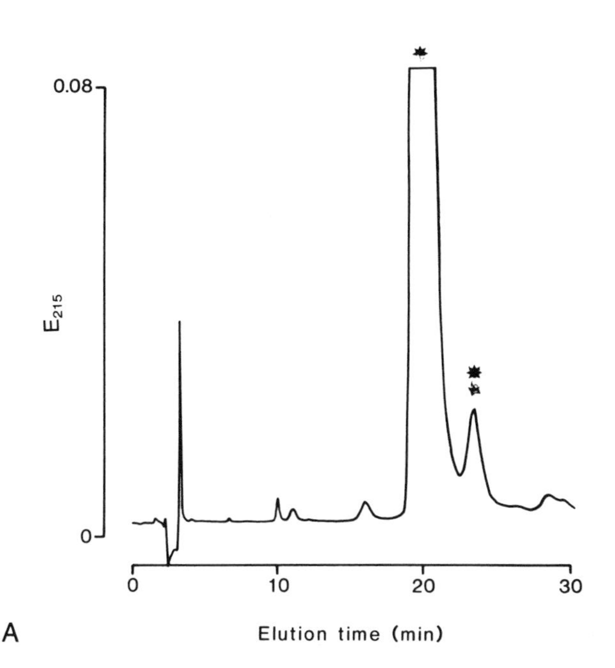

FIGURE 15–4. The elution pattern of insulin peptide* and monodesamidoinsulin** using a LiChrosorb RP-18 column (250 × 4.0 mm I.D.) eluted with an acetonitrile gradient in 0.125 *M* $(NH_4)_2SO_4$, pH 4.0, 45°C (A)

(*continued*)

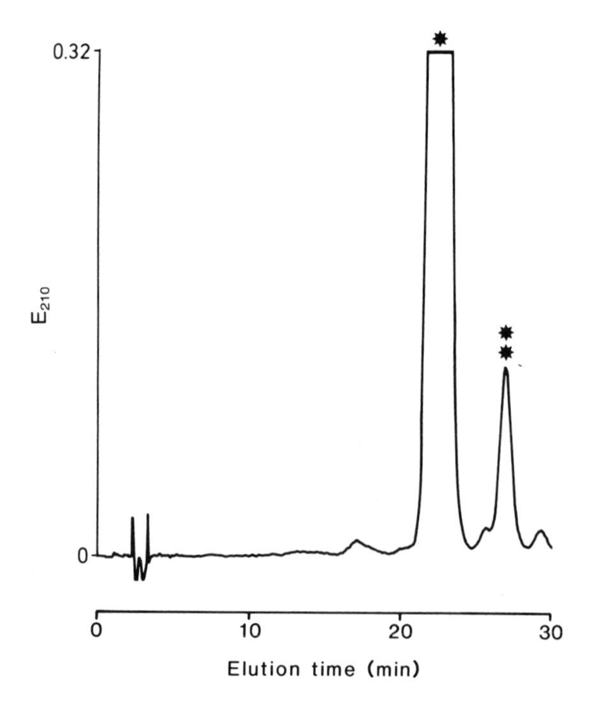

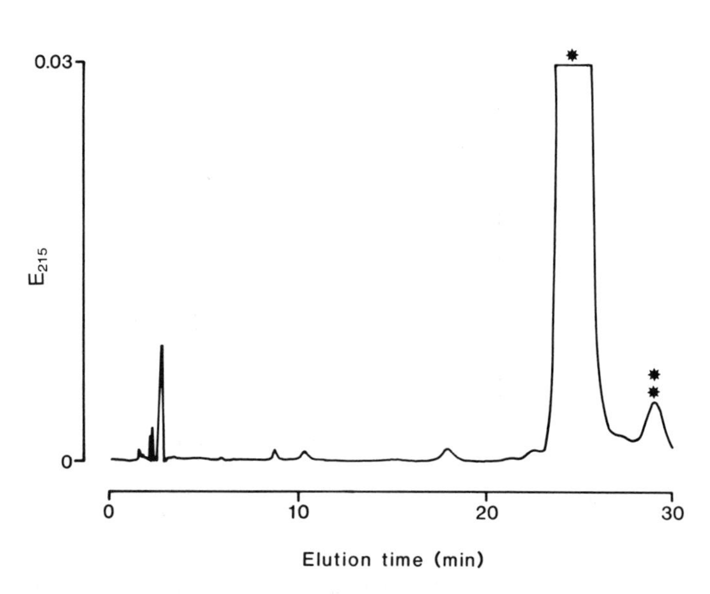

0.25 *M* TEAP, pH 3.0 (B), and 0.1 *M* NaH_2PO_4, pH 2.2, 45°C (C). Flow rate: 1.0 ml/min.

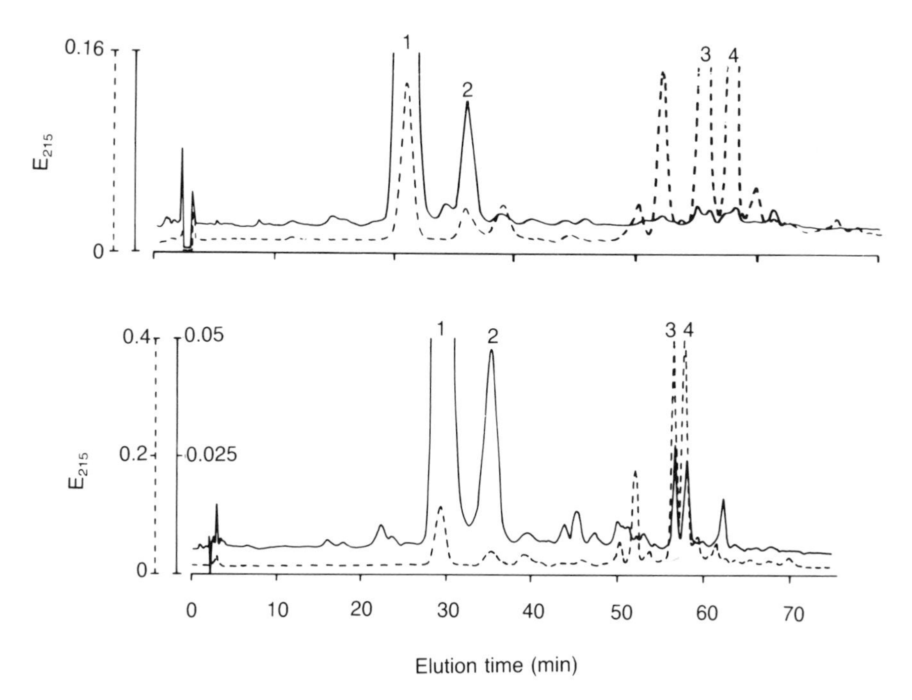

FIGURE 15–5. Gradient elution of 100 μg crystalline porcine insulin (solid line) or 100 μg b-component (primarily composed of proinsulin and insulin dimers; dotted line) using a LiChrosorb RP-18 (250 × 4.0 mm I.D.) column eluted with an acetonitrile gradient in 0.25 *M* TEAP, pH 3.0 (upper panel) or 0.125 *M* $(NH_4)_2SO_4$, pH 4.0 (lower panel). Flow rate 1.0 ml/min. The peaks marked with numbers correspond to insulin peptide (1), monodesamidoinsulin (2), proinsulin (3), and insulin dimer (4). (Reproduced with permission from ref. 125.)

A similar reverse elution order of A14 and B16 monoiodoinsulin was obtained if the separation temperature was lowered from ambient to 0°C using TEAP pH 4.0/acetonitrile as mobile phase,[129] indicating that temperature has a marked influence on the separation pattern of insulin and insulin-related substances. If the separation temperature in the $(NH_4)_2SO_4$/acetonitrile system (45°C) is lowered to 22°C, k' values are markedly reduced (Figure 15–10, A and B). If the acetonitrile concentration is lowered in order to obtain similar k' values for insulin peptide at the two temperatures, the two chromatograms are very similar, but the main peak (insulin peptide) is found to be broader at the lower temperature, i.e., mass transfer is slower at a lower temperature (Figure 15–10, A and C).

15.3.1.2 Human Growth Hormone (hGH)

Published RP-HPLC analyses of hGH are limited in number compared to RP-HPLC analyses of insulin,[128,130–148] reflecting the increasing difficulties in handling a 22-kDa hydrophobic protein under reversed-phase conditions. We have performed hGH analyses using Nucleosil C18 or TSK Phenyl 5 PW RP in order to separate the components present in pituitary-derived hGH (phGH) as

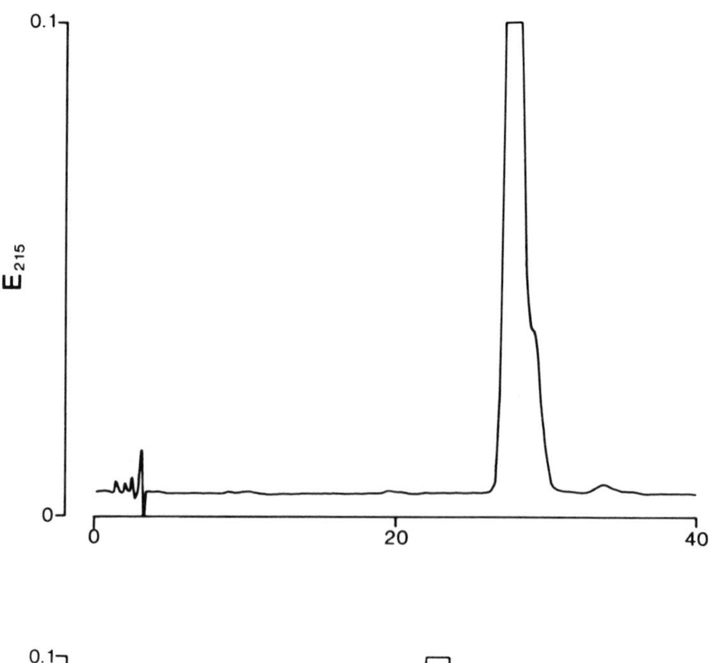

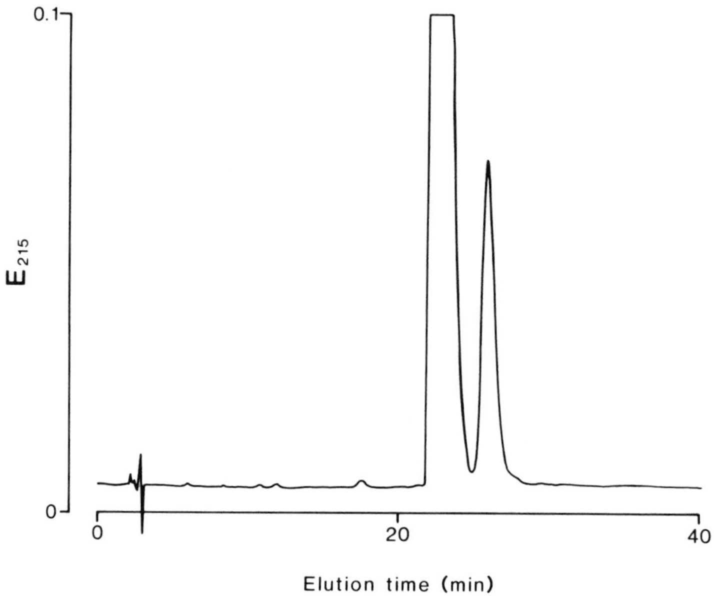

FIGURE 15–6. Isocratic elution of a mixture of 25 μg human insulin peptide (85%) and desalanineinsulin (15%) using a LiChrosorb RP-18 column (250 × 4.0 mm I.D.) eluted with 0.1 *M* NaH_2PO_4, pH adjusted to 2.2 with H_3PO_4/30% acetonitrile (upper panel) or 0.05 *M* NaH_2PO_4, pH adjusted to 2.5 with $HClO_4$/30% acetonitrile (lower panel). Flow rate: 1.0 ml/min. Separation temperature: 45°C.

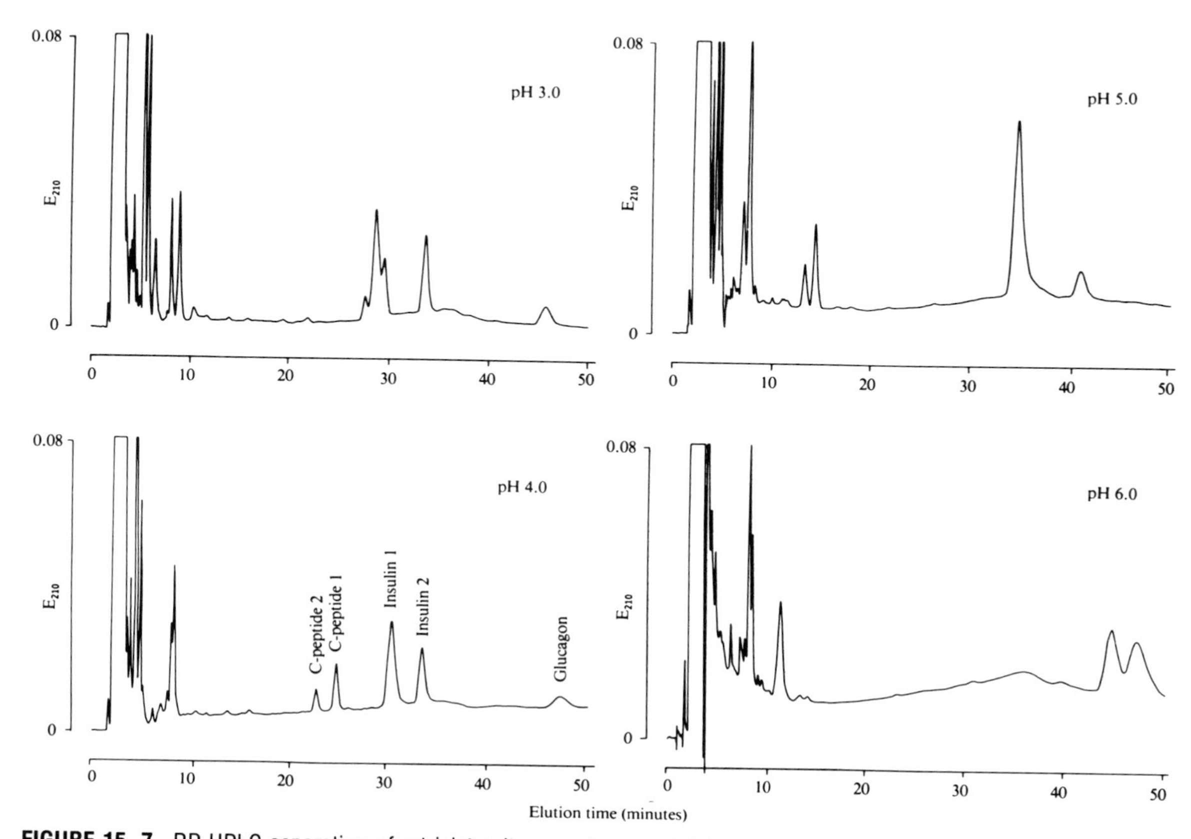

FIGURE 15–7. RP-HPLC separation of rat islet culture medium containing insulin I and II, C-peptide I and II, plus added glucagon using a LiChrosorb RP-18 (250 × 4.0 mm I.D.) column eluted at 1.0 ml/min with a linear acetonitrile gradient (25–30%) in 0.125 *M* TEAP adjusted to pH 3.0, 4.0, 5.0, or 6.0.

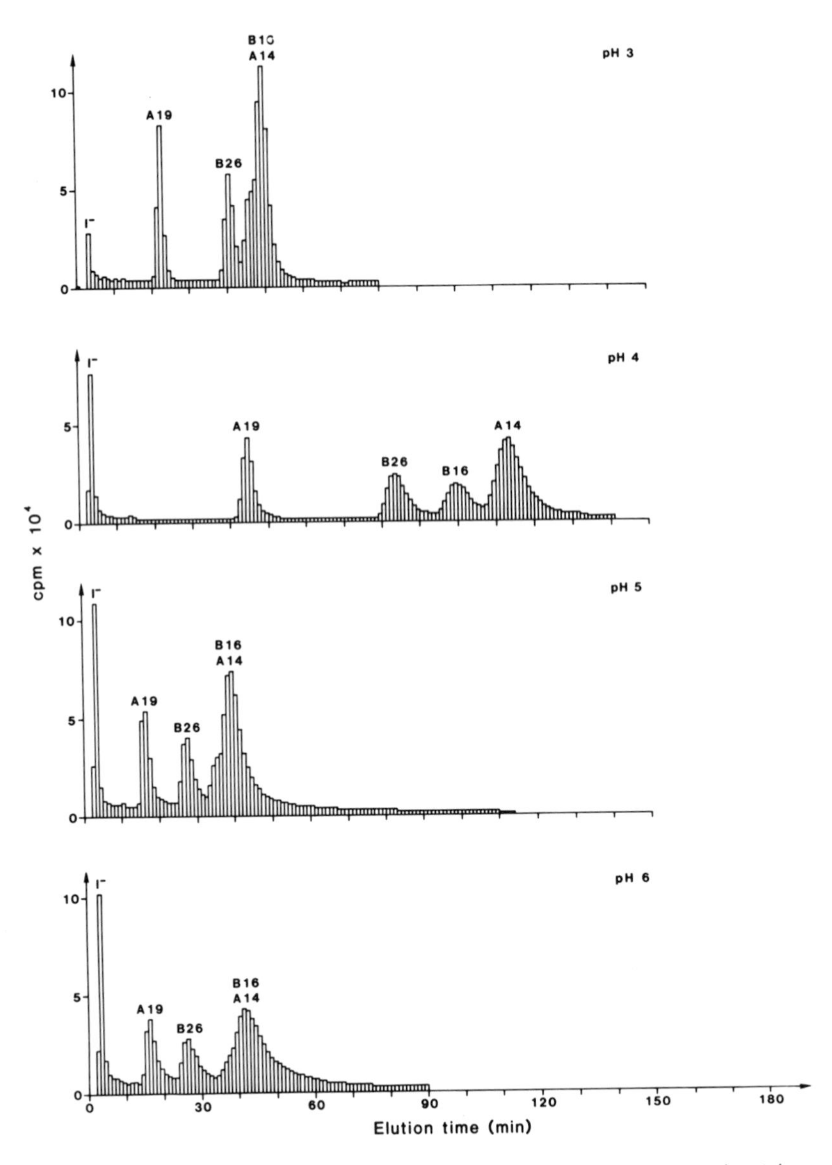

FIGURE 15–8. Isocratic elution of 50 μl of a diluted iodination mixture (containing 1–5 ng of the four ^{125}I-labeled monoiodoinsulins) using a LiChrosorb RP-18, 250 × 4.0 mm I.D. column eluted at 1.0 ml/min with 0.25 *M* TEAF/28% acetonitrile; pH was adjusted from 3 to 6 (top to bottom as indicated). The histograms represent the radioactivity in the collected fractions. (Reproduced with permission from ref. 129.)

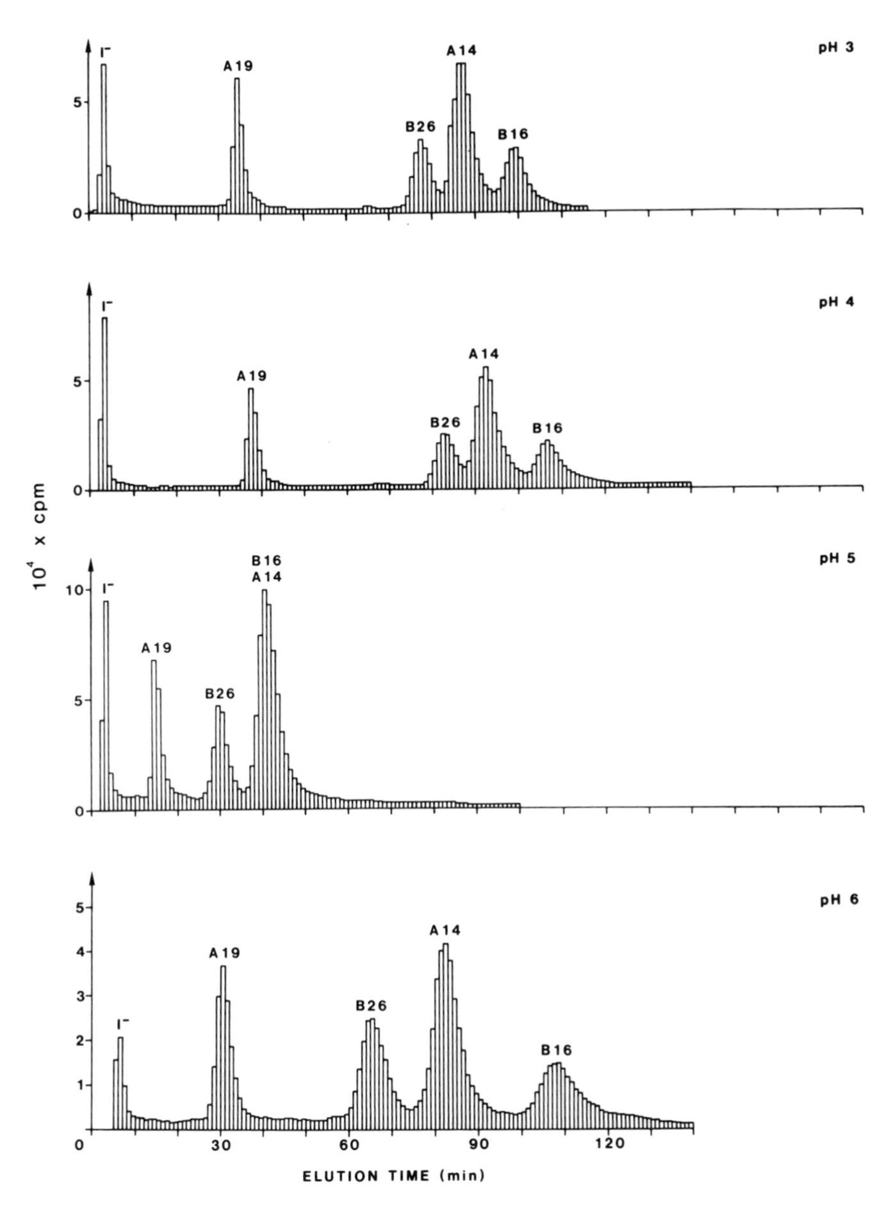

FIGURE 15–9. Sample and chromatographic conditions as in Figure 15–8, except that acetonitrile was replaced by 21.0% 2-propanol as organic modifier. (Reprinted with permission from ref. 129.)

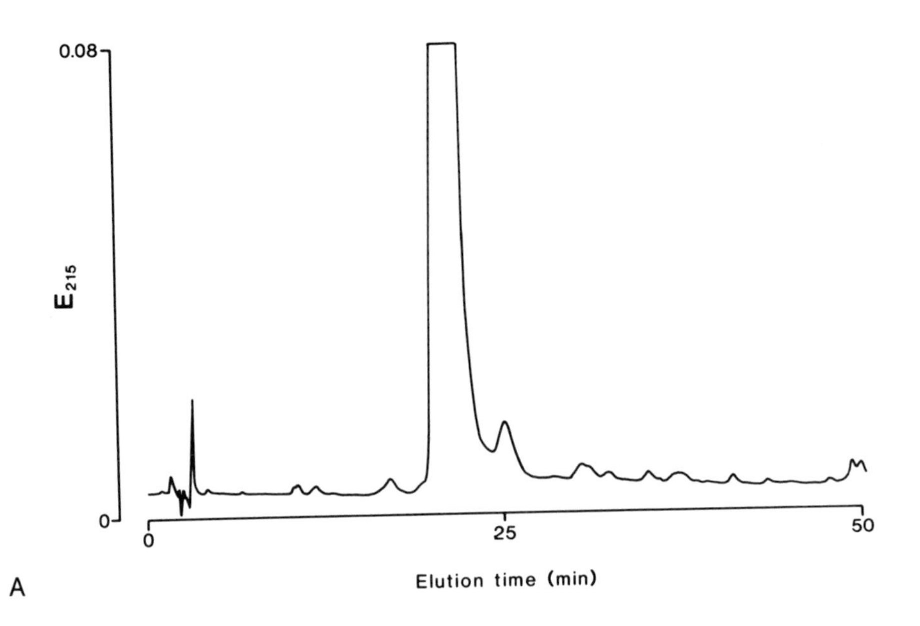

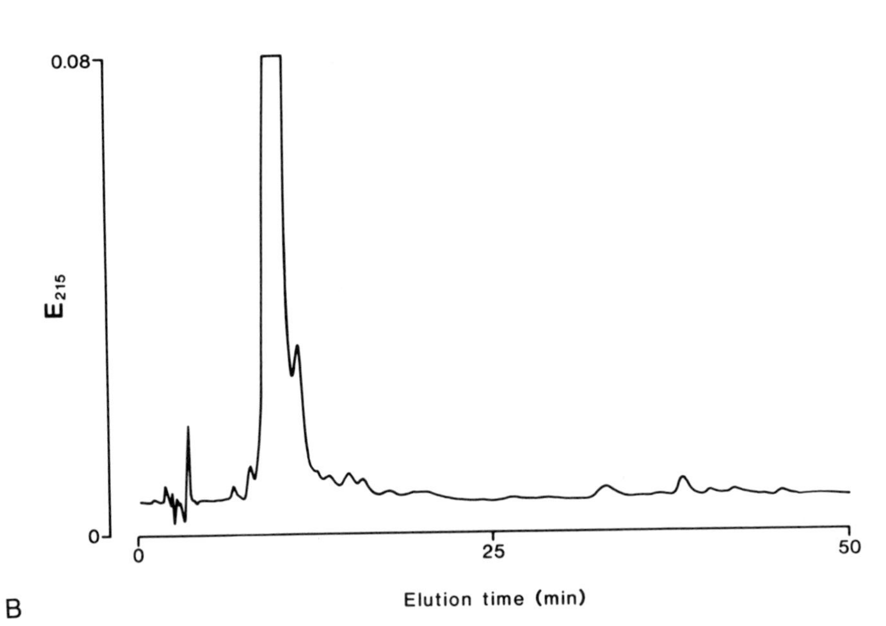

FIGURE 15–10. Isocratic elution of 75 μg crystalline porcine insulin using a LiChrosorb RP-18 column (250 × 4.0 mm I.D.) eluted at 1.0 ml/min with 0.125 *M* $(NH_4)_2SO_4$, pH 4.0, at 45°C (29.5% acetonitrile, A), at 22°C (29.5% acetonitrile, B), and

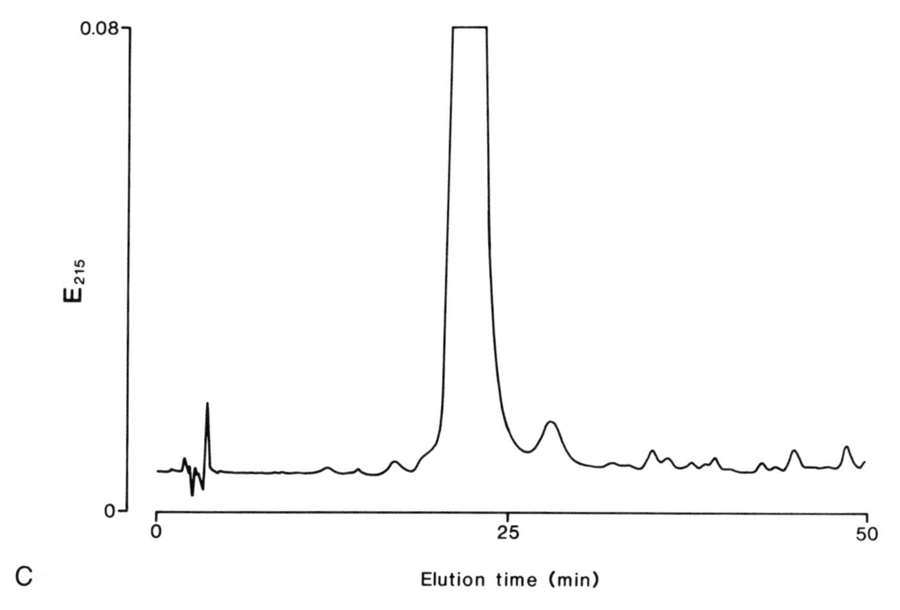

at 22°C (26% acetonitrile, C).

well as to distinguish between 22k hGH and methionyl-hGH (met-hGH), a possible product in the recombinant-derived production of hGH. The only difference between the two hGHs is an extension with a single methionine residue in the amino-terminal part of the hGH molecule.

Ammonium sulfate-based mobile phases were found to be the best choice for the Nucleosil C18-based separation of phGH (Figure 15–20, right panel), but only initial separation between met-hGH and biosynthetic hGH (bhGH) could be obtained under these acidic conditions, and the presence of perchlorate in the mobile phase was essential for any separation at all (Figure 15–11, upper panel). Much better separation could be obtained at pH 6.5 (ammonium phosphate/acetonitrile) although peak-broadening was noticed (Figure 15–11, middle panel), but if perchlorate was added to this mobile phase, the separation was lost completely (Figure 15–11, lower panel).

In the case of the resin-based TSK Phenyl 5 PW RP column, only neutral or slightly alkaline mobile phases resulted in separation of met-hGH and bhGH. Initial separation was obtained in ammonium bicarbonate/acetonitrile, and the separation was similar at pH 8.0 and 9.5 (Figure 15–12). In ammonium phosphate perchlorate, pH 7.0, very good resolution was obtained at 22°C as well as at 45°C (Figure 15–13, A and B). Baseline separation was obtained in this system when the separation temperature was increased from 20 to 45°C, and the slope of the acetonitrile gradient was decreased (Figure 15–13, C).

In the resin-based as well as the silica-based stationary phase, choice of organic modifier was essential, since the above-mentioned separations could be performed only in acetonitrile. A fairly good separation of the components

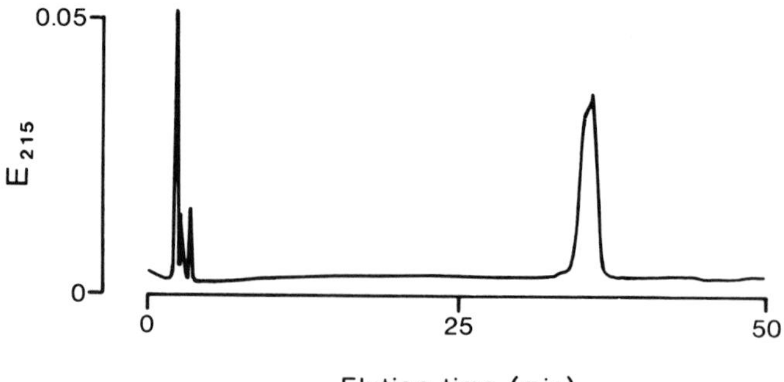

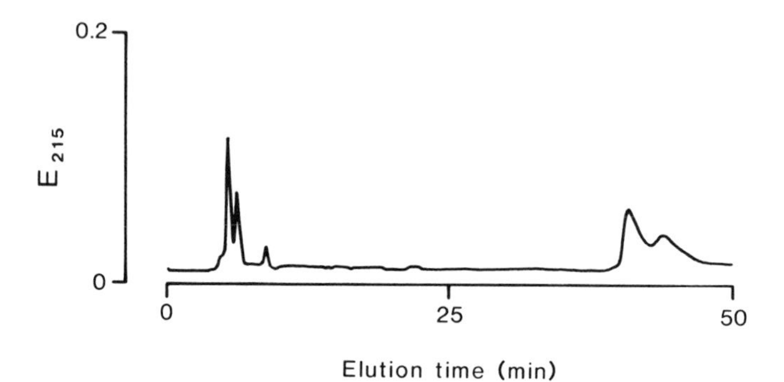

0.05
E_{215}
0
0
30
60
Elution time (min)

FIGURE 15–11. RP-HPLC analyses of 5 μg of a mixture of met-hGH and biosynthetic 22k hGH using a Nucleosil C18 (250 × 4.0 mm I.D.) eluted at 1.0 ml with an acetonitrile gradient (47–50% during 60 min) in 0.225 *M* $(NH_4)_2SO_4$/0.09 *M* NaH_2PO_4, pH adjusted to 2.5 with $HClO_4$ (upper panel), 0.2 *M* $(NH_4)_2HPO_4$, pH adjusted to 6.5 with H_3PO_4 (middle panel), or 0.2 *M* $(NH_4)_2HPO_4$/0.06 *M* $NaClO_4$, pH adjusted to 6.5 with H_3PO_4 (lower panel). Separation temperature: 45°C throughout. (Reproduced with permission from ref. 148.)

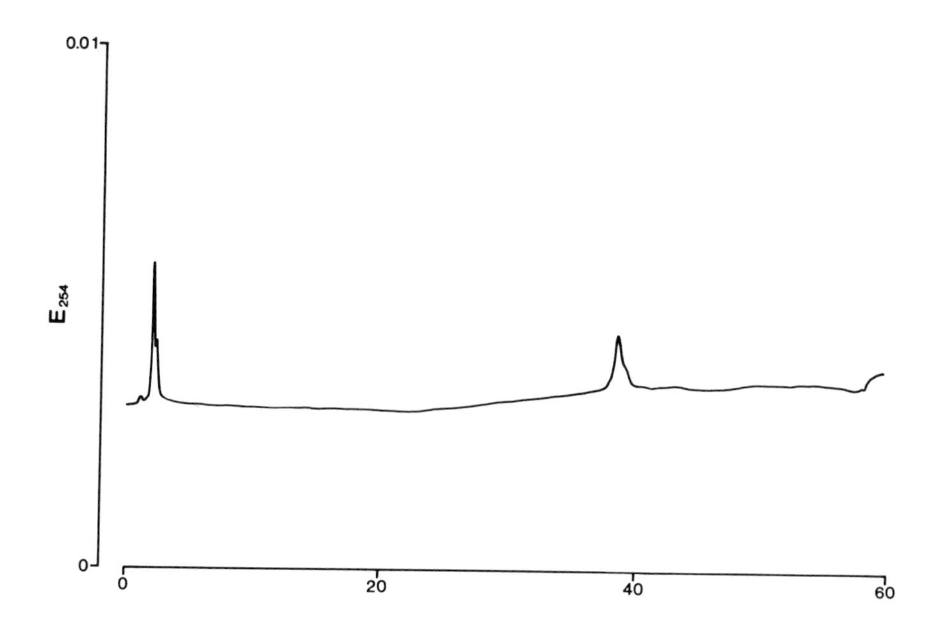

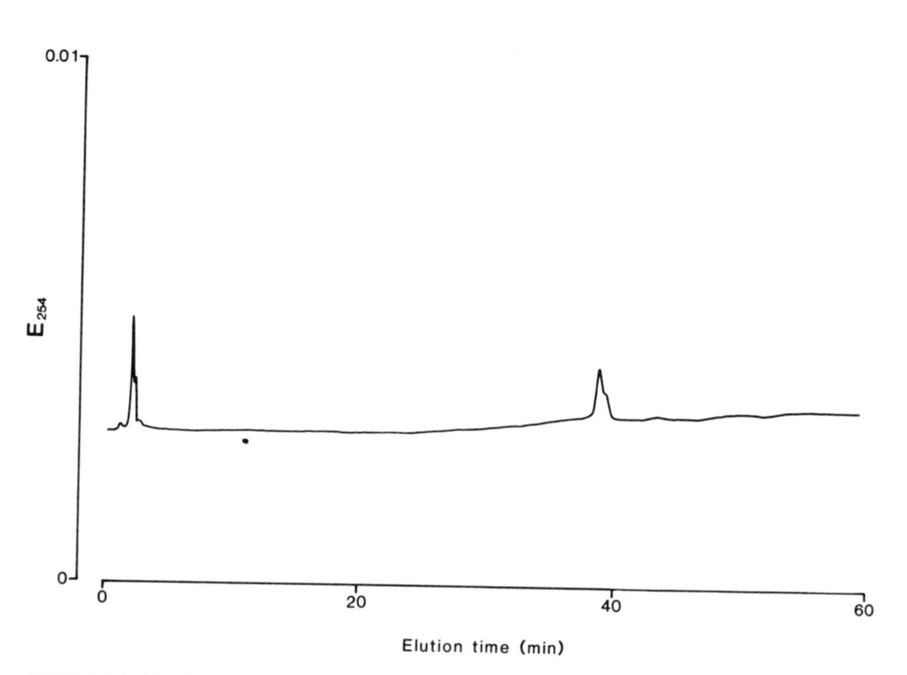

FIGURE 15–12. RP-HPLC analyses of 5 μg of a mixture of met-hGH and biosynthetic 22k hGH using a TSK Phenyl 5 PW RP (75 × 4.6 mm I.D.) eluted with an acetonitrile gradient (24–64% during 60 min) in 0.2 *M* NH_4HCO_3, pH 9.5 (upper panel) or 8.0 (lower panel). Flow rate 0.5 ml/min.

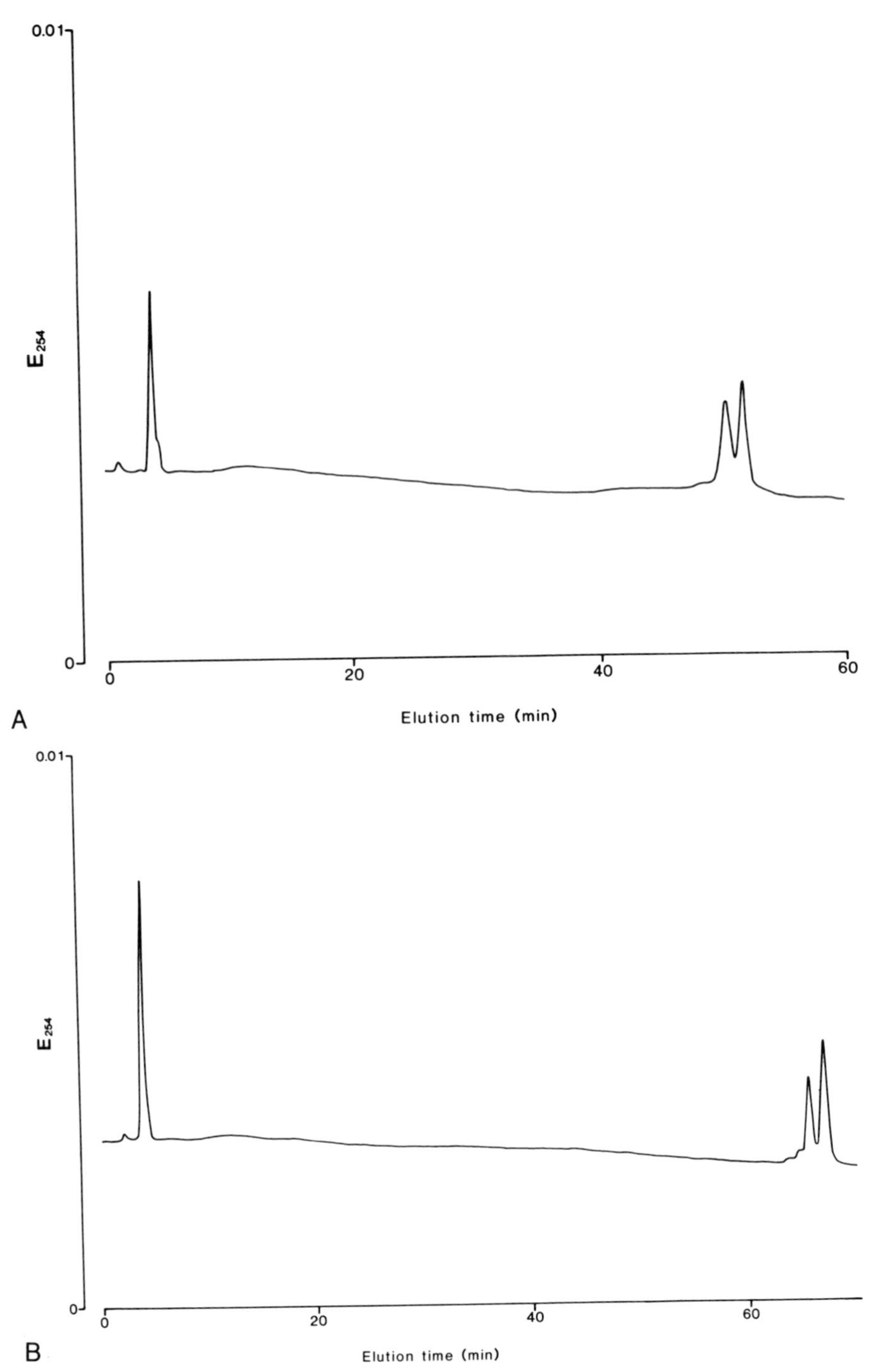

FIGURE 15–13. RP-HPLC analyses of 10 μg of a mixture of met-hGH and biosynthetic 22k hGH using a TSK Phenyl 5 PW RP (75 × 4.6 mm I.D.) eluted with an acetonitrile gradient (20–40% acetonitrile during 60 min) in 0.2 *M* $(NH_4)_2HPO_4$/0.1 *M* $NaClO_4$, pH 7.0, at 22°C (A) or 45°C (B).

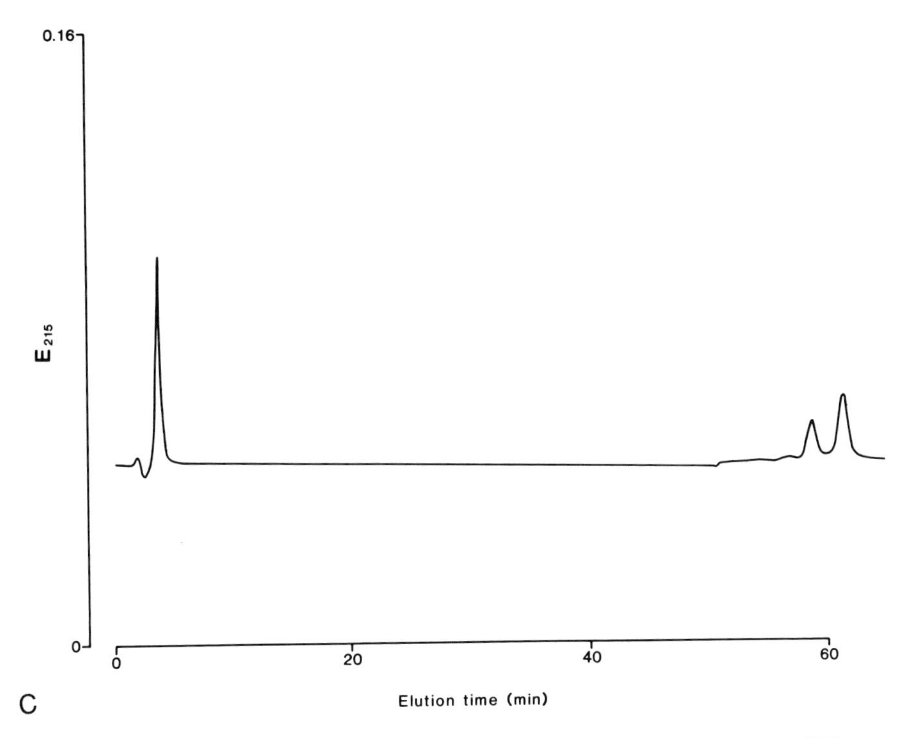

In C, the acetonitrile gradient was 32–40% during 60 min, separation temperature 45°C. Flow rate 0.3 ml/min throughout.

in phGH was obtained using TSK Phenyl 5 PW RP eluted with TEAP pH 5.0/acetonitrile, but if 2-propanol was used as modifier, the detailed separation of the minor components in phGH was lost, and the principal component (22k hGH) was eluted as a very broad peak (Figure 15–14). The separation pattern obtained in acetonitrile was found to be virtually identical at 22 and 45°C (Figure 15–14).

15.3.2 Stationary Phase Effects

The parameters available for variation in RP-HPLC of polypeptides and proteins may often not include the mobile phase, if specific demands are to be kept. Such demands may be that the mobile phase is UV-translucent, can be lyophilized, contains no additives harmful for a successive gas-phase sequencing, is nontoxic, can be reconciled with an eventual biological activity—or does not interfere with a specific assay for the sample components (i.e., RIA assay) or a general postcolumn reaction (i.e., fluorescence measurements). If the separation obtained with a specific mobile phase is inadequate, the separation may be optimized by variation in choice of stationary phase. The number of commercially available RP columns is enormous, and for economical reasons it is

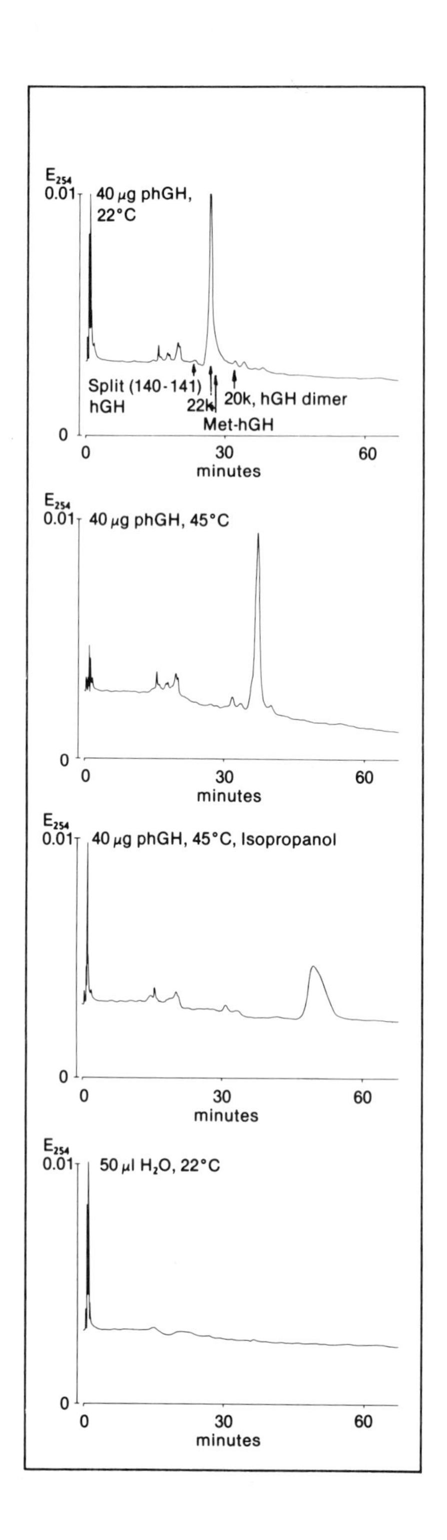

FIGURE 15–14. RP-HPLC analyses of phGH. Stationary phase as in Figures 15–12 and 15–13. Mobile phase: 0.25 *M* TEAP, pH 5.0 (H_3PO_4), 9–90% acetonitrile during 60 min, 1.0 ml/min. Other variations in mobile phase as indicated in the panels.

advisable to pack RP-HPLC columns in the laboratory—at least until some experience in the behavior of the most common stationary phases is obtained.

We present some examples of variation of chromatographic behavior of insulin and insulin-related substances as well as human growth hormone. In the case of insulin, the choice of stationary phase is limited to 80–120 Å silica-based C18 columns, since such columns have been found to be very useful for these separations.[1] Resin-based phenyl columns and silica-based C18 columns will be discussed for hGH analyses, and the problems with column-to-column variations for insulin as well as hGH analyses will be presented.

15.3.2.1 Insulin

As mentioned above, the separation of rat proinsulin I and II could be obtained if a LiChrosorb RP-18 column was eluted with TFA/acetonitrile, whereas TEAP/acetonitrile as mobile phase resulted in coelution of the two proinsulins (see Figure 15–3). However, separation of rat proinsulin I and II can also be obtained in TEAP/acetonitrile if the LiChrosorb column is replaced with an Ultrasphere ODS column (Figure 15–15). This difference in selectivity of the proinsulins is worth mentioning, since the separation pattern of rat insulin I and II, rat C-peptide I and II, glucagon, and rat pancreatic polypeptide was found to be very similar for the LiChrosorb and the Ultrasphere columns eluted with TEAP/acetonitrile (Figure 15–16).

The separation of insulin and the four monoiodinated insulin derivatives could be performed using three different narrow-pore silica C18 columns (LiChrosorb, Spherisorb, and TSK ODS, see Figure 15–17). This separation has been optimized with respect to mobile phase (pH, alkylammonium buffer, and organic modifier) using a LiChrosorb RP-18 column, and could not be

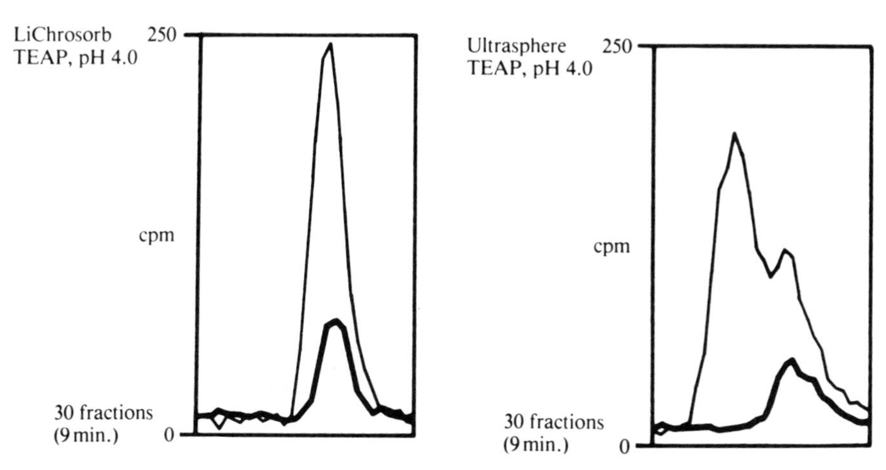

FIGURE 15–15. RP-HPLC separation of labeled rat proinsulin I and II from cultured rat islets using a LiChrosorb RP-18 (250 × 4.0 mm I.D.) or an Ultrasphere ODS (250 × 4.6 mm I.D.) eluted at 1.0 ml/min with a linear acetonitrile gradient (25–30% during 30 min) in 0.125 *M* TEAP, pH 4.0. The curves represent the later part of the chromatogram (from 35 min). Refer to Figure 15–3 for further details.

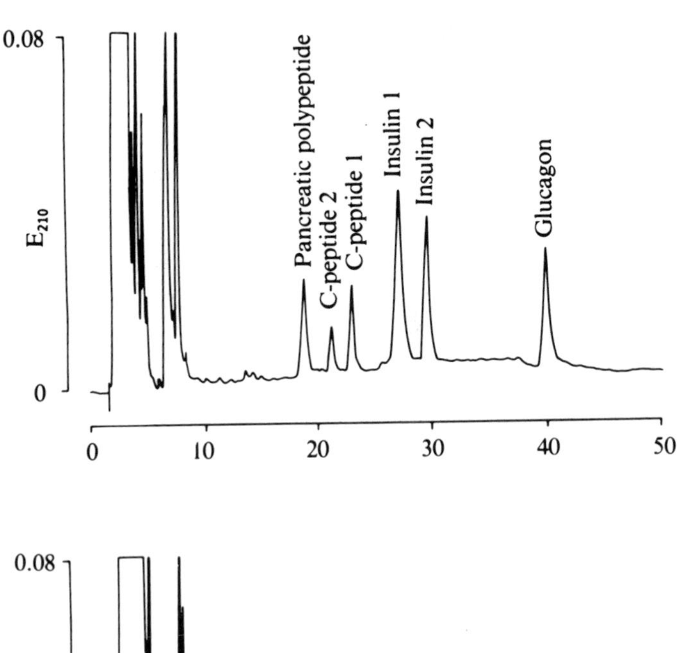

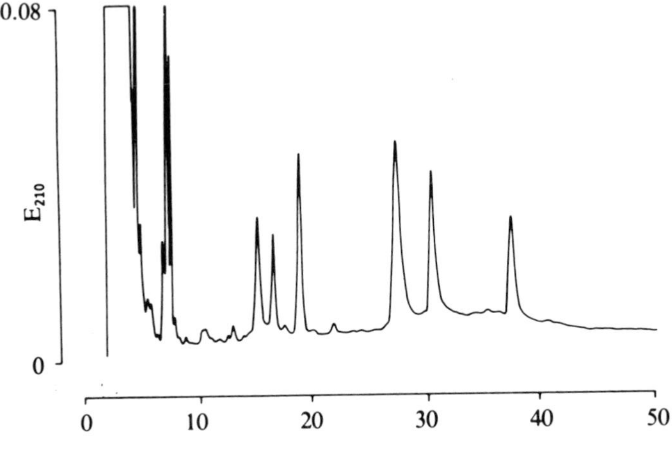

Elution time (minutes)

FIGURE 15–16. RP-HPLC of rat islet culture medium containing rat insulin I and II, C-peptide I and II, plus added glucagon and rat pancreatic polypeptide using a LiChrosorb RP-18 column upper panel and an Ultrasphere ODS column lower panel. Mobile phase conditions as in Figure 15–15.

performed with a number of similar stationary phases (Vydac C18, Techogel C18 and C4).[1] Although the separation pattern using the three narrow-pore size columns looks identical, it should be emphasized, that the elution order of A14 and B16 monoiodoinsulins is reversed when the LiChrosorb and Spherisorb columns (Figure 15–17, upper and middle panels) are compared to the TSK ODS column (Figure 15–17, lower panel).

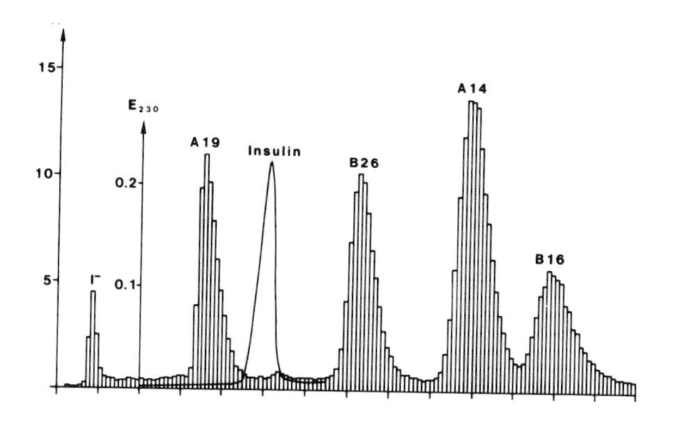

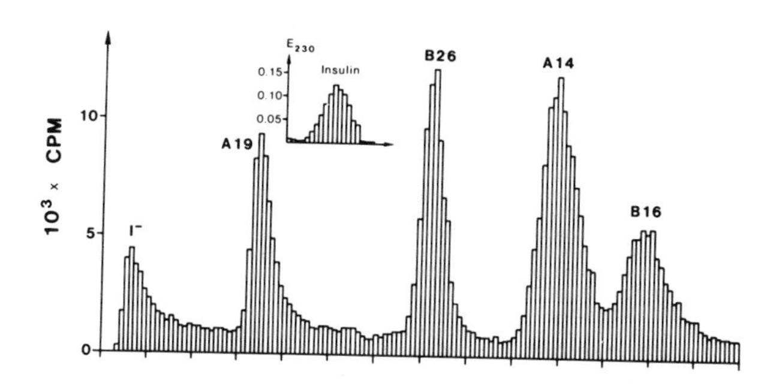

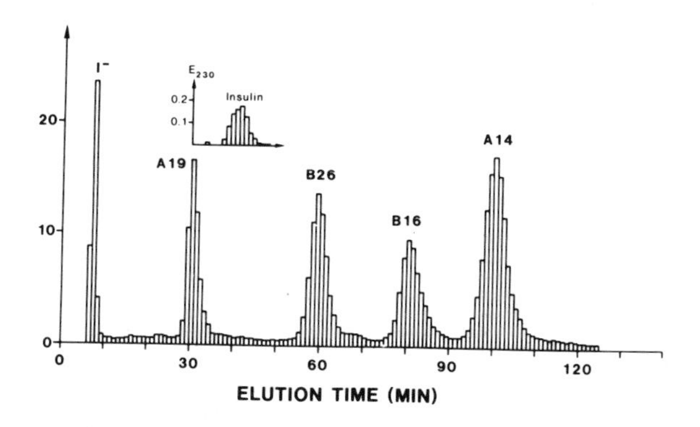

FIGURE 15–17. Isocratic separation of 50 μl diluted iodination mixture (containing 1–5 ng of the four ^{125}I-labeled monoiodoinsulins) using a 250 × 4.0 mm I.D. LiChrosorb RP-18 column (upper panel), a 150 × 4.0 mm I.D. Spherisorb ODS-2 column (middle panel), or a 250 × 4.6 mm I.D. TSK ODS 120T column (lower panel) eluted with 0.25 *M* TEAF, pH 6.0. 2-Propanol concentrations in the mobile phases were 21.5% (top), 21.5% (middle), and 20.5% (bottom). Flow rate 0.5 ml/min. (Reproduced with permission from ref. 1.)

The fact that a single reversed-phase column is useful for a polypeptide separation in no way guarantees that the next column will behave in an identical manner. Three randomly selected LiChrosorb RP-18 columns were analyzed with respect to the above-mentioned separation of the four monoiodoinsulins. One column behaved well, and two columns were not able to separate the monoiodoinsulins due to lack of selectivity, a reduced number of theoretical plates, as well as a too high asymmetrical factor (see Figure 15–18).

The same lack of identity in the separation pattern can be seen in the separation of rat insulin I and II, rat C-peptide I and II, and glucagon. Using three different LiChrosorb RP-18 columns eluted with TFA/acetonitrile, glucagon could be eluted after (Figure 15–19, upper panel) or before (Figure 15–19, lower panel) insulin II—or the two compounds could coelute (Figure 15–19, middle panel).

15.3.2.2 Human Growth Hormone

Since the number of published RP-HPLC analyses of hGH is limited, it is difficult to compare several types of columns. hGH is strongly bound to silica-based C18 columns, and the majority of published analyses utilizes wide-pore (i.e., pore size 300 Å or larger) silica-based C4 and C18 columns. We have investigated the recovery of biosynthetic human growth hormone from several Nucleosil C18 columns with pore size 120, 300, 500, and 1000 Å and surprisingly the 300 Å column had the highest recovery (90%). In contrast to this finding, the polymer-based PLRP-S columns were found to have similar recovery for the 100 and the 300 Å column (37%).[148]

Being a rather hydrophobic protein, RP separations of hGH require a carefully selected stationary phase if separation capacity similar to that obtained for insulin and insulin-related substances is needed. Optimized separations of phGH using a silica-based and a resin-based stationary phase are very similar: A main peak (22k hGH, 70–80%) is separated from 10–12 additional components (Figure 15–20), but if the optimized mobile phases are interchanged, the elution pattern is drastically changed, and the separation seriously deteriorated.[149] In contrast to RP-based insulin analyses, hGH analyses are strictly dependent on developmental work using a single RP column: If the Nucleosil C18 column is replaced with a LiChrosorb RP-18 column, no hGH material can be eluted from the column.[150] If the TSK Phenyl 5 PW RP column is exchanged with a resin-based PLRP-S column, the resulting separation of phGH is considerably deteriorated (Figure 15–21).

Being one of the first recombinant DNA-produced proteins, structural analyses of biosynthetic hGH are very important, and tryptic mapping has been applied intensively. Separation of the tryptic peptides are almost exclusively performed using silica-C18 columns eluted with TFA/acetonitrile, and the problems considering batch-to-batch variations in reversed-phase columns are as serious in this separation as mentioned for insulin separations. A satisfactory separation of hGH-derived tryptic peptides is shown in Figure 15–22, upper panel, but only approximately 5 of 100 columns will behave in this manner. The lower panel shows the same separation with a column of a different stationary phase batch, and although the columns will separate in an identical manner in the first half of the chromatogram, the last part of the chromatogram is very different and less detailed than that in the upper panel.

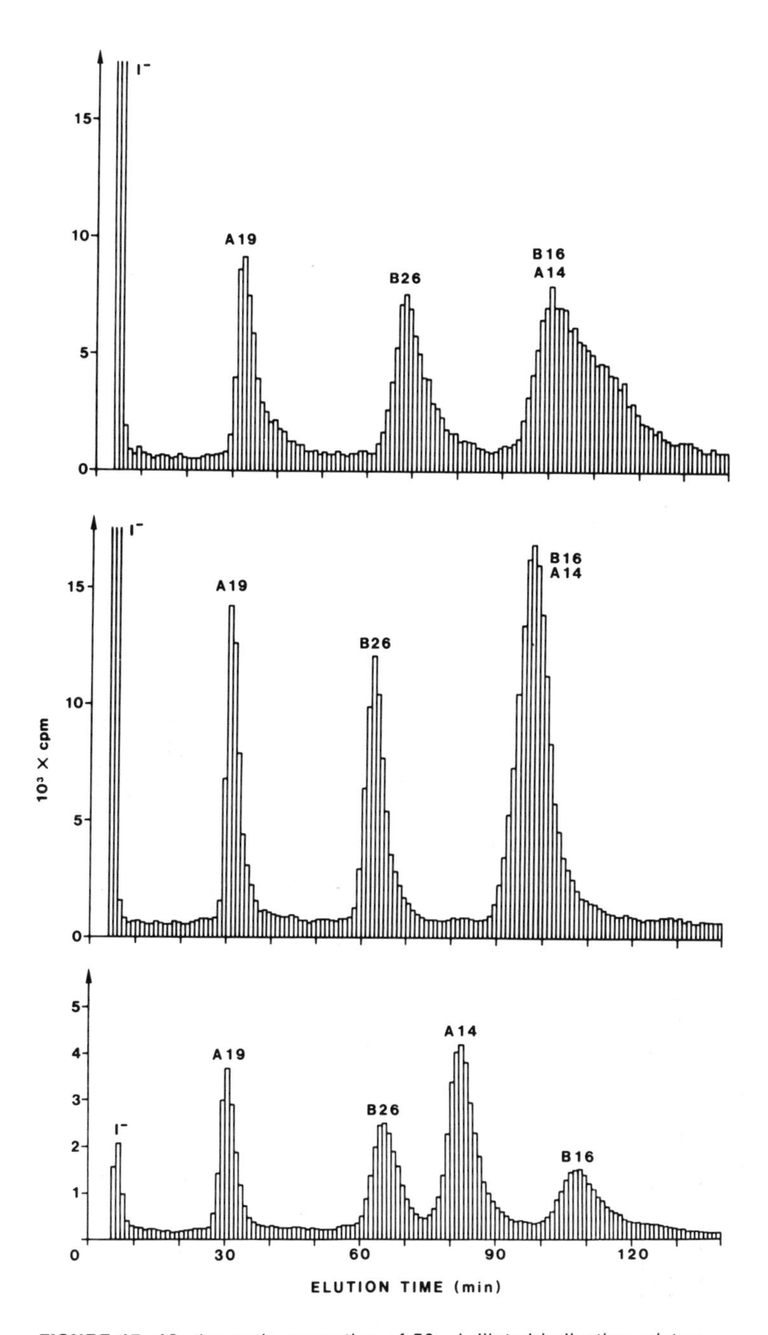

FIGURE 15–18. Isocratic separation of 50 μl diluted iodination mixture using three different LiChrosorb RP-18 columns (250 × 4.0 mm I.D.) eluted with 0.25 *M* TEAF, pH 6.0, containing (from top to bottom) 22.0, 21.0, and 21.0% 2-propanol. Flow rate 0.5 ml/min. (Reproduced with permission from ref. 1.)

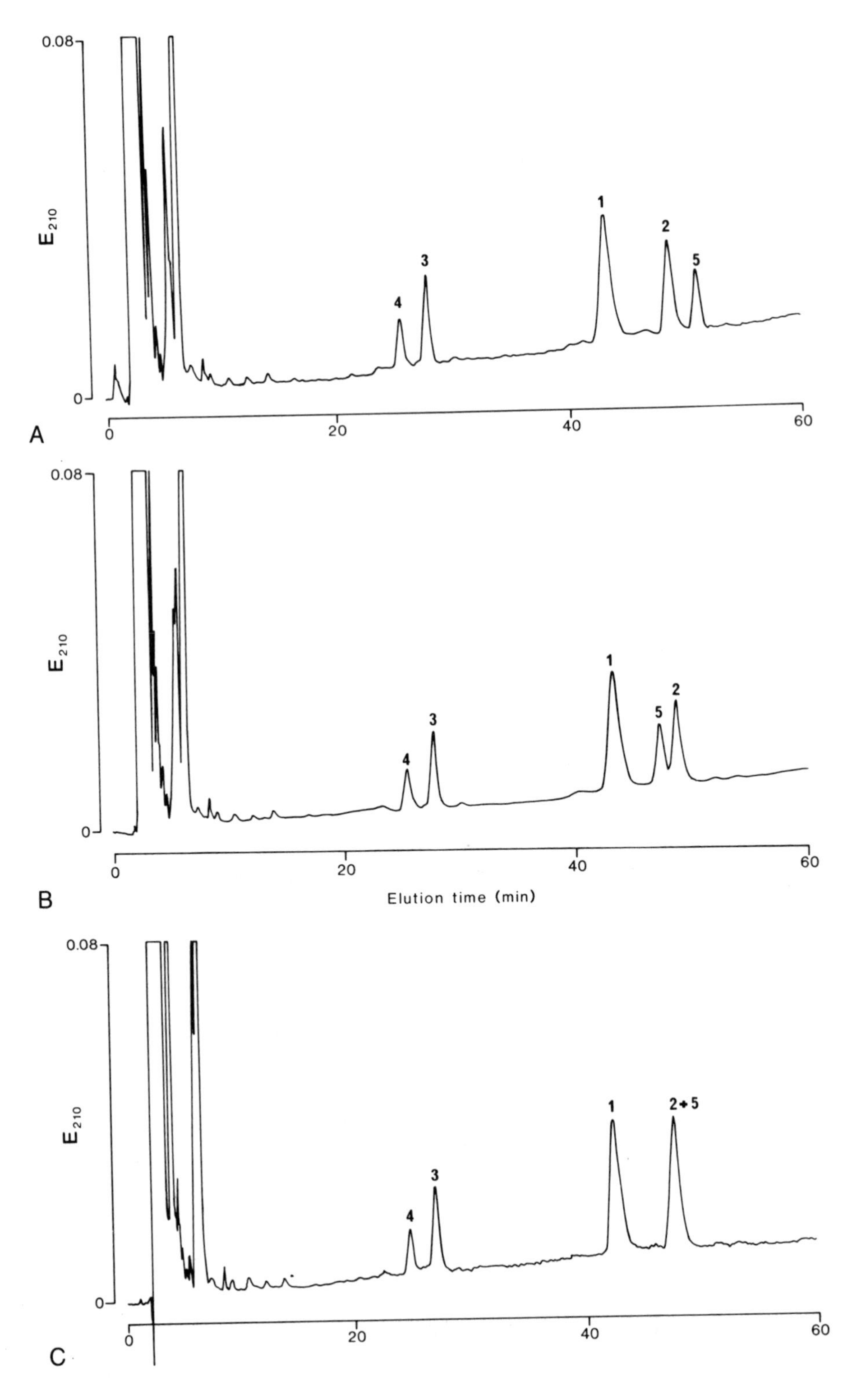
0.08
E210
0
4
3
1
2
5
0
20
40
60
A
0.08
E210
0
4
3
1
5
2
0
20
40
60
B
Elution time (min)
0.08
E210
0
4
3
1
2+5
0
20
40
60
C

15.4 HYDROPHOBIC-INTERACTION CHROMATOGRAPHY

With increasing molecular weight and/or hydrophobicity, reversed-phase columns become less usable for the separation of proteins. Combined with a constant demand for high-performance separations that can be performed under "physiological conditions," an increasing number of HIC columns, resin-based as well as silica-based, have become commercially available and we have investigated a number of such columns for the separation of insulin, hGH, ovalbumin, serum albumin, and β-lactoglobulin as well as the potential use of HIC columns eluted with detergent containing mobile phases for the separation of membrane proteins.

15.4.1 "Standard Proteins"

The HIC columns were eluted with a decreasing ammonium sulfate gradient in dilute phosphate buffer at neutral pH, as well as with a number of additives reported to be compatible with the stationary phase: glycerol, PEG, urea, and 2-propanol, and the schematic outlines of the results are given in Table 15–2. The best separation patterns of the five polypeptides are shown in Figure 15–23. In the case of insulin and growth hormone, they can be eluted from HIC columns in well-defined, sharp peaks, but none of the columns tested were able to separate either closely related insulins (i.e., insulin peptide and desamidoinsulin or human/porcine/bovine insulin) or hGH/met-hGH or hGH/desamido-hGH. Ovalbumin and serum albumin could be resolved in several components, whereas β-lactoglobulin was eluted as a broad peak without any sign of separation.

Addition of glycerol resulted in an unacceptable high back pressure, and addition of 7 *M* urea produced a highly distorted baseline. PEG and 2-propanol could be added without difficulties and low-UV detection could be sustained.

It should be emphasized that if low-UV detection is desirable in HIC, the initial 2 *M* ammonium sulfate must be based on a chemical of highest purity. Analytical grade ammonium sulfate may be used, but we have noticed serious baseline drift using this chemical purity, and batch-to-batch variation in the content of compounds with low-UV absorbance in analytical grade ammonium sulfate is not uncommon. Alternatively the ammonium sulfate solution may be purified on active carbon before use.

15.4.2 Membrane Proteins

Due to their high hydrophobicity, membrane proteins are difficult to purify and characterize in aqueous solution. Detergents are often a necessary additive

FIGURE 15–19. RP-HPLC separation of rat islet culture medium containing insulin I(1) and II(2), C-peptide I(3) and II(4), plus added glucagon(5) using three different LiChrosorb RP-18 columns (A, B, and C, 250 × 4.0 mm I.D.) eluted at 1 ml/min with TFA/acetonitrile as described in Figure 15–2.

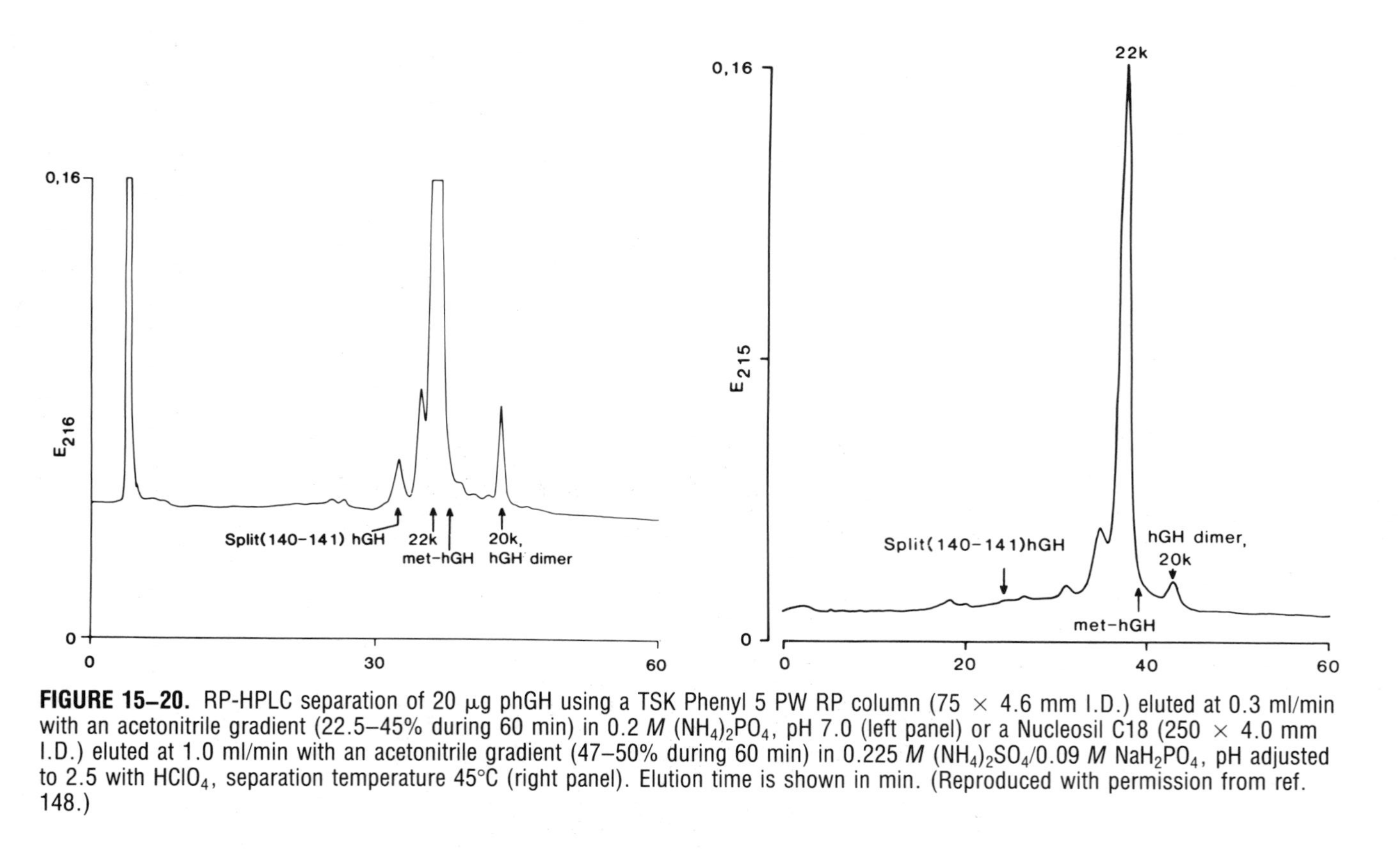

FIGURE 15–20. RP-HPLC separation of 20 μg phGH using a TSK Phenyl 5 PW RP column (75 × 4.6 mm I.D.) eluted at 0.3 ml/min with an acetonitrile gradient (22.5–45% during 60 min) in 0.2 *M* $(NH_4)_2PO_4$, pH 7.0 (left panel) or a Nucleosil C18 (250 × 4.0 mm I.D.) eluted at 1.0 ml/min with an acetonitrile gradient (47–50% during 60 min) in 0.225 *M* $(NH_4)_2SO_4$/0.09 *M* NaH_2PO_4, pH adjusted to 2.5 with $HClO_4$, separation temperature 45°C (right panel). Elution time is shown in min. (Reproduced with permission from ref. 148.)

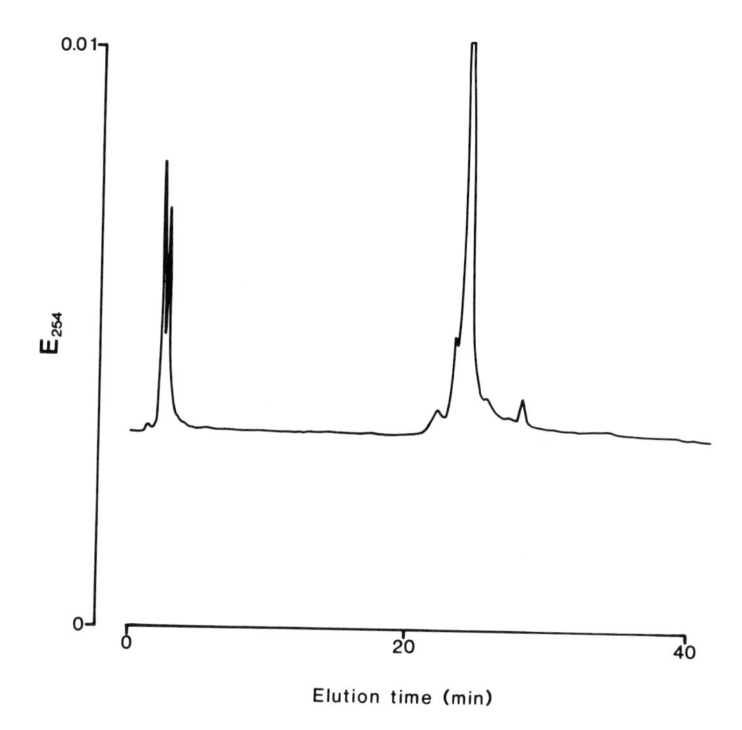

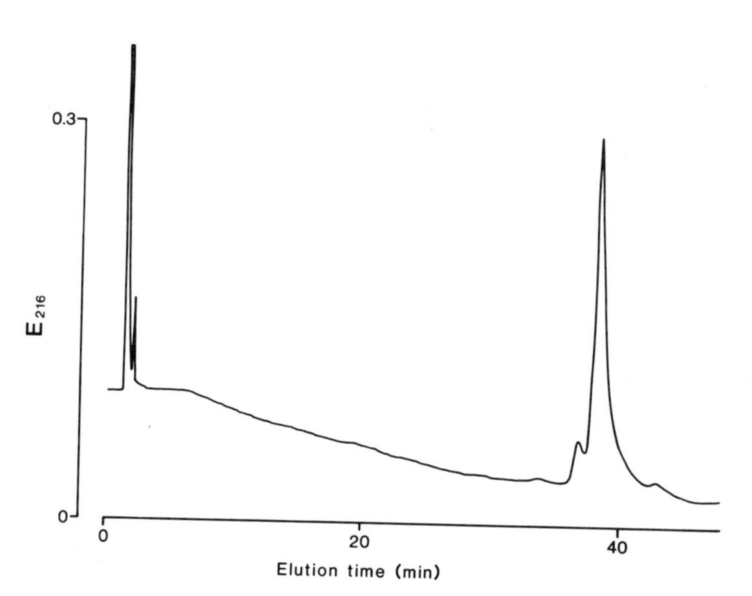

FIGURE 15–21. RP-HPLC separation of 20 μg phGH using a TSK Phenyl 5 PW RP column (75 × 4.6 mm I.D.) eluted with an acetonitrile gradient (21–42% during 30 min) in 0.2 *M* NH_4HCO_3, pH 8.0. Flow rate 0.5 ml/min (upper panel). Lower panel: RP-HPLC separation of 32 μg phGH using a 150 × 4.0 mm I.D. PLRP-S column eluted with an acetonitrile gradient (20–48% during 45 min) in 0.2 *M* $(NH_4)_2HCO_3$, pH 8.0. Flow rate: 1.0 ml/min.

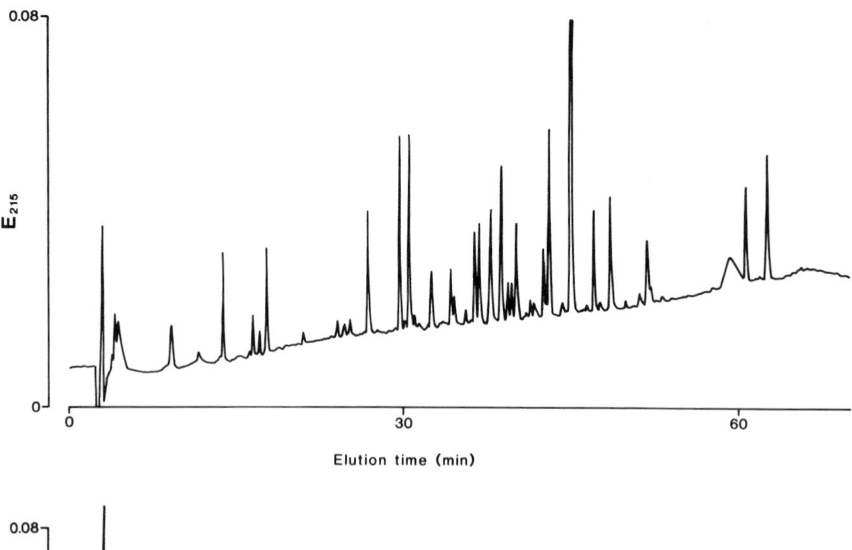

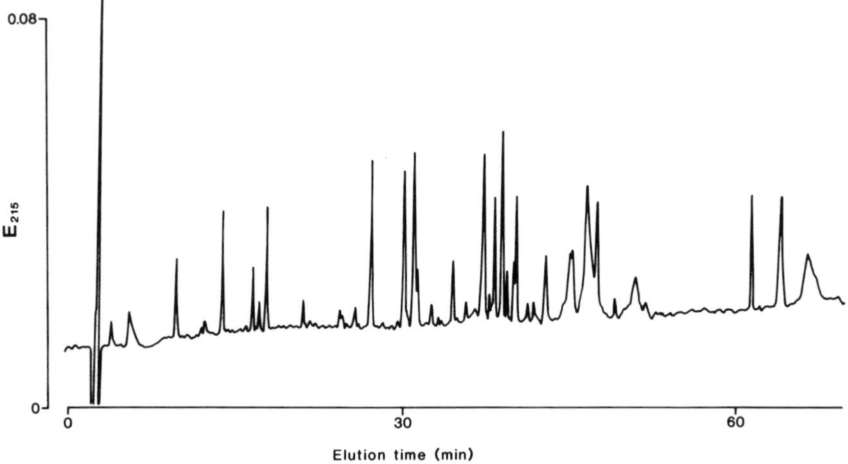

FIGURE 15–22. RP-HPLC of 50 μg tryptic digestion mixture of bhGH using two different LiChrosorb RP-18 columns (250 × 4.0 mm I.D.) eluted with an acetonitrile gradient (0–50% during 60 min) in 0.1% TFA. Flow rate 1.0 ml/min, separation temperature 45°C.

to the mobile phase, but this demand excludes the use of conventional RP columns. Size-exclusion chromatography in detergent-containing mobile phases as well as high-performance ion-exchange chromatography with nonionic detergents present in the buffers have been performed with some success.

We have evaluated three HIC columns as well as a hydroxylapatite column for their potential use in high-performance separation of membrane proteins. Erythrocyte ghost membrane proteins were chosen as "model membrane protein" and CHAPS, β-octylglucoside, or sulfobetaine was added in concentrations below the critical micelle concentration. The elution patterns of these membrane proteins obtained on such HIC columns are shown in Figure 15–24.

TABLE 15–2. Separation of Insulin, hGH, Ovalbumin, β-Lactoglobulin, and Human Serum Albumin[a,b]

	TSK Phenyl	TSK Ether	Propyl Aspart.	LC Hint	Beckman	Nucleosil-OH	Hydroxylapatite
Basic system							
Insulin	ne	1 (1) 2.0 (2) 1 (3)	ne	a 6.0 1	a 7.8 1	ne	a 6.0 1
hGH	a 2.6 1	a 2.4 1	i 1.6 1	a 6.4 1	a 4.6 1	ne	i 2.6 1
β-Lactoglobulin	nd	m 2.4 1	m 2.8 1	a 13.8 1	nr	a 5.6 1	m 11.4 1
HSA	m 10.0 1	a 1.2 2	m 7.0 1	a 14.2 1	a 4.6 2	a 4.4 2	a 5.6 2
Ovalbumin	a 3.7 1	a 3.5 1	m 4.0 1	a 6.0 1	a 3.6 2	a 3.8 4	i 2.8 2
Glycerol							
Insulin	ne	ne	m 5.0 1	m 11.4 1	nd	nd	nd
hGH	a 3.0 1	i 1.8 1	m 4.4 1	m 6.8 1	nd	nd	nd

(continued)

TABLE 15–2. Separation of Insulin, hGH, Ovalbumin, β-Lactoglobulin, and Human Serum Albumin[a,b] (*continued*)

	TSK Phenyl	TSK Ether	Propyl Aspart.	LC Hint	Beckman	Nucleosil-OH	Hydroxylapatite
β-Lactoglobulin	nd	nd	m 10.0 1	ne	nd	nd	nd
HSA	m 8.6 1	m 7.0 1	a 4.0 1	ne	nd	nd	nd
Ovalbumin	a 4.0 1	i 1.6 2	a 5.0 1	nr	nd	nd	nd
				Isopropanol			
Insulin	i 3.2 1	a 2.0 1	i 1.8 3	i 3.0 1	a 6.4 1	a 5.0 1	nd
hGH	i 3.0 1	i 1.6 1	i 1.8 1	i 4.6 1	m 5.6 1	a 4.6 2	nd
β-Lactoglobulin	nd	m 2.4 1	nd	m 8.6 1	nr	a 9.2 1	nd
HSA	a 4.0 1	a 2.0 1	a 3.0 2	a 4.6 1	a 4.6 2	a 3.2 1	nd

Ovalbumin	m 4.5 1	i 2.0 1	i 2.2 2	i 3.0 2	nd 3	a 3.6 3	nd
				Urea			
Insulin	i 1.3 1	nd	i 1.2 1	i 3.2 1	m 4.6 1	nd	nd
hGH	i 1.6 1	nd	i 1.0 1	i 2.2 2	i 2.2 1	nd	nd
β-Lactoglobulin	nd	nd	nd	m 8.2 1	nr	nd	nd
HSA	ne	nd	ne	m 4.6 1	a 3.0 2	nd	nd
Ovalbumin	a 2.4 1	nd	i 1.0 2	i 2.2 1	a 3.4 2	nd	nd
				PEG			
Insulin	ne	a 3.0 1	a 4.0 1	nd	nd	nd	nd
hGH	m 3.0 1	i 1.3 2	i 2.4 1	nd	nd	nd	nd

(*continued*)

TABLE 15–2. Separation of Insulin, hGH, Ovalbumin, β-Lactoglobulin, and Human Serum Albumin[a,b] *(continued)*

	TSK Phenyl	TSK Ether	Propyl Aspart.	LC Hint	Beckman	Nucleosil-OH	Hydroxylapatite
β-Lactoglobulin	nd	m 4.4 1	nd	nd	nd	nd	nd
HSA	m 7.8 2	a 1.2 2	m 6.2 2	nd	nd	nd	nd
Ovalbumin	a 4.0 3	i 4.5 1	i 1.3 4	nd	nd	nd	nd

[a] Using TSK Phenyl 5 PW (75 × 7.5 mm I.D.), TSK Ether 5 PW (75 × 7.5 mm I.D.), propyl aspartamide (200 × 4.6 mm I.D.), Supelco LC Hint (100 × 4.6 mm I.D.), Beckmann Spherogel CAA-HIC (100 × 4.6 mm I.D.), Nucleosil-OH (250 × 4.0 mm I.D.), or Pentax PEC 102 hydroxylapatite (100 × 7.5 mm I.D.). The HIC columns were eluted with a basic mobile phase [2 *M* $(NH_4)_2SO_4$ → 0 *M* $(NH_4)_2SO_4$ in 0.1 *M* Na_2HPO_4, pH 6.5, during 45 min, 0.5 ml/min). Additives: glycerol (20% in the A and B buffers), 2-propanol (20% in the B buffer), urea (7 *M* in the B buffer) or PEG-6000 (0.1% in the B buffer). The hydroxylapatite column was eluted with a phosphate gradient (0.01 *M* Na_2HPO_4/0.3 m*M* $CaCl_2$, pH 6.8 → 0.4 *M* Na_2HPO_4/0.0075 m*M* $CaCl_2$, pH 6.8, during 45 min; flow rate 0.5 ml/min).

[b] The separation has been characterized with respect to (1) Tailing factor: i = ideal (1–1.3), a = acceptable (1.3–2.0), or m = miserable (>2.0). (2) Peak width measured at 13.5% peak height (min). (3) Number of major components. ne, not eluted under these conditions; nd, not determined under these conditions; nr, not retained.

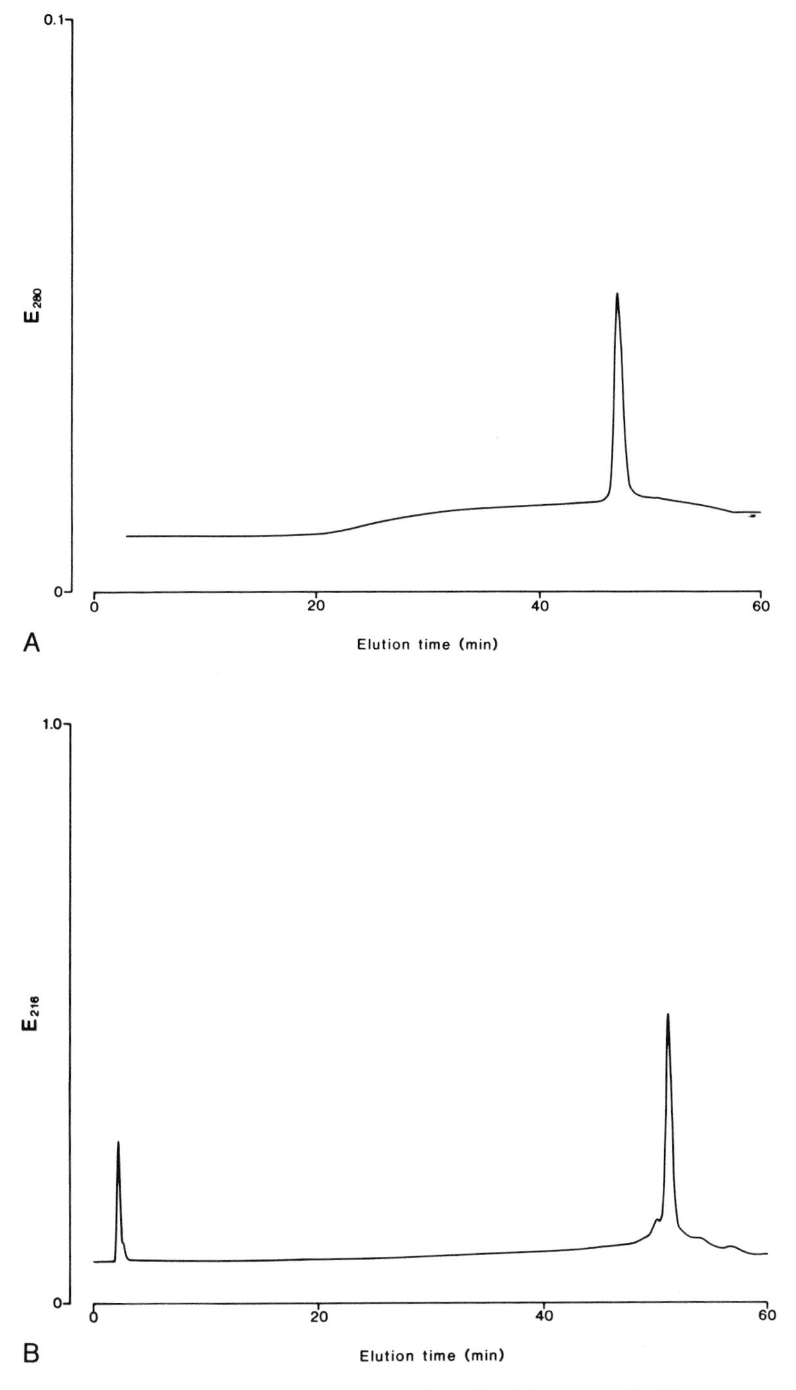

FIGURE 15–23. HIC of 50 μg porcine insulin (A), bhGH (B), ovalbumin (C), human serum albumin (D), and β-lactoglobulin (E). Columns: TSK Ether 5 PW, 75 × 7.5 mm i.d. (insulin and serum albumin), propyl aspartamide, 200 × 4.6 mm i.d. (bhGH and ovalbumin), (*continued*)

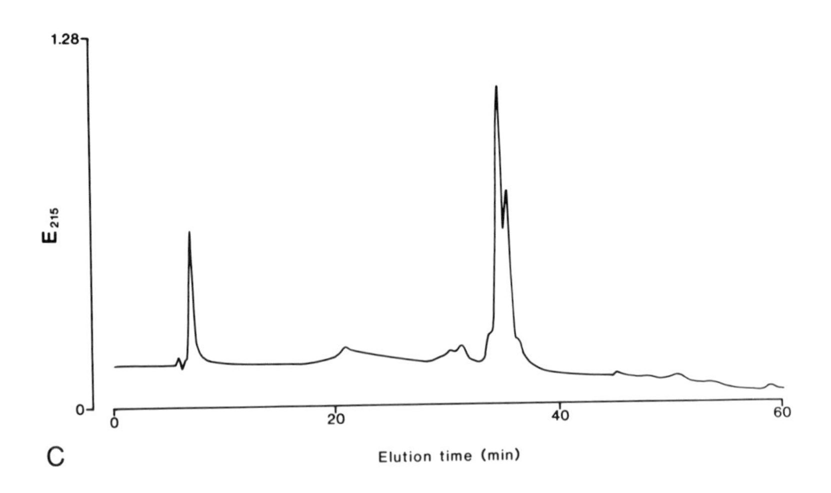

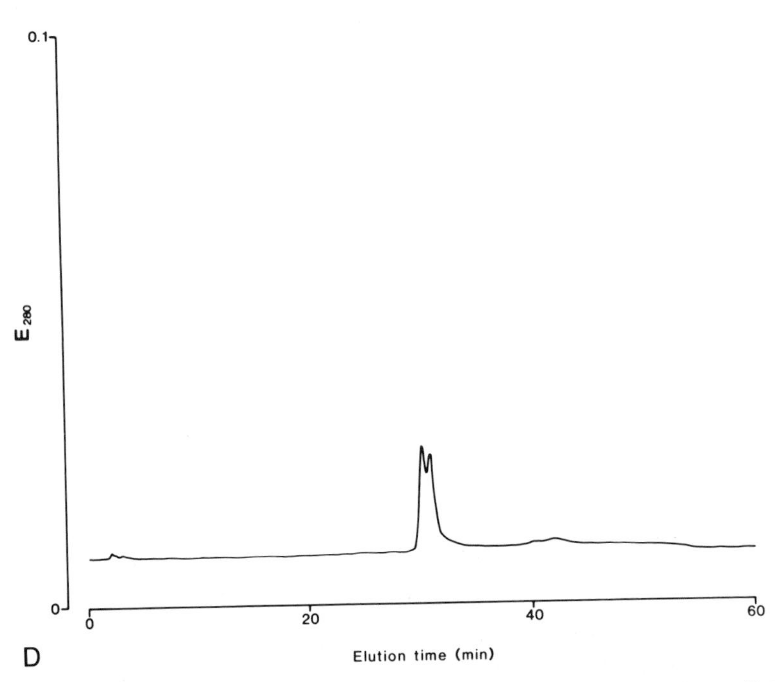

and LC Hint (β-lactoglobulin). The basal mobile phase was a reverse ammonium sulfate gradient (2–0 *M* during 45 min) in 0.1 *M* Na_2HPO_4, pH 6.5. Additives to the B buffer were

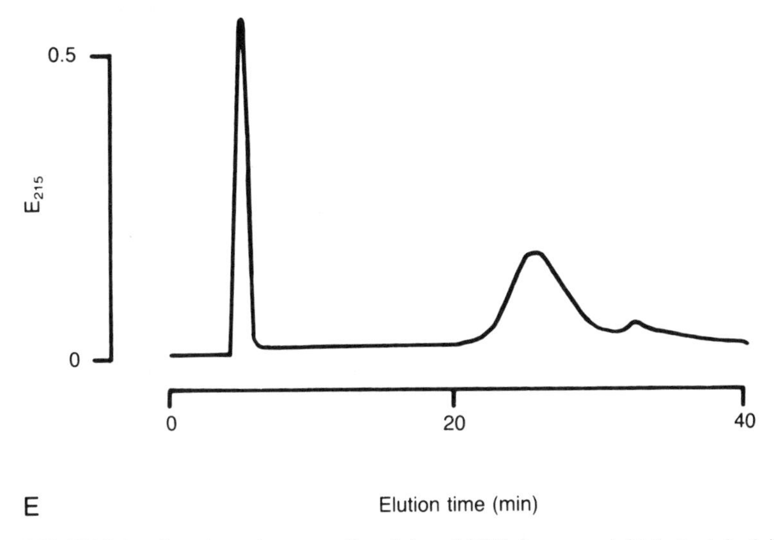

0.1% PEG 6000 (ovalbumin and serum albumin) and 20% 2-propanol (β-lactoglobulin). Flow rate 0.5 ml/min.

15.5 HIGH-PERFORMANCE SIZE-EXCLUSION CHROMATOGRAPHY

The content of protein dimers, oligomers, and polymers is important information, not only for analytical characterization but also for detection of a possible self-aggregation. Further, if size-exclusion chromatography is performed in disaggregating mobile phases, covalently bound protein aggregates may be distinguished from polymerization based on hydrophobic or ionic interaction.

15.5.1 HPSEC of Insulin and Human Growth Hormone

Analyses of the content of insulin and hGH dimers and polymers in pharmaceutical preparations are essential for their clinical use, since these aggregates are known to be antigenic and their biological activity is seriously reduced compared to insulin and hGH monomers.

Covalently bound insulin and hGH dimers may be separated in a number of RP analyses, but often the dimers will split (dimers, deamidated dimers, etc.) and the recovery of such insulin dimers is seriously reduced in C18 RP-HPLC analyses.[125] Higher oligomers of insulin as well as hGH (isolated from HPSEC analyses) are not eluted at all in common RP analyses.[150] Therefore, HPSEC remains the preferred HPLC method for quantitating a dimer/oligomer/polymer content in polypeptides.

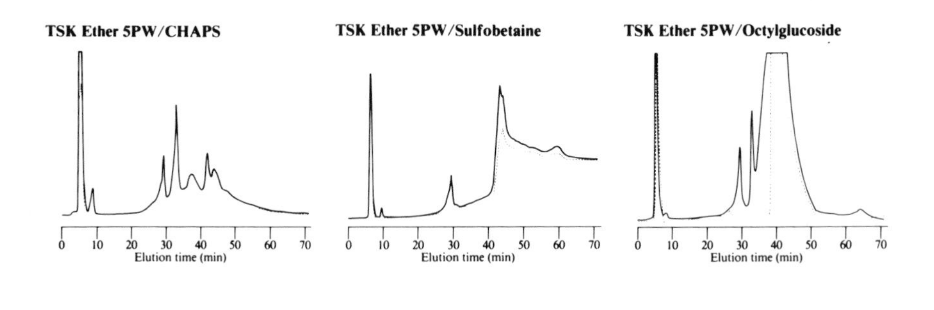

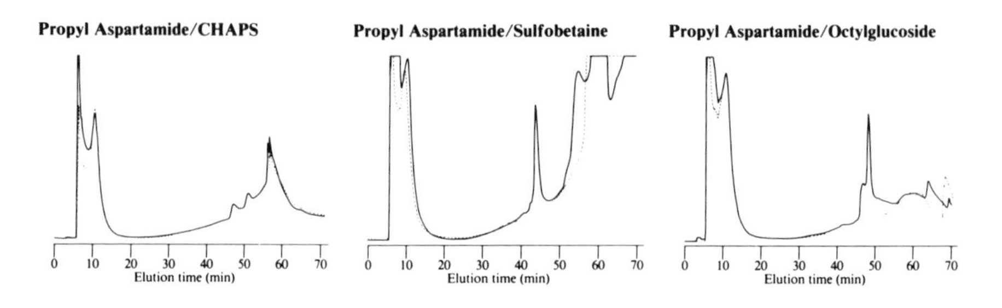

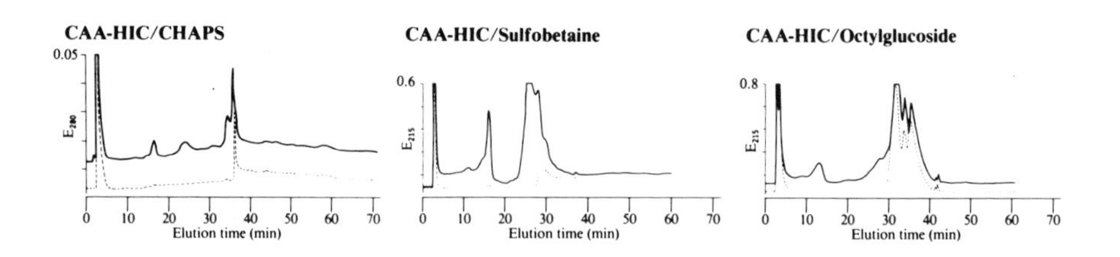

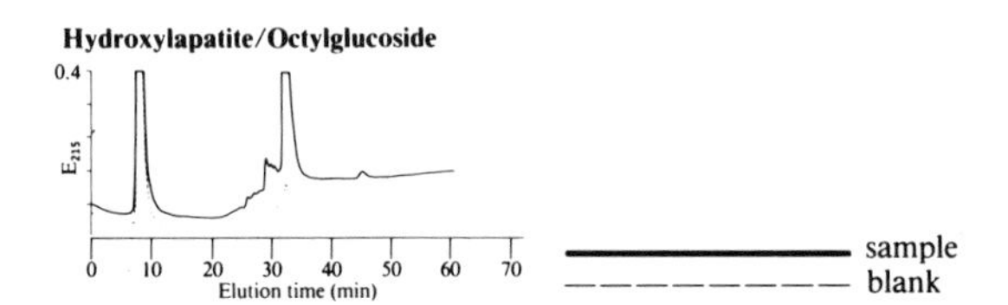

FIGURE 15–24. Separation of 50 μl detergent-solubilized erythrocyte ghost membrane proteins using a TSK Ether 5 PW (75 × 7.5 mm I.D.), propyl aspartamide (200 × 4.6 mm I.D.), Spherogel CAA-HIC (100 × 4.6 mm I.D.) or a 100 × 7.5 mm I.D. PEC 102 hydroxylapatite column eluted with the basal mobile phase described in Figure 15–23 containing 0.1% octylglucoside in A and B buffer, 0.3% CHAPS or sulfobetaine SB-12 in the B buffer as indicated in the figure. Flow rate 0.5 ml/min. The erythrocyte ghost membrane proteins were extracted in 10 m*M* Tris-HCl, 5 m*M* EDTA, pH 8.0 containing 1% octylglucoside, CHAPS, or sulfobetaine SB-12.

15.5.2 Mobile and Stationary Phase Effects

Commercially available high-performance size-exclusion columns are based on spherical 5- to 10-μm porous silica particles covered with a hydrophilic diol-like bonded phase. Although HPSEC is considered to be one of the simplest HPLC analyses with respect to optimization, precautions in choice of mobile and stationary phases must be taken in order to avoid ion exclusion (interaction between negatively charged groups in the polypeptide and residual silanol groups[151,152] and hydrophobic interaction between the sample and the stationary phase).

HPSEC of crystalline insulin using TSK 2000 SW (Toyo Soda) or I-125 (Waters) columns eluted with a disaggregating mobile phase (acetic acid/acetonitrile) are shown in Figure 15–25. Only the I-125 column was found to be capable of separating the c-components (MW 6000) and the b-components (MW 9000–12,000). The two components coeluted with considerable tailing using the 2000 SW column. In this mobile phase, insulin cannot be eluted from a GF-250 (Du Pont) column (data not shown).

The elution patterns of hGH from the TSK 2000 SW and GF-250 eluted with a "physiological" mobile phase are given in Figure 15–26. hGH could be eluted from both columns with approximately 100% recovery, but separation of hGH polymers, dimers, and hGH monomer could be achieved in a satisfactory manner only by using the TSK 2000 column. Initial separation was obtained using the GF-250 column, whereas no hGH material could be eluted from the I-125 column.

An example of mobile phase optimization is given in Table 15–3. Using the 2000 SW column eluted at neutral pH, increasing amounts of 2-propanol were added to the mobile phase, and the retention times of the polymer/dimer were found to be constant with more than 1% 2-propanol. The number of polymers was found to be constant over 3% 2-propanol, and these variations clearly demonstrate that hydrophobic interactions occur in GPC of polypeptides—and may be overcome by proper choice of mobile phase.

Addition of detergents—which often are used for solubilizing very hydrophobic proteins (i.e., membrane proteins)—reduces the effective usable MW range if the detergent binds to the protein molecule. Replacing the actual HPSEC column with one with a higher MW separation range often overcomes this problem (Figure 15–27).

15.6 HIGH-PERFORMANCE ION-EXCHANGE CHROMATOGRAPHY

Modern HPIEC columns offer high resolution and flow rates paired with short analytical run times for proteins in the MW range 5–300 kDa. The introduction of the new ion-exchange matrices has not only proven successful within the area of analytical techniques but has been an important tool in the design of downstream processing due to the high reproducibility and fast separation possible. It should be considered that although RP-HPLC was introduced several years ago, the technique is still mainly used for analytical purposes, thus

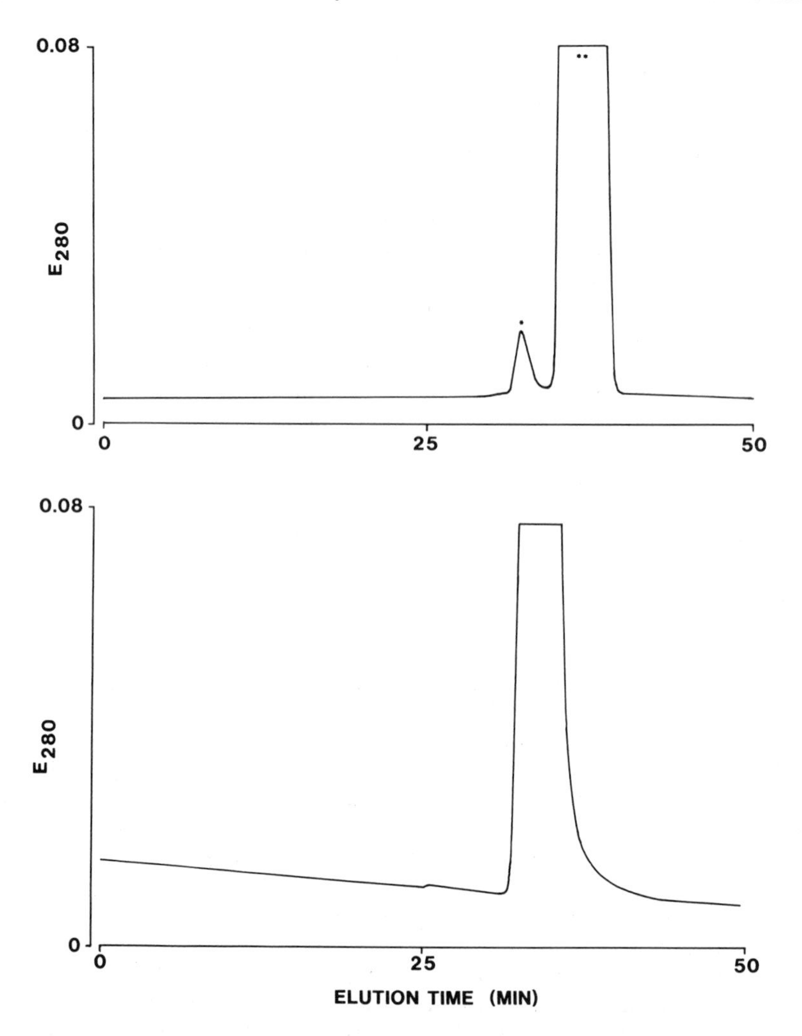

FIGURE 15–25. HPSEC of 500 μg crystalline porcine insulin using 2 × 300 × 7.5 mm I.D. Waters I-125 columns (upper panel) or a 600 × 7.5 mm I.D. TSK 2000 SW column (lower panel) eluted at 0.5 ml/min with 20% CH_3COOH in 20% acetonitrile. The major peaks are b-component* (proinsulin, insulin dimer) and c-component** (insulin peptide, desamidoinsulins, arginineinsulins, etc.).

leaving ion exchange (and gel chromatography) as the principle in large-scale chromatography.

This fact is partly explained by the considerable loss in resolution during up-scaling of RP columns due to the necessary changes in particle size (5 → 40 μm) and partly because of observed losses in specific biological activity in many molecules following RP-HPLC in organic solvents.[153]

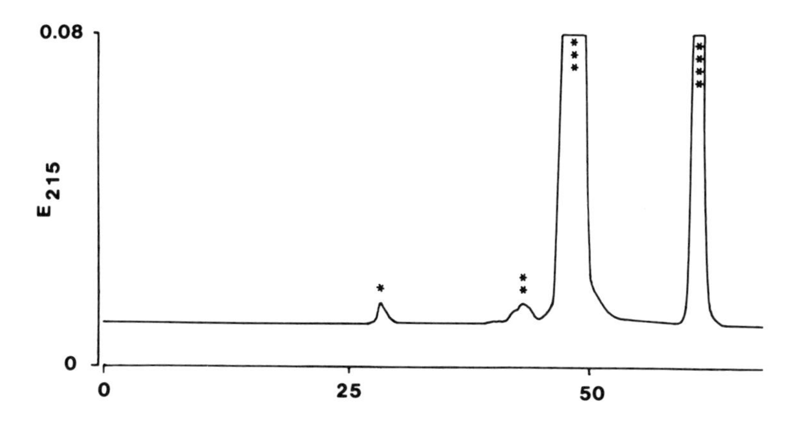

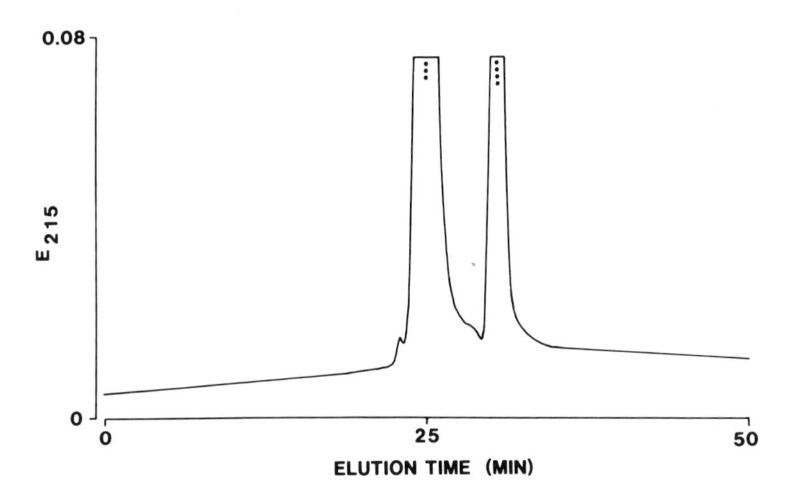

FIGURE 15–26. HPSEC of 25 μg bhGH using a 600 × 7.5 mm I.D. TSK 2000 SW column (upper panel) or a 250 × 9.0 mm I.D. Du Pont GF-250 column (lower panel) eluted at 0.4 ml/min with 0.1 *M* NaH_2PO_4, pH 7.3 containing 3% 2-propanol. The major peaks are hGH polymers*, hGH dimer/trimer**, hGH monomer***, and buffer components****.

TABLE 15–3. The Influence of Varying Amounts of 2-Propanol in the Mobile Phase on Retention Times and Content of hGH Dimers and Polymers[a]

2-Propanol in the Mobile Phase (%)	Retention Time (Dimer) (min)	Retention Time (Monomer) (min)	Dimer (%)	Polymer (%)
0	*x*	*y*	*z*	0
1	*x*—0.2	*y*—0.2	*z*	*a*
2	*x*—0.2	*y*—0.2	*z*	*a* + *b*
3	*x*—0.2	*y*—0.2	*z*	*a* + *b* + *c*
5	*x*—0.2	*y*—0.2	*z*	*a* + *b* + *c*
10	*x*—0.2	*y*—0.2	*z*	*a* + *b* + *c*

[a] Stationary phase: TSK 2000 SW. Basal mobile phase: 0.1 *M* Na_2PO_4, pH 7.3

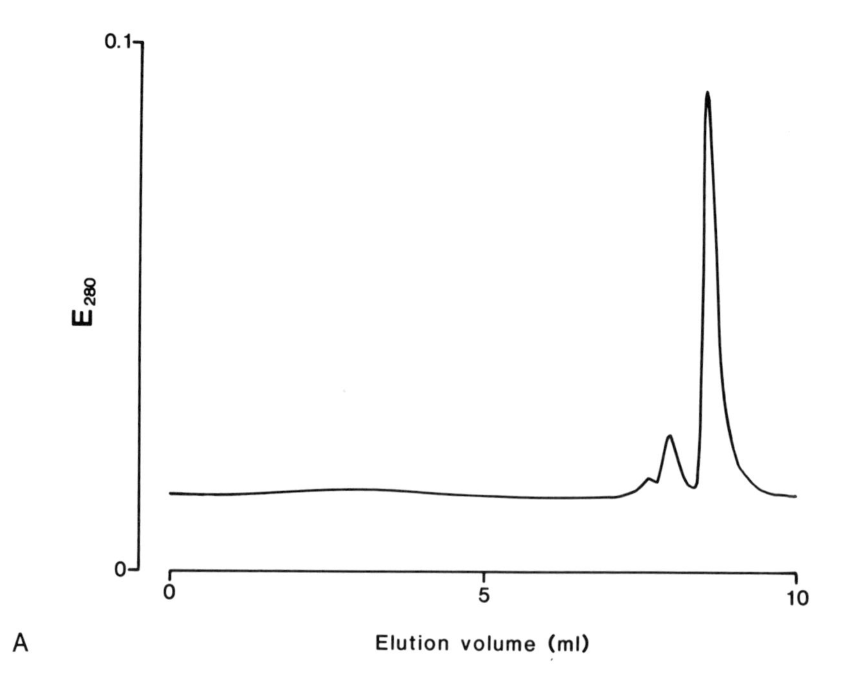

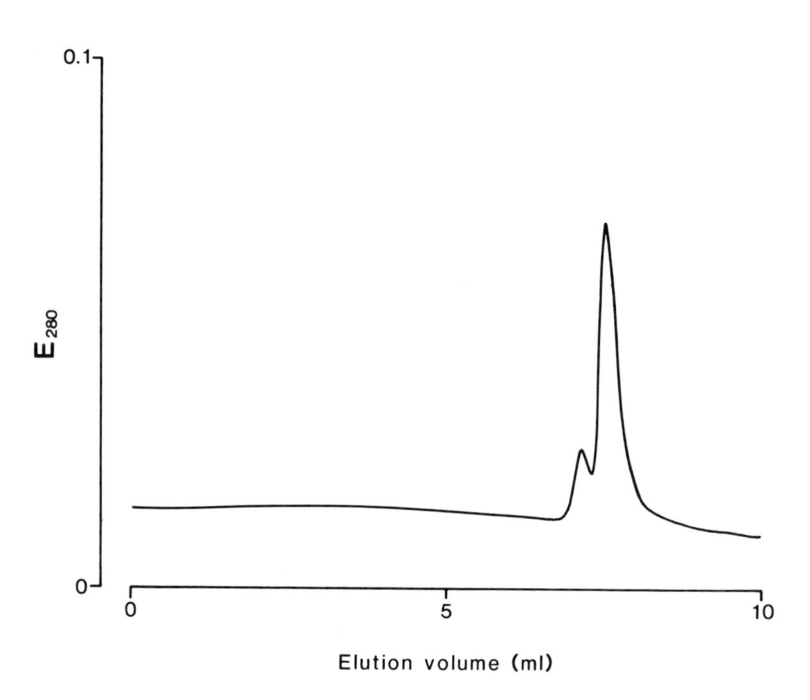

FIGURE 15–27. HPSEC of 50 μg human serum albumin using a 250 × 9.0 mm I.D. Du Pont GF-250 column eluted with 0.2 *M* NaH_2PO_4, pH 7.0 (A) or with the same mobile phase containing further 0.1% SDS and 0.02 *M* DTT (B).

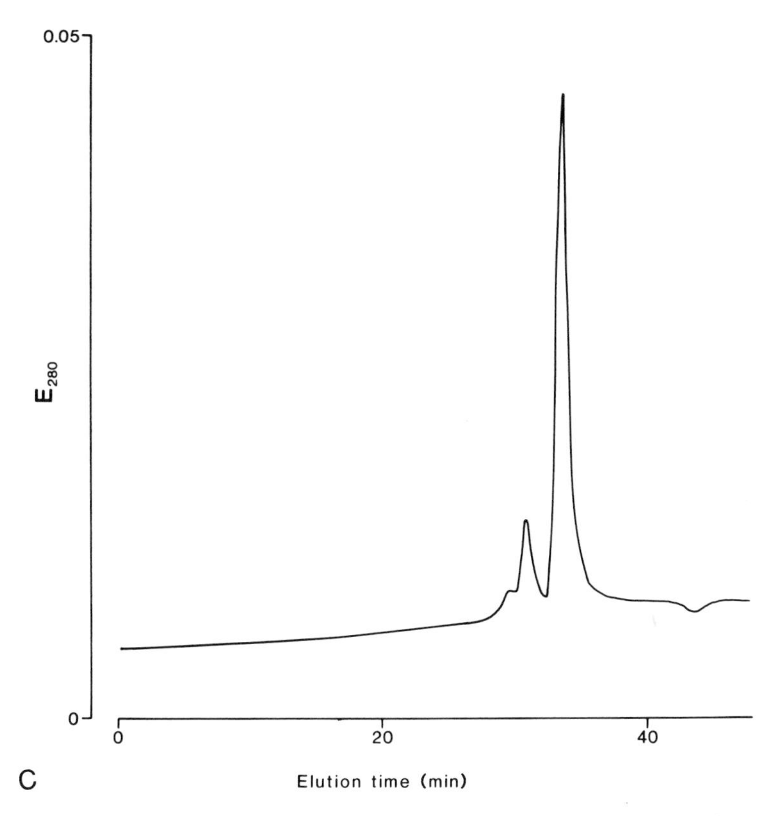

C shows the separation of the same sample using a 250 × 9.0 mm I.D. Du Pont GF-450 column eluted as described in B. Flow rate 0.25 ml/min.

Two of the most successful resins available are the Mono Q and the Mono S based on monodisperse Monobeads.[154] The matrix is a 10-μm hydrophilic resin that is completely stable in the pH range 2–12. A narrow particle size distribution and 500 Å pore size facilitates high loading capacity (25 mg protein per ml gel) and low back pressure (less than 200 psi for a 50 × 5 mm i.d. column at 1.0 ml/min).

In this section we demonstrate the use of Mono Q and Mono S for the analyses and purification of IL-1β from natural sources as well as recombinant DNA-derived fermentation broth, and that this purification can be transformed directly from microbore (2.0 mm i.d) to large-scale purification with exchange of the Monobeads (10 μm) to Fast Flow gels (90–130 μm). Further, nanogram amounts of IL-1β could be recovered from analytical as well as preparative columns with ~100% recovery and similar specific biological activity.

15.6.1 Interleukin-1β

IL-1β is a nonglycosylated protein comprising 153 amino acids with MW 17,359. Two free cysteine SH groups are present,[155] and p*I* is 7.[156] Its biological action is closely connected to the acute phase response of the immune system following infections. The specific biological activity has been measured to 3.2×10^8 units per mg in the leukocyte activating factor assay.[157]

As natural IL-1β is present in very low concentrations only (1–5 ng/ml), larger amounts of material have been isolated from an *E. coli* using recombinant technology.[155,158–160] Purification of minor amounts of the natural form has been reported.[156,157,161–163]

The recombinant material used here originates from an *E. coli* expressed precursor enzymatically cleaved with dipeptidyl aminopeptidase (DAP-1) to IL-1β utilizing the fact that proline being the second N-terminal amino acid was not recognized by the enzyme. This novel method to ensure a correct N-terminal sequence of proteins expressed in *E. coli* has been described earlier.[164]

Figure 15–28 shows the elution pattern of purified IL-1β using a Mono S or a Mono Q column, thus defining retention time, peak symmetry, and elution parameters. IL-1β is more strongly bound to the Mono S column, but in both cases symmetrical, well-defined peaks are obtained.

The resolution of the reaction mixture of DAP-1 cleavage of the amino-extended precursor to IL-1β is shown in Figure 15–29. The precursor comprising two glutamic acids was cleaved stepwise, and sequence analyses revealed that the three peaks observed in the Mono S chromatogram represented the precursor with two glutamic acid residues (elutes first), an intermediate form with one glutamic acid residue (eluted second), and the IL-1β molecule itself (eluted third). In agreement with theoretical considerations, a reverse elution order was observed for the Mono Q column (data not shown).

A micro, an analytical, and a preparative scale purification of the IL-1β precursor from an *E. coli* extract are shown in Figure 15–30. The elution patterns of the three diagrams are equal. Three main peaks were observed, identified as colored compounds, precursor, and lysozyme with the characteristic split peak. The resolutions on the microbore and the 50 × 5 mm i.d. columns were comparable, while the resolution on the FF-S resin (90–130 μm) was decreased markedly, as expected on expense of capacity.

Figure 15–31 shows the elution pattern of 39 ml supernatant from stimulated monocyte cultures containing 1.5 ng IL-1β/ml. Prior to sample loading monocyte culture medium was applied to the column in order to reduce nonspecific binding to the stationary phase. The recovery of ~60 ng natural IL-1β was 90–100%, and the specific biological activity of the natural IL-1β was found to be comparable before and after HPIEC purification (2.0×10^8 units/mg compared to 2.9×10^8 units/mg for HPIEC-purified recombinant IL-1β).

15.7 DISCUSSION

15.7.1 RP-HPLC

RP-HPLC separations of insulin and insulin-related compounds can be performed satisfactorily with several stationary phases (C18 being far the most popular), with few groups of mobile phase additives (neutral salts, alkylam-

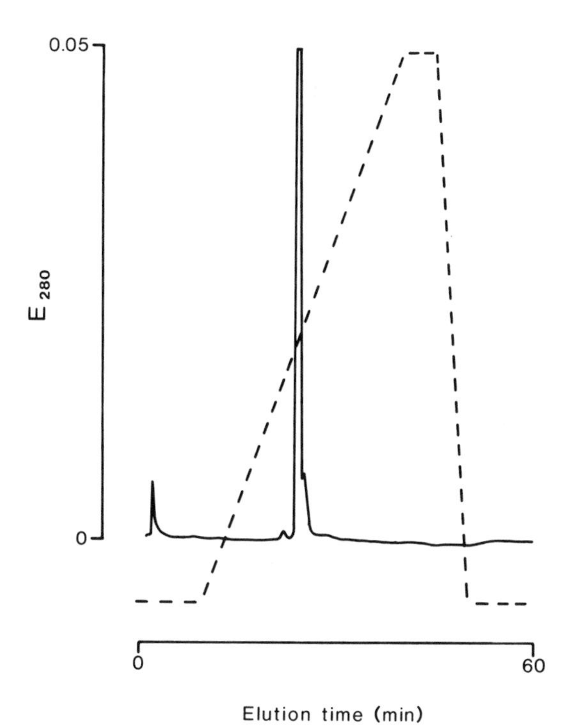

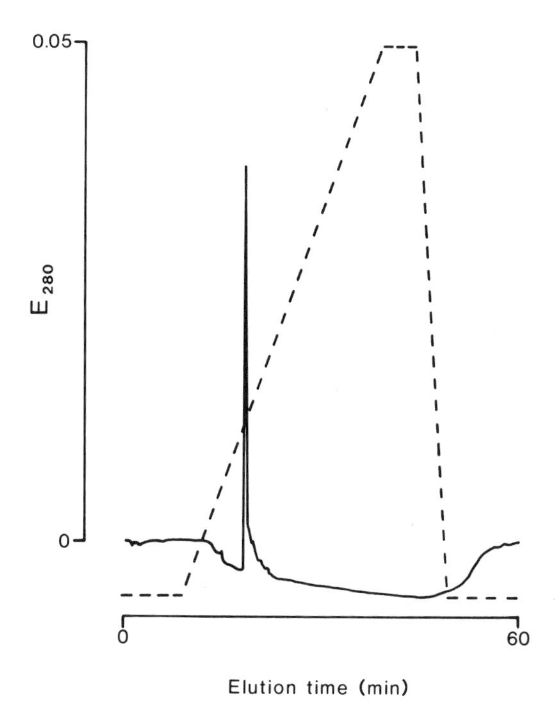

FIGURE 15–28. HPIEC of purified IL-1β using a 50 × 5.0 mm I.D. Mono S column eluted with a NaCl gradient (0–1 *M* during 40 min) in 0.03 *M* sodium citrate, pH 4.0 (upper panel) and a 50 × 5.0 mm I.D. Mono Q column eluted with a NaCl gradient (0–0.4 *M* during 40 min) in 0.05 *M* Tris, pH 9.5 (lower panel). Flow rate 1.0 ml/min. Temperature 4°C. The NaCl gradient is illustrated with a broken line.

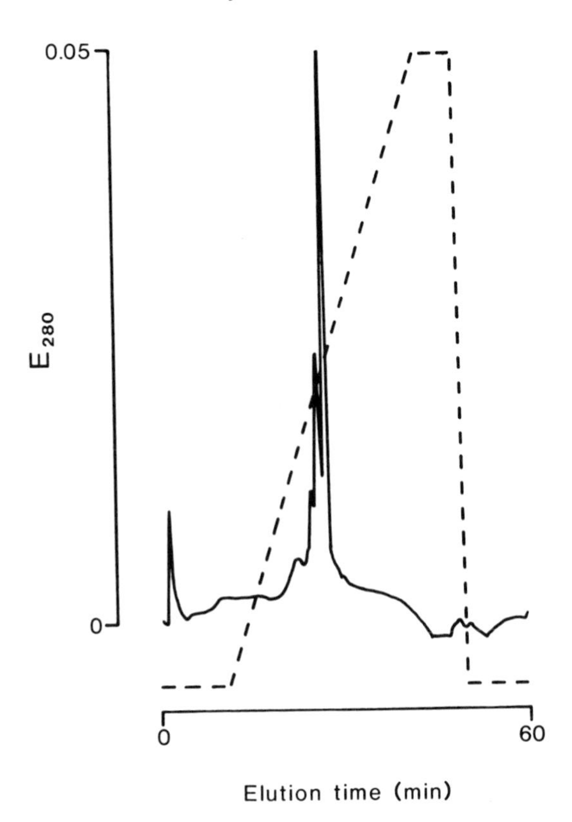

FIGURE 15–29. HPIEC of DAP-1-cleaved IL-1β precursor using a 50 × 5.0 mm I.D. Mono S column eluted as described in Figure 15–28, upper panel.

monium salts, TFA, or chaotropic agents) and primarily with acetonitrile as organic modifier. Minor modifications in a single of the 51 amino acids can be baseline separated from the native compound after some optimization of the mobile/stationary phase combination, and in this developmental process we have demonstrated the major influence of mobile phase composition using a single C18-silica column (Figures 15–1–15–10). Only minor variations in the separation pattern of insulin and insulin-related substances were noticed using a number of different narrow-pore silica-based C18 columns, whereas column-to-column and batch-to-batch variations in performance often constitute a major problem.

In the case of insulin, several stationary/mobile phase combinations result in very detailed separation patterns, a common experience for many polypeptides. With increasing MW and hydrophobicity, RP-HPLC analyses become less powerful and in the case of hGH the developmental work in optimizing the stationary and mobile phases was much more difficult. The majority of stationary and mobile phases did not result in any detailed separation (or in any elution at all), and for a single silica-based and a single resin-based stationary

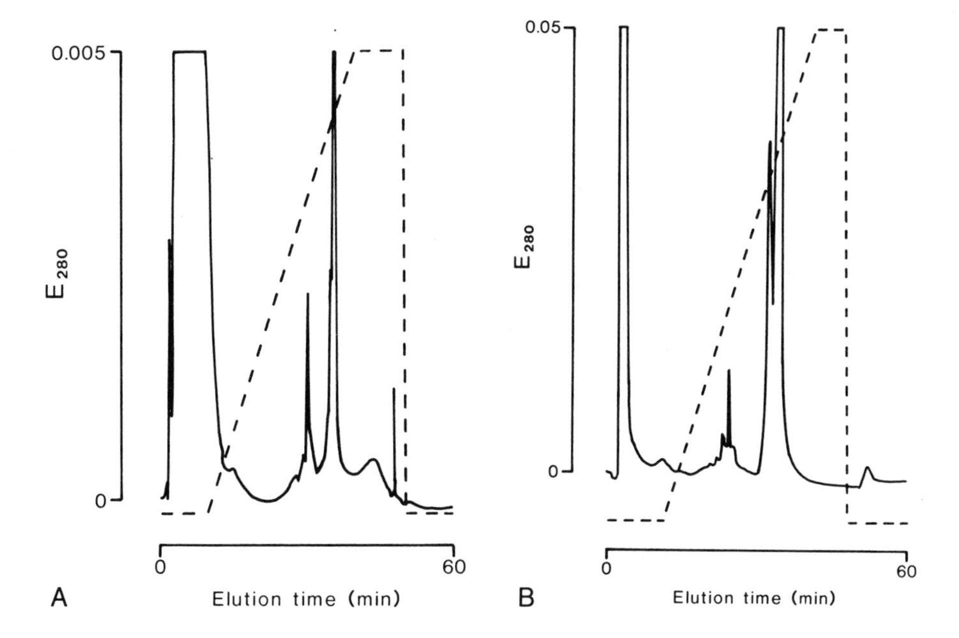

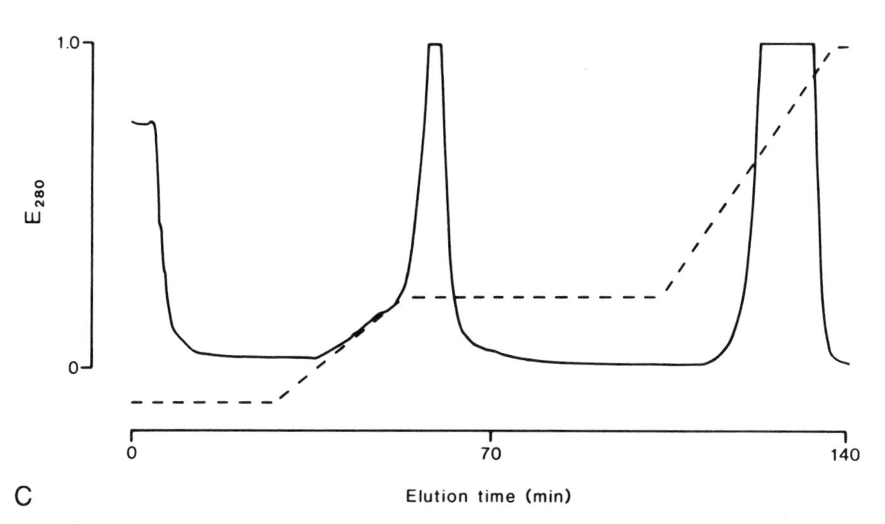

FIGURE 15–30. Ion-exchange chromatography of *E. coli* extract using the mobile phase described in Figure 15–28, upper panel. Columns: Mono S (30 × 2.0 mm I.D.), flow rate 0.1 ml/min at 4°C (A), Mono S (50 × 5.0 mm I.D.), flow rate 1.0 ml/min at 4°C (B) and FF-S Sepharose (100 × 10.0 mm I.D.), flow rate 1.0 ml/min at 4°C (C). Sample load: 100 μl (A), 200 μl (B), and 156 ml (C) *E. coli* extract. Peaks identified (increasing retention times: colored compounds, IL-1β precursor, lysozyme).

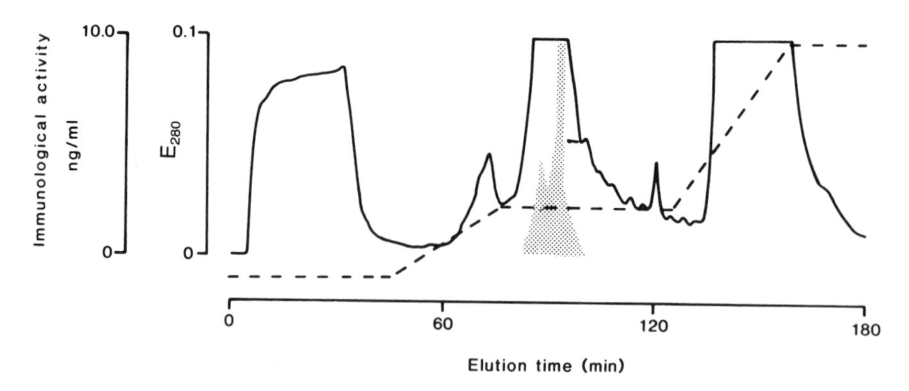

FIGURE 15–31. Ion-exchange chromatography of 39 ml monocyte culture medium using a 100 × 10.0 mm I.D. FF-S Sepharose column eluted at 1.0 ml/min as described in Figure 15–30, panel C. IL-1β immunoactivity is indicated by crosshatching.

phase it was necessary to develop two different mobile phases for the separation of hGH/met-hGH and the components in phGH (Figures 15–11 and 15–20). Contrary to RP analyses of insulin (where a single system may separate insulin and all insulin-related compounds), the separation of hGH and hGH-related substances demands a specific column/buffer optimization dependent on the type of hGH-related compound to be separated. Consequently, no published RP-HPLC analyses are able to separate hGH from the all common hGH-related substances.[148]

15.7.2 HIC

HIC may be classified as RP-HPLC performed at stationary phases with less ligand density than conventional RP columns or with alternative surface coverings, thereby creating less strong binding forces between the ligand and the sample molecule. The binding is normally established in a milieu with high ammonium sulfate concentration, and the desorbtion is performed with a reverse salt gradient. However, a number of mobile phase additives have been suggested in order to expand the useful separation range for HIC, but for polypeptides that can be separated with good or moderate efficiency using RP-HPLC, HIC is certainly no alternative. Insulin and human growth hormone may be eluted from HIC columns in well-defined peaks in a purely aqueous milieu, but no selectivity comparable to that described in RP analyses was obtained (Figure 15–23). For larger proteins HIC may offer an alternative since RP-HPLC of such proteins either cannot be performed at all (due to irreversible binding to the stationary phase) or the proteins lose their activity during the binding/elution procedure. HIC will probably be best suited for detecting changes in the three-dimensional structure of proteins, changes that will never be detected in RP analyses where the three-dimensional structure of most proteins probably is lost—totally or partially.

To expand the potential separation range of HIC columns, we have investigated the possible fractionation of a mixture of membrane proteins extracted from erythrocyte ghosts using octylglucoside, sulfobetaine, or CHAPS as mobile phase additives. As can be seen from Figure 15–24, a rather detailed separation could be obtained, but the need for optimizing the stationary as well as the mobile phase is evident.

15.7.3 HPSEC

Although size exclusion should be a "simple" chromatographic technique, only a very limited number of stationary phases are commercially available for HPSEC of polypeptides, essentially only three: TSK SW (Toyo Soda), I-125/250 (Waters), and GF 250/450 (Du Pont). All three stationary phases suffer from a number of drawbacks: They are very expensive, are only sold as prepacked columns, their chemical and physical stability are far from being ideal, batch-to-batch variations may be observed, the columns cannot be regenerated or repacked, and little information is provided concerning the bonded phase or the packing material in general. Consequently only a few literature reports deal with HPSEC of insulin[165,166] and hGH.[167–170]

This might be acceptable if the HPSEC columns behaved in an ideal or close-to-ideal manner, i.e., without mixed-mode separation effects, but as shown for hGH, establishment of stable chromatographic parameters depends on addition of organic solvent to the mobile phase (Table 15–3). From the comparative HPSEC of insulin and hGH using the three above-mentioned stationary phases, it can be seen that marked differences in elution pattern exist for the different columns (Figures 15–25 and 15–26). Actually insulin and hGH require different columns in order to obtain all potential information with respect to the sample composition.

For preparative chromatography, the limitation in loading capacity compared to HPIEC and RP-HPLC generally excludes this separation principle, at any rate as the initial purification step. After careful optimization of mobile and stationary phase, HPSEC may be a potential analytical alternative to RP-HPLC and HPIEC, but for the above-mentioned reasons its worldwide application will remain limited.

15.7.4 HPIEC

With the increasing number of polypeptides of biological interest present in extremely low concentrations *in vivo*, the demand for microscale chromatography and reliable up-scaling procedures has increased pointedly during the last few years. The introduction of the gas phase sequencer allows sequencing of polypeptides present in nanogram amounts, and this challenge has primarily been met by establishing microbore RP-HPLC purification strategies. However, if a biological activity must be retained—and kept constant—during a number of high-performance chromatographical procedures, HPIEC offers an attractive alternative. As shown in Figure 15–29, modern ion-exchange stationary phases operate according to electrostatic calculations; no extra-column effects are observed. It was possible to isolate minor amounts of IL-1β present in very complex mixtures using up-scaling parameters based on the analytical chromatography. The specific biological activity was constant before and after HPIEC.

Since recovery of polypeptides may be a limiting factor in RP-HPLC, especially at very low column loads,[128] HPIEC may become a more important separation principle in future purification strategies.

15.7.5 Comparison of Methods/Separation Strategy

Although we have analyzed only a few polypeptides/proteins, we think some general guidelines may be extracted. For hydrophobic polypeptides with MW 10,000 or less, RP-HPLC is a very suitable separation principle. A few variations in the mobile phase—as outlined for insulin—will probably lead to a satisfactory separation using conventional C18/C8 stationary phases. Acetonitrile is the choice for organic modifier, but since temperature effects may be unpredictable, this is not the first parameter to be varied. With increasing MW (and hydrophobicity), RP separation becomes increasingly difficult (as illustrated with hGH), and ion-exchange chromatography may be of similar value for the separation process.

To illustrate this point, we have performed RP-HPLC and HPIEC analyses of *in vitro* renatured biosynthetic hGH (22 kDa) and proinsulin (9 kDa). In the case of hGH, the two chromatograms are comparable (Figures 15–32 and 15–33), whereas RP-HPLC is clearly superior to HPIEC for the analyses of proinsulin and scrambled proinsulins (Figures 15–34 and 15–35). For larger proteins the choice will be HIC, HPIEC, or HPSEC, but it has to be accepted that the ability to distinguish between closely related molecules—so characteristic for RP-HPLC—is lost in either of the three separation principles.

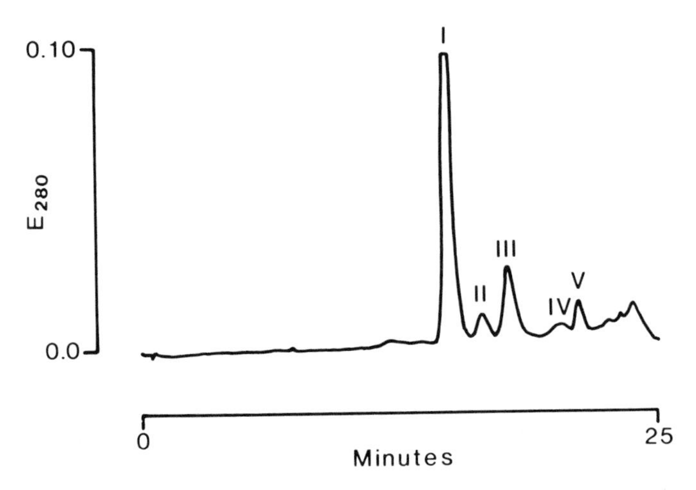

FIGURE 15–32. HPIEC of renatured biosynthetic hGH using a 50 × 5.0 mm I.D. Mono-Q column eluted with a NaCl gradient (0–0.04 *M* during 20 min, 0.04–0.4 *M* during 5 min) in 0.1 *M* histidine/7 *M* urea, pH 6.0. Flow rate 1.0 ml/min. The sample components were authentic hGH (peak I) and scrambled bhGH forms (peaks IV and V).

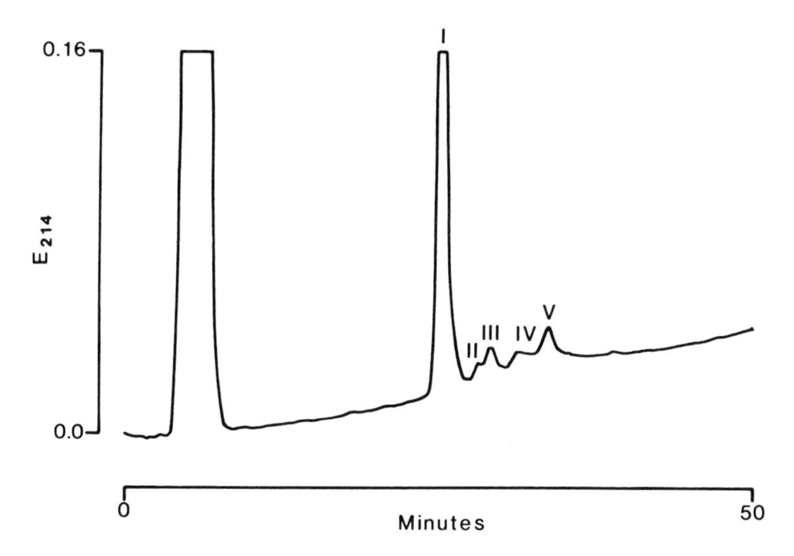

FIGURE 15–33. RP-HPLC of renatured biosynthetic hGH using a 250 × 4.0 mm I.D. Nucleosil C18 column eluted with an acetonitrile gradient (47–50% during 45 min) in 0.225 *M* $(NH_4)_2SO_4$/0.09 *M* NaH_2PO_4, pH 2.5 ($HClO_4$). Flow rate 1.0 ml/min, separation temperature 45°C. Peak identification as in Figure 15–32.

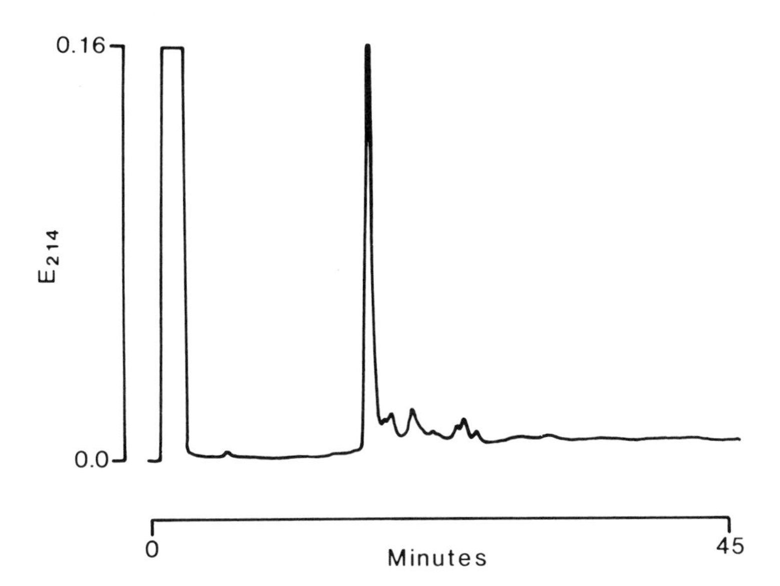

FIGURE 15–34. RP-HPLC of renatured biosynthetic human proinsulin using a 250 × 4.0 mm I.D. LiChrosorb RP-18 column eluted with an acetonitrile gradient in 0.125 *M* $(NH_4)_2SO_4$, pH 4.0. Flow rate 1.0 ml/min, separation temperature 45°C. The major peak at ~17 min is human proinsulin; following are scrambled proinsulin forms.

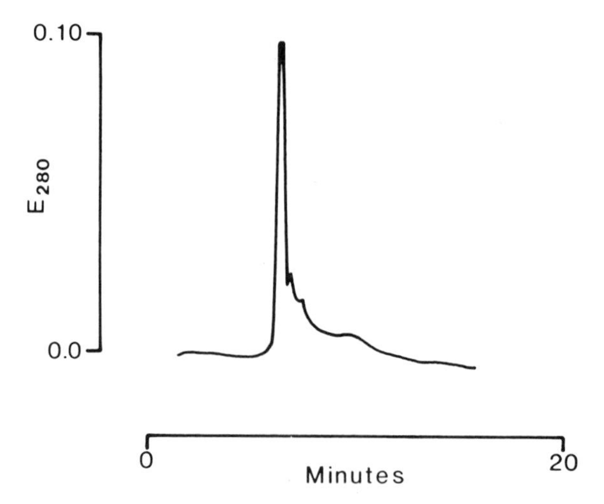

FIGURE 15–35. HPIEC of renatured biosynthetic human proinsulin using a 50 × 5.0 mm I.D. Mono-Q column eluted with a NaCl gradient (0–0.5 *M* during 20 min) in 0.02 *M* Tris/60% C_2H_5OH, pH 8.3. Flow rate 1.0 ml/min. The main peak is human proinsulin.

REFERENCES

1. B. S. Welinder, S. Linde, and B. Hansen, *J. Chromatogr.*, 348 (1985) 437.
2. U. Grau, *Diabetes*, 34 (1985) 1174.
3. L. Benzi, P. Marchetti, P. Cecchetti, F. Caricato, A. Masoni, and R. Navalesi, *J. Nucl. Med.*, 28 (1984) 81.
4. J. Markussen, K. H. Jørgensen, A. R. Sørensen, and L. Thim, *Int. J. Peptide Protein Res.*, 26 (1985) 70.
5. P. Marchetti, L. Benzi, V. Pezzino, D. Gullo, A. M. Ciccarone, P. Cecchetti, A. Masoni, R. Vigneri, and R. Navalesi, *J. Endocrinol. Invest.*, 1 (1985) 156.
6. D. J. Smith, R. M. Venable, and J. Collins, *J. Chromatogr. Sci.*, 23 (1985) 81.
7. J. P. Chang, W. R. Melander, and Cs. Horváth, *J. Chromatogr.*, 318 (1985) 11.
8. K. Hayakawa and H. Tanaka, *J. Chromatogr.*, 312 (1986) 476.
9. B. R. Srinisava, *J. Chromatogr.*, 295 (1984) 236.
10. R. Obermaier and G. Seipke, *Process Biochem.*, February (1984) 29.
11. J. Markussen, *Int. J. Peptide Protein Res.*, 25 (1985) 431.
12. M. N. Lioubin, M. D. Meier, and G. H. Ginsberg, *Prep. Biochem.*, 14 (1984) 303.
13. T. Tarvin, *Waters Lab. Highlights*, 0175 (7/1984).
14. M. Ohta, H. Tokunaga, T. Kimura, H. Satoh, and J. Kawamura, *Chem. Pharm. Bull.*, 32 (1984) 4641.
15. P. Marchetti, L. Benzi, P. Cecchetti, and T. Navalesi, *J. Nucl. Med.* 28 (1984) 31.
16. V. Lance, J. W. Hamilton, J. B. Rouse, J. K. R. Kimmel, and H. G. Pollock, *Gen. Comp. Endocrinol.*, 55 (1984) 112.
17. M. Knip, *Horm. Metab. Res.*, 16 (1984) 487.
18. H. W. Smith, L. M. Atkins, D. A. Binkley, W. G. Richardson, and D. J. Miner, *J. Liquid Chromatogr.*, 8 (1985) 419.

19. A. S. Chawla, I. Hinberg, P. Blais, and D. Johnson, *Diabetes*, 34 (1985) 420.
20. V. Pingoud and I. Trautschold, *Anal Biochem.*, 140 (1984) 305.
21. H. S. Tager, *Diabetes*, 33 (1984) 693.
22. B. H. Frank, A. H. Pekar, J. M. Pettee, E. M. Schirmer, M. G. Johnson, and R. E. Chance, *Int. J. Peptide Protein Res.*, 23 (1984) 506.
23. K. Hofmann, W. J. Zhang, H. Romovacek, F. M. Finn, A. A. Bothner-By, and P. K. Mishra, *Biochemistry*, 23 (1984) 2547.
24. P. S. L. Janssen, J. W. van Nispen, R. L. A. E. Hamelinck, P. A. T. A. Melgers, and B. C. Goverde, *J. Chromatogr. Sci.*, 22 (1984) 234.
25. B. H. Frank, P. J. Burck, F. F. Hutchins, and M. A. Root, in Neue Insuline (K.-G. Petersen and L. Kerp, eds.). Freiburger Graphische Betreibe, Freiburg, 1982, p. 45.
26. J. Rivier, R. McClintock, R. Galyean, and H. Anderson, *J. Chromatogr.*, 288 (1984) 303.
27. A. McLeod and S. P. Wood, *J. Chromatogr.*, 285 (1984) 319.
28. S. Shoelson, M. Fickowa, M. Haneda, A. Nahum, G. Musso, E. T. Kaiser, A. H. Rubenstein, and H. Tager, *Proc. Natl. Acad. Sci. U.S.A.*, 80 (1983) 7390.
29. M. Ohta, H. Togunaka, H. Satoh, and J. Kawamura, *Chem. Pharm. Bull.*, 31 (1984) 3566.
30. G. E. Tarr and J. W. Crabb, *Anal. Biochem.*, 131 (1983) 99.
31. K. Rose, H. De Pury, and R. E. Offord, *Biochem. J.*, 211 (1983) 671.
32. J. Rivier and R. McClintock, *J. Chromatogr.*, 268 (1983) 112.
33. H. Jaffe and D. K. Hayes, *J. Liquid Chromatogr.*, 6 (1983) 993.
34. J. W. Marsh, A. Nahum, and D. F. Steiner, *Int. J. Peptide Protein Res.*, 22 (1983) 39.
35. Supelco Reporter II, Supelco, Bellefonte, PA, (1983) 6.
36. A. U. Parmann and J. M. Rideout, *J. Chromatogr.*, 256 (1983) 283.
37. S. Shoelson, M. Haneda, P. Blix, A. Nanjo, T. Sanke, K. Inouye, D. Steiner, A. Rubenstein, and H. S. Tager, *Nature (London)*, 302 (1983) 540.
38. M. T. W. Hearn, B. Grego, and C. A. Bishop, *J. Liquid Chromatogr.*, 4 (1981) 1725.
39. W. S. Hancock, C. A. Bishop, R. L. Prestidge. D. R. K. Harding, and M. T. W. Hearn, *Science*, 200 (1978) 1168.
40. K. J. Wilson and G. J. Hughes, *Chimia*, 35 (1981) 327.
41. G. Vigh, Z. Varga-Puchony, J. Hlavay, and E. Pepp-Hites, *J. Chromatogr.*, 236 (1982) 51.
42. C. T. Wehr, L. Correla, and S. R. Abott, *J. Chromatogr. Sci.*, 20 (1982) 114.
43. G. Szepesi and M. Gazdag, *J. Chromatogr.*, 218 (1981) 597.
44. P. Rivaille, D. Raulais, and G. Milhaud, *Chromatogr. Sci.*, 12 (1979) 273.
45. M. J. O'Hare and E. C. Nice, *J. Chromatogr.*, 171 (1979) 209.
46. W. Mönch and W. Dehnen, *J. Chromatogr.*, 147 (1978) 415.
47. H. R. Morris, A. Dell, T. Etienne, and G. W. Taylor, in Frontiers in Protein Chemistry (T.-Y. Liu, G. Mamiya, and K. T. Yasunobu, eds.). Elsevier, New York, 1980, p. 193.
48. K. Morihari, T. Oka, H. Tsuzuki, Y. Tochino, and T. Kanaya, *Biochem. Biophys. Res. Commun.*, 92 (1980) 396.
49. J. Markussen and U. D. Larsen, in Insulin. Chemistry, Structure and Function of Insulin and Related Hormones (D. Brandenburg and A. Wollmer, eds.). Walter de Gruyter, Berlin, 1980, p. 161.
50. L. F. Lloyd and D. H. Calam, *J. Chromatogr.*, 237 (1982) 511.
51. L. F. Lloyd and H. Corran, *J. Chromatogr.*, 240 (1982) 445.
52. M. T. W. Hearn, W. S. Hancock, J. G. R. Hurrell, R. J. Fleming, and B. Kemp, *J. Liquid Chromatogr.*, 2 (1979) 919.
53. B. Grego and M. T. W. Hearn, *Chromatographia*, 14 (1981) 589.
54. M. Gazdag and G. Szepesi, *J. Chromatogr.*, 218 (1981) 603.
55. A. Dinner and L. Lorenz, *Anal. Chem.*, 51 (1979) 1872.
56. U. Damgaard and J. Markussen, *Horm. Metab. Res.*, 11 (1979) 580.

57. R. E. Chance, E. P. Kroeff, J. A. Hoffmann, and B. H. Frank, *Diabetes Care*, 4 (1981) 147.
58. D. H. Calam, *J. Chromatogr.*, 167 (1978) 91.
59. M. E. F. Biemond, W. A. Sipman, and J. Olivié, *J. Liquid Chromatogr.*, 2 (1979) 1407.
60. M. E. F. Biemond, W. A. Sipman, and J. Olivié, in Insulin. Chemistry, Structure and Function of Insulin and Related Hormones (D. Brandenburg and A. Wollmer, eds.). Walter de Gruyter, Berlin, 1980, p. 201.
61. H. P. J. Bennett, C. A. Browne, and S. Solomon, *J. Liquid Chromatogr.*, 3 (1980) 1353.
62. D. Bataille, J. Besson, C. Gespach, and G. Rosselin, in Hormone Receptors in Digestion and Nutrition (G. Rosselin, P. Gromageot, and S. Bonfils, eds.). Elsevier, Amsterdam, 1979, p. 79.
63. N. Asakawa, M. Tsuno, T. Hattori, M. Ueyama, A. Shinoda, and Y. Miyake, *J. Pharm. Soc.*, 101 (1981) 279.
64. N. Asakawa, M. Tsuno, Y. Saeki, M. Matsuda. T. Hattori. M. Ueyama, A. Shinoda, and Y. Miyake, *J. Pharm. Soc.*, 102 (1982) 43.
65. D. Kalant, J. C. Crawhall, and B. I. Posner, *Biochem. Med.*, 34 (1985) 230.
66. S. Seino, Z. Z. Fu, W. Marks, Y. Seino, H. Imura, and A. Vinik, *J. Clin. Endocrinol. Metab.*, 62 (1986) 64.
67. M. Haneda, M. Kobayashi, H. Maegawa, N. Watanabe, Y. Takata, O. Ishibashi, Y. Shigeta, and K. Inouye, *Diabetes*, 34 (1985) 568.
68. A. E. Kitabshi and F. B. Stentz, *Biochem. Biophys. Res. Commun.*, 128 (1985) 163.
69. J. M. Rideout, G. D. Smith, C. K. Lim, and T. J. Peters, *Biochem. Soc. Trans.*, 13 (1986) 1225.
70. F. G. Hamel, D. E. Peavy, M. P. Ryan, and W. C. Duckworth, *Endocrinology*, 118 (1986) 328.
71. O. Ladrón de Guervara, G. Estreda, S. Antonio, X. Alvarado, L. Guereca, F. Zamudio, and F. Bolivar, *J. Chromatogr.*, 349 (1985) 91.
72. P. S. Adams and R. F. Haines-Nutt, *J. Chromatogr.*, 351 (1986) 574.
73. D. Pearson, *Anal. Biochem.*, 152 (1986) 189.
74. B. S. Welinder and F. H. Andresen, in Hormone Drugs. Proceedings of the FDA-USP Workshop on Drug and Reference Standards for Insulin, Somatropins and Thyroid-Axis Hormones (J. L. Gueriguian, ed.). United States Pharmacopeial Convention, Rockville, MD, 1982, 163.
75. S. Seino, A. Funakoshi, Z. Z. Fu, and A. Vinik, *Diabetes*, 34 (1985) 1.
76. E. Schrader and E. Pfeiffer, *J. Liquid Chromatogr.*, 8 (1985) 1139.
77. S. Joshi, H. Ogawa, G. T. Burke, L. Y.-H. Tseng, M. M. Rechler, and P. G. Katsoyannis, *Biochem. Biophys. Res. Commun.*, 133 (1985) 133.
78. E. Plisetskaya, H. G. Pollock, J. B. Rouse, J. W. Hamilton, J. R. Kimmel, and A. Gorbmann, *Reg. Peptides*, 11 (1985) 105.
79. L. Benzi, V. Pezzino, R. Marchetti, D. Gullo, P. Cechetti, A. Masoni, R. Vigneri, and R. Navalesi, *J. Chromatogr.*, 378 (1986) 337.
80. D. C. Robbins, S. E. Shoelson, H. S. Tager, P. M. Mead, and D. H. Gaynor, *Diabetes*, 34 (1985) 510.
81. Z. Wang and Y. Qian, *Shengwu Huaxue Zazhi*, 1 (1985) 7.
82. S. M. Cutfield, C. G. Dodson, N. Ronco, and J. F. Cutfield, *Int. J. Peptide Protein Res.*, 27 (1986) 335.
83. H. Nakazawa and M. Nagase, *Yakugaku Zasshi*, 106 (1986) 398.
84. J. M. Conlon and L. Thim, *Gen. Comp. Endocrinol.*, 64 (1986) 199.
85. W. H. Fischer, D. Saunders, D. Brandenburg, C. Diaconescu, A. Wollmer, G. Dodson, P. de Meyts, and H. Zahn, *Biol. Chem. Hoppe-Seyl.*, 367 (1985) 999.
86. R. Ishii, K. Sato, and S. Murozomo, *Hormone Metabol. Res.*, 18 (1986) 830.
87. B. D. Given, R. M. Cohen, S. E. Shoelson, B. H. Frank, A. Rubenstein, and H. S. Tager, *J. Clin. Invest.*, 76 (1985) 1398.

88. G. Hallden, G. Gafvelin, V. Mutt, and H. Jørnvall, *Arch. Biochem. Biophys.*, 247 (1986) 20.
89. J. F. Cutfield, S. M. Cutfield, A. Carne, S. E. Emdin, and S. Falkmer, *Eur. J. Biochem.*, 158 (1986) 117.
90. B. V. Fischer and D. Smith, *J. Pharmaceut. Biomed. Res.*, 4 (1986) 377.
91. C.-C. Wang and C.-C. Tsou, *Biochemistry*, 25 (1986) 5336.
92. L. Thim, M. T. Hansen, K. Norris, I. Hoegh, E. Boel, J. Forstrom, G. Ammerer, and N. P. Fiil, *Proc. Natl. Acad. Sci. U.S.A.*, 83 (1986) 6766.
93. K. Sakina, Y. Ueno, T. Oka, and K. Morihara, *Int. J. Peptide Protein Res.*, 28 (1986) 411.
94. T. Kubiak and D. Cowburn, *Int. J. Peptide Protein. Res.*, 27 (1986) 514.
95. J. D. Rideout, G. D. Smith, C. K. Lina, and T. J. Peters, *Biochem. Soc. Trans.*, 13 (1986) 1225.
96. G. Vigh, Z. Varga-Puchony, G. Szepesi, and M. Gazdag, *J. Chromatogr.*, 386 (1987) 353.
97. H. Sakura, Y. Iwamoto, Y. Sakamoto, T. Kuzuya, and H. Hirata, *J. Clin. Invest.*, 78 (1986) 1666.
98. E. Chantelau, G. Lange, M. Gasthaus, M. Boxberger, and M. Berger, *Diabetes Care*, 10 (1987) 348.
99. J.-M. Selam, P. Zirinis, M. Mellet, and J. Mirouze, *Diabetes Care*, 10 (1987) 343.
100. Y. E. Tian, C.-C. Wang, and C.-L. Tsau, *Biol. Chem. Hoppe-Seyl.*, 368 (1987) 368.
101. P. A. Halban, *Diabetologia*, 29 (1986) 893.
102. R. Marchetti, L. Benzi, P. Cechetti, and R. Navalesi, *J. Nucl. Med. All. Sci.*, 30 (1986) 191.
103. J. M. Conlon, M. S. Davis, and L. Thim, *Gen. Comp. Endocrinol.*, 66 (1987) 203.
104. Y.-Q. Qian and C.-L. Tsou, *Biochem. Biophys Res. Commun.*, 146 (1987) 437.
105. J. M. Conlon, E. Dafgård, S. Falkmer, and L. Thim, *FEBS Lett.*, 208 (1986) 445.
106. Y. Yamada and G. Serrero, *J. Biol. Chem.*, 262 (1987) 209.
107. G. A. Spinas, B. S. Hansen, S. Linde, W. Kastern, J. Mølvig, T. Mandrup-Poulsen, C. A. Dinarello, J. H. Nielsen, and J. Nerup, *Diabetologia*, 30 (1987) 474.
108. L.-A. Savoy, R. L. M. Jones, S. Pochon, J. G. Davies, A. V. Muir, R. E. Offord, and K. Rose, *Biochem. J.*, 249 (1988) 215.
109. J. G. Davies, *Biochem. J.*, 249 (1988) 209.
110. U. Grau and C. D. Saudek, *Diabetes*, 36 (1987) 1453.
111. Y. I. Rusakov, V. S. Karasev, M. N. Pertseva, and Y. A. Pankow, *Biokhimiya*, 52 (1987) 247.
112. S. Seino, D. F. Steiner, and G. Bell, *Proc. Natl. Acad. Sci. USA*, 84 (1987) 7423.
113. T. Majewski, L. Thim, J. Izdebski, and J. Markussen. *Int. J. Peptide Protein Res.*, 30 (1987) 379.
114. G. P. Schwartz, G. T. Burke, and P. G. Katsoyannis, *Proc. Natl. Acad. Sci. U.S.A.*, 84 (1987) 6408.
115. M. de Gasparo and M. Faupel, *J. Chromatogr.*, 357 (1986) 139.
116. B. H. Frank, *J. Chromatogr.*, 266 (1983) 239.
117. M. Oimomi, H. Hatanaka, Y. Yoshimura, K. Yokomo, S. Baba, and Y. Taketoni, *Nephron*, 46 (1987) 63.
118. F. G. Hamel, D. E. Peavy, M. P. Ryan, and W. C. Duckworth, *Diabetes*, 36 (1987) 702.
119. W. C. Duckworth, F. G. Hamel, J. J. Liepuieks, D. E. Peavy, M. P. Ryan, M. A. Hermodson, and B. H. Frank, *Biochem. Biophys Res. Commun.*, 147 (1987) 615.
120. H. G. Pollock, J. R. Kimmel, J. W. Hamilton, J. B. Rouse, K. E. Ebner, V. Lance, and A. B. Rawitch, *Gen. Comp. Endocrinol.*, 67 (1987) 375.
121. A. Peter, G. Szepesi, L. Balaspiri, and K. Burger, *J. Chromatogr.*, 408 (1987) 43.
122. O. L. de Guevara, in Chromatography 85 (H. Kalaszand and L. S. Ettre, eds.). Budapest, 1986, p. 169.

123. T. Wasada, Y. Eguchi, S. Takayama, K. Yao, and Y. Hirata, *J. Clin. Metab.*, 66 (1988) 153.
124. F. B. Stentz and R. K. Wright, US Patent 4528134, 1985.
125. B. S. Welinder, H. H. Sørensen, and B. Hansen, *J. Chromatogr.*, 361 (1986) 357.
126. N. D. Danielson and J. J. Kirkland, *Anal. Chem.*, 59 (1987) 2501.
127. S. Linde, B. S. Welinder, B. Hansen, and O. Sonne, *J. Chromatogr.*, 369 (1986) 327.
128. B. S. Welinder, H. H. Sørensen, and B. Hansen, *J. Chromatogr.*, 408 (1987) 191.
129. B. S. Welinder, S. Linde, B. Hansen, and O. Sonne, *J. Chromatogr.*, 298 (1984) 41.
130. E. C. Nice, M. W. Capp, N. Cook, and M. J. O'Hare, *J. Chromatogr.*, 218 (1981) 569.
131. G. S. Baldwin, B. Grego, M. T. W. Hearn, J. A. Knessel, F. J. Morgan, and R. J. Simpson, *Proc. Natl. Acad. Sci. U.S.A.*, 80 (1983) 5276.
132. B. Grego, G. S. Baldwin, J. A. Knessel, R. J. Simpson, F. J. Morgan, and M. T. W. Hearn, *J. Chromatogr.*, 297 (1984) 21.
133. C. H. Lee and D. Chung, in Handbook of HPLC for the Separation of Amino Acids, Peptides and Proteins, Vol. II (W. S. Hancock, ed.). CRC Press, Boca Raton, FL, 1984, p. 435.
134. W. C. Chang, A. L. Y. Chen, C. K. Chu, and L. T. Hu, *Int. J. Peptide Protein Res.*, 23 (1984) 637.
135. K. Nakamura and Y. Kato, *J. Chromatogr.*, 333 (1985) 29.
136. W. J. Kore, R. Keck, and R. N. Harkins, *Anal. Biochem.*, 122 (1982) 348.
137. T. Christensen, J. J. Hansen, H. H. Sørensen, and J. Thomsen, in High Performance Liquid Chromatography in Biotechnology (W. S. Hancock, ed.). Wiley, New York, 1990 p. 191.
138. M. T. W. Hearn, B. Grego, and G. E. Chapman, *J. Liquid Chromatogr.*, 6 (1983) 215.
139. C. Secchi, P. A. Biondi, A. Negri, R. Borroni, and S. Ronchi, *Int. J. Peptide Protein Res.*, 28 (1986) 298.
140. B. Grego, F. Lambrou, and M. T. W. Hearn, *J. Chromatogr.*, 266 (1983) 89.
141. B. Grego and M. T. W. Hearn, *J. Chromatogr.*, 336 (1984) 25.
142. R. L. Patience and L. H. Rees, *J. Chromatogr.*, 324 (1985) 385.
143. R. L. Patience and L. H. Rees, *J. Chromatogr.*, 352 (1986) 241.
144. S. Lefort and P. Ferrara, *J. Chromatogr.*, 361 (1986) 209.
145. H. M. Hsiung, N. G. Mayne, and G. W. Becker, *Biotechnology*, 4 (1986) 991.
146. R. M. Riggin, G. K. Dorula, and D. J. Minor, *Anal. Biochem.*, 167 (1987) 199.
147. B. Mollerach-Gobbi, N. Vita, E. Poskus, and C. Pena, *Int. J. Peptide Protein Res.*, 29 (1987) 692.
148. B. S. Welinder, H. H. Sørensen, and B. Hansen, *J. Chromatogr.*, 398 (1987) 309.
149. B. S. Welinder and H. H. Sørensen, unpublished data.
150. H. H. Sørensen, unpublished data.
151. S. Mori and M. Kato, *J. Liquid Chromatogr.*, 10 (1987) 3113.
152. W. Kopaciewicz and F. E. Regnier, *Anal. Biochem.*, 126 (1982) 8.
153. B. S. Welinder, K. R. Hejnæs, and B. Hansen, in High Performance Liquid Chromatography in Biotechnology (W. S. Hancock, ed.). Wiley, New York, 1990 p. 79.
154. J. Uglestad, L. Søderberg, A. Berge, and J. Bergstroem, *Nature* (*London*), 303 (1983) 95.
155. P. Wingfield, M. Payton, J. Tavernier, B. Barnes, A. Shaw, K. Rose, M. G. Simona, S. Demczuk, K. Williamson, and J.-M. Dayer, *Eur. J. Biochem.*, 160 (1986) 491.
156. L. B. Lachmann, *Fed. Proc.*, 42 (1983) 2639.
157. S. R. Kronheim, C. J. March, S. K. Erb, P. J. Conlon, D. Y. Mochizuki, and T. P. Hopp, *J. Exp. Med.*, 161 (1985) 490.
158. S. R. Kronheim, M. A. Cantrell, M. C. Deeley, C. J. March, P. J. Glackin, D. M. Anderson, T. Hemenway, J. E. Merriam, D. Cosman, and T. P. Hopp, *Biotechnology*, 4 (1986) 1078.

159. C. A. Meyers, K. O. Johanson, L. M. Miles, P. J. McDevitt, P. L. Simon, R. L. Webb, M.-J. Chen, B. P. Holskin, J. S. Lillquist, and P. R. Young, *J. Biol. Chem.*, 262 (1987) 11176.
160. Y. Kikumoto, Y.-M. Hong, T. Nishida, S. Nakai, Y. Masui, and Y. Hirai, *Biochem. Biophys. Res. Commun.*, 147 (1987) 315.
161. J. A. Schmidt, *J. Exp. Med.*, 160 (1984) 772.
162. L. Rimsky, H. Wakasugi, P. Ferrara, P. Robin, J. Capdeville, T. Turtz, D. Fradelizi, and J. Bertoglio, *J. Immunol.*, 136 (1986) 3304.
163. P. Knudsen, C. A. Dinarello, and T. B. Strom, *J. Immunol.*, 136 (1986) 3311.
164. H. Dalbøge, H. H. M. Dahl, J. Pedersen, J. W. Hansen, and T. Christensen, *Biotechnology*, 5 (1987) 161.
165. B. S. Welinder, *J. Liquid Chromatogr.*, 3 (1980) 1399.
166. B. S. Welinder, in Handbook in HPLC for the Separation of Amino Acids, Peptides and Proteins, Vol. II (W. S. Hancock, ed.). CRC Press, Boca Raton, FL, 1984, p. 413.
167. T. F. Holzman, *Biochemistry*, 25 (1986) 6907.
168. R. M. Riggin, C. J. Shaar, G. K. Dorulla, D. S. Lefebre, and D. J. Minor, *J. Chromatogr.*, 435 (1988) 307.
169. G. W. Becker, R. R. Bowsher, W. C. Mackeller, M. L. Poor, P. M. Tackitt, and R. M. Riggin, *Biotechnol. Appl. Biochem.*, 9 (1987) 478.
170. G. Fairbanks, T. L. Steck, and D. F. H. Wallach, *Biochemistry*, 10 (1971) 2606.

CHAPTER 16

HPLC Purification of Detergent-Solubilized Membrane Proteins

Steven C. Goheen

CONTENTS

16.1 INTRODUCTION

High-performance liquid chromatography (HPLC) has become a powerful technique for the analysis and purification of proteins. The popular but complex subcategory of membrane proteins has recently received extensive recognition. This may be due to the realization that HPLC is one of the most effective tools for their purification and that many of the problems that were encountered in early studies have been overcome. This chapter was designed to be used as a guide for developing a purification scheme for all membrane proteins. Since every case will present unique problems, the information gleaned from this article may not always lead to success. However, it is hoped that for those rare examples, this chapter will at least provide a basis for further work. General discussions of membrane proteins and HPLC have been the subject of earlier reviews.[1–3]

The hydrophobic nature of membrane proteins forces their chromatography to be much more difficult than that of other (soluble) proteins. This barrier can be partially overcome by using various solubilizing techniques. Once membrane proteins are solubilized using organic modifiers, detergents, or other compounds, their chromatography is similar to that of hydrophilic macromolecules. These separations are nearly always carried out with either organic solvents or detergents to keep the amphiphilic proteins in solution. Due to the diversity of eluents that can be used, there are potentially more techniques for solubilizing and separating membrane proteins as there are chromatographers; however, some of the procedures that are most commonly successful will be emphasized.

HPLC is a fast and high-performance relative of open column chromatography. High-performance separations of membrane proteins have been reported for only a few proteins, using even fewer HPLC supports. Examples using HPLC will be emphasized here, but open column techniques will also be described when necessary.

The HPLC of membrane proteins involves several steps. These include disrupting the lipid bilayer to release components of the matrix. Then, determining if the protein of interest is solubilized, if it will freely flow through the HPLC system, and if it has been inserted into a micelle alone or into a mixed micelle containing other proteins. If all these conditions have been met and the protein remains in an acceptable (active) form, the next step is purification by HPLC. These procedures will be described in more detail.

16.2 DISRUPTING THE MEMBRANE

The first step in purifying a membrane protein involves the isolation of the organelle that it is bound to and rinsing away all the soluble components. This process of isolating membranes or organelles from one another often involves differential ultracentrifugation and will not be covered here, but can be investigated in other reviews.[4–6] Once the membrane has been isolated, the next step is to separate the lipophilic components from one another, such that the protein that is to be purified is in its own micelle and in solution. Ideally, each protein of interest will be bound to the detergent(s) in some manner so that the chromatographic support(s) can discriminate them from contaminants effectively.

To visualize some of the obstacles to solubilizing membrane proteins, imagine a plasma membrane (Figure 16–1). In the erythrocyte plasma membrane, for example, there are several major different proteins that are characterized by their mobility in sodium dodecyl sulfate polyacrylamide gel electrophoresis.[7]

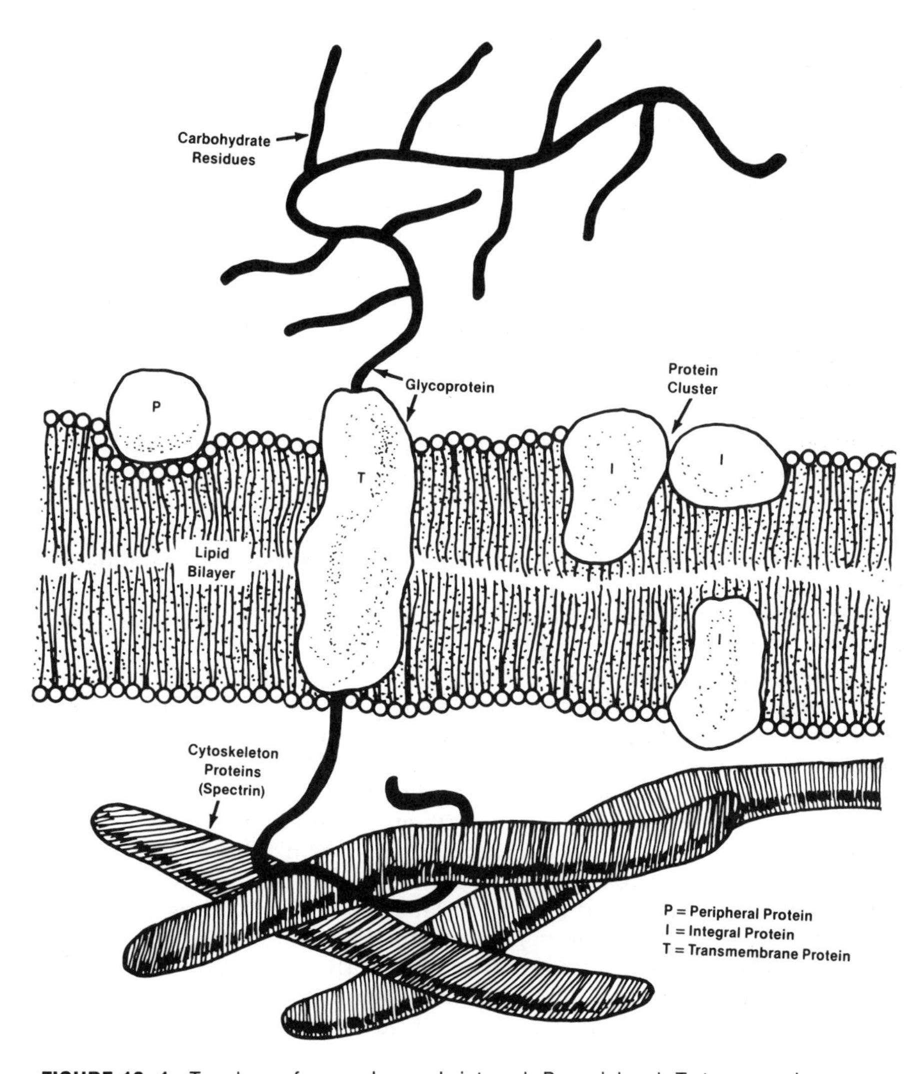

FIGURE 16–1. Topology of a membrane. I, integral; P, peripheral; T, transmembrane protein. (Reproduced from ref. 2 with permission.)

Electrophoretic bands that remain near the top of an electrophoresis gel are peripheral membrane proteins and are only weakly bound to the membrane. They are thought to be adsorbed to the hydrophilic interior membrane surface.[8] In contrast, both glycophorin and other integral membrane proteins penetrate all the way through the membrane. They contain relatively large hydrophobic regions that associate with the fatty acyl chains of neighboring phospholipids.[7] In the erythrocyte membrane, those proteins that are most loosely bound to the hydrophobic core of the phospholipid bilayer can be solubilized without the use of detergents or organic solvents. While sodium dodecyl sulfate (SDS) appears to be capable of solubilizing all the proteins of the erythrocyte membrane, some but not all can be solubilized using other detergents such as CHAPS.[9] An ideal situation for the purification of a membrane protein might be that the protein component would be solubilized alone leaving the contaminants to be removed by centrifugation. Although this is rare, solubilization or sample preparation conditions can be investigated for any membrane protein, which will limit the requirement for excessive purification steps. This saves time and improves yield.

There is no detergent or solvent known that will universally solubilize all membrane proteins. However, of the most commonly used detergents, SDS in dilute buffer is most effective. Nevertheless, SDS also generally destroys so much protein tertiary structure that activity is nearly always lost. Hjertén recently described the use of a detergent that will displace SDS and recover the activity of some soluble and insoluble proteins.[10] However, the usefulness of this detergent remains somewhat unclear. In some cases, it would be worthwhile to purify a membrane protein in the presence of SDS or other denaturing conditions, remove the denaturant by dialysis using a more gentle solvent such as a nonionic surfactant, and regain activity. Such a scheme has not yet become popular, but may be useful especially for smaller proteins that can more easily refold to their native conformation.

To understand the mechanism by which membrane proteins are solubilized (for reviews, see refs. 11–14), first consider their native environment. Each type of protein in a membrane may have slightly different surroundings. They may also have different affinities for each of the membrane components such as phospholipid, cholesterol, gangliosides, and other proteins, both membrane and nonmembrane bound. Some membrane proteins can be solubilized in aqueous buffers because they were only loosely associated with the hydrophobic core of the membrane in their native state. During the process of membrane disruption, their hydrophobic amino acids become engulfed through a change in tertiary structure or by aggregation with other (membrane) proteins. When detergents are introduced into a membrane, they begin at low concentrations by penetrating and eventually saturating the lipid bilayer. When the saturation condition has been exceeded, the membrane ruptures and forms membrane fragments. These form micelles, some of which contain membrane proteins. When proteins are purified from this condition, they are separated as aggregates or micelles. Each micelle may contain one or several different components.[15] If the micelles contain discrete categories of properties such as size or charge that can be distinguished by chromatography, then they can be separated. Often, distinct fractions containing several proteins will coelute,[16] suggesting that these components combine in mixed micelles. Solubilization conditions such as the choice of detergent(s), salt(s), temperature, or even mixing conditions may be important. For this reason, a general procedure is given in this chapter for determining the most effective solubilization procedure for maximum yield of protein mass and/or activity.

Before attempting HPLC separations, it is important to know not only whether the sample components have been solubilized, but also whether they will permeate through the HPLC column. It is helpful to visualize the sample as a mixture of micelles and mixed micelles that are suspended in a very complex solution containing water, proteins, lipids, detergents, and salts. During each purification step, the goal is to simplify the solution while retaining most if not all of the desired protein. The feasibility of using any chromatographic material can be tested by attempting some preliminary experiments on supports that are similar or identical to the support that will be used in the final purification steps. This screening procedure can be accomplished using gel filtration.[17] If the pore size of the gel filtration material is the same as that of supports used in other chromatographic steps, the solubility of the sample during gel filtration indicates whether subsequent separations are feasible.

16.3 PROCEDURES FOR MEMBRANE PROTEIN SOLUBILIZATION

The purification of membrane proteins by HPLC is possibly one of the most difficult problems in modern separation technology. Most membranes contain such a variety of components that the isolation of a single species seems nearly impossible. Then, to complicate the problem, samples are often extremely small and subject to rapid degradation from intrinsic proteolysis. Sometimes, solubilization may require several hours, as with the time-dependent monomerization of bactereorhodopsin in Triton X-100.[18] For these reasons, finding adequate solubilization and purification conditions can be frustrating. Unfortunately, there are no simple processes that can be followed with inevitable success. Josić et al. described a general procedure for the analysis of membrane proteins in which increasingly stronger solubilization conditions were used.[19] In this scheme, the sample was centrifuged after the addition of each solubilizing buffer, and the supernatant was analyzed by both gel filtration and reversed phase. This is a useful screening procedure that can be used with minimal material for rapidly analyzing a complex membrane sample. Below is a more general but tedious procedure, designed for the development of a gentle and effective purification technique (see Figure 16–2).

1. Carefully select a few detergents (e.g., SDS, Triton X-100, CHAPS) and follow this procedure for each. Dialyze the sample against buffered detergent, or add concentrated detergent to reach the desired dilution. One common buffer contains a detergent with 0.1 *M* sodium phosphate and 0.1 *M* KCl. Start with a detergent:protein ratio of 1:10 [detergent concentration should be around 1 to 5 times the critical micelle concentration

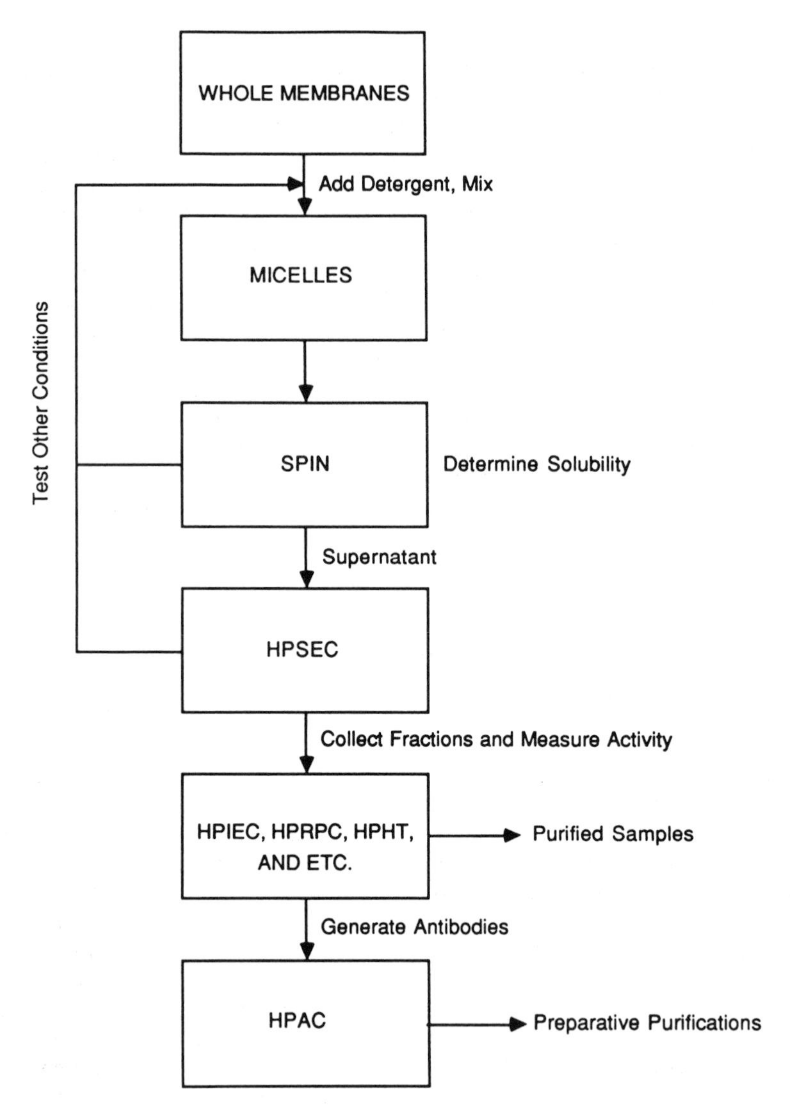

FIGURE 16–2. An outline of the procedure for solubilizing and separating membrane proteins by HPLC. Whole membranes are solubilized by adding a detergent and mixing. Micelles form and the mixture is centrifuged. The supernatant is analyzed for the membrane protein, and it is analyzed by high-performance size-exclusion chromatography (HPSEC). If the protein elutes, the solubilization and elution conditions qualify it for further purification. To maximize recovery, several conditions should be tested. The optimum procedure can be used in high-performance ion-exchange (HPIEC), reversed-phase (HPRPC), hydroxylapatite (HPHT), or other forms of chromatography. These samples can be used to generate antibodies for high-performance affinity chromatography (HPAC) if large quantities are desired.

(CMC)]. A list of detergents and their CMC can be found in a variety of reviews[9,20–23] and in Table 16–1.
2. Vortex or sonicate the sample to disrupt the membrane and form micelles in which proteins are incorporated.
3. Centrifuge and assay for the desired protein in the supernatant.*
4. Run a small portion of this sample in a gel filtration column with the same pore size as that of the desired analytical column in future purification steps, using the same detergent concentration for the eluting buffer as in the sample.
5. If the protein can be collected from the eluent, proceed. If not, change solubilization and elution conditions and repeat from step 1.
6. Collect the desired fraction and quantitate activity.
7. Repeat steps 1 to 6 with progressively higher concentrations of detergent until a ratio of 10:1, detergent:protein is achieved.†
8. Compile data and plot the amount (or percentage) of protein solubilized versus the detergent:protein ratio (or concentration of detergent).
9. Repeat steps 1–8 for the remaining detergents as described in step 1.†
10. Determine the best detergent solubilization conditions. If desired, alter pH, ionic strength, or other variables and repeat steps 1, 2, 4, 5, and 6 to try to improve recovery.†
11. Using the optimal conditions selected above, proceed to select appropriate isocratic or gradient procedures to be used during chromatography. Be sure that the sample stays soluble with the elution conditions. With this information, additional purification steps can be attempted by selecting a column and following steps 1, 2, 4 (using the analytical column), and 6 using the various procedures discussed in the sections that follow.

TABLE 16–1. Critical Micelle Concentrations (CMC) for Several Detergents in Water[a]

Detergent Name	CMC (m*M*)	Reference
CHAPS	1.4	21
Lubrol PX	0.1	21
Nonident P40	0.29	20
Octyl glucoside	25.0	21
SDS	8.2	20
Sodium deoxycholate	4–6	20
Sodium cholate	8.0	21
Triton X-100	0.240	20
Zwittergent	0.3	21

[a]The CMC of ionic surfactants is more strongly influenced by the presence of salt than those of nonionic detergents.

*If the protein is in the supernatant, proceed. If not, start again at step 1 with either another concentration of detergent or a different detergent.

†In most cases, there may not be enough sample to thoroughly follow these parts of the procedure. In that event, at least three data points should be attempted for each step.

16.4 GENERAL CHROMATOGRAPHY PROCEDURES

Once the solubilization conditions have been chosen, chromatography can proceed. Most chromatographic matrices will absorb some of the detergent that is passed through the column. The support can be saturated with detergent rapidly by eluting with the starting buffer, using twice the CMC of the detergent. Generally, about 3–5 column volumes of the eluting buffer should be passed over the column before introducing a sample. The eluting buffer will usually be the same as the ideal buffer that was determined from the solubilization experiments. Some new columns need to be conditioned before they provide reliable results. For these, several separations of standards (proteins) will indicate whether the support is ready for a more valuable (membrane) sample.

The most popular HPLC technique for purifying membrane proteins is reversed phase. However, reversed phase may destroy protein integrity. Other methods such as ion exchange, gel filtration, affinity, hydroxylapatite, and hydrophobic-interaction HPLC may be more useful, but fewer applications using these methods have been reported. Guidelines will be described for procedures in which the more common supports could be or have been used with some specific examples.

In gradient separations both the solvent concentrations and the CMC will change throughout the elution. This is the case in hydrophobic interaction, ion exchange, reversed phase, hydroxylapatite, and affinity chromatography. On the other hand, gel filtration involves a simple isocratic elution procedure that eliminates these variations. Consequently, this highly simplified technique should be attempted first. Some examples of how gel filtration has been used for membrane protein purifications follow.

16.4.1 Size Exclusion

Of all the HPLC techniques for purifying membrane proteins, high-performance size-exclusion chromatography (HPSEC) is probably the best. It provides the most information with the least effort. The molecular weight of a membrane protein can be calibrated by HPSEC when the proteins are dissolved in volatile solvents,[24] but not when detergents are used.[25] Another disadvantage of using detergents in HPSEC for these lipophilic proteins is the poor resolution. When micelles rich in membrane proteins elute in HPSEC, their corresponding peak widths are typically so much larger than for soluble proteins that an extra effort often needs to be made to improve resolution. This can be done by reducing flow rate and/or increasing the length of the column. This property of detergent-solubilized membrane proteins may be related to the nonspecific and nonstoichiometric relationship between the components of the micelles. Figure 16–3 shows a separation of whole human erythrocyte membrane proteins using HPSEC and SDS for solubilization. Figure 16–4 shows the same separation for an identical sample that had been solubilized in CHAPS. Sometimes it is advantageous to use a detergent that selectively solubilizes just a few membrane components to simplify the purification procedure.

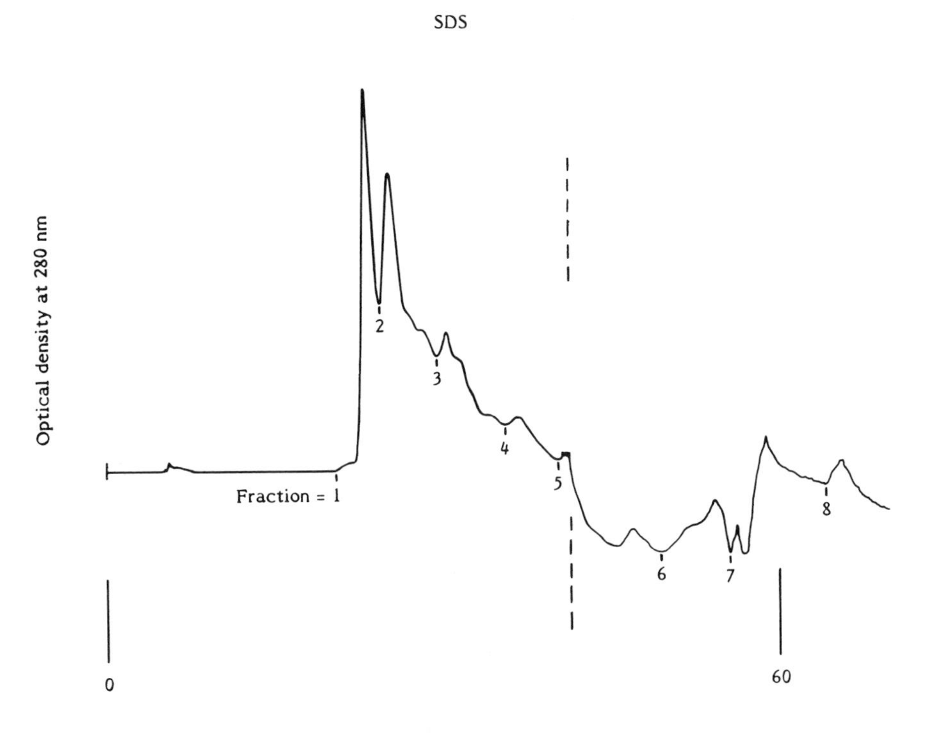

FIGURE 16–3. HPSEC of the human erythrocyte membrane proteins. SDS was used to solubilize the membranes in 0.1 *M* sodium phosphate, pH 6.5, and 10 times the CMC to a final concentration of 13 μg/ml protein. Sample was injected (200 μl) and eluted at 0.2 ml/min using a Bio-Sil 250 column (Bio-Rad), 0.1 *M* sodium phosphate, pH 6.5, and 0.8 times CMC of SDS. Absorbance was read at 280 nm and 0.32 AUFS (before fraction 4) and 0.02 AUFS (after fraction 4), as indicated by the dashed line. (Reproduced from ref. 14 with permission.)

Several other membrane proteins have been isolated by HPSEC. Sendai viral proteins were solubilized with Triton X-100, and separated using SDS in the eluent.[26] In another example, Lutensol and Brij 35 were evaluated for their abilities to solubilize a membrane protein using HPSEC. In this study SDS was used during elution to help characterize the usefulness of various buffers.[27] HPSEC and detergent solubilization have been used to separate membrane proteins from other, and sometimes more complex samples such as glycoproteins from human platelets[28] and tumors,[29] H-ATPase from the plasma membrane of *Neurospora crassa*,[30] liver extracts,[31] and the α-subunit of the acetylcholine receptor,[31] bactereorhodopsin,[18,32] β-glucocerebrosidase,[33] apolipoproteins from human serum[34,35] and insects,[36] membrane proteins from *Halobacterium halobium*,[37,38] and lung proteins.[39]

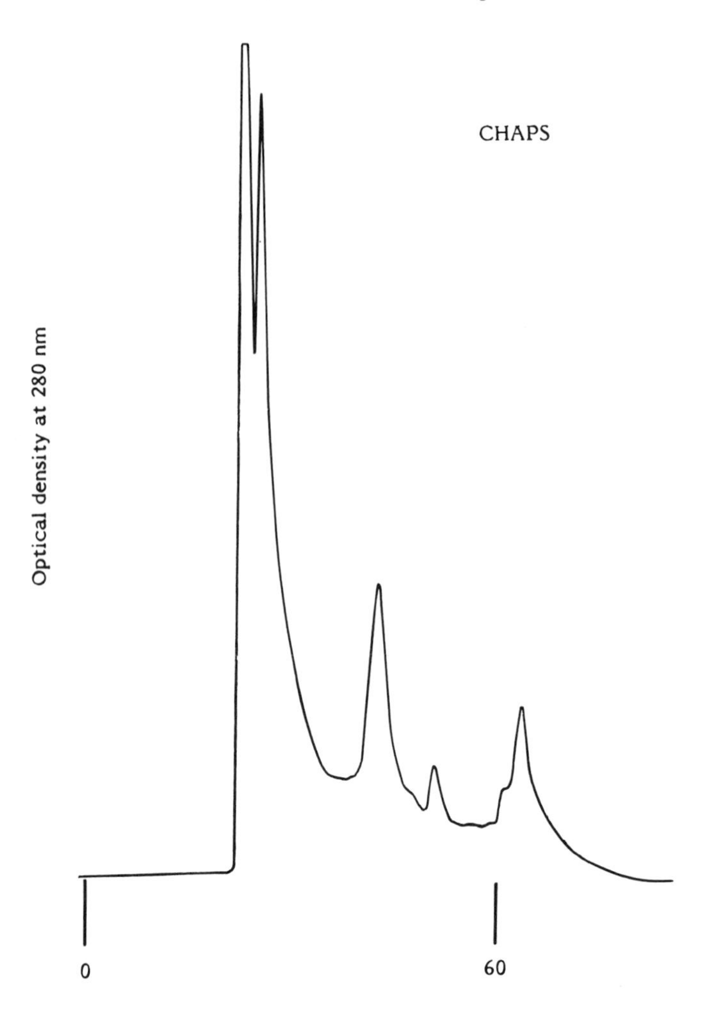

FIGURE 16–4. Separation of CHAPS solubilized erythrocyte membrane proteins by HPSEC. Membranes were solubilized in 5 times CMC of CHAPS and 0.1 *M* sodium phosphate, pH 6.5. They were then eluted using a Bio-Sil 250 column and 0.5 times CMC of CHAPS and 0.1 *M* sodium phosphate, pH 6.5 using a 0.2 ml/min flow rate. The sensitivity was set at 0.08 AUFS. (Reproduced from ref. 14 with permission.)

16.4.2 Ion Exchange

When membrane-bound proteins are separated with ion-exchange chromatography, elution is often carried out using nonionic detergents such as Tween-20, Triton X-100, or polyoxyethylene glycol alkyl ether.[26,40,41] In some cases, phosphate buffer, salt, and an organic modifier can be used for elution. In one example, influenza virus proteins were solubilized in 2% of the ionic surfactant, SDS, and isolated on a Bio-Gel DEAE-5PW (Bio-Rad) column using a salt gradient in the presence of 40% methanol and 2% SDS.[27] An example showing the high-performance ion-exchange chromatography (HPIEC) of the human erythrocyte membrane proteins is shown in Figure 16–5. Recently, new nonporous supports have been developed that offer some distinct advantages for the purification of proteins.[42–46] The nonporosity enables separations without trapping of large micelles and, generally, they provide better resolution then

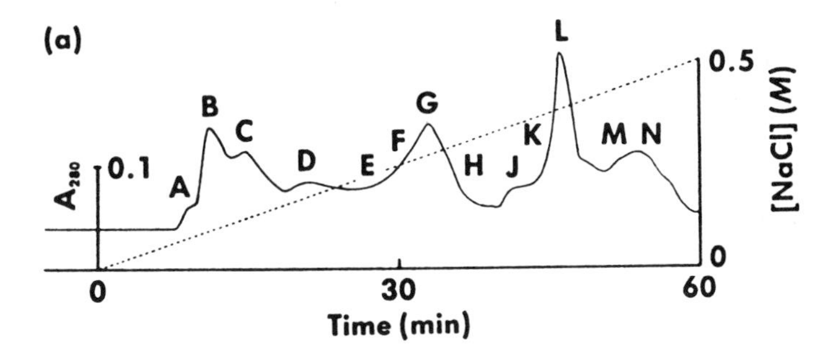

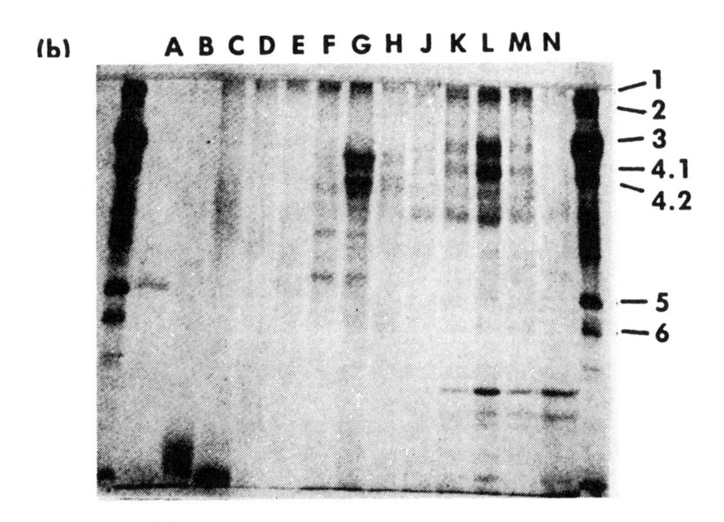

FIGURE 16–5. (a) HPIEC separation of erythrocyte membrane proteins using a DEAE HPLC column. Mobile phase, linear gradient, 0–0.5 *M* NaCl; detection, UV 280 nm; sample size, 12 mg protein solubilized in 1 ml of 1% poly(oxyethylene glycol alkyl ether)–5 m*M* EDTA–10 m*M* Tris-HCl, pH 8. (b) Electropherogram of fractions A–N from (a) in the presence of SDS using 10% polyacrylamide gel after heating at 100°C for 5 min in the solubilization buffer. HPIEC eluates were dialyzed overnight against a large excess of 50 m*M* Tris-HCl, pH 6.8, and concentrated. Right-hand numbers identify major protein fractions. (Reproduced with permission from ref. 40.)

porus ion exchangers with higher recovery. It is likely that, for the reasons outlined above, these columns will become increasingly popular for the purification of complex membrane samples.

16.4.3 Hydroxylapatite

Hydroxylapatite has been found to be useful for the purification of a number of membrane proteins.[47–53] Charles Hannum and his colleagues used high-performance hydroxylapatite (HPHT) for the separation of T-cell receptor polypeptides.[54,55] Their experiments indicated that this method would prove useful for the preparation of α- and β-chains of both mouse and human receptors. However, SDS is potentially one of the least compatible detergents for HPHT. In an extreme case, calcium from the hydroxylapatite can exchange with sodium in SDS and create an insoluble calcium dodecyl sulfate precipitate. However, this has not been reported. To the contrary, SDS has been used successfully in a number of separations with hydroxylapatite. One of the advantages of this support material for the purification of membrane proteins is its compatibility with nearly all detergents. One additional example is the purification of rhodopsin in which any of at least three detergents, tridecyltrimethylammonium bromide, Ammonyx LO, or Mega 9, can be used for solubilization and elution from HPHT.[56]

Hydroxylapatite (Bio-Gel HT or Bio-Gel HTP) has also been used to remove excess detergent from a sample. Examples using hydroxylapatite to concentrate, delipidate, and isolate protein–detergent complexes are given by Rivas et al.,[57] Riccio,[58] LeMarie et al,[59] and Sardet et al.[60] In these examples mixed micelles of nonionic detergents and lipids pass through a column packed with hydroxylapatite while solubilized protein remains adsorbed to the column material. Protein is most often released by eluting with high concentrations of sodium or potassium phosphate. An identical procedure could be applied to HPHT. When concentrations greater than 0.25 *M* sodium phosphate are required to release a protein from hydroxylapatite, cool temperatures ($\leq 10°C$) should be avoided to prevent precipitation.[58]

16.4.4 Reversed-Phase HPLC

Reversed-phase chromatography separates proteins by their hydrophobic character in the presence of organic solvents. Several membrane proteins have been successfully separated by high-performance reversed-phase chromatography (HPRPC).[36,61–64] However, proteins are sometimes lost on these columns and severe damage to the tertiary structure has been reported.[65,66] Recoveries of membrane proteins from reversed-phase columns have been reported to be low, especially when the pore size of the support was much less than 1000 Å.[67,68] Recently, reversed phase of membrane proteins using columns containing large (1000 Å) pores gave recoveries near 100% as shown in Table 16–2.[68] Resolution using this technique is generally superior to that of other methods. Reversed phase is generally an ideal method for analyzing membrane proteins, because the eluted fractions are often free of contaminants.

TABLE 16–2. Recovery of Erythrocyte Membrane Proteins with HPRPC Using 0.1% SDS for Solubilization and a 30 min Linear Gradient from 0 to 95% Acetonitrile in 0.05% TFA[a]

Column	Pore Size (Å)	Bonded Phase	Recovery (%)
Hi-Pore RP-318	330	C_{18}	31
Hi-Pore RP-304	330	C_4	26
Bio-Gel Phenyl RP+	1000	Phenyl	44
Bio-Gel Phenyl 5PW	1000	Phenyl	115

[a]Reproduced with permission from ref. 68.

Several efforts have been made to optimize HPRPC of membrane proteins.[69–72] Hukeshoven studied the use of several solvent systems including high concentrations of formic acid in *n*-propanol.[70] While these procedures may not be universally successful, reversed phase is a powerful high-resolution technique that should not be ruled out for the analysis or purification of membrane proteins.

16.4.5 Hydrophobic-Interaction HPLC

The separation mechanisms and the support matrices are similar for hydrophobic interaction (HPHIC) and HPRPC. However, HPHIC supports have much lower ligand densities and, in general, use ligands of lower hydrophobicity (C1 on phenyl in place of C18). These differences account for weaker hydrophobic interaction which probably yields the higher recoveries of membrane proteins from HPHIC than from HPRPC.[68] Generally, a decreasing ammonium sulfate gradient is used to elute sample components in HPHIC. Membrane proteins, however, may not desorb off any hydrophobic matrix under these aqueous conditions. In these cases, either detergents or other modifiers are required to encourage elution of lipophilic proteins.

Another advantage of HPHIC columns is their versatility. Some of the examples indicate that HPHIC columns can usually be used with either hydrophobic-interaction[74] or reversed-phase elution schemes. Whether a HPHIC column can be used for HPRPC separations can be determined from the manufacturer. Figure 16–6 shows the separation of viral extracts using a linear gradient from low to high concentrations of acetonitrile. In this example, recoveries were much higher than they were when a comparable reversed-phase column was used, and selectivities differed only slightly. With the HPHIC column, proteins eluted at an acetonitrile concentration approximately 10% less than with HPRPC, while retaining high activity. Similar separations of human erythrocyte membrane proteins have been reported with 100% recovery.[68]

Detergents are not commonly used in hydrophobic-interaction chromatography. However, one paper describes the separation of hydrophobic (but not membrane-bound) proteins using Brij 35 in the mobile phase. Human skin culture gelatinase was purified using a decreasing gradient of ammonium

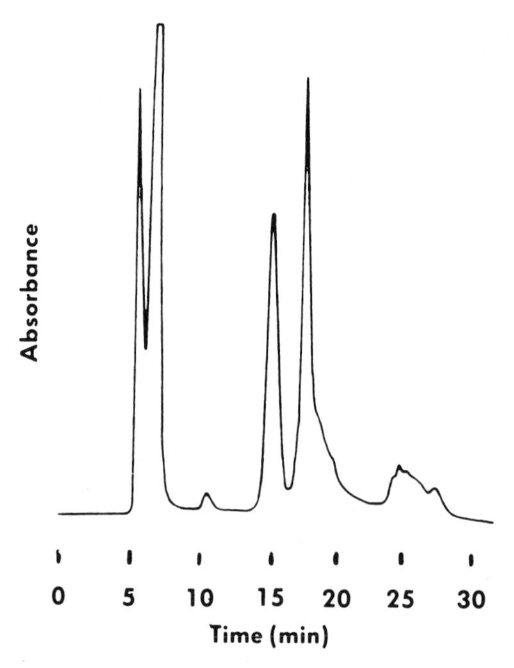

FIGURE 16–6. HPRPC separation of influenza virus proteins using an HPHIC column (Bio-Gel TSK Phenyl 5PW). Mobile phase, 25-min μl influenza virus polypeptides; sample size, 3 mg/ml protein. (From R. Mayner, N.I.H., personal communication.)

sulfate and an increasing gradient of Brij 35. The active fraction was collected near the end of the chromatogram, at about 0.08% detergent.[75]

If detergent remains in an HPHIC column, it may change the column's selectivity. The best way to remove the detergent is to first apply 1.0 or 0.5% SDS at a flow rate of 1 ml/min to remove bound proteins and detergents, followed by 50% methanol, and finally distilled water. This procedure can be used in lieu of, or in addition to, methods described previously.[76]

16.4.6 Affinity Chromatography

Affinity chromatography has been used in open column chromatography to bind ligands that will selectively adsorb a specific membrane protein. This procedure has been reported for EGF receptors,[77] muscarinic acetylcholine receptors from calf forebrain,[78] a local anesthetic binding protein from mammalian azonal membranes,[79] and the prolactin receptor from the rabbit mammary gland.[80] Recently, high-performance affinity chromatography (HPAC) columns have become available. These contain supports with either slow reacting (epoxides) or fast reacting (*n*-hydroxysuccinimide) groups that are covalently bound to the support. It is not clear from the literature whether one type or the other offers any distinct advantages for binding either membrane proteins or protein-binding ligands. However, the fast affinity materials are capable of binding ligands within a few minutes whereas covalent coupling to epoxides may take several hours. HPAC has been successfully used to purify human fibroblast membrane proteins.[81]

Affinity chromatography offers obvious advantages for the purification of membrane proteins since this technique removes the largest amount of contaminants most readily. The paradox is that antibodies are the preferred ligand, but they cannot be generated until the protein has been purified. Therefore, small quantities of membrane protein must first be isolated using ion exchange, gel filtration, hydroxylapatite or some other classical technique (see Figure 16–2). Antibodies are then generated and covalently coupled to the affinity support. The affinity column can then be used to purify large batches of membrane proteins.

16.5 CONCLUSION

There are some distinct advantages to using HPLC methods to purify membrane proteins. Some of these include speed and ease of separation. The isolated fractions are in a liquid suspension, ready for further analysis. However, largely because of the difficulties inherent in solubilizing these lipophilic materials, chromatography of membrane proteins is not trivial. This review provides a guide to assist in tailoring new separation schemes for membrane proteins by HPLC.

REFERENCES

1. F. E. Regnier, in Receptor Purification Procedures (J. Craig Venter and Len C. Harrison, eds.). Liss, New York, 1984, pp. 61–75.
2. R. S. Matson and S. C. Goheen, *LC/GC*, 4 (1986) 624.
3. S. Hjertén, H. Pan, and K. Yao, in Protides of the Biological Fluids, 29th Colloquium, 1981 (H. Peeters, ed.). Pergamon Press, New York, 1982, pp. 15–25.
4. P. Emmelot, C. J. Bos, R. P. van Hoeven, and W. J. van Blitterswijk, *Methods Enzymol.*, 31 (1974) 75.
5. J. V. Renswoule and C. Kempf, *Methods Enzymol.*, 104 (1984) 329.
6. N. N. Aronson and O. Touster *Methods Enzymol.*, 31 (1974) 90.
7. G. Fairbanks, T. L. Steck, and D. F. H. Wallach, *Biochemistry*, 10 (1971) 2606.
8. T. Steck and J. Yu, *J. Supramol. Struct.*, 1 (1974) 220.
9. L. M. Hjelmeland, *Methods Enzymol.*, 124 (1986) 135.
10. S. Hjertén, J.-L. Liao, and M. Sparrman, Membrane Protein Symposium, San Diego, California, August 3–6, 1986, abstract 201.
11. H. S. Penefsky and A. Tzagoloff, *Methods Enzymol.*, 22 (1971) 204.
12. D. A. W. Grant and S. Hjertén, *Biochem. J.*, 164 (1977) 465.
13. A. Tzagoloff and H. S. Penefsky, *Methods Enzymol.*, 22 (1971) 219.

14. C. Tanford and J. A. Reynolds, *Biochim. Biophys. Acta*, 457 (1976) 133.
15. S. Hjertén and H. Pan, *Biochim. Biophys. Acta*, 728 (1983) 281.
16. H. Ludi and W. Hasselbach, *J. Chromatogr.*, 297 (1984) 111.
17. R. S. Matson and S. C. Goheen, *J. Chromatogr.*, 359 (1986) 285.
18. R. Pabst, T. Nawroth, and K. Dose, *J. Chromatogr.*, 285 (1984) 333.
19. Dj. Josić, W. Schuett, R. Neumeier, and W. Reutter, *FEBS Lett.*, 185 (1985) 182.
20. A. Helenius and K. Simons, *Biochim. Biophys. Acta*, 415 (1975) 29.
21. L. M. Hjelmeland and A. Chrambach, *Methods Enzymol.*, 104 (1984) 305.
22. M. F. Emerson and A. Holtzer, *J. Phys. Chem.*, 71 (1967) 1898.
23. A. Helenius, D. McCaslin, E. Fries, and C. Tanford, *Methods Enzymol.*, 56 (1979) 734.
24. G. D. Swergold and C. S. Rubin, *Anal. Biochem.*, 131 (1983) 295.
25. M. LeMaire, L. P. Aggerbeck, C. Monteilhet, J. P. Andersen, and J. V. Moller, *Anal. Biochem.*, 154 (1986) 525.
26. G. W. Welling, J. R. J. Nijmeijer, R. Van der Zee, G. Groen, J. B. Wilterdink, and S. Welling-Wester, *J. Chromatogr.*, 297 (1984) 101.
27. D. H. Calam and J. Davidson, *J. Chromatogr.*, 296 (1984) 285.
28. P. J. Newman and R. A. Kahn, *Anal. Biochem.*, 132 (1983) 215.
29. P. Lambotte, J. van Snick, and T. Boon, *J. Chromatogr.*, 297 (1984) 139.
30. M. R. Sussman, *Anal. Biochem.*, 142 (1984) 210.
31. Dj. Josić, H. Baumann, and W. Reutter, *Anal. Biochem.*, 142 (1984) 473.
32. D. D. Muccio and L. J. DeLucas, *J. Chromatogr.*, 326 (1985) 243.
33. G. J. Murray, R. J. Youle, S. E. Gandy, G. C. Zirzow, and J. A. Barranger, *Anal. Biochem.*, 147 (1985) 301.
34. M. Kinoshita, M. Okazaki, H. Kato, T. Teramoto, T. Matsushima, C. Naito, H. Oka, and I. Hara, *J. Biochem.*, 94 (1983) 615.
35. D. Pfaffinger, C. Edelstein, and A. M. Scanu, *J. Lipid Res.*, 24 (1983) 796.
36. J. P. Shapiro, P. S. Keim, and J. H. Law, *J. Biol. Chem.*, 259 (1984) 3680.
37. T. Konishi and M. Sasaki, *Chem. Pharm. Bull.*, 30 (1982) 4308.
38. T. Konishi, *Methods Enzymol.*, 88 (1982) 202.
39. P. J. R. Phizackerley, M.-H. Town, and G. E. Newman, *Biochem. J.* 183 (1979) 731.
40. H. Ikigai, T. Nakae, and Y. Kato, *J. Chromatogr.*, 322 (1985) 212.
41. G. Berger, G. Girault, F. Andre, and J.-M. Galmiche, *J. Liquid Chromatogr.*, 10 (1987) 1507.
42. K. K. Unger, G. Jilge, R. Janzen, H. Giesche, and J. N. Kinkel, *Chromatographia*, 22 (1986) 379.
43. Y. Kato, T. Kitamura, A. Mitsue, and T. Hashimoto, *J. Chromatogr.*, 398 (1987) 327.
44. J. K. Duncan, A. J. C. Chen, and C. J. Siebert, *J. Chromatogr.*, 397 (1987) 3.
45. Dj. Josić, W. Hofmann, and W. Reutter, *J. Chromatogr.*, 371 (1986) 43.
46. D. J. Burke, J. K. Duncan, L. C. Dunn, L. Cummings, C. J. Siebert, and G. S. Ott, *J. Chromatogr.*, 353 (1986) 425.
47. R. S. Kaplan and P. L. Pedersen, *J. Biol. Chem.*, 260 (1985) 10293.
48. M. Kingenberg, P. Riccio, and H. Aquila, *Biochim. Biophys. Acta*, 503 (1978) 193.
49. P. Mende, H. V. J. Koble, B. Kadenbach, I. Stipani, and F. Palmieri, *Eur. J. Biochem.*, 128 (1982) 91.
50. J. P. Wehrle and P. L. Pedersen, *Arch. Biochem. Biophys.*, 223 (1983) 477.
51. C. S. Ricard and L. S. Sturman, *J. Chromatogr.*, 326 (1985) 191.
52. H. Wohlrab, A. Collins, and D. Costello, *Biochemistry* 23 (1984) 1057.
53. I. Stipani and F. Palmieri, *FEBS Lett.*, 161 (1984) 269.
54. C. Hannum, J. H. Freed, G. Tarr, J. Kappler, and P. Marrack, *Immunol. Rev.*, 81 (1984) 161.
55. Bio-Radiations, Bio Rad Laboratories, 51 (1984) 1.
56. P. A. Hargrave and J. Hugh McDowell, Department of Ophthalmology, University of Florida, Gainsville, personal communication.
57. E. Rivas, N. Pasdeloup, and M. LeMaire, *Anal. Biochem.*, 123 (1982) 194.

58. P. Riccio, in Chromatography in Biochemistry, Medicine and Environmental Research, Vol. 25(3) (A. Figero, ed.). Elsevier, New York, 1983, pp. 177–184.
59. M. LeMaire, K. E. Lind, K. E. Jorgensen, H. Roigaard, and JH. V. Moller, *J. Biol. Chem.*, 253 (1978) 7051.
60. C. Sardet, A. Tardieu, and V. Luzzati, *J. Mol. Biol.*, 105 (1976) 383.
61. K. R. Brunden, C. T. Berg, and J. F. Poduslo, *Anal. Biochem.*, 164 (1987) 474.
62. G. F. Wildner, C. Fiebig, N. Dedner, and H. E. Meyer, *Z. Naturforsch*, 42c (1987) 739.
63. B. G. Sharifi, C. C. Bascom, V. K. Khurana, and T. C. Johnson, *J. Chromatogr.*, 324 (1985) 173.
64. G. W. Welling, G. Groen, K. Slopsema, and S. Welling-Wester, *J. Chromatogr.*, 326 (1985) 173.
65. T. Takagaki, G. E. Gerber, K. Nihei, and H. G. Khurana, *J. Biol. Chem.*, 255 (1980) 1536.
66. H. G. Khorana, G. E. Gerber, W. C. Herlihy, C. P. Gray, R. J. Anderegg, K. Nihei, and K. Biemann, *Proc. Natl. Acad. Sci. U.S.A.*, 76 (1979) 5046.
67. S. C. Goheen and T. Chow, *J. Chromatogr.*, 359 (1985) 297.
68. S. C. Goheen, in Membrane Proteins (S. C. Goheen, ed.). Bio-Rad Laboratories, Richmond, CA, 1987, pp. 259–266.
69. J. Heukeshoven and R. Dernick, *Chromatographia*, 19 (1984) 95.
70. J. Heukeshoven and R. Dernick, *J. Chromatogr.*, 252 (1982) 241.
71. J. Heukeshoven and R. Dernick, *J. Chromatogr.*, 326 (1985) 91.
72. B. G. Sharifi, C. C. Bascom, U. K. Khurana, and T. C. Johnson, *J. Chromatogr.*, 324 (1985) 173–180.
73. S. C. Goheen and A. Stevens, *BioTechniques*, Jan/Feb (1985) 48.
74. S. Hjertén, *J Chromatogr.*, 159 (1978) 85.
75. J. L. Seltzer, M. L. Eschbach, and A. Z. Eisen, *J. Chromatogr.*, 326 (1985) 147.
76. Technical Bulletin 1153, Bio-Rad Laboratories, Richmond, California, 1984, pp. 1–4.
77. J. Downward, Y. Yarden, E. Mayes, G. Scrace, G. Totty, P. Stockwell, A. Ullrich, J. Schlessinger, and M. D. Waterfield, *Nature (London)*, 521 (1984) 307.
78. C. Andre, J. P. DeBacker, J. G. Guillet, P. Vanderhegden, G. Vauquelin, and A. D. Strosberg, *EMBO J.*, 2 (1983) 499.
79. M. Greenberg and T. Y. Tsony, *J. Biol. Chem.*, 259 (1984) 13241.
80. R. P. C. Shiu and H. G. Friesen, *J. Biol. Chem.*, 249 (1974) 7902.
81. J. N. Kinkel, B. Anspach, K. K. Unger, R. Wieser, and G. Brunner, *J. Chromatogr.*, 297 (1984) 167.

CHAPTER 17

Purification of Viral Proteins

Gjalt W. Welling and Sytske Welling-Wester

CONTENTS

17.1 INTRODUCTION

17.1.1 General Properties of Viruses

Viruses are among the smallest infectious microorganisms.[1] Most forms of life are susceptible to infection with the appropriate viruses. Although viral diseases have caused many plagues to mankind, most virus infections are inapparent, without signs and symptoms of clinical disease. Even with modern prevention and elimination of many of the more lethal viral diseases, infections remain the most common cause of a variety of disorders in man.

Three major properties distinguish viruses from other microorganisms: (1) the size, virus particles vary in size from 10 to 300 nm and are relatively small, while, for instance, bacteria have an approximate size of 1000 nm; (2) viruses have as genome either DNA or RNA, and do not contain both; the DNA or RNA may be double-stranded, single-stranded, and segmented; (3) virus particles are metabolically inert and are completely dependent on susceptible cells or organisms for their multiplication. They do not possess ribosomes, mitochondria, or a protein-synthesizing apparatus.

In the simpler viruses, the mature virus particle, the virion, consists of a single nucleic acid molecule surrounded by a protein coat, the capsid. The nucleic acid and the capsid together are called the nucleocapsid. More complex viruses may contain an electron-opaque center, the core. The core contains the viral DNA in the form of a torus, sometimes in association with viral proteins. The capsid is composed of a large number of capsomers. Each capsomer is made up of one or more polypeptide chains. The function of the capsid is probably to protect the nucleic acid from degradation by nucleases. Two kinds of symmetry have been recognized in capsids, icosahedral and helical. Poliovirus is an example of a virus with an icosahedral symmetry (Figure 17–1) and has been studied in detail by X-ray analysis.[2] The capsid is composed of four proteins, VP1, VP2, VP3, and VP4. The entire virus capsid consists of 60 copies of each of these proteins. The coat assembles from 12 compact aggregates, the pentamers, which contain 5 copies of each of the coat proteins. In each pentamer VP1 clusters at the top, VP2 and VP3 alternate around the foot, and VP4 provides the foundation.

A considerable number of viruses obtain a membrane or lipid bilayer by budding through the host cell surface. These viruses are called enveloped viruses. The envelope or the membrane surrounding the nucleocapsid contains virus specific glycoproteins. On electron micrographs of enveloped viruses these glycoproteins can often be seen as spikes, or outward oriented projections from the surface. The viral membrane proteins are anchored in the lipid bilayer of the envelope by a transmembrane region, a stretch predominantly consisting of 20 to 27 uncharged, hydrophobic amino acid residues. The number of membrane glycoproteins present in the envelope varies for different virus groups.

Sendai virus is an example of an enveloped virus (see Figure 17–2) and because its proteins are used as a model mixture in some of the next sections, it will be described in more detail. The virion envelope is composed of a lipid bilayer with a matrix protein (M) on the inside. Sendai virus belongs to the family of paramyxoviridea and to the genus of paramyxoviruses. Classified in

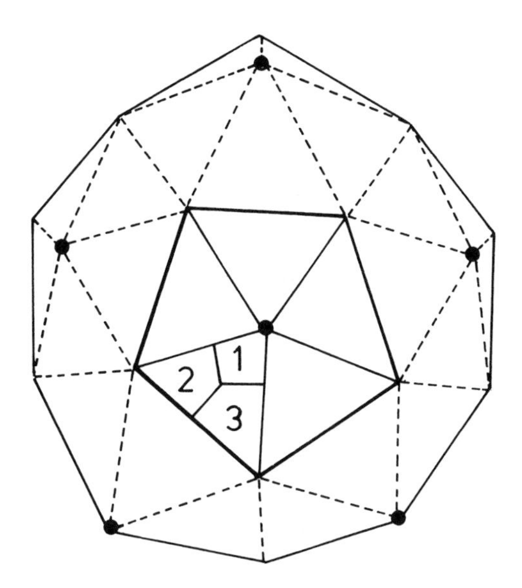

FIGURE 17–1. Schematic structure of a nonenveloped virus (poliovirus) with an icosahedral capsid. The capsomers are arranged as 60 trimers. Pentamers are indicated with a dot at the top. One pentamer is indicated in heavy lines; 1, 2, and 3, are the VP1, VP2, and VP3 proteins, respectively, of which five copies are present in each pentamer.

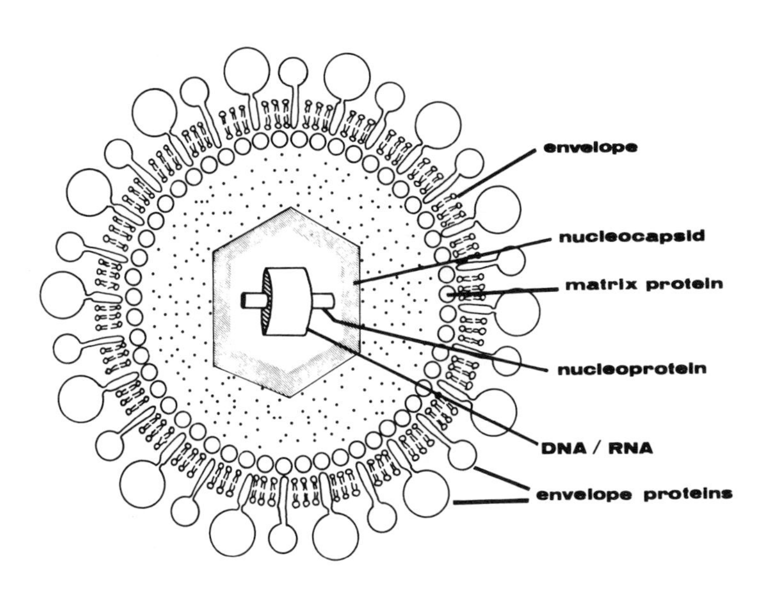

FIGURE 17–2. Schematic structure of an enveloped virus.

the same genus are four types of human parainfluenza virus, mumps virus, Newcastle disease virus, and Simian virus 5. Two glycoproteins, the hemagglutinin-neuraminidase protein (HN) and the fusion protein (F) are present in the envelope of the virus particles. The HN protein, the larger of the two, carries both hemagglutinating and neuraminidase activities. The F protein is involved in cell fusion, hemolysis, and virus penetration into the cell. During infection a precursor of the F protein, designated F_0, is produced. This biologically inactive precursor is cleaved by proteolysis into two biologically active subunits F_1 and F_2. The F_1 and F_2 subunits are linked by disulfide bridges. Both glycoproteins HN and F are able, like many other glycoproteins that are exposed on the outside of the virus particles, to induce the production of antibodies or other types of immune response. To elucidate the contribution of the individual glycoproteins to the immune response of the infected host, it is of importance to purify virual proteins. In addition, purified viral proteins can be used as vaccines.

17.1.2 Cultivation of Viruses

Viruses are intracellular parasites and can replicate only in living cells, and not in any cell-free system. In the laboratory, viruses are propagated in cell culture systems, embryonated eggs, and laboratory animals. The application of cell culture in virus research started after the discovery of antibiotics. By including antibiotics in cell culture media, contaminations were largely prevented. Prior to the 1950s, embryonated eggs and laboratory animals were the standard host for cultivation of viruses. Today, most viruses are grown in cell culture systems. However, the yield of some of the viruses (e.g., paramyxoviruses) is much higher after culturing in embryonated eggs than by growing in cell cultures. Also the purification of viruses grown in embryonated eggs is less complicated. Cell cultures, however, are essential for studies concerning replication and the regulation of virus multiplication. During virus multiplication in a susceptible cell, viral nucleic acid is replicated, virus-specific proteins are produced, and after assembly the progeny of virions are released. The virus-specific proteins produced during infection comprise basically three different functions. These proteins are involved in (1) the replication of the viral genome, i.e., virus-specific enzymes, polymerase; (2) the assembly into virions, the production of structural proteins of the virus particle; (3) the regulation of the host cell functions during virus multiplication, for instance, the presence of host-cell shutoff proteins. The proteins produced during multiplication, which are necessary as component of the virion, are called structural proteins; the remaining virus specified proteins are the nonstructural proteins.

17.1.3 Purification of Viruses

Depending on the virus protein of interest, the strategy for purification may be different. If it concerns a nonstructural protein a detergent extract of virus-infected cells can be used. For purification of structural proteins, virus particles are the preferred starting material, despite the fact that these proteins are abundantly present in infected cell extracts. Therefore, the first step in virus purification is to separate virions from the cells in which they were produced. Excreted virus from infected cells can be used or virus can be released from infected cells by controlled homogenization or by repeated freeze-thawing. Usually, virus particles are separated from contaminating cell components by several cycles of centrifugation. Low-speed centrifugation is carried out to remove the relatively large contaminating particles and rate zonal centrifugation through a gradient of sucrose or equilibrium gradient centrifugation in for instance cesium chloride or potassium tartrate separates virus particles from the remainder of the contaminants.

This classical approach to produce and isolate virus-specific proteins is gradually changing, influenced by new developments in molecular biology. Recombinant DNA techniques are employed to clone genes of virus-specific proteins in order to produce large quantities of these proteins. Virus proteins are expressed and produced in mainly four systems, prokaryotic organisms (of which *E. coli* is most widely used), yeast cells, mammalian cell cultures, and insect cell cultures. Although the amount of a particular virus protein produced by recombinant DNA techniques is much larger than during a natural infection, solubilization, and subsequent purification to separate the protein from contaminants of the expression system, is still required.

17.2 EXTRACTION AND SOLUBILIZATION OF VIRAL PROTEINS

Viral proteins are important as nonstructural or structural components of the virion. Structural viral proteins are often tightly associated with either a lipid bilayer envelope or as part of the nucleocapsid. The strongly hydrophobic character of these proteins contributes to a large extent to this strong interaction. In addition, electrostatic interactions may play a role. Although selective precipitation of a viral protein from a solution is a simple and rapid purification step, it is seldomly limited to one protein and washing steps or chromatography is necessary for final purification. To purify a protein by chromatographic methods, it has to be solubilized. Detergents, which are lipid-like substances, are often utilized for this purpose. Detergents are not only used to keep viral proteins in solution throughout a purification process but also as a first step in the purification of integral membrane proteins. Detergent molecules are able to compete with the lipids in the lipid bilayer envelope. This results in detergent–protein complexes (see Figure 17–3) that are soluble in aqueous solutions. Nonionic detergents generally do not affect the native conformation and the biological activity of the proteins and therefore they are often used for extraction but also as additive in elution buffers. Triton X-100 and the structurally rather similar detergent Nonidet P40 (NP-40) are the most popular nonionic detergents although others, like the relatively expensive octylglucoside, are also frequently used. Advantages of octylglucoside over Triton X-100 and Nonidet P40 are that it does not show UV absorbance at 280 nm and it can be removed easily by dialysis against water due to its relatively high critical

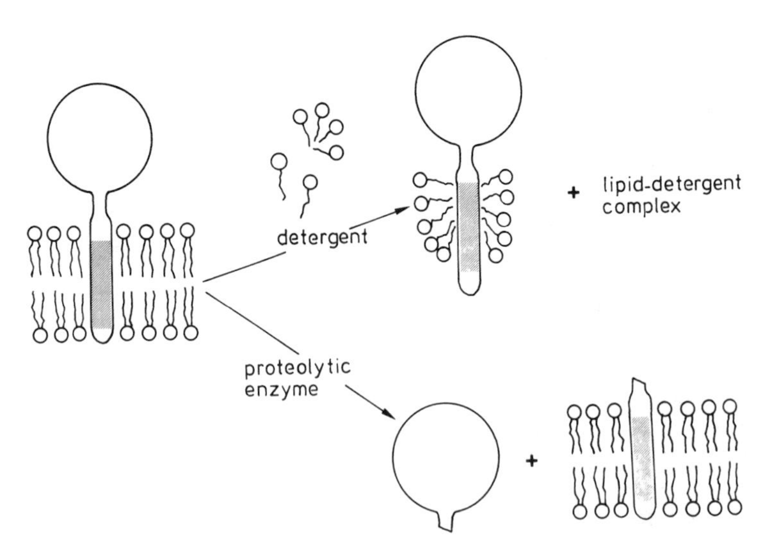

FIGURE 17–3. Detergent extraction of an integral membrane protein from a lipid bilayer envelope. A large relatively hydrophilic fragment of the protein and a complex of the hydrophobic membrane spanning region (shaded area) with the lipid bilayer may be the result of proteolytic activity present in the extract.

micelle concentration (CMC). The CMC is the concentration of a detergent monomer at which micelles, i.e., spherical bilayer aggregates of detergent molecules, begin to form. Table 17–1 lists a number of detergents.[3] In addition to the nonionic detergents, ionic detergents (e.g., sodium dodecyl sulfate and bile salts) and amphoteric detergents [e.g., 3[(3-cholamidopropyl) dimethylamino]-1-propane sulfonate (CHAPS)] can be used. During detergent extraction, proteolytic enzymes may be present originating from the preceding virus culturing. These enzymes may degrade the viral proteins to small fragments or in some cases also to large stable fragments. Proteolytic activity can be inhibited by adding protease inhibitors to the extraction medium. However, limited proteolysis can also be utilized to advantage, i.e., to obtain a large soluble fragment of the protein without its membrane-anchoring segment (see Figure 17–3). This soluble fragment may be still biologically active. Examples are the limited proteolysis of the HL-A antigen by papain treatment resulting in removal of a 10-kDa membrane anchoring fragment from the 44-kDa subunit,[9] the neuraminidase obtained by pronase treatment of influenza A virus, A2 (Singapore) 57,[10] and the hemagglutinin obtained by bromelain digestion of the X-31 strain influenza A2/Hong Kong/68.[11] A similar treatment of the 1968 influenza virus Aichi/68 resulted in a soluble trimer of the hemagglutinin. This soluble trimer was crystallized and its three-dimensional structure could be determined by X-ray crystallography.[12] In addition, organic solvents can be used to solubilize viral proteins or to extract them from a lipid bilayer. A two-phase system can be created, and proteins and viral lipids soluble in the organic phase can be separated from proteins in the aqueous phase.[13] For example, extraction of purified Rauscher murine leukemia virus suspensions with chlo-

TABLE 17–1. Critical Micelle Concentration and Micellar Molecular Weight of Detergents[a]

Detergent	Description	CMC (m*M*)	Micellar Molecular Weight
Ionic			
Sodium dodecyl sulfate		H_2O 8.13	17,000
		0.05 *M* NaCl 2.30	24,200
		0.5 *M* NaCl 0.51	38,100
Sodium cholate		13–15	900– 2,100
Sodium deoxycholate		4–6	1700–12,100
Sodium taurodeoxycholate		2–6	2,000
Nonionic			
Triton X-100	tert-$C_8\phi$ $E_{9.6}$	0.24–0.30	90,000
Nonidet P40	tert-$C_8\phi$ E_9	0.29	
Triton X-114	tert-$C_8\phi$ E_{7-8}	0.2	
Tween 80	$C_{18:1}$ sorbitan E_{20}	0.012	76,000
Emulphogen BC-720	$C_{12}E_8$	0.087	65,000
Octylglucoside	C_8 glycoside	25.0	8,000
Brij 35	$C_{12}E_{23}$	0.091	49,000
Dodecyl dimethylamineoxide		2.2	17,000
Amphoteric			
CHAPS	Bile acid derivative	4–6	6,150
Zwittergent 3-12	Sulfopropylammonium compound	3.6	

[a]Data are from refs. 4–8. C_xE_y, x refers to the number of C atoms in the alkyl chain and y to the average number of oxyethylene units; a phenyl ring is designated by ϕ; *tert*-C_8 refers to a tertiary octyl group and $C_{18:1}$ indicates an 18-carbon chain with one double bond. Reproduced from ref. 3 with permission.

roform–methanol, 2:1 (v/v) resulted in partitioning of the phosphoprotein p12 and the RNA into the aqueous phase and viral lipids to the organic phase.[14] Other viral proteins were present in the interphase layer. A similar extraction of the interphase layer in high ionic strength buffer selectively partitioned the protein p10 into the aqueous phase. The antigenicity of the proteins was preserved.

17.3 CHROMATOGRAPHIC PURIFICATION OF VIRAL PROTEINS

17.3.1 Introduction

The tendency of many viral proteins to aggregate determines the strategy for a chromatographic purification. Detergents, organic solvents, or denaturants like guanidine-HCl have to be present during chromatography to prevent aggregation. Even with these precautions, viral proteins often are eluted in broad peaks. Most chromatographic modes applicable to the more easily soluble hydrophilic proteins have been used for chromatographic purification of viral proteins, i.e., size-exclusion chromatography, ion-exchange chromatography, (bio)affinity chromatography, and reversed-phase chromatography. Gradually, high-performance liquid chromatography (HPLC) versions of these chromatographic modes became available. However, when a small amount of viral protein has to be purified from a large amount of starting material, e.g., infected cells, it is advisable to use a prepurification method, e.g., selective precipitation or extraction with or without subsequent conventional chromatography. HPLC would then be more useful in a later stage of the purification procedure.

For a variety of reasons, particular modes of chromatography are being used more often than others. Affinity chromatography with soft-gel supports are the most popular, either as immunoaffinity chromatography or as affinity chromatography with a lectin as ligand and occasionally with other ligands (see Table 17–5). High-performance affinity chromatography is less commonly used. In contrast to this, there are a considerable number of viral proteins that have been purified by HPLC (indicated by an a in Tables 17–2, 17–3, 17–4, and 17–6).

TABLE 17–2. Viral Proteins Purified by Size-Exclusion Chromatography

Proteins from	References
Borna disease virus	23[a]
Equine infectious anemia virus (EIAV)	19[a]
Influenza virus	20[a]
Sendai virus	15,[a] 18,[a] 21,[a] 24[a]
Sindbis virus	22
Tick-borne encephalitis virus	16,[a] 17[a]

[a]Viral proteins isolated by HPLC.

17.3.2 Size-Exclusion Chromatography

Two basically different approaches can be distinguished in size-exclusion chromatography. Either denaturing conditions are exploited for elution, e.g., SDS or organic solvents[15–20] or nondenaturing conditions are used, e.g., buffers with a nonionic detergent[21–23] or buffers without detergent. Viral proteins that have been purified by size-exclusion chromatography are listed in Table 17–2.

17.3.3 Ion-Exchange Chromatography

In ion-exchange chromatography, the elution conditions are generally mild. Buffers of near neutral pH containing a mild detergent (nonionic or zwitterionic) and an increasing concentration of NaCl are used for elution. Ion-exchange chromatography has been used for purification of a number of viral proteins, which are listed in Table 17–3. Sendai virus proteins have been purified both by conventional and high-performance chromatography and their purification will be discussed in more detail. To obtain an extract containing the HN, F, and M proteins, purified virions were treated with KCl-Triton X-100[38] and applied to a DEAE-BioGel A column.[35] Proteins were eluted stepwise with 0.1% Triton X-100 in 10 m*M* phosphate buffer, pH 7.2, containing 0.05 *M* NaCl or 0.5 *M* NaCl. HN protein was eluted with phosphate buffer with and without 0.05 *M* NaCl. With high salt, F protein was eluted, contaminated with HN protein. Cation-exchange chromatography on CM-Sepharose CL-6B has been exploited to purify the F protein.[36] In this case, the F protein was found in the unadsorbed fraction, while the HN protein, contaminated with F protein, was eluted between 0.15 and 0.20 *M* NaCl in 10 m*M* sodium acetate, pH 6.0, containing 0.25% Triton X-100. We have used anion-exchange HPLC on a Mono Q column for the purification of these proteins. They were eluted with a gradient from 0.15 to 1.5 *M* NaCl in 20 m*M* sodium phosphate, pH 7.2, containing 0.1% Triton X-100.[34] In contrast to the results with conventional anion-exchange chromatography, pure F protein could be eluted with the NaCl gradient. The HN protein was not adsorbed to the column under these conditions. Therefore, in a later study,[24] elution conditions were changed. As starting buffer,

TABLE 17–3. Viral Proteins Purified by Ion-Exchange Chromatography

Proteins from	References
Adenovirus	25, 26[a]
Avian myeloblastosis virus	27, 28
Bovine viral diarrhea virus	29[a]
Foot-and-mouth disease virus	30
Murine mammary tumor virus	31
Rous sarcoma virus	32
Rubella virus	33[a]
Sendai virus	24,[a] 34,[a] 35, 36
Simian foamy virus type 1	37

[a]Viral proteins isolated by HPLC.

20 m*M* Tris-HCl, pH 7.8 with 0.1% Triton X-100 was used and the proteins were eluted with a gradient to 0.5 *M* NaCl. These elution conditions allow chromatography of the HN protein and Figure 17–4 shows that it is present in fractions 4 and 5. The F protein is eluted as a broad peak, which might be due to different micellar forms or multimeric forms present in the extract, but probably also to differences in charge caused by the acidic carbohydrate chains attached to the protein. Since Triton X-100 adsorbs at 280 nm, other detergents might be preferred in the eluent. However, monitoring somewhat below or above 280 nm is a useful alternative. We have used other detergents in the eluent, e.g., 0.1% of Brij 35, octylglucoside, decylpolyethyleneglycol-300 ($C_{10}E_{5-9}$) and a similar separation was obtained. The high reactivity with monoclonal antibodies directed against the intact proteins showed that the conformation of the proteins was not affected by the chromatographic procedure (results not shown).

17.3.4 Reversed-Phase Chromatography

Reversed-phase chromatography is based on hydrophobic interaction between hydrophobic column ligands and hydrophobic sites on a protein. Proteins are generally unfolded on contact with the hydrophobic ligands and by being dissolved in an organic solvent of low pH. Therefore, in contrast to other modes of chromatography in which the protein conformation remains largely unaffected, not only surface-located interaction takes place but every hydrophobic amino acid residue and also the alkyl chain of lysine may interact. Since viral membrane proteins often are more hydrophobic than an average protein,[15,39] their elution will require relatively high concentrations of organic solvent. Viral proteins purified by reversed-phase chromatography are listed in Table 17–4. Since the hydrophobicity of a protein is related to the total number of hydrophobic groups, it is not unexpected that reversed-phase chromatography is more successful with small membrane proteins than with large membrane

TABLE 17–4. Viral Proteins Purified by Reversed-Phase Chromatography

Proteins from	References
Adenovirus	25[a]
Bovine leukemia virus	44[a]
Cytomegalovirus (CMV)	45[a]
Hepatitis A virus	43[a]
Herpes simplex cirus (HSV)	46[a]
Influenza virus	47[a]
Moloney murine leukemia virus	48[a]
Poliovirus	40,[a] 42,[a] 49[a]
Sendai virus	24,[a] 50[a]
Tick-borne encephalitis virus	17[a]

[a]Viral proteins purified by HPLC.

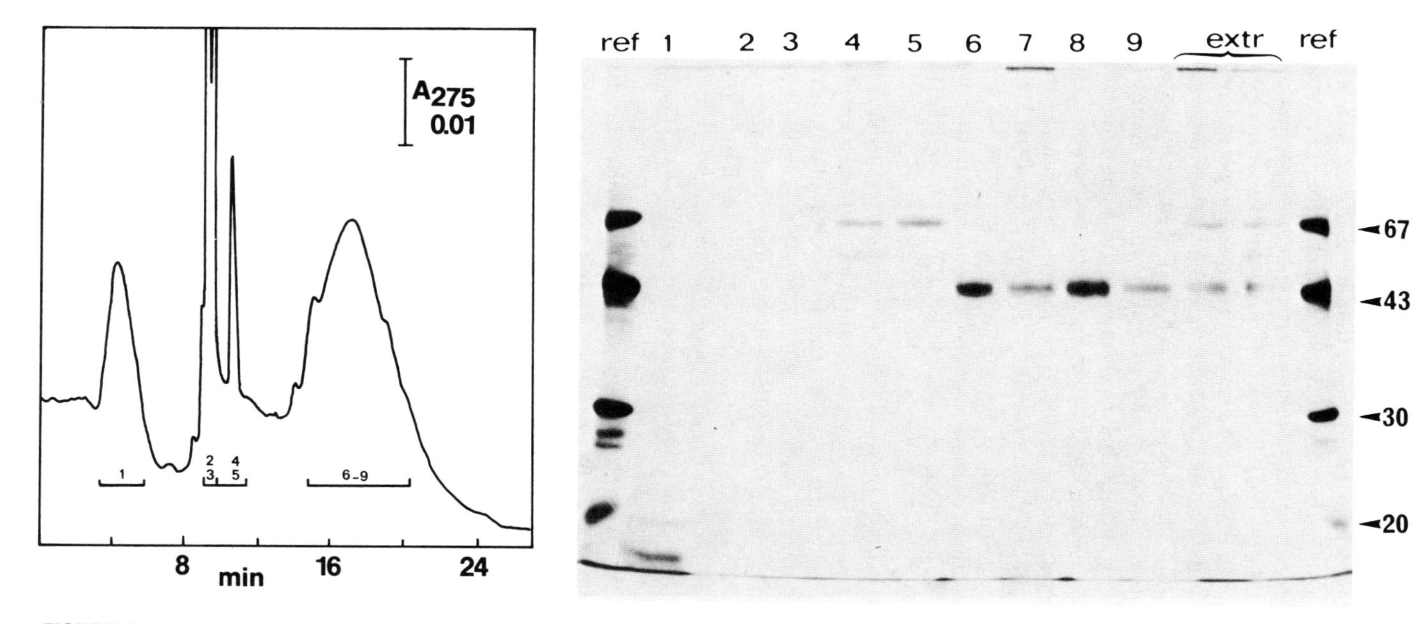

FIGURE 17–4. Anion-exchange HPLC of a Triton X-100 extract of purified Sendai virions. A Mono Q column (Pharmacia, Uppsala, Sweden) was eluted with a 24-min gradient from 20 m*M* Tris-HCl, pH 7.8, containing 0.5 *M* NaCl in the same buffer. The flow rate was 1 ml/min and the absorbance was monitored at 275 nm. Fractions 1–9 were analyzed by SDS-PAGE (10% gels). The molecular weight of reference proteins (ref) is indicated ($\times 10^{-3}$). extr, the Triton extract. (From ref. 24, reproduced with permission.)

proteins. This is illustrated by reversed-phase chromatography of a detergent extract of Sendai virus. The extract contained the fusion protein F (MW 65,000) and the dimer and tetramer of the HN protein (MW 136,000 and 272,000, respectively). These proteins could be eluted from a reversed-phase HPLC column with 100 nm pores, but broad peaks were observed.[39] This may be the result of repeated precipitation and dissolution of the proteins at the high concentration (around 50%) of acetonitrile at which they were eluted. Reduction of the proteins with dithiotreitol results in the monomeric form of the HN protein (MW 68,000) and because the disulfide bridge in the F protein is cleaved, in F_1 (MW 50,000) and F_2 (MW 13,000–15,000). The proteins present in this extract were also eluted as broad peaks, except for the small F_2 protein, which eluted as a sharp peak. In another experiment, the M protein (MW 38,000) was also present in the extract and similar results were obtained.[3] The smallest proteins, F_2 and M, were eluted as sharp peaks while the larger proteins were eluted as multiple broad peaks later in the acetonitrile gradient. These results should be taken into consideration when data are available on the size and the hydrophobicity of the protein to be purified. As a general rule, hydrophobic membrane proteins larger than 50,000 will be difficult to purify by reversed-phase chromatography.

Viral proteins may already be insoluble in the starting buffer and this is a frequently encountered problem in reversed-phase chromatography of these proteins. Although insolubility of a protein can be used in a purification procedure, chromatography requires that the proteins are soluble in the elution buffers. Not only the extreme hydrophobicity of viral membrane proteins but also other interactions, e.g., electrostatic interactions, play a role in tight structures as, for example, poliovirus (see Figure 17–1). The VP1, VP2, and VP3 proteins are tightly associated and partly intertwined. Twelve pentamers of these proteins form the capsid of poliovirus and the fourth protein VP4 lines the inner surface of the pentamers. Heukeshoven and Dernick[40] described an elegant though harsh procedure to purify these proteins by reversed-phase HPLC. Virus purified by cesium chloride-gradient centrifugation was precipitated by 10% trichloroacetic acid and redissolved in 70% formic acid. The solubilized virus preparation was applied to a C_{18} column that was eluted with a gradient of acetonitrile in 60% formic acid. Poliovirus proteins from either type 1, 2, or 3 could be purified in this way (see Figure 17–5). The high concentration of formic acid may affect the proteins. Aspartic acid–proline bonds may be cleaved and esterification of serine and threonine may occur. However, a short exposure appeared not to be harmful.[40,41] Antisera produced against VP1, VP2, and VP3 were bound by intact poliovirus and these antisera neutralized the virus at low titers.[42] It is expected that proteins from other, structurally similar picornaviruses, e.g., rhinovirus, hepatitis A virus (HAV), can be purified by this procedure. Gauss-Müller et al.[43] showed that from an HAV particle pool with a buoyant density of 1.20 g/ml they could purify HAV capsid proteins VP1, VP3, and VP0. VP0 is cleaved into VP2 and VP4 in the final assembly step. This particle pool presumably consists of immature virions that are composed of VP1, VP3, and the precursor VP0. Antibodies against the HPLC-purified proteins reacted positively in an immunofluorescence assay with HAV-infected cells but they did not neutralize the virus in cell culture assays.

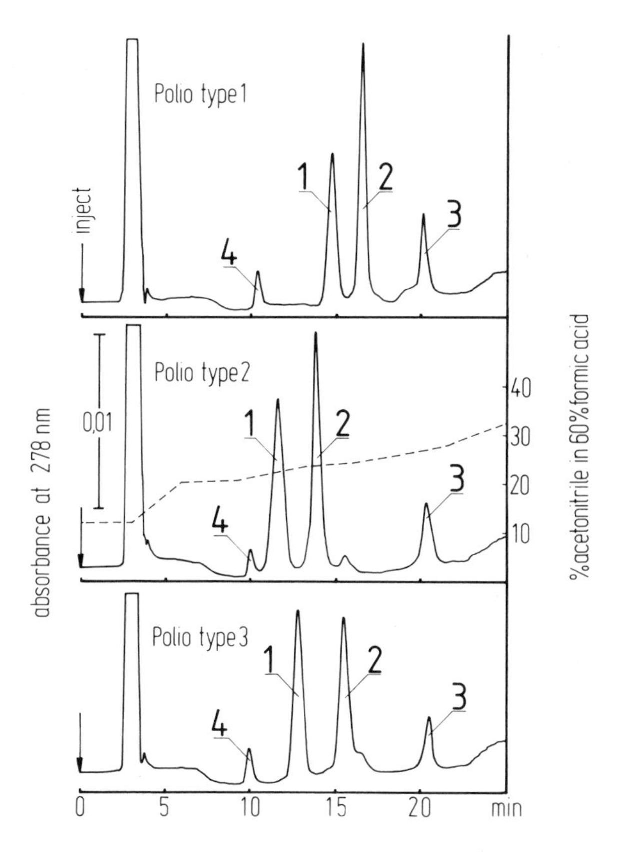

FIGURE 17–5. RP-HPLC of capsid proteins from poliovirus types 1, 2, and 3. Virus (30–40 μg) in 50 μl of 3 *M* CsCl was precipitated with trichloroacetic acid, redissolved in 50 μl 70% formic acid and injected. The column (a Baker widepore C_{18}, 250 × 4.6 mm) was eluted with 60% formic acid with an acetonitrile gradient as indicated by the dotted line. The flow rate was 1 ml/min and the absorbance was monitored at 278 nm. (From ref. 40, reproduced with permission.)

17.3.5 Affinity Chromatography

Viral proteins purified by affinity chromatography are listed in Table 17–5. In affinity chromatography, proteins are selectively adsorbed to a column ligand that may be any compound with a high affinity for the protein. For example, substrates of enzymes or enzyme inhibitors can be coupled as ligand and can be used to purify enzymes. A low-molecular-weight DNA binding protein of mouse mammary tumor virus (MMTV) was isolated in this way.[84] MMTV particles were disrupted in 6 *M* guanidine-HCl and the viral proteins were fractionated by size-exclusion chromatography on a BioGel column. Fractions that

TABLE 17–5. Viral Proteins Purified by Affinity Chromatography

Proteins from	References
Adenovirus	51, 52
Avian myeloblastosis virus	28
Avian sarcoma virus QV2	53
Borna disease virus	23[a]
Bovine herpesvirus type 1	54,[a] 55[a]
Bovine leukemia virus	56
Bovine viral diarrhea virus	57
Canine distemper virus	58[a]
Cytomegalovirus (CMV)	59,[a] 60,[a] 61[a]
Epstein–Barr virus (EBV)	62,[a] 63,[a] 64
Equine infectious anemia virus (EIAV)	65
Foot-and-mouth disease virus (FMDV)	66[a]
Friend leukemia virus	67, 68
Granulosis virus (GV)	69
Hepatitis A virus	70[a]
Hepatitis B virus	71[a]
Herpes simplex virus (HSV)	72,[a] 73,[a] 74,[a] 75,[a] 76,[a] 77[a]
Human immunodeficiency virus (HIV)	78[a]
Infectious bronchitis virus (IBV)	79,[a] 80
Measles virus	81,[a] 82, 83
Mouse mammary tumor virus	84
Murine leukemia virus	85, 86[a]
Myxoviruses	87, 88, 89, 90
Nuclear polyhedrosis virus	91
Polyoma virus	92[a]
Respiratory syncytial virus (RSV)	93[a]
Rous sarcoma virus	32[a]
Semliki forest virus (SFV)	97
Sendai virus	94,[a] 95,[a] 96
Simian foamy virus type 1	37
Sindbis virus	98
Vaccinia virus	99
Varicella zoster virus (VZV)	100,[a] 101,[a] 102[a]

[a]Viral proteins purified by immunoaffinity chromatography.

bound DNA were pooled and further purified by affinity chromatography on single-stranded calf thymus DNA Sepharose. Analysis of DNA-binding fractions revealed a single polypeptide of 14 kDa.

Lectins are proteins that naturally occur in plants and that have a high affinity for certain carbohydrate moieties of a protein. The first application of this type of affinity in glycoprotein fractionation was by Lloyd[103] and Donelly and Goldstein,[104] who prepared insoluble forms of concanavalin A as a column ligand. The interactions between carbohydrate groups and lectins are not affected by low concentrations of detergents, which makes this method suitable for the purification of membrane proteins. However, there is a lack of specificity, and a wide range of sugar residues generally binds to lectin columns with different affinities. Elution is achieved with buffers containing increasing concentrations of α-methylmannoside, glucose, mannose, fucose, lactose, *N*-acetylgalactosamine, etc. Besides the aspecific interactions of sugar residues with lectin columns, the presence of contaminating host cell glycoproteins in a virus preparation makes a multistep purification procedure for viral proteins necessary. By such an approach, a small glycoprotein E3 was purified from Sindbis virus-infected cells.[98] Virions were removed from the culture fluid by precipitation with polyethyleneglycol, and subsequent differential ethanol precipitation was applied to remove serum proteins and to precipitate the E3 protein. The E3 protein was resuspended and further purified by size-exclusion chromatography on an Ultrogel AcA-34 column that was eluted with 50 m*M* Tris buffer, pH 7.3, containing 0.1 *M* NaCl, 0.01% NaN_3, 60 μg/ml phenylmethylsulfonyl fluoride (PMSF), 0.1% SDS, and 0.1% 2-mercaptoethanol. The E3-containing fractions were precipitated with ethanol, resuspended, and subjected to ion-exchange chromatography on Sephadex DE-52. The elution was performed with a salt gradient (from 20 m*M* Tris buffer to 50 m*M* Tris buffer containing 450 m*M* NaCl, both in 0.5% Triton X-110, 0.01% NaN_3, 20 μg/ml PMSF, pH 7.2). After ethanol precipitation, E3 protein was dissolved in 50 m*M* Tris buffer, pH 7.3, containing 100 m*M* NaCl, 0.5% Triton X-100, 0.01% NaN_3, 0.1 m*M* $MnCl_2$, 20 μg/ml PMSF and loaded on a lentil lectin column. The column was extensively washed, 0.23 ml/min for 10 h. E3 protein was eluted with 100 m*M* α-methylmannoside in the same buffer as mentioned above. From 270 mg of culture fluid proteins, 4 mg of pure E3 was isolated with a recovery of 38%.

Immunoaffinity chromatography is one of the most specific ways to purify a particular protein. An antibody directed against a protein is used as a tool in its purification. Particularly useful in this respect are monoclonal antibodies. Monoclonal antibodies are monospecific and react not only with one particular protein, but binding is even restricted to a specific part of protein, called epitope. Binding of monoclonal antibodies to proteins may be protein conformation dependent, and the reaction site is then called a discontinuous epitope. If the monclonal antibodies bind to a linear part of the protein, the epitope is continuous and not dependent on the structure of the protein. The production and isolation of monoclonal antibodies do not require a purified protein. Mice can be immunized with a mixture of viral proteins, and screening and selection procedures will reveal hybridomas that produce monoclonal antibodies, only recognizing one specific protein. In this most widely used system for affinity chromatography monoclonal antibodies are coupled to a solid phase to isolate the antigen (protein) from a fluid phase. The disadvantages of this approach are that (1) the antibody specificity can be altered or inactivated during the coupling procedure, (2) leakage of the antibody from the solid phase may occur, and (3) steric hindrance of the antigen–antibody interaction may complicate the purification. An important advantage of immunoaffinity chromatography is that it combines a specific purfication step with a concentration step. This makes it especially suitable for the purification of virus proteins, which usually are present in relatively low quantities in extracts from virus-infected cells.

Buffers generally used for the elution in immunoaffinity chromatography are as follows:

1. high or low pH buffers,[23,54,55,58,59,61,62,74,81,93–95,102] e.g., ethanolamine (pH 11.2), glycine-HCl (pH 2–3);
2. chaotropic agents,[60,66,70–72,75–77,79,100,101] e.g., 3 *M* K-, Na-, NH_4-thiocyanate;
3. high salt concentrations,[63,78] e.g., 4 *M* $MgCl_2$, 3 *M* NaCl;
4. denaturant,[32] e.g., 6 *M* guanidine-HCl;
5. free ligand,[92] e.g., peptides, substrate proteins.

Most elutions are performed in the presence of a nonionic detergent.

Immunoaffinity chromatography was used to purify the two surface glycoproteins of measles virus, the hemagglutinin protein (H) and fusion protein (F), and the nonglycosylated matrix protein (M) from an extract of cells infected with the virus.[81] Cells that had been infected for 2–4 days with measles virus were disrupted in lysis buffer: 10 m*M* Tris buffer, pH 7.8, containing 150 m*M* NaCl, 600 m*M* KCl, 0.5 mM $MgCl_2$, 2% Triton X-100, 1 m*M* PMSF, and 1% aprotinin. The insoluble cellular debris was removed by ultracentrifugation, and the supernatant containing soluble viral and cellular proteins was subjected to immunoaffinity chromatography. Proteins were allowed to adsorb batchwise, to Sepharose 4B, to which monoclonal antibodies to H, F, or M protein were coupled. Columns were packed and washed three times (3 column volumes) with washing buffer: 10 m*M* Tris buffer, pH 8.0, 1 m*M* EDTA, 0.1% NP-40, or with 0.1% octyl glucoside. Elution was performed with 3 *M* KSCN and 0.1% NP-40 in washing buffer, or with 0.2 *M* glycine, pH 3.0, and 0.1% octylglucoside. Measles H and M protein were purified in one desorption step, as shown by SDS-PAGE. The purification of F protein required two steps. Elution with 3 *M* KSCN showed a strong enrichment of the F protein, but cellular actin and some other proteins were also present in the eluate. An additional washing step with 1 *M* KSCN removed the actin, while the F protein was eluted with 3 *M* KSCN in pure form, as judged by SDS-PAGE analysis. The effect of the elution conditions on the morphology of measles H and F proteins was studied by electron microscopy. The morphology of F peplomers could be recognized in material that was eluted with 3*M* KSCN, whereas H peplomers were found only in material eluted by 0.2 *M* glycine, pH 3.0. Removal of detergent of the H preparations caused the appearance of aggregates, but the F peplomer showed a tendency to aggregate in the presence of detergent. Antisera prepared by immunization with purified H, F, and M proteins showed that the anti-H and anti-F sera interfered with the biological properties of these proteins. Radioimmunoprecipitation confirmed the purity of the protein preparations since only the antigen used for immunization was precipitated.

17.3.6 Other Modes of Chromatography

Other modes of chromatography used for purification of viral proteins are listed in Table 17–6 and include chromatography on glass wool or controlled pore glass[44,108] and on hydroxylapatite.[105–107, 109] Two examples will be given. Schultz et al.[44] observed that siliconized controlled pore glass adsorbed preferentially proteins with molecular weights lower than 30,000. In this way, a bovine

TABLE 17–6. Viral Proteins Purified by Other Modes of Chromatography

Proteins from	References
Bovine leukemia virus	44
Corona virus	105[a]
Sendai virus	106
Vaccinia virus	107
Western equine encephalitis virus	108
Yellow fever virus	109

[a]Viral proteins purified by HPLC.

leukemia virus preparation was enriched for gp60, while p12, p15, and p24 were eluted from the glass beads with acetonitrile and p30 with 60% acetonitrile containing 0.1 *M* NaCl.

Ricard and Sturman[105] used high-performance hydroxylapatite chromatography to purify two distinct 90-kDa subunits of the envelope glycoprotein E_2 from a coronavirus (murine hepatitis virus). The polypeptides were separated by a linear gradient of 0.15 to 0.5 *M* sodium phosphate, pH 6.8, containing 0.1% SDS. To utilize SDS with hydroxylapatite, calcium was omitted from the phosphate buffer. This reduced column lifetime to 12 to 15 separations.

17.4 PRACTICAL EXAMPLE OF SIZE-EXCLUSION HPLC OF VIRAL PROTEINS

Despite the relatively low peak capacities in size-exclusion HPLC, it is possible to use this HPLC mode in the purification of viral membrane proteins by taking advantage of the special features of these proteins. Viral membrane proteins tend to aggregate, which is very plausible, because they generally exist as multimers in their natural environment. Hydrophobic interaction between nonpolar amino acid side chains plays an important role in this association. This type of interaction between the monomers of viral proteins can often be modulated by detergents. By varying the amount or type of detergent in a detergent extract of a virus preparation, multimers dissociate or associate. In addition, reduction of disulfide bridges between monomers may convert multimeric forms of a viral protein to its monomeric form. We have used this approach in the purification of Sendai virus proteins by size-exclusion HPLC. Reduction by 20 m*M* dithiothreitol converts the HN multimers to their monomeric form (MW 68,000) and the F protein to F_1 (MW 50,000) and F_2 (MW 13,000–15,000). The molecular weight of F_2 is sufficiently different to allow purification by size-exclusion HPLC, however, the 68-kDa and 50-kDa proteins are difficult to separate in this way. When the sample is made 4% in SDS and not reduced prior to chromatography in 0.1% SDS in 50 m*M* sodium phosphate, pH 6.5, the elution pattern shown in Figure 17–6 was obtained. SDS-PAGE showed that peaks a, b, and c contained the tetramer of HN (HN_4), the

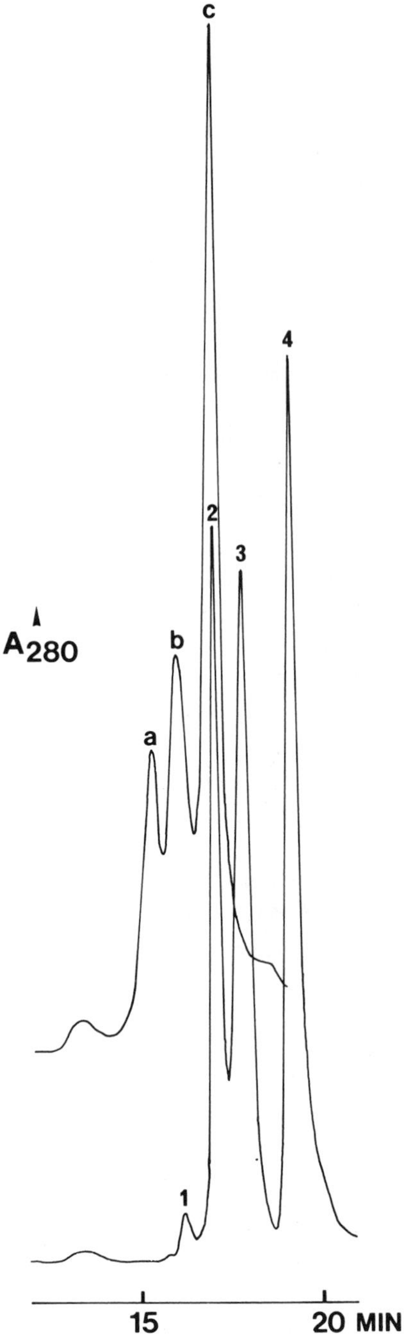

FIGURE 17–6. Size-exclusion HPLC of a detergent extract of Sendai virus. Purified virions (20 mg of virus protein) were extracted with decylpolyethyleneglycol-300 at a final concentration of 2% (w/w) for 20 min at room temperature. The detergent-to-viral-protein ratio was 2 (w/w). After centrifugation at 100,000 *g* (1 h), extracted viral proteins were present in the supernatant. Portions of 200 μl extract were made 4% in SDS, heated for 3 min in a boiling waterbath, and than applied to a Zorbax GF-450 column (two 25 cm × 9.4 mm columns in tandem) that was eluted with 50 m*M* sodium phosphate, pH 6.5, containing 0.1% SDS. The flow rate was 1 ml/min and the absorbance was monitored at 280 nm. (a) The tetramer of the HN protein; (b) the dimer of the HN protein; (c) the F protein. For comparison, the elution pattern of a mixture of reference proteins is also shown. (1) The dimer of bovine serum albumin (136 kDa); (2) bovine serum albumin (68 kDa); (3) ovalbumin (43 kDa); (4) trypsin inhibitor (20 kDa).

dimer of HN (HN_2), and the fusion protein F, respectively. For comparison, an elution pattern of reference proteins is given (MW: 1, 136,000; 2, 68,000; 3, 43,000; 4, 20,000). This procedure results in a satisfactory separation between HN_4, HN_2, and F. When the detergent extract is applied to the column without any pretreatment, i.e., no 4% SDS added, no boiling, no reduction, the elution pattern in Figure 17–7A is obtained. SDS-PAGE shows that all peaks that were eluted between 14 and 20 min contained F protein, while the first two peaks contained HN_4 and HN_2, respectively. Under such conditions, the F protein exists in multimeric forms with molecular weights similar to those of the dimeric and tetrameric form of HN. Preincubation for 1 h at 60°C results in the elution pattern shown in Figure 17–7B. The amount of monomeric F protein (the third peak) starts to increase. Boiling for 3 min at 100°C results in the pattern shown in Figure 17–7C. F protein, completely in its monomeric form, is present only in the third peak and the elution pattern is very similar to that shown in Figure 17–6. In all these examples, 0.1% SDS is present in the elution buffer. This may affect the structural integrity of the proteins. Studies with monoclonal antibodies directed against intact HN and F have shown that after chromatography, the F protein is still immunologically active, in contrast to the HN protein.[110] Higher immunological activities were observed

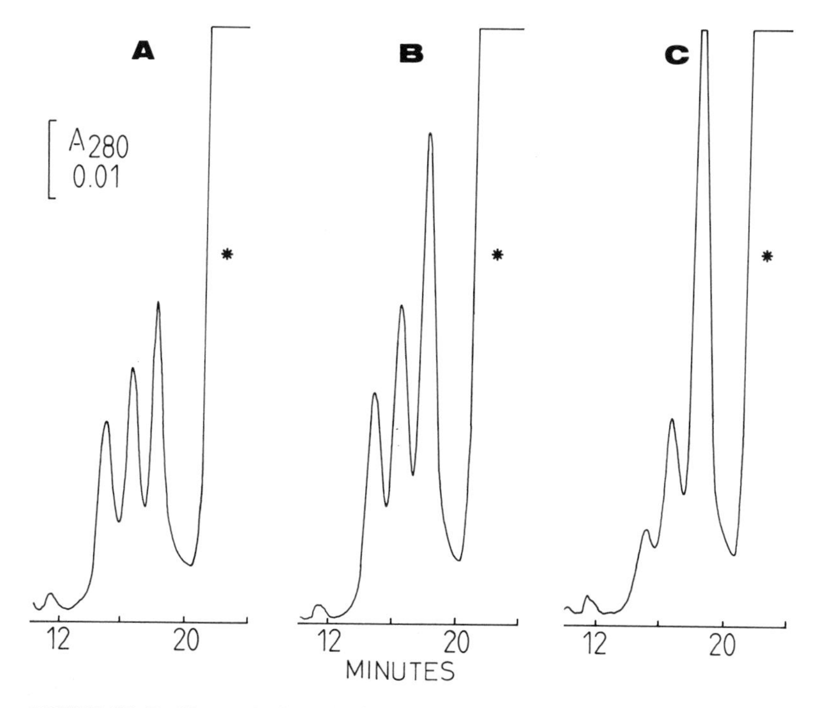

FIGURE 17–7. Size-exclusion HPLC of a Triton X-100 extract of purified Sendai virions on a TSK 4000SW column (60 cm × 7.5 mm). Elution conditions, see Figure 17–6. No SDS was added prior to chromatography. (A) Without any preincubation; (B) with preincubation at 60°C; (C) with 3 min boiling at 100°C. The Triton X-100 peak is indicated by an asterisk.

when 0.05% sarkosyl (dodecylmethylglycine sodium salt) or 0.1% octylglucoside was present in the elution buffer. However, in the latter case, proteins stayed together and could not be separated. In general, peaks are broader when nonionic detergents are present in the eluent, which means that their use in size-exclusion HPLC is limited to special cases. This is illustrated by the following example. A Triton X-100 extract of Sendai virus was applied to a TSK 4000SW column that was eluted with 0.1% Triton X-100 in 50 m*M* sodium phosphate, pH 6.5. Because of interference of the phenyl ring in Triton X-100 with detection at 280 nm, the absorbance was monitored at 286 nm. Under these mild conditions, broad peaks were observed (see Figure 17–8). SDS-PAGE showed that they contained multimeric forms of the F and the HN protein. The large peak of Triton X-100 is followed by a peak containing HN^-,

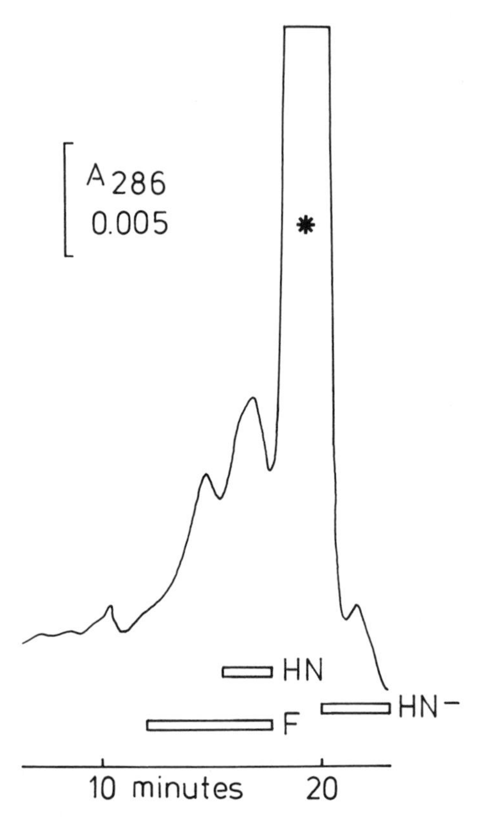

FIGURE 17–8. Size-exclusion HPLC of a Triton X-100 extract of Sendai virus on a TSK 4000SW column (60 cm × 7.5 mm) that was eluted with 50 m*M* sodium phosphate, pH 6.8, containing 0.1 *M* NaCl and 0.1% Triton X-100. The flow rate was 1 ml/min and the absorbance was monitored at 286 nm. The Triton X-100 peak is indicated by an asterisk.

which is an HN molecule without its membrane anchoring region and a monomeric molecular weight of 55,000. Presumably because it lacks this region that is rich in hydrophobic amino acid residues, it does bind fewer or no detergent molecules and is eluted relatively late. Fragments like HN^- are the result of limited proteolysis (see Figure 17–3), and this phenomenon is observed more often with integral membrane proteins.[9–12] Therefore, limited proteolysis studies of viral membrane proteins might be worthwhile to obtain large relatively hydrophilic fragments.

Size-exclusion HPLC may give unexpected results when detergent extracts of related viruses are analyzed. When different strains of Newcastle disease virus were studied by size-exclusion HPLC, Triton X-100 extracts of strain Mukteswar always contained multimeric HN, while such extracts from the vaccine strain LaSota always contained the monomeric form of HN (see Figure 17–9). This may be useful not only in the analysis of related virus strains but also in the purification of particular viral proteins.

17.5 CONCLUSIONS

So far, affinity chromatography, more specifically, immunoaffinity chromatography, has been the most popular method for purification of viral proteins. Before monoclonal antibodies became widely available as specific ligands in affinity chromatography, generally poor results were obtained with affinity chromatography alone. Multistep chromatographic procedures were necessary to purify a viral protein. However, it should be noted that also with monoclonal antibodies, it is not always possible to obtain a pure protein. An antibody molecule is a globular structure with a molecular weight of 150,000 and like any other protein molecule, its surface is composed of hydrophobic and hydrophilic regions. As a consequence, an immunoaffinity column may act as a hydrophobic column and an ion-exchange column. Other proteins, such as membrane proteins, may associate not only with the immunoglobulin ligand but also with the protein to which the monoclonal antibody is directed. This means that washing procedures are of paramount importance in order to remove aspecifically bound proteins. Even then it may be necessary to combine immunoaffinity chromatography with other modes of chromatography. Another aspect of immunoaffinity chromatography concerns the binding strength. In many cases, harsh denaturing conditions are necessary for elution of proteins, which may affect the biological activity of the protein. It may be worthwhile to explore the possibilities of other modes of chromatography.

Size-exclusion chromatography, preferably in its high-performance version, is useful only when the desired protein has a large difference in molecular mass compared to the other components in a mixture.[111] This may occur with integral membrane proteins as, for example, was shown for Sendai virus integral membrane proteins. In general, size-exclusion chromatography will be useful in multidimensional chromatography, i.e., combined with other modes of chromatography.

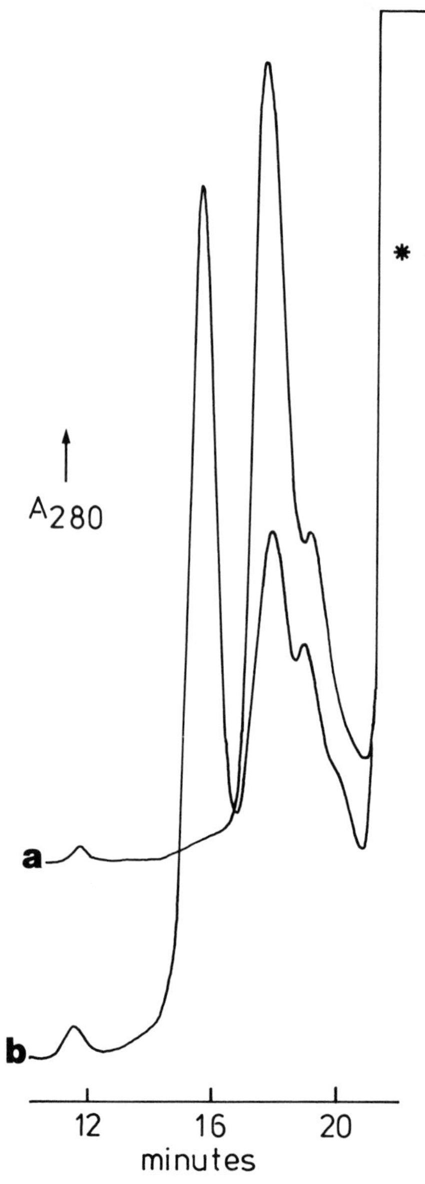

FIGURE 17–9. Size-exclusion HPLC of Triton X-100 extracts of Newcastle Disease virus strains. Elution conditions, see Figure 17–6. (a) Strain LaSota; (b) strain Mukteswar. The Triton X-100 peak is indicated by an asterisk.

The mild conditions employed in ion-exchange chromatography are attractive when the protein has to retain its biological activity, and the high-performance versions of this mode of chromatography will greatly facilitate the rapid determination of optimal elution conditions. When smaller amounts (micrograms) of protein have to be purified, nonporous columns for ion-exchange chromatography are recommended. Although the loading capacity is low, chromatography is rapid and yields are generally high, presumably because proteins interact only with the surface of the column particles.

Reversed-phase chromatography or rather reversed-phase HPLC, since the proteins in Table 17–4 are all purified by HPLC, has a denaturing effect on most proteins. Although antibodies produced against reversed-phase HPLC-purified proteins may still react with the intact virus or virus protein,[40] this is not the way to purify a biologically active protein in general. Larger viral membrane proteins (more than 50 kDa) are difficult to purify by reversed-phase HPLC,[3,25] which limits its use to the analysis of smaller viral proteins, for example, for amino acid sequence studies.

REFERENCES

1. B. N. Fields and D. M. Knipe, Fundamental Virology. Raven Press, New York, 1986.
2. M. Hogle, M. Chow, and D. J. Filman, *Science*, 229 (1985) 1358.
3. G. W. Welling, R. Van der Zee, and S. Welling-Wester, *J. Chromatogr.*, 418 (1987) 223.
4. A. Helenius and K. Simons, *Biochim. Biophys. Acta*, 415 (1975) 29.
5. C. Tanford and J. A. Reynolds, *Biochim. Biophys. Acta*, 457 (1976) 133.
6. A. Helenius, D. R. McCaslin, E. Fries, and C. Tanford, *Methods Enzymol.*, 56 (1979) 734.
7. L. M. Hjelmeland and A. Crambach, *Methods Enzymol.*, 104 (1984) 305.
8. A. Gonenne and R. Ernst, *Anal. Biochem.*, 87 (1978) 28.
9. T. Springer, J. Strominger, and D. Mann, *Proc. Natl. Acad. Sci. U.S.A.*, 71 (1974) 1539.
10. J. T. Seto, R. Drzeniek, and R. Rott, *Biochim. Biophys. Acta*, 113 (1966) 402.
11. C. M. Brand and J. J. Skehel, *Nature (London)*, 238 (1972) 145.
12. I. A. Wilson, J. J. Skehel, and D. C. Wiley, *Nature (London)*, 289 (1981) 366.
13. J. Van Renswoude and C. Kempf, *Methods Enzymol.*, 104 (1984) 329.
14. J. L. Olpin and S. Oroszlan, *Anal. Biochem.*, 103 (1980) 331.
15. G. W. Welling, K. Slopsema, and S. Welling-Wester, *J. Chromatogr.*, 397 (1987) 165.
16. G. Winkler, F. X. Heinz, and C. Kunz, *J. Chromatogr.*, 297 (1984) 63.
17. G. Winkler, F. X. Heinz, F. Guirakhoo, and C. Kunz, *J. Chromatogr.*, 326 (1985) 113.
18. G. W. Welling, G. Groen, K. Slopsema, S. Welling-Wester, *J. Chromatogr.*, 326 (1985) 173.
19. R. C. Montelaro, M. West, and C. J. Issel, *Anal. Biochem.*, 114 (1981) 398.
20. D. H. Calam and J. Davidson, *J. Chromatogr.*, 296 (1985) 285.
21. G. W. Welling, K. Slopsema, and S. Welling-Wester, *J. Chromatogr.*, 359 (1986) 307.
22. A. J. Crooks, J. M. Lee, and J. R. Stephenson, *Anal. Biochem.*, 152 (1986) 295.
23. B. Haas, H. Brecht, and R. Rott, *J. Gen. Virol.*, 67 (1986) 235.
24. G. W. Welling, J. R. J. Nijmeijer, R. Van der Zee, G. Groen, J. B. Wilterdink, and S. Welling-Wester, *J. Chromatogr.*, 297 (1984) 101.

25. M. Green and K. H. Brackmann, *Anal. Biochem.*, 124 (1982) 209.
26. M. Waris and P. Halonen, *J. Chromatogr.*, 397 (1987) 321.
27. D. J. Marciani and J. D. Papamatheakis, *J. Biol. Chem.*, 255 (1980) 1677.
28. K. Moelling, K.-W. Sykora, K. E. T. Dittmar, A. Scott, and K. F. Watson, *J. Biochem.*, 254 (1979) 3738.
29. P. Kårsnäs, J. Moreno-Lopez, and T. Kristiansen, *J. Chromatogr.*, 266 (1983) 643.
30. S. J. Shire, L. Bock, J. Ogez, S. Builder, D. Kleid, and D. M. Moore, *Biochemistry*, 23 (1984) 6474.
31. A. S. Dion, D. C. Farwell, A. A. Pomenti, and C. J. Williams, *Virology*, 135 (1984) 417.
32. A. Hizi, W. Wunderli, and W. K. Joklik, *Virology*, 93 (1979) 146.
33. L. Ho-Terry and A. Cohen, *Arch. Virol.*, 84 (1985) 207.
34. G. W. Welling, G. Groen, and S. Welling-Wester, *J. Chromatogr.*, 266 (1983) 629.
35. D. M. Urata and J. T. Seto, *Intervirology*, 6 (1975/76) 108.
36. Y. Fukami, Y. Hosaka, and K. Yamamoto, *FEBS Lett.*, 114 (1980) 342.
37. A. B. Benzair, A. Rhodes-Feuilette, J. Lasneret, R. Emanoil-Ravier, and J. Peries, *Arch. Virol.*, 87 (1986) 87.
38. A. Scheid and P. W. Choppin, *Virology*, 57 (1974) 475.
39. M. O. Dayhoff, L. T. Hunt, and S. Hurst-Calderone, Atlas of Protein Sequence; Structure, Vol. 5, Suppl. 3. National Biomedical Research Foundation, Washington, DC, 1978, p. 363.
40. J. Heukeshoven and R. Dernick, *J. Chromatogr.*, 326 (1985) 91.
41. G. E. Tarr and J. W. Crabb, *Anal. Biochem.*, 131 (1983) 99.
42. R. Dernick, J. Heukeshoven, and M. Hilbrig, *Virology*, 130 (1983) 243.
43. V. Gauss-Müller, F. Lottspeich, and F. Deinhardt, *Virology*, 155 (1986) 732.
44. A. M. Schultz, T. D. Copeland, and S. Oroszlan, *Virology*, 135 (1984) 417.
45. R. B. Clark, J. A. Zaia, L. Balce-Directo, and Y-P. Ting, *J. Virol.*, 49 (1984) 279.
46. S. Welling-Wester, T. Popken-Boer, J. B. Wilterdink, J. Van Beeumen, and G. W. Welling, *J. Virol.*, 54 (1985) 265.
47. M. A. Phelan and K. A. Cohen, *J. Chromatogr.*, 266 (1983) 55.
48. L. E. Henderson, R. Sowder, T. D. Copeland, G. Smythers, and S. Oroszlan, *J. Virol.*, 52 (1984) 492.
49. J. Heukeshoven and R. Dernick, *J. Chromatogr.*, 252 (1982) 241.
50. R. Van der Zee, S. Welling-Wester, and G. W. Welling, *J. Chromatogr.*, 266 (1983) 577.
51. R. Kornfeld and W. S. M. Wold, *J. Virol.*, 40 (1981) 440.
52. H. Persson, M. G. Katze, and L. Philipson, *J. Virol.*, 42 (1982) 905.
53. A. Ueno, M. Kohno, A. Ishihama, and K. Toyoshima, *J. Biochem.*, 86 (1979) 929.
54. S. Van Drunen Littel-van den Hurk and L. A. Babiuk, *Virology*, 144 (1985) 215.
55. S. Van Drunen Littel-van den Hurk and L. A. Babiuk, *Virology* 144 (1985) 204.
56. S. G. Devare and J. R. Stephenson, *J. Virol.*, 23 (1977) 443.
57. M. F. Coria, M. J. F. Schmerr, and A. W. McClurkin, *Arch. Virol.*, 76 (1983) 335.
58. E. Norrby, G. Utter, C. Örvell, and M. J. G. Appel, *J. Virol.*, 58 (1986) 536.
59. E. Gonczol, F. Hudecz, B. Ianacono, B. Dietzschold, S. Starr, and S. A. Plotkin, *J. Virol.*, 58 (1986) 661.
60. F. Hudecz, E. Gonczol, and S. A. Plotkin, *Vaccine*, 3 (1985) 300.
61. D. R. Gretch, M. Suter, and M. F. Stinski, *Anal. Biochem.*, 163 (1987) 270.
62. G. R. Nemerow, M. F. Siaw, and N. J. Cooper, *J. Virol.*, 58 (1986) 709.
63. B. Vroman, J. Luka, M. Rodriguez, and G. P. Pearson, *J. Virol.*, 53 (1985) 107.
64. B. Strnad, T. Schuster, R. Klein, and R. H. Neubauer, *Biochim. Biophys. Acta*, 98 (1981) 1121.
65. R. C. Montelaro, M. West, and C. J. Issel, *J. Virol. Methods*, 6 (1983) 337.
66. B. H. Robertson, D. O. Morgan, D. M. Moore, M. J. Grubman, J. Card, T. Fischer, G. Weddell, D. Dowbenko, and D. Yansura, *Virology*, 126 (1983) 614.

67. J. Schneider, H. Schwarz, and G. Hunsmann, *J. Virol.*, 29 (1979) 624.
68. J. Schneider, H. Falk, and G. Hunsmann, *J. Virol.*, 33 (1980) 597.
69. T. Yamamoto, H. Kita, and Y. Tanada, *J. Gen. Virol.*, 45 (1979) 371.
70. J. V. Hughes and L. W. Stanton, *J. Virol.*, 55 (1985) 395.
71. D. E. Wampler, E. B. Buynak, B. J. Harder, A. C. Herman, M. R. Hilleman, W. J. McAleer, and E. M. Scolnick, in Modern Approaches to Vaccines (R. M. Chanock and R. A. Lerner, eds.). Cold Spring Harbor Laboratory, Cold Spring Harbor, NY, 1984, pp. 251–254.
72. R. J. Eisenberg, M. Ponce de Leon, L. Pereira, D. Long, and G. H. Cohen, *J. Virol*, 41 (1982) 1099.
73. D. J. Vaughan, L. M. Banks, D. J. Purifoy, and K. L. Powell, *J. Gen. Virol.*, 65 (1984) 2033.
74. G. E. Kikuchi, S. A. Baker, S. D. Merajver, J. E. Coligan, M. Levine, J. C. Glorioso, and R. Nairn, *Biochemistry*, 26 (1987) 424.
75. Y. Kino, T. Eto, K. Nishiyama, N. Ohtomo, and R. Mori, *Arch. Virol.*, 89 (1986) 69.
76. R. B. Baucke and P. G. Spear, *J. Virol.*, 32 (1979) 779.
77. M. Zweig, S. D. Showalter, D. J. Simms, and B. Hampar, *J. Virol.*, 51 (1984) 430.
78. W. G. Robey, L. O. Arthur, T. J. Matthews, A. Langlois, T. D. Copeland, N. W. Lerche, S. Orozlan, D. P. Bolognesi, R. V. Gilden, and P. J. Fischinger, *Proc. Natl. Acad. Sci. U.S.A.*, 83 (1986) 7023.
79. A. Mockett, *J. Virol. Methods*, 76 (1983) 335.
80. J. A. Lancer and C. R. Howard, *J. Virol. Methods*, 1 (1980) 121.
81. T. M. Varsanyi, G. Utter, and E. Norrby, *J. Gen. Virol.*, 65 (1984) 355.
82. P. Casali, P. J. G. Sissons, R. S. Fujinami, and M. B. A. Oldstone, *J. Gen. Virol.*, 54 (1981) 161.
83. G. A. Lund and A. A. Salmi, *J. Gen. Virol.*, 56 (1981) 185.
84. L. O. Arthur, C. W. Long, G. H. Smith, and D. L. Fine, *Int. J. Cancer*, 22(1978) 433.
85. W. L. McLellan and J. N. Ihle, *Virology*, 89 (1978) 547.
86. O. Alaba, M. J. Rogers, and L. W. Law, *Int. J. Cancer*, 24 (1979) 608.
87. T. Kristiansen, M. Sparrman, and L. Heller, *J. Bioscience*, 5 (1983) *suppl. 1*, 149.
88. M. Sparrman, J. L. Ocho, and T. Kristiansen, *Protides Biol. Fluids*, 27 (1980) 431.
89. T. Kristiansen, *Protides Biol. Bluids*, 23 (1975) 663.
90. F. X. Bosch, A. Mayer, and R. T. C. Huang, *Med. Microbiol. Immunol.*, 168 (1980) 249.
91. C. C. Payne and J. Kalmakoff, *J. Virol.*, 26 (1978) 84.
92. G. Walter, A. M. Hutchinson, T. Hunter, and W. Eckhart, *Proc. Natl. Acad. Sci. U.S.A.*, 79 (1982) 4025.
93. E. E. Walsh, M. W. Brandriss, and J. J. Schlesinger, *J. Gen. Virol.*, 66 (1985) 409.
94. M. N. Al-Ahdal, I. Nakamura, and T. D. Flanagan, *J. Virol.*, 54 (1985) 53.
95. R. Van der Zee, G. W. Welling, and S. Welling-Wester, *J. Chromatogr.*, 327 (1985) 377.
96. M. J. Gething, J. M. White, and M. D. Waterfield, *Proc. Natl. Acad. Sci. U.S.A.*, 75 (1978) 2737.
97. K. Mattila, *Biochim. Biophys. Acta*, 579 (1979) 62.
98. J. T. Mayne, C. M. Rice, E. G. Strauss, M. W. Hunkapiller, and J. H. Strauss, *Virology*, 134 (1984) 338.
99. H. Shida and S. Dales, *Virology*, 111 (1981) 56.
100. Z. Wroblewska, D. Gilden, M. Green, M. Devlin, and A. Vafai, *J. Gen. Virol.*, 66 (1985) 1795.
101. W. E. Friedrich and C. Grose, *J. Virol.*, 49 (1984) 992.
102. K. Shiraki and M. Takahashi, *J. Gen. Virol.*, 61 (1982) 271.
103. K. O. Lloyd, *Arch. Biochem. Biophys.*, 137 (1970) 460.
104. E. H. Donelly and I. Goldstein, *Biochem. J.*, 118 (1970) 679.

105. C. S. Ricard and L. S. Sturman, *J. Chromatogr.*, 326 (1985) 191.
106. T. Semba, Y. Hosaka, and F. Sakiyama, *Biken J.*, 22 (1979) 71.
107. B. Moss and E. N. Rosenblum, *J. Biol. Chem.*, 247 (1972) 5194.
108. K. Yamamoto and B. Simizu, *Appl. Environ. Microbiol.*, 40 (1980) 240.
109. V. Deubel, V. Mouly, M. Girard, and J. P. Digoutte, *Ann. Virol.*, (*Inst. Pasteur*) 133E (1982) 429.
110. S. Welleing-Wester, C. Örvell, B. Kazemier, and G. W. Welling, *J. Chromatogr.*, 443 (1988) 255.
111. G. W. Welling and S. Welleing-Wester, in HPLC of Macromolecules (R. W. Oliver, ed.). IRL Press, Oxford, 1989, p. 77.

CHAPTER 18

HPLC Purification of Monoclonal Antibodies

Bohdan Pavlu

CONTENTS

18.1 INTRODUCTION

The development of different column materials for the separation of biomolecules has opened several possibilities for purifying monoclonal antibodies (mAb) by HPLC. Monoclonal antibodies are immunoglobulins of different classes, where IgG is the dominating class, produced by a single B lymphocyte cell raised against a single antigenic epitope (determinant). The immunoglobulins comprise a group of glycoproteins in which the basic unit consists of two identical light polypeptide chains (molecular weight 25,000) and two identical heavy polypeptide chains (molecular weight 50,000–77,000) linked together by disulfide bonds. Five distinct classes of immunoglobulins (Ig) are known, namely, IgG, IgA, IgM, IgD, and IgE. Some of these classes are further divided into several subclasses, IgG having four such subgroups.[1]

There is great and increasing interest in using mAb in various fields, such as medicine, diagnostics, immunopurification, and laboratory techniques. Since the techniques to produce mAb were first published by Kohler and Milstein in 1975, several reports on their isolation have appeared. The classical way to purify mAb is carried out on DEAE-anion exchanger and by protein A-Sepharose affinity chromatography.[2,3] During the last few years, however, a variety of new purification procedures have been reported, such as anion exchange,[4] hydroxyapatite,[5] hydrophobic interaction,[6] cation exchange,[7] protein-A affinity chromatography,[8] and chromatofocusing.[9]

For all the above-mentioned techniques, we now have highly efficient separation matrices that can be used together with automated chromatographic equipment such as HPLC (high-performance liquid chromatography), FPLC (fast protein liquid chromatography), and similar devices. The limitation for mAb purification by HPLC is the amount of material to be purified at each run. The definition of small-scale and large-scale purification is today difficult and largely depends on the purpose the purified antibodies are to be used for, as discussed by Oestlund.[10] The amount of mAb that can be purified depends to a large degree on how the sample was pretreated and what techniques were used for its purification. However, it can be stated that a suitable purification scale for laboratory scale HPLC techniques is up to 25 mg mAb. In our laboratory, we found that 1–5 mg of protein per ml of column gel matrix is a suitable amount. All the methods can of course be scaled up, but then some modifications of the sample injector are usually necessary for use with large sample volumes. We routinely use a 5-ml sample loop either once, or in several consecutive injections, with sample volumes up to 30 ml.

The choice of the purification method used is highly individual and may depend on the preferred column matrix, or on the equipment already available in the laboratory. A more correct method of selection is the degree of purification attainable, which varies with the properties of the individual antibodies. Methods based on general properties of proteins such as differences in charge and hydrophobicity can be highly successful in separating the mAb from major contaminants in one case but unsuccessful in another case.

The most prominent contaminants in ascitic fluid, which is a very concentrated sample (3–15 mg mAb/ml), are lipids, cell debris, albumin, transferrin, and host immunoglobulins. The ascites fluid can be purified preferably by ion-exchange techniques because the high loading capacity of anion and cation exchangers makes them eminently suitable. Hydroxyapatite should not be used as the first chromatographic step even though the matrix is known for very high protein binding capacity. When cell culture supernatant is used, the sample usually has a low mAb concentration (0.01–0.1 mg/ml) and is contaminated by albumin, transferrin, bovine IgG, and phenol red, used as an indicator dye. Cell culture supernatant should be concentrated before chromatography, if the sample volume causes some difficulties. Besides ion-exchange chromatography other chromatographic techniques could be used to concentrate the sample on the column. A convenient concentration procedure based on the high capacity of hydroxyapatite powder (HTP, Bio-Rad Laboratories) was reported by Juarez-Salinas et al.,[11] where HTP powder is added directly to the sample and adsorbing proteins on the gel with consecutive washing and desorption steps. Cell culture medium can even be concentrated by ultrafiltration.

Sample preparation is the most important step in the purification of mAb when high-performance liquid chromatographic methods are used. All the common HPLC columns used, e.g., Mono Q, Mono S, and Phenyl 5 PW, can be damaged by small particles and lipoproteins if they are not removed before application onto the column. The capacity for most column matrices is about 1–5 mg protein/ml gel except for the hydroxyapatite matrix whose capacity is about 50 mg protein/ml gel. By ammonium sulfate precipitation[12] as the first purification step, the total amount of impurities is decreased and consequently the separating capacity of the column is employed more efficiently for mAb itself.

18.2 SAMPLE PREPARATION

Before HPLC separation, an important step in the purification process is removal of small particles from the sample, as these can shorten the lifetime of the column. Lipoproteins are then removed and finally any IgG present is precipitated with ammonium sulfate prior to chromatography. These precautions should be taken despite the risk of losing antibody activity.[7,13,14,15] By this precipitating step, the immunoglobulin content of the sample is raised and the purification procedure on the column is more effective. The technique used for the preparation of the sample will depend to a larger extent on the subsequent chromatographic fractionation.

When dealing with ascitic fluids it is always advisable to remove lipid material, as this will rapidly clog the column, particularly if it is an anion exchanger. The methods for removing lipoproteins include dextran sulfate precipitation,[16] precipitation by polyvinylpyrrolidone (PVP), Plasdone K 26/28 (Povidone USP) (GAF Corp., 1361 Alps Road, Wayne, NJ 07470),[17] or by caprylic acid treatment.[18] Proteins that may coagulate are removed by calcium chloride treatment,[11] as described below.

18.2.1 Polyvinylpyrrolidone Treatment

The clarification procedure and lipoprotein precipitation can be more effective if the sample is frozen before PVP treatment. We use the following clarification procedures on samples first treated with ammonium sulfate and then frozen. After thawing, the sample was turbid. Solid polyvinylpyrrolidone (PVP) was added (3%, w/v) to the sample, which was then stirred at 4°C for 4 h. After centrifugation at 17,000 *g*, the supernatant was filtered through a Millipore filter, Millex-HV, or similar membrane. Sometimes we found desalting on small prepacked columns of Sephadex (PD 10 or NAP) very effective when sample turbidity was low, in which case we omitted PVP treatment, or, when PVP treatment was not effective, we used these columns after centrifugation. All these techniques must be tested individually for the different samples. The small prepacked columns of Sephadex mentioned above are also very effective for removing the phenol red that is added to the culture medium as a pH indicator. If not eliminated, it adsorbs to the HPLC column matrix and is difficult to remove.

18.2.2 Dextran Sulfate Treatment

Precipitation of lipoproteins with dextran sulfate was originally reported by van Dalen et al. and by Ballorad et al.[16,19] for IgM and IgG, respectively. The following procedure was used: for each milliliter of protein solution, 0.04 ml of 10% dextran sulfate, and 1 ml of 1 mol/liter $CaCl_2$ solution was added. The sample was then stirred for 15 min and centrifuged at 20,000 *g* for 15 min. The precipitate was discarded and the sample dialyzed against buffer A (the chromatographic buffer) used for the chosen chromatographic method.

18.2.3 Calcium Chloride Treatment

Sample preparation designed to remove lipoproteins and other proteins that can cause column clogging was reported by Juarez-Salinas et al.[11] After collection of the ascites fluid, conversion of fibrinogen to fibrin is promoted by adding calcium chloride solution (0.1 mol/liter) to a final concentration of 1 mmol/liter. This will accelerate the clotting process and allow clot removal before chromatography. The use of heparin to prevent clot formation is not recommended, since it may be inadvertantly removed during the sample preparation procedure or during the chromatography process, resulting in clot formation inside the column. Clot formation is completed by keeping the ascites at room temperature for 2 h, when the fibrin clot is detached and removed from the tube wall with a wooden applicator stick. The ascites fluid is then kept overnight at 4°C, and any new clots are then removed. Cell debris is then removed by centrifugation at 10,000 *g* for 30 min at 4°C and any remaining particular material by centrifugation at 100,000 *g* for 60 min at 4°C. The lipid layer can then be aspirated from the top of the sample whereafter the sample can be used for chromatography or for ammonium sulfate treatment after filtration through a 0.22-μm filter.

18.2.4 Ammonium Sulfate Treatment

Ammonium sulfate precipitation is very useful for all immunoglobulins as a first step in the purification procedure.[12] It brings about considerable enrichment and removes about 50% by weight of contaminating proteins, reducing the load in subsequent steps, though some mAbs are denatured by this procedure.[7,13–15]

However, ammonium sulfate precipitation can be omitted if a higher content of impurities in the sample can be accepted, or if an mAb purification method is used, where the precipitation step is unnecessary (e.g., affinity chromatography).

The ammonium sulfate precipitation procedure is done as follows. Dissolve 100 g of ammonium sulfate in 100 ml of water at room temperature and allow it to stand for 1–2 days. Make sure the solution is saturated. The ascitic fluid containing mAb is collected from the intraperitoneal cavity, centrifuged at 2500 *g* for 10 min to remove cells and other large particles, and finally diluted (1 + 1) with 0.15 mol/liter sodium chloride. The diluted ascites fluid can be stored at −20°C if not used immediately. Before the precipitating procedure, small amounts of buffer (stock solution, e.g., 1 mol/liter Tris-HC1, pH 8.0) are added to the ascitic fluid (1 part buffer stock solution + 9 parts ascites fluid) to maintain a stable pH during precipitation. The solution should be filtered or centrifuged if it contains particles. Precipitation should be performed at +4°C. To the diluted ascitic fluid, equal volumes of saturated ammonium sulfate solution (4°C) should be added slowly, under gentle stirring (avoid foaming) with a magnetic stirrer. At about 15–20% saturation, the solution starts to become turbid. Addition of saturated ammonium sulfate is continued until 50% saturation is reached. Stirring is continued for at least 1 h. Sometimes 50% saturation is not necessary and a lower degree of saturation can be sufficient to precipitate some specific immunoglobulins, but this of course must be tested experimentally.

The next step involves centrifugation for 20 min at 10,000 *g*. The supernatant is discarded and the sediment is washed twice with 50% (or weaker, see above) ammonium sulfate, and recentrifuged. If the liquid surface after centrifugation is covered by a film of lipoproteins, this should be removed with a Pasteur pipette. The sediment is dissolved in a small volume of buffer (preferably the one used for the subsequent chromatography), and ammonium sulfate is removed either by dialysis against the same buffer, or by gel filtration. Recently, techniques have been developed for removing salts (ammonium sulfate or others) by ultrafiltration through membrane filters, or by centrifugation with membrane cones, Centriflo (Amicon). Dialysis is very slow and inefficient as a method for adjusting the ionic strength, but because some antibodies, e.g., IgM, mouse IgG_{2b}, and IgG_3 in particular, are usually insoluble at low ionic strengths, it is the safest method.

Before purification of monoclonal antibodies by HPLC, the desalting and buffer exchange procedure with Sephadex G-25 or its equivalent is a very useful method, and even if some antibodies are precipitated by low ionic strength, this desalting method is rapid and effective. To avoid the risk of precipitation because of low ionic strength it is possible to use buffers of higher ionic strength and choose a chromatographic procedure that is compatible with these conditions. The Pharmacia prepacked PD 10 columns, which we have used frequently, are very convenient. For sample volumes exceeding 2.5 ml, several column passages are necessary or the use of several columns. If this procedure is used, Sephadex G-25 medium is the preferred packing gel.

18.2.5 Procedure for Desalting on Sephadex G-25 Medium

Swell the Sephadex G-25 in distilled water for 1 h using a boiling water bath. Avoid vigorous mechanical mixing (especially magnetic stirring), which can damage the beads. Each gram gives about 5 ml of swollen gel. Cool to operating temperature and prepare a slurry with about 75% settled gel. Pack the required volume of gel into a column. Use a short, wide bed whenever possible (1.6 × 20 cm, 2.6 × 40 cm, or 5.0 × 30 cm) since this will give the most rapid separation. Samples up to 20% of the bed volume can be applied with satisfactory desalting. Equilibrate the column with at least 2 bed volumes of buffer. Packing and equilibration of Sephadex G-25 medium can be performed at high flow rates by gravity feed using a reservoir located high above the column. Operate the column at up to 20 ml/cm^2 cross-sectional area/h. Apply the sample and proceed with the elution. The protein peak will start to elute after the void volume, i.e., about 30% of the total bed volume, and will be separated from small molecules, which typically will elute with a peak near the total bed volume. Do not use samples with very high viscosity (high protein concentration), otherwise zone distortion will occur.

When small sample volumes are utilized in analytical runs, the sample can be diluted to a salt concentration that will not interfere with the chromatographic technique (ion exchange, hydroxyapatite, or chromatofocusing). In some techniques, the presence of salt does not interfere (affinity chromatography), while for others salt has to be added to increase the polarity of the solution (hydrophobic-interaction chromatography).

18.3 CHOICE OF CHROMATOGRAPHIC METHOD FOR PURIFICATION OF IMMUNOGLOBULIN G AND M mAbs

Correct choice of the chromatographic method is the most critical step in the overall purification procedure. Examples of different procedures will be given, but it must be borne in mind that some optimization of conditions is always desirable, and sometimes essential. Monoclonal antibodies can vary to such a degree in their chromatographic properties that some methods may not even work. For example, a very acidic mAb may not bind to a cationic matrix or a very basic mAb may not bind to an anionic matrix. Too low or too high initial pH might destroy its activity. Furthermore, if a hydrophobic-interaction chromatography matrix is used and the mAb has a low hydrophobicity it is necessary to choose a more lipophilic matrix to avoid very high salt concentrations that can precipitate the mAbs. On the other hand, if a high lipophilic matrix is used and the mAbs have high hydrophobicity, sample recovery might be too low.

Purification of mAb using protein A affinity chromatography is very effective, but not all mouse mAb bind to protein A (IgG_3) and even those that do might only bind weakly (IgG_1) under chromatographic conditions of low ionic strength. To avoid adsorption problems, the samples and the chromatographic system should have high ionic strength.

18.3.1 Ion-Exchange Chromatography

In ion-exchange chromatography, the isoelectric point (p*I*) and charge density of the mAb govern the type of ion exchanger to be used. The p*I* for mAb can vary between the values 4.9 and 8.2. Anion-exchange chromatography can be successfully used in ascites fluid[5,10] for IgG mAb. The method is applicable in most cases but success in removing critical contaminants will vary from case to case, depending on the charge characteristics of the mAbs. It is strongly recommended that an electrophoretic titration curve be constructed where the net charge as a function of pH is plotted. This gives unique characteristics of the molecules and provides the basis for the selectivity of ion-exchange chromatography.

A pH titration curve provides valuable data about how the net charge on purified molecules varies with pH. The pH–net charge curve is a highly individual property of a given protein. At a pH value below its isoelectric point a protein is positively charged and will adsorb to a cation exchanger such as one containing sulfonate groups ($-CH_2-SO_3^-$). Conversely, above the p*I* a protein is negatively charged and will adsorb to an anion exchanger such as one containing quaternary amines ($-CH_2N^+(CH_3)_3$). A general rule is that the pH of the buffer system should have a value >1 pH unit above the mAb's isoelectric point for anion exchanger and <1 pH unit below the isoelectric point for cation exchanger. The choice of buffer is very important because buffers consist of ions that can also exchange and the pH equilibrium can be affected. To avoid these problems, "the rules of buffers" is applied: use cationic buffers with anionic exchangers and anionic buffers with cationic exchangers.

Ion-exchange chromatography of mAb against coagulation factor VIII was performed by Pavlu et al.[6] using a Mono Q HR 5/5 anion-exchange column (50×5 mm i.d.) (Pharmacia Fine Chemicals, Uppsala, Sweden) with starting buffer A, 0.020 mol/liter Tris-HCl (pH 8.0), and final buffer B, 0.020 mol/liter Tris-HCl (pH 8.0) containing 1.5 mol/liter sodium chloride. The gradient was generated over 50 min at a flow rate of 1 ml/min. All samples were freed from lipoproteins by treatment with PVP followed by filtration through a Millipore filter Milex-HV (Millipore Corp., Bedford, MA).

The chromatographic procedure was as follows for the above purification:

1. Convert the sample buffer to chromatographic buffer A, if it is different, either by desalting, gel filtration, or diluting 1:10, and filter through a membrane filter.
2. Follow the manufacturer's instructions for preparing the column.

It was found that the equilibration procedure should be prolonged with several column volumes to remove substances that could still remain on the column. Using modern diode array detector technology, where several signals can be monitored simultaneously and where continuous spectra can be taken even during the prerun procedure, it could be observed that the stabilization procedure of the baseline requires a longer period of column washing. The binding capacity of the Mono Q column is approx. 25 mg of protein, according to the manufacturer. Two experiments were done with 3.7 and 25 mg loads, which were pretreated with ammonium sulfate (Figures 18–1 and 18–2). The separation was almost as good in the high protein load (25 mg) experiment as in the low protein load (3.7 mg) experiment. To improve the separation of high protein loads, a different gradient was used (Figure 18–3), which gave a still better separation. The composition and purity of the chromatographic

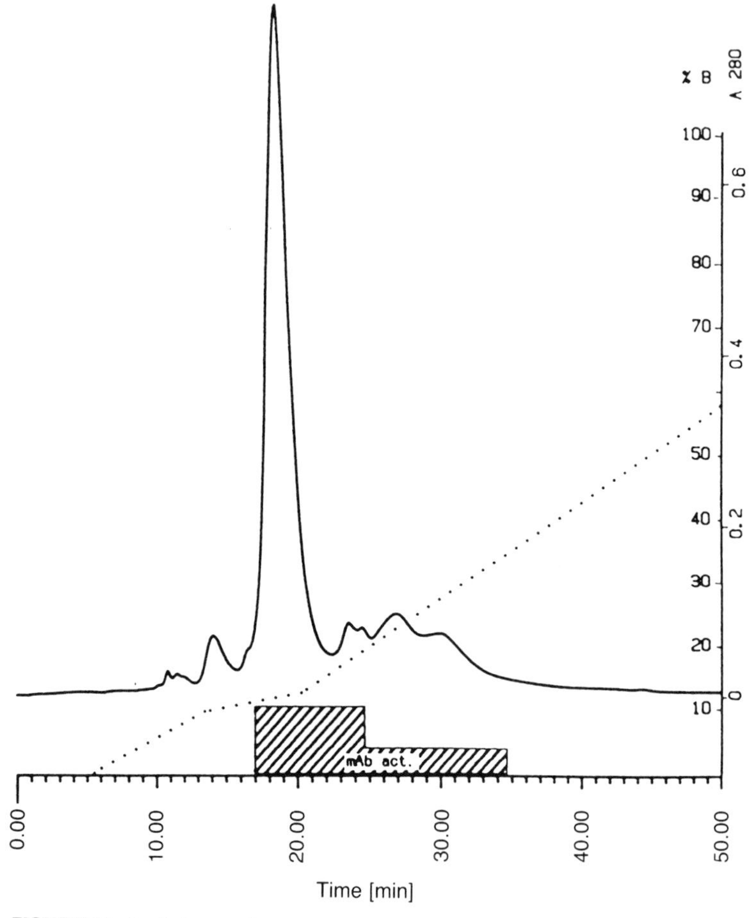

FIGURE 18–1. Anion-exchange chromatography of low sample load (3.1 mg protein) of ammonium sulfate-precipitated ascites fluid, containing antibodies against factor VIII. The cross-hatched area indicates the antibody activity. The solid line indicates detection by UV (280 nm) and the dotted line the salt gradient.

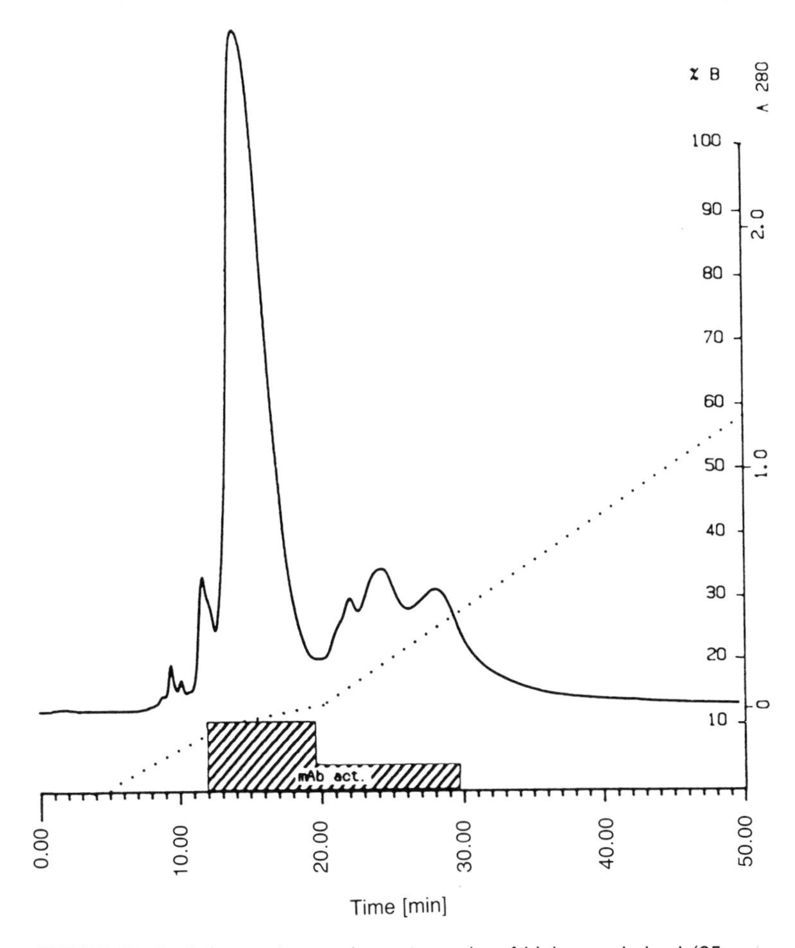

FIGURE 18–2. Anion-exchange chromatography of high sample load (25 mg protein) of ammonium sulfate-precipitated ascites fluid, containing antibodies against factor VIII. The cross-hatched area indicates the antibody activity. The solid line indicates detection by UV (280 nm) and the dotted line the salt gradient.

fractions were tested by sodium dodecyl sulfate-polyacrylamide gel electrophoresis (SDS-PAGE)[20] of the reduced samples. The total polyacrylamide concentration in the separating gel was 12%. Silver staining was used to visualize the protein bands.[21] The ammonium sulfate-precipitated ascites sample contains, in addition to the heavy and light chains of IgG, several contaminating proteins. These proteins can be efficiently removed by ion-exchange chromatography, except for one polypeptide, which migrates somewhat more slowly than the IgG heavy chain. When 25 mg of ammonium sulfate-precipitated ascites fluid was chromatographed on the anion-exchange column, the main IgG peak was only slightly more contaminated, but the extra polypeptides were effectively removed by changing the gradient profile for ion-exchange chromatography.

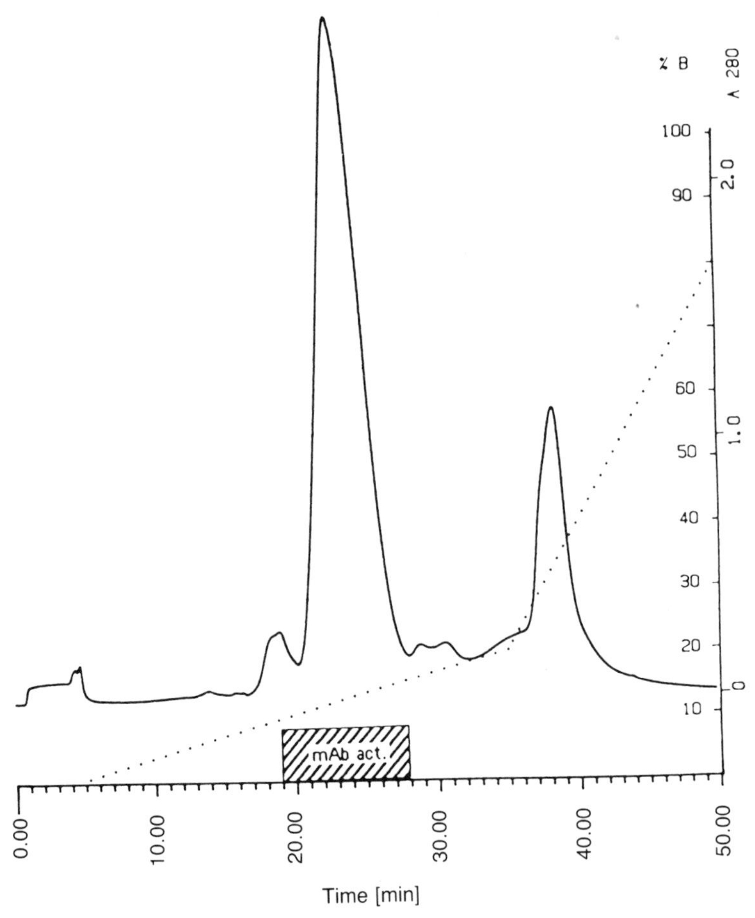

FIGURE 18–3. Anion-exchange chromatography of high sample load (25 mg protein) of ammonium sulfate-precipitated ascites fluid, containing antibodies against factor VIII. The cross-hatched area indicates the antibody activity. The solid line indicates detection by UV (280 nm) and the dotted line the improved salt gradient.

It has been reported that antibody activity can be partially lost during ammonium sulfate precipitation.[7,13–15] It was therefore of interest to investigate whether it was possible to obtain the same purity of mAb without previous ammonium sulfate precipitation. For the ion-exchange chromatography, the same conditions were used as in Figure 18–3. The result is shown in Figure 18–4. Here a much more complex picture is obtained, showing that the monoclonal antibody is not the main component of the unfractionated ascites fluid.

It must be pointed out that SDS-PAGE silver staining is about 50-to 100-fold more sensitive than SDS-PAGE Coomassie staining. If the purity of the material is to be checked properly, the silver staining SDS-PAGE gels should be used to detect all the impurities. If ammonium sulfate can be used as a first step, a single chromatographic procedure is sufficient for obtaining a highly pure mAb preparation. However, if ammonium sulfate precipitation must be avoided, ascites fluid can be used directly after separation of cell debris, lipoproteins etc., as starting material to isolate highly pure mAb by a two-step HPLC chromatographic procedure.

In anion-exchange chromatography, most proteins in the sample bind to the column matrix and this, in some cases, can reduce the column capacity and possibly cause increased contamination by transferrin (p*I* 5.1–5.8) and albumin (p*I* 4.9). An alternative method in ion-exchange chromatography is a cation exchanger where chromatographic conditions, pH, and ionic strength

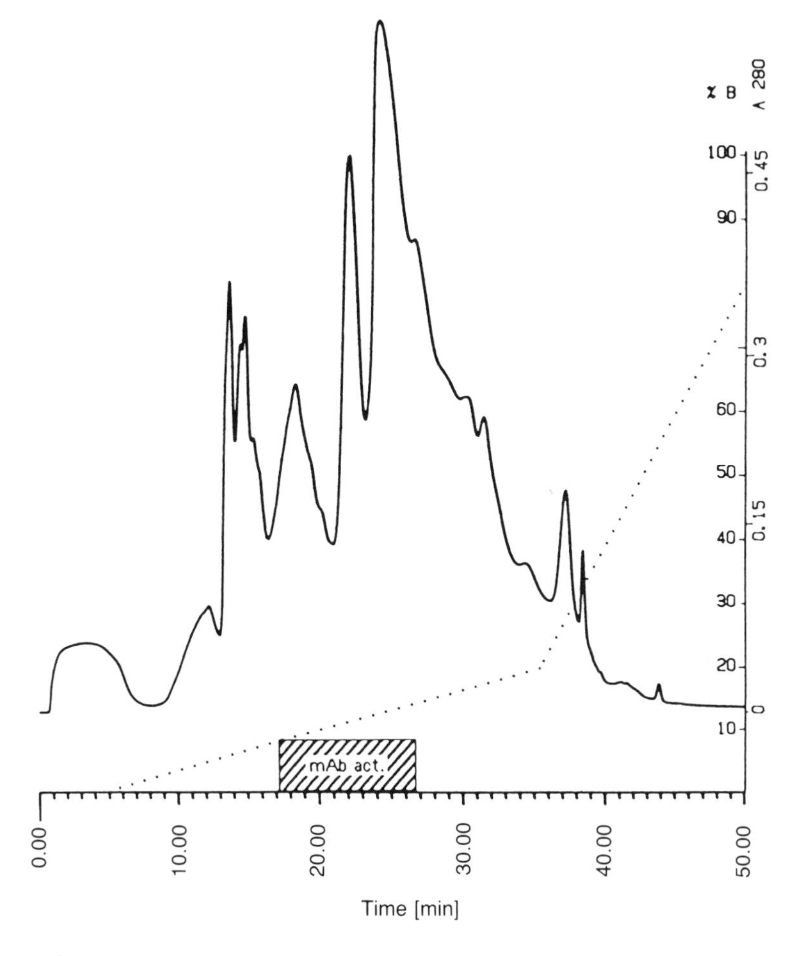

FIGURE 18–4. Anion-exchange chromatography of high sample load (25 mg protein) of unfractionated ascites fluid (no ammonium sulfate precipitation) containing antibodies against factor VIII. The cross-hatched area indicates the antibody activity. The solid line indicates detection by UV (280 nm) and the dotted line the salt gradient.

can be manipulated so that impurities can be removed directly during the sample loading,[22] because of the relatively low p*I* value of albumin and transferrin.

Ion-exchange chromatography of mAb (IgG_1) against apolipoprotein B was performed by Danielsson et al.[8] on a Mono S HR 5/5 cation-exchange column (50 × 5 mm i.d.) (Pharmacia Fine Chemicals, Uppsala, Sweden) with starting buffer A, 0.050 mol/liter 2-(*N*-morpholino) ethanesulfonic acid (MES) containing 0.020 mol/liter sodium chloride (pH 6.0), and final buffer B, 0.050 mol/liter MES containing 1.0 mol/liter sodium chloride (pH 6.0). The gradient was generated over 40 min at a flow rate of 1 ml/min. The sample was pretreated by the calcium procedure.[11] The solution was then diluted with buffer A after previous filtration through a 0.22-μm filter. The sample volume was 200 μl, corresponding to a protein load of 3.2 mg. The result of the separation can be seen in Figure 18–5, where the cross-hatched area indicates the antibody activity determined by enzyme-linked immunosorbent assay (ELISA).[23] The fractions were tested by SDS-PAGE silver staining, and the active fraction consisted of a homogeneous material.

The reason for the high salt concentrations in buffer B was to make unnecessary the injections of high concentrations of sodium chloride manually after the run. After long periods of usage (1 week) it is recommended that the column be washed with a small volume of 3–4 mol/liter sodium chloride solution. It is generally known that use of halide ions is undesirable because of corrosion risk to the steel components in the HPLC system. There are different views about how serious these risks are. Some of the HPLC manufacturers replace steel with titanium to obtain more resistant equipment. However, more serious for the whole system is still the buffer, and crystals that might be formed in the pump heads or on the sapphire pistons that could damage the sealings with resulting leakage. Replacing sodium sulfate (lower concentration in buffer B) with sodium chloride has been tried, but this salt gave even worse results due to lower selectivity of sodium sulfate. At the end of the run, or when operating overnight, the flow rate of the 50% B buffer should be lowered to 0.050 ml/min. For longer periods of use, the whole system should be washed out with distilled water rather than with the mixture of buffers A and B.

18.3.2 Hydrophobic-Interaction Chromatography

Hydrophobic-interaction chromatography is a separation technique that is very similar to reversed-phase HPLC, but in which the nonpolar mobile phase is replaced by polar buffer solutions. The column is packed with a porous hydrophilic support containing covalently bound lipophilic groups, e.g., phenyl or butyl. Proteins are adsorbed to the hydrophobic groups by the nonpolar amino acid chains located on the molecule surface. The protein adsorption to the matrix is reinforced by high salt concentration in the sample and buffer.

This technique was used by Pavlu et al.[6] for the purification of mAb against coagulation factor VIII. Hydrophobic-interaction chromatography was performed on a TSK gel Phenyl 5 PW column (75 × 7.5 mm i.d.) (Tosoh Corporation, Japan). The sample was loaded on the column in a solution of high ionic strength, e.g. (buffer A), 0.030 mol/liter Tris-HCl, 1.0 mol/liter sodium sulfate (pH 7.5). The salt concentration should be optimized for different mAbs

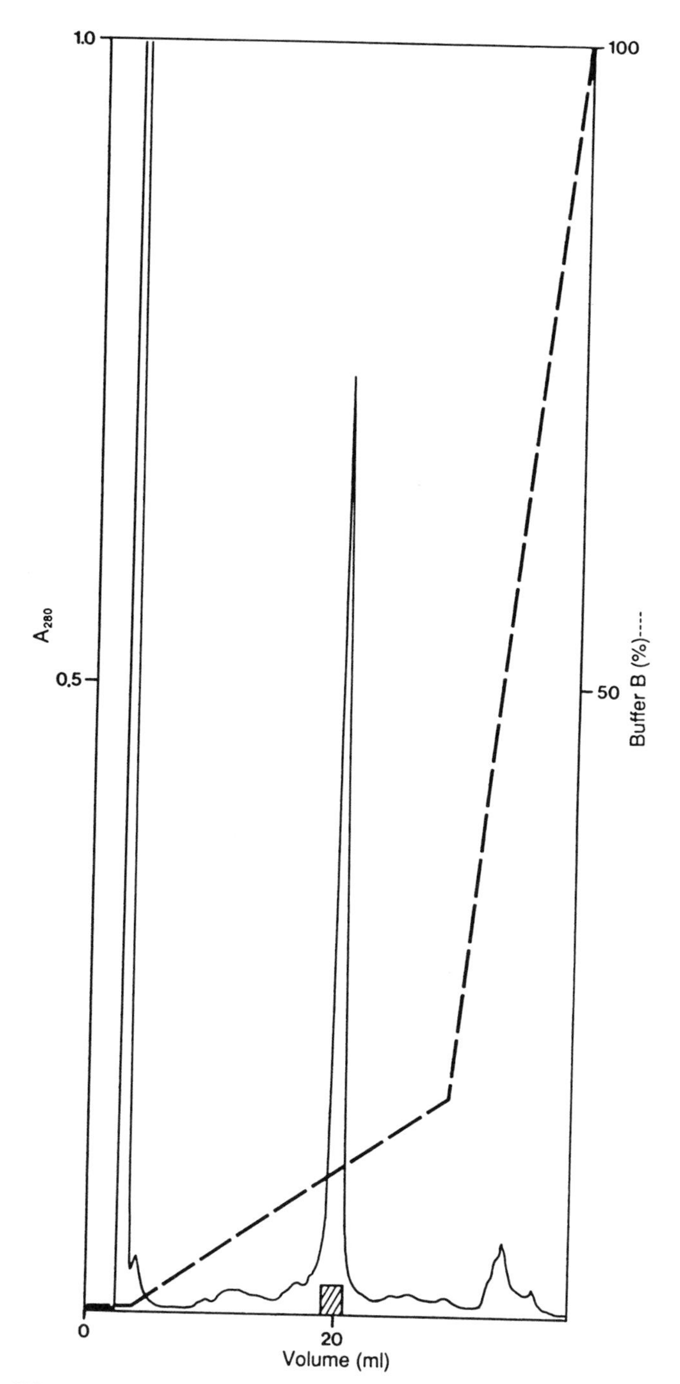

FIGURE 18–5. Cation-exchange chromatography of sample (3.2 mg protein) of calcium chloride-treated ascites fluid, containing antibodies (IgG_1) against apolipoprotein B. The cross-hatched area indicates the antibody activity. The solid line indicates detection by UV (280 nm) and the broken line the salt gradient.

depending on their hydrophobicity. Different salts have various selectivities. Ammonium sulfate, which is frequently used for protein purification on hydrophobic columns, was omitted because of the negative effect when mAb is used for affinity chromatography purposes and because of high UV absorbance at low wavelengths. Impurities in the salt can be removed by different methods, e.g., resin or charcoal treatment. Elution was accomplished by reducing the ionic strength and polarity of the mobile phase, e.g. (buffer B), 0.030 mol/liter Tris-HCl, containing 5% 2-propanol. This polarity-reducing step was achieved by using a linear gradient for 80 min at a flow rate of 1 ml/min. The sample load for this column was about 1 mg protein/ml gel. If there are several proteins of similar hydrophobicity, the column load must be reduced to avoid overlapping peaks, and if dealing with proteins of wide differences in hydrophobicity, the load could be larger. The temperature is an effective separational factor. The experiments should be performed preferably between 15 and 35°C but even below and above this temperature interval good results can be obtained. Consideration must be taken of salt solubility at low temperatures.

In the following experiment, the sample was a commercially available crude mAb preparation against factor VIII. Hydrophobic-interaction chromatography (Figure 18–6) was performed as described above, resulting in a very complex picture, indicating high resolving power. The mAb activity and purity in this experiment were not determined. In a second example of hydrophobic-interaction chromatography, an aliquot of fractions 18–24 from Figure 18–4, corresponding to 0.3 mg protein was applied to the hydrophobic column, which was then eluted (Figure 18–7). This step generated three main peaks, the mAb activity being associated with only one peak. The peaks eluted from the hydrophobic-interaction column (Figure 18–7) were also analyzed by SDS-PAGE. The peak containing the mAb activity was the only one that contained the heavy and light IgG polypeptides. This highly purified fraction still contained two contaminating polypeptide bands. However, it was only slightly less pure than the fraction obtained by ion-exchange chromatography from ammonium sulfate-precipitated ascites fluid. From these results it is apparent that the ammonium sulfate step gives a final mAb preparation of slightly higher purity than the one obtained if it is omitted. For separation improvement, the gradient can be changed in such a way as to give better separation over that part of the chromatogram at which there is a peak containing mAb activity but that is still contaminated by traces of albumin.

18.3.3 Chromatofocusing

Chromatofocusing is a chromatographic technique for separating biomolecules according to their isoelectric point (p*I*). After column equilibration, the sample is loaded on the column and eluted with a single buffer solution. Since the gradient is self-generating, there is no need for a mechanical mixer or dual pumping system.[24]

Purification of mouse ascites sample (IgG_{2a}) against lipoprotein A by chromatofocusing was reported by Danielsson et al.[9] They used a Mono P HR 5/20 column (200 × 5 mm i.d.) (Pharmacia Fine Chemicals, Uppsala, Sweden) with starting buffer A, 0.025 mol/liter triethanolamine (pH 8.3), and final buffer B, 3% (v/v) Polybuffer 96 + 7% Polybuffer 74.

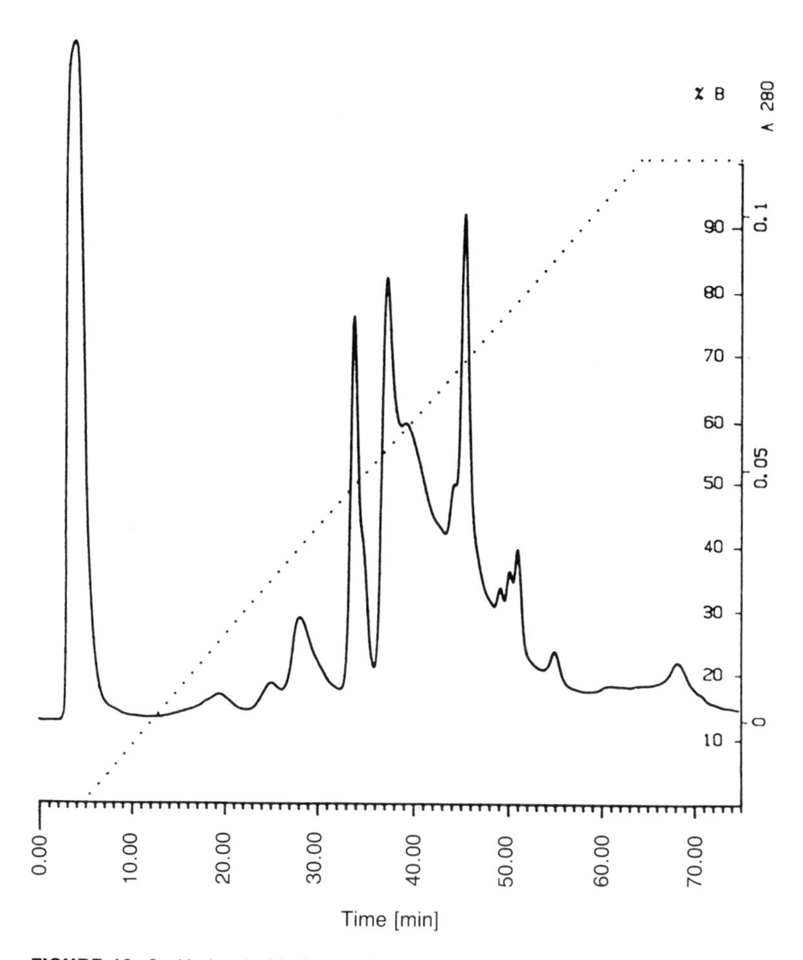

FIGURE 18–6. Hydrophobic interaction chromatography of commercially available crude monoclonal antibodies sample preparation against factor VIII. Sample load: 0.5 mg protein. The solid line indicates detection by UV (280 nm) and the dotted line %B buffer mixing.

The chromatographic sorbent, Mono P, is substituted with various tertiary and quaternary amines. Polybuffer contains numerous amphoteric buffering substances of different pK_a values. Linear pH gradients are developed during column elution with Polybuffer adjusted to a lower pH than that of the pre-equilibrated column. The mechanism of chromatofocusing is based on the buffering action of the charged groups on the Mono P and the fact that a molecule has a net negative charge at a pH above its p*I*. When the Mono P column is equilibrated to the initial pH, the sample is applied and any component with a net negative charge is retained on the column.

In the above investigation, the sample was centrifuged for 5 min, diluted 1 + 1 with buffer A, and finally filtered through a 0.22-μm filter. The sample, 200 μl (2.8 mg), was applied on the column after equilibration with 10 ml

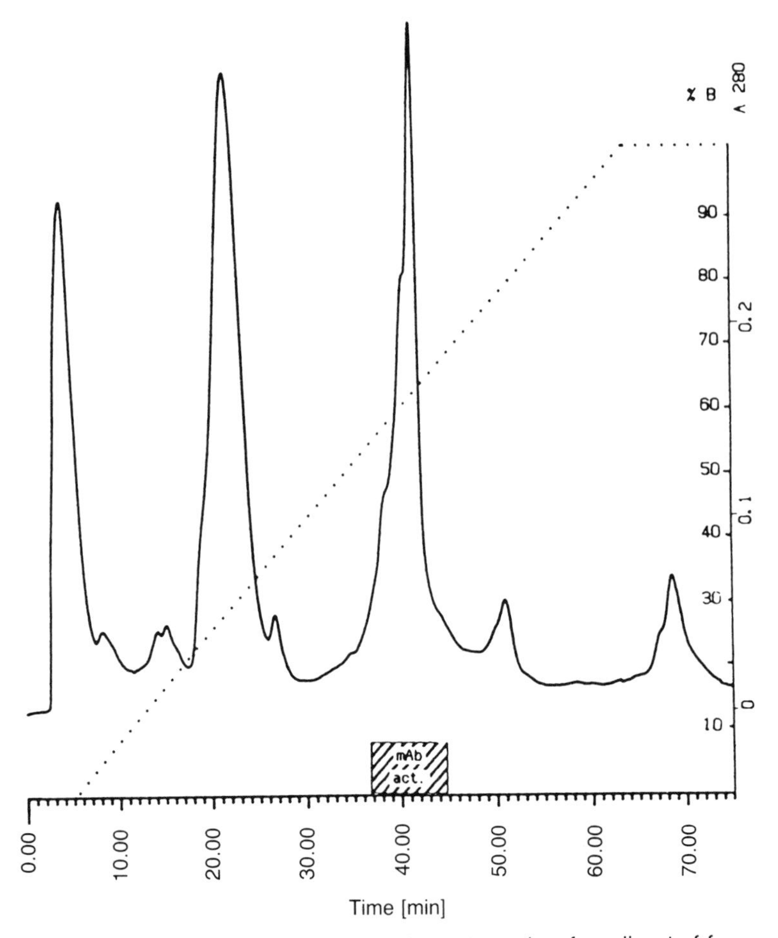

FIGURE 18–7. Hydrophobic-interaction chromatography of an aliquot of fractions 18–24 from Figure 18–4. Sample load: about 0.3 mg protein. The cross-hatched area indicates the antibody activity. The solid line indicates detection by UV (280 nm) and the dotted line %B buffer mixing.

buffer A. The elution procedure was accomplished with 50 ml of buffer B. The result of the separation can be seen in Figure 18–8, where the cross-hatched area indicates the antibody activity (ELISA). After the run, the column was washed with 2 mol/liter sodium acetate, to elute albumin. The fractions were tested by SDS-PAGE silver staining, which indicated approximately 80% purity. The contamination in the antibody-active fraction was transferrin.

18.3.4 Affinity Chromatography

Affinity chromatography is an effective separation technique for the purification and analysis of biomolecules. This separation is based on their specific interactions with other molecules (ligands).[25,26] The general approach is to attach the ligand of interest, e.g., an antigen, to a solid support and then use

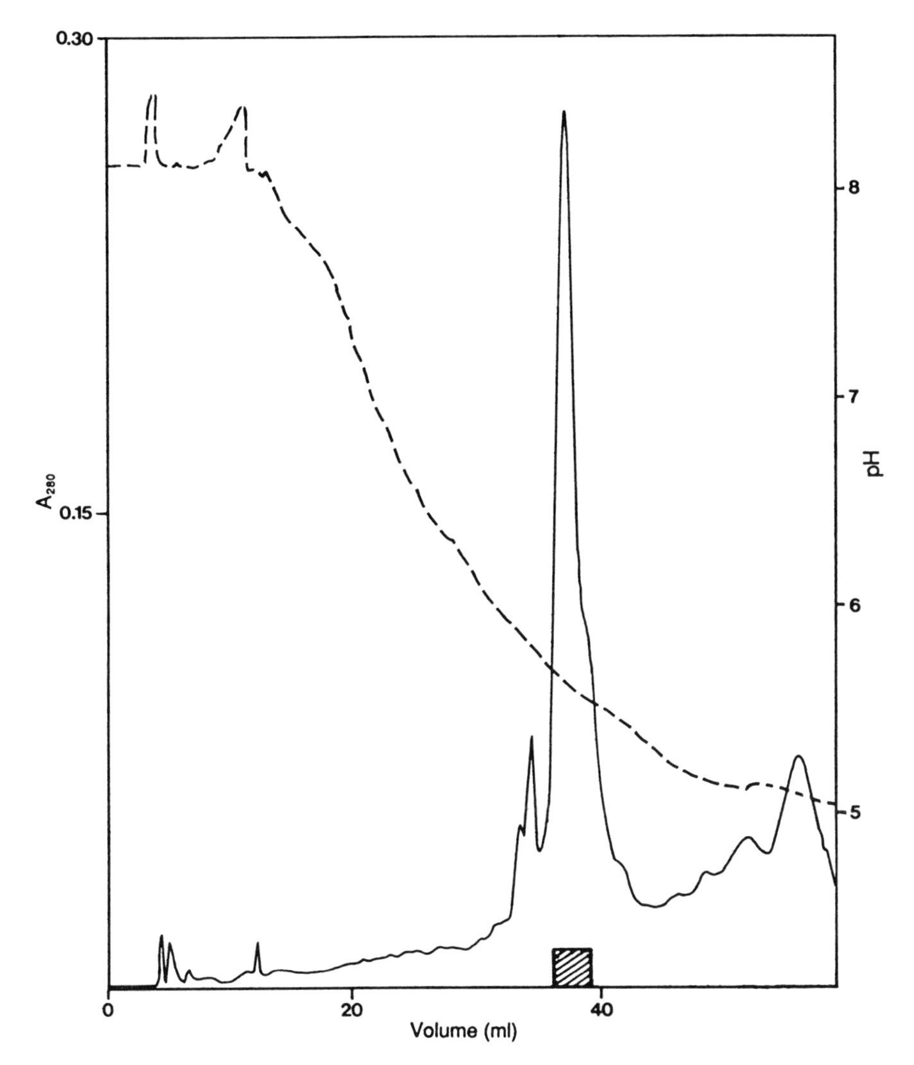

FIGURE 18–8. Chromatographic pattern for mouse monoclonal antibodies (IgG_{2a}) against lipoprotein A obtained by chromatofocusing on Mono P. The cross-hatched area indicates the antibody activity. The solid line indicates detection by UV (280 nm) and the broken line the formed pH gradient.

the matrix to selectively adsorb the molecules to be separated, e.g., an antibody. By this technique, specific molecules can be separated from crude mixtures of biological materials with a high degree of purity and biological activity.

The use of affinity techniques in HPLC, termed high-performance liquid affinity chromatography (HPLAC), high-performance affinity chromatography (HPAC), or some equivalent term, has now become an established tool for chromatographic separations of various biomolecules.[27,28] The advantages of this method include high speed of separation, improved resolution, and ease in scaling-up the operations. An area of lively interest and research is the purification and analysis of polyclonal and monoclonal antibodies from crude samples such as serum, ascites, and cell culture supernatants. HPLAC using bacterial receptor proteins such as protein A[29,30] and protein G, antigens, or antiantibodies[31,32] offers an attractive alternative to the separation and analysis of antibodies in various mixtures. To illustrate the potential of HPLAC for separations of mAb raised in cell culture supernatant, two typical applications, reported by Ohlson, using protein A[29] and protein G, are presented and discussed in detail below.

Bacterial receptors found in various strains of, e.g., *Staphylococci* and *Streptococci* have been widely used as reagents for immunoglobulins.[33,34] These bacterial proteins bind mainly to the constant (Fc) region of the immunoglobulin molecule. Earlier, the major focus was on protein A, derived from strains of *Staphylococcus aureus*, which was widely exploited for the analysis and purification of immunoglobulins.[33] Recently, however, another cell-wall protein (protein G) extracted from G strains of *Streptococci* has been studied in detail for its ability to bind immunoglobulins.[35] Protein G complements protein A by showing broader binding activity to IgG from various species.[35]

Separation of mAb by HPLAC with immobilized protein A and protein G can be performed on a SelectiSpher-10 Protein A column (50 × 5 mm, 10 μ, 300Å) and on a SelectiSpher-10 Protein G column (50 × 5 mm, 10 μm, 300 Å) (Perstorp Biolytica AB, S-223 70 Lund, Sweden). All the chromatographic separations were performed at room temperature (22°C) at flow rates of 1–3 ml/min with detection at 280 nm. After filtration (0.22 μm), the samples (3.2 ml) of cell culture fluid were injected. During chromatography, fractions were collected for subsequent immunological and electrophoretic analyses.

Mouse mAb (IgG_{2a}) was separated with the protein A column (Figure 18–9) in approx. 10 min. The recovery of activity was in this case approx. 90%, determined by ELISA.[23] Recovery varies from antibody to antibody and is sensitive to the selected experimental conditions. It is difficult to give a general rule on how to recover maximum activity. It is advisable, however, to strive for fast separations as the time spent at elution conditions, such as low pH, is thereby minimized. In addition, some mAbs can be recovered efficiently at milder elution conditions, e.g., pH 4 instead of pH 2 or 1 mol/liter KSCN instead of 2 mol/liter KSCN, etc. Affinity chromatography using specific ligands yields often highly purified samples; for instance, the purity of mouse mAb IgG_{2a} in the present case was estimated to be at least 95%. Minor contamination with albumin was detected when analyzed by SDS-PAGE, stained with silver.[21]

Many mAbs show no or limited binding to protein A. This is especially true for many mouse IgG_1, rat IgG_{2a}, and rat IgG_{2b}. By increasing the hydrophobic character of the binding between the protein and IgG by means of, e.g., high salt concentrations and high pH (e.g., 2 mol/liter NaCl, 2 mol/liter glycine pH 9.0), recovery of many mAbs can be increased significantly.

Mouse mAb (IgG_1) was separated with the protein G-HPLAC column within 10 min (Figure 18–10). Although mouse IgG_1 bound efficiently, 80% of its immunological activity could be recovered. A protein A column did not bind any mouse IgG under the same experimental conditions. This is a typical example of protein G's broader binding ability to various IgG, which do not generally exhibit any binding to protein A under physiological conditions. A number of different antibodies that usually do not bind to protein A, especially mouse IgG_1, rat IgG_{2a}, rat IgG_{2b}, goat IgG_1, and sheep IgG_1, have shown ef-

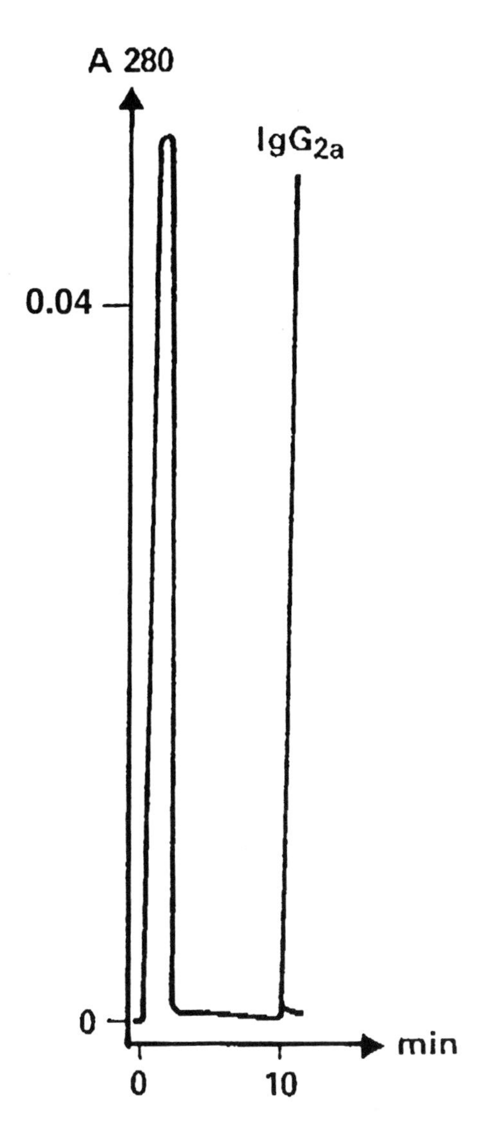

FIGURE 18–9. Chromatographic pattern for mouse monoclonal antibodies (IgG_{2a}) obtained by affinity chromatography on SelectiSpher-10 protein A. Chromatographic conditions were buffer A 0.050 mol/liter glycine pH 9.0, 0–10 min; buffer B 0.050 mol/liter glycine pH 3.0, 10–12 min. The solid line indicates detection by UV (280 nm).

ficient binding to protein G with high recovery of eluted activity (70–100%). However, it must be kept in mind that individual mAbs of the same subclass may vary considerably in the binding strength to both protein G and protein A. It is recommended that each individual antibody should be tested separately to decide whether it is suitable or not for protein A/protein G chromatography.

The HPLAC technique using protein G has also made it possible to isolate antibodies from crude extracts and to quantitatively analyze the mAb content by monitoring the absorbance at, e.g., 280 nm. In a preliminary study it has been shown that this technique can be used to follow the process of production of mAb as well as its subsequent purification. Generally, the binding capacity of mAb to protein A/protein G columns varies considerably but is normally in

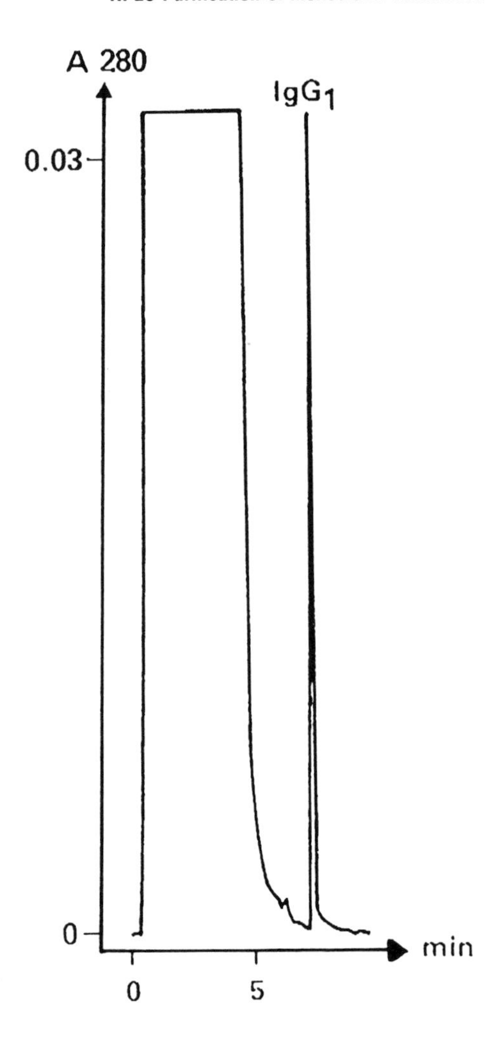

FIGURE 18–10. Chromatographic pattern for mouse monoclonal antibodies (IgG_1) obtained by affinity chromatography on SelectiSpher-10 protein G. Chromatographic conditions were buffer A 0.050 mol/liter sodium phosphate pH 6.5, 0–7.5 min; buffer B 0.050 mol/liter glycine pH 2.5, 7.5–10 min. The solid line indicates detection by UV (280 nm).

the range of 2–5 mg IgG/ml gel, depending on the species and subclasses of the IgG applied. When not in operation, the columns should be stored in buffers at neutral pH with addition of bacteriostatic agents such as 0.1 mol/liter sodium phosphate, pH 7.0, 0.05% sodium azide.

18.3.5 Hydroxyapatite Chromatography

Hydroxyapatite chromatography is a technique for separating biomolecules according to their adsorption to crystalline hydroxyapatite whose chemical composition is $Ca_{10}(PO_4)_6(OH)_2$. On the hydroxyapatite crystal surface are located positively charged adsorption sites, formed by two calcium ions. The other adsorption site on the crystalline hydroxyapatite is negatively charged, formed by six oxygen atoms belonging to three crystal phosphate ions. In the adsorption of proteins the carboxyl groups on the protein surface can be involved. When phosphoproteins adsorb to the matrix, the phosphate groups on the crystalline hydroxyapatite act as binding groups. Furthermore, biomolecules can even be adsorbed onto the sorbent by basic groups in the molecular structure (ϵ-amino and guanidinyl groups).[36] The high binding capacity of hydroxyapatite can be utilized for effective concentration of dilute protein solutions. Proteins with very small differences in configuration on their surface can be separated on this matrix.

The following example of the hydroxyapatite technique was reported by Pavlu et al.[6] for purification of mAb against coagulation factor VIII using a Bio-Gel HPHT column (100 $\times$ 7.8 mm i.d.) (Bio-Rad, Richmond, CA) with buffer A, 0.01 mol/liter sodium phosphate, 0.3 mmol/liter calcium chloride (pH 6.8), and final buffer B, 0.35 mol/liter sodium phosphate, 0.01 mmol/liter calcium chloride (pH 6.8). The gradient was generated over 70 min at a flow rate of 0.5 ml/min. The sample load was 4 mg protein. The sample for this example was first treated with ammonium sulfate and then with PVP to free it from lipoproteins. Just before chromatography, the sample was diluted and filtered through a 0.45-μm Millipore filter to reduce the salt concentration and to remove small particles. In Figure 18–11 a chromatographic pattern of mAb against factor VIII can be seen.

In a similar experiment, a commercially available crude mAb preparation against coagulation factor VIII was used as the sample (Figure 18–12), ammonium sulfate treatment being omitted. The sample load was 5 mg protein. The result was similar to the previous experiment (Figure 18–11). The chromatographic patterns for hydroxyapatite matrix indicated lower resolution for complex samples than was obtained by other methods. This observation was confirmed by Manil et al.[37] who state that hydroxyapatite chromatography was not very efficient.

The ability of hydroxyapatite to separate proteins with very small differences in configuration could be utilized for successful separation of different mAbs based on conformational variations in the light-chain composition.[38] This unique separation principle provides the possibility, when heterogeneous samples cannot be effectively separated, to use hydroxyapatite matrix as a second chromatographic step, e.g., after application on a protein A column, to separate contaminating host immunoglobulins and even inactive IgG, as was reported by Juarez-Salinas.[39] The use of hydroxyapatite columns appears to be a useful method for obtaining pure mAb with high specific activity. The loading capacity of the matrix is as high as 50 mg IgG and IgM/ml gel.[11] The above described examples illustrate a hydroxyapatite chromatographic technique, which is not sufficiently effective for purifying immunoglobulins from ascites fluid, but is very effective for separating IgG of different origins, and for removing active IgG from inactive.

Naturally, all these above described techniques can be combined into several consecutive purification steps by different methods. The combination of the purification steps that is actually used will depend on the nature of the starting material (ascites fluid or cell culture supernatant), on the immunoglobulin class, and the degree of specific activity required or the yield desired. However, it must be pointed out that, generally, the final step should consist of gel filtration, as this will give mAbs of high purity.

Immunoglobulin M (IgM) purifications require similar procedures to those described above for IgG mAbs. Monoclonal IgM is an antibody with high mo-

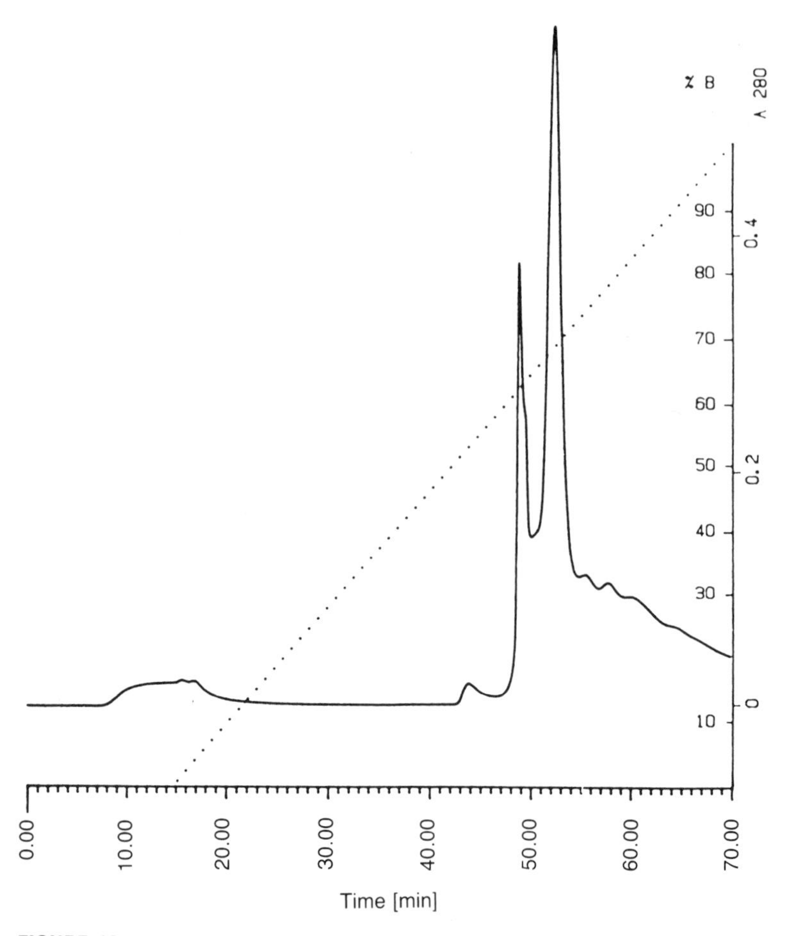

FIGURE 18–11. Hydroxyapatite chromatography of monoclonal antibodies sample preparation against factor VIII. Sample load: 4 mg protein. The solid line indicates detection by UV (280 nm) and the dotted line is the salt gradient.

lecular weight, approximately 970,000, and thus can be separated from most contaminants by gel filtration. Gel filtration is a technique that permits only a limited volume of sample to be loaded on the column. Consequently, ascites fluids with high protein concentration are suitable sample for this technique, but monoclonal IgM produced in cell culture with low protein concentration is not suitable. As was mentioned above in the section on affinity chromatography, some immunoglobulins, including IgM, have poor affinity for protein A. This limitation has been solved by the development of a new protein A binding buffer solution.[11] Juarez-Salinas et al.[11] describe the purification of mAb IgM produced in ascites fluid. The sample, containing 4 mg IgM, was diluted 1:1 with Affi-Prep protein A MAPS binding buffer A and injected into an Affi-Prep protein A column. Affi-Prep protein A chromatography gave rise

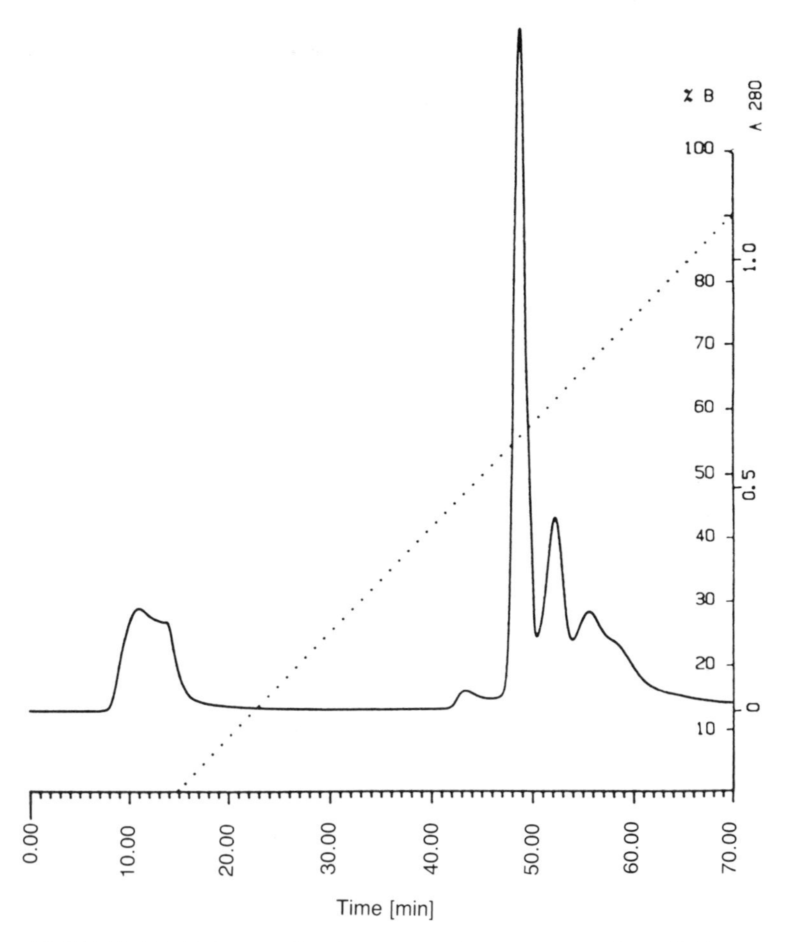

FIGURE 18–12. Hydroxyapatite chromatography of commercially available crude monoclonal antibodies sample preparation against factor VIII. Sample load: 5 mg protein. The solid line indicates detection by UV (280 nm) and the dotted line is the salt gradient.

to one large unretarded peak that was eluted with the binding buffer A. After changing the binding buffer A to eluting buffer B, the adsorbed IgM material was eluted giving a double peak pattern, indicating sample heterogeneity with respect to immunoglobulin composition. A second chromatographic step, performed on a hydroxyapatite matrix, can be performed if a highly purified IgM preparation is required.

Clezardin et al.[40] describe the purification of mAb IgM produced in cell culture. In the first step, the IgM antibodies were concentrated by running the sample through a Mono Q anion exchanger, thereafter it was subjected to gel-filtration on Superose 6 HR 10/30 (300 × 10 mm i.d.) (Pharmacia, Uppsala, Sweden). The monoclonal IgM obtained was highly purified, as determined by SDS-PAGE Coomassie staining, and immunoreactivity.

ACKNOWLEDGMENTS

I would like to express my gratitude to Drs. Eric Grund and Hector Juarez-Salinas for their valuable advice and to my two contributors Drs. Åke Danielsson and Sten Ohlson.

REFERENCES

1. I. Roitt, J. Brostoff, and D. Male, Immunology, Gower Medical Publishing, London, 1985.
2. P. L. Ey, S. J. Prowse, and C. R. Jenkins, *Immunochemistry*, 15 (1978) 429.
3. J. W. Goding, *J. Immunol. Methods*, 20 (1978) 241.
4. S. W. Burchiel, J. R. Billman, and T. R. Alber, *J. Immunol. Methods*, 69 (1984) 33.
5. L. H. Stanker, M. Vanderlaan, and H. Juarez-Salinas, *Immunol. Methods*, 76(1) (1985) 157.
6. B. Pavlu, U. Johansson, C. Nyhlén, and A. Wichman, *J. Chromatogr.*, 359 (1986) 449.
7. C. Bruck, D. Portelle, C. Glineur, and A. J. Bollen, *J. Immunol. Methods*, 53 (1982) 313.
8. J. R. Stephenson, J. M. Lee, and P. D. Wilton-Smith, *Anal. Biochem.*, 142 (1984) 189.
9. Å Danielsson, A. Ljunglöf, and H. Lindblom, *J. Immunol. Methods* (to be published).
10. C. Ostlund, *Tibtech*, 4 (1986) 288.
11. H. Juarez-Salinas, T. L. Brooks, G. S. Ott, R. E. Peters, and L. Stanker, Commercial Production of Monoclonal Antibodies, a Guide for Scale-Up (S. S. Seaver, ed.). New York.
12. J. W. Goding, In Monoclonal Antibodies: Principles and Practice, 1983.
13. P. Clezardin, J. L. MacGregor, M. Manach, H. Boucherche, and M. Dechavanne, *J. Chromatogr.*, 319 (1985) 67.
14. J. L. MacGregor, W. F. Brochier, M. C. Follea, M. C. Trzeciak, M. Dechavanne, and K. J. Clemetson, *Eur. J. Biochem.*, 131 (1983) 427.
15. S. W. Burchiel, *Methods Enzymol.*, 121 (1986) 596.
16. A. van Dalen, H. G. Seijen, and M. Gruber, *Biochim. Biophys. Acta*, 147 (1967) 421.
17. M. C. R. Burstein, *Acad. Sci.*, 244(26) (1957) 3189.
18. C. J. Russo, *Immunol. Methods*, 65 (1983) 269.
19. D. W. Ballard, D. M. Kranz, and E. W. Voss Jr., *Proc. Natl. Acad. Sci U.S.A.*, 80 (1983) 5071.
20. U. K. Laemmli, *Nature (London)*, 227 (1970) 680.
21. P. Tunón, K.-E. Johansson, *Biochem. Biophys. Methods*, 9 (1984) 171.
22. M. Carlsson, A. Hedin, M. Inganäs, B. Härfast, and F. Blomberg, *J. Immunol. Methods*, 79 (1985) 89.
23. E. Engvall and P. Perlman, *J. Immunol.*, (1972) 129.
24. FPLC Ion Exchange and Chromatofocusing, Principles and Methods. Pharmacia Laboratory Separation Division, S-751 82 Uppsala, Sweden.
25. W. B. Jacoby and M. Wilchek, *Methods Enzymol.*, 34 (1974).
26. C. R. Lowe, An Introduction to Affinity Chromatography, Vol 7/2 (T. S. Work and E. Work, eds.). North Holland, Amsterdam, 1979.
27. D. O. Larsson, M. Glad, L. Hansson, M. O. Månsson, S. Ohlson, and K. Mosbach, Advances in Chromatography, Vol. 21 (J. C. Giddings, E. Grushka, J. Cazes, and P. R. Brown, eds.). Dekker, New York, 1983, p. 41.

28. I. M. Chaiken, G. Fassina, and P. Caliceti, in High Performance Liquid Chromatography (P. R. Brown and R. H. Hartwick, eds.). Wiley Interscience, New York, 1989.
29. S. Ohlson and J. Wieslander, *J. Chromatogr.*, 397 (1987) 207.
30. S. C. Crowley and R. R. Walters, *J. Chromatogr.*, 266 (1983) 157.
31. T. M. Phillips, *LC Mag.*, 3 (1985) 962.
32. S. Ohlson, A. Lundblad, and D. Zopf, *Anal. Biochem.*, 169 (1988) 204.
33. A. Forsgren, V. Ghetie, R. Lindmark, and J. Sjöquist, in Staphylococci and Staphylococcal Infections (C. S. F. Easmon and C. Adlam, eds.). 1983, p. 429.
34. L. Björck and G. Kronvall, *J. Immunol.*, 133 (1984) 969.
35. B. Åkerström and L. Björck, *J. Biol. Chem.*, 261 (1986) 10240.
36. T. Kawasaki, S. Takahashi, and K. Ikeda, *Eur. J. Biochem.*, 152 (1985) 361.
37. L. Manil, P. Motte, P. Pernas, F. Troale, C. Bobuon, and D. Bellet, *J. Immunol. Methods*, 90 (1986) 25.
38. H. Juarez-Salinas, W. L. Bigbee, G. B. Lamotte, and G. S. Ott, *Int. Biotechnol. Lab.* April (1986) 20.
39. H. Juarez-Salinas, S. C. Engeehorn, W. L. Bigbee, M. A. Lowry, and L. H. Stanker, *BioTechniques, BioFeature*, May/June (1984) 164.
40. P. Clezardin, N. R. Hunter, I. R. MacGregor, J. L. MacGregor, D. S. Pepper, and J. J. Dawes, *Chromatography*, 358 (1986) 209.
41. Protean Dual-Slab Cell and Multi-Slab Cell, Operating Instructions, Bio-Rad, Richmond, CA.

CHAPTER 19

Application of High-Performance Liquid Chromatography to the Determination of Physiological Amino Acids

G. Ali Qureshi

CONTENTS

19.1 INTRODUCTION

Amino acids (AAs) are among the most important constituents of the human body with regard to assessing the nutritional requirements under various pathological states. More than 70 diseases are associated with defects in amino acid metabolism.[1–5] AAs are found mostly in living organisms in three different forms, free, conjugated with various unrelated compounds, or as the building blocks of proteins and peptides. Hence, the quantitation of AAs is one of the most informative while challenging tasks in the biomedical and biochemical fields.

In the last 40–50 years, the information on the steady-state concentrations of free AAs (FAAs) and total AAs (TAAs) in human biological samples has accumulated steadily, partly as the result of new methodology but also because of this information revealing metabolic disorders in various diseases.[1–7]

Two types of biological samples are generally subjected to AA analysis: (1) purified protein, i.e., acid or alkali hydrolyzed samples for the quantitative and qualitative analysis of the constituent AAs, and (2) biological samples, i.e., blood, urine, cerebrospinal fluid, or muscle to identify the known and unknown FAAs and TAAs to evaluate the levels for normal and patients under various pathological states. In biological samples a variety of AAs in addition to those used in protein synthesis are observed. Besides, these samples contain enormous numbers of other constituents such as lipids, polyamines, sugars, drugs, catecholamines, nucleosides and nucleotides, and small peptides. Hence, these complex samples place a higher demand on any method of quantitation. Once separated and quantitated, a physiological AA profile is used to provide the most valuable information on both metabolic status and genetic expression.

Among various applications, the role of AAs in hereditary disorders was first documented in 1946[8–10] and the studies provided an opportunity to study the impact of AAs under these disorders. In addition to diagnosis evaluation, the AA profiles also allowed prolonged dietary treatment of these disorders to be followed, which offered an excellent possibility to prevent genetic disorders in both pre- and postnatal stages.[4,11]

In the field of the nutritional sciences, the quantitation of AAs has been shown to be of important significance in assessing the status of malnutrition during various diseases.[12,13] Furthermore, the production of low- and high-protein dietetic products and their impact on correcting the metabolic disorders under various pathological states have been fields of interest for some time.[14–17]

AA profiles as a means for diagnostic purposes have also been used for various clinical purposes in plasma, amniotic fluid, feces, CSF, fibroblast cultures, liver cells, brain cells, erythrocytes, leukocytes, bone, muscle, and other tissues[18–28] to define the role of some of the AAs during disease and health.

Liquid chromatography (LC) as the method of choice for the quantitation of AAs was due to the availability of classical ion-exchange chromatography developed nearly 3 decades ago by S. Moore, W. H. Stein, and D. Spackman[29] and later automated by P. Hamilton.[30] During the last 20–25 years, this method has undergone dramatic and continual improvements resulting in the shortening of analysis time from 24 h to 30 min by using small particle size resins, small bore columns, stable high-pressure pumps, and injection valves, thus keeping the popularity of the method still alive. Furthermore, the use of fluorescence reagents instead of ninhydrin has improved the sensitivity of the method by 5–100 orders of magnitude. High-performance liquid chromatography (HPLC) is at present one of the fastest growing techniques and has successfully demonstrated its potential in the determination of AAs *in vivo* and *in vitro*. The purpose of this chapter is to give a general outline of the methods commonly used and their biological applications. The advantages and disadvantages in using these LC methods along with the treatment of biological samples are briefly discussed.

19.2 PRINCIPLE OF AMINO ACID SEPARATION BY LC METHODS

In most LC methods, the separation of AAs is based on the manipulation of two common parameters, i.e., charge and hydrophobicity differences. AAs are small amphoteric compounds with molecular weights between 70 and 250 with low UV-extinction coefficients. These AAs absorb light at a very low wavelength, i.e., 190 to 200 nm, and, therefore, UV detection is not suitable, since most organic solvents absorb light at a similar wavelength and the oxygen interference is also troublesome. Besides the sensitivity of detection is too low. Fluorescence and electrochemical detection could be alternatives, but there are only a few AAs having a natural fluorescence or which are detectable by electrochemical detector. Hence, it becomes necessary to derivatize AAs for quantitation purposes to achieve an adequate sensitivity.

The derivatization of AAs is performed before (precolumn) or after (postcolumn) the column separation. HPLC equipment can be used in either strategy enabling the AA quantitation in biological samples to be made with accuracy and reproducibility. But in practice the method of selection is more often than not based on tradition, personal preference where one is seeking the whole profile or a few interesting AAs, and the accuracy of the particular method.

19.2.1 Postcolumn Derivatization

In principle, reversed-phase and cation-exchange columns can be used, but most of the separations so far have been done on a strongly cation-exchanged column. The most commonly used resin is sulfonated polystyrene and the separation is performed using elution buffers of progressively increasing pH and/or ionic strength. The resolution of AAs on such a column is achieved according to the differential interaction between a positively charged AA and the negatively charged stationary phase (ionic interaction) in the order of acidic, hydroxylated, hydrophobic, and finally basic AAs.

Once the AA is separated, it is subjected to the derivatization procedure with a specific reagent for quantitation. The selection of the derivatizing reagent in this mode of separation is mainly based on its specific and selective reaction with AAs giving high extinction coefficients of the products resulting in low detection limits for quantitation.

19.2.2 Precolumn Derivatization

In this mode of separation, AAs are first derivatized to compounds with more hydrophobic characteristics then are separated on a reversed-phase (RP) siliconaceous packed column. In this procedure of separation, the hydrophobicity, selectivity, and stability of the reaction products are the main criteria in selection of a derivatizing agent.

The separation is performed on a C-chained silicon column in order to minimize the hydrophobic character and to eliminate ionic interaction due to free silanol groups in the supporting material. Among the various supports in the column, octandecyl silane hydrophobized sorbents are the most popular materials. On this column, elution order of AA and their derivatives is achieved, according to the variable polarity of the solutes interacting with the nonpolar stationary phase. The polar elution systems in most cases consist of H_2O/methanol or acetonitrile mixtures that are inexpensive, convenient, and often yield reproducible results. The purpose of derivatization reactions is primarily to modify α-amino and ϵ-amino groups in the amino acids, which cause extensive changes in the chromatographic properties of the AAs. The loss of the NH_2 group from the amino acid molecule following the derivatization means that the traditional cation-exchange columns are no longer applicable. The resultant change in polarity in the mobile phase means that the carboxylic acid group becomes the dominating factor for separation on RP-LC.

At the present time, precolumn derivatization procedures are the preferred method for AA analysis since they are more sensitive than postcolumn derivatization procedures and do not require elaborate systems. Furthermore, the precolumn instrument for AA analysis can easily be adopted for other applications as compared to postcolumn methods, giving it wide use for the quantitation of various groups of biological important substances.

19.2.3 Miscellaneous Separation Mechanisms

Two of the separation modes in LC, ion-pair liquid chromatography (IPLC) and chiral resolution by liquid chromatography (CRLC), are relatively new fields and have been shown to have various applications in biochemical, nutritional, and pharmaceutical sciences. Both of these modes are adaptable to pre- and postcolumn derivatization procedures.

19.2.3.1 Ion-Pair Liquid Chromatography (IPLC)

AAs, peptides, and proteins contain both cationic (RNH_3^+) and anionic ($RCOO^-$) groups (zwitterions) and in their underivatized form their separation on an RP-C_{18} column is dominated by their strength in polarity, i.e., the more polar a substance, the weaker is its interaction with the hydrophobic bonded stationary phase resulting in a shorter retention on the column. On addition of suitable hydrophobic ion additives to a mobile phase under controlled pH,[2,4] the retention of these polar substances can be delayed. Similarly in the case of a nonpolar substance that could have a long retention time on a C_{18} column, it may elute quicker on addition of a hydrophilic ion-pair reagent to a mobile phase with higher pH.[8–10] This theoretical possibility has already been applied in various separations of biologically important substances and has shown that the retention of AAs on an RP column can be enhanced in the presence of acrylsulfonate or tetraalkylammonium salts as hydrophobic ion additives in aqueous-organic solvent mobile phases.[31–40]

The separation of AAs on a C_{18} column after addition of acrylsulfonate to the mobile phase (pH < 4) is controlled by two major interactions caused by the formation of the acrylsulfonate salts of AAs and due to ion-exchange selectivity between the cationic AA and the RSO_3 countercation.

Walker and Pietrzyk[39] recently studied the separation of AA enantiomers by the use of various acrylsulfonate salts on a 5-μm LiChrosorb-C_8 column in aqueous–acetonitrile mobile phases. So far very few biological applications have been recorded.[34,36,38,40,41]

19.2.3.2 Chiral Liquid Chromatography

In applications to the separation of enantiomers in pharmaceutical and nutritional fields, chiral separation of L- and D-AAs has become a progressively more used HPLC method. Like IPLC, the technique is relatively new and so the potentials in the biological sciences are not yet explored.

The resolution of AA enantiomers can be achieved by three different methods: (1) chiral derivatization reagent,[42–44] (2) chiral eluents,[45,46] or (3) chiral stationary phases.[47–49] All of these methods have shown certain promise in separation of enantiomers, but as yet there have been few biological applications as the method of separation is still in the developmental stage.

19.3 INSTRUMENTATION FOR HPLC

Figure 19–1 consists of the essential components required to construct a postcolumn derivatization system. The following units are the important parts for a modern system:

1. solvent delivery
2. HPLC pump
3. gradient controller
4. automatic injector
5. pre- and analytical column
6. derivatizing unit or reaction coil

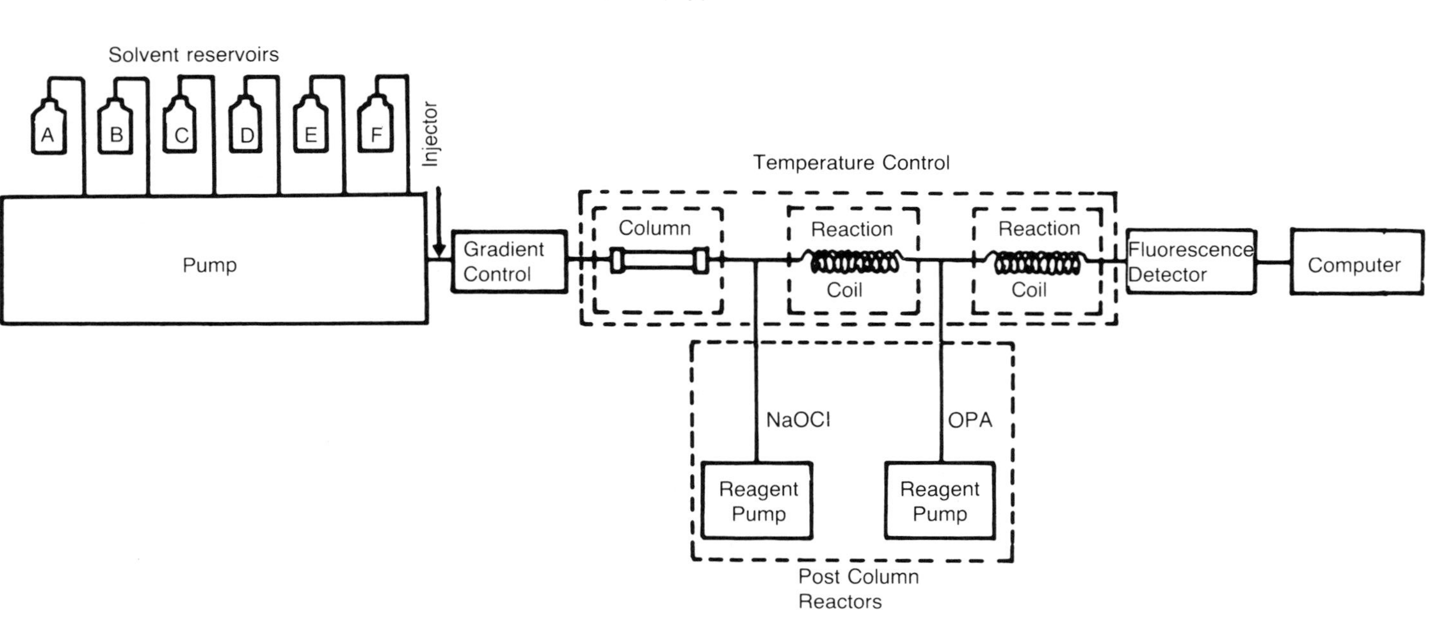

FIGURE 19–1. The components used for designing a modern HPLC system in the postcolumn derivatization mode.

7. detector
8. recorder or printer
9. integrator connected with microprocessor.

Three to five solvents (buffers) along with regeneration solvent are used with increasing pH and molarity to elute AAs from a biological sample. A constant flow pump is used to control the flow of the mobile phase by check-valves and the flow rate may easily be altered by adjustment of stroke rate.

There are various types of commercially available pumps, i.e., positive displacement, diaphragm, and pneumatic amplifier, but the use of a reciprocating piston pump is most commonly used. These pumps operate by displacement of solvents by a cam-driven piston. Pulsation of the pump should be minimized to maintain a steady baseline. Most of the recent available pump designs use more than one piston and are suitable for analysis.

A gradient controller is one of the important units in the system enabling one to record reproducible results. The gradient controller has two functions, to control the flow rate of one solvent at a time among various solvents (isocratic mode) and to mix two or more solvents according to their polarities, molarities, and pHs (gradient mode). In ion-exchange chromatography the first mode of running is more common than the latter, whereas in reverse-phase chromatography the latter mode is the most common. The mobile phase composition is generated by means of a gradient program that controls the delivery of one or more solvents according to a predetermined program. In modern HPLC instruments a multipump system is a suitable combination, although a single pump of low pressure is now widely used. Most of the commercial instruments include various hyperbolic curves for mixing the solvents, but based on the author's experience a linear curve is recommended for maintaining the reproducibility of the results. The reader is referred to ref. 50 for further details on the gradient controller.

The injector should be automatic to improve the efficiency and consistency of the chromatogram. Most of the injections are performed by introducing the sample through septum injection devices and injection valves. Comparing these two injection devices, septum designs are known to leak and the accuracy of the injected volume is always doubtful and septums need to be replaced more often. Addition of internal standards to be sample and standard mixer is a suitable method to overcome the above problems and would result in more accurate results. On the other hand injection valves offer small injection volumes, low pressure loading, and high injection precision with automatic capability. Combining the injection valve with an automatic system would increase the reliability of the injection system.

An analytical column is the heart of the chromatographic system and good or bad separation is mainly dependent on the characteristics of the packing material and its particle size. Pellicular packing materials with particle size of 30–40 μm were in common practice in the beginning of the LC revolution. These columns were relatively larger in length (1 m) and had low sample capacity and were easily overloaded. In recent years the concept of fast analysis has resulted in the development of microparticulate column-packing materials providing a high resolution and sensitivity for the analysis. These particles, which may be spherical or irregular, have narrow size distributions within a 5–10 μm range, a typical pore size of 3–10 nm providing a high efficiency.

In ion-exchange chromatography these resins are synthetic copolymers of styrene and divinylbenzene with the degree of cross-linking at 8–10%. In the use of these resins, the size distribution is actually more important for the resolution than the particle size, with the best resin having distributions of ±0.5 μm. In quantitation of AAs having an amount >10 pmol for each AA, it is possible to achieve reproducible results with the use of a one column system but when the levels for amino acids are <10 pmol, it is advisable to use two columns, one for the acidic and neutral AAs and the other entirely for the basic AAs.

In RP chromatography microparticulate silica of C_{18} or C_8 with 3–10 μm particle size is commonly employed. In dealing with the biological samples, the use of precolumn is recommended to protect the analytical column from various contaminants and to increase its durability.

In postcolumn derivatization systems, an additional pump is required for the derivatizing reagent to continuously add the reagent to the effluent after amino acid elution from the analytical column. Furthermore, a reaction coil is set to carry out the derivatization reaction under specific temperature control. The stability and the high yield of the reaction products are essential to provide high sensitivity and reproducibility of the method. To achieve this, the system should be maintained under constant flow rate of both reagent and mobile phases. Furthermore, the reaction coil, column, and injector should be kept under strictly controlled temperature.

Among the detectors, UV and fluorescence detection systems are the most frequently used in the postcolumn system whereas electrochemical, radioactive, NMR, and MS could also be used in the precolumn mode. The signals from a detector are recorded on a printer (recorder) or integrator, which could be connected with currently available computer systems for a rapid and accurate quantitation. This information could be stored on a disk.

In principle RP-LC is an extension of classical ion-exchange chromatography and is used in pre- and postcolumn derivatization modes. Figure 19–2 shows the commonly available design for the precolumn system. As compared to its counterpart, i.e., postcolumn, the mobile phases are each run with separate pumps and the mixing of these phases is controlled in a similar way to the previous mode but only in gradient elution. RP-C_8 or C_{18} columns are only employed in place of ion-exchange or RP columns.

The most common system employs two or three solvents in a gradient elution, but the separation of only certain amino acids could be achieved in an isocratic mode. The sensitivity of this mode is dependent on the reagent forming a single derivative with each AA to give high yield.

19.4 REAGENTS FOR POSTCOLUMN DERIVATIZATION PROCEDURES AND THEIR BIOLOGICAL APPLICATIONS

19.4.1 Ninhydrin

Most of the LC biological applications in various disciplines of biomedical sciences are done by the use of this reagent. It reacts with both primary and

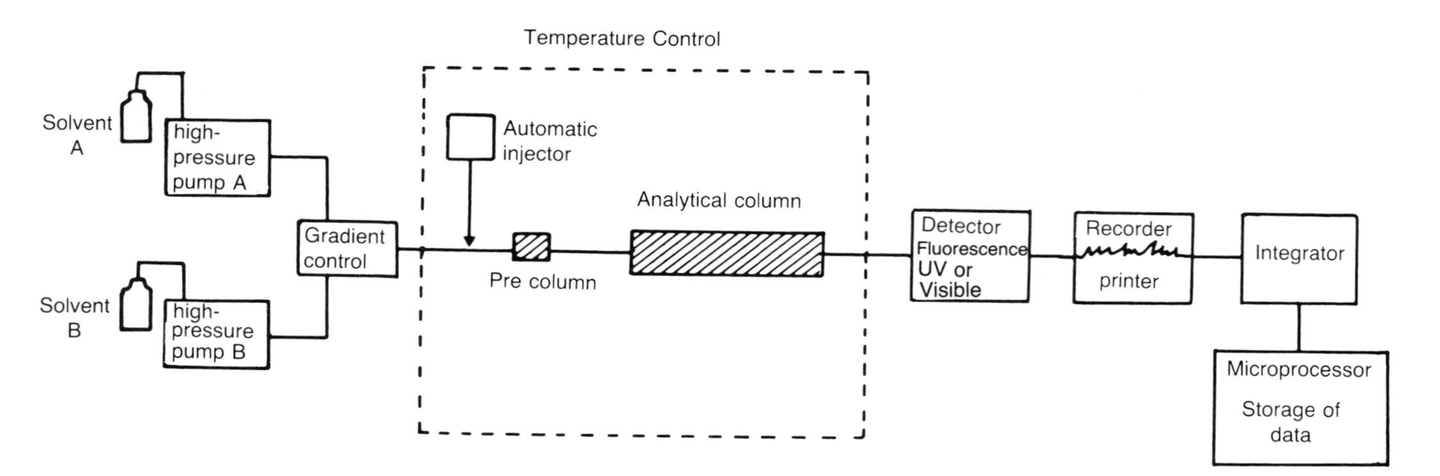

FIGURE 19–2. The components used for designing an HPLC system in the precolumn derivatization mode.

secondary AAs forming reaction products detectable at 470 and 550 nm, respectively. The reaction scheme is shown below.

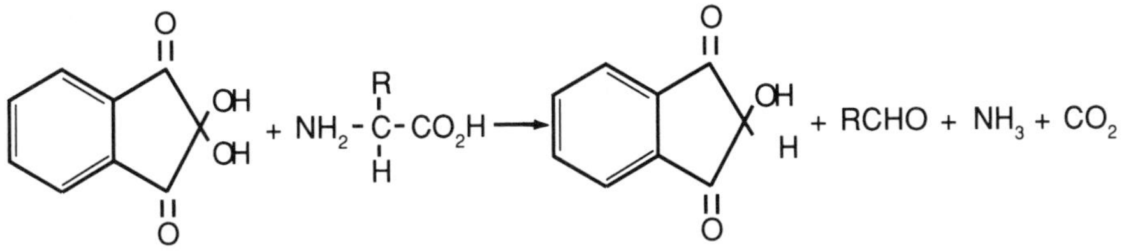

Ninhydrin + NH_2-C(R)(H)-CO_2H → Hydrindantin + RCHO + NH_3 + CO_2

Ninhydrin Amino acid Hydrindantin

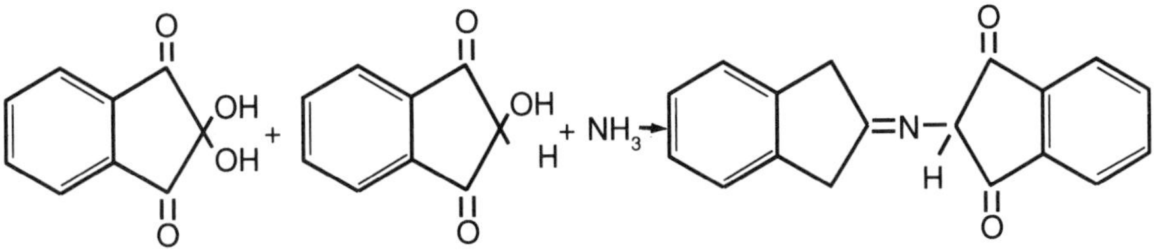

Ninhydrin + Hydrindantin + NH_3 → Ruhemann's Purple

Ninhydrin Hydrindantin Ruhemann's Purple

The reaction yield and kinetics for this reagent with AAs is temperature dependent, with high yields of the product at temperatures > 100°C within a few (2–3) minutes.

One of the main problems encountered in using this reagent is the difficulty in obtaining complete mixing with the eluting buffers due to the large viscosity differences. But, at present, ninhydrin reagents are considerably improved due to the commercial availability of the reagent, which is premixed, relatively stable, and nonprecipitating provided it is kept under oxygen-free conditions. Besides, the use of small reaction coils has also improved reagent performance. This could be one of the reasons that the reagent is still used in various clinical laboratories.

Figure 19–3 shows an ideal separation of 52 ninhydrin positive compounds on an (250 × 2.6 mm i.d.) ion-exchange column containing Hitachi-Custom ion-exchange resin 2619. The use of a precolumn (120 × 4 mm i.d.) packed with Hitachi-custom ion-exchange resin 2650 is shown as a suitable modification in the method to remove ammonia from the system.

The reagent has been utilized for an enormous number of applications in biological sciences in the past and is still in use for this purpose. The reader is referred to refs. 14, 15, 17, 23, 27, and 51–65 for further applications since 1970.

19.4.2 Fluorescamine

In the search for new reagents more sensitive than ninhydrin, fluorescamine was introduced by Underfield et al. in 1972.[66] The reagent is nonfluorescent

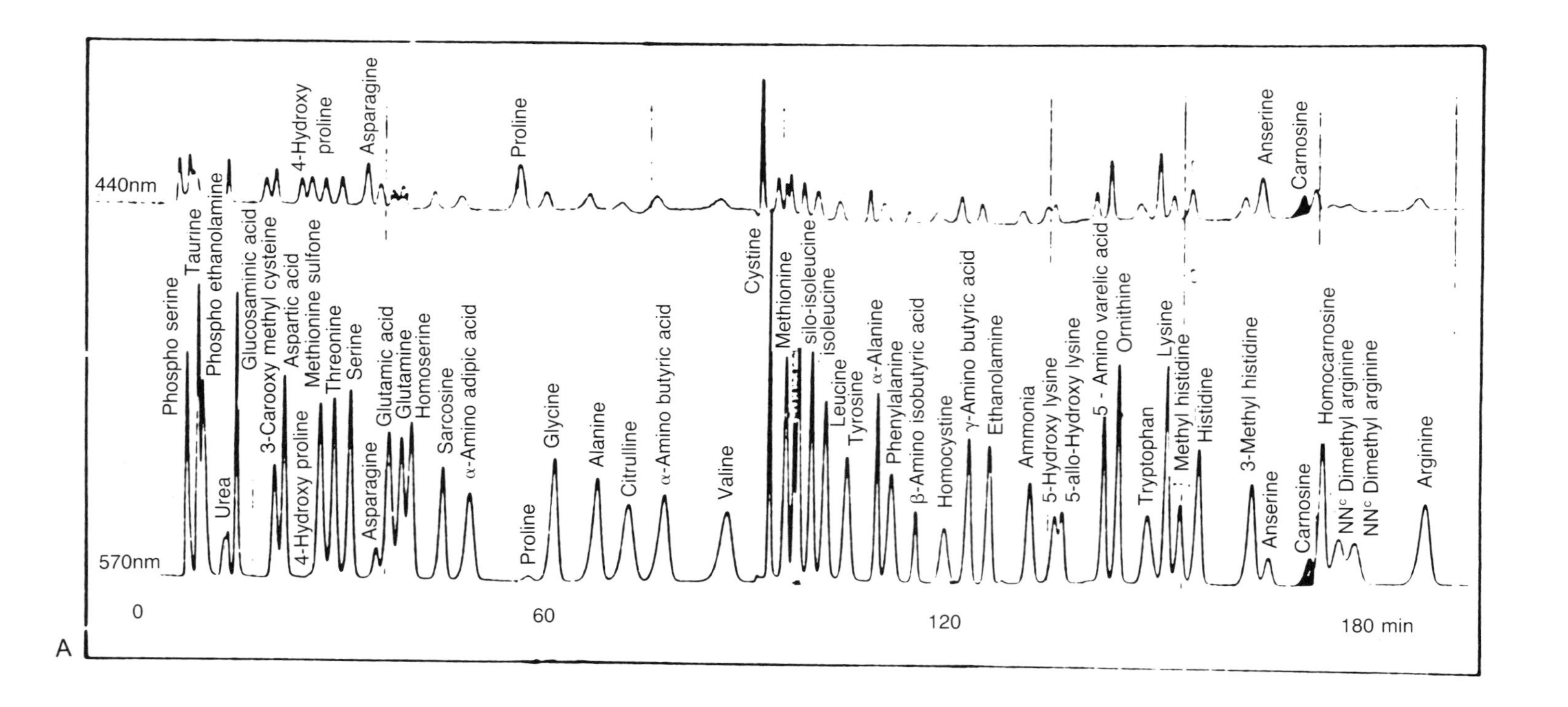
440nm
4-Hydroxy
proline
Asparagine
Proline
Anserine
Carnosine
570nm
Phospho serine
Taurine
Phospho ethanolamine
Urea
Glucosaminic acid
3-Carooxy methyl cysteine
Aspartic acid
4-Hydroxy proline
Methionine sulfone
Threonine
Serine
Asparagine
Glutamic acid
Glutamine
Homoserine
Sarcosine
α-Amino adipic acid
Proline
Glycine
Alanine
Citrulline
α-Amino butyric acid
Valine
Cystine
Methionine
silo-isoleucine
isoleucine
Leucine
Tyrosine
α-Alanine
Phenylalanine
β-Amino isobutyric acid
Homocystine
γ-Amino butyric acid
Ethanolamine
Ammonia
5-Hydroxy lysine
5-allo-Hydroxy lysine
5 - Amino varelic acid
Ornithine
Tryptophan
Lysine
Methyl histidine
Histidine
3-Methyl histidine
Anserine
Carnosine
Homocarnosine
NN^G Dimethyl arginine
NN^G Dimethyl arginine
Arginine
0
60
120
180 min
A

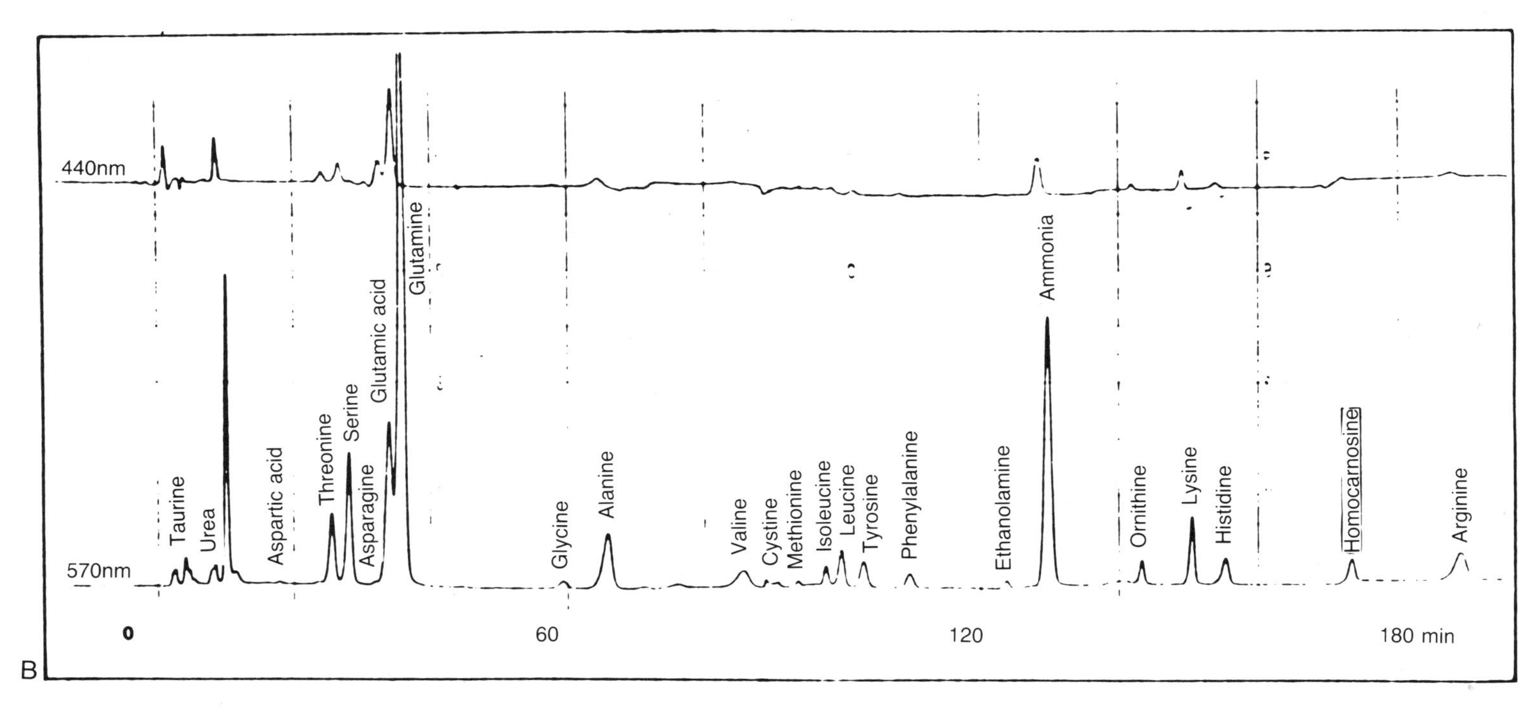

FIGURE 19–3. Typical chromatograms of (A) 52 standard ninhydrin-positive compounds separated on a stainless-steel column (250 × 2.6 mm i.d.) packed with Hitachi Custom ion-exchange resin 2619. Each AA represents concentrations of 2.5 nmol except for homoserine (0.625 nmol), cystathionine (1 nmol), *S*-carboxymethylcysteine, dimethylarginine (both 1.25 nmol), proline, sarcosine, β-alanine, and anserine (all 5 nmol), and urea (250 nmol). The separation was performed by the use of 5 lithium buffers with 0.155 to 1.2 *N* concentrations and a pH of 3–4.40. An application of the above method is shown in (B) a CSF sample under identical conditions shown with permission from the authors (ref. 51).

and reacts with primary AAs in akali medium, forming a sensitive fluorescence reaction product within a few minutes at ambient temperature. The reaction scheme is given below.

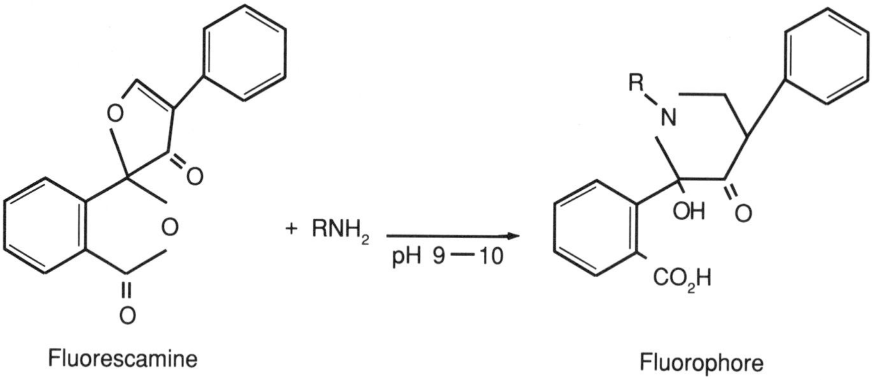

+ RNH_2 → pH 9—10

Fluorescamine Fluorophore

The detection of the reaction product (fluorophore) is performed at E_{ex} = 390 and E_{em} = 475 nm. The reagent does not react with secondary AAs, but the reaction chemistry could be modified by first reacting the secondary AAs with *N*-chlorosuccinimide thus converting these amines into aldehydes by oxidative carboxylation then reacting these aldehydes with the reagent.[67]

The reagent is far from ideal as it is almost instantaneously hydrolyzed by water and therefore is prepared in acetone. Hence, the utility of the reagent becomes limited in its use as the fluorescence intensity of the fluorophoric compound formed is reduced on its contact with aqueous buffers; in addition, acetone is sensitive to effluent temperature resulting in the problem of maintaining a steady baseline. Furthermore the reagent is too expensive as compared to other fluorescence reagents.

19.4.3 Orthophthalaldehyde (OPA)

Among all the reagents used in HPLC methodology, OPA is considered to be one of the most utilized. The reagent was first introduced by Roth in 1971 and later shown to be an alternative to ninhydrin in LC methods.[68,69]

Similar to fluorescamine, the reagent is nonfluorescent and reacts rapidly with primary amines under alkaline conditions. It is less expensive, readily soluble in aqueous solutions, and gives a 5- to 10-fold greater sensitivity than fluorescamine. The reaction of OPA with primary amines requires the presence of a reducing agent (thiol) to yield the reaction product. All primary amines form a single product with the reagent. The reaction chemistry is shown below.

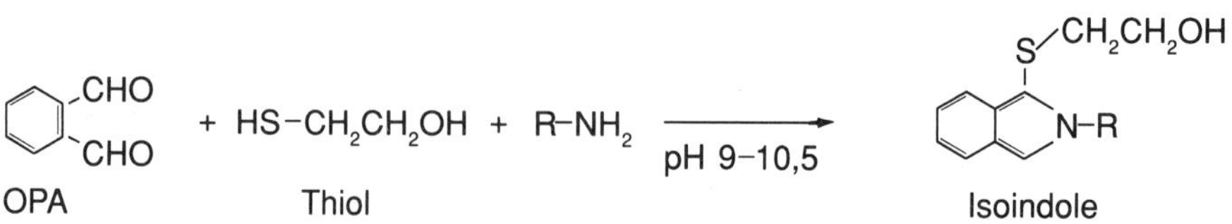

OPA + $HS-CH_2CH_2OH$ (Thiol) + $R-NH_2$ → pH 9–10,5 Isoindole

No reagent artifact peaks are observed and the highly fluorescent end-product, i.e., the 1-alkylthio-2-alkylisoindole derivative predisposes fluorescence detection with the detection limit < 1 pmol. The derivatives display a maximum excitation at 340 nm with an emission wavelength between 430 and 450 nm.

Among the primary AAs, cysteine (Cys) and lysine (Lys) give relatively low fluorescence responses with the reagent. The addition of iodoacetic acid or performic acid to the sample results in a better fluorescence yield for the Cys-OPA adduct,[70,71] whereas the addition of Brij-35 to the reagent results in an improved fluorescence response for Lys.[72]

The reagent has one more advantage over ninhydrin since the presence of ammonia in the mobile phase does not interfere with the quantitation of AAs (as the product of OPA-NH_3 gives 1000 times less fluorescence as compared to primary amines).

The reagent's disadvantage of not reacting with secondary AAs can be overcome by the use of an oxidizing agent such as sodium hypochloride[73] or sodium *N*-chloro-*p*-toluene sulfonamide (chloroamine-T).[74] At present, with the commercially available postcolumn systems, it is very possible to quantitate primary as well as secondary AAs in the same run with the use of an additional pump to oxidize secondary AAs before reacting them with the OPA reagent (see Figure 19–1). However, precautions should be taken to avoid continual use of the oxidizing agent as most of the primary AAs may be destroyed thus giving false quantitative results.

Another common problem with the OPA reagent is its susceptibility to air oxidation and its deterioration under light, which prevents its long-term use without removing oxygen and keeping the reagent in the dark. To achieve consistent results, the reagent should be prepared every 3 days and should be kept refrigerated under N_2 gas.

Figure 19–4 shows the separation of AAs in the postcolumn derivatization mode with the use of a 120-mm-long column containing 6 μm sulfonated ion-exchange resin. The separation of 18 amino acids is achieved by the use of two solvents and the separation of both primary and secondary AAs is shown by the authors[75] within 35 min with relative standard deviations (RSD) between 1 and 2.5% and all 18 amino acids at 100 pmol concentrations.

The method is also compared with the ninhydrin method in determining the molar ratios of AAs in soy protein hydrolysate and the result showed an agreeable comparison between the two procedures.[75]

Various other biological applications have been made[23,75,79] by the use of OPA/2-ME in the postcolumn mode but the reagent has shown more feasibility in its use in a precolumn mode, which is discussed under 19.5.4.

The use of an ion-pair reagent in the mobile phase to separate AAs on an RP-C_8 or C_{18} column has also been designed by various research groups[80,81] in conjunction with postcolumn derivatization using OPA/2-ME.

Figure 19–5 shows the separation of amino acids from normal human plasma on a (250×4 mm i.d.) LiChrosorb RP_8 column using a convex curve gradient between 0.05 *M* sodium lauryl sulfate (pH 3) and 0.05 *M* sodium lauryl sulfate–acetonitrile (55:45) with a flow rate of mobile phase and reagent (OPA) of 1.2 and 0.7 ml/min, respectively. In this separation, column and mixing coil were kept at ambient temperature.

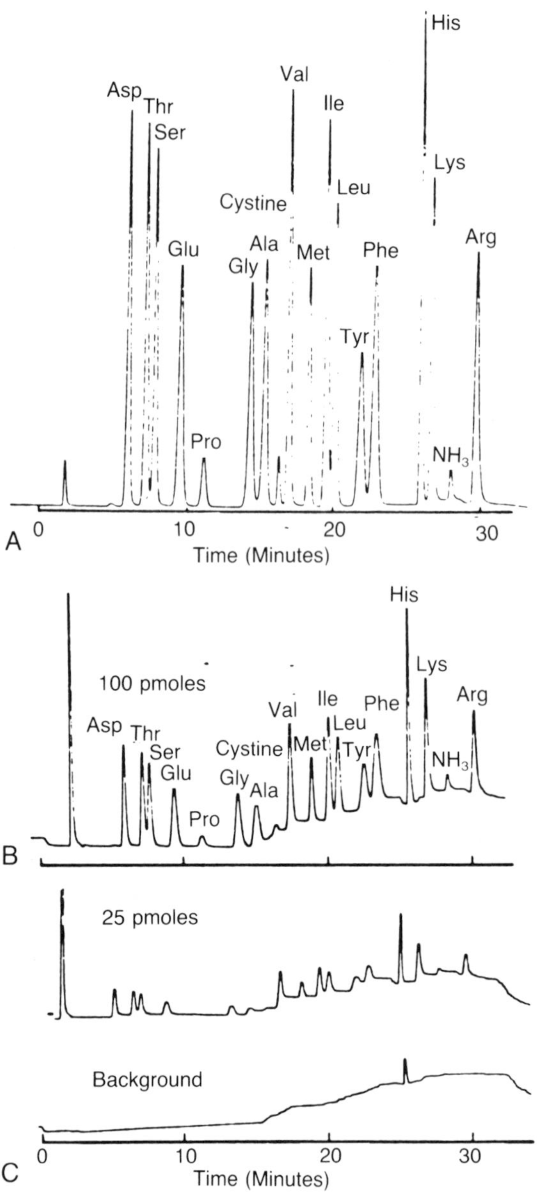

FIGURE 19–4. The separation of 18 amino acids is shown to demonstrate the high sensitivity of AAs determination at 500 (A), 100 (B), and 25 (C) pmol levels. The elution of AAs was performed on a Perkin-Elmer high-speed amino acid analysis column (120 $\times$ 4.6 mm i.d.) packed with 6-μm sulfonated ion-exchange resin by running a gradient with 3 solvents. The separation was performed in postcolumn derivatization mode, which is completed within 25 min. OPA/2ME was used as the reagent. Detection was made at E_{ex} = 340, E_{em} = 450 nm, shown with permission from the authors (ref. 75).

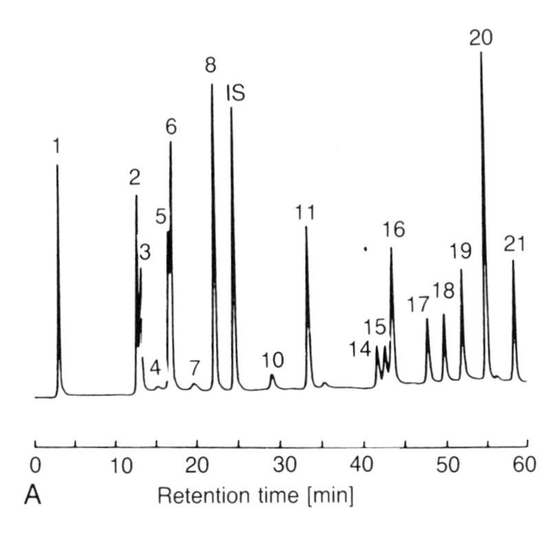

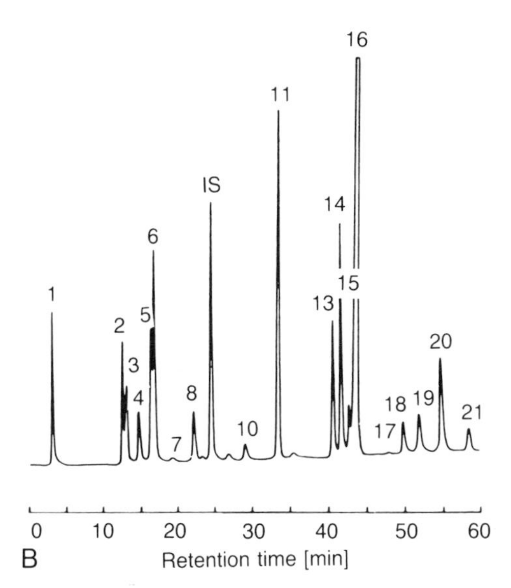

FIGURE 19–5. Separation of amino acids in human plasma from (A) normal and (B) MSUD patient by ion-pair HPLC. Peaks: 1, Tau; 2, Asp; 3, Ser; 4, Glu; 5, Thr; 6, Gly; 7, Cit; 8, Ala; 9, GABA (internal std); 10, Tyr; 11, Val; 13, Allo-Ise; 14, Ise; 15, Phe; 16, Leu; 17, Trp; 18, His; 19, Orn; 20, Lys; and 21, Arg. Operating conditions: Column (250 × 4 mm i.d.) LiChrosorb RP_8 (5 μm); mobile phase; solvent A, 0.05 *M* sodium lauryl sulfate (pH 3), solvent B, 0.05 *M* lauryl sulfate–acetonitrile (55:45); flow rate, 0.7 ml/min (mobile phase), 1.2 ml/min (reagent); injection volume 50 μl; column and mixing coil were kept at room temperature; fluorescence detection; E_{ex} = 365, E_{em} = 455 nm, shown with permission from the authors (ref. 80).

19.5 REAGENTS IN PRECOLUMN DERIVATIZATION PROCEDURES AND THEIR BIOLOGICAL APPLICATIONS

19.5.1 Dansyl Chloride (Dns-Cl)

Dansylation is one of the oldest precolumn derivatization procedures. Dansyl chloride (Dns-Cl), i.e., 1-dimethylamino naphthalene-5-sulfonyl chloride was first introduced in 1951[82] and later explored as a fluorescence labeling probe for the detection of amino acids by Gary and Hartley.[83,84] This Sanger-type reagent, which is itself fluorescent, reacts with both primary and secondary amines in alkaline media and generates strongly fluorescent reaction products. The reaction chemistry is shown below.

CH_3 CH_3 N — SO_2 Cl + RNH_2 $\xrightarrow{pH > 8 < 10}$ CH_3 CH_3 N — O=S=O — NHR + HCl

Dansyl chloride Dansyl amino acid

Earlier studies on the reagent have demonstrated that it is far from ideal since there are several problems encountered in the preparation of dansyl-amino acid (Dns-AAs) derivatives. The reagent not only reacts with the α-amino and imino groups but also reacts with some reactive side chains forming multiderivatives for the basic AAs such as histidine, lysine, tyrosine, and arginine. Besides, the yields for some of the AAs such as alanine and histidine are entirely dependent on the molar ratio of the reagent to the AA and on incubation conditions, especially at temperatures >60°C, which can also result in the loss of asparagine, glutamine, and tryptophan.

Tapuhi et al.[86] and Wiedmeier et al.[87] improved the derivatization procedure by conducting the reaction of Dns-Cl at room temperature to avoid conversion of Dns-AAs through reaction with Dns-Cl to form multiple derivatives with certain AAs. Furthermore, pH for the derivatization and the molar ratio between Dns-Cl and AA (>1000) have to be controlled rigorously to obtain the highest yield (>90%) of the reaction product. The reaction procedure is sensitive to light and must be performed in the dark both during the reaction and prior to subsequent quantitation. The quantitation of Dns-AAs is performed by UV absorption of 254 nm or fluorescence detection at E_{ex} = 385 nm and E_{em} = 460–500 nm.

Figure 19–6 shows the separation of amino acids of a sample from rat liver (from ref. 87).

The biological application on body tissues,[88] plasma and urine,[89] brain,[90] and infusion solutions[91] have been performed by some groups. All these studies make use of a multiple step gradient with acetate buffer (pH 3–4) and acetonitrile using either an RP-C_8 or RP-C_{18} column. In most of these studies, various experimental conditions for the derivatization procedures were adopted

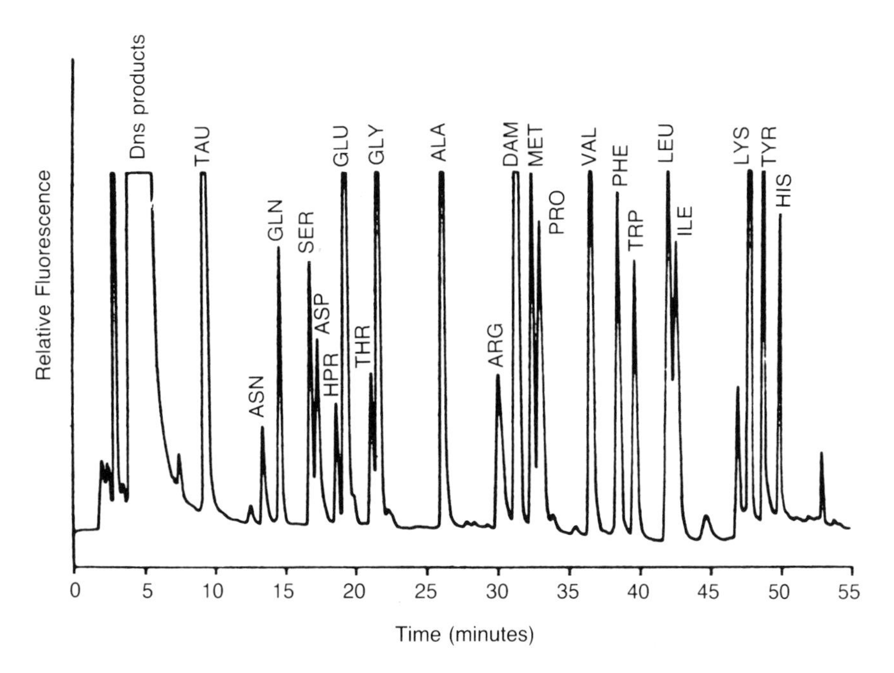

FIGURE 19–6. Chromatogram showing the separation of Dns-amino acid derivatives from a rat liver sample. Operating conditions: 5 μm ultrasphere-ODS (250 × 4.6 mm i.d.); mobile phase, solvent A, 10 m*M* sodium acetate buffer (pH 4.8)/tetrahydrofuran (95:5); solvent B, acetonitrile–tetrahydrofuran (90:10); flow rate, 1 ml/min; gradient used, the chromatographic run started with 10% B and was increased to 40% B over 30 min where it was kept for 15 min. Then %B was increased to 100% over 3 min and maintained there for 12 min. The column was reequilibrated with A/B (90:10) for 8 min before the next injection was made; injection volume, 50 μl; shown with permission from the authors (ref. 87).

to control the kinetics of the reaction between Dns-Cl and AAs resulting in a single derivative product for each AA.

19.5.2 Dimethylamino Azobenzene-4-sulfonyl Chloride (Dabsyl Chloride)

Lin and Chang[92] were the first in 1975 to use this reagent in HPLC methodology. The reaction chemistry is similar to Dns-Cl where the reagent products formed are more stable but less sensitive than Dns-Cl. The scheme for the reaction is as follows:

$$(CH_3)_2N\text{-}C_6H_4\text{-}N{=}N\text{-}C_6H_4\text{-}SO_2\text{-}Cl + RNH_2 \xrightarrow{\text{pH } 9} (CH_3)_2N\text{-}C_6H_4\text{-}N{=}N\text{-}C_6H_4\text{-}S(=O)_2\text{-}NH\text{-}R$$

Dabsyl—Cl DABS—Amino acid

The reaction of Dabsyl-Cl with AAs under carefully selected conditions (pH 9, 70°C) is complete within 10 min. The derivatives formed are strongly colored and are detectable at 425–436 nm. The authors have shown the separation of 20 amino acids within 30 min, utilizing an acetate–acetonitrile gradient system achieving a detection limit of 3–5 pmol.[92]

Very few biological applications have been recorded[92,93] using this reagent but in one of its applications, urine samples from cancer patients were shown to contain high concentrations of branched-chain amino acids and tryptophan compared to healthy persons.[93] The reaction procedure has also been applied to evaluate the levels of amino acids in a mouse brain under various pathological states.[92]

19.5.3 Phenylthiohydantoin (PTH)

Among PTH reagents (Edman reagents), phenylisothiocyanate (PITC) has been mostly used in the amino acid sequence analysis of a great majority of biologically active peptides and proteins. PITC has been known for 30 years. Its reaction with peptides and proteins employs the classical Edman's degradation procedure to subsequently cleave the N-terminal amino acids.[94] The following series of reactions form the basis of degradation as outlined by Edman et al.[95]

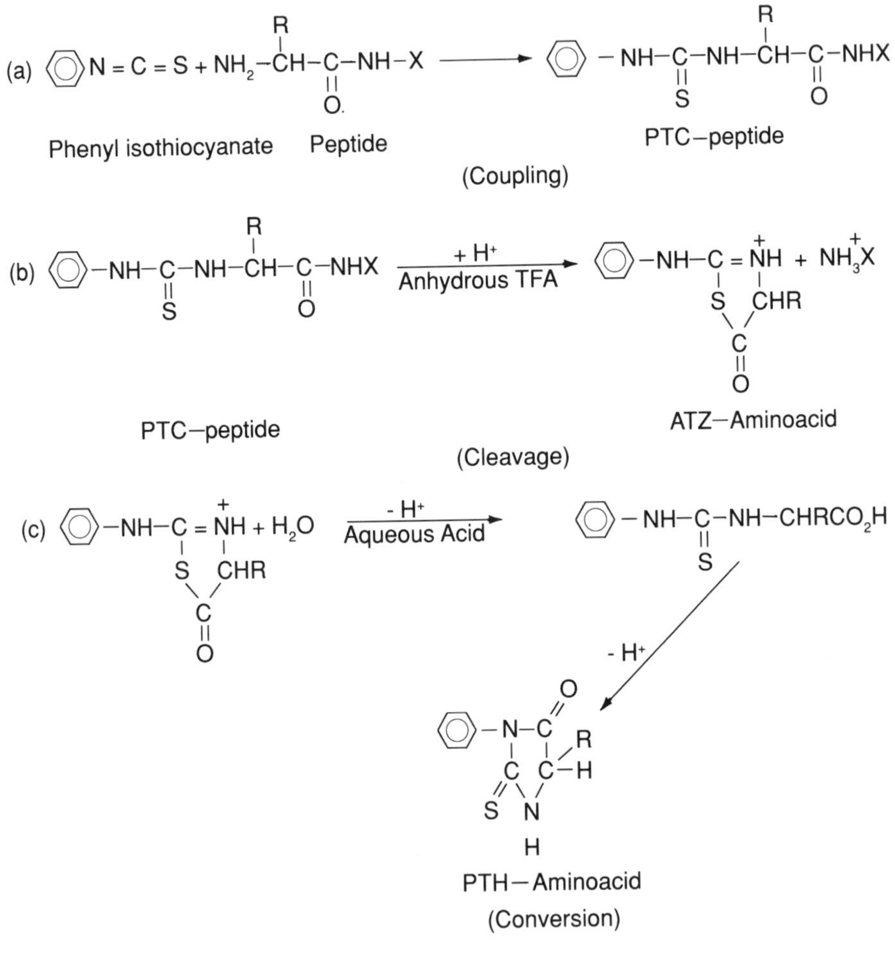

(a) C_6H_5–N=C=S + NH_2–CH(R)–C(=O)–NH–X ⟶ C_6H_5–NH–C(=S)–NH–CH(R)–C(=O)–NHX

Phenyl isothiocyanate Peptide PTC–peptide

(Coupling)

(b) C_6H_5–NH–C(=S)–NH–CH(R)–C(=O)–NHX $\xrightarrow[\text{Anhydrous TFA}]{+H^+}$ C_6H_5–NH–C=$\overset{+}{N}$H (ring: S, CHR, C=O) + $\overset{+}{N}H_3X$

PTC–peptide ATZ–Aminoacid

(Cleavage)

(c) C_6H_5–NH–C=$\overset{+}{N}$H (ring: S, CHR, C=O) + H_2O $\xrightarrow[\text{Aqueous Acid}]{-H^+}$ C_6H_5–NH–C(=S)–NH–CHRCO$_2$H $\xrightarrow{-H^+}$ PTH–Aminoacid (C_6H_5–N–C(=O)–C(R)(H)–NH–C(=S), ring)

PTH–Aminoacid

(Conversion)

The cycle of reaction is automatically performed using commercial equipment,[96] which enhances the speed and predictability with even lower amounts of proteins (<100 pmol).

Previously this scheme of reaction was common practice in analyzing AAs by paper, thin-layer, and gas chromatography and mass spectroscopy but the introduction of HPLC has shown many advantages over the previous methods in structure elucidation of proteins when small amounts of material are available. Furthermore, because PTH-AA derivatives lack volatile character and are thermally unstable, HPLC methods have an edge over other existing analytical methods and in addition HPLC is more sensitive by 3 orders of magnitude when compared to other methods.

Zimmerman et al.[97] showed the utility and potential of the reagent in the precolumn mode to separate 20 PTH-AA derivatives on a C_{18} column by use of a multiple gradient running between 0.01 *M* acetate buffer and acetonitrile. The derivatives were detected at UV 254–270 nm giving the same order of sensitivity as OPA.

The biological applications using this derivatization procedure, however, are very few and only a few research groups[98,100] have succeeded in showing some adequate separation of PTH-AA derivatives in biological fluids with reasonable reliability for their quantitations. The reason for this could be that the task of separating PTH-AA derivatives on an RP column is more complicated than the other prederivatizing reagents (such as OPA or DNS-Cl) due to the existence of two different polar groups within the derivatives, i.e., the hydrophobic groups such as Pro, Leu, Ile, Val, Phe, and Trp and hydrophilic groups such as Lys, Tyr, Thr, and acidic AAs making it difficult to resolve all AAs in one chromatographic run. But, perhaps the use of more than two solvents with varying pH, molarity, and a rise in column temperature would help in resolving problems. Recently Blajchand et al.[101] developed an HPLC method based on a ternary gradient containing phosphate buffer, methanol, and tetrahydrofuran as a mobile phase to separate 20 PTH-amino acids on a monofunctional dimethylphenyl modified silane column. Johansson and Isaksson[102] tackled the problem of separation by the use of the ion-pairing reagent 0.1% octane sulfate in acetate buffer and running a convex gradient against acetonitrile–tetrahydrofuran on a Pro RPC (20 × 0.46 cm i.d.) column from Pharmacia, Uppsala, Sweden. The method shows separation of 22 AAs in 20 min. In this separation the column temperature was kept at 41°C. Similar to PTH and PITC, new reagents such as dimethylaminobenzenethiohydantoin (DABTH), methylthiohydantoin (MTH), and diphenylindenonylthiohydantoin (ITH) are in use.[103–105] Among these reagents, ITH-AA showed better sensitivity by 3 orders of magnitude over PTH. Otherwise there are no other advantages in the use of these reagents over the more conventional PTH procedure. Figure 19–7 shows the separation of PITC-AAs in a plasma on Bio-Sil ODS-SS column with a stepwise gradient elution by the use of ammonium acetate (solvent A) and ammonium acetate–acetonitrile (50:50) (solvent B) with a flow rate of 1 ml/min.

19.5.4 Orthophthalaldehyde (OPA)

OPA is one of the reagents that can serve ideally both in pre-and postcolumn modes. The reaction chemistry is given in Section 19.4.3. Its excellent sen-

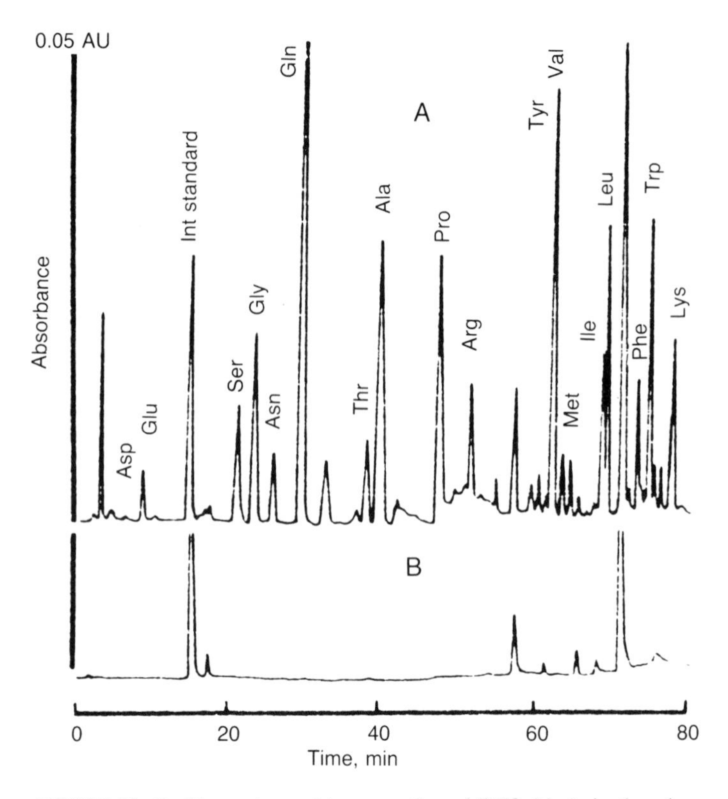

FIGURE 19–7. Chromatographic separation of PITC-AA derivatives in 50 μl (A) plasma; (B) blank sample after methanol extraction; 10 μl of the samples was injected. Operating conditions: 5 μm Bio-Sil-ODS (250 × 4 mm) (Bio-Rad); gradient: solvent A, 0.05 *M* ammonium acetate; solvent B, 50:50 buffer A:acetonitrile; detection wavelength, 254 nm; internal standard, α-amino adipate (2 nmol), shown with permission from the authors (ref. 98).

sitivity (<100 fmol) and rapid reaction make the reagent ideal for primary amines and AAs. Because the side chain of the primary AAs is incorporated into the isoindole structure, different OPA derivatives are formed from different AAs and hence the separation becomes an easier task than with other reagents. Furthermore the reducing agent (thiol) incorporates into the reaction product with different thiols such as 2-mercaptoethanol (2-ME), 3-mercaptopropionic acid (3-MPA), and ethanethiol (E) producing different structures with varying stabilities and chromatographic selectivities.[70] The main disadvantage of the reagent is that the OPA adducts are pH, time, and temperature dependent, but this limitation can be overcome by the use of an automatic system. Using an autosampler, aliquots of the sample and reagent are automatically mixed and hence the system can easily be automated to control the reaction kinetics with a controlled temperature and pH to provide reproducible results. In the author's laboratory using a Waters' WISP system Tables 19–1 and 19–2 are

TABLE 19–1. Reproducibility of the Data in Terms of Retention Times (t'_R) and Integrated Areas (A) Obtained HPLC Method Based on Precolumn Derivatization of Amino Acids with OPA/2-ME with Amino Acids. All the parameters are calculated after running the standard sample for 7 times. All amino acids corresponding to 5 μmol

	t'_R				$A \times 10^4$			
AA	MV	RSD	SEM	CV	MV	RSD	SEM	CV
Asp	5.93	0.008	0.003	0.14	4.37	0.031	0.012	0.73
Cys-S	7.62	0.024	0.090	0.31	3.71	0.052	0.020	1.41
Glu	10.76	0.021	0.008	0.20	4.12	0.033	0.011	0.74
Asn	19.14	0.201	0.076	1.05	4.04	0.051	0.021	1.37
Ser	20.67	0.202	0.076	0.97	4.76	0.104	0.038	2.12
Gln	23.33	0.397	0.150	1.70	2.59	0.108	0.037	3.79
His	24.84	0.499	0.189	2.05	2.90	0.180	0.068	6.22
Gly	26.18	0.396	0.150	1.51	3.32	0.183	0.069	5.53
Thr	26.70	0.410	0.155	1.54	5.00	0.130	0.049	2.58
3-MH	27.58	0.500	0.188	1.82	4.13	0.105	0.039	2.53
Arg	29.21	0.530	0.200	1.81	6.81	0.333	0.126	4.90
Ala	29.68	0.539	0.204	1.83	6.17	0.215	0.081	3.47
GABA	30.31	0.564	0.213	1.86	1.66	0.081	0.031	2.88
Tyr	31.58	0.564	0.212	1.85	5.70	0.172	0.065	2.02
Met	35.10	0.539	0.203	1.53	3.65	0.174	0.066	2.76
Val	35.43	0.505	0.191	1.42	5.94	0.283	0.107	4.76
Phe	36.21	0.434	0.164	1.20	4.22	0.585	0.221	3.85
Ile	37.04	0.377	0.142	1.02	3.96	0.152	0.057	3.84
Leu	37.47	0.362	0.137	0.97	4.57	0.037	0.014	0.81
Orn	38.35	0.252	0.095	0.66	1.31	0.028	0.011	2.18
Lys	38.85	0.237	0.090	0.61	2.02	0.034	0.013	1.65

[a] MV, mean value; RSD, relative standard deviation; SEM, standard error of mean; CV, coefficient of variation.

TABLE 19–2. Standard Curve Data for Amino Acids between the Concentrations of 5 and 50 μmol[a]

AA	Regression Equation	r^2	SEM	p
Asp	$Y = 0.22x + 0.11$	0.997	0.152	***
Cys-S	$Y = 0.15x + 0.11$	0.998	0.113	***
Glu	$Y = 0.05x + 0.12$	0.998	0.018	***
Asn	$Y = 0.58x + 0.16$	0.989	0.13	**
Ser	$Y = 0.22x + 0.11$	0.999	0.09	***
Gln	$Y = 0.10x + 0.16$	0.998	0.18	***
His	$Y = 0.23x + 0.10$	0.998	0.10	***
Gly	$Y = 0.22x + 0.11$	0.998	0.18	***
Thr	$Y = 0.13x + 0.15$	0.997	0.15	***
3-MH	$Y = 0.10x + 0.09$	0.999	0.06	***
Arg	$Y = 0.27x + 0.12$	0.999	0.09	***
Ala	$Y = 0.26x + 0.11$	0.999	0.09	***
GABA	$Y = 0.13x + 0.07$	0.999	0.05	***
Tyr	$Y = 0.31x + 0.12$	0.999	0.08	***
Met	$Y = 0.29x + 0.11$	0.998	0.13	***
Val	$Y = 0.38x + 0.15$	0.995	0.27	***
Phe	$Y = 0.23x + 0.11$	0.999	0.08	***
Ile	$Y = 0.22x + 0.13$	0.998	0.12	***
Leu	$Y = 0.19x + 0.11$	0.998	0.10	***
Orn	$Y = 0.16x + 0.04$	0.999	0.04	***
Lys	$Y = 0.18x + 0.06$	0.998	0.06	***

[a] p values: * <0.005, ** <0.01, *** <0.001. Regression equation: $Y = ax + b$ where Y = peak area $\times 10^4$, a = slope, x = concentration of amino acid, and b = the intercept on the y axis. SEM, standard error of mean.

constructed, which show the reliability of the OPA derivatization system in terms of retention times, integrated areas (Table 19–1), and regression data (Table 19–2).

The linearity of the fluorescence response for each amino acid is possible to maintain over a wide range of concentrations. However, it is important to use a 5- to 10-fold excess in concentration of OPA over the total amount of AAs. Most AA derivatives with OPA are separated either on C_8- or C_{18}-RP columns by a gradient elution using phosphate or acetate buffers (pH 5–7.5) and methanol or acetonitrile. The use of tetrahydrofuran (1–2%) does help to improve the separation of the Thr/Gly pair. An increase in effluent pH from 5 to 7.5 increases the fluorescence yield for most of the amino acids and hence the optimized pH would be between pH 6 to 7.2 within the pH constraints of the stationary phases.

The separation mechanism of OPA-AA derivatives on an RP column is believed to be a mixture of ionic (due to CO_2H group) and hydrophobic interactions.[106] With such a mechanism it is essential to use a well-buffered mobile phase such as phosphate buffer to maintain pH stability. Lindroth and Mopper[107] studied both OPA/2-ME and OPA/E-AAs and showed a dependence of retention parameters (t'_R and ln k') on PO_4^{3-} ion concentration. Furthermore, the column temperature showed an inverse relationship with retention parameters.

Hills et al.[108] demonstrated that by the use of a lower excitation wavelength (229 nm) as compared to the commonly used one of 340 nm, one can reach a sensitivity of 5 fmol for all amino acids. Besides in recent years, the use of electrochemical detection has shown a sensitivity in the same order of magnitude.[109] The applications of the OPA derivatization procedure combined with electrochemical detection have been made in the isocratic mode to evaluate the levels of amino acid neurotransmitters in brain homogenates and CSF.[110,111]

There are various biological applications recorded using this procedure of derivatization with fluorescence detection in analysis of protein hydrolysates, plasma, serum, urine, CSF, synaptosoma extract, tissues, culture cells, muscle, and inner ear fluids under various pathological states.[112–131] Figure 19–8 shows one of the applications of the OPA derivatization procedures on biological samples.[124]

The method was shown to separate 31 AAs within 40 min by the use of two solvents. Furthermore, the use of propionic acid in solvent A was shown to give good peak symmetry for 3-methylhistidine whereas the addition of dimethyl sulfoxide in solvent B improved the resolution of valine and methionine. Various applications have been made using the method with biological fluids.

Figure 19–9 shows another application[130] of OPA-2ME reaction with AAs in the quantitation of various AAs in liver tissue, brain, and gastrocnemius muscle by a more or less similar method.[125] The accuracy and reproducibility were shown to be much better than the previous method[125] by performing manual injection.

19.5.5 4-Fluoro-7-nitrobenzo-2,1,3-oxadiazole (NBD-F)

This is a relatively new reagent that had been introduced by Watanabe and Imai[132] in 1982. The reagent reacts with AAs at pH > 8 at 60°C within 1 min. The reaction chemistry is outlined below.

$$O_2N\text{-}C_6H_2(N_2O)\text{-}F + NH_2\text{-}CH(R)\text{-}CO_2H \xrightarrow{\text{pH } 8-9} O_2N\text{-}C_6H_2(N_2O)\text{-}NH\text{-}CH(R)\text{-}CO_2H + HF$$

7,Fluoro–4 nitro-
benzo oxa–1,3–dizole

NBD–Amino acid

The reagent reacts with both primary and secondary amines and is capable of being adopted for pre- as well as postcolumn derivatization modes. The sensitivity is 1 order of magnitude better than OPA.

The detection of the reaction product is made at E_{ex} = 470 and E_{em} = 550 nm. In this method the same authors performed a precolumn derivatization and with the use of 3 solvents, methanol, phosphate buffer (pH 6), and tetrahydrofuran, were able to resolve 18 common AAs within 80 min. From their chromatograms Gly/Gln, Ser/Asn, and Thr/Tau pairs overlapped each other

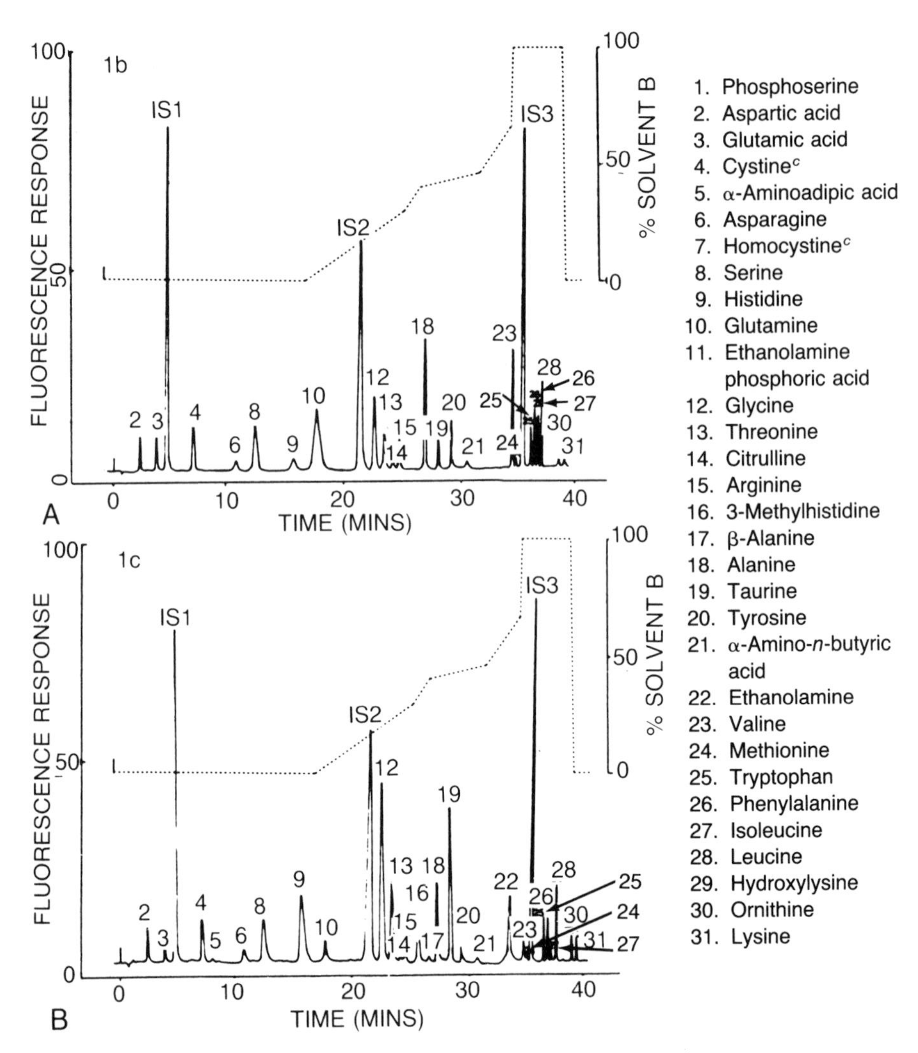

FIGURE 19–8. Separation of OPA/2-ME derivatized amino acids in (A) serum and (B) urine. Samples from a healthy person on 5-μm Ultrasphere-ODS (150 × 4.6 mm i.d.) by the use of the mobile phases, water–0.25 *M* sodium proprionate–acetonitrile (72:20:8) (solvent A) and water–acetonitrile–methanol–dimethyl sulfoxide (42:30:25:3 by vol) (solvent B). The gradient used is shown in the figure. A flow rate of 2 ml/min was maintained throughout the chromatographic run. The detection was made at E_{ex} = 230 and E_{em} = 418 nm, shown with permission from the authors (ref. 124).

through the application of this procedure has been applied to the quantitation of AAs in blood samples from newborns with phenylketonuria and syrup urine disease and from patients with tyrosinosis.

There has only been one more biological application recently[133] where the authors have improved the chromatographic methods to avoid the overlapping of the above mentioned AA pairs.

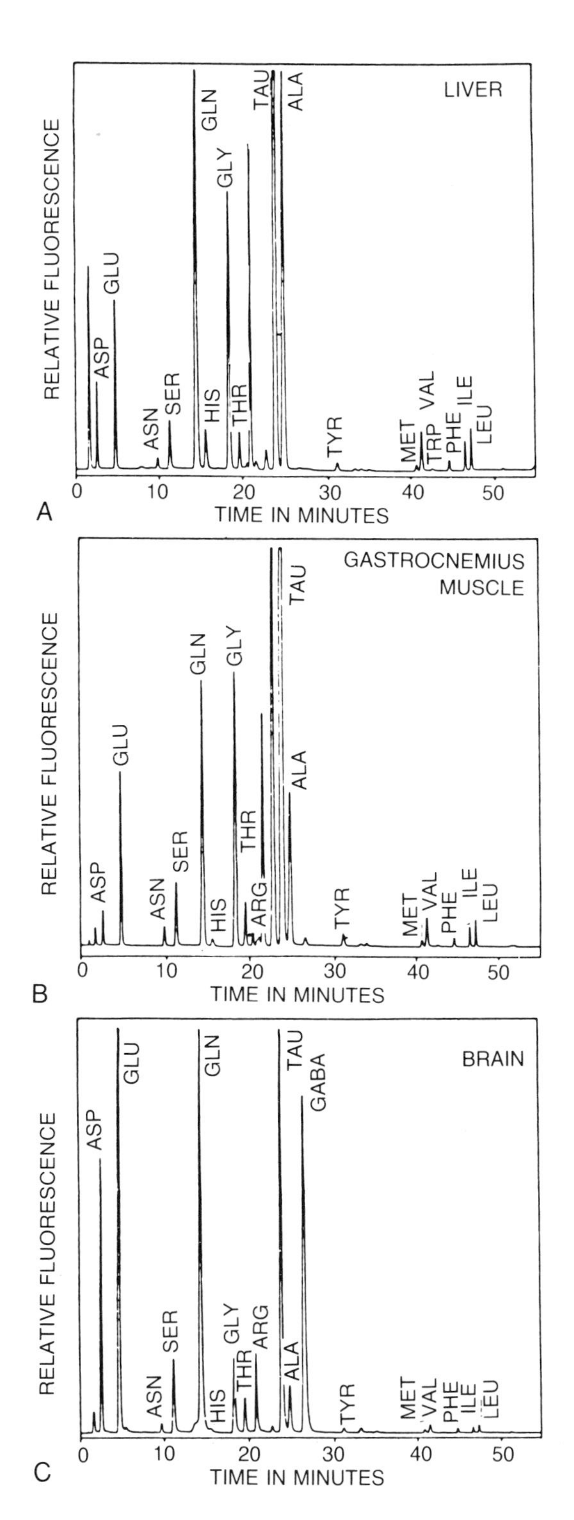

FIGURE 19–9. Chromatograms of (A) rat liver, (B) brain, and (C) gastrocnemius muscle amino acids as OPA/2-ME derivatives on 3-μm Ultrasphere-ODS (75 × 4.5 mm i.d.). Operating conditions: flow rate, 1.5 ml/min; solvent A, 0.1 *M* sodium acetate (pH 7.2); solvent B, methanol–tetrahydrofuran (97:3); gradient program, linear gradient from 10% (initial) to 18% B for 12 min, isocratic elution step at 18% B for 4 min, linear step to 28% B for 4 min, isocratic step at 28% B for 8 min, linear step to 45% B for 3.5 min, linear step to 70% B for 7.5 min, linear step to 100% B for 1 min, isocratic step at 100% B for 3 min, linear step 10% B (initial) for 1 min, isocratic at 10% B for 10 min; sample volume, 20 μl; detection, excitation at 338 nm, emission at 425 nm, shown with permission from the author (ref. 130).

19.5.6 9-Fluorenylmethylchloroformate (FMOC-Cl)

Various chloroformates are known to undergo very rapid condensation with amino groups in alkaline media resulting in the formation of carbonates in high yield.[134,135]

9-Fluorenylmethylchloroformate (FMOC-Cl) is one such chloroformate previously used as a protective reagent for the amino group in peptide synthesis.[136] Later, Anson Moye and Boning[137] demonstrated the use of the reagent in a fluorescence labeling procedure for both primary and secondary AAs. The reagent FMOC-Cl reacts with the amino group in AAs rapidly giving his yields within a short time, <1 min, under certain experimental conditions. The reaction chemistry is shown below.

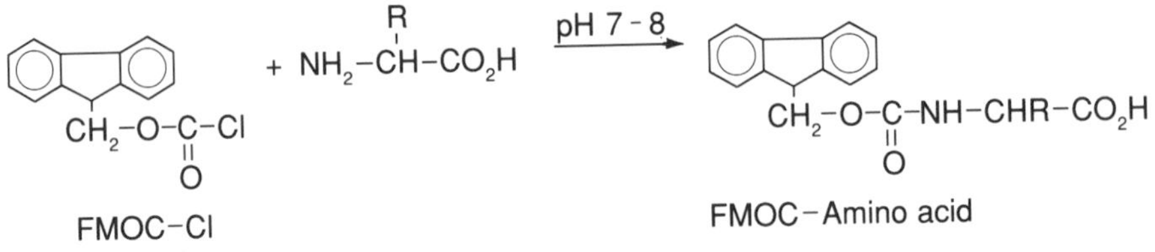

$$CH_2{-}O{-}\overset{\displaystyle O}{\overset{\|}{C}}{-}Cl \; + \; NH_2{-}\overset{\displaystyle R}{\overset{|}{C}}H{-}CO_2H \xrightarrow{\text{pH } 7-8} CH_2{-}O{-}\overset{\displaystyle O}{\overset{\|}{C}}{-}NH{-}CHR{-}CO_2H$$

FMOC–Cl FMOC–Amino acid

In contrast to OPA and fluorescamine, FMOC-Cl is itself fluorescent and has to be removed by liquid–liquid extraction (i.e., diethyl ether) after its reaction with AAs prior to HPLC analysis.

Einarsson et al.[138] developed an HPLC method and have shown the potential of the reagent in the quantitation of AAs in biological samples by the use of a 3-μm shandon Hypersil-ODS column (125 × 4.6 mm i.d.) by running a linear gradient between acetate buffer and acetonitrile. By this procedure the authors were able to separate 20 AAs within 20 min. The detection of FMOC amino acids was made at E_{ex} = 260 and E_{em} = 310 nm. The method of analysis by this derivatization procedure is claimed to give greater fluorescence sensitivity when compared to OPA and Dns-Cl.

Only two other biological applications of this derivatizing reagent are on record[139,140] and the author's opinion is that the reagent has a great potential which is yet to be seen.

19.6 RELIABILITY OF HPLC METHODS AND THE QUANTITATION OF AMINO ACIDS IN BIOLOGICAL SAMPLES (A CRITICAL VIEW)

There is no best method for AA analysis. In the literature various HPLC methods have been introduced, with each method claimed to be the best in terms of sensitivity, reproducibility, and reliability. But the task still remains to find a method that can overcome all the previously recorded disadvantages in AA quantitations.

LC based on an ion-exchange column has been developed since 1959 and is in use in most of the clinical laboratories for AA quantitation *in vivo* and *in vitro* despite the fact that RP-HPLC has shown within its few years of use a great potential and capacity for similar purposes. But not all or even a majority of research laboratories have shifted from ion-exchange HPLC to RP-HPLC or from a postcolumn to a precolumn derivatization mode or vice versa. A similar tendency is seen for the ninhydrin reagent for derivatization purposes, which is still regularly used despite the fact that many fluorescence reagents have been introduced giving highly sensitive reactions with AAs.

Furthermore, in AA quantitation a shift in the baseline, correct identification of amino acids, contamination of buffer used, interference caused by the presence of NH_3, and broadening of peaks are some of the problems associated with the postcolumn methodology.[141] The technical advancements in the method have indeed solved some of these problems but not completely. For example, two column systems and packed bed reactors have been introduced to minimize peak broadening and baseline shift.[142] On the other hand various limitations do exist in precolumn procedures.

There are various sources of error that should be controlled no matter what method is used. There are two main sources of discrepancies in AA quantitation in biological matrices caused by instrumental errors and performing the analysis. Both of these are discussed briefly.

19.6.1 Instrumental Errors

19.6.1.1 Validity and Reliability of the Selected Method for Analysis

Any optimized method of analysis is judged by its reproducibility and sensitivity under specific experimental conditions in recording the AA profile in normal or healthy and pathological states. The goal in most clinical studies is to refine and improve the understanding of a problem in a better way from the previous results. The improvement in the results is mainly achieved by the comparison of the present method with the previous method of analysis in terms of reproducibility obtained in a number of standard solutions on runs and its reliability in terms of standard deviation (SD), coefficient of variation (CV), and regression curve data in biological concentration range.

In this approach, it is vital that before any new method can be labeled as a good method it should meet the criteria in giving good reproducibility in reported runs with less than 3% SD and 1–2 CV having the value of r^2 from regression analysis in the biological concentration range near to unity. When any method fulfills all these requirements it should be put into practice to evaluate the levels of amino acids in biological samples. The reliability of the results is valid only when standards and the samples are treated and chromatographed under identical conditions.

19.6.1.2 Stability of the LC System

To achieve precision by any LC method of analysis, basic requirements should be made on the mechanical and electrical stability of the analyzing system, i.e., pump providing a constant flow, gradient control units ability to mix two or more solvents with precision, temperature variation during chromatographic runs, repeated performance by an analytical column, and the stability of the detector in terms of light source. Hence, errors caused by these variables should be avoided if these units are checked and when necessary repaired or replaced.

In most clinical laboratories, the people working with HPLC techniques have a medical education and lack technical know-how. In this situation perhaps courses on the technical aspects of HPLC might help to control these factors adequately.

19.6.1.3 Separation Phenomena and the Interpretation of the Results

In most ion-exchange HPLC, commercially available standard AA mixtures are used to score a complete separation depending on the geometry of the analytical column. The run time to resolve all amino acids varies from ½ to 2 h depending on the number of interesting amino acids one is interested in. On the other hand in RP-HPLC, most standards are prepared in the laboratory and efforts are made to resolve as many AAs as possible within a short time (10 min to 1 h).

In the fast growing field of HPLC, every effort is made to score the separation of AAs within the shortest possible time. When dealing with the assessment of the levels of AAs in biological samples under various pathological states and in nutritional and metabolic studies one often forces a quick separation and, thus, one is bound to face the overlap of 2 or more AAs or their metabolites in a chromatographic separation under experimental conditions. It is general practice in chromatographic sciences that one does not believe that the AA or AAs one is interested in could overlap with any other unknown or known substance and, hence, one might be subjected to wrong quantitation causing serious errors in the AA profile and their interpretations from a clinical point of view.

Second, when looking for accuracy in the results one should take into consideration the baseline shift that should be corrected before calculating the levels of AAs in biological samples.

Third, when a small peak runs quite near a big peak care must be taken to calculate the results according to heights as well as areas to be sure that the concentration for the small peak agrees by these two calculation methods.

Figure 19–10 shows the chromatograms of (A) standard mixture of AAs, (B) first plasma sample, (C) 47th plasma sample, and (D) 93rd plasma sample run on the same column. All the experimental conditions were identical. The separation of AAs becomes unreliable depending on the numbers of samples one has run. Hence, this could shift the baseline and not record peak areas if the AAs are badly resolved from each other and could cause tailing.

For the durability and prolonged use of any analytical column as a general rule the mobile phase should be free from heavy metals, microorganisms, and particulate matter. The use of 0.1% phenol in mobile phases can be useful in preventing bacterial growth.

In the author's experience, dilution of the biological sample prolongs the life of the analytical column.

Figure 19–11A and B shows a similar situation in ion-exchange HPLC where the deterioration in the column causes different results, as is evident by running the standard in the beginning when the column has just been packed and again when the column has been in use after running 200 to 500 biological

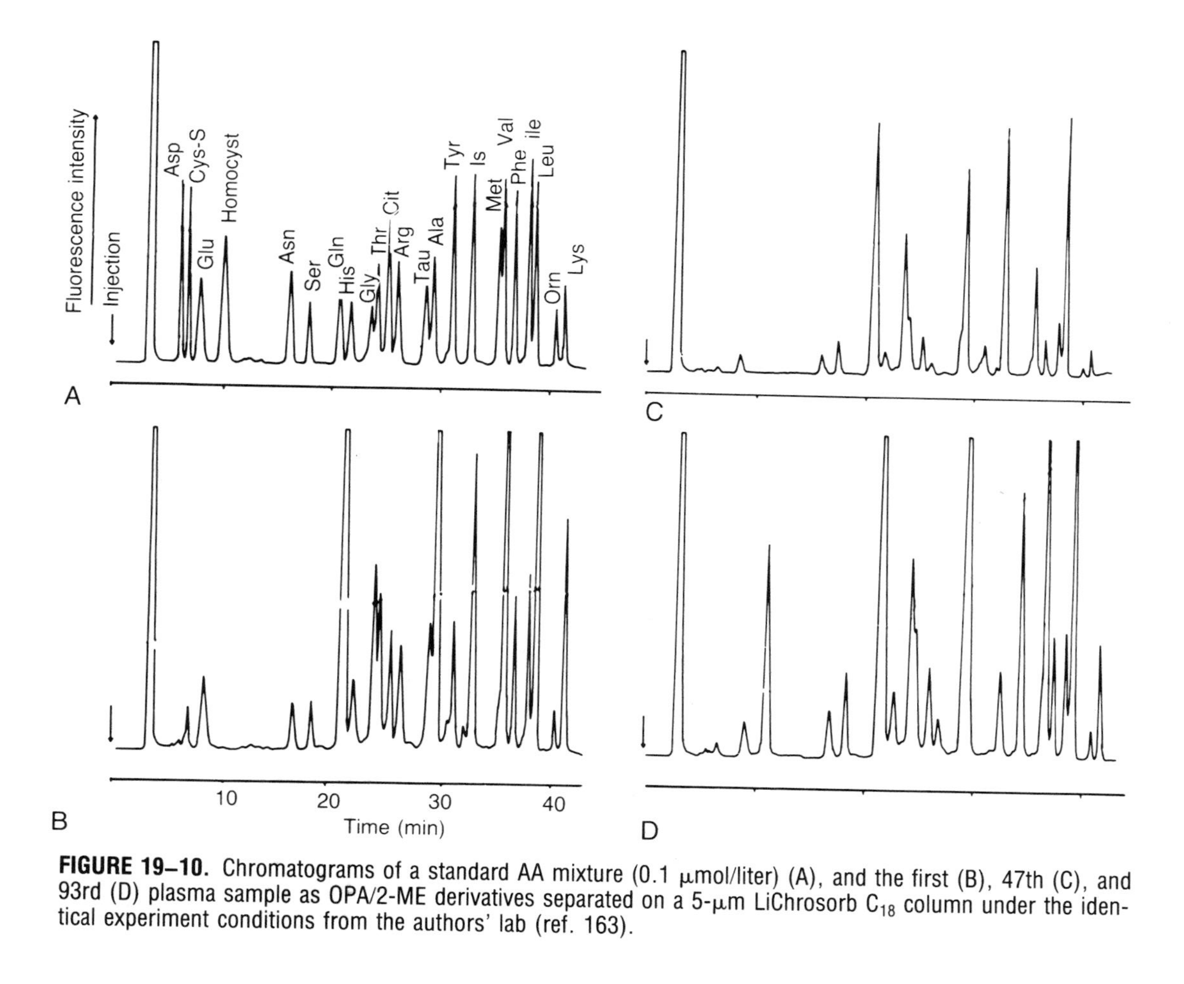

FIGURE 19–10. Chromatograms of a standard AA mixture (0.1 μmol/liter) (A), and the first (B), 47th (C), and 93rd (D) plasma sample as OPA/2-ME derivatives separated on a 5-μm LiChrosorb C_{18} column under the identical experiment conditions from the authors' lab (ref. 163).

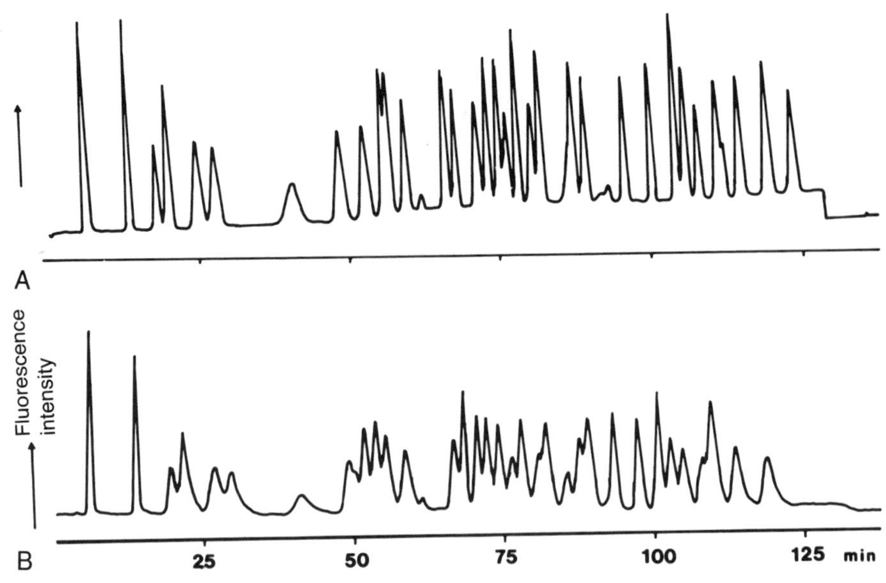

FIGURE 19–11. Aminogram of the standard mixture of AAs when the column is (A) newly packed with ion-exchange resin and (B) after running 350–400 biological samples under the identical experimental conditions from the authors' lab (ref. 163).

samples. In this situation the column should be washed with 0.2 *M* NaOH. On the other hand, it is vital to avoid bed compression and the flow rate should be maintained at <0.7 ml/min and pressure at 2500 psi.

19.6.2 Performing the Analysis on Biological Samples

19.6.2.1 Chemical Impurities

Artifacts are mainly caused by the use of impure chemicals giving rise to unknown peaks in the chromatograms, which sometimes create serious problems in AA identification. It is worth buying pure chemicals to avoid this problem in making the buffers and reagents. The present chemical firms sell most chemicals with varying percentages of purity and it is important to buy chemicals that are 98–100% analytically pure.

To maintain a low noise level of detection HPLC grade solvents are recommended. High precision can also be achieved by degassing the mobile phase to avoid air bubbles in the pumps. Insert gas purging and ultrasonic vacuum are some of the effective degassing techniques. Filtration of the solvents and samples is also recommended to prolong column life and maintain reproducible results. Both precolumn and postcolumn derivatization procedures are capable of producing reproducible results provided all these above-stated requirements are fulfilled. Water used in making the reagents and mobile phase should be doubly distilled and deionized. Dirt from hands, glassware, and oil used in pumps may also contribute to the inaccuracy of the results. Thus, hand gloves and acid-washed glass and the purging and storing of buffers under argon gas should minimize the appearance of unknown peaks in the chromatograms.

19.6.2.2 Collaboration Trials

There have been various research groups involved in collaboration trials since 1959 in an effort to standardize the pretreatment procedures for deproteinization and hydrolysis of biological or protein samples but to date no universal agreement has been found.[143–153] All these comparisons have been made by the use of a postcolumn derivatization procedure with either ninhydrin or OPA. The results of these findings are summarized below:

1. Sample handling along with the storage and selection of samples could be a cause of concern resulting in discrepancies in the levels of AAs.
2. At the higher temperatures necessary for performing hydrolysis of biological samples to evaluate the total concentration of AAs or to determine the purity of a protein or a peptide, a destruction of certain AAs such as Met, Glu, Asn, Cys, and Tryp may result.
3. Correct identification of AAs can be complicated due to the presence of impurities in samples, reagents, and mobile phases that can also increase the levels of AAs in biological samples.
4. Poor ion-exchange resins and tailing of certain peaks make for uncertainty in the quantitation of AAs. This can be true also in the case of an RP column.
5. A manual injection system provides more uncertain results and therefore the use of an automatic injector is recommended.
6. Under identical experimental conditions, the precision of AAs quantitation in plasma, protein, or peptide samples is more consistent than in urine.
7. Various standards from commercial sources give different results.

In the author's laboratory, three different derivatization procedures were used in evaluating the mean levels of AAs in 12 plasma samples that were handled and stored under identical conditions. The results are shown in Table 19–3.

Among the methods used, one was based on postcolumn derivatization with OPA/2-ME whereas the other two were prederivatization with OPA/2-ME and OPA/3-mercapthopropionic acid (3-MPA). Most of the amino acids shown have a comparable level except Asn, which has a higher, and Ser, Thr, Ala, Arg, Val, Ile, Leu, Orn, and Lys, which have lower concentrations in the postcolumn system than the other two precolumn systems. Comparing OPA/2-ME and OPA/3-MPA precolumn methods with each other, most of the amino acids agree well in both methods except Glu, Gln, Cit, Tau, Phe, and Leu, which are lower with the OPA/2-ME than the OPA/3-MPA procedure. In all these LC methods different standard mixtures were run and this could be the most likely reason for discrepancies.

19.6.2.3 Effects of Circadian Rhythms and Nutritional Status on the Levels of Amino Acids

In most clinical studies the assessment in variation of AA profiles in control (healthy) and patients with various pathological states is performed at a single time point and on the basis of the results, it is most commonly decided whether

TABLE 19–3. Levels of Amino Acids Mean Values[a]

Amino Acid	AAA (OPA/2-ME)[163]	HPLC (OPA/2-ME)[120]	HPLC (OPA/3-MPA)[127]
Asp	6.5 ± 0.5	5.6 ± 0.9	[b]
Glu	18.7 ± 7.2	19.7 ± 8.7	26.8 ± 2.2
Asn	81.4 ± 17.8	38.7 ± 3.9	39.0 ± 2.8
Ser	82.4 ± 4.8	118.5 ± 11.5	124.0 ± 5.7
Gln	592.0 ± 46.0	562.0 ± 73.0	808.0 ± 64.0
His	51.4 ± 4.9	56.3 ± 6.4	59.2 ± 7.7
Gly	153.0 ± 12.7	253.0 ± 10.4	268.0 ± 15.0
Thr	86.1 ± 9.3	120.0 ± 12.2	117.6 ± 12.3
Cit	22.6 ± 2.4	26.5 ± 2.4	38.6 ± 2.4
Ala	122.6 ± 11.8	180.2 ± 28.1	169.6 ± 22.1
Tau	33.6 ± 1.6	27.3 ± 1.6	41.4 ± 1.4
Arg	50.1 ± 10.2	68.2 ± 7.2	64.3 ± 7.1
Tyr	27.5 ± 1.7	28.7 ± 3.1	28.1 ± 2.0
Met	13.5 ± 1.0	16.6 ± 1.0	23.9 ± 2.1
Val	133.2 ± 14.0	205.3 ± 12.1	195.0 ± 13.0
Phe	32.4 ± 2.0	38.2 ± 3.7	74.6 ± 4.3
Ile	37.6 ± 2.7	51.2 ± 6.2	57.8 ± 6.7
Leu	80.5 ± 9.5	124.0 ± 22.0	146.0 ± 20.3
Ort	39.7 ± 1.1	49.1 ± 2.9	48.1 ± 3.1
Lys	102.6 ± 14.7	129.2 ± 10.8	136.7 ± 8.0

[a]Obtained from a postcolumn (AAA-OPA/2-ME) and two precolumn derivatization procedures, i.e., OPA/2-ME and OPA/3-MPA, from 12 plasma samples under identical conditions. The mean values are expressed in μmol/liter ±SD.

[b]Undetectable.

a subject manifests normal or abnormal amino acid metabolism even though the dynamics of amino acid metabolism in terms of circadian rhythm and nutritional status have not been fully evaluated.[152] AAs in steady-state conditions are regulated according to the following mechanism:

```
                              Intestinal lumen
                                     ↕
Metabolites ↔ Liver ←||→ Extracellular free ←||→ Nonhepatic ↔ Metabolites
              FAA        amino acids (FAA)        FAA
               ↕
         Cellular proteins ↔ Plasma proteins ↔ Cellular proteins
```

where ←||→ is the flow across the membrane.

This is the equilibrium system for FAAs in the extracellular space including plasma, which is a reflection of their inflow depending on various factors such as dietary intake, intestinal absorption, release of nonessential AAs from an endogenous system, and their outflow, which depends on uptake into liver and nonhepatic tissues, endogenous protein synthesis, and their catabolism.

Hence, to record the variation of free and/or total AA levels in biological matrices, the circadian rhythm and nutritional factors could generate intra-individual variation in levels of AAs.

19.6.2.4 Sample Collection

The most practical approach would be that the blood, CSF, and muscle biopsy samples should be collected after overnight fasting, between 6 and 9 A.M. for adults. For children, the fasting period could be reduced from 12 to 6–8 h. Blood samples should be collected in heparin-containing tubes to separate plasma by centrifuging the samples (blood) at 2500 *g* to 3000 *g* for 15 min. For serum samples, the blood samples are allowed to clot for some time (15–30 min) before separating the serum. In collecting plasma or serum samples, care must be practiced to separate the samples from platelets as contamination from thrombocytes or leukocytes may result in high values of Asp, Tau, and Gln.[154–156] Besides polypeptides present in platelets result in high values of AAs.[154–156] Plasma or serum samples should be deproteinized immediately and kept at −70°C. Urine samples should be collected from a subject (either healthy or patient) for a whole day and samples for analysis should be taken from the homogeneous 1 day collection. Various disposable devices such as C-loplasts, U-bags, Urinokol, or pediatric urine collectors are often used for collection purposes to avoid consumption from foreign sources. These samples could be preserved in 10% thymol, methiolate, or a mixture of toluene and chloroform. The urine sample could be preserved at −20 or −70°C but repeated freezing and thawing could cause discrepancies in AA levels, especially Gln, Asn, and Trp, which are sensitive to storage temperatures. Besides, decomposition of peptides from the epithelial cells and leukocytes do affect the levels of AAs.[153,157,158]

19.6.2.5 Handling of Biological Samples (Deproteinization Procedures)

For the separation of proteins from the biological samples, chemical precipitation is one of the most commonly used off-line procedures, whereas for on-line precipitation the use of a precolumn with a switch column system has been proposed recently.[159–162]

The main goal in this strategy irrespective of whichever method is adopted is to avoid the presence of protein that may be a cause of contamination to the analytical column. Various organic acids such as sulfosalicylic, perchlorotrichloacetic, and tungsten have been used. Besides the use of organic solvents such as diethyl ether, ethanol, methanol, and acetonitrile, mixed organic solvents are commonly used. Each one of these deproteinizing reagents has been shown to provide adequate reproducibility.

In the author's laboratory various deproteinizing procedures have been tried and among these reagents sulfosalicylic acid (SSA) was found to be the most convenient and suitable approach. For the plasma or serum samples, 30% SSA, 10% SSA for urine, dialysates or CSF samples, and 5–8% for muscle samples was sufficient to extract FAA from the samples. In addition to this, the samples could be kept for a year without effecting any remarkable change in their AA concentrations except for Trp, Cys, and Gln.[163]

The use of organic solvents is not recommended as the instability and hydrolysis of certain amino acids might give misleading results. Besides an addition of some organic solvents, thermally unstable amino acids such as Trp, His, 3-MH, Cys, Gin, and Asn are decreased from 10 to 50%.[163]

Pretreatment by the use of an ion-exchange column would also be a suitable alternative, but the dilution caused by this procedure may make it difficult to quantitate low concentrations of AAs.

19.6.2.6 Hydrolysis Procedures

Hydrolysis is the method of choice where the constituents of peptides and proteins are separated into units of AAs. In biological samples the AAs from the conjugated form bound to proteins or macromolecules are separated. In both cases alkali (NaOH) or acid (HNO_3 or HCl) is used to isolate the constituent AAs. Since these procedures are of long duration and are conducted at high temperatures the loss of certain AAs is a common phenomenon due to their degradation. Among the AAs Ser and Thr are destroyed under these procedures and their percentage loss is dependent on the method of hydrolysis. Losses of Trp, Gln, Asp, and Lys are more common in acidic than in akali hydrolysis.

Impurities present in the acid or alkali used for the hydrolyzing processes may also complicate the quantitation. Besides, the glassware should be cleaned thoroughly to eliminate contaminations that can be another cause of concern.

Care should also be taken to remove acid or alkali after the hydrolysis and the samples should be kept at room temperature prior to HPLC analysis.

ACKNOWLEDGMENTS

The author is thankful to Ms. Ann Hellström and Ingegerd Sidén for typing the manuscript and Dr. A. Rasheed Qureshi for his help in the collection of reference material. My special thanks go to Ms. Annelie Vestlund and Monica Eriksson for helping me in conducting some of the experiments.

REFERENCES

1. H. J. Bremmer, M. Duran, J. P. Kamerling, H. Przyremble, and S. D. Wadman, Disturbance of Amino Acid Metabolism, Clinical Chemistry and Diagnosis. Urban and Schwarzenberg, Baltimore, 1981.
2. J. B. Stanbury, J. B. Wyngaarden, and D. S. Fredrickson, The Metabolic Basis of Inherited Diseases, 4th ed. McGraw-Hill, New York, 1978.
3. J. P. Greenstein and M. Winitz, Chemistry of Amino Acids. Wiley, New York, 1961.
4. H. Galjaard, Genetic Metabolic Disorders. Elsevier North-Holland, Amsterdam, 1980.
5. C. R. Scriver and L. E. Rosenberg, Amino Acid Metabolism and Its Disorder. W.B. Saunders, Philadelphia, 1973.
6. J. M. G. Wilson and G. Junger, The Principle and Practice of Screening for Disease. World Health Organization, Public Health Paper No. 34, Geneva, 1968.

7. Report of a WHO Scientific Group, Screening for Inborn Errors of Metabolism. World Health Organization Technical Report No. 401, Geneva, 1968.
8. C. E. Dent, *Lancet*, ii (1946) 637.
9. C. E. Dent, *Biochem. J.*, 43 (1948) 169.
10. C. R. Schiver and E. Davies, *Lancet*, ii (1946) 230.
11. W. L. Nyhan, Heritable Disorders of Amino Acid Metabolism. Wiley, New York, 1974.
12. R. D. Feigin, *Am. J. Dis. Child.*, 117 (1969) 24.
13. C. R. Schiver, C. L. Clow, and P. Lamm, *Am. J. Clin. Nutr.*, 24 (1971) 876.
14. A. Alvestrand, M. Ahlberg, F. Furst, and J. Bergström, *Clin. Nephrol.*, 19 (1982) 67.
15. B. Lindholm and J. Bergström, in Continuous Ambulatory Peritoneal Dialysis (R. Gokal, ed.). Churchill Livingstone, London, 1986, pp. 228–264.
16. S. E. Snyderman, L. E. Holt, P. M. Norton, E. Rottman, and S. V. Phansalkar, *Paediat. Res.*, 2 (1968) 131.
17. D. V. Ashley, D. V. Barclay, F. A. Chauffard, D. Moennoz, and P. D. Leathwood, *Am. J. Clin. Nutr.*, 36 (1982) 143.
18. R. Jagenburg, *Scand. J. Clin. Lab. Invest.*, 11, Suppl. 43 (1974) 603.
19. A. E. H. Emery, D. Burt, and M. Nelson, *Lancet*, i (1979) 1307.
20. H. L. Levy, M. Madigan, and P. Lum, *Am. J. Clin. Pathol.*, 51 (1969) 765.
21. G. Biserte, K. Han, and P. Paysant, *Clin. Chim. Acta*, 8 (1963) 359.
22. J. T. Holden, Amino Acid Pools. Elsevier, Amsterdam, 1962.
23. T. N. Ferraro and T. A. Harey, *Brain Res.*, 338 (1985) 53.
24. H. L. Levy and E. Barkin, *J. Lab. Clin. Med.*, 78 (1971) 517.
25. Y. Houpert, P. Tarallo, and G. Siest, *Clin. Chem.*, 22 (1976) 1618.
26. J. Bergström, P. Furst, L. O. Noree, and E. Vinnars, *J. Appl. Physiol.*, 36 (1974) 693.
27. T. L. Hagenfeld and R. Andersson, *Clin. Chim. Acta*, 150 (1980) 133.
28. F. Cockburn, M. Giles, and S. P. Robins, *J. Obstet. Gynaecol. Br. Commonw.*, 80 (1973) 10.
29. D. Spackman, W. H. Stein, and S. Moore, *Anal. Chem.*, 30 (1958) 1190.
30. P. B. Hamilton, *Anal. Chem.*, 35 (1963) 2055.
31. M. T. W. Hearn, *Chromatogr. Sci.*, 31 (1985) 207.
32. J. H. Knox and R. A. Hartwich, *J. Chromatogr.*, 204 (1981) 3.
33. Z. Iskandarani and D. J. Pietrzyk, *Anal. Chem.*, 54 (1982) 2427.
34. J. Macek, L. Miterova, and M. Adam, *J. Chromatogr.*, 364 (1986) 253.
35. I. Molnar and C. Howarth, *J. Chromatogr.*, 142 (1977) 623.
36. M. K. Radjai and R. T. Hatch, *J. Chromatogr.*, 196 (1980) 319.
37. J. Crommen, B. Fransson, and G. Schill, *J. Chromatogr.*, 142 (1977) 283.
38. N. Seiler and B. Knodgen, *J. Chromatogr.*, 341 (1985) 11.
39. T. A. Walker and D. J. Pietrzyk, *J. Liquid Chromatogr.*, 8 (1985) 2047.
40. T. Hayashi, H. Tscuchiya, and H. Naruse, *J. Chromatogr.*, 274 (1983) 318.
41. S. L. Nissen, C. V. Huysen, and M. W. Haymond, *J. Chromatogr.*, 232 (1982) 170.
42. T. Tamegai, M. Ohmae, K. Kawabe, and M. Tomoeda, *J. Liquid Chromatogr.*, 2 (1979) 1229.
43. T. Numbara, S. Kiegawa, M. Hasegowe, and J. Gotb, *Anal. Chim. Acta*, 101 (1978) 111.
44. N. Niknura, A. Toyoma, and T. Kinoshita, *J. Chromatogr.*, 316 (1984) 547.
45. S. Lam and A. Karmen, *J. Chromatogr.*, 239 (1982) 451.
46. Y. Tapuhi, N. Miller, and B. L. Karger, *J. Chromatogr.*, 205 (1981) 325.
47. S. Lam, F. Chow, and A. Karmen, *J. Chromatogr.*, 199 (1980) 295.
48. G. Gubitz, W. Jellenz, and W. Santi, *J. Chromatogr.*, 203 (1981) 377.
49. J. Boue, R. Aubert, and C. Quivoron, *J. Chromatogr.*, 204 (1981) 185.
50. J. A. Schmit and R. Lehrer, in Handbook of HPLC for the Separation of Amino Acids, Peptides and Proteins, Vol. 1 (W. S. Hancock, ed.). CRC Press, Boca Raton, FL, 1984, pp. 61–78.
51. K. Murayama and T. Sugawara, *J. Chromatogr.*, 224 (1981) 315.

52. T. L. Perry, S. Hansen, K. Berry, C. Mole, and D. Lesk, *J. Neurochem.*, 18 (1971) 521.
53. C. Maillet and A. J. Garber, *Am. J. Clin. Nutr.*, 33 (1980) 1343.
54. L. Hoemorrhage, H. von Holst, and L. Hagenfelt, *Acta Neurochir.*, 78 (1985) 46.
55. E. Roth, F. Muhlbacher, J. Karner, G. Hamilton, and J. Furovies, *Metabolism*, 36 (1987) 7.
56. R. M. Flugel-Link, M. R. Jones, and J. D. Kopple, *J. Parenter. Enteral. Nutr.*, 7 (1983) 450.
57. F. Cockburn, M. Giles, S. P. Robins, and J. O. Forfar, *J. Obstet. Gynaecol., Br. Commun.*, 80 (1973) 10.
58. V. N. Liappis, *Z. Klin. Chem. Klin. Biochem.*, 11 (1975) 279.
59. V. N. Liappis and A. Jakel, *Mschr. Kinderheilk.*, 122 (1974) 6.
60. L. Hagenfeldt and A. Arvidsson, *Clin. Chim. Acta*, 100 (1980) 133.
61. H. L. Levy and T. Burkin, *J. Lab. Clin. Med.*, 78 (1971) 517.
62. M. D. Armstrong and U. Stave, *Metabolism*, 22 (1973) 571.
63. J. D. Dickinson, P. Rosenblum, and P. B. Hamilton, *Pediatrics*, 45 (1970) 606.
64. R. D. Feigin and W. W. Haymond, *Pediatrics*, 45 (1979) 782.
65. A. E. H. Emery, D. Burt, M. M. Nelson, and J. B. Serimgeour, *Lancet*, i (1979) 1307.
66. S. Udenfield, S. Stein, P. Bohlen, W. Dairman, W. Leimgruber, and M. Weigele, *Science*, 178 (1972) 871.
67. A. M. Felix and G. Terkelsen, *Anal. Biochem.*, 56 (1973) 610.
68. M. Roth, *Anal. Chem.*, 43 (1971) 880.
69. M. Roth and A. Hampai, *J. Chromatogr.*, 83 (1973) 353.
70. S. S. Simons Jr. and D. F. Johnson, *Anal. Biochem.*, 82 (1977) 250.
71. J. D. H. Cooper and D. C. Turnell, *J. Auto. Chem.*, 5 (1983) 36.
72. C. Schavabe and J. C. Celtie, *Anal. Biochem.*, 61 (1974) 302.
73. Y. Ishida, T. Fujita and K. Asai, *J. Chromatogr.*, 204 (1981) 143.
74. D. G. Drescher and K. S. Lee, *Anal. Biochem.*, 84 (1978) 559.
75. M. W. Dong and J. R. Gant, *J. Chromatogr.*, 327 (1985) 17.
76. B. V. R. Sastry, V. E. Janson, M. Horst, and C. C. Stephan, *J. Liquid Chromatogr.*, 9 (1986) 1689.
77. P. Böhlen and R. Schroeder, *Anal. Biochem.*, 126 (1982) 144.
78. M. Ogawa, A. Takahara, M. Ishijima, and S. Tazaki, *Jpn. Circ. J.*, 49 (1985) 1217.
79. C. G. Zarkadas, J. A. Rochemont, G. C. Zarkadas, C. N. Karatzas, and A. D. Khaliti, *Anal. Biochem.*, 160 (1987) 251.
80. T. Hayashi, H. Tsuchiya, and H. Naruse, *J. Chromatogr.*, 274 (1983) 318.
81. R. E. Major, in HPLC, Advances and Prospective, Vol. 1 (Cs. Horvath, ed.). Academic Press, New York, 1980, pp. 76–87.
82. G. Weber, *Biochem. J.*, 51 (1951) 155.
83. W. R. Gray and B. S. Hartley, *Biochem. J.*, 89 (1963) 59.
84. W. R. Gray and B. S. Hartley, *Biochem. J.*, 89 (1963) 379.
85. D. J. Neadle and R. J. Pollet, *Biochem. J.*, 97 (1965) 607.
86. Y. Tapuhi, D. E. Schmidt, W. Linder, and B. L. Karger, *Anal. Biochem.*, 52 (1973) 595.
87. V. T. Wiedmeier, S. P. Porterfield, and C. E. Hendrich, *J. Chromatogr.*, 231 (1982) 410.
88. D. C. Olson, G. J. Schmidt, and W. Slavin, *Chromatogr. Newslett.*, 7 (1979) 22.
89. R. Bongiovanni, A. R. Glass, and T. M. Boehm, *J. Chromatogr. Sci.*, 211 (1982) 211.
90. L. Zecca and P. Ferrario, *J. Chromatogr.*, 337 (1985) 391.
91. A. Herrndobler, *J. High Resolution Chromatogr. Chromatogr. Commun.*, 9 (1986) 602.
92. J. K. Lin and J. Y. Chang, *Anal. Chem.*, 47 (1975) 1634.
93. J. Y. Chang, P. Martin, R. Bernasconi, and D. G. Braun, *FEBS Lett.*, 132 (1981) 117.
94. P. Edman, *Acta. Chem. Scand.*, 4 (1950) 283.
95. P. Edman and A. Henscher, in Protein Sequence Determination (S. B. Needleman, ed.). Springer-Verlag, Berlin, 1975, p. 232.

96. A. P. Graffeo, A. Harg, and B. L. Karger, *Anal. Lett.*, 6 (1973) 505.
97. C. L. Zimmerman, E. Appella, and J. J. Rasano, *Anal. Biochem.*, 77 (1977) 369.
98. L. E. Lavi and J. S. Holcenberg, *J. Chromatogr.*, 377 (1986) 155.
99. J. Schreiber, W. Lohmann, F. Berthold, and F. Lampert, *Fresenius Anal. Chem.*, 325 (1986) 476.
100. H. G. Biggs and L. J. Gentilcore, *Clin. Chem.*, 30 (1984) 476.
101. J. L. Blajchand and J. J. Kirkland, *J. Chromatogr. Sci.*, 25 (1987) 4.
102. B. L. Johansson and K. Isaksson, *J. Chromatogr.*, 356 (1986) 383.
103. J. Y. Chang, *Biochem. J.*, 199 (1981) 557.
104. M. J. Horn, P. A. Hargrave, and J. K. Wang, *J. Chromatogr.*, 180 (1979) 111.
105. I. N. Mancheva, R. N. Nikolov, and J. Pfletschingar, *J. Chromatogr.*, 213 (1981) 99.
106. I. Molnar and Cs. Horvath, *J. Chromatogr.*, 142 (1977) 623.
107. P. Lindroth and K. Mopper, *Anal. Chem.*, 51 (1979) 1667.
108. D. W. Hills, F. H. Walter, T. D. Wilson, and J. D. Stuart, *Anal. Chem.*, 51 (1979) 1338.
109. M. H. Joseph and P. Davies, *J. Chromatogr.*, 277 (1983) 125.
110. L. A. Allison, G. S. Mayer, and R. E. Shoup, *Anal. Chem.*, 56 (1984) 1089.
111. H. R. Zielke, *J. Chromatogr.*, 347 (1985) 320.
112. C. R. Krishnamurti, A. M. Heindze, and G. Galzy, *J. Chromatogr.*, 315 (1984) 321.
113. R. J. Smith and K. A. Panico, *J. Liquid Chromatogr.*, 8 (1985) 1783.
114. M. H. Fernström and J. D. Fernström, *Life Sci.*, 92 (1981) 2219.
115. R. G. Elkin, *J. Agric. Food Chem.*, 32 (1984) 53.
116. M. Farrant, F. Zia-Gharib, and R. A. Webster, *J. Chromatogr.*, 417 (1987) 385.
117. G. A. Qureshi and P. Södersten, *J. Chromatogr.*, 400 (1987) 247.
118. G. A. Qureshi and P. Södersten, *Neurosci. Lett.*, 70 (1986) 374.
119. G. A. Qureshi and P. Södersten, *Neurosci. Lett.*, 75 (1987) 85.
120. G. A. Qureshi, L. Fohlin, and J. Bergström, *J. Chromatogr.*, 297 (1984) 91.
121. G. A. Qureshi, A. Gutierrez, and J. Bergström, *J. Chromatogr.*, 374 (1986) 363.
122. G. A. Qureshi, *J. Chromatogr.*, 400 (1987) 91.
123. G. A. Qureshi, A. R. Qureshi, and J. Bergström, in Abstract Book Int. Symp. on Pharmaceut. and Biomed. Analysis, Barcelona, Sept. 23–25, 1987.
124. D. C. Turnell and J. D. H. Cooper, *Clin. Chem.*, 28 (1982) 527.
125. B. N. Jones and J. P. Gilligan, *J. Chromatogr.*, 266 (1983) 471.
126. P. Kabus and G. Koch, *Biochem. Biophys. Res. Commun.*, 108 (1982) 783.
127. H. Godel, T. Graser, P. Földi, P. Pfaender, and P. Furst, *J. Chromatogr.*, 297 (1984) 49.
128. R. Thalmann, T. H. Comegys, and I. Thalmann, *Laryngoscope*, 92 (1982) 321.
129. D. L. Martin, *J. Anal. Biochem.*, 158 (1986) 79.
130. W. Rajendra, *J. Liquid Chromatogr.*, 10 (1987) 941.
131. D. L. Hogan, K. L. Kraemer, and J. I. Isenberg, *Anal. Biochem.*, 127 (1982) 17.
132. Y. Watanabe and K. Imai, *J. Chromatogr.*, 239 (1982) 723.
133. H. Kotaniguchi, M. Kawakatsu, T. Toyook, and K. Imai, *J. Chromatogr.*, 420 (1987) 141.
134. M. Matzer, R. P. Kurkjy, and R. H. Cotter, *Chem. Rev.*, 64 (1964) 645.
135. H. K. Hall, *J. Am. Chem. Soc.*, 79 (1957) 5439.
136. L. A. Carpino and G. Y. Han, *J. Org. Chem.*, 37 (1972) 3404.
137. H. Anson Moye and A. J. Boning, Jr., *Anal. Lett.*, 12 (1979) 25.
138. S. Einarsson, B. Josefsson, and S. Lagerqvist, *J. Chromatogr.*, 282 (1983) 609.
139. H. J. Schneider and P. Földi, *GIT. Fachz. Lab.*, 9 (1986) 873.
140. S. Einarsson, *J. Chromatogr.*, 348 (1985) 213.
141. A. P. Williams, *J. Chromatogr.*, 373 (1986) 175.
142. R. W. Freig, H. Jansen, and U. A. T. Brinckman, *Anal. Chem.*, 57 (1985) 1529.
143. A. E. Bender, J. A. Palgrave, and B. H. Doell, *Analysts*, 84 (1959) 526.
144. W. Matthias, *Tag. Ber. Akad. Landwirtsch, Wiss. DDR, Berlin*, 64 (1964) 7.
145. J. W. G. Porter, D. R. Westgarth, and A. P. Williams, *Br. J. Nutr.*, 22 (1968) 437.

146. A. P. Williams, D. Hewitt, J. E. Cockburn, D. A. Harris, R. A. Moore, and M. G. Davies, *J. Sci. Food Agric.*, 31 (1980) 474.
147. K. Weidner and B. O. Eggum, *Acta Agric. Scand.*, 16 (1966) 115.
148. J. Wunsche, *Sitzungsberichte*, 16 (1967) 17.
149. J. E. Knipfel, J. R. Aitken, D. C. Hill, B. E. McDonald, and B. D. Owen, *J. Ass. Off. Anal. Chem.*, 54 (1971) 777.
150. F. Mikoska, *Tag. Ber. Akad. Landwirtsch. Wiss., DDR, Berlin*, 124 (1974) 47.
151. T. Gerritsen, M. L. Rehiberg, and H. A. Waisman, *Anal. Biochem.*, 11 (1965) 460.
152. C. R. Scriver, C. L. Clow, and P. Lamm, *Am. J. Clin. Nutr.*, 24 (1971) 876.
153. R. Jagenburg, *Scand. J. Clin. Lab. Invest.*, 11, Suppl. 43 (1974) 603.
154. H. Ghadini, *Pediat. Res.*, 7 (1973) 169.
155. D. V. Ashley and D. V. Barclay, *Am. J. Clin. Nutr.*, 30 (1982) 143.
156. L. Hagenfeldt and A. Arvidsson, *Clin. Chim. Acta*, 100 (1980) 133.
157. P. Soupart, *Clin. Chim. Acta*, 4 (1959) 265.
158. M. E. Kornhuber, J. Kornhuber, A. W. Kornhuber, and M. Hartman, *Nuero. Sci. Lett.*, 69 (1986) 212.
159. P. O. Edlund and D. Westerlund, *J. Pharmaceut. Biomed. Anal.*, 2 (1984) 315.
160. A. Yamatodami and H. Wada, *Clin. Chem.*, 27 (1981) 1983.
161. M. Goto, G. Zou, and D. Ishi, *J. Chromatogr.*, 275 (1983) 271.
162. L. Hansson, M. Glad, and C. Hansson, *J. Chromatogr.*, 265 (1983) 37.
163. G. A. Qureshi, M. Eriksson, and A. Vestlund, unpublished results.

CHAPTER 20

HPLC of Oligonucleotides

Larry W. McLaughlin

CONTENTS

20.1 INTRODUCTION

Nucleic acids and oligonucleotides can be characterized as polymeric material containing anionic species (phosphodiesters) and hydrophobic residues (nucleobases/carbohydrates). In these respects, both anion-exchange chromatography and reversed-phase chromatography have been effective for the purification of these materials (for recent reviews see 1–8). The former relies on ion–ion interactions between the phosphodiesters and charged groups of the chromatographic matrix while the latter involves primarily nonpolar or hydrophobic interactions.

The fundamental mechanism of anion-exchange chromatography is the adsorption and desorption of the anionic solute on a positively charged stationary phase. Both phenomena are equilibrium processes and this equilibrium can be shifted to favor either adsorption or desorption by altering the parameters (commonly the anionic character or salt concentration) of the mobile phase. For a mixture of polyanionic solutes, the retention of an individual species will depend on its net charge. With oligonucleotides the net charge generally corresponds to the sequence length. Thus the separation of oligonucleotides by HPLC using an anion-exchange matrix resolves the mixture largely according to size.

Chromatographic separations that rely on nonpolar or hydrophobic interactions are commonly referred to as involving hydrophobic-interaction chromatography (HIC). Two forms of HIC can be used with oligonucleotides. In the more popular form, the mobile phase contains a low concentration of salt and uses an increasing gradient of organic solvent. This is more commonly known as reversed-phase chromatography. In the second form, the sample is introduced onto the matrix in the presence of mobile phase of high salt concentration and solutes are eluted by employing a decreasing salt gradient. This has also been referred to as "salting-out" chromatography.

Reversed-phase chromatography of oligonucleotides can be best understood by comparing the process with "normal-phase" adsorption chromatography. Traditional adsorption chromatography employs a polar stationary phase such as silica gel and a nonpolar mobile phase. Polar solutes interact more strongly with the polar stationary phase and are eluted later than nonpolar solutes.

Polar compounds can be eluted from the column by increasing the polarity of the mobile phase usually via a linear gradient. In reversed-phase chromatography, as the name implies, the process is reversed. The stationary phase is very nonpolar. Nonpolar solutes interact more strongly than polar solutes. Elution of a nonpolar solute is effected by lowering the polarity of the mobile phase. With oligonucleotides the mobile phase is typically an aqueous buffer solution and the polarity is reduced by the addition of an organic solvent.

Salting-out chromatography uses high concentrations of a neutral salt (such as ammonium sulfate) in the mobile phase. This appears to induce interfacial precipitation of the solute on a nonpolar stationary phase. As the salt concentration decreases, selective resolubilization and elution of the solutes occur.

The previously described chromatographic techniques primarily rely on a single mode of interaction between the solutes and the stationary/mobile phase. Mixed-mode chromatography, as the name implies, is the result of two or more simultaneous modes of chromatography. This is not a completely unknown process. Free silanol groups can affect resolution during reversed-phase chromatography,[9] electrostatic effects are present in size-exclusion chromatography[10] and hydrophobic interactions alter retention in ion-exchange and affinity chromatographies.[11,12] However, generally these effects are viewed as detrimental[13] and mobile phase characteristics are often designed to maximize the predominant solute/stationary phase interaction and minimize all others. Recently, my own research group[14,18] as well as others[19,21] have explored the preparation of stationary phases that specifically exploit multiple types of interaction, such as ionic and hydrophobic, simultaneously. In some cases the resolution of oligonucleotides and nucleic acids on these materials far exceeds that observed with single mode chromatography. The solute retention process in this case allows optimization of ion–ion as well as hydrophobic interactions. The pH, salt concentration, and organic solvent content of the mobile phase can all be varied to alter retention and resolution with these materials.

The remaining sections of this chapter will focus on recent reports employing these chromatographic techniques, the appropriate methodology, and some selected applications.

20.2 CHROMATOGRAPHIC METHODS

20.2.1 The Support

Traditional soft gel supports such as cellulose, polysaccharide, and polyacrylamide are not rigid enough to withstand the high mobile phase velocities used in HPLC. Silica gel has been principally used as a rigid support for anion-exchange, reversed-phase, and mixed-mode chromatographic matrices. With silica gel-based materials it is necessary to maintain the pH of the mobile phase within the range 2–8. However, this is not a limiting factor in oligonucleotide separations. Chromatographic matrices of this type are available in a variety of particle sizes and pore diameters. Spherical particles with diameters on the order of 5–10 μm appear optimal for oligonucleotide separations. Pore sizes are also an important consideration. With "normal" pore silica supports the pore sizes can vary from 10 to 120 Å depending on the manufacturer. It is also possible to obtain large pore supports from 300 to 4000 Å although the availability of specific bonded stationary phases is limited. We have found that chromatographic matrices with pore sizes on the order of 100 Å provide excellent resolution of oligonucleotides. Large pore supports appear on the other hand advantageous for high-molecular-weight nucleic acids.

20.2.2 Anion-Exchange Chromatography of Oligonucleotides

A positively charged or cationic matrix is necessary for effective anion-exchange chromatography of oligonucleotides. Primary, secondary, tertiary, or quaternary amines covalently bound to the silica support through a short carbaceous spacer and a siloxane linkage are usually employed in this respect.[22,23] Quaternary amines are charged regardless of the pH of the mobile phase and these materials are commonly referred to as "strong anion exchangers," often abbreviated as SAX. The remaining amine-containing matrices require protonation in order to generate the necessary cationic site. Resolution with these latter materials is in part dependent on the mobile phase insofar as the density of the cationic sites available for interaction with the oligonucleotide can be increased or decreased by corresponding alterations of the mobile phase pH.

In general, high-density cationic resins such as the SAX materials or the amine matrices (the later require relatively low pH buffers in order to generate high charge densities) are effective for the separation of oligonucleotides up to a sequence length of about 20. For longer fragments including in some cases plasmid DNA, the amine-containing matrices in combination with a mobile phase near neutral pH can in some cases provide successful separations.[24,25]

Another approach for the preparation of amine-containing matrices involves the adsorption and cross-linking of polyethyleneimine (PEI) on the appropriate silica gel particles.[26,27] These materials can be used directly or the amine residues can be quaternized with methyliodide. Because of the high carbaceous content of these materials, the mobile phase often contains a significant quantity of organic solvent to reduce nonspecific hydrophobic interactions. These materials have exhibited varying degrees of success for the resolution of oligonucleotides with sequence lengths greater than 30.

20.2.3 Chromatography of Oligonucleotides Involving Hydrophobic Interactions

20.2.3.1 Reversed-Phase Chromatography

Reversed-phase chromatography usually employs stationary phases containing alkyl groups bound via a siloxane linkage to the surface of the silica.[4] The degree of hydrophobic character can be varied with the alkyl group. Weakly hydrophobic materials contain trimethylsily, propyl, or butyl residues while more hydrophobic character is available with C_8 (octyl) or C_{18} (octadecyl) materials. It is also possible to employ phenyl or β-cyanoethyl materials as stationary phases for reversed-phase chromatography. By far the most commonly used material for oligonucleotide separations is the C_{18} or octadecylsilyl (ODS)-modified silica gel.

Reversed-phase chromatography using increasing gradients of methanol, acetonitrile, or isopropanol resolves oligonucleotides primarily according to sequence composition and is largely independent of sequence length.[28] The hydrophobic character of the nucleobases decreases in the order dA > dT > dG > dC. Thus, oligonucleotides rich in adenine residues will tend to elute much later than, for example, those rich in cytosine.

A second form of reversed-phase chromatography is that of ion-pairing chromatography.[28,31] In this case a positively charged ion-pairing reagent such as tetramethyl, tetraethyl, or tetrabutyl ammonium salt is added to the mobile phase. The ion-pairing reagent complexes with the negatively charged phosphodiester to increase the hydrophobic character of the oligonucleotide. The hydrophobic character of the complex will vary depending on the ion-pairing reagent. The use of tetrabutyl reagents results in better retention on the hydrophobic stationary phase and shifts the elution volume for a given species to much larger values than observed with corresponding tetramethyl reagents. For these types of materials the observed increase in hydrophobic character is roughly proportional to the number of phosphodiesters or, in effect, the sequence length. Thus with ion-pairing reagents the resolution of oligonucleotides is roughly proportional to sequence length with some resolution of sequence isomers.

20.2.3.2 Salting-Out Chromatography

Salting-out chromatography as a form of hydrophobic-interaction chromatography (HIC) has seen more widespread use in the resolution of proteins than oligonucleotides. It has, however, been successful in the resolution of tRNAs[32] and the separation of aminoacyl-tRNA, or tRNA carrying its cognate amino acid, from native tRNA.[25,26] In this case a weakly hydrophobic matrix is used, commonly C_1–C_3 residues.[32] However, more hydrophobic matrices can be used with corresponding changes in the character of the mobile phase.[22,23] The nucleic acid is introduced to the column in the presence of high concentration of salt (commonly ammonium sulfate). This results in retention of the solute by interfacial precipitation. As the ammonium sulfate concentration decreases via a linear gradient, selective resolubilization and elution occur. For additional details concerning this approach the reader is directed to other chapters of this book.

20.2.4 Mixed-Mode Chromatography of Oligonucleotides

Since nucleic acids can be resolved effectively using ionic interactions (anion-exchange chromatography) or hydrophobic interactions (reversed-phase chromatography), a matrix that could provide sites for simultaneous ionic/hydrophobic interactions should also provide effective oligonucleotide resolution. The concept is, however, deceptively simple, since effective mixed-mode chromatography must provide for variation and optimization of each chromatographic mode.

Two general approaches have been used to prepare mixed-mode materials. In one, silylchlorides of mixed functionality have been employed to modify silica gel.[19,21] Our own approach begins with a readily available ion-exchange or hydrophobic phase and introduces additional sites for the second set of interactions. In one case an ion-exchange matrix (aminopropylsilyl) was modified with phenylalanine.[15] The modified material, APS-PHE, contained a phenyl ring as a site for hydrophobic interactions and a primary amine as a pH-dependent site for ionic interactions. In test chromatograms, this material exhibited both ionic and hydrophobic character. Effective resolution of oligonucleotide mixtures using this matrix required some organic solvent in the mobile phase. Ten percent organic solvent appeared optimal when employing an increasing salt gradient. Optimization of a given separations problem can be, in this case, achieved by variations of the mobile phase pH. Changing the pH of the mobile phase alters the extent of protonation and thereby the number of ionic sites available to the solute. Since the number of hydrophobic sites remains constant, lowering the mobile phase pH will cause the matrix to take on a more ionic character while increasing the pH will make a more hydrophobic matrix.

In the second case, sites for ionic interactions were introduced onto a hydrophobic matrix.[14,18] As an example of this approach a C_{18}–modified silica gel has been noncovalently modified with a tetraalkylammonium salt (methyltrioctylammonium chloride). The resulting material exhibits both ionic and hydrophobic character. Chromatographic separations are performed using a mobile phase of high salt concentration. Using an increasing gradient of ammonium acetate this material can resolve a homopolymer digest of uridylic acid from the monomer UMP to $(Up)_{90}$. The high-resolution separation of tRNAs has been reported with this material.

20.3 METHODOLOGY

The methodology section of this chapter is divided into three parts: column packing and care, mobile phase considerations, and analytical vs. preparative separations. However, it should also be noted that these are general methodological techniques with application to many separations problems in addition to those involving oligonucleotides.

20.3.1 Column Packing and Care

The column, and more specifically, the stationary phase are the heart of any HPLC system used to solve purification problems. Columns are available from many manufacturers but often require significant financial investment particularly for preparative columns. It is therefore necessary that some care should be taken to extend column life. The most common problem with HPLC columns is high back pressures. Since the stationary phase is composed of silica particles usually 5–10 μm in diameter, which is held in the column between a 2-μm frit (column outlet) and a 5-μm frit (column inlet), it functions as an excellent filter. As it filters small particulates from the mobile phase, the back pressure builds up until the column becomes unusable. Column life can be extended by prefiltering all mobile phases through 0.45-μm membrane filters and using an additional "in line" filter or precolumn between the sample injection port and the column inlet. Either an in line filter or a precolumn can be renewed at minimal cost.

Degradation of the stationary phase can be a problem at pHs below 2 or about 8 or even at neutral pHs over a long period of time. In our hands column life can be extended by rigorously washing the column with distilled water at the end of each day. If a column is to be stored unused for long periods of time storage in an organic solvent such as methanol is often preferred.

One obvious approach to reduce the financial investment prepacked columns require is to use self-packed columns. Column packing is not a difficult technique (although manufacturers might disagree). The following procedure allows one to produce self-packed HPLC columns of high quality at a reasonable price. The columns are slurry packed in methanol followed by a wash with water. An HPLC pump that can generate a solvent flow of 10 ml/min at 200 bar is adequate. Column quality and life are somewhat better if a constant pressure packing pump is used (producing an initial flow of 100 ml/min and a pressure of 400 bar). The following column packing procedure includes the necessary equipment and is reproduced from ref. 33 with permission.

20.3.1.1 Equipment

The following hardware includes the column itself. High-quality stainless steel tubing can be purchased from a number of companies. The part numbers listed correspond to those from *Swagelok*. Other stainless-steel compression fittings can also be used but it is important not to mix fittings from different companies since the angles and tolerances will vary.

Packing column: stainless-steel 9.5-mm (3/8-in.) o.d., 5.7-mm i.d., 700-mm long column end fitting 3/8–1/16 in. SS-600-6-1ZV reducing union 3/8–1/4 in. SS-600-604.

Analytical HPLC column: stainless-steel 6.4-mm (1/4-in.) o.d., 4.6-mm i.d., 250-mm column end fittings 1/4–1/16 in. SS-400-6-1ZV-SA (5-μm frit), SS-400-6-1ZV-S5) (2-μm frit).

Pump: HPLC or column packing pump (see Shandon Southern Inc.) and 2 m of 1/16-in. o.d. stainless-steel tubing.

Assembly of the apparatus is illustrated in Figure 20–1. The packing column can be of other dimensions but should have an internal volume of at least 18 ml.

20.3.1.2 Packing Procedure

The column will be initially packed upwards as indicated by the relative positions of the columns in Figure 20–1. This is done for two reasons. It ensures that any air in either the packing or chromatographic column escapes and any large aggregates or dense contaminating material should sink to the bottom of the packing column and not be incorporated into the chromatographic column.

1. Assemble the apparatus as shown in Figure 20–1 allowing enough 1/16-in. stainless-steel tubing between the pump and the packing column and

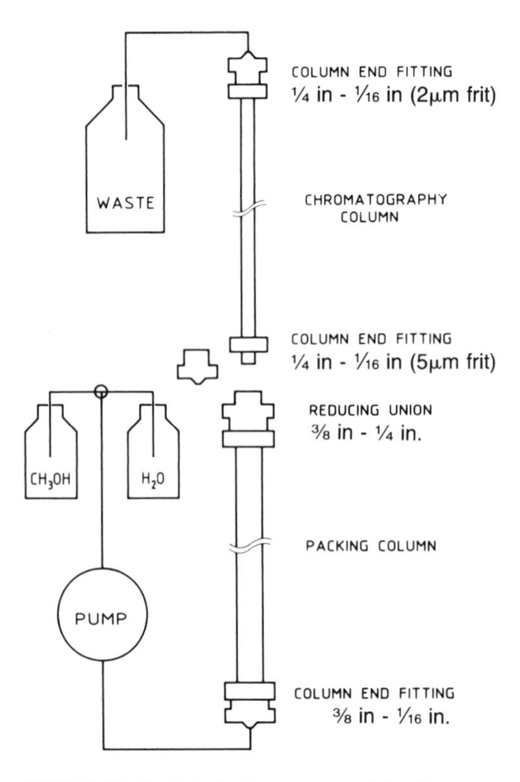

FIGURE 20–1. A typical arrangement for the preparation of self-packed columns. (Reprinted with permission from ref. 33.)

between the chromatographic column and the wash bottle that the two columns when coupled together can additionally be turned 180°.

2. To a small screw-top bottle (glass scintillation vials do nicely) with a minimum 20 ml volume add 3.3 g of the desired 5 μm column support and 15 ml of methanol. (**Caution:** manufacturers of microparticulate silicas recommend that dry material is weighed out in a fume hood since the danger of inhaled microparticulates of this type is at present unknown.)
3. Screw the bottle closed and shake to suspend the silica support.
4. To ensure suspension and the breakdown of large aggregate particles place the bottle in an ultrasonic bath of 2 min. (**Caution:** too long in the ultrasonic bath may result in fracturing of the silica support.)
5. Charge the pump with methanol and assemble the column apparatus as shown in Figure 20–1, such that the only connection that is still open is that between the chromatographic column and the packing column.
6. Add the silica suspension with a disposable pipette to the packing column.
7. Connect the chromatography column and the packing column together and start the pump (*wear safety glasses!*). It is recommended that the time between addition of the suspension to the packing column and starting of the pump be kept to a minimum.

8. Pack the column at 400 bar (constant pressure, packing pump) for 15 min or at 200 bar (HPLC pump 10 ml/min initial flow) for 30 min.
9. Rotate the joined columns 180° and continue packing with water for 15 or 30 min, respectively. Then stop the pump.
10. After the pressure has stabilized at 0 bar, loosen the compression fitting between the chromatography column and packing column.
11. Using a wrench on the outflow fitting of the chromatography column, rotate the entire column without removing it from the reducing union attached to the packing column. This ensures that the surface of the column support at the end of the chromatography column is cleanly broken off from excess material in the packing column.
12. Remove the chromatography column from the reducing union, repair the surface of the support with a spatula using excess column support from the packing column if necessary, and clean the outside of the compression fitting and attach the column end fitting to the chromatography column.
13. Mark the direction of flow and/or inlet and outlet of the column. The column is immediately useable.

    Larger HPLC columns (9.4 × 250 mm) can be packed using the same procedure with the following exceptions: use a packing pump with an initial solvent flow of approximately 100 ml/min at a pressure of 300 bar and a stainless-steel packing column with a 100 ml internal volume. For a 9.4 × 250 mm column, pack at 300 bar for 30 min with methanol following with water for 30 min.

20.3.1.3 Repacking the Same Column Support

In our experience with reversed-phase columns (ODS-Hypersil), poor resolution, broad peaks, or double peaks are generally related to disruption of the column bed or irreversibly bound material. In general, a large portion of the column support from a column that exhibits poor resolution is in good condition. To take advantage of this, particularly in the case of larger columns, and to extend the life of the column support, use the following procedure.

1. Wash the column with water and then methanol.
2. Open the inlet column fitting and attach the outlet fitting to a pump charged with methanol.
3. Increase the pump flow and/or pressure slowly until the column support is slowly extruded from the column.
4. Remove the material that is colored (usually varying from yellow to brown) from the end of the column (~1 cm).
5. Collect the remainder of the column support in a glass screw-top bottle.
6. Add enough new support to make up for that discarded, plus a slight excess (generally a total of 0.5 g for analytical columns and 2.0 g for preparative columns).
7. Treat this material as described above and repack into the column.

20.3.2 Mobile Phase Considerations

In addition to the stationary phase, variations in the mobile phase parameters are often the key to solving difficult separations. Problems associated with the mobile phase such as baseline drift and unknown peaks can be largely avoided by using high quality distilled water and organic solvents.

With reversed-phase chromatography bubble formation can occur during the gradient as the organic solvent and aqueous buffer are mixed. This can produce two types of problems depending on the type of HPLC system. If the gradient is formed by mixing the mobile phase on the low pressure side of the HPLC pump (usually with check valves), bubble formation reduces pumping efficiency and solute retention volumes are no longer reproducible. If the gradient is formed on the high-pressure side of the HPLC pump (usually two pumps are required, one for each mobile phase component), bubbles usually remain dissolved in the mobile phase until the pressure decreases (at the column outlet). The bubbles then show up in the detector as sharp spikes in the chromatogram. Both of these problems can usually be avoided if the organic solvent component of the mobile phase is not pure organic solvent but rather a high concentration (70–90%) in the aqueous component. Degassing the mobile phase using vacuum, ultrasonic treatment, or helium bubbling is often effective in removing such problems.

20.3.3 Analytical versus Preparative HPLC

Analytical and preparative terms are relative to a particular separations problem. For the present discussion, analytical refers to separations using columns no larger than 4.6 × 250 mm and usually involve less than 1 mg of total solute mixture. Preparative refers to larger columns and solute mixtures. The major consideration here involves the problems that might occur in scaling up a particular separation. For scaling up procedures we have commonly used 9.4 × 250 mm or 21.2 × 250 mm columns. One can obtain almost identical retention times for solutes if the gradient and the cross-sectional flow through the column remains the same. Thus a separation on a 4.6 × 250 mm column at 1 ml/min can be reproduced on a 9.4 mm column at 4.0 ml/min or a 21.2 mm column at 25 ml/min. This is not always feasible since HPLC pumps cannot commonly pump at more than 10 ml/min. Often it is possible to reduce the flow rate well below the optimum and obtain adequate resolution, although with different retention times. In some cases it may also be necessary to increase the time of the gradient.

Difficulties with preparative separations are more likely to arise with the detection system. Oligonucleotides exhibit a λ_{max} at 260 nm and UV detectors are commonly used to monitor column eluent. However, sensitive UV detectors can often be "blinded" by the quantity of material used in a preparative separation (Figure 20–2). Many HPLC detectors provide an optional preparative, or less sensitive (shorter pathlength), flow cell. This is the easiest approach for preparative isolations. If this is impossible or impractical, it is often feasible to detune the detector away from the λ_{max} (260 nm for oligonucleotides) and monitor the eluent at, for example, 290 nm. The relative peak heights in the chromatogram may differ significantly from those observed at 260 nm as a result of varying extinction coefficients. However, it is often still possible to effectively monitor the preparative separation in this manner.

Finally, after obtaining a pure oligonucleotide species from an HPLC column it may be desirable or necessary to remove the buffer salts from the mobile phase. This can be achieved, particularly after reversed-phase chromatogra-

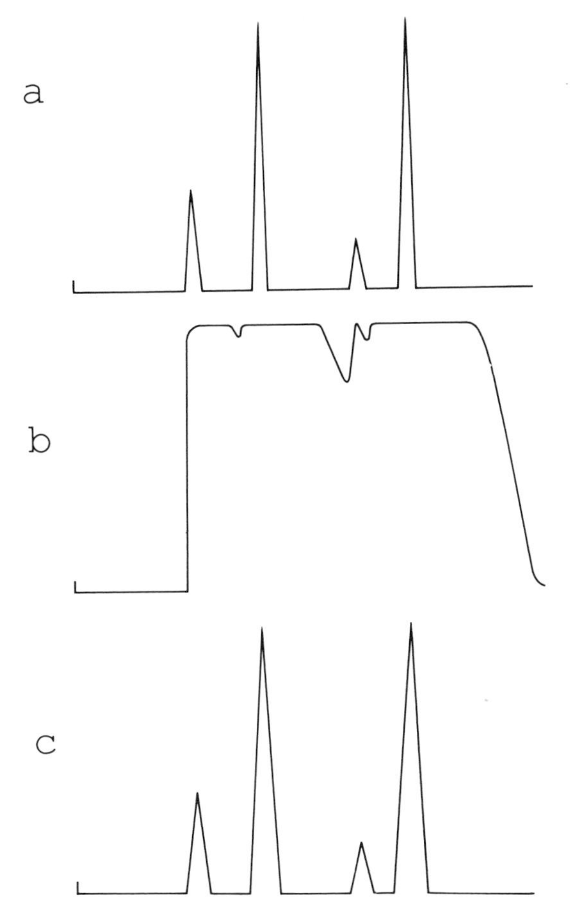

FIGURE 20–2. Illustrative chromatograms for (a) analytical separations at 260 nm, (b) a preparative separation using an analytical flow cell and UV monitoring at 260 nm, and (c) a preparative separation using a preparative flow cell. A chromatogram similar to (c) will result when using an analytical flow cell and detuning the detector 270–320 nm.

phy, by rotary evaporation or lyophilization if suitable volatile salts are used (e.g., triethylammonium acetate). Otherwise, soft gel size exclusion matrices such as BioGel P2 or Sephadex G-10 can be effective for "desalting" oligonucleotide samples.

20.4 SELECTED APPLICATIONS

The selected applications section for oligonucleotides will contain examples of anion-exchange, reversed-phase, and mixed-mode separations.

20.4.1 Anion-Exchange Separations

One of the primary applications of anion-exchange chromatography of oligonucleotides is the analysis of chemically synthesized nucleic acid fragments. Most chemically synthesized oligonucleotides are prepared on solid supports. The oligodeoxynucleotide is elongated by successive couplings of suitable nucleoside derivatives. After completion of a successful synthesis and deprotection of the oligonucleotides, the major species is the desired product oligonucleotide. However, the individual coupling reactions do not occur with 100% efficiency and small quantities of shorter "failed" sequences result. If an extremely poor coupling occurs, a much larger quantity of a failed sequence results. Anion-exchange chromatography is effective for the analysis of such synthetic procedures. The product oligonucleotide, having the longest sequence, thus the largest number of phosphate groups will elute latest. The illustrated example (Figure 20–3) of such an analysis employs a Whatman-SAX strong anion-exchange column (quaternary amine) in the presence of an increasing gradient of potassium phosphate.[34] The earliest peak contains the uncharged material—largely the chemical blocking groups. The "failed" sequences are then eluted according to the number of phosphates present and/or sequence length. The final peak is the product oligonucleotide. The analysis of Figure 20–3 illustrates a successful synthetic procedure. In a small scale

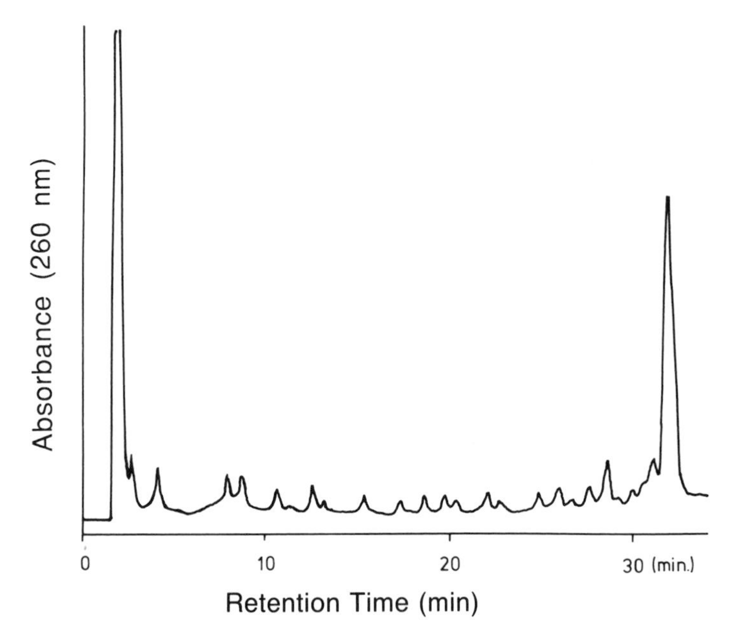

FIGURE 20–3. Analysis of the crude mixture containing a septadecamer (17-mer) after chemical synthesis on a solid support. Column: Whatman-SAX 4.6 × 250 mm. Buffer A: 0.001 *M* KH_2PO_4, pH 6.3, 60% formamide. Buffer B: 0.3 *M* KH_2PO_4, pH 6.3, 60% formamide. Gradient: 0–100% B in 60 min. Flow: 1.5 ml/min. Temperature: 45°C.

preparative procedure, it is also possible to collect the final peak of Figure 20–3 and, after desalting, a pure species is commonly obtained.

A second application for anion-exchange chromatography occurs in the analysis of enzyme reactions involving oligonucleotides. Often complex mixtures result from enzyme catalysis and include substrates, cosubstrates, intermediates, and products. For example, T_4 RNA ligase catalyzes the joining of single-stranded RNA fragments. The reaction requires a donor and acceptor oligonucleotide as well as ATP. In this case a primary amine matrix containing aminopropylsilyl residues has been employed for analysis of the reaction using anion-exchange chromatography (Figure 20–4). This analytical procedure allows monitoring of the amount of acceptor (UpApA) and donor (pUpUpUpCp) oligonucleotides as well as the extent of joining to form product (UpApApUpUpUpCp).[35] ATP is used by the enzyme to form the intermediate adenylated donor [A(5′)pp(5′)pUpUpUpCp]. On joining, AMP is released. Nonspecific ATPase activity produces ADP. The HPLC analysis of Figure 20–4 allows resolution of all the nucleic acid related species in this reaction.

Both the quaternary amine and primary amine anion-exchange matrices exhibit poor resolution of oligonucleotides with sequence lengths greater than 30. The PEI-based materials[26,27] show some promise in the resolution of oli-

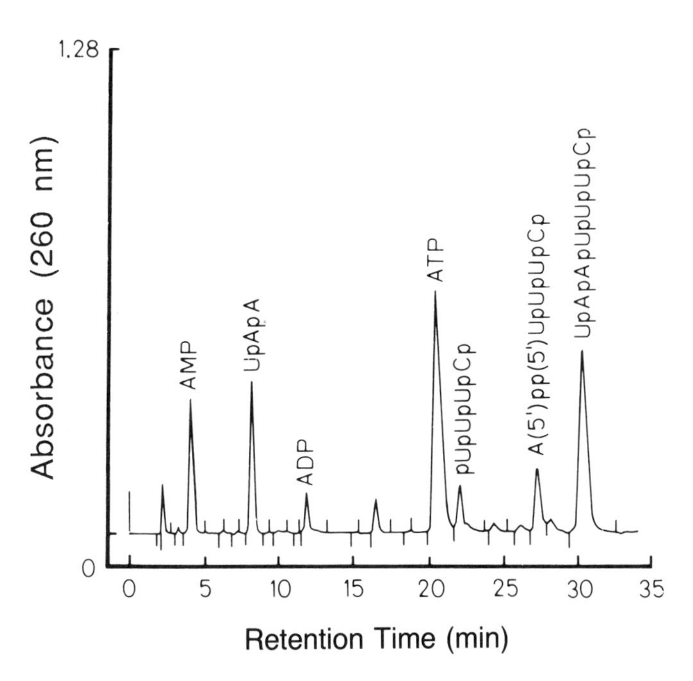

FIGURE 20–4. Analysis of the joining UpApA to pUpUpUpCp catalyzed by T_4 RNA ligase. Column: APS-HYPERSIL, 4.6 × 250 mm. Buffer A: 0.05 *M* KH_2PO_4, pH 4.5. Buffer B: 0.9 *M* KH_2PO_4, pH 4.5, 10% methanol. Gradient: 0–100% B in 60 min. Flow: 2 ml/min. Temperature 35°C. (Reprinted with permission from ref. 35.)

gonucleotides longer than 30-mers. The series of oligoadenylate fragments from $(Ap)_{40}$ to $(Ap)_{45}$ can be resolved with such a column (Figure 20–5).

Anion-exchange chromatography can also be used with large nucleic acids. Both viral RNA and plasmid DNA have been resolved using a tertiary amine anion-exchange matrix.[24,25]

20.4.2 Reversed-Phase Separations

Reversed-phase chromatography has been employed for a wide variety of separation problems involving nucleic acids. As with anion-exchange chromatography it is very useful in solving problems associated with the purification of chemically synthesized oligonucleotides. The protecting group commonly used for the 5′-hydroxyl of the nucleoside starting materials is the 4,4′-dimethoxytrityl (or 9-phenylxanthen-9-yl) group. After deprotection of the nucleobase and phosphate residues, only the 5′-terminal protecting group remains bound to the oligonucleotide. Trityl derivatives (triphenylmethyl species) are highly hydrophobic. Oligonucleotides carrying this protecting group will elute much later from a reversed-phase matrix than unmodified fragments.[28] By using a suitable "capping" step during the chemical synthesis procedures, the elongation procedure can be designed such that only the product oligonucleotide carries the trityl group. The shift in retention time for the trityl-containing species allows a rapid separation of the desired product[33,36] from failed sequences and protecting groups (Figure 20–6).

The selectivity available with reversed-phase chromatography of oligonucleotides is best illustrated with the mixture of decadeoxynucleotides (10-mers) resolved in Figure 20–7. Four 10-mers are present with the sequence

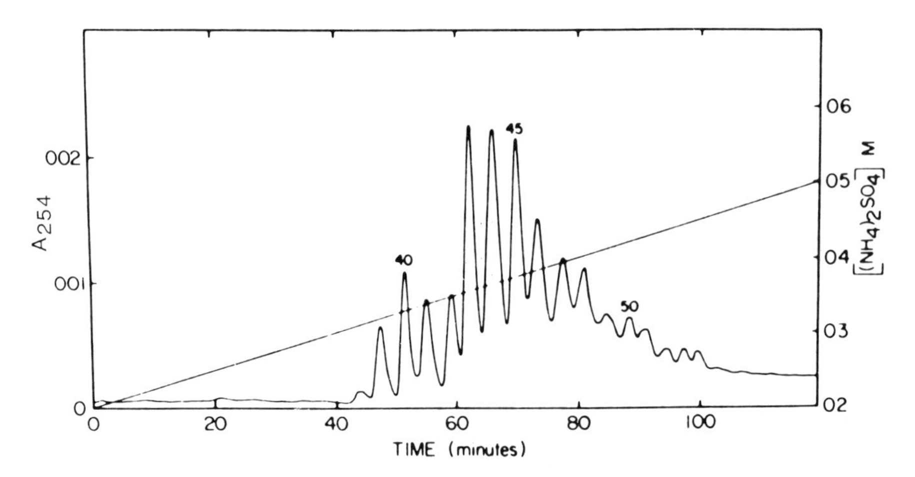

FIGURE 20–5. Resolution of a mixture of polyadenylate. Column: Cross-linked PEI adsorbed on silica gel, 4.6 × 250 mm. Buffer A: 50 m*M* KH_2PO_4, 15% acetonitrile, pH 5.9. Buffer B: 50 m*M* KH_2PO_4, 1.0 *M* NH_4SO_4, 15% acetonitrile, pH 5.9. Gradient: 0–50% B in 120 min. Flow: 0.5 ml/min. Temperature: ambient. (Reprinted with permission from ref. 27.)

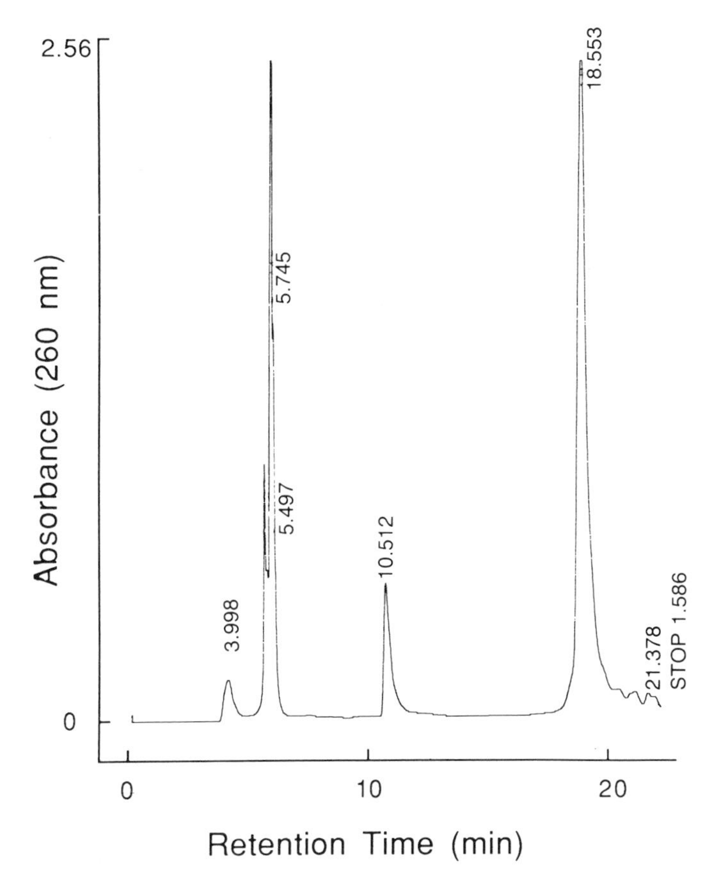

FIGURE 20–6. Isolation of a chemically synthesized decamer (10-mer) containing a 5′-terminal 4,4′-dimethoxytrityl protecting group. Column: 9.4 × 250 in ODS-Hypersil. Buffer A: 50 m*M* triethylammonium acetate, pH 7.0. Buffer B: 50 m*M* triethylammonium acetate, pH 7.0 containing 70% acetonitrile. Gradient: 20–65% B in 40 min. Flow: 4 ml/min. Temperature: ambient.

d(CpTpGpNpApTpCpCpApG). The base N in each case is one of the purines: guanine, hypoxanthine, 2-aminopurine, or purine. These bases differ only in the presence or absence of exocyclic carbonyl and amino groups at positions 2 and 6 of the purine base. Although these relatively subtle modifications occur at only one position in the decamer, the reversed-phase matrix is able to effectively resolve all four species (Figure 20–7). In the example illustrated (Figure 20–7), the order of elution, guanine, hypoxanthine, 2-amino purine followed by purine is observed for the four related decamers.

Typically, ionic compounds such as the phosphorylated derivatives of ATP elute relatively early from a reversed-phase column and in the order ATP, ADP, AMP. However, the use of a reversed-phase column in the ion-pairing mode[25–28] reverses this order. ATP, containing the largest number of phosphate residues, results in

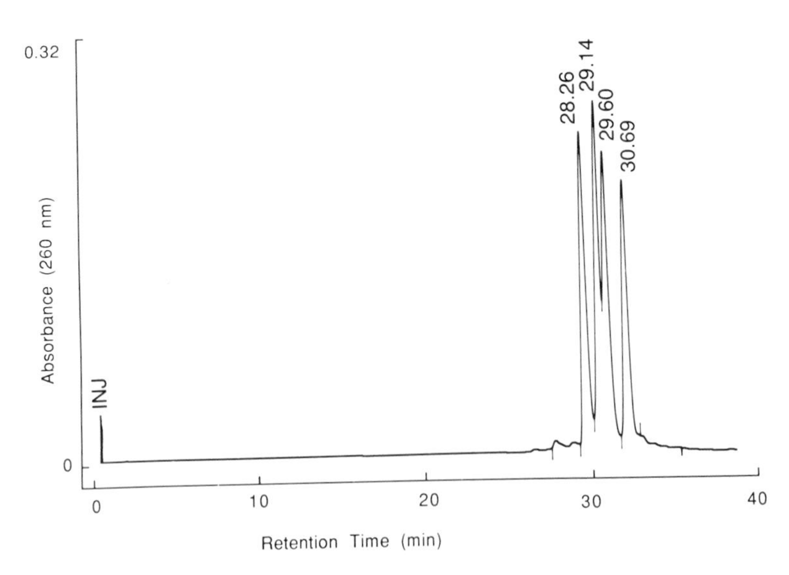

FIGURE 20–7. Resolution of four decamers where N is guanine, hypoxanthine, 2-aminopurine, and purine. Column: ODS-Hypersil, 4.6 × 250 mm. Buffer A: 20 m*M* KH_2PO_4, pH 5.5. Buffer B: 20 m*M* KH_2PO_4, pH 5.5 containing 70% methanol. Gradient: 0–30% B in 50 min. Flow: 1.5 ml/min. Temperature: 35°C.

the more hydrophobic ion-pair complex and the elution order for ATP, ADP, and AMP is reversed (Figure 20–8). Additionally, the chromatogram of Figure 20–8, illustrating the mixture obtained from a joining reaction catalyzed by T_4 RNA ligases, also resolves the nucleic acid material present according to sequence length.

20.4.3 Mixed-Mode Separations

As detailed earlier, mixed-mode chromatography employs both hydrophobic and ionic interactions. Multiple interactions of this type will allow separations by sequence as well as number of phosphodiester residues. One matrix successful in such separations is the APS-PHE material described earlier in this chapter. Resolution of mixed sequence isomers in the crude mixture obtained from chemical oligonucleotide synthesis is possible with this material using a mobile phase consisting of a salt gradient and a small quantity of organic solvent to mediate hydrophobic interactions (Figure 20–9). In this case the crude chemical synthesis containing the two undecamers, differing in sequence at only a single position, can be resolved. Optimization of mixed-mode chromatography can be best approached using techniques that allow variations in the ionic and hydrophobic content of the matrix. With the APS-PHE material, changes in pH will allow such variation in character that can optimize a particular separations problem. This is illustrated in Figure 20–10. In this case increasing the pH and allowing the matrix to take on a more hydrophobic

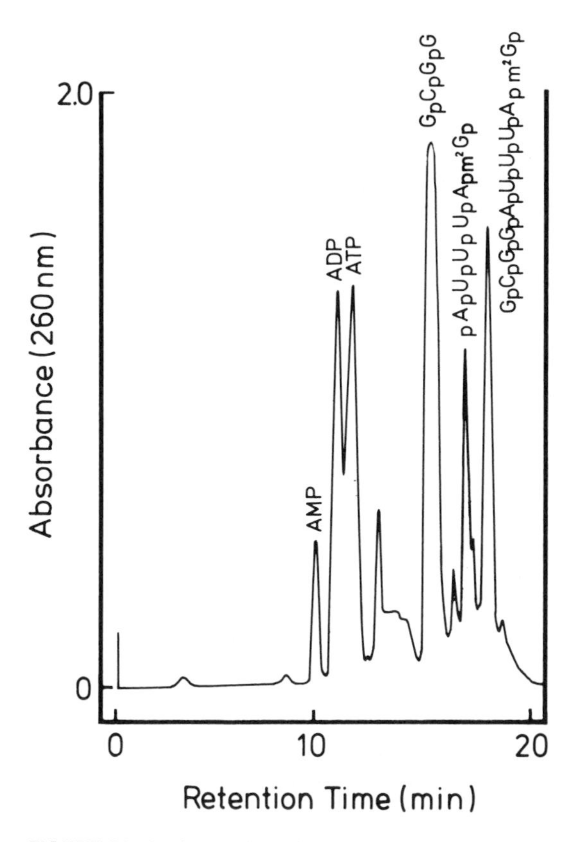

FIGURE 20–8. Separation of the mixture obtained from the T_4 RNA ligase catalyzed synthesis of GpCpGpGp-ApUpUpUpApm^{2}Gp from the corresponding donor and acceptor oligonucleotide. Column: 9.4 × 250 mm ODS-Hypersil. Buffer A: 50 m*M* triethylammonium acetate. Buffer B: 50 m*M* triethylammonium acetate, 70% acetonitrile. Gradient: 0–100% B in 30 min. Flow: 4 ml/min. Temperature: 35°C.

character results in a significant increase in resolution for a mixture of two hexamers and one octamer (Figure 20–10).

A mixed-mode support prepared by coating C_{18} material with a tetraalkylammonium salt[14,18] has been most successful for the resolution of nucleic acids such as tRNAs. However, the exceptional resolution obtained with a mixture of oligouridylic acid fragments (Figure 20–11) indicates this material may have great potential for the resolution of complex oligonucleotide mixtures. One application of this material to the resolution of such a complex mixture is illustrated in Figure 20–12. Ribonuclease T_1 hydrolyzes RNA fragments at guanine residues. It is possible to obtain specific RNA fragments, in this case arising from transfer RNA specific for phenylalanine, by allowing only a partial

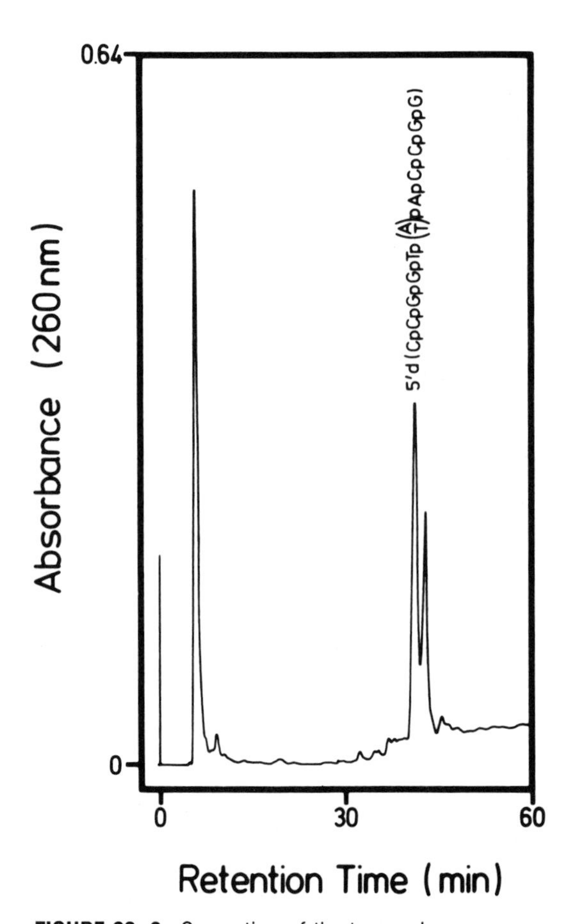

FIGURE 20–9. Separation of the two undecamers (11-mers) in the crude mixture obtained after chemical synthesis. Column: APS-PHE, 4.6 × 250 mm. Buffer A: 50 m*M* KH_2PO_4, pH 6.5, 10% acetonitrile. Buffer B: 0.9 *M* KH_2PO_4, pH 6.5, 10% acetonitrile. Gradient: 0–100% B in 60 min. Flow: 1.5 ml/min. Temperature: 35°C. (Reprinted with permission from ref. 15.)

hydrolysis of the tRNA by the enzyme. This reaction is difficult to control and thus results in a complex mixture of oligonucleotides. Using the mixed-mode matrix we were able to resolve a large number of these fragments ranging in length from 15 to 55 nucleoside residues (Figure 20–12).

A recent report[21] suggests that mixed-mode materials may also be of some value in the resolution of DNA restriction fragments. The separation of DNA restriction fragments is detailed elsewhere in this book.

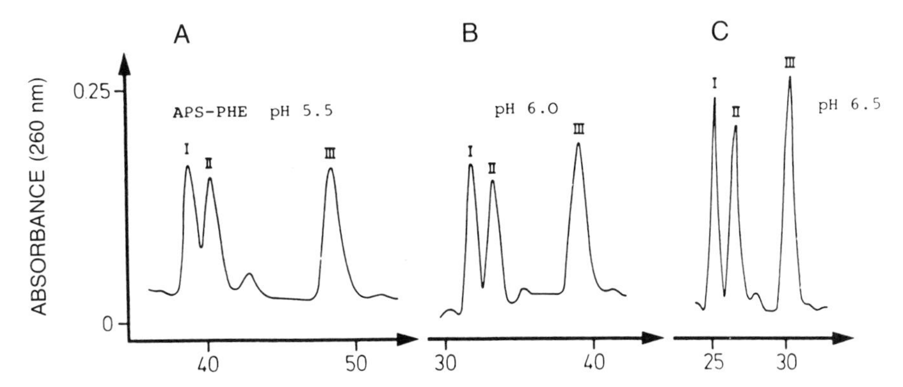

FIGURE 20–10. Resolution of three oligonucleotides ApApUpUpCpGp (I), ApUpUpUp-Apm^{2}Gp (II), and m^{1}ApUpCpCpApCpApGp (III). Column: APS-PHE, 4.6 × 250 mm. Buffer A: 0.5 *M* KH_2PO_4. Buffer B: 0.9 *M* KH_2PO_4, 10% methanol. Gradient: 0–100% B in 60 min. Flow: 1.5 ml/min. Temperature: 35°C. (A) pH 5.5, (B) pH 6.0, (C) pH 6.5.

20.4.4 Preparative Chromatography

HPLC of oliognucleotides on large columns differs from analytical separations only in those respects described earlier. Three of the preceding examples, Figures 20–6, 20–8, and 20–10 were performed on 9.4 × 250 mm, 9.4 × 250 mm, and 6.2 × 250 mm columns, respectively. One final example illustrates that the resolution that can be obtained from even larger columns (21.1 × 250 mm) often does not differ significantly from that experienced with analytical columns (Figure 20–13). In this case a reversed-phase matrix was used to resolve two hexamers that had coeluted on initial isolation from an anion-exchange column. Approximately 510 A_{260} units of the mixture were introduced to the column, which resulted in an isolated yield of greater than 200 A_{260} units of each fragment.

20.5 CONCLUSIONS

HPLC has superseded traditional liquid chromatography employing soft gel chromatography matrices as the method of choice for the resolution and isolation of oligonucleotides. At present the most effect HPLC matrices for olignucleotide separations exploit the known ionic (anion-exchange chromatography) and hydrophobic (reversed-phase chromatography) characteristics of the oligonucleotides. Recent advancements, such as the development of mixed-mode materials, suggest that significant advances in resolution and isolation techniques can be expected in the future.

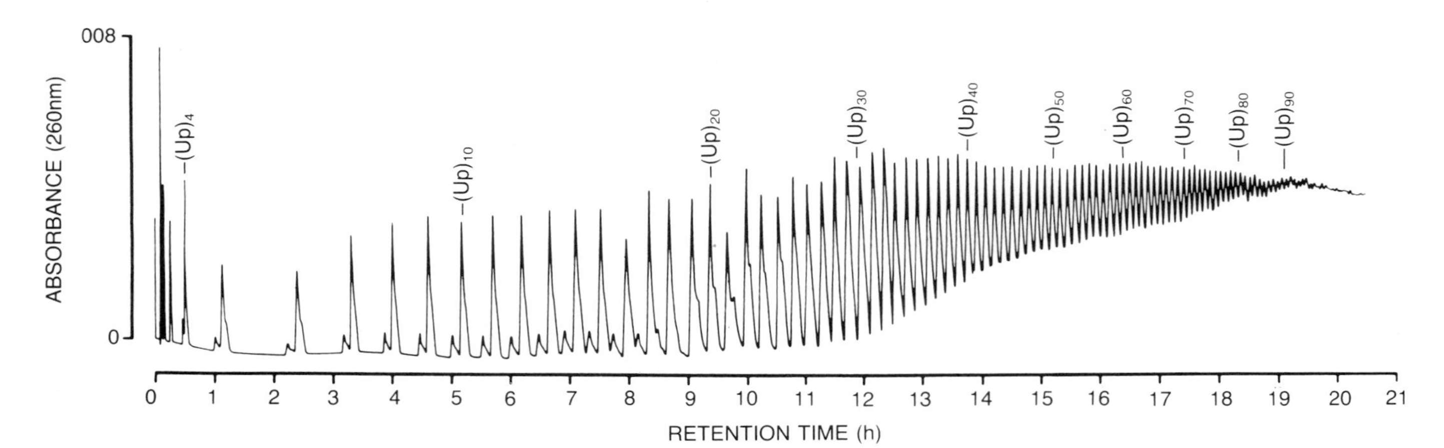

FIGURE 20–11. Resolution of 30 A_{260} units of a hydrolysate of polyuridylic acid. Column: methyltrioctylammonium chloride coated ODS-Hypersil, 4.6 × 250 mm. Buffer A: 0.5 *M* ammonium acetate, pH 4.5. Buffer B: 5.0 *M* ammonium acetate, pH 6.0. Gradient: 0–45% in 20 h. Flow: 0.5 ml/min. Temperature: 35°C. (Reprinted with permission from ref. 18.)

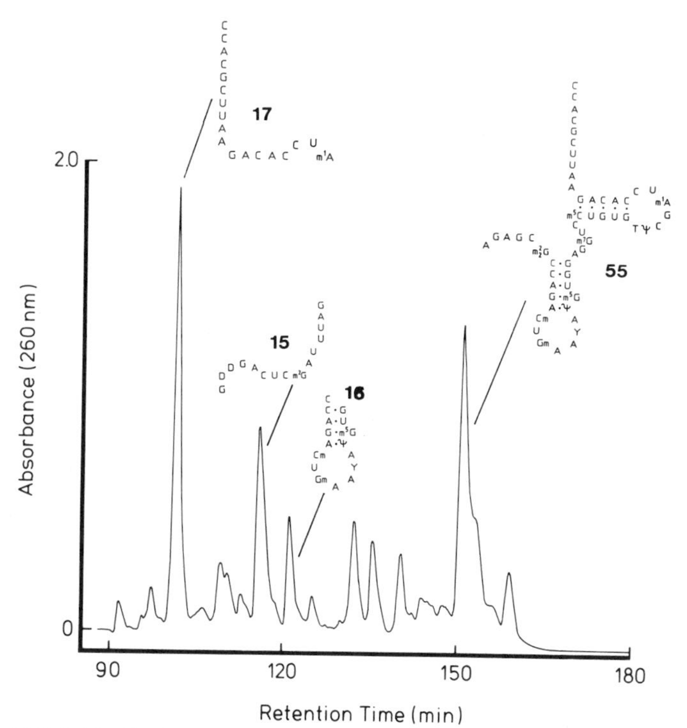

FIGURE 20–12. Resolution of the hydrolysis products obtained from a partial digest of $tRNA^{Phe}$ by ribonuclease T_1. Column: methyltrioctylammonium chloride coated ODS-Hypersil, 6.2 × 250 mm. Buffer A: 0.5 *M* ammonium acetate, pH 4.5. Buffer B: 5.0 *M* ammonium acetate, pH 6.0. Gradient: 0–50% in 2 h. Flow: 1.5 ml/min. Temperature: 50°C.

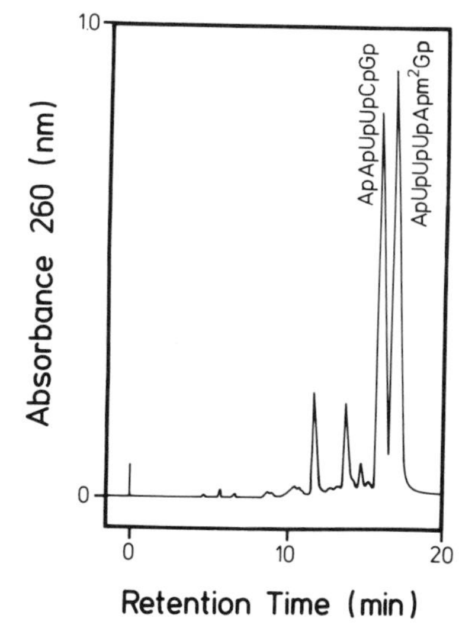

FIGURE 20–13. Resolution of 510 A_{260} units of ApApUpUpCpGp and ApUpUpUpApm^{2}Gp. Column: ODS-Hypersil, 21.2 × 250 mm. Buffer A: 20 m*M* KH_2PO_4, pH 5.5. Buffer B: 20 m*M* KH_2PO_4, pH 5.5, 70% methanol. Gradient: 0–100% B in 60 min. Flow: 40 ml/min. Temperature: 35°C.

REFERENCES

1. H. Schott, in High Performance Liquid Chromatography in Biochemistry (A. Henschen, K. P. Hupe, F. Lottspeich, and W. Volter, eds.). VCH Verlagsgesellschaft, Weinheim, F.R.G., 1982, p. 413.
2. F. Lottspeich and A. Henschen, in High Performance Liquid Chromatography in Biochemistry (A. Henschen, K. P. Hupe, F. Lottspeich, and W. Volter, eds.). VCH Verlagsgesellschaft, Weinheim, F.R.G., 1985, p. 141.
3. See P. R. Brown (ed.), Use of HPLC in Nucleic Acid Research. Dekker, New York, 1984, and references therein.
4. P. R. Brown and A. Krstulovic (eds.), Reversed Phase HPLC; Theory, Practice and Biomedical Applications. Wiley, New York, 1982.
5. L. W. McLaughlin, *Trends in Anal. Chem.*, 5 (1986) 215.
6. L. W. McLaughlin and R. Bischoff, *J. Chromatogr. Biomed Appl.*, 418 (1987) 51.
7. R. Bischoff and L. W. McLaughlin, in HPLC of Biological Macromolecules (F. Regnier and K. Gooding, eds.). Dekker, New York, Vol 51, p. 641.
8. R. Bischoff and L. W. McLaughlin, in Chromatography and Other Analytical Methods in Nucleic Acid Modification Research (C. Gehrke and K. Kuo, eds.). Elsevier, Amsterdam, in press.
9. M. T. W. Hearn, F. E. Regnier, and C. T. Wehr, *Am. Lab.*, 14 (1982) 18.
10. M. T. W. Hearn, in High Performance Liquid Chromatography: Advances and Perspectives, Vol. 3 (Cs. Horvath, ed.). Academic Press, New York, 1983, p. 87.
11. W. S. Hancock and J. T. Sparrow, in High Performance Liquid Chromatography: Advances and Perspectives, Vol. 3 (Cs. Horvath, ed.). Academic Press, New York, 1983, p. 49.
12. J. M. Bussolo, *Am. Biotechnol. Lab.*, June, 20 (1984) p. 131.
13. H. Engleshardt and H. Muller, *Chromatographia*, 19 (1984) 19.
14. R. Bischoff, E. Graeser, and L. W. McLaughlin, *J. Chromatogr.*, 257 (1983) 305.
15. R. Bischoff and L. W. McLaughlin, *J. Chromatogr.*, 270 (1983) 117.
16. R. Bischoff and L. W. McLaughlin, *J. Chromatogr.*, 269 (1984) 329.
17. R. Bischoff and L. W. McLaughlin, *J. Chromatogr.*, 317 (1984) 67.
18. R. Bischoff and L. W. McLaughlin, *Anal Biochem.*, 151 (1985) 526.
19. J. Crowther and R. Hartwick, *Chromatographia*, 16 (1982) 349.
20. J. Crowther, S. Fazio, and R. Hartwick, *J. Chromatogr.*, 282 (1983) 619.
21. T. R. Floyd, S. E. Cicero, S. D. Frazio, T. V. Raglione, S. H. Hsu, S. A. Winkle, and R. A. Hartwick, *Anal. Biochem.*, 154 (1986) 570.
22. M. J. Gait, H. W. D. Mathes, M. Singh, B. S. Spoat, and R. C. Titmas, *Nucl. Acids Res.*, 10 (1983) 6243.
23. L. W. McLaughlin, F. Cramer, and M. Spinzl, *Anal. Biochem.*, 112 (1981) 60.
24. R. Hecker, M. Coplan, and D. Riesner, *J. Chromatogr.*, 326 (1965) 251.
25. M. Coplan, J. Schumacher, W. Brugemann, H. L. Sanger, and D. Riesner, *Anal. Biochem.*, 131 (1983) 257.
26. A. Alpert and F. E. Regnier, *Anal. Biochem.*, 121 (1982) 156.
27. R. R. Drager and F. E. Regnier, *Anal. Biochem.*, 145 (1985) 47.
28. H.-J. Fritz, R. Belagaje, E. R. Brown, H. R. Fritz, R. A. Jones, R. G. Lees, and H. G. Khorana, *Biochemistry*, 17 (1978) 1259.
29. W. Jose, K. Unger, and G. Schill, *Anal. Biochem.*, 119 (1982) 214.
30. P. N. Nguyen, J. L. Bradley, and P. M. McGuire, *J. Chromatogr.*, 236 (1982) 508.
31. S. Eriksson, G. Glad, P. A. Pernemalm, and E. Westman, *J. Chromatogr.*, 359 (1986) 265.
32. J. D. Pearson, M. Mitchell, and F. E. Regnier, *J. Liquid Chromatogr.*, 6 (1983) 1441.
33. L. W. McLaughlin and N. Piel, in Oligonucleotide Synthesis, a. Practical Approach (M. J. Gait, ed.). IRL Press, Oxford, 1984, pp. 117–132.

34. M. J. Gait, H. W. D. Mathes, M. Singh, B. S. Sproat, and R. C. Titmas, *Nucl. Acids Res.*, 10 (1982) 6243.
35. L. W. McLaughlin and E. Romaniuk, *Anal. Biochem.*, 124 (1982) 37.
36. L. W. McLaughlin and J. Krusche, in Chemical and Enzymatic Synthesis of Gene Fragments (H. G. Gassen and E. Lang, eds.). Springer-Verlag, Berlin, 1982, pp. 199–217.

CHAPTER 21

HPLC of Plasmids, DNA Restriction Fragments, and RNA Transcripts

Detlev Riesner

CONTENTS

21.1 INTRODUCTION

Plasmids, DNA restriction fragments, and RNA transcripts form a class of nucleic acids that is the working material of molecular biology and gene technology. Common to these nucleic acids is the high molecular weight, mostly larger than several hundred thousand. In some special applications also other nucleic acids of high molecular weight are needed. Synthetic oligonucleotides, although smaller in size, belong to the tools in molecular biology and gene technology, too. The particular problems of preparation by HPLC are, however, different from those concerning the larger nucleic acids; therefore, they are treated in a different chapter of this volume.

However, the larger nucleic acids mentioned above are not only needed in gene technology or molecular biology but also in biochemistry and biophysics. These nucleic acids may serve for studies determining elementary parameters of nucleic structure, dynamics, and stability; in the case of plasmids, they are the subject of specialized studies about supercoiling and nucleic acid topology.[1,2] There are also other nucleic acids in the same molecular weight range, like ribosomal RNA, messenger RNA, and viral RNA. Although highly purified fractions of these nucleic acids have to be prepared for biochemical studies, they will be covered in lesser detail. As the title indicates the chapter concentrates on plasmids and nucleic acids that are made from plasmids such as restriction fragments and RNA transcripts. They have in common that they may be prepared from bacterial sources particularly selected for high yield or from *in vitro* synthesis mixtures.[3,4] Furthermore, these different nucleic acids are often prepared by the same researchers who probably prepare first plasmids, then select special restriction fragments for further cloning steps and finally purify the RNA of interest after transcription from a particular plasmid construct. In many procedures of molecular biology and gene technology, the nucleic acids mentioned above are required in high purity, and purity alone does not suffice as a specification; additionally, they are supposed to be highly active in a variety of enzymatic reactions and biological transformation. Another new field of HPLC of large nucleic acids is arising in diagnostic applications for medicine and phytopathology. In these new areas of application, too, highly purified probes of recombinant DNA or RNA will be required, e.g., for testing for infectious diseases or for genetically determined disorders.

21.2 NUCLEIC ACID STRUCTURES

Interactions of nucleic acids with the chromatographic resin are very much dependant on the structure of the nucleic acids. The nucleic acids, which are of interest in this chapter, belong to different but characteristic structural types, i.e., double-stranded linear DNA, single-stranded linear RNA, and supercoiled DNA. The characteristic structures are depicted in Figure 21–1. The DNA restriction fragments are linear DNA double strands, sometimes with four unpaired nucleotides on each 5′ end. The DNA double strands form a B-type double helix, the structure of which is known with atomic resolution (cf. textbook[2]). Particular sequences, in which purines and pyrimidines are strictly alternating, may form a left-handed double helix, the so-called Z-helix. All examples given in this chapter refer, however, to right-handed helices. Under the aspects of chromatographic interactions, the B-helix (cf. Figure 21–1A) is homogeneous with respect to charge density of the negatively charged backbone, hydrophobicity of the grooves of the helix, and hydrodynamic flexibility of the rod-like structure. The so-called persistence length of 600 Å for B-DNA means that around every segment of 200 base pairs (bp)* may be bent randomly in solution by 90°C. Therefore, the best structural model for a short restriction fragment (<100 bp) is a stiff rod, but for a long fragment (>500 bp) a flexible coil.

Very special forms of double-stranded DNA do occur, when both strands are covalently closed circles as in native plasmids. The resulting structure of native plasmids is a supercoil, in which different parts of the double-helical circle are wound around each other in a left-handed sense (cf. Figure 21–1B). An extended or a branched structure may be generated, and the local charge density is determined mostly by four charged backbones being in close contact.

Most single-stranded RNAs of natural origin may be considered as having a globular structure with a high degree of internal organization. Complementary sequences, which are closely neighbored, may form hairpin structures, and those with larger distances in between lead to a globular structure of the whole RNA. A well-known example the globular structure of tRNA is depicted in Figure 21–1C. If RNA transcripts are synthetic replicas of natural RNAs, the same structures have to be expected. In many cases, however, transcripts of messenger RNAs are synthesized, and the internal structure of messenger RNA,

*Abbreviations: bp, base pairs; ds, double-stranded; GPC, gel permeation chromatography; HIC, hydrophobic-interaction chromatography; IEC, ion-exchange chromatography; LLPC, liquid–liquid partition chromatography; nt, nucleotides; RPC, reversed-phase chromatography; SEC, size-exclusion chromatography; SPE, solid phase extraction; ss, single-stranded.

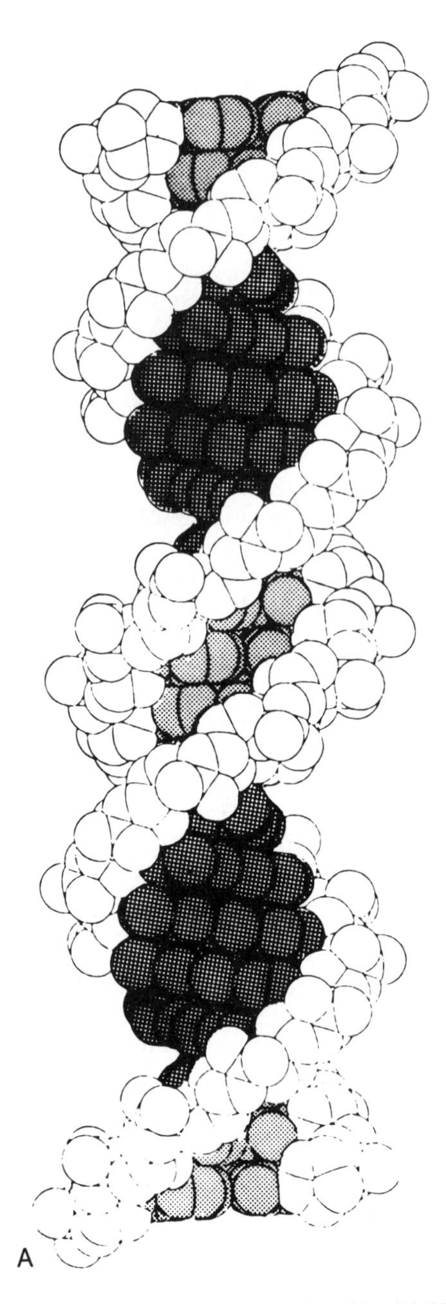

FIGURE 21–1. Typical structures of nucleic acids. **(A)** DNA double-helix in the B-form. The sugar-phosphate backbone is depicted as light model spheres, the stacked bases as shadowed spheres. One complete helical form is 10.4 Å in axial direction. (From ref. 5.)

B

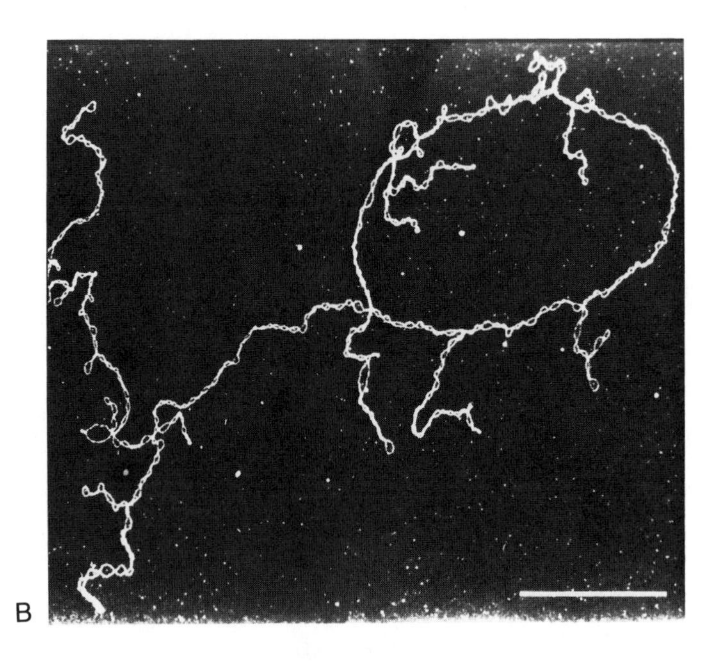

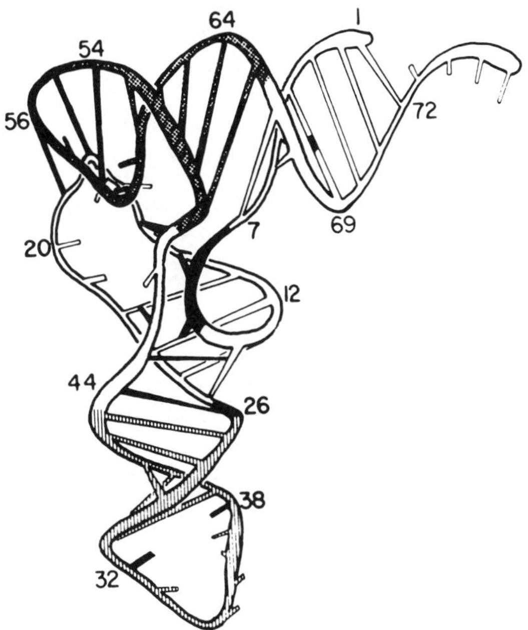

C

(B) Electron micrograph of a plasmid from *Halobacterium halobium* in the supercoil form. The bar is 1 μm. (Courtesy of Dr. G. Klotz, Ulm University.) **(C)** Schematic drawing of phenylalanine-specific tRNA from yeast in the L form. The sugar-phosphate backbone is represented as a continuous strand. The base pairs are shown as straight lines; the light and the shadowed lines represent Watson–Crick base pairs, the black lines hydrogen bridges between bases that are not of the Watson–Crick type. (From ref. 6.)

although not very well known, is assumed to be less pronounced than that of ribosomal RNA or tRNA, for example.

From the structural considerations above, it follows that mainly two parameters of nucleic acids are essential for interaction with an HPLC resin: total number of charges and a combination of size and shape in the form of the radius of gyration. The intrinsic hydrophobicity will not contribute much to a fractionation of nucleic acids of different molecular weight but may be essential, if double-stranded (ds) nucleic acids have to be separated from single-stranded (ss) nucleic acids. Consequently, size-exclusion, ion-exchange, and ion-pair chromatography are the most widely applied modes of HPLC for the nucleic acids of interest, whereas mixed-mode and hydrophobic-interaction chromatography are applied in special cases.

21.3 TECHNIQUES

21.3.1 Size-Exclusion Chromatography

Size-exclusion chromatography (SEC) or gel permeation chromatography (GPC) may be applied for biochemical separation problems wherever biopolymers of different size have to be fractionated. The chromatographic matrix consists of neutral and hydrophilic porous particles. Large molecules are excluded from the pores and eluted with the void volume V_0, whereas small molecules totally invade the pores and are eluted last. Between the extremes, there exists a large range of biopolymers with sizes that partially penetrate the support pores and have an elution volume V_e described by the equation $V_e = V_0 + K_D V_i$, with V_i being the pore volume and the distribution coefficient with values between 0 for exclusion and 1 for total penetration.

In addition to the general features of SEC, two aspects are of particular interest with nucleic acids. These are (1) the question, what means size, and (2) the problem of residual adsorptive interactions of the nucleic acids with the chromatographic matrix. In a recent systematic investigation[7] it was shown, that "size" as a universal calibration principle for SEC is determined by the viscosity radius, i.e., the molecular volume times a shape function that is defined by the intrinsic viscosity. Because of the different conformations of nucleic acids, a unique relationship between elution volume and molecular weight does not exist. If, however, nucleic acids with a homologous structure are separated, the elution volume is monotonic with the molecular weight. The most important example in this context are the DNA restriction fragments because they all have the solution structure of a rod, where the residual flexibility is characterized by a uniform persistence length. Exceptions from the homologous structure have been reported for peculiar sequences, which lead to a nonrandom bending of short double helices.[8] The bending effect seems to affect the retention more in IEC (see below) than in SEC. The properties of the most common SEC columns have been evaluated empirically for nucleic acids. They are the basis for choosing the appropriate column for a specific separation problem.

Most resins available for SEC may exhibit slightly hydrophobic interactions. These interactions are, however, barely detectable with nucleic acids, because nucleic acids are highly hydrophilic polyanions with a strong hydration shell, which protects them from hydrophobic contacts.

The columns are based on resins of a completely organic nature or on silica thinly coated with a hydrophilic surface. The hydrophilic surface coating of porous silica gels is either of the brush type carrying diol groups, or of the type of a hydrophilic polymeric phase. The commercially available chromatographic resins together with the available information about the type of resin, pore size, exclusion limit, and supplier are listed in Table 21–1. Only those that have been applied in the past to the fractionation of large nucleic acids have been included.

Flow rate and sample volume represent restrictions for scaling up. Large amounts of nucleic acid material need large sample volumes and, in consequence, large columns if the resolution is to be maintained. That means that a compromise between costs and resolution is necessary. The examples in the literature were always on an analytical scale. The low linear flow rate, typically 3-20 cm/h, is mainly a restriction on the separation time. Typically, the times of the whole elution process as reported were between 4 and 6 h. Higher flow rates diminish the resolution.

21.3.2 Anion-Exchange Chromatography

To fractionate polyanions, such as nucleic acids, anion-exchange chromatography (IEC) is the most obvious method. This principle has been applied as long as nucleic acids have been purified by means of chromatography. The introduction of high-performance anion-exchange matrices has led to an enormous increase in resolution and made it possible to tackle the problem of purifying high-molecular-weight nucleic acids. The negatively charged nucleic acids are adsorbed on positively charged groups of the anion-exchange resin. They are displaced from the resin by the ions of an increasing salt gradient, in a sequence corresponding to the number of their interacting charges.

As with SEC, two types of support materials are being used for IEC. Completely organic resins with surface charges as well as surface-modified silica-gel resins either polymer coated or brush-type coated are available. From the large number of commercially available columns, only those that have been applied successfully for the purification of high-molecular-weight nucleic acids are listed in Table 21–2. Several others have been reported in connection with oligo- and polynucleotides, with tRNA and mRNA, but are not within the scope of this chapter. A priori, one would not expect of the resins listed in Table 21–2 influences resulting from nonionic interactions. Available chromatographic data (see below), however, indicate slight hydrophobic interactions.

Most anion-exchange resins are based on porous supports. The pores have to meet two requirements, i.e., they have to enlarge the interacting surface, and they have to allow for a free penetration of nucleic acids in order to avoid size-exclusion effects. Consequently, only resins with larger pores (typically 500, 1000, and 4000 Å) may be used for plasmids, restriction fragments, and other large nucleic acids. Smaller pores have the advantage of a higher surface area and, thus, higher nucleic acid binding capacity; larger pores, on the other

TABLE 21–1. Columns for Size-Exclusion Chromatography (SEC)

Column	Material of the Chromatographic Resin	Pore Diameter (Å)	Exclusion Limit (Da)	Supplier
Superose 6	Cross-linked agarose			Pharmacia, Uppsala, Sweden
Superose 12				
TSK G 3000 PW	Hydrophilic polyether	200		Toyo Soda, Kyoto, Japan
TSK G 4000 PW		500		
TSK G 5000 PW		1000	1,000,000	
TSK G 6000 PW				
TSK G 2000 SW	Silica coated with hydrophilic polymer	125	50,000	Toyo Soda, Kyoto, Japan
TSK G 3000 SW		250	100,000	
TSK G 4000 SW		400	300,000	
Zorbax GF 150	Silica with diol groups on the surface	150		Du Pont, Wilmington, DE
Zorbax GF 250		250		
Zorbax GF 450		450		

TABLE 21–2. Columns for Anion-Exchange Chromatography (IEC)

Column	Material of the Chromatographic Resin	Functional Group for Anion Exchange	Pore Size (Å)	Supplier
Mono Q	Hydrophilic acrylic polymer	Quaternary amino	700	Pharmacia, Uppsala, Sweden
Nucleogen				
DEAE 60	Coated silica	Diethylaminoethyl	60	Macherey-Nagel, Düren, Germany
DEAE 500			500	Diagen, Düsseldorf, Germany
DEAE 4000			4000	
TSK DEAE 5PW	Hydroxylated polyether coated silica	Diethylaminoethyl	1000	Toyo Soda, Kyoto, Japan
TSK DEAE 3SW			250	
Gen-Pak FAX	Methacrylate polymer	Diethylaminoethyl	Unporous 2.5-μm particles	Waters, Milford, MA

hand, are always showing increased resolution. The user may be well advised to apply the largest pore size available in order to achieve the highest resolution and a medium-sized pore only if very high preparative capacity is needed. Recently, nonporous material was applied to large nucleic acid fractionation. It is a methacrylate polymer with a 2.5-μm particle size (see Table 21–2). In this case, the surface area needed for the nucleic acid binding capacity is not achieved by pores but by the small particle size.

Several mobile phases have been used for the elution of nucleic acids from anion-exchange columns. No systemic interpretation of the influence of the buffer–salt combination on the resolution has been given so far, but some of the empirical results are of practical importance. The most widely used combination, Tris-NaCl, is not always the best choice. Detailed investigations with Nucleogen columns have shown that phosphate buffer exhibits superior resolution with sodium chloride or potassium chloride as the eluting salt.[9] Addition of 4–6 *M* urea has been shown to achieve a further increase in resolution and to contribute significantly to the prevention of cross-contamination.[10] Under normal chromatographic conditions, the addition of urea does not denature the double helical structure of high-molecular-weight nucleic acid but eliminates residual interactions between different nucleic acid molecules as well as between nucleic acids and the resin. Hydrophobic interactions and hydrogen bonds are considered to contribute to these nonspecific interactions.

In contrast to SEC, the influence of flow rate on resolution is fairly minor. It is obvious that a higher flow rate and a shallower gradient will increase the peak volume and therefore decrease the detection limit. In Section 21.4.1 it will be shown that steep gradients (10 m*M*/min) are most appropriate for fast analysis, i.e., they give all the information needed in a very short time. For preparative applications, however, shallower gradients in some cases led to a better baseline separation and facilitate collection of the different peaks without cross-contamination.

The effect of an increase in the flow rate is similar to that caused by a decrease in the gradient, but the flow rate is limited by the increasing pressure. For the preparation of milligram amounts of restriction fragments, flow rates of 2–3 ml/min and gradients of 1–2 m*M*/min may be recommended (see below).

Variation of the temperature between room temperature and 60°C does not show a marked effect on the resolution. With Nucleogen-DEAE columns no change in resolution but only a slight shift to higher ionic strength (20 m*M* per 10°C) was observed.[9] It has been reported that Mono Q columns, however, show best resolution and reproducibility at 60°C.[11]

21.3.3 Reversed-Phase and Hydrophobic-Interaction Chromatography

Reversed-phase chromatography (RPC) and hydrophobic-interaction chromatography (HIC) are based on very similar types of interaction; in both techniques a hydrophobic surface of the chromatographic matrix represents the stationary phase, to which the nucleic acid is adsorbed. Different hydrophobic parts of the nucleic acid, however, are involved in the interaction.

In RPC, hydrophobicity is established by an alkyl chain that is bound in form of an alkylammonium ion to the negative phosphates of the nucleic acid.[12] Due to this ion-pair formation, RPC of nucleic acids is often called ion-pair chromatography. The adsorbed nucleic acids are eluted by an increasing gradient of organic solvents, typically acetonitrile or isopropanol. Furthermore, the hydrophobicity of the heterocyclic bases of the nucleic acids contribute to their overall hydrophobicity. These contributions, however, might be significant only in the case of ss nucleic acids. In the case of ds nucleic acids, hydrophobic interactions are being compensated by the intramolecular structure. Therefore, as a general rule ds nucleic acids are more weakly bound to hydrophobic surfaces and elute earlier than ss ones.

In HIC, nucleic acids are adsorbed to the hydrophobic surface by salting out from the aqueous mobile phase. The adsorbed nucleic acids are eluted by a decreasing salt gradient that redissolves the nucleic acids in the aqueous mobile phase. This type of chromatography is similar to the method of fractionated salt precipitation. Similarly as with salt precipitation, the adsorption is much stronger for ss as compared with ds nucleic acids. It increases with chain length. The hydrophobic surfaces for RPC are alkyl groups, typically C_8 and C_{18} phases, whereas for HIC, phenyl- and *t*-butyl phases are most common. The chromatographic supports for the hydrophobic surfaces are organic polymers or porous silica. The list of chromatographic resins as given in Table 21–3 is restricted to those that have been applied to large nucleic acids. Many more are available, for which, however, experience is available only with oligonucleotides.

Chromatographic parameters such as temperature, gradient slope, flow rate, and buffer conditions show only minor influence on resolution and capacity as long as different types of nucleic acids are separated, e.g., poly(U) from poly(A).[13,14] If, however, restriction fragments of different length have to be fractionated, the gradient has to be very shallow (see legend of Figure 21–4B).

21.3.4 RPC-5 and Mixed-Mode Chromatography

Although RPC stands for reversed-phase liquid chromatography, the chromatographic material RPC-5 is actually a material for mixed-mode chromatography. RPC-5 was the first chromatographic technique for the fractionation of high-molecular-weight nucleic acids, having been introduced more than 20 years ago.[15] The separation is based on ionic as well as on hydrophobic interactions. The resin applied originally consists of a charged reversed-phase matrix with a quaternary ammonium derivative being physically adsorbed on a nonporous polymer support, such as polychlorotrifluoroethylene beads (Plascon 2 300). More recently, resins with a covalently bound mixed-mode surface, which consists of partially modified aminopropylsilica with different alkyl chains and aryl groups,[16,17] have been synthesized. Because ionic interactions are prevalent in mixed-mode resins of this kind, elution of the adsorbed nucleic acid is achieved by a salt gradient.

In spite of the good results reported by Wells and co-workers on DNA restriction fragments[18–20] and by McLaughlin and co-workers on tRNA and larger

TABLE 21–3. Columns for Reversed-Phase (RPC) and Hydrophobic-Interaction (HIC) Chromatography

Column	Material for the Chromatographic Resin	Functional Group[a]	Pore Size (Å)	Supplier
μ-Bondapak	Coated silica	C_{18}	100	Waters, Milford, MA
Pep RPC	Coated silica			Pharmacia, Uppsala, Sweden
Pro RPC		C_8	300	
SynChropak RP-PC_8	Coated silica	C_8	300	SynChrom, Linden, IN
SynChropak RP-PC_{18}		C_{18}	300	
Varian MH 10	Coated silica	C_{18}		Varian, Walnut Creek, CA

[a] C_8, $(CH_2)_7\ CH_3$; C_{18}, $(CH_2)_{17}\ CH_3$.

oligonucleotides,[16,17,21] very few other authors reported on the application of mixed-mode chromatography to the fractionation of large nucleic acids. In this respect one has to keep in mind that RPC-5 was invented and applied before HPLC instrumentation was available to biochemists; the more recent trend to short separation times by HPLC techniques and easier handling of the newer chromatographic resins may have prompted most scientists to apply other techniques. Therefore, no detailed description of mixed-mode chromatography and no examples of application will be given.

21.3.5 Liquid–Liquid Partition Chromatography

Although liquid–liquid partition chromatography (LLPC) does not belong to the HPLC techniques in the normal sense, it should be included in this chapter, since successful experiments of the fractionation of large nucleic acids have been reported in recent years. LLPC was derived from countercurrent distribution as introduced by Martin and Synge,[22] in which the components of a mixture are separated according to their different partition coefficients in a two-phase system. If one of the two phases may be established as a stationary phase on a chromatographic matrix, it is in continuous contact and partially mixed with the other phase, which moves continuously in front of the mobile phase. Similarly as in SEC, a relationship exists between the elution volume V_e and the partition coefficient of the component m K_M according to $V_e = V_m + V_s \cdot 1/K_M$, with V_m and V_s being the volumes of the mobile and the stationary phase, respectively. K_M is defined according to Nernst as the quotient of the equilibrium concentrations of the component m in the mobile and the stationary phase.

For nucleic acid fractionation, an appropriate column chromatography technique could be developed only after Albertsson had described aqueous two-phase systems,[23] i.e., systems, both phases of which are native solvents for biopolymers. The different attempts to try different systems and to establish one phase as a stationary phase on a matrix will not be described here; only the system and the matrix that are presently available to the user will be discussed in some detail. The development was mainly the work of W. Müller.[24–26]

The aqueous-two phase system consists of polyethyleneglycol (PEG) and dextran (DX). Because the interactions between both of these are highly unfavorable, PEG and DX separate into two distinct phases, one heavier, DX-rich phase and one lighter, PEG-rich phase. The same exclusion effect was used to establish one phase stationary on a chromatographic matrix. It was found that polyacrylamide excludes PEG but not DX. Thereby, polyacrylamide bound covalently to a silica surface is able to bind the DX phase as a stationary phase. If a porous silica was used, it could be shown that the pores filled with the DX phase act as the stationary phase and the mobile phase uses most of the interstitial volume.

The PEG phase is slightly more hydrophobic than the DX phase. According to Bronstedt's semiempirical law of partitioning, the partition coefficient varies exponentially with the surface area of the solute. Since the surface area is proportional to the molecular weight of a homologous series of DNA molecules, e.g., restriction fragments, the partition coefficient is also related exponentially to the molecular weight. In Figure 21–2A this relationship is depicted in the form of the linear dependence of ln K on the sedimentation coefficient of DNA double strands. The sedimentation coefficient is used as the size parameter, but it should be noted that this parameter is not linearly related to the molecular weight of restriction fragment[27] and that therefore Bronstedt's formula does not hold quantitatively for the dependence of the partition coefficient on the surface area of DNA restriction fragments.

The partition coefficient may be varied by the molecular weight of the phase-forming polymer. An increase in the molecular weight decreases the solubility of the solute in that phase; the effect is not too large and is restricted to solutes of which the molecular weights are comparable to those of the phase-forming polymers.

The concentration and nature of ions in the two-phase systems exert more drastic effects. If the concentration of salt is higher than about 0.5 M, nucleic acids are dissolved much more in the DX than in the PEG phase. Smaller salt concentrations may markedly influence the partition coefficient in both directions. This effect is due to unequal distribution of anions and cations between the two phases. Thereby, an electrostatic potential difference between the phases is formed, which strongly influences the partition of charged macromolecules. Not only the salt concentration but also the activity coefficient affects the partition coefficient of the nucleic acid. This effect is used in practice,

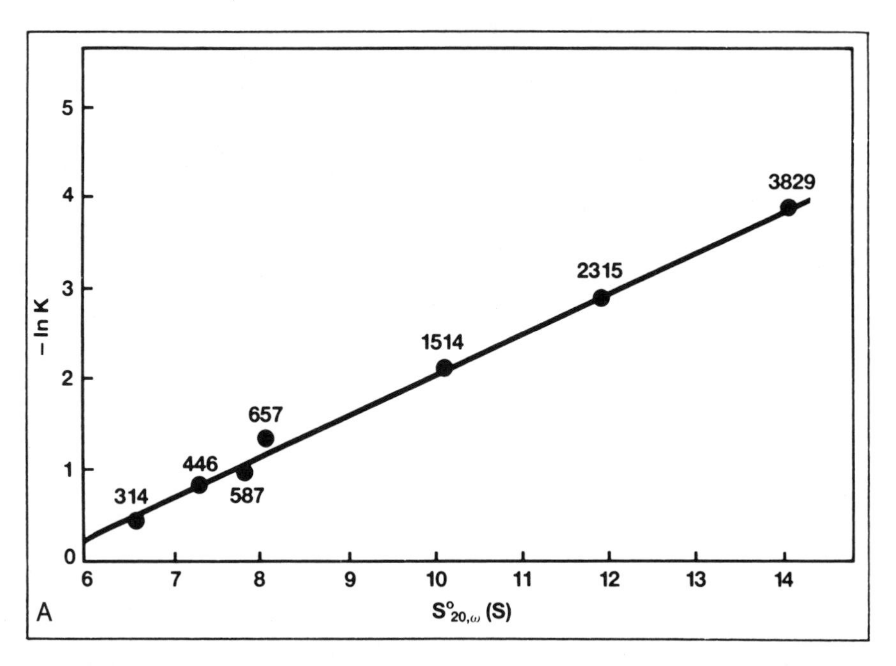

FIGURE 21–2. Partition coefficients of DNA restriction fragments. Partition coefficient K is defined as the ratio of concentrations of DNA in the mobile phase and in the stationary phase. (From ref. 25.) **(A)** Dependence of K on the sedimentation coefficient $S^{\circ}_{20,w}$ at 37°C in the standard PEG 8000/DX 500 system (cf. Table 21–4) in the presence of 0.2 M LiOAc.

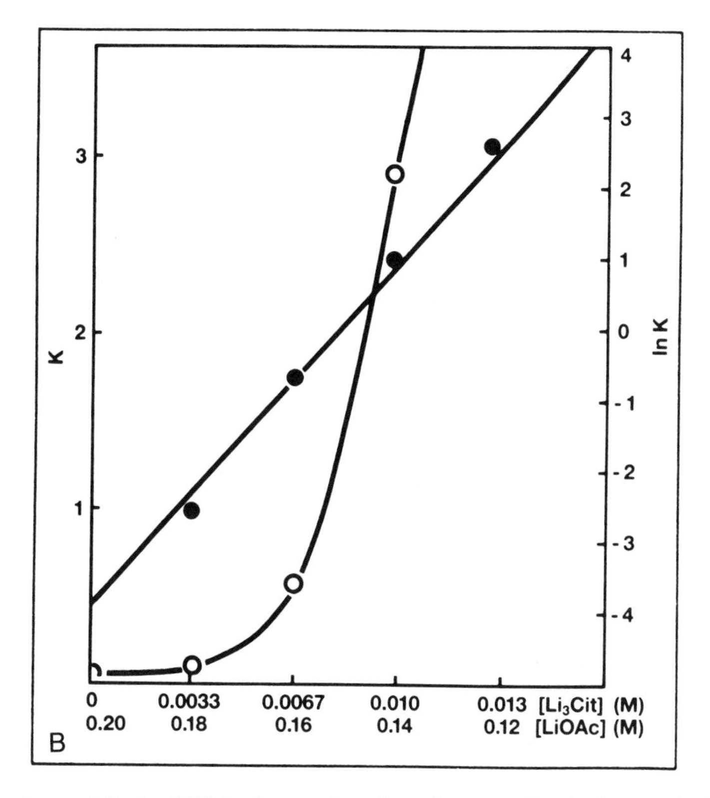

(B) Dependence of K of a 3829 bp fragment on the salt composition in the standard PEG 8000/DX 500 system. (○) Linear values of K; (•) logarithmic values of K.

if the elution of nucleic acid is carried out by forming a linear exchange of ions at constant ionic strength, e.g., of 0.2 M, from LiOAc to Li_3 citrate, or from NaOAc to LiOAc. An example of the variation of the partition coefficient as a function of the salt composition is given in Figure 21–2B. Due to this salt-exchange gradient the partition coefficient (K = concentration in the mobile phase/concentration in the stationary phase) is increased gradually, and the elution of nucleic acids of different molecular weights can be extended over larger elution volumes.

The details of preparing the two-phase system and the column with the stationary and the mobile phase are described in several reports by Müller.[24–26] The columns, uncoated as well as coated with both phases, are commercially available. They are listed in Table 21–4.

21.3.6 LC, HPLC, FPLC, and Solid Phase Extraction

Chromatographic procedures, which are based on the molecular interactions described in Sections 21.3.1–21.3.4, may be carried out in different technical performance. Liquid–liquid partition chromatography is a special develop-

TABLE 21–4. Columns for Liquid–Liquid Partition Chromatography

Column	Material of the Chromatographic Resin	Two-Phase System on the Column[a]	Pore size (Å)	Supplier
Li Par Gel 650 uncoated	Silica, surface modified with polyacrylamide	—	650	E. Merck, Darmstadt, Germany
Li Par Gel 650 (Dx 40/PEG 6000)	Silica, surface modified with polyacrylamide	Dx 40/PEG 6000	650	E. Merck, Darmstadt, Germany
Li Par Gel 650 (Dx 500/PEG 8000)	Silica, surface modified with polyacrylamide	Dx 500/PEG 8000	650	E. Merck, Darmstadt, Germany
Li Par Gel 750 uncoated	Silica, surface modified with polyacrylamide	—	750	E. Merck, Darmstadt, Germany
Li Par Gel 750 (Dx 500/PEG 8000)	Silica, surface modified with polyacrylamide	Dx 500/PEG 8000	750	E. Merck, Darmstadt, Germany

[a]DX 40, dextran of 40 kDa; DX 500, dextran of 500 kDa; PEG 6000, polyethyleneglycol of 6 kDa; PEG 8000, polyethyleneglycol of 8 kDa.

ment, which is commercially available only in one performance (cf. Table 21–4); it is therefore not considered further here.

Liquid chromatography (LC) is either used as the general description of chromatographic methods in solution or designates the conventional procedures, in which the chromatographic resin consists of large and soft particles, and the flow of the mobile phase is kept up by the hydrostatic pressure or peristaltic pumps. Agarose, dextran, cellulose, acrylates, and hydroxylapatite belong to these resins. The instruments needed are inexpensive, and the procedure is easy to carry out. The main disadvantage is the low chromatographic resolution mainly because of band broadening due to too large diffusion distances. LC is of very limited application for large nucleic acids. It is not recommended for trying to fractionate large nucleic acids but it may be applied for separating nucleic acids from other compounds as, for example, desalting, changing buffer, removing triphosphates, cleaning samples from gel residuals, and/or UV absorbing material.

The advantages of HPLC over conventional LC methods come mainly from small, pressure-resistant particles for the chromatographic resin and from more sophisticated equipment. The small particles with controlled diameters and pore sizes guarantee short diffusion distances and high capacity. A very constant flow at high pressure is achieved by special pumps and if needed by electronically controlled gradient generation. The development of both, chromatographic matrices and instruments, was a prerequisite for the fractionation of large nucleic acids. For the theory of the parameters mentioned above see other chapters. Instruments are equipped mostly with highly sensitive detection systems, which allow detection of nucleic acids in the concentration range of 100 ng/ml.

FPLC was originally a trade name for a particular instrument for fast protein LC, which worked at intermediate pressure (20 bars) and utilized only chemically inert materials in contact with the solutions. For example, the pumps were made from glass. At present, FPLC is used synonymously for HPLC of biopolymers under exclusion of any chemical impurities from the instrument as, for example, divalent metal ions. The importance of excluding divalent metal ions for HPLC of nucleic acids, particularly RNA, has been pointed out before FPLC came in use.[28]

Solid phase extraction (SPE) combines the development of new resins for HPLC with the unsophisticated instrumentation of LC. A one-way, low cost column is mounted on a syringe. These columns are appropriate for processing many samples on a small scale. The flow is due to hand-made pressure in the syringe, from the gravity of the solution, or from a simple vacuum box. The advantages are easy handling, low cost, and no demand for instruments. In most applications, i.e., with the exception of gel filtration, it is a chromatography carried out in the batch mode. The steps are equilibration, adsorption, washing, and desorption. SPE may generally be applied for the following procedures on large nucleic acids: desalting, concentration, recovery after gel elution, separation from small components such as oligonucleotides or triphosphates, extraction from cellular extracts, and others. SPE is not utilized for high resolution. The Qiagen system (cf. Section 21.4.5) is claimed to allow a moderate size fractionation; also the separation of ds and ss forms of M13 DNA may be carried out. A particular advantage of one-way columns is that cross-contaminations between different samples are excluded. The avoidance of contamination is particularly important for the use in microbiology. One-way columns, which are at present commercially available, are listed together with the mode of application in Table 21–5.

21.3.7 Sample Preparation and Recovery

Prior to chromatography the nucleic acids should be extracted with phenol or phenol/chloroform, respectively, precipitated with ethanol, and redissolved in low salt buffer. These are standard procedures described in laboratory guides.

The redissolved nucleic acids solutions are adjusted to the starting conditions of the chromatography by adding buffer from concentrated stock solution. In SEC, the sample volume has to be kept as small as possible, because a larger sample volume leads to a broader elution profile of a single component and thereby a decrease of resolution. Restrictions in the choice of the buffer nearly do not exist in SEC. In IEC, RPC-5, and mixed-mode chromatography, i.e., in all techniques that need an increasing salt gradient for elution, the ionic strength of the sample must not be higher than in the starting buffer. In RPC the eluting organic solvent has to be absent or low in the sample, and in HIC the salt concentration of the sample has to be higher than the starting concentration of the decreasing salt gradient. In LLPC the sample is dissolved in the mobile phase (PEG phase), or if the sample is present as a solution it is brought to the PEG concentration of the mobile phase by adding solid PEG. When the samples of large nucleic acids are injected into the HPLC instrument, shearing forces that may arise in a narrow needle of the injection syringe and could lead to a degradation of the nucleic acid, should be avoided.

After chromatography, the peak fractions are combined, and the nucleic acids have to be recovered from the combined fractions. In contrast to SEC and RPC, nucleic acids cannot be precipitated with ethanol after elution from IEC, HIC, mixed-mode chromatography, and LLPC, because coprecipitation of the vast excess of salt used in these chromatographic techniques would occur. The high salt content could potentially be removed by dialysis, but such procedure would be time consuming, and possibly degradation of the nucleic acids could lead to the loss of the sample.

Different procedures for recovery have been developed, which are adapted to the different chromatographic techniques and different nucleic acids. They are listed in Table 21–6.

21.4 APPLICATIONS

The applications of HPLC to different types of nucleic acids of interest are discussed by choosing particular examples from the literature. If possible, examples that have been documented extensively in the literature have been selected. In some cases the examples had to be taken from the application notes of the corresponding suppliers. The reader may also refer to a more complete listing of examples in a recent handbook.[29] The examples in the

TABLE 21–5. Prepurification and Recovery of Nucleic Acids by Solid-Phase Extraction in One-Way Columns[a]

Column	Mode of Separation	Recommended Application	Supplier
RDP	RPC-5	Recovery of dsDNA (88–50,000 bp) from gels after electrophoresis	Bio-Rad, Richmond, CA
Elutip d	RPC-5	Recovery of dsDNA from gels after electrophoresis	Schleicher und Schüll, Dassel, Germany
NACS PREPAC	RPC-5	Recovery of dsDNA from gels after electrophoresis; separation of large dsDNA from nucleotides and linkers; DNA concentration	Gibco-BRL, Bethesda, MD
NICK NAP	SEC (Sephadex G-25)	Desalting, buffer exchange	Pharmacia, Uppsala, Sweden
	SEC (Sephadex G-50)	Separation of nick-translated DNA and unincorporated nucleotides	
NENSORB	RPC, C_8	Separation of DNA or RNA from protein, salt, and unincorporated nucleotides	NEN Du Pont, Dreieich, Germany
QIAGEN-tip (5–20 μg nucleic acid binding capacity) Qiagen-pack (100–500 μg nucleic acid binding capacity)	IEC	Preparation of plasmid DNA and phage DNA; purification of mRNA, rRNA, viral RNA, and RNA transcript; separation of DNA or RNA from unincorporated nucleotides after nick translation, end labeling, or oligolabeling; separation of nucleic acids from dyes after dye labeling; removal of DNA linkers; recovery of nucleic acids from gels after electrophoresis; separation of nucleic acids with low resolution (cf. Figure 21–22)	Diagen, Düsseldorf, Germany
Geneclean	Reversible binding of DNA to glass beads	Recovery of DNA from gels after electrophoresis; removal of protein and small RNA from DNA; removal of unincorporated nucleotides in labeling reactions, desalting and concentrating of DNA	Bio 101, La Jolla, CA

[a]Detailed operational manuals are delivered by the corresponding suppliers.

TABLE 21–6. Recovery of Nucleic Acids from the Combined Peak Fractions after HPLC

	High-Molecular-Weight RNA	High-Molecular-Weight DNA
SEC, RPC	Precipitation by two volumes of ethanol at −20°C overnight	
IEC, HIC mixed-mode C	The sample is adsorbed on hydroxylapatite, washed with 20 m*M* potassium phosphate, pH 6.5, and eluted with 0.5 *M* potassium phosphate, pH 5.6. The RNA is precipitated with 0.1 volume of 1% cetyltrimethylammoniumbromide (CTAB), 1% NaCl, 0.1 m*M* EDTA for 1 h on ice. The pellet is dissolved in 7.5 *M* ammonium acetate, pH 7.4, diluted with 2 volumes H_2O to 2.5 *M*, and then precipitated with 2.5 volumes of ethanol. The precipitate is dissolved in low salt buffer and precipitated again with 2.5 volumes of ethanol.	Alternatively: (1) Solid polyethylene glycol (PEG 6000) is added and dissolved up to a final concentration of 10% (w/v); the DNA is allowed to precipitate on ice for 2 h or longer. (2) Samples are diluted with one volume of water, and the DNA is precipitated with one volume of 2-propanol at −20°C for 2 h or longer.
LLPC	RNA and DNA are treated as RNA after IEC (cf. above)	
	The pellets of the final precipitation are washed in 75% ethanol/25% water.	

following sections are not a complete review of the published data; they are only meant to give the reader an overview of the best possibilities for a variety of fractionation problems. All examples presented in the following sections are illustrated by elution profiles. In most cases the figure legends were taken from the original literature in order to pass on to the reader as much information as possible.

21.4.1 DNA Restriction Fragments

Although in daily laboratory work plasmids have to be purified first, and from these DNA restriction fragments are generated, the HPLC of the fragments will be presented first as the more general fractionation problem. First fractionations were carried out with RPC-5[20] and SEC.[30] In Figure 21–3 the elution profile of an example with SEC is given. The resolution is sufficient only up to a fragment size of a few hundred base pairs. More recently, reports in the literature concern examples obtained with IEC, RPC, and LLPC. The developments in these types of HPLC have resulted in superior qualities of resolution

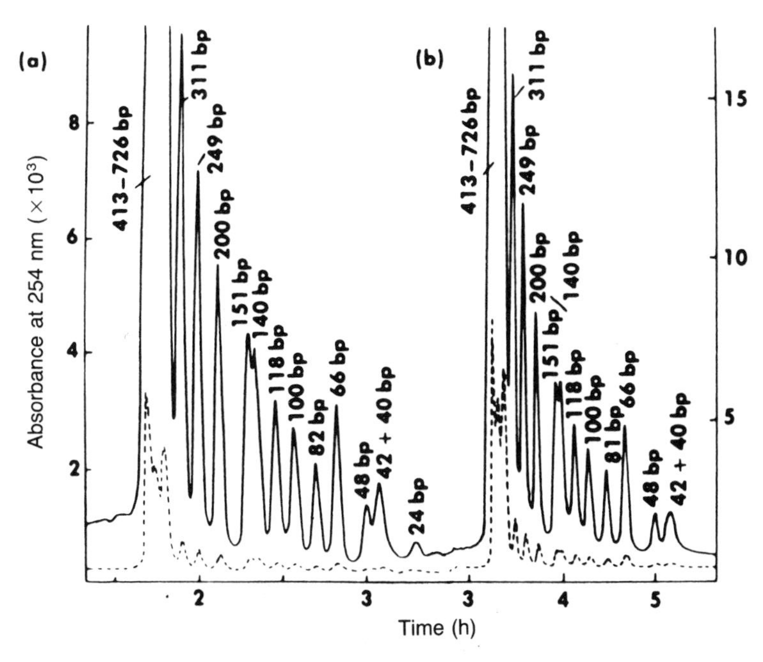

FIGURE 21–3. Size-exclusion HPLC of DNA restriction fragments. Column: (a) TSK-G 4000 SW (7.5 × 600 mm); (b) tandem TSK-G 4000 SW (7.5 × 600 mm) and TSK-G 3000 SW (7.5 × 600 mm). Sample: (a) 5 μg of DNA fragments from the phage φX174 after digestion of the RF DNA with *Hin*fI; the sizes of the fragments (in bp) are indicated in the figure; (b) 10 μg of sample (a). Chromatographic conditions: 50 m*M* triethylammonium acetate, pH 7.0; 6 ml/h; ambient temperature. (From ref. 30.)

and capacity of DNA restriction fragments. It should be emphasized that this judgment is meant particularly for restriction fragments and may be modified for other nucleic acids, for example, globular RNA. Very special utilization of SEC may be derived from the finding that large DNA fragments (>500 bp) are being retained on a Du Pont GF-250 column.[41]

In Figure 21–4 HPLC separations of a set of restriction fragments from 18 to about 600 bp are depicted, and the elution profiles obtained by IEC (Figure 21–4A), RPC (Figure 21–4B), and LLPC (Figure 21–4C) are compaired. The restriction fragments of Figure 21–4A and B are identical (*Hae*III digest of the plasmid pBR322), whereas those of Figure 21–4C are slightly different (*Bam*HI + *Hae*III + *Xba*I digest of the plasmid pDSI). Therefore, comparison of the elution profiles may elucidate the particular features of the different modes in HPLC.

The chromatographic resolution appears very similar in the three cases. Thus, no a priori differentiation can be made. Concerning the capacity, the example of LLPC is preparative (600 μg nucleic acid sample), whereas in the two other examples only 10 μg nucleic acid sample is applied. The elution time of 55 min with IEC appears superior to the hours with RPC and even more markedly to the 9 h with LLPC. This comparison needs several comments.

First, the times may be a consequence not only of the mode of HPLC but also of the special type of column used in the experiment. Second, longer elution times would have been needed with IEC and RPC, if preparative chromatographies similar to LLPC would have been carried out. Other examples with IEC (cf. below), however, have shown that a preparative fractionation of 10 or

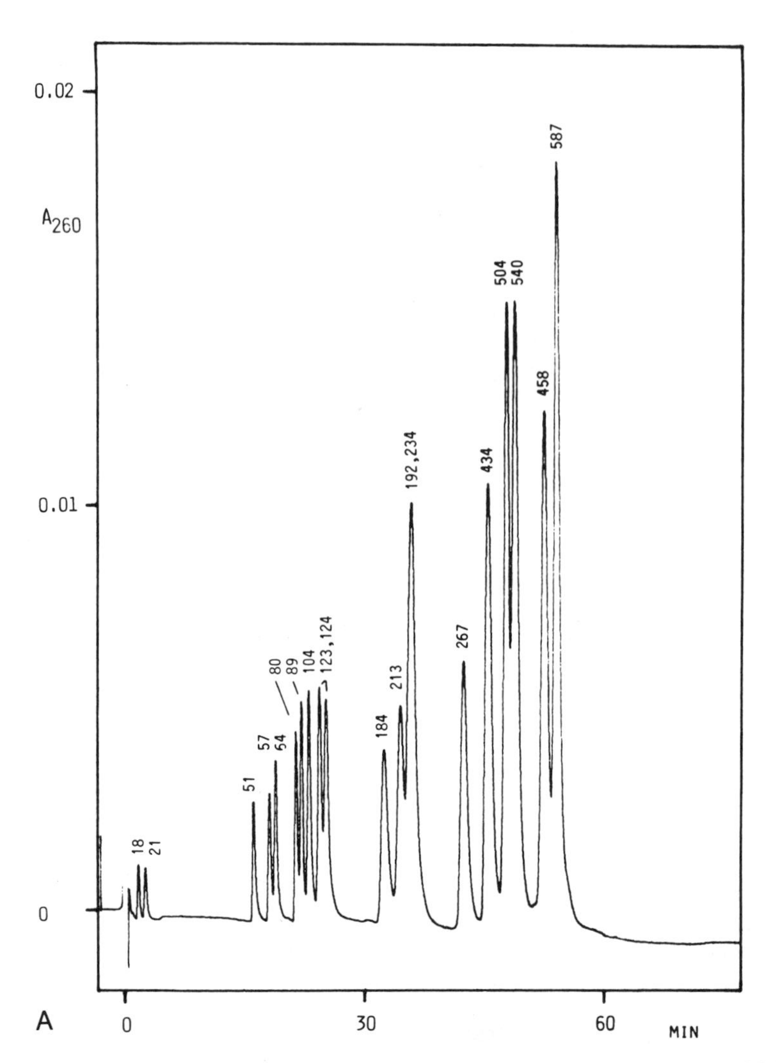

FIGURE 21–4. Separations of a set of DNA restriction fragments from 18 to about 600 bp. **(A)** Anion-exchange HPLC of DNA restriction fragments. Column: Nucleogen-DEAE 4000-7 (6 × 125 mm). Sample: 10 μg of DNA restriction fragments from the plasmid pBR322 cleaved with restriction endonuclease *Hae*III. The fragment sizes are indicated in base pairs. Chromatographic conditions: linear gradient from 0.5 to 0.8 *M* NaCl in 30 min; from 0.8 to 0.9 *M* NaCl in 50 min; 30 *M* Na-phosphate, pH 6.0, 6 *M* urea. Flow rate: 1.0 ml/min; temperature: 23°C. (From ref. 31.)

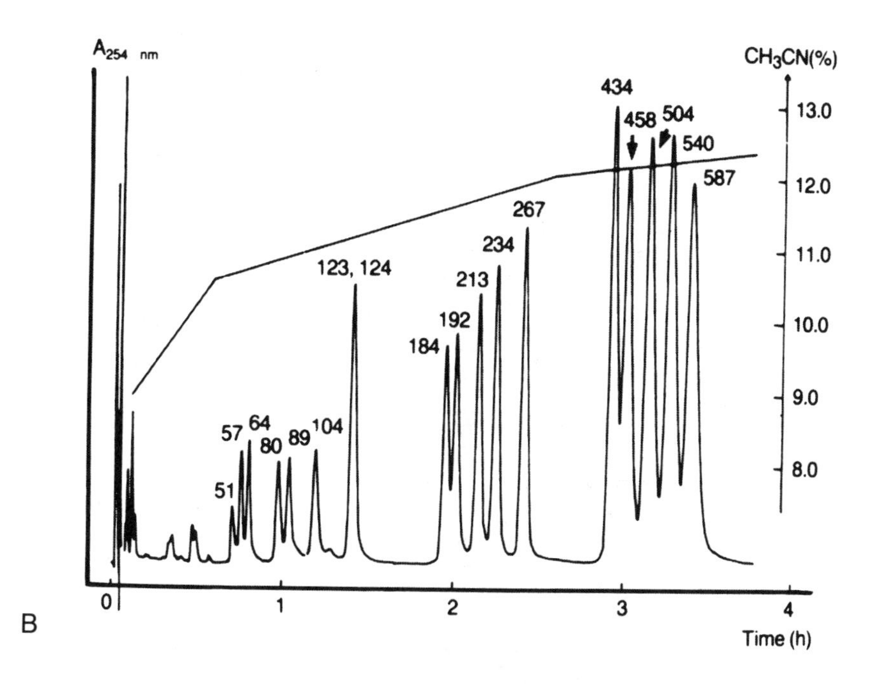

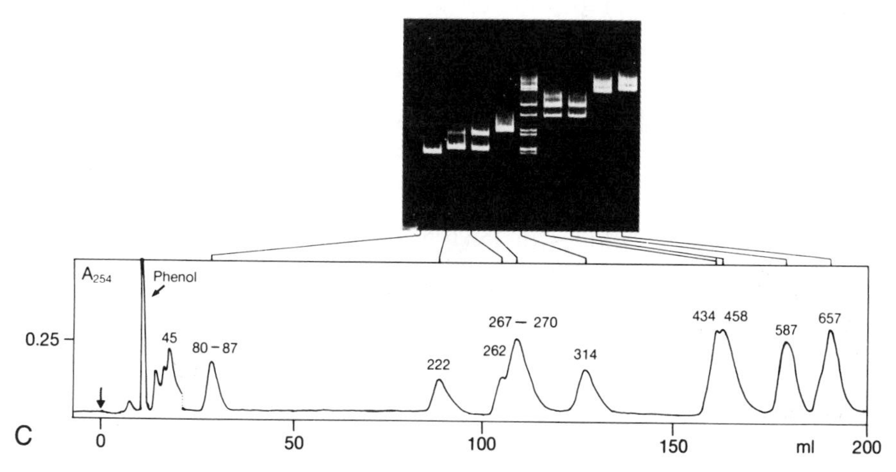

(B) Reversed-phase HPLC of DNA restriction fragments. Sample: 10 μg *Hae*III digested pBR322. Column: PepRPC HR 5/5. Flow rate: 0.5 ml/min. Buffer A: 40 m*M* triethylammonium acetate, pH 6.5, 8.5% acetonitrile. Buffer B: Buffer A with 12.3% acetonitrile. Gradient: 8.5–10.5% acetonitrile in 40 min; 10.5–12.0% acetonitrile in 120 min; 12.0–12.3% acetonitrile in 70 min. (From ref. 32.) **(C)** Liquid–liquid partition chromatography of DNA restriction fragments. Sample: 600 μg of plasmid pDSI digested with *Bam*HI, *Hae*III, and *Xba*I. Column: LiParSol (8000/500), 23 × 0.9 cm. Flow rate: 0.15 ml/min. Temperature: 37°C. Solution A: 0.2 *M* NaOAc in mobile phase. Solution B: 0.2 *M* LiOAc in mobile phase. Gradient: 0–10 ml: 0% B; 10–30 ml: 0–20% B; 30–250 ml: 20–100% B. The insert shows the analysis in a 5% polyacrylamide gel electrophoresis. (From ref. 26.)

20 components in one chromatographic run is not the method of choice. Furthermore, on an analytical scale, LLPC is not much faster.

The order of elution of the different fragments is not the same in the three modes of HPLC. Whereas in LLPC and RPC the elution is strictly in the order of increasing size (monotonic elution), several marked deviations from this order are observed with IEC (nonmonotonic elution). In the elution of Figure 21–4A the fragment with 192 bp elutes later than that with 213 bp and, even more drastically, the fragment with 458 bp elutes between the fragments with 540 and 587 bp. Similar deviations from the monotonic elution in IEC have been found in other high resolution HPLC of restriction fragments.[24,42] For an explanation one has to consider two possible effects. In IEC ligand-free DNA double strands interact with the charged surface of the chromatographic matrix under conditions that conserve the native structure of the double strand. Thus, a bent double strand may interact differently as compared with a non-bent molecule. Static bending of DNA double strands is a known effect, which is a consequence of particular nucleotide sequences (cf. the recent book on DNA bending[8]). One would not expect the same influence of bending on the elution profiles of RPC and LLPC. In the case of RPC the DNA double strands form ion-pairs with triethylammonium ions, possibly abolishing bending; in the case of LLPC the DNA double strands do not interact with a surface but are merely separated according to their solubility without significant influence of bending. The other effect, which could account for the nonmonotonic elution from the increase in size, is possibly the difference in counterion condensation to AT and GC base pairs, particularly to stretches of AT bp or to stretches of GC bp. This effect, however, seems to be of lesser influence, because if it were significant it should be so in IEC as well as in RPC and LLPC. The nonmonotonic elution makes the elution profiles less predictable but leads in some cases to an unexpectedly high resolution, if, for example, the low resolution of the fragments with 434 and 458 bp in RPC and LLPC is compared with the baseline separation of these fragments in IEC.

The fractionation of DNA restriction fragments was extended into the range of larger fragments. Examples (cf. Figure 21–5) may be given for all of the types of HPLC regarded so far. The discussion above also holds for those examples in which DNA fragments up to 5000 bp have been fractionated. Recently, a mixture of ligated 1 kb DNA fragments up to a size of 12,000 bp became commercially available as a size standard. This so-called 1 kb DNA ladder may be used for chromatographic test runs (Figure 21–6). As mentioned, chromatography as in Figure 21–6 serves as a test for very high resolution, it is not an example of a typical fractionation problem from gene technology or biochemistry.

For some applications very large amounts of restriction fragments of high purity are needed. This is the case for biophysical studies or for preparing DNA (or RNA) probes for routine tests. A general strategy for large-scale preparation does not consist of a mere scaling up of chromatographic runs, as in Figures 21–4 to 21–6, but involves an optimum combination of molecular biology and chromatography. Sometimes, a prefractionation by fractionated precipitation may be useful. The main idea is to reduce the purification of the wanted DNA restriction fragment from a complex mixture to a simple two-fragment separation. The general scheme is depicted in Figure 21–7. The DNA fragment of interest may first be obtained in analytical amounts (typically 10–100 ng) from a complex mixture by chromatography or by gel electrophoresis and gel elution. It may also be obtained by DNA synthesis or reverse transcription from a specific RNA. The DNA fragment is then subcloned in a high-copynumber plasmid, such as pUC18 or pWH802.[35–37] Under special conditions multiple inserts can be obtained.[38] The newly constructed plasmid is now used for a large-scale preparation of the specific piece of DNA in the form of a cloned DNA restriction fragment. For plasmid isolation a method is used that is fast and avoids cesium chloride gradient centrifugation (cf. next section). The plasmid is cut with the appropriate restriction endonuclease. This results in two fragments: the plasmid vector and the cloned DNA restriction fragment. If multiple insertions of the DNA fragment are made, the yield is higher. The vector and the inserted DNA fragment may be separated easily and rapidly by HPLC. An example of the purification by IEC of 1.1 mg of DNA restriction fragment from 7 mg of plasmid DNA is shown in Figure 21–8. In Figure 21–9 the separation by IEC of 26.5 mg insert DNA (80 bp) from the remaining vector DNA (3739 bp) is depicted. In this example the large excess of vector DNA was first removed by a fractionated PEG precipitation, and only the final purification was carried out by IEC.[39] Due to the prepurification step the capacity of the column could be utilized to a high ratio (50%) for the binding of the DNA fragment of interest. Also by LLPC, similar amounts of DNA insert (130 bp) have been separated from the vector DNA in the last step, after removing most of the vector DNA by a chloroform/phenol/water partition system in the presence of 4 m*M* spermidine.[40]

In summary, a number of reports in the literature describe the fractionation of DNA fragments up to a size of 12,000 bp with high resolution. As chromatographic modes IEC, RPC, and LLPC are applicable. Large-scale fractionation of a particular fragment has been achieved most successfully after recloning the fragment as a unique insert and separating the insert from the vector. The excess vector may be removed largely by a prepurification step.

21.4.2 Plasmids

Plasmids are used as cloning vectors for recombinant DNA studies. Either the complete plasmid will be used in further transformations, or particular inserts are of interest in analytical or preparative amounts. The plasmid may serve also as a template for RNA transcription. In some cases, plasmids have been isolated for biophysical studies on superhelical structures. Thus, the need for plasmid purification reaches from preparing many small samples up to purification of a single sample, but in an amount of several milligrams and in very high purity. The conventional method of plasmid preparation was banding them in a CsCl density gradient.[4] This procedure, however, needs prolonged ultracentrifugation at high speed and large amounts of CsCl. Furthermore, the ethidium bromide added for the centrifugation has to be removed afterward. Attempts at a chromatographic preparation of plasmids have been made for several years. The first successful protocol was given by Wells and co-workers with RPC-5,[20] which has, however, not been followed by others, probably because of the same difficulties in the continuous availability of RPC-5 as mentioned above.

In recent years several protocols have been reported for plasmid purification on commercially available HPLC columns. Most protocols are based on IEC and SEC. Cells, e.g., from *E. coli*, are homogenized and treated according to one of the standard procedures[4] yielding the so-called cleared cell lysate. Then the plasmid has to be separated by HPLC from the remaining small RNAs, from residual chromosomal DNA, and possibly from proteins.

In Figure 21–10 a typical elution profile obtained by IEC is depicted showing the elution of the plasmid as the last component. In the gel electrophoretic analysis of Figure 2–10 only the plasmid in the supercoiled form is detectable. According to the reports in the literature, plasmid preparation with IEC requires either a porous matrix with large pores[9,33] (4000 Å in the example of Figure 21–10) allowing the plasmids to penetrate, or a nonporous matrix[43] with the interaction on the surface. In the fractionation with SEC (cf. Figure 21–11) the plasmid elutes first, i.e., with the void volume. In this case, plasmids are separated from all components that are allowed to enter the pores. According to the gel electrophoretic analysis the purified plasmids contain a

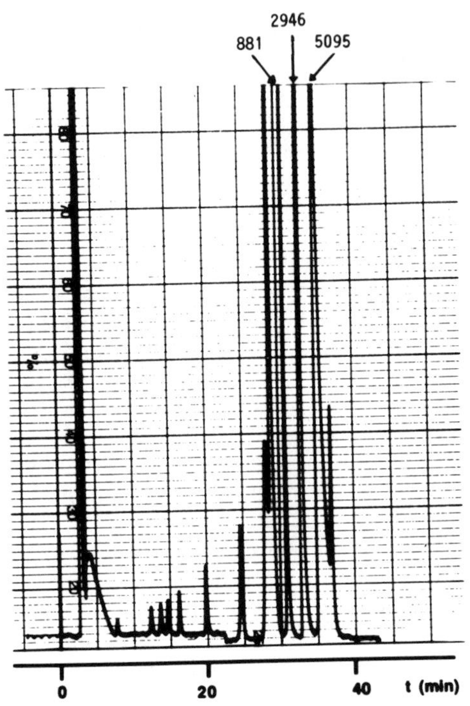

FIGURE 21–5. Separations of large DNA restriction fragments. **(A)** Anion-exchange HPLC of large DNA restriction fragments. Column: Nucleogen DEAE-4000 (46 × 125 mm). Sample: 10 μg of a mixture of DNA fragments with 19, 30, 34, 41, 45, 74, 168, 296, 4 × 344, 881, 2946, 5095 bp in the order of their elution; the small peak at 37 min is from switching the photometric sensitivity of the recorder. Chromatographic conditions: linear gradient from 250 to 750 m*M* KCl in 15 min and 750 to 1500 m*M* KCl in 50 min; 30 m*M* K-phosphate, 5 *M* urea, pH 6.6; 1 ml/min; 32 bar; ambient temperature. (From ref. 33.)

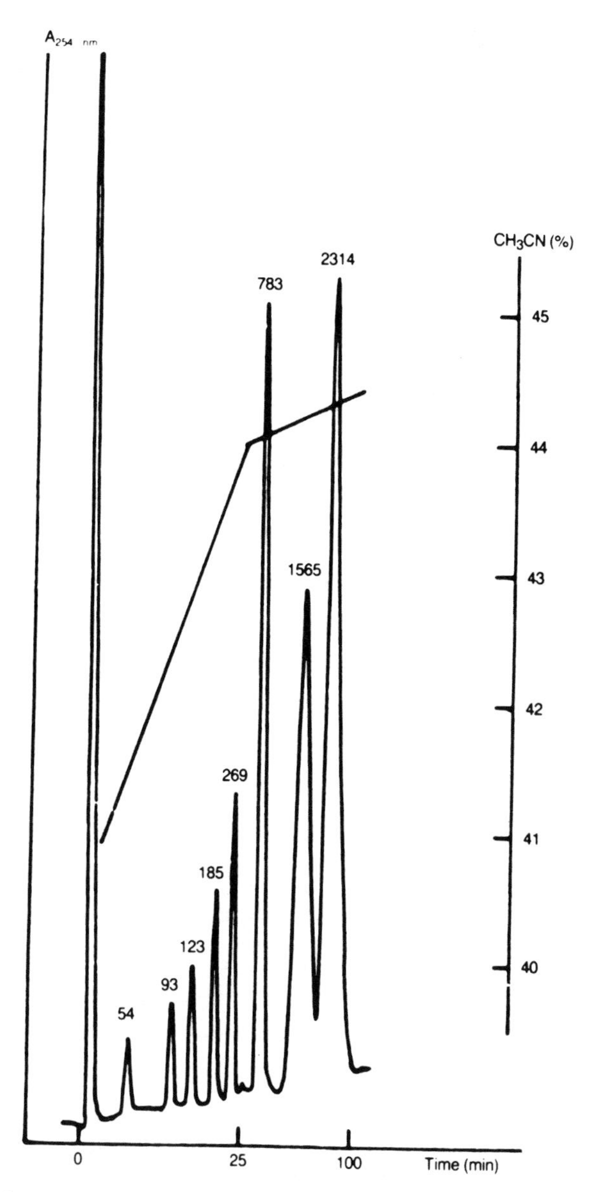

(B) Reversed-phase HPLC of large DNA restriction fragments. Sample: 5 μg *Hae*II digested ϕX174 RF. Column: PepRPC HR 5/5. Flow rate: 1.0 ml/min for 25 min, 0.2 ml/min for 75 min. Buffer A: 12 m*M* tetrabutylammonium bromide, 0.03 *M* phosphate, pH 6.5, 40.5% acetonitrile. Buffer B: Buffer A with 44.3% acetonitrile. Gradient: 40.5–44.0% acetonitrile in 25 min; 44.0–44.3% acetonitrile in 75 min. (From ref. 32.)

(*continued*)

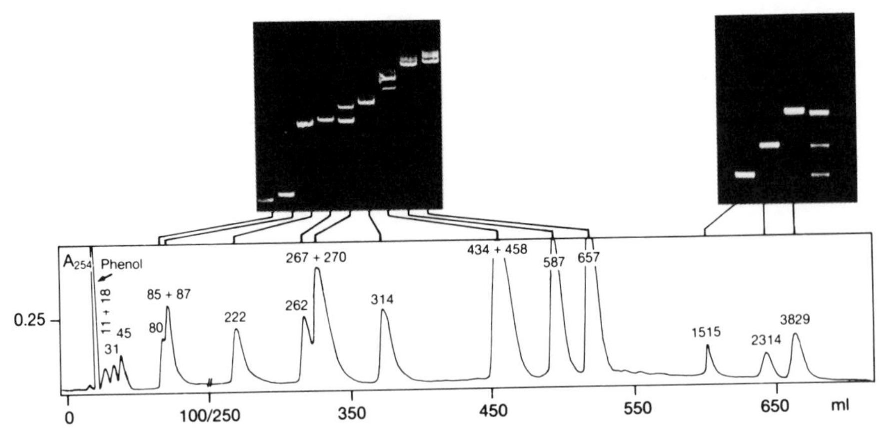

(C) Liquid–liquid partition chromatography of large DNA restriction fragments. Sample: 1.6 mg of *Hae*III digested pDSI, 100 μg *Xba*I digested pDSI, 80 μg of *Bam*HI linearized pDSI. Column: LiParSol (8000/500), 17 × 1.5 cm. Flow rate: 0.33 ml/min. Temperature: 37°C. Solution A: 0.2 *M* NaOAc in mobile phase. Solution B: 0.2 *M* LiOAc in mobile phase. Gradient: 0–80 ml: 0% B; 80–160 ml: 0–20% B; 160–600 ml: 20–85% B; 600–800 ml: 85–100% B. The inserts show the analysis in a 6% polyacrylamide gel electrophoresis (left) and 1% agarose gel electrophoresis (right). (From ref. 26.)

portion of relaxed circles. Successful plasmid preparation has been reported also with other commercially available SEC columns.[45–47]

As outlined with the restriction fragments, it is recommended that for a scaling-up of the plasmid preparation a prepurification step be introduced. This is easily achieved by an RNase digestion before HPLC, thereby eliminating all RNA. Then, a preparative purification of 3 mg plasmids in a single run is possible (Figure 21–12). As seen from the elution profile residual linear plasmid DNA may be separated from the supercoiled plasmid fraction.[48] The supercoiled plasmid fraction is also free of chromosomal DNA.

Plasmids excert highest biological activity if they are in the supercoiled form. Therefore, it is important either to prepare plasmids with a very high percentage of this form (cf. above) or to separate the different forms afterward. In IEC, the supercoiled plasmids could be resolved with a reduced gradient slope from their relaxed circular and their linear forms. In Figure 21–13 the separation of a mixture of the different forms is shown; in Figure 21–14 the different retention times of the supercoiled form and the relaxed form after topoisomerase treatment are compared. It is interesting to note that the relaxed circles elute later than the supercoils from the porous IEC matrix (Figure 21–13) but earlier from the nonporous matrix (Figure 21–14). Partial resolution of the different forms of plasmids was also achieved by SEC,[47] and separation of supercoiled and linear plasmids by RPC.[49]

The examples of HPLC of plasmids mentioned so far were selected to demonstrate that plasmids may be purified from cleared cell lysate without RNase digestion, in larger amounts after RNase digestion, and may even be fractionated into supercoiled, relaxed, and linear forms. Similarly to other application

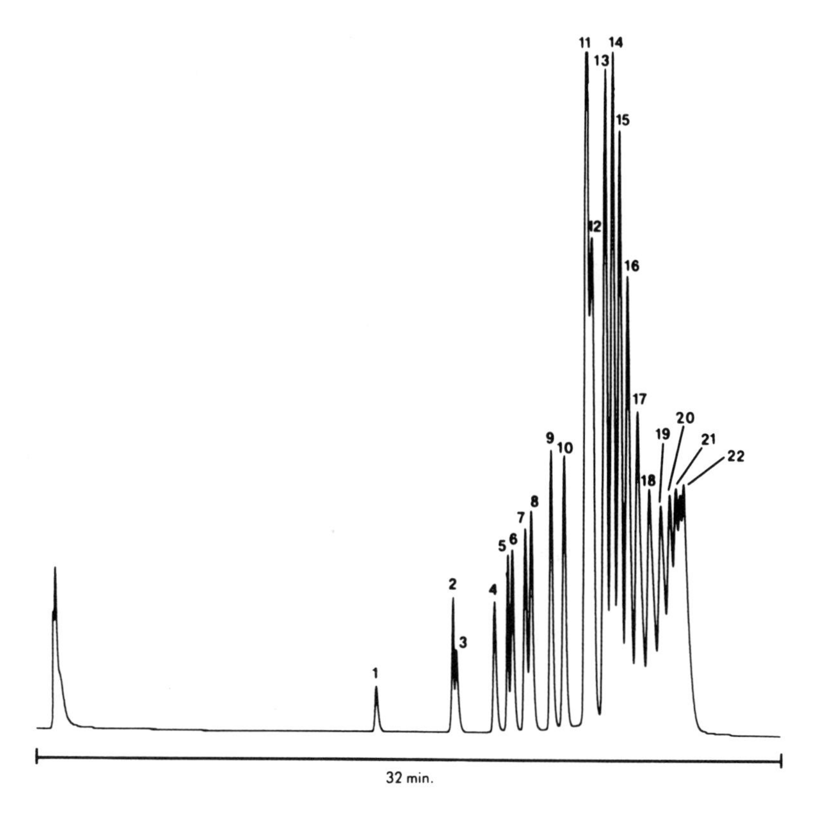

FIGURE 21–6. Anion-exchange of HPLC of the 1 kb ladder. Sample: 50 μg of the 1 kb ladder (Bethesda Research Labs, Rockville, MD; the number of the peaks in the elution profile refer to the following sizes: 1, 75 bp; 2, 134 bp; 3, 154 bp; 4, 201 bp; 5, 220 bp; 6, 298 bp; 7, 344 bp; 8, 396 bp; 9, 506/516 bp; 10, 1018 bp; 11, 2036 bp; 12, 1636 bp; 13, 3054 bp; 14, 4072 bp; 15, 5090 bp; 16, 6108 bp; 17, 7126 bp; 18, 8144 bp; 19, 9162 bp; 20, 10180 bp; 21, 11198 bp; 22, 12216 bp. Column: Gen-Pak FAX, 10 cm × 4.6 mm. Flow rate: 0.5 ml/min. Detection at 260 nm. Buffer A: 25 m*M* Na-phosphate, pH 7.0. Buffer B: A and 1 *M* NaCl.

examples, highest resolution and shortest elution time were achieved with IEC, whereas the recovery procedure is somewhat simpler with SEC. With IEC columns the problem of memory effects has been investigated; with the other columns these effects have not been described or not been studied. The memory effect, i.e., an elution of a small portion of plasmid from the previous run, is a particular problem of plasmid preparation, if different plasmids have to be prepared in consecutive runs. A minor cross-contamination from the previous run may be very disadvantageous in biological transformation experiments. The supplier of the columns are recommending particular reequilibration procedures in order to avoid cross-contamination. Mostly these are several washing gradient elutions in short times as, for example, 5 min. Particularly effective

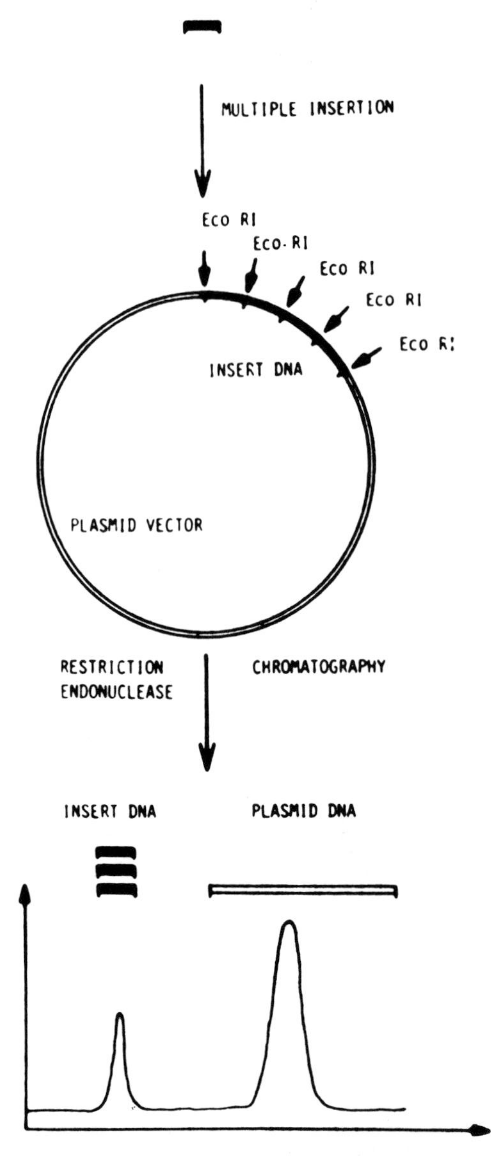

FIGURE 21–7. Large-scale preparation of a defined DNA restriction fragment. Procedure of recloning. The wanted DNA restriction fragment is cloned into a high copy number plasmid, if possible as multiple insert. The plasmid carrying the DNA restriction fragment is prepared in large amounts. The inserted DNA fragment is released by cleavage with the appropriate restriction endonuclease (in this scheme: *Eco*RI). The DNA restriction fragment is isolated by a single run with anion-exchange HPLC. (From ref. 31.)

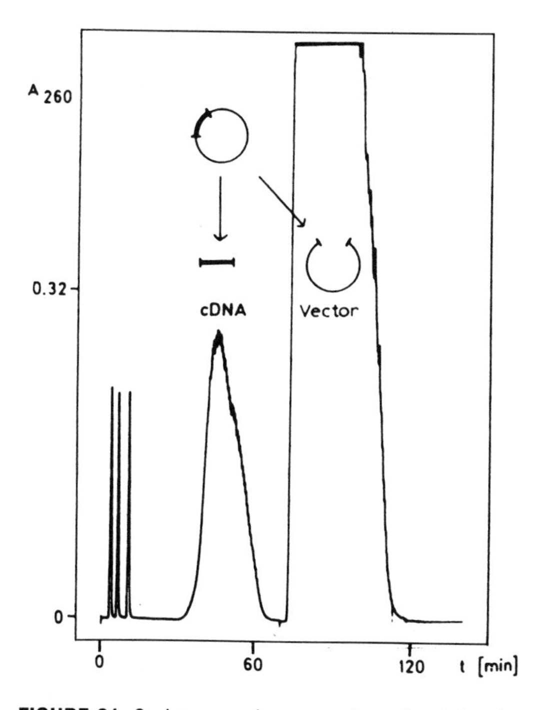

FIGURE 21–8. Large-scale preparation of a defined DNA restriction fragment. Anion-exchange HPLC. Column: Nucleogen DEAE 4000-10 (10 × 125 mm). Sample: 7 mg of plasmid pRH101 cleaved with restriction endonuclease *Bam*HI to release a DNA restriction fragment with 359 base pairs in size. The sample was applied by three injections. Chromatographic conditions: linear gradient from 0.84 to 1.2 *M* KCl in 360 min; 6 *M* urea, 20 m*M* K-phosphate, pH 6.7. Flow rate: 2.25 ml/min; temperature: 23°C. (From ref. 10.)

washing was achieved by a gradient from 10% acetic acid, 90% H_2O, without *i*-propanol to 10% acetic acid, 90% *i*-propanol (Colpan, personal communication). Small cross-contaminations do not play a significant role if plasmids are used for sequencing, restriction maps, or more generally biochemical or biophysical purposes. In general, one may recommend plasmid preparation by HPLC for biochemical and biophysical studies, whereas plasmids for microbiology may be prepared without any cross-contaminations by one-way columns (cf. Section 21.4.5).

21.4.3 RNA Transcripts and mRNA

DNA restriction fragments were of particular interest because they can be prepared in high purity and large amounts, and the sequence can be selected

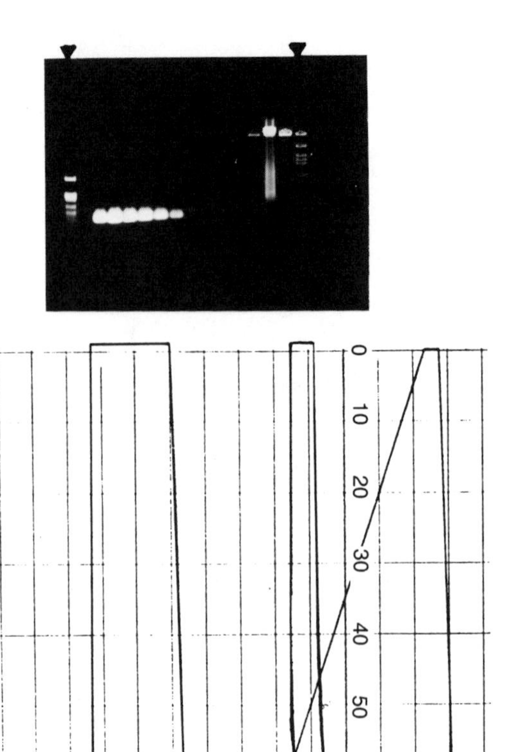

FIGURE 21–9. Large-scale HPLC of a defined DNA restriction fragment. Sample: 26.5 mg insert DNA (80 bp) and vector DNA (3739 bp) from pWH931. Column: Nucleogen DEAE 500-10, PTFE coated, 125 × 10 mm. Flow rate: 3 ml/min. Buffer A: 0.4 *M* NaCl, 30 m*M* K-phosphate, pH 6.0, 6 *M* urea. Buffer B: 1.2 *M* NaCl, 30 *M* K-phosphate, pH 6.0, 5.5 *M* urea. Gradient: 0–30% B in 6 min, 30–40% B in 30 min, 40–100% B in 24 min. The insert shows the analysis by 5% polyacrylamide gel electrophoresis. The slots belong to the corresponding fractions below the slots. The arrows indicate reference slots. (From ref. 39.)

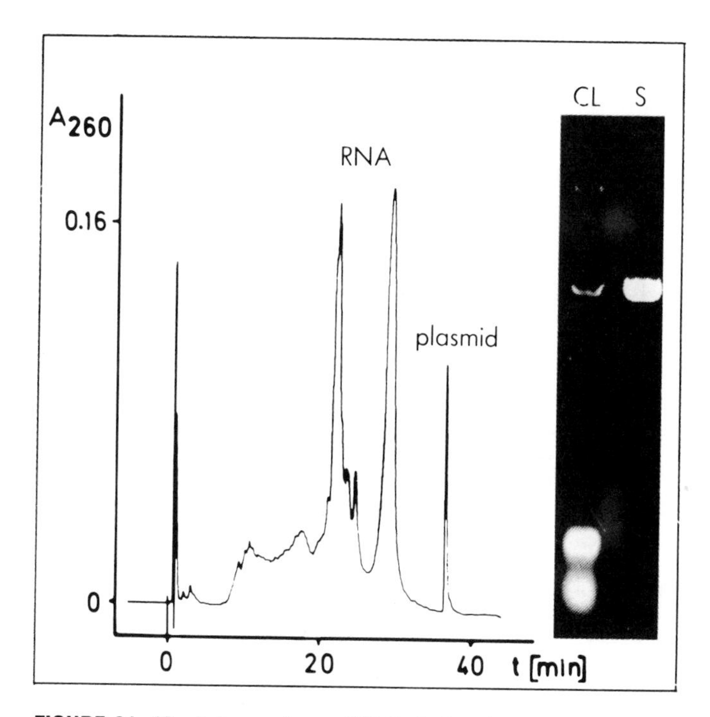

FIGURE 21–10. Anion-exchange HPLC of plasmids. Column: Nucleogen DEAE-4000 (6 × 125 mm). Sample: 5 μg plasmid pBR322 from a cleared lysate without RNase A digestion. Chromatographic conditions: linear gradient from 250 to 1250 m*M* KCl in 50 min; 30 m*M* K-phosphate, pH 6.5, 5.5 *M* urea; 1 ml/min; 36 bar; 22°C. The gel electrophoretic analysis shows the cleared lysate (CL) and the plasmid (S) in the supercoiled form. (From ref. 33.)

in advance. Due to the combination of molecular biology and chromatography RNA fragments became available that have the same properties and in addition some RNA-specific features. These RNA fragments are used today for biophysical studies, and particularly as hybridization probes, for the following reasons: (1) they are synthesized as single strands, i.e., they are strand-specific; (2) they may be synthesized containing radioactive labels as well as nonradioactive biotin labels; and (3) hybridization with RNA probes yields more stable hybridization complexes.

In principle, the RNA is transcribed from its DNA template by an *in vitro* transcription system derived from the bacteriophages SP6 or T7.[50,51] Depending on the length of the synthesized RNA two different strategies are possible (Figure 21–15). For long RNA sequences the corresponding DNA sequence is cloned into a plasmid behind the promotor specific for the RNA polymerase.[50,51] For short RNA sequences, i.e., if the DNA template may be synthesized in an automatic DNA synthesizer, two ssDNA fragments have to be synthesized: the template for the RNA transcript (including the promotor sequence) and a second strand consisting only of the promotor sequence. After hybridization of

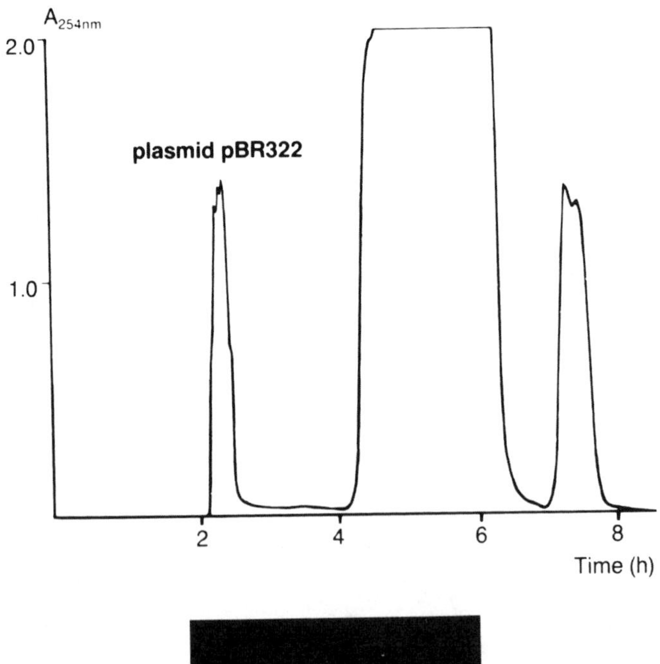

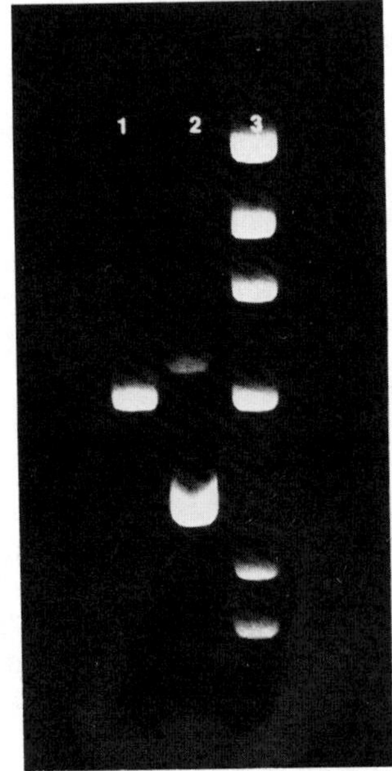

FIGURE 21–11. Size-exclusion HPLC of plasmids. Sample: 200 μg pBR322 from a cleared cell lysate without RNase digestion. Column: Superose 6 prep grade, HR 16/50. Flow rate: 0.25 ml/min. Buffer: 6 m*M* Tris-HCl, 6 m*M* NaCl, 0.2 m*M* EDTA, pH 8.0. The gel electrophoretic analysis on 0.8% agarose shows in lane 1: purified plasmid after linearization; lane 2: purified plasmid before linearization; lane 3: DNA after *Hin*dIII digestion as length standard. (From ref. 44.)

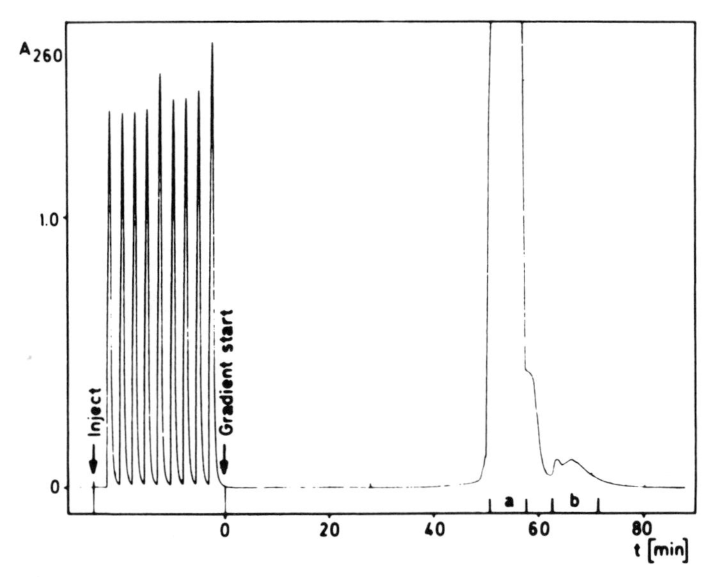

FIGURE 21–12. Large-scale anion-exchange HPLC of plasmids. Sample: 3 mg of plasmid pUC18 from a cleared lysate digested with RNase A. Column: Nucleogen DEAE-4000 (10 × 125 mm). Cleared lysate (18 ml) was injected 9 times in 2-ml aliquots on the column using a loop injector. Linear gradient from 750 to 1500 m*M* KCl in 100 min; 5.5 *M* urea; 30 m*M* K-phosphate buffer, pH 6.4. Flow rate: 3 ml/min; 45 bar; 22°C. As shown in agarose gel electrophoretic analysis of 5 μg of DNA of fraction (a) only supercoiled plasmid can be detected. The linear forms were eluted in fraction (b) without contaminating the peak of the supercoiled plasmids. (From ref. 48.)

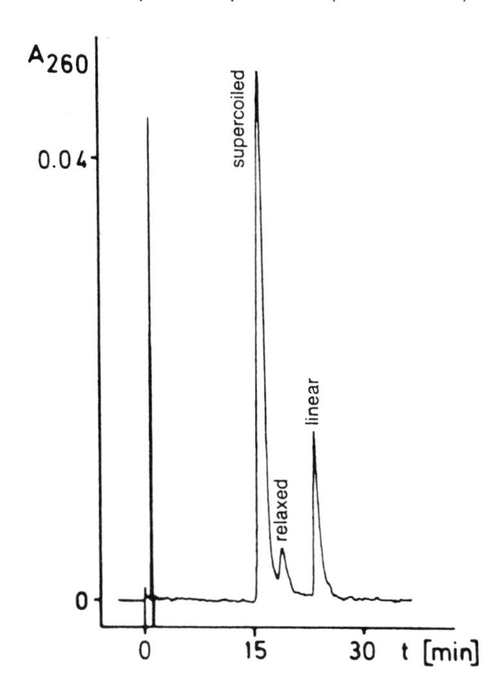

FIGURE 21–13. Anion-exchange HPLC of supercoiled, relaxed, and linear plasmid DNA. Column: Nucleogen DEAE-4000 (6 × 125 mm). Sample: 4 μg of supercoiled plasmid pBR322, 1.5 μg of the plasmid pBR322 linearized with *Bam*HI; the relaxed form is generated from the supercoiled form during storage. Chromatographic conditions: linear gradient from 750 to 1500 m*M* KCl in 120 min; 20 m*M* K-phosphate, 5 *M* urea, pH 6.6; 1.5 ml/min; 45 bar; ambient temperature. (From ref. 33.)

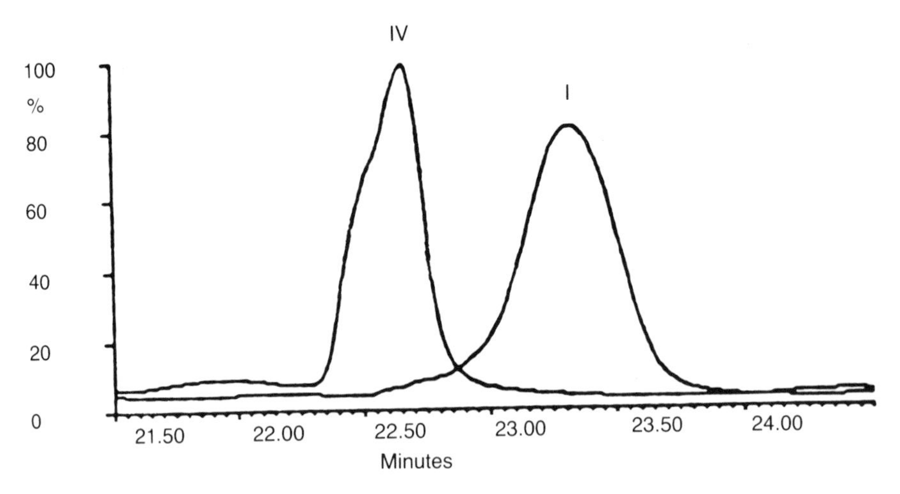

FIGURE 21–14. Anion-exchange HPLC of supercoiled and relaxed plasmid. The elution profiles of two different HPLC runs are drawn on the same time axis to show the difference in retention time. Sample I: 10 μg of supercoiled plasmid pUC19; sample II: 10 μg of plasmid pUC19 incubated for 30 min at 37°C with 10 units of *Xenopus laevis* DNA topoisomerase I. Column: Gen-Pak FAX, 10 cm × 4.6 mm. Flow rate: 0.5 ml/min. Ambient temperature. Buffer A: 20 m*M* Na-phosphate, pH 6.5. Buffer B: A and 1 *M* NaCl. Gradient: 40% B to 90% B in 30 min. The relaxed circular form (IV) is eluted earlier than the supercoiled form (I). (From ref. 43.)

both fragments a DNA template is obtained for transcription, which is double stranded only in the promotor region.[52] In some cases, particularly if the template forms a stable internal structure, it may be advantageous to synthesize both strands in their full length. After synthesis the RNA has to be separated from the DNA template, the RNA polymerase, and the nucleoside triphosphates. This may be done in a single HPLC run. An example of a chromatogram is shown in Figure 21–16. From the peak of the newly synthesized RNA an amplification of 100–500 RNA transcripts per DNA template can be calculated. The RNA was desalted by adsorption on hydroxylapatite, elution with 0.5 *M* potassium phosphate, and precipitated with cetyltrimethylammoniumbromide (CTAB).[28] The DNA template can be reisolated from the corresponding chromatographic peak by polyethyleneglycol precipitation[10] and used again for RNA synthesis.

From the chromatographic example in Figure 21–16 it is seen that the peak of the RNA transcript is not homogeneous but shows shoulders. Since in the gel electrophoresis under denaturing conditions only one RNA species was detectable, one has to conclude that the shoulders are from different conformers, which are stable under the high salt condition of IEC. The tendency to form conformational isomers is particularly expressed with ssRNA at high ionic strength. Although elution profiles may become complicated by this effect, there are no reports in the literature showing other modes of HPLC working more easily for the purification of RNA transcripts. If the transcription system produces RNA that is homogeneous and of full template length, i.e., without

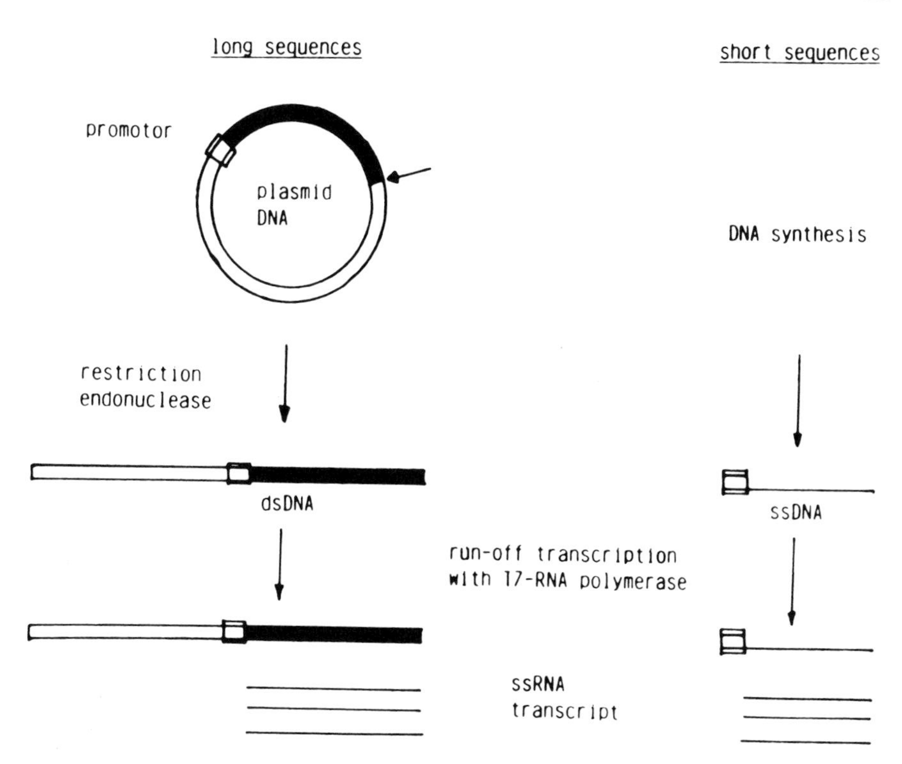

FIGURE 21–15. Preparation of RNA fragments. Depending on the length of the wanted RNA sequence, two strategies are possible. For long sequences, the DNA sequence of the wanted RNA fragment is cloned in a plasmid vector behind the promotor for the T7-RNA polymerase. The recombined plasmid is linearized behind the insert DNA with a restriction endonuclease. The RNA is synthesized by *in vitro* transcription from the plasmid template with the T7-RNA polymerase. The RNA fragment is isolated from the *in vitro* transcription reaction by anion-exchange HPLC. For short sequences, the DNA sequence complementary to the wanted RNA sequence, including the T7 promotor sequence, is synthesized in an automatic DNA synthesizer. The active T7 promotor region is obtained by hybridization with its complementary DNA oligonucleotide. The RNA is synthesized with the T7-RNA polymerase by *in vitro* transcription as for long sequences. The RNA fragment is isolated from the synthesis mixture by anion-exchange HPLC (cf. Figure 21–16). (From ref. 31.)

early chain terminations, the purification of the RNA may be achieved by one-way cartridges (cf. Section 21.4.5).

Messenger RNAs (mRNA) are similar to RNA transcripts in that they are single stranded, cover a range of a few hundreds to several thousands of nucleotides, and cannot be characterized by a uniform structure. In contrast to synthetic RNA transcripts, a major portion of natural mRNAs is polyadenylated at the 3′ side, and mRNA contains very many species. Thus, fractionation of mRNA would be highly desirable for consecutive cloning procedures. For fractionation of mRNA, SEC[53,54] and RPC[13,55] were employed, without, however, achieving high resolution. Best resolution was obtained when polyadenylated globin-mRNA was separated from poly(A)-free globin mRNA with RPC, as shown

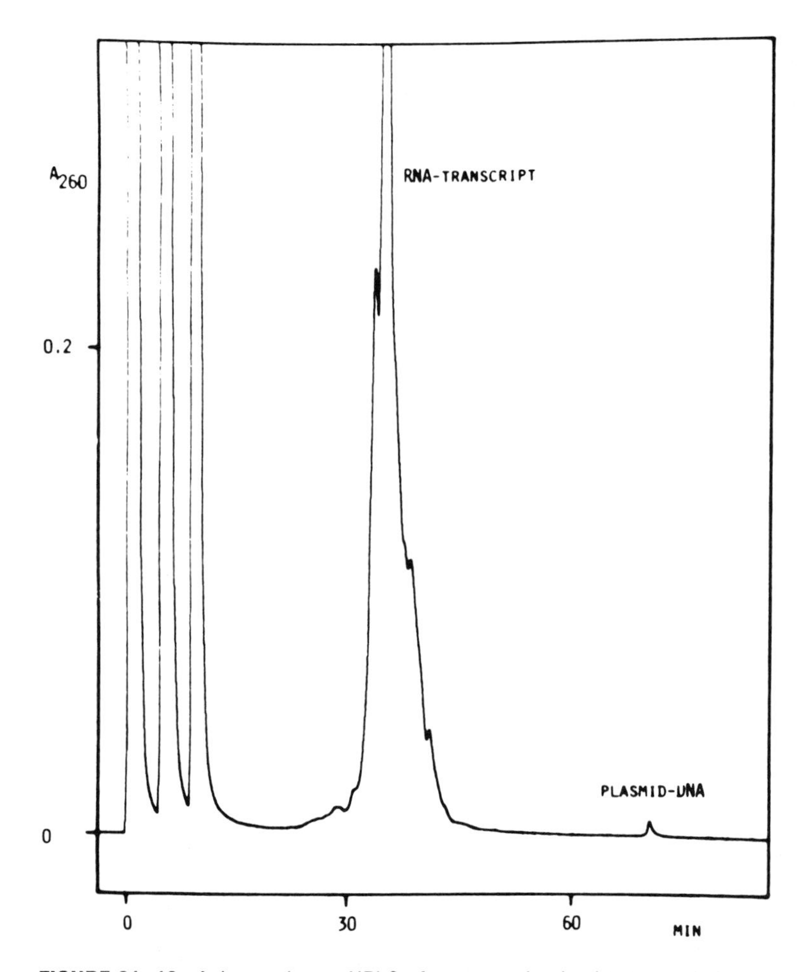

FIGURE 21–16. Anion-exchange HPLC of a preparative *in vitro* transcription for RNA synthesis. Column: Nucleogen-DEAE 4000-7 (6 × 125 mm). Sample: total *in vitro* transcription mixture containing 2 μg of linear plasmid pRH717/*Eco*RI as template. The amount of RNA fragment synthesized is 160 μg; the length is 725 nucleotides. It corresponds to a 500-fold transcription from each template DNA. The sample was applied by three injections. Chromatographic conditions: 0.5 *M* sodium chloride, 6 *M* urea, 25 m*M* sodium phosphate (pH 6.0) for 15 min; linear gradient from 0.5 to 0.7 *M* sodium chloride in 40 min, from 0.7 to 1.2 *M* sodium chloride in 25 min; 6 *M* urea, 25 m*M* sodium phosphate (pH 6.0). Flow rate: 2 ml/min; temperature, 22°C. The shoulders in the peak of the RNA transcript are due to different conformers. In gel electrophoresis under denaturing conditions only one RNA species was detectable. (From ref. 31.)

in Figure 21–17. In this example, the fractionation is more according to base composition and thereby to hydrophobicity than to size. Similar examples have been given also for total mRNA.[13]

The examples in this chapter have demonstrated that HPLC or ssRNA without a well-expressed and stable structure is a particularly difficult problem.

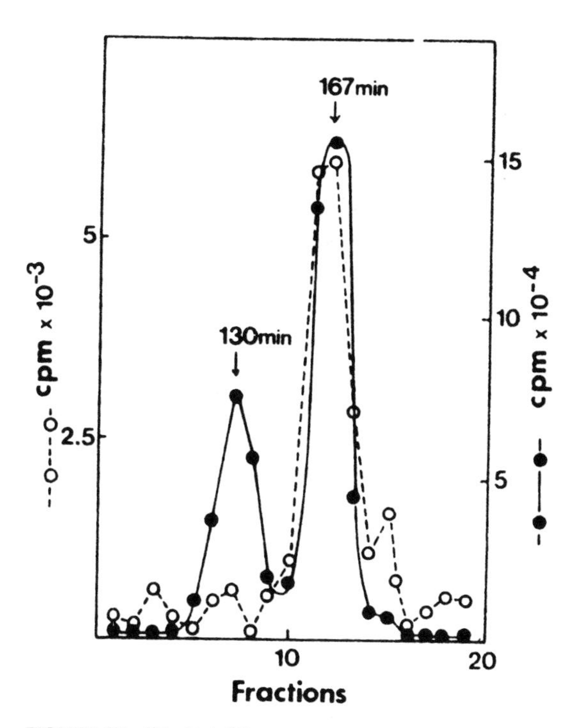

FIGURE 21–17. Poly(A) content of the globin mRNAs, separated by reversed-phase HPLC. Crude globin mRNA was chromatographed and mRNA translated. For each fraction, RNA was translated in the *in vitro* systems and hybridized to radioactive poly(U). (●) activity in the cell-free system; (○) poly(U) hybridized. Chromatographic conditions: Varian MH 10 (4 × 300 mm). Flow rate: 0.2 ml/min. Buffer A: 100 m*M* NH_4-acetate, pH 6.6. Buffer B: acetonitrile:water (1:1). Gradient: from 0 to 40% buffer B in 200 min. (From ref. 55.)

For RNA transcripts, IEC works well as long as the requirements for resolution are not too high. The situation of HPLC of large RNA is much more favorable, if RNAs of defined structure have to be fractionated. Ribosomal RNA has been fractionated successfully with SEC,[56] and viroid and viral RNAs have been purified in large amounts with IEC[9,28] (cf. also Figure 21–20).

21.4.4 Single- and Double-Stranded DNA, Single- and Double-Stranded RNA, RNA–DNA Hybrids

In the previous sections, all examples on DNA restriction fragments dealt with double-stranded nucleic acids and those on RNA transcripts with single-stranded nucleic acid. This is the general rule, but it would be wrong to give the impression that the other forms of nucleic acids such as ssDNA, dsRNA, or DNA–RNA hybrids would not be required in molecular biology. In particular cloning steps with phage M13 the double-stranded and single-stranded forms have to be separated. In studies with viral RNAs the genomic single-stranded form has to be isolated free of the replication intermediate in form of a RNA double strand. If DNA–RNA hybrids have to be formed, they should be freed from the excess single strands. In all these examples chromatographic steps are required that do not fractionate according to size but according to the different forms of nucleic acids.

The appropriate chromatographic procedures have been described in the literature. Single-stranded and double-stranded DNA are separated by RPC[57] and by IEC.[48] In RPC (Figure 21–18) the double-stranded form elutes earlier than the single-stranded form; in IEC (Figure 21–19) the elution is the other way around. This elution profile is obvious, because in RPC the single strands interact more strongly with the matrix because of their higher hydrophobicity, and in IEC the larger number of charges on the double strands is responsible for the higher affinity to the charged matrix. Furthermore, it is seen that in RPC the fractionation is not according to size, because the single- as well as the double-stranded fractions were highly inhomogeneous in size. The situation is different in the example with IEC, where both forms were of exactly

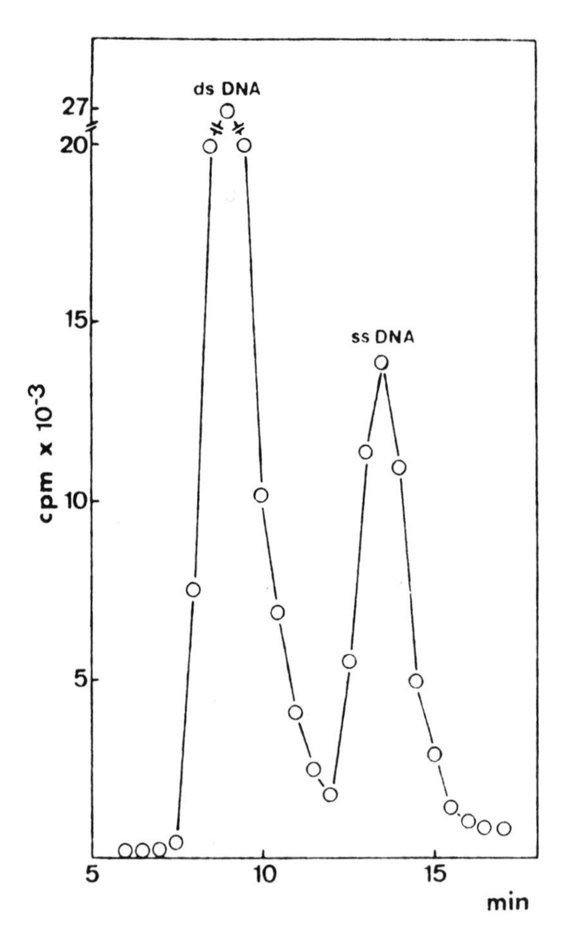

FIGURE 21–18. Reversed-phase HPLC of single-stranded and double-stranded DNA. A 100 μg amount of labeled DNA was treated with S1 nuclease (dsDNA) and mixed with 50 μg of DNA denatured by incubation for 15 min at 98°C (ssDNA). This mixture was applied to the octadecylsilane column [Varian MCH 10 (4 × 30 mm)] equilibrated with 100 m*M* ammonium acetate (pH 6.6) and eluted by increasing the concentration of acetonitrile solution (50% in water) from 0 to 50% in 15 min, then from 50 to 100% in 5 min. The flow rate was 1 ml/min. dsDNA eluted at 9 min and ssDNA at 13.5 min. (From ref. 57.)

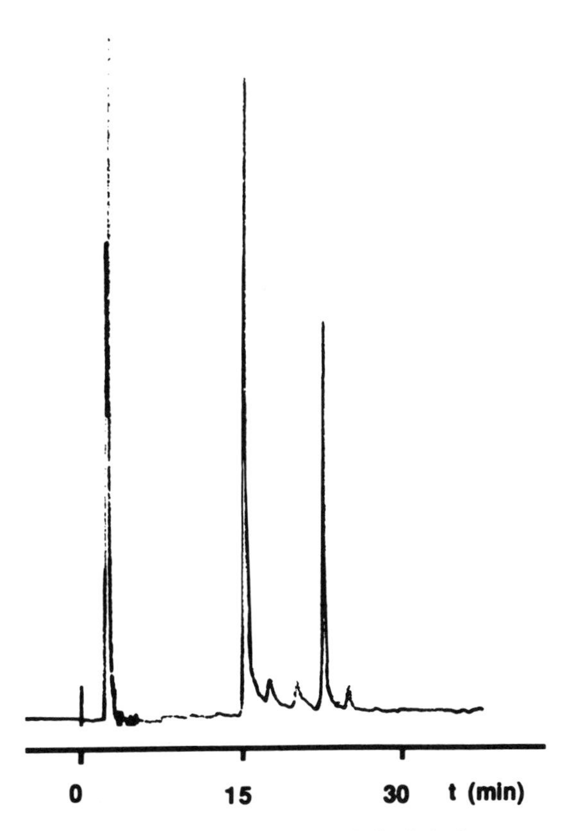

FIGURE 21–19. Anion-exchange HPLC of single-stranded and double-stranded M13 DNA. Sample: 10 μg of a mixture of both forms. Column: Nucleogen DEAE-4000 (6 × 125 mm). Linear gradient from 750 to 1500 m*M* KCl in 75 min; 30 m*M* K-phosphate buffer, pH 6.5, 5 *M* urea. Flow rate, 1.5 ml/min; 34 bar; 22°C. The ssM13 and dsM13 are well resolved from each other, with the single-stranded form eluting first without cross-contamination of both DNA fractions. (From ref. 48.)

the same DNA, i.e., from phage M13. Size inhomogeneity in the sample would have led to a drastic peak broadening in IEC. The result, that both forms may be separated in the case of a particular RNA, is seen in the IEC elution profile of Figure 21–20. Beside other RNA species such as the cellular tRNA, 5 S RNA, 7 S RNA, and the viroid RNA, the single-stranded form of the cucumber mosaic virus associated RNA (330 nt) is well resolved from its double-stranded form.

In Figure 21–21 the fractionation of RNA–DNA hybrids by IEC is shown. A dsDNA probe was incubated with viroid RNA. Besides the hybrid the excess dsDNA, the freed noncomplementary ssDNA, and the nonhybridized viroid RNA are visible. All components are well separated, but one should keep in mind that the DNA and its counterpart RNA are of different lengths and that in IEC nucleic acids are separated according to both strandedness and length.

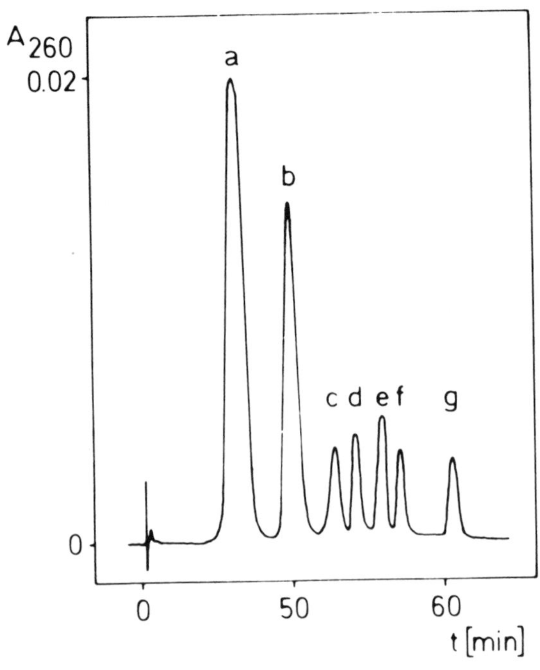

FIGURE 21–20. Anion-exchange HPLC of a mixture of viral and cellular RNA on a 12.7 × 50 mm Nucleogen-DMA-1000 glass column. Gradient: 250 m*M*–1.5 *M* KCl in 150 min, 20 m*M* potassium phosphate, pH 6.6, 5 *M* urea, 0.1 m*M* EDTA. Flow rate: 2 ml/min, 19 bar, 22°C. The peaks indicated in the figure are tRNA (a), 5 S RNA (b), 7 S RNA (c), single-stranded cucumber mosaic virus associated RNA 5 (d), viroid RNA (e), doubled-stranded cucumber mosaic virus associated RNA5 (f), and RNA from phage MS2 (g). (From ref. 9.)

21.4.5 Prepurification and Recovery of Nucleic Acids by Solid Phase Extraction in One-Way Columns

In Section 21.3.6 it has been indicated that most modes of LC are available today in the form of one-way columns. Because the elution is carried out batchwise, the term solid-phase extraction (SPE) was used for this type of chromatography. In Table 21–5 a list of commercially available one-way columns together with their mode of chromatography and their objects of application is given. SPE cannot be regarded as a type of chromatography competing with HPLC. In this section the complementarity of both is outlined for a few examples.

In most cases the classical type of LC was replaced by a one-way column, which is faster, easier to handle, and because of its one-way mode does not need any reequilibration or cleaning for subsequent utilization. Typically the high-molecular-weight nucleic acids are separated from smaller substances

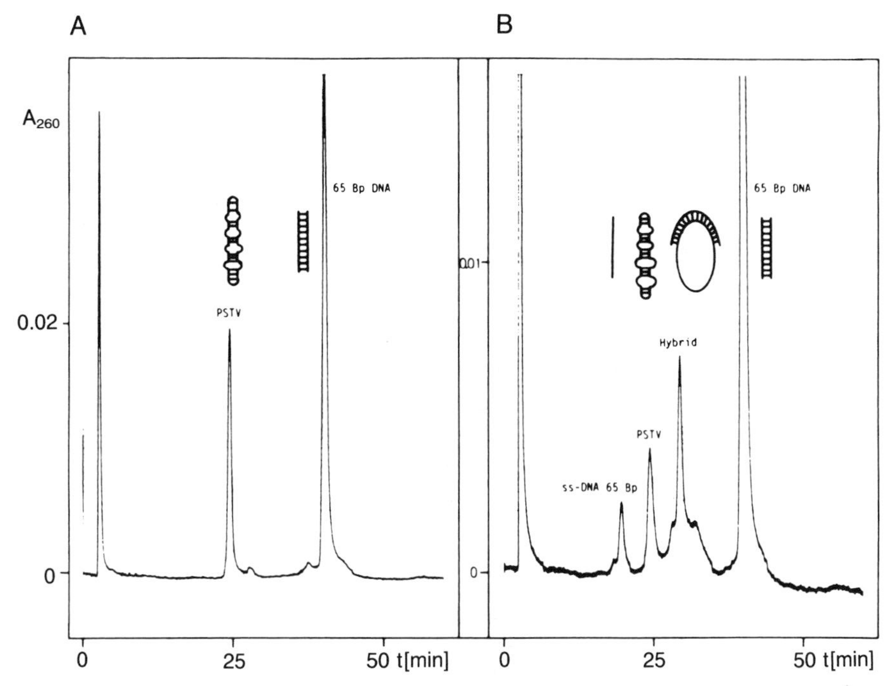

FIGURE 21–21. Anion-exchange HPLC of DNA–RNA hybrids. Chromatographic analysis of a hybridization of a viroid (PSTV) with a 65 bp restriction fragment from the PSTV-cDNA: (a) 1 μg of PSTV, 2 μg of 65 bp DNA; (b) hybridization of 1 μg of PSTV with 4 μg of 65 bp DNA. Conditions: column, Nucleogen-DEAE-4000-10 (6 × 125 mm). Flow rate: 1 ml/min. Pressure: 48 bar. Temperature: 24°C. Linear gradient: 500 to 1200 m*M* potassium chloride in 70 min (10 m*M*/min); 6 *M* urea, 25 m*M* potassium phosphate (pH 6.6). (From ref. 10.)

like salts, dyes, unincorporated nucleotides, small oligonucleotides, low-molecular-weight impurities after gel elution, and small proteins. For desalting, of course, only SEC one-way columns are appropriate; if, however, larger components have to be removed, the specific adsorption of the nucleic acids to the matrix in RPC-5, RPC, IEC, or glass bead adsorption is advantageous.

A size fractionation with moderate resolution has been described for Qiagen, a system of IEC cartridges. The schematic elution profiles of different nucleic acids in an NaCl gradient, which is depicted in Figure 21–22, is given by the supplier.[58] One should keep in mind that the elution profiles hold for a gradient elution, and that the resolution is lower in batchwise elution as is to be expected. For the laboratory routine the batchwise elution is most useful, and the most common applications should be mentioned here. Plasmids can be separated from proteins, RNA, and other impurities present in the cleared cell lysate. The resulting plasmid sample shows high activity in enzymatic reactions and in cell transformation. In this respect, the preparation may compete with the much more time consuming and more expensive CsCl density centrifugation. Small amounts of chromosomal DNA cannot be removed, however. As seen from Figure 21–12, a high-resolution HPLC is needed to separate

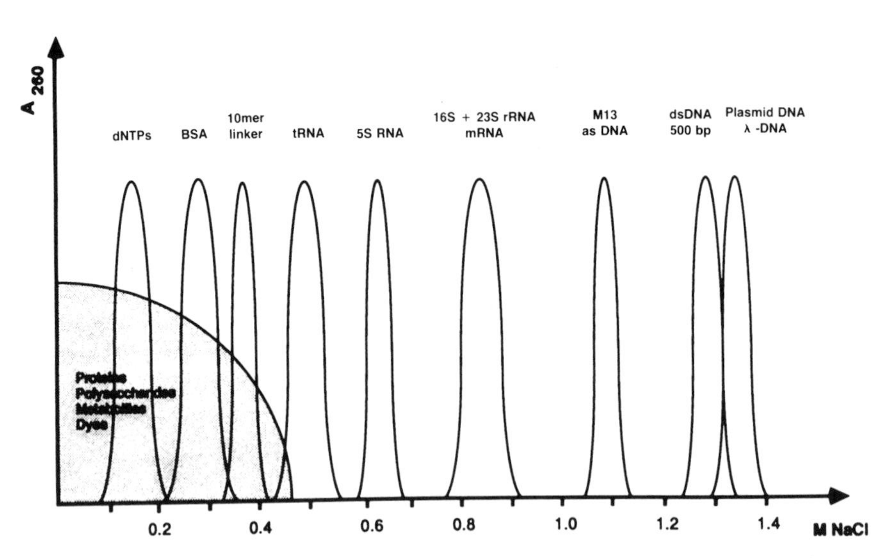

FIGURE 21–22. Separation range of solid-phase extraction on anion-exchange basis. One-way cartridge: Qiagen. A schematic elution profile for a gradient elution with NaCl at pH 7.0 is shown. Exact protocols for batchwise handling, including equilibration of the cartridge, adsorption of the sample, washing, and elution are given by the supplier. (From ref. 58.)

plasmids and residual chromosomal DNA. In the case of ss- and dsDNA from the phage M13 the elution conditions are sufficiently different that both forms may be eluted separately from Qiagen cartridges. The gel electrophoretic analysis showing this is given in Figure 21–23A. After synthesizing runoff RNA transcripts by T7- or SP6-polymerase, the RNA transcripts may be separated from the nonincorporated nucleotides and the DNA template. This is shown by gel electrophoresis in Figure 21–23B (from the author's laboratory). Comparing the results of fractionation of RNA transcripts by SPE and HPLC (cf. Figure 21–16), it is evident that for many applications a fractionation by SPE is sufficient; if early terminations, as seen in the transcript elution by SPE in Figure 21–23B, have to be removed from the full length transcript, a high resolution HPLC is needed.

21.5 CONCLUDING REMARKS

HPLC of nucleic acids has been developed on two tracks. The specialists in chromatography have extended their field of applications, and the users of chromatography in biochemistry and molecular biology have incorporated a new technique for their preparation problems. Still today, the different roots are visible, and one may ask, how far HPLC of nucleic acids has been developed as the playground for specialists or whether this technique has indeed become

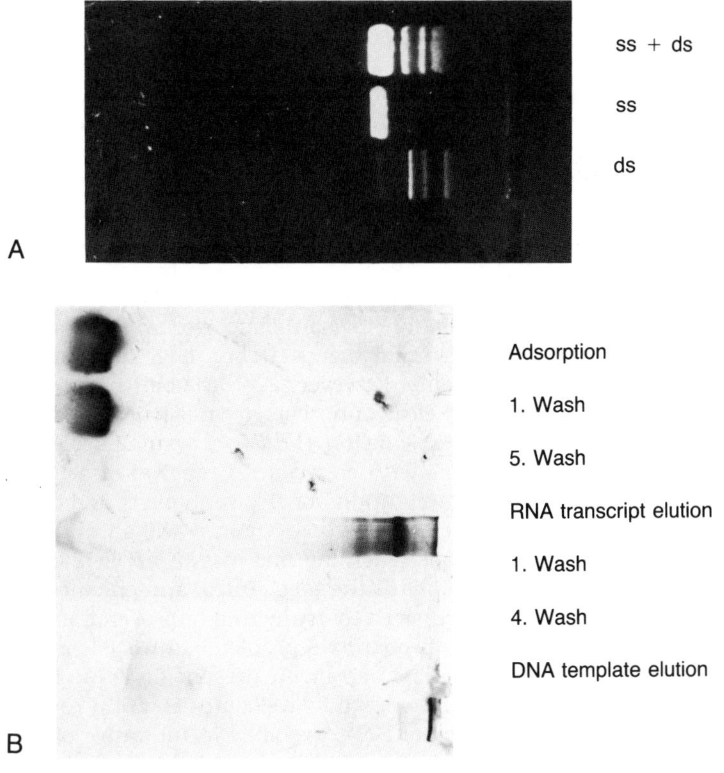

FIGURE 21–23. Application examples of solid-phase extraction. One-way cartridges: Qiagen-pack 100. (A) Separation of ss- and dsDNA from phage M13. Equilibration: 2 ml of 400 m*M* NaCl, 50 m*M* MOPS buffer, 15% ethanol, pH 7.0. Adsorption: 100 μg M13 DNA in 1.5 ml of 550 ml of 750 m*M* NaCl, 50 m*M* MOPS, 15% ethanol, pH 7.0. Elution of the ssDNA: 2 ml of 1100 m*M* NaCl, 50 m*M* MOPS, 4 *M* urea, 15% ethanol, pH 7.0. The dsDNA may be eluted with 1.5 *M* NaCl. The ssDNA is precipitated by adding 0.8 vol isopropanol for 30 min on ice. (B) Separation of RNA transcripts from nonincorporated nucleotides and the DNA template. Equilibration and washing with the same buffer, 400 m*M* NaCl, 50 m*M* MOPS, 15% ethanol, pH 7.0. Equilibration: 2 ml. Adsorption: 200 μg RNA in convenient volume. Washing: 5 ml. Elution: 2 ml of 1050 m*M* NaCl, 50 m*M* MOPS, 7.5% ethanol, 2 *M* urea, pH 7.0. To analyze the batchwise procedure in more detail, washing was carried out in this example in several steps (5 × 2 ml). No low-molecular-weight RNA was eluted from the cartridge with the fifth wash. After RNA transcript elution the cartridge was washed several times with elution buffer; no RNA or DNA was detected in these washes. The DNA template was eluted with 1.5 *M* NaCl, nearly free of any RNA.

a service method for many users. What is meant is seen best by the comparison of two chromatograms, the fancy elution profile of the 1 kb ladder (Figure 21–6) and the simple profile with only two peaks, one of an insert and one of the vector (Figure 21–9). It is the example in Figure 21–9 that really meets the requirements of the user. No other preparative technique than HPLC, in combination with particular cloning steps, is able to yield large amounts of nucleic acids with high biological quality in relatively short times. Biological quality does include not only high purity in the gel electrophoretic analysis but also high activity in enzymatic reactions and biological transformations. Also other examples like preparative plasmid preparation or preparation of viral RNA may be mentioned in this context. On the other hand, the high resolution profile of the 1 kb ladder, or the one of shorter restriction fragments (Figure 21–4), demonstrates the principal power of HPLC in respect to chromatographic resolution.

Although the progress during the last years is remarkable, one has to admit that the resolution of gel electrophoresis is still superior and the procedure is simpler and less expensive. Thus, many users cut out the DNA band of interest from the gel. The biological quality, however, is clearly better after HPLC purification. Therefore, HPLC and electrophoresis are not true alternatives; the real alternative for direct high-resolution HPLC on a small scale would be recovery from gel electrophoresis with consecutive removal of gel impurities by SPE (cf. Section 21.4.5). Combinations of electrophoresis and chromatography will gain more importance in the future, and it will always depend on the specific problem to determine which method may be applied favorably.

Future developments may deal with the mechanical and chemical qualities of the chromatographic matrices, with instrumental improvements, and with the application of HPLC to new preparative problems of nucleic acids. A few comments may be made on the last aspect. At present no DNAs larger than 20 kb have been dealt with. Hence, one would welcome the ability to fractionate whole phage DNA or large genomic DNA, probably in the range of up to 200 kb. Chromatographic resolution has not been extended into that size range. Except for that, one would not anticipate a problem, as, for example, from breaking of the DNA due to hydrodynamic shearing. Recent experience with SPE of genomic DNA has shown that chromatographic treatment of nucleic acids in that size range is possible in principal. Combining pulse field gel electrophoresis[59] and chromatographic techniques specially adapted to the large size of genomic DNA may be most promising for the future. Another area of interest is the fractionation of mRNA with higher resolution that has been achieved so far. This would facilitate the screening procedures in gene cloning. Finally, one may expect that HPLC of nucleic acids will be applied not only in the research laboratory but also in particular production processes. With a further spread of diagnostic techniques by DNA or RNA probes, these probes have to be produced on a larger scale and purified by HPLC.

ACKNOWLEDGMENTS

I am indebted to Drs. Colpan, Hecker, Hillen, Merion, and Tovar for stimulating discussions and allowing use of information prior to publication. I thank Ms. Gruber for help in preparing the manuscript. The work in the author's laboratory was supported by grants from the Deutsche Fondungsgemeinschaft and Fonds der Chemisden Industrie.

REFERENCES

1. V. Bloomfield, D. Crothers, and J. Tinoco, Jr., Physical Chemistry of Nucleic Acids. Harper & Row, New York, 1974.
2. W. Saenger (ed.), Principles of Nucleic Acid Structure. Springer-Verlag, New York, 1984.
3. (a) L. Grossman and K. Moldave (eds.), *Methods Enzymol.*, 65 (1980); (b) R. Wu (ed.), *Methods Enzymol.*, 68 (1979).
4. T. Maniatis, E. F. Fritsch, and J. Shambrock, Molecular Cloning, a Laboratory Manual. Cold Spring Harbor Laboratory, Cold Spring Harbor, NY, 1982.
5. Ch. J. Alden and S.-H. Kim, in Stereodynamics of Molecular Systems (R. H. Sarma, ed.). Pergamon Press, New York, 1979, Chap. IV, pp. 331–350.
6. S. R. Holbrook, J. L. Sussman, R. W. Warrant, and S.-H. Kim, *J. Mol. Biol.*, 123 (1978) 631.
7. M. Potschka, *Anal. Biochem.*, 162(1) (1987) 47.
8. W. K. Olson, M. H. Sarma, R. H. Sarma, and M. Sundaralingam (eds.), Structure and Expression, Vol. 3: DNA Bending and Curvature. Adenine Press, Schenectady, 1988.
9. M. Colpan and D. Riesner, *J. Chromatogr.*, 296 (1984) 339.
10. R. Hecker, M. Colpan, and D. Riesner, *J. Chromatogr.*, 326 (1985) 251.
11. W. Müller, *Eur. J. Biochem.*, 155 (1986) 203.
12. H.-J. Fritz, R. Belagaje, E. L. Brown, R. H. Fritz, R. A. Jones, R. G. Lees, and H. G. Khorana, *Biochemistry*, 17 (1978) 1257.
13. M. Simonian and M. W. Capp, *J. Chromatogr.*, 266 (1983) 351.
14. S. Garcia and J.-P. Liautard, *J. Chromatogr. Sci.*, 21 (1983) 398.
15. A. D. Kelmers, D. G. Novelli, and M. P. Stulberg, *J. Biol. Chem.*, 240 (1965) 3979.
16. R. Bischoff and L. W. McLaughlin, *J. Chromatogr.*, 270 (1983) 117.
17. R. Bischoff, E. Graeser, and L. W. McLaughlin, *J. Chromatogr.*, 257 (1983) 305.
18. J. E. Larson, S. C. Hardies, R. K. Patient, and R. D. Wells, *J. Biol. Chem.*, 254 (1979) 5535.
19. W. Hillen, R. D. Klein, and R. D. Wells, *Biochemistry*, 20 (1981) 3748.
20. R. D. Wells, S. C. Hardies, G. T. Horn, B. Klein, J. E. Larson, S. K. Neuendorf, N. Panagototos, R. K. Patient, and E. Selsing, *Methods Enzymol.*, 65 (1980) 327.
21. R. Bischoff and L. W. McLaughlin, *J. Chromatogr.*, 296 (1984) 329.
22. A. I. P. Martin and R. L. M. Synge, *Biochem. J.*, 35 (1941) 1358.
23. P.-Å. Albertsson and E. J. Nyns, *Nature (London)*, 184 (1969) 1456.
24. W. Müller, in Partitioning in Aqueous Two-Phase Systems (H. Walter, D. E. Brooks, and D. Fischer, eds.). Academic Press, New York, 1985, p. 227.
25. W. Müller, Kontakte (Merck, Darmstadt) (3) (1986) 3.
26. W. Müller, Kontakte (Merck, Darmstadt) (1) (1987) 45.
27. R. T. Kovacic and K. E. van Holde, *Biochemistry*, 16 (1977) 1490.
28. M. Colpan, J. Schumacher, W. Brüggemann, H. L. Sänger, and D. Riesner, *Anal. Biochem.*, 131 (1983) 257.
29. D. Riesner, in Landoldt-Börnstein, New Series, Biophysics-Nucleic Acids (W. Saenger, ed.) Vol. VII 1 d Springer Verlag, Berlin 31.
30. J. Kruppa, L. Graeve, A. Banche, and P. Földi, *Liquid Chromatogr. HPLC Mag.*, 2 (1984) 848.
31. D. Riesner, P. Klaff, G. Steger, and R. Hecker, in Endocytobiology III (J. J. Lee and F. Fredrick, eds.). Annals of the New York Academy of Sciences, New York, 1987.
32. S. Eriksson, G. Glad, P.-A. Pernemalm, and E. Westman, *J. Chromatogr.*, 359 (1986) 265.
33. M. Colpan and D. Riesner, in New Comprehensive Biochemistry, Modern Physical Methods in Biochemistry, Vol. 11 B (A. Neuberger and L. L. M. van Deenen, eds.). Elsevier, Amsterdam, 1988 85.

34. M. Merion, W. Warren, C. Stacey, and M. E. Dwyer, *BioTechniques*, 6(3) (1988) 246.
35. C. Yanisch-Perron, J. Vieira, and J. Messing, *Gene*, 22 (1985) 103.
36. J. Vieira and J. Messing, *Gene*, 19 (1982) 259.
37. B. Unger, G. Klock, and W. Hillen, *Nucleic Acids Res.*, 12 (1984) 7693.
38. A. Dugaiczyk, H. W. Boyer, and H. M. Goodman, *J. Mol. Biol.*, 96 (1975) 171.
39. H. Tovar and W. Hillen, personal communication.
40. H. Heumann, H. Lederer, W. Kammerer, P. Palm, W. Metzger, and G. Baer, *Biochim. Biophys. Acta*, 909 (1987) 126.
41. B. E. Boyes, D. G. Walter, and P. L. McGeer, *Anal. Biochem.*, 170(1) (1988) 127.
42. E. Westman, S. Eriksson, T. Laas, P. A. Pernemalm, and S. E. Skoeld, *Anal. Biochem.*, 166(1) (1987) 158.
43. D. J. Stowers, J. M. B. Keim, P. S. Paul, Y. S. Lyoo, M. Merion, and R. M. Benbow, *J. Liquid Chromatogr.*, in press.
44. Pharmacia FPLC: Application File, Plasmid DNA, 1987.
45. P. A. Edwardson, T. Atkinson, Ch. R. Lowe, and D. A. P. Small, *Anal. Biochem.*, 152 (1986) 215.
46. J. Gomez-Marquez, M. Freire, and F. Segade, *Gene*, 54(2–3) (1987) 255.
47. N. Morean, X. Tabary, and F. LeGoffic, *Anal. Biochem.*, 166(1) (1987) 188.
48. Nucleogen DEAE, Diagen 1986, Düsseldorf.
49. S. Colote, C. Ferraz, and J. P. Liautard, *Anal. Biochem.*, 154(1) (1986) 15.
50. D. A. Melton, P. A. Krieg, M. R. Rebagliati, T. Maniatis, K. Zinn, and M. R. Green, *Nucleic Acids Res.*, 12 (1984) 7035.
51. S. van der Werf, J. Bradley, E. Wimmer, F. W. Studier, and J. J. Dunn, *Proc. Natl. Acad. Sci. U.S.A.*, 83 (1986) 2330.
52. P. Lowary, J. Sampson, J. Milligan, D. Groebe, and O. C. Uhlenbeck, in Structure and Dynamics of RNA (P. H. van Knippenberg and C. W. Hilbers, eds.). Plenum, New York, 1986.
53. T. Ogishima, Y. Okada, and T. Omura, *Anal. Biochem.*, 138 (1984) 309.
54. L. Graeve, W. Goemann, P. Földi, and J. Kruppa, *Biochem. Biophys. Res. Commun.*, 107 (1982) 1559.
55. S. Garcia and J. P. Liautard, *J. Chromatogr.*, 296 (1984) 355.
56. LKB Application Note AP 101, 1982.
57. J. P. Liautard, *J. Chromatogr.*, 285 (1984) 221.
58. Application Protocols, in The Qiagenologist. Diagen, Düsseldorf, 1988.
59. D. C. Schwartz and C. R. Cantor, *Cell*, 37 (1984) 67.

CHAPTER 22

Separation of Proteins and Peptides by High-Performance Capillary Electrophoresis: A Versatile Analytical and Micropreparative Method

Stellan Hjertén

CONTENTS

22.1 INTRODUCTION

Carrier-free electrophoresis in capillaries has for decades attracted the interest of several researchers. The basic reason is that convection and thermal zone deformation are strongly suppressed in this type of electrophoresis. In 1960[1] and 1967[2] the present author described a free zone electrophoresis method in quartz capillaries with diameters of 1–6 mm (the stabilization against convection was improved by rotating the capillary tube around its long axis). The zones are located by a sophisticated UV-scanning technique. The method can be used for both analytical and micropreparative runs and is still the most accurate method for determination of mobilities. Typical run times are between

5 and 45 min. The apparatus, which is very simple to operate, permits studies of inorganic and organic ions, peptides, proteins, nucleic acids, virus, and whole cells.

The idea of electrophoresis in narrow-bore capillaries was suggested in 1967,[2] but the UV-monitors available at that time were not sensitive enough to detect solutes at low or moderate concentrations when the light path was only 0.05–0.1 mm (= the diameter of the capillary).

In 1968 Everaerts described an apparatus for displacement electrophoresis of weak acids and cations.[3] The zones in the glass capillary tube, which had a diameter around 0.6 mm, were detected when they passed a stationary thermocouple with low heat capacity. The detection sensitivity was relatively high due to the large diameter of the capillary and the relatively high solute concentrations typical of displacement electrophoresis. The disadvantage of a large diameter is the increased risk of convection and thermal zone deformation, although convection is partially compensated by the automatic zone-sharpening attending displacement electrophoresis. A somewhat modified apparatus, equipped with both a conductivity and a UV monitor, was ten years later used for zone electrophoresis of low-molecular-weight compounds.[4] The runs, performed in 0.2-mm polytetrafluoroethylene tubes, cannot be considered true free electrophoresis experiments, since they were conducted in a buffer containing a hydrophilic, nonionic polymer, which has the property of suppressing convection and electroendosmosis[5] (in buffers containing such polymers even the order of migration of solutes can differ from that in buffer alone). Five years earlier, Virtanen[6] had performed free zone electrophoresis experiments with inorganic ions in a 0.2-mm capillary of Pyrex. Fused silica tubing of an almost 3-fold smaller diameter was used by Jorgenson for electrophoretic analysis of low-molecular-weight compounds, including peptides.[7] Prelabeling of the solutes with fluorescamine was utilized for detection. UV monitoring[8–11] is, however, often more attractive since it has a broader application range, particularly when the detection system is designed so that it permits the use of wavelengths below 200 nm.[12]

The separation of small molecules by electrophoresis in capillaries involves in general no great problems. However, for electrophoresis of larger molecules, with which this chapter primarily deals, the situation is quite different, owing to their tendency to adsorb strongly onto the wall of the capillary. This problem was solved when Hjertén coated the tube wall with a hydrophilic polymer[8,13]—a technique originally introduced to eliminate disturbances caused by electroendosmosis.[2] In an analysis of the reasons why it is more difficult to separate biopolymers with the same high efficiency as low-molecular-weight compounds, Lauer et al.[14] found that the "most important contribution to band broadening (of biopolymers) arises from adsorption to the wall of the separating capillary" (see also ref. 15). This difference between small and large molecules regarding the strength of adsorption to the tube wall is due to the fact that macromolecules have a much larger number of adsorption sites. Analogous adsorption problems occur in HPLC on silica beads and therefore much effort has been devoted to attempts to eliminate the adsorption—particularly of macromolecules—by capping or by coating the beads with hydrophilic substances. Capillaries surface-modified by this technique are, however, still so negatively charged that both acidic and basic proteins are carried by the strong electroendosmosis toward the negative pole.[15] Green and Jorgenson[16] and Lauer and McManigill[13] made the same observation when they suppressed adsorption by using buffer ions that interact with the tube wall to give it a charge opposite to that of the proteins, thus accomplishing an electrostatic repulsion between these and the wall. As pointed out by the authors this approach is not applicable with all proteins.

With the introduction of the method for elimination of electroendosmosis and adsorption of all solutes, irrespective of their charge, by coating the capillary with a polymer such as methyl cellulose[2,7] or non-cross-linked polyacrylamide[11] the resolution of macromolecules (and smaller solutes) is now so high that free electrophoresis in capillary tubes (high-performance electrophoresis, HPE) in the near future can be expected to be an important tool for studies of biopolymers (and low-molecular-weight compounds), particularly since methods now are available to create very sharp starting zones[17]—a prerequisite for optimal utilization of the potential of this technique. These electroendosmosis-free capillaries also have the advantage that they permit absolute determinations of mobilities, although the accuracy is far less than that obtained with the capillary electrophoresis method described in ref. 2. Another advantage is that they can be considerably shorter than the noncoated tubes and still give the same effective electrophoretic migration distance (i.e., the same resolution) because the electroendosmotic mobility in the latter capillaries is considerably larger than the electrophoretic mobilities, causing all solutes, irrespective of their charge, to move cathodically. One should add that electroendosmosis is a disturbing factor in isoelectric focusing, too, and, in addition, makes it difficult to determine true values of theoretical plate numbers (see Section 22.6.1) in zone electrophoresis experiments.

High-performance electrophoresis of macromolecules can be conducted not only in free solution but also in nonsieving agarose gels[8,18] and in molecular-sieving gels of polyacrylamide both in the absence[8,9,11] and the presence of sodium dodecyl sulfate (SDS),[17–19] which facilitates the manipulation of the separation pattern and thereby the resolution. The great flexibility of the method is reflected also in that it can be employed for high-resolving isoelectric focusing by utilization of a method we recently developed for mobilization of the focused proteins.[20,21] Furthermore HPE can be used not only for analytical but also for micropreparative runs.[9,11,22]

Even if this book does not deal with the separation of small molecules I would like to point out that HPE has been successfully used by several authors for the fractionation of low-molecular-weight compounds.[4,6–13,16–18,22–28]

In Chapter 4, which deals with agarose-based high-performance liquid chromatography, the usefulness of HPE for rapid analyses of HPLC fractions is emphasized, particularly when adapted to zone electrophoresis in discontinuous buffer system or isoelectric focusing or displacement electrophoresis since these three methods afford an automatic zone sharpening and therefore permit investigation of dilute protein solutions without any preconcentration.

22.2 THEORETICAL AND PRACTICAL CONSIDERATIONS

22.2.1 Electrophoresis, Chromatography, Centrifugation—Three Analogous Separation Methods

These methods have in common that the separations obtained are based on differences in transport velocities of the solutes to be fractionated. In electrophoresis the transport is achieved by an electrical field, in centrifugation by a centrifugal field, and in chromatography by a hydrodynamical force (flow). The retarding forces originate from frictional resistance (electrophoresis and centrifugation) or affinity for the stationary phase (chromatography). These simple considerations indicate that electrophoresis, chromatography, and centrifugation have analogous separation mechanisms, which is still more evident from a comparison between Longsworth's classical equation for electrophoresis and an equation for chromatography that I have recently derived (see ref. 29 on p. 770). This means, for instance, that any sedimentation method has its electrophoretic and chromatographic counterpart. An example is isopycnic centrifugation, isoelectric focusing, and chromatofocusing; another is displacement centrifugation, displacement electrophoresis, and displacement chromatography. The method to be described in this chapter was developed with the aim of creating a technique that is the electrophoretic counterpart of high-performance liquid chromatography (HPLC) and has therefore been given an analogous designation: high-performance electrophoresis (HPE)—a notation also used by Mikkers et al.[4] In this connection it should be emphasized that the formulas used in chromatography for resolution, plate number, etc., also are employed in electrophoresis—with more or less obvious modifications (see Section 22.6.1). The fact that very few researchers are aware of the analogies between electrophoresis and chromatography has certainly hindered the development of both the methods. An example is the indirect detection method that has finally come into use in HPLC.[29] I believe that this detection technique would have been introduced into the field of chromatography much earlier if more chromatographers had realized the analogy between chromatography and electrophoresis (in the latter field it was introduced 20 years ago[2]). For similar reasons too many years elapsed between the introduction of isoelectric focusing[30,31] and chromatofocusing.[32,33]

22.2.2 Factors Causing Zone Broadening in Electrophoresis and Chromatography

In this section some analogous parameters affecting the resolution in electrophoresis and in chromatography will be discussed. Centrifugation is omitted in this comparison simply because this method often has a much lower resolution than electrophoresis and chromatography, partly due to the practical difficulties of designing durable rotors permitting the use of centrifuge tubes of the same height (= migration distance) as that commonly used in columns for electrophoresis and chromatography. The most important factors causing zone broadening in chromatography, electrophoresis, and centrifugation are listed in Table 22–1.

TABLE 22–1. Parameters Causing Zone Broadening

	Diffusion	Eddy Diffusion	Slow Mass Transfer	Thermal Zone Deformation	Disturbing Adsorption	Wall Effects[a]
Chromatography						
Porous beads	+	+	+	−	±	+
Nonporous beads	+	+	(+)	−	±	+
Electrophoresis						
Porous beads	+	+	+	+	±	+
Nonporous beads	+	+	(+)	+	±	+
Homogeneous gel	+	−	−	+	±	±
Free solution	+	−	−	+	−	±
Centrifugation	+	−	−	−	−	±

[a] In chromatography wall effects originate from differences in flow resistance at the tube wall and in the bulk of the bed; in free electrophoresis from charges at the wall of the electrophoresis chamber (electroendosmosis); in electrophoresis in granular media from charges at the surface of the granules (beads) making up the bed (electroendosmosis); in electrophoresis in homogeneous gels of polyacrylamide and agarose from differences in properties of the gel at the wall of the electrophoresis chamber and in the rest of the chamber.

Diffusion If the flow is stopped in a chromatography experiment, or the voltage switched off in an electrophoresis run the sample zone will become blurred by diffusion. This diffusional broadening caused by the Brownian motion of the molecules can be suppressed by lowering the temperature and shortening the run time.

Eddy Diffusion Zone broadening caused by Eddy diffusion[34] is illustrated schematically in Figure 22–1. The four molecules A, B, C, and D of the same solute form a sharp starting zone (I) but because they migrate along different paths and with different velocities in the granular bed the zone will broaden during the run (zone II). This phenomenon, called Eddy diffusion, is a consequence of the presence of a granular medium and will therefore not appear in electrophoresis in a carrier-free medium or in a coherent, homogeneous gel.

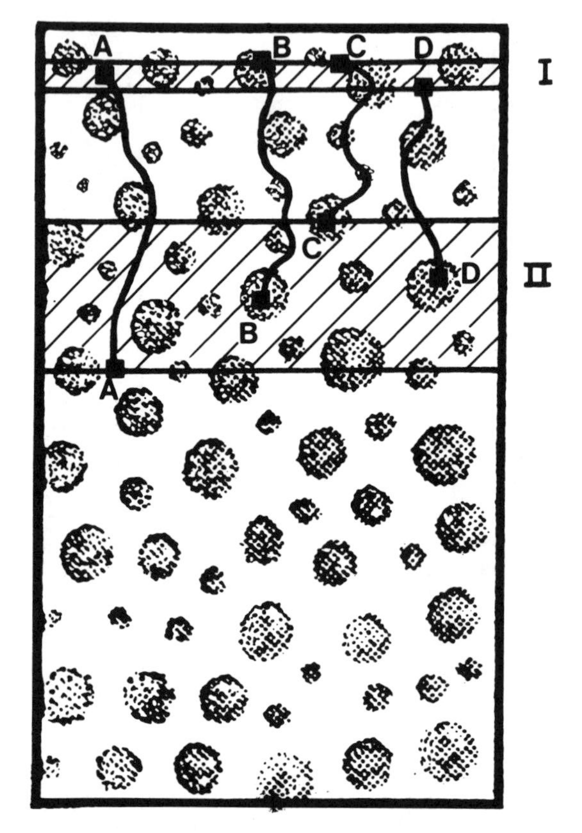

FIGURE 22–1. Zone broadening in a granular medium caused by Eddy diffusion. The solutes A, B, C, and D form a sharp starting zone (position I). Since they migrate (chromatographically or electorphoretically) with different velocities and along different paths the zone is much wider in position II.

Slow Mass Transfer In a chromatographic column made up of porous beads one can never attain true equilibrium in the partition of solutes between the stationary and mobile phases.[34] The conditions to approach equilibrium are, of course, much more favorable for nonporous beads. The situation is analogous in electrophoresis in granular media.

Thermal Zone Deformation This effect is of no importance in chromatography except at extremely high flow rates where the frictional heat may cause the temperature to become higher at the center of the column than at its periphery. Since the viscosity decreases with an increase in temperature the resistance to flow will be smaller in the center of the chromatographic tube than at its wall, i.e., the zone migrates faster in the center. This thermal zonal deformation is one of the most serious problems encountered in electrophoresis, where the current passing through the electrophoresis tube generates considerable Joule heat.

Disturbing Adsorption In chromatography the unspecific adsorption may be very disturbing, although it sometimes can be taken advantage of. An ideal electrophoretic supporting medium should exhibit no adsorption whatsoever. In free electrophoresis the adsorption onto the wall of the electrophoresis tube is an important factor only when the tube has a small diameter as in high-performance electrophoresis.

Wall Effects Since the flow resistance close to the wall of a chromatographic bed differs from that of the bulk of the bed (due to inevitable heterogeneities in the packing) the flow rates in these parts of the bed are not the same, which gives rise to zone deformation.

In electrophoresis another wall effect often appears namely electroendosmosis, a liquid flow originating from the presence of charges at the inner surface of the electrophoresis tube [electroendosmosis also occurs in a packed bed along the surface of the granules (beads), if they are charged]. The electroendosmosis itself will cause only a displacement of a zone without deformation, except in a thin layer (<100 Å) at the tube wall (Figure 22–2b). Such plug flow is observed in open capillaries. In closed capillaries the electroendosmosis is attended by a hydrodynamic counterflow that may give the zone a pronounced parabolic form (Figure 22–2c). An electrophoresis tube exhibiting electroendosmosis often causes adsorption of the solutes onto the tube wall. This adsorption is often of a complex nature (compare adsorption to untreated HPLC beads of silica) and includes electrostatic interactions, since electroendosmosis presupposes the existence of charges on the tube wall. Electroendosmosis can be taken advantage of to transport noncharged solutes and at the same time permit them to interact with a "stationary phase" (for instance the derivatized tube wall, a polymer, or a detergent micelle) and thereby achieve a separation.[23,25,26,28,35]

I want to stress that also for tubes with inside diameters of only 0.025–0.05 mm we have found that an electroendosmosis-free tube gives sharper zones, not only of cations but also of anions, than are obtainable in the presence of electroendosmosis. This probably reflects solute adsorption to the negatively charged wall of the tube, since electroendosmosis in such narrow capillaries should cause only a plug flow (which does not give rise to a significant zone deformation (Figure 22–2b) and not a disturbing counterflow (Figure 22–2c and d). However, one should expect somewhat broader zones when electroen-

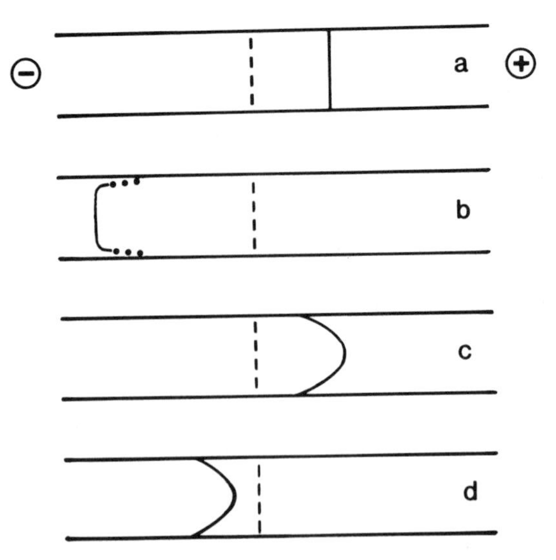

FIGURE 22–2. Electroendosmosis. The position and shape of a zone affected by electrophoresis (a) and electroendosmosis (b); the dots correspond to a very thin layer (<100 Å thick) in which the electroendosmotic velocity is lower than in the bulk of the medium; a hydrodynamic flow (c); electrophoresis, electroendosmosis, and a hydrodynamic flow (d), i.e., the combined effect of a, b, and c. The broken line corresponds to the starting zone.

dosmosis is superimposed on electrophoresis if the following statement of Tsuda et al.[23] is applicable: "These results provide further evidence that the flow rate pattern due to electroendosmosis is . . . less flat than that of plug flow."

Electrophoresis in polyacrylamide gels is not attended by electroendosmosis, whereas gels of even the highest quality agarose show some electroendosmosis, which, however, can be nullified by the addition of polymers, such as non-cross-linked polyacrylamide.[36] Wall effects can also occur if the tube wall affects the gel formation such that the gel in the immediate vicinity of the wall acquires a structure that differs from that of the bulk of the gel.

22.2.3 Selection of Experimental Electrophoresis Conditions to Suppress Zone Broadening Caused by Diffusion, Thermal Zone Deformation, Adsorption, and Wall Effects

Eddy diffusion and slow mass transfer are the factors that cause the most serious zone broadening in chromatography and in electrophoresis in granular media. Electrophoresis in free solution and in homogeneous gels have the great advantage of not being subject to these two types of zone broadening (see Table

22–1) and can accordingly be expected to give very high resolution. Therefore, only these two forms of electrophoresis will be considered in this section. Consequently, the discussion of optimization of the resolving power can be limited to a treatment of the parameters: diffusion, thermal zone deformation, adsorption, and wall effects, as is evident from Table 22–1.

Diffusional zone broadening is of less importance for macromolecules. It can be minimized, however, by lowering the temperature of the electrophoresis medium and by decreasing the run time, as mentioned above. The former alternative is not fruitful, since it brings about a decrease in the electrophoretic migration rate. The latter alternative can be realized by increasing the field strength F, since

$$v = uF \tag{22–1}$$

where v = migration rate and u = mobility (= the migration rate when $F = 1$). The field strength is determined by the relation

$$F = \frac{I}{q\kappa} \tag{22–2}$$

where I = current, q = the cross-sectional area of the electrophoresis tube, and κ = the electrical conductivity.

According to Eq. (22–2) an increase of the field strength can be achieved in two ways: by an increase in the current I or a decrease in the conductivity κ of the electrophoresis buffer. The latter approach cannot be pushed too far since the conductivity (and pH) in the zones will then differ so much from those of the buffer itself that the zones become asymmetrical, which is equivalent to zone broadening.[2,37] To increase the field strength by increasing the current has the disadvantage of increasing the heat developed and, thereby, the thermal zone deformation, as is evident from Figure 22–3 [the curves are based on an expression derived from Eq. (73) in ref. 2]. The zone deformation in this figure is defined as the percentage difference in migration velocity of solute molecules at the center of the tube and at its wall. The curves are accurate enough to allow a rough estimation of the zone deformation at different field strengths, even if the diffusional effects have not been considered.

For high resolution a thermal zone deformation of no more than one percent can be tolerated. According to Figure 22–3 one must then use tubes with diameters below 0.05 mm if field strengths as high as 800 V/cm are to be used in order to get short analysis times. This conclusion agrees with our experimental finding that tubes with diameters of 0.025 mm give higher resolution than do 0.05-mm tubes at this field strength. A more rigorous treatment of resolution in electrophoresis shows that in many experiments maximum resolution occurs when the plate height corresponding to diffusion is 4-fold that corresponding to thermal zone deformation (see ref. 29 on p. 770).

To minimize the wall effects occuring in *polyacrylamide gel* electrophoresis the inside wall of the electrophoresis tube should have a structure as similar as possible to that of the monomers constituting the polyacrylamide. This can be accomplished by coating the wall with a silane compound containing acrylamide (vinyl) groups. Such a compound is γ-methacryloxypropyltrimethoxy-

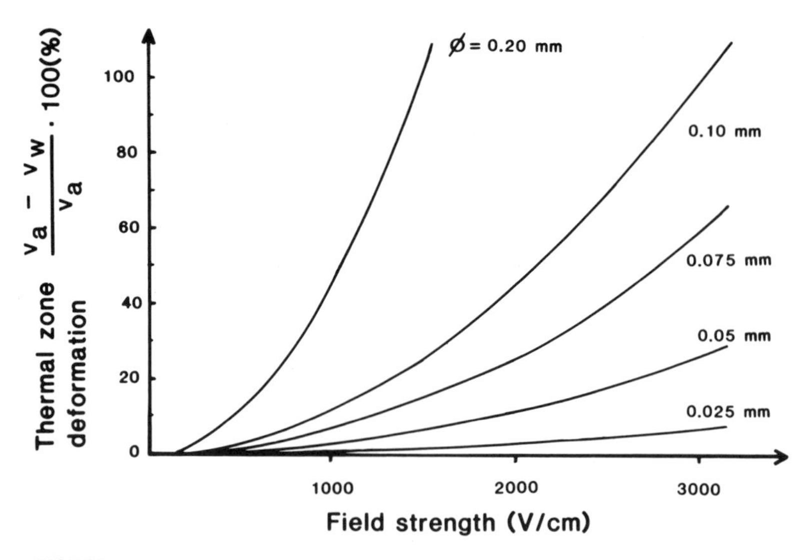

FIGURE 22–3. Thermal zone deformation as a function of the field strength at different diameters of the electrophoresis tube. The curves were drawn for a buffer with a conductivity $= 3.7 \times 10^{-3}\ \Omega^{-1}\ cm^{-1}$. The influence of diffusion has not been considered.

silane (Silane 174 from LKB, Bromma, Sweden), which also serves the purpose of covalently linking the polyacrylamide gel to the fused silica electrophoresis tube.[38]

In *free* electrophoresis we have to consider only one wall effect when disturbing adsorption is negligible: electroendosmosis. A theoretical treatment of this phenomenon could be summarized in the following formula[2]:

$$u_{eo} = \frac{\epsilon}{4\pi} \int_0^{\zeta} \frac{1}{\eta(x)} \, d\psi(x) \qquad (22\text{–}3)$$

where u_{eo} = the electroendosmotic mobility, ϵ = the dielectric constant, $\eta(x)$ = the viscosity at a distance x from the tube wall, $\psi(x)$ = the potential at a distance x from the tube wall, and ζ = the zeta potential of the tube wall. Observe that the viscosity, $\eta(x)$, is a function of x rather than constant as in Helmholtz' classical equation for electroendosmosis. From Eq. (22–3) one can conclude that for $1/\eta(x)$ and thereby the integral to approach zero it is sufficient to increase the viscosity only in a thin layer close to the tube wall. There is accordingly no prerequisite to increase the viscosity in the bulk of the buffer solution (which the Helmholtz equation requires). This conclusion is of importance, since an increase in viscosity throughout the buffer in the electrophoresis tube decreases not only the electroendosmotic migration velocity but also the electrophoretic migration velocity—and by the same factor.

In practice, the viscosity increase at the tube wall is achieved by coating it with non-cross-linked polyacrylamide, as described in ref. 13. Methyl cellulose can alternatively be used.[2] A solution of this polymer is, however, more viscous than a monomer solution of acrylamide and is therefore a little more difficult to suck into the extremely narrow capillaries (around 0.025 mm). The polyacrylamide (methyl cellulose) coating eliminates not only electroendosomosis but also adsorption, as judged from the finding that both acidic and basic proteins or low-molecular-weight compounds migrate as narrow, symmetrical peaks in coated tubes (no tailing). There are certainly several reasons why a polymer coating prevents interaction of solutes with the tube wall:

1. If the polymer is hydrophilic and nonionic like polyacrylamide one cannot expect hydrophobic or electrostatic interactions to take place.
2. If the concentration of the linked polymer (the ligand density) is high, macromolecules should be sterically excluded.
3. When using colored model proteins we have often observed that proteins migrate electrophoretically where they face the smallest resistance to migration. For instance, in a bed of porous gel beads the proteins seem to migrate between the beads. We have not observed that they enter the beads even if the pores in the beads are large enough to permit penetration of macromolecules. In other words, the separation pattern is similar to that obtained in free electrophoresis. We have no satisfactory explanation for this finding.

To summarize: zone broadening due to electroendosmosis and adsorption of solutes onto the tube wall can be eliminated by coating the wall with a polymer; zone broadening due to diffusion can be suppressed by performing the runs at high field strength and low conductivity (this zone broadening is often negligible for macromolecules, except when the sample zone has been sharpened to an extremely narrow band, for instance by the methods described in Section 22.2.6); the pronounced thermal zone deformation at these high field strengths can be minimized if the electrophoresis tubes have diameters around 25–50 μm and are thin walled and preferably actively cooled with water (or an organic liquid, for instance carbon tetrachloride, to minimize the risk of electrical shock).

We can thus now master the basic problems in electrophoresis in narrow capillaries (adsorption and electroendosmosis) and can roughly estimate for any experiment the maximum field strength that can be used as soon as we have decided how much thermal zone deformation can be tolerated (Figure 22–3). We are accordingly, in practice, close to the theoretically optimal degree of utilization of high-performance electrophoresis, provided that the starting zone is very narrow and that the peaks in the electropherogram are symmetrical (see ref. 29 on p. 770). These problems and different methods to apply the sample will be treated in the following sections.

22.2.4 Application of the Sample

There are several methods for the application of the sample. Only three techniques that do not require sophisticated equipment will be described. An application method analogous to that used in HPLC requires microvalves that can be designed and constructed only in a high-standard mechanical workshop.

22.2.4.1 Electrophoretic Application

The sample, preferably in a buffer of low concentration to get a zone-sharpening effect (see Section 22.2.6.1), is placed as a droplet, S, at the bottom of the glass capillary C of the application arrangement shown in Figure 22–4. When the voltage is switched on the solutes migrate electrophoretically into the capillary tube T. To eliminate the risk of denaturation of the sample by electrode reactions a gel G is placed between the electrode and the sample S. In this application technique the ratio between the amounts of the different solutes in the applied sample is not the same as in the original sample solution, since the lengths of the individual zones of the different solutes after application are roughly proportional to their mobilities (the electrophoresis pattern in the application stage corresponds to the pattern of the ascending boundaries in a moving boundary electrophoresis experiment). However, the areas of the peaks on the recorder chart are nevertheless roughly proportional to the concentrations of the solutes in the original sample when the on-tube detection method is used (see Figure 22–5). The basic reason for this is that a slowly migrating component spends a longer time in the detecting UV beam (and therefore gives a broader peak and consequently a larger area) than does a rapidly migrating compound—even if the zones in the electrophoresis tube have the same length, or more generally, the peak width (area) is proportional to the residence time of the zone in the UV beam and therefore inversely proportional to the speed with which the zone passes the UV beam.

22.2.4.2 Application with the Aid of the Capillary Forces

One end of the empty, dry electrophoresis tube is dipped into the buffer, which will automatically be sucked up into the coated tube by the capillary forces. The tube is lifted up from the buffer and touched into the sample solution when the buffer boundary is 1–3 mm from the far end of the tube (the sucking-in of the sample will automatically stop when the buffer reaches the far end). The filling of the electrophoresis tube with buffer can be speeded

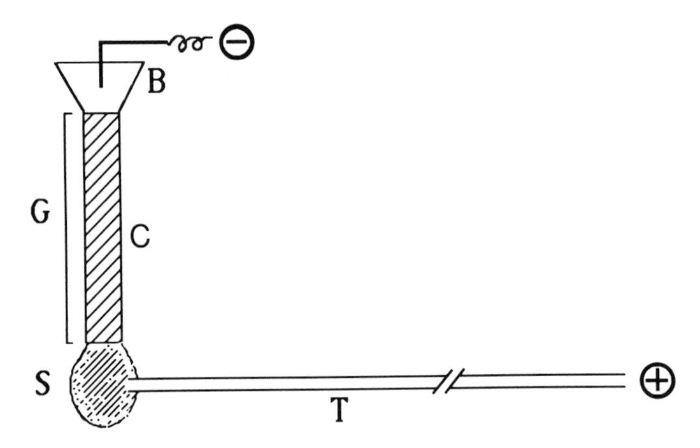

FIGURE 22–4. Electrophoretic application of the sample. T, electrophoresis tube; C, glass capillary; B, buffer; G, gel, prepared in buffer; S, a drop of the sample.

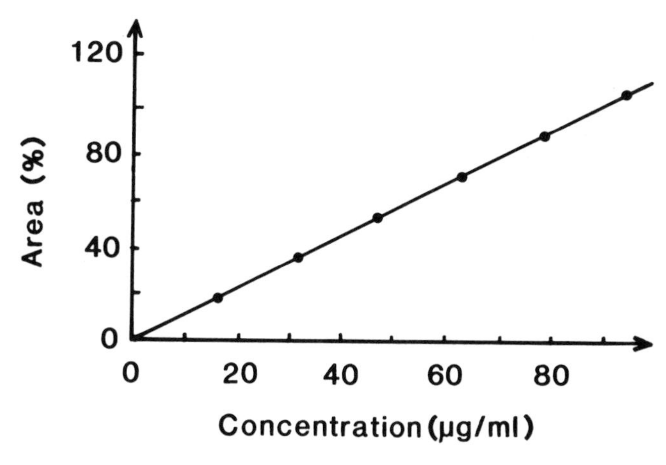

FIGURE 22–5. The relation between the concentration of a component in the sample and the peak area. The sample was electrophoretically applied. The on-tube detection method was used. Sample: Fragment 9–11 of substance P. Internal standard: Fragment 8–11. Dimensions of the fused silica electrophoresis tube: 0.025 (i.d.) × 140 mm. Buffer: 0.05 *M* sodium phosphate buffer, pH 2.6. Voltage: 6000 V. Detection wavelength: 200 nm. The area of the sample peak is expressed as percentage of the area of the internal standard peak. The experiment was performed by Drs. A. Chen and Zhu Ming-de.

up with the aid of a syringe or a water pump (this alternative must be used if the inside of the tube is moist).

Since this application method is based on a hydrodynamic flow of sample into the electrophoresis tube, the boundary between sample and buffer will have a parabolic shape. The sample zone will therefore be wider than the displaced air zone at the opposite end of the tube. By diffusion a smooth gradient in solute concentration will be formed.

In this application technique the concentration of a solute in the sample—as determined by the on-tube detection method—is approximately proportional to the area of the corresponding peak on the recorder chart divided by the retention time, since the more slowly a zone migrates in the tube, the longer time it will take for the zone to pass the detecting UV beam and the wider will become the peak on the recorder chart.[17] This application method differs from the electromigration technique in the respect that the ratios between the amounts of the different solutes in the original sample and in the applied sample zone are the same.

22.2.4.3 Application by Siphoning

This downhill flow method is simple, but has the drawback of giving a large uncertainty in the volume of the applied sample. An automatic sampler based on the siphon principle, seems, however, to give a high reproductivity, at least for capillaries of relatively large diameter (0.10–0.25 mm).[39] The discussion in the previous section is relevant also for application by siphoning. As an alternative to this application method the sample can be introduced by a pressure difference between the ends of the electrophoresis tube. This method requires, however, a relatively complicated equipment.

22.2.5 The Influence of Conductivity on Peak Asymmetry and Run Times

The concentration of the solute should be as small as the sensitivity of the detector permits, since the lower this concentration the lower the conductivity of the buffer that can be used without risk of getting asymmetrical peaks (see Eq. 34b in ref. 37); and a decrease in conductivity means shorter run times for two reasons: (1) electrophoretic mobilities increase with a decrease in ionic strength of the buffer[40] and (2) higher field strengths can be tolerated for any given, acceptable thermal zone deformation. The following mathematical treatment serves to express the latter statement in more exact terms.

The same degree of thermal zone deformation in two experiments 1 and 2 involves the same amount of heat developed per second, i.e.,

$$V_1 I_1 = V_2 I_2 \tag{22–4}$$

where V and I are voltage and current, respectively (the subscripts refer to experiments 1 and 2). Since $V = (l/q\kappa) \cdot I$ (l and q are the length and the cross-sectional area of the electrophoresis tube, respectively) Eq. (22–4) can be written

$$\frac{I_1^2}{\kappa_1} = \frac{I_2^2}{\kappa_2}$$

which in combination with Eq. (22–2) gives

$$F_2 = F_1 \sqrt{\kappa_1/\kappa_2} \tag{22–5}$$

This equation shows that if $\kappa_2 < \kappa_1$, then $F_2 > F_1$. For instance, if a run is performed in a buffer of a certain concentration (conductivity) and at a certain field strength, about the same thermal zone deformation will be obtained in another run in the same capillary if the buffer is diluted 4-fold and the field strength is increased 2-fold. Even without consideration of the increase in mobility with a decrease in ionic strength[40] the run time will accordingly be shortened by 50%.

22.2.6 Creation of Narrow Starting Zones

22.2.6.1 Zone Sharpening by Decreasing the Conductivity in the Sample

When the sample concentration is too low for the solutes to be detectable a preconcentration is an alternative method that, however, is difficult to perform with satisfactory yield when the sample volume is already small. A better and faster technique is instead to apply the nonconcentrated sample in a wide zone and then carry out the concentration in connection with the electrophoresis experiment. Two variants of this method can be utilized. If the conductivity of the sample is much lower (say, five times) than that of the buffer an automatic sharpening of the applied zone takes place[41,42] according to Eqs. (22–1) and (22–2) (a short zone of the diluted buffer should also be applied behind the sample). When the sample has too high a conductivity for this alternative to be applicable and is available only in a small volume it is rather difficult to decrease the conductivity of the sample (for instance by dialysis or chromatographic desalting) without substantial losses of the solutes of interest. In such cases zone sharpening with the aid of discontinuous buffer systems as described below is the method of choice, provided that the solute is compatible with the composition and the operating pH of the system.

22.2.6.2 Zone Sharpening by Discontinuous Buffer Systems

Following the pioneering work of Ornstein[43] a great number of such buffer systems have been developed for polyacrylamide gel electrophoresis of proteins. These systems are often not directly applicable for electrophoresis in free solution, since they are partly based on the zone-sharpening effect of the molecular-sieving polyacrylamide gel. Proteins with higher mobilities will thus not be destacked in a carrier-free medium, i.e., they will migrate very close to each other and be recorded as one peak. Therefore, I have developed new discontinuous buffer systems suitable for the separation in free solution of proteins of any mobilities. These buffer systems have been designed to have better destacking properties than those used for polyacrylamide gel electrophoresis. This has been accomplished by the following approach:

1. New types of terminators are used that on an increase in pH acquire higher mobilities than do conventional terminators, for instance glycine (yet they must have a very low mobility in the stacking phase). Polyaminopolycarboxylic (sulfonic) acids are suitable candidates. An example is diaminopimelic acid (there are other compounds of the same type which should be more suitable but they are apparently not commercially available).
2. An increase in the concentration of the leading ion (often chloride) decreases the mobilities of proteins more than those of low-molecular-weight compounds. This statement can be proven with the aid of the Debye–Hückel theory (see ref. 29 on p. 770). However, as pointed out in Section 22.2.5 one should avoid excessively high buffer concentrations since they cause long run times.

The following buffer systems, based on the above ideas, have been used successfully for the analysis of proteins by free high-performance electrophresis.

A. Anode buffer: 0.10 *M* HCl, titrated to pH 9.6 with Tris, tris-(hydroxymethyl)aminomethane. Separation buffer: the same. Stacking buffer: 0.10 *M* HCl, titrated to pH 6.7 with Tris. Cathode solution: 0.06 *M* diaminopimelic acid, titrated to pH 7.7 with Tris.
B. Anode and cathode buffer: 0.09 *M* diaminopimelic acid, titrated to pH 8.4 with Tris. Separation buffer: 0.75 *M* Tris, titrated to pH 9.7 with HCl. Stacking buffer: 0.25 *M* Tris, titrated to pH 6.8 with sulfuric acid.

C. Anode and cathode buffer: 0.19 *M* taurine, titrated to pH 8.1 with Tris. Separation buffer: 0.12 *M* HCl, titrated to pH 8.1 with Tris. Stacking buffer: 0.25 *M* Tris, titrated to pH 6.8 with sulfuric acid.

The inset in the legend to Figure 22–9 shows the initial position of the different buffers.

22.3 THE HIGH-PERFORMANCE ELECTROPHORESIS APPARATUS

22.3.1 On-Tube Detection

The apparatus for on-tube detection is outlined in Figure 22–6. A zone Z in the electrophoresis tube T migrating past the UV (or fluorescence) detector (M-P) is registered as a peak on the recorder chart. The tube T, made of fused silica or glass, has thin walls (0.05–0.10 mm) to permit rapid dissipation of the Joule heat and thereby minimize thermal zone deformation. The slit in the shutter S has a width of 0.1–0.4 mm and a height approximately equal to the inner (or sometimes outer) diameter of the tube. A fixed position of the tube is guaranteed by a horizontal V-groove in the shutter.

Fused silica tubing is available from several companies, for instance Scientific Glass Engineering Pty, Ltd., 7 Argent Plan, Ringwood, Victoria 3134, Australia. The outside polyimide coating, applied to make the tubing more mechanically strong, is burnt off on the section of the silica tubing where the light beam from the monochromator M is to pass. Glass tubes, which are less brittle than the uncoated part of the fused silica tubing, can with advantage be used for wavelengths down to about 265 nm (the small wall thickness makes them transparent to these short wavelengths). We also employ them for micropreparative runs (see Section 22.3.2). The glass tubes can be purchased from Modulohm I/S, 6-8 Vasekaer, DK-2730 Herlev, Denmark.

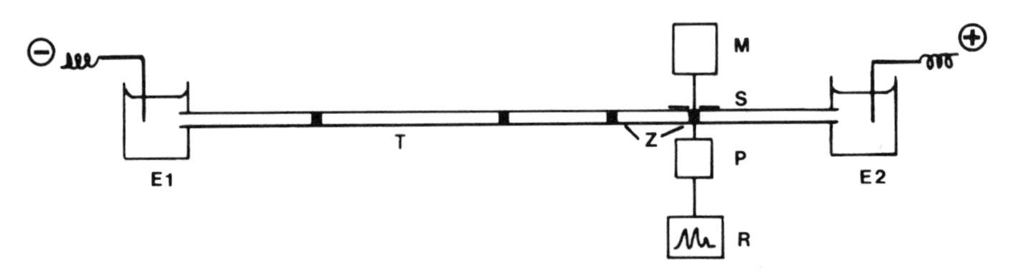

FIGURE 22–6. The analytical high-performance electrophoresis apparatus with on-tube monitoring. T, the (coated) electrophoresis tube (made from fused silica or glass); E1, E2, electrode vessels; M, monochromator; S, shutter with slit; P, photodiode with amplifier (or photomultiplier); R, recorder or an HPLC integrator; Z, solute zones.

Any laboratory that has an HPLC monitor or a spectrophotometer or equipment for scanning of gels in UV light (in all these the monochromator M and the detector D form one unit) can by a relatively simple attachment construct an apparatus for high-performance electrophoresis. A prerequisite is, however, that the light intensity in the UV beam is so high that the amount of light after passage of the small-dimension slit is large enough to give a recorder tracing without disturbing background noise.

22.3.2 Off-Tube Detection

The apparatus outlined in Figure 22–6 is designed for analytical purposes. For micropreparative runs we use the equipment depicted in Figure 22–7.[9,11,22] When the sample zones Z leave electrophoretically the glass capillary tube T they are transferred to an HPLC detector D and a fraction collector F by a stream of buffer delivered by the pump P. One might believe that the volume of the flow curvette in the HPLC detector must be much smaller than the volume of the zones in order not to impair the electrophoretic resolution of two adjacent zones. However, this condition need not be fulfilled if the pump speed (dilution factor) is so high that the two zones are not present at the same time in the

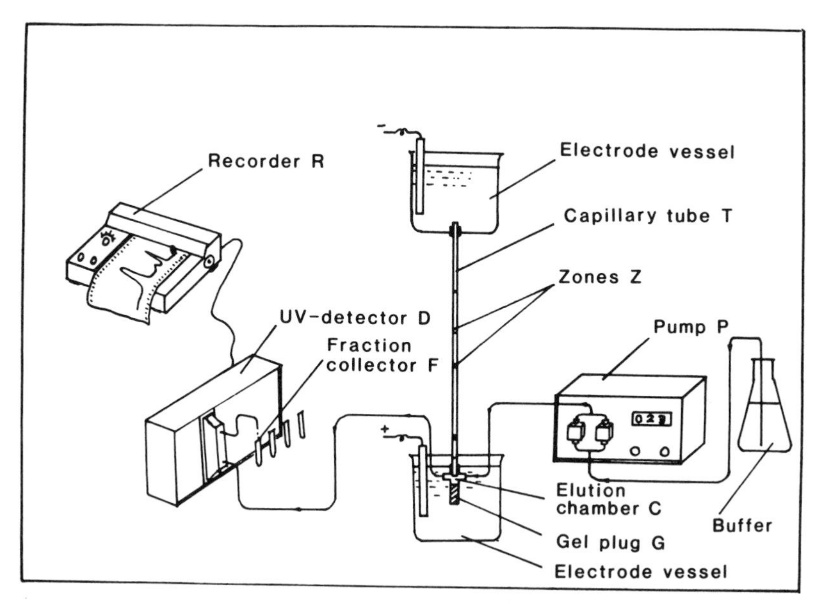

FIGURE 22–7. The micropreparative high-performance electrophoresis apparatus with off-tube monitoring. When the solute zones Z electrophoretically leave the capillary tube T and enter the elution chamber C they are transferred by a continuous buffer stream (delivered by the HPLC pump P) to the detector D (connected to a recorder R) and further to a fraction collector F. An interesting feature of the detection system is that the volume of the flow cuvette is considerably larger than that of the zone Z. The same detection method is applicable on microbore chromatography. (Reproduced with permission from ref. 22.)

flow cuvette of the HPLC monitor D (the cuvette volume is about 5 µl, i.e., larger than the volume of the whole capillary tube T). To emphasize again the analogies between electrophoresis and chromatography I would like to mention that this detection technique can be applied also in microbore HPLC. The advantage of this method is that any conventional HPLC detector based on absorption or fluorescence or other parameter can be used even if the volumes of the electrophoresis and chromatography columns are extremely small. A disadvantage in preparative runs, but not in analytical ones, is the dilution of the zones (the final zone volumes are still very small).

22.4 ISOELECTRIC FOCUSING

In isoelectric focusing the focused zones are stationary. To record them with the apparatus shown in Figures 22–6 and 22–7 they must be mobilized without distortion. This can be done either by pumping liquid through the electrophoresis tube without switching off the voltage applied to keep the zones sharp or by electrophoretic elution.[20] We prefer the latter method, which is treated theoretically in ref. 21 and which is the only alternative when the capillary tube is filled with a gel. In practice, this mobilization method is very simple and involves only addition of a salt, for instance 0.05 *M* sodium chloride to the anolyte (catholyte) for anodic (cathodic) elution. Another possibility is to replace the anolyte with the solution used as catholyte or vice versa.[20,21]

An inherent drawback of isoelectric focusing is that many proteins precipitate at their isoelectric points. In such cases the ampholyte solution should contain 10–30% ethylene glycol,[44,45] 1–3% of a neutral, non-UV-absorbing detergent,[46] for instance G 3707 (heptaoxyethylene lauryl ether),[47] or 6–8 *M* urea.[48]

Since the protein concentrations are very high (often 3–10%) in isoelectric focusing the detection of proteins can be performed without difficulty at 280 nm. Thin-walled capillaries made from glass instead of fused silica can therefore be used as separation tubes in the equipment outlined in Figure 22–6. Shorter wavelengths (and fused silica tubing) should not be used since the carrier ampholytes give a disturbing background absorption.

22.5 APPLICATIONS

22.5.1 High-Performance Carrier-Free Zone Electrophoresis

22.5.1.1 Peptide Separations, Including Manipulations of the Electropherogram with the Aid of Neutral Detergents

The fused silica electrophoresis tube had a length of 160 mm and an inner diameter of 0.05 mm. The sample consisted of the following peptides each at a concentration of 0.05 µg/µl: (1) α-neoendorphin (1–8), (2) dynorphin B, (3) Leu-enkephalin-Arg,[6] (4) Tyr-Gly-Gly, (5) contaminant from peptide 8, (6) Leu-enkephalin, (7) Met-enkephalin, and (8) D-Ala-D-Leu-enkephalin.

The run was conducted at 4000 V (12 μA) in 0.022 *M* sodium phosphate, pH 2.6. The sample, dissolved in the same buffer diluted 1:4 with water, was applied electrophoretically at 2000 V for 30 sec, corresponding to a load of about half a nanogram of peptide material. The detection was made on-tube at 185 nm.

The electropherogram in Figure 22–8a shows a very poor resolution between peptides 6, 7, and 8. However, when the experiment was repeated in the presence of 1% (w/v) G3707 (a neutral, non-UV-absorbing detergent[47]) they were well resolved (Figure 22–8b).

22.5.1.2 Peptide Separations: "Electrophoretic Mass Spectrometry"

A mixture of substance P and some of its degradation products was analyzed by HPE in 0.02 M sodium phosphate, pH 2.6 (the insert in Fig. 22–8c). The migration times (t) determined from the electropherogram were divided with that of substance P (t_o). A plot of these relative migration times (t/t_o) against $M^{2/3}/Z$ (M = the molecular weight of the peptide; Z = its valency) gave a straight line (Fig. 22–8c). Such calibration graphs permit the determination of the molecular weight (or the charge) of an unknown peptide from its migration time.

22.5.1.3 Analysis of Human Serum in a Discontinuous Buffer System

The fused silica tube had an inner diameter of 0.1 mm and a length of about 120 mm. The buffer system is described in detail in the legend to Figure 22–9. At a voltage of 3000 V the analysis was finished within 10 min. The detection was made at 215 nm.

22.5.2 High-Performance Polyacrylamide Gel Electrophoresis

22.5.2.1 Micropreparative Peptide Separations

Substance P, a putative neurotransmitter in sensory nerves, is built up of 11 amino acids. After synaptic release this peptide is inhibited—probably by enzymatic degradation. In a study of the degradation mechanism substance P was hydrolyzed with a peptidase and the cleavage products were identified by high-performance electrophoresis. The experiments were performed in the micropreparative equipment[9,11,22] depicted in Figure 22–7. The length of the electrophoresis tube, made of glass, was 200 mm and the inner diameter was 0.2 mm. A polyacrylamide gel of the total concentration $T = 3\%$ and the cross-linking concentration $C = 4\%$ was photopolymerized in the tube (for definition of C and T, see refs. 49 and 50). Phosphoric acid (0.01 *M*), titrated to pH 2.6 with sodium hydroxide, served as buffer. The sample was electrophoresed into the gel for 1 min at 1500 V. The pump speed was 0.08 ml/min and the monitoring was done at 220 nm. The following three samples were applied: Substance P (SP); SP treated for 60 min with the endopeptidase; and SP treated for 120 min with the endopeptidase. The electropherograms are shown in Figure 22–10a–c. The degradation products (peaks) could be identified by

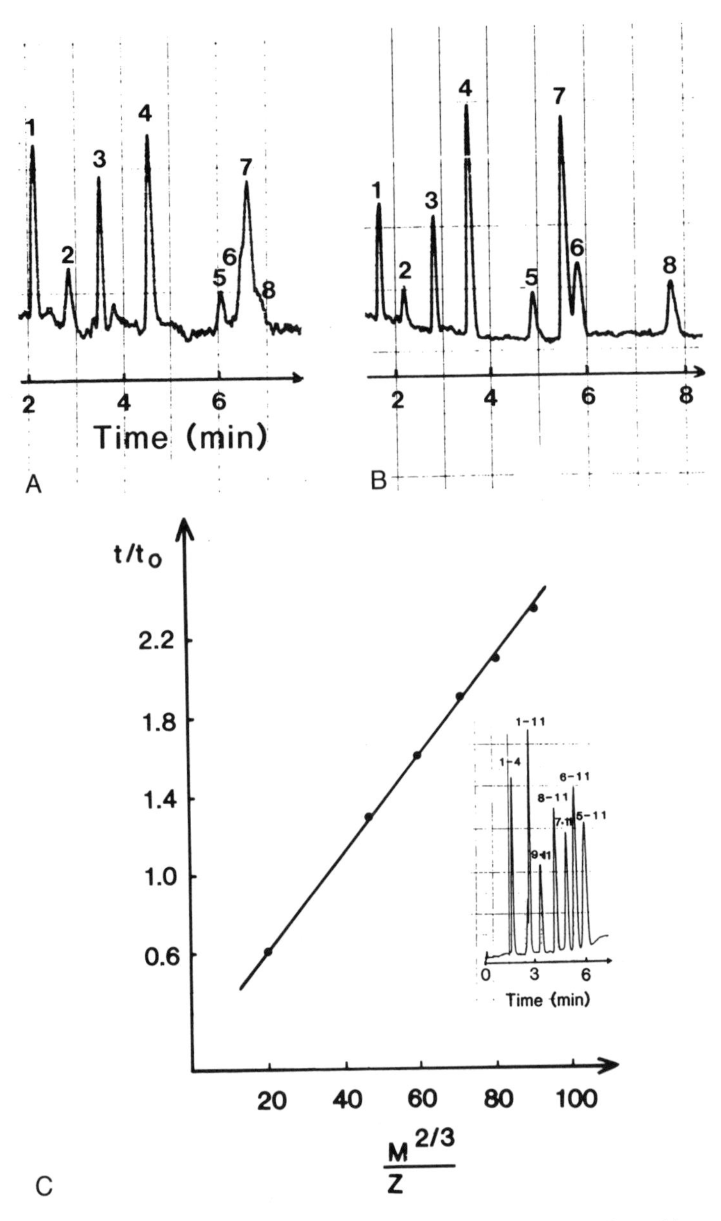

FIGURE 22–8. High-performance free zone electrophoresis of peptides. **a,b** Sample: endorphins. The experiments in a and b were performed in the absence and in the presence of G3707 (a nonionic detergent), respectively. Observe that peptides 6, 7, and 8 are much better resolved in experiment b than in a, due to hydrophobic interactions with the G3707 micelles. Also note that the order of migration of peptides 6 and 7 is different in a and b, owing to the higher hydrophobicity of peptide 6. The experiment was performed by Drs. J.-I. Liao and F. Nyberg, Biomedical Center, Uppsala. **c.** Sample: Substance P (1-11) and the fragments 1-4, 9-11, 8-11, 7-11, 6-11 and 5-11. The calibration curve was constructed from the electropherogram (the inset).

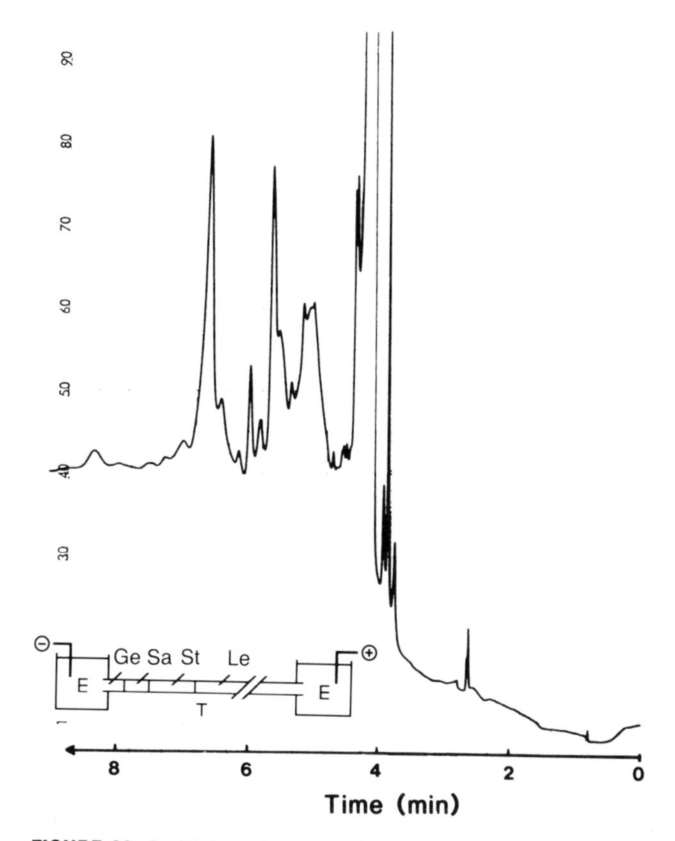

FIGURE 22–9. High-performance free electrophoresis of normal human serum. The inset shows the composition of the discontinuous buffer system at the start of the run. E, Electrode buffer (0.09 *M* diaminopimelic acid, titrated to pH 8.4 with Tris). Le, leading buffer (0.75 *M* Tris, titrated to pH 9.7 with hydrochloric acid). St, stacking solution (0.25 *M* Tris, titrated to pH 6.8 with sulfuric acid). Sa, sample of serum, diluted 1:1 with stacking solution, which was diluted 1:5 with water. Ge, gel plug, prepared in E. (Reproduced with permission from ref. 29 on p. 770.)

rerunning the third sample to which synthetic SP fragments of known structure had been added (spiking).

22.5.2.2 A Comparison of the Protein Patterns Obtained in Free Solution and in Polyacrylamide in the Presence of SDS

The fused silica electrophoresis tube had the length 130 mm and the inner diameter 0.1 mm. The sample consisted of the following model proteins, each at a concentration of 0.3 μg/μl: β-lactoglobulin (A), human transferrin (B), equine myoglobin (C), bovine carbonic anhydrase (D), and human carbonic anhydrase (E). The following discontinuous buffer system was used: Leading

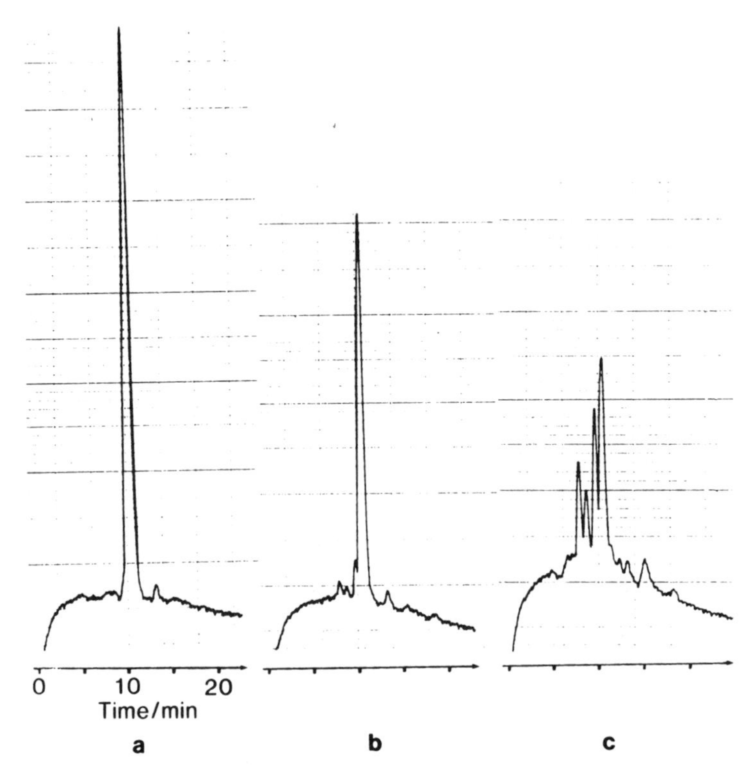

FIGURE 22–10. Micropreparative high-performance polyacrylamide gel electrophoresis of substance P and its degradation products. Sample: substance P (a) and the same substance after treatment with an endopeptidase for 60 min (b) and 120 min (c). The experiment was performed by Drs. F. Nyberg and M.-d. Zhu, Biomedical Center, Uppsala.

buffer: 0.06 *M* hydrochloric acid, titrated to pH 9.8 with Tris. Stacking buffer: 0.12 *M* Tris, titrated to pH 6.8 with sulfuric acid. Electrode buffer: 0.19 *M* glycine, titrated to pH 8.5 with Tris.

The sample was applied electrophoretically. The analysis was performed at 3000 V. The same model proteins were also subjected to polyacrylamide gel electrophoresis in 0.05 *M* sodium borate (pH 8.9) in the presence of 0.1% sodium dodecyl sulfate (SDS) in order to emphasize the difference in separation pattern obtained with this method (Figure 22–11b) and free electrophoresis (Figure 22–11a). The experiment was conducted at 1000 V, corresponding to a current of 5 μA. The polyacrylamide gel had the total concentration $T = 6\%$ and the cross-linking concentration $C = 3\%$. In the presence of SDS the proteins A, B, C, D and E have the approximate molecular weights of 18000, 80000, 17000, 30000, and 30000, respectively.

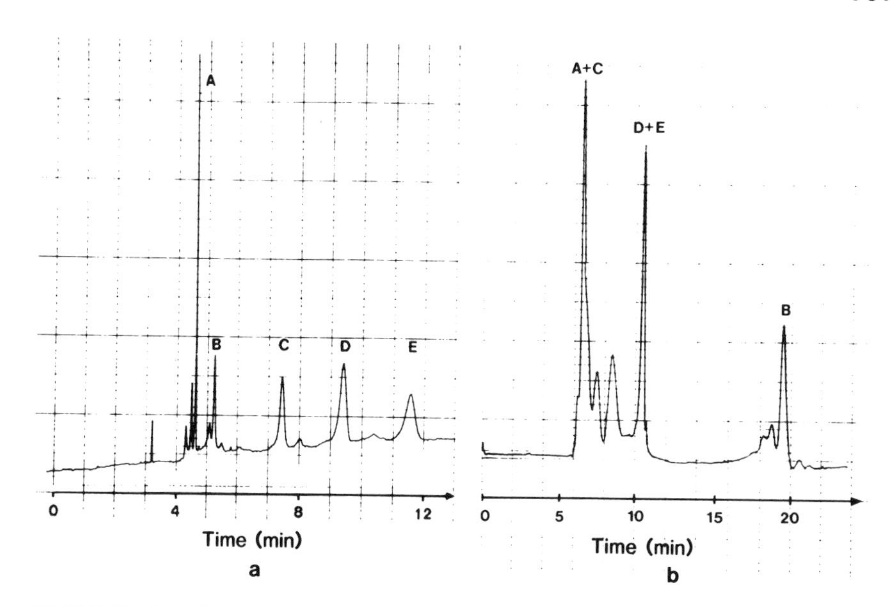

FIGURE 22–11. High-performance electrophoresis of proteins in free solution (a) and in a polyacrylamide gel in the presence of SDS (b). The same proteins (A–E) were used in a and b. This figure illustrates the difference in the separation mechanism between these two methods and the importance of utilizing both methods for analysis and purification of proteins. For details, see text. (Reproduced with permission from ref. 17.)

22.5.3 High-Performance Carrier-Free Isoelectric Focusing

22.5.3.1 Separation of Model Proteins

The run was performed in a fused silica tube with the length 120 mm and the inner diameter 0.1 mm. The sample, carbamylated carbonic anhydrase (carbamylyte™), was a gift from Dr. Jorge Lizana, Pharmacia, Uppsala, Sweden, and was delivered as a freeze-dried powder in a vial. The contents of the vial were dissolved in 50 μl of water. About 15 μl of this protein solution was added to 200 μl of a 1% (v/v) solution of Biolyte™ (pH 3–10) containing 8 *M* urea (Biolyte is a carrier ampholyte obtained from Bio-Rad Laboratories, Richmond, CA). The fused silica tube was filled with this mixture. Sodium hydroxide 0.02 *M* containing 8 *M* urea served as anolyte and 0.02 *M* phosphoric acid containing 8 *M* urea as catholyte. Following focusing for 7 min at 3000 V the anode solution was replaced by 0.02 *M* sodium hydroxide containing 8 *M* urea. Without deterioration of the resolution the focused protein bands then moved toward the anode and could be detected at 280 nm. The large number of peaks in the recorder tracing indicates a very high resolution (Figure 22–12).

Thormann et al.[51–54] described isoelectric focusing experiments in free solution in a 10-cm capillary of rectangular cross section. Their approach is very interesting, since it allows one to observe the dynamics of the electric field to be followed during focusing via the use of a linear array of potential gradient sensors.

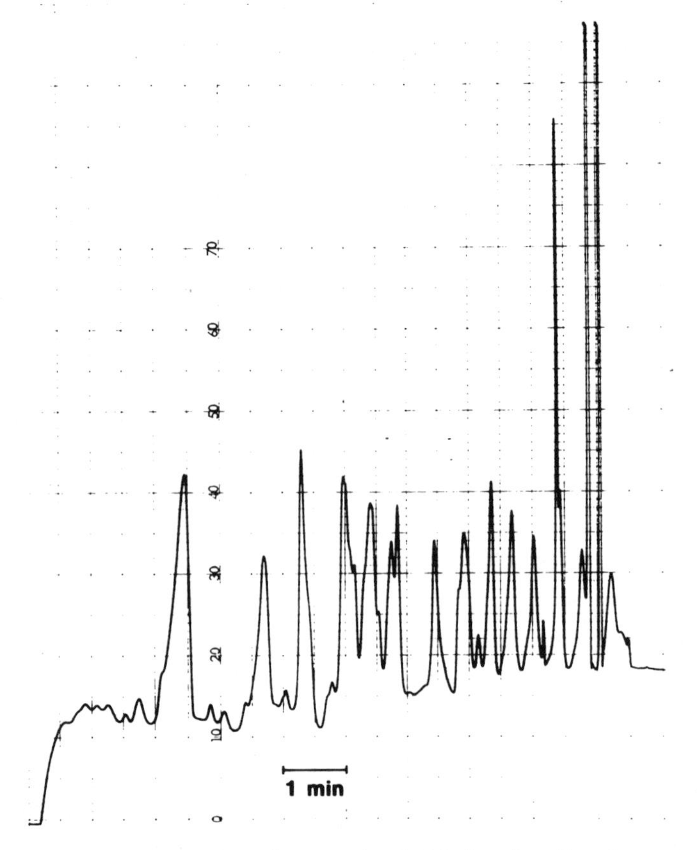

FIGURE 22–12. High-performance isoelectric focusing. Sample: Carbamylyte™ (carbamylated carbonic anhydrase). Dimensions of the fused silica electrophoresis tube: 0.1 (i.d.) × 120 mm. Carrier ampholyte: 1% Biolyte™ (pH 3–10) in 8 *M* urea. Following focusing for 7 min at 3000 V the focused proteins were mobilized to pass the detector by replacing the phosphoric acid at the anode with sodium hydroxide.

22.6 DISCUSSION

22.6.1 Resolution

A common way to increase the resolution in electrophoresis is to include in the buffer a substance that interacts more or less specifically with the solutes of interest. This approach was utilized to achieve a better separation between Leu-enkephalin, Met-enkephalin, and D-Ala-D-Leu-enkephalin by performing the run in the presence of the nonionic detergent G3707 (see Figure 22–8). As expected, in the presence of G3707 Leu-enkephalin migrated more slowly than Met-enkephalin, since it is more nonpolar and therefore should have a stronger hydrophobic interaction with the G3707 micelles. Since these micelles are nonionic they do not increase the ionic strength of the electrophoresis buffer, which is important in order to minimize the run times (see Section 22.2.5) and thereby zone broadening due to diffusion. In this respect the nonionic detergents are preferable to the ionic ones, for instance, sodium dodecyl sulfate (SDS), although even the latter can be used to give high resolution of low-molecular-weight compounds, as convincingly shown by Terabe et al.[25,35] and Cohen et al.[28] Electrophoresis in detergent—containing buffers corresponds to micellar chromatography—is another example of the analogy between electrophoresis and chromatography. Instead of detergents one can use polymers (for instance starch, dextran) to change the appearance of an electropherogram. Since every detergent and every polymer affects the separation pattern in a rather specific manner one should try different types of detergents and polymers to get optimal resolution.

Human serum is a very appropriate sample to test the resolving power of a new separation method, partly because many people from different disciplines are interested in this protein mixture, partly because the separation patterns obtained in a variety of chromatographic and electrophoretic analysis methods are well known and therefore can be easily compared with that given by the new method. Such a comparison with the electropherogram presented in Figure 22–9 shows that carrier-free HPE with automatic zone sharpening gives considerably higher resolution of proteins than any other method for free electrophoresis (or for electrophoresis in a nonsieving medium, for instance, agarose gels). The resolving power for serum proteins seems to be close to that typical of polyacrylamide gel electrophoresis and superior to that obtained in both high-performance ion-exchange and hydrophobic-interaction chromatography.

Isoelectric focusing might be the most highly resolving separation method for proteins (Figure 22–12). An obvious disadvantage is that several proteins precipitate at the pH corresponding to their isoelectric point. This precipitation can, however, be suppressed or eliminated if the focusing is run in the presence of a netural detergent, ethylene glycol or urea as mentioned in Section 22.4. The latter additive is very effective for keeping the proteins in solution but unfortunately denatures them. It is easy to decide whether a peak corresponds to a precipitate or a protein in solution, since the former peak is extremely sharp (like a spike).

In chromatography, separation efficiency is often calculated from the equation

$$N = 5.54 \left(\frac{t}{w_{1/2}}\right)^2 \qquad (22\text{–}6)$$

where N is the theoretical plate number, t the retention time, and $w_{1/2}$ the peak width at half the peak height (expressed in time units).

The same equation can be used in HPE in a straightforward way, provided that electroendosmosis is negligible. The situation is more complicated when this condition is not fulfilled, since electroendosmosis affects the peak width, as is evident from the following considerations.

As described in Section 22.2.4 the width of a peak on the recorder chart is inversely proportional to the speed with which the zone passes the slit in the UV detector. In an electroendosmosis-free capillary tube this speed is equal to the electrophoretic velocity, whereas in a noncoated glass or fused silica tube the speed is equal to the difference between the electroendosmotic and electrophoretic velocity. Since the latter speed is considerably lower than the former the peaks will be more narrow in the noncoated tube. The interesting conclusion is that the theoretical plate numbers reported in the literature for electrophoresis in noncoated glass and fused silica tubes are not true plate numbers, which are considerably lower. However, in the absence of adsorption and other disturbances the resolution between two adjacent peaks is the same in a coated (electroendosmosis-free) and noncoated tube, provided that the electrophoretic migration distances are identical in the two tubes. A mathematical treatment of plate numbers in the absence and presence of electroendosmosis will be published elsewhere (see ref. 29 on p. 770).

22.6.2 Run Times

In none of the experiments presented herein does the run time exceed 25 min. In this respect HPE thus competes favorably both with HPLC and with other electrophoresis techniques. The times can be shorter if the electrophoresis tube is surrounded by a streaming coolant. However, a cooling system requires a more complicated equipment and has not been utilized in the experiments described herein, since in this chapter I want to show what can be performed with the simplest possible apparatus.

22.6.3 Sensitivity

When the sample concentration is low and the detection is based on UV measurements wavelengths ranging from 185 to 205 nm must be used where the absorption coefficients of peptides and proteins (and many other substances) are very high. This detection technique requires that the electrophoresis buffer has negligible absorption at these wavelengths, and therefore we often use phosphate or borate buffers. The experiment shown in Figure 22–8 is an example. This experiment will now be used for calculation of the sensitivity of the detection method when a wavelength as short as 185 nm is utilized. Since the sample was applied by a preelectrophoresis, the lengths of the initial starting zones of the different components were different and roughly proportional to the mobilities of the components, as mentioned in Section 22.2.4. If we assume that the average length of the starting zones was 1 mm and that the sample was concentrated 5-fold (as a consequence of its low ionic strength) then the amount of a sample component in this zone is $5 \times 0.05 \times \pi \times 0.025^2 \times 1 = 0.0005\ \mu g = 0.5$ ng. The sensitivity at 185 nm is accordingly high enough to permit analysis of most peptide samples. In reversed-phase high-performance liquid chromatography the strong UV absorption of impurities in the organic solvents does in general not permit the use of a wavelength as short as 185 nm, at least not in gradient runs.

The peptide separation discussed was performed in the analytical apparatus shown in Figure 22–6. Also, the micropreparative equipment (Figure 22–7) permits isolation on a nanogram scale, as illustrated in ref. 12 by a fractionation of human growth hormone into species of the same molecular weight but different net surface charge densities.

HPE can be a complement to reversed-phase HPLC for peptide studies, particularly in the micropreparative version (Figure 22–7), which permits collection of peptide fractions for further experiments, for instance, amino acid analyses, sequence determinations, and mass spectrometry.

22.6.4 Adsorption

To suppress adsorption the tube wall can be coated with hydrophilic silanes—a method widely employed to decrease the nonspecific adsorption onto silica beads used as packing material in chromatography. However, the wall of these treated tubes is still negatively charged, as is revealed by the fact that electroendosmosis is so strong that anions migrate "backward" toward the cathode. In such electrophoresis tubes basic compounds will be adsorbed. Lauer and McManigill suggested that the tube should be coated with positively charged substances for analysis of these compounds to achieve repulsion between solute and tube wall and thus suppress adsorption.[15]

The polymer coating used in the experiments described herein has the advantage to be useful for both acidic and basic solutes.[13] Since these polymer-coated tubes are free from electroendosmosis they can be relatively short and still give high resolution (the electroendosmosis itself only transports the solutes but does not cause any separation in free electrophoresis except when the sample solutes interact reversibly and to a different degree with the tube wall). For a given field strength the short electrophoresis tubes require a relatively low voltage, which decreases the risk of electrical shock.

22.6.5 Polyacrylamide Gel Electrophoresis

The separation pattern obtained in free zone electrophoresis of proteins will in general not change on addition of detergents in such a way that the resolution increases, as is the case for low-molecular-weight substances (see Figure 22–8). In fact, in the presence of SDS all proteins acquire the same zeta-potential and accordingly migrate in free solution with about the same velocity. However, if the electrophoresis tube contains a molecular-sieving gel, for instance polyacrylamide, the proteins will separate roughly according to their molecular weights when SDS is included in the buffer (Figure 22–11b). The separation pattern in this figure differs markedly from that obtained on free electrophoresis of the same proteins in the absence of SDS (Figure 22–11a). Accordingly, if free electrophoresis does not give the desired protein separation one should investigate whether a polyacrylamide gel electrophoresis (with and without SDS) increases the resolution and vice versa. Since proteins have a tendency to precipitate on coming into contact with a polyacrylamide gel and therefore often clog the "pore" at the top of the gel (see ref. 45) a polyacrylamide-gel-containing electrophoresis tube has a limited lifetime. Sometimes it stands only one run. A prerun with reversed poles between each experiment often has a favorable effect, since this may "clear out" the pores. Dust and other particles in the buffer and sample should be removed by filtration, since they also can clog the gel pores. Below 280 nm the polyacrylamide gels have a relatively strong UV absorption, which is not constant during a run. The absorption is lower, however, if the tubes are used the day after the gel was prepared. The best way to get rid of the disturbing polyacrylamide gel absorption is to fill only part of the tube with gel and let the detecting UV beam pass through the section of the tube that contains only buffer (alternatively, one can connect two tubes, one containing only buffer and one containing buffer and gel). The tube section used for the free electrophoresis step must be coated with a polymer to eliminate electroendosmosis.[13] Otherwise, the proteins will migrate "backward" and cannot be detected. When a protein zone migrates out of the gel into free solution it broadens considerably, since the migration velocity is much faster in free buffer than in the polyacrylamide gel. However, this will not make the peaks on the recorder chart significantly broader, since the width of a peak is inversely proportional to the speed with which the corresponding zone in the tube passes the slit S (see Figure 22–6) in the UV detector.

As mentioned, in the presence of SDS all proteins migrate with the same velocity in free solution. Therefore, the appearance of the electropherograms will be the same independently of whether the detecting UV beam passes the gel section of the electrophoresis tube or the section containing buffer alone. The situation is different when the buffer does not contain SDS, since in this case proteins that migrate with similar velocities in the molecular-sieving polyacrylamide gel can migrate with quite different velocities in free solution, and vice versa. The resolution can accordingly be higher or lower when the detection is made in the free buffer section instead of in the gel section. However, if the proteins migrate only a short distance in the free solution the resolution is almost independent of which of the two detection methods is used. However, I recommend detection in free solution, since before we introduced it we could not reproducibly monitor proteins. This method is a prerequisite for detection at the extremely short wavelengths (185–210 nm) that must be used when the protein concentrations are low (polyacrylamide gels are only little permeable to these wavelengths).

22.6.6 HPLC–HPE

From being an important tool for the separation of low-molecular-weight compounds HPLC has been developed during the last 10 years to a high-resolution method for the fractionation of macromolecules, which should be evident from the articles in this book. This chapter shows that HPE is also a powerful method both for the separation of small molecules, such as peptides (see Figures 22–8 and 22–10) and of biopolymers (Figures 22–9, 22–11, and 22–12). HPE is therefore a good complement to HPLC—particularly when it has become automated and commercially available. Characteristic of both HPLC and HPE are high resolution; short experimental times; the capability of separating small amounts of material on both an analytical (Figures 22–8, 22–9, 22–11, and 22–12) and micropreparative scale (Figure 22–10); and no time-consuming staining procedures for detection of the analytes as in conventional agarose and polyacrylamide gel electrophoresis. The latter methods have, however, the advantage of permitting analysis of several samples in the same run. This possibility is of importance in routine analyses of a great number of samples, particularly when they are to be compared with each other.

High-performance electrophoresis in the form of isoelectric focusing or free zone electrophoresis in discontinuous buffer systems is ideal for fast analyses of HPLC fractions, since the zone-sharpening effect of these two methods makes it possible to apply relatively large volumes of dilute solutions and yet get high resolution. A preconcentration is thus not necessary. Displacement electrophoresis has the same advantage (see ref. 30 on p. 770).

ACKNOWLEDGMENTS

The author is much indebted to the following co-workers for their contribution in different forms to the development of high-performance electrophoresis: K. Elenbring, F. Kilàr, J.-l. Liao, C. Lindh, P.-A. Lidström, H. Pettersson, L. Valtcheva, K. Yao, and M.-d. Zhu. The work has been financially supported by the Swedish Natural Science Research Council and the Knut and Alice Wallenberg and Carl Trygger Foundations.

REFERENCES

1. S. Hjertén, in Protides of the Biological Fluids, Proceedings of the 7th Colloquium, Bruges, 1959 (H. Peeters, ed.). Elsevier, Amsterdam, 1960, pp. 28–30.
2. S. Hjertén, *Chromatogr. Rev.*, 9 (1967) 122.
3. F. M. Everaerts, Displacement Electrophoresis in Narrow Hole Tubes. Doctoral Thesis. Technical University of Eindhoven, 1968.
4. F. E. P. Mikkers, F. M. Everaerts, and Th. P. E. M. Verheggen, *J. Chromatogr.*, 169 (1979) 11.
5. S. Hjertén, *Arkiv Kemi*, 13 (1958) 151.
6. J. W. Jorgenson and K. D. Lukacs, *J. Chromatogr.*, 218 (1981) 209.
7. R. Virtanen, *Acta Polytech. Scand. Chem.*, 123 (1974) 1.
8. S. Hjertén, *J. Chromatogr.*, 270 (1983) 1.
9. M.-d. Zhu and S. Hjertén, in Electrophoresis '84 (V. Neuhoff, ed.). Verlag Chemie, Weinheim, 1984, pp. 110–113.
10. Y. Walbroehl and J. W. Jorgenson, *J. Chromatogr.*, 315 (1984) 135.
11. S. Hjertén and M.-d. Zhu, *J. Chromatogr.*, 327 (1985) 157.
12. S. Hjertén and M.-d. Zhu, in Protides of the Biological Fluids, Proceedings of the 33rd Colloquium, Brussels, 1985 (H. Peeters, ed.). Pergamon Press, Oxford, 1985, pp. 537–540.
13. S. Hjertén, *J. Chromatogr.*, 347 (1985) 191.
14. H. H. Lauer, D. McManigill, and T. A. Berger, Abstract no. 893, Pittsburgh Conference and Exposition, New Orleans, 1985.

15. H. H. Lauer and D. McManigill, *Anal. Chem.*, 58 (1986) 166.
16. J. W. Jorgenson and K. D. Lukacs, *Science*, 222 (1983) 266.
17. S. Hjertén, K. Elenbring, F. Kilàr, J.-l. Liao, A. J. C. Chen, C. J. Siebert, and M.-d. Zhu, *J. Chromatogr.*, 403 (1987) 47.
18. S. Hjertén, in Electrophoresis '83 (H. Hirai, ed.). Walter de Gruyter, Berlin, 1984, pp. 71–79.
19. A. S. Cohen and B. L. Karger, *J. Chromatogr.*, 397 (1987) 409.
20. S. Hjertén and M.-d. Zhu, *J. Chromatogr.*, 346 (1985) 265.
21. S. Hjertén, J.-l. Liao, and K. Yao, *J. Chromatogr.*, 387 (1987) 127.
22. S. Hjertén and M.-d. Zhu, in Physical Chemistry of Colloids and Macromolecules, Proceedings of the Svedberg Symposium in Uppsala, August 22–24, 1984 (B. Råby, ed.). Blackwell Scientific Publications, London, 1987, pp. 133–136.
23. T. Tsuda, K. Nomura, and G. Nakagawa. *J. Chromatogr.*, 248 (1982) 241.
24. P. Gebauer, M. Deml, P. Boček, and J. Janák, *J. Chromatogr.*, 267 (1983) 455.
25. S. Terabe, K. Otsuka, K. Ichikawa, A. Tsuchiya, and T. Ando, *Anal. Chem.*, 56 (1984) 111.
26. E. Gassmann, J. E. Kuo, and R. N. Zare, *Science*, 230 (1985) 813.
27. J. S. Green and J. W. Jorgenson, *J. Chromatogr.*, 352 (1986) 337.
28. A. S. Cohen, S. Terabe, J. A. Smith, and B. L. Karger, *Anal. Chem.*, 59 (1987) 1021.
29. G. Schill and J. Crommen, TrAC, 6 (1987) 111.
30. H. Svensson, *Acta Chem. Scand.*, 15 (1961) 325.
31. H. Svensson, *Acta Chem. Scand.*, 16 (1962) 456.
32. L. A. AE. Sluyterman and O. Elgersma, *J. Chromatogr.*, 150 (1978) 17.
33. L. A. AE. Sluyterman and J. Wijdenes, *J. Chromatogr.*, 150 (1978) 31.
34. J. C. Giddings, in Dynamics of Chromatography: Part I, Principles and Theory. Edward Arnold, London, and Dekker, New York, 1965.
35. S. Terabe, K. Otsuha, and T. Ando. *Anal. Chem.*, 57 (1985) 834.
36. B. G. Johansson and S. Hjertén, *Anal. Biochem.*, 59 (1974) 200.
37. S. Hjertén, in Topics in Bioelectrochemistry and Bioenergetics, Vol. 2 (G. Milazzo, ed.). Wiley, New York, 1978, pp. 271–333.
38. B. J. Radola, *Electrophoresis*, 1 (1980) 43.
39. S. Honda, S. Iwase, and S. Fujiwara, *J. Chromatogr.*, 404 (1987) 313.
40. A. Tiselius and H. Svensson, *Trans. Faraday Soc.*, 36 (1940) 16.
41. H. Haglund and A. Tiselius, *Acta Chem. Scand.*, 4 (1950) 957.
42. J. Porath, *Biochim. Biophys. Acta*, 22 (1956) 151.
43. L. Ornstein, *Ann. N.Y. Acad. Sci.*, 121 (1964) 321.
44. R. E. Jones, W. A. Hemmings, and W. Page Faulk, *Immunochemistry*, 8 (1971) 299.
45. S. Hjertén, H. Pan, and K. Yao, in Protides of the Biological Fluids, Proceedings of the 29th Colloquium, Brussels, 1981 (H. Peeters, ed.). Pergamon Press, Oxford, 1982, pp. 15–25.
46. A. D. Friesen, J. C. Jamieson, and F. E. Ashton, *Anal. Biochem.*, 41 (1971) 149.
47. D. A. W. Grant and S. Hjertén, *Biochem. J.*, 164 (1977) 465.
48. P. H. O'Farrel, *J. Biol. Chem.*, 250 (1975) 4007.
49. S. Hjertén, In "Methods of Immunochemistry," Vol. II. Chase, M. W. and Williams, C. A. Eds. Academic Press, Inc., 1968, pp. 142–150.
50. S. Hjertén, *Arch. Biochem. Biophys.*, Suppl. 1 (1962) 147.
51. W. Thormann, G. Twitty, A. Tsai, and M. Bier, in Electrophoresis '84 (V. Neuhoff, ed.). Verlag Chemie, Weinheim, 1984, pp. 114–117.
52. W. Thormann, R. A. Mosher, and M. Bier, *J. Chromatogr.*, 351 (1986) 17.
53. W. Thormann, N. B. Egen, R. A. Mosher, and M. Bier, *J. Biochem. Biophys. Methods*, 11 (1985) 287.
54. W. Thormann, A. Tsai, J.-P. Michaud, R. A. Mosher, and M. Bier, *J. Chromatogr.*, 389 (1987) 75.

RECENT DEVELOPMENTS

The progress in high-performance capillary electrophoresis (HPCE) is very rapid and therefore it is urgent to inform the reader about some of the advances published after this chapter was written. For that reason I have listed below some recent references on capillary electrophoresis of peptides and proteins. The titles of the papers are inserted to enable the reader to select what is of personal interest.

1. Hjertén, S.; Kilár, F.; Liao, J.-l. and Zhu, M.-d. "Use of high-performance electrophoresis apparatus for isoelectric focusing." In "Electrophoresis '86", Dunn, M. J. Ed.; VCH Verlagsgesellschaft; Weinheim, 1986, pp. 451–461.
2. Beckers, J. L.; Verheggen, Th. P. E. M. and Everaerts, F. M. "Use of a double-detector system for the measurement of mobilities in zone electrophoresis." *J. Chromatogr.* 1988, *452*, 591.
3. Verheggen, Th. P. E. M.; Beckers, J. L. and Everaerts, F. M. "Simple sampling device for capillary isotachophoresis and capillary zone electrophoresis." *J. Chromatogr.*, 1988, *452*, 615.
4. Thormann, W.; Firestone, M. A.; Dietz, M. L.; Cecconie, T. and Mosher, R. A. "Focusing counterparts of electrical field flow fractionation and capillary zone electrophoresis. Electrical hyperlayer field flow fractionation and capillary isoelectric focusing." *J. Chromatogr.*, 1989, *461*, 95.
5. Liu, J.; Cobb, K. A. and Novotny, M. "Separation of precolumn *ortho*-phthalaldehyde-derivatized amino acids by capillary zone electrophoresis with normal and micellar solutions in the presence of organic modifiers." *J. Chromatogr.*, 1989, *468*, 55.
6. Stover, F. S.; Haymore, B. L. and McBeath, R. J. "Capillary zone electrophoresis of histidine-containing compounds." *J. Chromatogr.*, 1989, *470*, 241.
7. Bruin, G. J. M.; Chang, J. P.; Kuhlman, R. H.; Zegers, K.; Kraak, J. C. and Poppe H. "Capillary zone electrophoretic separations of proteins in polyethylene glycol-modified capillaries." *J. Chromatogr.*, 1989, *471*, 429.
8. Nelson, R. J.; Paulus, A.; Cohen, A. S.; Guttman, A. and Karger, B. L. "Use of peltier thermoelectric devices to control column temperature in high-performance capillary electrophoresis." *J. Chromatogr.*, 1989, *480*, 111.
9. Wu, S. and Dovichi, N. J. "High-sensitivity fluorescence detector for fluorescein isothiocyanate derivatives of amino acids separated by capillary zone electrophoresis." *J. Chromatogr.*, 1989, *480*, 141.
10. Bushey, M. M. and Jorgenson, J. W. "Capillary electrophoresis of proteins in buffers containing high concentrations of zwitterionic salts." *J. Chromatogr.*, 1989, *480*, 301.
11. Zhu, M.; Hansen, D. L.; Burd, S. and Gannon, F. "Factors affecting free zone electrophoresis and isoelectric focusing in capillary electrophoresis." *J. Chromatogr.*, 1989, *480*, 311.
12. Kilár, F. and Hjertén, S. "Separation of the human transferrin isoforms by carrier-free high-performance zone electrophoresis and isoelectric focusing." *J. Chromatogr.*, 1989, *480*, 351.
13. Karger, B. L.; Cohen, A. S. and Guttman, A. "High-performance capillary electrophoresis in the biological sciences." *J. Chromatogr., Biomed. Appl.* 1989, *492*, 585.
14. Kilár, F. and Hjertén, S. "Fast and high resolution analysis of human serum transferrin by high-performance isoelectric focusing in capillaries." *Electrophoresis* 1989, *10*, 23.
15. Hjertén, S.; Valtcheva, L.; Elenbring, K. and Eaker, D. "High-performance electrophoresis of acidic and basic low-molecular-weight compounds and of proteins in the presence of polymers and neutral surfactants." *J. Liq. Chrom.*, 1989, *12 (13)*, 2471.

16. Rohlícek, V. and Deyl, Z. "Simple apparatus for capillary zone electrophoresis and its application to protein analysis." *J. Chromatogr., Biomed. Appl.* 1989, *494*, 87.
17. Mück, W. M. and Henion, J. D. "Determination of leucine enkephalin and methionine enkephalin in equine cerebrospinal fluid by microbore high-performance liquid chromatography and capillary zone electrophoresis coupled to tandem mass spectrometry." *J. Chromatogr., Biomed. Appl.* 1989, *495*, 41.
18. Kaniansky, D. and Marák, J. "On-line coupling of capillary isotachophoresis with capillary zone electrophoresis." *J. Chromatogr.*, 1990, *498*, 191.
19. Boček, P.; Deml, M. and Pospíchal, J. "New option in capillary zone electrophoresis. Use of a transient ionic matrix (dynamic pulse)." *J. Chromatogr.*, 1990, *500*, 673.
20. Towns, J. K. and Regnier, F. E. "Polyethyleneimine-bonded phases in the separation of proteins by capillary electrophoresis." *J. Chromatogr.*, 1990, *516*, 69.
21. Josic, D.; Zeilinger, K. and Reutter, W. "High-performance capillary electrophoresis of hydrophobic membrane proteins." *J. Chromatogr.*, 1990, *516*, 89.
22. Wu, S.-L.; Teshima, G.; Cacia, J. and Hancock, W. "Use of high-performance capillary electrophoresis to monitor charge heterogeneity in recombinant-DNA derived proteins." *J. Chromatogr.*, 1990, *516*, 115.
23. Zhu, M.-d.; Rodriguez, R.; Hansen, D. and Wehr, T. "Capillary electrophoresis of proteins under alkaline conditions." *J. Chromatogr.*, 1990, *516*, 123.
24. Tsuda, T.; Sweedler, J. V. and Zare, R. N. "Rectangular capillaries for capillary zone electrophoresis." *Anal. Chem.*, 1990, *62*, 2149.
25. Cobb, K. A.; Dolnik, V. and Novotny, M. "Electrophoretic separations of proteins in capillaries with hydrolytically stable surface structures." *Anal. Chem.*, 1990, *62*, 2478.
26. Liu, J.; Cobb, K. A. and Novotny, M. "Capillary electrophoretic separations of peptides using micelle-forming compounds and cyclodextrins as additives." *J. Chromatogr.*, 1990, *519*, 189.
27. Yin, H. F.; Lux, J. A. and Schomburg, G. "Production of polyacrylamide gel filled capillaries for capillary gel electrophoresis (CGE): Influence of capillary surface pretreatment on performance and stability." *J. High Resol. Chrom.*, 1990, *13*, 624.
28. Takigiku, R.; Keough, T.; Lacey, M. P. and Schneider, R. E. "Capillary-zone electrophoresis with fraction collection for desorption mass spectrometry." *Rapid Commun. Mas Spectrometry* 1990, *4*, 24.
29. Hjertén, S. "Zone broadening in electrophoresis with special reference to high-performance electrophoresis in capillaries: An interplay between theory and practice." *Electrophoresis* 1990, *11*, 665.
30. Hjertén, S. and Kiessling-Johansson M. "High-performance displacement electrophoresis in 0.025–0.050 mm capillaries coated with a polymer to suppress adsorption and electroendosmosis." *J. Chromatogr.*, 1991.

INDEX